BASIC CONTRACT LAW

CONCISE EDITION

Eleventh Edition

■ ■ ■

Lon L. Fuller
Late Carter Professor of General Jurisprudence
Harvard University

Melvin Aron Eisenberg
Jesse H. Choper Professor of Law Emeritus
University of California at Berkeley

Mark P. Gergen
Robert and Joann Burch D.P.
Professor of Tax Law and Policy
University of California at Berkeley

AMERICAN CASEBOOK SERIES®

WEST
ACADEMIC
PUBLISHING

American Casebook Series is a trademark registered in the U.S. Patent and Trademark Office.

© West, a Thomson business, 2006
© 2013 LEG, Inc. d/b/a West Academic Publishing
© 2018 LEG, Inc. d/b/a West Academic
© 2023 LEG, Inc. d/b/a West Academic
      860 Blue Gentian Road, Suite 350
      Eagan, MN 55121
      1-877-888-1330

West, West Academic Publishing, and West Academic are trademarks of West Publishing Corporation, used under license.

Printed in the United States of America

ISBN: 978-1-68561-031-9

ACKNOWLEDGMENTS

This book, *Basic Contract Law*, has a long and rich history. The first edition of the book, published in 1947, was authored by Lon Fuller, one of the greatest contracts and legal scholars of the twentieth century. Professor Robert Braucher, then of Harvard Law School and also the Reporter for the Restatement (Second) of Contracts, joined Fuller as a co-author of the second edition. Thereafter, however, Braucher left the book because he had been appointed as a judge on the Massachusetts Supreme Judicial Court, and Professor Melvin Eisenberg, of the University of California at Berkeley School of Law, took Braucher's place. Eisenberg then authored the third through the eighth editions. In 2012, Professor Mark Gergen, of the University of California at Berkeley School of Law, joined the book as a co-author of the ninth edition.

It is impossible to acknowledge all those scholars, students, and law-school staff members whose influence has made itself felt in this book. First and foremost is Lon Fuller. Although Fuller passed away after publication of the third edition of this book, his designation as co-author has been retained through all subsequent editions because the book continues to reflect his seminal views on contract law. For the present, eleventh, edition we also especially thank Jennifer McBride and Toni Mendicino for their terrific work in helping to get the materials in the book ready for publication and overseeing the production of the book. We also thank our dean at Berkeley Law, Erwin Chemerinsky, for his ongoing robust and generous support of our work.

MELVIN ARON EISENBERG
MARK P. GERGEN

June 2023

Summary of Contents

———————

PART 3. ASSENT

PART 4. WRITTEN CONTRACTS

PART 5. MISTAKE AND UNEXPECTED CIRCUMSTANCES

PART 6. CONDITIONS

TABLE OF CONTENTS

PART 2. REMEDIES FOR BREACH OF CONTRACT

PART 3. ASSENT

PART 4. WRITTEN CONTRACTS

PART 6. CONDITIONS

TABLE OF CASES

The principal cases are in bold type.

––––––––––

TABLE OF UNIFORM COMMERCIAL CODE CITATIONS

TABLE OF CITATIONS TO THE RESTATEMENT OF CONTRACTS

TABLE OF CITATIONS TO THE RESTATEMENTS OF RESTITUTION

BASIC CONTRACT LAW
CONCISE EDITION

Eleventh Edition

INTRODUCTION

■ ■ ■

The law of contracts is, broadly speaking, the law of voluntary obligations; that is, obligations that arise because of an express or implied commitment—in particular, a promise. (In contrast, the law of torts, broadly speaking, involves obligations that are imposed upon persons without regard to any commitment they have made.) A promise may be defined as an expression of an intention to act or refrain from acting in a specified way, so made as to justify the person to whom the expression is addressed in understanding that a commitment has been made to that person. Restatement, First, of Contracts § 2(1). A person who makes a promise is called a *promisor*. A person to whom a promise is made is called a *promisee.*

Because contract law normally does not get off the ground unless there is a promise, or at least a promissory matrix, it is useful to begin the study of contract law with a brief treatment of the moral obligation that a promise imposes. Although it is widely accepted that there is a moral obligation to keep a promise, there has been a continuing debate over how to justify that obligation. The next two selections are important contributions to that debate.

J. RAWLS, A THEORY OF JUSTICE
342–47 (1971).

... [T]he principle of fairness. ... holds that a person is under an obligation to do his part as specified by the rules of an institution whenever he has voluntarily accepted the benefits of the scheme or has taken advantage of the opportunities it offers to advance his interests, provided that this institution is just or fair. ...

... Now the principle of fidelity [to one's promise] is but a special case of the principle of fairness applied to the social practice of promising. ...

... [B]y making a promise one invokes a social practice and accepts the benefits that it makes possible. What are these benefits and how does the practice work? To answer this question, let us assume that the standard reason for making promises is to set up and to stabilize small-scale schemes of cooperation, or a particular pattern of transactions. The role of promises is analogous to that which Hobbes attributed to the sovereign. Just as the sovereign maintains and stabilizes the system of social cooperation by publicly maintaining an effective schedule of penalties, so men in the absence of coercive arrangements establish and stabilize their private ventures by giving one another their word. Such ventures are often hard to initiate and to maintain. This is especially evident . . . in those instances where one person is to perform before the other. For this person may believe that the second party will not do his part, and therefore the scheme never gets going. It is subject to [this kind of instability] . . . even though the person to perform later would in fact carry through. Now in these situations there may be no way of assuring the party who is to perform first except by giving him a promise, that is, by putting oneself under an obligation to carry through later. Only in this way can the scheme be made secure so that both can gain from the benefits of their cooperation. The practice of promising exists for precisely this purpose; and so while we normally think of moral requirements as bonds laid upon us, they are sometimes deliberately self-imposed for our advantage. Thus promising is an act done with the public intention of deliberately incurring an obligation the existence of which in the circumstances will further one's ends. We want this obligation to exist and to be known to exist, and we want others to know that we recognize this tie and intend to abide by it. Having, then, availed ourselves of the practice for this reason, we are under an obligation to do as we promised by the principle of fairness.

————

THOMAS M. SCANLON, PROMISES AND PRACTICES
19 Philosophy & Public Affairs 199 (1990).*

Consider the following example, which I will call the case of the Guilty Secret. Suppose that you are visiting for a [fifteen-week] term at a university where you know almost no one, and at a party shortly after your arrival you are surprised to encounter Harold, whom you have not seen for years. Long ago, when you were young together, Harold did something that at the time he regarded as perfectly all right but that he now recalls with shame and embarrassment. It was not really that bad (you would not be violating any duty to others by failing to tell them about it), but Harold has come to be extremely sensitive about the incident. So, when the two of you are having a brief conversation apart from the rest of the party, he brings the matter up. "Remember that awful night in Chicago?" he asks. "I'll never forget it. The thought of how I behaved that night has haunted me ever since. It would be terribly embarrassing for me if anyone here were to learn of it. I know it seems as if I'm excessively concerned with this, but will you promise not to mention it to anyone while you are here?" Suppose that you do promise and Harold, looking much relieved, moves off in the direction of

*   Copyright, and reprinted by permission of, Princeton University Press.

the bar. I assume that as a result of this encounter you now have two moral reasons not to tell the amusing story of that night in Chicago: you would be gratuitously injuring Harold, and you would be violating the obligation to him that you have just incurred. The question is how to account for this [second] obligation . . . It seems that Harold does not rely on the expectation you have created by taking or forgoing any action, because there is nothing he could do to shield himself from the embarrassment that would result from your telling the story. He can't leave town, and I am assuming that murder and bribery are ruled out. He's not that kind of guy. So there are no options that he is passing up as the days of your visit go by. There may have already been reliance of [some] kind. . . . If you had not promised so readily, Harold might have gotten down on his knees to plead with you or shown you pictures of his wife and children, whose happy lives, he believes, could be reduced to shambles by your loose lips. But, given that you promised to remain silent, he did not do these things. Even if there was reliance of this kind, however, it does not seem sufficiently important to be the basis of your obligation.

What is important is the value of assurance itself. It may seem that if you were to tell the Chicago story on the last night of your visit (having promised on the first night that you would not), your overall course of action would leave Harold better off than if you had told the story without having promised not to. After all, the promise gave him fifteen weeks of peace of mind. But this is to assume that the value of assurance is purely experiential, that it can be reduced to the values of freedom from worry, increased ability to sleep at night, and so on. I would maintain, however, that this assumption is false. What people in Harold's position, and many other positions, reasonably want is not mere freedom from worry; they also want certain things to happen (or, as in Harold's case, to not happen). They want to be given assurances, and they care about whether these assurances are genuine. One reason for caring is that they may rely on these assurances in deciding what to do. This is not, however, the only reason, as Harold's case demonstrates. Given the reasons which potential promisees have for wanting assurance, potential promisors have reason to want to be able to provide it. From the point of view of both potential promisees and potential promisors, then, it is reasonable to want a principle of fidelity that requires performance. . . . Such a principle can be stated as follows.

Principle F: If (1) A voluntarily and intentionally leads B to expect that A will do x (unless B consents to A's not doing x); (2) A knows that B wants to be assured of this; (3) A acts with the aim of providing this assurance, and has good reason to believe that he or she has done so; (4) B knows that A has the beliefs and intentions just described; (5) A intends for B to know this, and knows that B does know it; and (6) B knows that A has this knowledge and intent; then, in the absence of some special justification. A must do x unless B consents to x's not being done.

The fact that potential B's have reason to insist on such a duty of fidelity is in my view sufficient to establish it as a duty unless it would be reasonable for potential A's to reject such a principle. Would the duty described impose an unreasonable burden on those who create expectations in others? They could of course avoid bearing any burden at all simply by refraining from intentional creation of any expectations about their future conduct. This would be quite limiting if it meant that we could never tell people what we intend to do without being bound to seek their permission before changing course. But Principle F would not have this effect, since it applies only when A knows that B wants assurance, and when A has acted with the aim of supplying this assurance and has reason to believe that he or she has done so, and when this and other features of the situation are mutual knowledge. No one could reasonably object to a principle imposing, in such cases, at least a duty to warn at the time the expectation is created—to say, "This is my present intention, but of course I may change my mind," or to make this clear in some other way if it is not already clear in the context. Since the burden of such a duty to warn is so slight, one can hardly complain if failure to fulfill it leaves one open to the more stringent duty to perform or seek permission to substitute. But this is just the duty stated by Principle F, since the conditions of that principle specify that no such warning has been given and, indeed, that quite the opposite has occurred, since A has refrained from providing such a warning in situations in which he or she knows that the difference between an expectation qualified by that warning and one without that qualification is important to B.

When the conditions of Principle F are fulfilled, it would be wrong, in the absence of special justification, for the first party not to perform. In addition, the second party has a "right to rely" on this performance: that is, the second party has grounds for insisting that the first party fulfill the expectation he or she has created. . . .

Saying "I promise to . . . " normally binds one to do the thing promised, but it does not bind unconditionally or absolutely. It does not bind unconditionally because the binding force of promising depends on the conditions under which the promise is made: a promise may not bind if it was obtained by coercion or through deceit. It does not bind absolutely because, while a promise binds one against reconsidering one's intention simply on grounds of one's own convenience, it does not bind one to do the thing promised whatever the cost to oneself and others.

———

GARDNER, OBSERVATIONS ON THE
COURSE IN CONTRACTS

1934.

"The ethical problems involved in the law of contracts result as I see them from four elementary ideas:

"(1) *The Tort Idea,* i.e. that one ought to pay for the injuries he does to another. As applied to promises this means that one ought to pay for losses which others suffer in reliance on his promises.

"(2) *The Bargain Idea,* i.e. that one who gets anything of value by promising to pay an agreed price for it ought to pay the seller the price he agreed.

"(3) *The Promissory Idea,* i.e. that promises are binding in their own nature and ought to be kept in all cases.

"(4) *The Quasi-Contractual Idea,* i.e. that one who receives anything of value from another ought to pay for it unless it came to him as a voluntary gift.

"These ideas, which at first seem trite and wholly harmonious, are in fact profoundly in conflict. The first and fourth proceed from the premise that justice is to be known after the event, and that it is the business of the court to correct whatever consequences of voluntary intercourse between men may be found to have turned out unjustly. The second and third proceed from the premise that justice is to be known before the event in transactions voluntarily entered into, and that it is the parties' business to settle the justice and injustice of their voluntary transactions at the start. The conflict between these two standpoints is perennial; it can be traced throughout the history of the law of contracts and noted in nearly every debatable contact question; there is no reason to think that it can ever be gotten rid of or to suppose that the present compromises of the issue will be any more permanent than the other compromises that have gone before."

PART 1

WHAT PROMISES SHOULD THE LAW ENFORCE?—THE DOCTRINE OF CONSIDERATION

■ ■ ■

Part 1 introduces the doctrine of consideration and the first great question of contract law: What kinds of promises should be legally enforceable? As a matter of morality all promises should be kept, in the absence of a moral excuse such as duress. As a matter of law, however, not all promises are legally enforceable. The paradigm type of promise that is not legally enforceable is a simple donative promise, that is, a promise to give something to, or do something for, a promisee that is unaccompanied by a special element, such as reliance.

Promises that are legally enforceable generally are said to have consideration. The most important type of legally enforceable promise is a bargain promise. A bargain is an exchange of promises (referred to as a bilateral contract, or more simply a bargain contract) or an exchange of a promise for an act (referred to as unilateral contract) in which each party to the exchange views what she gives as the price of what she gets.

Under classical contract law, which prevailed from the middle of the nineteenth century to the middle of the twentieth, it was often said that consideration required either a gain to the promisor or a detriment to the promisee. That terminology still sometimes appears even today, but under modern contract law, and even in many cases under classical contract law, the term *consideration* is typically used to mean a bargain promise, although the term is sometimes used to mean any type of promise that is legally enforceable. Under the bargain principle in contract law, with a few exceptions bargains are enforceable according to their terms, in the absence of a defense, such as duress as mentioned.

Part I consists of three Chapters. Chapter 1 concerns bargain promises. Section 1 of Chapter 1 concerns cases that turn on whether a bargain has been made, and the consequences of a bargain having been made. Sections 2 and 3 concern two rules of classical contract law under which certain types of bargains lack consideration, and shows how those rules have been either attenuated or abolished under modern contract law.

7

Finally, Sections 4 and 5 concern two limits on the bargain principle; that the bargain was made under duress or is unconscionable.

Chapter 2 concerns reliance as a basis for enforcing a donative promise.

Chapter 3 concerns the limits of contract as a technique for social ordering.

———

CHAPTER 1

THE BARGAIN PRINCIPLE AND ITS LIMITS

∎ ∎ ∎

Contract law generally enforces promises made as part of a bargain according to their terms and without regard to the fairness of the bargain. Section 1 concerns the doctrine of consideration, which establishes this general principle. Sections 2 and 3 concern two types of bargains where the traditional requirement of consideration is not satisfied. Sections 4 and 5 concern limits placed on the bargain principle by rules on duress and unconscionability.

SECTION 1. THE BARGAIN PRINCIPLE

INTRODUCTORY NOTE

This section concerns the doctrine of consideration and the bargain principle. The leading definition of consideration requires that a promise be given in exchange for a return promise or a return act, or performance,* and that "the consideration and the promise bear a reciprocal relation of motive or inducement: the consideration induces the making of the promise and the promise induces the furnishing of the consideration." Restatement, Second, Contracts (hereafter Restatement Second) § 71, comment b. To put it more simply, the leading definition of consideration is that the promise be made as part of a bargain.

Under classical contract law it was often said that consideration required either a gain to the promisor or a detriment to the promisee. The motivational requirement ("reciprocal inducement") makes it clear that anything can be the subject matter of a bargain. On the promisor's side the motivational requirement is satisfied if an apparent purpose of the promisor in making the promise is to obtain a performance or a return promise from the promisee, this need not be the promisor's only purpose or even her dominant purpose. On the promisee's side the motivational requirement is satisfied if the promise may have influenced the promisee to do what the promisor requested.

---

* In some cases A makes a promise for B's *forbearance* to perform an act (for example, B's forbearance to bring a suit against A), rather than for B's *performance* of an act. In the context of unilateral contracts, in this book the term *a bargain for the performance of an act* will include a bargain to forbear from the performance of an act.

When a promise is made in a commercial context these rules usually ensure the consideration requirement clearly is satisfied, and the focus is on other issues. Sections 2 and 3 concern two major qualifications to this proposition. The consideration requirement may not be satisfied where the promisee gives the promisor nothing in exchange for the promise (or makes an illusory promise), or where a promise is made in exchange for the promisee performing a legal duty the promisee already owes to the promisor. One theme of Sections 2 and 3 is modern contract law has attenuated or abolished the rules in classical contract law that made promises unenforceable on these grounds.

The doctrine of consideration has a few flaws. Sections 2 and 3 show that the doctrine has been an impediment to enforcing some types of commercial promises that probably should be enforced. The doctrine does not provide much help in distinguishing a conditional bargain promise from a conditional donative promise in cases in which the promisor does not make her intent clear. The doctrine also cannot explain why there is not a contract when people exchange social promises, such as two people promising to meet for dinner. English law deals with these cases by imposing an additional requirement for a contract that there be an intent to create a legal relationship.

———

Westlake v. Adams, C.P.

5 C.B. (N.S.) 248, 265 (1858)

Byles, J., said: "It is an elementary principle, that the law will not enter into an inquiry as to the adequacy of the consideration. . . . The jury have, I think, made an end of the question [of consideration]; for they have found (as well they might) that the defendant received what he bargained for, and all that he bargained for."

———

HAMER V. SIDWAY
Court of Appeals of New York, 1891.
124 N.Y. 538, 27 N.E. 256.

Appeal from an order of the general term of the supreme court in the fourth judicial department, reversing a judgment entered on the decision of the court at special term in the county clerk's office of Chemung county on the 1st day of October, 1889. The plaintiff presented a claim to the executor of William E. Story, Sr., for $5,000 and interest from the 6th day of February, 1875. She acquired it through several mesne assignments from William E. Story, 2d. The claim being rejected by the executor, this action was brought. It appears that William E. Story, Sr., was the uncle of William E. Story, 2d; that at the celebration of the golden wedding of Samuel Story and wife, father and mother of William E. Story, Sr., on the

[handwritten top margin: Facts: a bargain b/w uncle & nephew]

20th day of March, 1869, in the presence of the family and invited guests, he promised his nephew that if he would refrain from drinking, using tobacco, swearing, and playing cards or billiards for money until he became 21 years of age, he would pay him the sum of $5,000. The nephew assented thereto, and fully performed the conditions inducing the promise. When the nephew arrived at the age of 21 years, and on the 31st day of January, 1875, he wrote to his uncle, informing him that he had performed his part of the agreement, and had thereby become entitled to the sum of $5,000.

The uncle received the letter, and a few days later, and on the 6th day of February, he wrote and mailed to his nephew the following letter: "Buffalo, Feb. 6, 1875, W.E. Story, Jr.—Dear Nephew: Your letter of the 31st ult. came to hand all right, saying that you had lived up to the promise made to me several years ago. I have no doubt but you have, for which you shall have five thousand dollars, as I promised you. I had the money in the bank the day you was twenty-one years old that I intend for you, and you shall have the money certain. Now Willie, I do not intend to interfere with this money in any way till I think you are capable of taking care of it, and the sooner that time comes the better it will please me. I would hate very much to have you start out in some adventure that you thought all right and lose this money in one year. The first five thousand dollars that I got together cost me a heap of hard work. . . . This money you have earned much easier than I did, besides, acquiring good habits at the same time, and you are quite welcome to the money. Hope you will make good use of it. I was ten long years getting this together after I was your age. . . . Truly yours, W.E. Story. P.S. You can consider this money on interest."

The nephew received the letter, and thereafter consented that the money should remain with his uncle in accordance with the terms and conditions of the letter. The uncle died on the 29th day of January, 1887, without having paid over to his nephew any portion of the said $5,000 and interest.

[handwritten: → executor]

PARKER, J. . . . The defendant contends that the contract was without consideration to support it, and therefore invalid. He asserts that the promisee, by refraining from the use of liquor and tobacco, was not harmed, but benefited; that that which he did was best for him to do, independently of his uncle's promise,—and insists that it follows that, unless the promisor was benefited, the contract was without consideration,—a contention which, if well founded, would seem to leave open for controversy in many cases whether that which the promisee did or omitted to do was in fact of such benefit to him as to leave no consideration to support the enforcement of the promisor's agreement. Such a rule could not be tolerated, and is without foundation in the law. The Exchequer Chamber in 1875 defined "consideration" as follows: "A valuable consideration, in the sense of the law, may consist either in some right, interest, profit, or benefit accruing to the one party, or some forbearance, detriment, loss, or responsibility

[handwritten right margin: executor claims no consid. b/c uncle not benefitted by bargain]

[handwritten left margin: Problem w/ defendant's argument]

given, suffered, or undertaken by the other." Courts "will not ask whether the thing which forms the consideration does in fact benefit the promisee or a third party, or is of any substantial value to any one. It is enough that something is promised, done, forborne, or suffered by the party to whom the promise is made as consideration for the promise made to him." Anson.Cont. 63. "In general a waiver of any legal right at the request of another party is a sufficient consideration for a promise." Pars.Cont. *444. "Any damage, or suspension, or forbearance of a right will be sufficient to sustain a promise." 2 Kent.Comm. (12th Ed.) *465. Pollock in his work on Contracts (page 166), after citing the definition given by the Exchequer Chamber, already quoted, says: "The second branch of this judicial description is really the most important one. 'Consideration' means not so much that one party is profiting as that the other abandons some legal right in the present, or limits his legal freedom of action in the future, as an inducement for the promise of the first."

Now, applying this rule to the facts before us, the promisee used tobacco, occasionally drank liquor, and he had a legal right to do so. That right he abandoned for a period of years upon the strength of the promise of the testator that for such forbearance he would give him $5,000. We need not speculate on the effort which may have been required to give up the use of those stimulants. It is sufficient that he restricted his lawful freedom of action within certain prescribed limits upon the faith of his uncle's agreement, and now, having fully performed the conditions imposed, it is of no moment whether such performance actually proved a benefit to the promisor, and the court will not inquire into it; but, were it a proper subject of inquiry, we see nothing in this record that would permit a determination that the uncle was not benefited in a legal sense. Few cases have been found which may be said to be precisely in point, but such as have been, support the position we have taken. . . .

Order appealed from reversed, and judgment of the special term affirmed.

———

NOTE ON THE STATUTE OF FRAUDS

William E. Story's original promise was not in writing. Did that affect the issue whether it was legally enforceable? The question, what promises must be in writing to be enforceable (or at least, to be enforceable in full), is addressed by a group of rules known as the Statute of Frauds. This casebook is designed so that Statute of Frauds problems are to be considered continuously, in the context of cases involving oral promises, rather than in one batch. To that end, an extended Note on the Statute of Frauds is set forth in the Appendix. You should study the Appendix at this point. Thereafter, whenever a case involves an oral promise you should turn to the relevant sections of the Appendix to consider the impact of the Statute of Frauds, if any, on that case.

————

RESTATEMENT, SECOND, CONTRACTS §§ 1, 17, 71, 79

[See Selected Source Materials Supplement*]

————

NOTE ON THE RESTATEMENT OF CONTRACTS

The American Law Institute (ALI) is an organization composed of lawyers, judges, and legal academics. The ALI's objective is to promote the clarification and simplification of the law and its better adaptation to social needs. It has sought to achieve this objective in part by preparing Restatements of various branches of the common law, including Contracts.

The theory of the Restatements has changed somewhat over time. The introduction to the Restatement [First] of Contracts stated that "The function of the Institute is to state clearly and precisely in the light of the [courts'] decisions the principles and rules of the common law." The present theory is that the ALI "should feel obliged in [its] deliberations to give weight to all of the considerations that the courts, under a proper view of the judicial function, deem it right to weigh in theirs." Wechsler, The Course of the Restatements, 55 A.B.A.J. 147, 156 (1969).

The first Restatement of Contracts (hereafter cited as Restatement First) was published by the ALI in 1932. The Reporter was Samuel Williston of Harvard Law School. Williston was one of the leaders of a school of thought that is now called classical contract law. This school treated contract law as a set of axioms that were deemed to be self-evident, together with a set of subsidiary rules that were purportedly deduced from the axioms. Among the axioms of classical contract law were that bargains, and only bargains, constituted consideration; that bargains were formed by offer and acceptance; and that the remedy for breach of an enforceable promise was expectation damages.

In 1981 Restatement First was superseded by Restatement Second. The Reporter for the first portion of Restatement Second was Robert Braucher, then of Harvard Law School. On Professor Braucher's appointment to the bench he was succeeded as Reporter by Professor Allan Farnsworth of Columbia Law School.

Arthur Corbin of Yale Law School was, until his death, Consultant to the Restatement Second. From the 1920s through the 1960s, Williston and Corbin were the two giants of contract law. Each authored famous multi-volume

---

* References in this casebook to "Selected Source Materials Supplement" are to S. Burton & M. Eisenberg, Contract Law: Selected Source Materials (West Publishing Co.).

treatises on contracts that are still in use. While Williston was a leader of the classical school of contract law, Corbin was instrumental in laying the foundation of modern contract law. To a significant extent, the differences in approach between Williston and Corbin are paralleled by differences in approach between Restatement First and Restatement Second. Restatement First had much that is admirable, and Restatement Second marks a considerable advance over Restatement First. However, both the theory of the Restatements and other factors often work to prevent a Restatement from setting out the best possible rule in any given area.

————

BATSAKIS V. DEMOTSIS

Court of Civil Appeals of Texas, 1949.
226 S.W.2d 673.

MCGILL, JUSTICE. This is an appeal from a judgment of the 57th judicial District Court of Bexar County. Appellant was plaintiff and appellee was defendant in the trial court. The parties will be so designated.

Plaintiff sued defendant to recover $2,000 with interest at the rate of 8% per annum from April 2, 1942, alleged to be due on the following instrument, being a translation from the original, which is written in the Greek language:

"Peiraeus

"April 2, 1942

"Mr. George Batsakis

Konstantinou Diadohou # 7

Peiraeus

"Mr. Batsakis:

"I state by my present (letter) that I received today from you the amount of two thousand dollars ($2,000.00) of United States of America money, which I borrowed from you for the support of my family during these difficult days and because it is impossible for me to transfer dollars of my own from America.

"The above amount I accept with the expressed promise that I will return to you again in American dollars either at the end of the present war or even before in the event that you might be able to find a way to collect them (dollars) from my representative in America to whom I shall write and give him an order relative to this. You understand until the final execution (payment) to the above amount an eight per cent interest will be added and paid together with the principal.

"I thank you and I remain yours with respects.

"The recipient,

(Signed) Eugenia The. Demotsis."

Trial to the court without the intervention of a jury resulted in a judgment in favor of plaintiff for $750.00 principal, and interest at the rate of 8% per annum from April 2, 1942 to the date of judgment, totaling $1163.83, with interest thereon at the rate of 8% per annum until paid. Plaintiff has perfected his appeal.

The court sustained certain special exceptions of plaintiff to defendant's first amended original answer on which the case was tried, and struck therefrom paragraphs II, III and V. Defendant excepted to such action of the court, but has not cross-assigned error here. The answer, stripped of such paragraphs, consisted of a general denial contained in paragraph I thereof, and of Paragraph IV, which is as follows:

"IV. That under the circumstances alleged in Paragraph II of this answer, the consideration upon which said written instrument sued upon by plaintiff herein is founded, is wanting and has failed to the extent of $1975.00, and defendant pleads specially under the verification hereinafter made the want and failure of consideration stated, and now tenders, as defendant has heretofore tendered to plaintiff, $25.00 as the value of the loan of money received by defendant from plaintiff, together with interest thereon.

"Further, in connection with this plea of want and failure of consideration defendant alleges that she at no time received from plaintiff himself or from anyone for plaintiff any money or thing of value other than, as hereinbefore alleged, the original loan of 500,000 drachmae. That at the time of the loan by plaintiff to defendant of said 500,000 drachmae the value of 500,000 drachmae in the Kingdom of Greece in dollars of money of the United States of America, was $25.00, and also at said time the value of 500,000 drachmae of Greek money in the United States of America in dollars was $25.00 of money of the United States of America. The plea of want and failure of consideration is verified by defendant as follows."

The allegations in paragraph II which were stricken, referred to in paragraph IV, were that the instrument sued on was signed and delivered in the Kingdom of Greece on or about April 2, 1942, at which time both plaintiff and defendant were residents of and residing in the Kingdom of Greece, and

"*Plaintiff* (emphasis ours) avers that on or about April 2, 1942 she owned money and property and had credit in the United

States of America, but was then and there in the Kingdom of Greece in straitened financial circumstances due to the conditions produced by World War II and could not make use of her money and property and credit existing in the United States of America. That in the circumstances the plaintiff agreed to and did lend to defendant the sum of 500,000 drachmae, which at that time, on or about April 2, 1942, had the value of $25.00 in money of the United States of America. That the said plaintiff knowing defendant's financial distress and desire to return to the United States of America, exacted of her the written instrument plaintiff sues upon, which was a promise by her to pay to him the sum of $2,000.00 of United States of America money."

Plaintiff specially excepted to paragraph IV because the allegations thereof were insufficient to allege either want of consideration or failure of consideration, in that it affirmatively appears therefrom that defendant received what was agreed to be delivered to her, and that plaintiff breached no agreement. The court overruled this exception, and such action is assigned as error. Error is also assigned because of the court's failure to enter judgment for the whole unpaid balance of the principal of the instrument with interest as therein provided.

Defendant testified that she did receive 500,000 drachmas from plaintiff. It is not clear whether she received all the 500,000 drachmas or only a portion of them before she signed the instrument in question. Her testimony clearly shows that the understanding of the parties was that plaintiff would give her the 500,000 drachmas if she would sign the instrument. She testified:

"Q. . . . who suggested the figure of $2,000.00?

"A. That was how he asked me from the beginning. He said he will give me five hundred thousand drachmas provided I signed that I would pay him $2,000.00 American money."

The transaction amounted to a sale by plaintiff of the 500,000 drachmas in consideration of the execution of the instrument sued on, by defendant. It is not contended that the drachmas had no value. Indeed, the judgment indicates that the trial court placed a value of $750.00 on them or on the other consideration which plaintiff gave defendant for the instrument if he believed plaintiff's testimony. Therefore the plea of want of consideration was unavailing. A plea of want of consideration amounts to a contention that the instrument never became a valid obligation in the first place. . . .

Mere inadequacy of consideration will not void a contract. 10 Tex.Jur., Contracts, Sec. 89, p. 150; Chastain v. Texas Christian Missionary Society, Tex.Civ.App., 78 S.W.2d 728, loc. cit. 731(3), Wr. Ref.

Nor was the plea of failure of consideration availing. Defendant got exactly what she contracted for according to her own testimony. The court should have rendered judgment in favor of plaintiff against defendant for the principal sum of $2,000.00 evidenced by the instrument sued on, with interest as therein provided. We construe the provision relating to interest as providing for interest at the rate of 8% per annum. The judgment is reformed so as to award appellant a recovery against appellee of $2,000.00 with interest thereon at the rate of 8% per annum from April 2, 1942. Such judgment will bear interest at the rate of 8% per annum until paid on $2,000.00 thereof and on the balance interest at the rate of 6% per annum. As so reformed, the judgment is affirmed.

Reformed and affirmed.

———

B. Sweet-Escott, Greece—A Political and Economic Survey 1939–1953

93–96 (1954)

"It has been said that Greece suffered more heavily during the war than any other Allied country except Soviet Russia. From 1941 to 1944 the country was visited by famine, destruction, and inflation. Greece normally requires to import some 600,000 tons of grain a year. Most of this comes by sea. As soon as the Axis occupied Greece the usual sea routes ceased to be available—except those from the Black Sea and the Adriatic. And in any case there were few ships on which the Axis could lay their hands for feeding the country. Moreover, the only other main line of communication, the railway to Belgrade and Sofia, was fully occupied in supplying the Axis armies of occupation. Even if the Axis had been determined to maintain the existing standard of nutrition in Greece, it would have been a difficult task. As things were, the standard fell disastrously. It is estimated that the average daily diet in 1941, the worst of the three war winters, fell to 900 calories per person, and that it never exceeded 1,400 calories during the occupation. As the daily diet of a healthy man should be in the region of 3,000 calories, it is hardly surprising that Greece fell a prey to famine, especially in the towns. At one period in the winter of 1941–2 people were dying daily in the streets of Athens by the score. It will probably never be known how many perished of malnutrition and the diseases occasioned thereby, but the figure may well run into hundreds of thousands. . . . "

———

HANCOCK BANK & TRUST CO. V. SHELL OIL CO.

Supreme Judicial Court of Massachusetts, 1974.
365 Mass. 629, 309 N.E.2d 482.

Before QUIRICO, BRAUCHER, KAPLAN and WILKINS, JJ.

RESCRIPT.

The plaintiff bank argues exceptions to a Superior Court judge's findings and rulings in an action of summary process. The defendant Shell Oil Company (Shell) occupied premises in Taunton under a written lease. The lease, executed on May 15, 1962, for a term of fifteen years commencing on August 1, 1962, with options to extend the term, contained a provision that "Shell may terminate this lease at any time by giving Lessor at least ninety (90) days' notice." The lease further provided for a fixed monthly rental, obligated Shell to make certain minor repairs, and required Shell to reimburse the lessor "for any amount by which the general taxes on the premises allocable to any full year of the term of this lease exceed . . . [$525]." The bank acquired the premises, subject to the lease agreement, at a public auction following foreclosure proceedings against the lessor. The bank asserts that a lease for fifteen years, with options in the lessee to extend the term for an additional fifteen years, which permits the lessee to terminate the lease on ninety days' notice, is "so lacking in mutuality as to be void as against public policy." The bank cites no authority for such a conclusion. Once it appears that there was consideration to support a contract, and in the absence of statute (see, e.g., G.L. c. 106, § 2–302; G.L. c. 255B, § 20; G.L. c. 255D, § 29, subsection C), courts have traditionally declined to relieve a party from the terms of a contract merely because he made what he regards as a bad or uneven bargain. See Shaw v. Appleton, 161 Mass. 313, 315, 37 N.E. 372 (1894); Manson v. Flanagan, 233 Mass. 150, 153, 123 N.E. 614 (1919); Eliopoulos v. Makros, 322 Mass. 485, 488, 77 N.E.2d 777 (1948); Graphic Arts Finishers, Inc. v. Boston Redevelopment Authy., 357 Mass. 40, 43, 255 N.E.2d 793 (1970). See also Williston, Contracts (3d ed.) § 115 (1957); Corbin, Contracts, § 127 (1963). On this record it is not clear that the original lessor made a bad bargain. In any event, there is no basis for treating the lease as void on public policy grounds. There was consideration to support the lessor's obligations under the lease. . . .

Exceptions overruled.

———

NOTE ON CONSIDERATION AND REMEDIES

The question, what types of promise should the law enforce, is inseparable from the issue, to what *extent* should a particular type of promise be enforced? This is not a problem when expectation, reliance, and restitutionary damages produce identical results. For example, suppose that Plumber P, whose normal rate is $60 an hour, agrees to perform a repair for Homeowner H, and spends one hour on the job. H fails to pay. P's expectation damages are $60, the value of H's promised performance. P's reliance damages are also probably $60, because the plumbing business being what it is, in accepting H's job, P probably gave up an opportunity to use his time doing plumbing repairs for someone else. Restitutionary damages may also be deemed to be $60, because H has received $60 worth of plumbing services.

Often, however, the three damage measures will differ. In *Batsakis v. Demotsis* the defendant argued in effect that the value of what she had received was much less than the value of what she had promised. She was willing to pay the value of what she had received—that is, restitutionary damages. What the defendant resisted was payment of the value of what she had promised— that is, expectation damages. Conversely, the plaintiff rejected restitutionary damages and insisted on expectation damages. In short, both parties admitted that the contract was enforceable to some extent; the question was, to what extent. In a very real way, therefore, when the court said that adequacy of consideration will not be reviewed, it was invoking a damages rule, namely, that when a bargain has been made the normal remedy for breach is expectation damages, and it is no defense that the value of one promised performance exceeded the value of the other.

———

CARLISLE V. T & R EXCAVATING, INC.
Ohio Court of Appeals, 1997.
123 Ohio App.3d 277.

DICKINSON, PRESIDING JUDGE.

I

Defendant T & R Excavating, Inc. is solely owned and operated by Thomas Carlisle. Plaintiff Janis Carlisle is the owner and director of Wishing Well, Inc. and trustee of The Enrichment Center of Wishing Well, Inc., both of which were also plaintiffs in this action.

Ms. Carlisle and Mr. Carlisle married in 1988. According to Ms. Carlisle's trial testimony, shortly after they were married, she began doing all of the bookkeeping for T & R, including organizing and modernizing its bookkeeping system. Mr. Carlisle allegedly offered to pay her for her work, but she refused. He then allegedly stated to her that he would, instead, "do [her] work for [her] on [her] building. . . ."

During 1992, Ms. Carlisle decided to build a preschool and kindergarten facility. . . .

On September 25, 1992, T & R presented a "Proposal" to Ms. Carlisle in which it proposed the following:

"We hereby propose to do all of the excavation and site work at the above new Location. The total amount budgeted for this portion of the new building is $69,800.00. All labor, equipment costs, overhead and profit, necessary for the completion of this project, totalling $40,000.00 will be provided at no cost to Wishing Well Preschool, Inc. The $29,800.00 allotted for materials will be billed to Wishing Well Preschool, Inc. at T & R Excavating's cost."

On that same date, Ms. Carlisle signed an "Acceptance of Proposal," which was printed at the bottom of the "Proposal":

"The above prices, specifications and conditions are satisfactory and are hereby accepted. You are authorized to do the work as specified. Payment will be made as outlined above."

During December 1992, Mr. Carlisle and Ms. Carlisle, in anticipation of a possible divorce, prepared a document . . . . [I]ncluded in that document was a paragraph regarding Ms. Carlisle's secretarial work and T & R's excavating work:

"In repayment to Jan for her secretarial services and computer programming to T & R Excavating, Inc., Tom agrees to do all the excavating and site work for The Enrichment Center in a timely manner, as set forth in his proposal dated September, 1992. In this proposal, Wishing Well Preschool, Inc., agrees to pay Tom for the materials used at his cost."

Mr. Carlisle never signed the document.

Sometime during early 1993, T & R began performing excavation and site work for the preschool. According to Mr. Carlisle's testimony at trial, Ms. Carlisle was no longer providing any bookkeeping or secretarial services to T & R after January 1993. They separated during March 1993, and T & R continued working on the project until it abandoned it in late May or early June 1993. By that time, Wishing Well Inc. had paid approximately $35,000 for materials used by T & R for excavation and site work. Ms. Carlisle hired other workers to finish the excavation and site work. . . .

II

T & R's sole assignment of error is that the trial court incorrectly found that there was a contract between the parties, because their agreement lacked sufficient consideration . . . . It has asserted that its offer to do the excavation and site work for the preschool was in the nature of a gift or a favor, and was not supported by any legally sufficient consideration. . . .

A contract consists of an offer, an acceptance, and consideration. . . . Without consideration, there can be no contract. . . . Under Ohio law, consideration consists of either a benefit to the promisor or a detriment to the promisee. . . . To constitute consideration, the benefit or detriment must be "bargained for. . . ." Something is bargained for if it is sought by the promisor in exchange for his promise and is given by the promisee in exchange for that promise. See Restatement of the Law 2d, Contracts (1981) 172, Section 71. . . .

Whether there is consideration at all . . . is a proper question for a court. Irving Leasing Corp. v. M & H Tire Co. (1984), 16 Ohio App.3d 191, 192, 16 OBR 205, 206–207, 475 N.E.2d 127, 129–130. Gratuitous promises are not enforceable as contracts, because there is no consideration. Restatement of Contracts, supra, 172–174, Section 71, Comments a and b. . . . A written gratuitous promise, even if it evidences an intent by the promisor to be bound, is not a contract. 2 Corbin, Contracts (Rev.1995) 20, Section 5.3. Likewise, conditional gratuitous promises, which require the promisee to do something before the promised act or omission will take place, are not enforceable as contracts. Restatement of Contracts, supra, 174, Section 71, Comment c. While it is true, therefore, that courts generally do not inquire into the adequacy of consideration once it is found to exist, it must be determined in a contract case whether any "consideration" was really bargained for. If it was not bargained for, it could not support a contract.

There is no evidence in the record of any benefit accruing to T & R or any detriment suffered by Ms. Carlisle due to their agreement that could constitute consideration for a contract. . . .

A desire to help cannot be consideration for a contract; rather, it is merely a motive. See Williston, Contracts, supra, 336–338, Section 7:17. . . .

Consideration was also not shown by Ms. Carlisle's testimony that Mr. Carlisle told her, after she refused payment for her bookkeeping services to T & R, that he would help her with her building. . . . If Mr. Carlisle made the statement after Ms. Carlisle had done the work for T & R, her services were "past consideration" and could not support a contract. See Gem Say. Assn v. Aqua Sportsman, Inc. (Aug. 12, 1992), Hamilton App. No. C-910361, unreported, 1992 WL 192500. See, also, Restatement of Contracts, supra, 173, Section 71, Comment a. This is because past consideration cannot be a bargained-for benefit or detriment, since it has already occurred or accrued. If T & R was merely repaying Ms. Carlisle for past services, its promise to do the excavation and site work was not legally enforceable. Similarly, if Mr. Carlisle offered to help her with her building out of mere gratitude and she accepted it as such, that also precluded her services from being consideration. . . .

III

T & R's assignment of error is sustained. The judgment of the trial court is reversed.

Judgment reversed and cause remanded.

QUILLIN and SLABY, JJ., concur.

––––––––

NOTE ON DISTINGUISHING A CONDITIONAL BARGAIN FROM A CONDITIONAL DONATIVE PROMISE

Bargain promises often are made in a conditional form. For example, A may say to B, "If you mow my lawn, I will pay you $20." Donative promises may also be made in conditional form. For example, C may say to D, "If you select a car costing no more than $20,000, I will buy it for you as a graduation present." What's the difference between a conditional bargain promise and a conditional donative promise? In the case of a bargain the parties view performance of the condition as the *price* of the promise. In the case of a gift the parties view performance of the condition as the *means* to make the gift, not as the price of the gift. Thus in the first example, B's act of mowing A's lawn is viewed by A and B as the price that B must pay to get $20 from A. (And, of course, $20 is viewed by A and B as the price that A must pay to get B to mow her lawn.) In contrast, in the second example, D's act of selecting a car is not viewed by C and D as a price D pays to get the gift, but as a the means for making the gift.

How do we know whether fulfillment of a condition to a conditional promise is a bargained-for price or simply the means for making the gift? We make a judgment based on all the circumstances and on our knowledge of how people normally act. All this was well put by Williston, who formulated a now-famous hypothetical:

> It is of course ... possible to make a gratuitous conditional promise. ... [A]ny event may be named in a promise as fixing the moment, on the happening of which a promisor (not as an exchange for the happening but as a mere coincidence in time) will perform a promise intended and understood to be gratuitous. The same thing, therefore, stated as the condition of a promise may or may not be consideration, according as a reasonable man would or would not understand that the performance of the condition was requested as the price or exchange for the promise. If a benevolent man says to a tramp, "if you go around the corner to the clothing shop there, you may purchase an overcoat on my credit," no reasonable person would understand that the short walk was requested as the consideration for the promise, but that in the event of the tramp going to the shop the promisor would make him a gift. Yet the walk to the shop is in its nature capable of being consideration. It is a legal detriment to the tramp to take the walk, and the only reason why the walk is not consideration is because on a reasonable interpretation, it must be

held that the walk was not requested as the price of the promise, but was merely a condition of a gratuitous promise.

Williston on Contracts § 112 (3d ed. 1957).

———

Pennsy Supply, Inc. v. American Ash Recycling Corp.

895 A.2d 595 (Pa. Superior Ct. 2006)

Defendant American Ash offered Treated Ash Aggregate ("AggRite') free of charge on a "first come, first served" basis to contractors such as Plaintiff, understanding the material would be used in paving work. Plaintiff's use of AggRite in paving saved Defendant the expense of disposing of AggRite, which was classified as hazardous waste material. Plaintiff's paving experienced cracking, which it attributed to defects in the AggRite, and Plaintiff was required to do remedial work, which included the removal and disposal of the AggRite. Plaintiff brought a breach of contract action against Defendant, seeking to recover the cost of removing and disposing of the AggRite. Defendant filed demurrers, which the trial court granted, finding that "any alleged agreement between the parties is unenforceable for lack of consideration" and that "the facts as pleaded do not support an inference that disposal costs were part of any bargaining process *or* that American Ash offered the AggRite with an intent to avoid disposal costs." Reversed:

> [W]e disagree with the trial court that the allegations of the Complaint show only that American Ash made a conditional gift of the AggRite to Pennsy. In paragraphs 8 and 9 of the Complaint, Pennsy alleged
>
> > American Ash actively promotes the use of AggRite as a building material to be used in base course of paved structures, and provides the material free of charge, in an effort to have others dispose of the material and thereby avoid incurring the disposal costs itself . . . American Ash provided the AggRite to Pennsy for use on the Project, which saved American Ash thousands of dollars in disposal costs it otherwise would have incurred.
>
> Compl. ¶¶ 8, 9. Accepting these allegations as true and using the Holmesian formula for consideration [i.e., that the promise and the consideration are in a relation of reciprocal inducement], it is a fair interpretation of the Complaint that American Ash's promise to supply AggRite free of charge induced Pennsy to assume the detriment of collecting and taking title to the material, and critically, that it was this very detriment, whether assumed by Pennsy or some other successful bidder to the paving subcontract, which induced American Ash to make the promise to provide free AggRite for the project. Paragraphs 8–9 of the Complaint simply belie the notion that American Ash offered AggRite as a conditional gift to the successful

bidder on the paving subcontract for which American Ash desired and expected nothing in return.

We turn now to whether consideration is lacking because Pennsy did not allege that American Ash's avoidance of disposal costs was part of any bargaining process between the parties. The Complaint does not allege that the parties discussed or even that Pennsy understood at the time it requested or accepted the AggRite that Pennsy's use of the AggRite would allow American Ash to avoid disposal costs. However, we do not believe such is necessary.

> The bargain theory of consideration does not actually require that the parties bargain over the terms of the agreement. . . . According to Holmes, an influential advocate of the bargain theory, what is required [for consideration to exist] is that the promise and the consideration be in 'the relation of reciprocal conventional inducement, each for the other.'

E. Allen Farnsworth, Farnsworth on Contracts § 2.6 (1990) (citing O. Holmes, The Common Law 293–94 (1881)); *see also* Restatement (Second) of Contracts § 71 (defining "bargained for" in terms of the Holmesian formula). Here, as explained above, the Complaint alleges facts which, if proven, would show the promise induced the detriment and the detriment induced the promise. This would be consideration.

———

Klockner v. Green

54 N.J. 230, 254 A.2d 782 (1969)

Plaintiffs Richard Klockner and Frances Klockner, the stepson and stepgranddaughter of Edyth Klockner, brought suit to enforce an alleged oral contract between Edyth and them to bequeath her estate to them in return for their services. The uncontradicted evidence at trial showed that Richard performed numerous services for his stepmother and that "Frances spent numerous nights with decedent when the latter felt fearful or alone, and also accompanied her on trips whenever she was needed." The evidence further showed that when Edyth discussed the disposition of her estate with Richard in June 1965 she "informed him that she wanted to compensate him for being so helpful, and that if he would agree to continue to look after her and continue to let Frances visit her, she would leave the real property to him and the balance of the estate to Frances." Edyth's long-time lawyer testified that she informed him of her decision, and that he redrafted her will in accordance with the decision in November 1965. Edyth died unexpectedly in 1966. She never signed the redrafted will out of a belief that it was a premonition of death. The trial court granted defendant's motion to dismiss at the conclusion of plaintiff's case, finding there was no consideration for Edyth's promise based on Richard and Frances' testimony "that they would have continued to perform the services for decedent even if she had not made the promises to compensate them." Reversed.

Although we recognize that alleged agreements to make a particular disposition of one's estate must be subjected to close scrutiny, we have no doubt that decedent here intended to obligate herself to bequeath her property to plaintiffs so long as they continued to serve her as they had prior to her promise. Such a promise, when acted upon, becomes a binding obligation. Decedent bargained for plaintiffs' services and obligated herself to bequeath the property to them when they performed. See 1 Corbin, Contracts, § 63 (1963).

The performance by plaintiffs need not have been induced solely by the offer of compensation. In the Restatement, Contracts § 55 (1932), it is indicated that if an act is requested by the offeror as consideration for a unilateral contract, the act need only be given with the intent of accepting the offer. The examples which illustrate that rule clearly encompass the instant case.

> "A offers a reward for information leading to the conviction of a criminal. . . . B, . . . induced by motives of fear or public duty, would have given the information without hope of reward, but as there is an offer of reward he intends when he gives the information to accept the offer. There is a contract."

In the only New Jersey case discussing this rule, the Court of Errors and Appeals noted that once the contract has been legally concluded, in giving effect to that contract "the motive which induced the party to make the contract or perform it must always be immaterial." Mayor, etc. of Hoboken v. Bailey, 36 N.J.L. 490, 497 (E. & A. 1873). See also 1 Corbin, Contracts § 58 (1963) (recognizing the complexity of motivating causes in human action); Restatement, Second, Contracts § 55 (Tent. Draft No. 1, April 13, 1964) and § 84 (Tent. Draft No. 2, April 30, 1965).

―――――

De Cicco v. Schweizer

221 N.Y. 431, 117 N.E. 807 (1917)

In 1902, the defendant Schweizer executed an agreement with his daughter's fiancée to pay his daughter an annuity of $2,500 annually for her life in consideration of the couple's engagement and marriage. The defendant stopped payment in 1912. The daughter and her husband assigned the claim to the plaintiff De Cicco. Cardozo, J., held consideration for the promise could be found in inducing the couple not to terminate the engagement or delay the marriage, and that this did not require any evidence they were actually considering this when the promise was made.

"It is enough that the natural consequence of the defendant's promise was to induce them to put the thought of rescission or delay aside. . . . 'If it is proved that the defendants with a view to induce the plaintiff to enter into a contract made a statement to the plaintiff of such a nature as would be likely to induce a person to enter into a contract, it is a fair inference of fact that he was induced to do so by the statement.' (Blackburn, L.J., in Smith v. Chadwick, 9 App. Cas. 187.) The same inference follows, not so inevitably, but still legitimately, where the statement is made to induce the preservation of a contract. It will not do to divert the minds of others from a given line of conduct, and then to urge that because of the diversion the opportunity has gone by to say how their minds would otherwise have acted. If the tendency of the promise is to induce them to persevere, reliance and detriment may be inferred from the mere fact of performance. The springs of conduct are subtle and varied. One who meddles with them must not insist upon too nice a measure of proof that the spring which he released was effective to the exclusion of all others.

"One other line of argument must be considered. The suggestion is made that the defendant's promise was not made animo contrahendi. It was not designed, we are told, to sway the conduct of any one; it was merely the offer of a gift which found its motive in the engagement of the daughter to the count. Undoubtedly, the prospective marriage is not to be deemed a consideration for the promise 'unless the parties have dealt with it on that footing.' Holmes, Common Law, p. 292. . . But here the very formality of the agreement suggests a purpose to effect the legal relations of the signers. One does not commonly pledge one's self to generosity in the language of a covenant. That the parties believed there was a consideration is certain. The document recites the engagement and the coming marriage. It states that these are the 'consideration' for the promise. The failure to marry would have made the promise ineffective. In these circumstances we cannot say that the promise was not intended to control the conduct of those whom it was designed to benefit. Certainly we cannot draw that inference as one of law. Both sides moved for the direction of a verdict, and the trial judge became by consent the trier of the facts. If conflicting inferences were possible, he chose those favorable to the plaintiff."

———

NOTE ON DONATIVE PROMISES, LEGAL FORMALITIES, AND NOMINAL CONSIDERATION

While the common law generally gives effect to a completed gift it generally does not enforce a promise to make a gift in the future absent a special ground such as reliance (this is covered in Chapter 2). The treatment of donative promises is fundamental to contract doctrine, particularly consideration. Under classical contract law, the basic fault line in consideration ran at the boundary between bargain promises and "gratuitous" (donative) promises, because classical contract law generally took the position that a promise not made as part of a bargain was unenforceable.

[margin notes: Process grounds; evidentiary safeguards; cautionary safeguards]

In Consideration and Form, 41 Colum. L. Rev. 799 (1941), Lon Fuller posited various substantive and formal grounds—we might now say process grounds—for enforcing promises so long as legally specified formal requirements ("legal formalities") are satisfied. Two process grounds were the provision of evidentiary safeguards that ensured that a promise had actually been made, and cautionary safeguards that prevented inconsiderate action by the promisor.

[margin note: process problems w/ donative promises]

Many donative promises fall short on both process grounds. This offers a partial justification for a policy of not enforcing donative promises. First, oral donative promises raise serious problems of proof: A false claim that an oral promise was made may often be found credible by a jury despite the absence of corroborating evidence. Second, often donative promises raise serious problems of deliberativeness, because characteristically a donative promisor is emotionally involved with the promisee, and therefore may tend to look mainly to the promisee's interests rather than her own.

[margin note: Channeling function]

Fuller posited legal formalities performed a third "channeling function." To explain this function he used an old rule (now largely abolished in the United States) enforcing a promise made in writing under seal (originally an impression made by a signet ring in hot wax). "The seal," Fuller explained, "not only insures a satisfactory memorial of the promise and induces deliberation in the making it. It serves also to mark or signalize the enforceable promise; it furnishes a simple and external test of enforceability." Fuller continued, "[t]o the business man who wishes to make his own or another's promise binding, the seal was at common law available as a device for the accomplishment of his objective. In this aspect form . . . offers channels for the legally effective expression of intention."

Prior to the 17th century, English courts generally only enforced promises made under seal or to pay for a benefit received in a half-completed exchange. When courts began to enforce promises made in wholly executory exchanges the doctrine of consideration became the primary test for the enforceability of a promise (with the statute of frauds adding a formal backstop for agreements within the statute).

[margin notes: false recital of consid; Nominal consid.]

Courts inevitably confronted the question whether a donative promise could be made enforceable by a false recital of consideration or a recital of nominal consideration. In Dougherty v. Salt, 227 N.Y. 200, 125 N.E. 94 (1919), an aunt gave her nephew a promissory note for $3,000 on a preprinted form that stated the note was for "value received." This is an example of a false recital of consideration. In Schnell v. Nell, 17 Ind. 29, 79 Am.Dec. 453 (1861), a widower executed an instrument promising three of his deceased wife's relatives $200 each in "consideration of," among other things, "one cent, received by him" from the promisees.* This is an example of nominal

---

*   The instrument in *Schnell v. Nell* also recited as consideration that the promisor's wife "has also been a dutiful and loving wife" to the promisor, "and has materially aided him in the acquisition of all property, real and personal, now possessed by him." The court rejected these as "past considerations." The rule that "past consideration" is no consideration sometimes is expressed as a rule that a pre-existing moral obligation is not consideration for a promise.

consideration. Both cases held the promises unenforceable on the ground the promise was unsupported by consideration.

The term nominal consideration plays off the bargain theory of consideration. A bargain is a substantive transaction, consisting of an exchange in which each party views what she gives up as the *price* of what she gets. A transaction is said to involve nominal consideration when it has the form of a bargain but not the substance of a bargain, because it is clear that the promisor does not view what she gives up as the price of what she gets. So, for example, it is clear that in *Schnell v. Nell* the promisor did not view one cent as the price of his promise to pay $600.

A basic axiom of the classical school of contract law was the bargain theory of consideration—that to constitute consideration a promise or performance must be bargained for. Ironically, however, as the bargain theory of consideration was actually elaborated by the classical school, it could be satisfied even though no bargain had been made: both Holmes and Restatement First took the view that the form of a bargain would suffice to make a promise enforceable. Holmes expressed his view in two well-known aphorisms:

Consideration is as much a form as a seal

and

[I]t is the essence of a consideration, that, by the terms of the agreement, it is given and accepted as the motive or inducement of the promise. Conversely, the promise must be made and accepted as the conventional motive or inducement for furnishing the consideration. The root of the whole matter is the relation of reciprocal conventional inducement, each for the other, between consideration and promise.

By the term *reciprocal inducement*, Holmes meant a bargain. By the term *conventional*, Holmes apparently meant a formal expression whose meaning and significance is artificially determined, like a bidding convention in the game of bridge. Thus, in Holmes's view, if the parties deliberately adopted the convention—that is, the form—of a bargain, the law would enforce their promises as though they had made an *actual* bargain.

Illustration 1 to Restatement First § 84 reflected the same idea:

A wishes to make a binding promise to his son B to convey to B Blackacre, which is worth $5000. Being advised that a gratuitous promise is not binding, A writes to B an offer to sell Blackacre for $1. B accepts. B's promise to pay $1 is sufficient consideration.

Restatement Second has retained the bargain definition of consideration. In two Illustrations, however, Restatement Second has reversed the position of Restatement First on nominal consideration, and adopted a test that requires a bargain in fact, rather than in form, to make a promise enforceable under the bargain principle:

4.   A desires to make a binding promise to give $1000 to his son B. Being advised that a gratuitous promise is not binding, A writes out and signs a false recital that B has sold him a car for $1000 and a promise to pay that amount. There is no consideration for A's promise.

5.   A desires to make a binding promise to give $1000 to his son B. Being advised that a gratuitous promise is not binding, A offers to buy from B for $1000 a book worth less than $1. B accepts the offer knowing that the purchase of the book is a mere pretense. There is no consideration for A's promise to pay $1000.

Although Restatement Second rejects the concept of nominal consideration as a general principle, it does provide that nominal consideration makes a promise enforceable in two specific areas—options and guaranties. (An option is an offer accompanied by an enforceable promise to hold the offer open. A guarantee is a promise by A to C that if B doesn't pay B's debt to C, A will.) Some cases require the nominal consideration actually be paid. See, e.g., Board of Control v. Burgess, 45 Mich.App. 183, 206 N.W.2d 256 (1973) ($1 nominal consideration not paid; option unenforceable; option would have been enforceable if the $1 had been paid). Why is not clear. If the consideration is really nominal, it is no less a form just because it is paid. Perhaps actual payment of nominal consideration is viewed as a better form than the mere recital of a bargain, because a physical transfer of money may have more psychological impact than a mere recital.

SECTION 2. THE DOCTRINE OF MUTUALITY AND THE ILLUSORY-PROMISE RULE

This section concerns promises made in anticipation of a future exchange where the promisor has not received a return-promise or performance. Technically the consideration requirement is not satisfied in these cases because the promisor has received nothing in exchange for the promise. Often the absence of consideration in these cases is described as an absence of "mutuality." When the promisee makes a return promise, but this promise is subject to a condition in the promisee's control, the return promise might be described as an "illusory promise," which does not constitute consideration.

These doctrines generally are viewed as unsound because often it is in a promisor's interest to bind herself to a promise made in anticipation of a future exchange because her commitment increases the probability the anticipated exchange will occur. Courts use several techniques to find consideration in these cases. One technique is to imply a return-promise and treat the implied promise as consideration. Another technique is to treat an act performed (or a commitment made) by the promisee as consideration for the promise although obtaining the act (or commitment) seems incidental to the promisor's objective in making the promise (which was to increase the probability of a future exchange). Another solution is to abolish the consideration requirement for these types of promises.

———

OFFICE PAVILION S. FLORIDA, INC. v. ASAL PRODS., INC.

District Court of Appeal of Florida, 2003.
849 So.2d 367.

ASAL Suing Pavillion

Warner, J. Appellee, ASAL Products, Inc. ("ASAL"), an office supply wholesaler, sued appellant, Office Pavilion, an office supply company, for breach of a contract to supply chairs. Office Pavilion contended that the contract was unenforceable, as it was not supported by consideration and was indefinite. The trial court denied all motions directed to the enforceability of the contract, and after trial, the jury returned a substantial verdict in favor of ASAL. We hold, however, that the contract for the purchase of chairs was not enforceable and reverse.

The agreement history

Office Pavilion ("Pavilion") is a subsidiary of Herman Miller, Inc., a corporation which manufactures and distributes office furniture throughout the United States and Europe and is the exclusive distributor of Herman Miller office products in South Florida. Bernd Stier is a German wholesaler and reseller of office furniture and equipment mainly in Germany but also in other parts of Europe. Stier hired Oliver Asel, a former employee of Pavilion, and the two formed ASAL in Florida in order to facilitate purchasing Herman Miller keyboard trays from Pavilion to resell to Stier's customers in Europe.

The contract

Asel contacted Pavilion's sales manager, Gary Kemp, to negotiate a contract for the sale of keyboards. After months of negotiations, on December 23, 1998, they entered into a two-year contract for keyboard trays. The contract provided, in part:

2.   Purpose of Contract:

The parties agree that the purpose for entering into this agreement is for Pavilion to supply and ASAL to purchase from Pavilion products known as keyboard trays, and accessories for those keyboard trays.

3.   Delivery Times:

Pavilion agrees to supply ASAL with keyboard trays & accessories ordered by ASAL within 30 days of receipt of any orders up to 2,000 units per month and any accessories ordered by ASAL to supplement ordered units. A "unit" is defined, for purposes of this contract as a keyboard tray. An accessory is not a "unit" for purposes of calculating minimum and maximum order quantities.

    4.   Quantities:

    ASAL agrees to order a minimum of 1,000 units per year. Pavilion agrees to supply ASAL with any and all quantities ordered by ASAL up to a maximum of 2,000 units per month plus the accessories for those ordered units.

The contract further provided that the unit price would be established by a separate writing, which included volume discounts. ASAL placed three orders for keyboard trays in amounts between 100 and 150, for which ASAL timely paid and Pavilion timely delivered.

Approximately a month after the contract was signed, ASAL became interested in expanding its contract to include Herman Miller's Aeron chair, and Asel commenced negotiations with Kemp for this modification. While these negotiations were proceeding, ASAL marketed the chair in January and February, in addition to the keyboard tray, to determine demand for the chair. On March 11, 1999, Kemp forwarded ASAL a letter regarding amending the parties' contract for the keyboard trays to include the Aeron chairs. The letter included the price for two Aeron chair models and indicated:

    The terms and conditions of the December 23, 1998 Contract and Amendment will apply to these chairs except for Paragraph 3 and 4, Delivery Times and Quantities. The following paragraph shall be added to the Contract and Amendment:

    Aeron Chair Delivery Times:

    Pavilion agrees to supply ASAL with Aeron chairs ordered by ASAL within its established manufacturing lead times. The lead time will normally be 6 weeks from receipt of orders until shipment to Pavilion. Shorter lead times are also available depending upon order quantity and fabric selection.

Like the keyboards, the attached price list allowed for volume discounts on the chairs. Later, the parties signed an addendum memorializing the pricing structure.

After the letter regarding the chairs was sent, ASAL purchased six chairs from Pavilion to display at a trade show in Germany. The show was such a success that ASAL immediately reevaluated its sales forecast and requested a meeting with Kemp. Asel wanted 2,450 chairs to cover sales orders from the show plus 30 chairs to use as samples. However, while ASAL wanted the chairs, it did not include a deposit with its order or specify model numbers for the chairs. Kemp replied that it could not fill the order because Herman Miller International would not approve the sale.

Pavilion had authority from Herman Miller to supply its products to ASAL only for sale in Germany, and ASAL was expanding outside of Germany, contrary to Kemp's understanding of their original contract negotiations.

ASAL filed a breach of contract action, claiming as damages its lost profits for all expected sales under the contract for its two-year duration. While Pavilion admitted the existence of the keyboard contract, it defended against the much larger chair contract, contending that the agreement lacked consideration.

At trial, Kemp testified that he drafted the letter and addendum to expand the contract between the parties to include the chairs. He explained that the quantity paragraph from the keyboard tray contract was specifically excluded in his March 11th letter because "there was no minimum order quantities that were promised or that we agreed to for pricing for discounting purposes." He further explained that:

> Furniture industry agreements to purchase. [sic] They are not—They don't require you to purchase unless it would specifically say you agree to by [sic] X amount. So historically what it is is [sic] it's a license—it's a hunting license, if you will, is what we used to call them in the industry, to try to go after business, but with no promise that you'd ever see any business from it.

However, Kemp said that even with the lack of a quantity term provision, if Pavilion received an order from ASAL, Pavilion would fill it "within whatever terms." Basically, with a hunting license, Pavilion "had no expectations of what would come from it." Based upon his negotiations with Asel, Kemp did not know when or if ASAL ever was going to place these orders because Asel had been indicating for several months that the "orders were coming."

Asel testified that he brought an order for 2,480 chairs and a check for $633,000 to the meeting with Kemp regarding the chairs. However, Kemp informed him that Herman Miller would not approve the agreement. Kemp then advised Asel to submit a smaller order, and Asel modified the amount to 1,000 chairs with a $255,000 deposit. However, that order also was not accepted. Kemp denied that Asel ever presented the $633,000 check at the meeting at which Kemp informed Asel of Herman Miller's rejection of his order. As to the smaller order, Asel's check for $255,000 was returned for insufficient funds, after which Pavilion rejected the order.

After the trial court denied Pavilion's motion for directed verdict with regard to the enforceability of the contract and on the speculative nature of the lost profits, the jury awarded ASAL $4,000,000 in damages. From this verdict and resulting judgment, Pavilion appeals.

Pavilion contends that the chair contract between the parties was legally unenforceable for lack of consideration. We agree. While the contract for keyboards obligated ASAL to purchase a minimum of 1,000 keyboards a year from Pavilion, there was no minimum quantity term for the chairs. Essentially, Pavilion agreed to fill orders as made by ASAL, but ASAL had no obligation to place any orders at all. As Kemp said, the "agreement" was a "hunting license" which allowed ASAL to look for customers of Pavilion's merchandise and then to place orders when it found them.

It is a fundamental principle of contract law that a promise must be supported by consideration to be enforceable. *See* Restatement (Second) of Contracts § 17 (1981) ("[T]he formation of a contract requires a bargain in which there is a manifestation of mutual assent to the exchange and a consideration.") Moreover, a modification of a contract must be supported with consideration. *See Wilson v. Odom,* 215 So.2d 37, 38 (Fla. 1st DCA 1968). In a contract where the parties exchange promises of performance, "[i]f either of those promises is illusory or unenforceable then there is no consideration for the other promise." *Allington Towers N., Inc. v. Rubin,* 400 So.2d 86, 87 (Fla. 4th DCA 1981). As stated by the Court of Appeals for the Eleventh Circuit applying Florida law:

> If, however, "one of the promises appears on its face to be so insubstantial as to impose no obligation at all on the promisor— who says, in effect, 'I will if I want to' "—then that promise may be characterized as an "illusory" promise . . . An illusory promise does not constitute consideration for the other promise, and thus the contract is unenforceable against either party.

Johnson Enter. of Jacksonville, Inc. v. FPL Group, Inc., 162 F.3d 1290, 1311 (11th Cir.1998) (citations omitted).

The Restatement of Contracts illustrates these contract principles. Section 75 acknowledges that "a promise which is bargained for is consideration if, *but only if,* the promised performance would be consideration." Restatement (Second) of Contracts § 75 (emphasis added). However, the Restatement further provides in Section 77, "[a] promise or apparent promise is not consideration if by its terms the promisor or purported promisor reserves a choice or alternative performances." The commentary to this section explains:

> Words of promise which by their terms make performance entirely optional with the "promisor" do not constitute a promise. . . Where the apparent assurance of performance is illusory, it is not consideration for the return promise.

Restatement, *supra* at § 77 cmt. a (citation omitted). As appellant noted in its brief, the Restatement contains an example of illusory promises explaining this principle which is analogous to the alleged contract between Pavilion and ASAL.

> A offers to deliver to B at $2 a bushel as many bushels of wheat, not exceeding 5,000 as B may choose to order within the next 30 days. B accepts, agreeing to buy at that price as much as he shall order from A within that time. B's acceptance involves no promise by him, and is not consideration.

Restatement, *supra* at § 77 cmt. a, illus. 1. Similarly, Pavilion agreed to sell to ASAL any chairs it chose to order at the price set forth in the price list. While ASAL may have agreed, its acceptance involved no promised performance and therefore did not constitute consideration to support the contract modification for the Aeron Chairs.

ASAL responds by maintaining that mutuality of obligation is unnecessary where other consideration is present in the contract; yet, it fails to point to any other consideration. It first cites to the parties' mutual promises in paragraph two of the contract for Pavilion to supply, and ASAL to buy, the chairs. Without the ensuing quantity term or price term, however, this "mutual promise" is illusory and unenforceable. Next, it maintains the consideration was the benefit Pavilion received from ASAL's ongoing marketing efforts and sales of the chairs. This "benefit" also does not constitute consideration. First, the contract does not obligate ASAL to market the chairs. Second, marketing the chairs actually benefits ASAL where it obtains orders from it. ASAL's marketing efforts did not obligate Pavilion to sell the chairs. *See, e.g., Gull Lab., Inc. v. Diagnostic Tech., Inc.,* 695 F.Supp. 1151, 1154 (D.Utah 1988) (holding agreement to actively market product did not supply consideration where contract failed to include requirement that purchaser had any obligation to buy a minimum quantity of product). Finally, ASAL asserts its implied promise to place future orders was consideration. Were that the case, then any promise to place orders with no obligation to do so would constitute consideration. The case law cited above rejects such an illusory promise.

Next, the parties' contract is unenforceable for lack of an essential term, the quantity of chairs ASAL must order. That a quantity term is essential to a contract for the sale of goods is illustrated by Florida's statute of frauds provisions adopted from the Uniform Commercial Code. [Section 2.201(a)], Florida Statutes (1997), provides that a contract for the sale of goods in excess of $500 must be in writing to be enforceable. "A writing is not insufficient because it omits or incorrectly states a term agreed upon but the contract is not enforceable under this paragraph *beyond the quantity of goods shown in such writing. "* ... (emphasis added) ... Therefore, without a quantity term, this contract would be unenforceable under this section. *See Merritt-Campbell, Inc. v. RxP Products, Inc.,* 164 F.3d 957, 962 (5th Cir.1999) ("[T]he only term that must appear in a writing to support an enforceable contract for the sale of goods is the quantity term."). Contrary to ASAL's argument, that pursuant to the statute the contract may still be enforceable if the parties admit the existence of the contract, the statute actually provides that a contract is enforceable, "[i]f the party against whom enforcement is sought admits in his or her pleading, testimony or otherwise in court that a contract for sale was made, but the contract is *not enforceable under this provision beyond the quantity of goods admitted.*" § 672.201(3)(b) (emphasis added). Not only did Pavilion not admit to an enforceable contract with respect to the sale of chairs, it did not admit any quantity of chairs governed by the contract. Therefore, the contract could not be enforceable under this exception.

Because the chair contract was illusory and unenforceable, and Pavilion did not breach the keyboard contract, the trial court erred in denying Pavilion's motion for directed verdict. We therefore reverse the final judgment and direct entry of a judgment in favor of Pavilion.

GUNTHER, J., and HARNAGE, HENRY H., ASSOCIATE JUDGE, concur.

NOTE ON THE UNIFORM COMMERCIAL CODE

Office Pavilion is your first encounter with a contract involving a sale of goods, which brings into play Article 2 of the Uniform Commercial Code. This note and the following notes provides background on Article 2 and explain its scope. The specific provision applied in the case is UCC § 2–201, which is the statute of frauds provision for a sale of goods. The court does not discuss another provision that might have been relevant if the plaintiff had limited its claim to damages for chairs ordered in the first 90 days after the receipt of the March 11 letter. The letter could be treated as a firm offer to sell chairs. UCC § 2–205 makes a firm offer irrevocable for a period no longer than 90 days even though there is no consideration for the offer. Section 2–205 is taken up in Chapter 9, Section 3.

The Uniform Sales Act is the forbearer to the Uniform Commercial Code ("UCC"). It was drafted by Professor Williston under the auspices of the National Conference of Commissioners on Uniform State Laws (NCCUSL), which consists of commissioners appointed by each state. NCCUSL recommends legislation to the states on subjects in which uniformity of law among the states is thought to be desirable.

In 1940, the idea of a Uniform Commercial Code was proposed to NCCUSL, to take the place of numerous disparate statutes, including the Uniform Sales Act, which had direct bearing on commercial transactions. Thereafter the UCC became a joint project of NCCUSL and the American Law Institute (ALI), with Karl N. Llewellyn of Columbia Law School, and later of the University of Chicago Law School, as the Chief Reporter. The UCC was adopted by NCCUSL and the ALI in 1952, and comprehensively revised in

1956; further amendments were promulgated thereafter. It has now been enacted in forty-nine states and the District of Columbia. (Louisiana, whose law is based on a civil code, has not adopted the UCC as such. However, it has adopted most Articles of the UCC other than Article 2 ("Sales") and it has incorporated many of the concepts of Article 2 into its Civil Code.)

Many provisions of the UCC are of major interest in the study of contract law, and will be referred to in this book. Most of these provisions are in Article 2. The direct applicability of that Article is set out in UCC § 2–102, which provides that "Unless the context otherwise requires, this Article applies to transactions in goods. . . . " UCC § 2–105(1) defines "goods" to mean "all things (including specially manufactured goods) which are movable at the time of identification to the contract for sale other than the money in which the price is to be paid, investment securities . . . and things in action." Other UCC provisions of interest in the study of contract law are contained in Article 1 ("General Provisions") and Article 9 ("Secured Transactions"). Articles 1 and 2, and selected portions of Articles 3 and 9, are set forth in the Selected Source Materials Supplement.

In considering the UCC provisions referred to in this book, it should be borne in mind that even where a UCC provision is not directly applicable to a transaction—for example, where the provision is in Article 2 and the transaction involves services—the *principle* embodied in the provision may be applicable, so that the provision may serve as a source of law. "[P]rovisions of the Uniform Commercial Code which do not conflict with statute or settled case law are entitled to as much respect and weight as courts have been inclined to give the various Restatements. It, like the Restatements, has the stamp of approval of a large body of American Scholarship." Fairbanks, Morse & Co. v. Consolidated Fisheries Co., 190 F.2d 817, 822 n. 9 (3d Cir.1951). See generally Murray, The Spreading Analogy of Article 2 of the Uniform Commercial Code, 39 Fordham L.Rev. 447 (1971). For general discussion of the use of statutes as a source of law, see Landis, Statutes and the Sources of Law, *in* Harvard Legal Essays 213 (R. Pound ed. 1934); Pound, Sources and Forms of Law, pt. III, 22 Notre Dame Law. 1, 36–45 (1946).

Conversely, the UCC itself rests on the foundation of general law. Section 1–103 of the UCC, "Supplementary General Principles of Law Applicable," provides that "Unless displaced by the particular provisions of this Act, the principles of law and equity, including the law merchant and the law relative to capacity to contract, principal and agent, estoppel, fraud, misrepresentation, duress, coercion, mistake, bankruptcy, or other validating or invalidating cause shall supplement its provisions." As stated in PEB Study Group, Uniform Commercial Code Article 2—Preliminary Report 22–23 (1990), Section 1–103 gives rise to two questions:

> . . . (1) Does the UCC displace the common law in a particular area: and, if not, (2) What common law principle should the court choose? A broader interpretive question is whether § 1–103 provides sufficient flexibility and guidance for the courts to develop principles

within the framework of the UCC, without having to find and integrate other "principles of law and equity."

For example, Article 2 uses but does not define the term "offer." See Sections 2–206(1) and § 2–207 (1). Arguably, under Section 1–103 the UCC sections that use the term offer do not displace the common law definition of the term. Is a court bound willy nilly by whatever concept of offer is applicable in the state or may the court develop a definition which is consistent with the formation policies found in Article 2, Part 2? This is an important question for which there is no clear answer.

NOTE ON THE COMMENTS TO THE UCC

Each section of the UCC is accompanied by an Official Comment. A Comment may simply state the background of the relevant Section or explain the way in which the Section is related to other sections. Often, however, the Comment plays a substantive role, by explaining the intention of the Section, putting a gloss on the language of the Section, providing examples of how the Section operates, or in other ways. The courts normally give deference to the Comments, but the exact legal status of the Comments is not completely clear. It has been said that "In the great majority of cases, courts cite the Comments to support the application or purpose described in them. In some cases, however, courts specifically reject the Comments as authority for their propositions." Note, The Jurisprudence and Judicial Treatment of the Comments to the Uniform Commercial Code, 75 Cornell L.Rev. 962, 975 (1990).

Pittsley v. Houser

125 Idaho 820, 875 P.2d 232 (App.1994)

This was a contract for the purchase and installation of residential carpeting. The single issue on appeal was whether the trial court erred in applying the UCC.

(Swanstrom, J.) "Although there is little dispute that carpets are 'goods,' the transaction in this case also involved installation, a service. Such hybrid transactions, involving both goods and services, raise difficult questions about the applicability of the UCC. Two lines of authority have emerged to deal with such situations.*

---

   * [Eds. note] Amendments to the UCC approved by NCCUSL in 2022 address the application of Article 2 to a "hybrid transaction." This is defined as a single transaction involving a sale of goods and the provision of services, a lease of goods, or "a sale, lease, or license of property other than goods." Amended § 2–106 (definition of "Hybrid Transaction"). Section 2–102 would be amended to make Article 2 applicable to the entire transaction "if the sales of goods aspects predominate" (unless the circumstances make it sensible not to apply Article 2 to a non-sales aspect of a transaction). On the other hand, "If the sales of goods aspects do not predominate, only

"The first line of authority, and the majority position, utilizes the 'predominant factor' test. The Ninth Circuit, applying the Idaho Uniform Commercial Code to the subject transaction, restated the predominant factor test as:

> The test for inclusion or exclusion is not whether they are mixed, but, granting that they are mixed, whether their predominant factor, their thrust, their purpose, reasonably stated, is the rendition of service, with goods incidentally involved (e.g., contract with artist for painting) or is a transaction of sale, with labor incidentally involved (e.g., installation of a water heater in a bathroom). . . .

"This test essentially involves consideration of the contract in its entirety, applying the UCC to the entire contract or not at all.

"The second line of authority . . . allows the contract to be severed into different parts, applying the UCC to the goods involved in the contract, but not to the nongoods involved, including . . . services as well as other nongoods assets and property. Thus, an action focusing on defects or problems with the goods themselves would be covered by the UCC, while a suit based on the service provided or some other nongoods aspect would not be covered by the UCC. . . .

"We believe the predominant factor test is the more prudent rule. Severing contracts into various parts, attempting to label each as goods or nongoods and applying different law to each separate part clearly contravenes the UCC's declared purpose 'to simplify, clarify and modernize the law governing commercial transactions.' . . . As the Supreme Court of Tennessee suggested in Hudson v. Town & Country True Value Hardware, Inc., 666 S.W.2d 51 (Tenn.1984), such a rule would, in many contexts, present 'difficult and in some instances insurmountable problems of proof in segregating assets and determining their respective values at the time of the original contract and at the time of resale, in order to apply two different measures of damages.' *Id.* at 54.

"Applying the predominant factor test to the case before us, we conclude that the UCC was applicable to the subject transaction. The record indicates that the contract between the parties called for '165 yds Masterpiece #2122—Installed' for a price of $4319.50. There was an additional charge for removing the existing carpet. The record indicates that Hilton paid the installers $700 for the work done in laying Pittsley's carpet. It appears that Pittsley entered into this contract for the purpose of obtaining carpet of a certain quality and color. It does not appear that the installation, either who would provide it or the nature of the work, was a factor in inducing Pittsley to choose Hilton as the carpet supplier. On these facts, we conclude that the sale of the carpet was

---

the provisions of this Article which relate primarily to the sales-of-goods aspects of the transaction apply." Proposed § 2–102(2)(a). The major changes approved in 2022 involve adding new rules, including a new Article 12 covering "Controllable Electronic Records", to address how digital assets, like virtual currencies and non-fungible tokens, are handled under the UCC.

the predominant factor in the contract, with the installation being merely incidental to the purchase."

———

NOTE ON THE ILLUSORY PROMISE RULE

In hundreds of American cases it has been asserted as a general rule of contract law that both parties must be bound or neither is bound. This is called the doctrine of mutuality. The doctrine often works in conjunction with the illusory promise rule. An illusory promise is an expression that seems like a promise, but isn't. A common form of the problem is as follows: two parties—call them A and B—enter into an agreement with the usual trappings of a contract. The agreement is in writing and has language that signifies an intent to be legally bound. The agreement will involve an exchange between A and B. A will commit to go through with the exchange at B's discretion. B will not commit to go through with the exchange, or B will make a promise that is illusory because he has the power to terminate the agreement. A breaches the contract. When B sues for breach of contract A will argue that the promise she made is unenforceable for want of mutuality or because the promise apparently made by B was illusory.

The Illustrations to Restatement Second of Contracts Section 77 show the rule in action:

1. A offers to deliver to B at $2 a bushel as many bushels of wheat, not exceeding 5,000, as B may choose to order within the next 30 days. B accepts, agreeing to buy at that price as much as he shall order from A within that time. B's acceptance involves no promise by him, and is not consideration. . . .

2. A promises B to act as B's agent for three years from a future date on certain terms; B agrees that A may so act, but reserves the power to terminate the agreement at any time. B's agreement is not consideration, since it involves no promise by him.

In Illustration 1, B makes no commitment because he only agrees to do whatever he may choose to do. In Illustration 2, B reserves the right to choose to terminate his apparent commitment at any time. In both cases B has not constrained his realm of choice.

The doctrine of mutuality and the illusory-promise rule are unsound because it often is a person's interest to commit to an exchange without a commitment from the other party. Williston acknowledged that for this reason the mutuality requirement did not follow from the bargain theory of consideration: "[That illusory promises] are frequently . . . so requested with intent to make a bargain cannot be successfully disputed. A contractor or seller is often so eager to obtain work, or a sale, that he will gladly subject himself to an absolute promise in return for one which leaves performance optional with the other party. This is most commonly illustrated in agreements to buy or sell goods where the quantity is fixed by the wishes of one of the parties." Williston on Contracts § 103b (Rev. ed. 1937). In Illustrations 1 and 2, the promisor, A, does not make a promise to B for nothing, as a gift. She makes it to advance her own interests, by increasing the probability of exchange. In Illustration 1, A must believe that B is unlikely to trade with her unless A agrees to allow B the choice of ordering as many bushels as he wants to at the stated price during the stated time. In Illustration 2, A must believe that B would be unlikely to retain her as his agent unless she agreed that B could terminate the arrangement at any time. In each Illustration, A presumably makes her promise because she believes that B's incentives to exchange with A, rather than with others, would be insufficient unless the promise is made. In effect, there is a disparity of information and incentives between A and B. A has confidence in the attractiveness of her performance, which she believes that B does not share. A therefore makes a promise to B that is intended to change B's incentives to exchange with A, so as to increase the probability of exchange. A does this by making a commitment that she believes will induce B to give A a *chance* to show that her performance is attractive, either by sampling A's performance or perhaps simply by giving more serious consideration to purchasing A's performance than he otherwise would be likely to do.

The value of a chance to increase the probability of exchange is widely evidenced: book clubs give free books for the opportunity to sell future books; developers give free vacations for the opportunity to present a sales pitch; retailers offer free prizes in promotional contests to induce customers to shop; direct sellers pay substantial amounts for mailing lists.

This proposition can be illustrated by the following hypothetical:

A, a third-year law student whose grades are only fair but whose confidence is great, interviews with the well-known Washington litigation firm, F, G & H. After the interview, which A feels went very well, she writes to F, G & H as follows:

Dear F, G & H:

I very much enjoyed meeting you at my recent interview. I know my grades are below the level F, G & H usually requires. However, I also know they are not a fair indicator of my skills, particularly in litigation. (As you may recall, I did exceptionally well in several moot court settings.) I am sure that if you gave me a chance you would be more than pleased with my work. In order to induce you to give me a chance I make the following offer: I will work for you for one year at $70,000 (one-half of your normal starting salary), beginning September 1. You may discharge me at any time, without notice, no questions asked.

Sincerely yours,

A

F, G & H concurs, and A begins work. After three months, however, A leaves for another job, over the firm's objection. F, G & H brings suit against A for breach of contract.

Under the doctrine of mutuality A would not be bound to her promise, because F, G & H made no promise to her. Clearly, however, A has made a bargain. If F, G & H had paid $500 for A's promise, her promise would clearly be enforceable. The act of giving A a chance to prove herself may be worth much more to A (and may cost F, G & H much more) than $500. A has received exactly what she bargained for, and should be bound by her promise.

The doctrine of mutuality is a creature of classical contract law. Although the rule is still on the books, it is being whittled away under modern contract law. One way to satisfy the requirement of mutuality is to characterize a transaction as a unilateral contract. In a bilateral contract, the parties exchange a promise for a promise. (For example, Seller promises to sell Buyer a used car for $2,000, delivery in three days, and Buyer promises to pay $2,000 on delivery.) In a unilateral contract, the parties exchange a promise for an act. (For example, A promises to pay B $50 for mowing A's lawn, and makes clear that only B's act of mowing the lawn, not B's promise to do so, will suffice.) In a unilateral contract, the party who exchanges an act for a promise (B, in the hypothetical) may never be bound, because he is not bound to do anything before he chooses to do the act and he may not be bound to do anything after he does the act. Thus suppose, in the hypothetical, that B mows the lawn. B was not bound to mow the lawn before he mowed it, and is not bound to A in any way after he mowed it. Nevertheless, A is bound to B. The requirement of mutuality is satisfied by B's performance. We begin with a case that illustrates another technique courts use to satisfy the requirement. After reading the following materials you should consider whether the court might have found the mutuality requirement satisfied in *Office Pavilion*, supra.

WOOD v. LUCY, LADY DUFF-GORDON

Court of Appeals of New York, 1917.
222 N.Y. 88, 118 N.E. 214.

CARDOZO, J. The defendant styles herself "a creator of fashions." Her favor helps a sale. Manufacturers of dresses, millinery, and like articles are glad to pay for a certificate of her approval. The things which she designs, fabrics, parasols, and what not, have a new value in the public mind when issued in her name. She employed the plaintiff to help her to turn this vogue into money. He was to have the exclusive right, subject always to her approval, to place her indorsements on the designs of others. He was also to have the exclusive right to place her own designs on sale, or to license others to market them. In return she was to have one-half of "all profits and revenues" derived from any contracts he might make. The exclusive right was to last at least one year from April 1, 1915, and thereafter from year to year unless terminated by notice of 90 days. The plaintiff says that he kept the contract on his part, and that the defendant broke it. She placed her indorsement on fabrics, dresses, and millinery without his knowledge and withheld profits. He sues her for the damages, and the case comes here on demurrer.

The agreement of employment is signed by both parties. It has a wealth of recitals. The defendant insists, however, that it lacks the elements of a contract. She says that the plaintiff does not bind himself to anything. It is true that he does not promise in so many words that he will use reasonable efforts to place the defendant's indorsements and market her designs. We think, however, that such a promise is fairly to be implied. The law has outgrown its primitive stage of formalism when the precise word was the sovereign talisman, and every slip was fatal. It takes a broader view to-day. A promise may be lacking, and yet the whole writing may be "instinct with an obligation," imperfectly expressed (Scott, J., in McCall Co. v. Wright, 133 App.Div. 62, 117 N.Y.S. 775; Moran v. Standard Oil Co., 211 N.Y. 187, 198, 105 N.E. 217). If that is so, there is a contract.

The implication of a promise here finds support in many circumstances. The defendant gave an exclusive privilege. She was to have no right for at least a year to place her own indorsements or market her own designs except through the agency of the plaintiff. The acceptance of the exclusive agency was an assumption of its duties. Phoenix Hermetic Co. v. Filtrine Mfg. Co., 164 App.Div. 424, 150 N.Y.S. 193; W.G. Taylor Co. v. Bannerman, 120 Wis. 189, 97 N.W. 918; Mueller v. Mineral Spring Co., 88 Mich. 390, 50 N.W. 319. We are not to suppose that one party was to be placed at the mercy of the other. Hearn v. Stevens & Bro., 111 App.Div. 101, 106, 97 N.Y.S. 566; Russell v. Allerton, 108 N.Y. 288, 15 N.E. 391. Many other terms of the agreement point the same way. We are told at the outset by way of recital that:

> "The said Otis F. Wood possesses a business organization adapted to the placing of such indorsements as the said Lucy, Lady Duff-Gordon, has approved."

The implication is that the plaintiff's business organization will be used for the purpose for which it is adapted. But the terms of the defendant's compensation are even more significant. Her sole compensation for the grant of an exclusive agency is to be one-half of all the profits resulting from the plaintiff's efforts. Unless he gave his efforts, she could never get anything. Without an implied promise, the transaction cannot have such business "efficacy, as both parties must have intended that at all events it should have." Bowen, L.J., in the Moorcock, 14 P.D. 64, 68. But the contract does not stop there. The plaintiff goes on to promise that he will account monthly for all moneys received by him, and that he will take out all such patents and copyrights and trade-marks as may in his judgment be necessary to protect the rights and articles affected by the agreement. It is true, of course, as the Appellate Division has said, that if he was under no duty to try to market designs or to place certificates of indorsement, his promise to account for profits or take out copyrights would be valueless. But in determining the intention of the parties the promise *has* a value. It helps to enforce the conclusion that the plaintiff *had* some duties. His promise to pay the defendant one-half of the profits and revenues resulting from the exclusive agency and to render accounts monthly was a promise to use reasonable efforts to bring profits and revenues into existence. For this conclusion the authorities are ample.

The judgment of the Appellate Division should be reversed, and the order of the Special Term affirmed, with costs in the Appellate Division and in this court.

CUDDEBACK, MCLAUGHLIN, and ANDREWS, JJ., concur. HISCOCK, C.J., and CHASE and CRANE, JJ., dissent.

Judgment reversed, etc.

———

RESTATEMENT, SECOND, CONTRACTS § 77

[See Selected Source Materials Supplement]

———

UCC § 2–306

[See Selected Source Materials Supplement]

———

NOTE ON REQUIREMENTS AND OUTPUT CONTRACTS

Many agreements for the sale of commodities take the form of requirements or output contracts. In a requirements contract (1) a seller promises to supply all of the buyer's requirements of a defined commodity at a stated price (or at a price determined under a stated formula) over a designated period of time, and (2) the buyer promises to purchase all of his requirements of the commodity during that time from the seller at the stated price. In an output contract (1) a buyer promises to buy all of a seller's output of a given commodity at a stated price (or at a price determined under a stated formula) over a designated period of time, and (2) the seller promises to sell all of her output of the commodity during that time to the buyer at the stated price.

In the era of classical contract law the courts often refused to enforce requirements contracts in cases where the buyer could choose to have no requirements because, for example, the buyer had no established business, or was a middleman or required the commodity only in a part of its operations that it could easily abandon.

However, even in cases where the buyer may choose to have no requirements, by making the agreement the seller reveals that in its view the value of the chance that the buyer will have requirements exceeds the cost to the seller of making a commitment. Furthermore, even when the buyer may choose to have no requirements, requirements contracts are bargains. The seller clearly shrinks her realm of choice. So does the buyer. Before the buyer enters into such a contract, he is morally free to purchase the commodity from anyone he chooses. After the buyer enters into such a contract, if he requires the commodity during the contract period he is morally obliged to purchase the commodity from the seller at the contract price. Since both parties have made real promises—have shrunk their realms of choice—and each has exchanged its promise as the price of the other's, courts that refused to enforce requirements contracts because the buyer might have no requirements violated the bargain principle.

UCC § 2–306(1) now provides that "A term which measures the quantity by the output of the seller or the requirements of the buyer means such actual output or requirements as may occur in good faith, except that no quantity unreasonably disproportionate to any stated estimate or in the absence of a stated estimate to any normal or otherwise comparable prior output or requirements may be tendered or demanded." The Official Comment adds that "Under this article, a contract for output or requirements . . . [does not] lack mutuality of obligation since, under this section, the party who will determine quantity is required to operate his plant or conduct his business in good faith and according to commercial standards of fair dealing in the trade so that his output or requirements will approximate a reasonably foreseeable figure." Although UCC § 2–306(1) applies only to the sale of goods, most requirements and output contracts fall into that category. In any event, a modern court would almost certainly hold that all requirements and output contracts have consideration.

———

Mattei v. Hopper

51 Cal.2d 119, 330 P.2d 625 (1958)

Plaintiff was a real-estate developer. He was planning to construct a shopping center on a tract adjacent to defendant's land, and wanted to acquire the defendant's land in connection with the development of the shopping center. For several months, a real-estate agent attempted to negotiate a purchase of defendant's land, on plaintiff's behalf, under terms agreeable to both parties. After several of plaintiff's proposals had been rejected by defendant because of the inadequacy of the price that plaintiff offered, defendant submitted an offer of $57,000, which plaintiff accepted.

The parties' written agreement was evidenced on a form of deposit receipt supplied by the real-estate agent. Under its terms, plaintiff was required to deposit $1000 with the real-estate agent, and was given 120 days to "examine the title and consummate the purchase." At the expiration of that period, the balance of the price was "due and payable upon tender of a good and sufficient deed of the property sold." The concluding paragraph of the deposit receipt provided: "Subject to Coldwell Banker & Company [a real-estate broker] obtaining leases satisfactory to the purchaser." Plaintiff wanted this clause, and the 120-day period, to make sure that he could arrange satisfactory leases of the shopping-center buildings prior to the time at which he was finally committed to pay the balance of the purchase price and take title to defendant's land.

Thereafter, defendant's attorney notified plaintiff that defendant would not sell her land under the terms contained in the deposit receipt. Subsequently, defendant was informed that satisfactory leases had been obtained by Coldwell Banker and that plaintiff offered to pay the balance of the purchase price. Defendant failed to tender the deed as provided in the deposit receipt. Plaintiff sued for damages, and defendant argued that the plaintiff's promise was illusory. Held, for plaintiff.

(Spence, J.) "While contracts making the duty of performance of one of the parties conditional upon his satisfaction would seem to give him wide latitude in avoiding any obligation and thus present serious consideration problems, such 'satisfaction' clauses have been given effect. They have been divided into two primary categories and have been accorded different treatment on that basis. First, in those contracts where the condition calls for satisfaction as to commercial value or quality, operative fitness, or mechanical utility, dissatisfaction cannot be claimed arbitrarily, unreasonably, or capriciously . . . and the standard of a reasonable person is used in determining whether satisfaction has been received. . . . Of the cited cases, two have expressly rejected the arguments that such clauses either rendered the contracts illusory . . . or deprived the promises of their mutuality of obligation. . . .

"[The] multiplicity of factors which must be considered in evaluating a lease shows that this case more appropriately falls within the second line of authorities dealing with 'satisfaction' clauses, being those involving fancy, taste, or judgment. Where the question is one of judgment, the promisor's determination that he is not satisfied, when made in good faith, has been held to be a defense to an action on the contract. . . . Although these decisions do not expressly discuss the issues of mutuality of obligation or illusory promises, they necessarily imply that the promisor's duty to exercise his judgment in good faith is an adequate consideration to support the contract. . . ."

———

Harris v. Time, Inc.

191 Cal.App.3d 449, 237 Cal.Rptr. 584 (1987)

Joshua Gnaizda, "the three-year-old son of a prominent Bay Area public interest attorney," received a letter from Time, Inc. The front of the envelope contained a small see-through window, which revealed part of the enclosed letter. The part of the letter that could be seen through the window contained a picture of a calculator watch under the following statement: "Joshua A. Gnaizda, I'll give you this versatile new calculator watch free just for opening this envelope before Feb. 15, 1985." However, the see-through window did not reveal the full text of the letter. Printed in the letter below the picture of the calculator watch, and not viewable through the see-through window, were the following additional words: "And mailing this certificate today!" The certificate required Joshua to purchase a subscription to *Fortune* magazine to receive the calculator watch.

Joshua's father demanded the calculator watch without purchasing a subscription to *Fortune*. Time refused. Joshua, acting through his father, then brought a class action for $15 million. Time argued there was no contract because the mere act of opening the envelope was valueless, and therefore did not constitute adequate consideration. The court rejected this argument.

(King, J.) " . . . It is basic modern contract law that, with certain exceptions not applicable here (such as illegality or preexisting legal duty), *any* bargained-for act or forbearance will constitute adequate consideration for a unilateral contract. . . . Courts will not require equivalence in the values exchanged or otherwise question the adequacy of the consideration. . . . If a performance is bargained for, there is no further requirement of benefit to the promisor or detriment to the promisee. . . .

"Moreover, the act at issue here—the opening of the envelope, with consequent exposure to Time's sales pitch—may have been relatively insignificant to the plaintiffs, but it was of great value to Time. At a time when our homes are bombarded daily by direct mail advertisements and solicitations, the name of the game for the advertiser or solicitor is to *get the recipient to open the envelope*. Some advertisers, like Time in the present case, will resort to ruse or trick to achieve this goal. From Time's perspective, the opening of the envelope was 'valuable consideration' in every sense of that phrase."

(The court nevertheless dismissed the action on the grounds that (i) members of the class other than Joshua had not given Time notice of performance, and (ii) Joshua fell within the legal maxim "de minimis non curat lex"—the law disregards trifles—embodied in Cal.Civil Code § 3533.)

———

Helle v. Landmark, Inc.

15 Ohio App.3d 1, 472 N.E.2d 765 (1984)

" 'The modern decisional tendency is against lending the aid of courts to defeat contracts on technical grounds of want of mutuality.' Texas Gas Utilities Co. v. Barrett (Tex.1970), 460 S.W.2d 409, 412. As a contract defense, the mutuality doctrine has become a faltering rampart to which a litigant retreats at his own peril."

––––––

NOTE ON CLASSICAL AND MODERN CONTRACT LAW

From the middle of the nineteenth century until the first part of the twentieth century, contract law was dominated by a school of thought, now known as classical contract law, which found its central inspiration in Christopher Columbus Langdell, Oliver Wendell Holmes, and Samuel Williston, and its central expression in Restatement First. Beginning in the middle of the twentieth century, modern contract law began to oust classical contract law. Today, classical contract law survives largely in the form of background rules that have been heavily eroded but not entirely superseded. The movement from classical to modern contract law has occurred in a variety of dimensions.

1.   *The nature of contract-law reasoning.* To begin with, there has been a shift in the nature of contract-law reasoning. Reasoning in common law areas, like contracts, may be substantive or formal. The premise of *substantive* legal reasoning is that the validity of a doctrine turns in part on normative considerations, that is, on the congruence of the doctrine with morals, policy, and experience. In contrast, the premise of *formal* legal reasoning is that law consists of doctrines that are autonomous from policy, morality, and experience—that doctrines are valid without regard to whether they are normatively justified.

Formal legal reasoning may be axiomatic, deductive, or both. *Axiomatic* legal reasoning takes as a premise that fundamental doctrines can be established on the ground that they are self-evident. In the strictest versions of axiomatic theories, such as classical contract law, no room is allowed for justifying doctrinal propositions on the basis of moral and policy propositions. So, for example, Langdell, speaking to the question whether an acceptance by mail was effective on dispatch or on receipt, said:

> The acceptance . . . must be communicated to the original offeror, and until such communication the contract is not made. It has been claimed that the purposes of substantial justice, and the interests of contracting parties as understood by themselves, will be best served by holding that the contract is complete the moment the letter of acceptance is mailed; and cases have been put to show that the

contrary view would produce not only unjust but absurd results. The true answer to this argument is that it is irrelevant.

Deductive legal reasoning is based on the idea that many or most doctrines can be established solely by deduction from other, more fundamental doctrines that are taken as the major premises of syllogisms. As Holmes observed, disparagingly, axiomatic theories may easily be coupled with deductive theories: "I sometimes tell students that the law schools pursue an inspirational combined with a logical method, that is, the postulates are taken for granted upon authority without inquiry into their worth, and then logic is used as the only tool to develop the results."

Classical contract law was based on just such a coupling. It conceived contract law as a small set of core doctrines—axioms—that were justified on the ground that they were self-evident, and as a larger set of doctrines that were justified largely on the ground that they could be deduced from the core axioms. For example, it was an axiom of classical contract law that only bargain promises had consideration, that is, were enforceable (although exceptions were recognized for certain kinds of promises, such as those under seal, that were considered to be enforceable on strictly precedential, rather than principled, grounds).

In contrast to the formal reasoning of classical contract law, modern contract-law reasoning seeks to justify doctrines on the basis of policy, morality, and experience. Doctrines have an important role to play even in substantive legal reasoning, because of the social value that underlies doctrinal stability, but that value must always be weighed against the value of normative justification.

2.   *The deep structure of contract-law rules.* A second aspect of the movement from classical to modern contract law concerns the deep structure of contract-law rules. Legal rules can be ranged along various spectra. Four such spectra, which are particularly salient in contract law, will be discussed in the balance of this Note.

a.   *Objectivity/subjectivity.* One of these spectra runs from objectivity to subjectivity. A contract-law doctrine lies at the objective end of this spectrum if its application depends on a directly observable state of the world, and lies at the subjective end if its application depends on a mental state. For example, the classical-law rule that nominal consideration made a promise enforceable was objective, because it asked only whether there was the objective form of a bargain. In contrast, the modern rule that nominal consideration does not make a promise enforceable allows the courts to inquire whether the parties were actually (subjectively) bargaining for the consideration that is recited in their contract.

b.   *Standardization/individualization.* A second spectrum runs from standardization to individualization. A contract-law doctrine lies at the standardized end of this spectrum if its application depends on an abstract variable that is unrelated to the intentions of the parties or the particular circumstances of the transaction. A contract-law doctrine lies at the individualized end of this spectrum if its application depends on situation-specific variables that *are* related to intentions and circumstances. For example, application of the classical doctrine that adequacy of consideration will not be reviewed depends on a single variable—the presence of a bargain—that is deliberately designed to screen out all information concerning intentions and circumstances. In contrast, application of the modern doctrine of unconscionability depends on a number of situation-specific variables that are wholly concerned with that sort of information.

    c.   *Static/dynamic.* A third spectrum runs from the static to the dynamic. A contract-law doctrine lies at the static end of this spectrum if its application turns entirely on what occurred at the moment in time when a contract was formed. A contract-law doctrine lies at the dynamic end if its application turns in significant part on a moving stream of events that precedes, follows, or constitutes the formation of a contract. For example, the bargain theory of consideration is static, because its application wholly depends on what occurs at the moment in time when the bargain was made. In contrast, the reliance principle is dynamic, because its application turns on events after the promise is made. Similarly, the classical-contract-law legal-duty rule, which made many or most contract modifications unenforceable (see Section 3, infra) was static, because all rights and duties were frozen at the moment of contract formation. In contrast, a regime under which modifications are enforceable is dynamic, because it takes account of the importance of voluntary reciprocity after contract formation.

    d.   *Binary/multi-faceted.* A fourth spectrum runs from the binary to the multi-faceted. Contract law doctrines are binary if they organize the experience within their scope into two categories. Contract law doctrines are multi-faceted if they organize the experience within their scope into several categories. For example, Williston argued that when it came to damages, the only choice in contract law was the binary choice between no damages and expectation damages. In contrast, modern contract law provides a multi-faceted menu of no damages, expectation damages, reliance damages, restitutionary damages, and disgorgement damages.

    Classical contract law was a rigid rather than a supple instrument. It gave overriding priority to objective, standardized, static, and binary rules, which were often responsive to neither the actual objectives of the parties, the actual facts and circumstances of the parties' transaction, nor the dynamic character of contracts. In contrast, modern contact law pervasively (although not completely) consists of principles that are individualized, dynamic, multi-faceted, and, in appropriate cases, subjective. Many of the Chapters in this book illustrate the movement from classical to modern contract law along one or more of these dimensions.

SECTION 3. THE LEGAL-DUTY RULE; MODIFICATIONS

Just as classical contract law excluded illusory promises from the operation of the bargain principle, so too it excluded promises to perform an act that the promisor was already obliged to do. Under the legal-duty rule such a promise is not consideration, so that a bargain in which one party only promises to perform an act that he is already obliged to perform is unenforceable. The application of that rule in cases involving contract modifications, and the rule's erosion under modern contract law, is the subject of this Section.

Pollock, Principles of Contract

196 (9th ed. 1921)

" . . . [N]either the promise to do a thing nor the actual doing of it will be a good consideration if it is a thing which the party is already bound to do either by the general law or by a subsisting contract with the other party. It seems obvious that an express promise by A. to B. to do something which B. can already call on him to do can in contemplation of law produce no fresh advantage to B. or detriment to A."

Shadwell v. Shadwell

30 L.J.C.P. 145 (1860)

BYLES, J., said in this case: "The reason why the doing what a man is already bound to do is no consideration, is not only because such a consideration is in judgment of law of no value, but because a man can hardly be allowed to say that the prior legal obligation was not his determining motive."

RESTATEMENT, SECOND, CONTRACTS § 73

[See Selected Source Materials Supplement]

LINGENFELDER V. WAINWRIGHT BREWERY CO.

Supreme Court of Missouri, 1891.
103 Mo. 578, 15 S.W. 844.

GANTT, P.J. This was an action by Phillip J. Lingenfelder and Leo Rassieur, executors of Edmund Jungenfeld against the Wainwright Brewery Company upon a contract for services as an architect. . . .

The controversy in the court below finally turned upon the single question whether or not, upon the facts found by the referee and the evidence returned by him, the deceased was entitled to commissions on the cost of the refrigerator plant. In considering the subject it should be borne in mind that Jungenfeld's contract with the brewery company was made on or about the 16th of June, 1883; that under and by it he undertook to design the buildings, and superintend their erection to completion; that the superintending or placing of machinery in the building was no part of his contract, and that the claim for commissions on the cost of the refrigerator plant is based solely on a subsequent promise, the facts of which are thus found and stated by the referee:

> "[The refrigerator plant] was ordered not only without Mr. Jungenfeld's assistance, but against his wishes. He was in no way connected with its erection. Plaintiff's claim as to this item rests on a distinct ground, as to which I make the following finding of facts:

> "Mr. Jungenfeld was president of the Empire Refrigerating Company, and was largely interested therein. The De la Vergne Ice-Machine Company was a competitor in business. Against Mr. Jungenfeld's wishes, Mr. Wainwright awarded the contract for the refrigerating plant to the De la Vergne Company. The brewery was at the time in process of erection, and most of the plans were made. When Mr. Jungenfeld heard that the contract was awarded he took away his plans, called off his superintendent on the ground, and notified Mr. Wainwright that he would have nothing more to do with the brewery. The defendant was in great haste to have its new brewery completed for divers reasons. It would be hard to find an architect to fill Mr. Jungenfeld's place, and the making of new plans and arrangements when another architect was found would involve much loss of time. Under these circumstances, Mr. Wainwright promised to give Mr. Jungenfeld five per cent on the cost of the De la Vergne ice machine if he would resume work. Mr. Jungenfeld accepted, and fulfilled the duties of superintending architect till the completion of the brewery.

> "It is not clear to me how plaintiffs can bring their claim for this extra compensation on special agreement under their

petition, which asks for the *quantum meruit* of Mr. Jungenfeld's labor; but I pass all questions of pleading, and treat the claim as properly before me, since it is desirable that this report should present findings as to the merits of all branches of the case.

"What was the consideration for defendant's promise to pay five per cent on the cost of the refrigerating plant, in addition to the regular charges?

"Plaintiffs submit two theories accounting for the consideration: (1) It is claimed that the transaction was the compromise of a doubtful claim. I do not find that Mr. Jungenfeld claimed that defendant had broken the contract, or intended to do so. I infer that Mr. Jungenfeld had confidently expected to get for his 'Empire Company' the contract for putting the refrigerating plant into the Wainwright brewery. When the De la Vergne machine was selected, he felt disappointed, aggrieved, angry; but I can find in the whole record no evidence that he ever claimed that any of his legal rights had been violated. With this understanding of the evidence, I find no basis for upholding defendant's promise to pay commission on this refrigerating plant as the compromise of any doubtful claim.

"(2) Plaintiffs also contend that the original contract between the parties was abrogated; that a new contract was entered into between the parties, differing from the old only in the fact that defendant was to pay a sum over and above the compensation agreed on in the discarded, original contract. The services to be performed (and thereafter actually performed) by Jungenfeld would, in this view, constitute a sufficient consideration. Such a principle has been recognized in a number of cases: Munroe v. Perkins, 9 Pick. 305; Holmes v. Doan, 9 Cush. 135; Lattimore v. Harsen, 14 Johns. 330; Peck v. Requa, 13 Gray 408. Without discussing the legal doctrine involved, (of the accuracy of which I may say, however, I am not convinced),* I do not think the case in

---

* [Authors' Note: There was good authority under classical contract law that parties could avoid the pre-existing duty rule by modifying a contract in two-steps. Step One is to agree to abrogate or rescind the old contract. Step Two is to enter into a new contract with the modified terms. This stratagem works if the rescission of the old contract relieves both parties of a legal obligation for this satisfies the consideration requirement with respect to the release. See Restatement First, § 406, Comment a (explaining "Where . . . there is a bilateral contract, and each party is still subject to some duty thereunder, the agreement of each party to surrender his rights under the contract affords sufficient consideration to the other for his corresponding agreement. . . . Adequacy of consideration is immaterial. . . . Therefore, since each party surrenders something which he might have retained, the agreement to rescind is effectual.") The release being effective, the reinstatement of whatever remaining obligation the beneficiary of the modification had under the old contract constitutes consideration because there is no pre-existing duty. For example, in Schwartzreich v. Bauman-Basch, Inc., 231 N.Y. 196, 131 N.E. 887 (1921), an agreement to increase an employee's weekly salary from $90 to $100 was held enforceable, with the jury being instructed that "the test question is whether by word or by act, either prior to or at

hand warrants its application. I find in the evidence no substitution of one contract for another. As I understand the facts, and as I accordingly formally find, defendant promised Mr. Jungenfeld a bonus to resume work, and complete the original contract under the original terms. This case seems to me analogous to that of seamen who, when hired for a voyage, under threats of desertion in a foreign port receive promises of additional compensation. It has been uniformly held they could not recover. I accordingly submit that in my view defendant's promise to pay Mr. Jungenfeld five per cent on the cost of the refrigerating plant was without consideration, and recommend that the claim be not allowed."

Referee: not enforceable

The referee's finding of fact is based on the testimony of Adolphus Busch, Philip Stock, Ellis Wainwright, and is amply borne out by the testimony. Upon this state of facts the referee was of opinion that the promise to pay the 5 per cent commissions on the cost of the refrigerator plant was void, and the claim should be rejected; whereas, the learned circuit judge was of opinion that the promise was good in law, and that the commission should be allowed; and this question of law is the sole matter presented by this record. . . .

C. Judge: enforceable

Was there any consideration for the promise of Wainwright to pay Jungenfeld the 5 per cent on the refrigerator plant? If there was not, plaintiffs cannot recover the $3,449.75, the amount of that commission. The report of the referee and the evidence upon which it is based alike show that Jungenfeld's claim to this extra compensation is based upon Wainwright's promise to pay him this sum to induce him, Jungenfeld, to complete his original contract under its original terms. It is urged upon us by respondents that this was a new contract. New in what? Jungenfeld was bound by his contract to design and supervise this building. Under the new promise he was not to do any more or anything different. What benefit was to accrue to Wainwright? He was to receive the same service from Jungenfeld under the new, that Jungenfeld was bound to render under the original, contract. What loss, trouble, or inconvenience could result to Jungenfeld that he had not already assumed? No amount of metaphysical reasoning can change the plain fact that Jungenfeld took advantage of Wainwright's necessities, and extorted the promise of 5 per cent on the refrigerator plant as the condition of his complying with his contract already entered into. Nor was there even the flimsy pretext that Wainwright had violated any of the conditions of the contract on his part. Jungenfeld himself put it upon the simple proposition that "if he, an architect, put up the brewery, and another company put up the refrigerating machinery, it would be a detriment to the Empire

Reasoning for D

the time of signing the $100 contract, these parties mutually agreed that the old contract from that instant should be null and void."]

Refrigerating Company," of which Jungenfeld was president. To permit plaintiff to recover under such circumstances would be to offer a premium upon bad faith, and invite men to violate their most sacred contracts that they may profit by their own wrong. "That a promise to pay a man for doing that which he is already under contract to do is without consideration" is conceded by respondents. The rule has been so long imbedded in the common law and decisions of the highest courts of the various states that nothing but the most cogent reasons ought to shake it. [Citation of cases omitted.] But "it is carrying coals to New Castle" to add authorities on a proposition so universally accepted, and so inherently just and right in itself.

The learned counsel for respondents do not controvert the general proposition. Their contention is, and the circuit court agreed with them, that when Jungenfeld declined to go further on his contract, that defendant then had the right to sue for damages, and, not having elected to sue Jungenfeld, but having acceded to his demand for the additional compensation, defendant cannot now be heard to say his promise is without consideration. While it is true Jungenfeld became liable in damages for the obvious breach of his contract we do not think it follows that defendant is estopped from showing its promise was made without consideration.

It is true that as eminent a jurist as Judge Cooley, in Goebel v. Linn, 47 Mich. 489, 11 N.W. 284, held that an ice company which had agreed to furnish a brewery with all the ice they might need for their business from November 8, 1879, until January 1, 1881, at $1.75 per ton, and afterwards, in May, 1880, declined to deliver any more ice unless the brewery would give it $3 per ton, could recover on a promissory note given for the increased price. Profound as is our respect for the distinguished judge who delivered that opinion, we are still of the opinion that his decision is not in accord with the almost universally accepted doctrine, and is not convincing, and certainly so much of the opinion as held that the payment by a debtor of a part of his debt then due would constitute a defense to a suit for the remainder is not the law of this state, nor, do we think, of any other where the common law prevails.

The case of <u>Bishop v. Busse</u>, 69 Ill. 403, is readily distinguishable from the case at bar. The price of brick increased very considerably, and the owner changed the plan of the building, so as to require nearly double the number. Owing to the increased price and change in the plans the contractor notified the party for whom he was building that he could not complete the house at the original prices, and thereupon a new arrangement was made and it is expressly upheld by the court on the ground that the change in the buildings was such a modification as necessitated a new contract.

Nothing we have said is intended as denying parties the right to modify their contracts, or make new contracts, upon new or different considerations, and binding themselves thereby. What we hold is that, when a party merely does what he has already obligated himself to do, he cannot demand an additional compensation therefor, and although by taking advantage of the necessities of his adversary he obtains a promise for more, the law will regard it as *nudum pactum,* and will not lend its process to aid in the wrong. So holding, we reverse the judgment of the circuit court of St. Louis to the extent that it allows the plaintiffs below (respondents here) the sum of $3,449.75, the amount of commission at 5 per cent on the refrigerator plant, and at the request of both sides we proceed to enter the judgment here which, in our opinion, the circuit court of St. Louis should have entered, and accordingly it is adjudged that the report of the referee be in all things approved, and that defendant have and recover of plaintiffs, as executors of Edmund Jungenfeld, the sum of $1,492.17, so found by the referee, with interest from March 9, 1887. All the judges of this division concur.

———

NOTE ON HOW PERFORMANCE OF A MODIFICATION ELIMINATES THE NEED FOR CONSIDERATION

The absence of consideration is not grounds for reversing a modification where the modification has been performed. Thus, if in *Lingenfelder v. Wainwright Brewery Company,* supra, the architect, Jungenfeld, had obtained the additional payment he demanded upfront, before he resumed work, Wainwright Brewery Company could not have recovered the additional payment on the ground that there was no consideration for the additional payment under the legal-duty rule.[1] To recover a payment that it had made Wainwright Brewery Company could argue duress. The doctrine of duress is covered in Section 4 infra. Technically, duress is grounds for avoiding a contract. A restitution claim is brought to recover a payment made under a void contract.

———

---

[1] In *Foakes v. Beer,* infra, the defendant had fully paid the judgment in installments, as he had promised, when the plaintiff sued to recover the interest that she had agreed to forebear to induce him to pay the principal. Thus the court could have enforced the agreement on the technical ground that the consideration was not required because the agreement had been fully performed. This argument was accepted in Schiffman v. Atlas Mill Supply, Inc., 193 Cal. App.2d 847, 14 Cal. Rptr. 708 (1961). The plaintiff orally agreed to forgive a $4,000 debt owed to her by a family-owned corporation with the understanding other family members would also forgive debts owed them by the corporation, as a part of a plan to facilitate sale of the corporation to a third party to help her sick brother, who held the majority of the stock in the corporation. The court held the agreement was fully executed when the family members cancelled the debts and the third party purchased the corporation, so the issue of consideration was immaterial.

Restatement, Second, Contracts § 73

Comment d: *"Contractual duty to third person.* The rule that performance of legal duty is not consideration for a promise has often been applied in cases involving a contractual duty owed to a person other than the promisor. In such cases, however, there is less likelihood of economic coercion or other unfair pressure than there is if the duty is owed to the promisee. In some cases consideration can be found in the fact that the promisee gives up his right to propose to the third person the rescission or modification of the contractual duty. But the tendency of the law has been simply to hold that performance of contractual duty can be consideration if the duty is not owed to the promisor. Relief may still be given to the promisor in appropriate cases under the rules governing duress and other invalidating causes. . . .

RESTATEMENT, SECOND, CONTRACTS § 89

[See Selected Source Materials Supplement]

ANGEL v. MURRAY

Supreme Court of Rhode Island, 1974.
113 R.I. 482, 322 A.2d 630.

ROBERTS, C.J. This is a civil action brought by Alfred L. Angel and others against John E. Murray, Jr., Director of Finance of the City of Newport, the city of Newport, and James L. Maher, alleging that Maher had illegally been paid the sum of $20,000 by the Director of Finance and praying that the defendant Maher be ordered to repay the city such sum. The case was heard by a justice of the Superior Court, sitting without a jury, who entered a judgment ordering Maher to repay the sum of $20,000 to the city of Newport. Maher is now before this court prosecuting an appeal.

The record discloses that Maher has provided the city of Newport with a refuse-collection service under a series of five-year contracts beginning in 1946. On March 12, 1964, Maher and the city entered into another such contract for a period of five years commencing on July 1, 1964, and terminating on June 30, 1969. The contract provided, among other things, that Maher would receive $137,000 per year in return for collecting and removing all combustible and noncombustible waste materials generated within the city.

In June of 1967 Maher requested an additional $10,000 per year from the city council because there had been a substantial increase in the cost

unexpected change of circumstances

of collection due to an unexpected and unanticipated increase of 400 new dwelling units. Maher's testimony, which is uncontradicted, indicates the 1964 contract had been predicated on the fact that since 1946 there had been an average increase of 20 to 25 new dwelling units per year. After a public meeting of the city council where Maher explained in detail the reasons for his request and was questioned by members of the city council, the city council agreed to pay him an additional $10,000 for the year ending on June 30, 1968. Maher made a similar request again in June of 1968 for the same reasons, and the city council again agreed to pay an additional $10,000 for the year ending on June 30, 1969.

contract modified

The trial justice found that each such $10,000 payment was made in violation of law. . . . [H]e found that Maher was not entitled to extra compensation because the original contract already required him to collect all refuse generated within the city and, therefore, included the 400 additional units. The trial justice further found that these 400 additional units were within the contemplation of the parties when they entered into the contract. It appears that he based this portion of the decision upon the rule that Maher had a preexisting duty to collect the refuse generated by the 400 additional units, and thus there was no consideration for the two additional payments. . . .

TC reasoning: Maher had preexisting duty

A.

As previously stated, the city council made two $10,000 payments. The first was made in June of 1967 for the year beginning on July 1, 1967, and ending on June 30, 1968. Thus, by the time this action was commenced in October of 1968, the modification was completely executed. That is, the money had been paid by the city council, and Maher had collected all of the refuse. Since consideration is only a test of the enforceability of executory promises, the presence or absence of consideration for the first payment is unimportant because the city council's agreement to make the first payment was fully executed at the time of the commencement of this action. . . . However, since both payments were made under similar circumstances, our decision regarding the second payment (Part B, infra) is fully applicable to the first payment.

B.

It is generally held that a modification of a contract is itself a contract, which is unenforceable unless supported by consideration. . . .

The primary purpose of the preexisting duty rule is to prevent what has been referred to as the "hold-up game." See 1A Corbin . . . § 171. A classic example of the "hold-up game" is found in Alaska Packers' Ass'n v. Domenico, 117 F. 99 (9th Cir.1902). There 21 seamen entered into a written contract with Domenico to sail from San Francisco to Pyramid Harbor, Alaska. They were to work as sailors and fishermen out of Pyramid Harbor during the fishing season of 1900. The contract specified that each man would be paid $50 plus two cents for each red salmon he caught. Subsequent to their arrival at Pyramid Harbor, the men stopped work and demanded an additional $50. They threatened to return to San Francisco if Domenico did not agree to their demand. Since it was impossible for Domenico to find other men, he agreed to pay the men an additional $50. After they returned to San Francisco, Domenico refused to pay the men an additional $50. The court found that the subsequent agreement to pay the men an additional $50 was not supported by consideration because the men had a preexisting duty to work on the ship under the original contract, and thus the subsequent agreement was unenforceable.

Another example of the "hold-up game" is found in the area of construction contracts. Frequently, a contractor will refuse to complete work under an unprofitable contract unless he is awarded additional compensation. The courts have generally held that a subsequent agreement to award additional compensation is unenforceable if the contractor is only performing work which would have been required of him under the original contract. See, e.g., Lingenfelder v. Wainwright Brewing Co., 103 Mo. 578, 15 S.W. 844 (1891), which is a leading case in this area. . . .

These examples clearly illustrate that the courts will not enforce an agreement that has been procured by coercion or duress and will hold the parties to their original contract regardless of whether it is profitable or unprofitable. However, the courts have been reluctant to apply the preexisting duty rule when a party to a contract encounters unanticipated difficulties and the other party, not influenced by coercion or duress, voluntarily agrees to pay additional compensation for work already required to be performed under the contract. For example, the courts have found that the original contract was rescinded, Linz v. Schuck, 106 Md. 220, 67 A. 286 (1907); abandoned, Connelly v. Devoe, 37 Conn. 570 (1871), or waived, Michaud v. McGregor, 61 Minn. 198, 63 N.W. 479 (1895).

Although the preexisting duty rule has served a useful purpose insofar as it deters parties from using coercion and duress to obtain additional compensation, it has been widely criticized as a general rule of law. . . .

The modern rule

The modern trend appears to recognize the necessity that courts should enforce agreements modifying contracts when unexpected or unanticipated difficulties arise during the course of the performance of a contract, even though there is no consideration for the modification, as long as the parties agree voluntarily.

Under the Uniform Commercial Code, § 2–209(1), which has been adopted by 49 states, "[a]n agreement modifying a contract [for the sale of goods] needs no consideration to be binding." See G.L.1956 (1969 Reenactment) § 6A–2–209(1). Although at first blush this section appears to validate modifications obtained by coercion and duress, the comments to this section indicate that a modification under this section must meet the test of good faith imposed by the Code, and a modification obtained by extortion without a legitimate commercial reason is unenforceable.

The modern trend away from a rigid application of the preexisting duty rule is reflected by [§ 89(a)] of the American Law Institute's Restatement, Second, Law of Contracts. . . .

We believe that [§ 89(a)] is the proper rule of law and find it applicable to the facts of this case.[2] It not only prohibits modifications obtained by coercion, duress, or extortion but also fulfills society's expectation that agreements entered into voluntarily will be enforced by the courts.[3] See generally Horwitz, The Historical Foundations of Modern Contract Law, 87 Harv.L.Rev. 917 (1974). Section [89(a)], of course, does not compel a modification of an unprofitable or unfair contract; it only enforces a modification if the parties voluntarily agree and if (1) the promise modifying the original contract was made before the contract was fully performed on either side, (2) the underlying circumstances which prompted the modification were unanticipated by the parties, and (3) the modification is fair and equitable.

Applying the modern Rule

---

[2]   The fact that these additional payments were made by a municipal corporation rather than a private individual does not, in our opinion, affect the outcome of this case. . . .

[3]   The drafters of [§ 89(a)] of the Restatement Second of the Law of Contracts use the following illustrations in comment (b) as examples of how this rule is applied to certain transactions:

"1.   By a written contract A agrees to excavate a cellar for B for a stated price. Solid rock is unexpectedly encountered and A so notifies B. A and B then orally agree that A will remove the rock at a unit price which is reasonable but nine times that used in computing the original price, and A completes the job. B is bound to pay the increased amount.

"2.   A contracts with B to supply for $300 a laundry chute for a building B has contracted to build for the government for $150,000. Later A discovers that he made an error as to the type of material to be used and should have bid $1,200. A offers to supply the chute for $1,000, eliminating overhead and profit. After ascertaining that other suppliers would charge more, B agrees. The new agreement is binding.

"3.   A is employed by B as a designer of coats at $90 a week for a year beginning November 1 under a written contract executed September 1. A is offered $115 a week by another employer and so informs B. A and B then agree that A will be paid $100 a week and in October execute a new written contract to that effect, simultaneously tearing up the prior contract. The new contract is binding.

"4.   A contracts to manufacture and sell to B 2,000 steel roofs for corn cribs at $60. Before A begins manufacture a threat of a nationwide steel strike raises the cost of steel about $10 per roof, and A and B agree orally to increase the price to $70 per roof. A thereafter manufactures and delivers 1,700 of the roofs, and B pays for 1,500 of them at the increased price without protest, increasing the selling price of the corn cribs by $10. The new agreement is binding.

"5.   A contracts to manufacture and sell to B 100,000 castings for lawn mowers at 50 cents each. After partial delivery and after B has contracted to sell a substantial number of lawn mowers at a fixed price, A notifies B that increased metal costs require that the price be increased to 75 cents. Substitute castings are available at 55 cents, but only after several months delay. B protests but is forced to agree to the new price to keep its plant in operation. The modification is not binding."

The evidence, which is uncontradicted, reveals that in June of 1968 Maher requested the city council to pay him an additional $10,000 for the year beginning on July 1, 1968, and ending on June 30, 1969. This request was made at a public meeting of the city council, where Maher explained in detail his reasons for making the request. Thereafter, the city council voted to authorize the Mayor to sign an amendment to the [1964] contract which provided that Maher would receive an additional $10,000 per year for the duration of the contract. Under such circumstances we have no doubt that the city voluntarily agreed to modify the 1964 contract.

Having determined the voluntariness of this agreement, we turn our attention to the three criteria delineated above. First, the modification was made in June of 1968 at a time when the five-year contract which was made in 1964 had not been fully performed by either party. Second, although the 1964 contract provided that Maher collect all refuse generated within the city, it appears this contract was premised on Maher's past experience that the number of refuse-generating units would increase at a rate of 20 to 25 per year. Furthermore, the evidence is uncontradicted that the 1967–1968 increase of 400 units "went beyond any previous expectation." Clearly, the circumstances which prompted the city council to modify the 1964 contract were unanticipated. Third, although the evidence does not indicate what proportion of the total this increase comprised, the evidence does indicate that it was a "substantial" increase. In light of this, we cannot say that the council's agreement to pay Maher the $10,000 increase was not fair and equitable in the circumstances.

The judgment appealed from is reversed, and the cause is remanded to the Superior Court for entry of judgment for the defendants.

———

Watkins & Son v. Carrig

91 N.H. 459, 21 A.2d 591 (1941)

"In common understanding there is, importantly, a wide divergence between a bare promise and a promise in adjustment of a contractual promise already outstanding. A promise with no supporting consideration would upset well and long-established human interrelations if the law did not treat it as a vain thing. But parties to a valid contract generally understand that it is subject to any mutual action they may take in its performance. Changes to meet changes in circumstances and conditions should be valid if the law is to carry out its function and service by rules conformable with reasonable practices and understandings in matters of business and commerce."

———

McCallum Highlands, Ltd. v. Washington Capital Dus, Inc.

66 F.3d 89 (5th Cir. 1995)

Susman and McCallum Highlands had a loan commitment from Washington Capital for $7,015,000 at an interest rate of 9.75% with an option to lower the interest rate through a buy-down process. Susman intended to use the loan to prepay an outstanding loan with a significantly higher interest rate. The lender agreed to waive a substantial prepayment penalty if Susman refinanced by April 30, 1991. After the commitment was made, Fannie Mae, a federal agency, criticized another loan Washington Capital had made to Susman as too risky. One month before closing, Washington Capital told Susman it wanted to reduce the loan amount because of Fannie Mae's criticism, and "that they thought they could get out of the commitment through a loophole." Susman told Washington Capital he expected them to honor the commitment. To qualify under a Fannie Mae program, Susman had to formally select an interest rate by April 19. On April 18, Washington Capital told Susman that it would allow him to select an interest rate only if he would agree to accept a loan limited to $6,400,000 with no buy-down provision. Susman accepted these terms because he believed he needed to refinance the old loan to avoid bankruptcy. He later sued to avoid certain amended portions of the loan agreement, arguing that it was obtained by duress or that there was no consideration for the modification. The trial court granted Washington Capital's motion for summary judgment. Reversed.

The court began by explaining why the plaintiff could not establish economic duress under Texas law. The defendant's conduct was not economic duress, as Texas law defines it, because the defendants threat did not involve "an illegal exaction or a fraudulent deception" and because the plaintiff could not establish the defendant had created his financial predicament.

Turning to the issue of consideration, the court explained that the district court erred in treating the reduction in the loan amount as consideration for the modification. It explained that the plaintiff had not bargained for this. Finally the court held that consideration could not be found in the defendant giving up the right to assert its claim the loan commitment was not binding because of the absence of the evidence that this was honestly in dispute. The court then turned to the question of whether the modification was enforceable in the absence of consideration:

(Stewart, J.) "Because no bargained-for consideration was granted to Susman in exchange for his agreement to modify the loan commitment, the issue then becomes whether one of the exceptions to the requirement of new consideration applies. Parties can agree to first rescind an original agreement, and subsequently enter into a new one, thus avoiding the new-consideration requirement. *See Blaylock v. Akin*, 619 S.W.2d 207, 209 (Tex.Civ.App.—Texarkana, 1981, writ ref'd n.r.e.); *Crossland v. Nelson Auction Service, Inc.*, 424 S.W.2d 318, 319 (Tex.Civ.App.—Amarillo, 1967, writ ref'd n.r.e.). However, where an alleged rescission is coupled with a simultaneous re-entry into a new contract and the terms of that new contract are more favorable to only one of the parties, doubt is created as to the mutuality of the agreement to rescind the original contract. 3 Williston on Contracts § 7:37 (1992). Lurking beneath the surface in such cases is an implied threat by the promisor to withhold performance unless he receives the additional compensation or other changes he wants. *See id.* Moreover, this exception is based on circular logic because the validity of the new agreement depends upon the rescission while the validity of the rescission depends upon the new agreement. 1A Corbin on Contracts § 186 (1963). As a result, the validity of this exception to the preexisting duty rule has been questioned by a number of authorities. *See e.g.,* 3 Williston on Contracts § 7:37; 1A Corbin on Contracts § 186 (1963), Restatement (Second) of Contracts § 89 comment b (1981); John D. Calamari & Joseph M. Perillo, Contracts 206 (3d ed. 1987). Because the rescission of the original commitment occurred simultaneously with the creation of the amended loan agreement, and because the terms were more favorable to Washington than McCallum, the facts of this case place it neatly into the category of cases where this exception is most criticized.

"A more appropriate exception to the preexisting duty rule is presented in § 89 of the Restatement Second of Contracts:

> A promise modifying a duty under a contract not fully performed on either side is binding
>
> (a) if the modification is fair and equitable in view of circumstances not anticipated by the parties when the contract was made.

Restatement (Second) of Contracts § 89 (1981). Whether a modification is fair and equitable goes beyond absence of coercion and requires an objectively demonstrable reason for seeking a modification. *Id.* at § 89 cmt. b. The reason for modification must rest in circumstances not anticipated when the contract was made. *Id.* When such a reason is present, the relative financial strength of the parties, the formality with which the modification is made, the extent to which it is performed or relied on and other circumstances may be relevant to show or negate imposition or unfair surprise. *Id.*

"This exception to the requirement of new consideration for a modified contract is integrated into Texas law. *See Wiedeman v. Howell,* 276 S.W.2d 380, 383 (Tex.Civ.App.—Austin, 1955, writ ref'd n.r.e.); *Allied Chemical Corporation v. DeHaven,* 752 S.W.2d 155, 159 (Tex.App.—Houston [14 Dist.], 1988, writ denied). Fannie Mae's criticism of the earlier loan was such an unforeseen circumstance, but we conclude that, to use the language in the Restatement, the modification was not "fair and equitable" to McCallum."

———

UCC § 2–209

[See Selected Source Materials Supplement]

———

CISG ART. 29

[See Selected Source Materials Supplement]

NOTE ON THE CISG

In 1969, the United Nations Commission on International Trade Law (UNCITRAL) appointed a Working Group to prepare a new draft of an international convention (treaty) on the sale of goods. The United States was an active participant in the Working Group. The ultimate result was the Convention for the International Sale of Goods (the CISG), which was adopted in 1980, and came into force in 1988 when it had been ratified by the requisite ten countries. The CISG is binding only in those countries that have ratified it. As of 2012, the CISG had been ratified by seventy-eight countries, including the United States, Canada, China, France, Germany, and Mexico.

Although in form the CISG is an international treaty, in substance it is a code, much like Article 2 of the UCC. Article 2 governs contracts for the sale of goods between a seller and a buyer in the United States. The CISG governs contracts for the sale of goods (with certain exclusions, such as consumer goods) between a seller and a buyer who have their places of business in different countries, both of which have ratified the CISG. Accordingly, if, for example, a seller with its place of business in the United States enters into a contract for the sale of goods to a buyer with its place of business in France, then unless the parties otherwise provide, the contract is governed by the provisions of the CISG.

Like the UCC, the CISG does not govern the issue whether a contract is substantively valid; that is, it does not govern matters such as fraud, capacity, duress, mistake, legality, or the like. However, the CISG does govern whether a contract satisfies requisite formal requirements, such as whether a contract is required to be in writing, and also governs such matters as whether a contract was formed and whether a contract is sufficiently definite to be enforceable.

FOAKES V. BEER
In the House of Lords, 1884.
[1884] 9 App.Cas. 605.

[Dr. Foakes owed Julia Beer, £2090.19s. on a judgment. The parties entered into an agreement which, as interpreted by the Court of Appeal, provided that if Dr. Foakes would pay Mrs. Beer £500 at once, and the remainder of the principal in certain installments, Mrs. Beer would forgive the interest on the debt. This is a suit for the interest brought by Mrs. Beer against Dr. Foakes, alleging that if any agreement to forgive the interest

P's
claim

was in fact entered, it was without consideration, since the consideration consisted only in Dr. Foakes' doing what he was already bound to do in paying the principal of the debt. Decision in the Court of Appeal went for Mrs. Beer.]

W.H. HOLL Q.C. for the appellant:—Apart from the doctrine of Cumber v. Wane [that £5 cannot be satisfaction of £15] there is no reason in sense or law why the agreement should not be valid, and the creditor prevented from enforcing his judgment if the agreement is performed. It may be much more advantageous to the creditor to obtain immediate payment of part of his debt than to wait to enforce payment, or perhaps by pressing his debtor to force him into bankruptcy with the result of only a small dividend. Moreover if a composition is accepted friends, who would not otherwise do so, may be willing to come forward to assist the debtor. And if the creditor thinks that the acceptance of part is for his benefit who is to say it is not? ... It is every day practice for tradesmen to take less in satisfaction of a larger sum, and give discount, where there is neither custom nor right to take credit. ... It has often been held that a sheet of paper or a stick of sealing wax is a sufficient consideration. ... Here the agreement is not to take less than the debt, but to give time for payment of the whole without interest. Mankind have never acted on the doctrine of Cumber v. Wane, but the contrary; nay few are aware of it. By overruling it the House will only declare the universal practice to be good law as well as good sense.

D's claim:
there was
consid b/c
agreemnt
benefitted P

[EARL OF SELBORNE, L.C. Whatever may be the ultimate decision of this appeal the House is much indebted to Mr. Holl for his exceedingly able argument.]

BOMPAS Q.C. (Gaskell with him) for the respondent: ... There is a strong current of authority that what the law implies as a duty is no consideration. Therefore where a debt is due part payment is no reason for giving up the residue. The doctrine is too well settled to be now overthrown. ... It is contrary to public policy to make the performance of a legal duty a good consideration. ...

P's claim

EARL OF SELBORNE L.C.: ... [T]he question remains, whether the agreement is capable of being legally enforced. Not being under seal, it cannot be legally enforced against the respondent, unless she received consideration for it from the appellant, or unless, though without consideration, it operates by way of accord and satisfaction, so as to extinguish the claim for interest. What is the consideration? On the face of the agreement none is expressed, except a present payment of £500, on account and in part of the larger debt then due and payable by law under the judgment. The appellant did not contract to pay the future instalments of £150 each, at the time therein mentioned; much less did he give any new security, in the shape of negotiable paper, or in any other form. The promise de futuro was only that of the respondent, that if the half-yearly payments

Only the P
gave consid

of £150 each were regularly paid, she would "take no proceedings whatever on the judgment." . . .

The question, therefore, is nakedly raised by this appeal, whether your Lordships are now prepared, not only to overrule, as contrary to law, the doctrine stated by Sir Edward Coke to have been laid down by all the judges of the Common Pleas in Pinnel's Case [that payment of a lesser sum on the day cannot be a satisfaction of a greater sum] . . . but to treat a prospective agreement, not under seal, for satisfaction of a debt, by a series of payments on account to a total amount less than the whole debt, as binding in law, provided those payments are regularly made. . . . The doctrine itself, as laid down by Sir Edward Coke, may have been criticised, as questionable in principle, by some persons whose opinions are entitled to respect, but it has never been judicially overruled; on the contrary I think it has always, since the sixteenth century, been accepted as law. If so, I cannot think that your Lordships would do right, if you were now to reverse, as erroneous, a judgment of the Court of Appeal, proceeding upon a doctrine which has been accepted as part of the law of England for 280 years. . . .

. . . It might be (and indeed I think it would be) an improvement in our law, if a release or acquittance of the whole debt, on payment of any sum which the creditor might be content to receive by way of accord and satisfaction (though less than the whole), were held to be, generally, binding, though not under seal; nor should I be unwilling to see equal force given to a prospective agreement, like the present, in writing though not under seal; but I think it impossible, without refinements which practically alter the sense of the word, to treat such a release or acquittance as supported by any new consideration. . . .

My conclusion is, that the order appealed from should be affirmed, and the appeal dismissed, with costs, and I so move your Lordships.

LORD BLACKBURN. . . .

What principally weighs with me in thinking that Lord Coke made a mistake of fact is my conviction that all men of business, whether merchants or tradesmen, do every day recognise and act on the ground that prompt payment of a part of their demand may be more beneficial to them than it would be to insist on their rights and enforce payment of the whole. Even where the debtor is perfectly solvent, and sure to pay at last, this often is so. Where the credit of the debtor is doubtful it must be more so. I had persuaded myself that there was no such long-continued action on this dictum as to render it improper in this House to reconsider the question. I had written my reasons for so thinking; but as they were not satisfactory to the other noble and learned Lords who heard the case, I do not now repeat them nor persist in them.

I assent to the judgment proposed, though it is not that which I had originally thought proper. . . .

LORD FITZGERALD. . . . I concur . . . that it would have been wiser and better if the resolution in Pinnel's Case had never been come to. . . . [but we] find the law to have been accepted as stated for a great length of time, and I apprehend that it is not now within our province to overturn it. . . .

———

Sugarhouse Finance Co. v. Anderson

610 P.2d 1369 (Utah 1980)

In December 1976, Sugarhouse recovered a judgment against Anderson for $2,423.86, plus interest, costs, and attorneys' fees, on account of an unpaid promissory note. Anderson failed to satisfy the judgment, and in January 1979 Sugarhouse served Anderson with an order in supplemental proceedings to collect the judgment. Two days after receiving this order, Anderson met with Petty, Sugarhouse's president, to discuss an alternative to full payment of the judgment. Anderson informed Petty of the existence of numerous outstanding obligations against him, including medical expenses incurred pursuant to treatment for injuries sustained in an automobile accident in 1978. He asserted that he was contemplating bankruptcy, which would result in Sugarhouse's judgment being discharged. The parties finally settled on a figure of $2,200 in full satisfaction of Sugarhouse's claim. Anderson agreed to borrow money from a third party to enable him to pay the $2,200. Anderson then gave Petty a check for this amount, but asked him not to negotiate the check immediately because there was some uncertainty as to the sufficiency of funds in Anderson's account to cover the check. Two days later, Anderson called to inform Sugarhouse that there were sufficient funds in the account to cover the check. Sugarhouse responded that it did not intend on going through with the settlement, and returned the check. Thereafter, Anderson filed a motion asking the court to order Sugarhouse to comply with the terms of the settlement. Held, for Anderson.

(Hall, J.) ". . . Where . . . the underlying claim is liquidated and certain as to amount, separate consideration must be found to support [an] accord; otherwise, the obligor binds himself to do nothing he was not already obligated to do, and the obligee's promise to accept a substitute performance is unenforceable. The original obligation in the present case being of a definite and undisputed amount, the question presented is whether or not separate consideration was given to support the accord reached by the parties. . . .

"It is to be noted that, in the present case, plaintiff held a judgment which had been outstanding for more than two years. Pursuant to the parties' conversation of January 31, 1979, defendant agreed that, for a release of the judgment upon payment of a lesser agreed amount, he would negotiate a loan with a third party to enable him to pay off the substitute obligation immediately. A check was given for the agreed amount at the conclusion of that conversation, and authorization to cash it followed two days later. In effect, defendant had agreed to transfer the debt, represented by plaintiff's judgment to a third party, thereby immediately satisfying the obligation owed to plaintiff. This was something defendant had no legal obligation to do; by law, plaintiff could only move by levy of execution against property already owned by the defendant—plaintiff could not legally require defendant to incur additional obligations to satisfy the judgment. By so doing, defendant deliberately incurred the detriment of surrendering his right to limit plaintiff's ability to obtain satisfaction of the underlying judgment, and bestowed upon plaintiff the benefit of immediate payment by means of the incurrence of additional indebtedness. We hold such action to constitute sufficient consideration to support the accord negotiated by the parties.

"We note, in addition, that this jurisdiction recognizes the doctrine of promissory estoppel, whereby an individual who has made a promise which the individual should reasonably expect to induce action or forbearance on the part of the promisee or a third person and which does induce such action or forbearance is estopped to deny or repudiate the promise should the promisee or some third party suffer detriment thereby. We note that, in the present case, defendant agreed to incur additional indebtedness pursuant to the terms of the accord, in reliance on plaintiff's promise to accept immediate payment of a lesser amount in full satisfaction of the underlying obligation. As such, plaintiff should now be estopped to deny or reject the promise made."

FURTHER NOTE ON THE LEGAL-DUTY RULE

The area of consideration manifests the shift from classical to modern contract law in a number of ways. Classical contract law held that as a matter of principle only bargains had consideration—that is, were enforceable. In contrast, the modern rules are that a promise is enforceable where a party has relied on it, or where the promise is to pay for a past benefit that gives rise to a moral obligation to make compensation (see Chapter 2). A striking movement from in the area of consideration involves the legal-duty rule. In an elegant article, Aivazian, Trebilock, and Penny argue that a regime under which modifications are enforceable would be based on static considerations, while the legal-duty rule (or more precisely, a rule under which modifications are presumptively unenforceable) reflects dynamic considerations:

> The nature of the apparent analytical paradox presented by contract modifications can be stated briefly. . . . If [most modification situations occur in a context in which one party seeks to exploit bargaining power he has obtained during the course of the relationship] . . . then it might be argued that the law should attempt to discourage extortionary, coercive, opportunistic or monopolistic behaviour by refusing to enforce most modifications, perhaps by means of a presumption of invalidity. . . . On the other hand, especially in commercial contexts where most litigated modification cases seem to arise, it might be argued that parties would typically not enter into modifications unless they both felt better off as a result relative to the position that would or might have been obtained

without a modification. Hence, the law should respect the parties' assessment of what course of action best advances their joint welfare and enforce modifications, that is, apply a presumption of validity.

    . . . The paradox described above is the product of a tension between two competing sets of efficiency considerations, which in some cases require difficult trade-offs. . . . Static efficiency considerations will generally require that contract modifications be enforced on the grounds that the immediate contracting parties perceive mutual gains from recontracting that cannot, at the time modification is proposed, be realized as fully by any alternative strategy. On the other hand, dynamic efficiency considerations focus on the long-run incentives for contracting parties at large. . . . In the modification context, these dynamic efficiency considerations adopt an ex ante perspective, rather than the ex post perspective implicit in the static efficiency considerations. Adopting the former perspective, rules that impose no constraints on recontracting may increase the over-all costs of contracting by creating incentives for opportunistic behavior in cases where "holdup" possibilities arise during contract performance. . . . Thus, what is in the best interests of two particular contracting parties ex post contract formation when a modification is proposed and what is in the interests ex ante of contracting parties generally in terms of legally ordained incentives and constraints that minimize the over-all costs of contracting may lead to divergent policy perspectives.

Varouj A. Aivazian, et al., The Law of Contract Modifications: The Uncertain Quest for a Bench Mark of Enforceability, 22 Osgoode Hall L.J. 173, 174–75 (1984).

    The authors use the terms "static" and "dynamic" in an economic sense. By static efficiency they mean the immediate welfare gains to the parties from a welfare-enhancing exchange that is made possible by enforcement of a modification. By dynamic efficiency they mean the general social welfare gains that result from a policy of not enforcing modifications when the prospect that a contract may be modified to their disadvantage deters people from exchange transactions that would be welfare enhancing. For example, it is in the immediate interest of both a creditor and a debtor for a creditor to have the legal power to take partial payment of a debt as satisfaction of the full debt. Using legal process to collect a debt imposes significant harms on a debtor and involves non-trivial costs to a creditor. But it may not be in the long-term interest of creditors and debtors generally for creditors to have this power, if the increase in the risk of less than full payment of a debt deters people who could extend credit and people who need credit from credit transactions that would be welfare enhancing.

    The concern for dynamic efficiency identified by Aivazian et al. applies to exploitative modifications. A seemingly one-sided modification may not be exploitative. When A and B have entered into a contract, and A requests a modification, it is often the case that B accedes to A's request for a modification out of either reciprocity or the hope of reciprocity. For example, B may agree to a modification that favors A for the purpose of reciprocating for past modifications, of either the same or other contracts, that favored B. Or, B may agree to a modification that favors A because he believes his agreement will increase the probability that A will consent to future modifications in B's favor when B is in A's position, under the same or other contracts. Therefore, modifications that appear to be one sided if examined in isolation will often be reciprocal when account is taken of the dynamic ebb and flow of the contractual stream in which the modification is located.

Certainly these considerations cannot justify a blunt a rule like the pre-existing duty rule that is insensitive to the circumstances of a modification. They might justify something like the modern rules that enforce a modification when it is justified by changed circumstances and when the modification is not obtained by the use of coercion.

SECTION 4. DURESS AND THE EXPLOITATION OF DISTRESS

INTRODUCTORY NOTE

Contract law generally allows a person to use a contract to exploit an advantage they have over another person so long as the other person freely consents to the contract. Thus in *Batsakis v. Demotsis*, supra Section 1, Batsakis could demand whatever Demotsis would agree to pay to borrow drachmae so she could buy desperately needed food.

This Section concerns the doctrine of duress, which gives a person the power to avoid certain types of coercive bargains. The principal case, *Totem Marine*, involves a challenge to a release of a contract claim on the ground the defendant obtained the release by duress. The relevant factors in determining whether there was duress are: Did the defendant have a legitimate reason to threaten not to perform? Was the defendant's threat not to perform coercive? And did the plaintiff have a reasonable alternative to succumbing, in particular could the plaintiff have protected herself by obtaining performance from another source and suing for damages?

The rule applied in *Totem Marine* does not prevent a person from using a superior bargaining position to drive a hard bargain with a stranger. The hypothetical Case of the Desperate Traveler is such a case. The hypothetical is similar to *Post v. Jones*, which was decided under a special rule in the law of salvage in admiralty law.

RESTATEMENT, SECOND, CONTRACTS §§ 175, 176

[See Selected Source Materials Supplement]

———

TOTEM MARINE TUG & BARGE, INC. v. ALYESKA
PIPELINE SERVICE COMPANY

Supreme Court of Alaska, 1978.
584 P.2d 15.

BURKE, J.

This appeal arises from the superior court's granting of summary judgment in favor of defendants-appellees Alyeska Pipeline Services, et al., in a contract action brought by plaintiffs-appellants Totem Marine Tug & Barge, Inc., Pacific, Inc., and Richard Stair.

The following summary of events is derived from the materials submitted in the summary judgment proceedings below.

Totem is a closely held Alaska corporation which began operations in March of 1975. Richard Stair, at all times relevant to this case, was vice-president of Totem. In June of 1975, Totem entered into a contract with Alyeska under which Totem was to transport pipeline construction materials from Houston, Texas, to a designated port in southern Alaska, with the possibility of one or two cargo stops along the way. In order to carry out this contract, which was Totem's first, Totem chartered a barge (The "Marine Flasher") and an ocean-going tug (the "Kirt Chouest"). These charters and other initial operations costs were made possible by loans to Totem from Richard Stair individually and Pacific, Inc., a corporation of which Stair was principal stockholder and officer, as well as by guarantees by Stair and Pacific.

By the terms of the contract, Totem was to have completed performance by approximately August 15, 1975. From the start, however, there were numerous problems which impeded Totem's performance of the contract. For example, according to Totem, Alyeska represented that approximately 1,800 to 2,100 tons of regular uncoated pipe were to be loaded in Houston, and that perhaps another 6,000 or 7,000 tons of materials would be put on the barge at later stops along the west coast. Upon the arrival of the tug and barge in Houston, however, Totem found that about 6,700 to 7,200 tons of coated pipe, steel beams and valves, haphazardly and improperly piled, were in the yard to be loaded. This situation called for remodeling of the barge and extra cranes and stevedores, and resulted in the loading taking thirty days rather than the three days which Totem had anticipated it would take to load 2,000 tons. The lengthy loading period was also caused in part by Alyeska's delay in assuring Totem that it would pay for the additional expenses, bad weather and other administrative problems.

The difficulties continued after the tug and barge left Houston. It soon became apparent that the vessels were travelling more slowly than anticipated because of the extra load. In response to Alyeska's complaints and with its verbal consent, on August 13, 1975, Totem chartered a second tug, the "N. Joseph Guidry." When the "Guidry" reached the Panama Canal, however, Alyeska had not yet furnished the written amendment to the parties' contract. Afraid that Alyeska would not agree to cover the cost of the second tug, Stair notified the "Guidry" not to go through the Canal. After some discussions in which Alyeska complained of the delays and accused Totem of lying about the horsepower of the first tug, Alyeska executed the amendment on August 21, 1975.

By this time the "Guidry" had lost its preferred passage through the Canal and had to wait two or three additional days before it could go through. Upon finally meeting, the three vessels encountered the tail of a hurricane which lasted for about eight or nine days and which substantially impeded their progress.

The three vessels finally arrived in the vicinity of San Pedro, California, where Totem planned to change crews and refuel. On Alyeska's orders, however, the vessels instead pulled into port at Long Beach, California. At this point, Alyeska's agents commenced off-loading the barge, without Totem's consent, without the necessary load survey, and without a marine survey, the absence of which voided Totem's insurance. After much wrangling and some concessions by Alyeska, the freight was off-loaded. Thereafter, on or about September 14, 1975, Alyeska terminated the contract. Although there was talk by an Alyeska official of reinstating the contract, the termination was affirmed a few days later at a meeting at which Alyeska officials refused to give a reason for the termination.

Following termination of the contract, Totem submitted termination invoices to Alyeska and began pressing the latter for payment. The invoices came to something between $260,000 and $300,000. An official from Alyeska told Totem that they would look over the invoices but that they were not sure when payment would be made perhaps in a day or perhaps in six to eight months. Totem was in urgent need of cash as the invoices represented debts which the company had incurred on 10–30 day payment schedules. Totem's creditors were demanding payment and according to Stair, without immediate cash, Totem would go bankrupt. Totem then turned over the collection to its attorney, Roy Bell, directing him to advise Alyeska of Totem's financial straits. Thereafter, Bell met with Alyeska officials in Seattle, and after some negotiations, Totem received a settlement offer from Alyeska for $97,500. On November 6, 1975, Totem, through its president Stair, signed an agreement releasing Alyeska from all claims by Totem in exchange for $97,500.

On March 26, 1976, Totem, Richard Stair, and Pacific filed a complaint against Alyeska, which was subsequently amended. In the amended complaint, the plaintiffs sought to rescind the settlement and release on the ground of economic duress and to recover the balance allegedly due on the original contract. In addition, they alleged that Alyeska had wrongfully terminated the contract and sought miscellaneous other compensatory and punitive damages.

Before filing an answer, Alyeska moved for summary judgment against the plaintiffs on the ground that Totem had executed a binding release of all claims against Alyeska and that as a matter of law, Totem could not prevail on its claim of economic duress. In opposition, plaintiffs contended that the purported release was executed under duress in that Alyeska wrongfully terminated the contract; that Alyeska knew that Totem was faced with large debts and impending bankruptcy; that Alyeska withheld funds admittedly owed knowing the effect this would have on plaintiffs and that plaintiffs had no alternative but to involuntarily accept the $97,500 in order to avoid bankruptcy. Plaintiffs maintained that they had thus raised genuine issues of material fact such that trial was necessary, and that Alyeska was not entitled to judgment as a matter of law. Alyeska disputed the plaintiffs' assertions.

On November 30, 1976, the superior court granted the defendant's motion for summary judgment. This appeal followed. . .

II

As was noted above, a court's initial task in deciding motions for summary judgment is to determine whether there exist genuine issues of material fact. In order to decide whether such issues exist in this case, we must examine the doctrine allowing avoidance of a release on grounds of economic duress.

This court has not yet decided a case involving a claim of economic duress or what is also called business compulsion. At early common law, a contract could be avoided on the ground of duress only if a party could show that the agreement was entered into for fear of loss of life or limb, mayhem or imprisonment. 13 Williston on Contracts, § 1601 at 649 (3d ed. Jaeger 1970). The threat had to be such as to overcome the will of a person of ordinary firmness and courage. Id., § 1602 at 656. Subsequently, however, the concept has been broadened to include myriad forms of economic coercion which force a person to involuntarily enter into a particular transaction. The test has come to be whether the will of the person induced by the threat was overcome rather than that of a reasonably firm person. Id., § 1602 at 657.

At the outset it is helpful to acknowledge the various policy considerations which are involved in cases involving economic duress. Typically, those claiming such coercion are attempting to avoid the consequences of a modification of an original contract or of a settlement and release agreement. On the one hand, courts are reluctant to set aside agreements because of the notion of freedom of contract and because of the desirability of having private dispute resolutions be final. On the other hand, there is an increasing recognition of the law's role in correcting inequitable or unequal exchanges between parties of disproportionate bargaining power and a greater willingness to not enforce agreements which were entered into under coercive circumstances.

There are various statements of what constitutes economic duress, but as noted by one commentator, "The history of generalization in this field offers no great encouragement for those who seek to summarize results in any single formula." Dawson, Economic Duress An Essay in Perspective, 45 Mich.L.Rev. 253, 289 (1947). Section 492(b) of the Restatement of Contracts defines duress as:

> any wrongful threat of one person by words or other conduct that induces another to enter into a transaction under the influence of such fear as precludes him from exercising free will and judgment, if the threat was intended or should reasonably have been expected to operate as an inducement.

Professor Williston states the basic elements of economic duress in the following manner:

> 1. The party alleging economic duress must show that he has been the victim of a wrongful or unlawful act or threat, and

> 2. Such act or threat must be one which deprives the victim of his unfettered will.

13 Williston on Contracts, § 1617 at 704 (footnotes omitted).

Many courts state the test somewhat differently, eliminating use of the vague term "free will," but retaining the same basic idea. Under this standard, duress exists where: (1) one party involuntarily accepted the terms of another, (2) circumstances permitted no other alternative, and (3) such circumstances were the result of coercive acts of the other party. Undersea Engineering & Construction Co. v. International Telephone & Telegraph Corp., 429 F.2d 543, 550 (9th Cir. 1970); Urban Plumbing and Heating Co. v. United States, 408 F.2d 382, 389, 187 Ct.Cl. 15 (1969); W. R. Grimshaw Co. v. Nevil C. Withrow Co., 248 F.2d 896, 904 (8th Cir. 1957); Fruhauf Southwest Garment Co. v. United States, 111 F.Supp. 945, 951, 126 Ct.Cl. 51 (1953). The third element is further explained as follows:

> In order to substantiate the allegation of economic duress or business compulsion, the plaintiff must go beyond the mere

showing of reluctance to accept and of financial embarrassment. There must be a showing of acts on the part of the defendant which produced these two factors. The assertion of duress must be proven by evidence that the duress resulted from defendant's wrongful and oppressive conduct and not by the plaintiff's necessities.

W. R. Grimshaw Co., supra, 111 F.Supp. at 904.

As the above indicates, one essential element of economic duress is that the plaintiff show that the other party by wrongful acts or threats, intentionally caused him to involuntarily enter into a particular transaction. Courts have not attempted to define exactly what constitutes a wrongful or coercive act, as wrongfulness depends on the particular facts in each case. This requirement may be satisfied where the alleged wrongdoer's conduct is criminal or tortious but an act or threat may also be considered wrongful if it is wrongful in the moral sense. Restatement of Contracts, § 492, comment (g); Gerber v. First National Bank of Lincolnwood, 30 Ill.App.3d 776, 332 N.E.2d 615, 618 (1975); Fowler v. Mumford, 48 Del. 282, 9 Terry 282, 102 A.2d 535, 538 (Del.Supr.1954).

In many cases, a threat to breach a contract or to withhold payment of an admitted debt has constituted a wrongful act. Hartsville Oil Mill v. United States, 271 U.S. 43, 49, 46 S.Ct. 389, 391, 70 L.Ed. 822, 827 (1926); Austin Instrument, Inc. v. Loral Corp., 29 N.Y.2d 124, 324 N.Y.S.2d 22, 25, 272 N.E.2d 533, 535 (1971); Capps v. Georgia Pacific Corporation, 253 Or. 248, 453 P.2d 935 (1969); See also 13 Williston, supra, § 1616A at 701. Implicit in such cases is the additional requirement that the threat to breach the contract or withhold payment be done in bad faith. See Louisville Title Insurance Co. v. Surety Title & Guaranty Co., 60 Cal.App.3d 781, 132 Cal.Rptr. 63, 76, 79 (1976); Restatement (Second) of Contracts, § 318 comment (e).

Economic duress does not exist, however, merely because a person has been the victim of a wrongful act; in addition, the victim must have no choice but to agree to the other party's terms or face serious financial hardship. Thus, in order to avoid a contract, a party must also show that he had no reasonable alternative to agreeing to the other party's terms, or, as it is often stated, that he had no adequate remedy if the threat were to be carried out. First National Bank of Cincinnati v. Pepper, 454 F.2d 626, 632–33 (2d Cir. 1972); Austin Instrument, supra, 324 N.Y.S.2d at 25, 272 N.E.2d at 535; Capps, supra; Ross Systems v. Linden Dari-Delite, Inc., 35 N.J. 329, 173 A.2d 258, 261 (1961); Leeper v. Beltrami, 53 Cal.2d 195, 1 Cal.Rptr. 12, 19, 347 P.2d 12, 19 (1959); Tri-State Roofing Company of Uniontown v. Simon, 187 Pa.Super. 17, 142 A.2d 333, 335–36 (1958). What constitutes a reasonable alternative is a question of fact, depending on the circumstances of each case. An available legal remedy, such as an action for breach of contract, may provide such an alternative. First National Bank of Cincinnati, supra; Austin Instrument, supra; Tri-State Roofing, supra. Where one party wrongfully threatens to withhold goods, services or money from another unless certain demands are met, the availability on the market of similar goods and services or of other sources of funds may also provide an alternative to succumbing to the coercing party's demands. Austin Instrument, supra; Tri-State Roofing, supra. Generally, it has been said that "(t)he adequacy of the remedy is to be tested by a practical standard which takes into consideration the exigencies of the situation in which the alleged victim finds himself." Ross Systems, 173 A.2d at 262. See also First National Bank of Cincinnati, supra at 634; Dalzell, Duress By Economic Pressure I, 20 N. Carolina L.Rev. 237, 240 (1942).

An available alternative or remedy may not be adequate where the delay involved in pursuing that remedy would cause immediate and irreparable loss to one's economic or business interest. For example, in Austin Instrument, supra, and Gallagher Switchboard Corp. v. Heckler Electric Co., 36 Misc.2d 225, 232 N.Y.S.2d 590 (N.Y.Sup.Ct.1962), duress was found in the following circumstances: A subcontractor threatened to refuse further delivery under a contract unless the contractor agreed to modify the existing contract between the parties. The contractor was unable to obtain the necessary materials elsewhere without delay, and if it did not have the materials promptly, it would have been in default on its main contract with the government. In each case such default would have had grave economic consequences for the contractor and hence it agreed to the modifications. In both, the courts found that the alternatives to agreeing to the modification were inadequate (i.e., suing for breach of contract or obtaining the materials elsewhere) and that modifications therefore were signed under duress and voidable.

Professor Dalzell, in Duress By Economic Pressure II, 20 N. Carolina L.Rev. 340, 370 (1942), notes the following with regard to the adequacy of legal remedies where one party refuses to pay a contract claim:

> Nowadays, a wait of even a few weeks in collecting on a contract claim is sometimes serious or fatal for an enterprise at a crisis in its history. The business of a creditor in financial straits is at the mercy of an unscrupulous debtor, who need only suggest that if the creditor does not care to settle on the debtor's own hard terms, he can sue. This situation, in which promptness in payment is vastly more important than even approximate justice in the settlement terms, is too common in modern business relations to be ignored by society and the courts.

This view finds support in Capps v. Georgia Pacific Corporation, 253 Or. 248, 453 P.2d 935 (1969). There, the plaintiff was owed $157,000 as a commission for finding a lessee for defendant's property but in exchange for $5,000, the plaintiff signed a release of his claim against defendant. The plaintiff sued for the balance of the commission, alleging that the release had been executed under duress. His complaint, however, was dismissed. On appeal, the court held that the plaintiff had stated a claim where he alleged that he had accepted the grossly inadequate sum because he was in danger of immediately losing his home by mortgage foreclosure and other property by foreclosure and repossession if he did not obtain immediate funds from the defendant. One basis for its holding was found in the following quote by a leading commentator in the area of economic duress:

> The most that can be claimed (regarding the law of economic duress) is that change has been broadly toward acceptance of a general conclusion that in the absence of specific countervailing factors of policy or administrative feasibility, restitution is required of any excessive gain that results, in a bargain transaction, from impaired bargaining power, whether the impairment consists of economic necessity, mental or physical disability, or a wide disparity in knowledge or experience.

Dawson, Economic—Duress An Essay In Perspective, 45 Mich.L.Rev. 253, 289 (1947).[4]

III

Turning to the instant case, we believe that Totem's allegations, if proved, would support a finding that it executed a release of its contract claims against Alyeska under economic duress. Totem has alleged that Alyeska deliberately withheld payment of an acknowledged debt, knowing that Totem had no choice but to accept an inadequate sum in settlement of that debt; that Totem was faced with impending bankruptcy; that Totem was unable to meet its pressing debts other than by accepting the immediate cash payment offered by Alyeska; and that through necessity,

---

[4]   This court expressed a similar view in Inman v. Clyde Hall Drilling Company, 369 P.2d 498, 500 (Alaska 1962). In response to a claim that a contract provision was unconscionable, it was said:

> In the absence of a constitutional provision or statute which makes certain contracts illegal or unenforceable, we believe it is the function of the judiciary to allow men to manage their own affairs in their own way. As a matter of judicial policy the court should maintain and enforce contracts, rather than enable parties to escape from the obligations they have chosen to incur.

> We recognize that 'freedom of contract' is a qualified and not an absolute right, and cannot be applied on a strict, doctrinal basis. An established principle is that a court will not permit itself to be used as an instrument of inequity and injustice. . . . In determining whether certain contractual provisions should be enforced, the court must look realistically at the relative bargaining positions of the parties in the framework of contemporary business practices and commercial life. If we find those positions are such that one party has unscrupulously taken advantage of the economic necessities of the other, then in the interest of justice as a matter of public policy we would refuse to enforce the transaction. But the grounds for judicial interference must be clear. Whether the court should refuse to recognize and uphold that which the parties have agreed upon is a question of fact upon which evidence is required. (footnotes omitted).

Totem thus involuntarily accepted an inadequate settlement offer from Alyeska and executed a release of all claims under the contract. If the release was in fact executed under these circumstances,[5] we think that under the legal principles discussed above that this would constitute the type of wrongful conduct and lack of alternatives that would render the release voidable by Totem on the ground of economic duress. We would add that although Totem need not necessarily prove its allegation that Alyeska's termination of the contract was wrongful in order to sustain a claim of economic duress, the events leading to the termination would be probative as to whether Alyeska exerted any wrongful pressure on Totem and whether Alyeska wrongfully withheld payment from Totem.

One purpose of summary judgment, however, is to pierce the allegations in the pleadings in an effort to determine whether genuine issues of fact exist. As the moving party, Alyeska had the burden of showing that there were no such genuine issues and that it was entitled to judgment as a matter of law. E. g., Brock v. Rogers and Babler, Inc., 536 P.2d 778, 782 (Alaska 1975). Alyeska showed that Totem had executed the release, that Totem had been represented by counsel at the negotiating session leading to the settlement and release and that appellant Stair, who actually signed the release on behalf of Totem, was fully aware of the consequences of such a release. Such evidence, by itself, would have entitled Alyeska to summary judgment in its favor. As a matter of law, there is no doubt that a valid release of all claims arising under a contract will bar any subsequent claims based on that contract.

To avoid summary judgment once the moving party meets its burden, the non-moving party must produce competent evidence showing that there are issues of material fact to be tried. Id. The respondent must set forth specific facts showing that it could produce admissible evidence reasonably tending to dispute the movants evidence or establish an affirmative defense. Id. The court then must draw all reasonable inferences in favor of the non-moving party and against the movant. E. g., Clabaugh v. Bottcher, 545 P.2d 172, 175 n.5 (Alaska 1976).

. . . Our examination of the materials presented by Totem in opposition to Alyeska's motion for summary judgment leads us to conclude that Totem has made a sufficient factual showing as to each of the elements of economic duress to withstand that motion. There is no doubt that Alyeska disputes many of the factual allegations made by Totem[7] and drawing all

---

[5]   By way of clarification, we would note that Totem would not have to prove that Alyeska admitted to owing the precise sum Totem claimed it was owed upon termination of the contract but only that Alyeska acknowledged that it owed Totem approximately that amount which Totem sought.

[7]   For example, Alyeska has denied that it ever admitted to owing any particular sum to Totem and has disputed the truthfulness of Totem's assertions of impending bankruptcy. Other factual issues which remain unresolved include whether or not Alyeska knew of Totem's financial

inferences in favor of Totem, we believe that genuine issues of material fact exist in this case such that trial is necessary. Admittedly, Totem's showing was somewhat weak in that, for example, it did not produce the testimony of Roy Bell, the attorney who represented Totem in the negotiations leading to the settlement and release. At trial, it will probably be necessary for Totem to produce this evidence if it is to prevail on its claim of duress. However, a party opposing a motion for summary judgment need not produce all of the evidence it may have at its disposal but need only show that issues of material fact exist. 10 C. Wright and A. Miller, Federal Practice and Procedure: Civil, § 2727 at 546 (1973). Therefore, we hold that the superior court erred in granting summary judgment for appellees and remand the case to the superior court for trial in accordance with the legal principles set forth above. . . .

REVERSED and REMANDED.

UNIDROIT PRINCIPLES OF INTERNATIONAL COMMERCIAL CONTRACTS ART. 3.9

[See Selected Source Materials Supplement]

NOTE ON UNIDROIT

In 1971, the governing council of the International Institute for the Unification of Private Law determined to include in its program a codification of the law of contracts. To this end, a Working Group consisting of academics, judges, and civil servants was created in 1980. The members of the Working Group were of different nationalities, but sat in their personal capacities, not to express the views of their governments. The ultimate result was the Unidroit Principles of International Commercial Contracts, which was finalized in 1994. The goal of the Unidroit Principles is to set forth general rules for international commercial contracts. The Principles are intended to enunciate communal principles and rules of existing legal systems, and to select the solutions that are best adapted to the special requirements of international commercial contracts. In preparing the Principles, particular attention was paid to recent codifications of contract and commercial law, including the UCC, the Restatement Second of Contracts, the Netherlands Civil Code, the 1985 Foreign Economic Contract Law of the People's Republic of China, the Draft New Civil Code of Quebec, and the Convention for the International Sale of Goods.

---

situation after termination of the contract and whether Alyeska did in fact threaten by words or conduct to withhold payment unless Totem agreed to settle.

The Unidroit Principles are not intended for adoption by any country, and are not legally binding. Instead, they are a sort of international Restatement of Contract Law.

————

PRINCIPLES OF EUROPEAN CONTRACT LAW § 4.108

————

NOTE ON THE PRINCIPLES OF EUROPEAN CONTRACT LAW

The Principles of European Contract Law are the product of the Commission on European Contract Law, a body of lawyers drawn from all the member States of the European Union, under the chairmanship of Professor Ole Lando. The Principles are a response to a perceived need for a European Union-wide infrastructure of contract law. They are intended to reflect the common core of solutions to problems of contract law. In preparing the Principles, the Commission drew on a wide range of legal materials from both within and outside Europe, including the Uniform Commercial Code and the Restatements of Contracts and of Restitution. Some of the provisions in the Principles reflect suggestions and ideas that have not yet materialized in the law of the European Union States. See Introduction, Principles of European Contract Law, parts I and II (1999).

————

Andreini v. Hultgren

860 P.2d 916 (Utah 1993)

After undergoing surgery on his right knee at Holy Cross Hospital, Andreini began to experience a "pins and needles" sensation in both hands, which also exhibited noticeable atrophy. His surgeon, Dr. Beck, told Andreini his condition was probably the result of lying in bed or hereditary. Another physician, Dr. Nord, diagnosed the source to be compression paralysis. Nord reported his findings to Beck, who offered to perform corrective surgery, and to get Holy Cross Hospital to waive its charges and to allow Andreini to pay Beck's fee over time. A week before the scheduled operation a nurse told Andreini the compression paralysis may have resulted from improper strapping of his wrists during surgery. The second operation was unsuccessful. Andreini sued Beck and Holy Cross for medical malpractice. They moved for summary judgment based on a release signed by Andreini before the second operation. The trial court found that Andreini had released both parties from liability and, as a matter of law, had not signed the form under duress. Reversed.

(Zimmerman, J.) "On July 9th, Andreini arrived at Holy Cross Hospital and was prepared for surgery. At some point between one-half to one hour before surgery was to begin, a Holy Cross employee presented Andreini with a

release form and asked him to sign it. Andreini refused. The employee then
arranged to have Beck talk to Andreini by phone. Beck told Andreini that he
would not perform the surgery unless Andreini released both him and Holy
Cross from future liability. Although visibly upset, Andreini signed the form
and underwent the operation. The procedure was unsuccessful. Andreini has
lost most of the dexterity in his hands and cannot perform any activity that
requires grasping or holding. . . .

"Andreini argues that he has put into issue sufficient material facts to
raise a jury question as to whether Beck's threat not to perform the corrective
surgery was a breach of the duty of good faith and fair dealing and therefore
constituted an improper threat. He also argues that he has raised a jury
question as to whether he had any reasonable alternatives to signing the
release. By making these arguments, Andreini hopes to meet the requirements
established in sections 175(1) and 176(1)(d) of the Restatement, which would
allow him to void the release.

"We first consider if Andreini adduced sufficient material facts as to
whether defendants made an improper threat by breaching the duty of good
faith and fair dealing. Under section 176(1)(d) of the Restatement, the breach
of the duty of good faith and fair dealing must be "under a contract with the
recipient." Id. § 176 & cmt. e, illus. 8–10. Therefore, to find a breach of the duty
of good faith and fair dealing, there must be some type of preexisting
contractual relationship. This is consistent with our case law. See Peterson v.
Browning, 832 P.2d 1280, 1284 (Utah 1992); Beck v. Farmers Ins. Exch., 701
P.2d 795, 798 (Utah 1985); cf. Brehaney v. Nordstrom, Inc., 812 P.2d 49, 55
(Utah 1991). Andreini, however, does not explicitly allege that he and
defendants entered into a contract before he was presented with and later
signed the release. Consequently, Andreini may not rely on an alleged breach
of good faith and fair dealing to claim duress for the first time on appeal.

"However, Andreini does make an argument that, fairly construed,
appears to constitute an improper threat under section 176(2)(b) of the
Restatement. Under this provision, an improper threat may be found when (i)
"the resulting exchange is not on fair terms," and (ii) "the effectiveness of the
threat in inducing the manifestation of assent is significantly increased by
prior unfair dealing by the party making the threat." Restatement (Second) of
Contracts § 176(2)(b) (1979). Andreini argues that Beck improperly induced
him into signing the release by promising that the corrective surgery would
fully restore the use of his hands. He avers that prior to entering the hospital
for the corrective surgery, Beck told him that patients with similar injuries
had recovered 50% use within two weeks and 100% use within two months as
a result of surgery similar to that proposed. Andreini also points to language
in the release itself suggesting full recovery: "I, EUGENE R. ANDREINI, will
receive surgery to correct ulnar nerve palsy. . . . " (Emphasis added.) This
evidence is sufficient to establish the legal possibility that the "resulting
exchange"—defendants' unfulfilled promise to correct Andreini's injury
exchanged for Andreini's release of all claims against defendants—is "not on
fair terms" within the meaning of section 176(2) of the Restatement.

"However, to avoid summary judgment under section 176(2)(b)'s formulation of an "improper threat," there must also be sufficient evidence to raise a factual issue as to whether defendants had engaged in unfair dealing and whether this significantly increased the impropriety of their threat. Andreini argues that defendants acted in bad faith by promising him that the corrective surgery would result in his full recovery while neglecting to inform him until just prior to surgery that he would have to waive any claims he might have against them.

"Viewing the evidence in the light most favorable to Andreini, there is sufficient evidence to take this argument to the jury. We have already recited the evidence suggesting that defendants promised Andreini full recovery, and in Andreini's deposition, he testifies that he was not told until after he had been placed in a gown, shaved, and prepared for surgery that he would have to relinquish his rights. Andreini also testified that defendants were purposely noncommittal about the paralysis in his hands and its possible causes, even after Dr. Nord diagnosed his condition as compression paralysis. Moreover, Andreini averred that when he signed the release, his hands "were getting progressively worse" and "seemed to get worse each day." An expert affidavit submitted by Andreini indicates that time was, in fact, crucial to his recovery and suggests that Beck may have been aware that immediate surgery was necessary. Dr. Masud Seyal stated in the affidavit that "[a]fter the onset of Andreini's bilateral ulnar neuropathy, as diagnosed by R. David Beck, prompt surgical intervention was the recommended procedure" and the two-month delay "in performing the nerve transposition on July 9, 1987, likely denied Mr. Andreini a more substantial recovery." (Emphasis added.)

"Based on this evidence, a jury could find that defendants engaged in unfair dealing that significantly increased the effectiveness of their threat to refuse to undertake the corrective surgery. This conclusion is consistent with the Restatement's official commentary. Comment "f" states that section 176(2)(b) "is concerned with cases in which the party making the threat has by unfair dealing achieved an advantage over the recipient that makes his [or her] threat unusually effective. Typical examples involve manipulative conduct during the bargaining stage that leaves one person at the mercy of the other." Restatement (Second) of Contracts § 176 cmt. f (1979).

"Having determined that Andreini has adduced sufficient facts to raise a jury question as to whether defendants made an improper threat, we now consider if Andreini has mustered sufficient facts as to whether he had any reasonable alternatives to signing the release. Again, viewing the evidence in the light most favorable to Andreini, we think that a jury could find that Andreini had no reasonable alternatives under the attendant circumstances. See id. § 175 cmt. b. We acknowledge, as the trial court found, that Andreini could have left the hospital and that he was not in a life-threatening situation. However, there is evidence from which a jury could find that his alternatives were not reasonable. As mentioned earlier, Andreini averred that he was aware that his hands were getting progressively worse each day when he was confronted with the release and an expert affidavit suggests that immediate corrective surgery was indeed necessary to prevent further irreversible damage. When Andreini initially refused to sign the release, Beck allegedly told him that if he did not sign, Beck was "going to play hard ball" with him, which Andreini took to mean that defendants would not provide the corrective surgery regardless of who would pay for it. This evidence is sufficient to convince us that while Andreini may have had alternatives to signing the release form, there is a question of material fact as to whether those alternatives were reasonable."

———

Chouinard v. Chouinard

568 F.2d 430 (5th Cir.1978)

Arc Corporation was owned by Fred Chouinard; Fred's father, Al Chouinard; and Fred's twin brother, Ed Chouinard. Fred was the president and apparently ran the business. Over the years, the parties were in dispute concerning the precise nature of the ownership interests of Ed and Al. At one point, Ed concluded that he and Al each owned 37½ percent of Arc, and that the value of each of their interests was close to $500,000. These conclusions were not shared by Fred. In 1974, Arc got into substantial financial difficulties due in part to a bad decision by Fred, and needed new financing. Fred was able to obtain a financing commitment from the Heller Company, a commercial lender, but when Heller learned that Ed and Al each claimed a stock-ownership interest, Heller made it clear that it would not make a loan until the stock-ownership dispute was settled. Fred's attorney drafted a proposed agreement under which all parties would agree that Heller could make the loan, but no one would acknowledge anyone else's ownership claim. This proposal was apparently never put on the table, because the attorney for Ed and Al informed Fred's counsel that this was a good occasion to settle the ownership issue. Fred's counsel labeled that approach as blackmail, but Fred realized that the Heller loan was essential. Accordingly, he agreed to pay Ed and Al $95,000 each, mostly in the form of promissory notes, in exchange for releases by Ed and Al of all their claims to ownership in Arc. Fred then closed the loan with Heller and Arc obtained the needed funds. Subsequently, Fred brought suit to set the promissory notes aside. Held, for Ed and Al.

(Thornberry. J.) "While there is ample evidence of economic necessity and financial peril, neither the 'threat of considerable financial loss' nor 'impending bankruptcy' establish economic duress. Such economic stress must be attributable to the party against whom duress is alleged. 'Mere hard bargaining positions, if lawful, and the press of financial circumstances, not caused by the [party against whom the contract is sought to be voided], will not be deemed duress.' Business Incentives Co. v. Sony Corp. of America, 397 F.Supp. 63, 69 (S.D.N.Y.1975).

"The only possible claim of duress is that Ed and Al, recognizing the weakened state of the company, seized that opportunity to settle the long-standing dispute regarding stock-ownership. Because duress may not be implied merely from the making of a hard bargain, the question becomes whether the conduct of Ed and Al was wrongful. The law in Georgia and other jurisdictions makes clear that it was not, for the two men were merely asserting a legal right, *i.e.*, their right to a certain share of the stock in the company. *See* Causey v. Matson, 215 Ga. 306, 110 S.E.2d 356 (1959); Williams v. Ruben, 216 Ga. 431, 117 S.E.2d 456 (1960). Fred admitted that Ed and Al were stockholders in the company, and the long-standing dispute was over the percentage of the company each owned. Thus, while there is no doubt that Fred was between the proverbial rock and a hard place, it is clear that his own actions put him there and that Ed and Al merely took advantage of the situation to insist upon settlement of the intrafamilial stock squabble. . . .

"We conclude, therefore, that there is simply no duress shown on this record, for one crucial element is missing: a wrongful act by the defendants to create and take advantage of an untenable situation. Ed and Al had nothing to do with the financial quagmire in which Fred found himself, and we cannot find duress simply because they refused to throw him a rope free of any 'strings.' "

———

Post v. Jones

60 U.S. (19 How.) 150, 15 L.Ed. 618 (1856)

The whaling vessel Richmond, with a nearly full cargo of whale oil, was inextricably run aground in a deserted area 5,000 miles from the nearest port of safety. Several days later, the whaling vessels Elizabeth Frith, Panama, and Junior came into the vicinity. These vessels did not have full cargoes, but the Richmond had more whale oil than the three vessels could take. At the instance of the Junior's captain, the Richmond's captain agreed to hold an auction for its oil. The Frith's captain bid $1 per barrel for as much as he needed, and the captains of the Panama and the Junior bid 75› per barrel. The three vessels took enough of the Richmond's oil to complete their cargoes, and returned to port with the oil and the Richmond's crew. The Richmond's owners then brought this action to recover part of the value of the oil taken by the Frith and the Panama, on the theory that while these vessels were entitled to salvage (a maritime concept under which one who saves property is entitled to a reward) for the oil they took, they were not entitled to keep the oil at the auction price. Held, for the owners of the Richmond.

(Grier, J.) "The contrivance of an auction sale, under such circumstances, where the master of the Richmond was hopeless, helpless, and passive—where there was no market, no money, no competition—where one party had absolute power, and the other no choice but submission where the vendor must take what is offered or get nothing—is a transaction which has no characteristic of a valid contract. It has been contended by the claimants that it would be a great hardship to treat this sale as a nullity, and thus compel them to assume the character of Salvors, because they were not bound to save this property, especially at so great a distance from any port of safety, and in a place where they could have completed their cargo in a short time from their own catchings, and where salvage would be no compensation for the loss of this opportunity. The force of these arguments is fully appreciated, but we think they are not fully sustained by the facts of the case. Whales may have been plenty around their vessels on the 6th and 7th of August, but, judging of the future from the past, the anticipation of filling up their cargo in the few days of the season in which it would be safe to remain, was very uncertain, and barely probable. The whales were retreating towards the North Pole, where they could not be pursued, and, though seen in numbers on one day, they would disappear on the next; and, even when seen in greatest numbers, their capture was uncertain. By this transaction, the vessels were enabled to proceed at once on their home voyage; and the certainty of a liberal salvage allowance for the property rescued will be ample compensation for the possible chance of greater profits, by refusing their assistance in saving their neighbor's property.

"It has been contended, also, that the sale was justifiable and valid, because it was better for the interests of all concerned to accept what was offered, than suffer a total loss. But this argument proves too much, as it would justify every sale to a salvor. Courts of admiralty will enforce contracts made for salvage service and salvage compensation, where the salvor has not taken advantage of his power to make an unreasonable bargain; but they will not tolerate the doctrine that a salvor can take the advantage of his situation, and avail himself of the calamities of others to drive a bargain; nor will they permit the performance of a public duty to be turned into a traffic of profit."

———

EISENBERG, THE BARGAIN PRINCIPLE AND ITS LIMITS
95 Harvard Law Review 741 (1982).

Suppose that A makes a bargain with B at a time when, through no fault of B, A is in a state of necessity that effectively compels him to enter into a bargain on any terms he can get—a condition that I shall refer to as distress. . . . [Take the following example:]

The Desperate Traveler. T, a symphony musician, has been driving through the desert on a recreational trip, when he suddenly hits a rock jutting out from the sand. T's vehicle is disabled and his ankle is fractured. He has no radio and little water, and will die if he is not soon rescued. The next day, G, a university geologist who is returning to Tucson from an inspection of desert rock formations, adventitiously passes within sight of the accident and drives over to investigate. T explains the situation and asks G to take him back to Tucson, which is sixty miles away. G replies that he will help only if T promises to pay him two-thirds of his wealth or $100,000, whichever is more. T agrees, but after they return to Tucson he refuses to keep his promise, and *G* brings an action to enforce it.

Under traditional contract doctrines, *T*'s promise would be enforceable to its full extent. He has made a bargain, and none of the orthodox contract defenses apply. The defense of duress might seem apposite, but traditionally that defense has required not only that the promisor was in distress, but that he was put in distress by a wrongful act or threat of the promisee. *G* did not put *T* in distress, and because the common law imposes no duty on strangers to rescue persons in distress even when life is at stake, *G*'s threat of refusing aid would probably not constitute a wrongful act within the meaning of this rule.

It seems clear, however, that [*T*'s promise, extracted through *G*'s distress,] should not be enforced to its full extent. Neither fairness nor efficiency, the two major props of the bargain principle, supports its application in such a case. In terms of fairness, our society posits, as part of its moral order, some degree of concern for others. In *The Desperate Traveler, G* has acted wrongly in treating *T* as simply an economic object.

The efficiency argument also fails. When a commodity is sold under perfect competition, the doctrine of distress would usually have no application, even to contracts for necessities. A sale at a perfectly competitive price would normally not be regarded as exploitive, because the price is generated by a mechanism that is conventionally regarded as fair, and normally equals the seller's opportunity cost and approximates the seller's marginal cost. Furthermore, traditional economic analysis suggests that such a price normally allocates supply to its highest-valued uses and encourages the appropriate amount of investment in productive capacity. *G*, however, is not a perfect competitor, but a monopolist. Full enforcement of promises like that made by *T* is not required to move rescue services to their highest-valued uses, and would have no measurable effect on the allocation of resources to rescue-capacity, since the rescue is adventitious, there are no other bidders for the rescue services at the time of the rescue, and prior to the accident there was no market on which the victim could have purchased a contingent contract to rescue. Indeed, there is an argument that full enforcement would be inefficient. If it were known that persons in distress could be required to pay the price demanded for adventitious rescue, however high, people either might be reluctant to engage in activity in which rescue is sometimes necessary or might spend on precautions an aggregate amount exceeding the cost of adventitious rescue.

 ... [O]ther mature legal systems ... allow the courts to review bargains made under distress for fairness of terms. For example, section 138(2) of the German Civil Code provides that a transaction is void "when a person [exploits] the distressed situation, inexperience, lack of judgmental ability, or grave weakness of will of another to obtain the grant or promise of pecuniary advantages ... which are obviously disproportionate to the performance given in return." French law is in accord. At home, it is well established in admiralty law that a contract for salvage services—that is, a contract to rescue a vessel or its cargo—is reviewable for fairness of terms if entered into while the promisor is in distress. . . . [as evidenced] in *Post v. Jones*. . . .

This . . . leaves open how to measure the promisee's recovery in such cases. Financial cost is one possibility. Such a solution, however, would often fail to recognize adequately the benefit conferred upon the promisor. Furthermore, a financial-cost rule might not provide a sufficient incentive to act. In *The Desperate Traveler,* for example, G's financial cost is close to zero. Assuming G is under no legal duty to rescue T, he would have no economic incentive to perform the rescue if his recovery were limited to financial cost. The need for an economic incentive in such cases should not be overemphasized; most individuals in G's position would be likely to rescue T whether they had an economic incentive to do so or not. Nevertheless, an economic incentive would probably be helpful at the margin. Admiralty again suggests a solution. Although it will not enforce unfair rescue contracts, it does provide ample compensation for rescuers under the principle of salvage. Recovery under this principle is viewed both as a reward and as an inducement. Accordingly, in measuring recovery the courts take into account the degree of danger to the rescued property; the value of the rescued property; the risk incurred by the salvors; their promptness, skill, and energy; the value of the property the salvor employed; the degree of danger to that property; and the salvor's time and labor. In more general terms, the recovery in distress cases involving an adventitious rescuer should not only compensate the promisee for all costs, tangible and intangible, but should also include a generous bonus to provide a clear incentive for action and compensation for the benefit conferred. Recovery measured in this way admits of no great precision, but that is not fatal in situations in which, by hypothesis, planning is not important. The viability of this approach is evidenced by the fact that it has stood the test of time in an area in which distress and adventitious rescue are common occurrences.

SECTION 5. UNCONSCIONABILITY AND PRICE GOUGING

WILLIAMS V. WALKER-THOMAS FURNITURE CO.

United States Court of Appeals, District of Columbia Circuit, 1965.
121 U.S.App.D.C. 315, 350 F.2d 445.

J. SKELLY WRIGHT, CIRCUIT JUDGE. Appellee, Walker-Thomas Furniture Company, operates a retail furniture store in the District of Columbia. During the period from 1957 to 1962 each appellant in these cases purchased a number of household items from Walker-Thomas, for which payment was to be made in installments. The terms of each purchase were contained in a printed form contract which set forth the value of the purchased item and purported to lease the item to appellant for a stipulated monthly rent payment. The contract then provided, in substance, that title would remain in Walker-Thomas until the total of all the monthly payments made equaled the stated value of the item, at which time appellants could take title. In the event of a default in the payment of any monthly installment, Walker-Thomas could repossess the item.

The contract further provided that "the amount of each periodical installment payment to be made by [purchaser] to the Company under this present lease shall be inclusive of and not in addition to the amount of each installment payment to be made by [purchaser] under such prior leases, bills or accounts; *and all payments now and hereafter made by [purchaser] shall be credited pro rata on all outstanding leases, bills and accounts* due the Company by [purchaser] at the time each such payment is made." (Emphasis added.) The effect of this rather obscure provision was to keep a balance due on every item purchased until the balance due on all items, whenever purchased, was liquidated. As a result, the debt incurred at the time of purchase of each item was secured by the right to repossess all the items previously purchased by the same purchaser, and each new item purchased automatically became subject to a security interest arising out of the previous dealings.

On May 12, 1962, appellant Thorne purchased an item described as a Daveno, three tables, and two lamps, having total stated value of $391.10. Shortly thereafter, he defaulted on his monthly payments and appellee sought to replevy all the items purchased since the first transaction in 1958. Similarly, on April 17, 1962, appellant Williams bought a stereo set of stated value of $514.95.[1] She too defaulted shortly thereafter, and appellee sought to replevy all the items purchased since December, 1957. The Court of General Sessions granted judgment for appellee. The District

---

[1]   At the time of this purchase her account showed a balance of $164 still owing from her prior purchases. The total of all the purchases made over the years in question came to $1,800. The total payments amounted to $1,400.

of Columbia Court of Appeals affirmed, and we granted appellants' motion
for leave to appeal to this court.

Appellants' principal contention, rejected by both the trial and the
appellate courts below, is that these contracts, or at least some of them, are
unconscionable and, hence, not enforceable. In its opinion in Williams v.
Walker-Thomas Furniture Company, 198 A.2d 914, 916 (1964), the District
of Columbia Court of Appeals explained its rejection of this contention as
follows:

> "Appellant's second argument presents a more serious
> question. The record reveals that prior to the last purchase
> appellant had reduced the balance in her account to $164. The last
> purchase, a stereo set, raised the balance due to $678.
> Significantly, at the time of this and the preceding purchases,
> appellee was aware of appellant's financial position. The reverse
> side of the stereo contract listed the name of appellant's social
> worker and her $218 monthly stipend from the government.
> Nevertheless, with full knowledge that appellant had to feed,
> clothe and support both herself and seven children on this
> amount, appellee sold her a $514 stereo set.

> "We cannot condemn too strongly appellee's conduct. It raises
> serious questions of sharp practice and irresponsible business
> dealings. A review of the legislation in the District of Columbia
> affecting retail sales and the pertinent decisions of the highest
> court in this jurisdiction disclose, however, no ground upon which
> this court can declare the contracts in question contrary to public
> policy. We note that were the Maryland Retail Installment Sales
> Act, Art. 83 §§ 128–153, or its equivalent, in force in the District
> of Columbia, we could grant appellant appropriate relief. We
> think Congress should consider corrective legislation to protect
> the public from such exploitive contracts as were utilized in the
> case at bar."

We do not agree that the court lacked the power to refuse enforcement
to contracts found to be unconscionable. In other jurisdictions, it has been
held as a matter of common law that unconscionable contracts are not
enforceable.[2] While no decision of this court so holding has been found, the
notion that an unconscionable bargain should not be given full enforcement
is by no means novel. In Scott v. United States, 79 U.S. (12 Wall.) 443, 445,
20 L.Ed. 438 (1870), the Supreme Court stated:

> " . . . If a contract be unreasonable and unconscionable, but
> not void for fraud, a court of law will give to the party who sues

---

[2] Campbell Soup Co. v. Wentz, 3 Cir., 172 F.2d 80 (1948); Indianapolis Morris Plan
Corporation v. Sparks, 132 Ind.App. 145, 172 N.E.2d 899 (1961); Henningsen v. Bloomfield Motors,
Inc., 32 N.J. 358, 161 A.2d 69, 84–96, 75 A.L.R.2d 1 (1960). Cf. 1 Corbin, Contracts § 128 (1963).

for its breach damages, not according to its letter, but only such as he is equitably entitled to. . . . "[3]

Since we have never adopted or rejected such a rule, the question here presented is actually one of first impression.

Congress has recently enacted the Uniform Commercial Code, which specifically provides that the court may refuse to enforce a contract which it finds to be unconscionable at the time it was made. 28 D.C.Code § 2–302 (Supp. IV 1965). The enactment of this section, which occurred subsequent to the contracts here in suit, does not mean that the common law of the District of Columbia was otherwise at the time of enactment, nor does it preclude the court from adopting a similar rule in the exercise of its powers to develop the common law for the District of Columbia. In fact, in view of the absence of prior authority on the point, we consider the congressional adoption of § 2–302 persuasive authority for following the rationale of the cases from which the section is explicitly derived.[2] Accordingly, we hold that where the element of unconscionability is present at the time a contract is made, the contract should not be enforced.

Unconscionability has generally been recognized to include an absence of meaningful choice on the part of one of the parties together with contract terms which are unreasonably favorable to the other party.[6] Whether a meaningful choice is present in a particular case can only be determined by consideration of all the circumstances surrounding the transaction. In many cases the meaningfulness of the choice is negated by a gross inequality of bargaining power.[7] The manner in which the contract was entered is also relevant to this consideration. Did each party to the contract, considering his obvious education or lack of it, have a reasonable

---

[3] See Luing v. Peterson, 143 Minn. 6, 172 N.W. 692 (1919); Greer v. Tweed, N.Y.C.P., 13 Abb.Pr., N.S., 427 (1872); Schnell v. Nell, 17 Ind. 29 (1861); and see generally the discussion of the English authorities in Hume v. United States, 132 U.S. 406, 10 S.Ct. 134, 33 L.Ed. 393 (1889).

[2] See Comment, § 2–302, Uniform Commercial Code (1962). Compare Note, 45 Va.L.Rev. 583, 590 (1959), where it is predicted that the rule of § 2–302 will be followed by analogy in cases which involve contracts not specifically covered by the section. Cf. 1 State of New York Law Revision Commission, Report and Record of Hearings on the Uniform Commercial Code 108–110 (1954) (remarks of Professor Llewellyn).

[6] See Henningsen v. Bloomfield Motors, Inc., supra Note 2; Campbell Soup Co. v. Wentz, supra Note 2.

[7] See Henningsen v. Bloomfield Motors, Inc., supra Note 2, 161 A.2d at 86, and authorities there cited. Inquiry into the relative bargaining power of the two parties is not an inquiry wholly divorced from the general question of unconscionability, since a one-sided bargain is itself evidence of the inequality of the bargaining parties. This fact was vaguely recognized in the common law doctrine of intrinsic fraud, that is, fraud which can be presumed from the grossly unfair nature of the terms of the contract. See the oft-quoted statement of Lord Hardwicke in Earl of Chesterfield v. Janssen, 28 Eng.Rep. 82, 100 (1751):

"... [Fraud] may be apparent from the intrinsic nature and subject of the bargain itself; such as no man in his senses and not under delusion would make. ... "

And cf. Hume v. United States, supra Note 3, 132 U.S. at 413, 10 S.Ct. at 137, where the Court characterized the English cases as "cases in which one party took advantage of the other's ignorance of arithmetic to impose upon him, and the fraud was apparent from the face of the contracts." See also Greer v. Tweed, supra Note 3.

opportunity to understand the terms of the contract, or were the important terms hidden in a maze of fine print and minimized by deceptive sales practices? Ordinarily, one who signs an agreement without full knowledge of its terms might be held to assume the risk that he has entered a one-sided bargain.[8] But when a party of little bargaining power, and hence little real choice, signs a commercially unreasonable contract with little or no knowledge of its terms, it is hardly likely that his consent, or even an objective manifestation of his consent, was ever given to all the terms. In such a case the usual rule that the terms of the agreement are not to be questioned[9] should be abandoned and the court should consider whether the terms of the contract are so unfair that enforcement should be withheld.[10]

In determining reasonableness or fairness, the primary concern must be with the terms of the contract considered in light of the circumstances existing when the contract was made. The test is not simple, nor can it be mechanically applied. The terms are to be considered "in the light of the general commercial background and the commercial needs of the particular trade or case."[11] Corbin suggests the test as being whether the terms are "so extreme as to appear unconscionable according to the mores and business practices of the time and place." 1 Corbin, op. cit. supra Note 2.[12] We think this formulation correctly states the test to be applied in those cases where no meaningful choice was exercised upon entering the contract.

Because the trial court and the appellate court did not feel that enforcement could be refused, no findings were made on the possible unconscionability of the contracts in these cases. Since the record is not sufficient for our deciding the issue as a matter of law, the cases must be remanded to the trial court for further proceedings.

---

[8] See Restatement, Contracts § 70 (1932); Note, 63 Harv.L.Rev. 494 (1950). See also Daley v. People's Building, Loan & Savings Ass'n, 178 Mass. 13, 59 N.E. 452, 453 (1901), in which Mr. Justice Holmes, while sitting on the Supreme Judicial Court of Massachusetts, made this observation:

" . . . Courts are less and less disposed to interfere with parties making such contracts as they choose, so long as they interfere with no one's welfare but their own. . . . It will be understood that we are speaking of parties standing in an equal position where neither has any oppressive advantage or power. . . . "

[9] This rule has never been without exception. In cases involving merely the transfer of unequal amounts of the same commodity, the courts have held the bargain unenforceable for the reason that "in such a case, it is clear, that the law cannot indulge in the presumption of equivalence between the consideration and the promise." 1 Williston, Contracts § 115 (3d ed. 1957).

[10] See the general discussion of "Boiler-Plate Agreements" in Llewellyn, The Common Law Tradition 362–371 (1960).

[11] Comment, Uniform Commercial Code [§ 2–302].

[12] See Henningsen v. Bloomfield Motors, Inc., supra Note 2; Mandel v. Liebman, 303 N.Y. 88, 100 N.E.2d 149 (1951). The traditional test as stated in Greer v. Tweed, supra Note 3, 13 Abb.Pr., N.S., at 429, is "such as no man in his senses and not under delusion would make on the one hand, and as no honest or fair man would accept, on the other."

So ordered.

DANAHER, CIRCUIT JUDGE (dissenting):

The District of Columbia Court of Appeals obviously was as unhappy about the situation here presented as any of us can possibly be. Its opinion in the *Williams* case, quoted in the majority text, concludes: "We think Congress should consider corrective legislation to protect the public from such exploitive contracts as were utilized in the case at bar."

My view is thus summed up by an able court which made no finding that there had actually been sharp practice. Rather the appellant seems to have known precisely where she stood.

There are many aspects of public policy here involved. What is a luxury to some may seem an outright necessity to others. Is public oversight to be required of the expenditures of relief funds? A washing machine, e.g., in the hands of a relief client might become a fruitful source of income. Many relief clients may well need credit, and certain business establishments will take long chances on the sale of items, expecting their pricing policies will afford a degree of protection commensurate with the risk. Perhaps a remedy when necessary will be found within the provisions of the "Loan Shark" law, D.C.Code § § 26–601 et seq. (1961).

I mention such matters only to emphasize the desirability of a cautious approach to any such problem, particularly since the law for so long has allowed parties such great latitude in making their own contracts. I dare say there must annually be thousands upon thousands of installment credit transactions in this jurisdiction, and one can only speculate as to the effect the decision in these cases will have.

I join the District of Columbia Court of Appeals in its disposition of the issues.

NOTE ON WILLIAMS V. WALKER-THOMAS

A number of states have adopted statutes that prohibit the type of provision that was at issue in *Williams v. Walker-Thomas*. After the decision in that case, the District of Columbia adopted such a statute, D.C. Code § 28–3805(a):

> If debts arising from two or more consumer credit sales other than sales pursuant to a revolving charge account . . . are secured by cross-collateral, or consolidated into one debt payable on a single schedule of payments, and the debt is secured by security interests taken with respect to one or more of the sales, payments received by the seller after the taking of the cross-collateral or the consolidation are deemed, for the purpose of determining the amount of the debt

secured by the various security interests, to have been first applied to the payment of the debts arising from the sales first made. To the extent debts are paid according to this section, security interests in items of property terminate as the debts originally incurred with respect to each item are paid.

———

Skilton & Helstad, Protection of the Installment Buyer of Goods Under the Uniform Commercial Code

65 Mich.L.Rev. 1465, 1476–81

"It appeared that from 1957 to 1962 Ora Lee Williams had made sixteen separate purchases of furniture and household appliances from the store, all on installment credit, and in each case had signed fine print bailment-lease contracts which provided for monthly rental payments and reserved title in the store until payment was made in full. Most of these purchases were made when a representative of the store came to her home. . . .

" . . . The seller maintained that it still had title to everything because, under the pro rata clause, a balance remained due on each item, despite Ora's payments of over $1,000. The store's records showed that of a combined total claim of $444 as of December 26, 1962, Ora still owed 25 cents on item 1, purchased December 23, 1957 (price $45.65); 3 cents on item 2, purchased December 31, 1957 (price $13.21); $2.34 on item 3, purchased August 12, 1958 (price $127.40); and similarly for subsequent purchases, with balances of $.96, $1.70, $2.86, $1.08, $7.21, $1.53, $2.38, $5.66, $10.32, and $1.61. The only claims which were significant in relation to the purchase price were for the last three purchases: an item for $254.95, on which a balance of $65.98 was claimed; the $514.95 stereo, on which a balance of $327.89 was claimed; and an item for $15.45, on which a balance of $12.60 was claimed. . . .

"Was there anything inherently wrong about what the seller did in Williams? Forget for the nonce that he was dealing with an impoverished buyer who asserted that she did not understand the pro rata plan and would not have bought the stereo had she known that the seller would continue to tie up all of her previous purchases. Is there any difference between this case and a case in which, to induce a loan or a credit sale, a person agrees to give the creditor a security interest in most of his personal property which he owns outright? Or in which he gives his creditor a security interest in all such property to secure the balance of a consolidated indebtedness? Is it simply the indirectness of what was done that raises questions? . . .

"The appellants in *Williams* . . . argued that to allow the store to utilize the pro-rata clause to enforce its claim upon so much of appellants' household goods would, in effect, subvert the policy of the statutes of the District of Columbia exempting household goods from attachment. Of course, the statutes on their face do not prevent creditors from taking security interests in such goods and then seizing them on default, but the point nevertheless has merit:

if our exemption statutes are to accomplish their patent purpose of protecting debtors from complete impoverishment as a result of creditor action, their provisions should be correlated with statutory provisions restricting the use of such property as security in certain kinds of transactions. . . ."

———

RESTATEMENT CONTRACTS, SECOND § 208

[See Selected Source Materials Supplement]

———

UCC § 2–302

[See Selected Source Materials Supplement]

———

UNIFORM CONSUMER CREDIT CODE §§ 1.301, 5.108

[See Selected Source Materials Supplement]

———

UNIDROIT PRINCIPLES OF INTERNATIONAL COMMERCIAL CONTRACTS ART. 3.10

[See Selected Source Materials Supplement]

———

PRINCIPLES OF EUROPEAN CONTRACT LAW §§ 4.109, 4.110

[See Selected Source Materials Supplement]

———

COMMISSION OF THE EUROPEAN COMMUNITIES, COUNCIL DIRECTIVE 93/13/EEC

[See Selected Source Materials Supplement]

———

MAXWELL v. FIDELITY FINANCIAL SERVICES, INC.

Supreme Court of Arizona, En Banc, 1995.
184 Ariz. 82, 907 P.2d 51.

FELDMAN, CHIEF JUSTICE.

Elizabeth Maxwell petitions us to review a court of appeals opinion affirming a trial court ruling that the doctrine of novation barred Maxwell's claim that a contract was unconscionable and therefore unenforceable. See Maxwell v. Fidelity Fin. Servs., Inc., 179 Ariz. 544, 880 P.2d 1090 (Ct.App.1993). We granted review . . .

FACTS AND PROCEDURAL HISTORY

The facts, taken in the light most favorable to Maxwell, against whom summary judgment was granted, are that in December 1984, Elizabeth Maxwell and her then husband, Charles, were approached by Steve Lasica, a door-to-door salesman representing the now defunct National Solar Corporation (National). Lasica sold the Maxwells a solar home water heater for a total purchase price of $6,512. Although National was responsible for installation, the unit was never installed properly, never functioned properly, and was eventually declared a hazard, condemned, and ordered disconnected by the City of Phoenix. Thus, although the unit may have been intrinsically worthless, the question of unconscionability is determined as of the time the contract was made. A.R.S. § 47–2302. [U.C.C. § 2–302].

Financing for the purchase was accomplished through a loan to the Maxwells from Fidelity Financial Services, Inc. (Fidelity). The sale price was financed for a ten-year period at 19.5 percent interest, making the total cost nearly $15,000.

At the time of the transaction, Elizabeth Maxwell earned approximately $400 per month working part-time as a hotel maid and her husband earned approximately $1,800 per month working for the local paper. At Fidelity's request, an appraisal was made of the Maxwells' South Phoenix home, where they had resided for the preceding twelve years. The appraisal showed that the Maxwells lived in a modest neighborhood, that their 1,539 square foot home was in need of a significant amount of general repair and maintenance, and that its market value was approximately $40,000.

In connection with the financing transaction, Elizabeth Maxwell signed numerous documents, including a loan contract, a deed of trust, a truth-in-lending disclosure form, and a promissory note and security agreement. The effect of these documents was not only to secure the deferred purchase price with a lien on the merchandise sold, but also to place a lien on Maxwell's house as additional security for payment on the water heater contract. The forms and their terms were unambiguous and clearly indicated that Maxwell was placing a lien on her house. Included in the consumer credit contract between Maxwell and Fidelity was a clause expressly stating that Fidelity was subject to all claims by and defenses that Maxwell could assert against National.

Despite the fact that the water heater was never installed or working properly, Maxwell made payments on it for approximately three and one-half years, reducing the deferred purchase balance to $5,733. In 1988, Maxwell approached Fidelity to borrow an additional $800 for purposes unrelated to the original loan. In making this second loan, Fidelity required Maxwell to again sign a bundle of documents essentially identical to those she signed in 1984. Instead of simply adding $800 to Maxwell's outstanding balance on the 1984 contract, Fidelity created a new contract that included the unpaid balance of $5,733 on the 1984 loan, a term life insurance charge of $313, as well as the new $800 loan. In all, Maxwell financed the sum of $6,976 with this second loan. The terms of this latest loan also included interest at 19.5 interest and payments for a period of six years, making Maxwell's new payments, including interest, total nearly $12,000. The combined amount Maxwell would pay under the two contracts for a non-functioning water heater and the additional $800 loan thus totals approximately $17,000, or nearly one-half the value of her home.

Maxwell continued to make payments until 1990, when she brought this declaratory judgment action seeking, *inter alia*, a declaration that the 1984 contract was unenforceable on the grounds that it was unconscionable.

Following discovery, Fidelity moved for summary judgment asserting, among other things, that the statute of limitations had run on Maxwell's claim of unconscionability and, if not, that the 1988 contract worked a novation, thereby barring any action by Maxwell on the 1984 contract. Maxwell filed a memorandum in opposition to this motion and pointed to sworn testimony in her deposition, which Fidelity submitted with its motion, as raising genuine issues of material fact.

In a brief order, the trial court granted Fidelity's motion on the theory of novation. . . .

The court of appeals affirmed [partly on procedural grounds]. . . .

On review from summary judgment, the appellate court views the record in a light most favorable to the party opposing summary judgment (Maxwell) and will affirm only if no genuine issue of material fact exists. We therefore review this record to determine whether it could support a finding that Maxwell's claim of unconscionability was barred by the 1988 loan.

PRELIMINARY ISSUES

Before discussing the merits of Maxwell's petition, we must address. . . . [the issue, must Maxwell show an agency relationship between Fidelity and National to defeat Fidelity's motion for summary judgment]. . . .

The court of appeals found that Maxwell failed to establish an agency relationship between National and Fidelity. The court reasoned that, absent such a relationship, Maxwell could not defeat Fidelity's motion for summary judgment on grounds of novation. We fail to see the relationship between establishing agency and defeating a claim of novation or pursuing a claim of unconscionability in this case. Fidelity stands in the shoes of National by virtue of both federal law and the terms of the contract to which it is a party. The 1984 and 1988 consumer credit contracts between Maxwell and Fidelity clearly state, in bold face, capital letters:

ANY HOLDER OF THIS CONSUMER CREDIT CONTRACT IS SUBJECT TO ALL CLAIMS AND DEFENSES WHICH THE DEBTOR COULD ASSERT AGAINST THE SELLER OF GOODS OR SERVICES OBTAINED WITH THE PROCEEDS HEREOF.

Thus, Maxwell need not establish an agency relationship between National and Fidelity to maintain a claim against Fidelity for unconscionability or to overcome Fidelity's claim of novation. . . .

Discussion

A. Unconscionability . . .

2.   The Test for Unconscionability

The court of appeals found the 1984 contract valid because Maxwell "failed to raise a material issue of fact that the agreement evidenced by [the contract documents] was beyond her reasonable expectations or was unconscionable." It is not clear why the court of appeals applied the test of "reasonable expectations" as this test is more correctly associated with contracts of adhesion, not claims of unconscionability, and the issue of adhesion contracts was neither before the trial court nor briefed or argued on appeal. This court previously has noted the rule that "reasonable expectations" and unconscionability are two distinct grounds for invalidating or limiting the enforcement of a contract and has stated that "even if [the contract provisions are] consistent with the reasonable expectations of the party" they are unenforceable if they are oppressive or unconscionable. Broemmer v. Abortion Serv. of Phoenix, 173 Ariz. 148, 151, 840 P.2d 1013, 1016 (1992) (quoting Graham v. Scissor-Tail, Inc., 28 Cal.3d 807, 171 Cal.Rptr. 604, 611–12, 623 P.2d 165, 172–73 (1981)).

3. The History of Unconscionability . . .

. . . Although U.C.C. § 2–302 recognized and codified the amorphous equitable doctrine [of unconscionability], it did little to provide a set of rules for analyzing claims of unconscionability. Also lacking in the statutory recognition of unconscionability is a definition of that term. Courts and respected commentators alike have grappled with defining and applying unconscionability under the Code since its adoption. To this day, both groups remain divided on the proper method for doing so, though they share some common ground on defining such a test.

Within this common area, the elements of unconscionability can be ascertained to fulfill the Code's obvious intent of protecting against unconscionable contracts while not unnecessarily denying parties the benefit of their bargain. Although no litmus test exists, the cases do provide a reasonable, workable analysis.

4. Divisions of Unconscionability under the U.C.C.

This court previously has acknowledged that the unconscionability principle involves an assessment by the court of

> whether, in the light of the general commercial background and the commercial needs of the particular trade or case, the clauses involved are so one-sided as to be unconscionable under the circumstances existing at the time of the making of the contract. . . . The principle is one of the prevention of oppression and unfair surprise . . . not of disturbance of allocation of risks because of superior bargaining power.

Seekings v. Jimmy GMC of Tucson, Inc., 130 Ariz. 596, 602, 638 P.2d 210, 216 (1981) (citations omitted). This somewhat circular articulation of the principle, however, is not readily applicable to the infinite variety of cases that may involve the doctrine of unconscionability.

The framework upon which the vast majority of courts construct their analysis consists of the well recognized division of unconscionability into substantive and procedural parts. See, e.g., James J. White & Robert S. Summers, 1 Uniform Commercial Code 204, N. 8 and cases cited therein; John D. Calamari & Joseph M. Perillo, Contracts 406 (3d ed. 1987). Professor Dobbs provides the following explanation of the difference between these two types:

> Procedural or process unconscionability is concerned with "unfair surprise," fine print clauses, mistakes or ignorance of important facts or other things that mean bargaining did not proceed as it should. Substantive unconscionability is an unjust or "one-sided" contract. Substantive unconscionability is important in two ways. First, substantive unconscionability sometimes seems sufficient in itself to avoid a term in the

contract. Second, substantive unconscionability sometimes helps confirm or provide evidence of procedural unconscionability.

Dobbs, supra at 706 (footnote omitted). This dichotomy evolved from a distinction made by the late Professor Leff in his oft-cited article Unconscionability and The Code—The Emperor's New Clause, 115 U.Pa.L.Rev. 485, 487 (1967). In his article, Professor Leff distinguished between "bargaining naughtiness" (procedural unconscionability) and overly harsh terms (substantive unconscionability). Id.

Over the years, courts have refined the two divisions of unconscionability and identified several factors that are indicative of each. Procedural unconscionability was well-explained in Johnson v. Mobil Oil Corp.:

> Under the procedural rubric come those factors bearing upon . . . the real and voluntary meeting of the minds of the contracting party: age, education, intelligence, business acumen and experience, relative bargaining power, who drafted the contract, whether the terms were explained to the weaker party, whether alterations in the printed terms were possible, whether there were alternative sources of supply for the goods in question.

415 F.Supp. 264, 268 (E.D.Mich.1976) (internal quotations omitted). As Professors White and Summers have noted, procedural unconscionability bears a strong resemblance to its "common-law cousins" of fraud and duress. White & Summers, supra at 204.

Substantive unconscionability concerns the actual terms of the contract and examines the relative fairness of the obligations assumed. Resource Management Co. v. Weston Ranch & Livestock Co., 706 P.2d 1028, 1041 (Utah 1985). Indicative of substantive unconscionability are contract terms so one-sided as to oppress or unfairly surprise an innocent party, an overall imbalance in the obligations and rights imposed by the bargain, and significant cost-price disparity. Id. (citations and internal quotations omitted).

We believe these authorities provide useful illustrations of both divisions of unconscionability under the U.C.C., although we do not restrict applicability of the doctrine to the factors outlined.

5. Application

The point of agreement by courts on the substantive-procedural elements also marks a point of departure in analyzing claims of unconscionability. See generally White & Summers, supra at 218–20. Many courts, perhaps a majority, have held that there must be some quantum of *both* procedural and substantive unconscionability to establish a claim, and take a balancing approach in applying them. Id. at 219. See also 2 William D. Hawkland, Uniform Commercial Code Series § 2–302:05

(1984) and cases cited therein. Other courts have held that it is sufficient if *either* is shown. See, e.g., Gillman v. Chase Manhattan Bank, N.A., 73 N.Y.2d 1, 537 N.Y.S.2d 787, 794, 534 N.E.2d 824, 829 (1988) ("While determinations of unconscionability are ordinarily based on the court's conclusion that both the procedural and substantive components are present . . . , there have been exceptional cases where a provision of the contract is so outrageous as to warrant holding it unenforceable on the ground of substantive unconscionability alone.") (citing State v. Wolowitz, 96 A.D.2d 47, 468 N.Y.S.2d 131 (1983)). In addition to the numerous courts holding that either procedural or substantive unconscionability is sufficient,[3] the leading commentators in this field have also endorsed this position. See White & Summers, supra at 220 (advocating the sufficiency of excessive price alone).

The cases that require a showing of both procedural and substantive unconscionability appear to be rather fact-specific, based more on the historical reluctance of courts to disturb contracts than on valid doctrinal underpinning.

In some cases substantive unconscionability is found because the contract price is grossly excessive (or sometimes grossly inadequate). Most of these cases present additional elements such as actual misrepresentations, gross mistreatment of people who are already disadvantaged, or a subject matter such as premarital settlements that calls for intense state scrutiny by judges. In some of them, the substantive unconscionability really seems to be evidentiary only, that is, as confirming the conclusion that the process of bargaining was itself defective.

Dobbs, supra at 707 (footnote omitted) (emphasis added); see also Calamari & Perillo, supra at 406 ("[C]ontracts involving grossly unequal exchanges almost always involve some impropriety in the negotiating process or disability of a party."); White & Summers, supra at 218 ("Almost all of [the cases finding substantively unconscionable terms] exhibit creditor

---

[3] See, e.g., Resource Management Co. v. Weston Ranch & Livestock Co., 706 P.2d 1028, 1043 (Utah 1985) ("Gross disparity in terms, absent evidence of procedural unconscionability, can support a finding of unconscionability."); American Home Improvement, Inc. v. MacIver, 105 N.H. 435, 201 A.2d 886, 889 (1964) (relying explicitly on U.C.S. § 2–302 and finding unconscionable, based on price-value disparity, a contract requiring payment of $1,609 for goods and services valued at "far less"); World Enter., Inc. v. Midcoast Aviation Serv., Inc., 713 S.W.2d 606, 610 (Mo.App.1986) ("Unconscionability is defined as either procedural or substantive."); Frank's Maintenance & Eng'g, Inc. v. C.A. Roberts Co., 86 Ill.App.3d 980, 42 Ill.Dec. 25, 31–32, 408 N.E.2d 403, 409–10 (1980) ("Unconscionability can be either procedural or substantive or a combination of both.") (emphasis added). Cf. Schroeder v. Fageol Motors, Inc., 86 Wash.2d 256, 544 P.2d 20, 23 (1975) (en banc) (recognizing that cases fall within the two classifications of procedural and substantive unconscionability). Indeed, it has long been recognized that gross disparity in terms may satisfy the standard for unconscionability by itself. See Marks v. Gates, 154 F. 481, 483 (9th Cir.1907) (inadequacy of consideration sufficient ground for withholding specific performance if it is so gross as to render the contract unconscionable).

behavior that may be regarded as both procedurally and substantively unconscionable.").

Additional evidence that the dual requirement position is more coincidental than doctrinal is found within the very text of the statute on unconscionability, which explicitly refers to "the contract *or any clause* of the contract." A.R.S. § 47–2302 (emphasis added). Conspicuously absent from the statutory language is any reference to procedural aspects. That the U.C.C. contemplated substantive unconscionability alone to be sufficient is the most plausible reading of the language in § 47–2302, given that the Code itself provides for *per se* unconscionability if there exists, without more, a substantive term in the contract limiting consequential damages for injury to the person in cases involving consumer goods. See A.R.S. § 47–2719(c) [U.C.C. § 2–719(c)]. It is wholly inconsistent to assert that unconscionability under § 47–2302 requires some procedural irregularity when unconscionability under § 47–2719 clearly does not.

Therefore, we conclude that under A.R.S. § 47–2302, a claim of unconscionability can be established with a showing of substantive unconscionability alone, especially in cases involving either price-cost disparity or limitation of remedies. If only procedural irregularities are present, it may be more appropriate to analyze the claims under the doctrines of fraud, misrepresentation, duress, and mistake, although such irregularities can make a case of procedural unconscionability. See Resource Management Co., 706 P.2d at 1043.

However, we leave for another day the questions involving the remedy for procedural unconscionability alone. We conclude further that this case presents a question of at least substantive unconscionability to be decided by the trial court. From the face of it, we certainly cannot conclude that the contract as a whole is not unconscionable, given the $6,500 price of a water heater for a modest residence, payable at 19.5 percent interest, for a total time-payment price of $14,860.43. These facts present at least a question of grossly-excessive price, constituting substantive unconscionability. See Dobbs, supra at 707; White & Summers, supra at § 4–5 and cases cited therein. This contract is made even more harsh by its security terms, which, in the event of non-payment, permit Fidelity not only to repossess the water heater but foreclose on Maxwell's home. The apparent injustice and oppression in these security provisions not only may constitute substantive unconscionability but also may provide evidence of procedural unconscionability. See Dobbs, supra at 706–07 (citing Williams v. Walker-Thomas Furniture Co., 350 F.2d 445 (D.C.Cir.1965)).

Under the U.C.C. as enacted in A.R.S. § 47–2302, the court may "refuse enforcement of the contract altogether." Dobbs, supra at 705; Restatement § 208. The present factual record, before the statutorily required evidentiary hearing, certainly contains some evidence that the entire 1984 contract, including sale price, security provisions, and remedies, is unenforceable. . . .

CONCLUSION

. . . [W]e vacate the court of appeals' opinion, reverse the trial court's judgment, and remand to the trial court for proceedings consistent with this opinion and A.R.S. § 47–2302.

MOELLER, V.C.J., and CORCORAN and ZLAKET, JJ., concur.

[The opinion of Judge Martone, concurring in the judgment, is omitted.]

———

NOTE ON THE RESTATEMENT OF THE LAW, CONSUMER CONTRACTS

The membership of the American Law Institute approved a tentative draft of the Restatement of the Law, Consumer Contracts, in June 2022. Revised Tentative Draft No. 2 (June 2022). Section 6 addresses the topic of unconscionability at length. It adopts a two-prong approach under which a court examines the basic factors of substantive unconscionability ("namely a fundamentally unfair or unreasonably one-sided contract or term") and procedural unconscionability ("namely a contract term that results in unfair surprise or results from the absence of meaningful choice"), to decide the ultimate question whether it is appropriate to "deny enforcement to contract terms that are fundamentally unfair." Comment 2 explains "the two prongs are viewed in tandem, and a sliding scale approach is applied: a large quantum of one prong means that a smaller quantum of the other is sufficient to establish unconscionability."

Comment 8 addresses the possibility of an unconscionable price:

"8. *Unconscionable price.* The substantive unconscionability test can be applied to scrutinize the contract price, but this should be done with extra care. An excessively high price, substantially in excess of the price at which similar products are obtainable in similar consumer transactions by like consumers, or bearing no reasonable relationship to the cost of providing the good or service, may be found to be substantively unconscionable. The procedural-unconscionability test may be more difficult to satisfy because the price is usually the most prominent element of a transaction and a critical factor in the consumer's contracting decision . . . Still, an egregiously high price may be held unconscionable by courts if it occurs in connection with unfair surprise or the absence of meaningful choice. A price term itself may surprise consumers, for example, when a product is sold via a complex pricing scheme. A consumer may be unfairly surprised when the price is multidimensional and certain price dimensions do not affect the contracting decisions. A consumer may also be unfairly surprised when the price is contingent or deferred and the consumer underestimates the likelihood of triggering the relevant price or the importance of certain deferred price dimensions (e.g., a long-term interest rate that replaces a low teaser rate after the introductory period, or the long-term, overall price of a repeatedly rolled-over, short-term loan), and thus underestimates the true cost of the contract. An egregiously high price may also result from absence of meaningful choice when there are market imperfections that make it less likely that the price was set by a freely competitive market to reflect the cost or the fair value of the product. And it may arise in situations in which the consumer's levels of literacy and numeracy or urgency of needs impede the exercise of the sophisticated, prudent judgment needed to evaluate the price. In those circumstances, a court might find that the price term is procedurally unconscionable. . . .

"Illustrations: . . .

"24. A set of cookware is sold, by home solicitation, for $375 in an area where a set of comparable quality is readily available for $125 or less. The high price satisfies the substantive-unconscionability test. The procedural-unconscionability test is satisfied if a high-pressure, door-to-door sales method prevented the consumer from obtaining information on the prevailing market price.

"25. A consumer borrows $5,000 under a three-year unsecured loan contract carrying an interest rate of 135 percent. The interest rate (the "price" of the loan) is substantively unconscionable if, under the facts of the case, it is excessive relative to the cost of credit the consumer can obtain on a comparable loan elsewhere, or relative to the expected cost for the business of supplying the credit, taking into account the risk of default. The procedural-unconscionability test is satisfied if the interest-rate term was obscured at the time of entering the contract, or if the consumer was under pressure to enter the contract."

———

NOTE ON PRICE-GOUGING STATUTES

Many states have statutes that seek to regulate price gouging during natural emergencies, like hurricanes. N.Y.Gen.Bus.Law § 396–r is an example. It empowers the New York attorney general to bring a civil action, and obtain an injunction, restitution, and civil penalties, to prevent "any party within the chain of distribution of consumer goods [and services] from taking unfair advantage of consumers during abnormal disruptions of the market" by demanding an "unconscionably excessive" price. Evidence of a gross disparity between the price demanded by the defendant during the emergency, and the price offered by the defendant immediately prior to the emergency, is treated as prima facie proof of a violation of the statute.

In People v. Two Wheel Corp., 71 N.Y.2d 693, 530 N.Y.S.2d 46, 525 N.E.2d 692 (1988), the Attorney General of New York charged that Two Wheel Corporation had violated N.Y.Gen.Bus.Law § 396–r by selling approximately

100 power generators at inflated prices—ranging from 4% to 67% over base prices—in anticipation of and during a hurricane that left much of Long Island without electrical power for around ten days. The trial court ordered Two Wheel to pay a civil penalty of $5000, to make restitution to thirteen consumers who had submitted affidavits, and to establish a $20,000 restitution fund for other consumers who had purchased generators from Two Wheel during the relevant period at prices exceeding the base prices. Affirmed.

"Respondents [Two Wheel] . . . contend that the prices charged were not unconscionably excessive. They note that, for some of the sales during the period, the sales price exceeded the base price by less than 5%; for others the differential fell between 5 and 15%. In fact, in the vast majority of the sales, the prices were inflated by less than 30%. In only five sales, according to the Attorney-General's figures, did the disparity reach as high as 60%. Even if some of the prices can be considered unconscionably excessive, they claim, others are clearly not, and they should not be required to make restitution to all consumers who were charged more than the base price.

"To support their argument, respondents point to General Business Law § 396–r(3), which provides in essence that evidence of a 'gross disparity' between the sales price at the time of the market disruption and the price charged before the disruption is prima facie proof of price gouging. From this provision and case law applying the unconscionability standard of the Uniform Commercial Code (UCC 2–302), respondents argue that the Legislature intended the price-gouging statute to apply only to extremely large price increases and that, accordingly, the majority of their sales did not offend the price-gouging prohibition.

"Respondents' argument places undue emphasis on the 'gross disparity' language of [§ 396–r(3)], treating it as a definition of price gouging. But the provision is procedural rather than definitional; it simply establishes a means of providing presumptive evidence that the merchant has engaged in price gouging. A showing of a gross disparity in prices, coupled with proof that the disparity is not attributable to supplier costs, raises a presumption that the merchant used the leverage provided by the market disruption to extract a higher price. The use of such leverage is what defines price gouging, not some arbitrarily drawn line of excessiveness.

"Furthermore, the term 'unconscionably excessive' does not limit the statute's prohibition to 'extremely large price increases', as respondents would have it. The doctrine of unconscionability, as developed in the common law of contracts and in the application of UCC 2–302, has both substantive and procedural aspects. . . . Respondents' argument focuses solely on the substantive aspect, which considers whether one or more contract terms are unreasonably favorable to one party. . . . The procedural aspect, on the other hand, looks to the contract formation process, with emphasis on such factors as inequality of bargaining power, the use of deceptive or high-pressure sales techniques, and confusing or hidden language in the written agreement (State of New York v. Wolowitz, 96 A.D.2d 47, 67, 468 N.Y.S.2d 131; see, Williams v.

Walker-Thomas Furniture Co., D.C.Cir., 350 F.2d 445, 449). Thus, a price may be unconscionably excessive because, substantively, the amount of the excess is unconscionably extreme, or because, procedurally, the excess was obtained through unconscionable means, or because of a combination of both factors. . . .

"Here, the Attorney-General's prima facie case established, at least presumptively, that respondents' price increases were attributable solely to their use of the bargaining advantage created by the natural disaster—that is, through means that are 'unconscionable according to the mores and business practices of the time and place' . . . because General Business Law § 396–r defines the mores governing this business setting and excises the use of such advantage from the repertoire of legitimate business practices. Furthermore, in this case, where the sales occurred over a relatively short period of time and were associated with a single market disruption, the presumption that the excess was unconscionably obtained, though established through proof of gross disparities, extends as well to the sales marked by lesser increases. The evidence, including the deposition testimony of two of respondents' employees, makes the inference inescapable that all of the price increases were tainted by respondents' use of the superior bargaining position attributable to the power outage."

See also People v. Beach Boys Equip. Co., 273 A.D.2d 850, 851, 709 N.Y.S.2d 729 (App.Div.2000) (trial court required restitution by a business that charged $1200 for generators following an ice storm, when other retailers were charging less than $600. The appellate court upheld the award of restitution, and announced that even a small increase in price may be unconscionably excessive under General Business Law § 396–r if "the excess was obtained through unconscionable means," which was held to be the case here); People v. Dame, 289 A.D.2d 997, 734 N.Y.S.2d 789 (App.Div.2001) (roofers who charged excessive prices when a storm was pending were ordered to pay restitution and penalties).

———

CHAPTER 2

RELIANCE AS A BASIS FOR ENFORCING A DONATIVE PROMISE

■ ■ ■

Bargained for consideration is not the only basis for enforcing a promise under modern contract law. This Section concerns reliance as an alternative basis for enforcing a donative promise. Reliance involves an injury to a promisee resulting from a change in position in reliance on the broken promise; in particular, a cost the promisee incurs in reliance on the promise.

KIRKSEY V. KIRKSEY

Supreme Court of Alabama, 1845.
8 Ala. 131.

Assumpsit by defendant, against the plaintiff in error.

The plaintiff was the wife of defendant's brother, but had for some time been a widow, and had several children. In 1840, the plaintiff resided on public land, under a contract of lease, she had held over, and was comfortably settled, and would have attempted to secure the land she lived on. The defendant resided in Talladega county, some sixty or seventy miles off. On the 10th October, 1840, he wrote to her the following letter:

> "Dear Sister Antillico,—Much to my mortification, I heard that brother Henry was dead, and one of his children. I know that your situation is one of grief and difficulty. You had a bad chance before, but a great deal worse now. I should like to come and see you, but cannot with convenience at present . . . I do not know whether you have a preference on the place you live on or not. If you had, I would advise you to obtain your preference, and sell the land and quit the country, as I understand it is very unhealthy, and I know society is very bad. If you will come down and see me, I will let you have a place to raise your family, and I have more open land than I can tend; and on the account of your situation, and that of your family, I feel like I want you and the children to do well."

Within a month or two after the receipt of this letter, the plaintiff abandoned her possession, without disposing of it, and removed with her family, to the residence of the defendant, who put her in comfortable houses, and gave her land to cultivate for two years, at the end of which time he notified her to remove, and put her in a house, not comfortable, in the woods, which he afterwards required her to leave.

A verdict being found for the plaintiff, for $200, the above facts were agreed, and if they will sustain the action, the judgment is to be affirmed, otherwise it is to be reversed.

ORMOND, J. The inclination of my mind is that the loss and inconvenience which the plaintiff sustained in breaking up and moving to the defendant's a distance of sixty miles is a sufficient consideration to support the promise to furnish her with a house and land to cultivate until she could raise her family. My brothers, however, think that the promise on the part of the defendant was a mere gratuity, and that an action will not lie for its breach.

The judgment of the court below must therefore be reversed, pursuant to the agreement of the parties.

———

Commonwealth v. Scituate Savings Bank

137 Mass. 301, 302 (1884)

(Holmes, J.) "It would cut up the doctrine of consideration by the roots, if a promisee could make a gratuitous promise binding by subsequently acting in reliance on it."

———

INTRODUCTORY NOTE ON PROMISSORY ESTOPPEL

From the middle of the nineteenth century to the middle of the twentieth, contract law was dominated by a school of thought now known as classical contract law. Classical contract law took it as axiomatic that only a bargain is consideration and that, accordingly, a donative promise could not be enforced. Cases like *Kirksey v. Kirksey* were based on this axiom.

Even during the classical era, however, courts often found a way to allow a claim where a donative promise had been relied upon. Some cases used the doctrine of equitable estoppel. Ricketts v. Scothorn, 57 Neb. 51, 77 N.W. 365 (1898), is a leading case. Testator was distressed because his granddaughter had to work in a store. To enable her to give up her job, he delivered to her a promissory note for $2,000, saying "I have fixed out something that you have not got to work any more." In reliance on the note, the granddaughter quit work. Testator died without either paying or repudiating the note. The granddaughter brought suit on the note against the grandfather's executor, and the court held for the granddaughter. The court side-stepped the issue of whether reliance constituted consideration by concluding that reliance estopped (prevented) the executor from pleading a lack of consideration. The approach taken in *Ricketts* drew on a doctrine known as *equitable estoppel* or *estoppel in pais*.

Today *Ricketts* would likely be treated as a promissory estoppel claim. The doctrine of promissory estoppel is distinct from the doctrine of equitable estoppel in two respects. First, equitable estoppel generally is based on a statement of past or present fact while promissory estoppel is based on a promise concerning the future. Second, equitable estoppel may only be used to prevent the other party from asserting a claim, or from asserting a defense to a claim, it is not recognized as a cause of action. In many states promissory estoppel is recognized as a cause of action.

Despite these differences, both doctrines turn on the core idea of reliance. More precisely, the two doctrines may be best understood as particular instances of a broader concept: When one person, A, uses words or actions that he knows or should know would induce another, B, to reasonably believe that A is committed to take a certain course of action, and A knows or should know that B will incur costs if A doesn't take action, A should take steps to ensure that if he doesn't take the action, B will not suffer a loss. See T.M. Scanlon, Promises and Practices, 19 Phil. & Pub. Affairs 199 (1990).

In many states, promissory estoppel is pled as a cause of action, typically in conjunction with a claim for breach of contract. For example, in Toscano v. Greene Music, 124 Cal. App. 4th 685 (Cal. App. 2004), Toscano quit his job as general manager of a piano store in reliance on the defendant's offer of employment as general manager of another store When the defendant withdrew the offer Toscano sued for breach of contract and promissory estoppel, as well as on other theories. The breach of contract claim was dismissed on a motion for summary judgment, but the promissory estoppel claim was allowed to proceed to a bench trial, where Toscano prevailed. The doctrine of promissory estoppel is important in contract litigation and contract law because a promissory estoppel claim (or the doctrine) can avoid several impediments to recovery on a breach of contract claim. One of these impediments is the requirement of bargained for consideration.

The Restatement of Contracts does not treat promissory estoppel as a claim or action that is distinct from an action for breach of contract. Instead the doctrine is accounted for by several provisions that make reliance a basis for overcoming an impediment to recovery on a breach of contract claim. The most important of these provisions is Section 90, which was included to account for cases like *Ricketts v. Scothorn* where the doctrine of equitable estoppel was used to overcome the impediment of the absence of bargained for consideration. As adopted in Restatement First, Section 90 provided as follows:

> A promise which the promisor should reasonably expect to induce action or forbearance of a definite and substantial character on the part of the promisee and which does induce such action or

forbearance is binding if injustice can be avoided only by enforcement of the promise.

The case that follows is a leading case applying Section 90 and the doctrine of promissory estoppel to enforce a donative promise. After you have read the next case, you may find it useful to go back to *Kirksey v. Kirksey* and ask how a promissory estoppel claim would have fared in that case, had it been considered.

RESTATEMENT, SECOND, CONTRACTS § 90

[See Selected Source Materials Supplement]

FEINBERG V. PFEIFFER CO.

Missouri Court of Appeals, 1959.
322 S.W.2d 163.

DOERNER, COMMISSIONER. This is a suit brought in the Circuit Court of the City of St. Louis by plaintiff, a former employee of the defendant corporation, on an alleged contract whereby defendant agreed to pay plaintiff the sum of $200 per month for life upon her retirement. A jury being waived, the case was tried by the court alone. Judgment below was for plaintiff for $5,100, the amount of the pension claimed to be due as of the date of the trial, together with interest thereon, and defendant duly appealed.

The parties are in substantial agreement on the essential facts. Plaintiff began working for the defendant, a manufacturer of pharmaceuticals, in 1910, when she was but 17 years of age. By 1947 she had attained the position of bookkeeper, office manager, and assistant treasurer of the defendant, and owned 70 shares of its stock out of a total of 6,503 shares issued and outstanding. Twenty shares had been given to her by the defendant or its then president, she had purchased 20, and the remaining 30 she had acquired by a stock split or stock dividend. Over the years she received substantial dividends on the stock she owned, as did all of the other stockholders. Also, in addition to her salary, plaintiff from 1937 to 1949, inclusive, received each year a bonus varying in amount from $300 in the beginning to $2,000 in the later years.

On December 27, 1947, the annual meeting of the defendant's Board of Directors was held at the Company's offices in St. Louis, presided over by Max Lippman, its then president and largest individual stockholder. The other directors present were George L. Marcus, Sidney Harris, Sol Flammer, and Walter Weinstock, who, with Max Lippman, owned 5,007 of the 6,503 shares then issued and outstanding. At that meeting the Board of Directors adopted the following resolution, which because it is the crux of the case, we quote in full:

"The Chairman thereupon pointed out that the Assistant Treasurer, Mrs. Anna Sacks Feinberg, has given the corporation many years of long and faithful service. Not only has she served the corporation devotedly, but with exceptional ability and skill. The President pointed out that although all of the officers and directors sincerely hoped and desired that Mrs. Feinberg would continue in her present position for as long as she felt able, nevertheless, in view of the length of service which she has contributed provision should be made to afford her retirement privileges and benefits which should become a firm obligation of the corporation to be available to her whenever she should see fit to retire from active duty, however many years in the future such retirement may become effective. It was, accordingly, proposed that Mrs. Feinberg's salary which is presently $350.00 per month, be increased to $400.00 per month, and that Mrs. Feinberg would be given the privilege of retiring from active duty at any time she may elect to see fit so to do upon a retirement pay of $200.00 per month for life, with the distinct understanding that the retirement plan is merely being adopted at the present time in order to afford Mrs. Feinberg security for the future and in the hope that her active services will continue with the corporation for many years to come. After due discussion and consideration, and upon motion duly made and seconded, it was—

"Resolved, that the salary of Anna Sacks Feinberg be increased from $350.00 to $400.00 per month and that she be afforded the privilege of retiring from active duty in the corporation at any time she may elect to see fit so to do upon retirement pay of $200.00 per month, for the remainder of her life."

At the request of Mr. Lippman his sons-in-law, Messrs. Harris and Flammer, called upon the plaintiff at her apartment on the same day to advise her of the passage of the resolution. Plaintiff testified on cross-examination that she had no prior information that such a pension plan was contemplated, that it came as a surprise to her, and that she would have continued in her employment whether or not such a resolution had been adopted. It is clear from the evidence that there was no contract, oral or written, as to plaintiff's length of employment, and that she was free to quit, and the defendant to discharge her, at any time.

Plaintiff did continue to work for the defendant through June 30, 1949, on which date she retired. In accordance with the foregoing resolution, the defendant began paying her the sum of $200 on the first of each month. Mr. Lippman died on November 18, 1949, and was succeeded as president of the company by his widow. Because of an illness, she retired from that office and was succeeded in October, 1953, by her son-in-law, Sidney M. Harris. Mr. Harris testified that while Mrs. Lippman had been president she signed the monthly pension check paid plaintiff, but fussed about doing so, and considered the payments as gifts. After his election, he stated, a new accounting firm employed by the defendant questioned the validity of the payments to plaintiff on several occasions, and in the Spring of 1956, upon its recommendation, he consulted the Company's then attorney, Mr. Ralph Kalish. Harris testified that both Ernst and Ernst, the accounting firm, and Kalish told him there was no need of giving plaintiff the money. He also stated that he had concurred in the view that the payments to plaintiff were mere gratuities rather than amounts due under a contractual obligation, and that following his discussion with the Company's attorney plaintiff was sent a check for $100 on April 1, 1956. Plaintiff declined to accept the reduced amount, and this action followed. Additional facts will be referred to later in this opinion.

Appellant's first assignment of error relates to the admission in evidence of plaintiff's testimony over its objection, that at the time of trial she was sixty-five and a half years old, and that she was no longer able to engage in gainful employment because of the removal of a cancer and the performance of a colocholecystostomy operation on November 25, 1957. Its complaint is not so much that such evidence was irrelevant and immaterial, as it is that the trial court erroneously made it one basis for its decision in favor of plaintiff. As defendant concedes, the error (if it was error) in the admission of such evidence would not be a ground for reversal, since, this being a jury-waived case, we are constrained by the statutes to review it upon both the law and the evidence, Sec. 510.310 RSMo 1949, V.A.M.S., and to render such judgment as the court below ought to have given. Section 512.160, Minor v. Lillard, Mo., 289 S.W.2d 1; Thumm v. Lohr, Mo.App., 306 S.W.2d 604. We consider only such evidence as is admissible, and need not pass upon questions of error in the admission and exclusion of evidence. Hussey v. Robison, Mo., 285 S.W.2d 603. However, in fairness to the trial court it should be stated that while he briefly referred to the state of plaintiff's health as of the time of the trial in his amended findings of fact, it is obvious from his amended grounds for decision and judgment that it was not, as will be seen, the basis for his decision.

Appellant's next complaint is that there was insufficient evidence to support the court's findings that plaintiff would not have quit defendant's employ had she not known and relied upon the promise of defendant to pay her $200 a month for life, and the finding that, from her voluntary retirement until April 1, 1956, plaintiff relied upon the continued receipt of the pension installments. The trial court so found, and, in our opinion, justifiably so. Plaintiff testified, and was corroborated by Harris, defendant's witness, that knowledge of the passage of the resolution was communicated to her on December 27, 1947, the very day it was adopted. She was told at that time by Harris and Flammer, she stated, that she could take the pension as of that day, if she wished. She testified further that she continued to work for another year and a half, through June 30, 1949; that at that time her health was good and she could have continued to work, but that after working for almost forty years she thought she would take a rest. Her testimony continued:

"Q. Now, what was the reason—I'm sorry. Did you then quit the employment of the company after you—after this year and a half?

"A. Yes.

"Q. What was the reason that you left?

"A. Well, I thought almost forty years, it was a long time and I thought I would take a little rest.

"Q. Yes.

"A. And with the pension and what earnings my husband had, we figured we could get along.

"Q. Did you rely upon this pension?

"A. We certainly did.

"Q. Being paid?

"A. Very much so. We relied upon it because I was positive that I was going to get it as long as I lived.

"Q. Would you have left the employment of the company at ✗ that time had it not been for this pension?

"A. No.

"Mr. Allen: Just a minute, I object to that as calling for a conclusion and conjecture on the part of this witness.

"The Court: It will be overruled.

"Q. (Mr. Agatstein continuing): Go ahead, now. The question is whether you would have quit the employment of the company at that time had you not relied upon this pension plan?

"A. No, I wouldn't.

"Q. You would not have. Did you ever seek employment while this pension was being paid to you—

"A. (interrupting): No.

Could have found other employment

"Q. Wait a minute, at any time prior—at any other place?

"A. No, sir.

"Q. Were you able to hold any other employment during that time?

"A. Yes, I think so.

"Q. Was your health good?

"A. My health was good."

It is obvious from the foregoing that there was ample evidence to support the findings of fact made by the court below.

We come, then, to the basic issue in the case. While otherwise defined in defendant's third and fourth assignments of error, it is thus succinctly stated in the argument in its brief: " . . . whether plaintiff has proved that she has a right to recover from defendant based upon a legally binding contractual obligation to pay her $200 per month for life."

Defendant's claim: merely donative promise b/c no consid.

It is defendant's contention, in essence, that the resolution adopted by its Board of Directors was a mere promise to make a gift, and that no contract resulted either thereby, or when plaintiff retired, because there was no consideration given or paid by the plaintiff. It urges that a promise to make a gift is not binding unless supported by a legal consideration; that the only apparent consideration for the adoption of the foregoing resolution was the "many years of long and faithful service" expressed therein; and that past services are not a valid consideration for a promise. Defendant argues further that there is nothing in the resolution which made its effectiveness conditional upon plaintiff's continued employment, that she was not under contract to work for any length of time but was free to quit whenever she wished, and that she had no contractual right to her position and could have been discharged at any time.

Plaintiff concedes that a promise based upon past services would be without consideration, but contends that there were two other elements which supplied the required element: First, the continuation by plaintiff in the employ of the defendant for the period from December 27, 1947, the date when the resolution was adopted, until the date of her retirement on June 30, 1949. And, second, her change of position, i.e., her retirement, and the abandonment by her of her opportunity to continue in gainful employment, made in reliance on defendant's promise to pay her $200 per month for life.

We must agree with the defendant that the evidence does not support the first of these contentions. There is no language in the resolution predicating plaintiff's right to a pension upon her continued employment. She was not required to work for the defendant for any period of time as a condition to gaining such retirement benefits. She was told that she could quit the day upon which the resolution was adopted, as she herself testified, and it is clear from her own testimony that she made no promise or agreement to continue in the employ of the defendant in return for its promise to pay her a pension. Hence there was lacking that mutuality of obligation which is essential to the validity of a contract. . . .

But as to the second of these contentions we must agree with plaintiff. . . .

Section 90 of the Restatement, Law of Contracts states that: "A promise which the promisor should reasonably expect to induce action or forbearance of a definite and substantial character on the part of the promisee and which does induce such action or forbearance is binding if injustice can be avoided only by enforcement of the promise." This doctrine has been described as that of "promissory estoppel," as distinguished from that of equitable estoppel or estoppel in pais, the reason for the differentiation being stated as follows:

> "It is generally true that one who has led another to act in reasonable reliance on his representations of fact cannot afterwards in litigation between the two deny the truth of the representations, and some courts have sought to apply this principle to the formation of contracts, where, relying on a gratuitous promise, the promisee has suffered detriment. It is to be noticed, however, that such a case does not come within the ordinary definition of estoppel. If there is any representation of an existing fact, it is only that the promisor at the time of making the promise intends to fulfill it. As to such intention there is usually no misrepresentation and if there is, it is not that which has injured the promisee. In other words, he relies on a promise and not on a misstatement of fact; and the term 'promissory' estoppel or something equivalent should be used to make the distinction." Williston on Contracts, Rev.Ed., Sec. 139, Vol. 1.

In speaking of this doctrine, Judge Learned Hand said in Porter v. Commissioner of Internal Revenue, 2 Cir., 60 F.2d 673, 675, that " . . . 'promissory estoppel' is now a recognized species of consideration."

As pointed out by our Supreme Court in In re Jamison's Estate, Mo., 202 S.W.2d 879, 887, it is stated in the Missouri Annotations to the Restatement under Section 90 that:

> " 'There is a variance between the doctrine underlying this section and the theoretical justifications that have been advanced for the Missouri decisions.' "

That variance, as the authors of the Annotations point out, is that:

> "This § 90, when applied with § 85, means that the promise described is a contract without any consideration. In Missouri the

same practical result is reached without in theory abandoning the doctrine of consideration. In Missouri three theories have been advanced as ground for the decisions (1) *Theory of act for promise.* The induced 'action or forbearance' is the consideration for the promise. . . . (2) *Theory of promissory estoppel.* The induced 'action or forbearance' works an estoppel against the promisor. . . . (3) *Theory of bilateral contract.* When the induced 'action or forbearance' is begun, a promise to complete is implied, and we have an enforceable bilateral contract, the implied promise to complete being the consideration for the original promise." (Citing cases.)

Was there such an act on the part of plaintiff, in reliance upon the promise contained in the resolution, as will estop the defendant, and therefore create an enforceable contract under the doctrine of promissory estoppel? We think there was. One of the illustrations cited under Section 90 of the Restatement is: "2. A promises B to pay him an annuity during B's life. B thereupon resigns a profitable employment, as A expected that he might. B receives the annuity for some years, in the meantime becoming disqualified from again obtaining good employment. A's promise is binding." This illustration is objected to by defendant as not being applicable to the case at hand. The reason advanced by it is that in the illustration B became "disqualified" from obtaining other employment *before* A discontinued the payments, whereas in this case the plaintiff did not discover that she had cancer and thereby became unemployable until *after* the defendant had discontinued the payments of $200 per month. We think the distinction is immaterial. The only reason for the reference in the illustration to the disqualification of A is in connection with that part of Section 90 regarding the prevention of injustice. The injustice would occur regardless of when the disability occurred. Would defendant contend that the contract would be enforceable if the plaintiff's illness had been discovered on March 31, 1956, the day before it discontinued the payment of the $200 a month, but not if it occurred on April 2nd, the day after? Furthermore, there are more ways to become disqualified for work, or unemployable, than as the result of illness. At the time she retired plaintiff was 57 years of age. At the time the payments were discontinued she was over 63 years of age. It is a matter of common knowledge that it is virtually impossible for a woman of that age to find satisfactory employment, much less a position comparable to that which plaintiff enjoyed at the time of her retirement.

The fact of the matter is that plaintiff's subsequent illness was not the "action or forbearance" which was induced by the promise contained in the resolution. As the trial court correctly decided, such action on plaintiff's part was her retirement from a lucrative position in reliance upon defendant's promise to pay her an annuity or pension. In a very similar case, Ricketts v. Scothorn, 57 Neb. 51, 77 N.W. 365, 367, 42 L.R.A. 794, the Supreme Court of Nebraska said:

> ". . . Having intentionally influenced the plaintiff to alter her position for the worse on the faith of the note being paid when due, it would be grossly inequitable to permit the maker, or his executor, to resist payment on the ground that the promise was given without consideration."

The Commissioner therefore recommends, for the reasons stated, that the judgment be affirmed.

PER CURIAM.

The foregoing opinion by DOERNER, C., is adopted as the opinion of the court. The judgment is, accordingly, affirmed.

WOLFE, P.J., and ANDERSON and RUDDY, JJ., concur.

———

Hayes v. Plantations Steel Co.

438 A.2d 1091 (R.I.1982)

Plantations Steel Co. was founded by Hugo R. Mainelli, Sr., and Alexander A. Dimartino. Hayes was employed by Plantations from 1947 to 1972. In January 1972, Hayes announced his intention to retire in July because he had worked continuously for fifty-one years. Hayes was then sixty-five, and was Plantation's general manager, a position of considerable responsibility. About a week before his actual retirement, Hayes spoke with Hugo R. Mainelli Jr., an officer and a shareholder of Plantations. Mainelli Jr. said that the company "would take care" of Hayes, although there was no mention of a sum of money or a percentage of salary that Hayes would receive. Mainelli Jr.'s father, Hugo R. Mainelli Sr., authorized the first payment "as a token of appreciation for the many years of [Hayes's] service." It was implied that payments would continue on an annual basis, and it was Mainelli Jr.'s personal intention that the payments would continue for as long as he was around. Four annual payments of $5,000 each were made.

After Hayes's retirement, he visited Plantations each year to say hello and renew old acquaintances. During the course of his visits, Hayes would thank Mainelli Jr. for the previous check, and ask how long the checks would continue, so that he could plan an orderly retirement. In 1976, the DiMartinos assumed full control of Plantations as a result of a dispute between the two founding families. After 1976, the payments to Hayes were discontinued. A succession of several poor business years and the takeover by the DiMartino family contributed to the decision to stop the payments. Hayes brought suit. Held, for Plantations.

(Shea, J.) "[T]he important distinction between *Feinberg* and the case before us is that in *Feinberg* the employer's decision definitely shaped the thinking of the plaintiff. In this case the promise did not. It is not reasonable to infer from the facts that Hugo R. Mainelli, Jr., expected retirement to result from his conversation with Hayes. Hayes had given notice of his intention seven months previously. Here there was thus no inducement to retire which would satisfy the demands of § 90 of the Restatement. Nor can it be said that Hayes's refraining from other employment was 'action or forbearance of a definite and substantial character.' The underlying assumption of Hayes's initial decision to retire was that upon leaving the defendant's employ, he would no longer work. It is impossible to say that he changed his position any more so because of what Mainelli had told him in light of his own initial decision. These circumstances do not lead to a conclusion that injustice can be avoided only by enforcement of Plantations's promise. Hayes received $20,000 over the course of four years. He inquired each year about whether he could expect a check for the following year. Obviously, there was no absolute certainty on his part that the pension would continue. Furthermore, in the face of his uncertainty, the mere fact that payment for several years did occur is insufficient by itself to meet the requirements of reliance under the doctrine of promissory estoppel."

NOTE ON THE PROMISSORY ESTOPPEL REMEDY

An unrelied-upon donative promise is normally unenforceable. Section 90 of the Restatement teaches that reliance may make a donative promise enforceable. But to what *extent* should a relied-upon promise be enforceable? Or, to put it differently, what injury to a relying donative promisee should the law compensate? Since a relied-upon donative promise is enforced because, and only because, it has been relied upon, in the normal case the promise should be enforced to the extent of the reliance, that is, the loss the promisee suffered because she changed her position in reliance on the broken promise. For reasons of policy or administrability, however, in at least some cases it might be desirable to enforce the promise, which is what the court did in *Feinberg v. Pfeiffer Co.* This was appropriate for the plaintiff's reliance loss was difficult to quantify while the sum she was promised was certain.

When Restatement First was being debated on the floor of the ALI, Samuel Williston, the Reporter, went much further, and took the position that the expectation measure should be used in all Section 90 cases:

> MR. WILLISTON: . . . Johnny says, "I want to buy a Buick car." Uncle says, "Well, I will give you $1000." . . . [Uncle] knows that that $1000 is going to be relied on by the nephew for the purchase of a car. . . .

> [MR.] PRICKETT: May I ask the Reporter if in the example he gave of Johnny and the car, his uncle's promise would be enforceable when Johnny buys the car?

[handwritten margin note: Relied-upon promise is enforceable to the extent that the promisee suffered a loss in reliance on a broken promise]

MR. WILLISTON: I should say so, because the promise was made as a direct reply to Johnny's expression of a desire for a car. . . .

MR. PRICKETT: Suppose Johnny pays no money down.

MR. WILLISTON: If he has got the car and is liable for the price he gets the $1000 under this Section. . . .

MR. PRICKETT: My idea is this: If he gets the car and pays no money down, if the car is taken away from him, has he suffered any substantial injury?

MR. WILLISTON: Oh, I think he has, as long as he is liable for the price. . . .

[MR.] TUNSTALL: . . . Suppose the car had been a Ford instead of a Buick, costing $600.

. . . Johnny says, "I want to buy a Ford" and . . . not being familiar with the market price of a Ford, the uncle says, "I will give you $1000." Now, is the uncle obligated for the $1000 or for the price of the Ford?

MR. WILLISTON: I think he might be bound for the $1000.

MR. COUDERT: . . . Please let me see if I understand it rightly. Would you say, Mr. Reporter, in your case of Johnny and the uncle, the uncle promising the $1000 and Johnny buying the car—say, he goes out and buys the car for $500—that uncle would be liable for $1000 or would he be liable for $500?

MR. WILLISTON: If Johnny had done what he was expected to do, or is acting within the limits of his uncle's expectation, I think the uncle would be liable for $1000; but not otherwise . . .

In Restatement Second, Section 90 was revised to explicitly negate Williston's view. This was accomplished by adding a new sentence to Section 90: "The remedy granted for breach may be limited as justice requires." In the hypothetical where Johnny purchases a car for $500 a court might only award Johnny $500 minus the resale value of the car, which would be Johnny's reliance damages (while Johnny is out-of-pocket $500 he now has a valuable asset, which he could sell). A court might also award $500 as expectation damages by interpreting Uncle's promise as a promise to pay *up to $1,000* to help Johnny buy a car.

————

Goldstick v. ICM Realty

788 F.2d 456 (7th Cir.1986)

(Posner, J.) "As a matter of strict logic one might suppose that the plaintiffs, even if they succeeded in establishing a promissory estoppel, would not necessarily be able to recover the value of the promise. . . . It would seem

Recovery based on damages, not value of the promise (what was lost)

they would have to show their actual damages: what they gave up . . . in reliance on [the] promise. . . .

"This approach treats promissory estoppel as a tort doctrine for purposes of damages, though it is conventionally classified as a contract doctrine. . . . Some cases do award just the tort measure of damages in promissory estoppel cases, rather than giving the plaintiff the value of the promise, which he would be entitled to in a breach of contract action. . . . In Gerson Electric Construction Co. v. Honeywell, Inc., 117 Ill.App.3d 309, 312–13, 72 Ill.Dec. 851, 853, 453 N.E.2d 726, 728 (1983), however, the Illinois Appellate Court held that a plaintiff in a promissory estoppel case could recover damages for the profits he would have made had the defendant kept his promise—provided such an award was necessary to do justice to the plaintiff.

"There is much to be said for using the value of the promise as the measure of damages, simply on grounds of simplicity. . . . In addition, an expectation measure of damages will frequently cover opportunity costs (which are real, but not out-of-pocket, costs), that the reliance measure would miss. . . . "

NOTE ON OTHER BASES FOR ENFORCING PROMISES WITHOUT CONSIDERATION

Other bases for enforcing a promise without bargained-for consideration include formality (e.g., a promise is in a sealed instrument) and a pre-existing moral obligation (e.g., a promise to pay a debt discharged by the statute of limitations). This note concerns these bases.

Most states have adopted statutes depriving the seal of its binding effect. As a consequence there is no longer available any legal device that can be employed with the certainty that it will bind a promisor to a promise when consideration is in doubt. The Uniform Commercial Code contains a number of provisions that dispense with consideration for certain types of contracts, including Section 2–205 on firm offers and Section 2–209(1) on contract modifications. Similarly, a series of New York statutes, enacted on the recommendation of the New York Law Revision Commission and now collected in N.Y. General Obligations Law §§ 5–1101 to 5–1115, 15–303, dispenses with consideration for certain types of promises—for example, promises to discharge a contract—if the promises are made in writing and signed.

As for a pre-existing moral obligation, Mills v. Wyman, 3 Pick. [20 Mass.] 207 (1825), illustrates the position of classical contract law. A father learned a distant inn-keeper had incurred substantial expenses caring for his ill son, who was poor and in distress, until the son's death. The father wrote a letter promising to reimburse the inn-keeper but failed to keep his promise. Parker, C.J., described the father's conduct as "disgraceful" but concluded the promise was unenforceable because it was not supported by consideration, while noting a few exceptions to the rule (basically covering a promise to repay a debt discharged by operation of law):

A deliberate promise, in writing, made freely and without any mistake, one which may lead the party to whom it is made into contracts and expenses, cannot be broken without a violation of moral duty. But if there was nothing paid or promised for it, the law, perhaps wisely, leaves the execution of it to the conscience of him who makes it. It is only when the party making the promise gains something, or he to whom it is made loses something, that the law gives the promise validity. And in the case of the promise of the adult to pay the debt of the infant, of the debtor discharged by the statute of limitations or bankruptcy, the principle is preserved by looking back to the origin of the transaction, where an equivalent is to be found. An exact equivalent is not required by the law; for there being a consideration, the parties are left to estimate its value: though here the courts of equity will step in to relieve from gross inadequacy between the consideration and the promise.

[margin note: promise w/o consid isn't enforceable]

Webb v. McGowin, 27 Ala. App. 82, 168 So. 196 (1935), and 232 Ala. 374, 168 So. 199 (1936), takes a more generous position. Webb seriously injured himself while rescuing McGowin. The grateful McGowin promised to pay Webb $15 every two weeks for maintenance for the rest of Webb's life. McGowin kept his promise but when he died his executor stopped payment. The courts stretched to find consideration in order to enforce the promise. This prompted Samford, J., to write in a concurring opinion: "The questions involved in this case are not free from doubt, and perhaps the strict letter of the rule . . . would bar a recovery by plaintiff, but I do not think that law ought to be separated from justice, where it is at most doubtful." Restatement Second Section 86 adopts a more generous rule. It provides "[a] promise made in recognition of a benefit previously received by the promisor from the promisee is binding to the extent necessary to prevent injustice." Occasions for applying this rule are rare.

[margin note: Restatement Sec. 86]

[margin note: prevention of injustice is a workaround to lack of consid]

———

CHAPTER 3

THE LIMITS OF CONTRACT

■ ■ ■

The term "contract" is ambiguous. The Restatement defines a contract as any legally enforceable promise. Under this definition, a relied-upon donative promise is a contract. For some purposes that is a useful definition, but in everyday life the term "contract" usually means an agreement—especially a legally enforceable agreement. The Chapters succeeding this one will deal for the most part with contracts consisting of commercial bargains, in which legal enforceability is pretty clearly appropriate. In contrast, the cases and materials in this Chapter concern situations in which contract—used in the sense of a legally enforceable bargain—may or may not be appropriate.

———

Balfour v. Balfour

2 K.B. 571, 578 (1919)

(Atkin, L.J.) "[I]t is necessary to remember that there are agreements between parties which do not result in contracts within the meaning of that term in our law. The ordinary example is where two parties agree to take a walk together, or where there is an offer and an acceptance of hospitality. Nobody would suggest in ordinary circumstances that those agreements result in what we know as a contract, and one of the most usual forms of agreement which does not constitute a contract appears to me to be the arrangements which are made between husband and wife. It is quite common, and it is the natural and inevitable result of the relationship of husband and wife, that the two spouses should make arrangements between themselves. . . . To my mind those agreements, or many of them, do not result in contracts at all, and they do not result in contracts even though there may be what as between other parties would constitute consideration for the agreement. The consideration, as we know, may consist either in some right, interest, profit or benefit accruing to one party, or some forbearance, detriment, loss or responsibility given, suffered or undertaken by the other. That is a well-known definition, and it constantly happens, I think, that such arrangements made between husband and wife are arrangements in which there are mutual promises, or in which there is consideration in form within the definition that I have mentioned. Nevertheless they are not contracts, and they are not contracts because the parties did not intend that they should be attended by legal consequences. . . . in respect of these promises each house is a domain into

which the king's writ does not seek to run, and to which his officers do not seek
to be admitted."

———————

IN RE THE MARRIAGE OF WITTEN

Supreme Court of Iowa, 2003.
672 N.W.2d 768.

TERNUS, JUSTICE.

The primary issue raised on appeal of the district court's decree in this
dissolution action is whether the court properly determined the rights of
Arthur (known as Trip) and Tamera Witten with respect to the parties'
frozen human embryos stored at a medical facility. While we agree with
Tamera that the informed consent signed by the parties at the request of
the medical facility does not control the current dispute between the donors
over the use or disposition of the embryos, we reject Tamera's request that
she be allowed to use the embryos over Trip's objection. Therefore, we
affirm the trial court's order that neither party may use or dispose of the
embryos without the consent of the other party. . . .

I.   BACKGROUND FACTS AND PROCEEDINGS.

The appellee, Arthur (Trip) Witten, and the appellant, Tamera Witten,
had been married for approximately seven and one-half years when Trip
sought to have their marriage dissolved in April 2002. One of the contested
issues at trial was control of the parties' frozen embryos. During the
parties' marriage they had tried to become parents through the process of
in vitro fertilization. Because Tamera was unable to conceive children
naturally, they had eggs taken from Tamera artificially fertilized with
Trip's sperm. Tamera then underwent several unsuccessful embryo
transfers in an attempt to become pregnant. At the time of trial seventeen
fertilized eggs remained in storage at the University of Nebraska Medical
Center (UNMC).[1]

Prior to commencing the process for in vitro fertilization, the parties
signed informed consent documents prepared by the medical center. These
documents included an "Embryo Storage Agreement," which was signed by
Tamera and Trip as well as by a representative of UNMC. It provided in
part:

———————

[1]   No medical testimony was introduced at trial with respect to the cell stage of the parties'
fertilized eggs. Therefore, while some cases refer to fertilized eggs in the early stages of division
as "pre-zygotes" or "preembryos," we use the term "embryo" in discussing the present appeal, since
that is the terminology used in the Wittens' contract with UNMC. This term is used
interchangeably with the term "fertilized egg." [Ed.: Compare A.Z. v. B.Z., 431 Mass. 150, 752
N.E.2d 1051 (2000), where the court said "We use the term 'preembryo' to refer to the four-to-eight
cell stage of a developing fertilized egg." *Id.* at footnote 1.]

Release of Embryos. The Client Depositors [Trip and Tamera] understand and agree that containers of embryos stored pursuant to this agreement will be used for transfer, release or disposition only with the signed approval of both Client Depositors. UNMC will release the containers of embryos only to a licensed physician recipient of written authorization of the Client Depositors.

The agreement had one exception to the joint-approval requirement that governed the disposition of the embryos upon the death of one or both of the client depositors. Another provision of the contract provided for termination of UNMC's responsibility to store the embryos upon several contingencies: (1) the client depositors' written authorization to release the embryos or to destroy them; (2) the death of the client depositors; (3) the failure of the client depositors to pay the annual storage fee; or (4) the expiration of ten years from the date of the agreement.

At trial, Tamera asked that she be awarded "custody" of the embryos. She wanted to have the embryos implanted in her or a surrogate mother in an effort to bear a genetically linked child. She testified that upon a successful pregnancy she would afford Trip the opportunity to exercise parental rights or to have his rights terminated. She adamantly opposed any destruction of the embryos, and was also unwilling to donate the eggs to another couple.

Trip testified at the trial that while he did not want the embryos destroyed, he did not want Tamera to use them. He would not oppose donating the embryos for use by another couple. Trip asked the court to enter a permanent injunction prohibiting either party from transferring, releasing, or utilizing the embryos without the written consent of both parties.

The district court decided the dispute should be governed by the "embryo storage agreement" between the parties and UNMC, which required both parties' consent to any use or disposition of the embryos. Enforcing this agreement, the trial court enjoined both parties "from transferring, releasing or in any other way using or disposing of the embryos . . . without the written and signed approval and authorization" of the other party.

Tamera has appealed the trial court's order, challenging only the court's resolution of the parties' dispute over the fertilized eggs. She claims the storage agreement is silent with respect to disposition or use of the embryos upon the parties' dissolution because there is no provision specifically addressing that contingency. Therefore, she argues, the court should have applied the "best interests [of the child]" test of Iowa Code chapter 598 (2001) and, pursuant to that analysis, awarded custody of the embryos to her. She makes the alternative argument that she is entitled to the fertilized eggs due to her fundamental right to bear children. Finally,

Tamera claims it would violate the public policy of this state if Trip were allowed to back out of his agreement to have children. She claims such an agreement is evidenced by his participation in the in vitro fertilization procedure. . . .

III. DISPOSITION OF EMBRYOS.

A. *Scope of storage agreement.* We first consider Tamera's contention that the storage agreement does not address the situation at hand. As noted earlier, the agreement had a specific provision governing control of the embryos if one or both parties died, but did not explicitly deal with the possibility of divorce. Nonetheless, we think the present predicament falls within the general provision governing "release of embryos," in which the parties agreed that the embryos would not be transferred, released, or discarded without "the signed approval" of both Tamera and Trip. This provision is certainly broad enough to encompass the decision-making protocol when the parties are unmarried as well as when they are married.

The only question, then, is whether such agreements are enforceable when one of the parties later changes his or her mind with respect to the proper disposition of the embryos. In reviewing the scarce case law from other jurisdictions on this point, we have found differing views of how the parties' rights should be determined. There is, however, abundant literature that has scrutinized the approaches taken to date. Some writers have suggested refinements of the analytical framework employed by the courts thus far; some have proposed an entirely new model of analysis. From these various sources, we have identified three primary approaches to resolving disputes over the disposition of frozen embryos, which we have identified as (1) the contractual approach, (2) the contemporaneous mutual consent model, and (3) the balancing test.

Tamera's argument that her right to bear children should override the parties' prior agreement as well as Trip's current opposition to her use of the embryos resembles the balancing test. As for Tamera's alternative argument, we have found no authority supporting a "best interests" analysis in determining the disposition of frozen embryos. Nonetheless, we will first consider whether chapter 598 requires application of that analysis under the circumstances presented by this case. Then, we will discuss and consider the three approaches suggested by decisions from other jurisdictions and the literature on this subject.

B. *"Best interests" test.* [The court began by considering the effect of an Iowa statute, § 598.41. This statute set forth various standards governing the award of child custody in a marital-dissolution case, including a requirement that any custody award reflect "the best interest of the child." The court held that the best-interest standard was not applicable to the issue at hand. "First, we note the purposes of the 'best interest' standard set forth in that statute are to 'assure the child the opportunity for the maximum continuing physical and emotional contact with both parents' and to 'encourage parents to share the rights and responsibilities of raising the child.' Iowa Code § 598.41(1)(a). The principles developed under this statute are simply not suited to the resolution of disputes over the control of frozen embryos. Such disputes do not involve maximizing physical and emotional contact between both parents and the child; they involve the more fundamental decision of whether the parties will be parents at all. Moreover, it would be premature to consider which parent can most effectively raise the child when the "child" is still frozen in a storage facility. The principles of section 598.41 do not fit because what is really at issue here is not the custody of children as that concept is generally viewed and analyzed in dissolution cases. Rather, the issue here is who will have decision-making authority with respect to the fertilized eggs." . . .

C. *Enforcement of storage agreement.* We now consider the appropriateness of the trial court's decision to allow Tamera and Trip's agreement with the medical center to control the current dispute between them. As we noted above, there are three methods of analysis that have been suggested to resolve disputes over frozen embryos. We will discuss them separately.

1. *Contractual approach.* The currently prevailing view—expressed in three states—is that contracts entered into at the time of in vitro fertilization are enforceable so long as they do not violate public policy. *See* [*Kass v. Kass*, 91 N.Y.2d 554, 673 N.Y.S.2d 350, 696 N.E.2d 174, 179 (1998)] (stating agreements between donors "regarding disposition of pre-zygotes should generally be presumed valid and binding"); [*Davis v. Davis*, 842 S.W.2d 588 (Tenn. 1992)], 842 S.W.2d at 597 (holding agreement regarding disposition of embryos "should be considered binding"); *In re Litowitz*, 146 Wash.2d 514, 48 P.3d 261, 271 (2002) (enforcing parties' contract providing for disposition of preembryos after five years of storage).[2] The New York Court of Appeals expressed the following rationale for this contractual approach:

---

[2] Application of the contractual approach in *Kass* resulted in enforcement of the parties' agreement that the fertilized eggs would be donated for research should the parties be "unable to make a decision regarding the disposition of [the] stored, frozen pre-zygotes." 696 N.E.2d at 176–77, 181. In *Litowitz*, the court permitted execution of the parties' previous agreement that the preembryos would be "disposed of" after five years. 48 P.3d at 271. The resolution of the divorcing couple's dispute was more complex in *Davis* because the parties did not have a contract addressing the disposition of any unused preembryos. 842 S.W.2d at 590. Noting that a "prior agreement concerning disposition should be carried out," the court concluded in the absence of such an agreement, "the relative interests of the parties in using or not using the preembryos must be weighed." *Id.* at 604. The court awarded the preembryos to the husband, concluding his interest in not becoming a parent outweighed his former wife's interest in donating the preembryos to another couple for implantation. *Id.* The court noted the issue might be closer if the wife had wanted to use the preembryos herself; but in view of the fact she had "a reasonable possibility of achieving parenthood by means other than use of the preembryos in question," she would not have prevailed even under those circumstances. *Id.*

[It is] particularly important that courts seek to honor the parties' expressions of choice, made before disputes erupt, with the parties' over-all direction always uppermost in the analysis. Knowing that advance agreements will be enforced underscores the seriousness and integrity of the consent process. Advance agreements as to disposition would have little purpose if they were enforceable only in the event the parties continued to agree. To the extent possible, it should be the progenitors—not the State and not the courts—who by their prior directive make this deeply personal life choice.

Kass, 673 N.Y.S.2d 350, 696 N.E.2d at 180.

This approach has been criticized, however, because it "insufficiently protects the individual and societal interests at stake":

First, decisions about the disposition of frozen embryos implicate rights central to individual identity. On matters of such fundamental personal importance, individuals are entitled to make decisions consistent with their contemporaneous wishes, values, and beliefs. Second, requiring couples to make binding decisions about the future use of their frozen embryos ignores the difficulty of predicting one's future response to life-altering events such as parenthood. Third, conditioning the provision of infertility treatment on the execution of binding disposition agreements is coercive and calls into question the authenticity of the couple's original choice. Finally, treating couples' decisions about the future use of their frozen embryos as binding contracts undermines important values about families, reproduction, and the strength of genetic ties.

[Carl H. Coleman, *Procreative Liberty and Contemporaneous Choice: An Inalienable Rights Approach to Frozen Embryo Disputes,*] 84 Minn. L.Rev. at 88–89. Another legal writer has echoed these concerns:

Binding a couple to a prior disposition agreement has its roots in contract law. The primary advantage of treating the disposition of preembryos as a contract dispute is that it binds individuals to previous obligations, even if their priorities or values change. This advantage, while maximizing the efficiency of commercial transactions, is ill-suited to govern the disposition of human tissue with the potential to develop into a child. The potential of the embryo requires that couples be allowed to make contemporaneous decisions about the fate of the embryo that reflect their current values.

Christina C. Lawrence, Note, *Procreative Liberty and the Preembryo Problem: Developing a Medical and Legal Framework to Settle the Disposition of Frozen Embryos,* 52 Case W. Res. L.Rev. 721, 729 (2002) [hereinafter "Lawrence Note"]; *accord J.B. v. M.B.*, 170 N.J. 9, 783 A.2d 707, 718–19 (2001). In response to such concerns, one commentator has suggested an alternative model requiring contemporaneous mutual consent. We now examine that approach.

2. *Contemporaneous mutual consent.* The contractual approach and the contemporaneous mutual consent model share an underlying premise: "decisions about the disposition of frozen embryos belong to the couple that created the embryo, with each partner entitled to an equal say in how the embryos should be disposed." Coleman, 84 Minn. L.Rev. at 81. Departing from this common starting point, the alternative framework asserts the important question is "at what time does the partners' consent matter?" *Id.* at 91. Proponents of the mutual-consent approach suggest that, with respect to "decisions about intensely emotional matters, where people act more on the basis of feeling and instinct than rational deliberation," it may "be impossible to make a knowing and intelligent decision to relinquish a right in advance of the time the right is to be exercised." *Id.* at 98; *see also* Sara D. Petersen, Comment, *Dealing With Cryopreserved Embryos Upon Divorce: A Contractual Approach Aimed at Preserving Party Expectations*, 50 UCLA L.REV. 1065, 1090 & n. 156 (2003) (stating "surveys of couples that have stored frozen embryos suggest that they may be prone to changing their minds while their embryos remain frozen" and citing a study that found " '[o]f the 41 couples that had recorded both a pre-treatment and post-treatment decision about embryo disposition, only 12(29%) kept the same disposition choice' " (citation omitted)). One's erroneous prediction of how she or he will feel about the matter at some point in the future can have grave repercussions. "Like decisions about marriage or relinquishing a child for adoption, decisions about the use of one's reproductive capacity have lifelong consequences for a person's identity and sense of self":

> When chosen voluntarily, becoming a parent can be an important act of self-definition. Compelled parenthood, by contrast, imposes an unwanted identity on the individual, forcing her to redefine herself, her place in the world, and the legacy she will leave after she dies. For some people, the mandatory destruction of an embryo can have equally profound consequences, particularly for those who believe that embryos are persons. If forced destruction is experienced as the loss of a child, it can lead to life-altering feelings of mourning, guilt, and regret.

Coleman, 84 Minn. L.Rev. at 96–97. To accommodate these concerns, advocates of the mutual-consent model propose "no embryo should be used by either partner, donated to another patient, used in research, or destroyed without the [contemporaneous] mutual consent of the couple that created the embryo." *Id.* at 110. Under this alternate framework,

advance instructions would not be treated as binding
contracts. If either partner has a change of mind about disposition
decisions made in advance, that person's current objection would
take precedence over the prior consent. If one of the partners
rescinds an advance disposition decision and the other does not,
the mutual consent principle would not be satisfied and the
previously agreed-upon disposition decision could not be carried
out. . . .

When the couple is unable to agree to any disposition
decision, the most appropriate solution is to keep the embryos
where they are—in frozen storage. Unlike the other possible
disposition decisions—use by one partner, donation to another
patient, donation to research, or destruction—keeping the
embryos frozen is not final and irrevocable. By preserving the
status quo, it makes it possible for the partners to reach an
agreement at a later time.

Id. at 110–12; *see also id.* at 89 (suggesting "the embryo would remain in
frozen storage until the parties reach a new agreement, the embryo is no
longer viable, or storage facilities are no longer available"); *accord*
Lawrence Note, 52 Case W. Res. L.Rev. at 742. Although this model
precludes one party's use of the embryos to have children over the objection
of the other party, the outcome under the contractual approach and the
balancing test would generally be the same. *See A.Z. v. B.Z.,* 431 Mass. 150,
725 N.E.2d 1051, 1057–58 (2000) ("As a matter of public policy, . . . forced
procreation is not an area amenable to judicial enforcement."); *J.B.,* 783
A.2d at 717 (evaluating relative interests of parties in disposition of
embryos, concluding husband should not be able to use embryos over wife's
objection); *Davis,* 842 S.W.2d at 604 ("Ordinarily, the party wishing to
avoid procreation should prevail."); Susan B. Apel, *Disposition of Frozen
Embryos: Are Contracts the Solution?,* Vermont Bar Journal, March 2001,
at 31 ("Some argue that the party seeking to avoid procreation should
prevail, and indeed, this appears to be the one harmonizing rationale of the
four reported cases.") [hereinafter "Apel"].

3.   *Balancing test.* The New Jersey Supreme Court appears to have
adopted an analysis regarding the disposition of frozen human embryos
that incorporates the idea of contemporaneous decision-making, but not
that of mutual consent. In *J.B.,* the New Jersey court rejected the *Kass* and
Davis contractual approach, noting public policy concerns in
"[e]nforcement of a contract that would allow the implantation of
preembryos at some future date in a case where one party has reconsidered
his or her earlier acquiescence." 783 A.2d at 718. The court stated:

We believe that the better rule, and the one we adopt, is to
enforce agreements entered into at the time in vitro fertilization

is begun, *subject to the right of either party to change his or her mind about disposition up to the point of use or destruction of any stored preembryos.*

Id. at 719 (emphasis added). The court based its decision on "[t]he public policy concerns that underlie limitations on contracts involving family relationships." *Id.; see also A.Z.,* 725 N.E.2d at 1057–58 (refusing, in light of the same public policy concerns, to enforce an agreement that allowed the wife, upon the parties' separation, to use the couple's preembryos for implantation).

The New Jersey court did not, however, adopt the requirement for mutual consent as a prerequisite for any use or disposition of the preembryos. Rather, that court stated that "if there is a disagreement between the parties as to disposition . . . , the interests of both parties must be evaluated" by the court. *J.B.,* 783 A.2d at 719. This balancing test was also the default analysis employed by the Tennessee Supreme Court in *Davis* where the parties had not executed a written agreement. *See Davis,* 842 S.W.2d at 604 (holding in the absence of a prior agreement concerning disposition, "the relative interests of the parties in using or not using the preembryos must be weighed" by the court).

The obvious problem with the balancing test model is its internal inconsistency. *See generally* Lawrence Note, 52 Case W. Res. L.Rev. at 738 (suggesting "[t]he premise of the balancing test . . . is flawed"). Public policy concerns similar to those that prompt courts to refrain from enforcement of contracts addressing reproductive choice demand even more strongly that we not substitute the courts as decision makers in this highly emotional and personal area. Nonetheless, that is exactly what happens under the decisional framework based on the balancing test because the court must weigh the relative interests of the parties in deciding the disposition of embryos when the parties cannot agree. *See J.B.,* 783 A.2d at 719.

D.   *Discussion.* With these alternative approaches in mind, we turn to the present case. . . .

[A]re prior agreements regarding the future disposition of embryos enforceable when one of the donors is no longer comfortable with his or her prior decision? We first note our agreement with other courts considering such matters that the partners who created the embryos have the primary, and equal, decision-making authority with respect to the use or disposition of their embryos. We think, however, that it would be against the public policy of this state to enforce a prior agreement between the parties in this highly personal area of reproductive choice when one of the parties has changed his or her mind concerning the disposition or use of the embryos.

Our statutes and case law evidence an understanding that decisions involving marital and family relationships are emotional and subject to change. For example, Iowa law imposes a seventy-two hour waiting period after the birth of a child before the biological parents can release parental rights. *See* Iowa Code § 600A.4(2)(*g*). In addition, although this court has not abolished claims for breach of promise to marry,[3] only recovery of monetary damages is permitted; the court will not force a party to actually consummate the marriage. *See* Herbert F. Goodrich, *Iowa Decisions on Breach of Marriage Promise,* 4 Iowa L. Bull. 166, 177 (1918). It has also long been recognized in this state that agreements for the purpose of bringing about a dissolution of marriage are contrary to public policy and therefore void. *Barngrover v. Pettigrew,* 128 Iowa 533, 535, 104 N.W. 904, 904 (1905) . . . .

This court has also expressed a general reluctance to become involved in intimate questions inherent in personal relationships. *See Miller v. Miller,* 78 Iowa 177, 179–80, 42 N.W. 641, 641 (1889). In *Miller,* we refused to enforce a contract between husband and wife that required, in part, each "to behave respectfully, and fairly treat the other." *Id.* at 180, 42 N.W. at 641. We explained our refusal on the following grounds:

> [J]udicial inquiry into matters of that character, between husband and wife, would be fraught with irreparable mischief, and forbidden by sound considerations of public policy.

> It is the genius of our laws, as well as of our civilization, that matters pertaining so directly and exclusively to the home, and its value as such, and which are so generally susceptible of regulation and control by those influences which surround it, are not to become matters of public concern or inquiry.

Id. at 182, 42 N.W. at 642; *accord Heacock v. Heacock,* 108 Iowa 540, 542, 79 N.W. 353, 354 (1899) ("Husband and wife cannot contract with each other to secure the performance of their marital rights and duties."). Certainly reproductive decisions are likewise not proper matters of judicial inquiry and enforcement.

We have considered and rejected the arguments of some commentators that embryo disposition agreements are analogous to antenuptial agreements and divorce stipulations, which courts generally enforce. *See* Apel, Vermont Bar Journal at 31. Whether embryos are viewed as having life or simply as having the potential for life, this characteristic or potential renders embryos fundamentally distinct from the chattels, real estate, and money that are the subjects of antenuptial agreements. Divorce stipulations are also distinguishable. While such agreements may address custody issues, they are contemporaneous with the implementation of the stipulation, an attribute noticeably lacking in disposition agreements.

---

[3]   This court has not had a breach-of-contract-to-marry case before it in over fifty years. *See Bearbower v. Merry,* 266 N.W.2d 128, 132 (Iowa 1978) (citing *Benson v. Williams,* 239 Iowa 742, 32 N.W.2d 813 (1948)).

In addition to decisional and statutory authority supporting a public policy against judicial enforcement of personal decisions concerning marriage, family, and reproduction, our statutes also anticipate the effect of a couple's dissolution on their prior decisions. For example, Iowa Code section 633.271 provides that if a testator is divorced after making a will, "all provisions in the will in favor of the testator's spouse" are automatically revoked. Similarly, Iowa Code section 633.3107 revokes all provisions in a revocable trust in favor of the settlor's spouse upon divorce or dissolution of the marriage. Similar considerations make enforcement of contracts between partners involving such personal decisions as the use and disposition of their combined genetic material equally problematic. As noted by one commentator, embryos are originally created as "a mutual undertaking by [a] couple to have children together." Coleman, 84 Minn. L.Rev. at 83. Agreements made in that context are not always consistent with the parties' wishes once the mutual undertaking has ended.

We think judicial decisions and statutes in Iowa reflect respect for the right of individuals to make family and reproductive decisions based on their current views and values. They also reveal awareness that such decisions are highly emotional in nature and subject to a later change of heart. For this reason, we think judicial enforcement of an agreement *between a couple* regarding their future family and reproductive choices would be against the public policy of this state.

Our decision should not be construed, however, to mean that disposition agreements *between donors and fertility clinics* have no validity at all. We recognize a disposition or storage agreement serves an important purpose in defining and governing the relationship between the couple and the medical facility, ensuring that all parties understand their respective rights and obligations. *See A.Z.,* 725 N.E.2d at 1057 n. 22 ("We also recognize that agreements among donors and IVF clinics are essential to clinic operations."). In fact, it is this relationship, between the couple on the one side and the medical facility on the other, that dispositional contracts are intended to address. *See generally* Ellen A. Waldman, *Disputing Over Embryos: Of Contracts and Consents,* 32 Ariz. St. L.J. 897, 918 (2000) (noting "courts and most scholarly authorities would transform documents designed to record the transmission of medical information from clinic to couple, and the couple's acceptance of medical treatment, into a binding agreement between the couple itself"). Within this context, the medical facility and the donors should be able to rely on the terms of the parties' contract. *See A.Z.,* 725 N.E.2d at 1057 n. 22 (noting court's decision not to enforce agreement between partners is not an "impediment to the enforcement of such contracts by the clinics or by the donors against the clinics"); *J.B.,* 783 A.2d at 719.

In view of these competing needs, we reject the contractual approach and hold that agreements entered into at the time in vitro fertilization is commenced are enforceable and binding on the parties, "subject to the right of either party to change his or her mind about disposition up to the point of use or destruction of any stored embryo." *J.B.*, 783 A.2d at 719. This decisional model encourages prior agreements that can guide the actions of all parties, unless a later objection to any dispositional provision is asserted. It also recognizes that, *absent a change of heart by one of the partners,* an agreement governing disposition of embryos does not violate public policy. Only when one person makes known the agreement no longer reflects his or her current values or wishes is public policy implicated. Upon this occurrence, allowing either party to withdraw his or her agreement to a disposition that person no longer accepts acknowledges the public policy concerns inherent in enforcing prior decisions of a fundamentally personal nature. In fairness to the medical facility that is a party to the agreement, however, any change of intention must be communicated in writing to all parties in order to reopen the disposition issues covered by the agreement. *Id.*

That brings us, then, to the dilemma presented when one or both partners change their minds and the parties cannot reach a mutual decision on disposition. We have already explained the grave public policy concerns we have with the balancing test, which simply substitutes the court as decision maker. A better principle to apply, we think, is the requirement of contemporaneous mutual consent. Under that model, no transfer, release, disposition, or use of the embryos can occur without the signed authorization of both donors. If a stalemate results, the status quo would be maintained. The practical effect will be that the embryos are stored indefinitely unless both parties can agree to destroy the fertilized eggs. Thus, any expense associated with maintaining the status quo should logically be borne by the person opposing destruction. *See* Coleman, 84 Minn. L.Rev. at 112 ("The right to insist on the continued storage of the embryos should be dependent on a willingness to pay the associated costs.").

Turning to the present case, we find a situation in which one party no longer concurs in the parties' prior agreement with respect to the disposition of their frozen embryos, but the parties have been unable to reach a new agreement that is mutually satisfactory. Based on this fact, under the principles we have set forth today, we hold there can be no use or disposition of the Wittens' embryos unless Trip and Tamera reach an agreement.[4] Until then, the party or parties who oppose destruction shall be responsible for any storage fees. Therefore, we affirm the trial court's ruling enjoining both parties from transferring, releasing, or utilizing the embryos without the other's written consent. . . .

---

[4]   We do not mean to imply that UNMC's obligation to store the embryos extends beyond the ten-year period provided in the parties' contract.

. . . DISPOSITION.

We affirm the trial court's decree [concerning the disposition of the embryos]. . . .

————

NOTE ON SURROGATE-PARENTING LEGISLATION

A number of states have adopted statutes concerning surrogacy. These statutes vary widely. For example, the District of Columbia, Indiana, Michigan, and North Dakota either prohibit surrogacy contracts or make such contracts void and unenforceable. Arkansas allows surrogacy contracts. Washington allows uncompensated surrogacy contracts. New Mexico allows uncompensated surrogacy contracts and payment of the surrogate's medical and similar expenses. Nebraska renders paid surrogacy contracts unenforceable, but says nothing about unpaid surrogacy. Nevada and Virginia allow unpaid surrogacy contracts but only where the prospective parents are married couples.

————

42 U.S. CODE § 274. PROHIBITION OF ORGAN PURCHASES

(a) *Prohibition.* It shall be unlawful for any person to knowingly acquire, receive, or otherwise transfer any human organ for valuable consideration for use in human transplantation if the transfer affects interstate commerce.

(b) *Penalties.* Any person who violates subsection (a) of this section shall be fined not more than $50,000 or imprisoned not more than five years, or both.

(c) *Definitions.* For purposes of subsection (a) of this section:

(1) The term "human organ" means the human (including fetal) kidney, liver, heart, lung, pancreas, bone marrow, cornea, eye, bone, and skin or any subpart thereof and any other human organ (or any subpart thereof, including that derived from a fetus) specified by the Secretary of Health and Human Services by regulation.

(2) The term "valuable consideration" does not include the reasonable payments associated with the removal, transportation, implantation, processing, preservation, quality control, and storage of a human organ or the expenses of travel, housing, and lost wages incurred by the donor of a human organ in connection with the donation of the organ. . . .

RADIN, MARKET-INALIENABILITY
100 Harvard L.Rev. 1849 (1987).*

Since the declaration of "unalienable rights" of persons at the founding of our republic, inalienability has had a central place in our legal and moral culture. Yet there is no one sharp meaning for the term "inalienable." Sometimes inalienable means nontransferable; sometimes only nonsalable.... In this Article I explore nonsalability, a species of inalienability I call market-inalienability. Something that is market-inalienable is not to be sold, which in our economic system means it is not to be traded in the market.

Controversy over what may be bought and sold—blood or babies—pervades our news.... About fifteen years ago, for example, Richard Titmuss advocated in his book, *The Gift Relationship,* that human blood should not be allocated through the market; others disagreed. More recently, Elisabeth Landes and Richard Posner suggested the possibility of a thriving market in infants, yet most people continue to believe that infants should not be allocated through the market....

In [one] important set of meanings, inalienability is ascribed to an entitlement, right, or attribute that cannot be voluntarily transferred from one holder to another. Inalienability in these uses may mean nongiveable, nonsalable, or completely nontransferable. If something is nontransferable, the holder cannot designate a successor holder. Nongiveability and nonsalability are subsets of nontransferability. If something is inalienable by gift, it might be transferred by sale; if it is inalienable by sale, it might be transferred by gift. This nonsalability is what I refer to as market-inalienability. In precluding sales but not gifts, market-inalienability places some things outside the marketplace but not outside the realm of social intercourse.

Market-inalienability negates a central element of traditional property rights, which are conceived of as fully alienable. But market-inalienability differs from the nontransferability that characterizes many nontraditional property rights—entitlements of the regulatory and welfare state—that are both nongiveable and nonsalable. [Examples are entitlements to social security and welfare benefits.] Market-inalienability also differs from the inalienability of other things, like voting rights, that seem to be moral or political duties related to a community's normative life; they are subject to broader inalienabilities that preclude loss as well as transfer. Unlike the inalienabilities attaching to welfare entitlements or

---

*   This article now forms the basis of a book, Margaret Jane Radin, Contested Commodities (1996). (Footnote by ed.)

political duties, market-inalienability does not render something inseparable from the person, but rather specifies that market trading may not be used as a social mechanism of separation. Finally, market-inalienability differs from the inalienability of things, like heroin, that are made nontransferable in order to implement a prohibition, because it does not signify that something is social anathema. Indeed, preclusion of sales often coexists with encouragement of gifts. For example, the market-inalienability of human organs does not preclude—and, indeed, may seek to foster—transfer from one individual to another by gift. . . .

Market-inalienability often expresses an aspiration for noncommodification. By making something nonsalable we proclaim that it should not be conceived of or treated as a commodity. When something is noncommodifiable, market trading is a disallowed form of social organization and allocation. We place that thing beyond supply and demand pricing, brokerage and arbitrage, advertising and marketing, stockpiling, speculation, and valuation in terms of the opportunity cost of production.

Market-inalienability poses for us more than the binary choice of whether something should be wholly inside or outside the market, completely commodified or completely noncommodified. Some things are completely commodified—deemed suitable for trade in a laissez-faire market. Others are completely noncommodified—removed from the market altogether. But many things can be described as incompletely commodified—neither fully commodified nor fully removed from the market. Thus, we may decide that some things should be market-inalienable only to a degree, or only in some aspects.

To appreciate the need to develop a satisfactory analysis of market-inalienability, consider the deeply contested issues of commodification that confront us. Infants and children, fetal gestational services, blood, human organs, sexual services, and services of college athletes are some salient things whose commodification is contested. Our division over whether to place a monetary equivalent on a spouse's professional degree or homemaker services in a divorce; or on various kinds of injuries in tort actions, such as loss of consortium, is another form of contest over commodification. Monetization—commodification—of clean air and water is likewise deeply contested. Moreover, debates about some kinds of regulation can be seen as contested incomplete commodification, with the contest being over whether to allow full commodification (a laissez-faire market regime) or something less. If we see the debates this way, residential rent control, minimum wage requirements, and other forms of price regulation, as well as residential habitability requirements, safety regulation, and other forms of product-quality regulation all become contests over the issue of commodification.

How are we to determine the extent to which something ought to be noncommodified, so that we can determine to what extent market-inalienability is justified? Because the question asks about the appropriate relationship of particular things to the market, normative theories about the appropriate social role of the market should be helpful in trying to answer it. We can think of such theories as ordered on a continuum stretching from universal noncommodification (nothing in markets) to universal commodification (everything in markets). On this continuum, Karl Marx's theory can symbolize the theoretical pole of universal noncommodification, and Richard Posner's can be seen as close to the opposite theoretical pole. . . .

Universal commodification undermines personal identity by conceiving of personal attributes, relationships, and philosophical and moral commitments as monetizable and alienable from the self. A better view of personhood should understand many kinds of particulars—one's politics, work, religion, family, love, sexuality, friendships, altruism, experiences, wisdom, moral commitments, character, and personal attributes—as integral to the self. To understand any of these as monetizable or completely detachable from the person—to think, for example, that the value of one person's moral commitments is commensurate or fungible with those of another, or that the "same" person remains when her moral commitments are subtracted—is to do violence to our deepest understanding of what it is to be human. . . .

———

PART 2

REMEDIES FOR BREACH OF CONTRACT

■ ■ ■

There are five possible remedies for breach of a bargain contract: expectation damages, reliance damages in lieu of expectation damages, restitution, disgorgement, and specific performance. These five remedies, and their limits, are considered in Chapters 4–7.

———

REMEDIES FOR BREACH
OF CONTRACT

* * *

CHAPTER 4

EXPECTATION DAMAGES: THE GENERAL PRINCIPLE

■ ■ ■

RESTATEMENT, SECOND, CONTRACTS § 344

[See Selected Source Materials Supplement]

HAWKINS V. MCGEE

Supreme Court of New Hampshire, 1929.
84 N.H. 114, 146 A. 641.

Assumpsit, against a surgeon for breach of an alleged warranty of the success of an operation. Trial by jury and verdict for the plaintiff. The writ also contained a count in negligence upon which a nonsuit was ordered, without exception.

[The defendant moved to have the verdict set aside on several grounds, one of them being that the damages awarded were excessive. The trial court ordered that the verdict be set aside unless the plaintiff would remit all damages in excess of $500. On the plaintiff's refusal to consent to a reduction, the trial court set the verdict aside as being "excessive and against the weight of the evidence." The plaintiff excepted to this ruling of the trial court; his exception and numerous exceptions taken by the defendant were transferred to the Supreme Court.]

BRANCH, J. The operation in question consisted in the removal of a considerable quantity of scar tissue from the palm of the plaintiff's right hand and the grafting of skin taken from the plaintiff's chest in place thereof. The scar tissue was the result of a severe burn caused by contact with an electric wire, which the plaintiff received about nine years before the time of the transactions here involved. There was evidence to the effect that before the operation was performed the plaintiff and his father went to the defendant's office, and that the defendant in answer to the question, "How long will the boy be in the hospital?" replied, "Three or four days, . . . not over four; then the boy can go home and it will be just a few days when he will go back to work with a perfect hand." Clearly this and other

139

testimony to the same effect would not justify a finding that the doctor contracted to complete the hospital treatment in three or four days or that the plaintiff would be able to go back to work within a few days thereafter. The above statements could only be construed as expressions of opinion or predictions as to the probable duration of the treatment and plaintiff's resulting disability, and the fact that these estimates were exceeded would impose no contractual liability upon the defendant. The only substantial basis for the plaintiff's claim is the testimony that the defendant also said before the operation was decided upon, "I will guarantee to make the hand a hundred per cent perfect hand" or "a hundred per cent good hand." The plaintiff was present when these words were alleged to have been spoken, and, if they are to be taken at their face value, it seems obvious that proof of their utterance would establish the giving of a warranty in accordance with his contention.

The defendant argues, however, that, even if these words were uttered by him, no reasonable man would understand that they were used with the intention of entering into any "contractual relation whatever," and that they could reasonably be understood only "as his expression in strong language that he believed and expected that as a result of the operation he would give the plaintiff a very good hand." It may be conceded, as the defendant contends, that, before the question of the making of a contract should be submitted to a jury, there is a preliminary question of law for the trial court to pass upon, i.e. "whether the words could possibly have the meaning imputed to them by the party who founds his case upon a certain interpretation," but it cannot be held that the trial court decided this question erroneously in the present case. It is unnecessary to determine at this time whether the argument of the defendant, based upon "common knowledge of the uncertainty which attends all surgical operations," and the improbability that a surgeon would ever contract to make a damaged part of the human body "one hundred per cent perfect," would, in the absence of countervailing considerations, be regarded as conclusive, for there were other factors in the present case which tended to support the contention of the plaintiff. There was evidence that the defendant repeatedly solicited from the plaintiff's father the opportunity to perform this operation, and the theory was advanced by plaintiff's counsel in cross-examination of defendant that he sought an opportunity to "experiment on skin grafting," in which he had had little previous experience. If the jury accepted this part of plaintiff's contention, there would be a reasonable basis for the further conclusion that, if defendant spoke the words attributed to him, he did so with the intention that they should be accepted at their face value, as an inducement for the granting of consent to the operation by the plaintiff and his father, and there was ample evidence that they were so accepted by them. The question of the making of the alleged contract was properly submitted to the jury.

2.   The substance of the charge to the jury on the question of damages appears in the following quotation: "If you find the plaintiff entitled to anything, he is entitled to recover for what pain and suffering he has been made to endure and for what injury he has sustained over and above what injury he had before." To this instruction the defendant seasonably excepted. By it, the jury was permitted to consider two elements of damage, (1) pain and suffering due to the operation, and (2) positive ill effects of the operation upon the plaintiff's hand. Authority for any specific rule of damages in cases of this kind seems to be lacking, but, when tested by general principle and by analogy, it appears that the foregoing instruction was erroneous.

Jury instruction

"By 'damages,' as that term is used in the law of contracts, is intended compensation for a breach, measured in the terms of the contract." Davis v. New England Cotton Yarn Co., 77 N.H. 403, 404, 92 A. 732, 733. The purpose of the law is "to put the plaintiff in as good a position as he would have been in had the defendant kept his contract." 3 Williston Cont. § 1338; Hardie-Tynes Mfg. Co. v. Easton Cotton Oil Co., 150 N.C. 150, 63 S.E. 676, 134 Am.St.Rep. 899. The measure of recovery "is based upon what the defendant should have given the plaintiff, not what the plaintiff has given the defendant or otherwise expended." 3 Williston Cont. § 1341. "The only losses that can be said fairly to come within the terms of a contract are such as the parties must have had in mind when the contract was made, or such as they either knew or ought to have known would probably result from a failure to comply with its terms." Davis v. New England Cotton Yarn Co., 77 N.H. 403, 404, 92 A. 732, 733, Hurd v. Dunsmore, 63 N.H. 171.

The present case is closely analogous to one in which a machine is built for a certain purpose and warranted to do certain work. In such cases, the usual rule of damages for breach of warranty in the sale of chattels is applied and it is held that the measure of damages is the difference between the value of the machine if it had corresponded with the warranty and its actual value, together with such incidental losses as the parties knew or ought to have known would probably result from a failure to comply with its terms. . . .

We therefore conclude that the true measure of the plaintiff's damage in the present case is the difference between the value to him of a perfect hand or a good hand, such as the jury found the defendant promised him, and the value of his hand in its present condition, including any incidental consequences fairly within the contemplation of the parties when they made their contract. 1 Sutherland, Damages (4th Ed.) § 92. Damages not thus limited, although naturally resulting, are not to be given.

The extent of the plaintiff's suffering does not measure this difference in value. The pain necessarily incident to a serious surgical operation was a part of the contribution which the plaintiff was willing to make to his joint undertaking with the defendant to produce a good hand. It was a legal detriment suffered by him which constituted a part of the consideration given by him for the contract. It represented a part of the price which he was willing to pay for a good hand, but it furnished no test of the value of a good hand or the difference between the value of the hand which the defendant promised and the one which resulted from the operation.

It was also erroneous and misleading to submit to the jury as a separate element of damage any change for the worse in the condition of the plaintiff's hand resulting from the operation, although this error was probably more prejudicial to the plaintiff than to the defendant. Any such ill effect of the operation would be included under the true rule of damages set forth above, but damages might properly be assessed for the defendant's failure to improve the condition of the hand, even if there were no evidence that its condition was made worse as a result of the operation.

It must be assumed that the trial court, in setting aside the verdict, undertook to apply the same rule of damages which he had previously given to the jury, and, since this rule was erroneous, it is unnecessary for us to consider whether there was any evidence to justify his finding that all damages awarded by the jury above $500 were excessive.

3.   Defendant's requests for instructions were loosely drawn, and were properly denied. A considerable number of issues of fact were raised by the evidence, and it would have been extremely misleading to instruct the jury in accordance with defendant's request No. 2, that "The only issue on which you have to pass is whether or not there was a special contract between the plaintiff and the defendant to produce a perfect hand." Equally inaccurate was defendant's request No. 5, which reads as follows: "You would have to find, in order to hold the defendant liable in this case, that Dr. McGee and the plaintiff both understood that the doctor was guaranteeing a perfect result from this operation." If the defendant said that he would guarantee a perfect result, and the plaintiff relied upon that promise, any mental reservations which he may have had are immaterial. The standard by which his conduct is to be judged is not internal, but external. . . . Defendant's request number 7 was as follows: "If you should get so far as to find that there was a special contract guaranteeing a perfect result, you would still have to find for the defendant unless you further found that a further operation would not correct the disability claimed by the plaintiff." In view of the testimony that the defendant had refused to perform a further operation, it would clearly have been erroneous to give this instruction. The evidence would have justified a verdict for an amount sufficient to cover the cost of such an operation, even if the theory underlying this request were correct. . . .

New trial.

MARBLE, J., did not sit: the others concurred.

———

BACKGROUND NOTE ON HAWKINS V. MCGEE

The following background facts concerning Hawkins v. McGee (based on interviews and correspondence with the Hawkins family and a local lawyer) are reported in Roberts, Hawkins Case: A Hair-Raising Experience, Harvard Law School Record, March 17, 1978, at 1, 7, 13.

. . . George Hawkins was born in January, 1904—the second of Rose Wilkinson and Charles Augustus Hawkins' six children. . . .

One morning in 1915, 11-year-old George burned his right hand while preparing breakfast for his father on the family's wood-burning stove. At the time, George was trying to turn on the kitchen light to illuminate the stove, but an electrical storm the night before had damaged the wiring so that George received a severe shock. One of George's younger brothers, Howard Hawkins, now an insurance agent in Berlin, described George's initial scar as a "small pencil-size scar" which was between his thumb and index finger and did not substantially affect his use of the hand. Nevertheless, Charles Hawkins took his son George to skin specialists in Montreal after the accident; but there the doctors advised the Hawkinses against doing anything to restore the hand.

During this period, the family physician, Edward McGee, while treating one of George's younger brothers for pneumonia, also became aware of George's scarred hand. Later, in 1919, after returning from several years of medical service in Europe during World War I, McGee requested George and his parents to let him operate on the hand in order to restore it to "perfect" condition.

According to Dorothy St. Hilaire, George's younger sister, McGee claimed to have done a number of similar skin grafts on soldiers in Germany during the war, although he later admitted that he had really only observed such operations.

St. Hilaire recollects that McGee, in persuading George to undergo the surgery, emphasized the social problems which his scarred hand might create. McGee encouraged the Hawkinses to allow him to operate on the hand for three years, until finally George agreed shortly after his 18th birthday. . . .

McGee operated on George's hand in the St. Louis Hospital in Berlin in March of 1922. The skin graft operation was supposed to be quick, simple, and effective, and to require only a few days of hospitalization. Instead, St. Hilaire recalls that her brother bled very badly for several days. . . .

. . . George was, in the words of his brother Howard, "in the throes of death" for quite a while after the operation because of his extensive bleeding and the ensuing infection. Moreover, the post-operation scar covered his thumb and two fingers and was densely covered with hair. Howard Hawkins remembers that George's hand was partially closed up and continued to bleed periodically throughout his life. . . .

The jury only awarded the Hawkinses $3,000 for damages, and the final settlement was for $1,400 and lawyers fees. St. Hilaire believes the jurors, while at heart solidly behind the Hawkinses' cause, were afraid to return heavier damages against McGee because he was one of the more prominent physicians in the area. Charles Hawkins took the $1,400 and his injured son back to Montreal to see if any subsequent operations would alleviate George's deformity, but the doctors there said that the grafted skin was so tough that nothing more could be done. . . .

Hawkins' crippled hand affected his employment and outlook throughout his lifetime. After the operation, George Hawkins never returned to high school, even though, in Howard's opinion, "George was very bright, learned quickly, and had a pleasing personality." He was encouraged by his parents to finish school, but would not because, in his siblings' view, he was embarrassed by his hand.

George also gave up tennis and riflery after the operation, although previously he had won several medals as a marksman for the State Home Guard. Because of his hand, George was unable to perform any heavy manual labor or learn to type. He worked for many years in the printing division of the Brown Company, a pulp and paper manufacturer in Berlin, and later in a tire store. . . .

. . . According to his family members, George was always very sensitive about his hand and suffered lifelong emotional distress. His parents also grieved until their deaths because of the tragic and unnecessary crippling of their son's hand.

The Hawkins family was unaware of the widespread study of Hawkins v. McGee in law schools until, in 1964, Howard and Edith Hawkins' daughter Gail encountered the case early in her contracts course at Boston University Law School. Moreover, the Hawkins family did not know about the case's use in "The Paper Chase" contracts class scene until Edith Hawkins happened to see the 1972 movie during its first run.

Howard Hawkins, however, believes that George was somewhat aware of the case's importance before his 1958 death. Howard states: "I think he became aware of the importance of his case through a lawyer friend, an O. (Ovide) J. Coulombe. I think it gave him a sense of importance, in that this was bringing the facts out in the public eye, but this was only temporary, as he really lived with this incapacity all his life, and he did suffer mentally as well as physically."

———

UNIDROIT PRINCIPLES OF INTERNATIONAL COMMERCIAL CONTRACTS ART. 7.4.2

[See Selected Source Materials Supplement]

———

COOTER & EISENBERG, DAMAGES FOR BREACH OF CONTRACT
73 Calif.L.Rev. 1434 (1985).*

We now consider whether reliance or expectation damages should be the preferred remedy for breach of a bargain contract. In examining this question, we turn from problems of definition to problems of fairness and policy.

Fairness seems to require that a person who breaches a contract should pay compensation to the victim of breach for the injury he suffers as a result. But the meanings of the terms "compensation" and "injury" are fundamentally ambiguous. Under a reliance conception, the uninjured state is the condition the victim would have been in if he had not made the contract with the breaching party. Under an expectation conception, the uninjured state is the condition the victim would have been in if the breaching party had performed the contract. Which conception should govern is far from obvious.

In many cases, the issue of selecting between reliance and expectation damages is not significant, because the two measures will yield virtually identical damages. In particular ... in a competitive market reliance damages normally will equal expectation damages [because the contract price promised by the wrongdoer will equal the forgone price at which the injured party could have contracted with a third party]. While it is true that few markets satisfy all the conditions of perfect competition, many come close enough so that the difference between expectation and reliance damages would be insignificant.

Often, however, the two measures may diverge significantly. This may occur, for example, in imperfectly competitive markets whose conditions differ materially from those of perfectly competitive markets.... The question of choice between competing conceptions of injury and compensation then becomes material. Traditionally, courts and

---

*   The text is somewhat reorganized from the original. (Footnote by ed.)

commentators were united in holding that the expectation conception of injury governed in such cases. In fact, prior to the 1930's the reliance principle operated in only a covert manner. However, with the promulgation in 1932 of section 90 of the Restatement of Contracts, and the publication in 1934 of Fuller and Perdue's landmark article *The Reliance Interest in Contract Damages,* the reliance principle began to undergo a process of steady and impressive growth. Until the last ten years or so, this growth served to expand liability in contract. Recently, however, some commentators have taken the position that the reliance principle should be used to reduce liability, by substituting the reliance conception for the expectation conception in the law of damages.

The reasons for this position are complex. Partly it is an attack on the very institution of contract: liability based on reliance may be conceptualized as liability in tort. It also results, however, from the apparent lack of a clear rationale for expectation damages. The reliance conception of injury reflects the basic intuition that if somebody is worse off than he was before, he has been hurt. The expectation conception reflects a much more subtle intuition, and indeed it is plausible to argue that the mere defeat of an expectation is not a very serious injury.

The question remains what measure of damages should be used in cases where expectation and reliance may materially diverge. We begin our analysis of that question with the concept of efficient contract terms.

Economists often distinguish between efficiency and distribution. For present purposes, efficiency concerns the amount of value created by a contract, and distribution concerns the division of that value between the parties. Economists say that a contract is efficient if its terms maximize the value that can be created by the contemplated exchange. Put differently, if a contract is inefficient, revising the inefficient terms can increase the value it creates.

The distinction between distribution and efficiency parallels a distinction between the price and nonprice terms of a contract. Adjusting *nonprice* terms often makes it possible to control a contract's efficiency. For example, suppose that a contract to make and sell a boat includes a term that imposes very high liquidated damages if Seller breaches. There are many types of precaution Seller can take to decrease the probability of breach, such as ordering materials well in advance, hiring extra workers to protect against someone's quitting or falling ill, and reserving dry-dock facilities needed in the final stages of construction. If the very high liquidated-damages term is enforceable, it may cause Seller to take excessive precaution, in the sense that the cost of the precaution to Seller is greater than the value to Buyer of the increased probability that Seller will perform. In that case, the liquidated damages term is inefficient. If, however, the term is modified by reducing the liquidated damages, the saving to Seller from taking less precaution would exceed the cost to Buyer of exposure to additional risk of nonperformance. This would result in a net increase in the value created by the contract.

The *price* term of a contract controls the distribution of the value that the contract creates. Revision of an inefficient nonprice term can produce an increase in value, and this increase can be distributed between the parties by adjusting the price term so that each party is better off. Thus in the boat case, an increase in value from adjusting the liquidated-damages provision, initially enjoyed by Seller, could be split with Buyer by lowering the price of the boat. The revised contract, containing lower liquidated damages and a lower price, would make both parties better off. Put differently, the original contract stipulates damages in the event of Seller's breach, thus creating a right in Buyer. If Seller is willing to pay more for a modification of this right than the price Buyer would demand, efficiency requires that the contract be modified. In this respect, the exchange of legal rights is no different than the exchange of ordinary commodities.

Under ideal conditions—that is, where negotiation and drafting are cost-free—self-interest compels a rational buyer and seller to create an efficient contract, so that the process of bargaining leads to the maximization of the value a contract creates. In practice, however, there are many obstacles to creating efficient contracts. For example, it is costly to write contract terms. Instead of including explicit terms covering all contingencies, therefore, most contracts leave many issues to be resolved by the courts in case an irreconcilable dispute should arise. Specifically, many contracts leave out terms covering damages for breach, and the courts, in effect, must fill in the contract with legal damages rules.

The damage rules that the courts apply to fill in contracts should be both fair and efficient. Contracts negotiated under ideal conditions will be efficient, and enforcing the terms of such contracts will usually be regarded as fair. Thus we take as a theorem that a damage rule is both fair and efficient if it corresponds to the terms that rational parties situated like the contracting parties would have reached when bargaining under ideal conditions.

The question then is, why might rational parties, who address the issue, choose an expectation measure over a reliance measure? One reason is administrative: it is usually easier to establish in court the value of performance than the extent of reliance. The very fact of reliance is often difficult to prove, as in cases where the reliance consists of passive inaction (such as failure to pursue alternatives) rather than a positive change of position. Even if the fact of reliance can be proved, reliance damages may be difficult to measure. In a noncompetitive market, for example, reliance damages would normally be calculated by the [victim's opportunity cost], which requires determining the forgone price. Often, however, the forgone price is very hard to determine, as where the buyer breaches and the commodity is so unusual that there is no way to establish exactly what the next-best alternative buyer would have paid. In contrast, expectation damages are based on the contract price, which is known, rather than the forgone price, which is speculative. This administrative consideration has implications for both fairness and efficiency. In terms of fairness, the difficulty of proving reliance damages might, paradoxically, result in a failure to protect the reliance interest unless an expectation measure is chosen. In terms of efficiency, a damage measure that was difficult to prove, and therefore unreliable, would undercut the goal of facilitating private planning.

An intimately related set of considerations has to do with the incentive effects of the expectation and reliance measures. Most contracts are made with the expectation of mutual gain. . . . The total gain to both parties—the surplus from exchange—is the value created by the contract. The terms of a contract have incentive effects upon behavior that influence how much value the contract will create. Accordingly, one index to whether a damage rule would have been agreed to by rational parties situated like the contracting parties, and bargaining under ideal conditions, is whether the rule provides incentives for efficient behavior. . . .

We begin with the incentive effects of damage measures on the decision whether to perform, that is, on the rate of breach. A contract involves a promise by at least one party, and it is always possible that events will induce a promisor to refuse to perform, either because performance has become unprofitable or because an alternative performance has become more profitable. If a promisor were liable only for the promisee's reliance damages, the value of the promisor's performance to the promisee would not enter into a purely self-interested calculation by the promisor whether to perform. In contrast, expectation damages place on the promisor the promisee's loss of his share of the contract's value in the event of breach, and thereby sweep that loss into the promisor's calculus of self-interest.

The effect of expectation damages on the promisor's calculations can be stated in terms of externalities. Economists say that an externality exists when one person imposes a cost upon another without paying for it. Incentives for performance are efficient if they compel a promisor to balance the cost to him of performing against the losses to himself and to others that will result if he does not perform. If the promisor does not perform, the promisee loses his share of the value of the contract. If the promisor is liable for that loss, he internalizes not only his own loss but the losses to the promisee that result from his failure to perform. In contrast, if the promisor is liable only for reliance damages, he will not internalize the full value of performance to the promisee. Thus expectation damages create efficient incentives for the promisor's performance, while reliance damages do not, unless they are identical to expectation damages.

By directly affecting the probability that the promisor will perform, the expectation measure has an indirect effect upon the promisee's behavior, which can be stated in terms of planning. Knowing that expectation damages give the promisor strong incentives to perform, the promisee will be more confident that his reliance on the promisor will not expose him to undue risk. The promisee can therefore plan more effectively, because once a contract is made he can order his affairs with the confidence that he will realize its value, whether by performance or damages. In contrast, under a regime of reliance damages, a promisee could plan only on the basis that if breach occurs the law will put him back to where he was when he started. Since planning is by nature forward-looking, this backward-looking nature of reliance damages would be a shaky foundation for ordering complex affairs. Furthermore, it is in the promisor's interest that the promisee be able to plan reliably, because the ability to do so will make the promisee willing to pay a higher price for the promise.

These ideas can also be expressed in institutional terms. The purpose of the social institution of bargain is to create joint value through exchange. In recognition of the desirability of creating value in this manner, the legal institution of contract supports the social institution of the bargain with official sanctions. It is rational to design the legal sanctions so that the joint value from exchange is maximized. This goal is achieved by protecting the expectation interest.

———

CHAPTER 5

EXPECTATION DAMAGES: SPECIFIC FORMULAS AND LIMITATIONS

■ ■ ■

When the general principle of expectation damages—that is, the principle that upon a promisor's breach of a bargain contract the promisee should be awarded damages that put her in the position she would have been in if the promisor had performed—is applied to recurring types of cases, such as breach of a contract for the provision of services, the courts apply formulas that implement the general principle, rather than the general principle itself. Section 1 considers buyer's remedies for breach of a contract to provide services and to provide goods. Section 2 considers seller's remedies for both types of contracts. Succeeding Sections consider certain limits on expectation damages, such as the requirement that such damages be proved with reasonable certainty and were reasonably foreseeable at the time the contract was made.

SECTION 1. BUYER'S REMEDIES

This Section considers the basic rules that define the damages recoverable by a buyer of a service or good when the seller fails to perform or renders deficient performance. The basic rules work best when the plaintiff obtains what he was promised from a third person through a reasonable substitute transaction—as by hiring a third person to perform the service, by purchasing the good from a third person, or by paying a third person to correct the deficiency in the service or the good. Expectation damages are measured by the difference between the price of the substitute and the contract price. These damages are easy to measure and give the plaintiff what he was promised if the substitute is equivalent to what he was promised. An equivalent substitute transaction can be thought of as a form of self-help specific performance: A buyer who seeks specific performance seeks an order from the court to compel the seller to perform her contract as promised. A buyer who engages in an equivalent substitute transaction obtains what he was promised in a voluntary transaction and then can be made close to whole by a damage award for the additional price he paid for the substitute.

When a reasonable substitute transaction is available to the buyer, and the buyer does not cover by buying the good from a third party, the basic damage rule gives the buyer the difference between the market price of the good and the contract price.

Problems arise when the buyer cannot obtain what he was promised through a reasonable substitute transaction. When the breach is of a contract to deliver a unique asset a court will award specific performance, ordering the seller to deliver the asset, if the seller has the asset in hand and is able to deliver. But courts are reluctant to compel a defendant to perform a service.

Many of the cases in Section A involve a related problem. Assume that the defendant's breach of a contract to perform a service leaves the plaintiff with property that has a defect. The defect can be repaired but at what appears to be an unreasonable cost because the repair cost is significantly greater than the reduction in the market value of the property caused by the defect. The basic damage rule that applies in this case generally requires that damages be measured either by the price of repairing the defect or by the reduction in the market value of the plaintiff's property caused by the defect. Often the plaintiff's actual loss (defined as the amount of money that would give the plaintiff the same satisfaction as repairing the defect) is an amount between the price of repairing the defect and reduction in the market value of the plaintiff's property caused by the defect.

———

(A) SERVICES CONTRACTS

LOUISE CAROLINE NURSING HOME, INC. v. DIX CONSTRUCTION CO.

Supreme Judicial Court of Massachusetts, 1972.
362 Mass. 306, 285 N.E.2d 904.

Before TAURO, C.J., and REARDON, QUIRICO, BRAUCHER and HENNESSEY, JJ.

QUIRICO, JUSTICE.

This is an action of contract in which Louise Caroline Nursing Home, Inc. (Nursing Home) seeks damages from Dix Construction Corp. (Dix) for breach of a contract to build a nursing home. . . .

The case was referred to an auditor for hearing pursuant to a stipulation of the parties that his findings of fact would be final. After hearing the parties, the auditor filed a report in which he found generally: (1) that the Nursing Home had fulfilled all of its contractual obligations to Dix; (2) that Dix had committed a breach of its contractual obligations to the Nursing Home by failing, without justification, to complete the contract within the time agreed. . . . However, he further found that the Nursing Home "suffered no compensable damages as a result of the breach by Dix . . . in that the cost to complete the nursing home . . . was within the contract price . . . less what had been paid to Dix. . . . " . . .

. . . Two of the Nursing Home's objections relate to the measure of the damages applied by the auditor in reaching his conclusion that it suffered no "compensable damages." The rule of damages applied by the auditor was that if the cost of completing the contract by the use of a substitute contractor is within the contract price, less what had already been paid on the contract, no "compensable damages" have occurred. The Nursing Home argues that the proper rule of damages would entitle it to the difference between the value of the building as left by Dix and the value it would have had if the contract had been fully performed. Under this rule the Nursing Home contends that it was entitled to the "benefits of its bargain," meaning that if the fair market value of the completed building would have exceeded the contractual cost of construction, recovery should be allowed for this lost extra value. It bases this argument primarily upon our statement in Province Sec. Corp. v. Maryland Cas. Co., 269 Mass. 75, 94, 168 N.E. 252, 257, that "[i]t is a settled rule that the measure of damages where a contractor has failed to perform a contract for the construction of a building for business uses is the difference between the value of the building as left by the contractor and its value had it been finished according to contract. In other words the question is how much less was the building worth than it would have been worth if the contract had been fully performed. Powell v. Howard, 109 Mass. 192. White v. McLaren, 151 Mass. 553, 24 N.E. 911. Norcross Brothers Co. v. Vose, 199 Mass. 81, 95, 96, 85 N.E. 468. Pelatowski v. Black, 213 Mass. 428, 100 N.E. 831." This statement was probably not necessary to the court's decision in the *Province Sec. Corp.* case and, in any event, must be read in light of the cases cited by the court in support of it. All of these cases involved failure of performance in the sense of defective performance, as contrasted with abandonment of performance. In one of the cases, Pelatowski v. Black, 213 Mass. 428, 431, 100 N.E. 831, 832, the court expressly distinguished "cases where a contractor has abandoned his work while yet unfinished."

The fundamental rule of damages applied in all contract cases was stated by this court in Ficara v. Belleau, 331 Mass. 80, 82, 117 N.E.2d 287, 289, in the following language: "It is not the policy of our law to award damages which would put a plaintiff in a better position than if the defendant had carried out his contract. . . . 'The fundamental principle upon which the rule of damages is based is compensation. . . . Compensation is the value of the performance of the contract, that is, what the plaintiff would have made had the contract been performed.' F.A.

Bartlett Tree Expert Co. v. Hartney, 308 Mass. 407, 412, 32 N.E.2d 237, 240. . . . The plaintiff is entitled to be made whole and no more."

Consonant with this principle we have held that in assessing damages for failure to complete a construction contract, "[t]he measure of the plaintiffs' damages (at least in the absence of other elements of damage, as, for example, for delay in construction, which the master has not found here) can be only in the amount of the reasonable cost of completing the contract and repairing the defendant's defective performance less such part of the contract price as has not been paid." Di Mare v. Capaldi, 336 Mass. 497, 502, 146 N.E.2d 517, 521. This principle was recently reiterated in Providence Washington Ins. Co. v. Beck, 356 Mass. 739, 255 N.E.2d 600. In the face of this principle the Nursing Home's arguments attempting to demonstrate the amount of alleged "benefits of its bargain" lost are to no avail. In any event, it should be noted that any such "benefits of its bargain" as would derive from obtaining a building worth much more than the actual costs of construction are preserved if the building can be completed at a total cost which is still within the contract price, less any amount which has already been paid on the contract. The auditor was correct in applying the "cost of completion" measure of damages which excluded any separate recovery for lost "benefits of its bargain."

The Nursing Home additionally contends that even under the rule of damages applied by the auditor they were entitled, in the words of the *DiMare* case, *supra,* to recover "other elements of damage, as, for example, for delay in construction." 336 Mass. at 502, 146 N.E.2d at 521. The short answer to this contention is the auditor's express statement, in his summary of the evidence, that "[t]here was no specific evidence as to the costs of delay, if any." . . .

. . . For the foregoing reasons the Nursing Home's exceptions to the denial of its motion to recommit the auditor's report and to the granting of Reliance's motion for entry of judgment in accordance with the auditor's report must be overruled.

Exceptions overruled.

———

PEEVYHOUSE V. GARLAND COAL & MINING CO.
Supreme Court of Oklahoma, 1962.
382 P.2d 109, cert. denied, 375 U.S. 906, 84 S.Ct. 196, 11 L.Ed.2d 145 (1963).

JACKSON, J. In the trial court, plaintiffs Willie and Lucille Peevyhouse sued the defendant, Garland Coal and Mining Company, for damages for breach of contract. Judgment was for plaintiffs in an amount considerably less than was sued for. Plaintiffs appeal and defendant cross-appeals.

In the briefs on appeal, the parties present their argument and contentions under several propositions; however, they all stem from the basic question of whether the trial court properly instructed the jury on the measure of damages.

Briefly stated, the facts are as follows: plaintiffs owned a farm containing coal deposits, and in November, 1954, leased the premises to defendant for a period of five years for coal mining purposes. A "strip-mining" operation was contemplated in which the coal would be taken from pits on the surface of the ground, instead of from underground mine shafts. In addition to the usual covenants found in a coal mining lease, defendant specifically agreed to perform certain restorative and remedial work at the end of the lease period. It is unnecessary to set out the details of the work to be done, other than to say that it would involve the moving of many thousands of cubic yards of dirt, at a cost estimated by expert witnesses at about $29,000.00. However, plaintiffs sued for only $25,000.00.

During the trial, it was stipulated that all covenants and agreements in the lease contract had been fully carried out by both parties, except the remedial work mentioned above; defendant conceded that this work had not been done.

Plaintiffs introduced expert testimony as to the amount and nature of the work to be done, and its estimated cost. Over plaintiffs' objections, defendant thereafter introduced expert testimony as to the "diminution in value" of plaintiffs' farm resulting from the failure of defendant to render performance as agreed in the contract—that is, the difference between the present value of the farm, and what its value would have been if defendant had done what it agreed to do.

[handwritten margin note: Reliance & expectation damages the same here]

At the conclusion of the trial, the court instructed the jury that it must return a verdict for plaintiffs, and left the amount of damages for jury determination. On the measure of damages, the court instructed the jury that it might consider the cost of performance of the work defendant agreed to do, "together with all of the evidence offered on behalf of either party".

It thus appears that the jury was at liberty to consider the "diminution in value" of plaintiffs' farm as well as the cost of "repair work" in determining the amount of damages.

It returned a verdict for plaintiffs for $5000.00—only a fraction of the "cost of performance", *but more than the total value of the farm even after the remedial work is done.*

On appeal, the issue is sharply drawn. Plaintiffs contend that the true measure of damages in this case is what it will cost plaintiffs to obtain performance of the work that was not done because of defendant's default. Defendant argues that the measure of damages is the cost of performance "limited, however, to the total difference in the market value before and after the work was performed".

It appears that this precise question has not heretofore been presented to this court. In Ardizonne v. Archer, 72 Okl. 70, 178 P. 263, this court held that the measure of damages for breach of a contract to drill an oil well was the reasonable cost of drilling the well, but here a slightly different factual situation exists. The drilling of an oil well will yield valuable geological information, even if no oil or gas is found, and of course if the well is a producer, the value of the premises increases. In the case before us, it is argued by defendant with some force that the performance of the remedial work defendant agreed to do will add at the most only a few hundred dollars to the value of plaintiffs' farm, and that the damages should be limited to that amount because that is all plaintiffs have lost.

Plaintiffs rely on Groves v. John Wunder Co., 205 Minn. 163, 286 N.W. 235, 123 A.L.R. 502. In that case, the Minnesota court, in a substantially similar situation, adopted the "cost of performance" rule as opposed to the "value" rule. The result was to authorize a jury to give plaintiff damages in the amount of $60,000, where the real estate concerned would have been worth only $12,160, even if the work contracted for had been done.

It may be observed that Groves v. John Wunder Co., supra, is the only case which has come to our attention in which the cost of performance rule has been followed under circumstances where the cost of performance greatly exceeded the diminution in value resulting from the breach of contract. Incidentally, it appears that this case was decided by a plurality rather than a majority of the members of the court.

Defendant relies principally upon Sandy Valley & E.R. Co., v. Hughes, 175 Ky. 320, 194 S.W. 344; Bigham v. Wabash-Pittsburg Terminal Ry. Co., 223 Pa. 106, 72 A. 318; and Sweeney v. Lewis Const. Co., 66 Wash. 490, 119 P. 1108. These were all cases in which, under similar circumstances, the appellate courts followed the "value" rule instead of the "cost of performance" rule. Plaintiff points out that in the earliest of these cases (Bigham) the court cites as authority on the measure of damages an earlier Pennsylvania *tort* case, and that the other two cases follow the first, with no explanation as to why a measure of damages ordinarily followed in cases sounding in tort should be used in contract cases. Nevertheless, it is of some significance that three out of four appellate courts have followed the diminution in value rule under circumstances where, as here, the cost of performance greatly exceeds the diminution in value.

The explanation may be found in the fact that the situations presented are artificial ones. It is highly unlikely that the ordinary property owner would agree to pay $29,000 (or its equivalent) for the construction of "improvements" upon his property that would increase its value only about ($300) three hundred dollars. The result is that we are called upon to apply principles of law theoretically based upon reason and reality to a situation which is basically unreasonable and unrealistic.

In Groves v. John Wunder Co., supra, in arriving at its conclusions, the Minnesota court apparently considered the contract involved to be analogous to a building and construction contract, and cited authority for the proposition that the cost of performance or completion of the building as contracted is ordinarily the measure of damages in actions for damages for the breach of such a contract.

In an annotation following the Minnesota case beginning at 123 A.L.R. 515, the annotator places the three cases relied on by defendant (Sandy Valley, Bigham and Sweeney) under the classification of cases involving "grading and excavation contracts".

We do not think either analogy is strictly applicable to the case now before us. The primary purpose of the lease contract between plaintiffs and defendant was neither "building and construction" nor "grading and excavation". It was merely to accomplish the economical recovery and marketing of coal from the premises, to the profit of all parties. The special provisions of the lease contract pertaining to remedial work were incidental to the main object involved.

Even in the case of contracts that are unquestionably building and construction contracts, the authorities are not in agreement as to the factors to be considered in determining whether the cost of performance rule or the value rule should be applied. The American Law Institute's Restatement of the Law, Contracts, Volume 1, Sections 346(1)(a)(i) and (ii) submits the proposition that the cost of performance is the proper measure of damages "if this is possible and does not involve *unreasonable economic waste*"; and that the diminution in value caused by the breach is the proper measure "if construction and completion in accordance with the contract would involve *unreasonable economic waste*". (Emphasis supplied.) In an explanatory comment immediately following the text, the Restatement makes it clear that the "economic waste" referred to consists of the destruction of a substantially completed building or other structure. Of course no such destruction is involved in the case now before us.

On the other hand, in McCormick, Damages, Section 168, it is said with regard to building and construction contracts that "... in cases where the defect is one that can be repaired or cured without *undue expense* "the cost of performance is the proper measure of damages, but where" ... the defect in material or construction is one that cannot be remedied without *an expenditure for reconstruction disproportionate to the end to be attained* "(emphasis supplied) the value rule should be followed. The same idea was expressed in Jacob & Youngs, Inc. v. Kent, 230 N.Y. 239, 129 N.E. 889, 23 A.L.R. 1429, as follows:

"The owner is entitled to the money which will permit him to complete, unless the cost of completion is grossly and unfairly out of proportion to the good to be attained. When that is true, the measure is the difference in value."

It thus appears that the prime consideration in the Restatement was "economic waste"; and that the prime consideration in McCormick, Damages, and in Jacob & Youngs, Inc. v. Kent, supra, was the relationship between the expense involved and the "end to be attained"—in other words, the "relative economic benefit".

In view of the unrealistic fact situation in the instant case, and certain Oklahoma statutes to be hereinafter noted, we are of the opinion that the "relative economic benefit" is a proper consideration here. This is in accord with the recent case of Mann v. Clowser, 190 Va. 887, 59 S.E.2d 78, where, in applying the cost rule, the Virginia court specifically noted that " . . . the defects are remediable from a practical standpoint and the costs *are not grossly disproportionate to the results to be obtained*" (Emphasis supplied).

23 O.S.1961 §§ 96 and 97 provide as follows:

"§ 96. . . . Notwithstanding the provisions of this chapter, no person can recover a greater amount in damages for the breach of an obligation, than he would have gained by the full performance thereof on both sides. . . .

"§ 97. . . . Damages must, in all cases, be reasonable, and where an obligation of any kind appears to create a right to unconscionable and grossly oppressive damages, contrary to substantial justice no more than reasonable damages can be recovered."

Although it is true that the above sections of the statute are applied most often in tort cases, they are by their own terms, and the decisions of this court, also applicable in actions for damages for breach of contract. It would seem that they are peculiarly applicable here where, under the "cost of performance" rule, plaintiffs might recover an amount about nine times the total value of their farm. Such would seem to be "unconscionable and grossly oppressive damages, contrary to substantial justice" within the meaning of the statute. Also, it can hardly be denied that if plaintiffs here are permitted to recover under the "cost of performance" rule, they will receive a greater benefit from the breach than could be gained from full performance, contrary to the provisions of Sec. 96.

An analogy may be drawn between the cited sections, and the provisions of 15 O.S.1961 §§ 214 and 215. These sections tend to render void any provisions of a contract which attempt to fix the amount of stipulated damages to be paid in case of a breach, except where it is impracticable or extremely difficult to determine the actual damages. This results in spite of the agreement of the parties, and the obvious and well known rationale is that insofar as they exceed the actual damages suffered, the stipulated damages amount to a penalty or forfeiture which the law does not favor.

23 O.S.1961 §§ 96 and 97 have the same effect in the case now before us. *In spite of the agreement of the parties,* these sections limit the damages recoverable to a reasonable amount not "contrary to substantial justice"; they prevent plaintiffs from recovering a "greater amount in damages for the breach of an obligation" than they would have "gained by the full performance thereof".

We therefore hold that where, in a coal mining lease, lessee agrees to perform certain remedial work on the premises concerned at the end of the lease period, and thereafter the contract is fully performed by both parties except that the remedial work is not done, the measure of damages in an action by lessor against lessee for damages for breach of contract is ordinarily the reasonable cost of performance of the work; however, where the contract provision breached was merely incidental to the main purpose in view, and where the economic benefit which would result to lessor by full performance of the work is grossly disproportionate to the cost of performance, the damages which lessor may recover are limited to the diminution in value resulting to the premises because of the non-performance.

We believe the above holding is in conformity with the intention of the Legislature as expressed in the statutes mentioned, and in harmony with the better-reasoned cases from the other jurisdictions where analogous fact situations have been considered. It should be noted that the rule as stated does not interfere with the property owner's right to "do what he will with his own" (Chamberlain v. Parker, 45 N.Y. 569), or his right, if he chooses, to contract for "improvements" which will actually have the effect of reducing his property's value. Where such result is in fact contemplated by the parties, and is a main or principal purpose of those contracting, it would seem that the measure of damages for breach would ordinarily be the cost of performance.

The above holding disposes of all of the arguments raised by the parties on appeal.

Under the most liberal view of the evidence herein, the diminution in value resulting to the premises because of nonperformance of the remedial work was $300.00. After a careful search of the record, we have found no evidence of a higher figure, and plaintiffs do not argue in their briefs that a greater diminution in value was sustained. It thus appears that the judgment was clearly excessive, and that the amount for which judgment should have been rendered is definitely and satisfactorily shown by the record.

We are asked by each party to modify the judgment in accordance with the respective theories advanced, and it is conceded that we have authority to do so. 12 O.S.1961 § 952; Busboom v. Smith, 199 Okl. 688, 191 P.2d 198; Stumpf v. Stumpf, 173 Okl. 1, 46 P.2d 315.

We are of the opinion that the judgment of the trial court for plaintiffs should be, and it is hereby, modified and reduced to the sum of $300.00, and as so modified it is affirmed.

WELCH, DAVISON, HALLEY, and JOHNSON, JJ., concur.

WILLIAMS, C.J., BLACKBIRD, V.C.J., and IRWIN and BERRY, JJ., dissent.

IRWIN, JUSTICE (dissenting).

By the specific provisions in the coal mining lease under consideration, the defendant agreed as follows:

"... 7b Lessee agrees to make fills in the pits dug on said premises on the property line in such manner that fences can be placed thereon and access had to opposite sides of the pits.

"[7]c Lessee agrees to smooth off the top of the spoil banks on the above premises.

"7d Lessee agrees to leave the creek crossing the above premises in such a condition that it will not interfere with the crossings to be made in pits as set out in 7b.

. . .

"7f Lessee further agrees to leave no shale or dirt on the high wall of said pits. ... "

Following the expiration of the lease, plaintiffs made demand upon defendant that it carry out the provisions of the contract and to perform those covenants contained therein.

Defendant admits that it failed to perform its obligations that it agreed and contracted to perform under the lease contract and there is nothing in the record which indicates that defendant could not perform its obligations. Therefore, in my opinion defendant's breach of the contract was wilful and not in good faith.

Although the contract speaks for itself, there were several negotiations between the plaintiffs and defendant before the contract was executed. Defendant admitted in the trial of the action, that plaintiffs insisted that the above provisions be included in the contract and that they would not agree to the coal mining lease unless the above provisions were included.

In consideration for the lease contract, plaintiffs were to receive a certain amount as royalty for the coal produced and marketed and in addition thereto their land was to be restored as provided in the contract.

Defendant received as consideration for the contract, its proportionate share of the coal produced and marketed and in addition thereto, the *right to use* plaintiffs' land in the furtherance of its mining operations.

The cost for performing the contract in question could have been reasonably approximated when the contract was negotiated and executed and there are no conditions now existing which could not have been reasonably anticipated by the parties. Therefore, defendant had knowledge, when it prevailed upon the plaintiffs to execute the lease, that the cost of performance might be disproportionate to the value or benefits received by plaintiff for the performance.

Defendant has received its benefits under the contract and now urges, in substance, that plaintiffs' measure of damages for its failure to perform should be the economic value of performance to the plaintiffs and not the cost of performance.

If a peculiar set of facts should exist where the above rule should be applied as the proper measure of damages, (and in my judgment those facts do not exist in the instant case) before such rule should be applied, consideration should be given to the benefits received or contracted for by the party who asserts the application of the rule.

Defendant did not have the right to mine plaintiffs' coal or to use plaintiffs' property for its mining operations without the consent of plaintiffs. Defendant had knowledge of the benefits that it would receive under the contract and the approximate cost of performing the contract. With this knowledge, it must be presumed that defendant thought that it would be to its economic advantage to enter into the contract with plaintiffs and that it would reap benefits from the contract, or it would have not entered into the contract.

Therefore, if the value of the performance of a contract should be considered in determining the measure of damages for breach of a contract, the value of the benefits received under the contract by a party who breaches a contract should also be considered. However, in my judgment, to give consideration to either in the instant action, completely rescinds and holds for naught the solemnity of the contract before us and makes an entirely new contract for the parties. . . .

In Great Western Oil & Gas Company v. Mitchell, Okl., 326 P.2d 794, we held:

> "The law will not make a better contract for parties than they themselves have seen fit to enter into, or alter it for the benefit of one party and to the detriment of the others; the judicial function of a court of law is to enforce a contract as it is written."

I am mindful of Title 23 O.S.1961 § 96, which provides that no person can recover a greater amount in damages for the breach of an obligation than he could have gained by the full performance thereof on both sides, except in cases not applicable herein. However, in my judgment, the above statutory provision is not applicable here.

In my judgment, we should follow the case of Groves v. John Wunder Company, 205 Minn. 163, 286 N.W. 235, 123 A.L.R. 502, which defendant agrees "that the fact situation is apparently similar to the one in the case at bar", and where the Supreme Court of Minnesota held:

"The owner's or employer's damages for such a breach (i.e. breach hypothesized in 2d syllabus) are to be measured, not in respect to the value of the land to be improved, but by the reasonable cost of doing that which the contractor promised to do and which he left undone."

The hypothesized breach referred to states that where the contractor's breach of a contract is wilful, that is in bad faith, he is not entitled to any benefit of the equitable doctrine of substantial performance.

In the instant action defendant has made no attempt to even substantially perform. The contract in question is not immoral, is not tainted with fraud, and was not entered into through mistake or accident and is not contrary to public policy. It is clear and unambiguous and the parties understood the terms thereof, and the approximate cost of fulfilling the obligations could have been approximately ascertained. There are no conditions existing now which could not have been reasonably anticipated when the contract was negotiated and executed. The defendant could have performed the contract if it desired. It has accepted and reaped the benefits of its contract and now urges that plaintiffs' benefits under the contract be denied. If plaintiffs' benefits are denied, such benefits would inure to the direct benefit of the defendant.

Therefore, in my opinion, the plaintiffs were entitled to specific performance of the contract and since defendant has failed to perform, the proper measure of damages should be the cost of performance. Any other measure of damage would be holding for naught the express provisions of the contract; would be taking from the plaintiffs the benefits of the contract and placing those benefits in defendant which has failed to perform its obligations; would be granting benefits to defendant without a resulting obligation; and would be completely rescinding the solemn obligation of the contract for the benefit of the defendant to the detriment of the plaintiffs by making an entirely new contract for the parties.

I therefore respectfully dissent to the opinion promulgated by a majority of my associates.

———

NOTE

In a petition for rehearing, plaintiffs argued that the trial court had wrongfully excluded evidence that the diminution in the value of their farm was greater than $300, because the farm consisted not merely of the 60 acres covered by the coal-mining lease, but other lands as well. The court held, 5–4, that the evidence was properly excluded because the complaint related only to the 60 acres covered by the lease and the case had been tried and argued by plaintiffs on a cost-of-completion theory rather than a diminished-value theory.

———

RESTATEMENT, SECOND, OF CONTRACTS § 348(2)

[See Selected Source Materials Supplement]

———

NOTE ON ADDITIONAL FACTS IN PEEVYHOUSE

In Peevyhouse v. Garland Coal & Mining Co. Revisited: The Ballad of Willie and Lucille, 89 Nw.U.L.Rev. 1341 (1995), Professor Judith Maute reports that the Peevyhouses were reluctant to allow mining on their land, while Garland needed immediate access to the land to divert a creek from a neighboring piece of land that it was already mining. Thus the Peevyhouses had a relatively strong bargaining position. What they negotiated for was Garland's promise to do the restorative work on their land. The standard strip-mining leases in the area did not contain provisions for restorative work. Instead, lessors typically received an up-front per-acre payment to compensate them for the damage that would be done to their land in the course of the mining. This amount would usually equal the total value of the land before mining began. The Peevyhouses were aware of this standard provision, and they had seen the damage done to their neighbors' land over the years. The Peevyhouses gave up the standard advance payment for surface damage, which in their case would have been $3,000, in return for Garland's promise to do the restorative work on their land.

Maute also questions Garland's claim that because the coal on the Peevyhouses' land was less accessible than Garland expected, the promised restoration was much more costly to implement than Garland expected.

———

H.P. Droher & Sons v. Toushin

250 Minn. 490, 85 N.W.2d 273 (1957)

This case was decided by the Minnesota court, which also decided Groves v. John Wunder Co., discussed in *Peevyhouse*. Droher agreed to build a house for the Toushins for an adjusted price of just under $44,000. When the house was completed, a steel post in the basement, which supported a beam on which the floor joists rested, was too low. As a result, the level of the floor, and of other parts of the house, sagged noticeably. To correct this defect it would have been necessary to jack up the beam. If that were done the plaster would crack and parts of the house would have to be rebuilt, so that the cost of repair would exceed $20,000. The diminution in the value of the house resulting from the defect was apparently much less than $20,000. Held, the diminished-value rule should be applied:

> . . . [The decision in Groves v. John Wunder Co.] was by a divided court, three members of the court concurring in the opinion, two dissenting, and two taking no part. The majority opinion is based, at least in part, on the fact that the breach of the contract was wilful and in bad faith. . . .
>
> It would seem that the better rule and the one followed by a majority of the courts is that, where there is a substantial good-faith effort to perform the contract but there are defects of such a nature that the contract has not been performed according to its terms, which defects can be remedied without the destruction of a substantial part of the building, the owner is entitled to recover the cost of making the work conform to the contract but, where it appears that the cost of remedying the defects is grossly disproportionate to the benefits to be derived therefrom, the owner is entitled to recover the difference between the value of the property as it would have been if the contract had been performed according to its terms and the value in its condition as constructed. Cases such as we have here, where the evidence establishes a substantial good-faith performance, are to be distinguished from those where there has been a wilful failure to perform at all, such as we had in Groves v. John Wunder Co. . . .

Eastern Steamship Lines, Inc. v. United States

125 Ct.Cl. 422, 112 F.Supp. 167 (1953)

During World War II, The United States Government chartered the steamship *Acadia* as a troop transport. The charter provided:

> Clause 7. . . . Before redelivery, the Charterer [that is, the Government], at its own expense, and on its time, shall restore the Vessel to at least as good condition and class as upon delivery, ordinary wear and tear excepted, and do all work and make all repairs necessary to satisfy any outstanding classification or steamboat inspection requirements necessary to place her in such condition and class. . . . [provided] that at the Charterer's option, redelivery of the Vessel to the Owner may be made prior to satisfying such requirements or prior to completion of such repairs or work, in

which event the Charterer shall pay to the Owner the amount reasonably expended to place the Vessel in such class and condition. . . .

After the war, the owner sued the government for $4,000,000, which the owner claimed to be due under Clause 7 as the estimated cost of restoring the *Acadia* to its pre-war condition. The Government claimed that it was not bound to pay more than $2,000,000, the estimated value of the ship after restoration. The court rejected the owner's claim:

[We will assume, based on the evidence] that after some $4,000,000 had been spent in restoring the ship, it would be worth $2,000,000. . . .

. . . According to the plaintiff's interpretation [of the charter] the Government has now become obligated to pay it $4,000,000. Candor compels the plaintiff to say that it will not feel obliged to spend the $4,000,000 when it gets it, to restore the *Acadia*. Common sense and reality tell us that it will not so spend the money, since after the expenditures it would have only a $2,000,000 ship. The result would be that the Government would pay out $2,000,000 more than the plaintiff had lost by the Government's chartering and use of its ship. The extra $2,000,000 would not be a subsidy to get ships built or sailing. The *Acadia* would still rust at anchor. We decline to . . . produce such a result.

. . . We think that neither party anticipated what actually happened, *viz.* that the market for old ships on the one hand, and the market for labor and materials, on the other, would be such as to make the restoration of old ships a useless and wasteful expenditure of public funds. . . .

The plaintiff has urged that, regardless of the waste of public money that would be entailed by compelling the Government to pay $4,000,000 when the plaintiff's loss is $2,000,000 the weight of authority is that what is "nominated in the bond" will be compelled, regardless of economic waste. We think that is not the law. . . .

. . . The case will be assigned to a commissioner of this court for trial upon the question of the value of the *Acadia*.

City School District of the City of Elmira v. McLane Construction Co.

85 A.D.2d 749, 445 N.Y.S.2d 258 (1981)

In 1976, the Elmira school district contracted with McLane Construction Company for the construction of a swimming-pool building, which was to feature a roof consisting of natural-wood decking supported by laminated-wood beams. The appearance of the beams was central to the aesthetics of the architectural scheme, which contrasted the natural beauty of the beams with the relatively stark unfinished concrete that comprised the balance of the structure. Even the effectiveness of the indirect lighting system employed in the building depended on the appearance of beams. Because the building was to be a showplace and the site of large regional swimming competitions, the design was intentionally dramatic. It was contemplated that the beams, properly treated, would be essentially maintenance-free. However, Weyerhauser Company, which supplied the beams, and was aware of the school district's plans and specifications, used a method of treating the beams that it knew would result in staining and discoloration, and the beams became permanently discolored.

The school district sued Weyerhauser and recovered a verdict of $357,000, based on the cost of replacing the beams. On appeal, Weyerhauser argued that damages should have been limited to $3,000, the difference between the value of the structure as built and its value if the beams had been as agreed upon. Held, for the school district.

"[W]here the contractor's performance has been incomplete or defective, the usual measure of damages is the reasonable cost of replacement or completion (*American Std. v. Schectman,* 80 A.D.2d 318, 321, 439 N.Y.S.2d 529). That rule does not apply if the contractor performs in good faith but defects nevertheless exist and remedying them could entail economic waste. Then, diminution in value becomes the proper measure of damages. A classic illustration of when the general rule is abandoned in favor of this exception is *Jacob & Youngs v. Kent,* 230 N.Y. 239, 129 N.E. 889, where the contractor did not use the brand of pipe specified in the contract, but other brands of like quality. Inasmuch as the cost of replacing the pipe was grievously out of proportion to any damages actually suffered by the house owner, the proper award was the nominal difference in value of the house with and without the specified brand of pipe.

"But Weyerhaeuser does not come within this exception, for here the defect, in relation to the entire project, was not of inappreciable importance. One of the school district's principal objectives was to have an aesthetically prepossessing structure, and that goal has by all accounts been frustrated. Moreover, as the facts already recited indicate, Weyerhaeuser's conduct cannot be said to be innocent oversight or inattention. . . . "

———

Advanced, Inc. v. Wilks

711 P.2d 524 (Alaska 1985)

(Rabinowitz, C.J.) "An owner's recovery is not necessarily limited to diminution in value whenever that figure is less than the cost of repair. It is true that in a case where the cost of repair exceeds the damages under the value formula, an award under the cost of repair measure may place the owner in a better economic position than if the contract had been fully performed, since he could pocket the award and then sell the defective structure. On the other hand, it is possible that the owner will use the damage award for its intended purpose and turn the structure into the one originally envisioned. He may do this for a number of reasons, including personal esthetics or a hope for increased value in the future. If he does this his economic position will equal the one he would have been in had the contractor fully performed. The fact finder is the one in the best position to determine whether the owner will actually complete performance, or whether he is only interested in obtaining the best immediate economic position he can. In some cases, such as where the property is held solely for investment, the court may conclude as a matter of law that the damage award can not exceed the diminution in value. Where, however, the property has special significance to the owner and repair seems likely, the cost of repair may be appropriate even if it exceeds the diminution in value."

NOTE ON DAMAGES WHEN THE PLAINTIFF COMPLETES WORK OR REPAIRS A DEFECT

When the plaintiff pays to complete work not finished by the defendant, courts routinely award the cost of completion without questioning the reasonableness of the plaintiff's decision to complete the work. See, e.g., Kirkpatrick v. Temme, 654 P.2d 1011 (Nev. 1982) (awarding $84,333.73 spent to complete construction where contract price was $175,000, despite defendant's testimony that the work was 80% compete and that he could have finished for $39,200, when the owner and the architect testified that the original plans and specifications were followed). While there is less authority for the point, the same seems to be true when the plaintiff repairs defective work. See, e.g., Hi-Valley Constructors, Inc. v. Heyser, 428 P.2d 354 (Colo. 1967) (awarding cost of repainting exterior of home). If the plaintiff does additional work, then only the amount the plaintiff would have paid for the original work, or to repair the defect, is recovered. See, e.g., Martin v. Phillips, 440 A.2d 1124 (N.H. 1982). Alternatively, the enhanced value from the additional work may be subtracted from the plaintiff's recovery. State Prop. & Bldg. Comm'n v. H.W. Miller Constr. Co., 385 S.W.2d 211 (Ky. 1964).

(B) SALE OF GOODS

NOTE ON BUYER'S REMEDIES UNDER THE UCC

The remedies for breach of a contract for the sale of goods are governed by the Uniform Commercial Code. A buyer's remedies for breach by the seller fall into two broad categories—specific relief (in which the buyer is awarded the actual goods) and damages. Specific relief will be covered in Chapter 6, infra.

The buyer's damage remedies, in turn, fall into several subcategories. One subcategory consists of the buyer's remedies when the seller fails to deliver or the buyer properly rejects the goods or rightfully revokes his acceptance (UCC §§ 2–712, 2–713). A second subcategory consists of the buyer's remedies when the buyer has accepted the goods, and cannot or does not want to rightfully revoke his acceptance, but the goods are defective (UCC § 2–714). Typically, such an action is for breach of warranty.

————

UCC §§ 2–711(1), 2–712, 2–713, 2–714, 2–715(1), 2–723, 2–724

[See Selected Source Materials Supplement]

————

CISG ARTS. 45, 49, 50, 74, 75, 76

[See Selected Source Materials Supplement]

————

Continental Sand & Gravel, Inc. v. K & K Sand & Gravel, Inc.

755 F.2d 87 (7th Cir.1985)

Defendant sold sand and gravel pit to plaintiff for a total price of $650,000. The sale included certain mobile equipment (front-loaders, cranes, and so forth) for a price of $50,000. Defendant made various express warranties concerning the equipment. The warranties were breached, and plaintiff sued for damages. The trial court awarded $104,206.75, the cost of repairs to bring the equipment up to the warranted condition. Affirmed.

(Cudahy, J.) "Defendants argue that, since the clear bargain of the parties was to sell and purchase the mobile equipment for $50,000, the plaintiff is only entitled to receive an amount of damages that represents the diminution in value from the purchase price as the result of the breach of warranty. In other words, defendants contend that the maximum amount of recoverable damages is the difference between the fair market value of the equipment as accepted, which they define as $50,000, and the fair market value of the equipment in the defective condition. Under this method of computing damages, Continental would be entitled to recover no more than the $50,000 purchase price, and as little as nothing, depending on the court's assessment of the value of the equipment in the defective condition. . . .

"The court below rejected this argument, and instead applied section 2–714 (2) of the Illinois Uniform Commercial Code, . . . which provides that damages generally should represent the difference between the value of the goods at the time of acceptance and the value they would have had if they had been as warranted. The court stated that under this section the cost of repair is the proper standard. This was the correct approach under Illinois law, as well as under the general commercial law. . . . As the district court noted, it is not unusual for damages in a breach of warranty case to exceed the purchase price of the goods. . . . This result is logical, since to limit recoverable damages by the purchase price, as defendants suggest, would clearly deprive the purchaser of the benefit of its bargain in cases in which the value of the goods as warranted exceeds that price. Thus we find that the district court properly computed the damages recoverable for the defendants' breach of the warranties."

———

Manouchehri v. Heim

123 N.M. 439, 941 P.2d 978 (N.M. Ct. App. 1997)

"Although [U.C.C. §] 2–714 (2) sets the measure of direct damages for breach of warranty as the difference between the value of the goods as warranted and the value of the goods as accepted, often that difference can be approximated by the cost to repair the goods so that they conform to the warranty. For example, if it costs $200 to fix [a] machine so that it performed as [warranted,] then one could assume that the unrepaired machine (the 'goods accepted') was worth $200 less than the repaired machine (the goods 'as warranted'). Thus, the cost of repair is commonly awarded as the direct damages."

———

EGERER V. CSR WEST, LLC

Court of Appeals of Washington, 2003.
116 Wash.App. 645, 67 P.3d 1128.

BECKER, C.J.

Appellant CSR West breached a contract to supply fill for land development. Issues on appeal include the calculation of damages based on "hypothetical cover". . . . We affirm in all respects.

According to unchallenged findings of fact entered after a bench trial, Robert Egerer owned a 10 acre parcel of land in Skagit County that he planned to develop into commercial property. The property required a considerable amount of fill to make it suitable for development.

Egerer first purchased fill material in 1995, when he contracted at the rate of $1.10 per cubic yard to have Wilder Construction haul to his property some material being excavated from the shoulders of Interstate 5 as a part of a highway improvement project. In its suitability to serve as structural fill, the shoulder material resembled a gravel known as "pit run", but it was cheaper than pit run because it contained asphalt grindings.

Beyond what Wilder Construction could supply, Egerer needed roughly 17,000 cubic yards of fill material. In May 1997, Egerer learned that CSR West had contracted with the Washington State Department of Transportation to excavate material from the shoulder areas of Interstate 5 near Lake Samish. He met with John Grisham, CSR's sales manager, and they reached an agreement to have CSR transport "all" the shoulder excavations from the project to Egerer's site at the rate of $.50 per cubic yard.

CSR brought fill material to Egerer's property on only two nights: July 9 and 10, 1997. Shortly thereafter, the Department of Transportation issued a change order that allowed CSR to use the excavated shoulder material in the reconstruction of the shoulder area. It was more profitable for CSR to supply the material for the State's use than to fulfill its contract with Egerer. CSR excavated a total of 16,750 cubic yards of material during its work on the shoulder project in 1997, and supplied virtually all of it to the Department of Transportation.

Egerer did not purchase replacement fill at the time of the breach in July 1997. Asked about this at trial, he explained that it would have been too expensive, and he also did not think there was time to find replacement fill and get it onto his property before the end of the summer. Egerer said that his window of opportunity to place fill on the property was June through September, before the weather became too wet. In January and February 1998, he obtained price quotes for pit run ranging from $8.25 per cubic yard to $9.00 per cubic yard. These prices exceeded Egerer's budget, and he did not contract for replacement fill at that time either.

In the summer of 1999, Egerer learned of an unexpected landslide at a gravel pit not far from his property. The company agreed to sell Egerer the unwanted slide material at a cost of $6.39 per cubic yard, including the cost of hauling and spreading.

Egerer filed suit in November 2000, alleging that CSR breached its contract by failing to deliver all the excavated shoulder material in the summer of 1997. After a bench trial, the court found breach. The court then turned to the Uniform Commercial Code to determine the measure of damages. CSR raises several legal issues with respect to the award of damages. . . .

Where a seller fails to make delivery of goods sold to a buyer, the buyer has two alternative remedies under the Uniform Commercial Code. One is the remedy of "cover": the buyer may purchase substitute goods and recover as damages the difference between the cost of this cover and the contract price, provided the buyer covers in good faith and without unreasonable delay. U.C.C. § 2–712.* The other, a complete alternative, is damages for

---

* For simplicity, citations to the UCC have been inserted in place of citations to the counterpart sections of the Washington UCC. (Footnote by eds.)

non-delivery, also known as "hypothetical cover"[1]: the buyer may recover as damages from the seller "the difference between the market price at the time when the buyer learned of the breach and the contract price". U.C.C. § 2–713. This measure applies only when and to the extent that the buyer does not cover. Uniform Commercial Code Comment 5, § 2–713. "The general baseline adopted in this section uses as a yardstick the market in which the buyer would have obtained cover had he sought that relief." U.C.C. Comment 1, § 2–713. "The market or current price to be used in comparison with the contract price under this section is the price for goods of the same kind and in the same branch of trade." U.C.C. Comment 2, § 2–713.

The court determined that Egerer was limited to damages for non-delivery under section 2–713: "Mr. Egerer is limited to damages reflecting the difference between CSR contract price and the price he could have obtained replacement material for at the time of the breach in 1997. *See* U.C.C. § 2–713(1) and Comment 3." The court found that Egerer could have obtained replacement material at the time of the breach for a cost of $8.25 per cubic yard—a price quoted to Egerer in early 1998. The court calculated his damages for the non-delivery of fill to be $129,812.50, which was the difference between the market price of $8.25 per cubic yard and the contract price of $.50 per cubic yard.

CSR accepts the trial court's decision to apply the remedy furnished by section 2–713, but contends the court erred by calculating damages based on a market price of $8.25 per cubic yard for pit run. CSR argues that $8.25 was not "the price for goods of the same kind" (as U.C.C. Comment 2 calls for) because pit run is a product superior to shoulder excavations containing asphalt grindings. CSR further argues that $8.25 was not "the market price at the time when the buyer learned of the breach" (as section 2–713 calls for) because the breach was in July 1997 and the $8.25 price was as of six months later—in January, 1998. CSR takes the position that the trial court should instead have used the $1.10 per cubic yard price reflected in Egerer's 1995 contract with Wilder Construction, because that was the only evidence in the record of a price for shoulder excavations. Use of the much higher price for pit run resulted in a windfall for Egerer, according to CSR.

The trial court expressly relied on Comment 3 to U.C.C. 2–713 in determining that $8.25 per cubic yard was the price for which Egerer could have obtained replacement material at the time of the breach. That comment states in part, "When the current market price under this section is difficult to prove the section on determination and proof of market price is available to permit a showing of a comparable market price or, where no

---

[1] *Allied Canners & Packers, Inc. v. Victor Packing Co.*, 162 Cal.App.3d 905, 911–12, 209 Cal.Rptr. 60, 61 (1984). (Note by eds. The more conventional name for the damages that the court refers to as "hypothetical cover" is "market-price damages.")

market price is available, evidence of spot sale prices is proper." U.C.C. Comment 3, § 2–713. The section on determination and proof of market price provides,

> If evidence of a price prevailing at the times or places described in this Article is not readily available the price prevailing within any reasonable time before or after the time described or at any other place which in commercial judgment or under usage of trade would serve as a reasonable substitute for the one described may be used, making any proper allowance for the cost of transporting the goods to or from such other place.

U.C.C. § 2–723 (2).

A court is granted a "reasonable leeway" in measuring market price under section 2–723. *Sprague v. Sumitomo Forestry Co., Ltd.,* 104 Wash.2d 751, 760, 709 P.2d 1200 (1985). Contrary to CSR's argument, a trial court may use a market price for goods different in quality from those for which the buyer contracted. That possibility is encompassed in the reference to "price . . . which in commercial judgment or under usage of trade would serve as a reasonable substitute for the one described". And section 2–723 expressly permits looking to a price "prevailing within any reasonable time before or after the time described."

We conclude the trial court did not misapply the law in concluding that the January 1998 price for pit run was the relevant market price. The court found the 1998 quotes for replacement material and hauling "were reasonable and customary", and noted that CSR "did not offer evidence that suitable replacement material was available at a lower price at the time of breach." There was testimony that shoulder excavation material, though cheap when available, is rarely available. John Grisham, CSR's sales manager, acknowledged that it would have been difficult for Egerer to locate an alternative supplier of shoulder excavations in 1997 because "quantities like that are few and far between". Grisham said he was unaware of any other pit in the area that would have had similar material available at a price anywhere near $.50 per cubic yard in the summer of 1997. Egerer's eventual purchase in 1999 was possible only because of the landslide that unexpectedly deposited unwanted fill material in a local gravel pit. If Egerer had covered at the time of the breach, higher-priced pit run would have been a reasonable substitute for the shoulder excavations. . . .

Affirmed.

WE CONCUR: SCHINDLER, COX, JJ.

———

J. White, R. Summers, D. Barnheiser, W. Barnes, & F. Snyder, Uniform Commercial Code

250 (7th ed. 2022)

"We come now to the problem of a buyer who has covered but who seeks to ignore 2–712 and sue for a larger contract-market differential under 2–713. On first reading, it seems that he can disregard 2–712; section 2–711 tells buyers that they can 'cover' or they can recover damages for nondelivery under 2–713. Commenting on the relationship between 2–712 and 2–713, Judge Peters argued that an aggrieved buyer who purchases goods 'in substitution' may disregard 2–712 and seek recovery under the contract-market differential of 2–713. However, this interpretation allows a buyer to learn of a breach on September 2 when the market is at $25,000, wait until September 15 to cover, when the market is at $23,000, and then sue under 2–713 for the higher damages of contract-market differential, all contrary to the general principle of 1–305(a)(2001) and its predecessor, 1–106 (2000)(in as good a position as if the other party had performed and no more). Moreover comment 5 to 2–713 indicates that a buyer who has covered may not use 2–713:

> The present section provides a remedy which is *completely alternative* to cover under the preceding section and applies only *when and to the extent that the buyer has not covered.* (Emphasis added.)

> If the Code's goal is to put the buyer in the same position as though there had been no breach, and if 2–712 will accomplish that goal but 2–713 will do so only by coincidence, why not force the covering buyer to use 2–712? There is no room for punitive damages here. . . . Notwithstanding Judge Peters' arguments concerning the statutory history . . . both the message of Comment 5 to 2–713 and the policy of the Code properly deny the covering buyer any use of 2–713. . . . Of course, whether purchases following seller's breach are cover purchases may be a disputed question of fact. If the facts at trial show cover, 2–712 applies. If the facts do not show cover, 2–713 applies.

––––––

SECTION 2. SELLER'S REMEDIES

This Section considers the basic rules that define the damages recovered by a seller of a service or good when the buyer breaches. When the plaintiff has fully performed he is entitled to the contract price as damages, plus interest when there is a statute providing pre-judgment interest. When the plaintiff has not fully performed damages generally are the contract price minus the cost avoided by the plaintiff as a result of not completing performance. Profit made by the plaintiff in another transaction may also be subtracted, if the plaintiff would not have made the profit but for the breach.

———

(A) SERVICES CONTRACTS

KEARSARGE COMPUTER, INC. v. ACME STAPLE COMPANY, INC.
Supreme Court of New Hampshire, 1976.
116 N.H. 705, 366 A.2d 467.

Opinion

KENISON, CHIEF JUSTICE.

This appeal results from cross actions by Kearsarge Computer, Inc., against Acme Staple Company, Inc., and by Acme against Kearsarge. Both actions relate to a certain data processing contract between the parties. Kearsarge sought payment for goods and services sold and delivered and damages for breach of contract. Acme also sued for breach of contract and alleged that, following termination of the contract, Kearsarge retained certain property owned by Acme. The cases were consolidated for a hearing on the merits before Master Earl J. Dearborn, Esquire, who held in favor of Kearsarge on all ultimate issues in both cases and awarded Kearsarge $12,313.22, plus interest and costs. Loughlin, J., approved the master's report and reserved and transferred the defendant's exceptions.

Under a one-year contract which began June 11, 1971, Kearsarge performed electronic data processing services for Acme for twenty-five dollars per computer hour or $2,000 per month whichever was greater. At a January 7, 1972 meeting between the parties, Acme terminated the contract on the grounds that Kearsarge's performance was unsatisfactory. In a letter dated January 10, 1972, Kearsarge requested information regarding the alleged data processing errors and any losses therefrom. Acme responded that such information had been sufficiently provided at the meeting. On April 12, 1972, Kearsarge served pretrial discovery interrogatories upon Acme one of which read:

'Please state in precise detail the alleged breaches by Kearsarge of the contract between it and Acme dated April 5, 1971, which resulted in Acme's alleged termination of said contract on January 7, 1972, giving the date of each alleged breach.'

In response, Acme listed eleven incidents of alleged breach in the degree of detail requested.

At trial the master refused to permit Acme to introduce evidence of any breaches other than those listed in the answer to the interrogatory. . . .

The first issue in this case is whether the master erred in excluding Acme's evidence. . . .

[The Court held the master did not err in excluding the evidence because "subjecting Kearsarge to the surprise of undisclosed evidence so late in the trial would be contrary to the purpose of pretrial discovery."]

The second issue is whether the master erred in awarding Kearsarge the full balance of the contract price. If the defendant's breach saves expense to the plaintiff, the plaintiff will recover the contract price minus the savings. McLaughlin v. Union Leader, 99 N.H. 492, 500, 116 A.2d 489, 496 (1955); Restatement of Contracts § 335 (1932); 5 A. Corbin, Contracts § 1038 (1964). The parties agree that if termination of the contract caused no savings or pecuniary advantage to Kearsarge, recovery is the full contract price.

Acme contends that Kearsarge did experience certain savings and that the master erred in not reducing the damages accordingly. However, Acme's breach did not result in substantial savings to Kearsarge. The plaintiff would not have spent significantly more on salaries, machine rental, or other overhead expenses if it continued to provide Acme with data processing services. With respect to labor costs, if a plaintiff cannot reduce his work force because of the breach, no savings result. 5 A. Corbin, supra at § 1038 at 239–40. Extensive testimony makes clear that no layoffs were possible in this case because each of Kearsarge's three employees performed separate functions. The payroll decrease subsequent to Acme's termination occurred only because the employees voluntarily accepted a drastic reduction in wages so that Kearsarge could stay in business. Such survival tactics cannot properly be classified as savings. Kearsarge's operating costs—notably the rentals on computers and other equipment—were substantially fixed. The reduction of output due to the breach did not result in savings. Id., R. Posner, Economic Analysis of the Law 59 n.7 (1972).

At the time of the breach, the only performance left on Kearsarge's part was the actual running of the data processing equipment and the delivery of the results to Acme. The cost of performance was the cost of paper, electricity and transportation of data to and from the offices of the parties. In suits for breach of contracts to sell advertising, courts hold that the costs of ink, paper and typographical composition are negligible and allow plaintiffs to recover the full contract price. Cases cited in Annot., 17 A.L.R.2d 968, 973 (1951). Similarly, the costs of performance [in this case] were trivial in relation to the contract price. Because the breach did not relieve Kearsarge of a costly burden, the master did not err in rewarding Kearsarge the full contract price. Restatement, supra at § 335, Comment b; 5 A. Corbin, supra at § 1038.

The fact that the plaintiff did not introduce evidence of the cost of paper, electricity and delivery of data does not bar recovery because the defendant has the burden of proving savings. Restatement, supra at § 335, Ill. 5. The general rule is:

> If the plaintiff's required expenditures are of cash or material, the tendency is to put the burden of allegation and proof of the amount thereof on him, but if his expenditures would be of time or labor, the burden is normally placed on the defendant. The court usually decides whether the plaintiff's performance requires an outlay of money or material from the nature of the contract, without a specific raising of the point by the parties. Annot., 17 A.L.R.2d 968, 972 (1951).

It is clear from the facts of this case that Kearsarge's performance did not require substantial cash outlays or materials as in the cases upon which the defendant relies.

After Acme terminated the contract, Kearsarge increased its efforts to secure new business. Acme's position is that at least some of the income from the new business should mitigate the damages. The general rule is that '(g)ains made by the injured party on other transactions after the breach are never to be deducted from the damages that are otherwise recoverable, unless such gains could not have been made, had there been no breach.' 5 A. Corbin, supra at § 1041; see D. Dobbs, Remedies § 3.6 at 183–84, § 12.6 at 827 (1973). In a suit for breach of a personal services contract, the wages obtained by the plaintiff-employee from a substitute job are deducted from the amount of damages if the earnings of the second income would not have been possible but for the breach. Id.; 11 Williston, Contracts § 1358 (3d ed. W. Jaeger 1968); Annot., 15 A.L.R. 751 (1921). In contrast, no deduction is allowed if the plaintiff sells to a third party a product that can be produced according to demand. The theory is that the second sale would have occurred even if the defendant did not breach his contract. See Locks v. Wade, 36 N.J.Super. 128, 114 A.2d 875 (App.Div.1955); J. Calamari & J. Perillo, Contracts § 217 (1970); 5 A. Corbin, supra at § 1041.

A contract for computer data processing services is neither a contract purely for personal services nor a contract for the sale of goods. It is an enterprise that involves a combination of personal skills and labor, materials, equipment and time. In these respects, a contract for data processing services is similar to a construction contract or a contract for the sale of advertising layouts. The law with respect to these contracts is clear. When a party refuses to allow a builder to perform, the builder's profits on contracts entered into after the breach do not mitigate the damages unless the first contract required the builder's personal services to such an extent that concurrent performance of another contract would be impossible. Olds v. Mapes-Reeves Const. Co., 177 Mass. 41, 58 N.E. 478 (1900); Sides v. Contemporary Homes, Inc., 311 S.W.2d 117 (Mo.App.1958); Restatement of Contracts § 346, Comment f on subsection (2) (1932); J. Calamari & J. Perillo, supra at § 217; Annot., 15 A.L.R. 751, 761 (1921). Likewise, when a purchaser of advertising space breaches his contract, the advertiser who is not limited by a specific number of pages recovers the full contract price. D. Dobbs, supra at § 3.6 at 183 n.2; Annot., 17 A.L.R.2d 968, 973 (1951). The reason is that, like manufacturing, these businesses are deemed to be expandable. The law presumes that they can accept a virtually unlimited amount of business so that income generated from accounts acquired after the breach does not mitigate the plaintiff's damages. 5 A. Corbin, Contracts § 1041 (1964). We hold that in the absence of evidence to the contrary a data processing contract does not involve unique personal services to such an extent that when the provider of such services seeks new business after a breach of contract, the income from such new business mitigates the damages owed to him by the breaching party. There is no evidence that Kearsarge could not render service to its new clients but for Acme's breach.

Finally, although the master found that Kearsarge's errors may have been justifiable, the contract unequivocally states that Kearsarge would be liable for its errors. Acme expended at least $837.75 in correcting mistakes in Kearsarge's work. Under the contract, Acme was entitled to this amount. Thus, Kearsarge's damages in the sum of $12,313.22 plus interest and costs shall be reduced by $837.75.

So ordered.

BOIS, J., did not sit; the others concurred.

Restatement, Second, Contracts
§ 347, Illustrations 6, 7

"6.   A contracts to build a house for B for $100,000. When it is partly built, B repudiates the contract and A stops work. A would have to spend $60,000 more to finish the house. The $60,000 cost avoided by A as a result of not having to finish the house is subtracted from the $100,000 price lost in determining A's damages. A has a right to $40,000 in damages from B, less any progress payments that he has already received.

"7.   The facts being otherwise as stated in Illustration 6, A has bought materials that are left over and that he can use for other purposes, saving him $5,000. The $5,000 cost avoided is subtracted in determining A's damages, resulting in damages of only $35,000 rather than $40,000."

Wired Music, Inc. v. Clark

26 Ill.App.2d 413, 168 N.E.2d 736 (1960)

Wired Music distributed recorded music to various locations, through direct wires rented from the telephone company. Clark executed a contract with Wired Music providing for three years of service at $24.30 per month. The contract provided that there could be no assignment without Wired Music's written consent.

After seventeen months, Clark moved his business and discontinued the service. The tenant who rented the space formerly occupied by Clark requested the right to take an assignment of Clark's contract, but Wired Music refused. Thereafter, the new tenant entered into a new contract for Wired Music's service at the same location and at a higher monthly charge. Wired Music sued Clark for its lost profits, based on the contract price to Clark minus Wired Music's costs for renting the telephone wires. Clark argued that Wired Music failed to show damages, because under the contract with the new tenant, Wired Music would realize more revenue from Clark's former location than it would have received from Clark. The trial court entered judgment for Wired Music in an amount that reflected the contract price for nineteen months minus the wire charges that Wired Music would have had to pay during that period to fulfill its contract with Clark. Affirmed.

"[T]he evidence is uncontradicted that plaintiff could supply any number of additional customers without incurring further expenses except for wire rental. If defendant's contention were adopted by this court, it would have the effect of denying to the plaintiff the benefit of his bargain. This case is not at all like the situation where a plaintiff has one house to rent or one car to sell or a fixed quantity of personal property or real estate. Here, plaintiff has so far as the evidence shows, an unlimited supply of music, limited in its distributions only by the number of contracts which plaintiff can secure."

––––––––

(B) SALE OF GOODS

UCC §§ 2–501(1), 2–703, 2–704(1), 2–706, 2–708, 2–709, 2–710, 2–723, 2–724

[See Selected Source Materials Supplement]

––––––––

CISG ARTS. 61, 62, 64, 74, 75, 76

[See Selected Source Materials Supplement]

––––––––

NOTE ON SELLER'S DAMAGES UNDER THE UCC

Where a buyer breaches a contract for the sale of goods the seller has several alternative remedies. Under UCC Section 2–706 the seller may resell the goods, and if the resale is made in good faith an in a commercially reasonable manner the seller may recover the difference between the contract price and the resale price together with incidental damages. Alternatively, under UCC Section 2–708(1) the seller can recover the difference between the contract price and the market price of the goods at the time and place for tender, together with incidental damages. Under UCC Section 2–708(2) if the measure of damages provided in UCC Section 2–708(1) is inadequate to put the seller in as good a position as performance would have done, the seller may recover the profit he would have made from full performance by the buyer together with incidental damages. Finally, under UCC Section 2–709 where the buyer fails to pay the price as it becomes due the seller may recover the price of goods accepted, or of goods the seller has identified to the contract if the seller is unable after reasonable efforts to resell them at a commercially reasonable price or the circumstances reasonably indicate that such effort would be unavailing.

NERI V. RETAIL MARINE CORP.

Court of Appeals of New York, 1972.
30 N.Y.2d 393, 334 N.Y.S.2d 165, 285 N.E.2d 311.

GIBSON, JUDGE. The appeal concerns the right of a retail dealer to recover loss of profits and incidental damages upon the buyer's repudiation of a contract governed by the Uniform Commercial Code. This is, indeed, the correct measure of damage in an appropriate case and to this extent the code (§ 2–708, subsection [2]) effected a substantial change from prior law, whereby damages were ordinarily limited to "the difference between the contract price and the market or current price".[1] Upon the record before us, the courts below erred in declining to give effect to the new statute and so the order appealed from must be reversed.

The plaintiffs contracted to purchase from defendant a new boat of a specified model for the price of $12,587.40, against which they made a deposit of $40. They shortly increased the deposit to $4,250 in consideration of the defendant dealer's agreement to arrange with the manufacturer for immediate delivery on the basis of "a firm sale", instead of the delivery within approximately four to six weeks originally specified. Some six days after the date of the contract plaintiffs' lawyer sent to defendant a letter rescinding the sales contract for the reason that plaintiff Neri was about to

---

[1] Personal Property Law, Consol.Laws, c. 41, § 145, repealed by Uniform Commercial Code, § 10–102 (L.1962, ch. 553, eff. Sept. 27, 1964); Lenobel, Inc. v. Senif, 252 App.Div. 533, 300 N.Y.S. 226.

undergo hospitalization and surgery, in consequence of which, according to the letter, it would be "impossible for Mr. Neri to make any payments". The boat had already been ordered from the manufacturer and was delivered to defendant at or before the time the attorney's letter was received. Defendant declined to refund plaintiffs' deposit and this action to recover it was commenced. Defendant counterclaimed, alleging plaintiffs' breach of the contract and defendant's resultant damage in the amount of $4,250, for which sum defendant demanded judgment. Upon motion, defendant had summary judgment on the issue of liability tendered by its counterclaim; and Special Term directed an assessment of damages, upon which it would be determined whether plaintiffs were entitled to the return of any portion of their down payment.

Upon the trial so directed, it was shown that the boat ordered and received by defendant in accordance with plaintiffs' contract of purchase was sold some four months later to another buyer for the same price as that negotiated with plaintiffs. From this proof the plaintiffs argue that defendant's loss on its contract was recouped, while defendant argues that but for plaintiffs' default, it would have sold two boats and have earned two profits instead of one. Defendant proved, without contradiction, that its profit on the sale under the contract in suit would have been $2,579 and that during the period the boat remained unsold incidental expenses aggregating $674 for storage, upkeep, finance charges and insurance were incurred. Additionally, defendant proved and sought to recover attorneys' fees of $1,250.

The trial court found "untenable" defendant's claim for loss of profit, inasmuch as the boat was later sold for the same price that plaintiffs had contracted to pay; found, too, that defendant had failed to prove any incidental damages; further found "that the terms of section 2–718, subsection 2(b), of the Uniform Commercial Code are applicable and same make adequate and fair provision to place the sellers in as good a position as performance would have done" and, in accordance with paragraph (b) of subsection (2) thus relied upon, awarded defendant $500 upon its counterclaim and directed that plaintiffs recover the balance of their deposit, amounting to $3,750. The ensuing judgment was affirmed, without opinion, at the Appellate Division, 37 A.D.2d 917, 326 N.Y.S.2d 984, and defendant's appeal to this court was taken by our leave.

The issue is governed in the first instance by section 2–718 of the Uniform Commercial Code which provides, among other things, that the buyer, despite his breach, may have restitution of the amount by which his payment exceeds: (a) reasonable liquidated damages stipulated by the contract or (b) absent such stipulation, 20% of the value of the buyer's total performance or $500, whichever is smaller (§ 2–718, subsection [2], pars. [a], [b]). As above noted, the trial court awarded defendant an offset in the amount of $500 under paragraph (b) and directed restitution to plaintiffs of the balance. Section 2–718, however, establishes, in paragraph (a) of subsection (3), an alternative right of offset in favor of the seller, as follows: "(3) The buyer's right to restitution under subsection (2) is subject to offset to the extent that the seller establishes (a) a right to recover damages under the provisions of this Article other than subsection (1)".

Among "the provisions of this Article other than subsection (1)" are those to be found in section 2–708, which the courts below did not apply. Subsection (1) of that section provides that "the measure of damages for non-acceptance or repudiation by the buyer is the difference between the market price at the time and place for tender and the unpaid contract price together with any incidental damages provided in this Article (Section 2–710), but less expenses saved in consequence of the buyer's breach." However, this provision is made expressly subject to subsection (2), providing: "(2) If the measure of damages provided in subsection (1) is inadequate to put the seller in as good a position as performance would have done then the measure of damages is the profit (including reasonable overhead) which the seller would have made from full performance by the buyer, together with any incidental damages provided in this Article (Section 2–710), due allowance for costs reasonably incurred and due credit for payments or proceeds of resale."

The provision of the code upon which the decision at Trial Term rested (§ 2–718, subsection [2], par. [b]) does not differ greatly from the corresponding provisions of the prior statute (Personal Property Law, § 145–a, subd. 1, par. [b]), except as the new act includes the alternative remedy of a lump sum award of $500. Neither does the present reference (in § 2–718, subsection [3], par. [a]) to the recovery of damages pursuant to other provisions of the article differ from a like reference in the prior statute (Personal Property Law, § 145–a, subd. 2, par. [a]) to an alternative measure of damages under section 145 of that act; but section 145 made no provision for recovery of lost profits as does section 2–708 (subsection [2]) of the code. The new statute is thus innovative and significant and its analysis is necessary to the determination of the issues here presented.

Prior to the code, the New York cases "applied the 'profit' test, contract price less cost of manufacture, only in cases where the seller [was] a manufacturer or an agent for a manufacturer" (1955 Report of N.Y.Law Rev.Comm., vol. 1, p. 693). Its extension to retail sales was "designed to eliminate the unfair and economically wasteful results arising under the older law when fixed price articles were involved. This section permits the recovery of lost profits in all appropriate cases, which would include all standard priced goods." (Official Comment 2, McKinney's Cons.Laws of N.Y., Book 62½, Part 1, p. 605, under Uniform Commercial Code, § 2–708.) Additionally, and "[i]n all cases the seller may recover incidental damages" (id., Comment 3). The buyer's right to restitution was established at Special Term upon the motion for summary judgment, as was the seller's right to proper offsets, in each case pursuant to section 2–718; and, as the parties concede, the only question before us, following the assessment of damages at Special Term, is that as to the proper measure of damage to be applied. The conclusion is clear from the record—indeed with mathematical certainty—that "the measure of damages provided in subsection (1) is inadequate to put the seller in as good a position as performance would have done" (Uniform Commercial Code, § 2–708, subsection [2]) and hence—again under subsection (2)—that the seller is entitled to its "profit (including reasonable overhead) . . . together with any incidental damages . . ., due allowance for costs reasonably incurred and due credit for payments or proceeds of resale."

It is evident, first, that this retail seller is entitled to its profit and, second, that the last sentence of subsection (2), as hereinbefore quoted, referring to "due credit for payments or proceeds of resale" is inapplicable to this retail sales contract.[2] Closely parallel to the factual situation now before us is that hypothesized by Dean Hawkland as illustrative of the operation of the rules: "Thus, if a private party agrees to sell his automobile to a buyer for $2,000, a breach by the buyer would cause the seller no loss (except incidental damages, i.e., expense of a new sale) if the seller was able to sell the automobile to another buyer for $2000. But the situation is different with dealers having an unlimited supply of standard-priced goods. Thus, if an automobile dealer agrees to sell a car to a buyer at the standard price of $2000, a breach by the buyer injures the dealer, even though he is able to sell the automobile to another for $2000. If the dealer has an inexhaustible supply of cars, the resale to replace the breaching buyer costs the dealer a sale, because, had the breaching buyer performed, the dealer would have made two sales instead of one. The buyer's breach, in such a case, depletes the dealer's sales to the extent of one, and the measure of damages should be the dealer's profit on one sale. Section 2–708 recognizes this, and it rejects the rule developed under the Uniform Sales Act by many courts that the profit cannot be recovered in this case." (Hawkland, Sales and Bulk Sales [1958 ed.], pp. 153–154; and see Comment, 31 Fordham L.Rev. 749, 755–756.)

---

[2]   The concluding clause, "due credit for payments or proceeds of resale", is intended to refer to "the privilege of the seller to realize junk value when it is manifestly useless to complete the operation of manufacture" (Supp. No. 1 to the 1952 Official Draft of Text and Comments of the Uniform Commercial Code, as Amended by the Act of the American Law Institute of the National Conference of Commissioners on Uniform Laws [1954], p. 14). The commentators who have considered the language have uniformly concluded that "the reference is to a resale as scrap under . . . Section 2–704" (1956 Report of N.Y.Law Rev.Comm., p. 397; 1955 Report of N.Y.Law Rev.Comm., vol. 1, p. 761; New York Annotations, McKinney's Cons.Laws of N.Y., Book 62½, Part 1, p. 606, under Uniform Commercial Code, § 2–708; 1 Willier and Hart, Bender's Uniform Commercial Code Service, § 2–708, pp. 1–180—1–181). Another writer, reaching the same conclusion, after detailing the history of the clause, says that " 'proceeds of resale' previously meant the resale value of the goods in finished form; now it means the resale value of the components on hand at the time plaintiff learns of breach" (Harris, Seller's Damages, 18 Stan.L.Rev. 66, 104).

The record which in this case establishes defendant's entitlement to damages in the amount of its prospective profit, at the same time confirms defendant's cognate right to "any incidental damages provided in this Article (Section 2–710)"[3] (Uniform Commercial Code, § 2–708, subsection [2]). From the language employed it is too clear to require discussion that the seller's right to recover loss of profits is not exclusive and that he may recoup his "incidental" expenses as well (Proctor & Gamble Distr. Co. v. Lawrence Amer. Field Warehousing Corp., 16 N.Y.2d 344, 354, 266 N.Y.S.2d 785, 792, 213 N.E.2d 873, 878). Although the trial court's denial of incidental damages in the uncontroverted amount of $674 was made in the context of its erroneous conclusion that paragraph (b) of subsection (2) of section 2–718 was applicable and was "adequate . . . to place the sellers in as good a position as performance would have done", the denial seems not to have rested entirely on the court's mistaken application of the law, as there was an explicit finding "that defendant completely failed to show that it suffered any incidental damages." We find no basis for the court's conclusion with respect to a deficiency of proof inasmuch as the proper items of the $674 expenses (being for storage, upkeep, finance charges and insurance for the period between the date performance was due and the time of the resale) were proven without objection and were in no way controverted, impeached or otherwise challenged, at the trial or on appeal. Thus the court's finding of a failure of proof cannot be supported upon the record and, therefore, and contrary to plaintiffs' contention, the affirmance at the Appellate Division was ineffective to save it.

The trial court correctly denied defendant's claim for recovery of attorney's fees incurred by it in this action. Attorney's fees incurred in an action such as this are not in the nature of the protective expenses contemplated by the statute (Uniform Commercial Code, § 1–106, subd. [1] ; § 2–710; § 2–708, subsection [2]) and by our reference to "legal expense" in Procter & Gamble Distr. Co. v. Lawrence Amer. Field Warehousing Corp. (16 N.Y.2d 344, 354–355, 266 N.Y.S.2d 785, 792–793, 213 N.E.2d 873, 878–879, supra), upon which defendant's reliance is in this respect misplaced.

It follows that plaintiffs are entitled to restitution of the sum of $4,250 paid by them on account of the contract price less an offset to defendant in the amount of $3,253 on account of its lost profit of $2,579 and its incidental damages of $674.

The order of the Appellate Division should be modified, with costs in all courts, in accordance with this opinion, and, as so modified, affirmed.

---

[3] Incidental damages to an aggrieved seller include any commercially reasonable charges, expenses or commissions incurred in stopping delivery, in the transportation, care and custody of goods after the buyer's breach, in connection with return or resale of the goods or otherwise resulting from the breach (Uniform Commercial Code, § 2–710).

FULD, C.J., and BURKE, SCILEPPI, BERGAN, BREITEL, and JASEN, JJ., concur.

Ordered accordingly.

———

Lazenby Garages Ltd. v. Wright

[1976] 2 All E.R. 770, [1976] 1 W.L.R. 459 (Ct.App. Eng. 1976)

(Lord Denning, M.R.) "Mr. Wright works on the land. On February 19, 1974 he went to the showrooms of motor dealers called Lazenby Garages Ltd. He saw some secondhand cars there. He agreed to buy a BMW 2002. He signed a contract to pay £1,670 for it. It was to be delivered to him on March 1, 1974. He went back home to his wife and told her about it. She persuaded him not to buy it. So next day he went back to the garage and said he would not have it after all. They kept it there offering it for re-sale. Two months later on April 23, 1974 they re-sold it for £1,770, that is, for £100 more than Mr. Wright was going to pay.

"Notwithstanding this advantageous re-sale, the garage sued Mr. Wright for damages. They produced evidence that they had themselves bought the car secondhand on 14th February 1974, that is five days before Mr. Wright had come in and agreed to buy it. They said that they had bought it for £1,325. He had agreed to buy it from them for £1,670. So they had lost £345 and they claimed that sum as damages.

"In answer Mr. Wright said: 'You haven't lost anything; you've sold it for a higher price.' The garage people said that they were dealers in secondhand cars; that they had had a number of cars of this sort of age and type, BMW 2002s; and that they had lost the sale of another car. They said that, if Mr. Wright had taken this car, they would have been able to sell one of those other cars to the purchaser. So they had sold one car less and were entitled to profit accordingly. . . .

". . . Now there is an appeal to this court. The cases show that if there are a number of new cars, all exactly of the same kind, available for sale, and the dealers can prove that they sold one car less than they otherwise would have done, they would be entitled to damages amounting to their loss of profit on the one car. . . .

"But it is entirely different in the case of a secondhand car. Each secondhand car is different from the next, even though it is the same make. The sales manager of the garage admitted in evidence that some secondhand cars, of the same make, even of the same year, may sell better than others of the same year. Some may sell quickly, others sluggishly. You simply cannot tell why. But they are all different.

"In the circumstances the cases about new cars do not apply. . . . "

———

SECTION 3. THE MITIGATION PRINCIPLE

SHIRLEY MACLAINE PARKER V. TWENTIETH CENTURY-FOX FILM CORP.

California Supreme Court, 1970.
3 Cal.3d 176, 89 Cal.Rptr. 737, 474 P.2d 689.

BURKE, J. Defendant Twentieth Century-Fox Film Corporation appeals from a summary judgment granting to plaintiff the recovery of agreed compensation under a written contract for her services as an actress in a motion picture. As will appear, we have concluded that the trial court correctly ruled in plaintiff's favor and that the judgment should be affirmed.

Plaintiff is well known as an actress, and in the contract between plaintiff and defendant is sometimes referred to as the "Artist." Under the contract, dated August 6, 1965, plaintiff was to play the female lead in defendant's contemplated production of a motion picture entitled "Bloomer Girl."* The contract provided that defendant would pay plaintiff a minimum "guaranteed compensation" of $53,571.42 per week for 14 weeks commencing May 23, 1966, for a total of $750,000. Prior to May 1966 defendant decided not to produce the picture and by a letter dated April 4, 1966, it notified plaintiff of that decision and that it would not "comply with our obligations to you under" the written contract.

By the same letter and with the professed purpose "to avoid any damage to you," defendant instead offered to employ plaintiff as the leading actress in another film tentatively entitled "Big Country, Big Man" (hereinafter, "Big Country"). The compensation offered was identical, as

---

* Victor Goldberg reports that *Bloomer Girl* was an adaptation of a stage musical written by Harold Arlen and Yip Harburg, which ran for 654 performances on Broadway in the mid-1940s. Harburg's son summarized the play's plot and political themes as follows:

> *Bloomer Girl* concerns the political activities of Amelia (renamed Dolly) Bloomer and the effect they have on a pre-Civil War family of her brother-in-law, hoopskirt king Horace Applegate, and his feminist daughter, Evalina. Evalina is the youngest and only remaining unmarried Applegate daughter; her older sisters are all married to company salesmen, and as *Bloomer Girl* begins, Horace is trying to unify business and family by encouraging his chief Southern salesman, Jefferson Calhoun, to court Evalina. On the eve of the Civil War, *Bloomer Girl* centers around Evalina's tutelage of Jeff in matters of gender and racial equality. Evalina, Dolly, and the other feminists of Cicero Falls not only campaign against Applegate's hoopskirts and sexism but also stage their own version of Uncle Tom's Cabin and conceal a runaway slave—Jeff's own manservant, Pompey. It was, said Yip, a show about "the indivisibility of human freedom."
>
> *Bloomer Girl* interweaves the issues of black and female equality and war and peace with the vicissitudes of courtship and pre-Civil War politics. . . . [I]t was at no point an escapist entertainment. . . .

[handwritten: A "serious" movie]

Goldberg, "Bloomer Girl Revisited or how to Frame an Unmade Picture," 1998 *Wisconsin Law Review* 1051 (1998) (quoting Harold Meyerson and Ernie Harburg, *Who Put the Rainbow in* The Wizard of Oz? *Yip Harburg, Lyricist* (1993). (Footnote by eds.)

were 31 of the 34 numbered provisions or articles of the original contract.[1] Unlike "Bloomer Girl," however, which was to have been a musical production, "Big Country" was a dramatic "western type" movie. "Bloomer Girl" was to have been filmed in California; "Big Country" was to be produced in Australia. Also, certain terms in the proffered contract varied from those of the original.[2] Plaintiff was given one week within which to accept; she did not and the offer lapsed. Plaintiff then commenced this action seeking recovery of the agreed guaranteed compensation.

The complaint sets forth two causes of action. The first is for money due under the contract; the second, based upon the same allegations as the first, is for damages resulting from defendant's breach of contract. Defendant in its answer admits the existence and validity of the contract, that plaintiff complied with all the conditions, covenants and promises and stood ready to complete the performance, and that defendant breached and "anticipatorily repudiated" the contract. It denies, however, that any money is due to plaintiff either under the contract or as a result of its breach, and pleads as an affirmative defense to both causes of action plaintiff's allegedly deliberate failure to mitigate damages, asserting that she unreasonably refused to accept its offer of the leading role in "Big Country."

Plaintiff moved for summary judgment under Code of Civil Procedure section 437c, the motion was granted, and summary judgment for $750,000

---

[1]   Among the identical provisions was the following found in the last paragraph of Article 2 of the original contract: "We [defendant] shall not be obligated to utilize your [plaintiff's] services in or in connection with the Photoplay hereunder, our sole obligation, subject to the terms and conditions of this Agreement, being to pay you the guaranteed compensation herein provided for."

[2]   Article 29 of the original contract specified that plaintiff approved the director already chosen for "Bloomer Girl" and that in case he failed to act as director plaintiff was to have approval rights of any substitute director. Article 31 provided that plaintiff was to have the right of approval of the "Bloomer Girl" dance director, and Article 32 gave her the right of approval of the screenplay.

Defendant's letter of April 4 to plaintiff, which contained both defendant's notice of breach of the "Bloomer Girl" contract and offer of the lead in "Big Country," eliminated or impaired each of those rights. It read in part as follows: "The terms and conditions of our offer of employment are identical to those set forth in the 'Bloomer Girl' Agreement, Articles 1 through 34 and Exhibit A to the Agreement, except as follows:

"1.   Article 31 of said Agreement will not be included in any contract of employment regarding 'Big Country, Big Man' as it is not a musical and it thus will not need a dance director.

"2.   In the 'Bloomer Girl' agreement, in Articles 29 and 32, you were given certain director and screenplay approvals and you had preapproved certain matters. Since there simply is insufficient time to negotiate with you regarding your choice of director and regarding the screenplay and since you already expressed an interest in performing the role in 'Big Country, Big Man,' we must exclude from our offer of employment in 'Big Country, Big Man' any approval rights as are contained in said Articles 29 and 32; however, we shall consult with you respecting the director to be selected to direct the photoplay and will further consult with you with respect to the screenplay and any revisions or changes therein, provided, however, that if we fail to agree . . . the decision of . . . [defendant] with respect to the selection of a director and to revisions and changes in the said screenplay shall be binding upon the parties to said agreement."

plus interest was entered in plaintiff's favor. This appeal by defendant followed.

The familiar rules are that the matter to be determined by the trial court on a motion for summary judgment is whether facts have been presented which give rise to a triable factual issue. The court may not pass upon the issue itself. Summary judgment is proper only if the affidavits or declarations in support of the moving party would be sufficient to sustain a judgment in his favor and his opponent does not by affidavit show facts sufficient to present a triable issue of fact. . . .

The general rule is that the measure of recovery by a wrongfully discharged employee is the amount of salary agreed upon for the period of service, less the amount which the employer affirmatively proves the employee has earned or with reasonable effort might have earned from other employment. . . . However, before projected earnings from other employment opportunities not sought or accepted by the discharged employee can be applied in mitigation, the employer must show that the other employment was comparable, or substantially similar, to that of which the employee has been deprived; the employee's rejection of or failure to seek other available employment of a different or inferior kind may not be resorted to in order to mitigate damages. (Gonzales v. Internat. Assn. of Machinists (1963) 213 Cal.App.2d 817, 822–824 [29 Cal.Rptr. 190]; Harris v. Nat. Union etc. Cooks, Stewards (1953) 116 Cal.App.2d 759, 761 [254 P.2d 673]. . . . de la Falaise v. Gaumont-British Picture Corp., 39 Cal.App.2d 46 [103 P.2d 447 (1940)]. . . .

In the present case defendant has raised no issue of *reasonableness of efforts* by plaintiffs to obtain other employment; the sole issue is whether plaintiff's refusal of defendant's substitute offer of "Big Country" may be used in mitigation. Nor, if the "Big Country" offer was of employment different or inferior when compared with the original "Bloomer Girl" employment, is there an issue as to whether or not plaintiff acted reasonably in refusing the substitute offer. Despite defendant's arguments to the contrary, no case cited or which our research has discovered holds or suggests that reasonableness is an element of a wrongfully discharged employee's option to reject, or fail to seek, different or inferior employment lest the possible earnings therefrom be charged against him in mitigation of damages.[5]

Issue

---

[5]   Instead, in each case the reasonableness referred to was that of the *efforts* of the employee to obtain other employment that was not different or inferior; his right to reject the latter was declared as an unqualified rule of law. Thus Gonzales v. Internat. Assn. of Machinists, supra, 213 Cal.App.2d 817, 823–824, holds that the trial court correctly instructed the jury that plaintiff union member, a machinist, was required to make "such *efforts* as the average [member of his union] desiring employment would make at that particular time and place" (italics added); but, further, that the court *properly rejected* defendant's *offer of proof of the availability of other kinds* of employment at the same or higher pay than plaintiff usually received and all outside the

Applying the foregoing rules to the record in the present case, with all intendments in favor of the party opposing the summary judgment motion—here, defendant—it is clear that the trial court correctly ruled that plaintiff's failure to accept defendant's tendered substitute employment could not be applied in mitigation of damages because the offer of the "Big Country" lead was of employment both different and inferior, and that no factual dispute was presented on that issue. The mere circumstance that "Bloomer Girl" was to be a musical review calling upon plaintiff's talents as a dancer as well as an actress, and was to be produced in the City of Los Angeles, whereas "Big Country" was a straight dramatic role in a "Western Type" story taking place in an opal mine in Australia, demonstrates the difference in kind between the two employments; the female lead as a dramatic actress in a western style motion picture can by no stretch of imagination be considered the equivalent of or substantially similar to the lead in a song-and-dance production.

Additionally, the substitute "Big Country" offer proposed to eliminate or impair the director and screenplay approvals accorded to plaintiff under the original "Bloomer Girl" contract (see fn. 2, ante), and thus constituted an offer of inferior employment. No expertise or judicial notice is required in order to hold that the deprivation or infringement of an employee's rights held under an original employment contract converts the available "other employment" relied upon by the employer to mitigate damages, into inferior employment which the employee need not seek or accept. (See Gonzales v. Internat. Assn. of Machinists, supra, 213 Cal.App.2d 817, 823–824; and fn. 5. . . .)

Statements found in affidavits submitted by defendant in opposition to plaintiff's summary judgment motion, to the effect that the "Big Country" offer was not of employment different from or inferior to that under the "Bloomer Girl" contract, merely repeat the allegations of defendant's answer to the complaint in this action, constitute only conclusionary assertions with respect to undisputed facts, and do not give rise to a triable factual issue so as to defeat the motion for summary judgment. . . .

---

jurisdiction of his union, as plaintiff could not be required to accept different employment or a non-union job.

In Harris v. Nat. Union etc. Cooks, Stewards, supra, 116 Cal.App.2d 759, 761, the issues were stated to be, inter alia, whether comparable employment was open to each plaintiff employee, and if so whether each plaintiff made a *reasonable effort* to secure such employment. It was held that the trial court *properly sustained an objection to an offer to prove a custom of accepting a job in a lower rank* when work in the higher rank was not available, as "The duty of mitigation of damages . . . . . . does not require the plaintiff 'to seek or to accept other employment of a different or inferior kind.' " . . .

See also: Lewis v. Protective Security Life Ins. Co. (1962) 208 Cal.App.2d 582, 584 [25 Cal.Rptr. 213]: "*honest effort* to find similar employment. . . . " (Italics added.) . . .de la Falaise v. Gaumont-British Picture Corp., supra, 39 Cal.App.2d 461, 469: "reasonable effort."

In view of the determination that defendant failed to present any facts showing the existence of a factual issue with respect to its sole defense— plaintiff's rejection of its substitute employment offer in mitigation of damages—we need not consider plaintiff's further contention that for various reasons, including the provisions of the original contract set forth in footnote 1, ante, plaintiff was excused from attempting to mitigate damages.

The judgment is affirmed.

MCCOMB, J., PETERS, J., TOBRINER, J., KAUS, J.,* and ROTH, J.,** concurred.

SULLIVAN, ACTING C.J. (dissenting). The basic question in this case is whether or not plaintiff acted reasonably in rejecting defendant's offer of alternate employment. The answer depends upon whether that offer (starring in 'Big Country, Big Man') was an offer of work that was substantially similar to her former employment (starring in 'Bloomer Girl') or of work that was of a different or inferior kind. To my mind this is a factual issue which the trial court should not have determined on a motion for summary judgment. The majority have not only repeated this error but have compounded it by applying the rules governing mitigation of damages in the employer-employee context in a misleading fashion. Accordingly, I respectfully dissent.

The familiar rule requiring a plaintiff in a tort or contract action to mitigate damages embodies notions of fairness and socially responsible behavior which are fundamental to our jurisprudence. Most broadly stated, it precludes the recovery of damages which, through the exercise of due diligence, could have been avoided. Thus, in essence, it is a rule requiring reasonable conduct in commercial affairs. This general principle governs the obligations of an employee after his employer has wrongfully repudiated or terminated the employment contract. Rather than permitting the employee simply to remain idle during the balance of the contract period, the law requires him to make a reasonable effort to secure other employment. He is not obliged, however, to seek or accept any and all types of work which may be available. Only work which is in the same field and which is of the same quality need be accepted.

Over the years the courts have employed various phrases to define the type of employment which the employee, upon his wrongful discharge, is under an obligation to accept. Thus in California alone it has been held that he must accept employment which is 'substantially similar' . . . 'comparable employment' . . . employment 'in the same general line of the first employment' . . . 'equivalent to his prior position' . . . 'employment in a

---

* Assigned by the Acting Chairman of the Judicial Council.
** Assigned by the Acting Chairman of the Judicial Council.

similar capacity' . . . employment which is 'not * * * of a different or inferior kind.' . . .

For reasons which are unexplained, the majority cite several of these cases yet select from among the various judicial formulations which contain one particular phrase, 'Not of a different or inferior kind,' with which to analyze this case. I have discovered no historical or theoretical reason to adopt this phrase, which is simply a negative restatement of the affirmative standards set out in the above cases, as the exclusive standard. Indeed, its emergence is an example of the dubious phenomenon of the law responding not to rational judicial choice or changing social conditions, but to unrecognized changes in the language of opinions or legal treatises. However, the phrase is a serviceable one and my concern is not with its use as the standard but rather with what I consider its distortion.

The relevant language excuses acceptance only of employment which is of a Different kind. . . . It has never been the law that the mere existence of Differences between two jobs in the same field is sufficient, as a matter of law, to excuse an employee wrongfully discharged from one from accepting the other in order to mitigate damages. Such an approach would effectively eliminate any obligation of an employee to attempt to minimize damage arising from a wrongful discharge. The only alternative job offer an employee would be required to accept would be an offer of his former job by his former employer. . . .

Difference b/w jobs isn't enough

I believe that the approach taken by the majority (a superficial listing of differences with no attempt to assess their significance) may subvert a valuable legal doctrine. The inquiry in cases such as this should not be whether differences between the two jobs exist (there will always be differences) but whether the differences which are present are substantial enough to constitute differences in the Kind of employment or, alternatively, whether they render the substitute work employment of an Inferior kind.

Case shouldn't be decided on summary judgement b/c requires weighing evidence

It seems to me that this inquiry involves, in the instant case at least, factual determinations which are improper on a motion for summary judgment. Resolving whether or not one job is substantially similar to another or whether, on the other hand, it is of a different or inferior kind, will often (as here) require a critical appraisal of the similarities and differences between them in light of the importance of these differences to the employee. This necessitates a weighing of the evidence, and it is precisely this undertaking which is forbidden on summary judgment. . . .

MOSK, J., did not participate.

———

RESTATEMENT, SECOND, CONTRACTS § 350

[See Selected Source Materials Supplement]

————

UNIDROIT PRINCIPLES OF INTERNATIONAL COMMERCIAL CONTRACTS ARTS. 7.4.7, 7.4.8

[See Selected Source Materials Supplement]

————

PRINCIPLES OF EUROPEAN CONTRACT LAW ARTS. 9.504, 9.505

[See Selected Source Materials Supplement]

————

Punkar v. King Plastic Corp.

290 So.2d 505 (Fla.App.1974)

"A wrongfully discharged employee is not necessarily obligated to mitigate damages by accepting alternative employment at a distance from his home. . . . Our research discloses that a majority of jurisdictions have confined the search required to the immediate community or neighborhood. 44 A.L.R.3d 629. We believe this to be the better view."

————

Mr. Eddie, Inc. v. Ginsberg

430 S.W.2d 5 (Tex.Civ.App.1968)

Ginsberg was wrongfully dismissed by defendant early in the term of a three-year employment contract. Immediately after the dismissal Ginsberg took another job, which he held for thirty-four weeks, earning $13,760. After Ginsberg left that job, he spent $1,340 unsuccessfully seeking further employment. Held, Ginsberg was entitled to recover his remaining salary under his contract with defendant, minus the $13,760 earned on the other job, but plus the $1,340 he unsuccessfully expended in looking for further employment. As to the $1,340 expense, the court said, "the rule in such cases is . . . as follows: 'The expenses for which a recovery may be had include necessary and reasonable disbursements made in an effort to avoid or mitigate the injurious consequences of the defendant's wrong. . . . if such expenses are the result of a prudent attempt to minimize damages they are recoverable even though the result is an aggravation of the damages rather than a mitigation.' "

————

Southern Keswick, Inc. v. Whetherholt

293 So.2d 109 (Fla.App.1974)

This was an action for breach of an employment contract. The jury was instructed, "[It is] the general rule that employment of different or inferior nature cannot be used in reduction of damages." Reversed. "While we would agree that a wrongfully discharged employee is not obliged to *seek* employment of a different or inferior nature, if he in fact *obtains* such employment within the contract period his earnings should be used in mitigation of damages. The foregoing charge was therefore clearly wrong. . . . " (Emphasis added.)

UCC §§ 2–704(2), 2–715(2)

[See Selected Source Materials Supplement]

CISG ART. 77

[See Selected Source Materials Supplement]

NOTE ON DAMAGES WHEN THE PLAINTIFF FAILS TO MITIGATE

A plaintiff who fails to mitigate does not recover damages for the avoidable loss. Rockingham County v. Luten Bridge Co., 35 F.2d 301 (1929), illustrates. Defendant county rescinded a contract for construction of bridge before the erection of the bridge was commenced. Plaintiff had spent $1,900 on labor and material at the time of the attempted rescission. Plaintiff ignored the attempted rescission, completed the bridge, and sued for the contract price of $18,301. The disputed issues in the case involved the validity of a series of conflicting actions taken by a divided board of county commissioners. The bridge contract had been approved by a 3–2 majority of the board. One member of the majority resigned and then tried to withdraw his resignation. The clerk ignored the withdrawal then appointed a new commissioner, who voted with the previous minority to rescind the contract. The court of appeal held that the rescission of the contract by the newly constituted majority of the board was valid and then turned to the issue of damages.

> . . . [W]e do not think that, after the county had given notice, while the contract was still executory, that it did not desire the bridge built and would not pay for it, plaintiff could proceed to build it and recover the contract price. It is true that the county had no right to rescind the contract, and the notice given plaintiff amounted to a breach on its part; but, after plaintiff had received notice of the breach, it was its duty to do nothing to increase the damages flowing

therefrom. If A enters into a binding contract to build a house for B, B, of course, has no right to rescind the contract without A's consent. But if, before the house is built, he decides that he does not want it, and notifies A to that effect, A has no right to proceed with the building and thus pile up damages. His remedy is to treat the contract as broken when he receives the notice, and sue for the recovery of such damages as he may have sustained from the breach, including any profit which he would have realized upon performance, as well as any other losses which may have resulted to him. In the case at bar, the county decided not to build the road of which the bridge was to be a part, and did not build it. The bridge, built in the midst of the forest, is of no value to the county because of this change of circumstances. When, therefore, the county gave notice to the plaintiff that it would not proceed with the project, plaintiff should have desisted from further work. It had no right thus to pile up damages by proceeding with the erection of a useless bridge. . . .

. . . It follows that there was error in directing a verdict for plaintiff for the full amount of its claim. The measure of plaintiff's damage, upon its appearing that notice was duly given not to build the bridge, is an amount sufficient to compensate plaintiff for labor and materials expended and expense incurred in the part performance of the contract, prior to its repudiation, plus the profit which would have been realized if it had been carried out in accordance with its terms. . . .

Bomberger v. McKelvey

35 Cal.2d 607, 220 P.2d 729 (1950)

(GIBSON, C.J) "It is the general rule in California and in practically all other jurisdictions that either party to an executory contract has the power to stop performance of the contract by giving notice or direction to that effect, subjecting himself to liability for damages, and upon receipt of such notice the other party cannot continue to perform and recover damages based on full performance. . . . This is an application of the principle that a plaintiff must mitigate damages so far as he can without loss to himself. See 5 Williston on Contracts, Rev.Ed.1937, § 1298, p. 3694.

"The reason for this rule is twofold: Ordinarily a plaintiff is interested only in the profit he will make from his contract, and if he receives this he obtains the full benefit of his bargain; on the other hand, performance by the plaintiff might be useless to the defendant, although he would have to pay the entire contract price if the plaintiff were permitted to perform, and this would inflict damage on the defendant without benefit to the plaintiff. See 5 Williston on Contracts, Rev.Ed.1937, § 1298, p. 3694; Dowling v. Whites Lumber & Supply Co., 170 Miss. 267, 154 So. 703, 705. If these reasons are not present, the rule is not applied. For example, where the plaintiff is not interested solely in profit from the agreement but must proceed with the work in order to fulfill contract obligations to others, or where refraining from performance might involve closing a factory, damages may be inadequate and the plaintiff may have a right to continue performance. Southern Cotton-Oil Co. v. Heflin, 5 Cir., 99 F. 339; 5 Williston on Contracts, Rev.Ed.1937, § 1299, p. 3696. It has likewise been held that where a contractor has started work and has reached a point where it would be impracticable to attempt to make a reasonable estimate of damages, or where to complete the work will diminish damages or at least not enhance them, the contractor may go forward and complete performance. Dowling v. Whites Lumber & Supply Co., 170 Miss. 267, 154 So. 703. In the Restatement of Contracts, Comment a on section 336, it is said that 'It is not reasonable to expect the plaintiff to avoid harm if at the time for action it appears that the attempt may cause other serious harm. He need not enter into other risky contracts, incur unreasonable inconvenience or expense, disorganize his business, or put himself in a humiliating position or in one involving loss of honor and respect.'

"The general rule is also subject to the jurisdiction of equity to order specific performance of the contract, and, apparently in recognition of this principle, it has been held that in cases where damages will not afford adequate compensation and where specific performance will lie, the plaintiff may continue to perform, in spite of a notice to stop, and thereafter recover on the basis of his continued performance. . . ."

NOTE ON THE DUTY TO MITIGATE AND THE POWER TO CONTINUE PERFORMANCE ON REPUDIATION

Usually when a buyer repudiates a contract for a personal service or for construction before a seller completes performance, the wronged seller will halt performance purely out of self-interest because the applicable damage rule will put him in as good or better position than performing and suing for the contract price. For example, if the repudiated contract is for a personal service, then the plaintiff is likely to recover the full contract price (unless he takes other work he could not have taken but for the breach). If the plaintiff prefers leisure to work, then he is better off stopping work and suing for the contract price.

But sometimes a wronged seller will find it in his self-interest to complete performance after repudiation. In such a case, a court will award the contract price if the seller had sufficient reason to perform to overcome the argument that the choice to perform was unreasonable. Bomberger v. McKelvey, 35 Cal.2d 607 (1950), canvasses the exceptions to the rule requiring a party to stop performance of a contract on repudiation and notes the common theme, which is that the plaintiff had to complete performance to avoid a loss that might not be adequately compensated with damages.

The case illustrates why the plaintiff may choose to complete performance, and recover the contract price. McKelvey bought a plot of land from Bomberger and agreed to pay Bomberger $3,500 to demolish a building on the land, with Bomberger being allowed to salvage what material he could from the existing building. After the land was conveyed, McKelvey decided to delay construction of the store it planned to build on the land, because it could not obtain needed materials due to wartime shortages. McKelvey ordered Bomberger not to proceed with the demolition. Bomberger ignored the order and demolished the building, asserting that he needed skylights salvaged from the building to complete another building. The skylights could have been replaced for a cost of $540 but with a three-month delay. The demolished building was worth around $26,000 and it was generating $300 monthly rent. The California Supreme Court affirmed the trial court's decision that Bomberger did not violate the duty to mitigate, and so was entitled to recover the agreed price for the demolition, because "[u]nder these circumstances the trial court could properly conclude that inability to obtain the salvage from the old building would seriously interfere with completion of the new building, that equivalent materials could not then be secured by plaintiffs, and that in an action for breach of contract damages would be difficult to ascertain and would be inadequate."

––––––––––

Madsen v. Murrey & Sons Co.

743 P.2d 1212 (Utah 1987)

Seller was in the business of manufacturing and selling pool tables. Buyer agreed to acquire 100 pool tables, to which it planned to add special electronic lighting-and-sound effects. To accommodate the electrical components that the buyer planned to install, Seller was to customize its pool tables by adding various holes, notches, and routings. Buyer encountered problems in developing the special effects, and notified Seller that he would be unable to take delivery of the pool tables. Seller then dismantled the 100 pool tables that it had customized, used part of the salvageable materials to manufacture other pool tables, and used the balance as firewood. Seller claimed that selling the tables, rather than dismantling them, would have damaged its reputation for quality, and that the special holes, notches, and routings weakened the structure of the pool tables and would have exposed Seller to potential liability if the tables were sold on the market. However, Buyer's expert testified that the customizing would not have adversely affected the quality or marketability of the 100 pool tables, and that the tables could have been sold at full value or at a discounted price.

In an opinion affirmed by the Utah Supreme Court, the trial court concluded that Seller had a duty to mitigate its damages and had failed to do so, because dismantling the tables for salvage and firewood, rather than attempting to sell or market the tables at full value or a discounted price, was not commercially reasonable.

In re Kellett Aircraft Corp.

186 F.2d 197 (3d Cir.1950)

Amerform entered into a contract with Kellett under which Kellett undertook to fabricate 5000 shower cabinets at $13.18 each, plus $3,331 for tooling costs. As Kellett knew, the cabinets were needed by Amerform to fulfill a government order calling for deliveries in July, August, and September, 1946. On September 16, 1946, Kellett stated in writing its inability to perform. Amerform immediately approached four or five companies located in various Pennsylvania and New Jersey cities in an effort to procure the cabinets as soon as possible. Cutler, which had previously made identical cabinets for Amerform, and already had the necessary dies and tools, offered to perform at a price of $18 per cabinet. Production was to be scheduled in accordance with the immediate availability of materials, and a night shift was to be added to accelerate production. Several days after the Cutler offer, still another company, Luscombe, proposed to make the cabinets at the price formerly agreed by Kellett, $13.18, plus an additional $500 for tooling. Luscombe, however, informed Amerform that it had to look to Kellett to fabricate the tools and dies, and promised to begin delivery of the cabinets four weeks after the tools and dies were to be delivered. Amerform awarded the contract to Cutler. The district court held that by contracting with Cutler rather than Luscombe, Kellett had failed to properly mitigate damages. Reversed.

(Hastie, J.) "Whether or not the buyer's obligation to mitigate damages has been discharged depends on the reasonableness of its conduct. In this connection, reasonable conduct is to be determined from all the facts and circumstances of each case, and must be judged in the light of one viewing the situation at the time the problem was presented. Where a choice has been required between two reasonable courses, the person whose wrong forced the choice can not complain that one rather than the other was chosen. The rule of mitigation of damages may not be invoked by a contract breaker as a basis for hypercritical examination of the conduct of the injured party, or merely for the purpose of showing that the injured person might have taken steps which seemed wiser or would have been more advantageous to the defaulter. One is not obligated to exalt the interests of the defaulter to his own probable detriment. . . .

". . . The claimant acted promptly and diligently. In all the circumstances, we consider it the exercise of prudent business judgment and in no way unreasonable conduct for Amerform to have awarded the contract at somewhat increased cost to one whose performance had on previous occasions proved satisfactory, who had at hand proper and adequate tools for the job, and who promised to get on with it at once."

SECTION 4. THE FORESEEABILITY PRINCIPLE AND OTHER LIMITING RULES

HADLEY V. BAXENDALE

In the Court of Exchequer, 1854.
9 Exch. 341.

. . . At the trial before Crompton, J., at the last Gloucester Assizes, it appeared that the plaintiffs carried on an extensive business as millers at Gloucester; and that, on the 11th of May, their mill was stopped by a breakage of the crank shaft by which the mill was worked. The steam-engine was manufactured by Messrs. Joyce & Co., the engineers, at Greenwich, and it became necessary to send the shaft as a pattern for a new one to Greenwich. The fracture was discovered on the 12th, and on the 13th the plaintiffs sent one of their servants to the office of the defendants, who are the well-known carriers trading under the name of Pickford & Co., for the purpose of having the shaft carried to Greenwich. The plaintiffs' servant told the clerk that the mill was stopped, and that the shaft must be sent immediately; and in answer to the inquiry when the shaft would be taken, the answer was, that if it was sent up by twelve o'clock any day, it would be delivered at Greenwich on the following day. On the following day the shaft was taken by the defendants before noon, for the purpose of being conveyed to Greenwich, and the sum of £2, 4s. was paid for its carriage for the whole distance; at the same time the defendants' clerk was told that a special entry, if required, should be made to hasten its delivery. The delivery of the shaft at Greenwich was delayed by some neglect; and the consequence was, that the plaintiffs did not receive the new shaft for several days after they would otherwise have done and the working of their mill was thereby delayed, and they thereby lost the profits they would otherwise have received.*

On the part of the defendants, it was objected that these damages were too remote, and that the defendants were not liable with respect to them. The learned Judge left the case generally to the jury, who found a verdict with £25 damages beyond the amount paid into Court.**

WHATELEY, in last Michaelmas Term, obtained a rule nisi for a new trial, on the ground of misdirection.

KEATING and DOWDESWELL (Feb. 1) showed cause. The plaintiffs are entitled to the amount awarded by the jury as damages. These damages

---

* In The Capability Problem in Contract Law (2d ed. 2004), Richard Danzig and Geoffrey R. Watson set out the following statement from the Assize Report in August 8, 1853, edition of The Times of London: "[I]nstead of being forwarded by wagon immediately, [the crankshaft] was kept for several days in London, and was at length forwarded by water on the 20th, along with many tons of iron goods which had been consigned to the same parties." Id. at 59 n. 5. (Footnote by eds.)

** According to the report of the case, the amount which the defendant had paid into court was £25. See 9 Exch.Rep. at 343. (Footnote by eds.)

are not too remote, for they are not only the natural and necessary consequence of the defendants' default, but they are the only loss which the plaintiffs have actually sustained. The principle upon which damages are assessed is founded upon that of rendering compensation to the injured party. . . .

[PARKE, B. The sensible rule appears to be that which has been laid down in France, and which is declared in their code—Code Civil, liv, iii, tit. iii. ss. 1149, 1150, 1151, and which is thus translated in Sedgwick [on Damages, p. 67]: "The damages due to the creditor consist in general of the loss that he has sustained, and the profit which he has been prevented from acquiring, subject to the modifications hereinafter contained. The debtor is only liable for the damages foreseen, or which might have been foreseen, at the time of the execution of the contract, when it is not owing to his fraud that the agreement has been violated. Even in the case of non-performance of the contract, resulting from the fraud of the debtor, the damages only comprise so much of the loss sustained by the creditor, and so much of the profit which he has been prevented from acquiring, as directly and immediately results from the non-performance of the contract."] If that rule is to be adopted, there was ample evidence in the present case of the defendants' knowledge of such a state of things as would necessarily result in the damage the plaintiffs suffered through the defendants' default. . . .

[. . . MARTIN, B. Take the case of the non-delivery by a carrier of a delicate piece of machinery, whereby the whole of an extensive mill is thrown out of work for a considerable time; if the carrier is to be liable for the loss in that case, he might incur damages to the extent of 10,000*l*. . . .] These extreme cases, and the difficulty which consequently exists in the estimation of the true amount of damages, supports the view for which the plaintiffs contend, that the question is properly for the decision of a jury, and therefore that this matter could not properly have been withdrawn from their consideration. . . .

WHATELEY, WILLES, and PHIPSON, in support of the rule (Feb. 2). It has been contended, on the part of the plaintiffs, that the damages found by the jury are a matter fit for their consideration; but still the question remains, in what way ought the jury to have been directed? It has been also urged, that, in awarding damages, the law gives compensation to the injured individual. But it is clear that complete compensation is not to be awarded; for instance, the non-payment of a bill of exchange might lead to the utter ruin of the holder, and yet such damage could not be considered as necessarily resulting from the breach of contract, so as to entitle the party aggrieved to recover in respect of it. Take the case of the breach of a contract to supply a rick-cloth, whereby and in consequence of bad weather the hay, being unprotected, is spoiled, that damage would not be recoverable. Many similar cases might be added. . . . Sedgwick says [p. 28], "In regard to the quantum of damages, instead of adhering to the term compensation, it would be far more accurate to say, in the language of Domat, which we have cited above, 'that the object is to discriminate between that portion of the loss which must be borne by the offending party and that which must be borne by the sufferer.' The law in fact aims not at the satisfaction but at a division of the loss." . . . This therefore is a question of law, and the jury ought to have been told that these damages were too remote; and that, in the absence of the proof of any other damage, the plaintiffs were entitled to nominal damages only. . . .

The judgment of the Court was now delivered by ALDERSON, B.

We think that there ought to be a new trial in this case; but, in so doing, we deem it to be expedient and necessary to state explicitly the rule which the Judge, at the next trial, ought, in our opinion, to direct the jury to be governed by when they estimate the damages.

It is, indeed, of the last importance that we should do this; for, if the jury are left without any definite rule to guide them, it will, in such cases as these, manifestly lead to the greatest injustice. The Courts have done this on several occasions; and, in Blake v. Midland Railway Company, 18 Q.B. 93, the Court granted a new trial on this very ground, that the rule had not been definitely laid down to the jury by the learned Judge at Nisi Prius.

"There are certain established rules," this Court says, in Alder v. Keighley, 15 M. & W. 117, "according to which the jury ought to find." And the Court, in that case, adds: "and here there is a clear rule, that the amount which would have been received if the contract had been kept, is the measure of damages if the contract is broken."

Now we think the proper rule in such a case as the present is this:— Where two parties have made a contract which one of them has broken, the damages which the other party ought to receive in respect of such breach of contract should be such as may fairly and reasonably be considered either arising naturally, i.e., according to the usual course of things, from such breach of contract itself, or such as may reasonably be supposed to have been in the contemplation of both parties, at the time they made the contract, as the probable result of the breach of it. Now, if the special circumstances under which the contract was actually made were communicated by the plaintiffs to the defendants, and thus known to both parties, the damages resulting from the breach of such a contract, which they would reasonably contemplate, would be the amount of injury which would ordinarily follow from a breach of contract under these special circumstances so known and communicated. But, on the other hand, if these special circumstances were wholly unknown to the party breaking the contract, he, at the most, could only be supposed to have had in his contemplation the amount of injury which would arise generally, and in the great multitude of cases not affected by any special circumstances, from such a breach of contract. For, had the special circumstances been known, the parties might have specially provided for the breach of contract by special terms as to the damages in that case; and of this advantage it would be very unjust to deprive them. Now the above principles are those by which we think the jury ought to be guided in estimating the damages arising out of any breach of contract. It is said, that other cases such as breaches of contract in the non-payment of money, or in the not making a good title to land, are to be treated as exceptions from this, and as governed by a conventional rule. But as, in such cases, both parties must be supposed to be cognizant of that well-known rule, these cases may, we think, be more properly classed under the rule above enunciated as to cases under known special circumstances, because there both parties may reasonably be presumed to contemplate the estimation of the amount of damages according to the conventional rule. Now, in the present case, if we are to apply the principles above laid down, we find that the only circumstances here communicated by the plaintiffs to the defendants at the time the contract was made, were, that the article to be carried was the broken shaft of a mill, and that the plaintiffs were the millers of that mill. But how do these circumstances [show] reasonably that the profits of the mill must be stopped by an unreasonable delay in the delivery of the broken shaft by the carrier to the third person? Suppose the plaintiffs had another shaft in their possession put up or putting up at the time, and that they only wished to send back the broken shaft to the engineer who made it; it is clear that this would be quite consistent with the above circumstances, and yet the unreasonable delay in the delivery would have no effect upon the intermediate profits of the mill. Or, again, suppose that, at the time of the delivery to the carrier, the machinery of the mill had been in other respects defective, then, also, the same results would follow. Here it is true that the shaft was actually sent back to serve as a model for a new one, and that the want of a new one was the only cause of the stoppage of the mill, and that the loss of profits really arose from not sending down the new shaft in proper time, and that this arose from the delay in delivering the broken one to serve as a model. But it is obvious that, in the great multitude of cases of millers sending off broken shafts to third persons by a carrier under ordinary circumstances, such consequences would not, in all probability, have occurred; and these special circumstances were here never communicated by the plaintiffs to the defendants. It follows, therefore, that the loss of profits here cannot reasonably be considered such a consequence of the breach of contract as could have been fairly and reasonably contemplated by both the parties when they made this contract. For such loss would neither have flowed naturally from the breach of this contract in the great multitude of such cases occurring under ordinary circumstances, nor were the special circumstances, which, perhaps, would have made it a reasonable and natural consequence of such breach of contract, communicated to or known by the defendants. The Judge ought, therefore, to have told the jury, that, upon the facts then before them, they ought not to take the loss of profits into consideration at all in estimating the damages. There must therefore be a new trial in this case.

Rule absolute.

———

BACKGROUND NOTE ON HADLEY V. BAXENDALE

Who was Hadley? Who was Baxendale? And what caused the delay? These and other questions concerning the players and the play are extensively addressed in Danzig, Hadley v. Baxendale: A Study in the Industrialization of the Law, 4 J.Leg.Stud. 249 (1975). A brief extract follows:

> In Gloucester, England, on Thursday, May 12, 1853, the engine shaft at City Flour Mills broke, preventing the further milling of corn. On May 13, the mill proprietors, Joseph and Jonah Hadley, dispatched an employee to Pickford and Co., "common carriers," to inquire as to the fastest means of conveying the shaft to W. Joyce and Co., Greenwich, where it would serve as a model for the crafting of a new shaft. . . . The shaft was delivered to Pickfords on Saturday, May 14, but it did not, in fact, reach W. Joyce and Co. until the 21st, because at the last stage of the voyage the shaft was shipped with a consignment of iron bound for Joyce and Co. by canal rather than by rail. . . . When Pickfords refused to make good these losses, the Hadleys brought suit . . . naming Joseph Baxendale, the London-based managing director of Pickford's, as the defendant. (Baxendale was personally liable for the failings of his unincorporated business.)
> . . .

Id. at 251.

———

Emerald Investments Ltd. Partnership v. Allmerican Financial Life Ins. and Annuity Co.

516 F.3d 612 (7th Cir. 2008)

(Posner, J.) ". . . *Hadley* and the cases following it . . . are cases about special handling. The Hadleys owned a flour mill. The millshaft broke, and the Hadleys hired Baxendale to transport the broken millshaft to a shop that, using the broken millshaft as a model, would make a new one. Because the Hadleys had no spare, the mill was shut down until the new millshaft arrived, and they incurred substantial losses. The receipt of the new shaft was delayed as a result of a breach by Baxendale of its contract of carriage. The court held that the Hadleys could not recover the profits they had lost because of the delay. Had they wanted Baxendale to take special care to get the new millshaft to them by the contractually specified deadline, they should have negotiated for that care, that special handling; undoubtedly Baxendale would have demanded a higher price.

"An Illinois case illustrates this point. The plaintiff in Siegel v. Western Union Telegraph Co., 312 Ill.App. 86, 37 N.E.2d 868 (1941), had delivered $200 to Western Union with instructions to transmit it to a friend of the plaintiff's. The money was to be bet (legally) on a horse, but this was not disclosed in the instructions to Western Union, which misdirected the money order; as a result it did not reach the friend until after the race was over-in which the horse that the plaintiff had intended to bet on won and would have paid $1650. The plaintiff sued Western Union for the $1450 in lost profit (which was conceded-there was no question that he would have bet on the horse that won), and failed on the authority of Hadley v. Baxendale, 37 N.E.2d at 871. Or imagine a professional photographer who after spending months in the Himalayas taking pictures to be used in advertising mountain-climbing gear drops off his roll of film at the nearest Walgreens when he returns to the United States and Walgreen loses it, and he sues Walgreen for his lost profits. He would lose. Had he wanted Walgreen to guarantee that the film would be properly developed and returned to him, he should have negotiated for such a guaranty; failing that, he should have taken an extra roll of film with him on his expedition or had the film developed by a firm catering to professional photographers.."

RESTATEMENT, SECOND, CONTRACTS § 351

[See Selected Source Materials Supplement]

UCC §§ 2–713, 2–715(2)

[See Selected Source Materials Supplement]

CISG ART. 74

[See Selected Source Materials Supplement]

UNIDROIT PRINCIPLES OF INTERNATIONAL COMMERCIAL CONTRACTS ART. 7.4.4

[See Selected Source Materials Supplement]

PRINCIPLES OF EUROPEAN
CONTRACT LAW ART. 9.503

[See Selected Source Materials Supplement]

NOTE ON THE REQUIREMENT OF REASONABLE CERTAINTY

To recover lost profits as consequential damages a plaintiff must present evidence that makes it possible to establish the amount of the loss with reasonable certainty. When a breach shuts down an on-going business evidence of the businesses' past profits is likely to be considered sufficient to establish lost profits with reasonable certainty. When the business is a new one "damages may be established with reasonable certainty with the aid of expert testimony, economic and financial data, market surveys and analyses, business records of similar enterprises, and the like." Restatement Second § 352, comment b.

Courts differ in how strictly they apply the requirement of reasonable certainty. Courts generally frown on a plaintiff who fails to present evidence the court considers relevant to estimating lost profits. For example, in ASK Chemicals, LP v. Computer Packages, Inc., 593 Fed. Appx. 506 (6th Cir. 2014), the claim was for lost profits from being denied the opportunity to exploit a patented technology in Japan. The plaintiff presented evidence of initial steps it had taken to establish demand for the technology in Japan (including internal projections of sales and the capital cost of a factory in Japan), and it presented evidence of its profits from exploiting the technology in Europe and North America. The court held the claim for lost profits was properly dismissed on a motion for summary judgment because the plaintiff failed to present data on the size of the Japanese market and costs the plaintiff would have incurred to exploit the opportunity in addition to the cost of building a plant.

Sometimes no amount of evidence will satisfy a court. Inevitable uncertainty on what a court will consider sufficient proof can make a claim for lost profits a high stakes wager when the plaintiff's potential lost profits are large but inherently speculative. Assembling the best available evidence (including expert testimony) is likely to be expensive but at the end of the day the evidence may not satisfy a court, Kenford Co. v. Erie County, 493 N.E.2d 234 (N.Y. 1986), illustrates the risk. The defendant breached a contract with the plaintiff for the construction and operation of what would have been the second domed stadium in the United States. Pretrial and preliminary proceedings took 10 years. The trial took nine months with the only issue being damages. This appeal concerned the plaintiffs' claim for lost profits on the management contract. The trial court allowed this claim to go to the jury, which awarded $25.6 million lost profits. The award did not survive appeal. The appeals court concluded "that despite the massive quantity of expert proof submitted by" the plaintiffs, the projections depended on too many assumptions that "require speculation and conjecture, making it beyond the capability of even the most sophisticated procedures to satisfy the legal requirements of proof with reasonable certainty."

―――――

UCC § 1–106(1)

[See Selected Source Materials Supplement]

―――――

RESTATEMENT, SECOND, CONTRACTS § 352

[See Selected Source Materials Supplement]

―――――

UNIDROIT PRINCIPLES OF INTERNATIONAL COMMERCIAL CONTRACTS ART. 7.4.3

[See Selected Source Materials Supplement]

―――――

Valentine v. General American Credit, Inc.

420 Mich. 256, 362 N.W.2d 628 (1984)

(Levin, J.) "Valentine may not recover mental distress damages for breach of the employment contract, although such damages may have been foreseeable and she might not be "made whole" absent an award of mental distress damages. . . .

"[T]he general rule, with few exceptions, is to "uniformly den[y]" recovery for mental distress damages although they are "foreseeable within the rule of *Hadley v. Baxendale.*" The rule barring recovery of mental distress damages— a gloss on the generality of the rule stated in *Hadley v. Baxendale*—is fully applicable to an action for breach of an employment contract.

"The denial of mental distress damages, although the result is to leave the plaintiff with less than a full recovery, has analogy in the law. The law does not generally compensate for all losses suffered. Recovery is denied for attorney's fees, for mental anguish not accompanied by physical manifestation, and "make-whole" or full recovery has been denied where the cost of performance exceeds the value to the promisee. The courts have not, despite "make whole" generalizations regarding the damages recoverable, attempted to provide compensation for all losses. Instead, specific rules have been established that provide for the calculation of the damages recoverable in particular kinds of actions. In contract actions, the market price is the general standard.

"In determining what damages are recoverable, the courts of this state have qualified the general rule, pursuant to which mental distress damages for breach of contract are not recoverable, with a narrow exception. Rather than look to the foreseeability of loss to determine the applicability of the exception, the courts have considered whether the contract "has elements of personality" and whether the "damage suffered upon the breach of the agreement is capable of adequate compensation by reference to the terms of the contract.

"The narrow scope of those verbal formulas appears on consideration of the limited situations in which this Court has allowed the recovery of mental distress damages for breach of contract. In *Vanderpool v. Richardson,* 52 Mich. 336, 17 N.W. 936 (1883), recovery was allowed for breach of a promise to marry. In *Stewart v. Rudner,* 349 Mich. 459, 84 N.W.2d 816 (1957), a doctor who failed to fulfill his promise to deliver a child by caesarean section was required to pay mental distress damages. In *Miholevich v. Mid-West Mutual Auto Ins. Co.,* 261 Mich. 495, 246 N.W. 202 (1933), the plaintiff, who was jailed for failure to pay a liability judgment, recovered mental distress damages from an insurer who had failed to pay the judgment.

"Loss of a job is not comparable to the loss of a marriage or a child and generally results in estimable monetary damages. In *Miholevich,* the breach resulted in a deprivation of personal liberty.

"An employment contract will indeed often have a personal element. Employment is an important aspect of most persons' lives, and the breach of an employment contract may result in emotional distress. The primary purpose in forming such contracts, however, is economic and not to secure the protection of personal interests. The psychic satisfaction of the employment is secondary.

"Mental distress damages for breach of contract have not been awarded where there is a market standard by which damages can be adequately determined. Valentine's monetary loss can be estimated with reasonable certainty according to the terms of the contract and the market for, or the market value of, her service. Mental distress damages are not awarded an employee found to have been wrongfully discharged in violation of a collective bargaining agreement.

"We conclude, because an employment contract is not entered into primarily to secure the protection of personal interests and pecuniary damages can be estimated with reasonable certainty, that a person discharged in breach of an employment contract may not recover mental distress damages."

RESTATEMENT, SECOND, CONTRACTS § 355

[See Selected Source Materials Supplement]

SECTION 5. LIQUIDATED DAMAGES

NPS, LLC v. MINIHANE

Supreme Judicial Court of Massachusetts, 2008.
451 Mass. 417, 886 N.E.2d 670.

COWIN, J.

In this case we decide whether an acceleration clause in a ten-year license agreement for luxury seats for New England Patriots professional football games at Gillette Stadium is enforceable. The agreement requires the purchaser of the license to pay, upon default, the amounts due for all years remaining on the license. The plaintiff contends that the clause is a lawful liquidated damages provision; the defendant, who defaulted in the first year of the agreement, argues that it is an unlawful penalty. A judge in the Superior Court agreed with the defendant and refused to enforce the provision. Because we conclude the provision is enforceable, we modify the judgment accordingly.

Background. The judge issued his ruling on the liquidated damages provision from the bench without detailed findings of fact. Most of the underlying facts, however, are not in dispute, as indicated by the joint stipulation of the parties. We supplement these facts with those that were found or implied by the judge. The plaintiff, NPS, LLC (NPS), is the developer of Gillette Stadium (stadium), the home field of the New England Patriots professional football team (Patriots). In 2002, while the stadium was still under construction, NPS entered into an agreement with the defendant, Paul Minihane, for the purchase of a ten-year license for two luxury seats in the Club Level III section. The agreement called for the defendant to pay $3,750 per seat annually for each of the ten seasons from 2002 to 2011. The agreement included a liquidated damages provision, set forth in the margin,[2] which provides that in the event of a default, including failure to pay any amount due under the license agreement, the payments would be accelerated so that the defendant would be required to pay the balance for all the years remaining on the contract. Upon executing the agreement, the defendant paid a $7,500 security deposit; he later made a

---

[2] "15. *Default.* The following shall constitute an 'Event of Default' under this Agreement: (i) Licensee fails to pay when due any amounts to be paid by Licensee pursuant to the Agreement . . . . In the event of any such Event of Default, Owner may, at its option: (a) withhold distribution of tickets to Licensee for games and/or other Stadium Events until such time as such default is cured; and/or (b) terminate the rights of Licensee under the Agreement after giving Licensee not less than twenty (20) days prior written notice of such default or breach . . . . In the event that Licensee shall not have cured the default or breach specified in said notice by the date specified in said notice, Owner may terminate the right of Licensee to the use and possession of the Club Seats and all other rights and privileges of Licensee under the Agreement and declare the entire unpaid balance of the License Fee (which for the purposes hereof shall include the total aggregate unpaid balance of the annual License Fees for the remainder of the Term) immediately due and payable, whereupon Owner shall have no further obligation of any kind to Licensee. Owner shall have no duty to mitigate any damages incurred by it as a result of a default by Licensee hereunder. . . . "

payment of $2,000 toward the license fee for the 2002 season. Although he or his guests attended all but one of the 2002 preseason and regular season Patriots games at the stadium using the tickets for the Club Seats, he made no further payments.

After giving notice to the defendant, NPS accelerated the payments and filed a complaint in the Superior Court seeking the full amount due under the contract. After a bench trial, the judge ruled that the liquidated damages provision was unenforceable because the amount due was "grossly disproportionate to a reasonable estimate of actual damages made at the time of contract formation." After taking further evidence on the issue of actual damages, the judge issued a memorandum of decision and order in which he awarded damages to NPS in the amount of $6,000. This appeal followed, and we transferred the case to this court on our own motion.

We accept the judge's findings of fact unless they are clearly erroneous. *Kendall v. Selvaggio*, 413 Mass. 619, 620, 602 N.E.2d 206 (1992). "On the other hand, to ensure that the ultimate findings and conclusions are consistent with the law, we scrutinize without deference the legal standard which the judge applied to the facts." *Id.* at 621, 602 N.E.2d 206. Whether a liquidated damages provision in a contract is an unenforceable penalty is a question of law. *Manganaro Drywall, Inc. v. Penn-Simon Constr. Co.*, 357 Mass. 653, 656, 260 N.E.2d 182 (1970). The burden of showing that a liquidated damages provision is unenforceable rests with the party challenging enforcement of the provision (here, the defendant), *TAL Fin. Corp. v. CSC Consulting, Inc.*, 446 Mass. 422, 423, 844 N.E.2d 1085 (2006), and we resolve reasonable doubts in favor of the aggrieved party (here, NPS). *Cummings Props., LLC v. National Communications Corp.*, 449 Mass. 490, 494, 869 N.E.2d 617 (2007).

It is well settled that "a contract provision that clearly and reasonably establishes liquidated damages should be enforced, so long as it is not so disproportionate to anticipated damages as to constitute a penalty." *TAL Fin. Corp. v. CSC Consulting, Inc., supra* at 431, 844 N.E.2d 1085. A liquidated damages provision will usually be enforced, provided two criteria are satisfied: first, that at the time of contracting the actual damages flowing from a breach were difficult to ascertain; and second, that the sum agreed on as liquidated damages represents a "reasonable forecast of damages expected to occur in the event of a breach." *Cummings Props., LLC v. National Communications Corp., supra* at 494, 869 N.E.2d 617. Where damages are easily ascertainable, and the amount provided for is grossly disproportionate to actual damages or unconscionably excessive, the court will award the aggrieved party no more than its actual damages. *A-Z Servicenter, Inc. v. Segall*, 334 Mass. 672, 675, 138 N.E.2d 266 (1956). Since there is "no bright line separating an agreement to pay a reasonable measure of damages from an unenforceable penalty clause," *TAL Fin. Corp.*

v. CSC Consulting, Inc., supra, the reasonableness of the measure of anticipated damages depends on the circumstances of each case. *A–Z Servicenter, Inc. v. Segall, supra.* In assessing reasonableness, we look to the circumstances at the time of contract formation; we do not take a "second look" at the actual damages after the contract has been breached. *Kelly v. Marx,* 428 Mass. 877, 878, 705 N.E.2d 1114 (1999).

In this case, the trial judge found that, at the time the parties entered into the license agreement, the harm resulting from a possible breach was difficult to ascertain. That finding was supported by the evidence, which indicated that the damages sustained by NPS would vary depending on the demand for tickets at the time of breach. Although the Patriots had won their first Super Bowl championship in 2002, shortly before the parties entered into their agreement, the demand for luxury stadium seats was then and remains variable and depends, according to the evidence, on the current performance of the team, as well as other factors, such as the popularity of the players and the relative popularity of other sports, that are unpredictable at the time of contract. Therefore, to predict at the time of contract how long it would take NPS to resell the defendant's seat license would be extremely difficult, if not impossible.

The judge went on to find, however, that the sum provided for in the agreement—acceleration of all payments for the remaining term of the contract—was "grossly disproportionate to a reasonable estimate of actual damages made at the time of contract formation." That finding was not supported by the evidence. It is the defendant's burden to show that the amount of liquidated damages is "unreasonably and grossly disproportionate to the real damages from a breach" or "unconscionably excessive." See *TAL Fin. Corp. v. CSC Consulting, Inc., supra* at 423, 844 N.E.2d 1085; *A–Z Servicenter, Inc. v. Segall, supra* at 675, 138 N.E.2d 266. Having presented little evidence beyond his assertion that the contract as a whole was unconscionable, the defendant in this case has not sustained that burden.

The liquidated damages provision here is similar to one we upheld in *Cummings Props., LLC v. National Communications Corp., supra* (*Cummings*). In that case, a tenant who defaulted on a commercial lease was required by the terms of the agreement to pay the entire amount of rent remaining under the lease. *Id.* at 491–492, 869 N.E.2d 617. The judge here did not have the benefit of our decision in *Cummings*, which was issued more than a year after the trial in this case; however, for present purposes, we see no meaningful distinction between the two provisions.

In upholding the liquidated damages provision in *Cummings,* we noted that "to the extent that the liquidated damages amount represented the agreed rental value of the property over the remaining life of the lease, decreasing in amount as the lease term came closer to expiration, it appears to be a reasonable anticipation of damages that might accrue from the nonpayment of rent." *Id.* at 496–497, 869 N.E.2d 617. The same is true here. This, like *Cummings,* is a case where the damages were difficult to estimate at the outset, and the defendant is required to pay no more than the total amount he would have paid had he performed his obligations under the agreement. The sum provided for therefore bears a reasonable relationship to the anticipated actual damages resulting from a breach. It anticipates a worst-case scenario, that is, NPS's inability to resell the seat for the remaining term of the license.[7] However, the defendant has not shown that this outcome is sufficiently unlikely that it renders the amount grossly disproportionate to a reasonable estimate of actual damages.

The defendant stood to receive a substantial benefit from this agreement: guaranteed luxury seating for all Patriots home games, as well as a hedge against future price increases over ten years. He was not deprived of an opportunity to learn and consider the terms of the agreement. Those terms may be harsh, especially when, as here, the breach occurred early in the life of the agreement. But the defendant has not shown that in the circumstances they are "unreasonably and grossly disproportionate to the real damages from a breach." *A–Z Servicenter, Inc. v. Segall,* 334 Mass. 672, 675, 138 N.E.2d 266 (1956).

On appeal, the parties have not raised the issue whether, if the liquidated damages provision is enforced, mitigation should be considered. However, because mitigation was raised (albeit obliquely) in the defendant's amended answer to the complaint, and because we hold that the liquidated damages provision is enforceable, we consider the issue, which appears to be one of first impression in Massachusetts.

We will follow the rule in many other jurisdictions and hold that, in the case of an enforceable liquidated damages provision, mitigation is irrelevant and should not be considered in assessing damages. When parties agree in advance to a sum certain that represents a reasonable estimate of potential damages, they exchange the opportunity to determine actual damages after a breach, including possible mitigation, for the "peace of mind and certainty of result" afforded by a liquidated damages clause. *Kelly v. Marx,* 428 Mass. 877, 881, 705 N.E.2d 1114 (1999), quoting *Kelly v. Marx,* 44 Mass.App.Ct. 825, 833, 694 N.E.2d 869 (1998) (Spina, J., dissenting). In such circumstances, to consider whether a plaintiff has mitigated its damages not only is illogical, but also defeats the purpose of liquidated damages provisions. See *Barrie School v. Patch,* 401 Md. 497, 513–514, 933 A.2d 382 (2007) (sum that stipulates damages in advance

---

[7]   We note in passing that there was evidence at trial that NPS in fact had not been able to resell the defendant's seat, some four years after the defendant committed a breach of the agreement. Although Kelly v. Marx, 428 Mass. 877, 878, 705 N.E.2d 1114 (1999), prevents our consideration of this fact, it suggests that it was not unduly pessimistic to think that NPS might have difficulty reselling the defendant's seat in the event of breach.

"replaces any determination of actual loss," so that if liquidated damages provision is enforceable, court need not consider mitigation). Since the liquidated damages provision at issue here is enforceable, the question is irrelevant.

Conclusion. The ruling of the Superior Court that the liquidated damages provision of the license agreement is unenforceable is set aside, and the judgment is modified to award NPS the total amount of unpaid license fees due under the agreement, $65,500, plus interest. As so modified, the judgment is affirmed.

So ordered.

———

Lee Oldsmobile, Inc. v. Kaiden

32 Md.App. 556, 363 A.2d 270 (1976)

Lee Oldsmobile dealt in Rolls-Royces as part of its business operations. Kaiden learned that Lee had on order, as a part of its allotted 1973 quota of ten or eleven Rolls-Royces, a car of the style and color she wanted, and in August 1973 she sent Lee a $5,000 deposit on the purchase of this car for $29,500. Lee then sent Kaiden an order form, which she signed and returned. The order form contained a clause providing that Lee had the right, upon failure or refusal of the purchaser to accept delivery of the motor vehicle, to retain as liquidated damages any cash deposit made by the purchaser. Apparently there was a dispute concerning the date of delivery, and on November 21, Kaiden notified Lee that she had purchased another Rolls elsewhere, and instructed that her order be canceled. On November 29, Lee notified Kaiden that the car was ready for delivery. She declined to accept and demanded the return of her deposit. Lee refused, and later sold the Rolls to another purchaser. Held, Kaiden was entitled to recover the amount of her deposit, minus actual damages.

"We reject the application of the liquidated damage clause in the present case . . . because it is clear that the actual damages are capable of accurate estimation. We do not say this from hindsight made possible because the actual figures claimed were in evidence. We say it because at the time the contract was made, it was clear that the nature of any damages which would result from a possible future breach was such that they would be easily ascertainable. . . . "

———

Norwalk Door Closer Co. v. Eagle Lock and Screw Co.

153 Conn. 681, 220 A.2d 263 (1966)

Norwalk and Eagle had a contract to manufacturer door closers exclusively for Norwalk, using tools, dies, patterns, and equipment provided by Norwalk. The contract had a seven-year term and provided that Eagle would pay $100,000 liquidated damages, if Eagle terminated the agreement, ceased operations, or there was a change in ownership. Eagle was acquired by new owners in breach of this term. Norwalk sued seeking liquidated damages. The trial court held the liquidated damage term was unenforceable, finding that Norwalk suffered no harm as a result of the change in ownership as the new owners employed the same local management and continued production "without loss to Norwalk of either business or time." Affirmed.

(Alcorn, J.) ". . . '[N]o provision in a contract for the payment of a fixed sum as damages, whether stipulated for as a penalty or as liquidated damages, will be enforced in a case where the court sees that no damage has been sustained.' See also King Motors, Inc. v. Delfino, supra, 136 Conn. 498, 72 A.2d 233. This principle finds approval in comment (e) of the Restatement, 1 Contracts § 339, where it is stated that '(i)f the parties honestly but mistakenly suppose that a breach will cause harm that will be incapable or very difficult of accurate estimation, when in fact the breach causes no harm at all or none that is incapable of accurate estimation without difficulty, their advance agreement fixing the amount to be paid as damages for breach * * * is not enforceable.' See also Priebe & Sons, Inc. v. United States, 332 U.S. 407, 412, 68 S.Ct. 123, 92 L.Ed. 32. This is not to say that any burden is placed on a plaintiff to prove actual damage in order to recover under a valid contract for liquidated damages. The proposition is only that equitable principles will be invoked to deny recovery when the facts make it apparent that no damage has been suffered.

"The principle is based on justice and fairness. 'The probable injury that the parties had reason to foresee is a fact that largely determines the question whether they made a genuine pre-estimate of that injury; but the justice and equity of enforcement depend also upon the amount of injury that has actually occurred.' 5 Corbin, contracts § 1063. For a collection of cases on the general subject see the annotation in 34 A.L.R. 1336.

"The circumstances which the parties might reasonably foresee at the time of making a contract could, in any given case, be vastly different from the circumstances which actually exist when a court is called upon to enforce the contract. It is not the function of the court to determine by hindsight the reasonableness of the expectation of the parties at the time the contract was made, but it is the function of the court at the time of enforcement to do justice. In the ordinary contract action the court determines the just damages from evidence offered. In a valid contract for liquidated damages, the parties are permitted, in order to avoid the uncertainties and time-consuming effort involved, to estimate in advance the reasonably probable foreseeable damages which would arise in the event of a default. Implicit in the transaction is the premise that the sum agreed upon will be within the fair range of those just damages which would be called for and provable had the parties resorted to proof. Consequently, if the damage envisioned by the parties never occurs, the whole premise of their agreed estimate vanishes, and, even if the contract was to be construed as one for liquidated damages rather than one for a penalty, neither justice nor the intent of the parties is served by enforcement. To enforce it would amount in reality to the infliction of a penalty. Massman Const. Co. v.

City Council of Greenville, Miss., 147 F.2d 925, 928 (5th Cir.); Northwest Fixture Co. v. Kilbourne & Clark Co., 128 F. 256, 261 (9th Cir.)

"Under the facts of the present case, where the court has found that Norwalk is continuing its business without having been harmed, and substantially as it did before the breach, neither justice nor reason permit it to recover $100,000 in damages."

UCC § 2–718(1)

[See Selected Source Materials Supplement]

RESTATEMENT, SECOND, CONTRACTS § 356

[See Selected Source Materials Supplement]

UNIDROIT PRINCIPLES OF INTERNATIONAL COMMERCIAL CONTRACTS ART. 7.4.13

[See Selected Source Materials Supplement]

PRINCIPLES OF EUROPEAN CONTRACT LAW ART. 9.509

[See Selected Source Materials Supplement]

NOTE ON LIQUIDATED DAMAGES

All courts agree on the principle that liquidated-damages provisions should be given special judicial scrutiny, although the formulation of the principle varies. In contrast, many commentators have criticized this principle. Most of the critiques have an implicit or explicit three-part structure: (1) They begin by assuming that the major justification for the principle that liquidated-damages provisions should be given special scrutiny is that such provisions lend themselves to blameworthy exploitation of one party by the other, and consequent one-sidedness, in a way that other types of contract provisions do not. (2) They then argue that this justification will not hold. (3) They conclude that the principle is therefore unjustified. So, for example, Goetz and Scott argue that the principle of special scrutiny of liquidated-damages provisions arose in a historical context in which protections against fraud and duress were not available. Given the modern development of unconscionability as a unifying unfairness principle, they suggest, the law should simply collapse the treatment of liquidated damages into that principle. Charles J. Goetz & Robert E. Scott, Liquidated Damages, Penalties and the Just Compensation Principle: Some Notes on an Enforcement Model and a Theory of Efficient Breach, 77 Colum. L. Rev. 554, 592 (1977).

The assumption that special scrutiny of liquidated-damages provisions is justified primarily by a special potential for blameworthy exploitation and one-sidedness does reflect the courts' rhetoric, which is cast in terms of whether or not such provisions are "penalties," and therefore suggests a concern with advantage-taking and oppression. In fact, however, the justification for the special scrutiny of liquidated-damages provisions is not that such provisions are specially amenable to blameworthy exploitation and one-sidedness, but that such provisions are systematically likely to reflect the limits of human cognition.

Classical contract law was based on a rational-actor model of psychology. Under this model, actors who make decisions in the face of uncertainty rationally maximize their subjective expected utility, with all future benefits and costs properly discounted to present value. A great body of theoretical and empirical work in cognitive psychology within the last thirty or forty years has shown that rational-actor psychology often lacks explanatory power. Although rational-actor psychology is the foundation of the standard economic model of choice, the empirical evidence shows that this model often diverges from the actual psychology of choice, due to limits of cognition. As Amos Tversky and Daniel Kahneman point out, expected-utility (rational-actor) theory "emerged from a logical analysis of games of chance rather than from a psychological analysis of risk and value. The theory was conceived as a normative model of an idealized decision maker, not as a description of the behavior of real people." Amos Tversky & Daniel Kahneman, Rational Choice and the Framing of Decisions, 59 J. Bus. S251 (1986).

In contrast to rational-actor psychology, modern cognitive psychology recognizes various limits of cognition. For purposes of contract law, three kinds of limits of cognition are especially salient: bounded rationality, irrational disposition, and defective capability.

1.   Bounded Rationality

To begin with, an actor may not even consider the choice that would maximize his utility, because actors limit their search for and their processing (evaluating and deliberating on) of choices. If the costs of searching for and processing information were zero, and human information-processing capabilities were perfect, then an actor contemplating a decision would make a comprehensive search for relevant information, would process perfectly all the information he acquired, and would then make the best possible substantive decision—the decision that, as of the time made, was better than all the alternative decisions the actor might have made if he had complete knowledge and perfect processing abilities, and which would therefore maximize the actor's subjective expected utility.

In reality, of course, searching for and processing information does involve costs, in the form of time, energy, and perhaps money. Most actors either do not want to expend the resources required for comprehensive search and processing or recognize that comprehensive search and processing would not be achievable at any realistic cost. Actors therefore put boundaries on the amount of search and processing they engage in before making decisions. To put it differently, actors often consciously choose to be in a state of *rational ignorance*—"rational," because the incremental cost of achieving complete knowledge concerning and deliberating on a decision would be more than the expected gain from making the decision with complete rather than partial knowledge. So, for example, a patient may seek a second or perhaps a third doctor's opinion about treatment, but no more, because he believes it unlikely that consulting an extra five, ten, or fifteen doctors will not improve the quality of his choice of treatment sufficiently to justify spending the extra time and money.

Furthermore, our abilities to process information and arrive at decisions are constrained by limitations of computational ability, ability to calculate consequences, ability to organize and utilize memory, and the like. Hence, actors will often process imperfectly even the information they do acquire. Such imperfections in human processing ability scale up as decisions become more complex and involve more permutations.

Accordingly, human rationality is normally bounded both by limited information and limited information-processing ability.

2.   *Irrational Disposition*

Next, actors are unrealistically optimistic as a systematic matter. (Lawyers do not realize this, because they are trained to be systematically pessimistic.) The dispositional characteristic of undue optimism is strikingly illustrated in a study by Lynn Baker and Robert Emery, appropriately titled, When Every Relationship Is Above Average, 17 Law and Hum. Behav. 439 (1993). Baker and Emery asked subjects who were about to get married to report on their own divorce-related prospects as compared to the divorce-related prospects of the general population. The disparities between perceptions concerning the prospects of the general population and the prospects of the subjects were enormous, and were almost invariably in the direction of optimism. For example, the subjects correctly estimated that fifty percent of American couples will eventually divorce. In contrast, the subjects estimated that their own chance of divorce was zero. Similarly, the subjects' median estimate of what percentage of spouses pay all court-ordered alimony was forty percent. In contrast, 100 percent of the subjects predicted that their own spouse would pay all court-ordered alimony.

3. *Defective Capability*

Finally, cognitive psychology has established that actors use certain decision-making rules (heuristics) that yield systematic errors: "[T]he deviations of actual behavior from the normative model are too widespread to be ignored, too systematic to be dismissed as random error, and too fundamental to be accommodated by relaxing the normative system." Tversky & Kahneman, supra, at S252. For example, actors make decisions on the basis of data that is readily available to their memory, rather than on the basis of all the relevant data. This is known as the availability heuristic. Accordingly, actors systematically give undue weight to instantiated evidence as compared to general statements, to vivid evidence as compared to pallid evidence, and to concrete evidence as compared to abstract evidence. Similarly, actors are systematically insensitive to sample size, and erroneously take small samples as representative samples.

Another defect in capability concerns the ability of actors to make rational comparisons between present and future states. For example, the sample consisting of present events is often wrongly taken to be representative, and therefore predictive, of future events. Actors also systematically give too little weight to future benefits and costs as compared to present benefits and costs. Thus Martin Feldstein concludes that "some or all individuals have, in Pigou's . . . words, a 'faulty telescopic faculty' that causes them to give too little weight to the utility of future consumption." Feldstein, The Optimal Level of Social Security Benefits, 100 Q. J. Econ. 303, 307 (1985).

A defect of capability related to faulty telescopic faculties is the systematic underestimation of risks. Based on the work of cognitive psychologists, Kenneth Arrow observes that "[i]t is a plausible hypothesis that individuals are unable to recognize that there will be many surprises in the future; in short, as much other evidence tends to confirm, there is a tendency to underestimate uncertainties." Arrow, Risk Perception in Psychology and Economics, 20 Econ. Inquiry 1, 5 (1982). In fact, empirical evidence shows that actors often not only underestimate but ignore low-probability risks.

4. *Liquidated-Damages Provisions*

The limits of cognition have a special bearing on liquidated-damages provisions. To begin with, bounded rationality and rational ignorance play an important role here. Contracting parties normally will find it relatively easy to evaluate proposed performance terms—terms that specify what performance the party is required to render—such as subject matter, quantity, and price. In contrast, at the time a contract is made it is often impracticable, if not impossible, to imagine all the scenarios of breach. Similarly, the inherent complexity of determining the application of a liquidated-damages provision to every possible breach scenario will often exceed actors' information-processing abilities.

Even on the doubtful assumption that a contracting party could imagine all breach scenarios, and determine the application of a liquidated-damages provision to every possible scenario, the benefits of extensive search and information processing on these issues will often seem to be very low as compared to the costs. A party who contracts to buy or sell a commodity normally expects to perform. Accordingly, the expected benefits of deliberating very carefully on performance terms are compelling, and the costs of such deliberation usually do not outweigh the expected benefits. In contrast, a party often will not expect that a liquidated-damages provision will ever come into play against him, partly because he intends to perform and partly because experience will tell him that in general there is a high rate of performance of contracts. For example, if contracts are performed at least ninety-five percent of the time (which observation suggests is likely), all the costs of processing the more remote applications of a liquidated-damages provision would have to be taken into account, but the benefits of such processing would have to be discounted by ninety-five percent. The resulting cost-benefit ratio will often provide a substantial disincentive for processing every possible application of a liquidated-damages provision, even if it were in fact possible to imagine every such application. As a result, contracting parties are often likely to not completely think through liquidated-damages provisions, and are therefore often unlikely to fully understand the full implications of such provisions.

The problem of irrational disposition also bears significantly on liquidated-damages provisions. Because actors tend to be unrealistically optimistic, a contracting party will probably believe that his performance is more likely, and his breach less likely, than is actually the case. Accordingly, unrealistic optimism will reduce even further the deliberation that actors give to liquidated-damages provisions.

Finally, defective capabilities have particular relevance to liquidated-damages provisions. The availability heuristic may lead a contracting party to give undue weight to his present intention to perform, which is vivid and concrete, as compared with the abstract possibility that future circumstances may lead him to breach. Because actors tend to take the sample of present evidence as unduly representative of the future, a contracting party is apt to overestimate the extent to which his present intention to perform is a reliable predictor of his future intention. Because actors have faulty telescopic faculties, a contracting party is likely to overvalue the benefit of the prospect of performance, which will normally begin to occur in the short term, as against the cost of breach, which will typically occur, if at all, only down the road. Because actors tend to underestimate risks, a contracting party is likely to underestimate the risk that a liquidated-damages provision will take effect.

The rationale for giving special scrutiny to liquidated-damages provisions affects the point of time on which the scrutiny is focused. If the justification for giving special scrutiny to liquidated-damages provisions is that such provisions are especially subject to blameworthy exploitation and one-sidedness, the scrutiny should be focused on the time the contract is made—a forward-looking test. In contrast, if the justification for special scrutiny is that parties often make cognitive errors in adopting such provisions, the scrutiny should be focused on the time of breach—a second-look test, which compares the liquidated damages with actual loss, on the ground that a gross discrepancy between forecast and result suggests that the liquidated-damages provision was a product of limited or defective cognition.

About half the states hold that the enforceability of liquidated-damages provisions is to be determined at the time the contract is made, and about half the states hold that enforceability of such provisions is to be determined, or also determined, at the time of the breach. See Kelly v. Marx, 44 Mass.App.Ct. 825, 694 N.E.2d 869 (1998), reversed, Kelly v. Marx, 428 Mass. 877, 705 N.E.2d 1114 (1999). However, even courts that purport to employ only a forward-looking test may apply a second-look test in the guise of relief against forfeiture, unconscionability, or the like. See, e.g., Hutchison v. Tompkins, 259 So.2d 129 (Fla. 1972).

NOTE ON ALTERNATIVE-PERFORMANCE TERMS

A contract may give the promisor the option to choose among alternative performances. This can include an option to pay a stipulated sum of money in lieu of some other performance. For example, a multi-year employment contract might give either party the option to buy out of the balance of the contract by paying a stipulated sum of money.

A genuine alternative-performance term is not subject to the rule prohibiting punitive liquidated damages. Best v. United States Bank, 303 Or. 557, 739 P.2d 554 (1987), gives the usual rationale. The plaintiffs challenged the fee charged by their bank for processing nonsufficient fund (NSF) checks. The bank had increased the fee from $3 to $5 per check. The plaintiffs presented evidence the new fee was two or three times the bank's NSF processing costs. Among the grounds for challenging the fee was that it was an unlawful penalty. This challenge failed because there was no agreement "not to write NSF checks. . . . There being no agreement, there could be no unlawful penalty for breach of the agreement."

In Carlyle Apartments Joint Venture v. AIG Life Ins. Co., 333 Md. 265, 635 A.2d 366 (1994), the borrower, Carlyle, sought to pre-pay a high interest commercial loan without paying a steep agreed prepayment fee, by arguing (i) prepayment was a breach because there was no right to prepay a fixed term loan under Maryland law, (ii) the fee was a liquidated damage term and (iii) as a liquidated-damage term it was void as a penalty. The court rejected the argument at the first step, holding prepayment was an option and not a breach. Among the authorities Carlyle relied upon was Whitman, Mortgage Prepayment Clauses: An Economic and Legal Analysis, 40 UCLA L. Rev. 851 (1993). Professor Whitman argued that "Essentially, prepayment fees are nothing more than liquidated damage clauses." Id. at 871. He went on to argue the fee should be enforced because it promotes economic efficiency, notwithstanding the legal rule. The court refused Carlyle's invitation to "give an economic interpretation to the loan contract in order to pronounce the prepayment clause a liquidated damage clause . . . " It continued: "[L]enders ordinarily should be able to predict the legal result that language employed by them in their loan contracts will achieve. No universal principle unifies the legal and economic analysis of all transactions, and the legal form selected for a transaction may control, despite its equivalency with some other form of transaction." 333 Md. at 279, 635 A.2d at 373.

Restatement, Second, Contracts § 356, Comment c ["Disguised penalties"] cautions:

> Sometimes parties attempt to disguise a provision for a penalty by using language that purports to make payment of the amount an alternative performance under the contract, that purports to offer a discount for prompt performance, or that purports to place a valuation on property to be delivered. Although the parties may in good faith contract for alternative performances and fix discounts or valuations, a court will look to the substance of the agreement to determine whether this is the case or whether the parties have attempted to disguise a provision for a penalty that is unenforceable under this Section. In determining whether a contract is one for alternative performances, the relative value of the alternatives may be decisive.

On the other hand, if a payment obligation is denominated as liquidated damages, then it seems it will be treated as such. In Brazen v. Bell Atlantic Corp., 695 A.2d 43 (Del. 1997), the termination-fee provisions in a corporate merger agreement stated that the $550 million fee "constitute liquidated damages and not a penalty." An attempt to characterize the fee as an alternative-performance term to avoid a challenge that it was a penalty was rejected: "counsel for Bell Atlantic explained that the liquidated damage language was 'boilerplate' terminology for termination fees in merger transactions such as this one. So be it . . . . [T]he parties to this merger cannot disown their own language." Id. at 48 n. 9. The form chosen was not fatal because the court went on to find the fee was not void as a penalty.

Whether a payment obligation is denominated as liquidated damages or as an alternative-performance term can matter for reasons other than whether the term will have to pass scrutiny under the penalty rule. If ordinary damages are inadequate, then the plaintiff can waive liquidated damages (assuming it was not agreed to be the exclusive remedy) and obtain an order compelling specific performance. Restatement § 361. Under an alternative-performance term the obligor has the power to choose between performance and payment. Another difference is that supervening events that make performance impracticable may absolve a party from liability to pay liquidated damages. They do not absolve a party from liability to render an alternative performance. This was the issue in American Soil Processing, Inc. v. Iowa Comprehensive Petroleum Underground Storage Tank Fund Board, 586 N.W.2d 325 (1998), which has an extended analysis of the difference between the two types of terms.

Similar issues are raised by the ability to cast a deposit paid towards the purchase of property as the price of an option to purchase the property. A term stating that a buyer forfeits the deposit on breach may be invalidated as a penalty. On the other hand, if the payment is the price of a genuine option, then there is no requirement that the amount be a reasonable estimate of the seller's anticipated or actual loss in the event the buyer allows the option to lapse. For an extended analysis of the proper characterization of a loan commitment fee, see Woodbridge Place Apartments v. Washington Square Capital, Inc., 965 F.2d 1249 (7th Cir. 1992).

———

CHAPTER 6

SPECIFIC PERFORMANCE

■ ■ ■

INTRODUCTORY NOTE

Chapter 6 concerns the remedy of specific performance. Under this remedy, the court, instead of ordering the breaching party to pay damages, orders the breaching party to perform the contract.

The historical background. For centuries the English administration of justice was characterized by the peculiarity that there were two systems of courts administering two different bodies of law. What may be called the "regular" court system consisted of the courts of common law, which had jurisdiction over "actions at law," and administered "regular" law. The other system consisted of courts of "equity" or "chancery," which had jurisdiction over "suits in equity," and applied a body of principles that came to be called "equity." (Note the double linguistic usages involved here. "Law" used: (1) in a broad sense to mean the principles for administering justice, which includes both common law and equity, or (2) in a narrower sense, to mean the principles applied by the common law courts. "Equity" used: (1) in a broad sense, to mean fairness, or (2) in a narrower sense, to mean the established principles administered by a specific system of courts.)

In general, the English equity or chancery courts acted to remedy defects in the rules administered by the common law courts. The equity courts did not have a general jurisdiction over all kinds of disputes; their function was to act in those cases where "the legal remedy was inadequate," that is, where according to the notions of the time, the regular or common law courts did not give the kind of relief that the plaintiff ought to have.

One of the great defects of common law courts was that except in certain extraordinary cases, the procedure in those courts did not contemplate *ordering* the defendant to do anything. If a creditor sued his debtor for £10 and was awarded a judgment at law, the judgment did not take the form of an order commanding the debtor to pay his debt. Instead, in its traditional form the judgment recited that it was "considered that the plaintiff do recover against the defendant his debt." Enforcement of the judgment was accomplished not by commanding the defendant to pay, but by directing the sheriff to levy execution on the defendant's property if the defendant did not pay, so that the plaintiff's claim could be satisfied out of this property.

Where the plaintiff was complaining of a breach of contract by the defendant, this defect prevented the courts from ordering the defendant to perform his promise. Thus, if Seller contracted to convey Blackacre to Buyer, and then broke his promise, there was no way in which Buyer, by appealing to the common law courts, could get a deed to Blackacre, even though Seller had a perfectly good title to the land and was wholly capable of carrying out her contract. Accordingly, the only relief Buyer could obtain from a common law court was an award of money damages. However, in such a case Buyer could successfully appeal to a court of equity, alleging that his legal remedy (money damages) was inadequate. The equity court would issue a decree ordering Seller to execute a deed in Buyer's favor. If Seller refused to obey this order, she would put herself in contempt of court and be subject to fine or imprisonment.

There are other situations, though, where an appeal to equity to enforce a contract would fail. To put the plainest kind of case, suppose that Seller had sold and delivered a horse to Buyer for $500, and that Buyer, although having ample funds to do so, refused to pay the promised price of the horse. Here conceivably Seller might get a certain spiritual satisfaction out of an order commanding Buyer to pay his debt—an order that the common law courts would not issue. On the other hand, the common law courts would ensure the promised price for Seller through a levy of execution on Buyer's goods. Accordingly in this case the legal remedy was deemed to be adequate, and a suit by Seller in an equity court would be denied.

In other cases, equity refused to enforce contracts not because the legal remedy was adequate, but because it was considered unwise for one or another reasons to attempt specific enforcement. For example, a famous opera singer agrees to sing in the plaintiff's opera house for three months and then breaks her contract. Here the opera-house proprietor may with much justice assert that his legal remedy of damages is inadequate; an award of money can scarcely be treated as an adequate substitute for actual performance. At the same time, there are obvious objections to attempting to compel a star to sing against her will. Accordingly, this is a case where a court of equity would deny specific performance despite a recognition that the monetary relief granted by the common law courts is an inadequate form of relief.

The relation of law and equity in the United States today. Specific performance is a type of injunction. It is usually said that a showing of irreparable injury is required for an injunction. Outside of contract law, some injuries—here, injury means no more than a violation of a legal right—are considered irreparable by their nature. Examples include a continuing trespass to land, a continuing nuisance, and a continuing violation of an individual's civil liberties. In contract law, specific performance of a contract generally requires a particularized showing of the inadequacy of damages. However, for certain types of contracts—in particular, contracts for the sale of land—such a showing is not required.

A plaintiff who establishes the inadequacy of damages is not *entitled* to specific performance. The remedy is discretionary. Discretionary factors include: performance would impose an undue burden on the defendant;

enforcement of the order would impose an undue burden on the court; performance or compulsion is contrary to public policy; or the contract is unconscionable.

Today, most American states no longer have separate courts of law and equity. Instead, in most states the same judges administer both bodies of law. This does not mean, however, that the two bodies of law are not to a considerable extent still kept distinct in the thinking of lawyers and judges. If a plaintiff asks the court to issue an order directing the defendant to perform her promise—say, to comply with a covenant not to compete—such a suit will be tested by principles and rules called "equity" and derived historically from the English chancery courts. In some jurisdictions, the suit will in fact be labeled as a "suit in equity" even though the judge who tries the suit has the power to try "actions at law" as well. Even in those jurisdictions where no label is attached to the suit to indicate whether it is "at law" or "in equity," the rules applied to the suit will be "equity" rules if the case involves a demand for an order directing the defendant to specifically perform. An important consequence in most states is that there is no right to a jury trial in a suit in equity.

LONDON BUCKET CO. v. STEWART

Court of Appeals of Kentucky, 1951.
314 Ky. 832, 237 S.W.2d 509.

STANLEY, COMMISSIONER. This is an appeal from a judgment decreeing specific performance of a contract to properly furnish and install a heating system for a large motel. The basic contention of the appellant, London Bucket Company, is that the remedy of specific performance will not lie for breach of this type of contract.

The chancellor overruled a demurrer to the petition and this is the first assignment of error. Stewart's petition set out the contract, the pertinent parts of which are as follows: "The parties of the first part agree and bind themselves to furnish and install (subletting installation) in said building the following equipment. . . . " The only standard as to the quality of work to be performed was that the defendant was to "guarantee to heat this said court to 75 degrees in winter, and to supervise all work," etc. The plaintiff alleged that the defendant "soon thereafter and within one year installed a plant in an incompleted, unskilled unworkmanlike manner, never finishing same, and of such size, type and inferior quality of materials that same does not to a reasonable degree perform the purpose contemplated." The petition further states: "Plaintiff here now demands of the court of equity that defendant be compelled to specifically perform the terms of said contract and complete said installation and furnish the type of furnace provided in said contract and all the things necessary to properly heat said building and rooms and same to be done forthwith, before the fall of cold weather."

The plaintiff prayed that "immediate specific performance be adjudged" and also asked $8,250 damages for faulty and negligent construction and resulting expense, loss of business, etc. On being required to elect his remedy, he chose specific performance and dismissed without prejudice his action for damages.

The defendant, among other defenses, pleaded there had been a mutual cancellation of the contract insofar as it covered the completion of the job. Upon sharply conflicting evidence, but with some documents strongly supporting the plaintiff's contention, the court found as a fact that there had been no such cancellation. This was an issue necessary to be decided before deciding there could be a decree of specific performance.

The court decreed: "The defendant is hereby mandatorily ordered and directed to comply with the terms of said contract, in its entirety. He shall proceed diligently so to do and continue its obligation, assumed by it under the said contract, therein specifically set out."

No matter what the evidence may have been, the plaintiff's legal right could be no greater than that which the basic facts pleaded authorized. So if the demurrer should have been sustained to his pleading which undertook to state his whole case, that is all the court need consider. In other words, if the plaintiff did not state a cause of action for specific performance, the demurrer should have been sustained instead of overruled. That is the way the trial court treated the case except to find that the work done was defective, the heating system was not properly functioning, and the job was incomplete. In his opinion, the court recognized the difficulty of the question whether the contract and the conditions were such as required specific performance. He considered the familiar principle that such an equitable decree will not be adjudged unless the ordinary common law remedy of damages for a breach of contract is an inadequate and incomplete remedy for injuries arising from the failure to carry out its terms. Edelen v. Samuels & Co., 126 Ky. 295, 103 S.W. 360. The court concluded, nevertheless, that this case was within Schmidt v. Louisville & N.R. Co., 101 Ky. 441, 41 S.W. 1015, 19 Ky.Law Rep. 666, 38 L.R.A. 809, and Pennsylvania Railroad Co. v. City of Louisville, 277 Ky. 402, 126 S.W.2d 840.

It seems to us the two cases are not altogether apt. In the *Schmidt* case it was held a decree of specific performance to operate the railroad under the terms of the lease for the benefit of both holders was proper since there was no adequate remedy at law. The *Pennsylvania Railroad* Case was a suit to declare the rights of the parties and to require several railroad companies to proceed with the elimination of grade crossings as they had contracted to do. Both cases involve matters of great magnitude and were of public interest and welfare. In each case the court in effect said, "Proceed to do what you contracted to do." There was no question of partial or incomplete or faulty performance of a building contract. The *Schmidt* case is distinguished in the leading case of Edelen v. Samuels & Co., supra. In the present case the decree was in effect to direct a building contractor to go back, correct defective work and complete its job. It is the general rule that contracts for building construction will not be specifically enforced because ordinarily damages are an adequate remedy and, in part, because of the incapacity of the court to superintend the performance. 9 Am.Jur., Building and Construction Contracts, § 124; 58 C.J. 1046. The case at bar is not within the exceptions to the rule or of the class where specific performance should be decreed. 49 Am.Jur., Specific Performance, § 12. That there may be difficulty in proving the damages as appellee suggests, is not enough to put the case within the exceptions.

Under our conclusion that specific performance should not have been decreed, the decision on the issue of cancellation of the contract must follow it. This will leave the question open in the common-law action for damages should it be filed.

Wherefore, the judgment is reversed.

————

RESTATEMENT, SECOND, CONTRACTS §§ 359, 360

[See Selected Source Materials Supplement]

————

UNIDROIT PRINCIPLES OF INTERNATIONAL COMMERCIAL CONTRACTS ARTS. 7.2.1, 7.2.2, 7.2.3

[See Selected Source Materials Supplement]

————

PRINCIPLES OF EUROPEAN CONTRACT LAW ARTS. 9.101, 9.102, 9.103

[See Selected Source Materials Supplement]

————

WALGREEN CO. v. SARA CREEK PROPERTY CO.

United States Court of Appeals, Seventh Circuit, 1992.
966 F.2d 273.

POSNER, CIRCUIT JUDGE.

This appeal from the grant of a permanent injunction raises fundamental issues concerning the propriety of injunctive relief. 775 F.Supp. 1192 (E.D.Wis.1991). The essential facts are simple. Walgreen has operated a pharmacy in the Southgate Mall in Milwaukee since its opening in 1951. Its current lease, signed in 1971 and carrying a 30-year, 6-month term, contains, as had the only previous lease, a clause in which the landlord, Sara Creek, promises not to lease space in the mall to anyone else who wants to operate a pharmacy or a store containing a pharmacy. . . .

In 1990, fearful that its largest tenant—what in real estate parlance is called the "anchor tenant"—having gone broke was about to close its store, Sara Creek informed Walgreen that it intended to buy out the anchor tenant and install in its place a discount store operated by Phar-Mor Corporation, a "deep discount" chain, rather than, like Walgreen, just a "discount" chain. Phar-Mor's store would occupy 100,000 square feet, of which 12,000 would be occupied by a pharmacy the same size as Walgreen's. The entrances to the two stores would be within a couple of hundred feet of each other.

Walgreen filed this diversity suit for breach of contract against Sara Creek and Phar-Mor and asked for an injunction against Sara Creek's letting the anchor premises to Phar-Mor. After an evidentiary hearing, the judge found a breach of Walgreen's lease and entered a permanent injunction against Sara Creek's letting the anchor tenant premises to Phar-Mor until the expiration of Walgreen's lease. He did this over the defendants' objection that Walgreen had failed to show that its remedy at law—damages—for the breach of the exclusivity clause was inadequate. Sara Creek had put on an expert witness who testified that Walgreen's damages could be readily estimated, and Walgreen had countered with evidence from its employees that its damages would be very difficult to compute, among other reasons because they included intangibles such as loss of goodwill.

Sara Creek reminds us that damages are the norm in breach of contract as in other cases. Many breaches, it points out, are "efficient" in the sense that they allow resources to be moved into a more valuable use. Patton v. Mid-Continent Systems, Inc., 841 F.2d 742, 750–51 (7th Cir.1988). Perhaps this is one—the value of Phar-Mor's occupancy of the anchor premises may exceed the cost to Walgreen of facing increased competition. If so, society will be better off if Walgreen is paid its damages, equal to that cost, and Phar-Mor is allowed to move in rather than being kept out by an injunction. That is why injunctions are not granted as a matter of course, but only when the plaintiff's damages remedy is inadequate. Northern Indiana Public Service Co. v. Carbon County Coal Co., 799 F.2d 265, 279 (7th Cir.1986). Walgreen's is not, Sara Creek argues; the projection of business losses due to increased competition is a routine exercise in calculation. Damages representing either the present value of lost future profits or (what should be the equivalent . . .) the diminution in the value of the leasehold have either been awarded or deemed the proper remedy in a number of reported cases for breach of an exclusivity clause in a shopping-center lease. . . . Why, Sara Creek asks, should they not be adequate here?

Sara Creek makes a beguiling argument that contains much truth, but we do not think it should carry the day. For if, as just noted, damages have been awarded in some cases of breach of an exclusivity clause in a shopping-center lease, injunctions have been issued in others. . . . The choice between remedies requires a balancing of the costs and benefits of the alternatives. Hecht Co. v. Bowles, 321 U.S. 321, 329, 64 S.Ct. 587, 591, 88 L.Ed. 754 (1944); Yakus v. United States, 321 U.S. 414, 440, 64 S.Ct. 660, 674, 88 L.Ed. 834 (1944). The task of striking the balance is for the trial judge, subject to deferential appellate review in recognition of its particularistic, judgmental, fact-bound character. K-Mart Corp. v. Oriental Plaza, Inc., 875 F.2d 907, 915 (1st Cir.1989). As we said in an appeal from a grant of a preliminary injunction—but the point is applicable to review of a permanent injunction as well—"The question for us [appellate judges] is whether the [district] judge exceeded the bounds of permissible choice in the circumstances, not what we would have done if we had been in his shoes." Roland Machinery Co. v. Dresser Industries, Inc., 749 F.2d 380, 390 (7th Cir.1984).

The plaintiff who seeks an injunction has the burden of persuasion— damages are the norm, so the plaintiff must show why his case is abnormal. . . . [W]hen, as in this case, the issue is whether to grant a permanent injunction, . . . the burden is to show that damages are inadequate. . . .

The benefits of substituting an injunction for damages are twofold. First, it shifts the burden of determining the cost of the defendant's conduct from the court to the parties. If it is true that Walgreen's damages are smaller than the gain to Sara Creek from allowing a second pharmacy into the shopping mall, then there must be a price for dissolving the injunction that will make both parties better off. Thus, the effect of upholding the injunction would be to substitute for the costly processes of forensic fact determination the less costly processes of private negotiation. Second, a premise of our free-market system, and the lesson of experience here and abroad as well, is that prices and costs are more accurately determined by the market than by government. A battle of experts is a less reliable method of determining the actual cost to Walgreen of facing new competition than negotiations between Walgreen and Sara Creek over the price at which Walgreen would feel adequately compensated for having to face that competition.

That is the benefit side of injunctive relief but there is a cost side as well. Many injunctions require continuing supervision by the court, and that is costly.... This ground was ... stressed in Rental Development Corp. v. Lavery, 304 F.2d 839, 841–42 (9th Cir.1962), a case involving a lease. Some injunctions are problematic because they impose costs on third parties. Shondel v. McDermott, 775 F.2d 859, 868 (7th Cir.1985). A more subtle cost of injunctive relief arises from the situation that economists call "bilateral monopoly," in which two parties can deal only with each other: the situation that an injunction creates. Goldstick v. ICM Realty, 788 F.2d 456, 463 (7th Cir.1986) ... The sole seller of widgets selling to the sole buyer of that product would be an example. But so will be the situation confronting Walgreen and Sara Creek if the injunction is upheld. Walgreen can "sell" its injunctive right only to Sara Creek, and Sara Creek can "buy" Walgreen's surrender of its right to enjoin the leasing of the anchor tenant's space to Phar-Mor only from Walgreen. The lack of alternatives in bilateral monopoly creates a bargaining range, and the costs of negotiating to a point within that range may be high. Suppose the cost to Walgreen of facing the competition of Phar-Mor at the Southgate Mall would be $1 million, and the benefit to Sara Creek of leasing to Phar-Mor would be $2 million. Then at any price between those figures for a waiver of Walgreen's injunctive right both parties would be better off, and we expect parties to bargain around a judicial assignment of legal rights if the assignment is inefficient. R.H. Coase, "The Problem of Social Cost," 3 J. Law & Econ. 1 (1960). But each of the parties would like to engross as much of the bargaining range as possible—Walgreen to press the price toward $2 million, Sara Creek to depress it toward $1 million. With so much at stake, both parties will have an incentive to devote substantial resources of time and money to the negotiation process. The process may even break down, if one or both parties want to create for future use a reputation as a hard bargainer; and if it does break down, the injunction will have brought about an inefficient result. All these are in one form or another costs of the injunctive process that can be avoided by substituting damages.

The costs and benefits of the damages remedy are the mirror of those of the injunctive remedy. The damages remedy avoids the cost of continuing supervision and third-party effects, and the cost of bilateral monopoly as well. It imposes costs of its own, however, in the form of diminished accuracy in the determination of value, on the one hand, and of the parties' expenditures on preparing and presenting evidence of damages, and the time of the court in evaluating the evidence, on the other. The weighing up of all these costs and benefits is the analytical procedure that is or at least should be employed by a judge asked to enter a permanent injunction, with the understanding that if the balance is even the injunction should be withheld. The judge is not required to explicate every detail of the analysis and he did not do so here, but as long we are satisfied that his approach is broadly consistent with a proper analysis we shall affirm; and we are satisfied here. The determination of Walgreen's damages would have been costly in forensic resources and inescapably inaccurate. . . . The lease had ten years to run. So Walgreen would have had to project its sales revenues and costs over the next ten years, and then project the impact on those figures of Phar-Mor's competition, and then discount that impact to present value. All but the last step would have been fraught with uncertainty.

. . . It is difficult to forecast the profitability of a retail store over a decade, let alone to assess the impact of a particular competitor on that profitability over that period. Of course one can hire an expert to make such predictions, Glen A. Stankee, "Econometric Forecasting of Lost Profits: Using High Technology to Compute Commercial Damages," 61 Fla.B.J. 83 (1987), and if injunctive relief is infeasible the expert's testimony may provide a tolerable basis for an award of damages. We cited cases in which damages have been awarded for the breach of an exclusivity clause in a shopping-center lease. But they are awarded in such circumstances not because anyone thinks them a clairvoyant forecast but because it is better to give a wronged person a crude remedy than none at all. It is the same theory on which damages are awarded for a disfiguring injury. No one thinks such injuries readily monetizable, City of Panama, 101 U.S. 453, 464, 25 L.Ed. 1061 (1880); McCarty v. Pheasant Run, Inc., 826 F.2d 1554, 1557 (7th Cir.1987); Marcus L. Plant, "Damages for Pain and Suffering," 19 Ohio St.L.J. 200, 205–06 (1958), but a crude estimate is better than letting the wrongdoer get off scot-free (which, not incidentally, would encourage more such injuries). Randall R. Bovbjerg et al., "Valuing Life and Limb in Tort: Scheduling 'Pain and Suffering,' " 83 Nw.U.L.Rev. 908 (1989). Sara Creek presented evidence of what happened (very little) to Walgreen when Phar-Mor moved into other shopping malls in which Walgreen has a pharmacy, and it was on the right track in putting in comparative evidence. But there was a serious question whether the other malls were actually comparable to the Southgate Mall, so we cannot conclude, in the face of the district judge's contrary conclusion, that the existence of comparative evidence dissolved the difficulties of computing damages in this case. Sara Creek complains that the judge refused to compel Walgreen to produce all the data that Sara Creek needed to demonstrate the feasibility of forecasting Walgreen's damages. Walgreen resisted, on grounds of the confidentiality of the data and the cost of producing the massive data that Sara Creek sought. Those are legitimate grounds; and the cost (broadly conceived) they expose of pretrial discovery, in turn presaging complexity at trial, is itself a cost of the damages remedy that injunctive relief saves.

Damages are not always costly to compute, or difficult to compute accurately. In the standard case of a seller's breach of a contract for the sale of goods where the buyer covers by purchasing the same product in the market, damages are readily calculable by subtracting the contract price from the market price and multiplying by the quantity specified in the contract. But this is not such a case and here damages would be a costly and inaccurate remedy; and on the other side of the balance some of the costs of an injunction are absent and the cost that is present seems low. The injunction here, like one enforcing a covenant not to compete (standardly enforced by injunction . . ., is a simple negative injunction—Sara Creek is not to lease space in the Southgate Mall to Phar-Mor during the term of Walgreen's lease—and the costs of judicial supervision and enforcement should be negligible. There is no contention that the injunction will harm an unrepresented third party. It may harm Phar-Mor but that harm will be reflected in Sara Creek's offer to Walgreen to dissolve the injunction. (Anyway Phar-Mor is a party.) The injunction may also, it is true, harm potential customers of Phar-Mor—people who would prefer to shop at a deep-discount store than an ordinary discount store—but their preferences, too, are registered indirectly. The more business Phar-Mor would have, the more rent it will be willing to pay Sara Creek, and therefore the more Sara Creek will be willing to pay Walgreen to dissolve the injunction.

The only substantial cost of the injunction in this case is that it may set off a round of negotiations between the parties. In some cases, illustrated by Boomer v. Atlantic Cement Co., 26 N.Y.2d 219, 309 N.Y.S.2d 312, 257 N.E.2d 870 (1970), this consideration alone would be enough to warrant the denial of injunctive relief. The defendant's factory was emitting cement dust that caused the plaintiffs harm monetized at less than $200,000, and the only way to abate the harm would have been to close down the factory, which had cost $45 million to build. An injunction against the nuisance could therefore have created a huge bargaining range (could, not would, because it is unclear what the current value of the factory was), and the costs of negotiating to a point within it might have been immense. If the market value of the factory was actually $45 million, the plaintiffs would be tempted to hold out for a price to dissolve the injunction in the tens of millions and the factory would be tempted to refuse to pay anything more than a few hundred thousand dollars. Negotiations would be unlikely to break down completely, given such a bargaining range, but they might well be protracted and costly. There is nothing so dramatic here. Sara Creek does not argue that it will have to close the mall if enjoined from leasing to Phar-Mor. Phar-Mor is not the only potential anchor tenant. . . .

To summarize, the judge did not exceed the bounds of reasonable judgment in concluding that the costs (including forgone benefits) of the damages remedy would exceed the costs (including forgone benefits) of an injunction. We need not consider whether, as intimated by Walgreen, exclusivity clauses in shopping-center leases should be considered presumptively enforceable by injunctions. Although we have described the choice between legal and equitable remedies as one for case-by-case determination, the courts have sometimes picked out categories of case in which injunctive relief is made the norm. The best-known example is specific performance of contracts for the sale of real property. Anderson v. Onsager, 155 Wis.2d 504, 455 N.W.2d 885 (1990); Okaw Drainage District v. National Distillers & Chemical Corp., 882 F.2d 1241, 1248 (7th Cir.1989); Anthony T. Kronman, "Specific Performance," 45 U.Chi.L.Rev. 351, 355 and n. 20 (1978). The rule that specific performance will be ordered in such cases as a matter of course is a generalization of the considerations discussed above. Because of the absence of a fully liquid market in real property and the frequent presence of subjective values (many a homeowner, for example, would not sell his house for its market value), the calculation of damages is difficult; and since an order of specific performance to convey a piece of property does not create a continuing relation between the parties, the costs of supervision and enforcement if specific performance is ordered are slight. The exclusivity clause in Walgreen's lease relates to real estate, but we hesitate to suggest that every contract involving real estate should be enforceable as a matter of course by injunctions. Suppose Sara Creek had covenanted to keep the entrance to Walgreen's store free of ice and snow, and breached the covenant. An injunction would require continuing supervision, and it would be easy enough if the injunction were denied for Walgreen to hire its own ice and snow remover and charge the cost to Sara Creek. Cf. City of Michigan City v. Lake Air Corp., 459 N.E.2d 760 (Ind.App.1984). On the other hand, injunctions to enforce exclusivity clauses are quite likely to be justifiable by just the considerations present here—damages are difficult to estimate with any accuracy and the injunction is a one-shot remedy requiring no continuing judicial involvement. So there is an argument for making injunctive relief presumptively appropriate in such cases, but we need not decide in this case how strong an argument.

AFFIRMED.

HARLINGTON WOOD, JR., SENIOR CIRCUIT JUDGE, concurring.

I gladly join in the affirmance reached in Judge Posner's expert analysis.

———

UCC §§ 2–709, 2–716

[See Selected Source Materials Supplement]

CISG ARTS. 46, 62

[See Selected Source Materials Supplement]

NOTE ON SPECIFIC PERFORMANCE OF CONTRACTS FOR THE SALE OF GOODS

The traditional, pre-UCC rule, inherited from the English legal system, was that in the case of a contract for the sale of goods neither the buyer nor the seller could ordinarily get specific performance unless the goods were unique. If goods were not unique then the buyer could cover, and damages for the cost of cover were deemed an adequate remedy. On the other hand, where a contract was for the sale of a unique item, such as a painting or an heirloom, cover on the market was by hypothesis not possible, and specific performance would be granted by a court of equity.

Today, specific performance of contracts for the sale of goods is largely governed by UCC § 2–716, which authorizes specific performance "where the goods are unique or in other proper circumstances." The Official Comment explains "this Article seeks to further a more liberal attitude than some courts have shown in connection with the specific performance of contracts of sale." Laclede Gas Co. v. Amoco Oil Co., 522 F.2d 33 (8th Cir. 1975), is an example. The case involved a contract to supply propane gas to Laclede for use in residential developments until the developments were supplied with natural gas, which might not occur for as much as 10 to 15 years. The court granted specific performance even though propane in and of itself is not unique:

"It is axiomatic that specific performance will not be ordered when the party claiming breach of contract has an adequate remedy at law. Jamison Coal & Coke Co. v. Goltra, 143 F.2d 889, 894 (8th Cir.), cert. denied, 323 U.S. 769, 65 S.Ct. 122, 89 L.Ed. 615 (1944). This is especially true when the contract involves personal property as distinguished from real estate.

"However, in Missouri, as elsewhere, specific performance may be ordered even though personalty is involved in the 'proper circumstances.' Mo.Rev.Stat. § 400.2–716 (1); Restatement, Contracts, supra, § 361. And a remedy at law adequate to defeat the grant of specific performance 'must be as certain, prompt, complete, and efficient to attain the ends of justice as a decree of specific performance.' . . .

"One of the leading Missouri cases allowing specific performance of a contract relating to personalty because the remedy at law was inadequate is Boeving v. Vandover, 240 Mo.App. 117, 218 S.W.2d 175, 178 (1949). In that case the plaintiff sought specific performance of a contract in which the defendant had promised to sell him an automobile. At that time (near the end of and shortly after World War II) new cars were hard to come by, and the court held that specific performance was a proper remedy since a new car 'could not be obtained elsewhere except at considerable expense, trouble or loss, which cannot be estimated in advance.'

"We are satisfied that Laclede has brought itself within this practical approach taken by the Missouri courts. As Amoco points out, Laclede has propane immediately available to it under other contracts with other suppliers. And the evidence indicates that at the present time propane is readily available on the open market. However, this analysis ignores the fact that the contract involved in this lawsuit is for a long-term supply of propane to these subdivisions. The other two contracts under which Laclede obtains the gas will remain in force only until March 31, 1977, and April 1, 1981, respectively; and there is no assurance that Laclede will be able to receive any propane under them after that time. Also it is unclear as to whether or not Laclede can use the propane obtained under these contracts to supply the Jefferson County subdivisions, since they were originally entered into to provide Laclede with propane with which to 'shave' its natural gas supply during peak demand periods.[4] Additionally, there was uncontradicted expert testimony that Laclede probably could not find another supplier of propane willing to enter into a long-term contract such as the Amoco agreement, given the uncertain future of worldwide energy supplies. And, even if Laclede could obtain supplies of propane for the affected developments through its present contracts or newly negotiated ones, it would still face considerable expense and trouble which cannot be estimated in advance in making arrangements for its distribution to the subdivisions."

NOTE ON SPECIFIC PERFORMANCE OF CONTRACTS FOR THE SALE OF LAND AND EMPLOYMENT CONTRACTS

1.   *Contracts for the sale of land.* It is well settled that in a contract for the sale of land the buyer can get a decree specifically ordering the seller to execute a deed in his favor. In most states, the seller can also get a decree ordering the buyer to take title to the land and pay the agreed price. Restatement Second § 360, Comment e.

The traditional rationale of the rule that a *buyer* of land can get specific performance is that damages are inadequate in such cases because: (1) The value of land is always to some extent conjectural, since land usually does not have a clearly defined market price; and (2) Every piece of land is to some extent unique, and therefore the buyer cannot with an award of money damages go out on the market and buy a piece of land exactly like that promised him by the defaulting seller. Statutes now provide for self-executing

---

[4]   During periods of cold weather, when demand is high, Laclede does not receive enough natural gas to meet all this demand. It, therefore, adds propane to the natural gas it places in its distribution system. This practice is called "peak shaving."

decrees in such cases; such a decree has the effect of a deed, and can be recorded in the Registry of Deeds.

Today, the concept that every piece of real property is unique seems questionable. A few cases recognize this reality and criticize the traditional rule. For example, in Watkins v. Paul, 95 Idaho 499, 511 P.2d 781 (1973), the court refused, on similar grounds, to order specific performance of an option to purchase a tract of land:

> The evidence fails to show that the plaintiffs need the land in question for any particular, unique purpose, which is one of the main reasons for granting specific performance; on the contrary, the plaintiffs' own evidence shows that they seek to obtain the land only so that they may resell it for profit. Under these circumstances, specific performance would bring the plaintiffs no greater relief than would damages in the amount of their lost profit.

However, although the right of a buyer of real property of specific performance is not soundly based on the ground that all real property is unique, the right can be justified on the ground of administrability, Some real property is unique, some is homogeneous, but most is moderately differentiated. Sorting through in every case which category the real property in question is not worth the time of litigants and courts: better to have a simple rule that a buyer of real property can always get specific performance.

Traditionally, a *seller* of land also is entitled to specific performance without a showing that damages are an inadequate remedy. Ordinarily, however, a decree in favor of the seller ordering the buyer to pay money is not enforced by contempt. Instead, the decree provides that if the purchase price is not paid by a certain time, the right of the buyer to "redeem" the land by paying the purchase price is cut off, or "foreclosed." If the buyer does not complete the purchase in the time ordered, then the seller retains the land and has a judgment for the purchase price.

Ash Park, LLC v. Alexander & Bishop, Ltd., 324 Wis.2d 703, 783 N.W.2d 294 (2010), takes a different approach to coercing the buyer. The trial court's order exposed the buyer to the possibility of being held in contempt if it did not complete the purchase. The buyer had argued this was unfair because it could not obtain financing. The Supreme Court instructed the buyer to raise this argument at the contempt hearing, under a long settled rule "that a person cannot be held in contempt of court for the failure to pay money unless the refusal is willful and contemptuous and not the result of his inability to pay."

2. *Employment contracts.* Employment contracts are not specifically enforced at the suit of either the employee or the employer. Restatement Second § 367(1). The objections to specific performance here do not lie in a notion that monetary relief is an adequate substitute for the promised performance. Rather, they stem from a belief that it is unwise to attempt to extract, from an unwilling party, a performance involving personal relations, and that ordering an employee to perform lies close to involuntary servitude.

In some cases the courts, although they will not order the employee to work for the employer, will enjoin the employee from working for a competitor. Often such an injunction could be tantamount to ordering specific performance, because if the employee cannot work for a competitor she will not be able to earn a living, and therefore will be indirectly forced to work for her original employer. Accordingly, Restatement Second § 367(2) adopts the rule that "[a] promise to render personal service exclusively for one employer will not be enforced by an injunction against serving another if its probable result will be to compel a performance involving personal relations the enforced continuance of which is undesirable or will be to leave the employee without other reasonable means of making a living."

———

CHAPTER 7

ALTERNATIVE DAMAGE MEASURES

■ ■ ■

This Chapter considers three damage measures that may be used in a bargain context as an alternative to the expectation measure.

Section 1 concerns the reliance measure as a remedy for breach in a bargain context. (Recall from Chapter 1 that the reliance measure may also be used in a donative context.) The name of this measure is something of a misnomer. Calling it the *cost* measure would be more accurate, and would make it easier to understand the measure's dynamics.

Section 2 concerns cases in which the aggrieved party elects to rescind the contract and bring a claim for restitutionary damages against the party in breach.

Section 3 concerns cases in which the aggrieved party has a claim for the profit the breaching party made by the breach. These are described as disgorgement damages.

———

SECTION 1. RELIANCE DAMAGES FOR BREACH OF A BARGAIN CONTRACT

SECURITY STOVE & MFG. CO. V. AMERICAN RYS. EXPRESS CO.
Kansas City Court of Appeals, Missouri, 1932.
227 Mo.App. 175, 51 S.W.2d 572.

BLAND, J. This is an action for damages for the failure of defendant to transport, from Kansas City to Atlantic City, New Jersey, within a reasonable time, a furnace equipped with a combination oil and gas burner. The cause was tried before the court without the aid of a jury, resulting in a judgment in favor of plaintiff in the sum of $801.50 and interest, or in a total sum of $1,000.00. Defendant has appealed.

The facts show that plaintiff manufactured a furnace equipped with a special combination oil and gas burner it desired to exhibit at the American Gas Association Convention held in Atlantic City in October, 1926. The president of plaintiff testified that plaintiff engaged space for the exhibit for the reason "that the Henry L. Dougherty Company was very much interested in putting out a combination oil and gas burner; we had just developed one, after we got through, better than anything on the market and we thought this show would be the psychological time to get in contact with the Dougherty Company"; that "the thing wasn't sent there for sale but primarily to show"; that at the time the space was engaged it was too late to ship the furnace by freight so plaintiff decided to ship it by express, and, on September 18th, 1926, wrote the office of the defendant in Kansas City, stating that it had engaged a booth for exhibition purposes at Atlantic City, New Jersey, from the American Gas Association, for the week beginning October 11th; that its exhibit consisted of an oil burning furnace, together with two oil burners which weighed at least 1,500 pounds; that, "In order to get this exhibit in place on time it should be in Atlantic City not later than October the 8th. What we want you to do is to tell us how much time you will require to assure the delivery of the exhibit on time."

Mr. Bangs, chief clerk in charge of the local office of the defendant, upon receipt of the letter, sent Mr. Johnson, a commercial representative of the defendant, to see plaintiff. Johnson called upon plaintiff taking its letter with him. Johnson made a notation on the bottom of the letter giving October 4th, as the day that defendant was required to have the exhibit in order for it to reach Atlantic City on October 8th.

On October 1st, plaintiff wrote the defendant at Kansas City, referring to its letter of September 18th, concerning the fact that the furnace must be in Atlantic City not later than October 8th, and stating what Johnson had told it, saying: "Now Mr. Bangs, we want to make doubly sure that this shipment is in Atlantic City not later than October 8th and the purpose of this letter is to tell you that you can *have your truck call for the shipment between 12 and 1 o'clock on Saturday, October 2nd for this.*" (Italics plaintiff's.) On October 2nd, plaintiff called the office of the express company in Kansas City and told it that the shipment was ready. Defendant came for the shipment on the last mentioned day, received it and delivered the express receipt to plaintiff. The shipment contained 21 packages. Each package was marked with stickers backed with glue and covered with silica of soda, to prevent the stickers being torn off in shipping. Each package was given a number. They ran from 1 to 21.

Plaintiff's president made arrangements to go to Atlantic City to attend the convention and install the exhibit, arriving there about October 11th. When he reached Atlantic City he found the shipment had been placed in the booth that had been assigned to plaintiff. The exhibit was set up, but it was found that one of the packages shipped was not there. This missing package contained the gas manifold, or that part of the oil and gas burner that controlled the flow of gas in the burner. This was the most important part of the exhibit and a like burner could not be obtained in Atlantic City.

Wires were sent and it was found that the stray package was at the "over and short bureau" of defendant in St. Louis. Defendant reported that the package would be forwarded to Atlantic City and would be there by Wednesday, the 13th. Plaintiff's president waited until Thursday, the day the convention closed, but the package had not arrived at the time, so he closed up the exhibit and left. About a week after he arrived in Kansas City, the package was returned by the defendant. . . .

The petition upon which the case was tried alleges that " . . . relying upon defendant's promise and the promises of its agents and servants, that said parcels would be delivered at Atlantic City by October 8th, 1926, if delivered to defendant by October 4th, 1926, plaintiff herein hired space for an exhibit at the American Gas Association Convention at Atlantic City, and planned for an exhibit at said Convention and sent men in the employ of this plaintiff to Atlantic City to install, show and operate said exhibit, and that these men were in Atlantic City ready to set up this plaintiff's exhibit at the American Gas Association Convention on October 8th, 1926." *[The reliance injury]*
. . .

Plaintiff asked damages, which the court in its judgment allowed as follows: $147.00 express charges (on the exhibit); $45.12 freight on the exhibit from Atlantic City to Kansas City; $101.39 railroad and pullman fares to and from Atlantic City, expended by plaintiff's president and a workman taken by him to Atlantic City; $48.00 hotel room for the two; $150.00 for the time of the president; $40.00 for wages of plaintiff's other employee and $270.00 for rental of the booth, making a total of $801.51. . . .

We think, under the circumstances in this case, that it was proper to allow plaintiff's expenses as its damages. Ordinarily the measure of damages where the carrier fails to deliver a shipment at destination within a reasonable time is the difference between the market value of the goods at the time of the delivery and the time when they should have been delivered. But where the carrier has notice of peculiar circumstances under which the shipment is made, which will result in an unusual loss by the shipper in case of delay in delivery, the carrier is responsible for the real damage sustained from such delay if the notice given is of such character, and goes to such extent, in informing the carrier of the shipper's situation, that the carrier will be presumed to have contracted with reference thereto. Central Trust Co. of New York v. Savannah & W.R. Co. (C.C.) 69 F. 683, 685. . . .

Defendant contends that plaintiff "is endeavoring to achieve a return of the status quo in a suit based on a breach of contract. Instead of seeking to recover what he would have had, had the contract not been broken, plaintiff is trying to recover what he would have had, had there never been any contract of shipment"; that the expenses sued for would have been incurred in any event. It is no doubt, the general rule that where there is a breach of contract the party suffering the loss can recover only that which he would have had, had the contract not been broken, and this is all the cases decided upon which defendant relies, including C., M. & St. P. Ry. v. McCaull-Dinsmore Co., 253 U.S. 97, 100, 40 S.Ct. 504, 64 L.Ed. 801. But this is merely a general statement of the rule and is not inconsistent with the holdings that, in some instances, the injured party may recover expenses incurred in relying upon the contract, although such expenses would have been incurred had the contract not been breached. See Morrow v. Railroad, 140 Mo.App. 200, 212, 213, 123 S.W. 1034; Bryant v. Barton, 32 Neb. 613, 616, 49 N.W. 331; Woodbury v. Jones, 44 N.H. 206; Driggs v. Dwight, 17 Wend. (N.Y.) 71, 31 Am.Dec. 283.

In Sperry et al. v. O'Neill-Adams Co. (C.C.A.) 185 F. 231, the court held that the advantages resulting from the use of trading stamps as a means of increasing trade are so contingent that they cannot form a basis on which to rest a recovery for a breach of contract to supply them. In lieu of compensation based thereon the court directed a recovery in the sum expended in preparation for carrying on business in connection with the use of the stamps. The court said, loc. cit. 239:

> "Plaintiff in its complaint had made a claim for lost profits, but, finding it impossible to marshal any evidence which would support a finding of exact figures, abandoned that claim. Any attempt to reach a precise sum would be mere blind guesswork. Nevertheless a contract, which both sides conceded would prove a valuable one, had been broken and the party who broke it was responsible for resultant damage. In order to carry out this contract, the plaintiff made expenditures which otherwise it would not have made. . . . The trial judge held, as we think rightly, that plaintiff was entitled at least to recover these expenses to which it had been put in order to secure the benefits of a contract of which defendant's conduct deprived it." . . .

The case at bar was [not] to recover damages for loss of profits by reason of the failure of the defendant to transport the shipment within a reasonable time, so that it would arrive in Atlantic City for the exhibit. There were no profits contemplated. The furnace was to be shown and shipped back to Kansas City. There was no money loss, except the expenses, that was of such a nature as any court would allow as being sufficiently definite or lacking in pure speculation. Therefore, unless plaintiff is permitted to recover the expenses that it went to, which were a total loss to it by reason of its inability to exhibit the furnace and equipment, it will be deprived of any substantial compensation for its loss. The law does not contemplate any such injustice. It ought to allow plaintiff, as damages, the loss in the way of expenses that it sustained, and which it would not have been put to if it had not been for its reliance upon the defendant to perform its contract. There is no contention that the exhibit would have been entirely valueless and whatever it might have accomplished defendant knew of the circumstances and ought to respond for whatever damages plaintiff suffered. In cases of this kind the method of estimating the damages should be adopted which is the most definite and certain and which best achieves the fundamental purpose of compensation. 17 C.J. p. 846; Miller v. Robertson, 266 U.S. 243, 257, 45 S.Ct. 73, 78, 69 L.Ed. 265. Had the exhibit been shipped in order to realize a profit on sales and such profits could have been realized, or to be entered in competition for a prize, and plaintiff failed to show loss of profits with sufficient definiteness, or that he would have won the prize, defendant's cases might be in point. But as before stated, no such situation exists here.

While it is true that plaintiff already had incurred some of these expenses, in that it had rented space at the exhibit before entering into the contract with defendant for the shipment of the exhibit and this part of plaintiff's damages, in a sense, arose out of a circumstance which transpired before the contract was even entered into, yet, plaintiff arranged for the exhibit knowing that it could call upon defendant to perform its common law duty to accept and transport the shipment with reasonable dispatch. The whole damage, therefore, was suffered in contemplation of defendant performing its contract, which it failed to do, and would not have been sustained except for the reliance by plaintiff upon defendant to perform it. It can, therefore, be fairly said that the damages or loss suffered by plaintiff grew out of the breach of the contract, for had the shipment arrived on time, plaintiff would have had the benefit of the contract, which was contemplated by all parties, defendant being advised of the purpose of the shipment.

The judgment is affirmed.

All concur.

Anglia Television Ltd. v. Reed

[1971] 3 All.E.R. 690 (C.A. 1971)

Anglia Television Ltd wanted to make a film for television entitled "The Man in the Wood," which portrayed an American man married to an English woman. Before Anglia selected the leading man, it arranged for a place where the filming was to occur; employed a director, a designer, and a stage manager; and involved itself in much expense. For the leading man, Anglia required a strong actor capable of holding the film together. It eventually decided upon Robert Reed, an American with a very high reputation as an actor, and by telephone conversation the parties agreed that Reed would come to England and star in the film for a fee of $581,050 and expenses. Reed later repudiated the contract because of a mixup in his bookings. Anglia tried hard to find a substitute but could not do so and abandoned the film. It then sued Reed for its out-of-pocket expenses on the film of $582,750, including almost $581,900 incurred before the contract was made. Held (per Denning, L.J.), Anglia was entitled to recover all of its expenses:

> [I]t is plain that, when Mr. Reed entered into this contract, he must have known perfectly well that much expenditure had already been incurred on director's fees and the like. He must have contemplated—or, at any rate, it is reasonably to be imputed to him— that if he broke his contract, all that expenditure would be wasted, whether or not it was incurred before or after the contract. He must pay damages for all the expenditure so wasted and thrown away. . . . It is true that, if the defendant had never entered into the contract, he would not be liable, and the expenditure would have been incurred by the plaintiff without redress; but, the defendant having made his contract and broken it, it does not lie in his mouth to say he is not liable, when it was because of his breach that the expenditure has been wasted.

————

L. Albert & Son v. Armstrong Rubber Co.

178 F.2d 182 (2d Cir.1949)

(L. HAND, J.) Seller agreed to sell to Buyer four machines designed to recondition old rubber. Seller breached the contract, and Buyer claimed as damages the expenses that it had incurred in reliance upon Seller's promise, including $3000 for the cost of a foundation it had laid for the machines. In the course of his opinion, Hand discussed as follows the issues involved by the possibility that if the contract had been completed it would have resulted in a loss to the plaintiff:

> . . . The Buyer . . . asserts that it is . . . entitled to recover the cost of the foundation upon the theory that what it expended in reliance upon the Seller's performance was a recoverable loss. In cases where the venture would have proved profitable to the promisee, there is no reason why he should not recover his expenses. On the other hand, on those occasions in which the performance would not have covered the promisee's outlay, such a result imposes the risk of the promisee's contract upon the promisor. . . . It is often very hard to learn what the value of the performance would have been; and it is a common expedient, and a just one, in such situations to put the peril of the answer upon that party who by his wrong has made the issue relevant to the rights of the other. On principle therefore the proper solution would seem to be that the promisee may recover his outlay in preparation for the performance, subject to the privilege of the promisor to reduce it by as much as he can show that the promisee would have lost, if the contract had been performed. . . .

————

SECTION 2. THE RESTITUTION MEASURE

If a breach of contract is material, then the promisee may elect to rescind the contract and recover the value of performance he rendered (less benefits received) through a restitutionary claim. This claim is unlike a claim for reliance damages in two respects. First, the measure of damages is the market price of the performance the plaintiff rendered. Other costs incurred by the plaintiff in preparing to perform are not recovered. Second, the defendant is not allowed to reduce damages by showing the plaintiff would not have recovered costs he incurred to perform had the contract not been breached. In some jurisdictions restitutionary damages may even exceed the contract price. Some jurisdictions cap restitutionary damages at the contract price.

———

OSTEEN V. JOHNSON
Colorado Court of Appeals, 1970.
473 P.2d 184.

DUFFORD, JUDGE . . . This was an action for breach of an oral contract. Trial was to the court, which found that the plaintiffs had paid the sum of $2,500. In exchange, the defendant had agreed to "promote" the plaintiffs' daughter, Linda Osteen, as a singer and composer of country-western music. More specifically, it was found that the defendant had agreed to advertise Linda through various mailings for a period of one year; to arrange and furnish the facilities necessary for Linda to record several songs; to prepare two records from the songs recorded; to press and mail copies of one of the records to disc jockeys throughout the country; and, if the first record met with any success, to press and mail out copies of the second record.

The trial court further found that the defendant did arrange for several recording sessions, at which Linda recorded four songs. A record was prepared of two of the songs, and 1,000 copies of the record were then pressed. Of the pressed records, 340 copies were mailed to disc jockeys, 200 were sent to the plaintiffs, and the remainder were retained by the defendant. Various mailings were made to advertise Linda; flyers were sent to disc jockeys throughout the country; and Linda's professional name was advertised in trade magazines. The record sent out received a favorable review and a high rating in a trade magazine.

Upon such findings the trial court concluded that the defendant had substantially performed the agreement. However, a judgment was entered in favor of the plaintiffs in the sum of $1.00 and costs on the basis that the defendant had wrongfully caused the name of another party to appear on the label of the record as co-author of a song which had been written solely by Linda. The trial court also ordered the defendant to deliver to the plaintiffs certain master tapes and records in the defendant's possession.

1.   RIGHT OF RESTITUTION

Although plaintiffs' reasons are not clearly defined, they argue here that the award of damages is inadequate, and that the trial court erred in concluding that the defendant had substantially performed the agreement. However, no evidence was presented during the trial of the matter upon which an award of other than nominal damages could be based. In our opinion, the remedy which plaintiffs proved and upon which they can rely is that of restitution. See 5 A. Corbin, Contracts § 996. This remedy is available where there has been a contract breach of vital importance, variously defined as a substantial breach or a breach which goes to the essence of the contract. See 5 A. Corbin, Contracts § 1104, where the author writes:

> "In the case of a breach by non-performance, . . . the injured party's alternative remedy by way of restitution depends upon the extent of the non-performance by the defendant. The defendant's breach may be nothing but a failure to perform some minor part of his contractual duty. Such a minor non-performance is a breach of contract and an action for damages can be maintained. The injured party, however, can not maintain an action for restitution of what he has given the defendant unless the defendant's non-performance is so material that it is held to go to the 'essence'. . . . A minor breach by one party does not discharge the contractual duty of the other party; and the latter being still bound to perform as agreed can not be entitled to the restitution of payments already made by him or to the value of other part performances rendered." . . .

2.   BREACH OF CONTRACT

The essential question here then becomes whether any breach on the part of the defendant is substantial enough to justify the remedy of restitution. Plaintiffs argue that the defendant breached the contract in the following ways: First, the defendant did not promote Linda for a period of one year as agreed; secondly, the defendant wrongfully caused the name of another party to appear on the label as co-author of the song which had been composed solely by Linda; and thirdly, the defendant failed to press and mail out copies of the second record as agreed.

The first argument is not supported by the record. Plaintiffs brought the action within the one-year period for which the contract was to run. There was no evidence that during this period the defendant had not continued to promote Linda through the use of mailings and advertisements. Quite obviously the mere fact that the one-year period had not ended prior to the commencement of the action does not justify the conclusion that the defendant had breached the agreement. Plaintiffs' second argument overlooks the testimony offered on behalf of the defendant that listing the other party as co-author of the song would make it more likely that the record would be played by disc jockeys.

The plaintiffs' third argument does, however, have merit. It is clear from the record and the findings of the trial court that the first record had met with some success. It is also clear that copies of the second record were neither pressed nor mailed out. In our opinion the failure of the defendant to press and mail out copies of the second record after the first had achieved some success constituted a substantial breach of the contract and, therefore, justifies the remedy of restitution. Seale v. Bates, 145 Colo. 430, 359 P.2d 356; Colorado Management Corp. v. American Founders Life Insurance Co., 145 Colo. 413, 359 P.2d 665; Bridges v. Ingram, 122 Colo. 501, 223 P.2d 1051. Both parties agree that the essence of their contract was to publicize Linda as a singer of western songs and to make her name and talent known to the public. Defendant admitted and asserted that the primary method of achieving this end was to have records pressed and mailed to disc jockeys. . . .

3.   DETERMINING DAMAGES

It is clear that the defendant did partially perform the contract and, under applicable law, should be allowed compensation for the reasonable value of his services. See 5 A. Corbin, Contracts § 1114, where the author writes:

> "[A]ll courts are in agreement that restitution by the defendant will not be enforced unless the plaintiff returns in some way what he has received as a part performance by the defendant."

It shall, therefore, be the ultimate order of this court that prior to restoring to the plaintiffs the $2,500 paid by them to the defendant further proceedings be held during which the trial court shall determine the reasonable value of the services which the defendant rendered on plaintiffs' behalf.

The judgment is reversed, and this case is remanded with directions that a new trial be held to determine the one issue of the amount to which the plaintiffs are entitled by way of restitution. Such amount shall be the $2,500 paid by plaintiffs to defendant less the reasonable value of the services which the defendant performed on behalf of plaintiffs.

COYTE and PIERCE, JJ., concur.

RESTATEMENT, SECOND, CONTRACTS §§ 344, 345, 370, 371

[See Selected Source Materials Supplement]

———

RESTATEMENT, SECOND, CONTRACTS § 370, ILLUSTRATIONS 2, 5

2.   A contracts to sell B a machine for $100,000. After A has spent $40,000 on the manufacture of the machine but before its completion, B repudiates the contract. A cannot get restitution of the $40,000 because no benefit was conferred on B. . . .

5.   A, a social worker, promises B to render personal services to C in return for B's promise to educate A's children. B repudiates the contract after A has rendered part of the services. A can get restitution from B for the services, even though they were not rendered to B, because they conferred a benefit on B. . . .

———

RESTATEMENT, THIRD, RESTITUTION AND UNJUST ENRICHMENT §§ 37, 38

[See Selected Source Materials Supplement]

———

NOTE ON RESTITUTIONARY AND RELIANCE DAMAGES

In theory, restitutionary and reliance damages are distinguishable: restitutionary damages are based on the market value of the performance rendered by the plaintiff; reliance damages are based on costs incurred by the plaintiff. Thus costs in preparing to perform may be recovered under the reliance measure in appropriate cases, but may not be recovered under the restitution measure. The frequent difficulty of distinguishing preparation from performance sometimes blurs this distinction.

Traditionally, restitutionary damages for breach have been viewed as benefit-based, that is, as based on the market value of the benefit rendered to the breaching party. However, under Restatement, Third, Restitution and Unjust Enrichment, restitutionary damages for breach of contract are not benefit-based. Instead, the measure of these damages is "the market value of the plaintiff's uncompensated contractual performance." Indeed, Restatement, Third, Restitution and Unjust Enrichment § 38(2)(b) avoids the term restitution to describe this type of damages, and instead describes them as performance-based damages. (Caution: This terminology is relatively new, although it accurately describes what courts tend to do. Many and perhaps most courts continue to use the benefit-based terminology.)

The market value of uncompensated performance is also sometimes used as the measure of damages when a restitution claim is brought because the defendant's promise to pay for the performance is unenforceable through a contract claim under the statute of frauds or on the ground of indefiniteness. For example, in Randolph v. Castle, 190 Ky. 776, 228 S.W. 418 (1921), defendant, the owner of a small coal mine, entered into an oral contract with plaintiffs whereby plaintiffs agreed to work defendant's mine for three years and defendant agreed to pay plaintiffs $2.10 per ton for coal removed. Defendant later repudiated the contract, and plaintiffs sued for damages. The court said, ". . . [T]he contract . . . was within the statute of frauds. . . . [and] plaintiffs were entitled to recover, if at all, on the *quantum meruit*. This necessitated plaintiffs showing the value of the services performed. . . . If the plaintiffs at the instance of defendant's mine foreman remained at the mine, ready, willing and able to work, but were assigned no duties, and thereby lost time, the defendant is liable to them for the reasonable value thereof. . . . "

Kearns v. Andree, 107 Conn. 181, 139 A. 695 (1928), illustrates both the distinction between reliance-based and performance-based damages and the difficulty of distinguishing preparation from performance. The defendant refused to honor an oral contract to purchase a house owned by the plaintiff. At the defendant's request, the plaintiff had made alterations in the house that reduced its value. The trial court held that the work done was sufficient to take the contract out of the statute of frauds but the agreement was unenforceable on the ground of indefiniteness. The Connecticut Supreme Court held that the plaintiff was entitled to recover the costs incurred in making the requested alterations, but not the costs incurred in repainting and replastering the house to restore it to its original condition to make it saleable. It rested the obligation to pay for the cost of making the requested alterations on "the underlying principle of implied contracts, which . . . places a legal obligation upon one to do that which in equity and good conscience he ought to do." It rejected the claim for the cost of restoring the house to its original condition on the ground that "this action would be, in effect, to permit a recovery upon an unenforceable contract, which may not be done."

NOTE ON CONTRACT PRICE AS A CAP ON RESTITUTIONARY DAMAGES

When a service provider sues for reliance damages the damage award can never exceed the contract price because this award would clearly put the plaintiff in a better position than the plaintiff would have been on full performance. Indeed, under the rule in Restatement Second § 349 and *L. Albert & Son v. Armstrong Rubber Co.*, Section 1, supra, if the defendant can prove the plaintiff would have suffered a loss on full performance because the cost to complete performance would have exceeded the contract price, then this loss is subtracted from the costs incurred by the plaintiff in preparing to perform and performing, putting the plaintiff in the position he would have been on full performance.

When a service provider sues for the market value of performance already rendered as restitution damages some cases do not cap the award at the contract price. United States v. Algernon Blair, Inc., 479 F.2d 638 (4th Cir. 1978), is a leading case. A subcontractor underbid work on a construction project. The general contractor breached. The subcontractor terminated the contract and sued for $37,000, which was the market value of the work it had done to date for which it had not yet been paid. The general contractor offered proof that the subcontractor would have lost more than this amount on full performance. The court held this was irrelevant to a restitution claim in quantum meruit:

> The impact of quantum meruit is to allow a promisee to recover the value of services he gave to the defendant irrespective of whether he would have lost money on the contract and been unable to recover in a suit on the contract. Scaduto v. Orlando, 381 F.2d 587, 595 (2d Cir.1967). The measure of recovery for quantum meruit is the reasonable value of the performance, Restatement of Contracts § 347 (1932); and recovery is undiminished by any loss which would have been incurred by complete performance. 12 Williston on Contracts § 1485, at 312 (3d ed. 1970). While the contract price may be evidence of reasonable value of the services, it does not measure the value of the performance or limit recovery. Rather, the standard for measuring the reasonable value of the services rendered is the amount for which such services could have been purchased from one in the plaintiff's position at the time and place the services were rendered.

Restatement Third, Restitution and Unjust Enrichment § 38(2)(b) rejects the result in *Algernon Blair*. Under the rule stated, restitutionary (performance-based) damages in a bargain contest may not exceed "the price of such performance as determined by reference to the parties' agreement." Comment d explains:

> . . . [S]ome authorities allow recovery 'off the contract,' unlimited by contract price; but this Restatement rejects that outcome. By capping the damage calculation at the contract rate (where such rate may be determined) § 38(2)(b) prevents these plaintiffs as well from electing performance-based damages as a means of escape from an unfavorable bargain.

> The contrary rule, allowing damages measured by the value of performance unlimited by the contract price, permits the injured party to reallocate or revalue risks that it is the function of contract to price and to assign. Such an outcome is contrary to fundamental objectives of contract law and inconsistent with the other remedies

for breach of contract, all of which take the parties' agreement as the benchmark by which the plaintiff's remedies are measured.

A contract-price cap is not the same as an expectation-damages-measure cap. If the market value of the plaintiff's partial performance prior to the defendant's breach is less than the contract price, then a contract-price cap does not limit damages, while an expectation cap does, if the defendant could prove the plaintiff would have incurred a loss had the plaintiff completed performance. The logic behind this is apparent if you consider the legal position of a contractor who has partially completed a construction contract at the time of the defendant's breach. The contractor has the option to sue for expectation damages if it can prove its cost to complete is less than the balance due (unpaid contract price minus expense saved). If the cost to complete is uncertain or difficult to prove, then the contractor may forgo a claim for expectation damages and either sue for the cost of preparing to perform and performance, through a reliance claim, or for the reasonable value of performance, through a restitution claim. The damages may not exceed the unpaid balance of the contract price. Furthermore, if the claim is restitutionary (performance-based), then under the rule in the Restatement Third of Restitution, the defendant cannot reduce damages by proving that the cost to complete exceeds the balance due. A restitution claim takes the issue of cost to complete off the table. Similarly, in *Osteen v. Johnson*, Johnson could not defeat the Osteens' claim to restitution of the money they paid him to produce a second record by showing that the second record would have been an embarrassment.

SECTION 3. DISGORGEMENT DAMAGES

UNITED STATES NAVAL INSTITUTE V. CHARTER COMMUNICATIONS, INC.
United States Court of Appeals, Second Circuit, 1991.
936 F.2d 692.

Before KEARSE, WINTER and ALTIMARI, CIRCUIT JUDGES.

KEARSE, CIRCUIT JUDGE:

This case returns to us following our remand in *United States Naval Institute v. Charter Communications, Inc.*, 875 F.2d 1044 (2d Cir.1989) ("*Naval I*"), to the United States District Court for the Southern District of New York, Pierre N. Leval, *Judge,* for the fashioning of relief in favor of plaintiff United States Naval Institute ("Naval") against defendant Charter Communications, Inc., and Berkley Publishing Group (collectively "Berkley"), for breach of an agreement with respect to the publication of the paperback edition of *The Hunt For Red October* ("*Red October*" or the "Book"). On remand, the district court awarded Naval $35,380.50 in damages, $7,760.12 as profits wrongfully received by Berkley, and

$15,319.27 as prejudgment interest on the damages awarded, plus costs. Naval appeals from so much of the judgment as failed to award a greater amount as profits, denied prejudgment interest on the profits awarded, and refused to award attorney's fees under the Copyright Act of 1976, 17 U.S.C. § 101 *et seq.* (1988) (the "Copyright Act" or the "Act"). Berkley cross-appeals from the judgment as a whole and from such parts of it as awarded moneys to Naval. For the reasons below, we reverse the award of profits; we affirm the award of damages, the award of prejudgment interest, and the denial of attorney's fees.

I.   BACKGROUND

The events leading to this action are fully set forth in *Naval I,* 875 F.2d at 1045–47, and will be summarized here only briefly. Naval, as the assignee of the author's copyright in *Red October,* entered into a licensing agreement with Berkley in September 1984 (the "Agreement"), granting Berkley the exclusive license to publish a paperback edition of the Book "not sooner than October 1985." Berkley shipped its paperback edition to retail outlets early, placing those outlets in position to sell the paperback prior to October 1985. As a result, retail sales of the paperback began on September 15, 1985, and early sales were sufficiently substantial that the Book was near the top of paperback bestseller lists before the end of September 1985.

Naval commenced the present action when it learned of Berkley's plans for early shipment, and it unsuccessfully sought a preliminary injunction. After trial, the district judge dismissed the complaint. He ruled that Berkley had not breached the Agreement because it was entitled, in accordance with industry custom, to ship prior to the agreed publication date. On appeal, we reversed. Though we upheld the district court's finding that the Agreement did not prohibit the early shipments themselves, we concluded that if the "not sooner than October 1985" term of the Agreement had any meaning whatever, it meant at least that Berkley was not allowed to cause such voluminous paperback retail sales prior to that date, and that Berkley had therefore breached the Agreement. *Naval I,* 875 F.2d at 1049–51. Accordingly, we remanded for entry of a judgment awarding Naval appropriate relief.

On the remand, Naval asserted that it was entitled to recovery for copyright infringement, and it sought judgment awarding it all of Berkley's profits from pre-October 1985 sales of the Book; it estimated those profits at $724,300. It also requested prejudgment interest, costs, and attorney's fees. Berkley, on the other hand, challenged Naval's right to any recovery at all, contending, *inter alia,* that Berkley could not be held liable for copyright infringement since the Agreement had made it the exclusive licensee of the paperback edition copyright as of September 14, 1984; it argued that Naval therefore had at most a claim for breach-of-contract but that Berkley could not be held liable on that basis because Naval had disavowed its pursuit of a contract claim. Berkley also argued that the profits attributed to it by Naval were inflated, and it opposed any award of prejudgment interest or attorney's fees.

In a Memorandum and Order dated July 17, 1990, 1990 WL 104027 ("July 17 Order"), the district judge rejected Berkley's claim that "its premature publication of the paperback edition constituted only a contract violation and not an infringement of Naval's copyright." *Id.* at 8. He found that Naval's copyright was infringed by the early publication because, though "the *extent* of the breach was a relatively trivial matter of two weeks of sales, the *term* breached was crucial to the scope of the license, as it governed when the license would take effect." *Id.* (emphasis in original). He concluded that Naval was entitled to recover damages for copyright infringement, comprising actual damages suffered by Naval plus Berkley's profits "attributable to the infringement," 17 U.S.C. § 504(b).

The court calculated Naval's "actual damages from Berkley's wrongful pre-October 'publication'" as the profits Naval would have earned from hardcover sales in September 1985 if the competing paperback edition had not then been offered for sale. July 17 Order at 8. Noting the downward trend of hardcover sales of the Book from March through August 1985, the court found that there was no reason to infer that Naval's September 1985 sales would have exceeded its August 1985 sales. The court calculated Naval's lost sales as the difference between the actual hardcover sales for those two months, and awarded Naval $35,380.50 as actual damages.

The district judge held that Berkley's profits "attributable to the infringement" were only those profits that resulted from "sales to customers who would not have bought the paperback but for the fact it became available in September." July 17 Order at 10. He found that most of the September paperback sales were made to buyers who would not have bought a hardcover edition in September, and therefore only those September sales that displaced hardcover sales were attributable to the infringement. Berkley's profit on the displacing copies totaled $7,760.12, and the court awarded that amount to Naval.

The court awarded Naval prejudgment interest (totaling $15,319.27) on the $35,380.50 awarded as actual damages but denied such interest on the award of Berkley's profits. It also denied Naval's request for attorney's fees.

Judgment was entered accordingly, and these appeals followed.

II. DISCUSSION . . .

A. *Naval's Claim of Copyright Infringement . . .*

The Agreement between Naval and Berkley, headed "Agreement made this 14th day of September 1984," granted Berkley, in & 1, "the exclusive right to publish and reproduce, distribute and sell English-language paperback editions" of the Book in the United States and certain other areas. Paragraph 2 of the Agreement stated that "[t]he term of this license will begin on the date written above"; it stated that the term of the license would continue until at least five years after the date of Berkley's "first publication" of the Book. Paragraph 4 provided that Berkley was to publish the paperback edition "not sooner than October 1985."

These provisions contradict the district court's finding that Berkley's publication date "governed when the license would take effect." Paragraph 2 provided that the license took effect on "the date written above"; since September 14, 1984, was the only date mentioned in the Agreement prior to & 3, the license term began on that date. Further, & 2's distinct references to (a) "the date written above" to define the start of the license term, and (b) Berkley's "first publication" date to anchor the continuation of the license term reveal that the parties deliberately did not define the start of the term by Berkley's first publication date. Thus, according to the express provisions of the Agreement, Berkley became the owner of the right to publish the paperback edition of the book in September 1984 and remained the owner of that right for at least five years after its first publication of that edition in 1985. Its publication of that edition in 1985 therefore could not constitute copyright infringement. . . .

B. Contract Damages

Our ruling that Naval is not entitled to recover under the Copyright Act does not, as Berkley would have it, require the entry of judgment in favor of Berkley. Though Berkley argues that Naval had abandoned its contract claim for money damages prior to trial, we thereafter ruled in *Naval I* that Naval was entitled to recover for breach of contract. . . . Our ruling in *Naval I* that Naval was entitled to recover for breach of the Agreement is the law of the case. . . .

As Naval has renounced any effort at rescission and has accepted Berkley's payments of substantial copyright royalties for paperback sales under the Agreement, plainly the relief to which Naval is entitled on its meritorious breach-of-contract claim is money damages.

The damages awarded by the district court on remand had two components: (1) Naval's lost profits resulting from Berkley's early publication of the paperback edition of the Book, and (2) Berkley's profits attributable to its assumed infringement. For the reasons discussed above, the latter component of the award cannot stand. The former component, however, may properly measure damages under a breach-of-contract theory.

Since the purpose of damages for breach of contract is to compensate the injured party for the loss caused by the breach, 5 *Corbin On Contracts* '1002, at 31 (1964), those damages are generally measured by the plaintiff's actual loss, *see, e.g., Restatement (Second) of Contracts* § 347 (1981). While on occasion the defendant's profits are used as the measure of damages, *see, e.g., Cincinnati Siemens-Lungren Gas Illuminating Co. v. Western Siemens-Lungren Co.*, 152 U.S. 200, 204–07, 14 S.Ct. 523, 525–26, 38 L.Ed. 411 (1894); *Murphy v. Lischitz*, 183 Misc. 575, 577, 49 N.Y.S.2d 439, 441 (Sup.Ct.N.Y. County 1944), *aff'd mem.*, 268 A.D. 1027, 52 N.Y.S.2d 943 (1st Dep't), *aff'd mem.*, 294 N.Y. 892, 63 N.E.2d 26 (1945), this generally occurs when those profits tend to define the plaintiff's loss, for an award of the defendant's profits where they greatly exceed the plaintiff's loss and there has been no tortious conduct on the part of the defendant would tend to be punitive, and punitive awards are not part of the law of contract damages. *See generally Restatement (Second) of Contracts* § 356 comment *a* ("The central objective behind the system of contract remedies is compensatory, not punitive."); *id.* comment *b* (agreement attempting to fix damages in amount vastly greater than what approximates actual loss would be unenforceable as imposing a penalty); *id.* § 355 (punitive damages not recoverable for breach of contract unless conduct constituting the breach is also a tort for which such damages are recoverable).

Here, the district court found that Berkley's alleged $724,300 profits did not define Naval's loss because many persons who bought the paperback in September 1985 would not have bought the book in hardcover but would merely have waited until the paperback edition became available. This finding is not clearly erroneous. . . .

[The court then held that Naval had proved with sufficient certainty the damages of $33,380.50 awarded by the trial court as the profits Naval would have earned on hardcover sales in September 1985 if the paperback edition had not then been offered for sale.]

CONCLUSION

. . . For the foregoing reasons, we reverse so much of the judgment as granted Naval $7,760.12 as an award of Berkley's profits. In all other respects, the judgment is affirmed.

No costs.

———

Laurin v. DeCarolis Construction Co.

372 Mass. 688, 363 N.E.2d 675 (1977)

In March 1971, the Laurins agreed to purchase a home that DeCarolis was then constructing. The home was situated on a well-wooded lot. Prior to the closing, the Laurins found that after the contract had been signed, DeCarolis had bulldozed many of the trees on the property. The Laurins ordered DeCarolis to desist, but DeCarolis continued to bulldoze trees and also removed gravel and loam worth $6480. The Laurins paid the purchase price of

$26,900 at the closing, and then sued DeCarolis for the value of the trees, gravel, and loam that DeCarolis had removed.

The case was tried by a master, who concluded that the Laurins were the "equitable owners" of the property from and after the signing of the agreement, so that DeCarolis had unlawfully converted the trees, gravel, and loam. In other words, the master reasoned that the Laurins were entitled to disgorgement under a property theory. The Massachusetts Supreme Judicial Court rejected this reasoning, on the ground that under Massachusetts law, "the rights of the purchaser of real property prior to closing are contract rights rather than property rights." Accordingly, the Court concluded, "[this] case must be decided, not as [an] action for injury to or conversion of property, but as a claim for a deliberate and willful breach of contract. . . . "

This left the contract theory. The problem was that taking the trees, gravel, and loam had not diminished the value of the property. Therefore, although DeCarolis had made a gain from breach, the Laurins had not suffered a loss. Nevertheless, the Court held that the Laurins were entitled to disgorgement, because DeCarolis should not be allowed to retain its gains from a willful breach of contract:

> . . . Particularly where the defendant's breach is deliberate and willful, we think damages limited to diminution in value of the premises may sometimes be seriously inadequate. "Cutting a few trees on a timber tract, or taking a few hundred tons of coal from a mine, might not diminish the market value of the tract, or of the mine, and yet the value of the wood or coal, severed from the soil, might be considerable. The wrongdoer would, in the cases instanced, be held to pay the value of the wood and coal, and he could not shield himself by showing that the property from which it was taken was, as a whole, worth as much as it was before." *Worrall v. Munn, 53 N.Y. 185, 190 (1873)*. This reasoning does not depend for its soundness on the holding of a property interest, as distinguished from a contractual interest, by the plaintiffs. Nor is it punitive; it merely deprives the defendant of a profit wrongfully made, a profit which the plaintiff was entitled to make. . . .

————

RESTATEMENT, THIRD, RESTITUTION AND UNJUST ENRICHMENT § 39

[See Selected Source Materials Supplement]

————

RESTATEMENT, THIRD, RESTITUTION AND UNJUST ENRICHMENT § 39, COMMENTS AND ILLUSTRATIONS

Comment b. Opportunistic breach. The common rationale of every instance in which restitution allows a recovery of profits from wrongdoing, in the contractual context or any other, is the reinforcement of an entitlement that would be inadequately protected if liability for interference were limited to provable damages. Cases in which restitution reaches the profits from a breach of contract are those in which the promisee's contractual position is vulnerable to abuse. Vulnerability in this context stems from the difficulty that the promisee may face in recovering, as compensatory damages, a full equivalent of the performance for which the promisee has bargained. A promisor who was permitted to exploit the shortcomings of the promisee's damage remedy could accept the price of the promised performance, then deliver something less than what was promised. Such an outcome results in unjust enrichment as between the parties. The mere possibility of such an outcome undermines the stability of any contractual exchange in which one party's performance may be neither easily compelled nor easily valued.

A promisor who recognizes this possibility and attempts to profit by it commits what is here called an "opportunistic breach." The label suggests the reasons why a breach of this character is condemned, but there is no requirement under this section that the claimant prove the motivation of the breaching party.

In countering this form of opportunism, the rule of § 39 reinforces the contractual position of the vulnerable party and condemns a form of conscious advantage-taking that is the equivalent, in the contractual context, of an intentional and profitable tort. A restitution claim in response to a profitable tort typically operates to protect property from deliberate interference: standard examples include the claim to profits from trespass or infringement. . . . The rule of § 39 extends an analogous protection to contract rights, where what the wrongdoer seeks to acquire is not "property" but the modification or release of his own contractual obligation. The two situations have much in common. Confronted with a situation—in either context—in which the appropriate course of action would be to negotiate regarding legal entitlements, the wrongdoer takes without asking. The opportunistic calculation in either setting is that the wrongdoer's anticipated liability in damages is less than the anticipated cost of the entitlement, were it to be purchased from the claimant in a voluntary transaction. Restitution (through the disgorgement remedy) seeks to defeat this calculation, reducing the likelihood that the conscious disregard of another's entitlement can be more advantageous than its negotiated acquisition. . . .

The broader function of disgorgement in the Illustrations that follow is not merely to frustrate conscious wrongdoers but to reinforce the stability of the contract itself, enhancing the ability of the parties to negotiate for a contractual performance that may not be easily valued in money. The result is to expand the range of transactions for which parties may effectively bargain. The point is seen by considering the position of the parties at the bargaining stage. Where the value of the promised performance is easily demonstrated—and substitutes are readily available—it may be plausible to attribute to the parties an understanding that the promisor shall be free, as a practical matter, to elect between performance and payment of damages. In other transactions ... the proposition that the promisor should be free to choose whether or not to perform would be incompatible with fundamental objectives of the promisee, ultimately making it impossible to fix a price for the promisor's contractual obligation. Absent an enforceable agreement on liquidated damages, the bargain in question is then less likely to be made.

Not by coincidence, the contractual entitlements that are vulnerable in the manner just described are those for which the promisee would most often be entitled to protection by injunction, or to a remedy by specific performance; or in which well-advised parties would most often provide by contract (where permitted to do so) for liquidated damages or specific enforceability. Disgorgement by the rule of this section serves the same contract-reinforcing objectives as the devices just mentioned, at a different stage of contractual performance.

    c.   Adequacy of a remedy in damages. If the promisee's contractual entitlement is adequately protected by a judgment for money damages, there is no claim to restitution by the rule of this section. (If the promisee's contractual entitlement is adequately compensated by an award of damages, there is no remedial vulnerability to be exploited, no opportunism, and no unjust enrichment.) The adequacy of a damage remedy in particular circumstances is a determination for the court, applying its governing law to its own understanding of the case before it; but § 39(2) provides the standard baseline of the inquiry. ...

Illustrations:

    . . .

    2.   Vendor and Purchaser agree on a sale of Blackacre for $100,000. The contract expressly provides that existing timber and gravel are to be conveyed with the property. Vendor removes timber and gravel which he sells for a net gain of $10,000. Purchaser takes title and commences an action against Vendor. Under local law, the contract of sale gives Purchaser no interest in the property prior to conveyance: accordingly, Purchaser has no action for conversion, being limited to the available remedies for breach of contract. Purchaser is entitled to recover $10,000 from Vendor by the

rule of this section. It is irrelevant that the removal of timber and gravel did not appreciably diminish the value of Blackacre. . . .

5.   Landowner and Mining Company enter a contract for strip-mining. The agreement authorizes Mining Company to remove coal from Blackacre in exchange for payment of a specified royalty per ton. A further provision of the agreement, included at Landowner's insistence, obliges Mining Company to restore the surface of Blackacre to its preexisting contours on the completion of mining operations. Mining Company removes the coal from Blackacre, pays the stipulated royalty, and repudiates its obligation to restore the land. In Landowner's action against Mining Company it is established that the cost of restoration would be $25,000, and that the diminution in the value of Blackacre if the restoration is not performed would be negligible. The contract is not affected by mistake or impracticability. The cost of restoration is in line with what Mining Company presumably anticipated, and the available comparisons suggest that Mining Company took this cost into account in calculating the contractual royalty. Landowner is entitled to recover $25,000 from Mining Company . . . . It is not a condition to Landowner's recovery in restitution that the money be used to restore Blackacre. . .

7.   City contracts with Firefighters' Association for fire protection services to be furnished during the ensuing 12 months. The contract specifies the number of men, horses, and wagons to be kept in readiness at specified times and places, and the contract price is negotiated as a function thereof. After the 12 months have elapsed and the full contract price has been paid, City discovers that Association consistently devoted fewer men, horses, and wagons to City's fire protection than the numbers required by contract. Association acted in deliberate breach of its contractual obligations, calculating—accurately as it turned out—that the resources specified by contract were in excess of City's firefighting needs. In consequence, Association saved $100,000 over the life of its contract with City; while City suffered no increased loss from fire as a result of Association's disregard of the contract specifications. City is entitled to recover $100,000 from Association by the rule of this section. . . .

9.   A licensing agreement between Coca-Cola and Bottler provides that products produced under license shall be manufactured in strict conformity to Coca-Cola's specifications, one of which calls for the use of cane sugar as the sweetening ingredient. In the course of renegotiating various aspects of the licensing agreement, Bottler asks to be allowed to substitute artificial sweeteners for sugar in the manufacture of certain licensed products. The parties fail to reach agreement on this point, and the amendment to the license resulting from their negotiations omits any modification of the product specifications. Acting in conscious disregard of its contractual obligations, Bottler substitutes low-cost artificial sweetener for sugar in the manufacture of licensed products. The products

manufactured from these different materials are for all practical purposes indistinguishable. By the time the practice comes to light, Bottler has saved $5 million by the use of the less expensive ingredients. Coca-Cola may require Bottler to disgorge $5 million by the rule of this section. It is not a condition of recovery that Coca-Cola prove damages as a result of Bottler's breach. . . .

––––––

Kansas v. Nebraska

574 U.S. 445, 135 S.Ct. 1042, 191 L.Ed.2d 1 (2015)

Nebraska was dilatory in implementing measures to decrease groundwater pumping that it knew were necessary to ensure it did not take more than its allotted share of water under an interstate compact with Kansas. The measures it took might have sufficed had there been prodigious amounts of rain. Instead there was drought. As a result the consumption of water by its residents exceeded its allocation under the compact with Kansas by 17 percent in 2005 and 2006. Kansas filed a claim in the U.S. Supreme Court, which has original jurisdiction over such matters. The Court appointed a special master who, after two years of proceedings, awarded Kansas $3.7 million compensatory damages and $1.8 million in "partial disgorgement" for the excess water taken by Nebraska in 2005–2006. Nebraska's gain from the breach exceeded Kansas' loss because "an acre-foot of water is substantially more valuable on farmland in Nebraska than in Kansas." The special master estimated Nebraska's gain was "several multiples" of Kansas' loss, which translates to a figure larger than $11.1 million. The special master found disgorgement to be appropriate because "Nebraska 'knowingly exposed Kansas to a substantial risk 'of receiving less water than the Compact provided, and so 'knowingly failed' to comply with the obligations." The master justified the $1.8 million award for disgorgement, and declined Kansas' request for an injunction, citing Nebraska's good faith efforts to bring itself into compliance with the compact after 2005–2006. Nebraska appealed, challenging the award of disgorgement damages. Kansas appealed asking for greater damages, among other things.

A divided Court affirmed the judgment. The majority held disgorgement damages were appropriate, though Nebraska did not deliberately breach the compact, because "Nebraska recklessly gambled with Kansas's rights, consciously disregarding a substantial probability that its actions would deprive Kansas of the water to which it was entitled." As for Kansas' request for full disgorgement, the majority held disgorgement need not be "all or nothing," and partial disgorgement will suffice when it "will serve to stabilize a compact by conveying an effective message to a breaching party that it must work hard to meet its future obligations." Three Justices dissented, arguing disgorgement was not justified because there was no "deliberate breach."

––––––

PART 3

ASSENT

■ ■ ■

The most common forms of contracts are bargains. A bargain requires mutual manifested assent. What constitutes mutual manifested assent for purposes of the law of contracts is sometimes a very difficult issue. That issue is considered in this Part.

Part 3 begins with Chapter 8, which concerns the basic principles of interpretation in contract law. Although problems of interpretation run through all areas of contract law, they are most salient when the issue is whether a person manifested assent to a contract or to a term.

Although bargains can be formed in more than one way, they are most commonly formed by an offer and an acceptance. Chapters 9 and 10 concern problems of offer and acceptance—problems such as what constitutes an offer, whether and when offers are revocable, and what kind of acceptance an offer requires.

Chapter 11 concerns the problems that arise where the terms of an agreement are indefinite or not final.

———

CHAPTER 8

AN INTRODUCTION TO INTERPRETATION

■ ■ ■

This Chapter concerns the interpretation of contractual language. It introduces the role of subjective and objective elements in contract interpretation. The subject of this Chapter could also be described as the general rules used to determine when a person assents to a contract or to a term of a contract. Special rules of interpretation often apply when people reduce an agreement to writing. These rules will be considered later, in Chapters 12 and 13, because they reflect policies that give primacy to written expressions of intent. Under these rules when a person assents to a writing they know (or should know) expresses terms of a contract they are likely to be held to a term in the writing even though they are unaware of the term.

LUCY V. ZEHMER
Supreme Court of Appeals of Virginia, 1954.
196 Va. 493, 84 S.E.2d 516.

BUCHANAN, JUSTICE. This suit was instituted by W.O. Lucy and J.C. Lucy, complainants, against A.H. Zehmer and Ida S. Zehmer, his wife, defendants, to have specific performance of a contract by which it was alleged the Zehmers had sold to W.O. Lucy a tract of land owned by A.H. Zehmer in Dinwiddie County containing 471.6 acres, more or less, known as the Ferguson farm, for $50,000. J.C. Lucy, the other complainant, is a brother of W.O. Lucy, to whom W.O. Lucy transferred a half interest in his alleged purchase.

The instrument sought to be enforced was written by A.H. Zehmer on December 20, 1952, in these words: "We hereby agree to sell to W.O. Lucy the Ferguson Farm complete for $50,000.00, title satisfactory to buyer," and signed by the defendants, A.H. Zehmer and Ida S. Zehmer.

The answer of A.H. Zehmer admitted that at the time mentioned W.O. Lucy offered him $50,000 cash for the farm, but that he, Zehmer considered that the offer was made in jest; that so thinking, and both he and Lucy having had several drinks, he wrote out "the memorandum" quoted above and induced his wife to sign it; that he did not deliver the memorandum to Lucy, but that Lucy picked it up, read it, put it in his pocket, attempted to offer Zehmer $5 to bind the bargain, which Zehmer refused to accept, and realizing for the first time that Lucy was serious, Zehmer assured him that he had no intention of selling the farm and that the whole matter was a joke. Lucy left the premises insisting that he had purchased the farm.

Depositions were taken and the decree appealed from was entered holding that the complainants had failed to establish their right to specific performance, and dismissing their bill. The assignment of error is to this action of the court.

W.O. Lucy, a lumberman and farmer, thus testified in substance: He had known Zehmer for fifteen or twenty years and had been familiar with the Ferguson farm for ten years. Seven or eight years ago he had offered Zehmer $20,000 for the farm which Zehmer had accepted, but the agreement was verbal and Zehmer backed out. On the night of December 20, 1952, around eight o'clock, he took an employee to McKenney, where Zehmer lived and operated a restaurant, filling station and motor court. While there he decided to see Zehmer and again try to buy the Ferguson farm. He entered the restaurant and talked to Mrs. Zehmer until Zehmer came in. He asked Zehmer if he had sold the Ferguson farm. Zehmer replied that he had not. Lucy said, "I bet you wouldn't take $50,000.00 for that place." Zehmer replied, "Yes, I would too; you wouldn't give fifty." Lucy said he would and told Zehmer to write up an agreement to that effect. Zehmer took a restaurant check and wrote on the back of it, "I do hereby agree to sell to W.O. Lucy the Ferguson Farm for $50,000 complete." Lucy told him he had better change it to "We" because Mrs. Zehmer would have to sign it too. Zehmer then tore up what he had written, wrote the agreement quoted above and asked Mrs. Zehmer, who was at the other end of the counter ten or twelve feet away, to sign it. Mrs. Zehmer said she would for $50,000 and signed it. Zehmer brought it back and gave it to Lucy, who offered him $5 which Zehmer refused, saying, "You don't need to give me any money, you got the agreement there signed by both of us."

The discussion leading to the signing of the agreement, said Lucy, lasted thirty or forty minutes, during which Zehmer seemed to doubt that Lucy could raise $50,000. Lucy suggested the provision for having the title examined and Zehmer made the suggestion that he would sell it "complete, everything there," and stated that all he had on the farm was three heifers.

December 20 was on Saturday. Next day Lucy telephoned to J.C. Lucy and arranged with the latter to take a half interest in the purchase and pay half of the consideration. On Monday he engaged an attorney to examine the title. The attorney reported favorably on December 31 and on January 2 Lucy wrote Zehmer stating that the title was satisfactory, that he was ready to pay the purchase price in cash and asking when Zehmer would be ready to close the deal. Zehmer replied by letter, mailed on January 13, asserting that he had never agreed or intended to sell.

Mr. and Mrs. Zehmer were called by the complainants as adverse witnesses. Zehmer testified in substance as follows.

He bought this farm more than ten years ago for $11,000. He had had twenty-five offers, more or less, to buy it, including several from Lucy, who had never offered any specific sum of money. He had given them all the same answer, that he was not interested in selling it. On this Saturday night before Christmas it looked like everybody and his brother came by there to have a drink. He took a good many drinks during the afternoon and had a pint of his own. When he entered the restaurant around eight-thirty Lucy was there and he could see that he was "pretty high." He said to Lucy, "Boy, you got some good liquor, drinking, ain't you?" Lucy then offered him a drink. "I was already high as a Georgia pine, and didn't have any more better sense than to pour another great big slug out and gulp it down, and he took one too."

After they had talked a while Lucy asked whether he still had the Ferguson farm. He replied that he had not sold it and Lucy said, "I bet you wouldn't take $50,000.00 for it." Zehmer asked him if he would give $50,000 and Lucy said yes. Zehmer replied, "You haven't got $50,000.00 in cash." Lucy said he did and Zehmer replied that he did not believe it. They argued "pro and con for a long time," mainly about "whether he had $50,000 in cash that he could put up right then and buy that farm."

Finally, said Zehmer, Lucy told him if he didn't believe he had $50,000, "you sign that piece of paper here and say you will take $50,000.00 for the farm." He, Zehmer, "just grabbed the back off of a guest check there" and wrote on the back of it. At that point in his testimony Zehmer asked to see what he had written to "see if I recognize my own handwriting." He examined the paper and exclaimed, "Great balls of fire, I got 'Firgerson' for Ferguson. I have got satisfactory spelled wrong. I don't recognize that writing if I would see it, wouldn't know it was mine."

After Zehmer had, as he described it, "scribbled this thing off," Lucy said, "Get your wife to sign it." Zehmer walked over to where she was and she at first refused to sign but did so after he told her that he "was just needling him [Lucy], and didn't mean a thing in the world, that I was not selling the farm." Zehmer then "took it back over there . . . and I was still looking at the dern thing. I had the drink right there by my hand, and I reached over to get a drink, and he said, 'Let me see it.' He reached and picked it up, and when I looked back again he had it in his pocket and he dropped a five dollar bill over there, and he said, 'Here is five dollars payment on it.' . . . I said, 'Hell no, that is beer and liquor talking. I am not going to sell you the farm. I have told you that too many times before.'" [Mrs. Zehmer's testimony was comparable to that of Mr. Zehmer. She added that after Lucy said, "All right, get your wife to sign it." Zehmer came back to where she was standing and said, "You want to put your name to this?" She said "No," but he said in an undertone, "It is nothing but a joke," and she signed it.] . . .

The defendants insist that the evidence was ample to support their contention that the writing sought to be enforced was prepared as a bluff or dare to force Lucy to admit that he did not have $50,000; that the whole matter was a joke; that the writing was not delivered to Lucy and no binding contract was ever made between the parties. . . .

In his testimony Zehmer claimed that he "was high as a Georgia pine," and that the transaction "was just a bunch of two doggoned drunks bluffing to see who could talk the biggest and say the most." That claim is inconsistent with his attempt to testify in great detail as to what was said and what was done. It is contradicted by other evidence as to the condition of both parties. . . . It was in fact conceded by defendants' counsel in oral argument that under the evidence Zehmer was not too drunk to make a valid contract. . . .

The appearance of the contract, the fact that it was under discussion for forty minutes or more before it was signed; Lucy's objection to the first draft because it was written in the singular, and he wanted Mrs. Zehmer to sign it also; the rewriting to meet that objection and the signing by Mrs. Zehmer; the discussion of what was to be included in the sale, the provision for the examination of the title, the completeness of the instrument that was executed, the taking possession of it by Lucy with no request or suggestion by either of the defendants that he give it back, are facts which furnish persuasive evidence that the execution of the contract was a serious business transaction rather than a casual, jesting matter as defendants now contend. . . .

If it be assumed, contrary to what we think the evidence shows, that Zehmer was jesting about selling his farm to Lucy and that the transaction was intended by him to be a joke, nevertheless the evidence shows that Lucy did not so understand it but considered it to be a serious business transaction and the contract to be binding on the Zehmers as well as on himself. . . .

Not only did Lucy actually believe, but the evidence shows he was warranted in believing, that the contract represented a serious business transaction and a good faith sale and purchase of the farm.

In the field of contracts, as generally elsewhere, "We must look to the outward expression of a person as manifesting his intention rather than to his secret and unexpressed intention. 'The law imputes to a person an intention corresponding to the reasonable meaning of his words and acts.'" First Nat. Exchange Bank of Roanoke v. Roanoke Oil Co., 169 Va. 99, 114, 192 S.E. 764, 770.

[margin note:] Evidence in favor of K's validity

At no time prior to the execution of the contract had Zehmer indicated to Lucy by word or act that he was not in earnest about selling the farm. They had argued about it and discussed its terms, as Zehmer admitted, for a long time. Lucy testified that if there was any jesting it was about paying $50,000 that night. The contract and the evidence show that he was not expected to pay the money that night. Zehmer said that after the writing was signed he laid it down on the counter in front of Lucy. Lucy said Zehmer handed it to him. In any event there had been what appeared to be a good faith offer and a good faith acceptance, followed by the execution and apparent delivery of a written contract. Both said that Lucy put the writing in his pocket and then offered Zehmer $5 to seal the bargain. Not until then, even under the defendants' evidence, was anything said or done to indicate that the matter was a joke. Both of the Zehmers testified that when Zehmer asked his wife to sign he whispered that it was a joke so Lucy wouldn't hear and that it was not intended that he should hear.

The mental assent of the parties is not requisite for the formation of a contract. If the words or other acts of one of the parties have but one reasonable meaning, his undisclosed intention is immaterial except when an unreasonable meaning which he attaches to his manifestations is known to the other party. Restatement of the Law of Contracts, Vol. I, § 71, p. 74. . . .

So a person cannot set up that he was merely jesting when his conduct and words would warrant a reasonable person in believing that he intended a real agreement. 17 C.J.S., Contracts, § 47, p. 390; Clark on Contracts, 4 ed., § 27, at p. 54.

Whether the writing signed by the defendants and now sought to be enforced by the complainants was the result of a serious offer by Lucy and a serious acceptance by the defendants, or was a serious offer by Lucy and an acceptance in secret jest by the defendants, in either event it constituted a binding contract of sale between the parties. *[handwritten: whether joke or serious, it is binding]*

Defendants contend further, however, that even though a contract was made, equity should decline to enforce it under the circumstances. These circumstances have been set forth in detail above. They disclose some drinking by the two parties but not to an extent that they were unable to understand fully what they were doing. There was no fraud, no misrepresentation, no sharp practice and no dealing between unequal parties. The farm had been bought for $11,000 and was assessed for taxation at $6,300. The purchase price was $50,000. Zehmer admitted that it was a good price. There is in fact present in this case none of the grounds usually urged against specific performance. . . . *[handwritten: very good price]*

The complainants are entitled to have specific performance of the contract sued on. The decree appealed from is therefore reversed and the cause is remanded for the entry of a proper decree requiring the defendants to perform the contract in accordance with the prayer of the bill.

Reversed and remanded.

RESTATEMENT, SECOND, CONTRACTS §§ 12, 16

[See Selected Source Materials Supplement]

RESTATEMENT, SECOND, CONTRACTS § 16, ILLUSTRATION 3 AND COMMENTS A AND B

Illustration 3. A has been drinking heavily. B, who has also been drinking, meets A, offers to buy A's farm for $50,000, a fair price, and offers A a drink which A accepts. In drunken exhilaration A, as a joke, writes out and signs a memorandum of agreement to sell, gets his wife to sign it, and delivers it to B, who understands the transaction as a serious one. A's intoxication is no defense to B's suit for specific performance...

Comment a. Because drunkenness has both voluntary and compulsive aspects, the courts have been ambivalent toward it as an incapacity defense. A way of avoiding the problem is to focus on the conduct of the other party and the fairness of the contract. This was the approach taken in Lucy v. Zehmer, 196 Va. 493, 84 S.E.2d 516 (1954). If one party takes advantage of the other's drunkenness and an unfair contract is entered into, a stronger case is made under the fraud, overreaching and unconscionability concepts than under capacity concepts, because the critical factor appears to be the conduct of the sober party, rather than the inability of the drunkard. In extreme cases, no manifestation of assent may occur, but otherwise, the problem seems closer to that of persons of mild mental retardation or dull normal intelligence where extra protection should be given rather than capacity denied....

b.   What contracts are voidable. The standard of competency in intoxication cases is the same as that in cases of mental illness. A contract made by a person who is so drunk he does not know what he is doing is voidable if the other party has reason to know of the intoxication. Where there is some understanding of the transaction despite intoxication, avoidance depends on a showing that the other party induced the drunkenness or that the consideration was inadequate or that the transaction departed from the normal pattern of similar transactions; if the particular transaction in its result is one which a reasonably competent person might have made, it cannot be avoided even though entirely executory.

———

Keller v. Holderman

11 Mich. 248, 83 Am.Dec. 737 (1863)

Suit against the maker of a check for $300, which had been given in return for an old silver watch, worth about $15. The court said, "when the court below found as a fact that 'the whole transaction between the parties was a frolic and a banter, the plaintiff not expecting to sell, nor the defendant to buy the watch at the sum for which the check was drawn,' the conclusion should have been that no contract was ever made by the parties, and the finding should have been that no cause of action existed upon the check to the plaintiff."

[handwritten margin note: If both parties think it is a joke, it is not binding]

———

RAFFLES V. WICHELHAUS
In the Court of Exchequer, 1864.
2 Hurl. & C. 906.

Declaration. For that it was agreed between the plaintiff and the defendants, to wit, at Liverpool, that the plaintiff should sell to the defendants, and the defendants buy of the plaintiff, certain goods, to wit, 125 bales of Surat cotton, guaranteed middling fair merchant's dhollorah, to arrive ex Peerless from Bombay; and that the cotton should be taken from the quay, and that the defendants would pay the plaintiff for the same at a certain rate, to wit, at the rate of 17¼ d. per pound, within a certain time then agreed upon after the arrival of the said goods in England. Averments: that the said goods did arrive by the said ship from Bombay in England, to wit, at Liverpool, and the plaintiff was then and there ready and willing and offered to deliver the said goods to the defendants, etc. Breach: that the defendants refused to accept the said goods or pay the plaintiff for them.

Plea. That the said ship mentioned in the said agreement was meant and intended by the defendant to be the ship called the Peerless, which sailed from Bombay, to wit, in October; and that the plaintiff was not ready and willing, and did not offer to deliver to the defendants any bales of cotton which arrived by the last-mentioned ship, but instead thereof was only ready and willing, and offered to deliver to the defendants 125 bales of Surat cotton which arrived by another and different ship, which was also called the Peerless, and which sailed from Bombay, to wit, in December.

[handwritten margin note: D says: different ship, different month, no k]

Demurrer, and joinder therein.

Milward, in support of the demurrer. The contract was for the sale of a number of bales of cotton of a particular description, which the plaintiff was ready to deliver. It is immaterial by what ship the cotton was to arrive, so that it was a ship called the Peerless. The words "to arrive ex Peerless," only mean that if the vessel is lost on the voyage, the contract is to be at an end. [Pollock, C.B. It would be a question for the jury whether both parties meant the same ship called the Peerless.] That would be so if the contract was for the sale of a ship called the Peerless; but it is for the sale of cotton on board a ship of that name. [Pollock, C.B. The defendant only bought that cotton which was to arrive by a particular ship. It may as well be said, that if there is a contract for the purchase of certain goods in warehouse A., that is satisfied by the delivery of goods of the same description in warehouse B.] In that case there would be goods in both warehouses; here it does not appear that the plaintiff had any goods on board the other Peerless. [Martin, B. It is imposing on the defendant a contract different from that which he entered into. Pollock, C.B. It is like a contract for the purchase of wine coming from a particular estate in France or Spain, where there are two estates of that name.] The defendant has no right to contradict by parol evidence, a written contract good upon the face of it. He does not impute misrepresentation or fraud, but only says that he fancied the ship was a different one. Intention is of no avail, unless stated at the time of the contract. [Pollock, C.B. One vessel sailed in October and the other in December.] The time of sailing is no part of the contract.

Mellish (Cohen with him), in support of the plea. There is nothing on the face of the contract to show that any particular ship called the Peerless was meant; but the moment it appears that two ships called the Peerless were about to sail from Bombay there is a latent ambiguity, and parol evidence may be given for the purpose of showing that the defendant meant one Peerless and the plaintiff another. That being so, there was no consensus ad idem, and therefore no binding contract. He was then stopped by the Court.

PER CURIAM. There must be judgment for the defendants.

Judgment for the defendants.

———

Simpson, Contracts for Cotton to Arrive: The Case of the Two Ships *Peerless*

11 Cardozo L. Rev. 287, 295 (1989)

"There were reports of at least eleven ships called *Peerless* sailing the seven seas at the time [of the *Peerless* case], for the name was a popular one. The *Mercantile Navy List* for 1863 lists nine British registered sailing vessels of that name, their ports of registration being London, Aberystwyth, Dartmouth, Greenock, Halifax, Windsor (Nova Scotia), Hull, and Liverpool, which boasted two such ships. There were also two American ships named

Peerless from Boston and Baltimore. The existence of so many vessels of the same or a similar name could obviously cause confusion in shipping movement reports. There was nothing unusual however in this state of affairs. Ships commonly shared the same name, particularly popular names such as *Annie*. But the two vessels with which we are concerned can readily be identified as the two which were registered at Liverpool. At the time it was the practice in the shipping press to differentiate vessels bearing the same name by the names of their captains, not, as one might expect, by using their unique registered number."

NOTE ON MUTUAL MISUNDERSTANDING

Raffles v. Wichelhaus generally is described as a case of mutual misunderstanding. In almost all of the cases covered in this chapter there is a misunderstanding either about the existence of a contract or about a material term. In *Raffles*, the misunderstanding was about a material term: whether the contract was for cotton on a vessel sailing from Bombay in October or in December. In *Lucy v. Zehmer*, if you believe Zehmer's testimony (the Virginia Supreme Court did not), the misunderstanding was about the existence of a contract: whether the sale was made in jest. *Lucy v. Zehmer* illustrates the law's usual way of handling a misunderstanding, which is to adopt the understanding of the party who is less at fault; this is the party who holds the more reasonable understanding. The label *mutual misunderstanding* is reserved for cases in which neither party is more at fault. *Raffles* illustrates the law's usual response in such cases.

Frigaliment Importing Co. v. B.N.S. Intern. Sales Corp., 190 F. Supp. 116 (S.D.N.Y. 1960), is a modern variation on *Raffles*. The contract was for the sale of chicken. The New York seller thought it could fill the contract with older and larger birds more precisely described as stewing chicken or fowl. The Swiss buyer thought it was buying younger and smaller birds more precisely described as broilers or fryers. The trial judge was Henry Friendly, one of the most respected jurists of the mid-20th century. His opinion carefully reviews the relevant evidence, including the correspondence between the parties, the parties' testimony of what they understood chicken to mean, the definition of chicken in authoritative sources, such as dictionaries and government regulations, and expert testimony on trade usage. The concluding passages in the opinion identify another relevant consideration and summarize the key factual findings:

> Defendant makes a further argument based on the impossibility of its obtaining broilers and fryers at the 33 cents price offered by plaintiff for the 2 1/2–3 lbs. birds. There is no substantial dispute that, in late April, 1957, the price for 2 1/2–3 lbs. broilers was between 35 and 37 cents per pound, and that when defendant entered into the contracts, it was well aware of this and intended to fill them by supplying fowl in these weights. It claims that plaintiff must likewise

have known the market since plaintiff had reserved shipping space on April 23, three days before plaintiff's cable to Stovicek, or, at least, that Stovicek was chargeable with such knowledge. It is scarcely an answer to say, as plaintiff does in its brief, that the 33 cents price offered by the 2 ½–3 lbs. "chickens" was closer to the prevailing 35 cents price for broilers than to the 30 cents at which defendant procured fowl. Plaintiff must have expected defendant to make some profit—certainly it could not have expected defendant deliberately to incur a loss. . . .

When all the evidence is reviewed, it is clear that defendant believed it could comply with the contracts by delivering stewing chicken in the 2 ½–3 lbs. size. Defendant's subjective intent would not be significant if this did not coincide with an objective meaning of "chicken." Here it did coincide with one of the dictionary meanings, with the definition in the Department of Agriculture Regulations to which the contract made at least oblique reference, with at least some usage in the trade, with the realities of the market, and with what plaintiff's spokesman had said. Plaintiff asserts it to be equally plain that plaintiff's own subjective intent was to obtain broilers and fryers; the only evidence against this is the material as to market prices and this may not have been sufficiently brought home. In any event it is unnecessary to determine that issue. For plaintiff has the burden of showing that "chicken" was used in the narrower rather than in the broader sense, and this it has not sustained.

The following year, Judge Friendly stated that *Frigaliment* might better have been placed on the ground of failure of the minds to meet, under *Raffles v. Wichelhaus*, "with the loss still left on the plaintiff because defendant's not unjustifiable change of position. . . . " Dadourian Export Corp. v. United States, 291 F.2d 178, 187 n. 4. (2d Cir.1961) (dissenting opinion). The reason the loss was left on the plaintiff (the buyer) was that it had paid the contract price for the first shipment of stewing hen and was seeking damages for breach of warranty. The plaintiff might have done better had it pled in the alternative that if the contract was not for broilers, then there was no contract (as in *Raffles*), and it was entitled to recover, in a restitution claim, the difference between the price it paid and the market price of fowl less the defendant's shipping costs. See Chapter 10, Section 5.

Oswald v. Allen

417 F.2d 43 (2d Cir.1969)

Oswald, a coin collector from Switzerland, was interested in Allen's collection of Swiss coins. In April 1964, Oswald was in the United States and the parties drove to the Newburgh Savings Bank, where two of Allen's coin collections were located. Oswald first examined the coins in Allen's Swiss Coin Collection, and was then shown several valuable Swiss coins from Allen's

Rarity Coin Collection. Oswald took notes on each collection. On the parties' return from the bank, a price of $50,000 was agreed upon for Allen's collection of Swiss coins. However, Oswald thought he was buying all of Allen's Swiss coins, while Allen thought she was selling only the Swiss Coin Collection, but not the Swiss coins in the Rarity Coin Collection. The evidence showed that each collection had its own key number, and was housed in a labeled cigar box. Oswald, however, testified that he did not know that some of the Swiss coins he examined were in a separate Collection. Held, no contract was formed. "Even though the mental assent of the parties is not requisite for the formation of a contract . . . the facts . . . clearly place this case within the small group of exceptional cases in which there is 'no sensible basis for choosing between conflicting understandings.' . . . The rule of Raffles v. Wichelhaus is applicable here."

Colfax Envelope Corp. v. Local No. 458-3M

20 F.3d 750 (7th Cir.1994)

"*Raffles* and *Oswald* were cases in which neither party was blameable for the mistake. . . . If neither party can be assigned the greater blame for the misunderstanding, there is no nonarbitrary basis for deciding which party's understanding to enforce, so the parties are allowed to abandon the contract without liability. . . . These are not cases in which one party's understanding is more reasonable than the other's. Compare Restatement . . . § 20(2)(b). If rescission were permitted in that kind of case, the enforcement of every contract would be at the mercy of a jury, which might be persuaded that one of the parties had genuinely held an idiosyncratic idea of its meaning, so that there had been, in fact, no meeting of the minds."

EMBRY V. HARGADINE, McKITTRICK DRY GOODS CO.

St. Louis Court of Appeals, Missouri, 1907.
127 Mo.App. 383, 105 S.W. 777.

Action by Charles R. Embry against the Hargadine-McKittrick Dry Goods Company. From a judgment for defendant, plaintiff appeals. Reversed and remanded.

GOODE, J. We dealt with this case on a former appeal (115 Mo.App. 130, 91 S.W. 170). It has been retried, and is again before us for the determination of questions not then reviewed. The appellant was an employee of the respondent company under a written contract to expire December 15, 1903, at a salary of $2,000 per annum. His duties were to attend to the sample department of respondent, of which he was given complete charge. It was his business to select samples for the traveling salesmen of the company, which is a wholesale dry goods concern, to use in selling goods to retail merchants.

Appellant contends that on December 23, 1903, he was re-engaged by respondent, through its president, Thos. H. McKittrick, for another year at the same compensation and for the same duties stipulated in his previous written contract. On March 1, 1904, he was discharged, having been notified in February that, on account of the necessity of retrenching expenses, his services and that of some other employees would no longer be required.

The respondent company contends that its president never re-employed appellant after the termination of his written contract, and hence that it had a right to discharge him when it chose. The point with which we are concerned requires an epitome of the testimony of appellant and the counter testimony of McKittrick, the president of the company, in reference to the alleged re-employment.

Appellant testified: That several times prior to the termination of his written contract on December 15, 1903, he had endeavored to get an understanding with McKittrick for another year, but had been put off from time to time. That on December 23d, eight days after the expiration of said contract, he called on McKittrick, in the latter's office, and said to him that as appellant's written employment had lapsed eight days before, and as there were only a few days between then and the 1st of January in which to seek employment with other firms, if respondent wished to retain his services longer he must have a contract for another year, or he would quit respondent's service then and there. That he had been put off twice before and wanted an understanding or contract at once so that he could go ahead without worry. That McKittrick asked him how he was getting along in his department, and appellant said he was very busy, as they were in the height of the season getting men out—had about 110 salesmen on the line and others in preparation. That McKittrick then said: "Go ahead, you're all right. Get your men out, and don't let that worry you." That appellant took McKittrick at his word and worked until February 15th without any question in his mind. It was on February 15th that he was notified his services would be discontinued on March 1st.

McKittrick denied this conversation as related by appellant, and said that, when accosted by the latter on December 23d he (McKittrick) was working on his books in order to get out a report for a stockholders' meeting, and, when appellant said if he did not get a contract he would leave, that he (McKittrick) said: "Mr. Embry, I am just getting ready for the stockholders' meeting to-morrow. I have no time to take it up now. I have told you before I would not take it up until I had these matters out of the way. You will have to see me at a later time. I said: 'Go back upstairs and get your men out on the road.' I may have asked him one or two other questions relative to the department, I don't remember. The whole conversation did not take more than a minute."

Embry also swore that, when he was notified he would be discharged, he complained to McKittrick about it, as being a violation of their contract, and McKittrick said it was due to the action of the board of directors, and not to any personal action of his, and that others would suffer by what the board had done as well as Embry. Appellant requested an instruction to the jury setting out, in substance, the conversation between him and McKittrick according to his version, and declaring that those facts, if found to be true, constituted a contract between the parties that defendant would pay plaintiff the sum of $2,000 for another year, provided the jury believed from the evidence that plaintiff commenced said work believing he was to have $2,000 for the year's work. This instruction was refused, but the court gave another embodying in substance appellant's version of the conversation, and declaring it made a contract "if you (the jury) find both parties thereby intended and did contract with each other for plaintiff's employment for one year from and including December 23, 1903, at a salary of $2,000 per annum." Embry swore that, on several occasions when he spoke to McKittrick about employment for the ensuing year, he asked for a renewal of his former contract, and that on December 23d, the date of the alleged renewal, he went into Mr. McKittrick's office and told him his contract had expired, and he wanted to renew it for a year, having always worked under year contracts. Neither the refused instruction nor the one given by the court embodied facts quite as strong as appellant's testimony, because neither referred to appellant's alleged statement to McKittrick that unless he was re-employed he would stop work for respondent then and there.

It is assigned for error that the court required the jury, in order to return a verdict for appellant, not only to find the conversation occurred as appellant swore, but that both parties intended by such conversation to contract with each other for plaintiff's employment for the year from December 1903, at a salary of $2,000. If it appeared from the record that there was a dispute between the parties as to the terms on which appellant wanted re-employment, there might have been sound reason for inserting this clause in the instruction; but no issue was made that they split on terms; the testimony of McKittrick tending to prove only that he refused to enter into a contract with appellant regarding another year's employment until the annual meeting of stockholders was out of the way. Indeed as to the proposed terms McKittrick agrees with Embry, for the former swore as follows: "Mr. Embry said he wanted to know about the renewal of his contract. Said if he did not have the contract made he would leave." As the two witnesses coincided as to the terms of the proposed re-employment, there was no reason for inserting the above mentioned clause in the instruction in order that it might be settled by the jury whether or not plaintiff, if employed for one year from December 23, 1903, was to be paid $2,000 a year. Therefore it remains to determine whether or not this part of the instruction was a correct statement of the law in regard to what was necessary to constitute a contract between the parties; that is to say, whether the formation of a contract by what, according to Embry, was said, depended on the intention of both Embry and McKittrick. Or, to put the question more precisely: Did what was said constitute a contract of re-employment on the previous terms irrespective of the intention or purpose of McKittrick?

Judicial opinion and elementary treatises abound in statements of the rule that to constitute a contract there must be a meeting of the minds of the parties, and both must agree to the same thing in the same sense. Generally speaking, this may be true; but it is not literally or universally true. That is to say, the inner intention of parties to a conversation subsequently alleged to create a contract cannot either make a contract of what transpired, or prevent one from arising, if the words used were sufficient to constitute a contract. In so far as their intention is an influential element, it is only such intention as the words or acts of the parties indicate; not one secretly cherished which is inconsistent with those words or acts. . . .

In Smith v. Hughes, L.R. 6 Q.B. 597, 607, it was said: "If, whatever a man's real intention may be, he so conducts himself that a reasonable man would believe that he was assenting to the terms proposed by the other party, and that other party upon that belief enters into the contract with him, the man thus conducting himself would be equally bound as if he had intended to agree to the other party's terms." . . .

In view of those authorities, we hold that, though McKittrick may not have intended to employ Embry by what transpired between them according to the latter's testimony, yet if what McKittrick said would have been taken by a reasonable man to be an employment, and Embry so understood it, it constituted a valid contract of employment for the ensuing year.

The next question is whether or not the language used was of that character, namely, was such that Embry, as a reasonable man, might consider that he was re-employed for the ensuing year on the previous terms, and act accordingly. We do not say that in every instance it would be for the court to pronounce on this question, because, peradventure, instances might arise in which there would be such an ambiguity in the language relied on to show an assent by the obligor to the proposal of the obligee that it would be for the jury to say whether a reasonable mind would take it to signify acceptance of the proposal. . . . Embry was demanding a renewal of his contract, saying he had been put off from time to time and that he had only a few days before the end of the year in which to seek employment from other houses, and that he would quit then and there unless he was re-employed. McKittrick inquired how he was getting along with the department, and Embry said they, i.e., the employees of the department, were very busy getting out salesmen. Whereupon McKittrick said: "Go ahead, you are all right. Get your men out, and do not let that worry you." We think no reasonable man would construe that answer to Embry's demand that he be employed for another year, otherwise than as an assent to the demand, and that Embry had the right to rely on it as an assent. . . . The answer was unambiguous, and we rule that if the conversation was according to appellant's version, and he understood he was employed, it constituted in law a valid contract of re-employment, and the court erred in making the formation of a contract depend on a finding that both parties intended to make one. . . .

The judgment is reversed, and the cause remanded. All concur.

RESTATEMENT, SECOND, CONTRACTS §§ 20, 201

[See Selected Source Materials Supplement]

CISG ART. 8

[See Selected Source Materials Supplement]

UNIDROIT PRINCIPLES OF INTERNATIONAL COMMERCIAL CONTRACTS ARTS. 4.1, 4.2, 4.3

[See Selected Source Materials Supplement]

PRINCIPLES OF EUROPEAN CONTRACT LAW ARTS. 5.101, 5.102

[See Selected Source Materials Supplement]

Morales v. Sun Constructors, Inc.

541 F.3d 218 (3d Cir. 2008)

As a condition to his employment, Juan Morales, "a Spanish-speaking welder who resided in St. Croix, United States Virgin Islands," was required to sign a 13-page hourly employment agreement that was presented to him at the end of a 2½-hour orientation conducted entirely in English. Morales was given some help at the orientation:

> The Sun employee who conducted the orientation, Mr. Langner, asked Jose Hodge (Hodge), a bilingual applicant who was also present at the orientation, and whom Morales knew, to explain to Morales what Langner was saying and help him fill out the documents. Hodge testified that he generally understands about eighty-five percent of what is said and written in English. He also stated that Morales did not ask him what he was signing and that he did not specifically explain the arbitration clause to Morales. Mr. Langner stated that he did explain the arbitration provisions in English and that, during the orientation, Hodge was speaking to Morales in a foreign language. . . .

Morales was fired by Sun after a year. When he brought a suit for wrongful termination in the District Court, Sun filed a motion to have the proceedings stayed pending arbitration. The District Court denied the motion, determining Morales had not assented to the arbitration clause. The Third Circuit reversed and remanded with instructions to enter a stay pending arbitration.

(Chagares, J.) "The Supreme Court has observed: "It will not do for a man to enter into a contract, and, when called upon to respond to its obligations, to say that he did not read it when he signed it, or did not know what it contained." *Upton v. Tribilcock,* 91 U.S. 45, 50, 23 L.Ed. 203 (1875). The "integrity of contracts demands" that this principle "be rigidly enforced by the courts." 1 Richard A. Lord, *Williston on Contracts* § 4:19 (4th ed.2008). As one noted treatise explains:

> According to the objective theory of contract formation, what is essential is not assent, but rather what the person to whom a manifestation is made is justified as regarding as assent. Thus, if an offeree, in ignorance of the terms of an offer, so acts or expresses itself as to justify the other party in inferring assent, and this action or expression was of such a character that a reasonable person in the position of the offeree should have known it was calculated to lead the offeror to believe that the offer had been accepted, a contract will be formed in spite of the offeree's ignorance of the terms of the offer. The most common illustration of this principle is the situation when one who is ignorant of the language in which a document is written, or who is illiterate, executes a writing proposed as a contract under a mistake as to its contents. Such a person is bound, in the absence of fraud, if the person does not require the document to be read to him. . .

Id. See New York Life Ins. Co. v. Kwetkauskas, 63 F.2d 890, 891 (3d Cir.1933) (recognizing that "[i]t is true that an illiterate man may bind himself by contract by negligently failing to learn the contents of an instrument which he has executed"); *Hoshaw v. Cosgriff,* 247 F. 22, 26 (8th Cir.1917) (holding that every contracting party has the duty "to learn and know the contents of a contract before he signs and delivers it"). . . .

"Morales, in essence, requests that this Court create an exception to the objective theory of contract formation where a party is ignorant of the language in which a contract is written. We decline to do so. In the absence of fraud, the fact that an offeree cannot read, write, speak, or understand the English language is immaterial to whether an English-language agreement the offeree executes is enforceable. *See Paper Express, Ltd. v. Pfankuch Maschinen,* 972 F.2d 753, 757 (7th Cir.1992) (addressing a contract dispute between an Illinois corporation and a German corporation and holding that parties should be held to contracts, even if the contracts are in foreign languages or the parties cannot read or understand the contracts due to blindness or illiteracy); *Shirazi v. Greyhound Corp.,* 145 Mont. 421, 401 P.2d 559, 562 (1965) (holding Iranian student subject to limitation contained in baggage receipt and stating that "[i]t was incumbent upon [the plaintiff], who knew of his own inability to read the English language, to acquaint himself with the contents of the ticket"); *Paulink v. Am. Express* Co., 265 Mass. 182, 163 N.E. 740, 741 (1928) (stating that "plaintiff was bound by the terms [of foreign bills of exchange], in the absence of deceit on the part of the defendant, even though not understanding their purport and ignorant of the English language"); *Wilkisius v. Sheehan,* 258 Mass. 240, 155 N.E. 5, 6 (1927) (holding that Lithuanian husband and wife, who did not speak or understand English and used an interpreter to contract for an exchange of real estate, were bound by the terms of the agreement because "their failure to understand these details was not due to fraudulent acts on the part of the defendant but to their own inability to read, write, speak or understand the English language, and to the incapacity of the interpreter").

"Morales is not claiming fraud, . . . and he is not alleging that Sun misrepresented the contents of the Agreement to him. . . ."

(Fuentes, J., dissenting) "No one disputes that Sun asked Hodge to translate the Employment Agreement for Morales, who did not read English. And no one disputes that Hodge failed to translate the arbitration clause in the Agreement. On this basis, I disagree with my colleagues' conclusion that the parties here manifested mutual assent to the arbitration clause of the Agreement, and I would therefore affirm the District Court's decision.

"The majority opens its opinion by asserting that this case "requires us to determine whether an arbitration clause is enforceable where one party is ignorant of the language in which the agreement is written." Maj. Op. at 220. The problem, however, is not simply Morales' ignorance of the language. The gravamen of this case is that Sun—the other party to the Agreement—took upon itself the task of translating the Agreement for Morales and, in doing so, failed to convey the entire contents of the Agreement. What we must determine is whether this failure resulted in a lack of mutual assent; I believe that it did.

"The law is clear that a party may not be relieved of his or her obligations pursuant to a contract solely because he or she cannot understand the language in which that contract is written. However, the law is also clear that there are certain circumstances where a person's inability to comprehend the language in which a contract is written may result in a lack of mutual assent. . . .

"The majority appears to agree that there can be such "special circumstances," but suggests that these circumstances exist *only* in a case where a fraud has been perpetuated. Maj. Op. at 223. I do not think that this is correct. In *New York Life,* the court noted that an illiterate signer will be held to a contract if he or she negligently failed to learn its contents; it does not automatically follow that an illiterate signer who is unaware of the contents of a contract but did not act in a negligent fashion will similarly be held to that contract unless he or she was a victim of fraud. 63 F.2d at 891. In *Pimpinello v. Swift & Co.,* another case cited by the majority, the court found that if a signer is "illiterate, or blind, or ignorant of the alien language of the writing" and the contents of a contract "are *misread or misinterpreted* to him" or her, the writing would be considered void unless the signer had acted negligently. 253 N.Y. 159, 163, 170 N.E. 530 (1930) (emphasis added). The court did not suggest that the contents would need to be *intentionally* "misread or misinterpreted" in order to void the writing. . . .

"Here, although Morales does not allege that Sun acted fraudulently, he does allege that Hodge, who was translating the document at Sun's direction, failed to inform Morales that the Agreement contained an arbitration clause. Importantly, Sun does not dispute the following factual findings made by the District Court: (1) Morales was unable to read the contract; (2) Sun assigned Hodge, a coworker who himself was not fluent in English, to translate the document for Morales; (3) Hodge, in translating the document, neglected to translate the arbitration clauses; and (4) as a result of Hodge's incomplete translation, Morales was not aware that the Agreement contained an arbitration clause. (App.3–5.) I also note, as does the majority, that the record demonstrates that Sun was under pressure to hire Morales in an expedient manner, and urged him to accept Hodge's translation and to sign the Agreement immediately. Maj. Op. at 220–221. . . .

"If the facts of this case were different, I might adopt the majority's position. For example, if Sun had simply handed the Agreement to Morales and indicated that it was Morales' responsibility to find a translator, and Morales had employed a incompetent translator who failed to translate the arbitration clause, I would agree that Morales was bound by the Agreement. However, when Sun made the decision to insert itself between Morales and the contract, it created a situation where lack of mutual assent could, and did, occur. Because I do not believe it was negligent or otherwise improper for Morales to rely upon the translation provided by Sun, and because Morales was not informed in the course of that translation that the Agreement contained an arbitration clause, I agree with the District Court that Morales did not "manifest an intention" to be bound by the arbitration clause."

NOTE ON OBJECTIVE AND SUBJECTIVE
ELEMENTS IN INTERPRETATION

Recall that one difference between classical contract law and modern contract law is that classical contract law tended to be objective and standardized, while modern contract law tends to include subjective and individualized elements as well. This difference is particularly striking in the area of interpretation. Classical contract law adopted a theory of interpretation that was purely, or almost purely, objective. As stated in Woburn National Bank v. Woods, 77 N.H. 172, 89 A. 491 (1914):

> A contract involves what is called a meeting of the minds of the parties. But this does not mean that they must have arrived at a common mental state touching the matter in hand. The standard by which their conduct is judged and their rights are limited is not internal but external. In the absence of fraud or incapacity, the question is: What did the party say and do? "The making of a contract does not depend upon the state of the parties' minds; it depends upon their overt acts."

The strict objectivism of classical contract law is also reflected in well-known passages by Williston and Learned Hand. According to Williston:

> It is even conceivable that a contract shall be formed which is in accordance with the intention of neither party. If a written contract is entered into, the meaning and effect of the contract depends on the construction given the written language by the court, and the court will give that language its natural and appropriate meaning; and, if it is unambiguous, will not even admit evidence of what the parties may have thought the meaning to be.

1 Samuel Williston, The Law of Contracts § 95, at 181–82 (1st ed. 1920.) And according to Learned Hand:

> A contract has, strictly speaking, nothing to do with the personal, or individual, intent of the parties. A contract is an obligation attached by the mere force of law to certain acts of the parties, usually words, which ordinarily accompany and represent a known intent. If, however, it were proved by twenty bishops that either party, when he used the words, intended something else than the usual meaning which the law imposes upon them, he would still be held, unless there were some mutual mistake, or something else of the sort. Of course, if it appear by other words, or acts, of the parties, that they attribute a peculiar meaning to such words as they use in the contract, that meaning will prevail, but only by virtue of the other words, and not because of their unexpressed intent.
>
> . . . [W]hatever was the understanding in fact of the banks [in this case] . . . of the legal effect of this practice between them, it is of not the slightest consequence, unless it took form in some acts or words, which, being reasonably interpreted, would have such

meaning to ordinary men. . . . Yet the question always remains for the court to interpret the reasonable meaning to the acts of the parties, by word or deed, and no characterization of its effect by either party thereafter, however truthful, is material. . . .

Hotchkiss v. National City Bank, 200 F. 287, 293–94 (S.D.N.Y.1911), aff'd 201 F. 664 (2d Cir.1912), aff'd 231 U.S. 50, 34 S.Ct. 20, 58 L.Ed. 115 (1913).

Restatement, First, Contracts § 231, comment *b* (1932), explains the thinking behind this approach to interpretation when people "integrate their agreement" (i.e., put it in writing):

> Where a contract has been integrated the parties have assented to the written words as the definite expression of their agreement. In ordinary oral negotiations and in many contracts made by correspondence the minds of the parties are not primarily addressed to the symbols which they are using, but merely to the things for which the symbols stand. Where, however, they integrate their agreement they have attempted more than to assent by means of symbols to certain things. They have assented to the writing as the expression of the things to which they agree, therefore the terms of the writing are conclusive, and a contract may have a meaning different from that which either party supposed it to have.

Morales v. Sun Constructors, supra, and the so-called duty to read rule give you a taste of the rules that apply when parties adopt a writing as an expression of the terms of their agreement. These rules are covered in detail later. Under classical contract law these contract law rules were qualified by rules in equity that enabled courts to correct mistakes and fraud regarding the content of a writing. One of these rules is the basis for the fraud exception to the duty to read rule.

Modern contract law pays greater attention to the parties' subjective intentions. There are four central modern principles of interpretation:

> *Principle I: If the parties subjectively attach different meanings to an expression, neither party knows that the other attaches a different meaning, and the two meanings are not equally reasonable, the more reasonable meaning prevails.*

Principle I is adopted in Restatement Second § 201(2)(b):

> Where the parties have attached different meanings to a promise or agreement or a term thereof, it is interpreted in accordance with the meaning attached by one of them if at the time the agreement was made. . . .

> (b) that party had no reason to know of any different meaning attached by the other, and the other had reason to know the meaning attached by the first party.

Principle I is based in significant part on the concept of liability for fault. If a reasonable person would have construed McKittrick's words as a promise of employment for the coming year, then McKittrick is at fault for leading Embry to believe his contract was extended. And McKittrick's negligence in speaking may have harmed Embry for he forewent other employment opportunities in the interim.

Although *Principle I* is primarily objective, it has a subjective element as well. For Embry to prevail he must establish that he actually believed his contract was extended, as well as that a reasonable person would have so construed McKittrick's words.

> *Principle II: If the parties subjectively attach different meanings to an expression, neither party knows that the other attaches a different meaning, and the two meanings are equally reasonable, neither meaning prevails.*

Principle II is adopted in the Restatement Second § 20(1):

> There is no manifestation of mutual assent to an exchange if the parties attach materially different meanings to their manifestations and
>
> > (a)   neither party knows or has reason to know the meaning attached by the other; or
> >
> > (b)   each party knows or each party has reason to know the meaning attached by the other.

Principle II is consistent with *Principle I*. If parties to a promissory transaction subjectively attach different meanings to their expressions, and in attaching these different meanings both parties are either equally fault-free or equally at fault, there is no reason why one meaning rather than the other should prevail. *Principle II* is associated with Raffles v. Wichelhaus, the *Peerless* case. To preserve the classical-school program, Holmes argued that the result in *Peerless* could be explained by objective theory. "The true ground of the decision was not that each party meant a different thing from the other . . . but that each said a different thing. The plaintiff offered one thing, the defendant expressed his assent to another." Holmes, The Common Law 309 (1881). But if both parties subjectively meant the December Peerless, Buyer should have been deemed in breach; and if both parties subjectively meant the October Peerless, Seller should have been deemed in breach. Holmes had it backwards: the result in *Peerless* is correct because the parties meant different things, not because the parties said different things.

> *Principle III: If the parties subjectively attach the same meaning to an expression, that meaning prevails even though it is unreasonable.*

Principle III squarely reverses the strict objectivism of classical contract law, under which the subjective intention of the parties was irrelevant even if mutually held. Where both parties attach the same unreasonable meaning to an expression, both parties may have been at fault in their use of language, but the fault caused no injury. Indeed, a party who in litigation presses a meaning that they did not attach to their expression at the time of contract-formation is at fault.

Principle III is adopted in Restatement Second § 201(1). That section provides that "[w]here the parties have attached the same meaning to a promise or agreement or a term thereof, it is interpreted in accordance with that meaning." Under section 201(1), reasonableness becomes relevant only where there is not a mutually held subjective meaning. Thus, Restatement Second stands the classical school's position on its head, by giving primacy to mutually held subjective interpretation, and resorting to an objective or reasonable meaning only in the absence of a mutually held subjective meaning. (Again in classical contract law a party could seek relief in equity on grounds of mistake when a writing did not reflect the parties' actual intent.)

> *Principle IV: If the parties, A and B, attach different meanings, Alpha and Beta, to an expression, and A knows that B attaches meaning Beta, but B does not know that A attaches meaning Alpha, the meaning Beta prevails even if it is less reasonable than the meaning Alpha.*

Principle IV is adopted in Restatement Second § 201(2):

> Where the parties have attached different meanings to a promise or agreement or a term thereof, it is interpreted in accordance with the meaning attached by one of them if at the time the agreement was made
>
> (a) that party did not know of any different meaning attached by the other, and the other knew the meaning attached by the first party. . . .

Principle IV, which is largely subjective, is supported by a fault analysis. B may have been at fault in attaching meaning Beta to the expression, but A was more at fault in allowing B to proceed on the basis of an interpretation that A knew B held, at least when B did not know that A held a different interpretation.

CHAPTER 9

THE MECHANICS OF A BARGAIN (I)— OFFER AND REVOCATION

■ ■ ■

Many bargains involving an exchange of promises are formed by the process of offer and acceptance. Because a bargain is enforceable by expectation damages at the moment it is formed, without regard to whether it has been relied upon, the rules that govern the offer-and-acceptance process often play a central role in contract disputes. These issues are the subject of Chapters 9 and 10.

Chapter 9 focuses on offers. It consists of three Sections:

Section 1 concerns the issue, what constitutes an offer. If it is determined that a party has made an offer, the legal consequence is to create in the offeree a power of acceptance—that is, a power to conclude a bargain, and therefore a legally enforceable contract, by accepting the offer. (In some of the cases in Section 1 the offer seeks performance and not a promissory acceptance so performance concludes a contract.) Section 2 concerns three kinds of events that can terminate a power of acceptance: lapse of the offer; rejection of the offer; and the making of a counter-offer (or some legal equivalent) by the offeree. Finally, Section 3 concerns the power of an offeror to terminate the offeree's power of acceptance by revoking the offer.

SECTION 1. WHAT CONSTITUTES AN OFFER

RESTATEMENT, SECOND, CONTRACTS § 24

[See Selected Source Materials Supplement]

CISG ART. 14(1)

[See Selected Source Materials Supplement]

UNIDROIT PRINCIPLES OF INTERNATIONAL COMMERCIAL CONTRACTS ART. 2.1.2

[See Selected Source Materials Supplement]

———

PRINCIPLES OF EUROPEAN CONTRACT LAW § 2.201(1)

[See Selected Source Materials Supplement]

———

LONERGAN V. SCOLNICK

California Court of Appeal, Fourth District, 1954.
129 Cal.App.2d 179, 276 P.2d 8.

BARNARD, PRESIDING JUSTICE. This is an action for specific performance or for damages in the event specific performance was impossible.

The complaint alleged that on April 15, 1952, the parties entered into a contract whereby the defendant agreed to sell, and plaintiff agreed to buy a 40-acre tract of land for $2,500; that this was a fair, just and reasonable value of the property; that on April 28, 1952, the defendant repudiated the contract and refused to deliver a deed; that on April 28, 1952, the property was worth $6,081; and that plaintiff has been damaged in the amount of $3,581. The answer denied that any contract had been entered into, or that anything was due to the plaintiff.

By stipulation the issue of whether or not a contract was entered into between the parties was first tried, reserving the other issues for a further trial if that became necessary. The issue as to the existence of a contract was submitted upon an agreed statement, including certain letters between the parties, without the introduction of other evidence.

The stipulated facts are as follows: During March, 1952, the defendant placed an ad in a Los Angeles paper reading, so far as material here, "Joshua Tree vic. 40 acres, . . . need cash, will sacrifice." In response to an inquiry resulting from this ad the defendant, who lived in New York, wrote a letter to the plaintiff dated March 26, briefly describing the property, giving directions as to how to get there, stating that his rock-bottom price was $2,500 cash, and further stating that "This is a form letter." On April 7, the plaintiff wrote a letter to the defendant saying that he was not sure he had found the property, asking for its legal description, asking whether the land was all level or whether it included certain jutting rock hills, and suggesting a certain bank as escrow agent "should I desire to purchase the land." On April 8, the defendant wrote to the plaintiff saying "From your description you have found the property"; that this bank "is O.K. for escrow agent"; that the land was fairly level; giving the legal description; and then saying, "If you are really interested, you will have to decide fast, as I expect to have a buyer in the next week or so." On April 12, the defendant sold the property to a third party for $2,500. The plaintiff received defendant's letter of April 8 on April 14. On April 15 he wrote to the defendant thanking him for his letter "confirming that I was on the right land", stating that he would immediately proceed to have the escrow opened and would deposit $2,500 therein "in conformity with your offer", and asking the defendant to forward a deed with his instructions to the escrow agent. On April 17, 1952, the plaintiff started an escrow and placed in the hands of the escrow agent $100, agreeing to furnish an additional $2,400 at an unspecified time, with the provision that if the escrow was not closed by May 15, 1952, it should be completed as soon thereafter as possible unless a written demand for a return of the money or instruments was made by either party after that date. It was further stipulated that the plaintiff was ready and willing at all times to deposit the $2,400.

The matter was submitted on June 11, 1953. On July 10, 1953, the judge filed a memorandum opinion stating that it was his opinion that the letter of April 8, 1952, when considered with the previous correspondence, constituted an offer of sale which offer was, however, qualified and conditioned upon prompt acceptance by the plaintiff; that in spite of the condition thus imposed, the plaintiff delayed more than a week before notifying the defendant of his acceptance; and that since the plaintiff was aware of the necessity of promptly communicating his acceptance to the defendant his delay was not the prompt action required by the terms of the offer. Findings of fact were filed on October 2, 1953, finding that each and all of the statements in the agreed statement are true, and that all allegations to the contrary in the complaint are untrue. As conclusions of law, it was found that the plaintiff and defendant did not enter into a contract as alleged in the complaint or otherwise, and that the defendant is entitled to judgment against the plaintiff. Judgment was entered accordingly, from which the plaintiff has appealed.

The appellant contends that the judgment is contrary to the evidence and to the law since the facts, as found, do not support the conclusions of law upon which the judgment is based. It is argued that there is no conflict in the evidence, and this court is not bound by the trial court's construction of the written instruments involved; that the evidence conclusively shows that an offer was made to the plaintiff by the defendant, which offer was accepted by the mailing of plaintiff's letter of April 15; that upon receipt of defendant's letter of April 8 the plaintiff had a reasonable time within which to accept the offer that had been made; that by his letter of April 15 and his starting of an escrow the plaintiff accepted said offer; and that the agreed statement of facts establishes that a valid contract was entered into between the parties. In his briefs the appellant assumes that an offer was made by the defendant, and confined his argument to contending that the evidence shows that he accepted that offer within a reasonable time.

There can be no contract unless the minds of the parties have met and mutually agreed upon some specific thing. This is usually evidenced by one party making an offer which is accepted by the other party. Section 25 of the Restatement, Law on Contracts reads:

> "If from a promise, or manifestation of intention, or from the circumstances existing at the time, the person to whom the promise or manifestation is addressed knows or has reason to know that the person making it does not intend it as an expression of his fixed purpose until he has given a further expression of assent, he has not made an offer."

The language used in Niles v. Hancock, 140 Cal. 157, 73 P. 840, 842, "It is also clear from the correspondence that it was the intention of the defendant that the negotiations between him and the plaintiff were to be purely preliminary," is applicable here. The correspondence here indicates an intention on the part of the defendant to find out whether the plaintiff was interested, rather than an intention to make a definite offer to the plaintiff. The language used by the defendant in his letters of March 26 and April 8 rather clearly discloses that they were not intended as an expression of fixed purpose to make a definite offer, and was sufficient to advise the plaintiff that some further expression of assent on the part of the defendant was necessary.

The advertisement in the paper was a mere request for an offer. The letter of March 26 contains no definite offer, and clearly states that it is a form letter. It merely gives further particulars, in clarification of the advertisement, and tells the plaintiff how to locate the property if he was interested in looking into the matter. The letter of April 8 added nothing in the way of a definite offer. It merely answered some questions asked by the plaintiff, and stated that if the plaintiff was really interested he would have to act fast. The statement that he expected to have a buyer in the next week or so indicated that the defendant intended to sell to the first-comer, and was reserving the right to do so. From this statement, alone, the plaintiff knew or should have known that he was not being given time in which to accept an offer that was being made but that some further assent on the part of the defendant was required. Under the language used the plaintiff was not being given a right to act within a reasonable time after receiving the letter; he was plainly told that the defendant intended to sell to another, if possible, and warned that he would have to act fast if he was interested in buying the land.

Regardless of any opinion previously expressed, the court found that no contract had been entered into between these parties, and we are in accord with the court's conclusion on that controlling issue. The court's construction of the letters involved was a reasonable one, and we think the most reasonable one, even if it be assumed that another construction was possible.

The judgment is affirmed.

GRIFFIN and MUSSELL, JJ., concur.

———

LEFKOWITZ V. GREAT MINNEAPOLIS SURPLUS STORE

Supreme Court of Minnesota, 1957.
251 Minn. 188, 86 N.W.2d 689.

MURPHY, JUSTICE. This is an appeal from an order of the Municipal Court of Minneapolis denying the motion of the defendant for amended findings of fact, or, in the alternative, for a new trial. The order for judgment awarded the plaintiff the sum of $138.50 as damages for breach of contract.

This case grows out of the alleged refusal of the defendant to sell to the plaintiff a certain fur piece which it had offered for sale in a newspaper advertisement. It appears from the record that on April 6, 1956, the defendant published the following advertisement in a Minneapolis newspaper:

"Saturday 9 A.M. Sharp
3 Brand New
Fur Coats
Worth to $100
First Come
First Served
$1 Each"

On April 13, the defendant again published an advertisement in the same newspaper as follows:

"Saturday 9 A.M.
2 Brand New Pastel
Mink 3-Skin Scarfs
Selling for $89.50
Out they go
Saturday.
Each. . . . $1.00
1 Black Lapin Stole
Beautiful,
worth $139.50. . . . $1.00

First Come
First Served"

The record supports the findings of the court that on each of the Saturdays following the publication of the above-described ads the plaintiff was the first to present himself at the appropriate counter in the defendant's store and on each occasion demanded the coat and the stole so advertised and indicated his readiness to pay the sale price of $1. On both occasions, the defendant refused to sell the merchandise to the plaintiff, stating on the first occasion that by a "house rule" the offer was intended for women only and sales would not be made to men, and on the second visit that plaintiff knew defendant's house rules.

The trial court properly disallowed plaintiff's claim for the value of the fur coats since the value of these articles was speculative and uncertain. The only evidence of value was the advertisement itself to the effect that the coats were "Worth to $100.00," how much less being speculative especially in view of the price for which they were offered for sale. With reference to the offer of the defendant on April 13, 1956, to sell the "1 Black Lapin Stole ... worth $139.50 ... " the trial court held that the value of this article was established and granted judgment in favor of the plaintiff for that amount less the $1 quoted purchase price.

1.   The defendant contends that a newspaper advertisement offering items of merchandise for sale at a named price is a "unilateral offer" which may be withdrawn without notice. He relies upon authorities which hold that, where an advertiser publishes in a newspaper that he has a certain quantity or quality of goods which he wants to dispose of at certain prices and on certain terms, such advertisements are not offers which become contracts as soon as any person to whose notice they may come signifies his acceptance by notifying the other that he will take a certain quantity of them. Such advertisements have been construed as an invitation for an offer of sale on the terms stated, which offer, when received, may be accepted or rejected and which therefore does not become a contract of sale until accepted by the seller; and until a contract has been so made, the seller may modify or revoke such prices or terms. . . .

The defendant relies principally on Craft v. Elder & Johnston Co. supra. In that case, the court discussed the legal effect of an advertisement offering for sale, as a one-day special, an electric sewing machine at a named price. The view was expressed that the advertisement was (38 N.E.2d 417, 34 Ohio L.A. 605) "not an offer made to any specific person but was made to the public generally. Thereby it would be properly designated as a unilateral offer and not being supported by any consideration could be withdrawn at will and without notice." It is true that such an offer may be withdrawn before acceptance. Since all offers are by their nature unilateral because they are necessarily made by one party or on one side in the negotiation of a contract, the distinction made in that decision between a unilateral offer and a unilateral contract is not clear. On the facts before us we are concerned with whether the advertisement constituted an offer, and, if so, whether the plaintiff's conduct constituted an acceptance.

There are numerous authorities which hold that a particular advertisement in a newspaper or circular letter relating to a sale of articles may be construed by the court as constituting an offer, acceptance of which would complete a contract. . . .

The test of whether a binding obligation may originate in advertisements addressed to the general public is "whether the facts show that some performance was promised in positive terms in return for something requested." 1 Williston, Contracts (Rev. ed.) § 27.

The authorities above cited emphasize that, where the offer is clear, definite, and explicit, and leaves nothing open for negotiation, it constitutes an offer, acceptance of which will complete the contract. The most recent case on the subject is Johnson v. Capital City Ford Co., La.App., 85 So.2d 75, in which the court pointed out that a newspaper advertisement relating to the purchase and sale of automobiles may constitute an offer, acceptance of which will consummate a contract and create an obligation in the offeror to perform according to the terms of the published offer.

Whether in any individual instance a newspaper advertisement is an offer rather than an invitation to make an offer depends on the legal intention of the parties and the surrounding circumstances. Annotation, 157 A.L.R. 744, 751; 77 C.J.S. Sales § 25b; 17 C.J.S. Contracts § 389. We are of the view on the facts before us that the offer by the defendant of the sale of the Lapin fur was clear, definite, and explicit, and left nothing open for negotiation. The plaintiff having successfully managed to be the first one to appear at the seller's place of business to be served, as requested by the advertisement, and having offered the stated purchase price of the article, he was entitled to performance on the part of the defendant. We think the trial court was correct in holding that there was in the conduct of the parties a sufficient mutuality of obligation to constitute a contract of sale.

2. The defendant contends that the offer was modified by a "house rule" to the effect that only women were qualified to receive the bargains advertised. The advertisement contained no such restriction. This objection may be disposed of briefly by stating that, while an advertiser has the right at any time before acceptance to modify his offer, he does not have the right, after acceptance, to impose new or arbitrary conditions not contained in the published offer. . . .

Affirmed.

SATERIALE V. R.J. REYNOLDS TOBACCO COMPANY
United States Court of Appeals, Ninth Circuit, 2012.
697 F.3d 777.

FISHER, CIRCUIT JUDGE.

R.J. Reynolds Tobacco Company (RJR) operated a customer rewards program, called Camel Cash, from 1991 to 2007. Under the terms of the program, RJR urged consumers to purchase Camel cigarettes, to save Camel Cash certificates included in packages of Camel cigarettes, to enroll in the program and, ultimately, to redeem their certificates for merchandise featured in catalogs distributed by RJR. The plaintiffs allege that, in reliance on RJR's actions, they purchased Camel cigarettes, enrolled in the program and saved their certificates for future redemption. They allege that in 2006 RJR abruptly ceased accepting certificates for redemption, making the plaintiffs' unredeemed certificates worthless. The plaintiffs brought this action for breach of contract, promissory estoppel and violation of two California consumer protection laws. The district court dismissed the action for failure to state a claim. We affirm in part, reverse in part and remand. We hold that the plaintiffs have adequately alleged claims for breach of contract and promissory estoppel, but affirm dismissal of the plaintiffs' claims under the Unfair Competition Law and the Consumer Legal Remedies Act.

I.   BACKGROUND

The plaintiffs appeal from a dismissal for failure to state a claim. *See* Fed.R.Civ.P. 12(b)(6). For purposes of a motion to dismiss, we accept all well-pleaded allegations of material fact as true and construe them in the light most favorable to the nonmoving party. *See Daniels-Hall v. Nat'l Educ. Ass'n,* 629 F.3d 992, 998 (9th Cir.2010). We thus recite the facts as they appear in the plaintiffs' third amended complaint. This factual background is based on the *allegations* of the plaintiffs' complaint. Whether the plaintiffs' allegations are true has not been decided.

RJR initiated the Camel Cash customer loyalty program in 1991. Compl. ¶ 24. RJR represented on Camel Cash certificates, packages of Camel cigarettes and in the media that customers who saved the certificates—called C-Notes—could exchange them for merchandise according to terms provided in a catalog. *Id.* The C-Notes stated:

> USE THIS NEW C-NOTE AND THE C-NOTES YOU'VE BEEN SAVING TO GET THE BEST GOODS CAMEL HAS TO OFFER. CALL 1-800-CAMEL CASH (1-800-266-3522) for a free catalog. Offer restricted to smokers 21 years of age or older. Value 1/1000 of 1¢. Offer good only in the USA, and void where restricted or prohibited by law. Check catalog for expiration date. Limit 5 requests for a catalog per household.

Id. ¶ 26. According to the complaint, "Certain (but not all) of the Camel Cash catalogs state[d] that Reynolds could terminate the Camel Cash program without notice." *Id.* ¶ 32.

The plaintiffs are 10 individuals who joined the Camel Cash program by purchasing RJR's products and filling out and submitting signed registration forms to RJR. *Id.* ¶¶ 27, 48. RJR sent each plaintiff a unique enrollment number that was used in communications between the parties. *Id.* ¶ 27. These communications included catalogs RJR distributed to the plaintiffs containing merchandise that could be obtained by redeeming Camel Cash certificates. *Id.*

From time to time, RJR issued a new catalog with merchandise offered in exchange for Camel Cash, either upon request, or by mailing catalogs to consumers enrolled in the program. *Id.* ¶ 28. The number of Camel Cash certificates needed to obtain merchandise varied from as little as 100 to many thousands. *Id.* ¶ 29. This encouraged consumers to buy more packages of cigarettes together with Camel Cash and also to save or obtain Camel Cash certificates to redeem them for more valuable items. *Id.*

RJR honored the program from 1991 to 2006, and during that time Camel's share of the cigarette market nearly doubled, from approximately 4 percent to more than 7 percent. *Id.* ¶¶ 3, 34. In October 2006, however, RJR mailed a notice to program members announcing that the program would terminate as of March 31, 2007. *Id.* ¶ 32. The termination notice stated:

> As a loyal Camel smoker, we [sic] wanted to tell you our Camel Cash program is expiring. C-Notes will no longer be included on packs, which means whatever Camel Cash you have is among the last of its kind.

> Now this isn't happening overnight—there'll be plenty of time to redeem your C-Notes before the program ends. In fact, you'll have from OCTOBER '06 through MARCH '07 to go to camelsmokes.com to redeem your C-Notes. Supplies will be limited, so it won't hurt to get there before the rush.

Id. ¶ 33 & ex. A.

The announcement advised members that they could continue to redeem their C-Notes until March 2007. Beginning in October 2006, however, RJR allegedly stopped printing and issuing catalogs and told consumers that it did not have any merchandise available for redemption. *Id.* ¶¶ 34, 48. Several of the plaintiffs attempted, without success, to redeem C-Notes or obtain a catalog during the final six months of the program. *Id.* ¶ 49. The plaintiffs had saved hundreds or thousands of Camel Cash certificates that they were unable to redeem. *Id.* ¶ 11.

In November 2009, the plaintiffs filed a class action complaint against RJR. They allege breach of contract, promissory estoppel and violations of two California consumer protection laws, the Unfair Competition Law (UCL), Cal. Bus. & Prof.Code § 17200 *et seq.*, and the Consumer Legal Remedies Act (CLRA), Cal. Civ.Code § 1750 *et seq.* The district court dismissed the action under Rule 12(b)(6), and the plaintiffs timely appealed.

II. JURISDICTION AND STANDARD OF REVIEW

We have jurisdiction under 28 U.S.C. § 1291. We review de novo a district court's order granting a Rule 12(b)(6) motion to dismiss. *See Cook v. Brewer,* 637 F.3d 1002, 1004 (9th Cir.2011). To survive a motion to dismiss, a complaint must contain sufficient factual matter to "state a claim to relief that is plausible on its face." *Ashcroft v. Iqbal,* 556 U.S. 662, 678, 129 S.Ct. 1937, 173 L.Ed.2d 868 (2009) (quoting *Bell Atl. Corp. v. Twombly,* 550 U.S. 544, 570, 127 S.Ct. 1955, 167 L.Ed.2d 929 (2007) (internal quotation marks omitted)). "We accept as true all well-pleaded allegations of material fact, and construe them in the light most favorable to the non-moving party." *Daniels-Hall,* 629 F.3d at 998. The parties agree that the plaintiffs' claims are governed by California law.

III. BREACH OF CONTRACT

We begin by addressing whether the plaintiffs have stated a claim for breach of contract. The plaintiffs do not dispute that RJR had the right to terminate the Camel Cash program effective March 31, 2007, but allege that RJR breached a contract by refusing to redeem C-Notes during the six months preceding program termination. Compl. ¶¶ 6–7. RJR challenges the plaintiffs' contract claim on four grounds: the absence of an offer, indefiniteness, lack of mutuality of obligation (premised on RJR's right to terminate its contractual obligations) and untimeliness. We address RJR's contentions in turn.

A. Existence of an Offer

"An offer is the manifestation of willingness to enter into a bargain, so made as to justify another person in understanding that his assent to that bargain is invited and will conclude it." *Donovan v. RRL Corp.,* 26 Cal.4th 261, 109 Cal.Rptr.2d 807, 27 P.3d 702, 709 (2001) (quoting *City of Moorpark v. Moorpark Unified Sch. Dist.,* 54 Cal.3d 921, 1 Cal.Rptr.2d 896, 819 P.2d 854, 860 (1991)) (internal quotation marks omitted). "The determination of whether a particular communication constitutes an operative offer, rather than an inoperative step in the preliminary negotiation of a contract, depends upon all the surrounding circumstances." *Id.* "[T]he pertinent inquiry is whether the individual to whom the communication was made had reason to believe that it was intended as an offer." *Id.* The issue here is whether the C-Notes, read in isolation or in combination with the catalogs, may have constituted an offer.

1. *Bilateral Contract*

As an initial matter, we are not persuaded that the plaintiffs have alleged the existence of an offer to enter into a *bilateral* contract. "A bilateral contract consists of mutual promises made in exchange for each other by each of the two contracting parties." *Sully-Miller Contracting Co. v. Gledson/Cashman Constr., Inc.*, 103 Cal.App.4th 30, 126 Cal.Rptr.2d 400, 403 (2002) (quoting Corbin on Contracts § 1.23 (rev. ed. 1993)) (internal quotation marks omitted). Both sides of the bargain must have made promises. Here, the plaintiffs have identified an alleged promise by RJR (to allow customers to redeem Camel Cash certificates for rewards), but they have not pointed to any promise they made to RJR. Nor do they argue that RJR sought a return promise in exchange for its own promise to allow consumers to exchange C-Notes for merchandise. They argue instead the requirements for a bilateral contract are met because they agreed to certain terms and conditions when they enrolled in the Camel Cash program. *See* Appellants' Reply Brief at 9; Compl. ¶ 26. Nothing in the complaint, however, suggests that these terms were anything more than *conditions* that the plaintiffs were required to satisfy to trigger RJR's duty to perform, as opposed to promises that the plaintiffs were bound to perform to avoid incurring their own contractual liability. "A condition is an event . . . which must occur . . . before performance under a contract becomes due." Restatement (Second) of Contracts (hereinafter Restatement) § 224 (1981). A promise, by contrast, "is an express or implied declaration in a contract that raises a duty to perform and subjects the promisor to liability for breach for failure to do so." 13 Richard A. Lord, *Williston on Contracts* (hereinafter Williston) § 38:5 (4th ed. 2012). The plaintiffs have not alleged that they were bound to do anything. They therefore have not alleged the existence of an offer to enter into a bilateral contract.[1]

2. *Unilateral Contract*

We reach a different conclusion as to the plaintiffs' theory that RJR made an offer to enter into a *unilateral* contract. In contrast to a bilateral contract, a unilateral contract involves the exchange of a promise for a performance. *See Harris v. Time, Inc.*, 191 Cal.App.3d 449, 237 Cal.Rptr. 584, 587 (1987). The offer is accepted by rendering a performance rather than providing a promise. *See* Restatement § 45 cmt. a. "Typical illustrations are found in offers of rewards or prizes. . . . " *Id.*

---

[1] It is, of course, possible for a consumer rewards program to involve a bilateral contract. Frequent flyer programs, for example, may be governed by membership agreements that impose contractual duties on both sides of the bargain, exposing airlines and travelers alike to potential contractual liability. *See, e.g., Ginsberg v. Northwest, Inc.*, 653 F.3d 1033, 1035, 1040 (9th Cir.2011); *Am. Airlines, Inc. v. Am. Coupon Exch., Inc.*, 721 F.Supp. 61, 63 (S.D.N.Y.1989). Here, however, the plaintiffs have not alleged an offer or contract involving reciprocal duties, and therefore they have not alleged a bilateral contract.

RJR argues that its C-Notes, whether read in isolation or in combination with the catalogs, were not offers, but invitations to make an offer. RJR relies on the common law's general rule that "[a]dvertisements of goods by display, sign, handbill, newspaper, radio or television are not ordinarily intended or understood as offers to sell." *Id.* § 26 cmt. b. RJR emphasizes that two judicial decisions have applied this general rule to customer rewards programs similar to the Camel Cash program, *see Leonard v. Pepsico, Inc.,* 88 F.Supp.2d 116, 122–27 (S.D.N.Y.1999); *Alligood v. Procter & Gamble Co.,* 72 Ohio App.3d 309, 594 N.E.2d 668, 668–70 (1991) (per curiam), and urges us to apply the rule here as well. We decline to do so.

First, it is not clear that the common law rule upon which RJR relies applies under California law. *See Donovan,* 109 Cal.Rptr.2d 807, 27 P.3d at 710 (stating that "[t]his court has not previously applied the common law rules upon which defendant relies, including the rule that advertisements generally constitute invitations to negotiate rather than offers," observing that "such rules . . . have been criticized on the ground that they are inconsistent with the reasonable expectations of consumers and lead to haphazard results," citing Melvin Aron Eisenberg, *Expression Rules in Contract Law and Problems of Offer and Acceptance,* 82 Cal. L. Rev. 1127, 1166–72 (1994), and concluding that "[i]n the present case . . . we need not consider the viability of the black-letter rule regarding the interpretation of advertisements").

Second, even assuming California law incorporates the common law rule, that rule includes an exception for offers of a reward, including offers of a reward for the redemption of coupons. As a leading contract law treatise explains,

> It is very common, where one desires to induce many people to action, to offer a reward for such action by general publication in some form. A statement that plausibly makes an offer of this kind must be reasonably interpreted according to its terms and the surrounding circumstances. If the statement, properly interpreted, calls for the performance or commencement of performance of specific acts, action in accordance with such an interpretation will close a contract or make the offer irrevocable. There are many cases of an offer of a reward for the capture of a person charged with crime, for desired information, for the return of a lost article, for the winning of a contest, or *for the redemption of coupons.* In addition, advertisements placed by buyers inviting sellers to ship goods without prior communication are clear cases of offers. The contracts so made are almost always unilateral.

Corbin on Contracts (hereinafter Corbin) § 2.4 (2012) (emphasis added) (footnotes omitted). RJR does not discuss this exception, relying instead on

Leonard and *Alligood*. Several courts, however, have applied the exception to customer rewards programs. *See, e.g., Payne v. Lautz Bros.,* 166 N.Y.S. 844, 845–46, 848 (N.Y.City Ct.1916) (reward coupons included with packages of soap wrappers), *aff'd without opinion,* 168 N.Y.S. 369 (N.Y.Sup.), *aff'd without opinion,* 185 A.D. 904, 171 N.Y.S. 1094 (1918), *cited with approval in* Corbin § 2.4 n.14; *Reynolds v. Philip Morris U.S.A., Inc.,* No. 05–cv–1876 (S.D.Cal. June 5, 2007) (order denying defendant's motion for summary judgment) (reward points obtained by purchasing Marlboro cigarettes), *rev'd on other grounds,* 332 Fed.Appx. 397 (9th Cir.2009); *Wolens v. Am. Airlines, Inc.,* 157 Ill.2d 466, 193 Ill.Dec. 172, 626 N.E.2d 205, 208 (1993) (reward miles awarded for flying on American Airlines), *rev'd on other grounds,* 513 U.S. 219, 115 S.Ct. 817, 130 L.Ed.2d 715 (1995).[2]

Like these courts, we see no justification for applying the general common law rule, rather than the common law exception, to circumstances such as those presented here. The common law rule that advertisements ordinarily do not constitute offers arose to address a specific problem—the potential for over-acceptance—not applicable here. Professor Farnsworth explains that an offer ordinarily does not exist

> when a proposal for a limited quantity has been sent to more persons than its maker could accommodate.... Otherwise, supposing a shopkeeper were sold out of a particular class of goods, thousands of members of the public might crowd into the shop and demand to be served, and each one would have a right of action against the proprietor for not performing his contract. A customer would not usually have reason to believe that the shopkeeper intended exposure to the risk of a multitude of acceptances resulting in a number of contracts exceeding the shopkeeper's inventory.

E. Allan Farnsworth, *Contracts* (hereinafter Farnsworth) § 3.10, at 134 (4th ed. 2004) (footnote and internal quotation marks omitted). This problem arises in the case of ordinary advertisements for the sale of goods or services, but not here. First, RJR's ostensible purpose in promoting the Camel Cash program was not to sell a limited inventory, but to induce as

---

[2] *Payne* found an enforceable unilateral contract where the defendant advertised that it would give a round-trip train ticket to consumers who collected 25 coupons from the defendant's soap packages and redeemed them for the train tickets (or other merchandise in the defendant's rewards catalogs) at the defendant's stores. *See* 166 N.Y.S. at 844–48. In *Reynolds,* the court held that a genuine issue of material fact existed regarding whether the plaintiff accepted an offer to enter into a unilateral contract by purchasing Marlboro cigarettes, clipping Marlboro Miles certificates, saving the certificates and eventually mailing a sufficient number of certificates to Philip Morris to exchange for products. *See Reynolds v. Philip Morris U.S.A., supra,* at 8. In *Wolens,* the Illinois Supreme Court recognized a contractual relationship between American Airlines and members of its frequent flyer program, stating, "When a member earns frequent flyer miles by flying on American or by doing business with American affiliates, a contractual relationship is formed which vests the frequent flyer with the right to earn specific travel awards." 193 Ill.Dec. 172, 626 N.E.2d at 208.

many consumers as possible to purchase Camel cigarettes. Second, RJR could not have been trapped into a situation in which acceptances exceeded inventory. RJR alone decided how many C-Notes to distribute, so it exercised absolute control over the number of acceptances. As Farnsworth explains, "if the very nature of a proposal restricts its maker's potential liability to a reasonable number of people, there is no reason why it cannot be an offer." *Id.* at 135.

For these reasons, we find no reason to presume that RJR's communications did not constitute an offer merely because they were addressed to the general public in the form of advertisements. The operative question under California law, therefore, is simply "whether the advertiser, in clear and positive terms, promised to render performance in exchange for something requested by the advertiser, and whether the recipient of the advertisement reasonably might have concluded that by acting in accordance with the request a contract would be formed." *Donovan*, 109 Cal.Rptr.2d 807, 27 P.3d at 710. Construing the complaint in the light most favorable to the plaintiffs, and drawing all reasonable inferences from the complaint in the plaintiffs' favor, *see Moss v. U.S. Secret Serv.*, 572 F.3d 962, 969 (9th Cir.2009); *Doe v. United States*, 419 F.3d 1058, 1062 (9th Cir.2005), we conclude that the plaintiffs have adequately alleged the existence of an offer to enter into a unilateral contract, whereby RJR promised to provide rewards to customers who purchased Camel cigarettes, saved Camel Cash certificates and redeemed their certificates in accordance with the catalogs' terms.

We reach this conclusion in light of the totality of the circumstances surrounding RJR's communications to consumers: the repeated use of the word "offer" in the C-Notes; the absence of any language disclaiming the intent to be bound; the inclusion of specific restrictions in the C-Notes ("Offer restricted to smokers 21 years of age or older"; "Offer good only in the USA, and void where restricted or prohibited by law"; "Check catalog for expiration date"; "Limit 5 requests for a catalog per household"); the formal enrollment process, through which consumers submitted registration forms and RJR issued enrollment numbers; and the substantial reliance expected from consumers.[3] *Donovan* explains that

---

[3] The plaintiffs' substantial reliance distinguishes this case from cases involving garden-variety advertisements. To take advantage of the Camel Cash program, consumers were expected to purchase Camel cigarettes and accumulate Camel Cash certificates for a period of weeks, months or even years. *See* Compl. ¶ 29 (alleging that "[t]he number of Camel Cash certificates needed to obtain merchandise . . . varied from as little as one hundred to many thousands," and noting that RJR "further encouraged plaintiffs and other Class members to collect their Camel Cash (as opposed to redeeming them as soon as possible) because merchandise listed in defendant's catalogs for redemption by a greater number of coupons was disproportionately more valuable than the merchandise which could be redeemed by fewer coupons"). Citing an offer for a reward as an example, Corbin explains that "a proposal is likely to be deemed to be an offer if it is foreseeable that the addressee of the proposal will rely upon it." Corbin § 2.2. This is so because a member of the public is unlikely to undertake substantial reliance in the absence of a binding commitment from the offeror—i.e., on the mere chance that the offeror will perform.

under the common law "advertisements have been held to constitute offers where they invite the performance of a specific act without further communication and leave nothing for negotiation." 109 Cal.Rptr.2d 807, 27 P.3d at 710. These requirements are satisfied here. RJR's alleged offer invited the performance of specific acts (saving C-Notes and redeeming them for rewards in accordance with the catalog) without further communication, and leaving nothing for negotiation.

RJR properly emphasizes that the alleged offer left aspects of RJR's performance to RJR's discretion. The offer did not specify when future catalogs would be issued, what rewards merchandise they would include, what quantities of merchandise would be available or how many C-Notes would be required to exchange for particular items. The plaintiffs, however, do not allege that these were essential terms. *See* Compl. ¶ 31 ("[I]t was not a contract to obtain a specific item or good, such as a 'Joe Camel' jacket or ashtray."). Instead, they allege a contract the essence of which was their general right to redeem their Camel Cash certificates, during the life of the program, for whatever rewards merchandise RJR made available, with RJR's discretion limited only by the implied duty of good faith performance. The presence of discretion thus does not preclude the existence of an offer.

[Section III-B of the opinion addressing the indefiniteness issue is set out in Chapter 11.]

C.   Mutuality of Obligation & RJR's Right to Terminate

RJR argues that the plaintiffs' contract claim must be dismissed for lack of mutuality of obligation because RJR had an unrestricted right to terminate the Camel Cash program at will, and without notice. The complaint discusses RJR's right to terminate the Camel Cash program in three paragraphs:

Plaintiffs do not dispute that defendant had the right to terminate the Camel Cash program. However, defendant made a deliberate and calculated choice to waive any right to terminate the program "without notice" and instead provided six months prior notice. Thus, during that six-month period, from approximately October 2006 through March 2007, defendant was obligated to comply with the terms of its contract with plaintiffs. . . .

Also, the breach of contract alleged is *not* that Reynolds was prohibited from terminating the program but that, during the program's duration, Reynolds had the obligation to perform through the program's termination date. Certain (but not all) of the Camel Cash catalogs state that Reynolds could terminate the Camel Cash program without notice. Defendant, however, waived any right to terminate without notice when, on or about October 1, 2006, it announced by mailing a notice to program members, that the program would terminate as of March 31, 2007. Namely, defendant gave notice of termination and represented that plaintiffs could redeem their Camel Cash certificates for six months. . . .

> 54. In or about October 2006, defendant announced that it was terminating the Camel Cash program as of March 31, 2007. Thus, the contract was in effect until March 31, 2007 when defendant terminated the program.

Compl. ¶¶ 6, 32, 54.

Given our conclusion that the plaintiffs have alleged an offer to enter into a unilateral rather than a bilateral contract, RJR's reliance on mutuality of obligation necessarily fails: that doctrine does not apply to unilateral contracts. *See, e.g., Asmus v. Pac. Bell,* 23 Cal.4th 1, 96 Cal.Rptr.2d 179, 999 P.2d 71, 78 (2000) ("In the unilateral contract context, there is no mutuality of obligation."). RJR's argument nonetheless raises important questions about the viability of the plaintiffs' contract claim. If, in fact, RJR reserved an *unrestricted* right to terminate the Camel Cash program, *without notice,* then the plaintiffs' contract claim may well be untenable.

First, a reservation of an unrestricted right to terminate could have precluded RJR's communications from constituting an offer. As Corbin explains, if an offeror expressly reserves not only the right to revoke the offer at will and without notice, but also the *unrestricted right not to perform,* then the offer is not legally effective as an offer at all: "A purported offer that reserves the power to withdraw at will even after an acceptance should not be described as an offer at all, but as an invitation to submit an offer." Corbin § 2.19.[8]

Second, if RJR reserved an unrestricted right to terminate the Camel Cash program at any time and without notice, then RJR's promise to perform could be deemed illusory, and hence unenforceable. As Farnsworth explains, when a promise "appears on its face to be so insubstantial as to impose no obligation at all on the promisor—who says, in effect, 'I will *if* I want to'"—the promise is not enforceable. Farnsworth § 2.13, at 75. Accordingly, an enforceable termination clause that gives a promisor an unrestricted power to terminate a contract at any time, without notice, renders the promise illusory and unenforceable, at least so long as the purported contract remains wholly executory.

Either of the foregoing principles could possibly serve to defeat the plaintiffs' contract claim here. The complaint, however, does not

---

[8] It does not appear that the plaintiffs' beginning of performance (by purchasing Camel cigarettes and saving C-Notes) would alter that result. It is true as a general matter that an offeree's part performance may render an offer to enter into a unilateral contract irrevocable. *See Steiner v. Thexton,* 48 Cal.4th 411, 106 Cal.Rptr.3d 252, 226 P.3d 359, 368 (2010); Restatement § 45(1). That default principle, however, does not apply when the offer expressly reserves the right to revoke notwithstanding the offeror's beginning of performance. *See* Restatement § 45 cmt. b.

definitively allege that RJR reserved an *unrestricted* right to terminate its duty to perform. The complaint alleges only that "[c]*ertain* (but not all) of the Camel Cash catalogs state that Reynolds could terminate the Camel Cash program without notice." Compl. ¶ 32 (emphasis added). The complaint, moreover, alleges that RJR "waived any right to terminate without notice when, on or about October 1, 2006, it announced by mailing a notice to program members, that the program would terminate as of March 31, 2007." *Id.* Dismissal is therefore unwarranted on the current record. . .

IV. PROMISSORY ESTOPPEL

Under California law, the elements of promissory estoppel are (1) a promise clear and unambiguous in its terms; (2) reliance by the party to whom the promise is made; (3) the reliance must be both reasonable and foreseeable; and (4) the party asserting the estoppel must be injured by his reliance. *See U.S. Ecology, Inc. v. State,* 129 Cal.App.4th 887, 28 Cal.Rptr.3d 894, 905 (2005).

Here, the parties chiefly dispute the first element—whether the plaintiffs have adequately alleged that RJR made a promise clear and unambiguous in its terms. We conclude this element is satisfied: the C-Notes promised consumers that if they saved C-Notes and redeemed them for rewards merchandise in accordance with the catalog, RJR would provide the merchandise. These terms are neither unclear nor ambiguous. *See Aceves v. U.S. Bank, N.A.,* 192 Cal.App.4th 218, 120 Cal.Rptr.3d 507, 514–15 (2011) (holding that a bank's promise—to work with the plaintiff on a mortgage reinstatement and loan modification if the plaintiff no longer pursued relief in bankruptcy court—was a clear and unambiguous promise to negotiate, even though it left open the terms of any loan modification agreement that might be discussed). RJR correctly points out that its communications were unspecific as to precisely what merchandise would be offered in future catalogs. The plaintiffs, however, do not rest their promissory estoppel claim on an alleged promise to provide particular merchandise.

The plaintiffs' promissory estoppel claim, though, is subject to the same definiteness requirement as their breach of contract claim. *See id.* at 514. This claim therefore rises or falls with the contract claim. Given that we have concluded that the alleged contract is sufficiently definite to survive a motion to dismiss, we vacate dismissal of the promissory estoppel claim as well. If further proceedings demonstrate that the contract claim fails for indefiniteness, the promissory estoppel claim will likely fail for the same reason. . . .

VIII. CONCLUSION

We affirm dismissal of the plaintiffs' UCL and CLRA claims. We reverse dismissal of the plaintiffs' breach of contract and promissory estoppel claims.

The parties shall bear their own costs on appeal.

AFFIRMED IN PART, REVERSED IN PART AND REMANDED.

———

RESTATEMENT, SECOND, CONTRACTS § 26

[See Selected Source Materials Supplement]

———

CISG ARTICLE 14(2)

[See Selected Source Materials Supplement]

———

PRINCIPLES OF EUROPEAN CONTRACT LAW ART. 2.201(2), (3)

[See Selected Source Materials Supplement]

———

NOTE ON OFFER AND ACCEPTANCE

Everyday life gives rise to recurring kinds of arrangements that might or might not be considered to be contracts. For example, a hotel reservation has been held to be a contract binding on the hotel, even where the guest has not guaranteed the reservation. Wells v. Holiday Inns, Inc., 522 F.Supp. 1023 (W.D.Mo.1981). On the other hand, in Glass Service Co. v. State Farm Mutual Auto. Ins. Co., 530 N.W.2d 867 (Minn.App.1995), the court held that appointments made by customers with an auto glass-repair company did not constitute contracts. In the course of its opinion the court said, "We do not believe people intend to be legally bound when they make reservations at a restaurant, or schedule appointments to have their car repaired, their hair cut, or their teeth checked. Nor is it likely that the providers of such services perceive the customers to be bound or intend to be legally bound themselves by scheduling appointments."

———

SECTION 2. TERMINATION OF THE OFFEREE'S POWER OF ACCEPTANCE: LAPSE, REJECTION, AND COUNTER-OFFER

AKERS v. J.B. SEDBERRY, INC.

Court of Appeals of Tennessee, 1955.
39 Tenn.App. 633, 286 S.W.2d 617, cert. denied by Tenn.S.Ct.

FELTS, JUDGE. These two consolidated causes are before us upon a writ of error sued out by J.B. Sedberry, Inc., and Mrs. M.B. Sedberry, defendants below, to review a decree of the Chancery Court, awarding a recovery against them in favor of each of the complainants, Charles William Akers and William Gambill Whitsitt, for damages for breach of a contract of employment. . . .

J.B. Sedberry, Inc., was a Tennessee corporation with its principal place of business at Franklin, Tennessee. Mrs. M.B. Sedberry owned practically all of its stock and was its president and in active charge of its affairs. It was engaged in the business of distributing "Jay Bee" hammer mills, which were manufactured for it under contract by Jay Bee Manufacturing Company, a Texas corporation, whose plant was in Tyler, Texas, and whose capital stock was owned principally by L.M. Glasgow and B.G. Byars.

On July 1, 1947, J.B. Sedberry, Inc., by written contract, employed complainant Akers as Chief Engineer for a term of five years at a salary of $12,000 per year, payable $1,000 per month, plus 1% of its net profits for the first year, 2% the second, 3% the third, 4% the fourth, and 5% the fifth year. His duties were to carry on research for his employer, and to see that the Jay Bee Manufacturing Company, Tyler, Texas, manufactured the mills and parts according to proper specifications. Mrs. M.B. Sedberry guaranteed the employer's performance of this contract.

On August 1, 1947, J.B. Sedberry, Inc., by written contract, employed complainant Whitsitt as Assistant Chief Engineer for a term of five years at a salary of $7,200 per year, payable $600 per month, plus 1% of the corporation's net profits for the first year, 2% for the second, 3% for the third, 4% for the fourth, and 5% for the fifth year. His duties were to assist in the work done by the Chief Engineer. Mrs. M.B. Sedberry guaranteed the employer's performance of this contract.

Under Mrs. Sedberry's instructions, Akers and Whitsitt moved to Tyler, Texas, began performing their contract duties in the plant of the Jay Bee Manufacturing Company, continued working there, and were paid under the contracts until October 1, 1950, when they ceased work, under circumstances hereafter stated. . . .

[After the employment contracts were made, Mrs. Sedberry acquired the stock of Jay Bee from Glasgow and Byars, and installed a new manager, A.M. Sorenson.] There soon developed considerable friction between Sorenson and complainants Akers and Whitsitt. The Jay Bee Manufacturing Company owed large sums to the Tyler State Bank & Trust Co.; and the bank's officers, fearing the company might fail under Sorenson's management, began talking to Akers and Whitsitt about the company's financial difficulties. . . .

While these matters were pending, Akers and Whitsitt flew to Nashville and went to Franklin to talk with Mrs. Sedberry about them. They had a conference with her at her office on Friday, September 29, 1950, lasting from 9:30 a.m. until 4:30 p.m. As they had come unannounced, and unknown to Sorenson, they felt Mrs. Sedberry might mistrust them; and at the outset to show their good faith, they offered to resign, but she did not accept their offer. Instead, she proceeded with them in discussing the operation and refinancing of the business.

Testifying about this conference, Akers said that, at the very beginning, to show their good faith, he told Mrs. Sedberry that they would offer their resignations on a ninety-day notice, provided they were paid according to the contract for that period; that she pushed the offers aside— "would not accept them", but went into a full discussion of the business; that nothing was thereafter said about the offers to resign; and that they spent the whole day discussing the business, Akers making notes of things she instructed him to do when he got back to Texas.

Whitsitt testified that . . . [Mrs. Sedberry]. . . . did not accept the offer, but proceeded with the business, and nothing further was said about resigning.

Mrs. Sedberry testified that Akers and Whitsitt came in and "offered their resignations"; that they said they could not work with Sorenson and did not believe the bank would go along with him; and that "they said if it would be of any help to the organization they would be glad to tender their resignation and pay them what was due them." She further said that she "did not accept the resignation", that she "felt it necessary to contact Mr. Sorenson and give consideration to the resignation offer." But she said nothing to complainants about taking the offer under consideration.

On cross-examination she said that in the offer to resign "no mention was made of any ninety-day notice". Asked what response she made to the offer she said, "I treated it rather casually because I had to give it some thought and had to contact Mr. Sorenson." She further said she excused herself from the conference with complainants, went to another room, tried to telephone Sorenson in Tyler, Texas, but was unable to locate him.

She then resumed the conference, nothing further was said about the offers to resign, nothing was said by her to indicate that she thought the offers were left open or held under consideration by her. But the discussion proceeded as if the offers had not been made. She discussed with complainants future plans for refinancing and operating the business, giving them instructions, and Akers making notes of them.

Following the conference, complainants, upon Mrs. Sedberry's request, flew back to Texas to proceed to carry out her instructions. . . .

On Monday, October 2, 1950, Mrs. Sedberry sent to complainants similar telegrams, signed by "J.B. Sedberry, Inc., by M.B. Sedberry, President", stating that their resignations were accepted, effective immediately. We quote the telegram to Akers, omitting the formal parts:

> "Account present unsettled conditions which you so fully are aware we accept your kind offer of resignation effective immediately. Please discontinue as of today with everyone employed in Sedberry, Inc., Engineering Department, discontinuing all expenses in this department writing." . . .

While this said she was "writing", she did not write. . . .

[Akers then wrote] that he was amazed to get her telegram, and called her attention to the fact that no offer to resign by him was open or outstanding when she sent the telegram; that while he had made a conditional offer to resign at their conference on September 29, she had immediately rejected the offer, and had discussed plans for the business and had instructed him and Whitsitt as to things she wanted them to do in the business on their return to Tyler.

This letter further stated that Akers was expecting to be paid according to the terms of his contract until he could find other employment that would pay him as much income as that provided in his contract, and that if he had to accept a position with less income, he would expect to be paid the difference, or whatever losses he suffered by her breach of the contract. [Whitsitt wrote a similar letter.] . . .

As it takes two to make a contract, it takes two to unmake it. It cannot be changed or ended by one alone, but only by mutual assent of both parties. A contract of employment for a fixed period may be terminated by the employee's offer to resign, provided such offer is duly accepted by the employer. . . .

An employee's tender of his resignation, being a mere offer is, of course, not binding until it has been accepted by the employer. Such offer must be accepted according to its terms and within the time fixed. The matter is governed by the same rules as govern the formation of contracts. . . .

An offer may be terminated in a number of ways, as, for example, where it is rejected by the offeree, or where it is not accepted by him within the time fixed, or, if no time is fixed, within a reasonable time. An offer terminated in either of these ways ceases to exist and cannot thereafter be accepted. 1 Williston on Contracts (1936), secs. 50A, 51, 53, 54; 1 Corbin on Contracts (1950), secs. 35, 36; 1 Restatement, Contracts, §§ 35, 40.

The question what is a reasonable time, where no time is fixed, is a question of fact, depending on the nature of the contract proposed, the usages of business and other circumstances of the case. Ordinarily, an offer made by one to another in a face to face conversation is deemed to continue only to the close of their conversation, and cannot be accepted thereafter.

The rule is illustrated by Restatement Contracts § 40, Illustration 2, as follows:

> "2. While A and B are engaged in conversation, A makes B an offer to which B then makes no reply, but a few hours later meeting A again, B states that he accepts the offer. There is no contract unless the offer or the surrounding circumstances indicate that the offer is intended to continue beyond the immediate conversation." . . .

Professor Corbin says:

> "When two negotiating parties are in each other's presence, and one makes an offer to the other without indicating any time for acceptance, the inference that will ordinarily be drawn by the other party is that an answer is expected at once. . . . If, when the first reply is not an acceptance, the offeror turns away in silence, the proper inference is that the offer is no longer open to acceptance." 1 Corbin on Contracts (1950), section 36, p. 111.

The only offer by Akers and Whitsitt to resign was the offer made by them in their conversation with Mrs. Sedberry. They made that offer at the outset, and on the evidence it seems clear that they expected an answer at once. Certainly, there is nothing in the evidence to show that they intended the offer to continue beyond that conversation; and on the above authorities, we think the offer did not continue beyond that meeting.

Indeed, it did not last that long, in our opinion, but was terminated by Mrs. Sedberry's rejection of it very early in that meeting. While she did not expressly reject it, and while she may have intended, as she says, to take the offer under consideration, she did not disclose such an intent to complainants; but, by her conduct, led them to believe she rejected the offer, brushed it aside, and proceeded with the discussion as if it had not been made.

> "An offer is rejected when the offeror is justified in inferring from the words or conduct of the offeree that the offeree intends not to accept the offer or to take it under further advisement (Rest. Contracts sec. 36)." 1 Williston on Contracts, section 51.

So, we agree with the Trial Judge that when defendants sent the telegrams, undertaking to accept offers of complainants to resign, there was no such offer in existence; and that this attempt of defendants to terminate their contract was unlawful and constituted a breach for which they are liable to complainants. . . .

Finally, defendants contend that if complainants are entitled to any recovery at all, such recovery should have been limited to the ninety-day period from and after October 2, 1950, because complainants themselves admitted that they had offered to resign upon ninety days notice with pay for that period.

The answer to this contention is that their offer to resign on ninety days notice was not accepted, but had terminated, and there was no offer in existence when Mrs. Sedberry undertook to accept their offers of resignation. Such attempt by defendants to terminate their contract was unlawful and was a breach for which they become liable for the measure of recovery as above stated. . . .

All of the assignments of error are overruled and the decree of the Chancellor is affirmed. . . .

The causes are remanded to the Chancery Court for further proceedings not inconsistent with this opinion.

HICKERSON and SHRIVER, JJ., concur.

———

RESTATEMENT, SECOND, CONTRACTS §§ 38, 41

[See Selected Source Materials Supplement]

———

CISG ART. 17

[See Selected Source Materials Supplement]

———

UNIDROIT PRINCIPLES OF INTERNATIONAL COMMERCIAL CONTRACTS ARTS. 2.1.5, 2.1.7

[See Selected Source Materials Supplement]

———

PRINCIPLES OF EUROPEAN CONTRACT LAW ARTS. 2.203, 2.206

[See Selected Source Materials Supplement]

NOTE ON THE EFFECT OF THE REJECTION OF AN OFFER

A recurring problem in the area of offer and acceptance concerns the issue whether an expression by an offeree in response to an offer terminates the offeree's power of acceptance. The underlying question in determining whether an offeree's response terminates his power of acceptance is whether the offeror would reasonably understand that the response serves to take the offer off the table. If an offer is taken off the table the offeree has nothing to accept, any more than if the offer had never been made or had lapsed. Furthermore, an offeror is likely to rely on his understanding that the offer has been taken off the table. For example, suppose an offer states that it will be open for ten days. During those ten days, the offeror may begin steps to prepare for performance based on his assessment of the probability of acceptance by the offeree. Suppose now that as a result of an expression used by the offeree on the second day, the offeror reasonably believes the offer has been taken off the table. In that case, the offeror will take no further steps to prepare for performance, and may arrange his affairs on the basis that he will not be entering into the proposed contract. Alternatively, the offeror may make a new offer to a third party that he would not have made in the absence of the offeree's expression. If the offeree then tries to accept on the tenth day, the offeror would be caught short. Moreover, it would be difficult if not impossible for the offeror to prove that he would have acted differently in the absence of the offeree's expression, because the offeror's response to the offeree's expression may consist of nonaction or of action that is not related to the expression in an obvious way.

The issue then is, what kinds of expressions by an offeree will lead an offeror to reasonably believe that the offer is off the table. To a very large extent, the law of offer and acceptance deals with this issue through a series of categorical rules, rather than by application of the general principles of interpretation on a case-by-case basis. Under one of these rules, a rejection terminates the offeree's power of acceptance even if the rejection is communicated before the offer would otherwise have lapsed. It is easy to justify this rule, because it seems virtually certain that under the general principles of interpretation a rejection would be understood by the offeror to take the offer off the table. Although it is conceivable that in a few cases the general principles of interpretation would lead to a different result—because, for example, neither party subjectively viewed the rejection as taking the offer off the table—such a scenario is so unlikely that a categorical rule is supported by administrative considerations. It should be stressed, however, that even in this relatively easy case, the categorical rule represents a choice. A rejection terminates the power of acceptance, not because a rejection must logically terminate the power of acceptance, but because giving that effect to a rejection is justified by prudential considerations.

ARDENTE V. HORAN

Supreme Court of Rhode Island, 1976.
117 R.I. 254, 366 A.2d 162.

DORIS, JUSTICE. Ernst P. Ardente, the plaintiff, brought this civil action in Superior Court to specifically enforce an agreement between himself and William A. and Katherine L. Horan, the defendants, to sell certain real property. The defendants filed an answer together with a motion for summary judgment pursuant to Super.R.Civ.P. 56. Following the submission of affidavits by both the plaintiff and the defendants and a hearing on the motion, judgment was entered by a Superior Court justice for the defendants. The plaintiff now appeals.

In August 1975, certain residential property in the city of Newport was offered for sale by defendants. The plaintiff made a bid of $250,000 for the property which was communicated to defendants by their attorney. After defendants' attorney advised plaintiff that the bid was acceptable to defendants, he prepared a purchase and sale agreement at the direction of defendants and forwarded it to plaintiff's attorney for plaintiff's signature. After investigating certain title conditions, plaintiff executed the agreement. Thereafter plaintiff's attorney returned the document to defendants along with a check in the amount of $20,000 and a letter dated September 8, 1975, which read in relevant part as follows:

> "My clients are concerned that the following items remain with the real estate: a) dining room set and tapestry wall covering in dining room; b) fireplace fixtures throughout; c) the sun parlor furniture. I would appreciate your confirming that these items are a part of the transaction, as they would be difficult to replace."

The defendants refused to agree to sell the enumerated items and did not sign the purchase and sale agreement. They directed their attorney to return the agreement and the deposit check to plaintiff and subsequently refused to sell the property to plaintiff. This action for specific performance followed.

In Superior Court, defendants moved for summary judgment on the ground that the facts were not in dispute and no contract had been formed as a matter of law.[1] The trial justice ruled that the letter quoted above

---

[1]   Although the contract would appear to be within the statute of frauds, defendants did not raise this defense in the trial court, nor do they raise it here. Where a party makes no claim to the benefit of the statute, the court sua sponte will not interpose it for him. Conti v. Fisher, 48 R.I. 33, 36, 134 A. 849, 850 (1926).

constituted a conditional acceptance of defendants' offer to sell the property and consequently must be construed as a counteroffer. Since defendants never accepted the counteroffer, it followed that no contract was formed, and summary judgment was granted. . . .

The plaintiff assigns several grounds for appeal in his brief. He urges first that summary judgment was improper because there existed a genuine issue of fact. The factual question, according to plaintiff, was whether the oral agreement which preceded the drafting of the purchase and sale agreement was intended by the parties to take effect immediately to create a binding oral contract for the sale of the property.

We cannot agree with plaintiff's position. A review of the record shows that the issue was never raised before the trial justice. The plaintiff did not, in his affidavit in opposition to summary judgment or by any other means, bring to the attention of the trial court any facts which established the existence of a relevant factual dispute. Indeed, at the hearing on the motion plaintiff did not even mention the alleged factual dispute which he now claims the trial justice erred in overlooking. The only issue plaintiff addressed was the proper interpretation of the language used in plaintiff's letter of acceptance. This was solely a question of law. . . .

The plaintiff's second contention is that the trial justice incorrectly applied the principles of contract law in deciding that the facts did not disclose a valid acceptance of defendants' offer. Again we cannot agree.

The trial justice proceeded on the theory that the delivery of the purchase and sale agreement to plaintiff constituted an offer by defendants to sell the property. Because we must view the evidence in the light most favorable to the party against whom summary judgment was entered, in this case plaintiff, we assume as the trial justice did that the delivery of the agreement was in fact an offer.[3]

The question we must answer next is whether there was an acceptance of that offer. The general rule is that where, as here, there is an offer to form a bilateral contract, the offeree must communicate his acceptance to the offeror before any contractual obligation can come into being. A mere mental intent to accept the offer, no matter how carefully formed, is not sufficient. The acceptance must be transmitted to the offeror in some overt manner. Bullock v. Harwick, 158 Fla. 834, 30 So.2d 539 (1947); Armstrong v. Guy H. James Constr. Co., 402 P.2d 275 (Okl.1965); 1 Restatement, Contracts § 20 (1932). See generally 1 Corbin, Contracts § 67 (1963). A review of the record shows that the only expression of acceptance which was communicated to defendants was the delivery of the executed purchase

---

[3]   The conclusion that the delivery of the agreement was an offer is not unassailable in view of the fact that defendants did not sign the agreement before sending it to plaintiff, and the fact that plaintiff told defendants' attorney after the agreement was received that he would have to investigate certain conditions of title before signing the agreement. If it was not an offer, plaintiff's execution of the agreement could itself be no more than an offer, which defendants never accepted.

and sale agreement accompanied by the letter of September 8. Therefore it is solely on the basis of the language used in these two documents that we must determine whether there was a valid acceptance. Whatever plaintiff's unexpressed intention may have been in sending the documents is irrelevant. We must be concerned only with the language actually used, not the language plaintiff thought he was using or intended to use.

There is no doubt that the execution and delivery of the purchase and sale agreement by plaintiff, without more, would have operated as an acceptance. The terms of the accompanying letter, however, apparently conditioned the acceptance upon the inclusion of various items of personalty. In assessing the effect of the terms of that letter we must keep in mind certain generally accepted rules. To be effective, an acceptance must be definite and unequivocal. "An offeror is entitled to know in clear terms whether the offeree accepts his proposal. It is not enough that the words of a reply justify a probable inference of assent." 1 Restatement, Contracts § 58, comment a (1932). The acceptance may not impose additional conditions on the offer, nor may it add limitations. "An acceptance which is equivocal or upon condition or with a limitation is a counteroffer and requires acceptance by the original offeror before a contractual relationship can exist." John Hancock Mut. Life Ins. Co. v. Dietlin, 97 R.I. 515, 518, 199 A.2d 311, 313 (1964). Accord, Cavanaugh v. Conway, 36 R.I. 571, 587, 90 A. 1080, 1086 (1914).

However, an acceptance may be valid despite conditional language if the acceptance is clearly independent of the condition. Many cases have so held. Williston states the rule as follows:

> "Frequently an offeree, while making a positive acceptance of the offer, also makes a request or suggestion that some addition or modification be made. So long as it is clear that the meaning of the acceptance is positively and unequivocally to accept the offer whether such request is granted or not, a contract is formed." 1 Williston, Contracts § 79 at 261–62 (3d ed.1957).

Corbin is in agreement with the above view. 1 Corbin, supra, § 84 at 363–65. Thus our task is to decide whether plaintiff's letter is more reasonably interpreted as a qualified acceptance or as an absolute acceptance together with a mere inquiry concerning a collateral matter.

In making our decision we recognize that, as one text states, "The question whether a communication by an offeree is a conditional acceptance or counter-offer is not always easy to answer. It must be determined by the same common-sense process of interpretation that must be applied in so many other cases." 1 Corbin, supra § 82 at 353. In our opinion the language used in plaintiff's letter of September 8 is not consistent with an absolute acceptance accompanied by a request for a gratuitous benefit. We interpret the letter to impose a condition on plaintiff's acceptance of defendants' offer. The letter does not unequivocally state that even without the enumerated items plaintiff is willing to complete the contract. In fact, the letter seeks "confirmation" that the listed items "are a part of the transaction". Thus, far from being an independent, collateral request, the sale of the items in question is explicitly referred to as a part of the real estate transaction. Moreover, the letter goes on to stress the difficulty of finding replacements for these items. This is a further indication that plaintiff did not view the inclusion of the listed items as merely collateral or incidental to the real estate transaction.

A review of the relevant case law discloses that those cases in which an acceptance was found valid despite an accompanying conditional term generally involved a more definite expression of acceptance than the one in the case at bar. E.g., Moss v. Cogle, 267 Ala. 208, 101 So.2d 314 (1958); Jaybe Constr. Co. v. Beco, Inc., 3 Conn.Cir. 406, 216 A.2d 208, 212 (1965); Katz v. Pratt Street Realty Co., 257 Md. 103, 262 A.2d 540 (1970); Nelson v. Hamlin, 258 Mass. 331, 155 N.E. 18 (1927); Duprey v. Donahoe, 52 Wash.2d 129, 323 P.2d 903 (1958).

Accordingly, we hold that since the plaintiff's letter of acceptance dated September 8 was conditional, it operated as a rejection of the defendants' offer and no contractual obligation was created.

The plaintiff's appeal is denied and dismissed, the judgment appealed from is affirmed and the case is remanded to the Superior Court.

PAOLINO, J., did not participate.

––––––––

Rhode Island Dep't of Transportation v. Providence & Worcester R.R.

674 A.2d 1239 (R.I.1996)

P & W owned a parcel of waterfront property in East Providence, Rhode Island. There were railroad tracks on the property. A statute, Rhode Island G.L. § 39–6.1–9, provided that "All rail properties within the state offered for sale by any railway corporation . . . shall be offered for sale to the state in the first instance at the lowest price at which the railway corporation is willing to sell. . . . The state shall have a period of not more than thirty (30) days from receipt of the notification to accept the offer." P & W entered into a Real Estate Sales Agreement to sell the property to Promet for $100,000, subject to the State's option. Under the agreement with Promet, P & W was required to remove the tracks from the property. Pursuant to the statute, P & W then offered the property to the State for $100,000. The relevant State official accepted the offer in writing, but added, "Of course, you understand that certain wording in the Real Estate Sales Agreement [with Promet] relating to 'buyer' and obligations concerning the removal of track would be inappropriate to the purpose of the State's purchase." P & W claimed that no contract had been formed because the State's response was a conditional acceptance. Held, for the State:

This Court has held that a valid acceptance "must be definite and unequivocal," Ardente v. Horan, 117 R.I. 254, 259, 366 A.2d 162, 165 (1976), and that an "acceptance which is equivocal or upon condition or with a limitation is a counteroffer and requires acceptance by the original offeror before a contractual relationship can exist." John Hancock Mutual Life Insurance Co. v. Dietlin, 97 R.I. 515, 518, 199 A.2d 311, 313 (1964). It is not equivocation, however, "if the offeree merely puts into words that which was already reasonably implied in the terms of the offer." 1 Corbin on Contracts, § 3.32 at 478–79 (rev. ed.1993). It is further the case that "an acceptance must receive a reasonable construction" and that "the mere addition of a collateral or immaterial [matter] will not prevent the formation of a contract." Raydon Exploration, Inc. v. Ladd, 902 F.2d 1496, 1500 (10th Cir.1990). See also Hoyt R. Matise Co. v. Zurn, 754 F.2d 560, 566 (5th Cir.1985) ("[t]o transmogrify a purported acceptance into a counteroffer, it must be shown that the acceptance differs in some material respect from the offer").

The state's letter of acceptance points out that the name of the buyer in the original agreement would have to be changed. In our opinion, this statement simply reflected the obvious necessity to replace "the state" for "Promet" as the named buyer in the deed. Moreover, the letter's reference to P & W's obligation to Promet to remove tracks from the property as "inappropriate to the purpose of the State's purchase" did not add any terms or conditions to the contract but, instead, constituted a clear benefit to P & W. In pointing out that the "wording" that obligated P & W to remove tracks would be "inappropriate" in an agreement between P & W and the state, the state, in fact, relieved P & W from the obligation and expense it otherwise would have incurred in selling the property to Promet. When an offeree, in its acceptance of an offer, absolves the offeror of a material obligation, the "rules of contract construction and the 'rules of common sense'" preclude construing that absolution as an additional term that invalidates the acceptance. Textron, Inc. v. Aetna Casualty and Surety Co., 638 A.2d 537, 541 (R.I.1994). . . .

Therefore, we concur with the trial justice who found that the state validly accepted the option extended to it by P & W.

———

RESTATEMENT, SECOND, CONTRACTS § 39

[See Selected Source Materials Supplement]

———

RESTATEMENT, SECOND, CONTRACTS
§ 39, ILLUSTRATIONS 1–3

1.　A offers B to sell him a parcel of land for $5,000, stating that the offer will remain open for thirty days. B replies, "I will pay $4800 for the parcel," and on A's declining that, B writes, within the thirty day period, "I accept your offer to sell for $5,000." There is no contract unless A's offer was [an option supported by consideration], or unless A's reply to the counter-offer manifested an intention to renew his original offer.

2.　A makes the same offer to B as that stated in Illustration 1, and B replies, "Won't you take less?" A answers, "No." An acceptance thereafter by B within the thirty-day period is effective. B's inquiry was not a counter-offer, and A's original offer stands.

3.　A makes the same offer to B as that stated in Illustration 1. B replies "I am keeping your offer under advisement, but if you wish to close the matter at once I will give you $4800." A does not reply, and within the thirty-day period B accepts the original offer. B's acceptance is effective.

RESTATEMENT, SECOND, CONTRACTS § 59

[See Selected Source Materials Supplement]

CISG ART. 19

[See Selected Source Materials Supplement]

UNIDROIT PRINCIPLES OF INTERNATIONAL
COMMERCIAL CONTRACTS ART. 2.1.11

[See Selected Source Materials Supplement]

PRINCIPLES OF EUROPEAN
CONTRACT LAW ART. 2.208

[See Selected Source Materials Supplement]

NOTE ON THE MIRROR-IMAGE RULE

Under classical contract law, the rule that a conditional acceptance terminates the power of acceptance was accompanied by a closely connected rule known as the mirror-image or ribbon-matching rule. Under that rule if a purported acceptance varied from the offer in any respect, no matter how minor, no contract was formed. Under modern contract law, the bite of this rule has been softened in two respects. First, UCC § 2–207 applies a special rule in the case of contracts for the sale of goods. Although section 2–207 is not limited in terms to form offers and form acceptances, it is obviously designed primarily to deal with the problems presented by forms, and normally is applied only to forms. UCC § 2–207 will be considered in Chapter 15, infra. Second, Comment a to Restatement Second § 59, which builds on UCC § 2–207, and is supported by some case law, provides that "a definite and seasonal expression of acceptance is operative despite the statement of additional or different terms if the acceptance is not made to depend on assent to the additional or different terms." This leaves open how a court is to determine whether in any given case the acceptance is or is not made to depend on assent to the additional or different terms.

SECTION 3. TERMINATION OF THE OFFEREE'S POWER OF ACCEPTANCE: REVOCATION

DICKINSON V. DODDS

In the Court of Appeal, Chancery Division, 1876.
2 Ch.Div. 463.

On Wednesday, the 10th of June, 1874, the defendant John Dodds signed and delivered to the plaintiff, George Dickinson, a memorandum, of which the material part was as follows:

> "I hereby agree to sell to Mr. George Dickinson the whole of the dwellinghouses, garden ground, stabling, and outbuildings thereto belonging, situate at Croft, belonging to me, for the sum of £800. As witness my hand this tenth day of June, 1874.

[Signed] John Dodds."

"P.S.—This offer to be left over until Friday, 9 o'clock a.m. J.D. (the twelfth), 12th June, 1874.

[Signed] J. Dodds."

The bill alleged that Dodds understood and intended that the plaintiff should have until Friday, 9 a.m., within which to determine whether he would or would not purchase, and that he should absolutely have until that time the refusal of the property at the price of £800, and that the plaintiff in fact determined to accept the offer on the morning of Thursday, the 11th of June, but did not at once signify his acceptance to Dodds, believing that he had the power to accept it until 9 a.m. on the Friday.

In the afternoon of the Thursday the plaintiff was informed by a Mr. Berry that Dodds had been offering or agreeing to sell the property to Thomas Allan, the other defendant. Thereupon the plaintiff, at about half past seven in the evening, went to the house of Mrs. Burgess, the mother-in-law of Dodds, where he was then staying, and left with her a formal acceptance in writing of the offer to sell the property. According to the evidence of Mrs. Burgess this document never in fact reached Dodds, she having forgotten to give it to him.

On the following (Friday) morning, at about seven o'clock, Berry, who was acting as agent for Dickinson, found Dodds at the Darlington railway station, and handed to him a duplicate of the acceptance by Dickinson, and explained to Dodds its purport. He replied that it was too late, as he had sold the property. A few minutes later Dickinson himself found Dodds entering a railway carriage, and handed him another duplicate of the notice of acceptance, but Dodds declined to receive it, saying: "You are too late. I have sold the property."

It appeared that on the day before, Thursday, the 11th of June, Dodds had signed a formal contract for the sale of the property to the defendant Allan for £800, and had received from him a deposit of £40.

The bill in this suit prayed that the defendant Dodds might be decreed specifically to perform the contract of the 10th of June, 1874; that he might be restrained from conveying the property to Allan; that Allan might be restrained from taking any such conveyance; that, if any such conveyance had been or should be made, Allan might be declared a trustee of the property for, and might be directed to convey the property to, the plaintiff; and for damages.

The cause came on for hearing before Vice Chancellor Bacon on the 25th of January, 1876. [It was his opinion that Dodds could withdraw only by giving notice to Dickinson, in spite of Cooke v. Oxley, 3 T.R. 653, and that the contract took effect by the doctrine of relation back as of the time of the offer and hence was prior to the sale to Allan. He therefore decreed specific performance in favor of the plaintiff. From the decision both of the defendants appealed.]

JAMES, L.J., after referring to the document of the 10th of June, 1874, continued:

The document, though beginning "I hereby agree to sell," was nothing but an offer, and was only intended to be an offer, for the plaintiff himself tells us that he required time to consider whether he would enter into an agreement or not. Unless both parties had then agreed, there was no concluded agreement then made; it was in effect and substance only an offer to sell. The plaintiff, being minded not to complete the bargain at that time, added this memorandum: "This offer to be left over until Friday, 9 o'clock a.m. 12th June, 1874." That shows it was only an offer. There was no consideration given for the undertaking or promise, to whatever extent it may be considered binding, to keep the property unsold until 9 o'clock on Friday morning; but apparently Dickinson was of opinion, and probably Dodds was of the same opinion, that he (Dodds) was bound by that promise, and could not in any way withdraw from it, or retract it, until 9 o'clock on Friday morning, and this probably explains a good deal of what afterwards took place. But it is clear settled law, on one of the clearest principles of law, that this promise, being a mere nudum pactum, was not binding, and that at any moment before a complete acceptance by Dickinson of the offer, Dodds was as free as Dickinson himself.

Well, that being the state of things, it is said that the only mode in which Dodds could assert that freedom was by actually and distinctly saying to Dickinson, "Now I withdraw my offer." It appears to me that there is neither principle nor authority for the proposition that there must be an express and actual withdrawal of the offer, or what is called a retraction. It must, to constitute a contract, appear that the two minds were at one, at the same moment of time, that is, that there was an offer continuing up to the time of the acceptance. If there was not such a continuing offer, then the acceptance comes to nothing. Of course it may well be that the one man is bound in some way or other to let the other man know that his mind with regard to the offer has been changed; but in this case, beyond all question, the plaintiff knew that Dodds was no longer minded to sell the property to him as plainly and clearly as if Dodds had told him in so many words, "I withdraw the offer." This is evident from the plaintiff's own statements in the bill.

The plaintiff says in effect that, having heard and knowing that Dodds was no longer minded to sell to him and that he was selling or had sold to some one else, thinking that he could not in point of law withdraw his offer, meaning to fix him to it, and endeavoring to bind him: "I went to the house where he was lodging, and saw his mother-in-law, and left with her an acceptance of the offer, knowing all the while that he had entirely changed his mind. I got an agent to watch for him at 7 o'clock the next morning, and I went to the train just before 9 o'clock, in order that I might catch him and give him my notice of acceptance just before 9 o'clock, and when that occurred he told my agent, and he told me, 'You are too late,' and he then threw back the paper." It is to my mind quite clear that before there was any attempt at acceptance by the plaintiff, he was perfectly well aware that Dodds had changed his mind, and that he had in fact agreed to sell the property to Allan. It is impossible, therefore, to say there was ever that existence of the same mind between the two parties which is essential in point of law to the making of an agreement. I am of opinion, therefore, that the plaintiff has failed to prove that there was any binding contract between Dodds and himself. . . .

[The bill] will be dismissed with costs.

[The concurring opinion of Mellish, L.J., is omitted.]

RESTATEMENT, SECOND, CONTRACTS §§ 42, 43

[See Selected Source Materials Supplement]

CISG ART. 16

[See Selected Source Materials Supplement]

UNIDROIT PRINCIPLES OF INTERNATIONAL COMMERCIAL CONTRACTS ART. 2.1.4

[See Selected Source Materials Supplement]

PRINCIPLES OF EUROPEAN CONTRACT LAW ART. 2.202

[See Selected Source Materials Supplement]

NOTE ON WHAT CONSTITUTES RECEIPT OF A WRITTEN ACCEPTANCE

What was the legal effect of leaving a written acceptance with Dodds's mother-in-law, assuming Dickinson still had power to accept? Restatement, Second, Contracts § 68 provides that "A written revocation, rejection, or acceptance is received when the writing comes into the possession of the person addressed, or of some person authorized by him to receive it for him, or when it is deposited in some place which he has authorized as the place for this or similar communications to be deposited for him." Illustration 1 to § 68 is as follows:

A sends B by mail an offer dated from A's house and states as a condition of the offer that an acceptance must be received within three days. B mails an acceptance which reaches A's house and is delivered to a servant or is deposited in a mail box at the door within three days; but A has been called away from home and does not personally receive the letter for a week. There is a contract.

Under UCC § 1–201(27), "a notice or notification received by an organization is effective for a particular transaction from the time when it is brought to the attention of the individual conducting that transaction, and in any event from the time when it would have been brought to his attention if the organization had exercised due diligence. . . ."

See also Note on Electronic Commerce, Chapter 10, infra.

———

RESTATEMENT, SECOND, CONTRACTS § 87(1)

[See Selected Source Materials Supplement]

———

1464-EIGHT, LTD. & MILLIS MANAGEMENT CORP. v. JOPPICH

Supreme Court of Texas, 2004.
154 S.W.3d 101.

COLEMAN, J. The question presented is whether section 87(1)(a) of the Restatement (Second) of Contracts should be incorporated into the common law of Texas. *See* 3 Williston & Lord, A Treatise on the Law of Contracts § 7:23 (4th ed. 1992) ("As far as option contracts are concerned, the Restatement (Second) has taken the position, adopted by some common law courts, that a false recital of nominal consideration is sufficient to support the irrevocability of an offer so long as the underlying exchange is fair and the offer is to be accepted within a reasonable time.").

The petitioners, citing section 87(1)(a) of the Restatement (Second) of Contracts, assert that the respondent's offer to sell real property should be binding as an option contract because the offer was in writing and signed by the respondent, acknowledged the receipt of a nominal consideration of ten dollars, and proposed an exchange on fair terms within a reasonable time. The respondent, contending that the parties' written option agreement is unenforceable, asserts that the agreement lacks consideration because the recited nominal consideration was never actually paid, and that the offer was revoked before it was properly accepted.

In this case of first impression, we agree with the petitioners that the nonpayment of the recited nominal consideration does not preclude enforcement of the parties' written option agreement. Therefore, we will reverse and remand.

I

In July 1997, Gail Ann Joppich entered into an earnest money contract with 1464-Eight, Ltd. and Millis Management Corporation (collectively "Millis") under which Joppich agreed to buy, and Millis agreed to convey, an undeveloped residential lot located in a subdivision being developed by Millis. The purchase price was $65,000. An addendum attached to the earnest money contract provided:

> All Lots being sold in Shiloh Lake Estates Subdivision are being sold pursuant to an Option Agreement to be executed by Buyer and Seller at closing that shall survive closing and provide Seller with an option to purchase the Property from the Buyer at a price equal to 90% of the sale price herein if Buyer fails to commence construction of a private residence on the Property within 18 months from the date of closing.

At the closing later the same month, Millis executed a special warranty deed conveying the lot to Joppich. In addition, the parties executed a separate four-page document entitled "Option Agreement." The notarized document, which was signed by both Joppich and Millis, provided:

1. *Grant of Option.* In consideration of the sum of Ten and No/100 ($10.00) Dollars ("Option Fee") paid in cash by Developer, the receipt and sufficiency of which is hereby acknowledged and confessed, Purchaser hereby grants to Developer the exclusive right and option to purchase [the Property]. This Option may be exercised at any time from and after January 21, 1999.

2. *Purchase Price.* The total purchase price for the Property shall be [$58,500] and shall be due and payable at closing.

3. *Expiration Date.* This Option shall automatically expire at 5:00 o'clock p.m. on the date which is five (5) years after the date of execution and recording in the Office of the County Clerk of Fort Bend County, Texas unless prior to the expiration date this Option is exercised by Developer.

4. *Termination.* This Option shall automatically terminate on the date that Purchaser, or Purchaser's assigns, commence construction of a primary residence which has been approved by [the appropriate committee].

The Option Agreement did not contain an express statement regarding whether the parties intended the offer to sell real property to be revocable or irrevocable. . . .

[Joppich initiated litigation when she sought a declaratory judgment that the Option Agreement was unenforceable for lack of consideration or failure of consideration. In the trial court and the court of appeals, Millis argued that nominal consideration was sufficient under Texas law as a general matter. Neither party ever mentioned Restatement Second Section 87(1)(a). Millis prevailed in the trial court but lost in the court of appeals. Millis belatedly argued in the court of appeals that the property itself was consideration for the option. The Texas Supreme Court held this argument could not considered because it was not raised in the trial court.]

In this Court, Millis asserts that "[t]he court of appeals' holding that failure to deliver the nominal consideration recited in an option contract precludes its enforcement directly conflicts with the modern view reflected in the Restatement (Second) of Contracts." In response, Joppich argues that "[t]he Restatement shows that its view is not the modern view but is in fact the minority view consisting of one and possibly two states." Joppich does not dispute Millis's contention, made in both its petition for review and its brief on the merits, that the Option Agreement satisfies section 87(1)(a) of the Restatement (Second) of Contracts, including its requirement that an offer propose an exchange on fair terms within a reasonable time.

II

"[A] promise to give an option is valid if supported by an independent consideration. For example, if a sum of money be paid for the option, the promisee may, at his election, enforce the contract." *Nat'l Oil & Pipe Line Co. v. Teel,* 95 Tex. 586, 68 S.W. 979, 980 (1902); *see also* Restatement (Second) of Contracts § 25 (1981) ("An option contract is a promise which meets the requirements for the formation of a contract and limits the promisor's power to revoke an offer."). . .

Section 87(1) of the Restatement (Second) of Contracts provides:

(1)   An offer is binding as an option contract if it

(a)   is in writing and signed by the offeror, recites a purported consideration for the making of the offer, and proposes an exchange on fair terms within a reasonable time; or

(b)   is made irrevocable by statute.

Restatement (Second) of Contracts § 87(1) (1981).

The official comment to section 87 states:

b.   Nominal consideration. Offers made in consideration of one dollar paid or promised are often irrevocable under Subsection (1)(a). . .

[A] nominal consideration is regularly held sufficient to support a short-time option proposing an exchange on fair terms. The fact that the option is an appropriate preliminary step in the conclusion of a socially useful transaction provides a sufficient substantive basis for enforcement, and a signed writing taking a form appropriate to a bargain satisfies the desiderata of form. In the absence of statute, however, the bargaining form is essential: a payment of one dollar by each party to the other is so obviously not a bargaining transaction that it does not provide even the form of an exchange.

    c.   False recital of nominal consideration. A recital in a written agreement that a stated consideration has been given is evidence of that fact as against a party to the agreement, but such a recital may ordinarily be contradicted by evidence that no such consideration was given or expected. See § 218. In cases within Subsection (1)(a), however, the giving and recital of nominal consideration performs a formal function only. The signed writing has vital significance as a formality, while the ceremonial manual delivery of a dollar or a peppercorn is an inconsequential formality. In view of the dangers of permitting a solemn written agreement to be invalidated by oral testimony which is easily fabricated, therefore, the option agreement is not invalidated by proof that the recited consideration was not in fact given. A fictitious rationalization has sometimes been used for this rule: acceptance of delivery of the written instrument conclusively imports a promise to make good the recital, it is said, and that promise furnishes consideration. Compare § 218. But the sound basis for the rule is that stated above.

Id. § 87 cmts. b–c (illustrations omitted).

The illustration following comment c states:

    3.   A executes and delivers to B a written agreement "in consideration of one dollar in hand paid" giving B an option to buy described land belonging to A for $15,000, the option to expire at noon six days later. The fact that the dollar is not in fact paid does not prevent the offer from being irrevocable.

Id. § 87 cmt. c, illus. 3.

The authors of the national treatises on contracts have generally endorsed section 87(1)(a) of the Restatement (Second) of Contracts. For example, *Corbin on Contracts* states:

    [Restatement (Second)] has synthesized [cases upholding nominal consideration for options] into a new doctrine, categorizing . . . option contracts—where the formal requisites are met—as enforceable contracts without consideration. The reason for giving special treatment to options and guaranties is their presumptive utility as ancillaries to bargain transactions. . .

    Consideration is designed primarily to protect promisors from their own donative promises. Options, however, are one commercial step in a commercial deal. A number of cases have followed the forthright approach taken by the Restatement (Second). Indeed, it may be urged that the Restatement fails to lead the way to more progressive reform. Having recognized the value of the enforceability of options as commercial devices, it still insists on the fictional recital of a purported consideration. Such fictional charades should not be a part of a mature legal system. Commercial promises such as options and credit guaranties should be enforceable without consideration.

2 Perillo & Bender, Corbin on Contracts § 5.17 (rev. ed.1995). . .

In addition, the authors of law review commentary have agreed that the nonpayment of a recited nominal consideration should not preclude enforcement of a written option agreement. . .

III

The position taken by section 87(1)(a) of the Restatement (Second) of Contracts is admittedly the minority position among the limited number of state supreme courts that have addressed the question. *See, e.g., Lewis v. Fletcher,* 101 Idaho 530, 617 P.2d 834, 835 (1980) (holding that a written option agreement that contains a fictional recital of a nominal consideration is unenforceable for lack of consideration) . . . Nevertheless, we are persuaded that the position of the Restatement (Second) of Contracts, which is supported by a well-articulated and sound rationale, represents the better approach. *See, e.g.,* Restatement (Second) of Contracts § 87 cmt. b (1981) ("The fact that the option is an appropriate preliminary step in the conclusion of a socially useful transaction provides a sufficient substantive basis for enforcement, and a signed writing taking a form appropriate to a bargain satisfies the desiderata of form."); Gordon, *Consideration and the Commercial-Gift Dichotomy,* 44 Vand. L.Rev. 283, 293–94 (1991) ("Option contracts are related to economic exchanges— transactions based on self-interest, not altruism. Moreover, people expect that option contracts are serious and binding commitments.") (footnote omitted).

IV

Based on the foregoing analysis, we reverse the court of appeals's judgment and remand the case to the court of appeals for further proceedings.

[The concurring opinion of Chief Justice Jefferson and Justice Brister are omitted.]

———

UCC § 2–205

[See Selected Source Materials Supplement]

———

Dodge, Teaching the CISG in Contracts

50 J. Leg. Ed. 72 (2000)

"Under the common law, an offer is freely revocable, even if the offeror has promised to hold it open, unless that promise is supported by consideration or reliance. The UCC, of course, changes this rule, allowing a merchant to make an irrevocable offer—a "firm offer"—without the need for consideration. But the UCC's firm-offer rule contains a number of restrictions: the offeror must be a merchant; the offer must be in a signed writing; the offer must contain an "assurance that it will be held open"; and the period of irrevocability may not exceed three months.

"CISG Article 16 allows an offeror to make a firm offer without these limitations:

    (1)   Until a contract is concluded an offer may be revoked if the revocation reaches the offeree before he has dispatched an acceptance.

    (2)   However, an offer cannot be revoked:

        (a) if it indicates, whether by stating a fixed time for acceptance or otherwise, that it is irrevocable; or

        (b) if it was reasonable for the offeree to rely on the offer as being irrevocable and the offeree has acted in reliance on the offer.

"As one can see, Article 16 does not require that the offeror be a merchant or that the offer be in a signed writing, and there is no limit on the period of irrevocability. Article 16 does not even require an express assurance that the offer will be held open. It requires only that the offer 'indicate that it is irrevocable' and it makes clear that an offer may do this 'by stating a fixed time for acceptance.' If an offer simply stated that it would expire after thirty days, the UCC would not treat the offer as 'firm' and would allow the offeror to revoke before the thirty days were up. The CISG, on the other hand, would treat the offer as being irrevocable during the thirty-day period. Article 16(2)(b), like Restatement (Second) § 87(2), provides for an offer to become irrevocable because of the offeree's reliance.

"Article 16 reflects a compromise between the civil law tradition, which presumes that offers are irrevocable, and the common law tradition, which presumes the opposite. Article 16(1) provides that offers are revocable, as under the common law, but Article 16(2) creates broad exceptions that will lead many offers to be irrevocable in practice."

RESTATEMENT, SECOND, CONTRACTS § 45

[See Selected Source Materials Supplement]

RAGOSTA V. WILDER

Supreme Court of Vermont, 1991.
156 Vt. 390, 592 A.2d 367.

Before ALLEN, C.J., and PECK, GIBSON, DOOLEY and MORSE, JJ.

PECK, JUSTICE.

Defendant appeals from a judgment ordering him to convey to plaintiffs a piece of real property known as "The Fork Shop." Defendant argues that the court improperly found that a binding contract existed and that it misapplied the doctrine of equitable estoppel. He also contends that the ruling cannot be upheld under promissory estoppel principles since the court failed to examine the extent to which enforcement of defendant's promise to sell was required to prevent injustice. Because the trial court's ruling cannot stand on contract or equitable estoppel grounds and because the court's analysis of promissory estoppel is inextricably bound in its contractual analysis, we reverse and remand the cause for further proceedings consistent with the principles expressed herein.

In 1985, plaintiffs became interested in purchasing "The Fork Shop" from defendant, but preliminary negotiations between the parties were fruitless. In 1987, plaintiffs learned that defendant was again considering selling "The Fork Shop," [and] mailed him a letter offering to purchase the property along with a check for $2,000 and began arrangements to obtain the necessary financing. By letter dated September 28, 1987, defendant returned the $2,000 check explaining that he had two properties "up for sale" and that he would not sign an acceptance to plaintiffs' offer because "that would tie up both these properties until [there was] a closing." In the letter, he also made the following counter-offer:

> I will sell you The Fork Shop and its property as listed in book 35, at page 135 of the Brookfield Land Records on 17 April 1972, for $88,000.00—(Eighty-eight thousand dollars), at anytime up until the 1st of November 1987 that you appear with me at the Randolph National Bank with said sum. At which time they will give you a certified deed to this property or to your agent as directed, providing said property has not been sold.

On October 1st, the date plaintiffs received the letter, they called defendant. The court found that during the conversation plaintiffs told defendant that "the terms and conditions of his offer were acceptable and that they would in fact prepare to accept the offer." Defendant assured plaintiffs that there was no one else currently interested in purchasing "The Fork Shop."

On October 6th, plaintiffs informed defendant that they would not close the sale on October 8th as discussed previously but that they would come to Vermont on October 10th. On October 8th, defendant called plaintiffs and informed them that he was no longer willing to sell "The Fork Shop." The trial court found that, at that time, defendant was aware plaintiffs "had processed their loan application and were prepared to close." Plaintiffs informed defendant that they would be at the Randolph National Bank at 10:00 a.m. on October 15th with the $88,000 purchase price and in fact appeared. Defendant did not. Plaintiffs claim they incurred $7,499.23 in loan closing costs.

Plaintiffs sued for specific performance arguing that defendant had contracted to sell the property to them. They alleged moreover that defendant knew they would have to incur costs to obtain financing for the purchase but assured them that the sale would go through and that they relied on his assurances.

The trial court concluded that defendant "made an offer in writing which could only be accepted by performance prior to the deadline." It concluded further that defendant could not revoke his offer on October 8th because plaintiffs, relying on the offer, had already begun performance and that defendant should be estopped from revoking the offer on a theory of equitable estoppel. It ordered defendant to convey to plaintiffs "The Fork Shop" for $88,000. This appeal followed.

I.

Plaintiffs claim that defendant's letter of September 28, 1987 created a contract to sell "The Fork Shop" to them unless the property was sold to another buyer. Rather, defendant's letter contains an offer to sell the property for $88,000, which the trial court found could only be accepted "by performance prior to the deadline," and a promise to keep the offer open unless the property were sold to another buyer. Defendant received no consideration for either promise. In fact, defendant returned plaintiffs' check for $2,000 which would have constituted consideration for the promise to keep the offer open, presumably because he did not wish to make a firm offer. Thus, the promise to keep the offer to sell open was not enforceable and, absent the operation of equitable estoppel, defendant could revoke the offer to sell the property at any time before plaintiffs accepted it. See *Buchannon v. Billings*, 127 Vt. 69, 75, 238 A.2d 638, 642 (1968) ("An option is a continuing offer, and *if supported by a consideration*, it cannot be withdrawn before the time limit.") (emphasis added).

Plaintiffs argue that the actions they undertook to obtain financing, which were detrimental to them, could constitute consideration for the promise to keep the offer to sell open. Their argument is unconvincing. Although plaintiffs are correct in stating that a detriment may constitute consideration, they ignore the rule that "[t]o constitute consideration, a performance or a return promise must be bargained for." Restatement (Second) of Contracts § 71(1) (1981). "A performance or return promise is bargained for if it is sought by the promisor in exchange for his promise and is given by the promisee in exchange for that promise." *Id.* at § 71(2). Plaintiffs began to seek financing even before defendant made a definite offer to sell the property. Whatever detriment they suffered was not in exchange for defendant's promise to keep the offer to sell open.

The trial court ruled that the offer to sell "The Fork Shop" could only be accepted by performance but concluded that in obtaining financing plaintiffs began performance and that therefore defendant could not revoke the offer to sell once plaintiffs incurred the cost of obtaining financing. Section 45 of the Restatement (Second) of Contracts provides that "[w]here an offer invites an offeree to accept by rendering a performance and does not invite a promissory acceptance, an option contract is created when the offeree tenders or begins the invited performance or tenders a beginning of it." However, "[w]hat is begun or tendered must be part of the actual performance invited in order to preclude revocation under this Section." *Id.* at comment f.

Here, plaintiffs were merely engaged in preparation for performance. The court itself found only that "plaintiffs had changed their position in order to tender performance." At most, they obtained financing and assured defendant that they would pay; plaintiffs never tendered to defendant or even began to tender the $88,000 purchase price. Thus, they never accepted defendant's offer and no contract was ever created. See *Multicare Medical Center v. State Social & Health Services,* 114 Wash.2d 572, 584, 790 P.2d 124, 131 (1990) ("under a unilateral contract, an offer cannot be accepted by promising to perform; rather, the offeree must accept, if at all, by performance, and the contract then becomes executed").*

II.

Defendant claims next that the court was not justified in applying equitable estoppel in this case. We agree.

One who invokes the doctrine of equitable estoppel has the burden of establishing each of its constituent elements. Four essential elements must be established: first, the party to be

---

* Because defendant specified that the manner of acceptance would be performance, plaintiffs' argument that they accepted defendant's offer over the telephone must fail. In fact, plaintiffs admitted in their depositions that they were very worried that the property would be sold to someone else prior to closing. Thus, they should have understood that they had no enforceable contract until closing.

estopped must know the facts; second, the party being estopped must intend that his conduct shall be acted upon or the acts must be such that the party asserting the estoppel has a right to believe it is so intended; third, the latter must be ignorant of the true facts; and finally, the party asserting the estoppel must rely on the conduct of the party to be estopped to his detriment.

Fisher v. Poole, 142 Vt. 162, 168, 453 A.2d 408, 411–12 (1982) (citations omitted).

Equitable estoppel is inapplicable here because there were no facts known to defendant but unknown to plaintiffs. Plaintiffs cannot have acted on an understanding that defendant would definitely convey the property to them. On its face, defendant's offer stated only that he would convey the property to plaintiffs if he did not convey it to another party first. The trial court acknowledged that if defendant had sold "The Fork Shop" to another party plaintiffs would not have been entitled to relief. Thus, plaintiffs had no assurance that defendant would definitely convey the property to them even if on October 1st defendant told them that there was no one else interested in buying the property at that time. Moreover, plaintiffs engaged in obtaining financing for the purchase even before defendant made any offer to them whatsoever. They understood, at the time they obtained financing for the transaction, that they were assuming a risk that they would be unable to purchase the property in question. Since the plaintiffs had not tendered performance and did not establish the elements for the application of equitable estoppel, defendant was entitled to withdraw his offer when he did.

III.

In the course of analyzing the case under part performance and equitable estoppel theories, the trial court cited promissory estoppel principles. It noted, "Plaintiffs relied on the conduct of the Defendant to their detriment when they prepared for and tendered performance" and concluded that defendant's conduct induced plaintiffs to begin performance by obtaining financing.

A promise which the promisor should reasonably expect to induce action or forbearance on the part of the promisee or a third person and which does induce such action or forbearance is binding if injustice can be avoided only by enforcement of the promise. The remedy granted for breach may be limited as justice requires.

Restatement (Second) of Contracts § 90(1). This principle is distinct from part performance since the action or forbearance involved need not constitute part performance. While the court's order cannot be upheld under a part performance theory, its ruling may be appropriate on promissory estoppel grounds. We cannot affirm the order on those grounds, however, because the trial court, in ruling that the promise must be enforced, erroneously relied on a part performance theory. Cf. *Price v. Price,* 149 Vt. 118, 122, 541 A.2d 79, 82 (1987) (order must be reversed and remanded where court may have relied on inappropriate considerations for its ruling). Under promissory estoppel, plaintiffs are entitled to enforcement of defendant's promise only if the promise induced them to take action "of a definite and substantial character," and if "injustice [*can*] *be avoided only* by enforcement of the promise." *Stacy v. Merchants Bank,* 144 Vt. 515, 521, 482 A.2d 61, 64 (1984) (emphasis added) (citing Restatement (Second) of Contracts § 90).

On remand the court shall consider the case under promissory estoppel only and determine what remedy, if any, is necessary to prevent injustice. In making this determination the court should consider the fact that plaintiffs incurred the expense of obtaining financing although they could not be certain that the property would be sold to them. . . .

Reversed and the cause remanded for further proceedings consistent with the principles expressed herein.

———

NOTE ON OFFERS FOR UNILATERAL CONTRACTS

The court in *Ragosta* drew a sharp distinction between *preparing* to perform an act pursuant to an offer for a unilateral contract and *beginning* to perform the act. To understand why the court drew this distinction, it is necessary to briefly trace the doctrinal history concerning an offer for a unilateral contract—that is, an offer for a contract to be formed by the exchange of a promise (in the form of an offer) and an act, rather than an offer for a contract to be formed by an exchange of promises.

It was a rule of classical contract law that an offer for a unilateral contract could be revoked at any time before the designated act had been completed, even if performance of the act had begun. This rule was exemplified in a pair of famous hypotheticals. In one, A says to B, "I will give you $100 if you walk across the Brooklyn Bridge." After B has walked halfway across the bridge, A overtakes B and revokes. In the other, A offers B $50 to climb a flagpole. After B has climbed halfway up the flagpole, A calls out to B and revokes. The result under classical contract law was the same in both hypotheticals: the revocation was effective, on the ground that an offer for a unilateral contract is revocable until performance of the act has been completed even if performance had begun. Too bad for B.

The rule that an offer for a unilateral contract is revocable until the act has been completed was justified almost exclusively on the basis of deductive reasoning. The major premises of this reasoning were that only a bargained-for promise was enforceable, and that an offer could be revoked at any time prior to acceptance unless the offeror had made a bargained-for promise to hold the offer open. The minor premises were that an offer for a unilateral contract is not bargained for, and is not accepted until the performance that the offer calls for has occurred, that is, has been completed. The deductive conclusion was that an offer for a unilateral contract is revocable until performance has been completed.

The unilateral-contract rule defeated the reasonable expectations of offerees. Tiersma has put this point very well:

> [N]o reasonable person would intentionally create the sort of agreement that the traditional theory of unilateral contracts assumes. Suppose that a person, asserting his freedom to contract and his mastery over his offer, specifically intends to make a promise that will bind him not at the time he makes it, but only after the other party has completed a particular act in exchange. In other words, this promisor wishes to create the traditional unilateral contract. For example, he might tell the offeree that if she paints his house, he will—once she is finished—commit himself to paying her $1000. He makes it clear that he does not wish to be bound until she is completely finished, explaining to her that before she is finished he may revoke with impunity. What rational person would even buy the paint if she believed the speaker had not committed himself? The fact of the matter . . . is that very reasonable people spend substantial time and money doing the sorts of things that unilateral contracts attempt to induce them to do. The only rational explanation for such behavior is that people believe the speaker is in fact committed then and there to paying the price if the conditions of the offer are met.

Peter Meijes Tiersma, Reassessing Unilateral Contracts: The Role of Offer, Acceptance and Promise, 26 U.C. Davis L. Rev. 1, 29 (1992).

Furthermore, the unilateral-contract rule was against the interests of offerors as a class. An actor makes an offer for a unilateral contract because she thinks her interests are best served by such an offer. It is in the interests of an actor who makes an offer for a unilateral contract that the offeree act under the offer—otherwise, the offer would not be made—and correspondingly that the offeree begin acting as quickly as reasonably possible. If, however, offers for unilateral contracts were revocable before performance was completed, offerees would not act under such offers, or at least would act at a much lower rate, because of the substantial risks of forfeiture that such action would entail if the offeror revokes before the act has been completed.

The framers of Restatement First—in particular, Williston, as the Reporter—understood that the unilateral-contract rule was unsatisfactory. However, because classical contract law was conceived as an axiomatic system, and the unilateral-contract rule seemed to flow inexorably from some of the axioms, Williston had trouble in figuring out how to break away from the rule without breaking away from the axioms on which he conceived contract law rested. Williston was willing to bend, but not to break. The result was Section 45 of the First Restatement, which provided:

If an offer for a unilateral contract is made, and part of the consideration requested in the offer is given or tendered by the offeree in response thereto, the offeror is bound by a contract, the duty of immediate performance of which is conditional on the full consideration being given or tendered within the time stated in the offer, or, if no time is stated therein, within a reasonable time.

Despite the fact that under Section 45 liability was triggered only if the offeree took a certain kind of action, Section 45 was conceptualized as bargain-based, not reliance based. If it had been conceptualized as reliance-based, then the Section would have been unnecessary, because the problem it addressed could have been solved by its even more famous cousin, Section 90. Instead, the beginning of performance was—and under Restatement Second still is—conceptualized as completing an option contract, enforceable by expectation damages. The theory is as follows: an offer for a unilateral contract carries with it an implied promise that if part of the requested performance is given or tendered, the offeror will not revoke the offer. Rendering (or tendering) part performance completes a bargain for that promise. This makes the promise enforceable as an option under the bargain theory of consideration.

In order to maintain this conceptualization, the text and comment of Section 45, as formulated in both the First and Second Restatements, drew a sharp distinction between beginning to perform and preparing to perform. Under Section 45 of Restatement First, beginning to perform completed a bargain and therefore made the offeror's promise to hold the offer open enforceable. In contrast, action by the offeree other than beginning to perform had no effect under Section 45, because it would not complete a Section 45 bargain—although the Comment to Restatement First added that such action could have an effect under Section 90, which is not bargain based:

> The main offer [for a unilateral contract] includes as a subsidiary promise, necessarily implied, that if part of the requested performance is given, the offeror will not revoke his offer. . . . Part performance . . . may thus furnish consideration for the subsidiary [promise]. Moreover, merely acting in justifiable reliance on an offer may in some cases serve as sufficient reason for making a promise binding (see § 90).

Section 45 of Restatement Second carries forward the approach of Restatement First.

The distinction between beginning to perform and preparing to perform is not easy to justify. For example, suppose A offers B $10,000 to B if B produces a solution to a famous mathematical problem. B begins by developing some new techniques that will be needed to solve the problem, but will also have independent significance. Has B prepared to perform or has he begun to perform? And why should it matter? As James Gordley observes, under the preparation-versus-performance distinction, if the offeree takes one step on the Brooklyn Bridge the offeror is bound, but if the offeree engages in massive preparations to get ready to cross the Bridge, the offeror is not bound. James Gordley, Enforcing Promises, 82 Cal. L. Rev. 547, 605 (1995).

––––––––––

DRENNAN V. STAR PAVING CO.

Supreme Court of California, 1958.
51 Cal.2d 409, 333 P.2d 757.

TRAYNOR, JUSTICE. Defendant appeals from a judgment for plaintiff in an action to recover damages caused by defendant's refusal to perform certain paving work according to a bid it submitted to plaintiff.

On July 28, 1955, plaintiff, a licensed general contractor, was preparing a bid on the "Monte Vista School Job" in the Lancaster school district. Bids had to be submitted before 8:00 p.m. Plaintiff testified that it was customary in that area for general contractors to receive the bids of subcontractors by telephone on the day set for bidding and to rely on them in computing their own bids. Thus on that day plaintiff's secretary, Mrs. Johnson, received by telephone between fifty and seventy-five subcontractors' bids for various parts of the school job. As each bid came in, she wrote it on a special form, which she brought into plaintiff's office. He then posted it on a master cost sheet setting forth the names and bids of all subcontractors. His own bid had to include the names of subcontractors who were to perform one-half of one per cent or more of the construction work, and he had also to provide a bidder's bond of ten per cent of his total bid of $317,385 as a guarantee that he would enter the contract if awarded the work.*

Late in the afternoon, Mrs. Johnson had a telephone conversation with Kenneth R. Hoon, an estimator for defendant. He gave his name and telephone number and stated that he was bidding for defendant for the paving work at the Monte Vista School according to plans and specifications and that his bid was $7,131.60. At Mrs. Johnson's request he repeated his bid. Plaintiff listened to the bid over an extension telephone in his office and posted it on the master sheet after receiving the bid form from Mrs. Johnson. Defendant's was the lowest bid for the paving. Plaintiff computed his own bid accordingly and submitted it with the name of defendant as the subcontractor for the paving. When the bids were opened on July 28th, plaintiff's proved to be the lowest, and he was awarded the contract.

On his way to Los Angeles the next morning plaintiff stopped at defendant's office. The first person he met was defendant's construction

––––––––––

* Under a "bidder's" or "bid" bond, a Surety promises the person who is receiving bids (the "Obligee"), that if the bidder is awarded the contract but refuses to enter into it, the Surety will pay damages up to a stipulated amount (called "the penalty") that is set in the bond. (Footnote by ed.)

engineer, Mr. Oppenheimer. Plaintiff testified: "I introduced myself and he immediately told me that they had made a mistake in their bid to me the night before, they couldn't do it for the price they had bid, and I told him I would expect him to carry through with their original bid because I had used it in compiling my bid and the job was being awarded them. And I would have to go and do the job according to my bid and I would expect them to do the same."

Defendant refused to do the paving work for less than $15,000. Plaintiff testified that he "got figures from other people" and after trying for several months to get as low a bid as possible engaged L & H Paving Company, a firm in Lancaster, to do the work for $10,948.60.

The trial court found on substantial evidence that defendant made a definite offer to do the paving on the Monte Vista job according to the plans and specifications for $7,131.60, and that plaintiff relied on defendant's bid in computing his own bid for the school job and naming defendant therein as the subcontractor for the paving work. Accordingly, it entered judgment for plaintiff in the amount of $3,817.00 (the difference between defendant's bid and the cost of the paving to plaintiff) plus costs.

Defendant contends that there was no enforceable contract between the parties on the ground that it made a revocable offer and revoked it before plaintiff communicated his acceptance to defendant.

There is no evidence that defendant offered to make its bid irrevocable in exchange for plaintiff's use of its figures in computing his bid. Nor is there evidence that would warrant interpreting plaintiff's use of defendant's bid as the acceptance thereof, binding plaintiff, on condition he received the main contract, to award the subcontract to defendant. In sum, there was neither an option supported by consideration nor a bilateral contract binding on both parties.

Plaintiff contends, however, that he relied to his detriment on defendant's offer and that defendant must therefore answer in damages for its refusal to perform. Thus the question is squarely presented: Did plaintiff's reliance make defendant's offer irrevocable?

Section 90 of the Restatement of Contracts states: "A promise which the promisor should reasonably expect to induce action or forbearance of a definite and substantial character on the part of the promisee and which does induce such action or forbearance is binding if injustice can be avoided only by enforcement of the promise." This rule applies in this state. . . .

Defendant's offer constituted a promise to perform on such conditions as were stated expressly or by implication therein or annexed thereto by operation of law. (See 1 Williston, Contracts [3rd ed.], § 24A, p. 56, § 61, p. 196.) Defendant had reason to expect that if its bid proved the lowest it would be used by plaintiff. It induced "action ... of a definite and substantial character on the part of the promisee."

Had defendant's bid expressly stated or clearly implied that it was revocable at any time before acceptance we would treat it accordingly. It was silent on revocation, however, and we must therefore determine whether there are conditions to the right of revocation imposed by law or reasonably inferable in fact. In the analogous problem of an offer for a unilateral contract, the theory is now obsolete that the offer is revocable at any time before complete performance. Thus section 45 of the Restatement of Contracts provides: "If an offer for a unilateral contract is made, and part of the consideration requested in the offer is given or tendered by the offeree in response thereto, the offeror is bound by a contract, the duty of immediate performance of which is conditional on the full consideration being given or tendered within the time stated in the offer, or, if no time is stated therein, within a reasonable time." In explanation, comment *b* states that the "main offer includes as a subsidiary promise, necessarily implied, that if part of the requested performance is given, the offeror will not revoke his offer, and that if tender is made it will be accepted. Part performance or tender may thus furnish consideration for the subsidiary promise. Moreover, merely acting in justifiable reliance on an offer may in some cases serve as sufficient reason for making a promise binding (see § 90)."

Whether implied in fact or law, the subsidiary promise serves to preclude the injustice that would result if the offer could be revoked after the offeree had acted in detrimental reliance thereon. Reasonable reliance resulting in a foreseeable prejudicial change in position affords a compelling basis also for implying a subsidiary promise not to revoke an offer for a bilateral contract.

The absence of consideration is not fatal to the enforcement of such a promise. It is true that in the case of unilateral contracts the Restatement finds consideration for the implied subsidiary promise in the part performance of the bargained-for exchange, but its reference to section 90 makes clear that consideration for such a promise is not always necessary. The very purpose of section 90 is to make a promise binding even though there was no consideration "in the sense of something that is bargained for and given in exchange." (See 1 Corbin, Contracts 634 et seq.) Reasonable reliance serves to hold the offeror in lieu of the consideration ordinarily required to make the offer binding. In a case involving similar facts the Supreme Court of South Dakota stated that "we believe that reason and justice demand that the doctrine [of section 90] be applied to the present facts. We cannot believe that by accepting this doctrine as controlling in the state of facts before us we will abolish the requirement of a consideration in contract cases, in any different sense than an ordinary estoppel abolishes some legal requirement in its application. We are of the opinion, therefore, that the defendants in executing the agreement [which was not supported by consideration] made a promise which they should have reasonably expected would induce the plaintiff to submit a bid based thereon to the Government, that such promise did induce this action, and that injustice can be avoided only by enforcement of the promise." Northwestern Engineering Co. v. Ellerman, 69 S.D. 397, 408, 10 N.W.2d 879, 884; see also, Robert Gordon, Inc. v. Ingersoll-Rand Co., 7 Cir., 117 F.2d 654, 661; cf. James Baird Co. v. Gimbel Bros., 2 Cir., 64 F.2d 344.

When plaintiff used defendant's offer in computing his own bid, he bound himself to perform in reliance on defendant's terms. Though defendant did not bargain for this use of its bid neither did defendant make it idly, indifferent to whether it would be used or not. On the contrary it is reasonable to suppose that defendant submitted its bid to obtain the subcontract. It was bound to realize the substantial possibility that its bid would be the lowest, and that it would be included by plaintiff in his bid. It was to its own interest that the contractor be awarded the general contract; the lower the subcontract bid, the lower the general contractor's bid was likely to be and the greater its chance of acceptance and hence the greater defendant's chance of getting the paving subcontract. Defendant had reason not only to expect plaintiff to rely on its bid but to want him to. Clearly defendant had a stake in plaintiff's reliance on its bid. Given this interest and the fact that plaintiff is bound by his own bid, it is only fair that plaintiff should have at least an opportunity to accept defendant's bid after the general contract has been awarded to him.

It bears noting that a general contractor is not free to delay acceptance after he has been awarded the general contract in the hope of getting a better price. Nor can he reopen bargaining with the subcontractor and at the same time claim a continuing right to accept the original offer. See, R.J. Daum Const. Co. v. Child, Utah, 247 P.2d 817, 823. In the present case plaintiff promptly informed defendant that plaintiff was being awarded the job and that the subcontract was being awarded to defendant.

Defendant contends, however, that its bid was the result of mistake and that it was therefore entitled to revoke it. It relies on the rescission cases of M.F. Kemper Const. Co. v. City of Los Angeles, 37 Cal.2d 696, 235 P.2d 7, and Brunzell Const. Co. v. G.J. Weisbrod, Inc., 134 Cal.App.2d 278, 285 P.2d 989. See also, Lemoge Electric v. San Mateo County, 46 Cal.2d 659, 662, 297 P.2d 638. In those cases, however, the bidder's mistake was known or should have been known to the offeree, and the offeree could be placed in status quo. Of course, if plaintiff had reason to believe that defendant's bid was in error, he could not justifiably rely on it, and section 90 would afford no basis for enforcing it. Robert Gordon, Inc. v. Ingersoll-Rand, Inc., 7 Cir., 117 F.2d 654, 660. Plaintiff, however, had no reason to know that defendant had made a mistake in submitting its bid, since there was usually a variance of 160 per cent between the highest and lowest bids for paving in the desert around Lancaster. He committed himself to performing the main contract in reliance on defendant's figures. Under these circumstances defendant's mistake, far from relieving it of its obligation, constitutes an additional reason for enforcing it, for it misled plaintiff as to the cost of doing the paving. Even had it been clearly understood that defendant's offer was revocable until accepted, it would not necessarily follow that defendant had no duty to exercise reasonable care in preparing its bid. It presented its bid with knowledge of the substantial possibility that it would be used by plaintiff; it could foresee the harm that would ensue from an erroneous underestimate of the cost. Moreover, it was motivated by its own business interest. Whether or not these considerations alone would justify recovery for negligence had the case been tried on that theory (see Biakanja v. Irving, 49 Cal.2d 647, 650, 320 P.2d 16), they are persuasive that defendant's mistake should not defeat recovery under the rule of section 90 of the Restatement, Contracts. As between the subcontractor who made the bid and the general contractor who reasonably relied on it, the loss resulting from the mistake should fall on the party who caused it. . . .

There is no merit in defendant's contention that plaintiff failed to state a cause of action, on the ground that the complaint failed to allege that plaintiff attempted to mitigate the damages or that they could not have been mitigated. Plaintiff alleged that after defendant's default, "plaintiff had to procure the services of the L & H Co. to perform said asphaltic paving for the sum of $10,948.60." Plaintiff's uncontradicted evidence showed that he spent several months trying to get bids from other subcontractors and that he took the lowest bid. Clearly he acted reasonably to mitigate damages. In any event any uncertainty in plaintiff's allegation as to damages could have been raised by special demurrer. Code Civ.Proc. § 430, subd. 9. It was not so raised and was therefore waived. Code Civ.Proc. § 434.

The judgment is affirmed.

GIBSON, C.J., and SHENK, SCHAUER, SPENCE and McCOMB, JJ., concur.

RESTATEMENT, SECOND, CONTRACTS § 87(2)

[See Selected Source Materials Supplement]

NOTE ON RESTATEMENT SECOND § 87(2)

At first glance, it is not easy to see how the operation of Restatement Second § 87(2) differs from that of Section 45, since both sections concern offers that have been relied upon. In the view of those who prepared Restatement Second, the difference is rooted in the distinction discussed in the Note on Offers for Unilateral Contracts, supra, between beginning to perform and preparing to perform. According to the Comment to Section 45, that section (which applies only to offers for unilateral contracts) is applicable to beginning to perform, but not to preparing to perform. The Comment goes on to say, however, that "Preparations to perform may . . . constitute justifiable reliance sufficient to make the offeror's promise binding under Section 87(2)."

Thus the framers of the Restatement apparently believed that where an offeree has actually begun to perform pursuant to an offer for a unilateral contract, he should automatically be entitled to expectation damages, while in other cases of reliance on an offer, the offeree may appropriately be limited to reliance damages. According to the Comment to Section 87(2), "[i]f the beginning of performance is a reasonable mode of acceptance, it makes the offer *fully enforceable* under § 45 . . .; if not, the offeror commonly has no reason to expect part performance before acceptance. But circumstances may be such that the offeree must undergo substantial expense, or undertake substantial commitments, or forego alternatives, in order to put himself in a position to accept by either promise or performance. . . . Full-scale enforcement of the offered contract is not necessarily appropriate in such cases." (Emphasis added.)

———

Pavel Enterprises, Inc. v. A.S. Johnson Co.

342 Md. 143, 674 A.2d 521 (1996)

(Karwacki, J.) "The *Drennan* decision has been very influential. Many states have adopted the reasoning used by Justice Traynor. . . .

"Despite the popularity of the *Drennan* reasoning, the case has subsequently come under some criticism. The criticism centers on the lack of symmetry of detrimental reliance in the bid process, in that subcontractors are bound to the general, but the general is not bound to the subcontractors. The result is that the general is free to bid shop,[13] bid chop,[14] and to encourage bid peddling,[15] to the detriment of the subcontractors. One commentator described the problems that these practices create:

> 'Bid shopping and peddling have long been recognized as unethical by construction trade organizations. These "unethical," but

---

[13] Bid shopping is the use of the lowest subcontractor's bid as a tool in negotiating lower bids from other subcontractors post-award.

[14] "The general contractor, having been awarded the prime contract, may pressure the subcontractor whose bid was used for a particular portion of the work in computing the overall bid on the prime contract to reduce the amount of the bid." . . .

[15] An unscrupulous subcontractor can save estimating costs, and still get the job by not entering a bid or by entering an uncompetitive bid. After bid opening, this unscrupulous subcontractor, knowing the price of the low sub-bid, can then offer to perform the work for less money, precisely because the honest subcontractor has already paid for the estimate and included that cost in the original bid. This practice is called bid peddling.

common practices have several detrimental results. First, as bid shopping becomes common within a particular trade, the subcontractors will pad their initial bids in order to make further reductions during post-award negotiations. This artificial inflation of subcontractor's offers makes the bid process less effective. Second, subcontractors who are forced into post-award negotiations with the general often must reduce their sub-bids in order to avoid losing the award. Thus, they will be faced with a Hobson's choice between doing the job at a loss or doing a less than adequate job. Third, bid shopping and peddling tend to increase the risk of loss of the time and money used in preparing a bid. This occurs because generals and subcontractors who engage in these practices use, without expense, the bid estimates prepared by others. Fourth, it is often impossible for a general to obtain bids far enough in advance to have sufficient time to properly prepare his own bid because of the practice, common among many subcontractors, of holding sub-bids until the last possible moment in order to avoid pre-award bid shopping by the general. Fifth, many subcontractors refuse to submit bids for jobs on which they expect bid shopping. As a result, competition is reduced, and, consequently, construction prices are increased. Sixth, any price reductions gained through the use of post-award bid shopping by the general will be of no benefit to the awarding authority, to whom these price reductions would normally accrue as a result of open competition before the award of the prime contract. Free competition in an open market is therefore perverted because of the use of post-award bid shopping.'

". . . These problems have caused at least one court to reject promissory estoppel in the contractor-subcontractor relationship. Home Elec. Co. v. Underdown Heating & Air Conditioning Co., 86 N.C.App. 540, 358 S.E.2d 539 (1987). . . . But other courts, while aware of the limitations of promissory estoppel, have adopted it nonetheless. . . . "

Preload Technology, Inc. v. A.B. & J. Construction Co., Inc.

696 F.2d 1080, 1089 (5th Cir.1983)

(Garwood, J.) "Another limitation on the doctrine of promissory estoppel in [suits by a general contractor alleging reliance on a subcontractor's bid] is the prohibition against 'bid shopping,' 'bid chiseling' and related practices sometimes engaged in by general contractors after they have been awarded the general contract and before they subcontract the particular part of the work in dispute. . . . 'Bid shopping' commonly refers to a general contractor's seeking of bids from subcontractors other than the one whose bid amount the general used in calculating its own bid, and often involves the general's informing the other subcontractors of the amount of the low bid and inviting them to undercut it. 'Bid chiseling' usually refers to the general contractor's attempt to negotiate a lower price than that bid from the subcontractor whose bid figure the general employed in calculating its own bid, frequently by threatening to subcontract the work to a third party. . . . When these practices are engaged in, recovery by the general contractor under § 90 may be denied on a variety of theories, viz: that the general contractor did not in fact rely on the subcontractor's bid, or failed to accept it within a reasonable time, or rejected it by a counter-offer, or, perhaps more persuasively, because in such circumstances there is a failure to meet § 90's requirement that 'injustice can be avoided only by enforcement of the promise.' "

————

Allen M. Campbell Co. v. Virginia Metal Industries, Inc.

708 F.2d 930 (4th Cir.1983)

Campbell, a general contractor, proposed to bid on a contract to construct housing. Virginia Metal telephoned Campbell and quoted a price to supply hollow metal doors and frames required by the contract plans and specifications. Campbell was awarded the contract, but Virginia Metal backed out of its bid. Campbell sued. The case was governed by North Carolina law. Held, Virginia Metal was bound to its bid under the theory of promissory estoppel. Although the bid was oral, the UCC Statute of Frauds was not a defense, because under North Carolina law promissory estoppel overcomes the Statute of Frauds.

————

CHAPTER 10

THE MECHANICS OF A BARGAIN (II)—ACCEPTANCE

■ ■ ■

INTRODUCTORY NOTE

This Chapter concerns the rules on acceptance and some related issues. Under classical contract law the fundamental requirement for a response to an offer to be treated as an acceptance is that the response must unequivocally manifest the offeree's assent to the offeror's terms. See *Ardente v. Horan*, supra Chapter 9. Section 1 of this Chapter concerns additional issues involving the form of acceptance and the requirement that acceptance be communicated to the offeror. Section 2 concerns when an acceptance is effective. This is the subject of the "mail box" rule. Section 3 concerns the rules that determine when silence is acceptance. A contract that is based on the parties' actions, and not their expressions, is sometimes described as an "implied-in-fact contract." Section 4 concerns the action in the law of restitution when the plaintiff renders a benefit to the defendant in the mistaken belief in the existence of a contract.

———

SECTION 1. FORM OF ACCEPTANCE

INTERNATIONAL FILTER CO. V. CONROE GIN, ICE & LIGHT CO.

Commission of Appeals of Texas, 1925.
277 S.W. 631.

State of the Case.

NICKELS, J.

Plaintiff in error, an Illinois corporation, is a manufacturer of machinery, apparatus, etc., for the purification of water in connection with the manufacture of ice, etc., having its principal office in the city of Chicago. Defendant in error is a Texas corporation engaged in the manufacture of ice, etc., having its plant, office, etc., at Conroe, Montgomery county, Tex.

On February 10, 1920, through its traveling solicitor, Waterman, plaintiff in error, at Conroe, submitted to defendant in error, acting through Henry Thompson, its manager, a written-instrument, addressed to defendant in error, which (with immaterial portions omitted) reads as follows:

"Gentlemen: We propose to furnish, f. o. b. Chicago, one No. two Junior (steel tank) International water softener and filter to purify water of the character shown by sample to be submitted. * * * Price: Twelve hundred thirty ($1,230.00) dollars. * * * This proposal is made in duplicate and becomes a contract when accepted by the purchaser and approved by .an executive officer of the International Filter Company, at its office in Chicago. Any modification can only be made by duly approved supplementary agreement signed by both parties.

"This proposal is submitted for prompt acceptance, and unless so accepted is subject to change without notice.

'(Respectfully submitted,

"International Filter Co.

"W. W. Waterman."

On the same day the "proposal" was accepted by defendant in error through notation made on the paper by Thompson reading as follows:

"Accepted Feb. 10, 1920.

"Conroe Gin, Ice & Light Co.,

"By Henry Thompson, Mgr."

The paper as thus submitted and "accepted" contained the notation, "Make shipment by Mar. 10." The paper, in that form, reached the Chicago office of plaintiff in error, and on February 13, 1920, P. N. Engel, its president and vice president, indorsed thereon: "O. K. Feb. 13, 1920, P. N. Engel." February 14, 1920, plaintiff in error wrote and mailed, and in due course defendant in error received, the following letter:

"Feb. 14, 1920.

"Attention of Mr. Henry Thompson, Manager.

"Conroe Gin, Ice & Light Co., Conroe, Texas—Gentlemen: This will acknowledge and thank you for your order given Mr. Waterman for a No. 2 Jr. steel tank International softener and filter, for 110 volt, 60 cycle, single phase current—for shipment March. 10th.

"Please make shipment of the sample of water promptly so that we may make the analysis and know the character of the water before shipment of the apparatus. Shipping tag is inclosed, and please note the instructions to pack to guard against freezing.

"Yours very truly,

"International Filter Co.,

"M. B. Johnson."

By letter of February 28, 1920, defendant in error undertook to countermand the "order," which countermand was repeated and emphasized by letter of March 4, 1920. By letter of March 2, 1920 (replying to the letter of February 28th), plaintiff in error denied the right of countermand, etc., and insisted upon performance of the "contract." The parties adhered to the respective positions thus indicated, and this suit resulted.

Plaintiff in error sued for breach of the contract alleged to have been made in the manner stated above. The defense is that no contract was made because: (1) Neither Engel's indorsement of "O. K.," nor the letter of February 14, 1920, amounted to approval "by an executive officer of the International Filter Company, at its office in Chicago." (2) Notification of such approval, or acceptance, by plaintiff in error was required to be communicated to defendant in error; it being insisted that this requirement inhered in the terms of the proposal and in the nature of the transaction and, also, that Thompson, when he indorsed "acceptance" on the paper stated to Waterman, as agent of plaintiff in error, that such notification must be promptly given; it being insisted further that the letter of February 14, 1920, did not constitute such acceptance or' notification of approval, and therefore defendant in error, on February 28, 1920, etc., had the right to withdraw, or countermand, the unaccepted offer. Thompson testified in a manner to support' the allegation of his statement to Waterman. There are other matters involved in the suit which must be ultimately determined, but the foregoing presents the issues now here for consideration.

The case was tried without a jury, and the judge found the facts in favor of defendant in error on all the issues indicated above, and upon other material issues. The judgment was affirmed by the Court of Civil Appeals, 269 S. W. 210.

Opinion.

We agree with the honorable Court of Civil Appeals upon the proposition that Mr. Engel's indorsement of "O. K." amounted to an approval "by an executive officer of the International Filter Company, at its office 'in Chicago," within the meaning of the so-called ' "proposal" of February 10th. The paper then became a "contract," according to its definitely expressed terms, and it became then, and thereafter it remained, an enforceable contract, in legal contemplation, unless the fact of approval by the filter company was-required to be communicated to the other party and unless, in that event, the communication was not made.

We are not prepared to assent to the ruling that such communication was essential. There is no disposition to question the justice of the general rules stated in support of that holding, yet the existence of contractual capacity imports the right of the offerer to dispense with notification; and he does dispense with it "if the form of the offer," etc., "shows that this was not to be required." 9 Cyc. 270, 271; Carlill v. Carbolic Smoke Ball Co., 1 Q. B. 256 (and other references in note 6, 9 Cyc. 271). The case just cited, it seems to us, correctly states the rule:

"As notification of acceptance is required for the benefit of the person who makes the offer, the person who makes the offer may dispense with notice to himself if he thinks it desirable to do so, and I suppose there can be no doubt that where a person in an offer made by him to another person, expressly or impliedly intimates a particular mode of acceptance as sufficient to make the bargain binding, it is only necessary for the other person to whom such offer is made to follow the indicated method of acceptance; and if the person making the offer, expressly or impliedly intimates in his offer that it will be sufficient to act on the proposal without communicating acceptance of it to himself, performance of the condition is a sufficient acceptance without notification."

See, also, Fort v. Barnett, 23 Tex. 460, 464. The Conroe Gin, Ice & Light Company executed the paper for the purpose of having it transmitted, as its offer, to the filter company at Chicago. It was so transmitted and acted upon. Its terms embrace the offer, and nothing else, and by its terms the question of notification must be judged, since those terms are not ambiguous.

The paper contains two provisions which relate to acceptance by the filter company. One is the declaration that the offer shall "become a contract * * * when approved by an executive officer of the International Filter Company, at its Chicago office." The other is thus stated: "This proposal is submitted for prompt acceptance, and unless so accepted is subject to change without notice." The first provision states "a particular mode of acceptance as sufficient to make the bargain binding," and the filter company (as stated above) followed "the indicated method of acceptance." When this was done, so the paper declares, the proposal "became a contract." The other provision does not in any way relate to a different method of acceptance by the filter company. Its sole reference is to the time within which the act of approval must be done; that is to say, there was to be a "prompt acceptance," else the offer might be changed "without notice." The second declaration merely required the approval thereinbefore stipulated for to be done promptly; if the act was so done, there is nothing in the second provision to militate against, or to conflict with, the prior declaration that, thereupon, the paper should become "a contract."

A holding that notification of that approval is to be deduced from the terms of the last-quoted clause is not essential in order to give it meaning or to dissolve ambiguity. On the contrary, such a construction of the two provisions would introduce a conflict, or ambiguity, where none exists in the language itself, and defeat the plainly expressed term wherein it is said that the proposal "becomes a contract * * * when approved by an executive officer'." There is not anything in the language used to justify a ruling that this declaration must be wrenched from its obvious meaning and given one which would change both the locus and time prescribed for the meeting of the minds. The offerer said that the contract should be complete if approval be promptly given by the executive officer at Chicago; the court cannot properly restate the offer so as to make the offerer declare that a contract shall be made only when the approval shall have been promptly. given at Chicago and that fact shall have been communicated to the offerer at Conroe. In our; opinion, therefore, notice of the approval was not required.

The letter of February 14th, however, sufficiently communicated notice, if it was required. . . .

CURETON, C. J.

Judgment of the Court of Civil Appeals reversed, and cause remanded to the Court of Civil Appeals for further consideration by that court, as recommended by the Commission of Appeals.

RESTATEMENT, SECOND, CONTRACTS §§ 30, 56, 60

[See Selected Source Materials Supplement]

UCC § 2–206

[See Selected Source Materials Supplement]

NOTE ON ACCEPTANCE BY PROMISE OR PERFORMANCE

Restatement Second § 32 provides that "In case of doubt an offer is interpreted as inviting the offeree to accept either by promising to perform what the offer requests or by rendering the performance, as the offeree chooses." Relatedly, UCC § 2–206(1)(b) provides that "an order or other offer to buy goods for prompt or current shipment shall be construed as inviting acceptance either by a prompt promise to ship or by the prompt or current shipment of conforming or non-conforming goods." When the offeree accepts an offer of a bilateral contract by rendering performance she undertakes an obligation to perform in accordance with the offer. An offeree who ships non-conforming goods can avoid the shipment being treated as both an acceptance and a breach by seasonably notifying the buyer that the shipment "is offered only as an accommodation to the buyer."

Bishop v. Eaton

161 Mass. 496, 37 N.E. 665 (1894)

In December, 1886, defendant in a letter to plaintiff said "If Harry needs more money, let him have it, or assist him to get it, and I will see that it is paid." Harry was defendant's brother and was connected in business with plaintiff. Defendant lived in Nova Scotia; Harry and plaintiff lived in Illinois. On January 7, 1887, plaintiff signed a $200 note for Harry as surety. Plaintiff immediately sent a letter to defendant stating that the note had been given and the amount. Defendant testified that he never received the letter.

(Knowlton, J.) "[T]his was not a proposition which was to become a contract only upon the giving of a promise for the promise, and it was not necessary that the plaintiff should accept it in words, or promise to do anything before acting upon it. It was an offer which was to become effective as a contract upon the doing of the act referred to. It was an offer to be bound in consideration of an act to be done, and in such a case the doing of the act constitutes the acceptance of the offer and furnishes the consideration. Ordinarily there is no occasion to notify the offerer of the acceptance of such an offer, for the doing of the act is a sufficient acceptance, and the promisor knows that he is bound when he sees that action has been taken on the faith of his offer. But if the act is of such a kind that knowledge of it will not quickly come to the promisor, the promisee is bound to give him notice of his acceptance within a reasonable time after doing that which constitutes the acceptance. In such a case it is implied in the offer that, to complete the contract, notice shall be given with due diligence, so that the promisor may know that a contract has been made. But where the promise is in consideration of an act to be done, it becomes binding upon the doing of the act so far that the promisee cannot be affected by a subsequent withdrawal of it, if within a reasonable time afterward he notifies the promisor. In accordance with these principles, it has been held in cases like the present, where the guarantor would not know of himself, from the nature of the transaction, whether the offer has been accepted or not, that he is not bound without notice of the acceptance, seasonably given after the performance which constitutes the consideration. Babcock v. Bryant, 12 Pick. 133; Whiting v. Stacy, 15 Gray, 270; Schlessinger v. Dickinson, 5 Allen, 47.

"In the present case the plaintiff seasonably mailed a letter to the defendant, informing him of what he had done in compliance with the defendant's request, but the defendant testified that he never received it, and there is no finding that it ever reached him. The judge ruled, as matter of law, that upon the facts found, the plaintiff was entitled to recover, and the question is thus presented whether the defendant was bound by the acceptance when the letter was properly mailed, although he never received it.

"When an offer of guaranty of this kind is made, the implication is that notice of the act which constitutes an acceptance of it shall be given in a reasonable way. What kind of a notice is required depends upon the nature of the transaction, the situation of the parties, and the inferences fairly to be drawn from their previous dealings, if any, in regard to the matter. If they are so situated that communication by letter is naturally to be expected, then the deposit of a letter in the mail is all that is necessary. If that is done which is fairly to be contemplated from their relations to the subject-matter and from their course of dealing, the rights of the parties are fixed, and a failure actually to receive the notice will not affect the obligation of the guarantor.

"The plaintiff in the case now before us resided in Illinois, and the defendant in Nova Scotia. The offer was made by letter, and the defendant must have contemplated that information in regard to the plaintiff's acceptance or rejection of it would be by letter. It would be a harsh rule which would subject the plaintiff to the risk of the defendant's failure to receive the letter giving notice of his action on the faith of the offer. We are of opinion that the plaintiff, after assisting Harry to get the money, did all that he was required to do when he seasonably sent the defendant the letter by mail informing him of what had been done."

————

NOTE ON REQUIREMENT TO COMMUNICATE ACCEPTANCE

As a general rule, when an offeree accepts by promise she is expected to make a reasonable effort to communicate the acceptance to the offeror. *International Filter*, supra, discusses one exception to this rule: when the offeror expressly dispenses with notice of acceptance. Restatement Second § 54(1) provides that "Where an offer invites an offeree to accept by rendering a performance, no notification is necessary to make such an acceptance effective unless the offer requests such a notification." The rule in § 54(2) qualifies this by requiring the offeree to "exercise reasonable diligence to notify the offeror of acceptance" when the offeree "has reason to know that the offeror has no adequate means of learning of the performance with reasonable promptness and certainty." UCC § 2–206(2) is similar.

————

Restatement, Second, Contracts § 56, Illustration 2

"A makes written application for life insurance through an agent for B Insurance Company, pays the first premium, and is given a receipt stating that the insurance "shall take effect as of the date of approval of the application" at B's home office. Approval at the home office in accordance with B's usual practice is an acceptance of A's offer even though no steps are taken to notify A."

————

SECTION 2. WHEN AN ACCEPTANCE IS EFFECTIVE (THE MAILBOX RULE)

The issue often arises in contract law whether a given type of communication is effective when it is dispatched or when it is received. The rules that govern this issue were formulated when the basic modes of communication were face to face and by mail or, somewhat later, by telephone and telegram. The rules that developed were as follows: Except for acceptances, contractual communications are normally effective when received. If an acceptance is given face to face or "by telephone or other medium of substantially instantaneous two-way communication," it is also effective when received. See Restatement Second § 64. However, if an acceptance is transmitted through a medium, such as regular mail, that is not substantially instantaneous two-way communication then the acceptance is effective when dispatched unless the offeror specifies otherwise. (Presumably, the same rule would be applied to private express-mail services, such as FedEx.) This rule is known as the *mailbox rule* or the *dispatch rule*. The rule is often associated with a famous English case, Adams v. Lindsell, 1 Barn. & Ald. 681 (K.B. 1818).

Application of the mailbox rule arises in a variety of contexts. Two follow:

1. *Crossed revocation and acceptance.* The paradigm case for application of the mailbox rule is a crossed revocation and acceptance. For example, assume that A makes an offer by mail to B on June 1. The course of post is two days, so that B receives the offer on June 3. B promptly accepts by mail that day, and his acceptance reaches A on June 5. Meanwhile, on June 2, A has sent B a revocation, which reaches B on June 4. Here A's revocation was dispatched before B's acceptance was dispatched, and was received before B's acceptance was received. Nevertheless, under the mailbox rule a contract is formed, because a revocation is effective only when received (on June 4) while an acceptance is effective when dispatched (on June 3).

An argument in favor of the mailbox rule in this context is that it pushes up the beginning of performance to the earliest possible date. Suppose, for example, that as in the hypothetical, the course of post is two days, and the offeree is to perform before the offeror. Under the mailbox rule, an offeree can safely begin to perform as soon as he dispatches his acceptance. If we assume that, as seems likely, most offerors do not revoke, then offerors as a class may prefer the mailbox rule, because it is usually in the interests of offerors that performance begin as soon as possible.

2. *Delay or failure of transmission.* A different question is presented when a mailed acceptance is either delayed or fails to reach the offeror. For example, suppose that Seller offers by mail to sell Blackacre to Buyer, and gives Buyer five days in which to accept. Buyer promptly dispatches a letter

of acceptance, but the letter miscarries and never reaches Seller. Seller waits ten days, and having had no word from Buyer, assumes that Buyer is no longer interested and sells Blackacre to someone else. Buyer, who has no reason to anticipate that his acceptance will fail to reach Seller, disposes of the premises now in his possession, in the expectation of occupying Blackacre. Is there a contract?

Delay or failure cases are commonly dealt with under the mailbox rule, on the theory that the cases turn on the same issue as crossed-revocation-and-acceptance cases—namely, when does an acceptance take effect. It is apparent, however, that delay and failure cases involve different considerations than those involved in the crossed-revocation-and-acceptance context. In crossed-revocation-and-acceptance cases, the offeror knows that the offeree decided to accept. In delay or failure cases, the offeror is likely to believe that the offeree decided not to accept. Accordingly, if an acceptance takes effect on dispatch in the delay and failure cases, it must either be for reasons other than those that apply to the crossed-revocation-and-acceptance case, or because it is thought wise to avoid nuances and complexities by establishing a categorical rule to cover all types of cases in which the issue is when an acceptance takes effect.

———

RESTATEMENT, SECOND, CONTRACTS §§ 30, 49, 60, 63–68

[See Selected Source Materials Supplement]

———

UCC § 2–206(1)

[See Selected Source Materials Supplement]

———

CISG ARTS. 15, 16, 18(2), 20, 22, 23, 24

[See Selected Source Material Supplement]

———

UNIDROIT PRINCIPLES OF INTERNATIONAL COMMERCIAL CONTRACTS ARTS. 2.1.3, 2.1.6(2), 2.1.7, 2.1.8, 2.1.10

[See Selected Source Materials Supplement]

PRINCIPLES OF EUROPEAN CONTRACT LAW ARTS. 2.205(1), 2.206

[See Selected Source Materials Supplement]

Dodge, Teaching the CISG in Contracts

50 J. Leg. Ed. 72 (2000)

"Under the common law, acceptances are effective upon dispatch, even if they never reach the offeror. This rule performs two functions: it protects the offeree against the possibility of revocation once the acceptance is dispatched, and it places the risk of a lost communication on the offeror. In contrast to the common law mailbox rule, Article 18(2) of the CISG adopts a receipt rule: 'An acceptance of an offer becomes effective at the moment the indication of assent reaches the offeror.' But this provision must be read in conjunction with Article 16(1), which says that 'an offer may be revoked if the revocation reaches the offeree before he has dispatched an acceptance' (emphasis added). In other words, once the offeree has dispatched an acceptance, the offeror may no longer revoke, but if the acceptance is lost in the mail there is no contract. So the CISG and the common law both protect the offeree against the possibility of revocation once the acceptance is dispatched, but the CISG places the risk of a lost communication on the offeree rather than the offeror."

SECTION 3. SILENCE AS ACCEPTANCE

This section concerns the rules that treat an offeree's silence in response to an offer as acceptance of the offer. In the principal case the question is whether an offeror's silence in response to a counter-offer is acceptance of a changed term in the counter-offer when the original offeror did not read the counter-offer. You will see this issue again in Chapter 15 when we take up the battle of the forms. The rules in Restatement Section 69 on when silence constitutes acceptance generally focus on a simpler problem, defining when a party who takes property or services tacitly agrees to pay.

MCGURN V. BELL MICROPRODUCTS, INC.
United States Courts of Appeals, First Circuit, 2002.
284 F.3d 86.

LIPEZ, CIRCUIT JUDGE.

This case requires us to evaluate the district court's application of an exception to the general rule that silence does not constitute acceptance of the terms of a contract offer.

I.

Bell Microproducts, Inc. (Bell) mailed George R. McGurn a signed offer of employment, which stipulated that if McGurn was terminated without cause during the first twelve months of his employment with Bell he would receive a severance package worth $120,000. In countersigning and returning the offer letter, McGurn crossed out the word "twelve" and replaced it with "twenty-four." McGurn initialed his alteration, but otherwise did nothing to call it to Bell's attention. Bell terminated McGurn thirteen months later and refused to pay him the severance package on the ground that the twelve-month period stipulated in the offer letter had passed, and that McGurn's replacement of "twelve" with "twenty-four" was a counteroffer which Bell had never accepted.

McGurn filed an action in the Massachusetts Superior Court to collect the compensation he claimed Bell owed him under the contract, and Bell removed the case to federal district court on the basis of diversity of citizenship. The parties agree that Massachusetts law governs this dispute. Presented with cross-motions for summary judgment, the district court granted summary judgment for McGurn, finding that Bell's silence in response to McGurn's counteroffer constituted an acceptance of the 24-month termination clause. We find that conclusion premature. The import of Bell's silence cannot be decided as a matter of law on a motion for summary judgment because of genuine issues of material fact about whether Bell knew or should have known of McGurn's counteroffer. We therefore vacate the district court's judgment and remand for further proceedings.

II.

Except as noted, the following facts are undisputed. Bell Microproducts is a distributor of semiconductor parts and components with headquarters in San Jose, California. McGurn is a resident of Massachusetts. In March of 1997, Bell's President, Donald Bell, met with McGurn, who at the time was gainfully employed elsewhere, to discuss the position of Vice President for the Eastern Region at Bell. McGurn said that if he came to work for Bell he would require a written contract that included a "termination clause" stipulating that he would receive six months salary and half his commissions in the event that he was fired.

During the next few months McGurn communicated several times with Bill Murphy, the Bell official to whom McGurn would report, and expressed interest in pursuing the position.

Based on these discussions, Murphy's secretary prepared an offer letter and delivered it to Linda Teague, Bell's Director of Human Resources. Teague dated the letter June 10, 1997, signed it, and mailed it to McGurn. Upon receipt of the letter, McGurn telephoned Murphy to discuss the offer and the absence of a termination clause. McGurn then had a series of telephone conversations with Donald Bell in which a termination clause was discussed. On June 29, McGurn requested a termination clause that would remain in force as long as he worked for Bell. However, he also said to Donald Bell that he would consider one that was limited to the first twenty four months of his employment. According to McGurn, Donald Bell replied that a twenty-four month termination clause would be acceptable.

Teague then drafted a second offer letter, in consultation with Donald Bell, which she signed and dated July 1, 1997. The letter included a termination clause stipulating that "[i]f your status as an employee with Bell Microproducts is terminated within the first 12 months of employment for any reason other than gross misconduct, upon termination you will receive a six-month severance package." In response, McGurn drafted his own proposed offer letter, dated July 2, 1997, which included a paragraph on termination "for cause," defined as conviction of a felony or gross negligence or misconduct on the job, and a paragraph on termination "without cause," which was open-ended:

> [T]he Company may terminate your employment without cause. In such event, you will continue to receive your base salary for a period of six (6) months following your termination of employment, [and] . . . you will receive an additional lump-sum amount equal to $40,000 or 50% of annual incentive.

McGurn faxed his proposed offer letter to Murphy.

McGurn's next contact with Bell was his receipt of an offer letter dated July 3, 1997, signed by Teague. The letter included the following paragraph on termination without cause (we have underlined the material change from McGurn's July 2 proposal):

> [T]he Company may terminate your employment without cause. In *the event that this occurs within your first twelve months of employment,* you will continue to receive your base salary for a period of six (6) months following your termination of employment, [and] . . . you will receive an additional lump-sum amount equal to $40,000 or 50% of annual incentive.

The letter concluded with Teague's request that McGurn "sign an acknowledgment of this offer of employment and return to me for our files." The following appeared under Teague's signature:

I acknowledge my acceptance of the offer as described above and my start date will be _____.

Signed _____ Date _____

McGurn signed his name and entered "7–8–97" in the other two blank spaces. In addition, he crossed out the word "twelve" in the termination clause, inserted "twenty four" directly above it, and initialed the change. The alteration was in the center of the second page of the two-page letter, five inches above McGurn's signature. McGurn returned the letter to Teague (or possibly to Murphy), and started work on July 8, 1997.

McGurn advised no one at Bell that he had modified the July 3 offer letter, and Teague, Murphy, and Donald Bell all deny having viewed the letter upon its return. The Human Resources Department did receive the letter, but Teague testified that she herself would only have been notified if the letter had *not* been received, as McGurn could not have been paid unless a countersigned copy of the offer letter was in Bell's files. Although there is no direct evidence that anyone in the Human Resources Department examined the returned letter, there was evidence that it was Bell's practice to check that returned offer letters had been signed by the employee.

In or around April of 1998, Brian Clark (Murphy's successor at Bell) concluded that McGurn's performance was not satisfactory. At some point after Clark made this determination, but before he fired McGurn on August 3, 1998, Murphy discovered McGurn's alteration of the offer letter, and discussed it with Teague and Donald Bell. Upon learning of his termination on August 3, 1998, after approximately 13 months at Bell, McGurn conveyed to Clark his belief that his contract included a two-year termination clause. Clark disagreed, and Bell refused to pay the amounts specified in the termination clause.

McGurn sued Bell for breach of contract in the Superior Court of Middlesex County, Massachusetts. Based on diversity of citizenship, Bell removed the case to federal district court. 28 U.S.C. § 1332(a)(1). The parties filed cross-motions for summary judgment. In a Memorandum and Order dated February 15, 2001, the district court granted McGurn's motion and denied Bell's motion. The district court found that McGurn's alteration of the July 3 offer letter constituted a counteroffer which, in the circumstances of this case, Bell had accepted by its silence. The court entered judgment for McGurn in the amount of $120,000 plus interest, and Bell filed a timely notice of appeal.

III.

The parties agree that McGurn's alteration of Bell's offer letter
constituted a rejection of that offer and created a counteroffer. *See
Restatement (Second) of Contracts* § 59 (1981) ("A reply to an offer which
purports to accept it but is conditional on the offeror's assent to terms
additional to or different from those offered is not an acceptance but is a
counter-offer."). What is in dispute is whether Bell accepted McGurn's
counteroffer. The district court concluded that it did because Bell should
have known about the change made by McGurn, and hence its silence
constituted an acceptance of McGurn's counteroffer:

> Although no one on behalf of the defendant signed McGurn's
> counteroffer, the defendant admits it received the offer and
> accepted McGurn's services for thirteen months. A presumably
> sophisticated employer who receives a signed letter of engagement
> from a prospective employee and fails to read the letter,
> particularly after weeks of negotiation, does so at its own peril.
> Thus, in the circumstances of this case, the defendant's failure to
> read the terms of the offer [does] not preclude the formation of a
> contract. The defendant accepted the terms of the plaintiff's offer
> when it decided to and did employ the plaintiff for thirteen
> months.

Urging a different theory than the "should have known" theory
adopted by the district court, McGurn argues that Bell's silence in the face
of his counteroffer amounted to an acceptance because Bell knew that
McGurn had amended the termination clause, but gave no indication that
it rejected the change. Bell denies that it knew about McGurn's alteration
of the offer letter.

As a general rule, silence in response to an offer to enter into a contract
does not constitute an acceptance of the offer. *See Restatement (Second) of
Contracts* § 69 cmt. a ("Acceptance by silence is exceptional."); *Polaroid
Corp. v. Rollins Envtl. Servs. (NJ), Inc.*, 416 Mass. 684, 624 N.E.2d 959,
964 (1993) (noting that "silence does not ordinarily manifest assent").
There is, however, an exception to the rule against acceptance by silence
"[w]here an offeree takes the benefit of offered services with reasonable
opportunity to reject them and reason to know that they were offered with
the expectation of compensation."[2] *Restatement (Second) of Contracts*
§ 69(1)(a).

In *Gateway Co. v. Charlotte Theatres, Inc.*, 297 F.2d 483 (1st Cir.1961),
a case in many respects similar to this one, the defendant had sent the

---

[2] Although the *Restatement* exception, by its terms, addresses a situation in which the
offeree advances no payment at all in exchange for the offeror's services, the district court
concluded correctly that the exception also applies when there is a dispute about the nature or
extent of required compensation. *See Polaroid*, 624 N.E.2d at 964 (applying the exception to a
dispute over whether a waste disposal contract included an indemnification clause).

plaintiff two copies of a document which reduced to writing an oral agreement for the defendant to install air conditioning in the plaintiff's movie theater, with one copy to be countersigned and returned. *Id.* at 485. The plaintiff signed, but also inserted a provision that the work would be performed by a certain date. *Id.* The plaintiff returned the countersigned contract with a cover letter noting its "understanding" that the work would be performed by that date (although the letter made no reference to the alteration of the contract itself). *Id.* at 485–86. We stated that "[i]n the absence of actual knowledge [of the alteration of the contract], the test is whether there was reason for [the defendant] to suppose that such addition might have been made." *Id.* at 486. We held that because of the cover letter flagging the issue, defendant's silence could constitute acceptance of plaintiff's counteroffer.

Importantly, we also noted in *Gateway* that "absent the [cover] letter, the case would seem more like" *Kidder v. Greenman*, 283 Mass. 601, 187 N.E. 42 (1933). *Gateway,* 297 F.2d at 486. In *Kidder,* a tenant had signed and returned a lease to her landlord with the understanding that the landlord would fill in certain blank spaces pursuant to an oral agreement. The landlord then completed the lease so as to include a term contrary to the oral understanding, signed it, and returned it to the tenant, who "did not look at the lease at the time she received it except to slit the envelope and see it contained a lease." *Kidder,* 187 N.E. at 45 (internal quotation marks omitted). The court declined to enforce the disputed term against the tenant on the ground that she "had no reason to think that the [landlord] had not completed the lease in the authorized manner and, therefore, [had] no occasion to examine it, when it was returned to her, to see if he had done so." *Id.* at 48. The *Kidder* court concluded that "[i]n these circumstances the doctrine that a person who accepts an instrument . . . without reading it . . . is charged with knowledge of [its] contents is not applicable." *Id.* (citations omitted).

We distill from the *Restatement* and the *Gateway* and *Kidder* precedents the legal rule in Massachusetts that silence in response to an offer may constitute an acceptance if an offeree who takes the benefit of offered services knew or had reason to know of the existence of the offer, and had a reasonable opportunity to reject it. *See Restatement (Second) of Contracts* § 69(1)(a); *Gateway,* 297 F.2d at 485–86; *Kidder,* 187 N.E. at 48. We turn now to the application of that rule in this case.

IV.

Under Federal Rule of Civil Procedure 56(c), a court may enter summary judgment if the record "show[s] that there is no genuine issue as to any material fact and that the moving party is entitled to a judgment as a matter of law." We review the district court's grant of summary judgment de novo, and examine the record in the light most favorable to the party against whom summary judgment had been entered, drawing all reasonable inferences in that party's favor. *Barreto-Rivera v. Medina-Vargas*, 168 F.3d 42, 45 (1st Cir.1999). We note that "disputes about whether a contract has or has not been formed as the result of words and conduct over a period of time . . . present interpretive issues traditionally understood to be for the trier of fact." *Charbonnages de France v. Smith*, 597 F.2d 406, 414–15 (4th Cir.1979). This is so unless "the manifestations of intention of both parties to be bound, or of either not to be bound, are so unequivocal as to present no genuine issue of fact." *Id.* at 415.

A.   The District Court's Opinion

In response to Bell's assertion that it did not notice McGurn's alteration of the offer letter until just before his termination, the district court observed that "absent fraud, a party to a contract is bound by the terms of the contract whether or not he read them." The court added: "It will not do for a man to enter into a contract, and, when called upon to respond to its obligations, to say that he did not read it when he signed it, or did not know what it contained." The district court's legal proposition is sound, but inapposite to this case. The disputed term was added to the offer *after Bell had signed it.* The relevant question is why, as a matter of law, Bell should be expected to *re-read* an offer it had written and signed, upon its return with McGurn's countersignature.

In response to that question, the district court declared that "[a] presumably sophisticated employer who receives a signed letter of engagement from a prospective employee and fails to read the letter, particularly after weeks of negotiation, does so at its own peril." Although the logic of this generalization has some appeal, its generality is an insurmountable problem. Unless the record establishes that Bell knew or had reason to know that McGurn had modified what Bell had written—and the district court points to no facts in the record that would support such a conclusion—we cannot say that Bell's silence, as a matter of law, constituted an acceptance of McGurn's counteroffer.

Although we decline to endorse the district court's generalization, "we may affirm [a summary judgment] order on any ground revealed by the record." *Houlton Citizens' Coalition v. Town of Houlton*, 175 F.3d 178, 184 (1st Cir.1999). We therefore examine the record to see if, drawing all reasonable inferences in Bell's favor, the evidence nevertheless compels the conclusion that responsible officials at Bell knew or should have known about McGurn's counteroffer far enough in advance of his termination that Bell had a reasonable opportunity to reject the 24-month termination clause if it wished to avoid being bound. Summary judgment for McGurn would be proper if Bell had actual or constructive knowledge of McGurn's counteroffer at the time he returned the offer letter, or if, when Clark discovered the counteroffer, he had a "reasonable opportunity to reject" it before he fired McGurn, but instead continued to "take[ ] the benefit of [McGurn's] services" without speaking up. *Restatement (Second) of Contracts* § 69(1)(a).

There are three possible grounds for affirmance suggested by the record, two involving alleged actual knowledge and one involving constructive knowledge. We examine them in turn.

B.   Prominence of the Alteration

McGurn argues that Bell had actual knowledge of the alteration of the offer letter at the time of its return. Although McGurn advances no direct evidence that anyone at Bell noticed his revision of the termination clause, he points out that the alteration was made on the same page that bore his signature, which Bell acknowledges an unknown employee checked pursuant to company policy. McGurn infers from this that the unknown employee "had to have seen the change" in the duration of the termination clause, because "one's eyes are immediately drawn to the change made by McGurn and his initials above that change."

While an inference that Bell "had to have seen the change" would be permissible based on the evidence in the record—the alteration was in the center of the very page McGurn had signed—we cannot say that a factfinder would be required to conclude that the Bell employee who checked for McGurn's signature must have noticed McGurn's alteration of the termination clause half-way up the page. That is, the evidence that a Bell employee must have seen McGurn's alteration is not "so one-sided that [McGurn] must prevail as a matter of law." *Anderson v. Liberty Lobby, Inc.,* 477 U.S. 242, 252, 106 S.Ct. 2505, 91 L.Ed.2d 202 (1986).

C.   Clark's Discovery

Clark declared that he examined the countersigned offer letter and discovered what McGurn had done "[a]t some point after making [the] decision [to terminate McGurn], but before the actual termination." The record only establishes that this discovery was made during or after April of 1998, and before McGurn was fired in August of 1998. McGurn argues that once Bell discovered his counteroffer it had an obligation to speak up if it wished to reject it. Bell points out, however, that Clark "could have discovered the altered document as late as the day before" he fired McGurn. Whatever the merits of McGurn's legal argument on this point—a matter as to which we take no view—this factual uncertainty precludes summary judgment for McGurn based on Clark's actual knowledge of McGurn's counteroffer.

D.   Teague's Responsibility

We also examine the record for evidence that Teague (Bell's Director of Human Resources), or an employee in her department acting on her behalf, should have determined if the returned offer letter had been modified. Teague had participated in the negotiations with McGurn. She stated at her deposition that "Bill Murphy and I worked together on all of these offer letters," and Donald Bell testified that he "consult[ed] with Linda [Teague]" during the drafting of the letter. The July 3 offer letter from Bell to McGurn was signed by Teague, and indicated that McGurn should return the countersigned copy *to her*. Under these circumstances, a jury might conclude that McGurn could reasonably have expected Teague (or Murphy) to inspect the document upon its return. Moreover, the offer set out in Bell's letter was not a mere reduction to writing of a previous oral agreement; it was a step in a negotiation which Bell had no reason to assume had been concluded. Although Teague requested that McGurn simply sign and return the letter unamended, the evidence supports the inference that she had no basis for assuming he would do so. Instead, she should have checked the document to ensure that he had not made further changes.

Although an inference that Teague should have examined the returned offer letter with greater care would be permissible based on the evidence in the record, the evidence, again, does not compel such an inference. Bell disputes the notion that Teague (or her subordinates) had any reason to check the returned offer letter for unauthorized modifications, and a factfinder might conclude that Teague had no reason to inspect the letter absent any indication from McGurn that he had revised a material term.[5]

We have stated that "[o]rdinarily the question of whether a contract has been made . . . is for the jury," *Ismert & Assocs., Inc. v. New England Mut. Life Ins. Co.*, 801 F.2d 536, 541 (1st Cir.1986), except where "[t]he words and actions that allegedly formed a contract [are] so clear themselves that reasonable people could not differ over their meaning," *Bourque v. FDIC*, 42 F.3d 704, 708 (1st Cir.1994) (internal quotation marks omitted). When, as is the case here, "the facts support plausible but conflicting inferences on a pivotal issue in the case, the judge may not choose between those inferences at the summary judgment stage." *Coyne v. Taber Partners I*, 53 F.3d 454, 460 (1st Cir.1995); *accord* 10A Charles Alan Wright, Arthur R. Miller & Mary Kay Kane, *Federal Practice and Procedure* § 2725 at 433–37 (3d ed. 1998) ("[I]f the evidence presented on [a] motion [for summary judgment] is subject to conflicting interpretations,

---

[5]   Because the July 3 offer letter was signed by Teague, and McGurn returned it to Teague (or Bill Murphy), we need not be detained by Bell's argument that the low-level employee who examined the returned letter lacked the authority to bind the corporation (with his silence) on the question of McGurn's termination clause. Teague having requested that McGurn return the letter *to her*, it would be no defense for her to say that a subordinate in her office who lacked the authority to bind the corporation opened the letter and failed to show it to her. *See Gateway*, 297 F.2d at 486 & n. 4 (holding corporation responsible for contents of letter addressed to its president but read by a secretary). To accept Bell's argument on this point would be to penalize McGurn for Teague's failure to read her own mail. The same logic applies if McGurn returned the letter to Murphy, as he suggested he might have done.

or reasonable people might differ as to its significance, summary judgment is improper.") (footnotes omitted).

<h1 style="text-align:center">V.</h1>

In sum, drawing all reasonable inferences in Bell's favor, as we must in reviewing the district court's entry of summary judgment against Bell, we cannot say that the facts in the record compel a conclusion that Bell noticed or should have noticed McGurn's modification of Bell's offer letter, and that its silence, therefore, constituted an acceptance of McGurn's offer. Instead, those issues must be resolved by the factfinder at a trial.

Judgment vacated. Remanded for further proceedings consistent with this opinion. Each party to bear his or its own costs.

SELYA, CIRCUIT JUDGE (dubitante).

I write separately because I doubt that the court's opinion reflects either the practicalities of the case at hand or the result that the Supreme Judicial Court (SJC) would reach.

The critical facts are undisputed. McGurn's counteroffer—the letter containing his modification of the termination clause—was received at Bell's headquarters in the ordinary course and routed by it to its human resources department. That letter formed the basis for the company's treatment of McGurn as an employee and remained part of the corporate personnel records for the duration of his employment. Given these facts, the case turns on whether Bell should be said to have accepted McGurn's counteroffer.

While no official of the company ever said "I accept" in so many words, acceptance can occur by silence under certain circumstances. *See, e.g., Ismert & Assocs., Inc. v. New Engl. Mut. Life Ins. Co.,* 801 F.2d 536, 541–42 (1st Cir.1986); *Polaroid Corp. v. Rollins Envtl. Servs. (NJ), Inc.,* 416 Mass. 684, 624 N.E.2d 959, 964 (1993); *see also* Restatement (Second) of Contracts § 69 (1981). One such set of circumstances, pertinent here, is when an offeree fails to reply to an offer yet takes the benefit of the offered services with reasonable opportunity to reject them and reason to know that they were tendered in the expectation of a particular consideration. *See* Restatement (Second) of Contracts § 69(1). In such a situation, it would be manifestly unjust for an offeree to reap the benefit of the services without letting the offeror know that it had no intention of paying the remuneration that the offeror expected to receive. *Id.,* cmt. b. Thus, fundamental fairness permits silence to operate as an acceptance.

This principle is part of the warp and woof of Massachusetts contract law. *See Polaroid,* 624 N.E.2d at 964; *Bump v. Robbins,* 24 Mass.App.Ct. 296, 509 N.E.2d 12, 18–19 (1987). On the facts of record here, I think it likely that the SJC would find, as did the able district judge, that Bell implicitly assented to (and, therefore, should be bound by) the terms of

McGurn's counteroffer. After all, Bell unreservedly accepted McGurn's services, having reason to know *from its own files* that those services were being rendered with an expectation that the terms of the counteroffer (including the amended termination clause) would be fulfilled.

To be sure, Bell tells us that, even though it employed McGurn for thirteen months *pursuant to the letter that set out the terms of his counteroffer,* no one in its employ noticed the modification. But there is no hint here of chicanery on McGurn's part, and I doubt that ignorance induced by a party's own negligence or lassitude is a basis for escaping from contractual obligations. To the contrary, the acceptance of offered services, under circumstances in which the beneficiary of those services ought to have known that the provider expected to be compensated for them in a certain way, is the functional equivalent of express assent. *See Bump,* 509 N.E.2d at 18–19. This case seems to fit within the contours of that rule.

To sum up, I believe that a party should not be able to insulate itself from ex contractu liability by professing that it neglected to read the very document essential for the formation of the contract, especially when that document has reposed in its own files at all relevant times. Were the law otherwise and the majority's view taken to its logical extreme, an offeree could completely redefine its responsibilities by the simple expedient of claiming that it was not aware of what its own records plainly showed. I doubt that the SJC would countenance so counterintuitive a result. *Cf. Upton v. Tribilcock,* 91 U.S. 45, 50, 23 L.Ed. 203 (1875) (observing that "[i]t will not do for a man to enter into a contract, and, when called upon to respond to its obligations, to say that he did not . . . know what it contained. If this were permitted, contracts would not be worth the paper on which they are written"). Given this doubt, I respectfully decline to join the court's opinion.

RESTATEMENT, SECOND, CONTRACTS § 69

[See Selected Source Materials Supplement]

CISG ART. 18(1), (3)

[See Selected Source Materials Supplement]

UNIDROIT PRINCIPLES OF INTERNATIONAL COMMERCIAL CONTRACTS ART. 2.1.6(3)

[See Selected Source Materials Supplement]

PRINCIPLES OF EUROPEAN
CONTRACT LAW ART. 2.204(2)

[See Selected Source Materials Supplement]

Kukuska v. Home Mut. Hail-Tornado Ins. Co.

204 Wis. 166, 235 N.W. 403 (1931)

On July 3, Kukuska, a farmer, applied to an agent of the Home Mutual Hail-Tornado Insurance Company for hail insurance. Kukuska received no communication from the company or its agent until 11 A.M. on August 1, when he was informed that his application was declined. That afternoon, Kukuska's crops were severely damaged by hail. "Other insurance companies were writing hail insurance, and, if the plaintiff had been notified of the rejection of his application within a reasonable time, he could have protected himself against such loss. It is well known that the months of July and August constitute the most hazardous period for hailstorms in the locality where plaintiff's crops were situated." Kukuska brought suit against the company for the loss occasioned by the hailstorm. Held, for Kukuska:

It is significant that the insured does not take the first step in the process which leads to the making of a contract of insurance. . . . [The insurer in this case] required the application to be made upon blanks furnished by it. By the terms of the application, which was required to be made according to the by-laws, the applicant agreed to pay all just assessments and to be governed and abide by the rules, regulations, and by-laws of the company. He was required to pay the amount of the premium in advance. If the application were accepted, he agreed that the policy should run from the date of the application, July 2, 1928, rather than from the date of the acceptance when made. By the soliciting, making and receiving of the application, the parties had entered into some kind of a consensual relationship. . . .

Under such circumstances, having in view the nature of the risk against which the insurer seeks protection, is there not a duty upon the insurer to act upon the application within a reasonable time? Can the insurer, having preempted the field, retain control of the situation and the applicant's funds indefinitely? Does not the very nature of the transaction impose upon the insurer a duty to act? It is considered that there is a duty. If the insurer is under such a duty and fails to perform the duty within a reasonable time and, as a consequence, the applicant sustains damage, it is not vastly important that the legal relationship be placed in a particular category. If we say it is contractual, that is, there is an implied agreement under the circumstances on the part of the insurer to act within a reasonable time, or, having a duty to act, the insurer negligently fails in the performance of that duty, or that the duty springs out of a consensual relationship, and is therefore in the nature of a quasi contractual liability, is not vitally important. Each view finds some support in the cases. . . .

————

Hobbs v. Massasoit Whip Co.

158 Mass. 194, 33 N.E. 495 (1893)

Without receiving any specific order for them, the plaintiff had on four or five occasions shipped eelskins to the defendant, for which the defendant had paid. The plaintiff then shipped further eelskins. The defendant retained these eelskins for some months without communicating with the plaintiff, but after a destruction of the skins, the defendant refused to pay for them. The plaintiff sued for the price of the skins. Held, for the plaintiff. The past dealings of the parties were such that the plaintiff had a kind of "standing offer" for eelskins. ". . . Even if the offer was not such that the contract was made as soon as skins corresponding to its terms were sent, sending them did impose on the defendant a duty to act about them; and silence on its part, coupled with a retention of the skins for an unreasonable time, might be found by the jury to warrant the plaintiff in assuming that they were accepted, and thus to amount to an acceptance."

————

Louisville Tin & Stove Co. v. Lay

251 Ky. 584, 65 S.W.2d 1002 (1933)

Mrs. Lay operated Lay's Variety Store. Her husband, who was insolvent and without credit, operated an independent business known as Lay's Electric Shop. Mr. Lay ordered goods from the plaintiff to be consigned to Lay's Variety Store. When Mrs. Lay was informed that the goods consigned to her store had arrived at the railway depot, she "became angry and said it was her husband's doings." Mrs. Lay directed a drayman to take the goods from the depot to Lay's Electric Shop. Held, when Mrs. Lay assumed control over the disposition of the goods, her acts constituted an acceptance of the shipment, and she became liable to the plaintiff for the price of the goods.

————

Austin v. Burge

156 Mo.App. 286, 137 S.W. 618 (1911)

This was an action for the subscription price of a newspaper. The defendant's father-in-law had given him a two-year subscription to the newspaper, but the publisher continued mailing the newspaper to defendant after the subscription expired. The defendant twice paid bills for the subscription price, but each time he directed the newspaper to be stopped. The publisher nevertheless continued to mail the newspaper to the defendant, and the defendant continued to receive and read the newspaper, until finally he moved to another state. The trial court gave judgment for the defendant. Reversed:

> It is certain that one cannot be forced into contractual relations with another and that therefore he cannot, against his will, be made the debtor of a newspaper publisher. But it is equally certain that he may cause contractual relations to arise by necessary implication from his conduct.... In this case defendant admits that, notwithstanding he ordered the paper discontinued at the time when he paid a bill for it, yet plaintiff continued to send it, and he continued to take it from the post office to his home. This was an acceptance and use of the property, and, there being no pretense that a gratuity was intended, an obligation arose to pay for it. . . .

> The preparation and publication of a newspaper involves much mental and physical labor, as well as an outlay of money. One who accepts the paper, by continuously taking it from the post office, receives a benefit and pleasure arising from such labor and expenditure as fully as if he had appropriated any other product of another's labor, and by such act he must be held liable for the subscription price.

---

39 U.S.C. § 3009 [MAILING OF UNORDERED MERCHANDISE]

[See Selected Source Materials Supplement]

NOTE ON NEGATIVE-OPTION PLANS

A negative-option plan is a promotional technique that is similar in some respects to the sending of unordered merchandise. This type of plan is defined in a Federal Trade Commission rule to mean "a contractual plan or arrangement under which a seller periodically sends to subscribers an announcement which identifies merchandise (other than annual supplements to previously acquired merchandise) it proposes to send to subscribers to such plan, and the subscribers thereafter receive and are billed for the merchandise identified in each such announcement, unless by a date or within a time specified by the seller with respect to each such announcement the subscribers, in conformity with the provisions of such plan, instruct the seller not to send the identified merchandise." 16 C.F.R. § 425.1. Among the most familiar examples are book and record clubs. In contract-law terms, negative-option plans differ significantly from the sending of unordered merchandise, because the consumer normally contracts in advance, for consideration (in the form of a bonus for joining), to be bound by the plan's terms. The FTC's rule does not prohibit such plans. Instead, the rule requires clear disclosure of the plan's material terms and imposes certain minimal regulation, such as a requirement that the subscriber be given at least ten days in which to instruct the seller not to mail the current selection.

DAY V. CATON
Supreme Judicial Court of Massachusetts, 1876.
119 Mass. 513.

Contract to recover the value of one-half of a brick party wall built by the plaintiff upon and between the adjoining estates, 27 and 29 Greenwich Park, Boston.

At the trial in the Superior Court, before Allen, J., it appeared that, in 1871, the plaintiff, having an equitable interest in lot 29, built the wall in question, placing one half of it on the vacant lot 27, in which the defendant then had an equitable interest. The plaintiff testified that there was an express agreement on the defendant's part to pay him one half the value of the wall when the defendant should use it in building upon lot 27. The defendant denied this, and testified that he never had any conversation with the plaintiff about the wall; and there was no other direct testimony on this point.

The defendant requested the judge to rule that: "(1) The plaintiff can recover in this case only upon an express agreement. (2) If the jury find there was no express agreement about the wall, but the defendant knew that the plaintiff was building upon land in which the defendant had an equitable interest, the defendant's rights would not be affected by such knowledge, and his silence and subsequent use of the wall would raise no implied promise to pay anything for the wall."

The judge refused so to rule, but instructed the jury as follows: "A promise would not be implied from the fact that the plaintiff, with the defendant's knowledge, built the wall and the defendant used it, but it might be implied from the conduct of the parties. If the jury find that the plaintiff undertook and completed the building of the wall with the expectation that the defendant would pay him for it, and the defendant had reason to know that the plaintiff was so acting with that expectation, and allowed him so to act without objection, then the jury might infer a promise on the part of the defendant to pay the plaintiff."

The jury found for the plaintiff, and the defendant alleged exceptions.

DEVENS, J. The ruling that a promise to pay for the wall would not be implied from the fact that the plaintiff, with the defendant's knowledge, built the wall, and that the defendant used it, was substantially in accordance with the request of the defendant, and is conceded to have been correct. Chit.Cont. (11th Ed.) 86; Wells v. Banister, 4 Mass. 514; Knowlton v. Plantation No. 4, 14 Me. 20; Davis v. School Dist., 24 Me. 349.

The [defendant], however, contends that the presiding judge incorrectly ruled that such promise might be inferred from the fact that the plaintiff undertook and completed the building of the wall with the expectation that the defendant would pay him for it, the defendant having reason to know that the plaintiff was acting with that expectation, and allowed him thus to act without objection.

The fact that the plaintiff expected to be paid for the work would certainly not be sufficient of itself to establish the existence of a contract, when the question between the parties was whether one was made. Taft v. Dickinson, 6 Allen, 553. It must be shown that in some manner the party sought to be charged assented to it. If a party, however, voluntarily accepts and avails himself of valuable services rendered for his benefit, when he has the option whether to accept or reject them, even if there is no distinct proof that they were rendered by his authority or request, a promise to pay for them may be inferred. His knowledge that they were valuable, and his exercise of the option to avail himself of them, justify this inference. Abbot v. Hermon, 7 Greenl. (Me.) 118; Hayden v. Madison, 7 Greenl. (Me.) 76. And when one stands by in silence, and sees valuable services rendered upon his real estate by the erection of a structure (of which he must necessarily avail himself afterwards in his proper use thereof), such silence, accompanied with the knowledge on his part that the party rendering the services expects payment therefor, may fairly be treated as evidence of an acceptance of it, and as tending to show an agreement to pay for it.

The maxim, "Qui tacet consentire videtur," is to be construed indeed as applying only to those cases where the circumstances are such that a party is fairly called upon either to deny or admit his liability.* But, if silence may be interpreted as assent where a proposition is made to one which he is bound to deny or admit, so also it may be if he is silent in the face of facts which fairly call upon him to speak. Lamb v. Bunce, 4 Maule & S. 275; Connor v. Hackley, 2 Metc. (Mass.) 613; Preston v. Linen Co., 119 Mass. 400.

If a person saw day after day a laborer at work in his field doing services, which must of necessity inure to his benefit, knowing that the laborer expected pay for his work, when it was perfectly easy to notify him if his services were not wanted, even if a request were not expressly proved,

---

* According to Black's Law Dictionary, the Latin maxim "Qui tacet consentire videtur, ubi tractatur de ejus commodo" means "He who is silent is considered as assenting, when his interest is at stake." (Footnote by ed.)

such a request, either previous to or contemporaneous with the performance of the services, might fairly be inferred. But if the fact was merely brought to his attention upon a single occasion and casually, if he had little opportunity to notify the other that he did not desire the work and should not pay for it, or could only do so at the expense of much time and trouble, the same inference might not be made. The circumstances of each case would necessarily determine whether silence with a knowledge that another was doing valuable work for his benefit and with the expectation of payment indicated that consent which would give rise to the inference of a contract. The question would be one for the jury, and to them it was properly submitted in the case before us by the presiding judge.

Exceptions overruled.

SECTION 4. RESTITUTION FOR A BENEFIT CONFERRED IN THE MISTAKEN BELIEF OF THE EXISTENCE OF A CONTRACT

Q: What if plaintiff knew Dobos too poor to pay

NURSING CARE SERVICES, INC. V. DOBOS

District Court of Appeal of Florida, Fourth District, 1980.
380 So.2d 516.

Q: What if Dobos died? (like Mills)

HURLEY, JUDGE.

Posture / holding

Plaintiff, Nursing Care Services, Inc., appeals from that part of a final judgment which disallowed compensation for certain nursing care services. Our review of the record reveals substantial uncontradicted testimony supporting plaintiff's theory of recovery and thus we remand for entry of an amended final judgment.

Mary Dobos, the defendant, was admitted to Boca Raton Community Hospital with an abdominal aneurysm. Her condition was sufficiently serious to cause her doctor to order around-the-clock nursing care. The hospital implemented this order by calling upon the plaintiff which provides individualized nursing services.

Mrs. Dobos received nursing care which in retrospect can be divided into three periods: (1) two weeks of in-hospital care; (2) forty-eight hour post-release care; and (3) two weeks of at-home care. The second period of care (the forty-eight hour post-release care) was removed as an issue at trial when Mrs. Dobos conceded that she or her daughter authorized that period of care. The total bill for all three periods came to $3,723.90; neither the reasonableness of the fee, the competency of the nurses, nor the necessity for the services was contested at trial.

The gist of the defense was that Mrs. Dobos never signed a written contract nor orally agreed to be liable for the nursing services. Testifying about the in-hospital care, she said, "Dr. Rosen did all the work. I don't know what he done (sic), and he says, I needed a nurse." It is undisputed that Mrs. Dobos was mentally alert during her at-home recuperation period. Asked if she ever tried to fire the nurses or dispense with their care, she replied, "I didn't. I didn't know who—I thought maybe if they insist, the doctors insist so much, I thought the Medicare would take care of it, or whatever. I don't know."

After a non-jury trial, the court granted judgment for the plaintiff in the sum of $248.00, the cost of the forty-eight hour post-release care. It declined to allow compensation for the first and third periods of care, saying,

[Handwritten margin note: Trial court ruled for plaintiff – but only $248.00]

> "... [T]here certainly was a service rendered, but based on the total surrounding circumstances, I don't think there is sufficient communications and dealings with Mrs. Dobos to make sure that she knew that she would be responsible for those services rendered. ... "

[Handwritten margin note: Trial court: Dobos didn't know she'd be responsible]

We concur in the trial court's determination that the plaintiff failed to prove an express contract or a contract implied in fact. It is our view, however, that the uncontradicted testimony provided by plaintiff and defendant alike, clearly established a contract implied in law which entitles the plaintiff to recover.

[Handwritten margin note: ★ Holding]

Contracts implied in law, or as they are more commonly called "quasi contracts", are obligations imposed by law on grounds of justice and equity. Their purpose is to prevent unjust enrichment. Unlike express contracts or contracts implied in fact, quasi contracts do not rest upon the assent of the contracting parties. See generally, 28 Fla.Jur., Restitution and Implied Contracts.

[Handwritten margin note: Quasi Contract]

One of the most common areas in which recovery on a contract implied in law is allowed is that of work performed or services rendered. The rationale is that the defendant would be unjustly enriched at the expense of the plaintiff if she were allowed to escape payment for services rendered or work performed. There is, however, an important limitation. Ordinarily liability is imposed to pay for services rendered by another only when the person for whose benefit they were rendered requested the services or knowingly and voluntarily accepted their benefits. *Yeats v. Moody,* 128 Fla. 658, 175 So. 719 (1937); *Strano v. Carr & Carr, Inc.,* 97 Fla. 150, 119 So. 864 (1929); *Taylor v. Thompson,* 359 So.2d 14 (Fla. 1st DCA 1978); and *Tobin & Tobin Insurance Agency, Inc. v. Zeskind,* 315 So.2d 518 (Fla. 3d DCA 1975).

The law's concern that needless services not be foisted upon the unsuspecting has led to the formulation of the "officious intermeddler

officious intermeddler doctrine (OID)

doctrine." It holds that where a person performs labor for another without the latter's request or implied consent, however beneficial such labor may be, he cannot recover therefor. *Tipper v. Great Lakes Chemical Company,* 281 So.2d 10 (Fla.1973). A notable exception to this rule, however, is that of emergency aid:

emergency aid exception to OID

> A person who has supplied things or services to another, although acting without the other's knowledge or consent, is entitled to restitution therefore from the other if he acted unofficiously and with intent to charge therefore, and the things or services were necessary to prevent the other from suffering serious bodily harm or pain, and the person supplying them had no reason to know that the other would not consent to receiving them, if mentally competent, and it was impossible for the other to give consent or, because of extreme youth or mental impairment, the other's consent would have been immaterial. 66 Am.Jur.2d, Restitution and Implied Contract, § 23.

In the case at bar it is unclear whether Mrs. Dobos, during the period of in-hospital care, understood or intended that compensation be paid. Her condition was grave. She had been placed in the hospital's intensive care unit and thereafter had tubes and other medical equipment attached to her body which necessitated special attention. She was alone, unable to cope and without family assistance. It is worthy of note that at no point during the litigation was there any question as to the propriety of the professional judgment that the patient required special nursing care. To the contrary, the record demonstrates that the in-hospital nursing care was essential to Mrs. Dobos' health and safety. Given these circumstances it would be unconscionable to deny the plaintiff recovery for services which fall squarely within the emergency aid exception. *Tipper v. Great Lakes Chemical Company,* supra.

The third period of care is less difficult. It is unquestioned that during the at-home recuperation, Mrs. Dobos was fully aware of her circumstances and readily accepted the benefits conferred. Given such facts, we believe the rule set down in *Symon v. J. Rolfe Davis, Inc.,* 245 So.2d 278, 279 (Fla. 4th DCA 1971) must govern:

> It is well settled that where services are rendered by one person for another which are knowingly and voluntarily accepted, the law presumes that such services are given and received in expectation of being paid for, and will imply a promise to pay what they are reasonably worth.

A patient's unannounced misconception that the cost of accepted services will be paid by an insurer or Medicare does not absolve her of responsibility to bear the cost of the services.

Just b/c she thought she didn't have to pay doesn't mean she didn't have to pay

As a postscript we note that Mrs. Dobos' home recuperation was interrupted by her readmission to the hospital with an apparent heart attack. In this age of burgeoning malpractice actions it is not idle conjecture to ponder what her legal position might have been had the plaintiff unilaterally terminated its services at a time of vital need. To its credit, it did not and therefore it is entitled to just compensation. Accordingly, we remand the cause to the trial court with instructions to enter an amended final judgment for the plaintiff in the sum of $3,723.90 plus interest and court costs.

It is so ordered.

ANSTEAD and LETTS, JJ., concur.

Court rules in favor of plaintiff — Dobos should pay

NOTE ON TERMINOLOGY AND HISTORY

Various names are used to denote the non-contractual claim in the principal case: quasi-contract, implied-in-law contract, quantum meruit, restitution, and unjust enrichment. There is a great deal of history behind this welter of names.

At an early time, the English common law settled into a *formulary* system. Under this system, a plaintiff could obtain a judicial remedy only if the transaction giving rise to his grievance came within (or could, through a legal fiction, be made to come within) an established form of action or *writ*. Until the late 16th century, the principal writs for enforcing what we think of as a contract were *covenant* and *debt*. These actions were available only if a promise was under seal or if a promise was to pay a "sum certain" for a performance already received.

Over time these actions were gradually superseded by a new form of action, known as *assumpsit*, originally using the writ *trespass on the case*.* The pleading of assumpsit also became formulaic using what were referred to as the common counts. *Quantum meruit* ("as much as he deserved") is one of the common counts. It was a claim for the value of work and labor. Originally this count was used in cases where the promise to pay was explicit or reasonably implicit. But the fictitious nature of the promise that was pled gave the count a broader range. For example, in a case reported in 1744 a home builder was unable to recover on his contract because the house did not comply with the promised specifications. The court allowed the claim on quantum meruit, leaving it to the jury to decide a fair payment for the work done.

A claim for money lent was pled as *indebitatus assumpsit* and eventually as an action for *money had and received*. While these claims were originally

---

*   The modern tort of negligence also grew out of cases using this writ. The non-formulaic character of the writ lent itself to pleading a novel claim. The heart of the writ was a description of the defendant's harmful conduct. This was preceded by a "whereas" cause that explained why the harmful conduct should be actionable.

used in cases where the promise was explicit or reasonably implicit they came to cover claims to recover mistaken payments and the like. In a landmark decision, Moses v. Macferlan, 2 Burr. 1005, 1 W Bl 219 (1760), Lord Mansfield described the action as "founded in the equity of the plaintiff's case, as it were upon a contract ('quasi ex contractu' as the Roman law expresses it)." This case is thought of as the fountainhead of the law of unjust enrichment.

The recognition of restitution or unjust enrichment as a general field of obligation alongside contract and tort is a relatively recent development. The titles of a few canonical works on the topic reflect the welter of names. The first common law treatise on the topic is Keener, Treatise on the Law of Quasi-Contracts (1893). The full title of the first restatement on the subject is Restatement of the Law of Restitution, Quasi-Contracts, and Constructive Trusts (1936). The concept of unjust enrichment appears in Section 1: "A person who has been unjustly enriched at the expense of another is required to make restitution to the other." There is no second restatement, but following the American Law Institute's practice concerning the titles of Restatements, the successor to the first restatement is Restatement, Third, Restitution and Unjust Enrichment (2011). The term *unjust enrichment* appears in the title and throughout Restatement Third. However, Comment *b* to Section 1 urges against treating unjust enrichment as a principle, while suggesting another name for the field: "The concern of restitution is not, in fact, with unjust enrichment in any such broad sense, but with a narrower set of circumstances giving rise to what might more appropriately be called *unjustified enrichment.* Compared to the open-ended implications of the term 'unjust enrichment,' instances of unjustified enrichment are both predictable and objectively determined, because the justification in question is not moral but legal." The wisdom of trying to detach this area of law from morality is doubtful.

––––––

NOTE ON THE TWO TYPES OF RESTITUTION CLAIMS IN THE PRINCIPAL CASE

Two different types of restitution and unjust enrichment claims are involved in *Dobos.*

1.   *The two weeks of in-hospital care.* This claim is covered by the rule embodied in Restatement, Third, Restitution and Unjust Enrichment § 20, which allows a claim for the reasonable market price of "professional services required for the protection of another's life or health . . . if the circumstances justify the decision to intervene without request." Generally when one person voluntarily confers an unrequested benefit to another person the benefactor has no claim in restitution against the beneficiary. Thus Restatement, Third, Restitution and Unjust Enrichment § 2(3) provides: "There is no liability in restitution for an unrequested benefit voluntarily conferred, unless the circumstances of the transaction justify the claimant's intervention in the absence of a contract." The incapacity of Dobos during the two weeks justified the unrequested intervention.

2.   *The two weeks of at-home care.* This claim presents a much more difficult issue under the law of restitution. The plaintiff's claim would be that it provided Dobos this care in the mistaken belief it had a contract with Dobos to pay for the service. The trial court found that Dobos did not know that she was expected to pay for the at-home care. Thus this is a case of misunderstanding. As you have seen, when there is a misunderstanding about the existence or terms of an agreement, the objective principle of interpretation resolves the misunderstanding against the party who is more at fault. For example, Painter paints the exterior of Owner's house while Owner is absent, reasonably believing that Owner has ordered him to proceed. Actually Owner did not intend to order the work and was undecided about the color. The principle of objective interpretation casts the loss from the misunderstanding on Owner by finding a contract to pay for the work if Owner reasonably appeared to order Painter to proceed. If nothing was said about price, then a reasonable price will be implied.

But what if Painter was more at fault because he was unreasonable in thinking Owner had ordered the work? Painter does not have a contract claim. But Painter may have a restitution claim to avoid unjust enrichment. The principle precluding restitution for unrequested benefits voluntarily conferred does not bar the claim. Benefits conferred by mistake are not considered voluntarily conferred. For example, a restitution claim is available to recover a mistaken payment of cash so long as the recipient has not changed his position in the good faith belief the cash was his, such as by spending the cash on something other than a necessity. That a mistake is a product of carelessness or negligence does not preclude a restitution claim.

Two other limiting principles in Restatement, Third, Restitution and Unjust Enrichment § 2 potentially apply when a plaintiff seeks restitution for the value of a benefit conferred in the mistaken belief of the existence of a contract. Section 2(2) provides: "A valid contract defines the obligation of the parties as to matters within its scope, displacing to that extent any inquiry into unjust enrichment." In *Dobos*, this principle would cut off the plaintiff's restitution claim for the two weeks of at-home care if the court had found there was a contract absolving Dobos from an obligation to pay for the at-home care because the plaintiff had reason to know Dobos contracted for the service on the assumption that Medicare (and not she) would pay for it.

Sometimes a contract will not dispose of a possible unjust enrichment claim. For example. Painter has a contract with Owner's next-door neighbor but he gets the address wrong and mistakenly paints the exterior of Owner's house while Owner is absent. There is no contract between Painter and Owner so the claim is not barred by the principle in § 2(2). But the claim may still run afoul of the principle in Restatement, Third, Restitution and Unjust Enrichment § 2(4): "Liability in restitution may not subject an innocent recipient to a forced exchange: in other words, an obligation to pay for a benefit that the recipient should have been free to refuse." Unless there are unusual facts that make the benefit to Owner clear and quantifiable, this principle casts the loss from the mistake on Painter so long as Owner is "an innocent recipient."

The plaintiff's claim against *Dobos* for the in-home care would be covered by the principle in § 2(4) if the court found there was no contract either obligating Dobos to pay for the in-home care or absolving Dobos from obligation to pay for the in-home care. This is possible if Dobos did not know or have reason to know the plaintiff expected to be paid by her, and if the plaintiff did not know or have reason to know Dobos expected she would not be charged for the service. Restatement, Third, Restitution and Unjust Enrichment § 9 (Benefits Other Than Money) provides rules to implement the principle in § 2(4). These rules would require either that Dobos "has revealed a willingness to pay for the benefit" or that Dobos "has been spared an otherwise necessary expense."

Vickery v. Ritchie, 202 Mass. 247, 88 N.E. 835 (1909), illustrates the application of the first of these two rules in a case of mutual misunderstanding. An architect duped a property owner and a contractor to proceed with a project to construct a bath house on the owner's land. The architect misled the owner to believe that the price was $23,200 and the contractor to believe that the price was $33,721. The deception was discovered after the work was completed. At trial, the value of the improvement was established to be $22,000 and the "fair value" of the contractor's labor and materials was established to be $33,499.30. Today an architect generally acts as agent for the owner so the loss would be cast on the owner. In the case the architect was considered an agent for both parties so it was a case of mutual misunderstanding. The court awarded $33,499.30, treating the claim as a run-of-the-mill quantum-meruit claim. Restatement First and Restatement Third take the position that the appropriate measure of damages is $23,200, which is what the owner agreed to pay for the building. The Restatement Third explains this does not impose a "forced exchange" on the owner for he agreed to pay this price. See id. § 10, Illustration 27. Query whether the result subjects the architect to a "forced exchange" of his services for $23,200 rather than $33,721?

CHAPTER 11

INDEFINITENESS, PRELIMINARY NEGOTIATIONS, AND THE DUTY TO BARGAIN IN GOOD FAITH

■ ■ ■

One of the axioms of classical contract law was that a contract is formed by offer and acceptance. This axiom was at the center of several clusters of rules. One of these clusters concerned preliminary negotiations, indefiniteness, further-document-to-follow provisions, agreements to agree, and the duty to negotiate in good faith. The rules in this cluster are the subject of this Chapter.

One set of the rules in this cluster concerned the characterization and effect of expressions looking toward the formation of a bargain. Under classical contract law, such expressions were characterized as either an offer or acceptance, on the one hand, or as preliminary negotiations, on the other. This was a binary, static characterization, in which an expression either had an immediate legal effect or no legal effect. An offer had the immediate legal effect of creating a power of acceptance in the offeree, and an acceptance had the immediate legal effect of concluding a contract. In contrast, preliminary negotiations had no legal effect. This binary characterization was reflected in binary outcomes: no liability up to the time at which an acceptance of an offer occurred; full liability for expectation damages thereafter.

Another set of rules in this cluster concerned the indefiniteness of agreements. The relationship between the basic rules of offer and acceptance and the rules concerning indefiniteness was not always clear. A basic rule of offer and acceptance is that an expression will not constitute an offer unless it is sufficiently definite. But why then should contract law have another rule about the indefiniteness of *agreements*? If an expression is not sufficiently definite to constitute an offer, no contract can be formed. If an expression is sufficiently definite to constitute an offer, and the offeree assents, what room is left to argue that a resulting agreement is too indefinite?

One possible answer to this question is that the concept of indefiniteness of agreements reflects the brute fact that many contracts are not formed by an offer-and-acceptance sequence, but by simultaneous actions, like signing a contract, shaking hands, concurring that "It's a deal," or the like. In such cases, whether one of the parties used an expression that was sufficiently definite to constitute an offer is usually irrelevant. Instead, indefiniteness bears on whether parties to a joint expression that looks like an agreement reasonably believed that they had concluded the bargaining process, or were still in preliminary negotiations—preliminary, that is, to the conclusion of an agreement. In addition, indefiniteness may be relevant because even if the parties believed they had concluded the bargaining process, the resulting agreement may be too indefinite to allow the courts to determine the existence of a breach and a remedy.

Still another set of rules in this cluster involved fact patterns in which the parties made an agreement that would look as if it were a completed bargain except for the fact that the parties included in the agreement a provision that contemplated a further, more elaborate document. Often, the original agreement would be sufficiently definite to be enforceable but for the presence of such a provision. The question then is, what is the legal significance of the provision? The rule of classical contract law again was binary and static: If the parties intended the further document to be only an evidentiary memorial of the terms of their original agreement (for example, to tie together various pieces of correspondence), and the original agreement was otherwise sufficiently definite, then the original agreement was enforceable. If, however, the parties intended not to be bound unless and until the further document was executed, so that the further document was to be the consummation of their negotiations, then the original agreement was unenforceable. Accordingly, the parties' contemplation of a further document, which did not eventuate either (1) prevented the formation of a contract, in which case there was no liability, or (2) did not, in which case there was a contract on the terms of the original agreement.

Finally, classical contract law did not recognize a duty to negotiate in good faith. On the contrary, it adopted the rule that an agreement to agree was unenforceable, which by implication precluded an obligation to negotiate in good faith.

As will be seen in this Chapter, in regard to these issues modern contract law has made important dynamic departures from the binary, static offer-and-acceptance model of classical contract law.

ACADEMY CHICAGO PUBLISHERS V. CHEEVER
Supreme Court of Illinois, 1991.
144 Ill.2d 24, 161 Ill.Dec. 335, 578 N.E.2d 981.

JUSTICE HEIPLE delivered the opinion of the court:

This is a suit for declaratory judgment. It arose out of an agreement between the widow of the widely published author, John Cheever, and

Academy Chicago Publishers. Contact between the parties began in 1987 when the publisher approached Mrs. Cheever about the possibility of publishing a collection of Mr. Cheever's short stories which, though previously published, had never been collected into a single anthology. In August of that year, a publishing agreement was signed which provided, in pertinent part:

> "Agreement made this 15th day of August 1987, between Academy Chicago Publishers or any affiliated entity or imprint (hereinafter referred to as the Publisher) and Mary W. Cheever and Franklin H. Dennis of the USA (hereinafter referred to as Author).

> Whereas the parties are desirous of publishing and having published a certain work or works, tentatively titled *The Uncollected Stories of John Cheever* (hereinafter referred to as the Work):

* * *

> 2.   The Author will deliver to the Publisher on a mutually agreeable date one copy of the manuscript of the Work as finally arranged by the editor and satisfactory to the Publisher in form and content.

* * *

> 5.   Within a reasonable time and a mutually agreeable date after delivery of the final revised manuscript, the Publisher will publish the Work at its own expense, in such style and manner and at such price as it deems best, and will keep the Work in print as long as it deems it expedient; but it will not be responsible for delays caused by circumstances beyond its control."

Academy and its editor, Franklin Dennis, assumed the task of locating and procuring the uncollected stories and delivering them to Mrs. Cheever. Mrs. Cheever and Mr. Dennis received partial advances for manuscript preparation. By the end of 1987, Academy had located and delivered more than 60 uncollected stories to Mrs. Cheever. Shortly thereafter, Mrs. Cheever informed Academy in writing that she objected to the publication of the book and attempted to return her advance.

Academy filed suit in the circuit court of Cook County in February 1988, seeking a declaratory judgment: (1) granting Academy the exclusive right to publish the tentatively titled, "The Uncollected Stories of John Cheever"; (2) designating Franklin Dennis as the book's editor; and (3) obligating Mrs. Cheever to deliver the manuscript from which the work was to be published. The trial court entered an order declaring, *inter alia:* (1) that the publishing agreement executed by the parties was valid and enforceable; (2) that Mrs. Cheever was entitled to select the short stories to be included in the manuscript for publication; (3) that Mrs. Cheever would comply with her obligations of good faith and fair dealing if she delivered a manuscript including at least 10 to 15 stories totaling at least 140 pages; (4) Academy controlled the design and format of the work to be published, but control must be exercised in cooperation with Mrs. Cheever.

Academy appealed the trial court's order, challenging particularly the declaration regarding the minimum story and page numbers for Mrs. Cheever's compliance with the publishing agreement, and the declaration that Academy must consult with defendant on all matters of publication of the manuscript.

The appellate court affirmed the decision of the trial court with respect to the validity and enforceability of the publishing agreement and the minimum story and page number requirements for Mrs. Cheever's compliance with same. The appellate court reversed the trial court's declaration regarding control of publication, stating that the trial court erred in considering extrinsic evidence to interpret the agreement regarding control of the publication, given the explicit language of the agreement granting exclusive control to Academy. (200 Ill.App.3d 677, 146 Ill.Dec. 386, 558 N.E.2d 349.) Appeal is taken in this court pursuant to Supreme Court Rule 315(a) (134 Ill.2d R. 315(a)).

The parties raise several issues on appeal; this matter, however, is one of contract and we confine our discussion to the issue of the validity and enforceability of the publishing agreement.

While the trial court and the appellate court agreed that the publishing agreement constitutes a valid and enforceable contract, we cannot concur. The principles of contract state that in order for a valid contract to be formed, an "offer must be so definite as to its material terms or require such definite terms in the acceptance that the promises and performances to be rendered by each party are reasonably certain." (1 Williston, Contracts §§ 38 through 48 (3d ed. 1957); 1 Corbin, Contracts §§ 95 through 100 (1963).) Although the parties may have had and manifested the intent to make a contract, if the content of their agreement is unduly uncertain and indefinite no contract is formed. 1 Williston § 37; 1 Corbin § 95.

The pertinent language of this agreement lacks the definite and certain essential terms required for the formation of an enforceable contract. (*Midland Hotel Corp. v. Reuben H. Donnelley Corp.* (1987), 118 Ill.2d 306, 113 Ill.Dec. 252, 515 N.E.2d 61.) A contract "is sufficiently definite and certain to be enforceable if the court is enabled from the terms and provisions thereof, under proper rules of construction and applicable principles of equity, to ascertain what the parties have agreed to do." (*Morey v. Hoffman* (1957), 12 Ill.2d 125, 145 N.E.2d 644.) The provisions of the subject publishing agreement do not provide the court with a means of determining the intent of the parties.

Trial testimony reveals that a major source of controversy between the parties is the length and content of the proposed book. The agreement sheds no light on the minimum or maximum number of stories or pages necessary for publication of the collection, nor is there any implicit language from which we can glean the intentions of the parties with respect to this essential contract term. The publishing agreement is similarly silent with respect to who will decide which stories will be included in the collection. Other omissions, ambiguities, unresolved essential terms and illusory terms are: No date certain for delivery of the manuscript. No definition of the criteria which would render the manuscript satisfactory to the publisher either as to form or content. No date certain as to when publication will occur. No certainty as to style or manner in which the book will be published nor is there any indication as to the price at which such book will be sold, or the length of time publication shall continue, all of which terms are left to the sole discretion of the publisher.

A contract may be enforced even though some contract terms may be missing or left to be agreed upon, but if the essential terms are so uncertain that there is no basis for deciding whether the agreement has been kept or broken, there is no contract. (*Champaign National Bank v. Landers Seed Co.* (1988), 165 Ill.App.3d 1090, 116 Ill.Dec. 742, 519 N.E.2d 957, Restatement (Second) of Contracts § 33 (1981).) Without setting forth adequate terms for compliance, the publishing agreement provides no basis for determining when breach has occurred, and, therefore, is not a valid and enforceable contract.

An enforceable contract must include a meeting of the minds or mutual assent as to the terms of the contract. (*Midland Hotel,* 118 Ill.2d at 313, 113 Ill.Dec. 252, 515 N.E.2d 61.) It is not compelling that [whether?] the parties share a subjective understanding as to the terms of the contract; the parties' conduct may indicate an agreement to the terms of same. (*Steinberg v. Chicago Medical School* (1977), 69 Ill.2d 320, 13 Ill.Dec. 699, 371 N.E.2d 634.) In the instant case, however, no mutual assent has been illustrated. The parties did not and do not share a common understanding of the essential terms of the publishing agreement.

In rendering its judgment, the trial court supplied minimum terms for Mrs. Cheever's compliance, including story and page numbers. It is not uncommon for a court to supply a missing material term, as the reasonable conclusion often is that the parties intended that the term be supplied by implication. However, where the subject matter of the contract has not been decided upon and there is no standard available for reasonable implication, courts ordinarily refuse to supply the missing term. (1 Williston § 42; 1 Corbin § 100.) No suitable standard was available for the trial court to apply. It is our opinion that the trial court incorrectly supplied minimum compliance terms to the publishing agreement, as the agreement did not constitute a valid and enforceable contract to begin with. As noted above, the publishing agreement contains major unresolved uncertainties. It is not the role of the court to rewrite the contract and spell out essential elements not included therein.

In light of our decision that there was no valid and enforceable contract between the parties, we need not address other issues raised on appeal. For the foregoing reasons, the decisions of the trial and appellate courts in this declaratory judgment action are reversed.

Reversed.

JUSTICES CLARK and FREEMAN took no part in the consideration or decision of this opinion.

————

Peter Kurth, Book Review of Anita Miller, Uncollecting Cheever, the Family of John Cheever v. Academy Chicago Publisher

Salon, November 25, 1998

" 'Uncollecting Cheever' is the blow-by-blow account of the Cheevers' famous legal battle with Academy Chicago, a small Midwestern publishing house owned and run by [Anita] Miller and her husband, Jordan, who in 1988 hoped to publish a volume of Cheever's previously uncollected short stories. The idea for the book came from Franklin Dennis, a New York book publicist who did work for the Millers and was also a neighbor of the Cheevers in Ossining. Mary Cheever at first agreed to the project, signing a contract and receiving half of a $1,500 token advance for what she later insisted she had envisioned as 'a small edition for libraries, for students,' and not a major commercial work. Only when Franklin Dennis had unearthed more than 60 Cheever stories from magazines and anthologies, and when paperback rights to the collection were sold for $225,500 in advance of publication, did the Cheevers—and, for that matter, the Millers—realize that they might have 'a gold mine' on their hands. Mary Cheever tried to break the contract; the Millers responded with a lawsuit to enforce its terms; the Cheevers countered with a suit to protect their copyright, and one of the great literary court battles was born."

————

Ridgway v. Wharton

6 Clark's H.L. Cases 238, 305–306 (1856)

Lord Wensleydale said: "An agreement to be finally settled must comprise all the terms which the parties intend to introduce into the agreement. An agreement to enter into an agreement upon terms to be afterwards settled between the parties is a contradiction in terms. It is absurd to say that a man enters into an agreement till the terms of that agreement are settled. Until those terms are settled he is perfectly at liberty to retire from the bargain."

————

Rego v. Decker

482 P.2d 834 (Alaska 1971)

(Rabinowitz, J.) "Regarding the rule requiring reasonable certainty and its application to particular factual situations, [our cases] demonstrate that:

> The dream of a mechanical justice is recognized for what it is—only a dream and not even a rosy or desirable one.

"In general it has been said that the primary underlying purpose of the law of contracts is the attempted 'realization of reasonable expectations that have been induced by the making of a promise.' In light of this underlying purpose, two general considerations become relevant to solution of reasonable certainty-specific performance problems. On the one hand, courts should fill gaps in contracts to ensure fairness where the reasonable expectations of the parties are fairly clear. The parties to a contract often cannot negotiate and draft solutions to all the problems which may arise. Except in transactions involving very large amounts of money or adhesion contracts to be imposed on many parties, contracts tend to be skeletal, because the amount of time and money needed to produce a more complete contract would be disproportionate to the value of the transaction to the parties. Courts would impose too great a burden on the business community if the standards of certainty were set too high. On the other hand, the courts should not impose on a party any performance to which he did not and probably would not have agreed. Where the character of a gap in an agreement manifests failure to reach an agreement rather than a sketchy agreement, or where gaps cannot be filled with confidence that the reasonable expectations of the parties are being fulfilled, then specific enforcement should be denied for lack of reasonable certainty.

"Several other considerations affect the standard of certainty. A greater degree of certainty is required for specific performance than for damages, because of the difficulty of framing a decree specifying the performance required, as compared with the relative facility with which a breach may be perceived for purposes of awarding damages. Less certainty is required where the party seeking specific performance has substantially shifted his position in reliance on the supposed contract, than where the contract is wholly unperformed on both sides."

————

Saliba-Kringlen Corp. v. Allen Engineering Co.

15 Cal.App.3d 95, 92 Cal.Rptr. 799 (1971)

Saliba, a general contractor, was awarded a freeway-construction contract. Allen, an electrical subcontractor, had submitted the low bid to Saliba for the electrical work, but refused to honor its bid, and Saliba was forced to subcontract out the electrical work at a price in excess of Allen's bid. Saliba sued Allen, who defended on the ground that its bid was too indefinite to form the basis of a contract, since it stated only the price. Held, for Saliba:

It is undisputed that the customary practice in the construction industry is for the general contractor who is awarded a contract to enter into a written contract with the subcontractor, which written contract embraces far more than the price which the subcontractor has bid by telephone. The additional matters would include such things as whether the subcontractor would furnish a bond, who would provide for insurance, how payments would be made and many other matters. Although the provisions other than price are not identical in all subcontracts generally or in electrical subcontracts particularly, price is the principal item as is evident from the fact (as shown by the evidence) that seldom does a general contractor fail to reach an agreement with the subcontractor whose bid is low. Defendant asserts that it should not be held to its bid price because the general contractor could not have known that the general contractor and defendant would have reached an agreement on the terms of the subcontract.

While a prospective subcontractor could submit a bid by way of a written proposed subcontract including not only the price but all other details, we are not aware that this is ever done. The customary bid is made, as it was here, by a brief telephone call in which only the price is stated. If defendant's position is correct, there would never be an occasion to invoke section 90 of the Restatement, Contracts by a general contractor against a prospective subcontractor. Even a subcontractor who did not make a mistake in his bid price but who desired to avoid doing the work because of increased costs, other commitments or any other reason could claim that his bid is not binding because it is incomplete. But California has not taken that position. In *Drennan* the bid was one of price only and it is obvious that the general contractor would have entered into a written subcontract with the prospective subcontractor containing terms other than price. The Supreme Court nevertheless held that the subcontractor's bid was binding. The same rule must be applied here.

It should be noted that here the lack of an electrical subcontract between the general contractor and defendant was not due to the failure of the parties negotiating in good faith to arrive at the terms other than price. We do not intimate what our conclusion would be had that been the case. Here, as in *Drennan,* the parties did not get around to discussing contract provisions because defendant made it clear that it would not do the work at the price bid regardless of the other contractual provisions.

———

Mears v. Nationwide Mutual Ins. Co.

91 F.3d 1118 (8th Cir. 1986)

Mears won a contest in which the prize was two Mercedes-Benz automobiles. The promoter of the contest contended that the contract was too indefinite to enforce because there was a very wide range of Mercedes-Benz used and new models and no model had been specified. Held, for Mears:

> There is, as the district court notes, a wide range of values for Mercedes, depending largely on the model and year. This uncertainty, however, is not fatal. First, contract terms are interpreted with strong consideration for what is reasonable... Under a reasonable interpretation of the contest contract, the jury could expect the automobiles to be new.

> Second, when a minor ambiguity exists in a contract, Arkansas law allows the complaining party to insist on the reasonable interpretation that is least favorable to him... These two factors, taken together, are sufficient to support the jury's conclusion that Nationwide owed Mears two of Mercedes-Benz's least expensive new automobiles as his contest prize.

———

RESTATEMENT, SECOND, CONTRACTS §§ 33, 34

[See Selected Source Materials Supplement]

———

UCC §§ 2–204, 2–305, 2–308, 2–309, 2–310

[See Selected Source Materials Supplement]

———

CISG ARTS. 14(1), 31, 33, 55, 57, 58

[See Selected Source Materials Supplement]

———

UNIDROIT PRINCIPLES OF INTERNATIONAL COMMERCIAL CONTRACTS ARTS. 2.1.2, 2.1.13, 2.1.14, 5.1.7, 5.1.8, 6.1.1, 6.6.6

[See Selected Source Materials Supplement]

PRINCIPLES OF EUROPEAN CONTRACT LAW §§ 2.201(1), 6.104, 6.109, 7.01, 7.102

[See Selected Source Materials Supplement]

NOTE ON GAP-FILLERS

The UCC provisions cross-referenced above are generally referred to as gap-fillers, because they fill gaps that parties may leave in a contract for the sale of goods. The UCC gap-filler provisions are default rules; that is, background rules that the law reads into a contract in the absence of, but only in the absence of, the parties' actual agreement on the relevant issues. (In contrast, mandatory rules, such as the principles of consideration, cannot be supplanted by the parties' agreement.)

The theory of how default rules should be constructed is contested. Most commentators take the position that with certain exceptions, default rules should be based on the agreement parties probably would have reached if they had addressed the relevant issues. This approach leaves open two possible conceptions. Under one conception, the default rule should be the term that reasonable persons in the positions of the parties probably would have agreed to if they had addressed the relevant issue when they made their contract. Under an alternative conception, the default rule should be the term that the actual parties probably would have agreed to if they had addressed the issue. The second conception takes into account the bargaining power and risk-averseness of the actual parties, the intensity with which the parties hold their positions, and the like. The first conception is much more attractive, because it would be extremely difficult to determine the actual parties' relative bargaining power, degree of risk-averseness, intensity, and the like at the time they made their contract, and even if those elements could be determined, it would be highly problematic how those elements would have played out in the negotiation of any given issue.

Hawkland, Sales Contract Terms Under the UCC

17 U.C.C.L.J. 195, 207 (1985)

"The rationale underlying the use of statutory [gap-filler] terms is that they represent ordinary understanding about common matters and therefore most likely would have been used by the parties had they considered the term when they made their agreement. In short, statutory terms presuppose that the parties have omitted, through haste, ignorance, or forgetfulness, a routine term that subsequently has become important and that the fairest method to fill that missing term is to impose upon them the kind of term that normally is used by most parties in common, unexceptional deals."

SATERIALE V. R.J. REYNOLDS TOBACCO COMPANY

United States Court of Appeals, Ninth Circuit, 2012.
697 F.3d 777.

[Other parts of the opinion are in Chapter 9, supra.]

RJR argues that, even if there was an offer, any contract arising from it would be too indefinite to be enforced. To be enforceable under California law, a contract must be sufficiently definite "for the court to ascertain the parties' obligations and to determine whether those obligations have been performed or breached." *Bustamante v. Intuit, Inc.,* 141 Cal.App.4th 199, 45 Cal.Rptr.3d 692, 699 (2006) (quoting *Ersa Grae Corp. v. Fluor Corp.,* 1 Cal.App.4th 613, 2 Cal.Rptr.2d 288, 294 (1991)) (internal quotation marks omitted). "The terms of a contract are reasonably certain if they provide a basis for determining the existence of a breach and for giving an appropriate remedy." *Id.* (quoting Restatement § 33(2)) (internal quotation marks omitted).

1. *Existence of a Breach*

The first of these requirements is satisfied here. The plaintiffs do not claim that they were entitled to particular merchandise, but that RJR was required to make reasonable quantities of rewards merchandise available during the life of the Camel Cash program—a duty RJR allegedly breached by failing to make *any* merchandise available after October 1, 2006. This alleged breach is readily discernible. *See* Restatement § 33 cmt. b ("[T]he degree of certainty required may be affected by the dispute which arises and by the remedy sought. Courts decide the disputes before them, not other hypothetical disputes which might have arisen.").[5]

---

[5]   That the alleged contract afforded RJR some discretion in performing does not compel the conclusion that the alleged contract is too indefinite to be enforced. *See* Restatement § 34 cmt. a ("If the agreement is otherwise sufficiently definite to be a contract, it is not made invalid by the fact that it leaves particulars of performance to be specified by one of the parties."); Corbin § 4.4 ("[T]he fact that one of the parties reserves the power of fixing or varying the price or other

2. *Giving an Appropriate Remedy*

The second requirement—that the contract provide a basis for giving an appropriate remedy—presents a closer question. As noted, RJR exercised considerable discretion in deciding what rewards would be offered. We cannot know precisely what merchandise the plaintiffs might have received had RJR fully performed its obligations, an uncertainty that could inhibit the process of determining a remedy. *See Bustamante,* 45 Cal.Rptr.3d at 699 ("[T]he limits of performance must be sufficiently defined to provide a rational basis for the assessment of damages." (quoting *Ladas v. Cal. State Auto. Ass'n,* 19 Cal.App.4th 761, 23 Cal.Rptr.2d 810, 814 (1993)) (internal quotation marks omitted)).

It is not clear, however, that damages could not be rationally assessed here. RJR's internal documents assigned C-Notes values, such as 15 cents per $1 note, that might afford a basis for assessing damages. In the alternative, RJR's final rewards catalog and pre-breach performance might provide a basis for giving an appropriate remedy.

We should not lightly conclude, especially at this early stage in the proceedings, that there is no basis for determining an appropriate remedy where, as here, the allegations suggest that the parties intended to contract. *See Cal. Lettuce Growers,* 289 P.2d at 790 ("The law does not favor, but leans against, the destruction of contracts because of uncertainty; and it will, if feasible, so construe agreements as to carry into effect the reasonable intentions of the parties if that can be ascertained." (*quoting McIllmoil v. Frawley Motor Co.,* 190 Cal. 546, 213 P. 971, 972 (1923))); Corbin § 4.1 ("If the parties have concluded a transaction in which it appears that they intend to make a contract, the court should not frustrate their intention if it is possible to reach a fair and just result, even though this requires a choice among conflicting meanings and the filling of some gaps that the parties have left."). Here, the allegations of the complaint support the inference that the parties intended to contract. The plaintiffs enrolled in the Camel Cash program, purchased Camel cigarettes and collected Camel Cash certificates. RJR accepted the plaintiffs' registration forms, issued them enrollment numbers, performed under the program for 15 years and, according to internal RJR documents, treated outstanding C-Notes as a binding obligation and an outstanding financial liability. According to the documents, RJR closely monitored its exposure under the program, and even went so far as to create a financial reserve to cover that exposure—actions consistent with a legally binding commitment.

---

performance is not fatal if the exercise of this power is subject to prescribed or implied limitations, as that the variation . . . must be reasonable or in good faith." (footnote omitted)); *Cal. Lettuce Growers, Inc. v. Union Sugar Co.,* 45 Cal.2d 474, 289 P.2d 785, 791 (1955) ("[W]here a contract confers on one party a discretionary power affecting the rights of the other, a duty is imposed to exercise that discretion in good faith and in accordance with fair dealing.").

We also consider the plaintiffs' substantial reliance on RJR's promises, as well as the substantial benefits RJR accrued by virtue of consumers' reliance on the Camel Cash program. Corbin explains that, "[i]f one party has greatly benefited by part performance or if one party has relied extensively on the agreement, the court should go to great lengths to find a construction of the agreement that will salvage it." Corbin § 4.3 (footnotes omitted). For these reasons, dismissal for indefiniteness is unwarranted.

———

Arbitron, Inc. v. Tralyn Broadcasting, Inc.

400 F.3d 130 (2d Cir. 2005)

Arbitron had a five-year license agreement (1997 to 2002) to provide listener-demographics data to Trayln for its single radio station at a monthly rate of $1,729.57. The data would be more valuable to Trayln if it acquired additional stations in the same market or an adjacent market. The agreement covered this possibility with an escalation clause, which gave Arbitron the right to increase the fee in the event Trayln (or its successor) acquired additional stations. Trayln also agreed to inform Arbitron in this event. In June 1999, JMD purchased Trayln's station. The purchase agreement assigned the Arbitron license agreement to JMD. JMD and Trayln did not inform Arbitron of the assignment, as required by the license agreement. Nor did they inform Arbitron that JMD owned four additional radio stations in the same market. In June 2000, Arbitron learned of these events. It notified JMD that it was exercising its right to increase the monthly licensing fee by five to reflect the five JMD stations that could now share Arbitron's listener data. JMD refused to pay. Arbitron sued for breach, seeking the quintupled fee from June 1999 to the end of the contract's five year term. The district court granted summary judgment for JMD, concluding that because "[n]either the escalation clause in ¶ 11, nor any other section of the Agreement, contains any basis for determining the new rate to be paid Arbitron in the event changes in ownership occur, the License Agreement's escalation clause was unenforceably vague under New York law." Reversed.

(Calabresi, J.) "[W]e conclude that the escalation clause is enforceable under the common law of New York. This is so because the clause before us is not an "agreement to agree," under which future negations between the parties must occur, but is instead an acknowledgment that, if certain conditions arise in the future, *no* new agreement is required before Arbitron may set new license terms. Such an agreement is not unenforceably vague under New York's common law.

"The seminal New York precedent on unenforceably indefinite contracts is *Joseph Martin, Jr., Delicatessen, Inc. v. Schumacher,* 52 N.Y.2d 105, 436 N.Y.S.2d 247, 417 N.E.2d 541 (1981). There, the Court of Appeals was faced with an agreement between a landlord and a tenant to lease a commercial space for five years at a monthly rate beginning at $500 and escalating over five years to $650, with the option to renew the lease for another five-year term at a rent to be determined by the parties. At the close of the lease's five-year term, the landlord sought to increase the rent from $650 to $900 monthly. Surprised, the tenant employed an assessor, who appraised the market value of the premises at no more than $550 per month. The tenant sued for specific performance, seeking a new five-year lease at the fair market rate of $550. *Id.* at 108, 436 N.Y.S.2d 247, 417 N.E.2d 541. In resolving the case, the *Delicatessen* majority recognized that the U.C.C., as implemented by the New York legislature, counseled in favor of supplying missing price terms to save and enforce the agreement, and that the terms supplied by a court under the U.C.C. would correspond to a good's fair market value. *Id.* at 111, 436 N.Y.S.2d 247, 417 N.E.2d 541 (discussing predecessors to N.Y. U.C.C. § 2–305 in New York law). Nevertheless, because the New York statute's terms made clear that leases or contracts for the sale of real property were not covered by the U.C.C., the Court of Appeals refused to enforce the agreement. It concluded that

> it is rightfully well settled *in the common law of contracts in this State that a mere agreement to agree, in which a material term is left for future negotiations, is unenforceable.* This is *especially true* of the amount to be paid for the sale or lease of real property. The rule applies *all the more,* and not the less, when, as here, the extraordinary remedy of specific performance is sought.

52 N.Y.2d at 109–10, 436 N.Y.S.2d 247, 417 N.E.2d 541 (all emphases added) (internal citations omitted). . . .

"The escalation clause, unlike the promise to set a future rent rate collectively in *Delicatessen,* does not require the parties to reach an "agreement" on price at some point in the future. That is, the escalation clause is not an "agreement to agree." *Delicatessen,* 52 N.Y.2d at 109, 436 N.Y.S.2d 247, 417 N.E.2d 541. Instead, like the contract in *Cobble Hill,* it is a mechanism for objectively setting material terms in the future without further negotiations between both parties. It does so, moreover, with "sufficient evidence that both parties intended that [pricing] arrangement." *Express Indus.,* 93 N.Y.2d at 590, 693 N.Y.S.2d 857, 715 N.E.2d 1050. The escalation clause clearly and unambiguously states that, in the event that Tralyn or its successors acquired new radio stations in the same (or an adjacent) geographic market, "Arbitron may redetermine its Gross Annual Rate for the Data, Reports and Services licensed hereunder . . . effective the first of the month following [the acquisition]." The escalation clause further provides, in unambiguous language, that Arbitron may exercise this power to "redetermine" the license fee "[n]otwithstanding Station's failure to notify Arbitron" that an acquisition had occurred.

"The intent of the parties is manifest in the language of the agreement. Both Arbitron and Tralyn explicitly agreed that Arbitron was authorized to adjust the license fee in the event that Tralyn or its successors began to operate additional stations. This fact makes the instant case very different from those disputes in which courts are faced with "no objective evidence" of a shared intent to permit one party to set prices in the future. *See [In Re Express Indus. & Terminal Corp.,* 93 N.Y.2d 584, 693 N.Y.S.2d 857, 715 N.E.2d 1050 (1999)] And it in no way leads a court enforcing the contract to "impos[e] its own conception of what the parties should or might have undertaken." *Delicatessen,* 52 N.Y.2d at 109, 436 N.Y.S.2d 247, 417 N.E.2d 541. Accordingly, we conclude that the district court erred in holding the License Agreement's escalation clause "impenetrably vague" under New York law. . .

"It is not clear whether, under New York law, a license agreement of the sort at issue in this case constitutes a contract for the sale of goods, or is otherwise governed by the U.C.C. We note, however, that were this section of New York's commercial code applied to the License Agreement, then the escalation clause would undoubtedly be a valid contract term under New York law; it would simply establish "[a] price to be fixed by the seller," and would be enforceable so long as that price was fixed "in good faith." N.Y. U.C.C. § 2–305. But the applicability of the U.C.C. to the license agreement before is not something we need to decide today.

"Because we believe that the License Agreement's escalation clause is not inconsistent with New York law, we conclude that the district court erred in granting summary judgment to JMD. We therefore vacate the district court's order and remand the case for further proceedings. On remand, the district court may wish to consider whether Arbitron has exercised its authority under the escalation clause in "good faith" within the meaning of N.Y. U.C.C. § 2–305 (which, as we have previously noted, may or may not apply to a "license" of this sort), or more generally, in a manner consistent with Arbitron's implied duty of fair dealing under New York law. *See, e.g., Carvel Corp. v. Diversified Mgmt. Group, Inc.,* 930 F.2d 228, 230 (2d Cir.1991) ("Under New York law, every contract contains an implied covenant of good faith and fair dealing."). We express no opinion on either question."

Moolenaar v. Co-Build Companies Inc.

354 F.Supp. 980 (D.V.I. 1973)

In October 1967, Moolenaar, a sheep-and-goat farmer, leased 150 acres of land from Correa. The lease was to run for a period of five years, and Moolenaar had an option to renew for an additional five years. Moolenaar was to pay $375 per month during the initial term. The lease provided that the rent for the renewal period "shall be renegotiated." Later, Correa sold the land to Co-Build Companies. Co-build purchased the land subject to Moolenaar's rights under the lease.

In April 1972, six months before expiration of the first five-year term, Moolenaar informed Co-Build of his intention to exercise the renewal option. Co-Build expressed its willingness to extend the lease at a "renegotiated" rent of $17,000 per month. Co-Build justified this figure by the high price it had paid for the land and the land's unquestionably great value if put to industrial use. Such a rent, however, was beyond the resources of the less profitable Moolenaar's husbandry business. Moolenaar therefore proposed a considerably lower figure, and indicated his desire to meet for direct negotiations. All such offers were declined. Upon Co-Build's refusal to recede from its initial position, Moolenaar filed an action for a declaratory judgement of the rights of the parties under the lease. Held, Moolenaar had a right to renew at a reasonable rent:

(Young, J.) "The threshold question is, of course, whether Moolenaar possesses a renewal option at all. A number of jurisdictions would hold that he does not, reasoning that a clause which neglects to stipulate the rent is void for uncertainty and indefiniteness. . . . The better view, however, would hold that such a clause intends renewal at a 'reasonable' rent, and would find that market conditions are ascertainable with sufficient certainty to make the clause specifically enforceable. A number of policy considerations support this result. First, it will probably effectuate the intent of the parties better than would striking out the clause altogether. A document should be construed where possible to give effect to every term, on the theory that the signatories inserted each for a reason and if one party had agreed to the clause only in the secret belief that it would prove unenforceable, he should be discouraged from such paths. Secondly, a renewal option has a more sympathetic claim to enforcement than do most vague contractual terms, since valuable consideration will often have already been paid for it. The option of renewal is one factor inducing the tenant to enter into the lease, or to pay as high a rent as he did during the initial period. To this extent the landlord benefited from the tenant's reliance on the clause, and so the tenant has a stronger claim to receive the reciprocal benefit of the option.[3] . . .

". . . The rule which I have followed here is admittedly the minority view. . . . I think it is appropriate to give greater weight to recent decisions rather than weighing the authorities on a strictly numerical basis. . . . Briefly, the common law is in a state of perpetual evolution and recent decisions will more accurately reflect the current understanding on an issue. For the issue at hand the minority view is nonetheless a widely followed one, . . . and has been gaining adherents at a rate which indicates that the common law is moving in that direction. Compare, e. g., 30 A.L.R. 572 (1924) (few cases cited for minority view) with 6 A.L.R.2d 448, 454 (1949) (many such cases). And while, of course, not controlling here, the U.C.C. provisions on the Sale of Goods also illustrate the approach of the modern law, with its emphasis on reasonable commercial dealings and its rejection of technical requirements."

---

[3]   Contrary to Co-Build's assertion that such a clause may benefit either the landlord or the tenant, depending on market conditions, it benefits only the tenant. He has the choice of whether or not to exercise the option, while the landlord would be in a corresponding position only if he could elect to renew the lease and thereby bind the tenant for rent during the additional period.

CHANNEL HOME CENTERS V. GROSSMAN

United States Court of Appeals, Third Circuit, 1986.
795 F.2d 291.

Before WEIS, HIGGINBOTHAM, BECKER, CIRCUIT JUDGES.

Opinion of the Court

BECKER, CIRCUIT JUDGE.

This diversity case presents the question whether, under Pennsylvania law, a property owner's promise to a prospective tenant, pursuant to a detailed letter of intent, to negotiate in good faith with the prospective tenant and to withdraw the lease premises from the marketplace during the negotiation, can bind the owner for a reasonable period of time where the prospective tenant has expended significant sums of money in connection with the lease negotiations and preparation and where there was evidence that the letter of intent was of significant value to the property owner. We hold that it may. We therefore vacate and reverse the district court's determination that there was no enforceable agreement, and remand the case for trial.

I.

Appellant Channel Home Centers ("Channel"), a division of Grace Retail Corporation, operates retail home improvement stores throughout the Northeastern United States, including Philadelphia and its suburbs. Appellee Frank Grossman, a real estate broker and developer, with his sons Bruce and Jeffrey Grossman, either owns or has a controlling interest in appellees Tri-Star Associates ("Tri-Star"), Baker Investment Corporation ("Baker"), and Cedarbrook Associates, a Pennsylvania Limited Partnership ("Cedarbrook").

Between November, 1984 and February, 1985, the Grossmans, through Baker, were in the process of acquiring ownership of Cedarbrook Mall ("the mall") located in Cheltenham Township, Pennsylvania, a northern suburb of Philadelphia. During these months, Baker was the equitable owner of the mall, Tri-Star was acting as the mall's leasing agent, and legal title was in Equitable Life Assurance Society. It was anticipated that, upon closing in February, 1985, Baker would become both legal and equitable owner of the mall. App. at 218a–219a, 496a. The Grossmans intended to revitalize the mall, which had fallen on hard times prior to their acquisition, through an aggressive rehabilitation and leasing program.

In the third week of November, 1984, Tri-Star wrote to Richard Perkowski, Director of Real Estate for Channel, informing him of the availability of a store location in Cedarbrook Mall which Tri-Star believed Channel would be interested in leasing. Perkowski expressed some interest, and met the Grossmans on November 28, 1984. After Perkowski was given a tour of the premises, the terms of a lease were discussed. App. at 457a, 496a. Frank Grossman testified that "we discussed various terms, and these terms were, some were loose, some were more or less terms." App. at 364a, 496a–497a.

In a memorandum dated December 7, 1984, to S. Charles Tabak, Channel's senior vice-president for general administration, Perkowski outlined the salient lease terms that he had negotiated with the Grossmans. App. at 97a. On or about the same date, Tabak and Leon Burger, President of Channel, visited the mall site with the Grossmans. They indicated that Channel desired to lease the site. App. at 413a–415a. Frank Grossman then requested that Channel execute a letter of intent that, as Grossman put it, could be shown to "other people, banks or whatever." App. at 366a–367a. Tabak testified that the Grossmans wanted to get Channel into the site because it would give the mall four "anchor" stores. App. at 414a. Apparently, Frank Grossman was anxious to get Channel's signature on a letter of intent so that it could be used to help Grossman secure financing for his purchase of the mall. App. at 366a–367a, 497a.

On December 11, 1984, in response to Grossman's request, Channel prepared, executed, and submitted a detailed letter of intent setting forth a plethora of lease terms which provided, *inter alia,* that

> [t]o induce the Tenant [Channel] to proceed with the leasing of the Store, you [Grossman] will withdraw the Store from the rental market, and only negotiate the above described leasing transaction to completion.

Please acknowledge your intent to proceed with the leasing of the store under the above terms, conditions and understanding by signing the enclosed copy of the letter and returning it to the undersigned within ten (10) days from the date hereof.

App. at 31a.[2]

---

[2]   The full December 11, 1984 letter, on Channel stationery, reads as follows:

Dear Mr. Grossman:

The Channel Home Centers Division of Grace Retail Corporation has approved the leasing of a store at the above described location subject to the terms and conditions of this letter. The purpose of this letter is to express the understanding under which an Agreement of Lease, prepared by Tenant, but in a mutually satisfactory form, is to be executed by the owner of the Shopping Center, as Landlord and Grace Retail Corporation, as Tenant.

The Landlord will lease to the Tenant the following described Store located in the captioned Shopping Center, all as shown and described on the copy of your leasing brochure attached to this letter and on the following terms:

1. *Store:* Existing 70,400 sq. ft. area designated in the attached leasing brochure as space "1" on lower level of mall beneath Jamesway Department Store, together with use of outdoor area for storage and sales. Such area located in portion of parking lot adjacent to space "1".

2. *Term & Rent:* Term of twenty-five (25) years commencing the date Tenant opens for business during which Tenant will pay Annual Rent in the amounts set forth below plus

Very truly yours,

s/s/

S.C. Tabak

Percentage Rent of two (2) percent of Gross Sales during each lease year in excess of the Gross Sales Break Point set forth below:

Lease Year	Annual Rent	Gross Sales Break Point
1–5	$112,500	$10.0 MM
6–10	137,500	11.0 MM
11–15	162,500	12.1 MM
16–20	187,500	13.3 MM
20–25	212,500	14.6 MM

3. *Option Periods:* Tenant's right to extend for four (4) option periods of five (5) years each, on the same terms as during the initial term, except that during each exercised option period, the Annual Rent shall be increased once by $25,000 per year, and the Gross Sales Break Point shall be increased by 10% over the sums in effect for the prior 5-year period (i.e. during Lease Years 26–30 of first option period, Annual Rent shall be $237,500 per year and Gross Sales Break Point shall be $16.06 million);

4. *Real Estate Taxes:* Landlord's obligation, Tenant does not make contributions;

5. *Common Area Maintenance:* Landlord's obligation to maintain and repair existing 850 car parking lot in northeast portion of Shopping Center, which will be the Tenant's primary parking area, and other common areas of the Shopping Center; Tenant does not make contributions;

6. *Landlord's Pre-term Responsibilities:* Landlord will deliver Store empty and broom clean including the removal of all partitions, and with HVAC system in working order. The Landlord will submeter and locate the major electric service to the area of the Store, as Channel designates. Landlord will remove the existing escalator and provide escape stairs as per fire code, and will insure that the building is free of any asbestos hazard. The service elevator and two receiving bays on the lower level, will be boxed-out from the Tenant's Store, to serve the upper levels of the Shopping Center.

7. *Maintenance & Repairs:* Landlord will maintain repair and replace if necessary the HVAC system, roof and structural and exterior portions of the building. Tenant responsible for building interior and store front and will pay its prorate share of HVAC usage.

Execution of the Agreement of Lease by Landlord and Tenant is specifically subject to each of the following:

a. *Tenant's authority:* Approval by Tenant's parent corporation, W.R. Grace & Co., and its Retail Group, of the essential business terms of the Agreement of Lease;

b. *Legal Title:* Approval by the Tenant of the status of title for the site, including any access easements.

c. *Sign Contingency:* The Tenants obtaining all necessary permits with the [Landlord's] cooperation (including obtaining any sign variances) for the erection of Tenant's identification signs, on two (2) pylons located on Cheltenham Ave. and Easton Ave., respectively, and two building signs on the front of the mall and the front of the Store.

The Tenant has and will not incur any brokerage fees in connection with this proposed lease. Any expenditure by the Landlord or Tenant prior to execution of the Agreement of Lease shall be at the party's own risk.

A store opening date during the first half of 1985 is planned. Lease preparation, obtaining the sign permits and approvals described above and delivery of possession of the Store to Tenant would commence immediately and proceed to achieve that estimated opening date. To induce the Tenant to proceed with the leasing of this Store, you will withdraw the Store from the rental market, and only negotiate the above described leasing transaction to completion.

Please acknowledge your intent to proceed with the leasing of the captioned store under the above terms, conditions and understanding by signing the enclosed copy of this letter and returning it to the undersigned within ten (10) days from the date hereof.

App. at 29a–31a.

Senior Vice President
Channel Home Center Division

Frank Grossman promptly signed the letter of intent and returned it to Channel. App. at 499a. Grossman contends that Perkowski and Tabak also agreed orally that a draft lease be submitted within thirty (30) days. App. at 331a–332a, 365–366a. Perkowski and Tabak denied telling Grossman that a lease would be forthcoming within 30 days or any finite period of time. App. at 445a, 473a.

Thereafter, both parties initiated procedures directed toward satisfaction of lease contingencies. The letter of intent specified that execution of the lease was expressly subject to each of the following: (1) approval by Channel's parent corporation, W.R. Grace & Company ("Grace"), of the essential business terms of the lease; (2) approval by Channel of the status of title for the site; and (3) Channel's obtaining, with Frank Grossman's cooperation, all necessary permits and zoning variances for the erection of Channel's identification signs. App. at 30a; *see supra* note 2.

On December 14, 1984, Channel directed the Grace legal department to prepare a lease for the premises. Channel's real estate committee approved the lease site on December 20, 1984. App. at 472a. Channel planning representatives visited the premises on December 21, 1984, to obtain measurements for architectural alterations, renovations and related construction. App. at 379a. Detailed marketing plans were developed, building plans drafted, delivery schedules were prepared and materials and equipment deemed necessary for the store were purchased. App. at 91a–96a, 99a–135a, 422a–423a, 517a–547a. The Grossmans applied to the Cheltenham Township building and zoning committee for permission to erect commercial signs for Channel and other tenants of the mall. App. at 15a.

On January 11, 1985, Frank Shea, Esquire, of the Grace legal department sent to Frank Grossman two copies of a forty-one (41) page draft lease and, in a cover letter, requested copies of several documents to be used as exhibits to the lease. App. at 43a–44a. On January 16, 1985, Frank Shea received the following letter from Bruce Grossman:

Dear Mr. Shea:

As you requested, enclosed please find the following documents:

1) A copy of a recent title report for the Cedarbrook Mall (the "Mall"),

2) A legal description of the Mall,

3) A site plan of the Mall, and

4) A description of the Landlord's construction.

As we discussed, we have commenced work on the Channel location at the Mall and would, therefore, appreciate your assistance in expediting the execution of the Channel lease.

I look forward to hearing from you soon.

> VERY TRULY YOURS,
> BAKER INVESTMENT
> CORPORATION
> /S/
> BRUCE S. GROSSMAN,
> EXECUTIVE VICE PRESIDENT

App. at 16a. On January 21, 1985, Frank Shea received a copy of a letter from Frank Grossman to Richard Perkowski dated January 17, 1985. It provided:

> At Frank Shea's request, enclosed is a site plan for the Cedarbrook Mall and also a copy of the proposed pylon sign design.
>
> We look forward to executing the lease agreement in the very near future. If you have any questions, please feel free to call me.

App. at 46a.

Bruce Grossman called Shea on January 23, 1985 to discuss the lease. The only item Grossman could recall discussing pertained to the "use" clause in the lease, specifically whether Channel could use the site for warehouse facilities at some future point. App. at 286a–287a, 502a. Apparently, Grossman then related other areas of concern and Shea suggested that a telephone conference be arranged with all parties the following week. App. at 382a, 502a. Grossman agreed. According to Grossman, Shea was supposed to initiate the conference call; however, when the call was not forthcoming, Grossman did not attempt to reach Shea or anyone else at Channel. App. at 389a–390a. Shea understood that the Grossmans were going to discuss the lease among themselves and get back to him. App. at 448a.

On or about January 22, 1985, Stephen Erlbaum, Chairman of the Board of Mr. Good Buys of Pennsylvania, Inc. ("Mr. Good Buys"), contacted Frank Grossman. Like Channel, Mr. Good Buys is a corporation engaged in the business of operating retail home improvement centers; it is a major competitor of Channel in the Philadelphia area. App. at 20a–21a. Erlbaum advised Grossman that Mr. Good Buys would be interested in leasing space at Cedarbrook Mall, and sent Grossman printed information about Mr. Good Buys. App. at 202a.

On January 24, 1985, construction representatives from Channel met at the mall site to go over building alterations and designs. App. at 287a–288a, 503a. The next day, January 25, 1985, Erlbaum and other representatives from Mr. Good Buys met with the Grossmans and toured Channel's proposed lease location. App. at 503a. When Erlbaum expressed an interest in leasing this site, lease terms were discussed. *Id.*

On February 6, 1985, Frank Grossman notified Channel that "negotiations terminated as of this date" due to Channel's failure to submit a signed and mutually acceptable lease for the mall site within thirty days of the December 11, 1984 letter of intent. App. at 42a. (This was the first and only written evidence of the purported thirty-day time limit. The letter of intent contained no such term. . . .) On February 7, 1985, Mr. Good Buys and Frank Grossman executed a lease for the Cedarbrook Mall. App. at 147a–196a. Mr. Good Buys agreed to make base-level annual rental payments which were substantially greater than those agreed to by Channel in the December 11, 1984 letter of intent. App. at 147a.[3] Channel's corporate parent, Grace, approved the terms of Channel's proposed lease on February 13, 1985. App. at 443a–444a.

II.

Channel commenced this diversity action, 28 U.S.C. § 1332(a), in the district court for the Eastern District of Pennsylvania on February 15, 1985. Count I of Channel's complaint alleged that appellees' conduct violated the December 11, 1984 letter of intent and constituted a breach of contract. . . . In a supporting affidavit, S. Charles Tabak averred that Channel had substantially completed all tasks necessary to meet the opening date contemplated in the letter of intent and that it had made out-of-pocket expenditures to this end in the sum of $25,000. . . .

Thereafter, on March 26, 1985, the district court filed a Memorandum Opinion and Order. . . .

In its opinion, the district court rejected Channel's arguments that the letter of intent constituted either a valid unilateral or a valid bilateral agreement. The court concluded that the letter of intent (1) did not bind the parties to any obligation; (2) was unenforceable for lack of consideration. . . .

IV.

[Channel contends] that the district court erred in holding that the letter of intent was unenforceable and did not bind the parties to any obligation. Channel argues that the letter, coupled with the surrounding

---

[3] Channel had agreed to rental payments of $112,500 for years 1–5; $137,500 for years 6–10; $162,500 for years 11–15; $187,500 for years 16–20, and $212,500 for years 20–25. Additionally, Channel agreed to pay percentage rent of two (2) percent of gross sales above the following gross sales break points: $10,000,000 for years 1–5; $11,000,000 for years 6–10; $12,100,000 for years 11–15; $13,300,000 for years 16–20, and $14,600,000 for years 20–25. *See supra* note 3. Mr. Good Buys agreed to rental payments of $249,750 for years 1–5; $360,750 for years 6–10; $388,500 for years 11–15; $416,250 for years 6–20; and $444,000 for years 21–25. App. at 147a. Mr. Good Buys did not have to pay additional percentage rent based on gross sales, however. *Id.*

circumstances, constitutes a binding agreement to negotiate in good faith. Appellees rejoin that a promise to negotiate in good faith or to use best efforts to reduce to formal writing an agreement between the parties is enforceable only if the parties have in fact reached agreement on the underlying transaction. Because it is conceded that the letter of intent did not constitute a final agreement between the parties, appellees contend that it is merely evidence of preliminary negotiations and, as such, is unenforceable at law. Appellees further argue that even if the agreement were an otherwise enforceable contract, the letter of intent and any promises contained therein are unenforceable by virtue of Channel's lack of consideration. The parties agree that Pennsylvania law applies to the case.

It is hornbook law that evidence of preliminary negotiations or an agreement to enter into a binding contract in the future does not alone constitute a contract. *See Goldman v. McShain,* 432 Pa. 61, 68, 247 A.2d 455, 458 (1968); *Lombardo v. Gasparini Excavating Co.,* 385 Pa. 388, 392, 123 A.2d 663, 666 (1956); *Kazanjian v. New England Petroleum Corp.,* 332 Pa.Super. 1, 7, 480 A.2d 1153, 1157 (1984); *see* Restatement (Second) of Contracts § 26 (1979). Appellees believe that this doctrine settles this case, but, in so arguing, appellees misconstrue Channel's contract claim. Channel does not contend that the letter of intent is binding as a lease or an agreement to enter into a lease. Rather, it is Channel's position that this document is enforceable as a mutually binding obligation *to negotiate in good faith.*[7] By unilaterally terminating negotiations with Channel and precipitously entering into a lease agreement with Mr. Good Buys, Channel argues, Grossman acted in bad faith and breached his promise to "withdraw the Store from the rental market and only negotiate the above-described leasing transaction to completion." *See supra* note 2.

Under Pennsylvania law, the test for enforceability of an agreement is whether both parties have manifested an intention to be bound by its terms and whether the terms are sufficiently definite to be specifically enforced. *Lombardo v. Gasparini Excavating Co.,* 385 Pa. 388, 393, 123 A.2d 663, 666; *Linnet v. Hitchcock,* 324 Pa.Super. 209, 214, 471 A.2d 537, 540. Additionally, of course, there must be consideration on both sides. *Stelmack v. Glen Alden Coal Co.,* 339 Pa. 410, 14 A.2d 127 (1940); *Cardamone v. University of Pittsburgh,* 253 Pa.Super. 65, 384 A.2d 1228 (1978). Consideration "confers a benefit upon the promisor or causes a detriment to the promisee and must be an act, forbearance or return promise

---

[7]   Because Channel does not argue that the letter of intent is enforceable as a lease between the parties, appellees' reliance upon the district court's conclusion that the letter of intent is insufficient to satisfy the Pennsylvania Statute of Frauds for Leases, Pa.Stat.Ann. tit. 68, §§ 250.202–203 (Purdon 1965 & Supp.1986), is misplaced. The district court therefore erred in holding that the letter of intent was insufficient to satisfy the Statute of Frauds for leases.

bargained for and given in exchange for the original promise." *Curry v. Estate of Thompson*, 332 Pa.Super. 364, 371, 481 A.2d 658, 661 (1984).

Although no Pennsylvania court has considered whether an agreement to negotiate in good faith may meet these conditions, the jurisdictions that have considered the issue have held that such an agreement, if otherwise meeting the requisites of a contract, is an enforceable contract. *See, e.g., Thompson v. Liquichimica of America, Inc.*, 481 F.Supp. 365, 366 (E.D.N.Y.1979); ("Unlike an agreement to agree, which does not constitute a closed proposition, an agreement to use best efforts [or to negotiate in good faith] is a closed proposition, discrete and actionable."); *accord Reprosystem, B.V. v. SCM Corp.*, 727 F.2d 257, 264 (2d Cir.1984); *Chase v. Consolidated Foods Corp.*, 744 F.2d 566, 571 (7th Cir.1984); *Arnold Palmer Golf Co. v. Fuqua Industries Inc.*, 541 F.2d 584 (6th Cir.1976); *Itek Corp. v. Chicago Aerial Industries, Inc.*, 248 A.2d 625 (Del.1968); Restatement (Second) of Contracts § 205 comment (c) (1979) ("Good faith in negotiation"); *see generally* Kessler and Fine, *Culpa in Contrahendo, Bargaining in Good Faith, and Freedom of Contract; a Comparative Study,* 77 Harv.L.Rev. 401 (1964).[8] We are satisfied that Pennsylvania would follow this rule. Applying Pennsylvania law, then, we must ask (1) whether both parties manifested an intention to be bound by the agreement; (2) whether the terms of the agreement are sufficiently definite to be enforced; and (3) whether there was consideration.

In determining the parties' intentions concerning the letter of intent, we must examine the entire document and the relevant circumstances surrounding its adoption. *United Refining Co. v. Jenkins*, 410 Pa. 126, 137, 189 A.2d 574, 580 (1963); *Hillbrook Apartments, Inc. v. Nyce Crete Co.*, 237 Pa.Super. 565, 572, 352 A.2d 148, 151 (1975). The letter of intent, signed by both parties, provides that "[t]o induce the Tenant [Channel] to proceed with the leasing of the Store, you [Grossman] will withdraw the Store from the rental market, and only negotiate the above described leasing transaction to completion." *See supra* note 2. The agreement thus contains an unequivocal promise by Grossman to withdraw the store from the rental market and to negotiate the proposed leasing transaction with Channel to completion.

Evidence of record supports the proposition that the parties intended this promise to be binding. After the letter of intent was executed, both Channel and the Grossmans initiated procedures directed toward satisfaction of lease contingencies. Channel directed its parent corporation

---

[8] Good faith in the bargaining or formation stages of the contracting process is distinguishable from the common law duty to perform in good faith. *See* Restatement of Contracts (Second) § 205 (1979) ("Every contract imposes upon each party a duty of good faith and fair dealing in its performance and its enforcement."); *Baker v. Lafayette College*, 350 Pa.Super. 68, 84, 504 A.2d 247, 255 (1986); *Germantown Manufacturing Co. v. Rawlinson*, 341 Pa.Super. 42, 60, 491 A.2d 138, 148 (1985); *see generally* Burton, *Breach of Contract and the Common Law Duty to Perform in Good Faith,* 94 Harv.L.Rev. 369 (1980).

to prepare a draft lease; Channel planning representatives visited the lease premises to obtain measurements for architectural alterations, renovations, and related construction. Channel developed extensive marketing plans; delivery schedules were prepared and material and equipment deemed necessary for the store were purchased. The Grossmans applied to the township zoning committee for permission to erect Channel signs at various locations on the mall property. Channel submitted a draft lease on January 11, 1985, and the parties, through correspondence and telephone conversations and on-site visits, exhibited an intent to move toward a lease as late as January 23, 1985. . . . Accordingly, the letter of intent and the circumstances surrounding its adoption both support a finding that the parties intended to be bound by an agreement to negotiate in good faith.

We also believe that Grossman's promise to "withdraw the Store from the rental market and only negotiate the above described leasing transaction to completion," viewed in the context of the detailed letter of intent (which covers most significant lease terms, *see supra* n. 2), is sufficiently definite to be specifically enforced, provided that Channel submitted sufficient legal consideration in return.

Appellees argue that "[n]o money or thing of value was paid, either at the time of the letter or at any other time that would convert an agreement to negotiate into some enforceable type of contract." Brief of Appellees at 16. We disagree. It seems clear that the execution and tender of the letter of intent by Channel was of substantial value to Frank Grossman. At the time the letter of intent was executed, Grossman was in the process of obtaining financing for his purchase of the mall. When it became apparent to Grossman that Channel—a major corporate tenant—was seriously interested in leasing the mall site, he requested that Channel sign a letter of intent which, as Grossman put it, could be shown to "other people, banks or whatever with a view to getting permanent financing." App. at 366a–367a. Fully aware of Grossman's desire to obtain financing, Channel sought to solidify its bargaining position by requesting that Grossman also sign the letter of intent and promise to "withdraw the store from the rental market and only negotiate the above-described leasing transaction to completion." There being evidence that value passed from each party to the other, we conclude that the record would support a finding that Channel's execution and tender of the letter of intent conferred a bargained for benefit on Grossman which was valid consideration for Grossman's return promise to negotiate in good faith.

V.

In sum, we agree with Channel that the record contains evidence that supports a finding that the parties intended to enter into a binding agreement to negotiate in good faith. We further hold that the agreement had sufficient specificity to make it an enforceable contract if the parties so intended, and that consideration passed between the parties. We will therefore remand this case to the district court for trial.

At least two significant issues must be resolved at trial. First, although our review of the record reveals that there is sufficient evidence to support a finding that the parties intended to be bound by the letter of intent, we do not hold that the evidence requires this conclusion. At trial, evidence will presumably be brought to light that will aid the trier of fact in deciding this issue.

As noted above, there is also some dispute over whether there was a time limit on the negotiations that was not specified in the letter of intent. Because the district court erroneously concluded that the letter of intent was unenforceable as a matter of law, it made no factual findings with regard to this critical term. If, as appellees suggest, Channel orally agreed to forward a draft lease within 30 days of the date on which the letter of intent was executed, Channel's failure to do so could have terminated the agreement. Alternatively, if, as Channel argues, the parties did not fix a definite time for the duration of negotiations, then a reasonable time would be applicable. *See Darlington v. General Electric Corp.*, 350 Pa.Super. 183, 192–93, 504 A.2d 306, 310–11 (1986), and a determination must be made as to what constitutes a reasonable time under all the circumstances.

The judgment of the district court will therefore be reversed, and the case remanded for further proceedings consistent with this opinion.

UNIDROIT PRINCIPLES OF INTERNATIONAL COMMERCIAL CONTRACTS ART. 2.1.15

[See Selected Source Materials Supplement]

PRINCIPLES OF EUROPEAN CONTRACT LAW ART. 2.301

[See Selected Source Materials Supplement]

TEACHERS INSURANCE AND ANNUITY ASSOCIATION
OF AMERICA v. TRIBUNE CO.

Southern District of New York, 1987.
670 F.Supp. 491.

LEVAL, DISTRICT JUDGE.

[Tribune Company sought a large loan that would be backed by mortgage received by Tribune from LaSalle Partners in a sale-leaseback of the iconic News Building. Tribune hoped to use offset accounting so the loan would not appear on its balance sheet. Tribune identified six institutions, including Teachers Insurance and Annuity Association of America (Teachers or TIAA) that Tribune believed would have the means and flexibility to make such a loan. All the institutions except Teachers promptly rejected the deal. On August 20, 1982, Scott Smith, Tribune's Vice President and Treasurer, sent Martha Driver, a Teachers executive, an Offering Circular term sheet describing the proposed transaction. For tax reasons Tribune wanted to complete the transaction during 1982. Accordingly, Smith's letter stated that "While we are flexible on funds delivery, our objective is to have a firm commitment from a lender by September 15, 1982. Consequently, we need to move the due diligence and negotiation process along very quickly." 670 F. Supp. at 493. On September 16 Teachers' Finance Committee met and approved the loan to Tribune, and Driver told Smith that Teachers would promptly issue a commitment letter.

Teachers' commitment letter included a two-page Summary of Proposed Terms, which was drawn from Tribune's term sheet and the parties' ensuing conversations. The commitment letter covered all the basic economic terms of the proposed loan. Neither Tribune's term sheet nor Teachers' commitment letter referred to Tribune's using offset accounting. Instead, the commitment letter stated that the agreement between Teachers and Tribune was "contingent upon the preparation, execution and delivery of instruments . . . in form and substance satisfactory to TIAA and to TIAA's special counsel," *Id.* at 494, and that the transaction documents would contain the usual and customary representations and warranties, closing conditions, other covenants, and events of default "as we and our special counsel may deem reasonably necessary to accomplish this transaction." *Id.* The letter concluded by inviting Tribune to "evidence acceptance of the conditions of this letter by having it executed below by a duly authorized officer" *Id.* and added that "Upon receipt by TIAA of an accepted counterpart of this letter, our agreement to purchase from you and your agreement to issue sell and deliver to us . . . the [described] securities, shall become a binding agreement between us." *Id.*

The "binding agreement" language in Teachers' commitment letter caused serious concern to Tribune's lawyers. Tribune's outside counsel advised Smith not to sign a letter that contained this language,[1] but having been turned down by five other institutions Smith did not want to risk losing Teachers' commitment. Therefore, he did not question the binding-agreement language. Instead, he executed the commitment letter on Tribune's behalf and added a notation that the commitment letter was subject to certain modifications outlined in his covering letter. In the covering letter Smith wrote that "[O]ur acceptance and agreement is subject to approval by the [Tribune] Company's Board of Directors and the preparation and execution of legal documentation satisfactory to the Company." *Id.* at 500. The cover letter, like the commitment letter, made no mention of offset accounting.

On October 28, Tribune's board authorized its officers to effect the borrowing "with all of the actual terms and conditions to be subject to the prior approval by resolution of the Finance Committee." *Id.* at 495. Meanwhile, however, interest rates had dropped rapidly and were substantially below the rates that prevailed when Teachers and Tribune had entered into the commitment letter, and therefore the rate Tribune was obliged to pay. In addition, Tribune became concerned that its accountants would not approve Tribune's proposed use of offset accounting.

On December 6, Tribune and LaSalle closed the sale of the News Building. Teachers grew worried that Tribune, which could now borrow at substantially lower rates, was seeking to back out of the transaction, and pressed Tribune to put the loan agreements into final form. To this end Teachers dropped a demand it had made for conditions on Tribune's ability to exercise an option under the loan agreement, and asked for a meeting to iron out all open issues. But the fall in interest rates together with doubts as to the availability of offset accounting now made the deal much less attractive to Tribune. Smith replied to Teachers that there was no point in meeting unless Teachers first agreed that Tribune's obligation to close the loan would be conditional on Tribune's ability to use offset accounting. Teachers responded that Tribune's accounting was not part of the deal. When Tribune exhibited no further interest in pursuing the transaction, Teachers brought suit.]

Discussion

The primary contested issue is as to the nature of the obligations that arose out of the commitment letter agreement:

Tribune contends that although the commitment letter was an undertaking to negotiate, it did not obligate either side to enter into a loan contract that was adverse to its interest. Pointing out that the commitment letter agreement left many terms open, that both sides had reserved the

---

[1] A few days before, Tribune had entered into a letter of intent with LaSalle for the sale of the building which, in contrast, expressly provided that it was "not a binding agreement." *Id.* at 494 n.1.

right of approval of satisfactory documentation, and that Tribune had furthermore made its obligation conditioned on the approval of its Board of Directors, it argues that it had no binding commitment to the loan agreement, especially if it found the terms adverse to its interests.

Teachers argues that although the commitment letter did not constitute a concluded loan agreement, it was nonetheless a binding commitment which obligated both sides to negotiate in good faith toward a final contract conforming to the agreed terms; it thus committed both sides not to abandon the deal, nor to break it by a demand that was outside the scope of the agreement. Although Teachers recognizes that the letter agreement left many points unspecified, it argues that the open terms were of minor economic significance and were covered by the provision that "[t]he documents shall contain such representations and warranties, closing conditions, other covenants, events of default and remedies, requirements for delivery of financial statements, and other information and provisions *as are usual and customary in this type of transaction. . . .*" (Emphasis supplied.) It argues that these minor open terms did not render the contract illusory or unenforceable. Nor did they indicate an intention of the parties not to be bound when taken together with the express language of "binding agreement." Although it was of course possible for the deal to break without liability on either side by reason of inability of the parties to reach agreement on the open terms, Teachers argues that neither side was free to break the deal over conditions which were either inconsistent with the agreed terms or outside the scope of provisions that would be "usual and customary in this type of transaction."

There has been much litigation over preliminary agreements. It is difficult to generalize about their legal effect. They cover a broad scope ranging in innumerable forms and variations from letters of intent which presuppose that no binding obligations will be placed upon any party until final contract documents have been signed, to firm binding commitments which, notwithstanding a need for a more detailed documentation of agreement, can bind the parties to adhere in good faith to the deal that has been agreed. As is commonly the case with contract disputes, prime significance attaches to the intentions of the parties and to their manifestations of intent. Labels such as "letter of intent" or "commitment letter" are not necessarily controlling although they may be helpful indicators of the parties' intentions. Notwithstanding the intention of the parties at the time, if the agreement is too fragmentary, in that it leaves open terms of too fundamental importance, it may be incapable of sustaining binding legal obligation. Furthermore, the conclusion that a preliminary agreement created binding obligations does not necessarily resolve disputes because it leaves open the further question of the nature, scope and extent of the binding obligations.

A primary concern for courts in such disputes is to avoid trapping parties in surprise contractual obligations that they never intended. Ordinarily in contract negotiation, enforceable legal rights do not arise until either the expression of mutual consent to be bound, or some equivalent event that marks acceptance of offer. Contractual liability, unlike tort liability, arises from consent to be bound (or in any event from the manifestation of consent). It is fundamental to contract law that mere participation in negotiations and discussions does not create binding obligation, even if agreement is reached on all disputed terms. More is needed than agreement on each detail, which is overall agreement (or offer and acceptance) to enter into the binding contract. Nor is this principle altered by the fact that negotiating parties may have entered into letters of intent or preliminary agreements if those were made with the understanding that neither side would be bound until final agreement was reached. The Court of Appeals in several recent cases has stressed the importance of recognizing the freedom of negotiating parties from binding obligations, notwithstanding their having entered into various forms of non-binding preliminary assent. Those decisions have underlined various indicia that can be helpful in making the determination whether a manifestation of preliminary assent amounted to a legally binding agreement.

Notwithstanding the importance of protecting negotiating parties from involuntary judicially imposed contract, it is equally important that courts enforce and preserve agreements that were intended as binding, despite a need for further documentation or further negotiation. It is, of course, the aim of contract law to gratify, not to defeat, expectations that arise out of intended contractual agreement, despite informality or the need for further proceedings between the parties.

Preliminary contracts with binding force can be of at least two distinct types. One occurs when the parties have reached complete agreement (including the agreement to be bound) on all the issues perceived to require negotiation. Such an agreement is preliminary only in form only in the sense that the parties desire a more elaborate formalization of the agreement. The second stage is not necessary; it is merely considered desirable. As the Court of Appeals stated with respect to such preliminary agreements in V'Soske v. Barwick, 404 F.2d 495, 499 (2d Cir.), cert. denied, 394 U.S. 921, 89 S. Ct. 1197, 22 L. Ed. 2d 454 (1969), "the mere fact that the parties contemplate memorializing their agreement in a formal document does not prevent their informal agreement from taking effect prior to that event. . . . Restatement (Second) of Contracts, § 26 (then Tert. Draft No. 1, 1964); 1 Corbin on Contracts § 30 (1950); 1 Williston on Contracts § 28 (3d ed. 1957)."

The second and different sort of preliminary binding agreement is one that expresses mutual commitment to a contract on agreed major terms, while recognizing the existence of open terms that remain to be negotiated. Although the existence of open terms generally suggests that binding agreement has not been reached, that is not necessarily so. For the parties can bind themselves to a concededly incomplete agreement in the sense that they accept a mutual commitment to negotiate together in good faith in an effort to reach final agreement within the scope that has been settled in the preliminary agreement. To differentiate this sort of preliminary agreement from the first, it might be referred to as a binding preliminary commitment. Its binding obligations are of a different order than those which arise out of the first type discussed above. The first type binds both sides to their ultimate contractual objective in recognition that that contract has been reached, despite the anticipation of further formalities. The second type the binding preliminary commitment does not commit the parties to their ultimate contractual objective but rather to the obligation to negotiate the open issues in good faith in an attempt to reach the alternate objective within the agreed framework. In the first type, a party may lawfully demand performance of the transaction even if no further steps have been taken following the making of the "preliminary" agreement. In the second type, he may not. What he may demand, however, is that his counterparty negotiate the open terms in good faith toward a final contract incorporating the agreed terms. This obligation does not guarantee that the final contract will be concluded if both parties comport with their obligation, as good faith differences in the negotiation of the open issues may prevent a reaching of final contract. It is also possible that the parties will lose interest as circumstances change and will mutually abandon the negotiation. The obligation does, however, bar a party from renouncing the deal, abandoning the negotiations, or insisting on conditions that do not conform to the preliminary agreement.

It may often be difficult for a court to determine whether a preliminary manifestation of assent should be found to be a binding commitment. The factors mentioned by the Court of Appeals in Winston, 777 F.2d 78,* and [R.G. Group v. Horn & Hardart Co., 751 F.2d 69 (2d Cir.1984)], as relevant to a determination whether final contracts had been reached in preliminary form are also relevant to determination whether preliminary commitments are to be considered binding. But, for this different inquiry, the factors must be applied in a different way. For example, in R.G. Group, 751 F.2d at 76, the court identified the third factor as "whether there was literally nothing left to negotiate or settle, so that all that remained to be

---

* [These factors were summarized as follows in *Winston v. Mediafare Entertainment Corp.*, 777 F.2d 78 (2d Cir.1985).

. . . We have articulated several factors that help determine whether the parties intended to be bound in the absence of a document executed by both sides. The court is to consider (1) whether there has been an express reservation of the right not to be bound in the absence of a writing; (2) whether there has been partial performance of the contract; (3) whether all of the terms of the alleged contract have been agreed upon; and (4) whether the agreement at issue is the type of contract that is usually committed to writing. (Footnote by eds.)]

done was to sign what had already been fully agreed to." The existence of open terms is always a factor tending against the conclusion that the parties have reached a binding agreement. But open terms obviously have a somewhat different significance where, unlike R.G. Group, the nature of the contract alleged is that it commits the parties in good faith to negotiate the open terms. To consider the existence of open terms as fatal would be to rule, in effect, that preliminary binding commitments cannot be enforced. That is not the law.

In seeking to determine whether such a preliminary commitment should be considered binding, a court's task is, once again, to determine the intentions of the parties at the time of their entry into the understanding, as well as their manifestations to one another by which the understanding was reached. Courts must be particularly careful to avoid imposing liability where binding obligation was not intended. There is a strong presumption against finding binding obligation in agreements which include open terms, call for future approvals and expressly anticipate future preparation and execution of contract documents. Nonetheless, if that is what the parties intended, courts should not frustrate their achieving that objective or disappoint legitimately bargained contract expectations.

Giving legal recognition to preliminary binding commitments serves a valuable function in the marketplace, particularly for relatively standardized transactions like loans. It permits borrowers and lenders to make plans in reliance upon their preliminary agreements and present market conditions. Without such legal recognition, parties would be obliged to expend enormous sums negotiating every detail of final contract documentation before knowing whether they have an agreement, and if so, on what terms. At the same time, a party that does not wish to be bound at the time of the preliminary exchange of letters can very easily protect itself by not accepting language that indicates a "firm commitment" or "binding agreement."

* * *

Upon careful consideration of the circumstances and the express terms of this commitment letter, I conclude that it represented a binding preliminary commitment and obligated both sides to seek to conclude a final loan agreement upon the agreed terms by negotiating in good faith to resolve such additional terms as are customary in such agreements. I reject Tribune's contention that its reservation of the right of approval to its Board of Directors left it free to abandon the transaction.

Expression of Intent

The Court of Appeals' first and most important factor looks to the language of the preliminary agreement for indication whether the parties considered it binding or whether they intended not to be bound until the conclusion of final formalities. This factor strongly supports Teachers. The exchange of letters constituting the commitment was replete with the terminology of binding contract, for example:

> If the foregoing properly sets forth your understanding of this transaction, please evidence acceptance of the conditions of this letter by having it executed below by a duly authorized officer . . . and by returning one executed counterpart. . . .

> Upon receipt by [Teachers] of an accepted counterpart of this letter, our agreement to purchase from you and your agreement to issue, sell and deliver to us . . . the captioned securities, shall become a binding agreement between us.

In signing, Tribune used the words "Accepted and agreed to." Tribune's additional letter of acceptance began "Attached is an executed copy of the Commitment Letter . . . for a $76 million loan." The intention to create mutually binding contractual obligations is stated with unmistakable clarity, in a manner not comfortably compatible with Tribune's contention that either side was free to walk away from the deal if it decided its interests were not served thereby.

Tribune argues that this language of binding agreement was effectively contradicted by its statement that "our acceptance and agreement is subject to approval by the Company's Board of Directors and the preparation and execution of legal documentation satisfactory to the Company," as well as by similar reservations in Teachers' letter.

Contracts of preliminary commitment characteristically contain language reserving rights of approval and establishing conditions such as the preparation and execution of documents satisfactory to the contracting party. Although such reservations, considered alone, undoubtedly tend to indicate an intention not to be finally bound, they do not necessarily require that conclusion. Such terms are not to be considered in isolation, but in the context of the overall agreement. Such terms are by no means incompatible with intention to be bound. Since the parties recognize that their deal will involve further documentation and further negotiation of open terms, such reservations make clear the right of a party, or of its Board, to insist on appropriate documentation and to negotiate for or demand protections which are customary for such transactions. In Reprosystem, 727 F.2d at 262, and R.G. Group, 751 F.2d at 75, the court reasoned that a term stating the agreement would be effective "when executed" could conclusively establish that no binding force was intended prior to execution. That reasoning is of diminished force, however, where the inquiry is not whether the parties had concluded their deal, but only whether they had entered into a binding preliminary commitment which required further steps. Here, the reservation of Board approval and the expressed "contingen[cy] upon the preparation, execution and delivery of documents" did not override and nullify the acknowledgement that a "binding agreement" had been made on the stated terms; those reservations merely recognized that various issues and documentation remained open which also would require negotiation and approval. If full consideration of the circumstances and the contract language indicates that there was a mutual intent to be bound to a preliminary commitment, the presence of such reservations does not free a party to walk away from its deal merely because it later decides that the deal is not in its interest.

The Context of the Negotiations

These conclusions are further reinforced by the particular facts of the negotiation. As Smith's proposal letter of August 20 advised Teachers, Tribune wanted "to have a firm commitment from a lender by September 15, 1982." If such a "firm commitment" meant nothing more than Tribune now contends it does, such a commitment would have been of little value, as the lender would have remained free to abandon the loan if it decided at anytime that the transaction did not suit its purposes, whether because of changed interest rates or for any reason: Tribune wanted a firm commitment because it felt it needed to be sure the transaction would be concluded by the end of the year.

This same thinking governed Tribune's conduct a month later when it received the Teachers' commitment letter. Tribune's lawyers, recognizing that the form of agreement committed Tribune to a "binding" obligation, warned about the consequences of signing it. Tribune, however, wanted Teachers' binding commitment to make the loan. Tribune had been turned down by the five other lenders it considered eligible, and it did not want to risk losing Teachers' commitment. Accordingly, Smith refrained from raising any question about the "binding agreement" language. If he intended by adding the reservation of approval of Tribune's Board of Directors to change the deal fundamentally by freeing Tribune from binding obligations without Teachers noticing the change, he did not accomplish this. Tribune remained committed, as Teachers did. That is to say each was obligated to seek in good faith to conclude a final agreement within the terms specified in the commitment letter, supplemented by such representations, warranties and other conditions as are customary in such transactions. Teachers would not have been free to walk away from the loan by reason of a subsequent decision that the transaction was not in Teachers' interest. Nor could Tribune.

Partial Performance

The factor of partial performance slightly favors Teachers. The evidence shows that for Teachers, its "commitment" to lend involved a budgeting of the funds, albeit somewhat informal. Teachers was in the business of lending its funds. The amount it had available for placement in long-term loans was finite, if large. In its loan budgeting process, Teachers would informally allocate funds which had been so committed. Such allocation reduced the net amount considered available for commitments to new loans. In fact, Teachers advised Tribune that it had only $25 million remaining available to be advanced in 1982 and that the rest would be advanced in 1983.

Tribune argues that because there was no formal segregation, it was of no significance. This misses the point. However informally it was done, the allocation of the loan commitment effectively reserved the funds for the Tribune loan. It reduced the amount of Teachers' funds that it would consider available to competing borrowers. It meant that Teachers would forego opportunities to procure commitments from other borrowers when its own commitments exhausted its available funds.

In urgently seeking Teachers' "firm commitment" by September 15, Tribune well understood that the commitment would involve a partial performance on Teachers' part. By virtue of the commitment given in September, Tribune was assured that when the time came in December for concluding final documents and drawdown, it would not be told that Teachers had nothing left to lend. Tribune was negotiating to reserve those funds. Teachers acceded and issued the commitment. That constituted a partial performance.

A party's partial performance does not necessarily indicate a belief that the other side is bound. A party may make some partial performance merely to further the likelihood of consummation of a transaction it considers advantageous. This factor was not the subject of highly focused evidence. I have not attached great importance to it and mention it primarily because it is listed among the factors suggested by the Court of Appeals in R.G. Group and Winston. I conclude, however, that this factor favors the conclusion that both sides considered the commitment binding.

The Customary Form for Such Transactions

The fourth factor mentioned in R.G. Group, and Winston, is "whether the agreement at issue is the type of contract that is usually committed to writing." 777 F.2d at 80. See also 751 F.2d at 77. Of course, the agreement here, unlike those cases, was in writing, but that does not dispose of the issue. To give this factor a broader application, it would better be put in terms of whether in the relevant business community, it is customary to accord binding force to the type of informal or preliminary agreement at issue. The evidence on that question tends to favor Teachers.

Of course it is true, as Tribune argues, that $80 million loans involving mortgages are generally not concluded by means of a four-page letter. But that is not the issue. The question is rather whether the customary practices of the relevant financial community include according such binding force as Teachers here advocates to such preliminary commitment agreements. Teachers' expert evidence showed that it is within the recognized practices of the financial community to accept that preliminary commitments can be binding. Not all preliminary commitments are binding. Some are not. Some are binding on only one side: Where, for example, the borrower pays a commitment fee for the purpose of binding the lender, the agreement may be in the nature of an option to the borrower to decide by a specified date whether to go ahead with the transaction. In such cases the seller has been paid for its one-sided commitment. Some such preliminary agreements are properly seen as merely letters of intent which leave both sides free to abandon the transaction. The point is that the practices of the marketplace are not rigid or uniform. They encompass a considerable variety of transactions negotiated to suit the needs of the parties, including mutually binding preliminary commitments. Each transaction must be examined carefully to determine its characteristics. . . .

> * * *

Judgment is granted to the plaintiff.

SO ORDERED.

———

Cambridge Capital, LLC v. Ruby Has, LLC

565 F. Supp.3d 420 (S.D.N.Y. 2021)

Plaintiff Cambridge Capital is a private equity firm. Defendant Ruby Has is an e-commerce fulfillment company. In June 2020 the parties executed a six-page Letter of Intent ("LOI") that described a contemplated transaction in which Cambridge would provide $40 million capital to Ruby in exchange for a controlling interest in the company. The LOI included an exclusivity term that prevented Ruby from seeking other sources of capital as well as other terms. The deal eventually fell apart and Cambridge sued Ruby claiming Rudy had breached its duty to negotiate in good faith. The parties told very different stories in their pleadings. According to Cambridge, while there were a few bumps and delays in the process the parties had completed transaction documents when Ruby significantly increased the price of a controlling interest and solicited another buyer. According to Ruby, negotiations were tense and Cambridge repeatedly tried to renegotiate terms until Ruby finally gave up and looked for capital elsewhere. In a motion to dismiss, Ruby argued the following term in LOI precluded the claim for breach of the duty to negotiate in good faith:

> ***Non-Binding Agreement*** This letter is not intended to be a binding contract (other than with respect to the section herein titled *Exclusivity Period*), and the parties understand that no obligation exists on behalf of either Cambridge to pay the Purchase Price or on behalf of the Company to sell the units prior to entering into the share purchase agreement. This letter is an expression of mutual intent to proceed with the drafting of the share purchase agreement and

collateral documents contemplated hereby in accordance with the principles stated herein.

(Liman, J.) "The parties stake out opposing positions on the enforceability of the LOI. Ruby Has argues that the LOI is non-binding and creates no legal obligations on either side except for those based on the exclusivity provision. Cambridge Capital argues that the LOI constitutes a Type II agreement—"a contract that expresses mutual commitment to a contract on certain agreed terms, with others to be negotiated," *Siga Techs., Inc. v. PharmAthene, Inc.*, 132 A.3d 1108, 1141 (Del. 2015) ("*SIGA II*") (internal quotation marks omitted)—thereby imposing an obligation to negotiate in good faith. Cambridge Capital also argues that both the exclusivity provision and the expenses provision of the LOI create enforceable obligations.

"Delaware law applies to the interpretation of the LOI. Delaware law follows New York law in recognizing that parties can create between themselves an obligation to negotiate in good faith. . . .

"Drawing all reasonable inferences in favor of Cambridge Capital, as it must on a motion to dismiss, the Court concludes that enough has been pleaded to establish that the LOI is a Type II preliminary agreement. In other words, Cambridge Capital has sufficiently pleaded that the LOI bound the parties to negotiate open terms in good faith under the LOI's framework but did not bind them to the LOI's terms (except for the exclusivity provision) or to reaching the ultimate contractual objective prior to entering into a share purchase agreement.

"[The] first and most important factor looks to the language of the preliminary agreement for indication whether the parties considered it binding or whether they intended not to be bound until the conclusion of final formalities." [*TIAA v. Tribune Co.*], 670 F. Supp. at 499. There is language in the LOI that supports Cambridge Capital's argument that the parties intended it to reflect a binding Type II agreement, with open terms to be worked out in good faith.

"The LOI is striking in the detail it provides. It contains the parties' agreement on many major terms, including the purchase price, the transaction structure, the agreed percentage of the company that Cambridge Capital receives for its capital infusion, and a due diligence process. LOI at 2–3. It even includes governance provisions for the future after Cambridge Capital has completed its investment. *Id.* at 3. The governance provision states that Cambridge Capital will pursue acquisitions only if a super majority, including the CEO and Cambridge Capital, agree to do so. *Id.* It further sets forth the specific annual management fee that Ruby Has agrees to pay Cambridge Capital. *Id.*

"Nothing on those general terms appears to be left open. They each are expressed in concrete terms. Indeed, the LOI goes forward to reflect that the high interest debt on Ruby Has's balance sheet will be paid off and refinanced only upon mutual agreement, *id.* at 2, and that there will be a working capital adjustment subject to certain parameters, i.e., "consistent with historical working capital requirements of the Company, including consideration of historic seasonality," *id.* at 3.

"In words that are mandatory and not merely aspirational, the LOI also sets forth a process each party is required to follow to reach final agreement and then closing. Both parties have obligations and not just goals with respect to diligence. While Cambridge Capital must conduct a due diligence review and select an independent chartered accountant to perform "[a] review of [Ruby Has's] historical financial statements Quality of Earnings analysis," *id.* at 3, Ruby Has "*will* use their best efforts to make available all documents, facilities and personnel as requested so that [Cambridge Capital] can properly due diligence the Company during the exclusivity period," *id.* at 5 (emphasis added). The LOI sets a deadline that Cambridge Capital "*will* complete" the due diligence requirements "within 90 days of the execution of this [LOI]." *Id.* at 3 (emphasis added). It goes on to reflect Cambridge Capital's "intent is to move forward to a *closing* as quickly as possible," not just to negotiation and consummation of final transaction documents. *Id.* at 3 (emphasis added). These details of the LOI weigh in favor finding that it is a Type II agreement. . . .

"Notably, the LOI also expressly states that it is "an expression of mutual intent to proceed with the drafting of the share purchase agreement and collateral documents contemplated hereby in accordance with the principles stated herein." LOI at 5. . . Additionally, the LOI was "Agreed and Accepted" by Ruby Has and signed by both parties. . . Together with the agreed upon major terms and the framework established by the LOI, this language suggests that the parties intended to be bound—not to the specific terms contained in the LOI or to the "ultimate contractual objective," *Tribune*, 670 F. Supp. at 498, but rather to the LOI's framework in which the parties would negotiate the final deal in good faith.

"Ruby Has puts dispositive weight on a section entitled "Non-Binding Agreement," which provides in part: "This [LOI] is not intended to be a binding contract (other than with respect to the section herein titled *Exclusivity Period*) . . . ." LOI at 5. Although that language can be read to support Ruby Has's argument that the LOI should not be read to create even Type II obligations, the Court cannot conclude that it eliminates all ambiguity and entitles Ruby Has to dismissal of Cambridge Capital's claim on this motion.

"In the first instance, it is a fundamental precept of contract law that agreements must be read in their entirety and that no provision of a contract draws the entirety of its meaning from examining is language in isolation. "In determining whether a letter of intent is sufficient to give rise to a duty to negotiate in good faith, [the Court] must examine the entire document and the relevant circumstances surrounding its adoption." *Bennett v. Itochu Int'l, Inc.*, 682 F. Supp. 2d 469, 482 (E.D. Pa. 2010) (citing *Channel Home Centers, Div. of Grace Retail Corp. v. Grossman*, 795 F.2d 291, 298 (3d Cir. 1986)). Under Delaware law, language that an agreement's terms are non-binding does not alone relieve a party of an obligation otherwise created to negotiate in good faith. . . . Although the language of the "Non-Binding Agreement" section thus weighs in favor of a conclusion that the agreement creates no obligations whatsoever (save for those imposed on Ruby Has with respect to exclusivity), there are other provisions that point in the other direction.

"Moreover, even when read in isolation, the language of the "Non-Binding Agreement" provision is not as definitive as Ruby Has would have it be. The provision states that the LOI "is not intended to be a binding contract," not that it is intended not to create any obligation. It thus plausibly could be read to reflect the parties' agreement that the LOI does not create any binding obligations of a Type I variety. Under that reading, the parties would not ultimately be committed even to the terms that are reflected in the LOI (other than with respect to the section titled *Exclusivity Period*). Ruby Has need not, for example, conduct its business in the ordinary course during the time until negotiation and consummation of final papers on pain of a breach of contract claim if it fails to comply. But they are not relieved of the obligation to negotiate the open terms in good faith within the framework of the terms agreed in the LOI. . . .

"The language of the LOI here thus is strikingly different from the "non-binding" language in *CKSJB Holdings LLC v. EPAM Sys., Inc.*, 837 F. App'x 901 (3d Cir. 2020), upon which Ruby Has relies. In that case, the indication of interest ("IOI") at issue stated: "This proposal does not constitute and *will not give rise to any legally binding obligation* whatsoever on the part of [the party expressing the indication of interest]." *Id.* at 902. It also went on to state:

> [E]xcept as expressly provided in any binding written agreement that [the parties] may enter into the future, *no past, present or future action*, course of conduct, or failure to act relating to the transaction . . . and/or by this proposal *will give rise to or serve as the basis for any obligation* or other liability on the part of such entities or any of their respective affiliates.

Id. at 902–03. The clause thus notably precluded either side from relying on any past action, including the kinds of action that could provide parol evidence, to create an obligation on either party.

"In those circumstances, and confronted with a letter that stated that the party expressing the interest would provide a "definitive list" of conditions to closing upon completing its due diligence and that as the process moved forward it might require a commitment of exclusivity, *id.* at 903, the Third Circuit held that the language alone that the putative purchaser would "work diligently" with the target "to close the transaction in an expedient manner" was mere "optimistic language" that did not create any obligation to negotiate in good faith and that the claim was dismissable at the pleadings stage. *Id.* at 903–04.

"Here, unlike in *CKSJB Holdings*, the LOI expressly contemplates that there could be such "obligations arising out of or in connection with" the LOI. And the LOI could be read to specify the subjects on which the parties do *not* agree—the ultimate agreement by Ruby Has to sell units to Cambridge Capital and by Cambridge Capital to infuse capital into Ruby Has in exchange for those units. The language of the IOI in *CKSJB Holdings*, by contrast, expansively disclaims "any obligation" arising from "past, present or future action, course of conduct, or failure to act relating to the transaction." The language of the LOI here is not akin to that of the IOI's expansive disclaimer.

"In addition, in this case, unlike in *CKSJB Holdings*, there is an exclusivity provision, and there is language that can be read to set forth the conditions upon which Cambridge Capital will continue to conduct due diligence—and if it has completed due diligence, will continue to the signing of a final agreement—and that expresses a "mutual" intent of the parties to move forward with "the drafting of the share purchase agreement and collateral documents." This is more than just the separate aspirational intent of each party or the "negotiation" of an agreement. Among other things, under the LOI, Ruby Has commits—in language all agree to be binding—that it will take itself out of the market for the Exclusivity Period (during which it alleges it was in critical need of capital). If it breached that agreement, Cambridge Capital would be entitled to damages even if no final agreement were reached, including, for example, its incurred due diligence costs. That is why the LOI states that Cambridge Capital "will defer other projects, deploy significant resources, and incur material expenses in order to promptly try to consummate the Potential Transaction." LOI at 5. The LOI also establishes what are plainly expressed to be conditions to Cambridge Capital moving forward. The results of the accounting review and quality of earnings analysis must be "satisfactory" to Cambridge Capital, and so too must the due diligence review, "including that the Company is on track to achieve its forecasted revenue" for 2020. *Id.* at 3. And Ruby Has must conduct its business in the ordinary course "[u]ntil the execution and delivery of the share purchase agreement or such earlier date as negotiations may terminate." *Id.* at 4.

"In the face of all of these provisions, it is plausible that Cambridge Capital had a duty to negotiate in good faith and that Ruby Has would have had a claim of a Type II variety if it were revealed, at the end of the Exclusivity Period and after Ruby Has had limited itself to business in the ordinary course, that Cambridge Capital never had an intent to negotiate in good faith. That would be so notwithstanding what Ruby Has claims is the clear language of the first clause of the Non-Binding Agreement provision. The language conditioning Cambridge Capital's obligation to move forward on Ruby Has's cooperation in due diligence and on the results of the accounting review and quality of earnings analysis would be mere surplusage if Cambridge Capital could walk from the transaction (or never have intended to negotiate it in good faith) for reasons entirely independent on those set forth in the LOI.

"It necessarily follows that, at least at this stage of the proceedings, the language of Non-Binding Agreement cannot bear the weight Ruby Has puts on it. The Non-Binding Agreement section, by its terms, is indifferent to party. If the LOI as a whole can be read to admit of an obligation on Cambridge Capital to negotiate in good faith, notwithstanding the language of Non-Binding

Agreement, so too it can be read to admit of such an obligation on the part of Ruby Has.

"Finally, Cambridge Capital's argument that the LOI gave rise to Type II obligations also gains force, at least at the pleading stage, by the context of the negotiations and by each parties' partial performance—factors not considered by the court in *CKSJB Holdings* due to the unambiguous language in the IOI. . . . Before entering into the LOI, the parties engaged in "in-person meetings and deep discussions over the past year." LOI at 1. This fact favors finding an obligation to negotiate in good faith. . . .

"Regarding partial performance, Cambridge Capital performed due diligence as promised, and Ruby Has made diligence materials available as promised. . . . When Ruby Has fell short of its working capital and cash balance forecasts, the parties negotiated an adjustment for working capital as contemplated by the LOI. Compl. ¶ 60. These allegations are suggestive of the conclusions both that the LOI reflects the agreement of the parties on the major terms of the transaction and that each party understood it was obligated to negotiate in good faith within the confines of the agreed framework created by the LOI. . . .

"Of course, it is conceivable that the LOI could be read another way and that the language regarding non-binding agreement could be read to eliminate any obligations of either side save for those imposed on Ruby Has with respect to exclusivity. But on this motion, all that Cambridge Capital has to establish to go forward with discovery is that there is an ambiguity and that its reading is plausible. . . . Cambridge Capital has done so."

Venture Associates Corp. v. Zenith Data Systems Corp.

96 F.3d 275 (7th Cir.1996)

(Posner, J.) "Damages for breach of an agreement to negotiate may be, although they are unlikely to be, the same as the damages for breach of the final contract that the parties would have signed had it not been for the defendant's bad faith. If, quite apart from any bad faith, the negotiations would have broken down, the party led on by the other party's bad faith to persist in futile negotiations can recover only his reliance damages—the expenses he incurred by being misled, in violation of the parties' agreement to negotiate in good faith, into continuing to negotiate futilely. But if the plaintiff can prove that had it not been for the defendant's bad faith the parties would have made a final contract, then the loss of the benefit of the contract is a consequence of the defendant's bad faith, and, provided that it is a foreseeable consequence, the defendant is liable for that loss—liable, that is, for the plaintiffs consequential damages. . . . The difficulty, which may well be insuperable, is that since by hypothesis the parties had not agreed on *any* of the terms of their contract, it may be impossible to determine what those terms would have been and hence what profit the victim of bad faith would have had. . . . But this goes to the practicality of the remedy, not the principle of it. Bad faith is deliberate misconduct, whereas many breaches of 'final' contracts are involuntary— liability for breach of contract being, in general, strict liability. It would be a paradox to place a lower ceiling on damages for bad faith than on damages for a perfectly innocent breach, though a paradox that the practicalities of proof may require the courts in many or even all cases to accept."

Kansas Municipal Gas Agency v. Vesta Energy Co.

843 F.Supp. 1401 (D. Kan. 1994)

In early April 1992, Vesta Energy Co. entered into three letter agreements to begin supplying gas to Kansas Municipal Gas Agency (KMGA) from three designated pipelines at agreed-upon prices. The letter agreements were for one-year terms, but each agreement provided that "This Letter Agreement shall remain valid until the execution of a mutually agreeable contract. Should Buyer and Seller fail to reach a mutually agreeable contract, this Letter Agreement shall become null and void." Following the execution of the letter agreements, the parties entered into negotiations for a finalized written contract. Over the next several months, the parties exchanged several draft contracts and had numerous telephone contacts in an attempt to arrive at a mutually agreeable contract. Several issues remained unresolved. On August 17, 1992, KMGA prepared yet another draft contract and sent it to Vesta. On September 8, Vesta sent a letter to KMGA declaring the letter agreements null and void due to the parties' failure to reach agreement on a mutually acceptable contract. KMGA brought suit. The court held that Vesta had violated an obligation to negotiate in good faith and was liable for expectation damages.

(Lungstrom, J.) "The court is persuaded that Vesta terminated the agreement because it was a bad business deal and it could not extricate itself otherwise. Its stated reasons for terminating were pretextual. The evidence on which the court relies in arriving at this conclusion is best understood in the context of Vesta's demand for a force majeure clause in the final contract that was not limited to conditions generally accepted in the natural gas supply business, but rather one which would have provided it with a way out of the contract in the event of a broadly defined 'loss of supply.'

"The RFP [request for proposal] sent out by KMGA specifically set forth that KMGA was seeking a 'firm supply' of gas. Having a firm supply of gas was of the utmost importance to KMGA. This is due to the fact that its member cities use the gas for residential heating and cooling, and an interruption of gas supply would have a traumatic effect on the member cities. It made this point clear to Vesta and the court has no difficulty finding as a matter of fact that the mutual intention of the parties was that the letter agreements were for a firm supply. Within the natural gas industry, 'firm supply' generally means that the supplier guarantees that it will meet its supply requirements. This is typically done by providing specific well dedications in the case of a producer or, in the case of a marketer such as Vesta, by warranting that it has gas supply in sufficient quantities to meet its obligations under a gas supply contract. In contrast, a 'best efforts' arrangement requires that a gas supplier use its 'best efforts' to supply gas, but typically imposes no penalty for a failure to do so. A firm supply contract creates a much greater commitment on the part of a supplier to supply gas than does a best efforts contract.

"Although a firm supply contract puts a great onus on the supplier to deliver the specified quantity of gas, firm supply contracts typically contain a provision limiting the supplier's obligation in cases of 'force majeure.' A contractual force majeure provision provides that a supplier is not obligated to supply gas when certain events, beyond the control of a supplier, make such supply impossible. Typical force majeure events in a gas supply contract consist of various events that are beyond the supplier's control, including, among other things, such conditions as acts of God, strikes, lockouts, wars, blockades, government regulatory intervention, explosions, sabotage, freezeup and line collapse. As one of its reasons for canceling the letter agreements, Vesta points to the failure of KMGA to agree to force majeure language in the contract to the effect that Vesta would not be obligated to produce gas in cases of 'failure of supply.' The court finds that this broad loss of supply provision demanded by Vesta is totally contradictory to the notion of a firm supply contract, and the court relies on the testimony of expert witness William Giese that such a provision would not be generally accepted force majeure language in a firm supply contract. . . .

". . . Natural gas is covered by the definition of 'goods' contained in [UCC §] 2–105. There can be no doubt that, at the time of the execution of the letter agreements, the parties fully intended that performance under the letter agreements included attempting to arrive at a mutually agreeable final written contract governing the gas purchase. The parties were therefore obligated under . . . [UCC §] 1–203 to conduct themselves in good faith in endeavoring to negotiate and finalize the final written contract. Because the parties fit the UCC definition of merchants contained in . . . UCC § 2–104(1), the duty of good faith applicable here is defined in . . . [§] 2–103(b).

". . . Vesta's demand for a broad 'failure of supply provision' in the force majeure section of the contract was totally contradictory to the notion of a firm supply contract and . . . such a provision would not be generally accepted language in a firm supply contract. Consequently, the court finds that Vesta's insistence on such a broad force majeure provision was not consistent with 'the observance of reasonable commercial standards of fair dealing in the trade,' as required by [§] 2–103(b) and therefore was not a valid justification for Vesta's termination of the letter agreements. . . .

"Following Vesta's breach of the letter agreements, KMGA proceeded to purchase substitute gas from another supplier. Pursuant to [UCC §] 2–712(1), following a breach by a seller the buyer may 'cover' by making in good faith and without unreasonable delay any reasonable purchase of or contract to purchase goods in substitution for those from the seller. The buyer is then

entitled to recover from the seller as damages the difference between the cost
of cover and the contract price."

NOTE ON THE AVAILABILITY OF A PROMISSORY ESTOPPEL CLAIM OR A RESTITUTION CLAIM WHEN A CONTRACT IS INDEFINITE

Under classical contract law the rigorous nature of the requirement of
definiteness could result in a court finding an agreement insufficiently definite
to be enforced as a contract even though the parties intended to enter into a
contract and one party had performed, or prepared to perform, in reliance on
the existence of the contract. From early on courts used the law of restitution
to allow the plaintiff to recover performance-based damages in these cases.
Once the doctrine of promissory estoppel was developed courts used it to allow
the plaintiff to recover reliance-based damages.

Wheeler v. White, 398 S.W.2d 93 (1965), illustrates the use of promissory
estoppel. White promised to provide money to Wheeler to finance construction
of improvements on land owned by Wheeler, either by procuring a loan from a
third party or lending his own money The parties executed a written
agreement stating the amount of the loan, the term, the maximum interest
rate, and the commission Wheeler was to pay White. Relying on the agreement,
and acting on White's advice to get started with the project, Wheeler
demolished an old structure on the property. White refused to perform his
agreement. Wheeler tried to borrow money elsewhere but could not. He sued
for breach of contract. The court held the agreement was insufficiently definite
to be "specifically enforceable," but that the doctrine of promissory estoppel
could be used to estop White "from denying the enforceability of the promise."

Kearns v. Andree, 107 Conn. 181, 139 A. 695 (1928), illustrates the use of
restitution. The defendant refused to honor an oral agreement to purchase a
house owned by the plaintiff. At the defendant's request, the plaintiff had made
alterations in the house that reduced its value. The court held that the work
done was sufficient to take the contract out of the statute of frauds but the
agreement was unenforceable on the ground of indefiniteness. The parties had
agreed the defendant would finance part of the purchase price with a mortgage
from a third party but they did not specify the mortgagee or the terms of the
mortgage. The plaintiff was held entitled to recover damages for his costs in
making the requested alterations on a restitution claim. But he was not
allowed to recover his cost in restoring the house to its original condition. The
plaintiff would have recovered these costs as well on a promissory estoppel
claim (assuming he acted reasonably in restoring the house to its original
condition).

Under modern contract law a court should find the contracts in these cases
to be sufficiently definite to determine the defendant had breached his
contract. The indefiniteness of the contract might still bear on the court's

choice of a remedy. For example, in *Kearns* a court might decline to grant the plaintiff specific performance because of the absence of an agreement on the terms of the mortgage to finance part of the purchase price. The inability of the plaintiff in *Wheeler* to cover by borrowing money elsewhere might well lead to the same result with the plaintiff recovering reliance damages as a surrogate for speculative expectation damages.

———

D&G STOUT, INC. v. BACARDI IMPORTS, INC.
United States Court of Appeals, Seventh Circuit, 1991.
923 F.2d 566.

CUDAHY, CIRCUIT JUDGE. D & G Stout, Inc., operating at all relevant times under the name General Liquors, Inc. (General), was distributing liquor in the turbulent Indiana liquor market in 1987. When two of its major suppliers jumped ship in early 1987, General faced a critical dilemma: sell out at the best possible price or continue operating on a smaller scale. It began negotiating with another Indiana distributor on the terms of a possible sale. Bacardi Imports, Inc. (Bacardi), was still one of General's remaining major suppliers. Knowing that negotiations were ongoing for General's sale, Bacardi promised that General would continue to act as Bacardi's distributor for Northern Indiana. Based on this representation, General turned down the negotiated selling price it was offered. One week later, Bacardi withdrew its account. Realizing it could no longer continue to operate, General went back to the negotiating table, this time settling for an amount $550,000 below the first offer. The question is whether General can recover the price differential from Bacardi on a theory of promissory estoppel. The district court believed that as a matter of law it could not, and entered summary judgment for defendant Bacardi. We disagree, and so we remand for trial.

I.

General was (and D & G Stout, Inc., is) an Indiana corporation with its main place of business in South Bend. Bacardi is a corporation organized in New York and doing business primarily in Miami, Florida. General served at Bacardi's will as its wholesale distributor in Northern Indiana for over 35 years. During the 1980s, liquor suppliers in Indiana undertook an extensive effort to consolidate their distribution, the effect of which was to reduce the number of distributors in the state from approximately twenty in 1980 to only two in 1990.

General weathered the storm until April 1987, when two of its major suppliers withdrew their lines, taking with them the basis of more than fifty percent of General's gross sales. By June, General recognized that it must choose between selling out and scaling back operations in order to stay in business. Despite the recent setbacks, General calculated that remaining operational was possible as long as it held on to its continuing two major suppliers, Bacardi and Hiram Walker.

About this time (and probably in connection with the same forces concentrating distribution) Bacardi lost its distributor in Indianapolis and southern Indiana. Bacardi decided to convene a meeting on July 9, 1987, of applicants for the open distributorship. General's president, David Stout, attended the meetings as an observer, with no designs on the new opening. Stout did intend to seek assurances from Bacardi about its commitment to General in Northern Indiana. While in Indianapolis, Stout was approached by National Wine & Spirits Company (National), which expressed an interest in buying General. Stout agreed to begin negotiations the following weekend. Stout also received the assurances from Bacardi he sought: after listening to Stout's concerns and hearing about his contemplated sale of General, Bacardi emphatically avowed that it had no intention of taking its line to another distributor in Northern Indiana. This promise was open-ended—no one discussed how long the continuing relationship might last.

During the ensuing two weeks, General carried on negotiations with National to reach a price for the purchase of General's assets. Bacardi kept in close contact with General to find out whether it would indeed sell. The negotiations yielded a final figure for Stout to consider. On July 22 and again on July 23—with negotiations concluded and only the final decision remaining—Stout again sought assurances from Bacardi. The supplier unequivocally reconfirmed its commitment to stay with General, and Stout replied that, as a result, he was going to turn down National's offer and would continue operating. Later on the 23rd, Stout rejected National's offer. That same afternoon, Bacardi decided to withdraw its line from General.

General learned of Bacardi's decision on July 30. The news spread quickly through the industry, and by August 3, Hiram Walker had also pulled its line, expressing a belief that General could not continue without Bacardi on board. By this time, sales personnel were abandoning General for jobs with the two surviving distributors in Indiana (one of which was National). General quickly sought out National to sell its assets, but National's offer was now substantially reduced. The ensuing agreement, executed on August 14 and closed on August 28, included a purchase price $550,000 lower than the one National offered in mid-July. Stout's successor company brought suit under the diversity jurisdiction against Bacardi, claiming that the supplier was liable by reason of promissory estoppel for this decline in the purchase price. Judge Miller entered summary judgment for Bacardi, holding that the promises plaintiff alleged were not the type upon which one may rely under Indiana law. Plaintiff appeals.

II.

. . . Before us . . . is the legal question whether the plaintiff has alleged any injury which Indiana's law of promissory estoppel redresses.

Indiana has adopted the Restatement's theory of promissory estoppel:

A promise which the promisor should reasonably expect to induce action or forbearance on the part of the promisee and a third person and which does induce such action or forbearance is binding if injustice can be avoided only by the enforcement of the promise. The remedy for breach may be limited as justice requires.

Restatement (Second) of Contracts Sec. 90(1) (1981); Eby v. York-Division, Borg-Warner, 455 N.E.2d 623, 627 (Ind.App.1983); Pepsi-Cola General Bottlers, Inc. v. Woods, 440 N.E.2d 696, 698 (Ind.App.1982). The district judge dismissed the complaint on the ground that Bacardi's alleged promise was not one on which it should reasonably have expected General to rely.

The district court first noted that the relationship between General and Bacardi had always been terminable at will. Because Bacardi's promises that it would continue to use General as its distributor contained no language indicating that they would be good for any specific period,[1] the court reasoned that the relationship remained terminable at will. It then concluded that the promise was not legally enforceable, and thus was not one on which General reasonably might rely. We agree with each of these conclusions but the last. Notwithstanding the continuation of an at-will relationship between Bacardi and General, the promises given between July 9 and July 23 were not without legal effect.

In Indiana, as in many states, an aspiring employee cannot sue for lost wages on an unfulfilled promise of at-will employment. Pepsi-Cola, 440 N.E.2d 696; accord Ewing v. Board of Trustees of Pulaski Memorial Hosp., 486 N.E.2d 1094, 1098 (Ind.App.1985) (employment contract for indefinite tenure is unenforceable for future employment). Because the employer could have terminated the employee without cause at any time after the employment began, the promise of a job brings no expectation of any determinable period of employment or corresponding amount of wages. The promise is therefore unenforceable under either a contract or a promissory estoppel theory in an action for lost wages. Nevertheless, lost wages are not the only source of damages flowing from a broken promise of employment, enforceable or not. Indiana courts acknowledge certain damages as recoverable when the employer breaks a promise of employment, even if the employment is to be terminable at will. For example, in Eby v. York-Division, Borg-Warner, 455 N.E.2d at 627, a plaintiff who gave up a job and moved from Indiana to Florida on a promise of employment sued for recovery of preparation and moving expenses incurred on the basis of the promise. The Indiana appellate court reversed the lower court's summary judgment for the defendant employer, holding that the plaintiff employee had stated a cause of action for promissory estoppel. The court found that the defendant could have expected the plaintiff and his wife to move in reliance on the promise of employment and therefore might be liable for reneging. See also Pepsi-Cola, 440 N.E.2d 696; accord Lorson v. Falcon Coach, 214 Kan. 670, 522 P.2d 449 (1974).

Our review of Indiana law thus leaves us a simple if somewhat crude question: are the damages plaintiff seeks here more like lost future wages or like moving expenses? We can better answer the question if we determine why Indiana draws this distinction. Unlike lost wages, moving expenses represent out-of-pocket losses; they involve a loss of something already possessed. It would be plausible, although not very sophisticated, to distinguish between the loss of something yet to be received and the loss of something already in hand. But this is not precisely where Indiana draws the distinction, nor where we would draw it if it were our choice to make. Eby itself involved not only moving expenses, but wages lost at plaintiff's old job during the few days plaintiff was preparing to move. 455 N.E.2d at 625. Those wages were not out-of-pocket losses: plaintiff had no more received those wages than he had received wages from his promised employment.

In fact, the line Indiana draws is between expectation damages and reliance damages. In future wages, the employee has only an expectation of income, the recovery of which promissory estoppel will not support in an at-will employment setting. In wages forgone in order to prepare to move, as in moving expenses themselves, the employee gave up a presently determinate sum for the purpose of relocating. Both moving expenses and forgone wages were the hopeful employee's costs of positioning himself for his new job; moving expenses happen to be out-of-pocket losses, while forgone wages are opportunity costs. Both are reliance costs, not expectancy damages.

Thus, the question has become whether the loss incurred from the price drop was attributable to lost expectations of future profit or resulted from an opportunity forgone in reliance on the promise. At first blush, the injury might seem more like the loss of future wages. Bacardi was a major supplier whose business was extremely valuable to General. While the loss of this "asset" might cause a decline in General's market value as measured by the loss of future income from the sale of Bacardi's products, this loss is not actionable on a promissory estoppel theory. Those damages would presumably be measured by the present value of General's anticipated profit from the sale of Bacardi's products, and Indiana will not grant relief based on promissory estoppel to compensate an aggrieved party for such expectancy damages. Lost future income expected from an at-will relationship, whether from wages or from profits, is not recoverable on a theory of promissory estoppel, and neither is the present value of such losses.

But the fact is that recovery of lost profits is not a question before us. Bacardi's account was never an "asset" that National could acquire by purchasing General. As counsel for the defendant candidly but carefully explained, National never assumed that it would retain the Bacardi account by buying General; in fact, National assumed the opposite. Bacardi's major competitor in the rum distilling business distributed through National, and the two top distillers in a given category of liquor would not choose the same distributor. Both before and after Bacardi decided to withdraw its products, all National wanted from General were its assets other than the Bacardi account. But Bacardi's repudiation of its promise ostensibly affected the price of General's business so drastically because, as everyone in the industry understood, General's option to stay in business independently was destroyed by Bacardi's withdrawal of its account. Thus, through its repudiation, Bacardi destroyed General's negotiating leverage since General no longer had the alternative of continuing as an independent concern. Presumably, after Bacardi's withdrawal General's only alternative to selling to National was to liquidate. Thus, Bacardi's repudiation turned General's discussions with National from negotiations to buy a going concern into a liquidation sale. Instead of bargaining from strength, knowing it could reject a junk-value offer and carry on its business, General was left with one choice: sell at any price.

Under these facts, General had a reliance interest in Bacardi's promise. General was in lively negotiations with National, and it repeatedly informed Bacardi of this fact. A price was agreed upon, and based on that figure, Stout had to decide whether to close his doors or continue operating. General had a business opportunity that all parties knew would be devalued once Bacardi announced its intention to go elsewhere. The extent of that devaluation represents a reliance injury, rather than an injury to General's expectation of future profit. The injury is analogous to the cost of moving expenses incurred as a result of promised employment in Eby and Pepsi-Cola.

Nor were these promises merely meaningless restatements of an understood at-will relationship. With its current business opportunity, General stood at a crossroads. Circumstances foreshadowed a costly demise for the company, but it was able to negotiate an alternative. Far from confirming the obvious, Bacardi wrote its assurances on a clean slate with full knowledge that General was just as likely to reject the offered relationship as embrace it. That this was the situation is indicated most clearly by Bacardi's repeated calls to check on Stout's impending decision. Bacardi reassured Stout of its commitment in full knowledge that he planned to reject National's offer and with the reasonable expectation that an immediate pull out would severely undermine General's asking price. Like the plaintiffs in Eby who moved based on the promise of a job, General incurred a cost in rejecting the deal that was non-recoverable once Bacardi's later decision became known.

There may always exist the potential for a quandary in a promissory estoppel action based on a promise of at-will employment. When could Bacardi terminate the relationship with General without fear of liability for reliance costs, once it made the assurances in question? Obviously we do not hold that General and Bacardi had formed a new, permanent employment relationship. How long an employee can rely on the employer's promise is not a matter we can decide here. The issue is one of reasonable reliance, and to the extent that there might be questions, they should be for trial.

We have, of course, reviewed this case in the posture of summary judgment. General's allegations still must be proven at trial. However, under Indiana law, we think that Bacardi's promise was of a sort on which General might rely, with the possibility of damages for breach. For that reason the judgment of the district court is

Reversed and Remanded.

––––––

GARWOOD PACKAGING, INC. V. ALLEN & COMPANY, INC.
United States Court of Appeals, Seventh Circuit, 2004.
378 F.3d 698.

POSNER, CIRCUIT JUDGE.

This is a diversity suit, governed by Indiana law, in which substantial damages are sought on the basis of promissory estoppel. The suit pits Garwood Packaging, Inc., which created a packaging system designed to increase the shelf life of fresh meat, and its two principals, Garwood and McNamara, against Allen & Company (an investment company) and a vice-president of Allen named Martin. We shall refer to the plaintiffs collectively as "GPI" and the defendants collectively as "Allen." The district court granted summary judgment in favor of Allen and dismissed the suit. . . .

GPI had flopped in marketing its food-packaging system and by 1993 had run up debts of $3 million and was broke. It engaged Martin to help find investors. After an initial search turned up nothing, Martin told GPI that Allen (Martin's employer, remember) would consider investing $2 million of its own money in GPI if another investor could be found who would make a comparable investment. The presence of the other investor would reduce the risk to Allen not only by augmenting GPI's assets but also by validating Allen's judgment that GPI might be salvageable, because it would show that someone else was also willing to bet a substantial sum of money on GPI's salvation. To further reduce its risk Allen decided to off-load half its projected $2 million investment on other investors.

Martin located a company named Hobart Corporation that was prepared to manufacture $2 million worth of GPI packaging machines in return for equity in the company. Negotiations with Hobart proved arduous, however. There were two sticking points: the amount of equity that Hobart would receive and the obtaining of releases from GPI's creditors. Hobart may have been concerned that unless the creditors released GPI the company would fail and Hobart wouldn't be able to sell the packaging systems that it manufactured. Or it may have feared that the creditors would assert liens in the systems. All that is clear is that Hobart insisted on releases. They were also important to the other investors whom Allen wanted to bring into the deal, the ones who would contribute half of Allen's offered $2 million.

Martin told Garwood and McNamara (GPI's principals) that he would see that the deal went through "come hell or high water." Eventually, however, Allen decided not to invest, the deal collapsed, and GPI was forced to declare bankruptcy. The reason for Allen's change of heart was that the investors who it thought had agreed to put up half of "Allen's" $2 million had gotten cold feet. When Allen withdrew from the deal, no contract had been signed and no agreement had been reached on how much stock either Allen or Hobart would receive in exchange for their contributions to GPI. Nor had releases been obtained from the creditors.

GPI's principal claim on appeal, and the only one we need to discuss (the others fall with it), is that Martin's unequivocal promise to see the deal through to completion bound Allen by the doctrine of promissory estoppel, which makes a promise that induces reasonable reliance legally enforceable. *Brown v. Branch,* 758 N.E.2d 48, 52 (Ind.2001); *First National Bank of Logansport v. Logan Mfg. Co.,* 577 N.E.2d 949, 954 (Ind.1991); *Consolidation Services, Inc. v. KeyBank National Ass'n,* 185 F.3d 817, 822 (7th Cir.1999) (Indiana law); *Restatement (Second) of Contracts* § 90(1) (1981); 1 E. Allan Farnsworth, *Farnsworth on Contracts* § 2.19 (3d ed.2004). If noncontractual promises were never enforced, reliance on their being enforceable would never be reasonable, so let us consider why the law might want to allow people to rely on promises that do not create actual contracts and whether the answer can help GPI.

The simplest answer to the "why" question is that the doctrine merely allows reliance to be substituted for consideration as the basis for making a promise enforceable. *First National Bank of Logansport v. Logan Mfg. Co., supra,* 577 N.E.2d at 954; *Workman v. United Parcel Service, Inc.,* 234 F.3d 998, 1001 (7th Cir.2000); *Consolidation Services, Inc. v. KeyBank National Ass'n, supra,* 185 F.3d at 822; *Porter v. Commissioner,* 60 F.2d

673, 675 (2d Cir.1932) (L.Hand, J.). On this view promissory estoppel is really just a doctrine of contract law. The most persuasive reason for the requirement of consideration in the law of contracts is that in a system in which oral contracts are enforceable—and by juries, to boot—the requirement provides some evidence that there really *was* a promise that was intended to be relied on as a real commitment. *Gibson v. Neighborhood Health Clinics, Inc.,* 121 F.3d 1126, 1131 (7th Cir.1997); *Scholes v. Lehmann,* 56 F.3d 750, 756 (7th Cir.1995); *Krell v. Codman,* 154 Mass. 454, 28 N.E. 578 (Mass.1891) (Holmes, J.); Lon L. Fuller, "Consideration and Form," 41 *Colum. L.Rev.* 799, 799–801 (1941). Actual reliance, in the sense of a costly change of position that cannot be recouped if the reliance turns out to have been misplaced, is substitute evidence that there may well have been such a promise. *Consolidation Services, Inc. v. KeyBank National Ass'n, supra,* 185 F.3d at 822; *Yontz v. BMER Interprises, Inc.,* 91 Ohio App.3d 202, 632 N.E.2d 527, 530 (1993). The inference is especially plausible in a commercial setting, because most businesspeople would be reluctant to incur costs in reliance on a promise that they believed the promisor didn't consider himself legally bound to perform.

   In other words, reasonable reliance is seen as nearly as good a reason for thinking there really was a promise as bargained-for reliance is. In many such cases, it is true, no promise was intended, or intended to be legally enforceable; in those cases the application of the doctrine penalizes the defendant for inducing the plaintiff to incur costs of reliance. The penalty is withheld if the reliance was unreasonable; for then the plaintiff's wound was self-inflicted—he should have known better than to rely.

   A relevant though puzzling difference between breach of contract and promissory estoppel as grounds for legal relief is that while the promise relied on to trigger an estoppel must be definite in the sense of being clearly a promise and not just a statement of intentions, *Security Bank & Trust Co. v. Bogard,* 494 N.E.2d 965, 968–69 (Ind.App.1986); *Wood v. Mid-Valley Inc.,* 942 F.2d 425, 428 (7th Cir.1991) (Indiana law); *Major Mat Co. v. Monsanto Co.,* 969 F.2d 579, 582–83 (7th Cir.1992), its terms need not be as clear as a contractual promise would have to be in order to be enforceable. E.g., *Janke Construction Co. v. Vulcan Materials Co.,* 527 F.2d 772, 777 (7th Cir.1976) (Wisconsin law); *Hawkins Construction Co. v. Reiman Corp.,* 245 Neb. 131, 511 N.W.2d 113, 117 (1994); *Neiss v. Ehlers,* 135 Or.App. 218, 899 P.2d 700, 707 (1995). Indiana may go furthest in this direction: "Even though there were insufficient terms for the enforcement of an express oral contract, and unfulfilled pre-existing conditions prohibiting recovery for breach of a written contract . . ., we are not precluded from finding a promise under these circumstances. Indeed, it is precisely under such circumstances, where a promise is made but which is not enforceable as a 'contract,' that the doctrine of promissory estoppel is recognized." *First National Bank of Logansport v. Logan Mfg. Co., supra,* 577 N.E.2d at 955.

The reason for this difference between breach of contract and promissory estoppel is unclear. A stab at an explanation is found in *Rosnick v. Dinsmore,* 235 Neb. 738, 457 N.W.2d 793, 800 (1990), where the court said that "promissory estoppel only provides for damages as justice requires and does not attempt to provide the plaintiff damages based upon the benefit of the bargain. The usual measure of damages under a theory of promissory estoppel is the loss incurred by the promisee in reasonable reliance on the promise, or 'reliance damages.' Reliance damages are relatively easy to determine, whereas the determination of 'expectation' or 'benefit of the bargain' damages available in a contract action requires more detailed proof of the terms of the contract." The only problem with this explanation is that its premise is mistaken; if the promise giving rise to an estoppel is clear, the plaintiff will usually be awarded its value, which would be the equivalent of the expectation measure of damages in an ordinary breach of contract case. *Goldstick v. ICM Realty,* 788 F.2d 456, 463–64 (7th Cir.1986); *Restatement, supra,* § 90 comment d. The rationale in both cases is that the benefit of the contract to the promisee is a good proxy for the opportunities that he forewent in making the contract. *Walters v. Marathon Oil Co.,* 642 F.2d 1098, 1100–01 (7th Cir.1981); L.L. Fuller & William R. Perdue, Jr., "The Reliance Interest in Contract Damages: 1," 46 *Yale L.J.* 52, 60 (1936) ("physicians with an extensive practice often charge their patients the full office call fee for broken appointments. Such a charge looks on the face of things like a claim to the promised fee; it seems to be based on the 'expectation interest'. Yet the physician making the charge will quite justifiably regard it as compensation for the loss of the opportunity to gain a similar fee from a different patient"). Of course, if the promise is unclear, damages will be limited to expenses incurred in reasonable reliance on the vague promise, *First National Bank of Logansport v. Logan Mfg. Co., supra,* 577 N.E.2d at 952, 955–56, but that would be equally true in a breach of contract case in which the promise that the defendant had broken was unclear.

But even though the court is "not precluded from finding a promise" by its vagueness, *id.* at 955, the vaguer the alleged promise the less likely it is to be found to *be* a promise. *Mays v. Trump Indiana, Inc.,* 255 F.3d 351, 358–59 (7th Cir.2001) (Indiana law); *All-Tech Telecom, Inc. v. Amway Corp.,* 174 F.3d 862, 868–69 (7th Cir.1999); *Restatement, supra,* § 33(3) and comment f. And if it is *really* vague, the promisee would be imprudent to rely on it—he wouldn't know whether reliance was worthwhile. The broader principle, which the requirement that the promise be definite and at least minimally clear instantiates, is that the promisee's reliance must be reasonable; if it is not, then not only is he the gratuitous author of his own disappointment, but probably there wasn't really a promise, or at least a promise intended or likely to induce reliance. The "promise" would have been in the nature of a hope or possibly a prediction rather than a commitment to do something within the "promisor's" power to do ("I promise it will rain tomorrow"); and the "promisee" would, if sensible, understand this. He would rely or not as he chose but he would know that he would have to bear the cost of any disappointment.

We note, returning to the facts of this case, that there was costly reliance by GPI, which forewent other opportunities for salvation, and by Garwood and McNamara, who moved from Indiana to Ohio to be near Hobart's plant where they expected their food-packaging system to be manufactured, and who forgave their personal loans to GPI and incurred other costs as well. The reliance was on statements by Martin, of which "come hell or high water" was the high water mark but is by no means an isolated example. If GPI's evidence is credited, as it must be in the procedural posture of the case, Martin repeatedly confirmed to GPI that the deal would go through, that Allen's commitment to invest $2 million was unconditional, that the funding would be forthcoming, and so on; and these statements induced the plaintiffs to incur costs they would otherwise not have done.

But were these real promises, and likely to be understood as such? Those are two different questions. A person may say something that he intends as merely a prediction, or as a signal of his hopes or intentions, but that is reasonably understood as a promise, and if so, as we know (this is the penal or deterrent function of promissory estoppel), he is bound. *Tipton County Farm Bureau Cooperative Ass'n, Inc. v. Hoover,* 475 N.E.2d 38, 42 (Ind.App.1985). But what is a reasonable, and indeed actual, understanding will often depend on the knowledge that the promisee brings to the table. McNamara, with whom Martin primarily dealt, is a former investment banker, not a rube. He knew that in putting together a deal to salvage a failing company there is many a slip 'twixt cup and lips. Unless blinded by optimism or desperation he *had* to know that Martin could not mean *literally* that the deal would go through "come hell or high water," since if Satan or a tsunami obliterated Ohio that would kill the deal. Even if Allen had dug into its pockets for the full $2 million after the investors who it had hoped would put up half the amount defected, the deal might well not have gone through because of Hobart's demands and because of the creditors. GPI acknowledges that the Internal Revenue Service, one of its largest creditors, wouldn't give a release until paid in full. Some of GPI's other creditors also intended to fight rather than to accept a pittance in exchange for a release. Nothing is more common than for a deal to rescue a failing company to fall apart because all the creditors' consent to the deal cannot be obtained—that is one of the reasons for bankruptcy law. Again these were things of which McNamara was perfectly aware.

The problem, thus, is not that Martin's promises were indefinite, which they were not if GPI's evidence is credited, but that they could not have been reasonably understood by the persons to whom they were addressed (mainly McNamara, the financial partner in GPI) to *be* promises rather than expressions of optimism and determination. *Security Bank & Trust Co. v. Bogard, supra,* 494 N.E.2d at 968–69; *Workman v. United Parcel Service, Inc., supra,* 234 F.3d at 1001–02; *Wood v. Mid-Valley Inc., supra,* 942 F.2d at 428; *Major Mat Co. v. Monsanto Co., supra,* 969 F.2d at 582–83. To move to Ohio, to forgive personal loans, to forgo other searches for possible investors, and so forth were in the nature of gambles on the part of GPI and its principals. They may have been reasonable gambles, in the sense that the prospects for a successful salvage operation were good enough that taking immediate, even if irrevocable, steps to facilitate and take advantage of the expected happy outcome was prudent. But we often reasonably rely on things that are not promises. A farmer plants his crops in the spring in reasonable reliance that spring will be followed by summer rather than by winter. There can be reasonable reliance on statements as well as on the regularities of nature, but if the statements are not reasonably understood as legally enforceable promises there can be no action for promissory estoppel.

Suppose McNamara thought that there was a 50 percent chance that the deal would go through and believed that reliance on that prospect would cost him $100,000, but also believed that by relying he could expect either to increase the likelihood that the deal would go through or to make more money if it did by being able to start production sooner and that in either event the expected benefit of reliance would exceed $100,000. Then his reliance would be reasonable even if not induced by enforceable promises. The numbers are arbitrary but the example apt. GPI and its principals relied, and may have relied reasonably, but they didn't rely on Martin's "promises" because those were not promises reasonably understood as such by so financially sophisticated a businessman as McNarama. *McInerney v. Charter Golf, Inc.,* 176 Ill.2d 482, 223 Ill.Dec. 911, 680 N.E.2d 1347, 1352–53 (1997); *Gruen Industries, Inc. v. Biller,* 608 F.2d 274, 281–82 (7th Cir.1979); *Clardy Mfg. Co. v. Marine Midland Business Loans Inc.,* 88 F.3d 347, 358, 360–61 (5th Cir.1996). So we see now that the essence of the doctrine of promissory estoppel is not that the plaintiff have reasonably relied on the defendant's promise, but that he have reasonably relied on its *being* a promise in the sense of a legal commitment, and not a mere prediction or aspiration or bit of puffery.

One last point. Ordinarily the question whether a plaintiff reasonably understood a statement to be a promise is a question of fact and so cannot be resolved in summary judgment proceedings. But if it is clear that the question can be answered in only one way, there is no occasion to submit the question to a jury. See *Mason & Dixon Lines, Inc. v. Glover,* 975 F.2d

1298, 1303–05 (7th Cir.1992); *J.C. Wyckoff & Associates, Inc. v. Standard Fire Ins. Co.*, 936 F.2d 1474, 1493 (6th Cir.1991). This, we believe, is such a case.

Affirmed.

Hoffman v. Red Owl Stores, Inc.

26 Wis.2d 683, 133 N.W.2d 267 (1965)

Plaintiff Hoffman owned and operated a successful bakery in Wautoma, Wisconsin. Defendant Red Owl's divisional manager, Lukowitz, persuaded Hoffman to apply for a Red Owl grocery store franchise in a larger town. Hoffman repeatedly told Lukowitz that he had only $18,000 capital to invest in a store. Lukowitz repeatedly assured him this amount would be sufficient. To get experience in running a grocery store, Hoffman bought the assets of a small grocery in Wautoma, which he ran successfully for several months in 1961 before selling the store. In September 1961, Hoffman paid $1,000 for an option on a lot for a grocery store in Chilton. In November 1961, Hoffman sold his bakery on Lukowitz's advice, retaining the equipment for the grocery. He also moved his family. All of this Hoffman did on Lukowitz's advice. During Fall and early Winter 1961 Hoffman met with Red Owl's people to negotiate the terms of the franchise agreement. During these meetings a credit manager informed Hoffman that he would need more than the $18,000 capital Lukowitz had assured him would suffice. Hoffman borrowed $13,000 from his father-in-law to obtain the additional capital. Initially Red Owl's credit manager told Hoffman this could be treated as a lowest-priority unsecured loan, but at the last minute he was told it had to be a gift. When Hoffman refused to ask his father-in-law to make a gift of the money negotiations terminated. Hoffman sued Red Owl for breach of contract, seeking as damages his expenses and lost income. The jury awarded Hoffman $20,000 damages, the major element of which was a $16,735 loss on the sale of Wautoma store. The trial court granted a new trial on damages with respect to this loss. Affirmed, instructing that on retrial damages with respect to the loss on the sale of the Wautoma store should be measured by the difference between the sales price and the fair market value.

(Currie, C.J.) "We determine that there was ample evidence to sustain the answers of the jury to the questions of the verdict with respect to the promissory representations made by Red Owl, Hoffman's reliance thereon in the exercise of ordinary care, and his fulfillment of the conditions required of him by the terms of the negotiations had with Red Owl.

"There remains for consideration the question of law raised by defendants that agreement was never reached on essential factors necessary to establish a contract between Hoffman and Red Owl. Among these were the size, cost, design, and layout of the store building; and the terms of the lease with respect to rent, maintenance, renewal, and purchase options. This poses the question of whether the promise necessary to sustain a cause of action for promissory estoppel must embrace all essential details of a proposed transaction between promisor and promisee so as to be the equivalent of an offer that would result in a binding contract between the parties if the promisee were to accept the same.

"Originally the doctrine of promissory estoppel was invoked as a substitute for consideration rendering a gratuitous promise enforceable as a contract. See Williston, Contracts (1st ed.), p. 307, sec. 139. In other words, the acts of reliance by the promisee to his detriment provided a substitute for consideration. If promissory estoppel were to be limited to only those situations where the promise giving rise to the cause of action must be so definite with respect to all details that a contract would result were the promise supported by consideration, then the defendants' instant promises to Hoffman would not meet this test. However, sec. 90 of Restatement, 1 Contracts, does not impose the requirement that the promise giving rise to the cause of action must be so comprehensive in scope as to meet the requirements of an offer that would ripen into a contract if accepted by the promisee. Rather the conditions imposed are:

(1)   Was the promise one which the promisor should reasonably expect to induce action or forbearance of a definite and substantial character on the part of the promisee?

(2)   Did the promise induce such action or forbearance?

(3)   Can injustice be avoided only by enforcement of the promise?

"We deem it would be a mistake to regard an action grounded on promissory estoppel as the equivalent of a breach of contract action. As Dean Boyer points out, it is desirable that fluidity in the application of the concept be maintained. 98 University of Pennsylvania Law Review (1950), 459, at page 497. While the first two of the above listed three requirements of promissory estoppel present issues of fact which ordinarily will be resolved by a jury, the third requirement, that the remedy can only be invoked where necessary to avoid injustice, is one that involves a policy decision by the court. Such a policy decision necessarily embraces an element of discretion.

"We conclude that injustice would result here if plaintiffs were not granted some relief because of the failure of defendants to keep their promises which induced plaintiffs to act to their detriment."

———

Gruen Industries, Inc. v. Biller

608 F.2d 274 (7th Cir.1979)

Biller and Hersch owned 340,000 of Windsor's 400,000 outstanding shares. In early 1975, Gruen Industries, represented by Evans, its Vice President, approached Biller and Hersch to discuss a possible acquisition of

Windsor. In May, Biller and Hersch orally agreed to a sale of their stock. At the time of the oral agreement, Gruen informed Hersch that it would not incur the expenses for preparation of the written agreement unless he would assure Gruen that it had a firm commitment. Hersch assured Gruen that it did. Gruen then retained lawyers and the drafting process began. The date to sign the written agreement was set for the middle of July.

The drafting of the agreement was virtually complete by early July. However, on July 17 a third party, PCA, made a written proposal to purchase the Windsor shares for a higher price. Biller and Hersch sold their shares to PCA, and the draft agreement with Gruen was never signed. Gruen sued in federal court for expectation damages on the ground of breach of contract, and alternatively for reliance damages on the ground of promissory estoppel. The suit was governed by the law of Wisconsin. The Seventh Circuit first held that the breach of contract claim was barred by the Statute of Frauds. It then turned to the claim based on promissory estoppel, which had been dismissed by the trial court on a motion for summary judgment.

(Pell, J.) ". . . The plaintiffs seek to recover various preparation expenses incurred, comprising primarily substantial attorneys' fees for drafting the agreement and supplemental documents. As the basis for this theory of recovery the plaintiff has alleged that the defendants orally assured them that they had a firm commitment and then consented to the plaintiffs' procuring legal counsel for the purpose of drafting the necessary documents.

"In *Hoffman v. Red Owl Stores, Inc.*, 26 Wis.2d 683, 133 N.W.2d 267 (1965), the Wisconsin Supreme Court established three conditions for application of promissory estoppel:

(1)   Was the promise one which the promisor should reasonably expect to induce action or forbearance of a definite and substantial character on the part of the promisee?

(2)   Did the promise induce such action or forbearance?

(3)   Can injustice be avoided only by enforcement of the promise?

The first two conditions present questions of fact; the third presents a policy question for the court to decide, and necessarily embraces an element of discretion. . . .

"More recently, in *Silberman v. Roethe*, 64 Wis.2d 131, 218 N.W.2d 723 (1974), the Wisconsin Supreme Court discussed in detail for the first time the factors to be considered by the trial court in deciding whether a plaintiff has satisfied the third condition. The factor receiving primary consideration in *Silberman* was the certainty 'that the plaintiff has actually suffered from his action in reliance.' In *Silberman* the plaintiff reduced a debt owed to him by a corporation in reliance on a promise by the defendant to purchase the corporation and to strengthen it financially. The defendant did not keep its promise, and the corporation failed. Nevertheless, the plaintiff did not prevail against the defendant because it was speculative that the plaintiff ever could have collected the full debt had it tried.

"Similarly, the alleged agreement here was subject to numerous conditions, some of which were under the control of third parties. If any of these conditions were not satisfied, the buyers or sellers would have been able to terminate the agreement unilaterally prior to the sale and purchase of the stock. Had the defendants kept the alleged promises, as they are embodied in the unsigned Agreement, the sale may very well have failed on the basis of the many contingencies, and the plaintiffs would not have been entitled to any reimbursement of their expenses. We agree with the district court that summary judgment is appropriate here. To avoid injustice, it clearly is not necessary that plaintiffs be placed in a better position for the alleged breach than they may have been had the promise been kept. The conditional promise alleged is not a reasonable basis for reliance and thus not a proper basis for estoppel. . . .

"In addition to the conditional nature of the promise, other circumstances of this case militate against recovery on an estoppel theory. The alleged promises were made informally; indeed even under the plaintiffs' theory of the case, the written Agreement was intended as a formal and more detailed record of the agreement of the parties. *See Silberman, supra,* 64 Wis.2d at 146, 218 N.W.2d at 730. Furthermore, the plaintiffs were represented by sophisticated businessmen, and therefore '[t]his is not a situation of an individual taken advantage of by a corporation or individual with superior knowledge of legal and business practices.' *Id.* Finally, there is no allegation that the defendants were in any way unjustly enriched because of the plaintiff's reliance. In fact, the defendants also retained attorneys in connection with the preparation of the agreement and no doubt paid a substantial sum for their services."

————

Classic Cheesecake Company, Inc. v. JP Morgan Chase Bank, N.A.

546 F.3d 839 (7th Cir. 2008)

Plaintiff Classic sought a loan from defendant bank to establish a distribution center in Las Vegas to serve hotels and casinos. Classic's principals met with Dowling, a vice president of a local loan office of the bank, on July 27, 2004, to pitch the loan. On September 17 Dowling told Classic the loan was a "go," while asking for additional documents to speed up the confirmation process. Dowling did not tell Classic that her superior had initially declined to approve the loan on August 19, citing various concerns. Dowling continued to assure Classic that the loan would be approved until October 12, when she told them the loan had been turned down. Classic sued for breach of an oral promise to make a loan, claiming "the breach delayed it from seeking loans elsewhere for a critical two and a half months and that as a result of the delay it . . . . incurred in the aggregate a loss of more than $1 million." The district court granted defendant's motion to dismiss because of an absence of a writing to satisfy a provision of the Indiana statute of frauds requiring that agreements to lend money be in writing. Ind.Code § 26–2–9–5. Affirmed.

(Posner, J.) "[T]he question becomes whether the bank's conduct could have been found to inflict an "unjust and unconscionable injury and loss" and so trump the bank's defense based on the statute of frauds. To answer the question requires us to explore the provenance of a phrase at once vague (what does "unjust and unconscionable" mean?) and redundant (how does "injury" differ from "loss"?).

"The statute of frauds has long been controversial. The Farnsworth treatise says that "it has been the subject of constant erosion." 2 E. Allan Farnsworth, *Farnsworth on Contracts* § 6.1, p. 107 (3d ed.2004). The particular erosive process that culminates in the doctrine of "unjust and unconscionable injury and loss" began—where else?—in an opinion by Justice Traynor, *Monarco v. Lo Greco*, 35 Cal.2d 621, 220 P.2d 737 (1950), that allowed the statute of frauds to be circumvented by a claim of promissory estoppel. . . . Importantly, however, Justice Traynor limited the use of promissory estoppel to defeat the statute of frauds: only if "either an unconscionable injury or unjust enrichment would result from refusal to enforce" an oral promise would a defense based on the statute of frauds be negated. 220 P.2d at 741.

"The *Monarco* opinion, like so many of Justice Traynor's innovations, caught on. 2 Farnsworth, *supra*, § 6.12, p. 206. Eventually it was picked up— and expanded—by the *Restatement (Second) of Contracts* (1981), which in section 139(1) allows promissory estoppel to defeat the statute of frauds "if injustice can be avoided only by enforcement of the [oral] promise." This notably loose formulation has been influential too, 2 Farnsworth, *supra*, § 6.12, pp. 206–13—but not in Indiana. "Indiana courts have declined to embrace § 139 [of the *Restatement*], but have recognized the possibility of relief for 'injustice' in limited circumstances, while defining it much more narrowly than in § 139." *Coca-Cola Co. v. Babyback's Int'l, Inc.*, 841 N.E.2d 557, 569 (Ind.2006).

"Indiana's formula is as follows:

In order to establish an estoppel to remove the case from the operation of the Statute of Frauds, the party must show [ ] that the other party's refusal to carry out the terms of the agreement has resulted not merely in a denial of the rights which the agreement was intended to confer, but the infliction of an unjust and unconscionable injury and loss.

In other words, neither the benefit of the bargain itself, nor mere inconvenience, incidental expenses, etc. short of a reliance injury so substantial and independent as to constitute an unjust and unconscionable injury and loss are sufficient to remove the claim from the operation of the Statute of Frauds.

Id., quoting *Brown v. Branch, supra*, 758 N.E.2d at 52, which in turn was quoting *Whiteco Industries, Inc. v. Kopani*, 514 N.E.2d 840, 845 (Ind.App.1987).

"The formula itself—"unjust and unconscionable injury and loss"—does not tell us much, and it has not been further elaborated by the Indiana courts. Comparison with Justice Traynor's formula—"either an unconscionable injury or unjust enrichment"—deepens the mystery. The Traynor formula suggests two grounds for getting around the statute of frauds: unjust gain to the promisor or "unconscionable" injury to the promisee. . . .

"We can at least set aside any issue of unjust enrichment in this case. The bank made no money in its dealings with Classic and gained no other advantage; all it gained was this lawsuit against it. And anyway, to invoke the doctrine of unconscionability Classic would have to show that it had been taken advantage of because of its obvious ignorance or desperate circumstances, e.g., *Weaver v. American Oil Co.,* 257 Ind. 458, 276 N.E.2d 144, 146 (1971), and there is nothing like that here. . . .

"We can get some help from the case law. In *Monarco,* the *fons et origo* of the doctrine that the Indiana courts call "unjust and unconscionable injury and loss," there was both a big loss and unjust enrichment. When the plaintiff reached 18 and wanted to leave home and make his own way in the world, his mother and stepfather promised him that if he stayed and worked on the family farm they would leave almost all their property (which was in joint tenancy) to him. He stayed, and worked hard, receiving in exchange only room and board and spending money. The farm prospered. But when the stepfather died 20 years later, he left his half interest in the farm to his own grandson. 220 P.2d at 738–39. The element of unjust enrichment lay in the fact that the plaintiff had worked the farm for slight compensation for 20 years (giving up among other things the opportunity to obtain an education beyond high school) in the expectation that he would be well compensated when either his mother or his stepfather died. The farm had done well, in part no doubt because of the plaintiff's undercompensated efforts—his "sweat equity." So the grandson was indeed unjustly enriched. The plaintiff's having the rug pulled out from under him after working for 20 years for slight remuneration faintly echoed Laban's fraud on his son-in-law Jacob. After promising the hand of his younger daughter, Rachel, to Jacob in marriage in return for seven years' service to him, Laban tricked Jacob—whose work had enriched Laban—into marrying Laban's elder daughter, Leah, instead. Jacob was compelled to serve Laban for another seven years in order to be permitted to marry Rachel. As in *Monarco,* there was both unjust enrichment of the oral promisor and heavy loss to the promisee—seven more years of unpaid labor. . . .

"Only two cases (one a federal district court diversity case governed by Indiana law) have allowed a claim based on the Indiana formula to survive a motion for summary judgment, though in neither case did the plaintiff ultimately prevail. . . .

"In the diversity case, *Madison Tool & Die, Inc. v. ZF Sachs Automotive of America, Inc.,* 2007 WL 2286130 (S.D.Ind. Aug.7, 2007), the defendant orally agreed to make the plaintiff its auto parts supplier. To induce the plaintiff to retool its facilities so that it could supply the parts, the defendant announced that it was not working with any other suppliers and would therefore need the plaintiff to begin production within 30 days. So the plaintiff went out and bought a special machine for $415,000 to produce the parts for the defendant. The plaintiff made test parts for the defendant with the new machine, but rather than ordering any parts the defendant assured the plaintiff for three years that it would begin ordering parts soon. Yet it never did, and at the end of the period declared that it would not be using the plaintiff as a supplier after all.

"In the other case, *Keating v. Burton,* 545 N.E.2d 35 (Ind.App.1989), the defendant orally agreed to hire the plaintiff as a full-time employee with an option to purchase 49 percent of the defendant's company after three years of employment. In reliance on the agreement the plaintiff went to work for the defendant and claimed to have shut down his own company, which had been growing. (The court eventually found that the plaintiff had not abandoned his business entirely. But for purposes of getting a fix on Indiana law, all that matters is the evidence that was before the court when it decided not to grant summary judgment to the defendant.) After the plaintiff had been working for the defendant's company for a year and a half, the defendant so limited the plaintiff's responsibilities that he quit.

"These cases are not as dramatic as *Monarco* or *Genesis* 29 and do not involve (so far as appears) substantial gain to the (oral) promisor. But there is a family resemblance, which helps us to understand the scope and operation of the Indiana formula as elaborated in the second paragraph of the indented quotation from *Babyback's* and as paraphrased in *Spring Hill Developers, Inc. v. Arthur,* 879 N.E.2d 1095, 1103 (Ind.App.2008), as follows: the "injury must be not only (1) independent from the benefit of the bargain and resulting incidental expenses and inconvenience, but also (2) so substantial as to constitute an unjust and unconscionable injury." The benefit of the bargain would be what the promisee hoped to gain from the promise, which in *Madison* would have been the profit from selling auto parts to the defendant and in *Keating* the 49 percent share of the defendant's company. The plaintiffs lost those expectancies of course, but they suffered other losses as well—the cost of the machine in *Madison* that the plaintiff would not have bought had it not been for the oral promise and in *Keating* the plaintiff's alleged loss of his company. And those losses were significant in relation to the plaintiffs' net worth, satisfying the second part of the Indiana formula.

"But what these cases really show is the mercury-like slipperiness of the Indiana formula, as of the *Monarco* formula as well. The "benefit of the bargain" is contract-speak for the expected profit from performing a contract; the "independent" loss of which the *Spring Hill* opinion spoke is the reliance loss—the expenses a party incurs to perform the contract. The plaintiff in *Madison* incurred the expense of the machine in reliance on the defendant's promise, and likewise with the plaintiff's giving up his business in *Keating*. A promise plus a reliance loss is what you need for promissory estoppel, yet the Indiana Supreme Court refused in *Babyback's* to endorse a *general* exception to the statute of frauds for promissory estoppel. 841 N.E.2d at 568–70; see

Spring Hill Developers, Inc. v. Arthur, supra, 879 N.E.2d at 1100–04. So the whole weight of the doctrine of "unjust and unconscionable injury and loss" falls on the gravity of the injury, and the decisive distinction between *Monarco, Madison,* and *Keating* (and for that matter Jacob's grievance) on the one hand and the present case on the other hand is simply the duration of the injury in those cases relative to this one: 20 years, 3 years, 1.5 years, and 7 years (Jacob's case), versus in our case at most 2.5 months but more likely 3.5 weeks—the time that elapsed between Dowling's telling Classic on September 17 that the deal was a "go" and on October 12 that the loan application had been rejected. The more protracted the period during which reliance costs are being incurred, the stronger the inference that the oral promise was as the plaintiff represents it to be; for had there been no promise the plaintiff's conduct—his immense reliance cost relative to his resources—would have been incomprehensible.

"Remember that the objection to placing promissory estoppel outside the statute of frauds is that it is too easy for a plaintiff to incur reliance costs in order to bolster his claim of an oral promise. The objection is attenuated if the reliance is so extensive that it is unlikely that the plaintiff would have undertaken it (buying an expensive specialized machine or giving up a growing company) merely to bolster a false claim. He might of course have misunderstood the "promisor" or been gambling on getting a contract, but courts seem not to think those possibilities likely enough to warrant a sterner rule. The compromise that the courts strike between the value of protecting reasonable reliance and the policy that animates the statute of frauds is to require a party that wants to get around the statute of frauds to prove an *enhanced* promissory estoppel, and the enhancement consists of proving a kind or amount of reliance unlikely to have been incurred had the plaintiff not had a good-faith belief that he had been promised remuneration.

"This seems to us a better understanding of the "unjust and unconscionable" rule than ascribing it to judicial indignation at dishonorable behavior by promisors. It is a strength rather than a weakness of contract law that it generally eschews a moral conception of transactions. Liability for breach of contract is strict, rather than based (as tort liability generally is) on fault; punitive damages are unavailable even for deliberate breaches (and again note the contrast with tort law); and specific performance is exceptional—and when the only remedy for a breach of contract is compensatory damages, a promisor has in effect an option to perform or pay damages rather than a duty to perform (the duty the civil law expresses by the phrase *pacta sunt servanda*). Even such contract doctrines as "good faith," "best efforts," and "duress," which have a moral ring, seem aimed not at vindicating the moral law but at protecting each party to a contract from the other party's taking advantage of a temporary monopoly (not in an antitrust sense) that contracts often create when the performance of the parties is not simultaneous. . . .

"Even though the behavior of the defendants in *Monarco* and the other cases we have discussed may well shock the conscience, the outcomes of those cases are defensible on the practical ground of protecting reasonable reliance in situations (and this is key) in which the contention that the reliance was induced by an oral promise is credible. The formulas the cases use to describe these situations, however, are not illuminating. Holmes warned that "the law is full of phraseology drawn from morals, and by the mere force of language continually invites us to pass from one domain to the other without perceiving it, as we are sure to do unless we have the boundary constantly before our minds." O.W. Holmes, "The Path of the Law," 10 *Harv. L.Rev.* 457, 459–60 (1897). Ruminating on the meaning of "unjust" and "unconscionable" will not separate the cases we have discussed from this case; reflection on reliance will.

"The duration of reliance in the present case was much shorter than in the other cases that we have discussed, and the reliance is more easily imagined as based on hope than on a promise. And not all of it could be considered *reasonable* reliance, which is the only kind that can support a claim of promissory estoppel and *a fortiori* an invocation of the enhanced promissory-estoppel doctrine of the Indiana cases. The only reasonable reliance that the plaintiffs placed on Dowling's assurances was to cure (for less than $20,000) a delinquency somewhat earlier than they would otherwise have been forced to do. For the plaintiffs to treat the bank loan as a certainty because they were told by the bank officer whom they were dealing with that it would be approved was unreasonable, especially if, as the plaintiffs' damages claim presupposes, the need for the loan was urgent. Rational businessmen know that there is many a slip 'twixt cup and lips, that a loan is not approved until it is approved, that if a bank's employee tells you your loan application will be approved that is not the same as telling you it has been approved, and that if one does not have a loan commitment in writing yet the need for the loan is urgent one had better be negotiating with other potential lenders at the same time. The level of reliance that could be thought to have been reasonable in this case was not comparable to that involved in the other cases. In the end, this case turns out to be a routine promissory estoppel case, and that is not enough in Indiana to defeat a defense of statute of frauds."

———

PART 4

WRITTEN CONTRACTS

■ ■ ■

This Part takes up issues that generally arise when there is a written contract.

Chapter 12 concerns cases in which A and B have entered into a written contract, and A claims that prior to, or contemporaneously with, making the written contract, the parties entered into a separate agreement that concerned the same subject matter as the written contract, but was not intended to be superseded by the written contract. The treatment of such alleged separate agreements—and more specifically, the issue whether evidence concerning such agreements is admissible—is governed by the *parol evidence rule*.

Chapter 13 concerns several issues that broadly relate to the interpretation of a written contract. The Chapter begins with the differences between textualist and contextualist approaches to interpretation of a writing. The Chapter also concerns the use of trade usage, course of performance, and course of dealing both to interpret a writing and as a source of implied terms; implication and purposive interpretation; and the obligation to perform in good faith.

Chapter 14 concerns how conduct subsequent to the execution of a written contract can operate as a waiver of rights under the contract. It also concerns the effect of a contract having a no oral modification clause when there is an oral modification.

Chapter 15 and 16 concerns issues that are generally associated with commercial and consumer form contracts. Chapter 15 concerns what is called "the battle of the forms." This refers to the situation in which two firms trade forms in a transaction and neither party signifies assent to doing business based on terms in the other party's form. Chapter 16 concerns consumer form contracts. In these cases a firm typically presents an individual consumer or employee with a form with boilerplate terms. The individual may or may not sign the form. Invariably, the individual does not read boilerplate terms in the form. As you will see, American law tilts in favor of the firm and against the individual in this situation.

———

CHAPTER 12

THE PAROL EVIDENCE RULE

■ ■ ■

Section 1 of this Chapter takes up the parol evidence rule. Section 2 concerns uses of parol evidence not precluded by the rule.

SECTION 1. THE RULE

MITCHILL V. LATH
Court of Appeals of New York, 1928.
247 N.Y. 377, 160 N.E. 646, 68 A.L.R. 239.

Action by Catherine C. Mitchill against Charles Lath and another. Judgment of Special Term in plaintiff's favor, directing specific performance of an agreement to remove an icehouse, was affirmed by the Appellate Division (220 App.Div. 776, 221 N.Y.S. 864), and defendants appeal. Judgments of Appellate Division and Trial Term reversed, and complaint dismissed.

ANDREWS, J. In the fall of 1923 the Laths owned a farm. This they wished to sell. Across the road, on land belonging to Lieutenant Governor Lunn, they had an icehouse which they might remove. Mrs. Mitchell looked over the land with a view to its purchase. She found the icehouse objectionable. Thereupon "the defendants orally promised and agreed, for and in consideration of the purchase of their farm by the plaintiff, to remove the said icehouse in the spring of 1924." Relying upon this promise, she made a written contract to buy the property for $8,400, for cash and a mortgage and containing various provisions usual in such papers. Later receiving a deed, she entered into possession, and has spent considerable sums in improving the property for use as a summer residence. The defendants have not fulfilled their promise as to the icehouse, and do not intend to do so. We are not dealing, however, with their moral delinquencies. The question before us is whether their oral agreement may be enforced in a court of equity.

This requires a discussion of the parol evidence rule—a rule of law which defines the limits of the contract to be construed. Glackin v. Bennett, 226 Mass. 316, 115 N.E. 490. It is more than a rule of evidence, and oral testimony, even if admitted, will not control the written contract (O'Malley

v. Grady, 222 Mass. 202, 109 N.E. 829), unless admitted without objection (Brady v. Nally, 151 N.Y. 258, 45 N.E. 547). It applies, however, to attempts to modify such a contract by parol. It does not affect a parol collateral contract distinct from and independent of the written agreement. It is, at times, troublesome to draw the line. Williston, in his work on Contracts (section 637) points out the difficulty. "Two entirely distinct contracts," he says, "each for a separate consideration, may be made at the same time, and will be distinct legally. Where, however, one agreement is entered into wholly or partly in consideration of the simultaneous agreement to enter into another, the transactions are necessarily bound together. . . . Then if one of the agreements is oral and the other in writing, the problem arises whether the bond is sufficiently close to prevent proof of the oral agreement." That is the situation here. It is claimed that the defendants are called upon to do more than is required by their written contract in connection with the sale as to which it deals.

The principle may be clear, but it can be given effect by no mechanical rule. As so often happens, it is a matter of degree, for, as Prof. Williston also says, where a contract contains several promises on each side it is not difficult to put any one of them in the form of a collateral agreement. If this were enough, written contracts might always be modified by parol. Not form, but substance, is the test.

In applying this test, the policy of our courts is to be considered. We have believed that the purpose behind the rule was a wise one, not easily to be abandoned. Notwithstanding injustice here and there, on the whole it works for good. Old precedents and principles are not to be lightly cast aside, unless it is certain that they are an obstruction under present conditions. New York has been less open to arguments that would modify this particular rule, than some jurisdictions elsewhere. Thus in Eighmie v. Taylor, 98 N.Y. 288, it was held that a parol warranty might not be shown, although no warranties were contained in the writing.

Under our decisions before such an oral agreement as the present is received to vary the written contract, at least three conditions must exist: (1) The agreement must in form be a collateral one; (2) it must not contradict express or implied provisions of the written contract; (3) it must be one that parties would not ordinarily be expected to embody in the writing, or, put in another way, an inspection of the written contract, read in the light of surrounding circumstances, must not indicate that the writing appears "to contain the engagements of the parties, and to define the object and measure the extent of such engagement." Or, again, it must not be so clearly connected with the principal transaction as to be part and parcel of it.

The respondent does not satisfy the third of these requirements. It may be, not the second. We have a written contract for the purchase and sale of land. The buyer is to pay $8,400 in the way described. She is also to pay her portion of any rents, interest on mortgages, insurance premiums, and water meter charges. She may have a survey made of the premises. On their part, the sellers are to give a full covenant deed of the premises as described, or as they may be described by the surveyor, if the survey is had, executed, and acknowledged at their own expense; they sell the personal property on the farm and represent they own it; they agree that all amounts paid them on the contract and the expense of examining the title shall be a lien on the property; they assume the risk of loss or damage by fire until the deed is delivered; and they agree to pay the broker his commissions. Are they to do more? Or is such a claim inconsistent with these precise provisions? It could not be shown that the plaintiff was to pay $500 additional. Is it also implied that the defendants are not to do anything unexpressed in the writing?

That we need not decide. At least, however, an inspection of this contract shows a full and complete agreement, setting forth in detail the obligations of each party. On reading it, one would conclude that the reciprocal obligations of the parties were fully detailed. Nor would his opinion alter if he knew the surrounding circumstances. The presence of the icehouse, even the knowledge that Mrs. Mitchill thought it objectionable, would not lead to the belief that a separate agreement existed with regard to it. Were such an agreement made it would seem most natural that the inquirer should find it in the contract. Collateral in form it is found to be, but it is closely related to the subject dealt with in the written agreement—so closely that we hold it may not be proved. . . .

We do not ignore the fact that authorities may be found that would seem to support the contention of the appellant. Such are Erskine v. Adeane (1873) L.R. 8 Ch.App. 756, and Morgan v. Griffith (1871) L.R. 6 Exch. 70, where although there was a written lease a collateral agreement of the landlord to reduce the game was admitted. In this state, Wilson v. Deen might lead to the contrary result. Neither are they approved in New Jersey. Naumberg v. Young, 44 N.J.Law, 331, 43 Am.Rep. 380. Nor in view of later cases in this court can Batterman v. Pierce, 3 Hill, 171, be considered an authority. A line of cases in Massachusetts, of which Durkin v. Cobleigh, 156 Mass. 108, 30 N.E. 474, 17 L.R.A. 270, 32 Am.St.Rep. 436, is an example, have to do with collateral contracts made before a deed is given. But the fixed form of a deed makes it inappropriate to insert collateral agreements, however closely connected with the sale. This may be cause for an exception. Here we deal with the contract on the basis of which the deed to Mrs. Mitchill was given subsequently, and we confine ourselves to the question whether its terms may be modified. . . .

It is argued that what we have said is not applicable to the case as presented. The collateral agreement was made with the plaintiff. The contract of sale was with her husband, and no assignment of it from him appears. Yet the deed was given to her. It is evident that here was a transaction in which she was the principal from beginning to end. We must treat the contract as if in form, as it was in fact, made by her.

Our conclusion is that the judgment of the Appellate Division and that of the Special Term should be reversed and the complaint dismissed, with costs in all courts.

[The dissenting opinion of Lehman, J., is omitted.]

CARDOZO, C.J., and POUND, KELLOGG and O'BRIEN, JJ., concur with ANDREWS, J.

LEHMAN, J., dissents in opinion in which CRANE, J., concurs.

Judgment accordingly.

———

Von Mehren, Civil Law Analogues to Consideration: An Exercise in Comparative Analysis

72 Harv.L.Rev. 1009, 1011–1012 (1959)

"One or more of the interested parties often think that a contractual obligation will be more readily enforced if it is formally divorced from the environment and the motives that produced it. Civil-law theorists, especially the German writers, have discussed such a divorcement in terms of whether the legal system permits an 'abstract' obligation. . . . [I]n all jurisdictions, a transaction can also be rendered partially abstract by embodying it in an integrating agreement."

———

James Bradley Thayer, A Preliminary Treatise on Evidence

428–429 (1898)

Commenting on an opinion of Chief Justice Holt, Thayer remarked: "The Chief Justice here retires into that lawyer's Paradise where all words have a fixed, precisely ascertained meaning; where men may express their purposes, not only with accuracy, but with fulness; and where, if the writer has been careful, a lawyer, having a document referred to him, may sit in his chair, inspect the text, and answer all questions without raising his eyes. Men have dreamed of attaining for their solemn muniments of title such an absolute security; and some degree of security they have encompassed by giving strict definitions and technical meanings to words and phrases, and by rigid rules of construction. But the fatal necessity of looking outside the text in order to identify persons and things, tends steadily to destroy such illusions and to reveal the essential imperfection of language, whether spoken or written."

———

CALAMARI & PERILLO, A PLEA FOR A UNIFORM PAROL EVIDENCE RULE AND PRINCIPLES OF INTERPRETATION
42 Indiana L.J. 333 (1967).

Any reader of advance sheets is well aware that most of the contract decisions reported do not involve offer and acceptance or other subjects usually explored in depth in a course in contracts but rather involve the parol evidence rule and questions of interpretation, topics given scant attention in most courses in contracts. . . . Much of the fog and mystery surrounding these subjects stems from the fact that there is basic disagreement as to the meaning and effect of the parol evidence rule and as to the appropriate goals to be achieved by the process of contractual interpretation. The cases and treatises of the contract giants tend to conceal this conflict. While frequently masking disagreement by using the same terminology, Professors Williston and Corbin are often poles apart in the meaning they attach to the same term. Often starting from what superficially appear to be the same premises, they frequently advocate different results in similar fact situations. The polarity of their views reflects conflicting value judgments as to policy issues that are as old as our legal system and that are likely to continue as long as courts of law exist. Although many writers and courts have expressed their views on the subject and have made major contributions to it, concentration on the analyses of Professors Williston and Corbin will point up the fundamental bases upon which the conflicting cases and views rest.

THE AREA OF SUBSTANTIAL AGREEMENT

There is a rule of substantive law which states that whenever contractual intent is sought to be ascertained from among several expressions of the parties, an earlier tentative expression will be rejected in favor of a later expression that is final. More simply stated, the contract made by the parties supersedes tentative promises made in earlier negotiations. Consequently, in determining the content of the contract, the earlier tentative promises are irrelevant.

The parol evidence rule comes into play only when the last expression is in writing. Professor Corbin states the rule as follows: "When two parties have made a contract and have expressed it in a writing to which they have both assented as the complete and accurate integration of that contract, evidence, whether parol or otherwise, of antecedent understandings and negotiations will not be admitted for the purpose of varying or contradicting the writing." Professor Williston's formulation is not to the contrary: "Briefly stated," he writes, "this rule requires, in the absence of fraud, duress, mutual mistake, or something of the kind, the exclusion of extrinsic evidence, oral or written, where the parties have reduced their agreement to an integrated writing." Both agree that this, too, is a rule of substantive law that also operates as an exclusionary rule of evidence merely because prior understandings are irrelevant to the process of determining the content of the final contract. The similarity between the parol evidence rule and the rule stated in the preceding paragraph is obvious. The main and important difference is that where the last expression is not in writing the jury determines whether the parties intended the second expression to supersede the first. This is to say that this question of intention is determined as is any other question of intention stemming from oral transactions. Where the later expression is in writing, however, this question is usually determined by the trial judge. At an early date it was felt (and the feeling strongly remains) that writings require the special protection that is afforded by removing this issue from the province of unsophisticated jurors.

THE PAROL EVIDENCE RULE: THE MAJOR AREA OF CONFLICT

Apparent agreement by Professors Williston and Corbin, except as noted, on the rules stated above conceals real conflict. The battleground upon which they express disagreement is a major one: the concept of total integration. This, of course, is the area in which most of the cases arise. Both assert that the existence of a total integration depends on the intention of the parties. . . . It appears, however, that in this context they use the term "intent" in ways that are remarkably dissimilar. A typical fact situation will illustrate this. *A* agrees to sell and *B* agrees to purchase Blackacre for $10,000. The contract is in writing and in all respects appears complete on its face. Prior to the signing of the contract *A*, in order to induce *B's* assent, orally promises him in the presence of a number of reputable witnesses that if *B* will sign the contract, *A* will remove an unsightly shack on *A's* land across the road from Blackacre. May this promise be proved and enforced? This depends upon whether the writing is a total integration.

Williston argues that if the intention to have a total integration were to be determined by the ordinary process of determining intention, the parol evidence rule would be emasculated. He points out that the mere existence of the collateral oral agreement would conclusively indicate that the parties intended only a partial integration and that the only question that would be presented is whether the alleged prior or contemporaneous agreement was actually made. This would be a question of fact for the jury, thus eliminating the special protection which the trial judge should afford the writing. . . .

. . . [Williston therefore suggests that] where the writing appears to be a complete instrument expressing the rights and obligations of both parties, it is deemed a total integration unless the alleged additional terms were such as might naturally be made as a separate agreement by parties situated as were the parties to the written contract.

Professor Corbin has an easy task in demolishing the Willistonian approach. In treating the matter of integration as a question of intent, as

Professor Williston purports to do, he shows the absurdity of excluding all relevant evidence of intent except the writing itself. But . . . Williston, and [courts that follow his view] are unconcerned about the true intention of the parties. Rather, shorn of rote language of fiction indicating a search for intention, they are advocating and applying a rule of form. Since (and even before) the common law had its genesis, there has been a deeply-felt belief that transactions will be more secure, litigation will be reduced, and the temptation to perjury will be removed, if everyone will only use proper forms for his transactions. The Statute of Wills and the Statute of Frauds are but examples of this belief. Professor Corbin, by attacking the apparent arguments of Williston's position has not expressly come to grips with the substance of his position. This is not to suggest that either he or Professor Williston have been unaware of the true nature of their disagreement. Rather, they seem for the most part to have been content not to make explicit the basis of their differing views. . . .

The debate involves the question: is the public better served by giving effect to the parties' entire agreement written and oral, even at the risk of injustice caused by the possibility of perjury and the possibility that superseded documents will be treated as operative, or does the security of transactions require that, despite occasional injustices, persons adopting a formal writing be required, on the penalty of voidness of their oral and written side agreements, to put their entire agreement in the formal writing. . . .

––––––

RESTATEMENT, SECOND, CONTRACTS
§§ 209, 210, 213, 214, 215, 216

[See Selected Source Materials Supplement]

––––––

Braucher, Interpretation and Legal Effect in the Second Restatement of Contracts

81 Colum.L.Rev. 13, 17 (1981)

"The core of the 'parol evidence rule' is stated in section 213: a binding integrated agreement discharges inconsistent prior agreements, and a binding completely integrated agreement discharges prior agreements within its scope. These statements, however, merely point to the obvious conclusion; the difficulties arise in determining whether there is an integrated agreement, whether, if so, it is completely or only partially integrated, and whether the prior agreement is consistent with the integrated agreement or within its scope. Those determinations are made in accordance with all relevant evidence, and require interpretation both of the integrated agreement and of the prior agreement. They are made by the court, not by the trier of fact."

Interform Co. v. Mitchell Constr. Co.

575 F.2d 1270, 1275–77 (9th Cir.1978)

(Sneed, J.) "In practice ... the difference between the [Corbin and Williston] views is less significant than one might imagine. A writing, which ordinarily and naturally would be an integrated one, generally is one the parties thereto intended to be integrated. Also, the meaning to which the reasonably intelligent person would subscribe generally is that to which the parties did subscribe. . . .

"There are, however, significant differences between the two views. To suggest none exist would reduce the debate between their respective leading protagonists, Williston with regard to the first and Corbin the second, to a triviality. The debate is not that. It relates, as indicated, to the attitude with which judges should approach written contracts. Williston requires the judge to ascertain the legal relations between the parties by reference to those associated with the 'forms' (that is, the natural and normal integration practices and the meaning of words that reasonably intelligent people would employ) to which they should adhere and from which they depart at their peril. Calamari & Perillo 104–05; Williston §§ 633, 638–39. Corbin, on the other hand, directs the judge to fix the legal relations between the parties in accordance with their intention even when the 'forms' they employed suggest otherwise. Corbin §§ 538–42A. A judge, guided by Williston ... would impose upon the parties the terms of the [contractual documents] as understood by the reasonably intelligent person if [those documents] appear complete and any additional terms ordinarily and naturally would have been included therein. Williston §§ 638–39; Calamari & Perillo 105. A judge, guided by Corbin, would impose upon the parties the agreement that the evidence indicates they in fact reached. . . .

"It is unlikely that any jurisdiction will inflexibly adopt one approach to the exclusion of the other; each is likely to influence the conduct of judges and the disposition of cases. However, it must be acknowledged that the influence of Corbin's way is stronger now ..., than when he and Williston grappled during the drafting of the American Law Institute's first Restatement, Contracts. . . . "

Murray, The Parol Evidence Process and Standardized Agreements Under the Restatement, Second, Contracts

123 U.Pa.L.Rev. 1342 (1975)

"The first indication of the test suggested in the *Restatement, Second* is found in comment *c* to the first section of topic three, [section 209]: 'Whether a writing has been adopted as an integrated agreement is a question of fact to be determined in accordance with all relevant evidence.' That the question is 'one of fact' has long been generally conceded. The significance of the statement is its direction that the integration determination be made 'in accordance with all relevant evidence.' The flavor of Corbin is here so strong as to mask any others. Professor Corbin has suggested that '[o]n this issue of fact, no relevant testimony should be excluded.' Here, at the outset of the *Restatement, Second,* Corbin appears to win the first and probably the decisive battle. . . . "

CISG ART. 8(3)

[See Selected Source Materials Supplement]

Dodge, Teaching the CISG in Contracts

50 J. Leg. Ed. 72 (2000)

"Under the parol evidence rule found in both the common law and the UCC, the parties may not contradict the terms of a final written agreement with evidence of prior or contemporaneous negotiations or agreements. CISG Article 8(3), by contrast, directs a court interpreting a contract to give 'due consideration . . . to all relevant circumstances of the case including the negotiations, any practices which the parties have established between themselves, usages and any subsequent conduct of the parties.' In other words, the CISG lacks a parol evidence rule and allows a court interpreting a written contract to consider not just trade usage, course of dealing, and course of performance, but even the parties' prior negotiations."

UNIDROIT PRINCIPLES OF INTERNATIONAL LAW ART. 4.3

[See Selected Source Materials Supplement]

MASTERSON V. SINE
Supreme Court of California, 1968.
68 Cal.2d 222, 65 Cal.Rptr. 545, 436 P.2d 561.

TRAYNOR, CHIEF JUSTICE.

Dallas Masterson and his wife Rebecca owned a ranch as tenants in common. On February 25, 1958, they conveyed it to Medora and Lu Sine by a grant deed "Reserving unto the Grantors herein an option to purchase the above described property on or before February 25, 1968" for the "same consideration as being paid heretofore plus their depreciation value of any improvements Grantees may add to the property from and after two and a half years from this date." Medora is Dallas' sister and Lu's wife. Since the conveyance Dallas has been adjudged bankrupt. His trustee in bankruptcy and Rebecca brought this declaratory relief action to establish their right to enforce the option.

The case was tried without a jury. Over defendants' objection the trial court admitted extrinsic evidence that by "the same consideration as being paid heretofore" both the grantors and the grantees meant the sum of $50,000 and by "depreciation value of any improvements" they meant the depreciation value of improvements to be computed by deducting from the total amount of any capital expenditures made by defendants grantees the amount of depreciation allowable to them under United States income tax regulations as of the time of the exercise of the option.

The court also determined that the parol evidence rule precluded admission of extrinsic evidence offered by defendants to show that the parties wanted the property kept in the Masterson family and that the option was therefore personal to the grantors and could not be exercised by the trustee in bankruptcy.

The court entered judgment for plaintiffs, declaring their right to exercise the option, specifying in some detail how it could be exercised, and reserving jurisdiction to supervise the manner of its exercise and to determine the amount that plaintiffs will be required to pay defendants for their capital expenditures if plaintiffs decide to exercise the option.

Defendants appeal. They contend that the option provision is too uncertain to be enforced and that extrinsic evidence as to its meaning should not have been admitted. The trial court properly refused to frustrate the obviously declared intention of the grantors to reserve an option to repurchase by an overly meticulous insistence on completeness and clarity of written expression. (See California Lettuce Growers v. Union Sugar Co. (1955) 45 Cal.2d 474, 481, 289 P.2d 785, 49 A.L.R.2d 496; Rivers v. Beadle (1960) 183 Cal.App.2d 691, 695–697, 7 Cal.Rptr. 170.) It properly admitted extrinsic evidence to explain the language of the deed. . . . to the end that the consideration for the option would appear with sufficient certainty to permit specific enforcement. . . . The trial court erred, however, in excluding the extrinsic evidence that the option was personal to the grantors and therefore nonassignable.

Parol ev. should have been included

When the parties to a written contract have agreed to it as an "integration"—a complete and final embodiment of the terms of an agreement—parol evidence cannot be used to add to or vary its terms. . . . When only part of the agreement is integrated, the same rule applies to that part, but parol evidence may be used to prove elements of the agreement not reduced to writing. . . .

California cases have stated that whether there was an integration is to be determined solely from the face of the instrument . . . and that the question for the court is whether it "appears to be a complete . . . agreement. . . ." . . . Neither of these strict formulations of the rule, however, has been consistently applied. The requirement that the writing must appear incomplete on its face has been repudiated in many cases where parol evidence was admitted "to prove the existence of a separate oral agreement as to any matter on which the document is silent and which is not inconsistent with its terms"—even though the instrument appeared to state a complete agreement. . . . Even under the rule that the writing alone is to be consulted, it was found necessary to examine the alleged collateral agreement before concluding that proof of it was precluded by the writing alone. (See 3 Corbin, Contracts (1960) § 582, pp. 444–446.) It is therefore evident that "The conception of a writing as wholly and intrinsically self-determinative of the parties' intent to make it a sole memorial of one or seven or twenty-seven subjects of negotiation is an impossible one." (9 Wigmore, Evidence (3d ed. 1940) § 2431, p. 103.) For example, a promissory note given by a debtor to his creditor may integrate all their present contractual rights and obligations, or it may be only a minor part of an underlying executory contract that would never be discovered by examining the face of the note.

In formulating the rule governing parol evidence, several policies must be accommodated. One policy is based on the assumption that written evidence is more accurate than human memory. . . . This policy, however, can be adequately served by excluding parol evidence of agreements that directly contradict the writing. Another policy is based on the fear that fraud or unintentional invention by witnesses interested in the outcome of the litigation will mislead the finder of facts. . . .

Evidence of oral collateral agreements should be excluded only when the fact finder is likely to be misled. The rule must therefore be based on the credibility of the evidence. One such standard, adopted by section 240(1)(b) of the Restatement [First] of Contracts, permits proof of a collateral agreement if it "is such an agreement as might *naturally* be made as a separate agreement by parties situated as were the parties to the written contract." (Italics added; see McCormick, Evidence (1954) § 216, p. 441; see also 3 Corbin, Contracts (1960) § 583, p. 475, § 594, pp. 568–569; 4 Williston, Contracts (3d ed. 1961) § 638, pp. 1039–1045.) The draftsmen of the Uniform Commercial Code would exclude the evidence in still fewer instances: "If the additional terms are such that if agreed upon, they would *certainly* have been included in the document in the view of the court, then evidence of their alleged making must be kept from the trier of fact." (Com. 3, § 2–202, italics added.)[1]

---

[1] Corbin suggests that, even in situations where the court concludes that it would not have been natural for the parties to make the alleged collateral oral agreement, parol evidence of such

The option clause in the deed in the present case does not explicitly provide that it contains the complete agreement, and the deed is silent on the question of assignability. Moreover, the difficulty of accommodating the formalized structure of a deed to the insertion of collateral agreements makes it less likely that all the terms of such an agreement were included. (See 3 Corbin, Contracts (1960) § 587; 4 Williston, Contracts (3d ed. 1961) § 645; 70 A.L.R. 752, 759 (1931); 68 A.L.R. 245 (1930).) The statement of the reservation of the option might well have been placed in the recorded deed solely to preserve the grantors' rights against any possible future purchasers and this function could well be served without any mention of the parties' agreement that the option was personal. There is nothing in the record to indicate that the parties to this family transaction, through experience in land transactions or otherwise, had any warning of the disadvantages of failing to put the whole agreement in the deed. This case is one, therefore, in which it can be said that a collateral agreement such as that alleged "might naturally be made as a separate agreement." *A fortiori,* the case is not one in which the parties "would certainly" have included the collateral agreement in the deed.

It is contended, however, that an option agreement is ordinarily presumed to be assignable if it contains no provisions forbidding its transfer or indicating that its performance involves elements personal to the parties. (Mott v. Cline (1927) 200 Cal. 434, 450, 253 P. 718; Altman v. Blewett (1928) 93 Cal.App. 516, 525, 269 P. 751.) The fact that there is a written memorandum, however, does not necessarily preclude parol evidence rebutting a term that the law would otherwise presume. In American Industrial Sales Corp. v. Airscope, Inc., supra, 44 Cal.2d 393, 397–398, 282 P.2d 504, we held it proper to admit parol evidence of a contemporaneous collateral agreement as to the place of payment of a note, even though it contradicted the presumption that a note, silent as to the place of payment, is payable where the creditor resides. (For other examples of this approach, see Richter v. Union Land etc. Co. (1900) 129 Cal. 367, 375, 62 P. 39 [presumption of time of delivery rebutted by parol evidence]; Wolters v. King (1897) 119 Cal. 172, 175–176, 51 P. 35 [presumption of time of payment rebutted by parol evidence]; Mangini v. Wolfschmidt, Ltd., supra, 165 Cal.App.2d 192, 198–201, 331 P.2d 728 [presumption of duration of an agency contract rebutted by parol evidence]; Zinn v. Ex-Cell-O Corp. (1957) 148 Cal.App.2d 56, 73–74, 306 P.2d 1017; see also Rest., Contracts, § 240, com. c.)[3] Of course a statute may preclude

an agreement should nevertheless be permitted if the court is convinced that the unnatural actually happened in the case being adjudicated. (3 Corbin, Contracts, § 485, pp. 478, 480; cf. Murray, The Parol Evidence Rule: A Clarification (1966) 4 Duquesne L.Rev. 337, 341–342.) This suggestion may be based on a belief that judges are not likely to be misled by their sympathies. If the court believes that the parties intended a collateral agreement to be effective, there is no reason to keep the evidence from the jury.

[3] Counsel for plaintiffs direct our attention to numerous cases that they contend establish that parol evidence may never be used to show a collateral agreement contrary to a term that the

parol evidence to rebut a statutory presumption. . . . Here, however, there is no such statute. In the absence of a controlling statute the parties may provide that a contract right or duty is nontransferable. . . . Moreover, even when there is no explicit agreement—written *or* oral—that contractual duties shall be personal, courts will effectuate a presumed intent to that effect if the circumstances indicate that performance by substituted person would be different from that contracted for. . . .

In the present case defendants offered evidence that the parties agreed that the option was not assignable in order to keep the property in the Masterson family. The trial court erred in excluding that evidence.

The judgment is reversed.

PETERS, TOBRINER, MOSK, and SULLIVAN, JJ., concur.

Dissenting Opinion

BURKE, JUSTICE.

I dissent. . . .

The opinion permits defendants to establish by parol testimony that their grant to their brother (and brother-in-law) of a written option, absolute in terms, was nevertheless agreed to be nonassignable by the grantee (now a bankrupt), and that therefore the right to exercise it did not pass, by operation of the bankruptcy laws, to the trustee for the benefit of the grantee's creditors.

And how was this to be shown? By the proffered testimony of the bankrupt optionee himself! Thereby one of his assets (the option to purchase defendants' California ranch) would be withheld from the trustee in bankruptcy and from the bankrupt's creditors. Understandably the trial court, as required by the parol evidence rule, did not allow the bankrupt by parol to so contradict the unqualified language of the written option. . . .

[T]he majority assert that 'There is nothing in the record to indicate that the parties to this family transaction, through experience in land transactions or otherwise, had any warning of the disadvantages of failing to put the whole agreement in the deed.' (Italics added.) The facts of this case, however, do not support such claim of naivete. The grantor husband (the bankrupt businessman) testified that as none of the parties were attorneys 'we wanted to contact my attorney * * * which we did. * * * The wording in the option was obtained from (the attorney). * * * I told him what my discussion was with the Sines (defendant grantees) and he wanted * * * a little time to compose it * * *. And, then this (the wording provided by the attorney) was taken to the title company at the time Mr.

law presumes in the absence of an agreement. In each of these cases, however, the decision turned upon the court's belief that the writing was a complete integration and was no more than an application of the rule that parol evidence cannot be used to vary the terms of a completely integrated agreement. . . .

and Mrs. Sine and I went in to complete the transaction.' The witness was an experienced businessman who thus demonstrated awareness of the wisdom of seeking legal guidance and advice in this business transaction, and who did so. Wherein lies the naive family transaction postulated by the majority? . . .

McComb, J., concurs.

Rehearing denied; McComb and Burke, JJ., dissenting.

———

UCC § 2–202

[See Selected Source Materials Supplement]

———

Interform v. Mitchell Constr. Co.

575 F.2d 1270, 1277 (9th Cir. 1978)

(Sneed, J.) ". . . [UCC § 2–202] reflects Corbin's influence. It precludes contradiction of 'confirmatory memoranda' by prior or contemporaneous oral agreements when the writing was 'intended by the parties as a final expression of their agreement' and permits the introduction of consistent additional terms 'unless the court finds the writing to have been *intended* also as a complete and exclusive statement of the terms of the agreement.' (Italics added). The focus plainly is on the intention of the parties, not the integration practices of reasonable persons acting normally and naturally. This is Corbin's focus. Furthermore, [Official Comment 1 rejects] certain rules more applicable to Williston's approach than to Corbin's. . . . "

———

NOTE ON MERGER CLAUSES

Many written contracts contain provisions that state that the written contract is the entire contract between the parties. These provisions are known as "merger" or "integration" clauses because they say, in effect, that all agreements between the parties have been merged or integrated into the writing. Typically these are boilerplate provisions—that is, they are standardized provisions that are routinely inserted by the drafting lawyer into every contract the lawyer writes—even when the principals have not specifically negotiated such a provision—and usually appear at the end of the contract with other standardized provisions, like provisions that set out the addresses to which notices should be sent.

The law on what effect should be given to merger clauses is messy. In some cases they have been given a great deal of weight; in some they have been given little weight; and in some the courts have said that the weight to be given such provisions depends on the circumstances. The muddiness of the case law is reflected in the muddiness of Restatement Second § 216, Comment e:

> e. *Written term excluding oral terms ("merger" clause).* Written agreements often contain clauses stating that there are no representations, promises or agreements between the parties except those found in the writing. Such a clause may negate the apparent authority of an agent to vary orally the written terms, and if agreed to is likely to conclude the issue whether the agreement is completely integrated. Consistent additional terms may then be excluded even though their omission would have been natural in the absence of such a clause. But such a clause does not control the question whether the writing was assented to as an integrated agreement, the scope of the writing if completely integrated, or the interpretation of the written terms.

UNIDROIT PRINCIPLES OF INTERNATIONAL COMMERCIAL CONTRACTS ART. 2.1.17

[See Selected Source Materials Supplement]

SECTION 2. USES OF PAROL EVIDENCE NOT PRECLUDED BY THE RULE

SNYDER V. LOVERCHECK

Supreme Court of Wyoming 1999.
992 P.2d 1079.

TAYLOR, JUSTICE, Retired.

Believing himself to have been shortchanged in the purchase of a wheat farm, appellant filed suit against the sellers, both real estate agents, and his agent's employer. The district court granted summary judgment in favor of all defendants on all of appellant's claims. The district court awarded costs to all defendants, and awarded attorney's fees to the sellers. Finding the district court's disposition on the motions for summary judgment to be correct, we affirm. . .

In the fall of 1995, Snyder began searching for a suitable wheat farm. To facilitate his search, he contacted and employed Hayek, a real estate agent employed by The Property Exchange. Hayek contacted Ron Lovercheck of Bear Mountain Land Company (Ron) and discussed O.W. and Margaret Lovercheck's (the Loverchecks) farm in Goshen County. Hayek, Ron, and Snyder toured the farm on November 5, 1995. The crops were planted but not growing when they toured the farm. Ron did mention that there had been some problems with rye in the past, expressing his belief that the problem was minor. Snyder left the meeting with the understanding that the problem was confined to about 100 of the 1,960 acres.

The following day, Ron, through Hayek, informed Snyder that he had spoken with the former owner of the farm, Ray Headrick (Headrick). Headrick stated that the acreage in question had always produced more wheat than the county average. Headrick also showed Ron the areas where the rye problem was at its worst. Those areas comprised about 100 acres total, and Headrick said that those areas could grow as much as twenty to twenty-five percent rye. Snyder returned to view the property on ten to twelve occasions after the initial tour.

Eventually, Snyder made an offer on the property, and negotiations ensued. On February 16, 1996, Snyder and the Loverchecks entered into a contract for sale of the farm. The contract, drafted by Hayek on Wyoming Real Estate Commission Forms, expressly provided that:

> Purchaser is not relying upon any representations of the Seller or Seller's agents or sub-agents as to any condition which Purchaser deems to be material to Purchaser's decision to purchase this property[.]

This language mirrors the language in a statement of condition of the property completed by the Loverchecks at Snyder's request. The contract also contained an "as is" clause, a merger clause, a liberal inspection clause, and a specific objection procedure. Snyder stated in his deposition that he read parts of the contract, but not the above-quoted language.

The purchase price for the farm was $526,500.00, and the parties closed on May 10, 1996. According to Snyder, when the crops came up the rye problem was not minor, but rather he estimates that there is rye on 1,800 acres, over a third of which was 100% infected. The affidavit of Snyder's expert stated that the extensive rye problem decreased the value of the farm to only $392,000.00.

Snyder filed suit alleging that the Loverchecks breached the contract for sale, that Ron and the Loverchecks negligently and fraudulently misrepresented the extent of the rye problem, that Ron's fraudulent misrepresentations entitled Snyder to punitive damages, and that Hayek and The Property Exchange breached their duty to delete and/or explain the waiver language quoted above. The district court granted summary judgment in favor of all appellees. The district court awarded the Loverchecks $12,811.09 in attorney's fees and $819.90 in costs, and awarded $8,746.12 in costs to Ron. This timely appeal followed. . .

The district court found that neither Ron nor the Loverchecks had breached the contract, and that the punitive damages claim fell with the underlying claims. Snyder makes no argument to this Court that such determinations were erroneous; rather, he relies solely on the contention that the Loverchecks, through Ron, negligently and fraudulently represented to Snyder that the rye problem was minor and manageable. The Loverchecks respond that the disclaimer clause in the contract for sale precludes Snyder from asserting such claims. The district court considered the common elements of both causes of action,[1] and held that Snyder could not assert reliance upon the representations of either Ron or the Loverchecks. We, however, find the two causes of action sufficiently distinguishable to merit independent analysis.

... FRAUDULENT MISREPRESENTATION

The effect of merger and disclaimer clauses on pre-contractual misrepresentations poses significant questions of public policy. There are two prevailing views on the subject. One school of thought focuses on the sanctity of the right to contract, and holds that a party is bound by a specific disclaimer even if the contract was fraudulently obtained. The other school of thought latches on to the age-old proposition that fraud vitiates all contracts, and holds that a party to a contract is not bound by a disclaimer if it was fraudulently obtained. Wyoming subscribes to the latter view.

The Loverchecks ask us to adopt the reasoning of *Danann Realty Corp. v. Harris,* 184 N.Y.S.2d 599, 5 N.Y.2d 317, 157 N.E.2d 597, 598 (1959), where the New York Court of Appeals considered "whether the plaintiff can possibly establish from the facts alleged in the complaint * * * reliance upon the misrepresentations * * *." In *Danann Realty Corp.,* the contract provided:

"The Purchaser has examined the premises agreed to be sold and is familiar with the physical condition thereof. The Seller has not made and does not make any representations as to the physical condition, rents, leases, *expenses, operation* or any other matter or thing affecting or related to the aforesaid premises, except as herein specifically set forth, and the Purchaser hereby *expressly acknowledges that no such representations have been made, and the Purchaser further acknowledges that it has inspected the premises and agrees to take the premises 'as is'* * * *. It is understood and agreed that all understandings and agreements heretofore had between the parties hereto are merged

---

[1] The elements of a negligent misrepresentation claim are: false information supplied in the course of one's business for the guidance of others in their business; failure to exercise reasonable care in obtaining or relating the information; and pecuniary loss resulting from justifiable reliance thereon. *Richey v. Patrick,* 904 P.2d 798, 802 (Wyo.1995); *Duffy v. Brown,* 708 P.2d 433, 437 (Wyo.1985); Restatement of Torts (Second) § 552 at 126–27 (1977).

The elements of a claim for fraud are: "a false representation made by the defendant which is relied upon by the plaintiff to his damage, the asserted false representation must be made to induce action, and the plaintiff must reasonably believe the representation to be true." *Duffy,* 708 P.2d at 437.

in this contract, which alone fully and completely expresses their agreement, *and that the same is entered into after full investigation, neither party relying upon any statement or representation*, not embodied in this contract, made by the other. The Purchaser has inspected the buildings standing on said premises and is thoroughly acquainted with their condition."

Danann Realty Corp., 184 N.Y.S.2d 599, 157 N.E.2d at 598 (emphasis in original). That court recognized a difference between a general merger clause and a specific disclaimer of reliance, noting that general merger clauses do not preclude a claim of fraud in the inducement. The New York Court of Appeals went on to say:

> Here, however, plaintiff has in the plainest language announced and stipulated that it is not relying on any representations as to the very matter as to which it now claims it was defrauded. Such a specific disclaimer destroys the allegations in plaintiff's complaint that the agreement was executed in reliance upon these contrary oral representations * * *.

and,

> If the language here used is not sufficient to estop a party from claiming that he entered the contract because of fraudulent representations, then no language can accomplish that purpose. To hold otherwise would be to say that it is impossible for two businessmen dealing at arm's length to agree that the buyer is not buying in reliance on any representations of the seller as to a particular fact.

Danann Realty Corp., 184 N.Y.S.2d 599, 157 N.E.2d at 599, 600.

Danann Realty Corp. has been followed by other courts, but has been limited in its applicability to situations where the disclaimer is specifically tailored. In *LaFazia v. Howe,* 575 A.2d 182, 186 (R.I.1990), the Supreme Court of Rhode Island applied the reasoning of *Danann Realty Corp.* to a disclaimer specifically denying reliance upon the seller's representations as to the profitability of the business being sold. However, in *Travers v. Spidell,* 682 A.2d 471, 473 (R.I.1996) (per curiam), the court found that a merger-and-disclaimer clause was insufficient to invoke the rule where it did not specifically discuss the location or boundaries of the well in issue. Another path of evolution has been to dilute *Danann Realty Corp.* into a balancing test where the disclaimer is a factor to be considered in determining reliance. *See Flakus v. Schug,* 213 Neb. 491, 329 N.W.2d 859, 863 (1983), *overruled on other grounds sub nom., Nielsen v. Adams,* 223 Neb. 262, 388 N.W.2d 840 (1986).

Although not cited by the parties, we found that this issue is not unprecedented in Wyoming, and we choose to follow our long-established rule. Our decision to do so is not solely based on consideration of the doctrine of stare decisis, but also our finding that the rule in Wyoming more appropriately balances the competing interests of justice and freedom of contract.

In *Baylies v. Vanden Boom,* 40 Wyo. 411, 278 P. 551, 552 (1929), the parties negotiated an exchange of a hotel in Kansas City, Missouri for a ranch in Uinta County. The parties entered into a agreement which provided:

> "In the telegram of acceptance of proposition of the exchange of properties said telegram mentioned certain representations made by Bert L. Cook, Henry J. Vanden Boom, having no way of knowing whether to concur in his agents' representations, said representations are herewith set out, and constitute the only representations made."

Baylies, 278 P. at 553–54. The memorandum went on to list several representations, and was signed by both parties. *Id.* at 554. After taking over management of the hotel, Baylies discovered that several of the representations made to him, and not contained within the agreement, were untrue. *Id.* at 552. Baylies sued to rescind the contract, and Vanden Boom asserted that Baylies was precluded from asserting reliance upon any representations not contained within the memorandum. *Id.* at 551–52.

We considered the rule analogous to *Danann Realty Corp.* that was in use at the time in several jurisdictions, and exemplified by Massachusetts cases.

> "The Massachusetts cases emphasize the desirability of certainty in the contractual relations of those who have made a definite agreement, and if they say that they contract without regard to prior representations and that prior utterances have not been an inducement to their consent, any occasional damage to the individual caused by antecedent fraud is thought to be outweighed by the advantage of certainty and freedom from attacks, which would in the majority of cases be unfounded where such provisions were in the agreement."

Baylies, 278 P. at 555 (*quoting Arnold v. National Aniline & Chemical Co.,* 20 F.2d 364 (2nd Cir.1927)). We found, however, that competing considerations outweighed any interest in certainty. " 'A perpetrator of fraud cannot close the lips of his innocent victim by getting him blindly to agree in advance not to complain against it.' " *Baylies,* 278 P. at 556 (*quoting Webster v. Palm Beach Ocean Realty Co.,* 16 Del.Ch. 15, 139 A. 457 (1927)). We held that Baylies was not precluded from proving that he relied upon the fraudulent misrepresentations notwithstanding the fact that he had signed the memorandum. *Baylies,* 278 P. at 557.

The Massachusetts Supreme Court has subsequently adopted the rule to which we subscribe, and has succinctly stated the policy behind the rule:

> In the realm of fact it is entirely possible for a party knowingly to agree that no representations have been made to him, while at the same time believing and relying upon representations which in fact have been made and in fact are false but for which he would not have made the agreement. To deny this possibility is to ignore the frequent instances in everyday experience where parties accept, often without critical examination, and act upon agreements containing somewhere within their four corners exculpatory clauses in one form or another, but where they do so, nevertheless, in reliance upon the honesty of supposed friends, the plausible and disarming statements of salesmen, or the customary course of business. To refuse relief would result in opening the door to a multitude of frauds and in thwarting the general policy of the law.

Bates v. Southgate, 308 Mass. 170, 31 N.E.2d 551, 558 (1941).

Moreover, such a rule comports with the well-established exceptions to the parol evidence rule. That rule dictates that when the meaning of a contract is unambiguous, extrinsic evidence is not admitted to contradict the plain meaning of the terms used by the parties. *Union Pacific Resources Co. v. Texaco, Inc.,* 882 P.2d 212, 220 (Wyo.1994). We depart from the parol evidence rule only if parol evidence is used to establish a separate and distinct contract, a condition precedent, *fraud*, mistake or repudiation. *Applied Genetics Intern., Inc. v. First Affiliated Securities, Inc.,* 912 F.2d 1238, 1245 (10th Cir.1990); Restatement of Contracts (Second) § 214 (1981).

Therefore, we decline to adopt the reasoning of *Danann Realty Corp.,* and hold that Snyder is not precluded from asserting a claim for fraudulent misrepresentation by either the merger or disclaimer clauses. While the district court's decision on this issue was incorrect, it is well established that a district court judgment may be affirmed on any proper legal grounds supported by the record. *Bird v. Rozier,* 948 P.2d 888, 892 (Wyo.1997).

"A plaintiff who alleges fraud must do so clearly and distinctly, and fraud will not be imputed to any party when the facts and circumstances out of which it is alleged to arise are consistent with honesty and purity of intention." *Duffy v. Brown,* 708 P.2d 433, 437 (Wyo.1985). Fraud must be established by clear and convincing evidence, and will never be presumed. *Id.*

In the present case, Snyder presented no evidence to the district court consistent with fraud. Ron expressed his belief about the extent of the rye problem, and immediately sought a more informed opinion. No accusation has been made that Headrick's appraisal of the rye problem was based on anything other than his observations or was intentionally misleading. No one prevented Snyder from inspecting the land, and, in fact, he visited the land at least ten times before he agreed to the purchase. The facts of this case do not even approach the elevated burden of proof necessary to establish a claim of fraud. Summary judgment was properly granted on this issue. . . .

[The court affirmed summary judgment for the defendants on the negligent misrepresentation claim, adopting a rule that a seller owes no duty of care to a buyer to ensure the accuracy of a representation made by the seller, or to warn the buyer not to rely, when the contract clearly and unambiguously allocates the risk in question to the buyer. The court also affirmed summary judgment for the broker Hayek on Snyder's malpractice claim. The court declined to affirm on the ground pressed by Hayek, which was "that Snyder waived the breach of duty by signing the contract." The opinion observes: "It is inconceivable to this Court that a broker can escape liability for failing to advise his client of the consequences of signing a document by allowing the client to sign the very document that the broker failed to explain . . . [S]uch a rule . . . provides no protection for the unsophisticated and unwary consumer who places his trust in his paid agent." The court instead affirmed on the ground that "the undisputed facts in this case are such that no genuine question of material fact could be raised. Snyder is not the typical first-time home buyer who might benefit from a detailed explanation of all the terms contained in a contract for sale. Snyder fancies himself a sophisticated purchaser... Snyder read the document, and expressed neither concern nor confusion about the language. Hayek was justified in believing that . . . the contract was understandable and acceptable to Snyder."]

. . . Summary judgment was properly granted as to all claims . . . By this decision, the balance of rights between sellers, buyers, and broker is maintained. Buyers may assert claims if they have been defrauded in their purchase; however, simple negligence will not relieve a buyer from a poor bargain. Brokers, entrusted with great responsibility to protect their client's interests, must explain the contracts they present in a manner commensurate with the sophistication of their clients. Accordingly, the judgment of the district court is affirmed on the motions for summary judgment . . .

———

RESTATEMENT, SECOND, CONTRACTS § 214

[See Selected Source Materials Supplement]

———

NOTE ON EXCEPTIONS TO THE PAROL EVIDENCE RULE

The disagreement between Corbin and Williston discussed in the excerpt from Calamari & Perillo, *supra*, was over whether a court should consider all relevant evidence in deciding whether the written contract was intended to be an integration. Williston sided with the majority in *Mitchill v. Lath*; Corbin with the dissent. It is uncontroversial that the rule does not preclude the use of parol evidence for a variety of other purposes, including to establish fraud, mutual misunderstanding, or mistake, to establish a basis for reformation, or for purpose of interpretation. Within each of these bodies of law there are rules that enable judges to screen out dubious claims to protect the integrity of written contracts. Rules on interpretation are considered in Chapter 13.

————

Sisneros v. Citadel Broadcasting Co.

140 N.M. 266, 142 P.3d 34 (N.M. App. 2006)

Plaintiff Sisneros worked as a radio personality for defendant Citadel for over twenty years under a series of employment agreements. The last of these agreements was entered in September 2002. When presented with a draft of this agreement Sisneros demanded and Citadel agreed to eliminate a provision (paragraph 26(h)) requiring arbitration of disputes. Sisneros did not object to another provision (paragraph 22) that required arbitration of disputes "in accordance with, and to the extent provided in, the standard arbitration procedure in the Company's employee handbook." The handbook included a term requiring arbitration of all disputes between an employee and the company. In 2003 Citadel terminated Sisneros without cause. Sisneros filed a lawsuit asserting various claims, including breach of contract and misuse of his name and persona for commercial gain. The trial court granted Citadel's motion to compel arbitration. Reversed.

(Fry, J.) "Plaintiff contends that the parties expressly agreed they would not be compelled to arbitrate their disputes. He claims that even though paragraph 22 of the employment agreement sets forth an agreement to arbitrate, this paragraph does not reflect the understanding of the parties before they entered into the agreement.

"Plaintiff claims the parties agreed that language referring to compulsory arbitration would be removed from the final employment agreement. To support this claim before the district court, Plaintiff submitted two affidavits stating that (1) during negotiations over the employment agreement, Plaintiff objected to the draft agreement's paragraph 26(h), which waived his right to litigate in court any disputes arising out of the agreement, and told Citadel's representatives that compulsory arbitration would be a "deal breaker"; (2) Citadel agreed to remove all language referring to compulsory arbitration; (3) Citadel's representatives provided Plaintiff with a revised employment agreement and told him that the compulsory arbitration requirement had been removed; and (4) based on these representations and his review of paragraph

26(h) of the revised agreement, which no longer required compulsory arbitration, Plaintiff agreed to the revised agreement. Based on these affidavits, Plaintiff argues that the evidence was insufficient that the parties intended to enter into an arbitration agreement or, in the alternative, the contract was ambiguous on the subject. He contends that Citadel misrepresented its agreement to remove the arbitration requirement in order to induce him to sign the contract.

"Citadel counters that paragraph 22 remained part of the final agreement and clearly set forth an agreement to arbitrate according to the standard arbitration procedures in the handbook. Citadel claims that (1) evidence extrinsic to the employment agreement is not admissible to establish any understandings reached before the parties signed the agreement; (2) Plaintiff had a duty to ascertain the contents of what he was signing and cannot now object to the writing that he signed; (3) Plaintiff failed to establish an element of his claim, which is that Citadel intentionally deceived Plaintiff; and (4) even if a misrepresentation induced Plaintiff to sign the agreement, Plaintiff affirmed or ratified the agreement by accepting six months of paychecks after he was terminated, as provided in the agreement. We address each of Citadel's arguments in turn.

"1. Extrinsic Evidence

"Citadel contends that "evidence outside of the 'four corners' of a written contract . . . is *only* admissible at this stage to show the language actually used by the parties in a contract is ambiguous." Therefore, Citadel continues, Plaintiff cannot rely on evidence of what occurred prior to the signing of the agreement in order to support his claim that Citadel misrepresented the substance of the agreement. We do not agree. "Extrinsic evidence is admissible to establish that the [contract] did not express the true agreement of the parties, even if the inconsistency cannot be detected on the face of the [contract] and becomes clear only in light of surrounding circumstances." *Twin Forks Ranch, Inc. v. Brooks,* 120 N.M. 832, 835, 907 P.2d 1013, 1016 (Ct.App.1995). If Citadel's argument were correct, it would be virtually impossible to show mistake or misrepresentation in the contract context.

"2. Duty to Read Before Signing

"It is the general rule that a person has a duty to read a contract and familiarize himself with its contents, *see Ballard v. Chavez,* 117 N.M. 1, 3, 868 P.2d 646, 648 (1994), and Plaintiff does not contend that he had no opportunity to review the final version of the contract prior to signing it. However, this general rule is not absolute. In order to understand the limitations on the general rule, we first review the law regarding misrepresentation in the contract context.

"Misrepresentations by one party as to a writing can make a contract voidable by the other party. *See Restatement* § 164 (describing the circumstances under which a misrepresentation makes a contract voidable). In order for this to occur, the recipient of the misrepresentation must show that

(1) there was a misrepresentation that was (2) material or fraudulent and which (3) induced the recipient to enter into the agreement, and that (4) the recipient's reliance on the misrepresentation was justified. *See Robison v. Katz,* 94 N.M. 314, 319, 610 P.2d 201, 206 (Ct.App.1980) (stating that rescission of a contract "should be granted a party who, in entering a contract, justifiably relied on a misrepresentation of a material fact"); *Restatement* ch. 7 at 425 (listing similar elements to support voiding a contract). Citadel's argument regarding Plaintiff's duty to read the agreement involves the first and third elements—whether there was a misrepresentation and if so, whether Plaintiff justifiably relied on it.

"A misrepresentation is an assertion that is not in accord with the facts." *Id.* at 424. A misrepresentation includes the situation where one party knows that the other party is mistaken as to the content of a writing and yet fails to correct this mistake. *Id.* § 161 cmt. E. (stating that a party is expected to correct the mistaken understanding of the other party as to the contents of a writing); *Chromo Mountain Ranch P'ship v. Gonzales,* 101 N.M. 298, 299, 681 P.2d 724, 725 (1984); *see also* I E. Allan Farnsworth, *Farnsworth on Contracts* § 4.11 (3d ed.2004) (explaining that a misrepresentation can include a false representation "as to the contents or legal effect of a writing that is to evidence or embody the contract"). Plaintiff's affidavits about the pre-contract negotiations reasonably give rise to an inference that Citadel knew Plaintiff was unwilling to agree to compulsory arbitration and told Plaintiff the employment agreement had been changed to remove the arbitration provision even though the stated change had not been made. It is for the fact finder to determine whether to accept or reject this inference after considering all the evidence.

"As for whether Plaintiff was justified in relying on Citadel's statements, a contract may be voidable even when a party fails to use care in reading the writing and thus does not discover the mistake, depending on the circumstances. *Restatement* § 161 cmt. E; *see also Godfrey, Bassett & Kuykendall Architects, Ltd. V. Huntington Lumber & Supply Co.,* 584 So.2d 1254, 1259 (Miss.1991) (stating that "[w]here one party's false representations induce another party to contract, negligence of the second party cannot be raised to bar relief to him"). "A recipient's fault in not knowing or discovering the facts before making the contract does not make his reliance unjustified unless it amounts to a failure to act in good faith and in accordance with reasonable standards of fair dealing." *Restatement* § 172. Our Supreme Court, in a case involving mutual mistake, recognized this notion that failure to read a writing does not necessarily bar a contracting party from a remedy. *Ballard,* 117 N.M. at 3, 868 P.2d at 648 ("[A] mutual mistake . . . can be subject to reformation . . . despite the fact that each party to a contract has a duty to read and familiarize himself with the contents of the contract.").

"The *Restatement's* discussion of misrepresentation and fault contains an illustration closely tracking Plaintiff's allegations:

A and B reach an understanding that they will execute a written contract containing terms on which they have agreed. A prepares a writing containing essential terms different from those agreed upon and induces B to sign it by telling him that it contains the agreed terms and that it is not necessary for him to read it. [B's] . . . reliance is justified since his fault does not amount to a failure to act in good faith . . . [or] fair dealing. The contract is voidable by B. In the alternative he may have the writing reformed.

"§ 172 cmt. a, illus. 1. The evaluation of fault and the recipient's failure to discover a mistake in the writing is fact-specific and includes consideration of the conduct of both parties. The inquiry includes a consideration of the recipient's "peculiar qualities and characteristics" and whether he knew the representation was false. *Id.* § 172 cmt. b.

"Thus, contrary to Citadel's argument, the existence of Plaintiff's duty to read the agreement before signing it does not end the inquiry. Plaintiff has produced evidence giving rise to factual inferences that could reasonably support the determination that his failure to read the agreement was justified by Citadel's conduct. It was improper for the district court to resolve these factual issues by entering summary judgment.

"3. Intentional Fraud

"Citadel argues that Plaintiff must prove that Citadel intentionally deceived Plaintiff to survive summary judgment. We are not persuaded. As we have already noted, Plaintiff does not appear to claim that Citadel's misrepresentations were fraudulent. In addition, our case law makes it clear that a misrepresentation can result in the voiding or rescission of a contract "irrespective of the good or bad faith of the party making the misrepresentation." *Robison,* 94 N.M. at 319, 610 P.2d at 206; *see also Maxey v. Quintana,* 84 N.M. 38, 41, 499 P.2d 356, 359 (Ct.App.1972) ("Rescission may be effected without regard to the good faith with which a misrepresentation is made."). The *Restatement* explains that the recipient of a misrepresentation may void the contract regardless of whether the misrepresentation was intentionally made to mislead. *See* § 164(1) (stating that a contract is voidable "[i]f a party's manifestation of assent is induced by *either a fraudulent or a material misrepresentation* by the other party upon which the recipient is justified in relying" (emphasis added)); § 162 cmt. a (explaining that a fraudulent misrepresentation "must not only be consciously false but must also be intended to mislead another"). However, if a misrepresentation is non-fraudulent, the recipient is entitled to void the contract only if the misrepresentation is material. *Id.* cmt. c. Thus, the question for the fact finder in the present case, assuming Citadel made a misrepresentation, is whether the misrepresentation was material, not whether it was intentional."

NOTE ON THE AVAILABILITY OF EQUITABLE RELIEF FOR A MISTAKE REGARDING THE CONTENT OF A WRITING

During the heyday of classical contract law equity was a separate body of law. Rules in equity operated as a safety valve to prevent a person from exploiting another person's mistake regarding the content of a writing. The rule on misrepresentation applied in *Sisneros* comes from equity. The fraud exception to the duty to read rule mentioned in *Morales*, supra Chapter 8, also comes from equity. Chapter 17 covers rules on reformation and unilateral mistake that allow a party to correct an error regarding the content of the writing, if the other party knew or had reason to know of the error. These rules also come from equity.

CHAPTER 13

THE INTERPRETATION OF WRITTEN CONTRACTS

■ ■ ■

Section 1 concerns a significant point of difference between classical contract law and modern contract law. The difference involves the interpretation of a contractual writing. Classical contract law started from the premise that when parties "integrate their agreement they . . . have assented to the writing as the expression of the things to which they agree, therefore the terms of the writing are conclusive, and a contract may have a meaning different from that which either party supposed it to have." Restatement, First, Contracts § 230, comment *b*. Modern contract law starts from the premise that a court's goal in interpreting a writing is to determine the parties' actual intent. Under classical contract law, a court did not consider many types of extrinsic evidence bearing on the parties actual intent unless a writing was ambiguous on its face. Under modern contract law, a court will consider all relevant evidence bearing on parties' actual intent even if a writing seems unambiguous on its face.

Section 2 concerns the use of evidence of usage, course of dealing, and course of performance for purposes both of interpretation of a writing and of implying terms. Section 3 concerns implication more generally and its relationship to purposive interpretation. Section 4 concerns the obligation to perform in good faith.

———

SECTION 1. TEXTUALISM V. CONTEXTUALISM

INTRODUCTORY NOTE

The parol evidence rule does not preclude the use of extrinsic evidence (that is, evidence that is outside the four corners of a written agreement) for the purpose of *interpreting* a written agreement. However, classical contract law used another rule, the plain meaning (or four corners) rule to limit the use of many types of extrinsic evidence in interpreting written agreements. Some courts continue to adhere to the plain meaning rule. Other courts have abandoned the rule and adopted a rule that instructs a judge to give effect to the parties intent, and to consider all relevant evidence of what the parties' intended.

There are substantive differences between the parol evidence rule and the plain meaning rule, because the two rules preclude the use of different types of evidence. The parol evidence rule precludes evidence of certain prior or contemporaneous separate agreements. The plain meaning rule precludes many other types of extrinsic evidence when a writing is deemed unambiguous. This category is broader than prior or contemporaneous separate agreements. For example, evidence of course of performance is never precluded by the parol evidence rule but is likely to be precluded by the plain meaning rule.

Holmes, The Theory of Legal Interpretation

12 Harv.L.Rev. 417 (1899)

"I do not suppose that you could prove, for purposes of construction as distinguished from avoidance, an oral declaration or even an agreement that words in a dispositive instrument making sense as they stand should have a different meaning from the common one; for instance, that the parties to a contract orally agreed that when they wrote five hundred feet it should mean one hundred inches, or that Bunker Hill Monument should signify Old South Church."

Williston on Contracts

3d ed., § 95

"It is even conceivable that a contract may be formed which is in accordance with the intention of neither party. If a written contract is entered into, the meaning and effect of the contract depends on the interpretation given the written language by the court. The court will give that language its natural and appropriate meaning; and, if the words are unambiguous, will not even admit evidence of what the parties may have thought the meaning to be."

Restatement, First, Contracts § 231

Illustration 2: "A and B are engaged in buying and selling shares of stock from one another and agree orally for the purpose of concealing the nature of their dealings that in transactions between them the word 'buy' shall be used to mean 'sell,' and that the word 'sell' shall be used to mean 'buy.' A sends a written offer to B to 'sell' certain shares of stock. B, having in mind the oral agreement, accepts the offer and tenders the shares to A. On A's refusal to accept the tender, B brings an action against him. B cannot recover, unless reformation is had of the writings. The private oral agreement cannot make 'buy' mean 'sell,' though a private agreement may give to a word which has no inconsistent meaning, a meaning in accordance with the agreement."

———

Corbin on Contracts

Supp. § 572b (1971)

"No contract should ever be interpreted and enforced with a meaning that neither party gave it."

———

Restatement, Second, Contracts § 212

Illustration 4: "A and B are engaged in buying and selling shares of stock from each other, and agree orally to conceal the nature of their dealings by using the word 'sell' to mean 'buy' and using the word 'buy' to mean 'sell.' A sends a written offer to B to 'sell' certain shares, and B accepts. The parties are bound in accordance with the oral agreement."

———

STEUART V. MCCHESNEY
Supreme Court of Pennsylvania, 1982.
498 Pa. 45, 444 A.2d 659.

Before O'BRIEN, C.J., and ROBERTS, NIX, LARSEN, FLAHERTY, MCDERMOTT and HUTCHINSON, JJ.

OPINION OF THE COURT

FLAHERTY, JUSTICE.

This is an appeal from an Order of the Superior Court which reversed a Decree of the Court of Common Pleas of the Thirty-Seventh Judicial District construing a Right of First Refusal affecting the sale of certain real property.

On June 8, 1968, the appellant, Lepha I. Steuart, and her husband, James A. Steuart (now deceased), executed an agreement granting to the appellees, William C. McChesney and Joyce C. McChesney, husband and wife, a Right of First Refusal on a parcel of improved farmland. The agreement provided:

(a) During the lifetime of said Steuarts, should said Steuarts obtain a Bona Fide Purchaser for Value, the said McChesneys may exercise their right to purchase said premises at a value equivalent to the market value of the premises according to the assessment rolls as maintained by the County of Warren and Commonwealth of Pennsylvania for the levying and assessing of real estate taxes; provided, however, that the date of valuation shall be that upon which the said Steuarts notify said McChesneys, in writing, of the existence of a Bona Fide Purchaser.

On July 6, 1977, the subject property was appraised by a real estate broker at a market value of $50,000. Subsequently, on October 10, 1977 and October 13, 1977 respectively, appellant received bona fide offers of $35,000 and $30,000 for the land. Upon receiving notice of these offers, the appellees sought to exercise their right to purchase the property by tendering $7,820. This amount was exactly twice the assessed value of the property as listed on the tax rolls maintained in Warren County, it being the practice in that County to value real estate for tax assessment purposes at 50% of market value. The tender was refused, however, by appellant, who then commenced an action in equity seeking to cancel the Right of First Refusal, or, in the alternative, to have the agreement construed as requiring that the exercise price be that of a bona fide third party offer or fair market value as determined independently of assessed value. Appellees, requesting a conveyance of the subject premises for $7,820, sought specific performance.

The primary issue on appeal concerns the price at which the Right of First Refusal may be exercised. The Court of Common Pleas, after hearing testimony, held that the formula of twice the assessed value was intended to serve as "a mutual protective minimum price for the premises rather than to be the controlling price without regard to a market third party offer." The agreement was, therefore, construed as granting appellees a preemptive right to purchase the land for $35,000, the amount of the first bona fide offer received. The Superior Court reversed, holding that the plain language of the agreement required that assessed market value, alone, determine the exercise price. We agree.

It is well established that the intent of the parties to a written contract is to be regarded as being embodied in the writing itself, and when the words are clear and unambiguous the intent is to be discovered only from the express language of the agreement. *Estate of Breyer,* 475 Pa. 108, 379 A.2d 1305 (1977); *Felte v. White,* 451 Pa. 137, 302 A.2d 347 (1973). . . . As this Court stated in *East Crossroads Center, Inc. v. Mellon-Stuart Co.,* 416 Pa. at 230–231, 205 A.2d at 866, "[w]hen a written contract is clear and unequivocal, its meaning must be determined by its contents alone. It speaks for itself and a meaning cannot be given to it other than that expressed. Where the intention of the parties is clear, there is no need to resort to extrinsic aids or evidence." Hence, where language is clear and unambiguous, the focus of interpretation is upon the terms of the agreement as *manifestly expressed,* rather than as, perhaps, silently intended.

Application of the plain meaning rule of interpretation has, however, been subjected to criticism as being unsound in theory. "The fallacy consists in assuming that there is or ever can be *some one real* or absolute meaning." 9 Wigmore, *Evidence* § 2462 (Chadbourn rev. 1981). "[S]ome of the surrounding circumstances always must be known before the meaning of the words can be plain and clear; and proof of the circumstances may make a meaning plain and clear when in the absence of such proof some other meaning may also have seemed plain and clear." 3 Corbin, *Contracts* § 542 (1960). "It is indeed desirable that it be made as difficult as is reasonably feasible for an unscrupulous person to establish a meaning that was foreign to what was in fact understood by the parties to the contract. However, this result can be achieved without the aid of an inflexible rule." Murray, *Contracts,* § 110 (1974).

While adhering to the plain meaning rule of construction, this Court, too, has cautioned:

> We are not unmindful of the dangers of focusing only upon the words of the writing in interpreting an agreement. A court must be careful not to "retire into that lawyer's Paradise where all words have a fixed, precisely ascertained meaning; where men may express their purposes, not only with accuracy, but with fullness; and where, if the writer has been careful, a lawyer, having a document referred to him, may sit in his chair inspect the text, and answer all questions without raising his eyes." Thayer, Preliminary Treatise on Evidence 428, quoted in 3 Corbin on Contracts § 535 n. 16 (1960).

Estate of Breyer, 475 Pa. at 115, 379 A.2d at 1309 n. 5 (1977). Indeed, whether the language of an agreement is clear and unambiguous may not be apparent without cognizance of the context in which the agreement arose:

> The flexibility of or multiplicity in the meaning of words is the principal source of difficulty in the interpretation of language. Words are the conduits by which thoughts are communicated, yet scarcely any of them have such a fixed and single meaning that they are incapable of denoting more than one thought. In addition to the multiplicity in meaning of words set forth in the dictionaries there are the meanings imparted to them by trade customs, local uses, dialects, telegraphic codes, etc. One meaning crowds a word full of significance, while another almost empties the utterance of any import.

Hurst v. Lake & Co., Inc., 141 Or. 306, 310, 16 P.2d 627, 629 (1932), quoted in 4 Williston, *Contracts* § 609 (3d ed. 1961).

Nevertheless, the rationale for interpreting contractual terms in accord with the plain meaning of the language expressed is multifarious, resting in part upon what is viewed as the appropriate role of the courts in the interpretive process: "[T]his Court long ago emphasized that '[t]he parties [have] the right to make their own contract, and it is not the function of this Court to re-write it, or to give it a construction in conflict with . . . the accepted and plain meaning of the language used.' *Hagarty v. William Akers, Jr. Co.,* 342 Pa. 236, 20 A.2d 317 (1941)." *Felte v. White,* 451 Pa. at 144, 302 A.2d at 351. " 'It is not the province of the court to alter a contract by construction or to make a new contract for the parties; its duty is confined to the interpretation of the one which they have made for themselves, without regard to its wisdom or folly.' [13 C.J. § 485, p. 524]" *Moore v. Stevens Coal Co.,* 315 Pa. 564, 568, 173 A. 661, 662 (1934).

In addition to justifications focusing upon the appropriate role of the courts in the interpretive process, the plain meaning approach to construction has been supported as generally best serving the ascertainment of the contracting parties' mutual intent. "When the parties have reduced their agreement to writing, the writing is to be taken to be the final expression of their intention." 17A C.J.S. *Contracts* § 296(2). "Where the contract evidences care in its preparation, it will be presumed that its words were employed deliberately and with intention." 17A C.J.S. *Contracts* § 296(2). "In determining what the parties intended by their contract, the law must look to what they clearly expressed. Courts in interpreting a contract do not assume that its language was chosen carelessly." *Moore v. Stevens Coal Co.,* 315 Pa. at 568, 173 A. at 662. Neither can it be assumed that the parties were ignorant of the meaning of the language employed. *See Fogel Refrigerator Co. v. Oteri,* 391 Pa. 188, 137 A.2d 225, 231 (1958).

Accordingly, the plain meaning approach enhances the extent to which contracts may be relied upon by contributing to the security of belief that the final expression of *consensus ad idem* will not later be construed to import a meaning other than that clearly expressed. *Cf.* McCormick, *The Parol Evidence Rule as a Procedural Device for Control of the Jury,* 41 Yale L.J. 365, 365–366 (1932). Likewise, resort to the plain meaning of language hinders parties dissatisfied with their agreement from creating a myth as to the true meaning of the agreement through subsequently exposed extrinsic evidence. Absent the plain meaning rule, nary an agreement could be conceived, which, in the event of a party's later disappointment with his stated bargain, would not be at risk to having its true meaning obfuscated under the guise of examining extrinsic evidence of intent. Even if the dissatisfied party in good faith believed that the agreement, as manifest, did not express the *consensus ad idem,* his post hoc judgment would be inclined to be colored by belief as to what should have been, rather than what strictly was, intended. Hence, the plain meaning approach to interpretation rests upon policies soundly based, and the judiciousness of that approach warrants reaffirmation.

In the instant case, the language of the Right of First Refusal, viewed in context, is express and clear and is, therefore, not in need of interpretation by reference to extrinsic evidence. The plain meaning of the agreement in question is that if, during the lifetime of the appellant, a bona fide purchaser for value should be obtained, the appellees may purchase the property "at a value equivalent to the market value of the premises according to the assessment rolls as maintained by the County of Warren and Commonwealth of Pennsylvania for the levying and assessing of real estate taxes." Indeed, a more clear and unambiguous expression of the Right of First Refusal's exercise price would be onerous to conceive. By conditioning exercise of the Right of First Refusal upon occurrence of the triggering event of there being obtained a bona fide offer, protection was afforded against a sham offer, made not in good faith, precipitating exercise of the preemptive right. The clear language of the agreement, however, in no manner links determination of the exercise price to the magnitude of the bona fide offer received through that triggering mechanism.

Were the present agreement to be regarded as ambiguous, so as to enable a court to consider extrinsic evidence of the meaning intended, as was done in the Court of Common Pleas, the policy of resorting to extrinsic evidence only when confronted with unclear or ambiguous language would be enervated. Certainly, the words of the Right of First Refusal are not indefinite, doubtful, or uncertain in their signification, so as to be regarded as unclear. Nor is the language reasonably or fairly susceptible to being understood in more than one sense so as to be regarded as ambiguous. "A patent ambiguity is that which appears on the face of the instrument, and arises from the defective, obscure, or insensible language used." *Black's Law Dictionary* 105 (rev. 4th ed. 1968). In contrast, a latent ambiguity arises from extraneous or collateral facts which make the meaning of a written agreement uncertain although the language thereof, on its face, appears clear and unambiguous. *Easton v. Washington County Insurance Co.,* 391 Pa. 28, 137 A.2d 332 (1957). "The usual instance of a latent ambiguity is one in which a writing refers to a particular person or thing and is thus apparently clear on its face, but upon application to external objects is found to fit two or more of them equally." *Id.* at 35, 137 A.2d at 336. In holding that an ambiguity is present in an agreement, a court must not rely upon a strained contrivancy to establish one; scarcely an agreement could be conceived that might not be unreasonably contrived into the appearance of ambiguity. Thus, the meaning of language cannot be distorted to establish the ambiguity. *Anstead v. Cook,* 291 Pa. 335, 337, 140 A. 139, 140 (1927). The instant agreement, not being reasonably susceptible to being understood in more than one sense, whether by patent or latent ambiguity, does not present language in need of extrinsic clarification.

By construing the clause in question to merely signify that the exercise price be, *in effect, "not less than"* the market value of the premises according to the assessment rolls, the Court of Common Pleas ignored the clearly expressed intent that the exercise price be "*equivalent* to the market value of the premises according to the assessment rolls." To no extent is the term "equivalent", meaning "equal",[3] interchangeable with "not less than", and, since the parties specified the former, they shall be deemed to have intended the same. Hence, any divergence between the exercise price and the bona fide offer cannot be eliminated by construction where no ambiguity exists. Nor is there freedom, under the guise of construction, to redraft the Right of First Refusal simply because of the realization, at the time when rights under the agreement are to be exercised, that the market price according to the assessment rolls falls substantially short of the bona fide offers received.

Appellant contends that, based upon equitable considerations, specific performance at the assessed market value of $7,820 should be denied; in particular, the divergence between assessed market value and the amount of the bona fide offers assertedly renders an award of specific performance inequitable. As this Court has established, however, " '[i]nadequacy of consideration is not ground for refusing to decree specific performance of a contract to convey real estate, unless there is evidence of fraud or unfairness in the transaction sufficient to make it inequitable to compel performance . . .' *Welsh v. Ford,* 282 Pa. 96, 99, 127 A. 431, 432 (1925). . . . " . . . . Appellant alleges that an attorney employed solely by the appellees drafted the Right of First Refusal agreement, and that she was unfairly induced to enter the agreement without representation of her interests. This position ignores, however, an express finding of fact by the Court of Common Pleas, amply supported by testimony of record, that at the time of the preliminary negotiation and drafting of the agreement the parties were all represented by the same attorney. Hence, appellant's assertion is without merit.

Order affirmed.

ROBERTS, J., files a dissenting opinion in which LARSEN, J., joins.

ROBERTS, JUSTICE, dissenting.

I dissent. Although the contract at issue mandates that appellees may purchase appellant's property at "the market value of the premises according to the assessment rolls as maintained by the County of Warren

---

[3] "Equivalent carries with it the idea of value in some way (Latin *aequus,* equal, plus *valere,* to be strong or valuable). When something adds up to something else in value or worth or significance or importance, the two are said to be equivalent the one to the other; when two or more things are exactly the same they are properly said to be equal. *Equal* is the simpler term, and applies to simpler considerations." J.B. Opdycke, *Mark My Words,* at 568–569 (1940).

. . .," it is by no means clear that $7,820 is the price which appellees should pay.

The omission from the contract of a specific future purchase price was intentional because, according to the draftsman, the parties "wanted to reflect either increase or decrease of the assessed value as of [the] time" of appellees' exercise of the option to buy. To assure the accuracy and currency of this "reflection" of the change in assessed value, the parties provided that "the date of valuation shall be that upon which the said Steuarts notify said McChesneys, in writing, of the existence of a Bona Fide purchaser."

Written notice of appellant's receipt of an offer for the property was delivered to appellees on or about October 25, 1977. At that time, the assessed value of the property, as recorded on the tax rolls of Warren County, was $3,910, or 50% of the "market value" of $7,820. However, from the testimony of the draftsman, it would appear that the property had not been reassessed since 1972, when the assessed value was increased by only $405.

Section 602 of the Fourth to Eighth Class County Assessment Law provides:

> "It shall be the duty of the chief assessor to assess, rate and value all subjects and objects of local taxation . . . according to the actual value thereof. . . . [R]eal property shall be assessed at a value based upon an established predetermined ratio . . . not exceeding seventy-five per centum (75%) of its actual value or the price for which the same would separately bona fide sell. . . ."

72 P.S. § 5453.602(a) (1964). As this Court stated in *Brooks Building Tax Assessment Case,* 391 Pa. 94, 97, 137 A.2d 273, 274 (1958),

> "[t]he term 'actual value' means 'market value' [citing cases]. And market value has been defined as the price which a purchaser, willing but not obliged to buy, would pay an owner, willing but not obliged to sell, taking into consideration all uses to which the property is adapted and might in reason be applied."

Accord, *Buhl Foundation v. Board of Property Assessment,* 407 Pa. 567, 570, 180 A.2d 900, 902 (1962).

Here, where appellant received bona fide offers of $30,000, $35,000, and $50,000 for her property, there can be no doubt that the actual value of appellant's property in 1977 was at least four times greater than the value according to the outdated assessment on the Warren County tax rolls. It is the height of unfairness to grant appellees' requested decree for specific performance at a price based on a valuation which took place in 1972. In effect, appellees are receiving a substantial windfall simply because Warren County has apparently failed to maintain accurate assessments "according to the actual value" of appellant's property, as required by law.

In these circumstances, I would remand this case to the Court of Common Pleas of Warren County for a determination of what the proper assessed value of appellant's property would have been on October 25, 1977, the "date of valuation," with directions to enter a decree of specific performance in favor of appellees at a "market value" based upon that determination.

LARSEN, J., joins in this dissenting opinion.

———

PACIFIC GAS & ELECTRIC CO. v. G.W. THOMAS DRAYAGE & RIGGING CO.

Supreme Court of California, 1968.
69 Cal.2d 33, 69 Cal.Rptr. 561, 442 P.2d 641.

TRAYNOR, CHIEF JUSTICE. Defendant appeals from a judgment for plaintiff in an action for damages for injury to property under an indemnity clause of a contract.

In 1960 defendant entered into a contract with plaintiff to furnish the labor and equipment necessary to remove and replace the upper metal cover of plaintiff's steam turbine. Defendant agreed to perform the work "at [its] own risk and expense" and to "indemnify" plaintiff "against all loss, damage, expense and liability resulting from . . . injury to property, arising out of or in any way connected with the performance of this contract." Defendant also agreed to procure not less than $50,000 insurance to cover liability for injury to property. Plaintiff was to be an additional named insured, but the policy was to contain a cross-liability clause extending the coverage to plaintiff's property.

During the work the cover fell and injured the exposed rotor of the turbine. Plaintiff brought this action to recover $25,144.51, the amount it subsequently spent on repairs. During the trial it dismissed a count based on negligence and thereafter secured judgment on the theory that the indemnity provision covered injury to all property regardless of ownership.

Defendant offered to prove by admissions of plaintiff's agents, by defendant's conduct under similar contracts entered into with plaintiff, and by other proof that in the indemnity clause the parties meant to cover injury to property of third parties only and not to plaintiff's property.[1] Although the trial court observed that the language used was "the classic

---

[1] Although this offer of proof might ordinarily be regarded as too general to provide a ground for appeal . . . since the court repeatedly ruled that it would not admit extrinsic evidence to interpret the contract and sustained objections to all questions seeking to elicit such evidence, no formal offer of proof was required. . . .

language for a third party indemnity provision" and that "one could very easily conclude that . . . its whole intendment is to indemnify third parties," it nevertheless held that the "plain language" of the agreement also required defendant to indemnify plaintiff for injuries to plaintiff's property. Having determined that the contract had a plain meaning, the court refused to admit any extrinsic evidence that would contradict its interpretation.

When a court interprets a contract on this basis, it determines the meaning of the instrument in accordance with the " . . . extrinsic evidence of the judge's own linguistic education and experience." (3 Corbin on Contracts (1960 ed.) [1964 Supp. § 579, p. 225, fn. 56].) The exclusion of testimony that might contradict the linguistic background of the judge reflects a judicial belief in the possibility of perfect verbal expression. (9 Wigmore on Evidence (3d ed. 1940) § 2461, p. 187.) This belief is a remnant of a primitive faith in the inherent potency and inherent meaning of words.

The test of admissibility of extrinsic evidence to explain the meaning of a written instrument is not whether it appears to the court to be plain and unambiguous on its face, but whether the offered evidence is relevant to prove a meaning to which the language of the instrument is reasonably susceptible. . . .

A rule that would limit the determination of the meaning of a written instrument to its four-corners merely because it seems to the court to be clear and unambiguous, would either deny the relevance of the intention of the parties or presuppose a degree of verbal precision and stability our language has not attained.

Some courts have expressed the opinion that contractual obligations are created by the mere use of certain words, whether or not there was any intention to incur such obligations.[4] Under this view, contractual obligations flow, not from the intention of the parties but from the fact that they used certain magic words. Evidence of the parties' intention therefore becomes irrelevant.

In this state, however, the intention of the parties as expressed in the contract is the source of contractual rights and duties.[5] A court must ascertain and give effect to this intention by determining what the parties meant by the words they used. Accordingly, the exclusion of relevant, extrinsic evidence to explain the meaning of a written instrument could be

---

[4]   "A contract has, strictly speaking, nothing to do with the personal, or individual, intent of the parties. A contract is an obligation attached by the mere force of law to certain acts of the parties, usually words, which ordinarily accompany and represent a known intent." (Hotchkiss v. National City Bank of New York (S.D.N.Y.1911) 200 F. 287, 293. . . .)

[5]   "A contract must be so interpreted as to give effect to the mutual intention of the parties as it existed at the time of contracting, so far as the same is ascertainable and lawful." (Civ.Code, § 1636 . . .)

justified only if it were feasible to determine the meaning the parties gave to the words from the instrument alone.

If words had absolute and constant referents, it might be possible to discover contractual intention in the words themselves and in the manner in which they were arranged. Words, however, do not have absolute and constant referents. "A word is a symbol of thought but has no arbitrary and fixed meaning like a symbol of algebra or chemistry,. . . . " (Pearson v. State Social Welfare Board (1960) 54 Cal.2d 184, 195, 5 Cal.Rptr. 553, 559, 353 P.2d 33, 39.) The meaning of particular words or groups of words varies with the " . . . verbal context and surrounding circumstances and purposes in view of the linguistic education and experience of their users and their hearers or readers (not excluding judges). . . . A word has no meaning apart from these factors; much less does it have an objective meaning, one true meaning." (Corbin, The Interpretation of Words and the Parol Evidence Rule (1965) 50 Cornell L.Q. 161, 187.) Accordingly, the meaning of a writing " . . . can only be found by interpretation in the light of all the circumstances that reveal the sense in which the writer used the words. The exclusion of parol evidence regarding such circumstances merely because the words do not appear ambiguous to the reader can easily lead to the attribution to a written instrument of a meaning that was never intended. [Citations omitted.]" (Universal Sales Corp. v. Cal. Press Mfg. Co., supra, 20 Cal.2d 751, 776, 128 P.2d 665, 679 (concurring opinion); see also, e.g., Garden State Plaza Corp. v. S.S. Kresge Co. (1963) 78 N.J.Super. 485, 189 A.2d 448, 454. . . .

Although extrinsic evidence is not admissible to add to, detract from, or vary the terms of a written contract, these terms must first be determined before it can be decided whether or not extrinsic evidence is being offered for a prohibited purpose. The fact that the terms of an instrument appear clear to a judge does not preclude the possibility that the parties chose the language of the instrument to express different terms. That possibility is not limited to contracts whose terms have acquired a particular meaning by trade usage, but exists whenever the parties' understanding of the words used may have differed from the judge's understanding.

Accordingly, rational interpretation requires at least a preliminary consideration of all credible evidence offered to prove the intention of the parties.[7] (Civ.Code, § 1647; Code Civ.Proc. § 1860; see also 9 Wigmore on Evidence, op. cit. supra, § 2470, fn. 11, p. 227.) Such evidence includes

---

[7]   When objection is made to any particular item of evidence offered to prove the intention of the parties, the trial court may not yet be in a position to determine whether in the light of all of the offered evidence, the item objected to will turn out to be admissible as tending to prove a meaning of which the language of the instrument is reasonably susceptible or inadmissible as tending to prove a meaning of which the language is not reasonably susceptible. In such case the court may admit the evidence conditionally by either reserving its ruling on the objection or by admitting the evidence subject to a motion to strike. (See Evid.Code, § 403.)

testimony as to the "circumstances surrounding the making of the agreement . . . including the object, nature and subject matter of the writing . . . " so that the court can "place itself in the same situation in which the parties found themselves at the time of contracting." (Universal Sales Corp. v. Cal. Press Mfg. Co., supra, 20 Cal.2d 751, 761, 128 P.2d 665, 671; Lemm v. Stillwater Land & Cattle Co., supra, 217 Cal. 474, 480–481, 19 P.2d 785.) If the court decides, after considering this evidence, that the language of a contract, in the light of all the circumstances, is "fairly susceptible of either one of the two interpretations contended for. . . . " . . . extrinsic evidence relevant to prove either of such meanings is admissible.[8]

In the present case the court erroneously refused to consider extrinsic evidence offered to show that the indemnity clause in the contract was not intended to cover injuries to plaintiff's property. Although that evidence was not necessary to show that the indemnity clause was reasonably susceptible of the meaning contended for by defendant, it was nevertheless relevant and admissible on that issue. Moreover, since that clause was reasonably susceptible of that meaning, the offered evidence was also admissible to prove that the clause had that meaning and did not cover injuries to plaintiff's property.[9] Accordingly, the judgment must be reversed. . . .

---

[8]   Extrinsic evidence has often been admitted in such cases on the stated ground that the contract was ambiguous (e.g., Universal Sales Corp. v. Cal. Press Mfg. Co., supra, 20 Cal.2d 751, 761, 128 P.2d 665). This statement of the rule is harmless if it is kept in mind that the ambiguity may be exposed by extrinsic evidence that reveals more than one possible meaning.

[9]   The court's exclusion of extrinsic evidence in this case would be error even under a rule that excluded such evidence when the instrument appeared to the court to be clear and unambiguous on its face. The controversy centers on the meaning of the word "indemnify" and the phrase "all loss, damage, expense and liability." The trial court's recognition of the language as typical of a third party indemnity clause and the double sense in which the word "indemnify" is used in statutes and defined in dictionaries demonstrate the existence of an ambiguity. (Compare Civ.Code, § 2772, "Indemnity is a contract by which one engages to save another from a legal consequence of the conduct of one of the parties, or of some other person," with Civ.Code, § 2527, "Insurance is a contract whereby one undertakes to indemnify another against loss, damage, or liability, arising from an unknown or contingent event." Black's Law Dictionary (4th ed. 1951) defines "indemnity" as "A collateral contract or assurance, by which one person engages to secure another against an anticipated loss or to prevent him from being damnified by the legal consequences of an act or forbearance on the part of one of the parties or of some third person." Stroud's Judicial Dictionary (2d ed. 1903) defines it as a "Contract . . . to indemnify against a liability. . . . " One of the definitions given to "indemnify" by Webster's Third New Internat. Dict. (1961 ed.) is "to exempt from incurred penalties or liabilities.")

Plaintiff's assertion that the use of the word "all" to modify "loss, damage, expense and liability" dictates an all inclusive interpretation is not persuasive. If the word "indemnify" encompasses only third-party claims, the word "all" simply refers to all such claims. The use of the words "loss," "damage," and "expense" in addition to the word "liability" is likewise inconclusive. These words do not imply an agreement to reimburse for injury to an indemnitee's property since they are commonly inserted in third-party indemnity clauses, to enable an indemnitee who settles a claim to recover from his indemnitor without proving his liability. (Carpenter Paper Co. v. Kellogg (1952) 114 Cal.App.2d 640, 651, 251 P.2d 40. . . .

The provision that defendant perform the work "at his own risk and expense" and the provisions relating to insurance are equally inconclusive. By agreeing to work at its own risk defendant may have released plaintiff from liability for any injuries to defendant's property arising out of the contract's performance, but this provision did not necessarily make defendant an insurer

PETERS, MOSK, BURKE, SULLIVAN, and PEEK, JJ., concur.

MCCOMB, J., dissents.

———

Joy v. Hay Group, Inc.

403 F.3d 875 (2005)

In 1996, defendant HGI hired Bassick and Joy to create an executive-compensation consulting practice, giving both an employment contract promising one year's base salary ($210,000 in Joy's case) as severance pay if they were terminated "for reasons other than cause." Bassick, who was Joy's supervisor, testified that he asked Lacey, a senior manager at HGI, what cause meant, and that Lacey replied that it meant serious wrongdoing. Lacey corroborated this testimony. Bassick also testified that he told Joy she was not expected to bring in new business. In 2002, HGI terminated Joy, stating as cause her failure to meet a quota of $398,000 in annual billings. Joy sued for severance pay. The trial court granted HGI's motion for summary judgment, finding the term "cause" to unambiguously include the reason for her termination. Reversed.

(Posner, J.) "HGI's position . . . it is that the word "cause" in Joy's employment contract unambiguously denotes unsatisfactory performance as judged by HGI. Cases have upheld discharges on the basis of such an interpretation of "cause." . . . But there may be a difference between "cause" for discharge and "cause" for denial of severance pay. Business firms almost always reserve the right to fire an employee (unless the employee is protected by a collective bargaining agreement) if the firm decides that the employee's performance is unsatisfactory. But it is precisely because of the insecurity of such employment—the determination that Joy's performance was unsatisfactory was based on a criterion selected by the firm after she went to work for it, rather than being specified in her employment contract—that employment contracts often provide for severance pay. Joy was leaving a good job to go to work for HGI and in doing so may have been taking a risk (though, with her mentor leaving Hewitt, maybe there would have been a risk in her remaining there), especially since she was going to be working in what was a new line of business for HGI. If she lost her job she would need money to tide her over while she looked for a new job. Hence the severance-pay provision in her employment contract with HGI. . . .

"HGI . . . argues . . . that the only situation in which firing Joy would not have been for cause would have been if a decline in business had required laying off workers. So narrow an interpretation would leave Joy unprotected in the common situation in which, because the new employee does not make a satisfactory adjustment to her new job, the employer is dissatisfied with her

against injuries to plaintiff's property. Defendant's agreement to procure liability insurance to cover damages to plaintiff's property does not indicate whether the insurance was to cover all injuries or only injuries caused by defendant's negligence.

performance and fires her. It is uncertain whether an exception for "cause" to a contractual right to severance pay would extend to that situation. The precise meaning that the word bears in the contract cannot be determined just from reading the contract, as HGI argues. It is a considerable irony that a firm that is in the business of consulting on executive compensation failed to draft a contract that clearly specified the compensation rights of one of its own executives.

"For completeness we note that even if a contract is clear "on its face"— which is to say, even if someone who knew nothing of the contract's background or commercial context would think its meaning clear—extrinsic evidence, which is to say evidence besides just the written contract itself, is admissible to demonstrate that the contract may not mean what it says, provided the evidence used to show this is "objective" in the sense of not being merely self-serving, unverifiable testimony. . . . The proviso is important. Bassick and Lacey are not disinterested witnesses. Neither is employed any longer by HGI; Bassick has sued HGI; and Lacey left because of disagreements with management. Testimony by disgruntled former employees is not the kind of evidence that may be used to establish that a seemingly clear contract actually is ambiguous. The examples that we and other courts have given of the kind of evidence that is sufficiently "objective" to be allowed to upend the "four corners" rule do not include evidence given by former employees.

"But the present case is not one in which the written contract appears to have a clear meaning and dubious evidence is presented in an effort to blur that meaning. When as in this case the written contract is unclear, *any* evidence admissible under the rules of evidence is usable to establish the contract's meaning. The cases do not actually say this; but when they rule that because a contract is ambiguous extrinsic (or parol) evidence of its meaning is admissible, they don't place any special restrictions on admissibility. . . . So Joy is entitled to a trial at which she can call Bassick and Lacey as witnesses. Whether they will be believed is, of course, another matter."

NOTE ON THE NEW LITERALISM

Are tacos, burritos, and quesadillas "sandwiches"? Antonin Scalia and Brian Garner, Reading Law: The Interpretation of Legal Texts (2012), use a case that turns on this question to argue that courts often need only consult a dictionary to interpret a legal document. Richard Posner, Reflections on Judging (2013), challenges their account of the case. Mitch Berman, Judge Posner's Simple Law, 113 Mich. L. Rev. 777, 785–786, 790–791 (2015), tells the story:

> The first case involved the question of whether tacos, burritos, and quesadillas are "sandwiches" for purposes of a lease between a shopping center and a restaurant. The lease forbade the shopping center from renting space to any other restaurant that would be

expected to derive more than 10 percent of its income from the sale of "sandwiches."[32] Scalia and Garner describe the decision as follows:

> *Sandwiches* not being a defined term in the lease, the court sensibly relied on a reputable dictionary, which defined a sandwich as "two thin pieces of bread, usually buttered, with a thin layer (as of meat, cheese, or savory mixture) spread between them." . . . The injunction was properly denied on grounds that no reasonable speaker of English would call a taco, a burrito, or a quesadilla a "sandwich."

"Scalia and Garner stop there," says Posner, "as if that dictionary reference were the court's entire decision and therefore establishes the utility and propriety of judges' using dictionaries as a guide to the meaning of legal documents. But the court had not stopped with the dictionary; it had begun there" (pp. 199–200).

After quoting the dictionary, the court went on to observe that the plaintiff restaurant had drafted the exclusivity clause, that it had known, prior to executing the lease, that other restaurants in the vicinity sold Mexican food, and that it had offered no evidence that the parties intended for the clause to cover burritos and the like. "These," Posner opines, "are more persuasive points than the dictionary's definition of 'sandwich'"—all the more so because "the court got the definition wrong" (p. 200):

> A sandwich does not have to have two slices of bread; it can have more than two (a club sandwich), and it can have just one (an open-faced sandwich). The slices of bread do not have to be thin, and the layer between them does not have to be thin either. The slices do not have to be slices of bread: a hamburger is generally regarded as a sandwich, as is also a hot dog—and some people regard tacos and burritos as sandwiches, and a quesadilla is even more sandwich-like. (p. 200)

Posner's conclusion? "Dictionaries are mazes in which judges are soon lost. A dictionary-centered textualism is hopeless" (p. 200). . . .

So, has Posner caught Scalia and Garner in such errors? Not, I have already said, as often as he thinks. And yet more often than his critics recognize.

Take the sandwich case. I understand Posner to be making two related points. First, he takes issue with the (descriptive) statements that the court "relied" on the dictionary and that it denied the injunction "on grounds that no reasonable speaker of English would call a taco, a burrito, or a quesadilla a 'sandwich.'" Posner claims, in effect, that the court's reliance on the dictionary was only partial and therefore that Scalia and Garner misleadingly characterize the

---

[32] White City Shopping Ctr., LP v. PR Rests., LLC, No. 2006196313, 2006 WL 3292641 (Mass. Super. Ct. Oct. 31, 2006).

"grounds" of the ruling. His second and related point is that the other considerations the court invoked weren't incidental. Rather, reliance on extratextual considerations is made proper and frequently necessary by the seductive imprecision of dictionary definitions—even of so seemingly straightforward and concrete a word as "sandwich." The dictionary definition, Posner argues, is highly infirm—even if it is plausible enough at first glance that its defects escape the attention of our most textualist Supreme Court justice and the country's foremost legal lexicographer. Hirsch,* Garner's chosen impartial arbitrator, mocks this claim, but Posner is right and Hirsch wrong.

Posner's observation that a sandwich can have more or fewer than two slices of bread "ignores the fact[s]." Hirsch objects,

> [A]s everyone knows, burritos, tacos, and quesadillas are made on tortillas, not bread. Tortillas are not "slices" of bread because they are not sliced from a larger loaf. And tortillas are ground meal that is pounded flat .... They are about as much like sandwich bread as matzo crackers are. One wonders whether Judge Posner has ever eaten Mexican food or watched it being prepared.

Fine, tortillas are like matzos. But that *supports* Posner's point. One wonders whether Hirsch has ever been to a Passover seder or heard of the Hillel sandwich. Hirsch also objects that, the fact that the slices of bread do not have to be thin "is of no relevance to deciding the *White City* case, since tortillas are, by any measure, thin." It might not be relevant to deciding the case; it *is* relevant to the adequacy of the dictionary definition.

Hirsch also ridicules Posner's observation that hamburgers and hot dogs are "generally regarded as . . . sandwich[es]" and that some people think that burritos and tacos are too. Hirsch does so by protesting that, in "normal conversation," neither a customer nor a waiter would refer to, for example, a "burrito sandwich[ ]" or a "hamburger sandwich[ ]." But Hirsch confuses whether something *is* a "sandwich" with whether it is idiomatic to refer to the thing by a name that includes the word "sandwich." A negative answer to the second question does not entail a negative answer to the first. Hirsch's imagined customer might request a "club sandwich" or a "pastrami sandwich" (and so on), but she would never request (if she's a native speaker of American English) a "reuben sandwich"; she'd just ask for "a reuben." But reubens are still sandwiches. The same might be true of hamburgers, hot dogs, and even quesadillas.

---

*   [Steven Hirsch is a California attorney who was asked by Brian Garner to evaluate Posner's charges of misrepresentation. Hirsch's report is available on Garner's blog, www.lawprose.org. (Footnote by eds.)]

So we have to do better than ask whether it is idiomatic to speak of a "hamburger sandwich." (Compare: poodles are dogs, although it's nonidiomatic to refer to "poodle dogs.") For instance, it might be more revealing to look at actual restaurant menus. A Google image search for "sandwich menus" returns many that list hamburgers and even hot dogs under the heading "sandwiches." It's probably more usual still for menus to have separate categories captioned "sandwiches" and "hamburgers" or a single category captioned "sandwiches and burgers." But the important points are that listing hamburgers and hot dogs under "sandwiches" is plenty common and that in no case is the inclusion jarring—not as it would be if the list of "sandwiches" included, say, salads or pastas or steak.

In short, Posner shows that the dictionary definition is actually pretty bad, and bad in lots of ways, all of which were overlooked by Scalia and Garner (and later also by Hirsch). The point of this showing is that *Reading Law* describes some of the opinions that it discusses in tendentious ways designed to pump readers' intuitions that textual originalism, and it alone, produces sensible results.

NOTE ON SURROUNDING CIRCUMSTANCES

The plain meaning rule allows a court to consider evidence of surrounding circumstances in interpreting a writing without a prior finding the writing is ambiguous. Many versions of the rule also allow a court to consider evidence of "operative usages." Thus Restatement First Section 230 defines the objective meaning of a writing as "the meaning that would be attached to the integration by a reasonably intelligent person acquainted with all operative usages and knowing all the circumstances prior to and contemporaneous with the making of the integration, other than oral statements by the parties of what they intended it to mean."

URI, Inc. v. Kleburg County

543 S.W.3d 755 (Tex. 2018)

A 2004 settlement agreement between URI and Kleburg County conditioned URI's right to commence uranium mining operations in an area designated PAA 3 on showing that at least 90 percent of the wells in an area designated PAA 1, which was already mined by URI, had water that was suitable for drinking, livestock, or irrigation. This requirement only applied to wells that had water suitable for drinking, livestock, or irrigation before URI began mining operations in PAA 1 in 1988. During public hearings on the settlement agreement in 2004 it was explained that this qualification did not make the restoration obligation meaningless because one well (Well I-11) in PAA 1 fit this description. This was based on 1985 baseline data.

In 2007, URI commenced mining operations in PAA 3, taking the position that it had satisfied other requirements in the settlement agreement and that the restoration obligation did not apply to Well I-11 because it had baseline data from 1987 that, when averaged with the 1985 baseline data, showed the water was not suitable for drinking, livestock, or irrigation. The trial court found the 1987 baseline data was valid but that it was irrelevant because "this additional data on Well I-11 was not public data and was not known to the County at the time of the execution of the Agreement; and thus, would not have been contemplated by the County at the time it entered the Agreement in 2004." Nevertheless the trial court allowed URI to continue mining in PAA 3 while it worked to restore Well I-11 to make the water suitable for irrigation. The court of appeals affirmed on the first point but held the trial court abused its discretion in not ordering URI to halt mining in PAA-3 until the water in Well I-11 was restored to being suitable for irrigation. Held, reversed.

(Guzman, J.) "We have long articulated a principle of contract construction that permits courts to consult the facts and circumstances surrounding a negotiated contract's execution to aid the interpretation of its language. Despite expounding on this principle from time to time, and as recently as last term, it remains susceptible to confusion and inconsistency when applied to unambiguous contract terms. The principle's limitations are, however, clear: surrounding facts and circumstances cannot be employed to "make the language say what it unambiguously does not say" or "to show that the parties probably meant, or could have meant, something other than what their agreement stated." In other words, extrinsic evidence may only be used to aid the understanding of an unambiguous contract's language, not change it or "create ambiguity."

"When interpreting a written contract, the prime directive is to ascertain the parties' intent as expressed in the instrument. "[O]bjective, not subjective, intent controls," so the focus is on the words the parties chose to memorialize their agreement. But language is nuanced, and meaning is often context driven. Contract language is thus construed in its lexical environment, which may include objectively determinable facts and circumstances that contextualize the parties' transaction. Surrounding facts and circumstances can inform the meaning of language but cannot be used to augment, alter, or contradict the terms of an unambiguous contract. . . .

"The central issue here is the role evidence of "surrounding circumstances" plays in the construction of section 11.1 of the Settlement Agreement. Consideration of surrounding circumstances is limited by the parol evidence rule,* which prohibits a party to an integrated written contract from presenting extrinsic evidence "for the purpose of creating an ambiguity or to give the contract a meaning different from that which its language imports." "Only where a contract is ambiguous may a court consider the parties' interpretation and 'admit extraneous evidence to determine the true meaning of the

___
* [The opinion should refer to the plain meaning rule here (in Texas law this is often referred to as the four corners rule), and not to the parol evidence rule. (Footnote by eds.)]

instrument.' " "[N]o issue regarding the parties' intentions is raised *unless* the [contract] is ambiguous—and evidence of those intentions cannot be used to create an ambiguity."

"The parol evidence rule does not, however, prohibit courts from considering extrinsic evidence of the facts and circumstances surrounding the contract's execution as "an aid in the construction of the contract's language," but the evidence may only "give the words of a contract a meaning consistent with that to which they are reasonably susceptible, i.e., to 'interpret' contractual terms." This is true even if doing so reveals a latent ambiguity in a contract's terms. But whether a court is considering if an ambiguity exists or construing the terms of an unambiguous contract, surrounding facts and circumstances can only provide context that elucidates the meaning of the words employed, and nothing else. As we have often stated in one way or another, "[u]nderstanding the context in which an agreement was made is essential in determining the parties' intent *as expressed in the agreement*, but it is the parties' *expressed intent* that the court must determine."

"If a written contract is so worded that it can be given a definite or certain legal meaning when so considered and as applied to the matter in dispute, then it is not ambiguous. But if contract language is susceptible to more than one reasonable interpretation when so viewed, an ambiguity exists.

"Contract ambiguity comes in two flavors: patent or latent. "A patent ambiguity is evident on the face of the contract" while a "latent ambiguity arises when a contract which is unambiguous on its face is applied to the subject matter with which it deals and an ambiguity appears by reason of some collateral matter," such as the circumstances present when the contract was entered. Allowing that surrounding circumstances may reveal a latent ambiguity seems conceptually at odds with the proscription against employing extrinsic evidence to create an ambiguity. But to say extrinsic evidence may not create an ambiguity but may reveal one means only that "[t]he ambiguity must become evident when the contract is read in context of the surrounding circumstances, not after parol evidence of intent is admitted to create an ambiguity."

"A classic example of a latent ambiguity is when a contract requires goods to be delivered to "the green house on Pecan Street," but there were, in fact, two green houses on Pecan Street. When surrounding circumstances reveal an ambiguity about the intent embodied in the contract's language, as in the "green house" example, extrinsic evidence of the parties' true intent will then— and only then—be admissible to settle the matter. But, when the contextual evidence discloses no ambiguity, extrinsic evidence that the parties actually intended for the goods to be delivered to the blue house on Pecan Street would not be admissible to alter unambiguous contract language requiring delivery to the green house. Nor would the contract's *meaning* be informed by extrinsic evidence that the parties intended additional requirements or constraints that were not expressed in the agreement—such as delivery by 5:00 p.m. or only on Sundays. . . .

"What "facts and circumstances" may be consulted will naturally vary from case to case, but reasonably well-defined contours can be mined from our jurisprudence. Because objective intent controls the inquiry, only circumstantial evidence that is objective in nature may be consulted. We have accordingly described surrounding circumstances as including " 'the commercial or other setting in which the contract was negotiated and other *objectively determinable* factors that give a context to the transaction between the parties.' " Setting can be critical to understanding contract language, as we found in cases involving the lawyer-client relationship and construction of an arbitration agreement. We have also cited trade custom as bearing on the parties' objective intent when provisions were stricken from a form insurance contract. Similarly, trade usage can illuminate the meaning of contract language because "the meaning to which a certain term or phrase is most reasonably susceptible is the one which [is] so regularly observed in place, vocation, trade or industry so 'as to justify an expectation that it will be observed with respect to a particular agreement.' " Facts attending the execution may or may not shed light on contract meaning and may or may not cross the parol-evidence line. In deciding what facts and circumstances are informative, rather than transformative, ascertaining objective meaning is the touchstone.

"A certain degree of latitude is inherent in the inquiry, but absolute limits on the use of surrounding circumstances are abundantly clear. Parties cannot rely on extrinsic evidence to "give the contract a meaning different from that which its language imports," "add to, alter, or contradict" the terms contained within the agreement itself, "make the language say what it unambiguously does not say," or "show that the parties probably meant, or could have meant, something other than what their agreement stated."

"Here, the court of appeals impermissibly relied on extrinsic evidence of Kleberg County's subjective intent to construe the unambiguous language in section 11.1 of the Settlement Agreement. While evidence of the commercial setting necessarily contextualizes and informs the meaning of some of the contract terms (for example, "baseline wells," "baseline" data, and "before URI's mining in PAA 1"), the court of appeals went too far in looking beyond the Settlement Agreement's language to interlineate limitations and specific results not expressed in the instrument itself. Construing the contract in light of the surrounding circumstances here does not support the conclusion that section 11.1 precludes URI's reliance on the 1987 baseline data, and we may not rely on extrinsic evidence for the purpose of modifying, enlarging, or curtailing its terms. . . .

"By its plain terms, section 11.1(1)(ii) imposes a well-restoration requirement contingent on an alteration of suitability that emanated from PAA 1 mining operations as determined by "baseline" data and the water quality that existed "before URI's mining in PAA 1." According to TCEQ regulations, "[b]aseline quality" refers to "[t]he parameters and their concentrations that describe the local groundwater quality of an aquifer prior to the beginning of injection operations." Section 11.1 does not refer to any particular set of baseline data, prescribe the use of particular data, place limitations on the data that may be considered in determining pre-mining suitability, or require restoration of any well, let alone a particular well.

"The trial court found the 1987 baseline data URI relied on is valid, and the evidence at trial establishes that the TCEQ accepted the 1987 data as accurately reflecting baseline quality. Per the trial court's express findings, the 1987 baseline data shows the water in Well I-11 was unsuitable for any of the contractually specified uses before URI began mining in PAA 1 in 1988. The trial court's findings are unchallenged. Accordingly, under a plain reading of section 11.1(1)(ii), URI had no obligation to ensure the water in Well I-11 was suitable for drinking, livestock watering, or irrigation before resuming mining in PAA 3.

"The lower courts concluded, however, that URI could not use the 1987 baseline data, alone or in combination with the 1985 baseline data, precisely because this outcome would ensue from a plain and objective reading of the Settlement Agreement. Even though the contract admits no ambiguity, the lower courts engrafted limitations that are entirely external to the instrument and directed to fulfilling Kleberg County's unexpressed subjective intent. This is not a proper use of surrounding facts and circumstances. "[C]ourts cannot rewrite the parties' contract or add to or subtract from its language. . . .""

NOTE ON PURPOSIVE INTERPRETATION

Arguments about interpretation generally focus on the question, what evidence a court ought to consider in interpreting a writing. Recent scholarship shifts the focus to the question what type of meaning a court ought to ascribe to the contents of a writing.* Possibilities include authorial meaning, semantic or textual meaning, and purposive or pragmatic meaning.

A commitment to objective interpretation does not preclude purposive interpretation. Under New York law, "a court should accord that language its plain meaning giving due consideration to 'the surrounding circumstances [and] apparent purpose which the parties sought to accomplish.'" Cable Science Corp. v. Rochdale Village, Inc., 920 F.2d 147, 151 (2d Cir. 1990), quoting William C. Atwater & Co. v. Panama R.R. Co., 246 N.Y. 519, 524, 159 N.E. 418 (1927).

For example, in Outlet Embroidery Co. v. Derwent Mills, 172 N.E. 462 (N.Y. 1930), the issue was whether a seller committed to deliver yarn for $3.10 per box when its acceptance said the price "is subject to change pending tariff revision." The seller argued there was no commitment because it clearly reserved the power to change the price. Cardozo brushed this argument off,

---

*   Peter M. Gerhart and Juliet P. Kostritsky, Efficient Contextualism, 76 U. Pitt. L. Rev. 509 (2015); Gregory Klass, Contracts, Constitutions, and Getting the Interpretation-Construction Distinction Right, 18 Geo. J.L. & Pub. Policy 13 (2021); Shahar Lifshitz and Elad Finkelstein, A Hermeneutic Perspective on the Interpretation of Contracts, 54 American Bus. L.J. 519 (2017).

noting "the letters between plaintiff and defendant were from one merchant to another. They are to be read as business men would read them, and only as a last resort are to be thrown out altogether as meaningless futilities." Id. at 463. He took judicial notice of a debate in Congress over a possible future tariff increase when the agreement was made, and explained that in this context the qualification obviously meant the price was contingent on no tariff increase.

___

NOTE—IS THE INTERPRETATION OF WRITTEN CONTRACTS A QUESTION FOR THE JUDGE OR FOR THE JURY?

It is commonly said that questions of fact are for the jury and questions of law are for the judge. A more realistic statement would be that questions that the legal system assigns to the jury are *called* questions of fact, and questions that the legal system assigns to the judge are *called* questions of law. Within this verbal framework, it has long been the general rule that the interpretation of written contracts is a question of law even though "in actuality [such interpretation involves] a factual, not a legal, decision. . . . This fact-finding function exercised by the court is denominated a 'question of law' . . . not because analytically it is a question of law but rather to indicate that it is the trial judge, not the jury, to whom the law assigns the responsibility for deciding the matter." Community College v. Community College, Society of the Faculty, 473 Pa. 576, 375 A.2d 1267 (1977).

Traditionally, there has been an exception to this general rule—that is, the interpretation of written contracts has been given to the trier of fact—where the court deems the agreement ambiguous; the meaning of the agreement turns on evidence extrinsic to the agreement; and the credibility of that evidence is at issue. In Meyers v. Selznick Co., 373 F.2d 218 (2d Cir.1966), Judge Friendly forcefully supported a liberalization of this exception under which questions of interpretation are for the trier of fact *whenever* evidence extrinsic to the written instrument is relevant to its interpretation, even though there is no issue as to the credibility of the evidence, but merely as to its significance:

> Whether determination of meaning be regarded as a question of fact, a question of law, or just itself, reliance on the jury to resolve ambiguities in the light of extrinsic evidence seems quite as it should be, save where the form or subject-matter of a particular contract outruns a jury's competence. . . . Resolution of [issues involving the determination of meaning] may hinge in no small degree on notions of fairness—the very kind of decision laymen are ideally equipped to make.

This view is adopted in Restatement Second § 212(2), which provides that "A question of interpretation of an integrated agreement is to be determined by the trier of fact if it depends on the credibility of extrinsic evidence or on a choice among reasonable inferences to be drawn from extrinsic evidence.

Otherwise a question of interpretation of an integrated agreement is to be determined as a question of law."

SECTION 2. THE ROLE OF USAGE, COURSE OF DEALING, AND COURSE OF PERFORMANCE IN INTERPRETATION

FOXCO INDUSTRIES, LTD. v. FABRIC WORLD, INC.

United States Court of Appeals, Fifth Circuit, 1979.
595 F.2d 976.

TJOFLAT, CIRCUIT JUDGE:

In this diversity action Foxco Industries, Ltd. (Foxco), a Delaware corporation, following a jury trial recovered a $26,000 judgment against Fabric World, Inc. (Fabric World), an Alabama corporation, for breaching a contract to purchase certain knitted fabric goods and refusing to pay for merchandise previously purchased. [On appeal, Fabric World argues that] the district court erred in admitting into evidence published standards of the Knitted Textile Association to establish the meaning of a disputed contract term. For the reasons set forth below, we reject the [argument] of Fabric World and affirm.

I

Foxco is in the business of manufacturing knitted fabrics for sale to retail fabric stores and the garment industry. Foxco's principal place of business is in New York City; it has never formally qualified to do business in Alabama. Fabric World is engaged in the retail fabric business and operates a chain of stores in a number of states; its headquarters is in Huntsville, Alabama.

There are two seasons in the fabric industry, a spring season and a fall season. Before the beginning of each season Foxco displays for customers samples of the line of fabrics it will manufacture that season. Customer orders are accepted only from the fabric shown on display. Foxco's manufacturing operation is limited to filling these orders; no fabrics are manufactured merely to be held as inventory. There was some conflict in the testimony as to whether fabric specially knit for one customer, such as Fabric World, could be resold to another customer.

Foxco sells some of its goods to retail fabric stores through manufacturers' representatives, operating on a commission basis, who sell the lines of numerous manufacturers. Foxco furnishes each representative with samples and a price list. Larger retail store customers, such as Fabric World, are handled personally by Foxco's sales manager, Allen Feller, a salaried employee, who supervises all retail fabric store sales. He has responsibility over the approximately twenty-six manufacturers' representatives carrying the Foxco line.

Foxco has never maintained an office in Alabama. At the time of the transactions giving rise to this action, its manufacturers' representative in Alabama was a resident of the state. Foxco's sales manager, Feller, made periodic trips to Alabama to meet with this representative and to obtain orders from Fabric World and Kennemer Company, another large fabric retailer. At the beginning of each season Feller would meet with the manufacturers' representative for two or three days so that the new line of fabrics could be previewed and discussed. In 1974, Foxco's gross sales approximated $14,000,000; Alabama accounted for in excess of $100,000 of that amount. A substantial portion of the Alabama business was with Fabric World, from which three separate orders were obtained.

On April 22, 1974, Feller traveled to Huntsville to show Fabric World the new fall line. His meeting with Glenn Jameson, Fabric World's president, culminated in a written order for "first quality" goods. A dispute subsequently arose regarding the quality of the goods sent to fill the order, and Fabric World refused to pay for the portion of the goods it considered defective.

On October 21, 1974, Feller returned to Huntsville to show Jameson the line for the following spring season. Jameson voiced no complaint about the quality of the goods received pursuant to the previous April 22 order. In fact, he gave Feller a new order, in writing, for 12,000 yards of first quality fabric, at a price of $36,705, to be delivered by January 15, 1975.

A few weeks after the October 21 order was placed, the textile industry began to experience a precipitous decline in the price of yarn. Because of a drop in the price of finished goods, Fabric World wrote Foxco on November 15, 1974, and cancelled its October 21 order. Foxco immediately replied, stating that the manufacture of the order was substantially completed and that it could not accept the cancellation. On November 27, 1974, Foxco's attorney wrote Fabric World that if the goods were not accepted they would be finished and sold and Fabric World sued for the difference between the contract price and the sales price received by Foxco. On December 3, 1974, Fabric World agreed to accept the order, but threatened to return the entire shipment if it contained one flaw. Foxco, believing that it was impossible to produce an order of this magnitude without a single flaw, decided it would not ship the order (which was completed a short time later).

Fabric World established that in December 1974 the fair market value of the October order was approximately 20% less than the contract price. However, Foxco made no attempt to sell the goods from the time Fabric World cancelled the order until September 1975, when the goods had dropped 50% In value. In that month Foxco sold at a private sale without notice to Fabric World approximately 7,000 yards from the order for an average price of between $1.50 and $1.75 per yard, a total consideration of $10,119.50. By the time of trial in April 1976, Foxco had on hand about 5,000 yards of the order worth between $1.25 and $1 per yard, or about $6,250.

During the course of the trial there was much testimony regarding the meaning of the term first quality goods used in the contracts between Foxco and Fabric World. The testimony on behalf of Fabric World was that it meant fabric containing no flaws. Foxco introduced evidence, over the objection of Fabric World, in the form of an exhibit containing standards for finished knitted goods promulgated by the Knitted Textile Association, a large textile industry group to which Foxco belongs. These standards indicated that certain types and amounts of flaws were permissible in first quality fabric. Fabric World is not a member of that association and claimed it had no knowledge of the standards adopted by the association's members. One ground for Fabric World's present appeal is its contention that the standards of a trade association of which it had no knowledge are not admissible to show the meaning of the undefined and disputed contract term "first quality" goods. . . .

Fabric World's [claims] that the district court erred in admitting into evidence the definition of first quality goods contained in the Standards for Finished Knitted Fabrics of the Knitted Textile Association. It contends that it is not a member of the Knitted Textile Association, was unaware of its existence until the time of trial, and that that group's standards were inadmissible because they were a custom or usage of the trade of which Fabric World had no knowledge. We find no error in the trial court's ruling.

A major issue in this case is what was meant by the term "first quality." Under the traditional application of the parol evidence rule, Fabric World's contention may have merit: the private, subjective intent of one party to a contract may well be irrelevant in determining the meaning of a contract term unless it is shown that that intent was communicated to the other party. See Levie, Trade Usage and Custom under the Common Law and the Uniform Commercial Code, 40 N.Y.U.L.Rev. 1101 (1965). In this case there is no direct evidence, as Fabric World argues, that it was put on notice that usage and custom, as embodied in the industry standards, would be used to define the meaning of first quality. Under Alabama sales law, however, that Fabric World did not know of the industry's usage and custom or of the standards in question is of no moment; the parties to a contract such as the one in issue are presumed to have intended the incorporation of trade usage in striking their bargain. U.C.C. section 2–202, Ala.Code tit. 7, § 7–2–202 (1977), explicitly provides that trade usages may help explain or supplement contract terms.[8] As stated in the comment to that provision,

> [Section 2–202(a)] makes admissible evidence of course of dealing, usage of trade and course of performance to explain or supplement the terms of any writing stating the agreement of the parties in order that the true understanding of the parties as to the agreement may be reached. *Such writings are to be read on the assumption that* the course of prior dealings between the parties *and the usages of trade were taken for granted when the document was phrased. Unless carefully negated they have become an element of the meaning of the words used.*

Id., Official Comment (emphasis added). Section 1–205(2) . . . defines trade usages. It provides in part that

> A usage of trade is any practice or method of dealing having such regularity of observance in a place, vocation or trade as to justify an expectation that it will be observed with respect to the transaction in question. The existence and scope of such a usage are to be proved as facts.

It further states: "A course of dealing between parties and any usage of trade in the vocation or trade in which they are engaged or of which they are or should be aware give particular meaning to and supplement or qualify terms of an agreement." . . . There was uncontroverted testimony that the Knitted Textile Association is an industry group with over 1500 members. Its standards could certainly qualify as trade usages, and thus were admissible notwithstanding Fabric World's unawareness of them. Loeb & Co. v. Martin, 295 Ala. 262, 327 So.2d 711, 715 (1976). See Columbia Nitrogen Corp. v. Royster Co., 451 F.2d 3 (4th Cir. 1971); Chase Manhattan Bank v. First Marion Bank, 437 F.2d 1040 (5th Cir. 1971); Southern Concrete Services, Inc. v. Mableton Contractors, Inc., 407 F.Supp. 581 (N.D.Ga.1975), aff'd 569 F.2d 1154 (5th Cir. 1978).

. . . Accordingly, the judgment of the district court is AFFIRMED.

---

[8]   Section 2–202 states:

Final written expression: Parol or extrinsic evidence.

Terms with respect to which the confirmatory memoranda of the parties agree or which are otherwise set forth in a writing intended by the parties as a final expression of their agreement with respect to such terms as are included therein may not be contradicted by evidence of any prior agreement or of a contemporaneous oral agreement but may be explained or supplemented:

(a) By course of dealing or usage of trade (section 7–1–205) or by course of performance (section 7–2–208); and

(b) By evidence of consistent additional terms unless the court finds the writing to have been intended also as a complete and exclusive statement of the terms of the agreement.

RESTATEMENT, SECOND, CONTRACTS
§ 221, ILLUSTRATION 2

2. A, an ordained rabbi, is employed by B, an orthodox Jewish congregation, to officiate as cantor at specified religious services. At the time the contract is made, it is the practice of such congregations to seat men and women separately at services, and a contrary practice would violate A's religious beliefs. At a time when it is too late for A to obtain substitute employment, B adopts a contrary practice. A refuses to officiate. The practice is part of the contract, and A is entitled to the agreed compensation.

RESTATEMENT, SECOND, CONTRACTS § 222

[See Selected Source Materials Supplement]

RESTATEMENT, SECOND, CONTRACTS § 222,
ILLUSTRATIONS 1–3

1. A contracts to sell B 10,000 shingles. By usage of the lumber trade, in which both are engaged, two packs of a certain size constitute 1,000, though not containing that exact number. Unless otherwise agreed, 1,000 in the contract means two packs.

2. A contracts to sell B 1,000 feet of San Domingo mahogany. By usage of dealers in mahogany, known to A and B, good figured mahogany of a certain density is known as San Domingo mahogany, though it does not come from San Domingo. Unless otherwise agreed, the usage is part of the contract. . . .

3. A and B enter into a contract for the purchase and sale of "No. 1 heavy book paper guaranteed free from ground wood." Usage in the paper trade may show that this means paper not containing over 3% ground wood.

Hurst v. W.J. Lake & Co.

141 Or. 306, 16 P.2d 627 (1932)

Buyer and Seller made a contract for the sale of 350 tons of horse meat scraps, "minimum 50% protein," for $50 per ton. Under the contract, if any of the scraps tested at "less than 50% of protein" Buyer was to receive a discount of $5.00 per ton. About 170 tons contained less than 50% protein; of these, 140 tons contained 49.53 to 49.96% protein. Buyer took a $5.00 discount on the entire 170 tons. Seller claimed that Buyer was entitled to a discount on only 30 tons, because under a usage of trade the terms "minimum 50% protein" and "less than 50% protein," when used in a contract for the sale of horse meat scraps, meant that a protein content of not less than 49.5% was equal to a content of 50% protein. The trial court granted Buyer's motion for judgment on the pleadings. Reversed.

(Bean, C.J.) "The flexibility of or multiplicity in the meaning of words is the principal source of difficulty in the interpretation of language. Words are the conduits by which thoughts are communicated, yet scarcely any of them have such a fixed and single meaning that they are incapable of denoting more than one thought. In addition to the multiplicity in meaning of words set forth in the dictionaries there are the meanings imparted to them by trade customs, local uses, dialects, telegraphic codes, etc. One meaning crowds a word full of significance, while another almost empties the utterance of any import. The various groups above indicated are constantly amplifying our language; in fact, they are developing what may be called languages of their own. Thus one is justified in saying that the language of the dictionaries is not the only language spoken in America. For instance, the word, 'thousand' as commonly used has a very specific meaning; it denotes ten hundreds or fifty scores, but the language of the various trades and localities has assigned to it meanings quite different from that just mentioned. Thus in the bricklaying trade a contract which fixes the bricklayer's compensation at "$5.25 a thousand" does not contemplate that he need lay actually one thousand bricks in order to earn $5.25 but that he should build a wall of a certain size: Brunold v. Glasser, 25 Misc. 285 (53 N.Y.S. 1021); Walker v. Syms, 118 Mich. 183 (76 N.W. 320). In the lumber industry a contract requiring the delivery of 4,000 shingles will be fulfilled by the delivery of only 2,500 when it appears that by trade custom two packs of a certain size are regarded as 1,000 shingles and that, hence, the delivery of eight packs fulfills the contract, even though they contain only 2,500 shingles by actual count: Soutier v. Kellerman, 18 Mo. 509. And where the custom of locality considers 100 dozen as constituting a thousand, one who has 19,200 rabbits upon a warren under an agreement for their sale at the price of 60 pounds for each thousand rabbits will be paid for only 16,000 rabbits: Smith v. Wilson, 3 Barn. & Adol. 728. . . .

". . . We believe that it is safe to assume, in the absence of evidence to the contrary, that when tradesmen employ trade terms they attach to them their trade significance. If, when they write their trade terms into their contracts, they mean to strip the terms of their special significance and demote them to their common import, it would seem reasonable to believe that they would so state in their agreement. Otherwise, they would refrain from using the trade term and express themselves in other language."

———

Restatement, Second, Contracts § 220

Illustration 9: ". . . A promises to sell and B to buy a certain quantity of 'white arsenic' for a stated price. The parties contract with reference to a usage of trade that 'white arsenic' includes arsenic colored with lamp black. The usage is part of the contract."

———

UCC §§ 1–201(3), (12), 1–303, 2–208

[See Selected Source Materials Supplement]

———

RESTATEMENT, SECOND, CONTRACTS §§ 219–223

[See Selected Source Materials Supplement]

———

CISG ART. 9

[See Selected Source Materials Supplement]

———

UNIDROIT PRINCIPLES OF INTERNATIONAL COMMERCIAL CONTRACTS ART. 1.9

[See Selected Source Materials Supplement]

———

PRINCIPLES OF EUROPEAN CONTRACT LAW ART. 1.105

[See Selected Source Materials Supplement]

———

Dennis Patterson, Good Faith, Lender Liability, and Discretionary Acceleration: Of Llewellyn, Wittgenstein, and the Uniform Commercial Code

68 Tex. L. Rev. 169, 187–192 (1989)

" . . .Williston and Llewellyn differed fundamentally on the proper role and function of law in regulating commerce. For Williston, contract was the apotheosis of theory, a pure conceptual edifice. By the 1930s, the Uniform Sales Act (Williston's statute) was to Llewellyn's mind hopelessly antiquated both in form and substance. Llewellyn's goal, first manifested in three successive drafts of a revised Uniform Sales Act and ultimately realized (with some compromises) in the Code, was to replace the offer—acceptance-consideration model of contract with one more in keeping with the realities of commercial practice. The cornerstone of the new conceptualism of the Code was the concept of agreement. . .

"In the Code concept of agreement, Llewellyn reacted against two salient aspects of Willistonian formalism: (1) that contract terms might have a plain meaning, and (2) that written contract terms have priority over all unwritten expressions of agreement. . . In Llewellyn's view . . . the meaning of the agreement did not depend, in the first instance, on the existence or content of a writing. Instead, meaning derived from an interpretation of 'language and by implication from other circumstances, including course of dealing or usage of trade or course of performance,' considered together, each an aspect of the total context. The context, and not an a priori rule, determined the weight accorded any one aspect.

"Llewellyn's embrace of the commercial context challenged . . . common-law sales doctrine. Under the common law, neither custom nor trade usage could be introduced as evidence to contradict the written terms of an agreement. The Uniform Sales Act afforded little relief from this orthodoxy, providing merely that trade usage could displace express terms only if the parties intended it to. The argument is viciously circular. Resort to terms or sources of meaning outside the express terms of the contract was allowable only if the parties intended such reference. The language of the agreement, however, was the sole expression of the parties' intent.

"In the 1941 draft of the Revised Uniform Sales Act, Llewellyn sought to put the confusion to rest. The 1941 Act provided that trade usage and course of dealing were no longer the stepchildren of the writing: their significance for the question of contract interpretation was now guaranteed.

'Between merchants, the usage of trade, or of a particular trade, and any course of dealing between the parties, are presumed to be the background which the parties have presupposed in their bargaining and have intended to read into the particular contract; and express words are to be construed, where that is reasonable, as consistent with, rather than as a displacement of, such usage and course of dealing.'

"Llewellyn's concept of agreement thus integrated trade usage and course of dealing with the written terms of the parties. Now, a court could not answer the question of what the parties meant by their agreement without first understanding the meaning of the commercial practice from which their agreement arose.

"Llewellyn's conceptual revolution was not universally embraced. After the completion of the New York Law Revision Commission hearings, Professor Edwin Patterson of the Columbia University Law School prepared a report recommending 'amendment of section 1–205(4) to insure that express terms would always dominate usage of trade and course of dealing.' . . .

"Professor Patterson never gave up in his attempt to reorient judicial thinking to the classical model. In 1964, fully eight years after having his perspective rejected by the New York Law Revision Commission, Patterson wrote the following:

'The Commercial Code seeks to express the requirement of reasonableness along with a statement as to which source of interpretation prevails when they are in conflict with each other: [text of section 1–205(4)]. An alleged usage which contradicts express terms of the contract is to be rejected. A course of dealing between these parties is more likely to express their expectations than a conflicting usage that may be the practice of other persons.' "

NANAKULI PAVING AND ROCK CO. V. SHELL OIL CO.

United States Court of Appeals, Ninth Circuit, 1981.
664 F.2d 772.

Before BROWNING, CHIEF JUDGE, and KENNEDY, CIRCUIT JUDGE, and HOFFMAN,* DISTRICT JUDGE.

HOFFMAN, DISTRICT JUDGE:

[Prior to 1963, there were two major paving contractors on Oahu: Nanakuli and Hawaiian Bitumals ("H.B."). Of these, H.B. was by far the largest, in part because it had a special relationship with Chevron, which supplied asphalt, a major element in paving construction. Shell Oil, like Chevron, was a major worldwide oil company, but partly because of the relationship between H.B. and Chevron, Shell had only a small percentage of the asphalt market in Hawaii and had no asphalt terminals in Hawaii.

In 1963, Nanakuli and Shell entered into a five-year contract under which Nanakuli agreed to buy its asphalt requirements from Shell, and Shell agreed to supply these requirements. The contract gave Nanakuli an assured source of supply, so that it could compete on equal terms with H.B., and gave Shell the potential for drastically expanding its asphalt sales in Hawaii. In 1969, a new contract was executed. The term of this contract was until December 31, 1975, at which point each party had an option to cancel on 6 months' notice.

In February 1976, Nanakuli sued Shell for breach of the 1969 contract. That contract provided that the price of asphalt to Nanakuli would be "Shell's posted price at the time of delivery"—that is, the price Shell posted,

---

* Honorable Walter E. Hoffman, Senior United States District Judge for the Eastern District of Virginia, sitting by designation.

at the time of delivery, for sale to all buyers. Nanakuli argued that notwithstanding this price term, Nanakuli was entitled to "price protection" under both trade usage and course of performance, and that Shell had breached the contract by refusing to give such protection. "Price protection" means that a supplier will not increase the price charged to a contractor, despite an increase in the supplier's posted price, without advance notice, and instead will apply the posted price that is in place at the time the contractor made a bid, and that is incorporated by the contractor into its bid, long enough to allow the contractor to order the asphalt needed on the job. Nanakuli claimed that Shell breached the 1969 contract in January 1974 by failing to price protect Nanakuli on 7,200 tons of asphalt when Shell raised the price for asphalt from $44 to $76. The jury returned a verdict of $220,800 for Nanakuli. The district court set aside this verdict, and granted Shell's motion for judgment n.o.v.]

. . . We reinstate the jury verdict because we find that, viewing the evidence as a whole, there was substantial evidence to support a finding by reasonable jurors that Shell breached its contract by failing to provide protection for Nanakuli in 1974. . . .

[W]e hold that, under the facts of this case, a jury could reasonably have found that Shell's acts on two occasions to price protect Nanakuli were not ambiguous and therefore indicated Shell's understanding of the terms of the agreement with Nanakuli rather than being a waiver by Shell of those terms.[8]

[We also] hold that, although the express price terms of Shell's posted price of delivery may seem, at first glance, inconsistent with a trade usage of price protection at time of increases in price, a closer reading shows that the jury could have reasonably construed price protection as consistent with the express term. We reach this holding for several reasons. First, we are persuaded by a careful reading of the U.C.C., one of whose underlying purposes is to promote flexibility in the expansion of commercial practices and which rather drastically overhauls this particular area of the law. The Code would have us look beyond the printed pages of the contract to usages and the entire commercial context of the agreement in order to reach the "true understanding" of the parties. Second, decisions of other courts in similar situations have managed to reconcile such trade usages with seemingly contradictory express terms where the prior course of dealings between the parties, trade usages, and the actual performance of the contract by the parties showed a clear intent by the parties to incorporate those usages into the agreement or to give to the express term the

---

[8] In addition, Shell's Bohner volunteered on direct for Shell that Shell price protected Nanakuli again after 1974 on the only two occasions of later price increases in 1977 and 1978. Although not constituting a course of performance, since the occasions took place under different contracts, these two additional instances of price protection could have reinforced the jury's impression that Shell's earlier actions were a carrying out of the price term.

particular meaning provided by those usages, even at times varying the apparent meaning of the express terms. Third, the delineation by thoughtful commentators of the degree of consistency demanded between express terms and usage is that a usage should be allowed to modify the apparent agreement, as seen in the written terms, as long as it does not totally negate it. We believe the usage here falls within the limits set forth by commentators and generally followed in the better reasoned decisions. The manner in which price protection was actually practiced in Hawaii was that it only came into play at times of price increases and only for work committed prior to those increases on non-escalating contracts. Thus, it formed an exception to, rather than a total negation of, the express price term of "Shell's Posted Price at time of delivery." Our decision is reinforced by the overwhelming nature of the evidence that price protection was routinely practiced by all suppliers in the small Oahu market of the asphaltic paving trade and therefore was known to Shell; that it was a realistic necessity to operate in that market and thus vital to Nanakuli's ability to get large government contracts and to Shell's continued business growth on Oahu; and that it therefore constituted an intended part of the agreement, as that term is broadly defined by the Code, between Shell and Nanakuli. . . .

II

Trade Usage Before and After 1969

The key to price protection being so prevalent in 1969 that both parties would intend to incorporate it into their contract is found in one reality of the Oahu asphaltic paving market: the largest paving contracts were let by government agencies and none of the three levels of government—local, state, or federal—allowed escalation clauses for paving materials. If a paver bid at one price and another went into effect before the award was made, the paving company would lose a great deal of money, since it could not pass on increases to any government agency or to most general contractors. Extensive evidence was presented that, as a consequence, aggregate suppliers routinely price protected paving contractors in the 1960's and 1970's, as did the largest asphaltic supplier in Oahu, Chevron. Nanakuli presented documentary evidence of routine price protection by aggregate suppliers as well as two witnesses: Grosjean, Vice-President for Marketing of Ameron H.C. & D., and Nihei, Division Manager of Lone Star Industries for Pacific Cement and Aggregate (P.C. & A.). Both testified that price protection to their knowledge had always been practiced: at H.C. & D. for many years prior to Grosjean's arrival in 1962 and at P.C. & A. routinely since Nihei's arrival in 1960. Such protection consisted of advance notices of increases, coupled with charging the old price for work committed at that price or for enough time to order the tonnage committed. The smallness of the Oahu market led to complete trust among suppliers and pavers. H.C. & D. did not demand that Nanakuli or other pavers issue purchase orders or sign contracts for aggregate before incorporating its aggregate prices into bids. Nanakuli would merely give H.C. & D. a list of projects it had bid at the time H.C. & D. raised its prices, without documentation. "Their word and letter is good enough for us," Grosjean testified. Nihei said P.C. & A. at the time of price increases would get a list of either particular projects bid by a paver or simply total tonnage bid at the old price. "We take either one. We take their word for it." None of the aggregate companies had a contract with Nanakuli expressly stating price protection would be given; Nanakuli's contract with P.C. & A. merely set out that P.C. & A. would not charge Nanakuli more than it charged its other customers.

The evidence about Chevron's practice of price protection came in the form of an affidavit by Bery Jameyson, Chevron's Division Manager-Asphalt in California. He stated that Chevron had routinely price protected H.B. on work bid for many years, the last occasion prior to the signing of the 1969 contracts between Nanakuli and Shell being a price increase put into effect on March 7, 1969, with the understanding that H.B. would be protected on work bid, which amounted to 12,000 tons. In answer to Shell's protest that such evidence was not relevant without the contract itself, Nanakuli introduced the contract into evidence. Much like the contract at issue here, it provided that the price to H.B. would be a given percentage of the price Chevron set for a specified crude oil in California. No mention was made of price protection in the written contract between H.B. and Chevron.

In addition to evidence of trade usages existing in 1969 when the contract at issue was signed, the District Judge let in evidence of the continuation of that trade usage after 1969, over Shell's protest. He stated that, giving a liberal reading to Section 1–205, he felt that later evidence was relevant to show that the expectation of the parties that a given usage would be observed was justified. The basis for incorporating a trade usage into a contract under the U.C.C. is the justifiable expectation of the parties that it will be observed. That later evidence consisted here of more price protection by the aggregate companies on Oahu, as well as continued asphalt price protection. Chevron after 1969 continued price protecting H.B. on Oahu and, on raising prices in 1979, price protected Nanakuli on the island of Molokai, where Nanakuli purchased its asphalt from Chevron. Additionally, Shell price protected Nanakuli in 1977 and 1978 on Oahu.[17]

---

[17] We do not need to decide whether usage evidence after a contract was signed is admissible to show that a party's reliance on a given usage was justifiable, given its continuation, because part of that evidence dealing with asphalt prices was admissible to show the reasonably commercial standards of fair dealing prevalent in the trade in 1974 and the part dealing with the continuation of price protection by aggregate suppliers, after 1969 was not so extensive as to be prejudicial to Shell. . . .

III

Shell's Course of Performance of the 1969 Contract

The Code considers actual performance of a contract as the most relevant evidence of how the parties interpreted the terms of that contract. In 1970 and 1971, the only points at which Shell raised prices between 1969 and 1974, it price protected Nanakuli by holding its old price for four and three months, respectively, after announcing a price increase. In the late summer of 1970, Shell had announced a price increase from $35 to $40 a ton effective September 1, 1970. When Nanakuli protested to Bohner [Shell's Hawaiian representative] that it should be price protected on work already committed, Blee [a Shell asphalt official in San Francisco, to whom Bohner reported] wrote Bohner an in-house memo that, if Bohner could not "convince" Nanakuli to go along with the price increase on September 1, he should try to "bargain" to get Nanakuli to accept the price raise by at least the first of the year, which was what was finally agreed upon. During that four-month period, Nanakuli bought 3,300 tons. Shell announced a second increase in October, 1970, from $40 to $42 effective December 31st. Before that increase went into effect, on November 25 Shell increased the [amount of the] raise to $4, making the price $44 as of the first of the year.[18] Shell again agreed to price protect Nanakuli by holding the price at $40, which had been the official price since September 1, for three months from January to March, 1971. Shell did not actually raise prices again until January, 1974, but at several points it believed that increases would be necessary and gave several months' advance notice of those possible increases. Those actions were in accord with Shell's own policy, as professed by Bohner, and that of other asphalt and aggregate suppliers: to give at least several months' advance notice of price increases. On January 14, 1971, Shell wrote its asphalt customers that the maximum 1971 increase would be to $46. On July 9, 1971, another letter promised the price would not go over $50 in 1972. In addition, Bohner volunteered on direct the information that Shell price protected Nanakuli on the only two occasions of price increases after 1974 by giving 6 months' advance notice in 1977 and 3 or 4 months' advance notice in 1978, a practice he described as "in effect carryover pricing," his term for price protection. By its actions, Bohner testified, Shell allowed Nanakuli time to make arrangements to buy up tonnage committed at the old price, that is, to "chew up" tonnage bid or contracted. Shell apparently offered this testimony to impress the jury with its subsequent good faith toward Nanakuli. In fact, it also may have reinforced the impression of the universality of price protection in the asphaltic paving trade on Oahu and, by showing Shell's adherence to that practice on every relevant occasion except 1974, have highlighted for the

---

[18] That November letter also announced a "new pricing policy" of Shell, setting out a requirement that firm contractual commitments be made with Shell within 15 days of accepting a bid.

CH. 13   THE INTERPRETATION OF WRITTEN CONTRACTS   499

jury what was the commercially reasonable standard of fair dealing in effect on Oahu in 1974. . . .

VI

Waiver or Course of Performance

Course of performance under the Code is the action of the parties in carrying out the contract at issue, whereas course of dealing consists of relations between the parties *prior* to signing that contract. Evidence of the latter was excluded by the District Judge; evidence of the former consisted of Shell's price protection of Nanakuli in 1970 and 1971. Shell protested that the jury could not have found that those two instances of price protection amounted to a course of performance of its 1969 contract, relying on two Code comments. First, one instance does not constitute a course of performance. "A single occasion of conduct does not fall within the language of this section. . . . " Haw.Rev.Stat. § 490:2–208, Comment 4. Although the Comment rules out one instance, it does not further delineate how many acts are needed to form a course of performance. The prior occasions here were only two, but they constituted the only occasions before 1974 that would call for such conduct. In addition, the language used by a top asphalt official of Shell in connection with the first price protection of Nanakuli indicated that Shell felt that Nanakuli was entitled to some form of price protection. On that occasion in 1970 Blee, who had negotiated the contract with Nanakuli and was familiar with exactly what terms Shell was bound to by that agreement, wrote of the need to "bargain" with Nanakuli over the extent of price protection to be given, indicating that some price protection was a legal right of Nanakuli's under the 1969 agreement.

Shell's second defense is that the Comment expresses a preference for an interpretation of waiver.

> 3.   Where it is difficult to determine whether a particular act merely sheds light on the meaning of the agreement or represents a waiver of a term of the agreement, the preference is in favor of "waiver" whenever such construction, plus the application of the provisions on the reinstatement of rights waived . . ., is needed to preserve the flexible character of commercial contracts and to prevent surprise or other hardship.

Id., Comment 3. The preference for waiver only applies, however, where acts are ambiguous. It was within the province of the jury to determine whether those acts were ambiguous, and if not, whether they constituted waivers or a course of performance of the contract. The jury's interpretation of those acts as a course of performance was bolstered by evidence offered by Shell that it again price protected Nanakuli on the only two occasions of post-1974 price increases, in 1977 and 1978.[31]

VII

Express Terms as Reasonably Consistent With Usage In Course of Performance

Perhaps one of the most fundamental departures of the Code from prior contract law is found in the parol evidence rule and the definition of an agreement between two parties. Under the U.C.C., an agreement goes beyond the written words on a piece of paper. " 'Agreement' means the bargain of the parties in fact as found in their language or by implication from other circumstances including course of dealing or usage of trade or course of performance as provided in this chapter (sections 490:1–205 and 490:2–208)." *Id.* § 490:1–201 (3). Express terms, then, do not constitute the entire agreement, which must be sought also in evidence of usages, dealings, and performance of the contract itself. The purpose of evidence of usages, which are defined in the previous section, is to help to understand the entire agreement.

> [Usages are] a factor in reaching the commercial meaning of the agreement which the parties have made. The language used is to be interpreted as meaning what it may fairly be expected to mean to parties involved in the particular commercial transaction in a given locality or in a given vocation or trade.... Part of the agreement of the parties ... is to be sought for in the usages of trade which furnish the background and give particular meaning to the language used, and are the framework of common understanding controlling any general rules of law which hold only when there is no such understanding.

Id. § 490:1–205, Comment 4. Course of dealings is more important than usages of the trade, being specific usages between the two parties to the contract. "[C]ourse of dealing controls usage of trade." *Id.* § 490:1–205(4). It "is a sequence of previous conduct between the parties to a particular transaction which is fairly to be regarded as establishing a common basis of understanding for interpreting their expressions and other conduct." *Id.* § 490:1–205(1). Much of the evidence of prior dealings between Shell and Nanakuli in negotiating the 1963 contract and in carrying out similar earlier contracts was excluded by the court.[32]

---

[31] Bohner testified on direct for Shell at the 1978 trial that the two later instances of price protection occurred "this" year and "last" year, by which he could have meant 1976 and 1977. Bohner's testimony was that on those later occasions Shell gave Nanakuli six and three or four months' notice of an increase to allow Nanakuli to buy tonnage it had committed at the old price. He defined Shell's actions as "in effect carryover pricing." The jury's finding was reasonable in light of the circumstances of universal price protection by asphalt and aggregate suppliers, as well as by Shell on all price increases except 1974.

[32] *See* footnote 31, *supra.*

A commercial agreement, then, is broader than the written paper and its meaning is to be determined not just by the language used by them in the written contract but "by their action, read and interpreted in the light of commercial practices and other surrounding circumstances. The measure and background for interpretation are set by the commercial context, which may explain and supplement even the language of a formal or final writing." *Id.,* Comment 1. Performance, usages, and prior dealings are important enough to be admitted always, even for a final and complete agreement; only if they cannot be reasonably reconciled with the express terms of the contract are they not binding on the parties. "The express terms of an agreement and an applicable course of dealing or usage of trade shall be construed wherever reasonable as consistent with each other; but when such construction is unreasonable express terms control both course of dealing and usage of trade and course of dealing controls usage of trade." *Id.* § 490:1–205(4).

Of these three, then, the most important evidence of the agreement of the parties is their actual performance of the contract. *Id.* The operative definition of course of performance is as follows: "Where the contract for sale involves repeated occasions for performance by either party with knowledge of the nature of the performance and opportunity for objection to it by the other, any course of performance accepted or acquiesced in without objection shall be relevant to determine the meaning of the agreement." *Id.* § 490:2–208(1) . "Course of dealing ... is restricted, literally, to a sequence of conduct between the parties previous to the agreement. However, the provisions of the Act on course of performance make it clear that a sequence of conduct after or under the agreement may have equivalent meaning (Section 2–208)." *Id.* 490:1–205, Comment 2. The importance of evidence of course of performance is explained: "The parties themselves know best what they have meant by their words of agreement and their action under that agreement is the best indication of what that meaning was. This section thus rounds out the set of factors which determines the meaning of the 'agreement' . . . " *Id.* § 490:2–208, Comment 1. "Under this section a course of performance is always relevant to determine the meaning of the agreement." *Id.,* Comment 2.

Our study of the Code provisions and Comments, then, form the first basis of our holding that a trade usage to price protect pavers at times of price increases for work committed on nonescalating contracts could reasonably be construed as consistent with an express term of seller's posted price at delivery. Since the agreement of the parties is broader than the express terms and includes usages, which may even add terms to the agreement,[34] and since the commercial background provided by those

---

[34] "The agreement of the parties includes that part of their bargain found in course of dealing, usage of trade, or course of performance. These sources are relevant not only to the interpretation

usages is vital to an understanding of the agreement, we follow the Code's mandate to proceed on the assumption that the parties have included those usages unless they cannot reasonably be construed as consistent with the express terms.

Federal courts usually have been lenient in not ruling out consistent additional terms or trade usage for apparent inconsistency with express terms. The leading case on the subject is *Columbia Nitrogen Corp. v. Royster Co.,* 451 F.2d 3 (4th Cir.1971). Columbia, the buyer, had in the past primarily produced and sold nitrogen to Royster. When Royster opened a new plant that produced more phosphate than it needed, the parties reversed roles and signed a sales contract for Royster to sell excess phosphate to Columbia. The contract terms set out the price that would be charged by Royster and the amount to be sold. It provided for the price to go up if certain events occurred but did not provide for price declines. When the price of nitrogen fell precipitously, Columbia refused to accept the full amount of nitrogen specified in the contract after Royster refused to renegotiate the contract price. The District Judge's exclusion of usage of the trade and course of dealing to explain the express quantity term in the contract was reversed. Columbia had offered to prove that the quantity set out in the contract was a mere projection to be adjusted according to market forces. Ambiguity was not necessary for the admission of evidence of usage and prior dealings.[35] Even though the lengthy contract was the result of long and careful negotiations and apparently covered every contingency, the appellate court ruled that "the test of admissibility is not whether the contract appears on its face to be complete in every detail, but whether the proffered evidence of course of dealing and trade usage reasonably can be construed as consistent with the express terms of the agreement." *Id.* at 9. The express quantity term could be reasonably construed as consistent with a usage that such terms would be mere projections for several reasons: (1) the contract did not expressly state that usage and dealings evidence would be excluded; (2) the contract was silent on the adjustment of price or quantities in a declining market; (3) the minimum tonnage was expressed in the contract as Products Supplied, not Products Purchased; (4) the default clause of the contract did not state a penalty for failure to take delivery; and (5) apparently most important in the court's view, the parties had deviated from similar express terms in earlier contracts in times of

---

of express contract terms, but may themselves constitute contract terms." White & Summers, *supra,* § 3–3 at 84.

[35] As discussed earlier, the District Judge here mistakenly equated ambiguity with admissibility. He said, "I think this is a close case. On the face of the contract it would seem to be unambiguous," although acknowledging that liberal commentators on the Code would let in evidence of usage and performance even without ambiguity. He only let in usage evidence because Shell's answer to interrogatory 11 provided some ambiguity, . . . saying "I think if these can be consistently used to explain the apparently unambiguous terms, they should be allowed in." In fact, this court has ruled that ambiguity is not necessary to admit usage evidence. *Board of Trade of San Francisco v. Swiss Credit Bank,* 597 F.2d 146, 148 (9th Cir.1979).

declining market. *Id.* at 9–10. As here, the contract's merger clause said that there were no oral agreements. The court explained that its ruling "reflects the reality of the marketplace and avoids the overly legalistic interpretations which the Code seeks to abolish." *Id.* at 10. The Code assigns dealing and usage evidence "unique and important roles" and therefore "overly simplistic and overly legalistic interpretation of a contract should be shunned." *Id.* at 11. . . .

. . . Here the evidence was overwhelming that all suppliers to the asphaltic paving trade price protected customers under the same types of circumstances. Chevron's contract with H.B. was a similar long-term supply contract between a buyer and seller with very close relations, on a form supplied by the seller, covering sales of asphalt, and setting the price at seller's posted price, with no mention of price protection. . . .

> Because the stock printed forms cannot always reflect the changing methods of business, members of the trade may do business with a standard clause in the forms that they ignore in practice. If the trade consistently ignores obsolete clauses at variance with actual trade practices, a litigant can maintain that it is reasonable that the courts also ignore the clauses. . . .

Kirst, [Usage of Trade and Course of Dealing: Subversion of the UCC Theory, [1977] U.Ill.L. Forum 811] at 824. *Levie,* [Trade Usage and Custom . . ., 40 N.Y.U.L.Rev. 1101 (1965)], at 1112, writes, "Astonishing as it will seem to most practicing attorneys, under the Code it will be possible in some cases to use custom to contradict the written agreement. . . . Therefore usage may be used to 'qualify' the agreement, which presumably means to 'cut down' express terms although not to negate them entirely." Here, the express price term was "Shell's Posted Price at time of delivery." A total negation of that term would be that the buyer was to set the price. It is a less than complete negation of the term that an unstated exception exists at times of price increases, at which times the old price is to be charged, for a certain period or for a specified tonnage, on work already committed at the lower price on nonescalating contracts. Such a usage forms a broad and important exception to the express term, but does not swallow it entirely. Therefore, we hold that, under these particular facts, a reasonable jury could have found that price protection was incorporated into the 1969 agreement between Nanakuli and Shell and that price protection was reasonably consistent with the express term of seller's posted price at delivery. . . .

[The court also held that in light of the universal practice in the asphaltic paving trade of giving advance notice of a price increase, Shell could not have exercised good faith in raising its price by $32, effective January 1, in a letter written on December 31 and only received on January 4.]

Because the jury could have found for Nanakuli on its price protection claim under either theory, we reverse the judgment of the District Court and reinstate the jury verdict for Nanakuli in the amount of $220,800, plus interest according to law.

REVERSED AND REMANDED WITH DIRECTIONS TO ENTER FINAL JUDGMENT.

KENNEDY, CIRCUIT JUDGE, concurring specially:

The case involves specific pricing practices, not an allegation of unfair dealing generally. Our opinion should not be interpreted to permit juries to import price protection or a similarly specific contract term from a concept of good faith that is not based on well-established custom and usage or other objective standards of which the parties had clear notice. Here, evidence of custom and usage regarding price protection in the asphaltic paving trade was not contradicted in major respects, and the jury could find that the parties knew or should have known of the practice at the time of making the contract. In my view, these are necessary predicates for either theory of the case, namely, interpretation of the contract based on the course of its performance or a finding that good faith required the seller to hold the price. With these observations, I concur.

C-Thru Container Corp. v. Midland Mfg. Co.

533 N.W.2d 542 (Iowa 1995)

C-Thru and Midland entered into a contract under which Midland purchased bottle-making equipment from C-Thru. Under the contract, Midland could pay for the equipment by supplying commercially acceptable bottles to C-Thru. If Midland failed to supply the bottles, C-Thru could demand the purchase price of the equipment in cash. C-Thru claimed that Midland had breached the contract by being incapable of producing commercially acceptable bottles, and demanded that Midland pay the purchase price of the equipment. Midland contended that it had not breached the contract because C-Thru had not ordered any bottles. C-Thru responded that the practice in the bottling industry was that before the purchaser places an order, the bottle manufacturer provides sample bottles to verify that it is capable of producing commercially acceptable bottles, and that C-Thru had not provided such samples. C-Thru argued that evidence of this practice was inadmissible under the parol evidence rule, because the contract was complete and unambiguous. Held, evidence that there was such a practice was admissible.

We first reject Midland's argument that evidence of trade usage is admissible only when the contract is ambiguous. There is no such requirement in [UCC § 2–202]. Moreover, the official comment to [§ 2–202] ... states that this section "definitely rejects" a requirement that the language of the contract be ambiguous as a condition precedent to the admission of trade-usage evidence. . . .

We also hold that even a "complete" contract may be explained or supplemented by parol evidence of trade usages.[1] . . . As the official comment to section 2–202 states, commercial sales contracts "are to be read on the assumption that the course of prior dealings between the parties and the usages of trade were taken for granted when the document was phrased." U.C.C. § 2–202 cmt. 2 (1977). Therefore, even a completely integrated contract may be supplemented by practices in the industry that do not contradict express terms of the contract.

That brings us to the remaining argument made by Midland— that C-Thru may not use parol evidence to add a new term to the agreement. Section [2–202] says that when parol evidence shows a usage of trade that does not contradict a contract term, the evidence is admissible to "supplement" the contract. We look to the common meaning of the word "supplement." . . . "Supplement" means "to add . . . to." Webster's Third New Int'l Dictionary 2297 (1993). Consequently, the trade-usage evidence upon which C-Thru relies is admissible even though it adds a new term to the contract. White & Summers, § 3–3 (usage of trade may itself constitute a contract term).

SECTION 3. IMPLICATION AND PURPOSIVE INTERPRETATION

WILLIAMS, LANGUAGE AND THE LAW—PART IV
61 L.Q.Rev. 384, 400–404 (1945).

[A distinction must] be made between (a) the literal or primary meaning of the words, and (b) the ulterior meaning i.e., the meaning, other than the literal meaning, intended to be conveyed by the speaker when he uttered the words, or the meaning, other than the literal meaning, attributed by a hearer to the speaker. . . .

. . . For example a tactless host looks out of the window and says to his guest: "It has stopped raining." The guest mistakenly takes this to be an oblique hint that he is desired to leave. Here it may be said that while the meaning of the words to the host is "It has stopped raining" . . . the meaning to the guest is both this . . . and also "Please go". . . .

It has already been remarked that the Courts will generally enforce consequences logically implied in the language of contracts, wills, statutes,

---

[1]   The contract here stated that "[t]his agreement constitutes the entire agreement between C-Thru and Midland and supersedes any and all prior agreements between them."

and other legal documents and transactions. The point now to be noticed is that the legal doctrine of implied terms goes much farther than this. Judges are accustomed to read into documents and transactions many terms that are not logically implied in them. As an academic matter non-logical implication may be classified into three kinds: (i) of terms that the parties (the plural shall throughout include the singular) probably had in mind but did not trouble to express; (ii) of terms that the parties, whether or not they actually had them in mind, would probably have expressed if the question had been brought to their attention; and (iii) of terms that the parties, whether or not they had them in mind or would have expressed them if they had foreseen the difficulty, are implied by the Court because of the Court's view of fairness or policy or in consequence of rules of law. Of these three kinds of non-logical implication (i) is an effort to arrive at actual intention; (ii) is an effort to arrive at hypothetical or conditional intention— the intention that the parties would have had if they had foreseen the difficulty; (iii) is not concerned with the intention of the parties except to the extent that the term implied by the Court may be excluded by an expression of positive intention to the contrary.

. . . [O]nly in case (i) does the implication amount to a declaration by the Court of ulterior meaning in the sense already defined; in the other two cases the so-called implication is in reality an addition by the Court to the meaning of the parties. . . .

We pass to a consideration of . . . types (ii) and (iii). It is common form among judges to deny that they ever read into a contract or other document anything other than what, in their view, the parties actually intended; and occasionally they have even gone so far as to say that the implication must be collected from the words of the document itself. These statements cannot be taken seriously. It is true that the declaration of presumed actual intention is the commonest form of implication; but it is not the only form. Courts frequently import into a document terms that are not logically implied in it, and that the parties probably did not think about: or, to say the least, such terms are imported whether or not in the particular case it is probable that the parties thought about them. . . .

The view may perhaps be held that this particular process is not very happily called "implication." It is not so much the interpretation of a pre-existing and expressed intent as legislation amending or supplementing the expressed intent. Terms so read into the contract might better be called "constructive" than "implied." However, this is simply a question of nomenclature; and in any case no fixed nomenclature can be maintained in practice, because terms of classes (i) (ii) and (iii) merge into each other. . . .

This brings me to my last point, which is that it is a matter of taste whether implied terms of classes (ii) and (iii) be styled implied terms or rules of law. They are in fact merely rules of law that apply in the absence of an expression of contrary intent: whether we choose to call them implied terms or not is simply a matter of terminology. . . .

———

FISH, NORMAL CIRCUMSTANCES, LITERAL LANGUAGE, DIRECT SPEECH ACTS, THE ORDINARY, THE EVERYDAY, THE OBVIOUS, WHAT GOES WITHOUT SAYING, AND OTHER SPECIAL CASES
4 Critical Inquiry 625 (Summer 1978).

. . . [A]s Kenneth Abraham observes,

> A statute without a purpose would be meaningless . . . to speak of the literal meaning of a statute . . . is already to have read it in the light of some purpose, to have engaged in an interpretation.

In other words, any reading that is plain and obvious in the light of some assumed purpose (and it is impossible not to assume one) is a literal reading, but no reading is *the* literal reading in the sense that it is available apart from any purpose whatsoever.

A sentence is never not in a context. We are never not in a situation. . . . A set of interpretive assumptions is always in force. A sentence that seems to need no interpretation is already the product of one. . . .

[Suppose student X says to student Y, "Let's go to the movies tonight," and student Y replies, "I have to study for an exam." The statement by student X seems to be a proposal, and the statement by student Y seems to be rejection of the proposal. Now suppose student Y replies instead, "I have to eat popcorn tonight" or "I have to tie my shoes." In most circumstances, those statements would not be regarded as a rejection of the proposal. But] is it possible to imagine a set of circumstances in which "I have to eat popcorn tonight" would immediately and without any chain of inference be heard as a rejection of X's proposal? It is not only possible; it is easy. Let us suppose that student Y is passionately fond of popcorn and that it is not available in any of the local movie theaters. If student X knows these facts (if he and student Y mutually share background information), then he will hear "I have to eat popcorn tonight" as a rejection of his proposal. Or, let us suppose that student Y is by profession a popcorn taster; that is, he works in a popcorn manufacturing plant and is responsible for quality control. Again if student X knows this, he will hear "I have to eat popcorn tonight" as a rejection of his proposal because it will mean "Sorry, I have to work." Or, let us suppose that student Y owns seventy-five pairs of shoes and that he has been ordered by a dormitory housemother to retrieve them from various corners, arrange them neatly in one place, and tie them together in pairs so that they will not again be separated and scattered. In such a situation "I have to tie my shoes" will constitute a rejection of student X's proposal and will be so heard. Moreover it is not just "I have to eat popcorn" and "I have to tie my shoes" that could be heard as a rejection of the proposal; given the appropriate circumstances *any* sentence ("The Russians are coming," "My pen is blue," "Why do you behave like that?") could be so heard. . . .

The argument will also hold for "Let's go to the movies tonight." . . . Thus if speakers X and Y are trapped in some wilderness, and one says to the other, "Let's go to the movies tonight," it will be heard not as a proposal, but as a joke; or if student X is confined to his bed or otherwise immobilized, and student Y says, "Let's go to the movies tonight," it will be heard not as a proposal, but as a dare. . . .

It is important to realize what my argument does *not* mean. It does not mean that [a] sentence can mean anything at all. . . . A sentence . . . is never in the abstract; it is always in a situation, and the situation will already have determined the purpose for which it can be used. So it is not that any sentence can be used as a request to open the window, but that given any sentence, there are circumstances under which it would be heard as a request to open the window. A sentence neither means anything at all, nor does it always mean the same thing; it always has the meaning that has been conferred on it by the situation in which it is uttered.

————

RESTATEMENT, SECOND, CONTRACTS § 204

[See Selected Source Materials Supplement]

————

UNIDROIT PRINCIPLES OF INTERNATIONAL COMMERCIAL CONTRACTS ART. 4.8

[See Selected Source Materials Supplement]

————

BEANSTALK GROUP, INC. v. AM GENERAL CORPORATION

United States Court of Appeals, Seventh Circuit, 2002.
283 F.3d 856.

POSNER, J. Beanstalk, which serves owners of intellectual property by negotiating licenses of their property, brought this diversity suit for breach of its contract with AM General; the substantive issues are governed by the law of Indiana. The contract, called a "representation agreement," appointed Beanstalk an agent of AM General to obtain licenses to use the latter's "HUMMER" trademark. When the contract was made in 1997, AM General was the manufacturer of the Humvee, a military vehicle that is the successor to the jeep and like the jeep is also sold in a version intended for the civilian market, under the name "Hummer." Beanstalk named General Motors as an additional defendant for reasons that will appear in a moment. The district judge granted the defendants' motion to dismiss the complaint (to which Beanstalk had attached the representation agreement) for failure to state a claim. Fed.R.Civ.P. 12(b)(6). Since the representation agreement was part of a pleading rather than submitted separately, the judge could consider it without converting the defendants' motion to one for summary judgment. Fed.R.Civ.P. 12(c); *Berthold Types Ltd. v. Adobe Systems Inc.*, 242 F.3d 772, 775 (7th Cir.2001).

The agreement made Beanstalk AM General's "sole and exclusive nonemployee representative" for the purpose of licensing the Hummer trademark and entitled Beanstalk to 35 percent of the "gross receipts . . . received on Owner's [AM General's] behalf . . . under any License Agreements" made while the representation agreement was in force. Each license agreement "shall provide for all payments thereunder to be made to Beanstalk on Owner's behalf," and Beanstalk is required to account quarterly to AM General for "all gross receipts actually received during the preceding calendar quarter under any License Agreements." AM General is given "the absolute right to veto, without cause and at its sole discretion," any proposed license, including renewals. "License agreement" is defined as "any agreement or arrangement, whether in the form of a license or otherwise, granting merchandising or other rights in the Property," which in turn is defined to mean trademarks and related rights. The contract, which is assignable (though by Beanstalk only with AM's consent) and contains an integration clause, was to continue until the end of 2000.

The agreement was drafted by Beanstalk, but this fact has little interpretive significance since AM General is a commercially sophisticated party represented by counsel. Most courts now agree with this exception to the principle that contracts are to be construed against the party that drafted it. . . There are holdouts, illustrated by *Eastern Bus Lines, Inc. v. Board of Education*, 7 Conn.App. 581, 509 A.2d 1071, 1073–74 (1986), where the court, quoting an earlier opinion, said that "the party who actually does the writing of an instrument will presumably be guided by his own interests and goals in the transaction. He may choose shadings of expression, words more specific or more imprecise, according to the dictates of these interests." No doubt; but the other party, if commercially sophisticated and represented by counsel, will insist on clarification. Indiana has yet to take a stand on the exception . . . No matter . . . We add that the rule is in practice a makeweight rather than a tie breaker.

Beanstalk set about obtaining agreements for the licensing of the Hummer trademark. In 1999, however, two years into the representation agreement with Beanstalk, AM General entered into a joint-venture agreement with General Motors under which GM would design and engineer a new version of the Hummer, would make an interest-free loan of $235 million to AM General for the construction of a factory to manufacture the new version, would promise to buy a minimum number of the new vehicles, would obtain an option to buy up to 40 percent of AM General's common stock—and would acquire the Hummer trademark. GM informed Beanstalk that it had not assumed any of AM General's obligations under the representation agreement and that it would not compensate Beanstalk for any license agreements made or renewed after the effective date of the joint-venture agreement.

Beanstalk argues that the agreement between AM General and GM, although of course not labeled a license agreement, was one because it transferred the Hummer trademark to GM and thus was an "agreement or arrangement, whether in the form of a license or otherwise, granting merchandising or other rights in the Property"; for the transfer gave GM the right, indeed the exclusive right, to merchandise the Hummer trademark, that is, the "Property." The contract thus is clear, Beanstalk argues—the joint venture was an "agreement" that "grant[ed]" GM "merchandising . . . rights" in the Hummer trademark and it did not have to be "in the form of a license" because the representation agreement says "in the form of a license *or otherwise* "-and under accepted principles of contract law we should look no further. Beanstalk wants 35 percent of so much of the consideration running from GM to AM General as represents the value of the Hummer trademark. We do not know what the consideration was, or what that value is, because no evidence has been taken—in fact, the joint-venture agreement is not even in the record, though the sketch we have just given of its terms is not contested.

Beanstalk is correct that written contracts are usually enforced in accordance with the ordinary meaning of the language used in them and without recourse to evidence, beyond the contract itself, as to what the parties meant. This presumption simplifies the litigation of contract disputes and, more important, protects contracting parties against being blindsided by evidence intended to contradict the deal that they thought they had graven in stone by using clear language. It is a strong presumption, motivated by an understandable distrust in the accuracy of litigation to reconstruct contracting parties' intentions, but it is rebuttable—here by two principles of contract interpretation that are closely related in the setting of this suit. The first is that a contract will not be interpreted literally if doing so would produce absurd results, in the sense of results that the parties, presumed to be rational persons pursuing rational ends, are very unlikely to have agreed to seek. . .

This is an interpretive principle, not a species of paternalism. "The letters between plaintiff and defendant were from one merchant to another. They are to be read as businessmen would read them, and only as a last resort are to be thrown out altogether as meaningless futilities... If literalness is sheer absurdity, we are to seek some other meaning whereby reason will be instilled and absurdity avoided." *Outlet Embroidery Co. v. Derwent Mills,* 254 N.Y. 179, 172 N.E. 462, 463 (1930) (Cardozo, C.J.). "There is a long tradition in contract law of reading contracts sensibly; contracts—certainly business contracts of the kind involved here—are not parlor games but the means of getting the world's work done... True, parties *can* contract for preposterous terms. If contract language is crystal clear or there is independent extrinsic evidence that something silly was actually intended, a party may be held to its bargain, absent some specialized defense." *Rhode Island Charities Trust v. Engelhard Corp.,* 267 F.3d 3, 7 (1st Cir.2001); see also *Dispatch Automation, Inc. v. Richards,* 280 F.3d 1116, 1118–19 (7th Cir.2002). The second principle is that a contract must be interpreted as a whole... Sentences are not isolated units of meaning, but take meaning from other sentences in the same document.

The second principle thus is linguistic; the first reflects the fact that interpretation is a cultural as well as a linguistic undertaking. To interpret a contract or other document, it is not enough to have a command of the grammar, syntax, and vocabulary of the language in which the document is written. One must know something about the practical as well as the purely verbal context of the language to be interpreted. In the case of a commercial contract, one must have a general acquaintance with commercial practices. This doesn't mean that judges should have an M.B.A. or have practiced corporate or commercial law, but merely that they be alert citizens of a market-oriented society so that they can recognize absurdity in a business context. A blinkered literalism, a closing of one's eyes to the obvious, can produce nonsensical results, as this case illustrates. Beanstalk is in the business of merchandising trademarks. If, while the representation agreement was in effect, a toy company wanted to make a toy Hummer, Beanstalk was authorized to grant the toy company a license in exchange for a fee that it would split 35/65 with AM General. The joint-venture agreement was not that kind of arrangement. It was not an arrangement for the promotion of AM General's trademark. By the agreement creating the joint venture, AM General essentially transferred the Hummer business to General Motors, retaining a role limited to manufacturing, in a factory built with GM's money, a vehicle designed by, engineered by, and to be marketed by (that is the significance of the transfer of the trademark) GM. Quite apart from the option that GM also received to buy a large, doubtless controlling interest in AM General, it's as if AM General had sold its entire business, including its manufacturing assets and all its trademarks, to GM.

Beanstalk is not a business broker. It had nothing to do with the joint venture and indeed didn't even know about it until after it took place. The parties could hardly have intended that Beanstalk should get a commission if AM General decided, as in effect it did, to get out of the Hummer business. A business would not contract to pay an agent for work that the agent did not do but that the business did itself. Beanstalk and AM General must have known when they signed the representation agreement that if AM General ever sold its Hummer business, the trademark would go with it, as the purchaser would need it in order to identify the product, while AM General would no longer have any need or use for it. Indeed, AM General would have nothing to attach the trademark to—and a trademark is an identifier, not a freestanding piece of intellectual property; hence the rule that a trademark cannot be sold in gross, that is, without the assets that create the product that it identifies. 15 U.S.C. § 1060; *United Drug Co. v. Theodore Rectanus Co.*, 248 U.S. 90, 97, 39 S.Ct. 48, 63 L.Ed. 141 (1918); *In re Cult Awareness Network, Inc.*, 151 F.3d 605, 608 n. 1 (7th Cir.1998); *Green River Bottling Co. v. Green River Corp.*, 997 F.2d 359, 362 (7th Cir.1993); *Sands, Taylor & Wood Co. v. Quaker Oats Co.*, 978 F.2d 947, 956 (7th Cir.1992); *Beauty Time, Inc. v. VU Skin Systems, Inc.*, 118 F.3d 140, 150 (3d Cir.1997). The parties would hardly have intended Beanstalk to obtain a commission on the sale of the business merely because the sale would *inevitably* include the trademark. And they would not have wanted to burden the sale with the added cost of allocating the purchase price between the trademark and the other assets involved in the sale, as Beanstalk claims they must do in order to compute the commission to which it is entitled on the joint venture. (Such allocations may be required for tax purposes. See *Thrifticheck Service Corp. v. Commissioner,* 287 F.2d 1, 2, 3–4 (2d Cir.1961) (Friendly, J.). We are not told whether that was the case with the AM General-GM joint venture.)

The unreasonableness of Beanstalk's position can be seen most clearly by imagining that the joint venture had taken place the day after the representation agreement between Beanstalk and AM General went into effect. Then on Beanstalk's interpretation it would be entitled to 35 percent of the entire value of the Hummer trademark even though it had made absolutely no contribution to that value. That makes no sense; it is apparent that the definition of "License Agreement" in the representation agreement covers any agreement that has the function or character of a trademark licensing agreement even if the word "license" or a cognate term does not appear; the sale of a business is an agreement of an entirely different character. "[The] issue of whether a transfer of the use of a trademark is a sale or a license for tax purposes is a thorny one, and has not always been consistently solved in the courts. The basic problem is to determine the extent to which the transferor retains proprietary rights in the transferred asset. If the transferor retains sufficient proprietary rights, the transfer must be considered a license rather than a sale . . . We do not suggest that [the] nomenclature [used in the contract] should be finally determinative of the distinction between a license and a sale." *Consolidated Foods Corp. v. United States,* 569 F.2d 436, 437, 442 (7th Cir.1978). Indeed not.

Beanstalk ignores relevant provisions of the contract, one of which engages Beanstalk to be AM General's "sole and exclusive *non-employee* representative," implying that AM General's employees can negotiate license agreements without going through Beanstalk. Beanstalk agrees with this interpretation, as it must (there is no possible ambiguity), but claims that even when an employee of AM General negotiates such an agreement with no involvement by Beanstalk, Beanstalk is entitled to 35 percent of the revenues that AM General obtains under the agreement. No reason is given why AM General would compensate Beanstalk for services rendered wholly by AM General's own employees, whom it must compensate. That would be paying double for the same service.

Further ignored are the provisions keying Beanstalk's commissions to gross receipts "received"—obviously by Beanstalk—"on Owner's [that is, AM General's] behalf" and requiring Beanstalk to account to AM General periodically for the gross receipts of the license agreements. This implies that Beanstalk would receive receipts only for license agreements that it negotiated. The implication is reinforced by the fact that the representation agreement contains no provision for compensating Beanstalk out of receipts received directly by AM General, for example under a license agreement negotiated by an employee of AM General.

Beanstalk goes so far as to argue that, whoever negotiates the license agreement, the receipts generated by it must be paid in the first instance to Beanstalk to enable it to take its 35 percent cut off the top. Beanstalk thus is arguing that not 35 percent but 100 percent of the consideration that GM paid AM General for the joint-venture agreement that represented the value of the Hummer trademark had to be paid to Beanstalk. Beanstalk's argument amounts to saying that if Chrysler hired it to license the Chrysler trademarks and then sold its entire automobile business to Daimler for $10 billion, Beanstalk would be entitled to an immediate cash receipt of $10 billion, from which it would deduct 35 percent of the value of the Chrysler trademarks and then remit the balance to Chrysler. Absurd.

Against all this it might be argued that to disregard a contractual term, whether on the basis that interpreting it literally would yield absurd results or that other terms in the contract alter the disputed term's apparent meaning, requires evidence and thus cannot be done on a motion to dismiss. Not so. For when we said earlier that the interpretation of a contract is a cultural as well as a linguistic undertaking, we did not add that the materials of interpretation are limited to literal meanings on the one hand and trial-type evidence on the other. The cultural background that a judge brings to the decision of a contract case includes as we said a general knowledge of how the world operates, including the commercial world, and this knowledge, precisely because it is general rather than being knowledge of the specific facts of the case ("adjudicative facts"), can show that the literal interpretation of a particular contractual term would be unsound, in which event no evidence need be taken. *Unelko Corp. v. Prestone Products Corp.,* 116 F.3d 237, 240 (7th Cir.1997).

It would be different if Beanstalk, instead of standing on the literal terms of the representation agreement—on quicksand, in other words—wanted to present evidence to show that the agreement means what it says it means. The only evidence it wants to present is that before selling the Hummer business to GM, AM General approached Beanstalk and asked for an express exclusion from the representation agreement of any agreement "for the purpose of producing motor vehicles" even if such an agreement included a transfer of trademark rights. But of course. It was simple prudence for AM General to try to head off this lawsuit. It doesn't follow that the lawsuit has any merit. Indeed, to penalize AM General for attempting an amicable resolution of a potential dispute in advance would violate the spirit of the rule that makes settlement offers inadmissible in an adjudication on the merits. See Fed.R.Evid. 408.

With our conclusion that there was no breach of contract, Beanstalk's other claims collapse . . .

As for GM's having told Beanstalk that it will not pay any commissions on license agreements that are renewed, GM was entitled as the owner of the "Property" to veto any license agreements, including renewals, that Beanstalk might propose. Even if GM remains bound by the representation agreement, which it does not, because the agreement did not require AM General to assign its duties under it to an assignee of the "Property" covered by the agreement, the veto power granted the represented party excuses GM from any duty to renew any license agreements negotiated by Beanstalk.

[The dissenting opinion of Rovner, J., is omitted]

———

SECTION 4. THE OBLIGATION TO PERFORM IN GOOD FAITH

SEGGEBRUCH V. STOSOR

Appellate Court of Illinois, 1941.
309 Ill. App. 385, 33 N.E.2d 159.

O'CONNOR, J. June 29, 1939, plaintiff filed a forcible detainer suit against defendant to recover possession of certain premises in Chicago Heights which were improved with a brick building used as a gasoline station. In the complaint it is alleged defendant was to pay 1 1/4 cents for each gallon of gasoline sold as rental for the premises; that defendant had performed all the covenants of the lease, paid the monthly rent which was approximately $140 a month up to May 1, 1939; that shortly prior to that date defendant acquired an adjoining lot and erected another gasoline station thereon which he continued to operate from May 1, and abandoned the operation of the gas station on plaintiff's premises, except occasionally defendant sold a few gallons of gasoline. Plaintiff claimed $1000 was due under the terms of the lease.

Defendant filed his answer in which he set up the lease entered into between the parties June 24, 1937, covering a period from July 1, 1937, to June 30, 1942; denied he had ceased operating the gasoline station; admitted he operated a gasoline station on the adjoining premises but denied that in doing so he had breached any of covenants of the lease; averred he had maintained a full time attendant every day who operated the gasoline station on plaintiff's premises from 7:30 o'clock in the morning to 7:30 o'clock in the evening; denied plaintiff was entitled to possession of the premises or that plaintiff was entitled to recover any damages.

March 6, 1940, plaintiff filed a "Separate Action in Chancery" in which, among other things, she alleged that a short time prior to May 1, 1939, defendant, intending to cheat and defraud plaintiff, acquired adjoining real estate and erected a gasoline station thereon; that since May 1, 1939, defendant had refused to have an attendant at the gasoline station located on plaintiff's premises, except that he sold about 200 gallons of gasoline a month from that station while prior to May 1, he had sold approximately 12,000 gallons a month; that defendant was financially insolvent and plaintiff was without an adequate remedy at law; that she was entitled to recover the reasonable rental of the premises which was $150 a month; that the lease be canceled and plaintiff be given a decree for the amount found due.

Defendant filed his answer in which he alleged he kept an attendant who operated the gasoline station on plaintiff's premises every day, substantially as alleged in his answer to the forcible detainer suit; admitted he sold approximately 12,000 gallons of gasoline per month prior to May 1,

1939; alleged he had asked plaintiff to "enclose the grease and oil rack so that he could more completely service his customers," which plaintiff refused to do, and thereupon he was compelled to erect a gasoline station on the adjoining premises; denied he was insolvent; denied that the reasonable rental value of the premises was $150 per month, and denied that plaintiff was entitled to recover damages.

April 23, 1940, the case was heard before the court without a jury and a decree entered which found the equities in favor of plaintiff; that defendant had maliciously failed and refused to operate the gasoline station on plaintiff's premises for the purpose of defrauding her; that there was due and owing plaintiff $147.50 a month from May 1, 1939, to the date of the entry of the decree. The decree further found the court had theretofore entered judgment at law in the forcible detainer case in plaintiff's favor and against defendant that she recover possession of the premises and it was decreed that plaintiff recover from defendant $1696.25. Defendant appeals from that part of the decree awarding plaintiff $1696.25. No appeal was taken from the judgment entered in the forcible detainer case.

Defendant contends he had a right to construct and conduct a station on the adjoining premises because, as stated by counsel, "No minimum rental is fixed and there is no agreement that the defendant will not conduct the same business at any other address"—that since the lease contained no provision on this question defendant was at liberty to conduct the gasoline station on the adjoining premises.

In deciding the case the chancellor said: "The parties hereto entered into a written lease for the premises and as a rental it is provided" that defendant would pay plaintiff 1 1/4 cents for each gallon of gasoline "sold from the premises each month during the term * * * During the term created by the lease the Defendant built another station immediately adjoining this particular station and began to operate the new place.

"The pleadings admit that prior to his occupation of the new station there was sold an average of 12,000 gallons of gas at the station operated under the lease and that immediately after the new station began to be operated the sale of gas in the old place dropped to some 200 gallons a month. The Defendant on the witness stand admits there was no change in the volume of sale at the place so that since the operation of the new station the sales in the two places have reached about the same as the sales in the old place when it was operated alone.

"In an undertaking such as we have here the lessee undertakes to operate the premises in such a way as to reasonably produce the rental contemplated by the parties at the time the contract was entered into, and that he will not by his own act deprive the Plaintiff of her share of the bargain to which she would be reasonably entitled if the premises continued in the condition in which it was rented without hinderance on the part of the Defendant.

"Here the Defendant willfully and deliberately and purely with the intention of injuring the Plaintiff built himself a station right next door and transferred to the new place. Now he stands before the Court and says there is nothing in my contract that I will not cheat the Plaintiff by building my own station next door thereby depriving her of income under the lease. Of course, there is not. Certainly the Plaintiff could not foresee such a possibility and the law will not stand by and allow such an evident wrong to be committed without finding some remedy. The law will treat the income from the new place as belonging to the old, especially since the evidence clearly shows there was no change in the volume."

We agree with the statement of the chancellor and while there was no express covenant in the lease, it was clearly implied that defendant would use reasonable diligence in operating the gas station on plaintiff's premises.

In Thebest Laundry & Cleaning Co. v. Duffy, 293 Ill.App. 252, 12 N.E.2d 235, in passing on a contract we said: "In Grossman v. Schenker, 206 N.Y. 466 [100 N.E. 39], the court said (p. 469 [p. 40]): 'A contract includes not only what the parties said but also what is necessarily to be implied from what they said. (Milliken v. Western Union Tel. Co., 110 N.Y. 403, 408 [18 N.E. 251, 1 L.R.A. 281].) Thus the words "cash on delivery" with no other promise to pay "imply a promise and create an obligation" to make payment upon delivery. (Justice v. Lang, supra [42 N.Y. 493, 1 Am.Rep. 576].) So the word "sold" in a written agreement implies not only a contract to sell but also a contract to buy (Butler v. Thomson, 92 U.S. 412, 414 [23 L.Ed. 684]); and a contract to buy with no express promise to sell implies the latter obligation. ([Delaware &] Hudson Canal Co. v. Penn. Coal Co., 75 U.S. (8 Wall.) 276, 289 19 L.Ed. 349].) "What is implied in an express contract is as much a part of it as what is expressed" (Bishop on Contracts (2d Ed.), sec. 241); for "the law is a silent factor in every contract." (Long v. Straus, 107 Ind. 94, 95 [6 N.E. 123, 7 N.E. 763, 57 Am.Rep. 87].)' "

And our Supreme Court many years ago announced the law as above stated. Daughetee v. Ohio Oil Co., 263 Ill. 518, 105 N.E. 308; Stoddard v. Ill. Imp. Co., 275 Ill. 199, 113 N.E. 913.

In the Daughetee case, the court construed an oil and gas lease, by which the lessee was given the exclusive right to explore plaintiff's land for gas and oil, to mean that the lessee was required to use reasonable diligence to develop oil and gas on the lands. And in the Stoddard case where lands were leased for a stone quarry it was held that the lessee should quarry stone with reasonable diligence for a term covered by the lease if the stone could be found and quarried at a profit, and that if the lessee retained possession of the property but quarried no stone he was liable in damages for the amount of stone at the price fixed in the lease which could by reasonable diligence have been quarried and sold at a profit.

The decree of the Circuit Court of Cook County is affirmed.

Decree affirmed.

NOTE ON IMPLIED STANDARDS OF PERFORMANCE

The rent of 1 and $1/4$ cent per gallon of gasoline sold is an example of an open performance term. If the contract had simply said nothing at all about the amount of the rent, and it was clear the parties intended to be bound, then a court that follows principles of modern contract law will imply an obligation to pay a reasonable rent. (A court that follows principles of classical contract law might find the contract unenforceable on ground of indefiniteness.) In *Seggebrush* the contract based the rent on the volume of gas sold but it said nothing about how much gas was to be sold. The court implied an obligation to use "reasonable diligence" to sell gas.

Contracts that define quantity as a seller's "output" or a buyer's "requirements" of a good raise a similar issue. UCC § 2–306(1) provides such a term means "such actual or output or requirements as may occur in good faith." The statute further provides the quantity cannot be "unreasonably disproportionate" to "normal or otherwise comparable prior output or requirements." UCC § 2–306(2) applies to a contract "for exclusive dealing in the kind of goods concerned." When the buyer has an exclusive right to resale the goods there is "an obligation . . . by the buyer to use best efforts to promote their sale." Official Comment 5 equates "best efforts" with "reasonable diligence as well as good faith."

Bloor v. Falstaff Brewing Corp., 601 F.2d 609 (2nd Cir. 1979), involves a claim by the seller of the Ballantine beer brand against the buyer of the brand, Falstaff, for breach of an express promise to use "best efforts" to sell Ballantine beer. Falstaff paid $4 million for the brand and related assets plus a royalty of 50 cents for each barrel of Ballantine sold for a six year period. Falstaff lost money for the first few years as sales of both Ballantine and Falstaff declined in the face of competition from national brands. New owners took over Falstaff in 1975. The new owners made changes that returned Falstaff to profitability but that resulted in plummeting sales of Ballantine during a period in which sales of regional beers also declined but much less dramatically. The case was tried to a judge who did not clearly spell out the standard he applied in finding a breach of contract and awarding damages. The Court of Appeals had the following to say about the standard of performance required under New York law as well as the degree of certainty required in fixing damages:

> . . . [A]ppellate counsel for Falstaff contend that the judge read the best efforts clause as requiring Falstaff to maintain Ballantine's

volume by any sales methods having a good prospect of increasing or maintaining sales or, at least, to continue lawful methods in use at the time of purchase, no matter what losses they would cause. Starting from this premise, counsel reason that the judge's conclusion was at odds with New York law, stipulated by the contract to be controlling, as last expressed by the Court of Appeals in Feld v. Henry S. Levy & Sons, Inc., 37 N.Y.2d 466, 373 N.Y.S.2d 102, 335 N.E.2d 320 (1975). . . . Falstaff argues from this that it was not bound to do anything to market Ballantine products that would cause "more than trivial" losses.

We do not think the judge imposed on Falstaff a standard as demanding as its appellate counsel argues that he did. . . . [H]e did not in fact proceed on the basis that the best efforts clause required Falstaff to bankrupt itself in promoting Ballantine products or even to sell those products at a substantial loss. . .

. . . With respect to its own brands, management was entirely free to exercise its business judgment as to how to maximize profit even if this meant serious loss in volume. Because of the obligation it had assumed under the sales contract, its situation with respect to the Ballantine brands was quite different. The royalty of $.50 a barrel on sales was an essential part of the purchase price. Even without the best efforts clause Falstaff would have been bound to make a good faith effort to see that substantial sales of Ballantine products were made, unless it discontinued under clause 2(a)(v) with consequent liability for liquidated damages. Cf. Wood v. Duff-Gordon, 222 N.Y. 88, 118 N.E. 214 (1917) (Cardozo, J.). Clause 8 imposed an added obligation to use "best efforts to promote and maintain a *high* volume of sales. . . . " (emphasis supplied). Although we agree that even this did not require Falstaff to spend itself into bankruptcy to promote the sales of Ballantine products, it did prevent the application to them of Kalmanovitz' philosophy of emphasizing profit *über alles* without fair consideration of the effect on Ballantine volume. Plaintiff was not obliged to show just what steps Falstaff could reasonably have taken to maintain a high volume for Ballantine products. It was sufficient to show that Falstaff simply didn't care about Ballantine's volume and was content to allow this to plummet so long as that course was best for Falstaff's overall profit picture, an inference which the judge permissibly drew. The burden then shifted to Falstaff to prove there was nothing significant it could have done to promote Ballantine sales that would not have been financially disastrous.

Having correctly concluded that Falstaff had breached its best efforts covenant, the judge was faced with a difficult problem in computing what the royalties on the lost sales would have been. There is no need to rehearse the many decisions that, in a situation like this, certainty is not required; "[t]he plaintiff need only show a 'stable foundation for a reasonable estimate of royalties he would have earned had defendant not breached' "... . After carefully considering other possible bases, the court arrived at the seemingly sensible conclusion that the most nearly accurate comparison was with the combined sales of Rheingold and Schaefer beers, both, like Ballantine, being "price" beers sold primarily in the northeast, and computed what Ballantine sales would have been if its brands had suffered only the same decline as a composite of Rheingold and Schaefer. . . .

... It is true ... that the award may overcompensate the plaintiff since Falstaff was not necessarily required to do whatever Rheingold and Shaefer did. But that is the kind of uncertainty which is permissible in favor of a plaintiff who has established liability in a case like this. . . .

———

UCC § 2–306

[See Selected Source Materials Supplement]

———

RESTATEMENT, SECOND, CONTRACTS § 205

[See Selected Source Materials Supplement]

———

PRE-2001 UCC ARTICLE 1, §§ 1–201(19), 1–203, UCC § 2–103(1)(b)

2001 VERSION OF ARTICLE 1, § 1–201(20)

[See Selected Source Materials Supplement]

———

NOTE ON THE UCC DEFINITIONS OF GOOD FAITH

The UCC is promulgated by the National Conference of Commissioners on Uniform State Law (NCCUSL) and the American Law Institute (ALI). However, the UCC is only effective to the extent it is adopted by state legislatures. Prior to 2001, Section 1–201(19) of Article 1 (General Provisions) defined good faith narrowly, to mean "honesty in fact in the conduct or transaction concerned." In contrast, Section 2–201 of Article 2 (Sale of Goods) defined good faith broadly, to mean, in the case of a merchant, "honesty in fact and the observance of reasonable commercial standards of fair dealing in the trade."

In 2001, NCCUSL and the ALI promulgated a revised official version of UCC Article 1. Section 1–201 (20) of the revised official version of Article 1 defined good faith broadly, for all Articles of the UCC except Article 5, to mean "honesty in fact and the observance of reasonable commercial standards of fair dealing." The adoption of this broad definition in the revised official version of Article 1 rendered superfluous the broad definition of good faith in the official version of Article 2. Accordingly, that definition was deleted from the official version of Article 2. Prof. Keith Rowley reports that as of July 1, 2011, forty states had adopted the revised official version of Article 1. Of these forty, eleven did not adopt the definition of good faith in revised Article 1 and retained the prior definition of good faith in Article 2.

CISG ART. 7(1)

[See Selected Source Materials Supplement]

UNIDROIT PRINCIPLES OF INTERNATIONAL COMMERCIAL CONTRACTS ART. 1.7

[See Selected Source Materials Supplement]

PRINCIPLES OF EUROPEAN CONTRACT LAW ART. 1.201

[See Selected Source Materials Supplement]

NOTE ON CRITICISM OF THE DOCTRINE

Young Living Essential Oils, LC v. Marin, 366 P.3d 814 (Utah 2011), warns that "judicial inference of contract terms is also fraught with peril, as its misuse threatens commercial certainty and breeds costly litigation." The opinion continues:

> With these concerns in mind, we have set a high bar for the invocation of a new covenant. Under our cases, the court may recognize a covenant of good faith and fair dealing where it is clear from the parties' "course of dealings" or a settled custom or usage of trade that the parties undoubtedly would have agreed to the covenant if they had considered and addressed it. No such covenant may be invoked, however, if it would create obligations "inconsistent with express contractual terms." These limitations likewise protect the reliance interests of the parties to a contract and foreclose the

imposition of a code of commercial morality rooted merely in judicial sensibilities. Where the court adopts a covenant enshrined in a settled custom or usage of trade, it is simply endorsing a universal standard that the parties would doubtless have adopted if they had thought to address it by contract. Where the parties themselves have agreed to terms that address the circumstance that gave rise to their dispute, by contrast, the court has no business injecting its own sense of what amounts to "fair dealing." By enforcing these standards and limitations, our cases preserve the core role of the covenant of good faith while controlling against its misuse to the detriment of commercial security and reliance.

Marin was a distributor of Young Living products. He argued Young Living had breached a promise to provide him promotional materials, and that this breach excused his failure to meet performance guarantees. Young Living prevailed in the district court on a motion for summary judgment with "the court holding that the parol-evidence rule barred extrinsic evidence of a condition not set forth in the parties' integrated contract and that such a condition could not be inferred through the covenant of good faith and fair dealing." The rejected evidence was an affidavit from Marin attesting to repeated representations and a shared understanding that promotional materials would be supplied. Marin argued the representations, some of which were subsequent to the execution of the distributorship agreement, constituted a "course of dealing." The court replied:

> Marin misperceives the kind of "course of dealing" evidence that is relevant to establishing a covenant of good faith and fair dealing. The covenant is not a license for the judiciary to codify standards of altruism that a party may have held itself to in the course of its contract performance. Young Living may have expressed a willingness to provide marketing materials to Marin, but that does not itself establish a binding legal covenant to do so. To sustain a new covenant, evidence of "course of dealing" would have to conform to the core terms of the legal doctrine, by demonstrating a settled, longstanding pattern of dealing that the parties unquestionably would have relied on (but failed to memorialize) in entering into their contract. If Young Living for years provided new product to its distributors on the first of every month, for example, but suddenly withheld such product until the 20th of the month despite the existence of a monthly sales quota, it might make sense to deem Young Living to have breached a covenant informed by the parties' longstanding course of dealing. That is not at all what is presented by Marin here, however, and his claim fails despite his invocation of the "course of dealing" terminology.

English v. Fischer, 660 S.W.2d 521, 522 (Tex. 1983), rejects the doctrine entirely:

A basis for the judgments below was the adoption of a novel theory of law enunciated only by California courts. That theory holds that in every contract there is an implied covenant that neither party will do anything which injures the right of the other party to receive the benefits of the agreement. The courts below call this a covenant of "good faith and fair dealing."

This concept is contrary to our well-reasoned and long-established adversary system which has served us ably in Texas for almost 150 years. Our system permits parties who have a dispute over a contract to present their case to an impartial tribunal for a determination of the agreement as made by the parties and embodied in the contract itself. To adopt the laudatory sounding theory of "good faith and fair dealing" would place a party under the onerous threat of treble damages should he seek to compel his adversary to perform according to the contract terms as agreed upon by the parties. The novel concept advocated by the courts below would abolish our system of government according to settled rules of law and let each case be decided upon what might seem "fair and in good faith," by each fact finder. This we are unwilling to do.

Some of this criticism appears to be directed at the <u>tort</u> of bad faith breach of contract. California law at the time was unusual in allowing a tort claim with possible punitive damages for bad faith breach outside the insurance context, and in particular for bad faith termination of an at-will employee.

MARKET STREET ASSOCIATES V. FREY

United States Court of Appeals, Seventh Circuit, 1991.
941 F.2d 588.

[Market Street Associates acquired the leasehold interest in a shopping center owned by General Electric Pension Trust under a 25-year sale leaseback agreement. Market Street Associates acquired the property in 1987 when there were six years left to run on the lease. Under the sale leaseback agreement, the lessee could request the lessor (the pension trust) finance improvements costing at least $250,000. If such a request was made, then the pension trust agreed to negotiate in good faith to provide financing, and, if negotiations failed, then after 60 days, the lessee had an option to purchase the property for the original price increased 6% per annum. In 1988 Market Street Associates sought to buy the property from the pension trust, acting through its General Partner, Orenstein. David Erb, the responsible official at the pension trust, failed to return Orenstein's calls, and eventually quoted a price ($3 million) that Orenstein thought was much too high. At this point Orenstein made a formal request for $2 million financing, but never mentioning the lease nor the relevant provision of the lease providing the contingent buy-out option. Erb peremptorily rejected this request, explaining that the pension trust was not interested in financing projects of less than $7 million. Orenstein replied that he would look elsewhere for financing. The next communication from Orenstein to Erb was sent immediately after the 60 day period ended. It was a notice that Market Street Associates was exercising the buy-out option at a price of $1 million.]

POSNER, CIRCUIT JUDGE . . . .

The pension trust refused to sell, and this suit to compel specific performance followed. Apparently the price computed by the formula in paragraph 34 is only $1 million. The market value must be higher, or Market Street Associates wouldn't be trying to coerce conveyance at the paragraph 34 price; whether it is as high as $3 million, however, the record does not reveal.

The district judge granted summary judgment for the pension trust on two grounds that he believed to be separate although closely related. The first was that, by failing in its correspondence with the pension trust to mention paragraph 34 of the lease, Market Street Associates had prevented the negotiations over financing that are a condition precedent to the lessee's exercise of the purchase option from taking place. Second, this same failure violated the duty of good faith . . . . In support of both grounds the judge emphasized a statement by Orenstein in his deposition that it had occurred to him that Erb mightn't know about paragraph 34, though this was unlikely (Orenstein testified) because Erb or someone else at the pension trust would probably check the file and discover the paragraph and realize that if the trust refused to negotiate over the request for financing, Market Street Associates, as Penney's assignee, would be entitled to walk off with the property for (perhaps) a song. The judge inferred that Market Street Associates didn't want financing from the pension trust—that it just wanted an opportunity to buy the property at a bargain price and hoped that the pension trust wouldn't realize the implications of turning down the request for financing. Market Street Associates should, the judge opined, have advised the pension trust that it was requesting financing pursuant to paragraph 34, so that the trust would understand the penalty for refusing to negotiate. . . .

So we must consider the meaning of the contract duty of "good faith." The Wisconsin cases are cryptic as to its meaning though emphatic about its existence, so we must cast our net wider. We do so mindful of Learned Hand's warning, that "such words as 'fraud,' 'good faith,' 'whim,' 'caprice,' 'arbitrary action,' and 'legal fraud' . . . obscure the issue." Thompson-Starrett Co. v. La Belle Iron Works, 17 F.2d 536, 541 (2d Cir.1927). Indeed they do. . . . The particular confusion to which the vaguely moralistic overtones of "good faith" give rise is the belief that every contract establishes a fiduciary relationship. A fiduciary is required to treat his principal as if the principal were he, and therefore he may not take advantage of the principal's incapacity, ignorance, inexperience, or even naivete. . . . Meinhard v. Salmon, 249 N.Y. 458, 463–64, 164 N.E. 545, 546 (1928) (Cardozo, C.J.). If Market Street Associates were the fiduciary of General Electric Pension Trust, then (we may assume) it could not take advantage of Mr. Erb's apparent ignorance of paragraph 34, however exasperating Erb's failure to return Orenstein's phone calls was and however negligent Erb or his associates were in failing to read the lease before turning down Orenstein's request for financing.

But it is unlikely that Wisconsin wishes, in the name of good faith, to make every contract signatory his brother's keeper, especially when the brother is the immense and sophisticated General Electric Pension Trust, whose lofty indifference to small (= < $7 million) transactions is the signifier of its grandeur. In fact the law contemplates that people frequently will take advantage of the ignorance of those with whom they contract, without thereby incurring liability. Restatement, supra, § 161, comment d. The duty of honesty, of good faith even expansively conceived, is not a duty of candor. You can make a binding contract to purchase something you know your seller undervalues. Laidlaw v. Organ, 15 U.S. (2 Wheat.) 178, 181 n. 2, 4 L.Ed. 214 (1817); . . . Anthony T. Kronman, "Mistake, Disclosure, Information, and the Law of Contracts," 7 J. Legal Stud. 1 (1978).

That of course is a question about formation, not performance, and the particular duty of good faith under examination here relates to the latter rather than to the former. But even after you have signed a contract, you are not obliged to become an altruist toward the other party and relax the terms if he gets into trouble in performing his side of the bargain. Kham & Nate's Shoes No. 2, Inc. v. First Bank, 908 F.2d 1351, 1357 (7th Cir.1990). Otherwise mere difficulty of performance would excuse a contracting party—which it does not. Northern Indiana Public Service Co. v. Carbon County Coal Co., 799 F.2d 265, 276–78 (7th Cir.1986). . . .

But it is one thing to say that you can exploit your superior knowledge of the market—for if you cannot, you will not be able to recoup the investment you made in obtaining that knowledge—or that you are not required to spend money bailing out a contract partner who has gotten into trouble. It is another thing to say that you can take deliberate advantage of an oversight by your contract partner concerning his rights under the contract. Such taking advantage is not the exploitation of superior knowledge or the avoidance of unbargained-for expense; it is sharp dealing. Like theft, it has no social product, and also like theft it induces costly defensive expenditures, in the form of overelaborate disclaimers or investigations into the trustworthiness of a prospective contract partner, just as the prospect of theft induces expenditures on locks. See generally

Steven J. Burton, "Breach of Contract and the Common Law Duty to Perform in Good Faith," 94 Harv.L.Rev. 369, 393 (1980).

The form of sharp dealing that we are discussing might or might not be actionable as fraud or deceit. That is a question of tort law and there the rule is that if the information is readily available to both parties the failure of one to disclose it to the other, even if done in the knowledge that the other party is acting on mistaken premises, is not actionable. . . . Before the contract is signed, the parties confront each other with a natural wariness. Neither expects the other to be particularly forthcoming, and therefore there is no deception when one is not. Afterwards the situation is different. The parties are now in a cooperative relationship the costs of which will be considerably reduced by a measure of trust. So each lowers his guard a bit, and now silence is more apt to be deceptive. Cf. AMPAT/Midwest, Inc. v. Illinois Tool Works Inc., 896 F.2d 1035, 1040–41 (7th Cir.1990).

Moreover, this is a contract case rather than a tort case, and conduct that might not rise to the level of fraud may nonetheless violate the duty of good faith in dealing with one's contractual partners and thereby give rise to a remedy under contract law. Burton, supra, at 372 n. 17. This duty is, as it were, halfway between a fiduciary duty (the duty of *utmost* good faith) and the duty merely to refrain from active fraud. Despite its moralistic overtones it is no more the injection of moral principles into contract law than the fiduciary concept itself is. Tymshare, Inc. v. Covell, 727 F.2d 1145, 1152 (D.C.Cir.1984). . . It would be quixotic as well as presumptuous for judges to undertake through contract law to raise the ethical standards of the nation's business people. The concept of the duty of good faith like the concept of fiduciary duty is a stab at approximating the terms the parties would have negotiated had they foreseen the circumstances that have given rise to their dispute. The parties want to minimize the costs of performance. To the extent that a doctrine of good faith designed to do this by reducing defensive expenditures is a reasonable measure to this end, interpolating it into the contract advances the parties' joint goal.

It is true that an essential function of contracts is to allocate risk, and would be defeated if courts treated the materializing of a bargained-over, allocated risk as a misfortune the burden of which is required to be shared between the parties (as it might be within a family, for example) rather than borne entirely by the party to whom the risk had been allocated by mutual agreement. But contracts do not just allocate risk. They also (or some of them) set in motion a cooperative enterprise, which may to some extent place one party at the other's mercy. "The parties to a contract are embarked on a cooperative venture, and a minimum of cooperativeness in the event unforeseen problems arise at the performance stage is required even if not an explicit duty of the contract." AMPAT/Midwest, Inc. v. Illinois

Tool Works, Inc., supra, 896 F.2d at 1041. The office of the doctrine of good faith is to forbid the kinds of opportunistic behavior that a mutually dependent, cooperative relationship might enable in the absence of rule. " 'Good faith' is a compact reference to an implied undertaking not to take opportunistic advantage in a way that could not have been contemplated at the time of drafting, and which therefore was not resolved explicitly by the parties." Kham & Nate's Shoes No. 2, Inc. v. First Bank, supra, 908 F.2d at 1357. The contractual duty of good faith is thus not some newfangled bit of welfare-state paternalism or (pace Duncan Kennedy, "Form and Substance in Private Law Adjudication," 89 Harv.L.Rev. 1685, 1721 (1976)) the sediment of an altruistic strain in contract law, and we are therefore not surprised to find the essentials of the modern doctrine well established in nineteenth-century cases . . .

The emphasis we are placing on postcontractual versus precontractual conduct helps explain the pattern that is observed when the duty of contractual good faith is considered in all its variety, encompassing not only good faith in the *performance* of a contract but also good faith in its *formation*, Summers, supra, at 220–32, and in its enforcement. Harbor Ins. Co. v. Continental Bank Corp., 922 F.2d 357, 363 (7th Cir.1990). The formation or negotiation stage is precontractual, and here the duty is minimized. It is greater not only at the performance but also at the enforcement stage, which is also postcontractual. "A party who hokes up a phony defense to the performance of his contractual duties and then when that defense fails (at some expense to the other party) tries on another defense for size can properly be said to be acting in bad faith." Id.; see also Larson v. Johnson, 1 Ill.App.2d 36, 46, 116 N.E.2d 187, 191–92 (1953). At the formation of the contract the parties are dealing in present realities; performance still lies in the future. As performance unfolds, circumstances change, often unforeseeably; the explicit terms of the contract become progressively less apt to the governance of the parties' relationship; and the role of implied conditions—and with it the scope and bite of the good-faith doctrine—grows.

We could of course do without the term "good faith," and maybe even without the doctrine. We could, as just suggested, speak instead of implied conditions necessitated by the unpredictability of the future at the time the contract was made. Farnsworth, "Good Faith Performance and Commercial Reasonableness under the Uniform Commercial Code," 30 U.Chi.L.Rev. 666, 670 (1963). Suppose a party has promised work to the promisee's "satisfaction." As Learned Hand explained, "he may refuse to look at the work, or to exercise any real judgment on it, in which case he has prevented performance and excused the condition." Thompson-Starrett Co. v. La Belle Iron Works, supra, 17 F.2d at 541. See also Morin Building Products Co. v. Baystone Construction, Inc., 717 F.2d 413, 415 (7th Cir.1983). That is, it was an implicit condition that the promisee examine the work to the extent necessary to determine whether it was satisfactory; otherwise the performing party would have been placing himself at the complete mercy of the promisee. The parties didn't write this condition into the contract either because they thought such behavior unlikely or failed to foresee it altogether. In just the same way—to switch to another familiar example of the operation of the duty of good faith—parties to a requirements contract surely do not intend that if the price of the product covered by the contract rises, the buyer shall be free to increase his "requirements" so that he can take advantage of the rise in the market price over the contract price to resell the product on the open market at a guaranteed profit. Empire Gas Corp. v. American Bakeries Co., 840 F.2d 1333 (7th Cir.1988). If they fail to insert an express condition to this effect, the court will read it in, confident that the parties would have inserted the condition if they had known what the future held. Of similar character is the implied condition that an exclusive dealer will use his best efforts to promote the supplier's goods, since otherwise the exclusive feature of the dealership contract would place the supplier at the dealer's mercy. Wood v. Duff-Gordon, 222 N.Y. 88, 118 N.E. 214 (1917) (Cardozo, J.).

But whether we say that a contract shall be deemed to contain such implied conditions as are necessary to make sense of the contract, or that a contract obligates the parties to cooperate in its performance in "good faith" to the extent necessary to carry out the purposes of the contract, comes to much the same thing. They are different ways of formulating the overriding purpose of contract law, which is to give the parties what they would have stipulated for expressly if at the time of making the contract they had had complete knowledge of the future and the costs of negotiating and adding provisions to the contract had been zero.

. . . The dispositive question in the present case is simply whether Market Street Associates tried to trick the pension trust and succeeded in doing so. If it did, this would be the type of opportunistic behavior in an ongoing contractual relationship that would violate the duty of good faith performance however the duty is formulated. There is much common sense in Judge Reynolds' conclusion that Market Street Associates did just that. The situation as he saw it was as follows. Market Street Associates didn't want financing from the pension trust (initially it had looked elsewhere, remember), and when it learned it couldn't get the financing without owning the property, it decided to try to buy the property. But the pension trust set a stiff price, so Orenstein decided to trick the pension trust into selling at the bargain price fixed in paragraph 34 by requesting financing and hoping that the pension trust would turn the request down without noticing the paragraph. His preliminary dealings with the pension trust made this hope a realistic one by revealing a sluggish and hidebound bureaucracy unlikely to have retained in its brontosaurus's memory, or to be able at short notice to retrieve, the details of a small lease made twenty years earlier. So by requesting financing without mentioning the lease Market Street Associates might well precipitate a refusal before the pension trust woke up to paragraph 34. It is true that Orenstein's second letter requested financing "pursuant to the lease." But when the next day he received a reply to his first letter indicating that the pension trust was indeed oblivious to paragraph 34, his response was to send a lulling letter designed to convince the pension trust that the matter was closed and could be forgotten. The stage was set for his thunderbolt: the notification the next month that Market Street Associates was taking up the option in paragraph 34. Only then did the pension trust look up the lease and discover that it had been had.

The only problem with this recital is that it construes the facts as favorably to the pension trust as the record will permit, and that of course is not the right standard for summary judgment. The facts must be construed as favorably to the nonmoving party, to Market Street Associates, as the record permits (that Market Street Associates filed its own motion for summary judgment is irrelevant, as we have seen). When that is done, a different picture emerges. On Market Street Associates' construal of the record, $3 million was a grossly excessive price for the property, and while $1 million might be a bargain it would not confer so great a windfall as to warrant an inference that if the pension trust had known about paragraph 34 it never would have turned down Market Street Associates' request for financing cold. And in fact the pension trust may have known about paragraph 34, and either it didn't care or it believed that unless the request mentioned that paragraph the pension trust would incur no liability by turning it down. Market Street Associates may have assumed and have been entitled to assume that in reviewing a request for financing from one of its lessees the pension trust would take the time to read the lease to see whether it bore on the request. Market Street Associates did not desire financing from the pension trust initially—that is undeniable—yet when it discovered that it could not get financing elsewhere unless it had the title to the property it may have realized that it would have to negotiate with the pension trust over financing before it could hope to buy the property at the price specified in the lease.

On this interpretation of the facts there was no bad faith on the part of Market Street Associates. It acted honestly, reasonably, without ulterior motive, in the face of circumstances as they actually and reasonably appeared to it. The fault was the pension trust's incredible inattention, which misled Market Street Associates into believing that the pension trust had no interest in financing the improvements regardless of the purchase option. We do not usually excuse contracting parties from failing to read and understand the contents of their contract; and in the end what this case comes down to—or so at least it can be strongly argued—is that an immensely sophisticated enterprise simply failed to read the contract.

On the other hand, such enterprises make mistakes just like the rest of us, and deliberately to take advantage of your contracting partner's mistake during the performance stage (for we are not talking about taking advantage of superior knowledge at the formation stage) is a breach of good faith. To be able to correct your contract partner's mistake at zero cost to yourself, and decide not to do so, is a species of opportunistic behavior that the parties would have expressly forbidden in the contract had they foreseen it. The immensely long term of the lease amplified the possibility of errors but did not license either party to take advantage of them.

The district judge jumped the gun in choosing between these alternative characterizations. The essential issue bearing on Market Street Associates' good faith was Orenstein's state of mind, a type of inquiry that ordinarily cannot be concluded on summary judgment, and could not be here. If Orenstein believed that Erb knew or would surely find out about paragraph 34, it was not dishonest or opportunistic to fail to flag that paragraph, or even to fail to mention the lease, in his correspondence and (rare) conversations with Erb, especially given the uninterest in dealing with Market Street Associates that Erb fairly radiated. To decide what Orenstein believed, a trial is necessary. As for the pension trust's intimation that a bench trial (for remember that this is an equity case, since the only relief sought by the plaintiff is specific performance) will add no illumination beyond what the summary judgment proceeding has done, this overlooks the fact that at trial the judge will for the first time have a chance to see the witnesses whose depositions he has read, to hear their testimony elaborated, and to assess their believability.

The judgment is reversed and the case is remanded for further proceedings consistent with this opinion.

REVERSED AND REMANDED.

———

CHAPTER 14

WAIVER AND NO ORAL MODIFICATION TERMS

■ ■ ■

This Chapter concerns the waiver doctrine and the effect of a provision in a written contract that the contract cannot be modified except by a writing. An express waiver of a contract right is similar to a contract modification relinquishing a right in that both involve an expression by the right-holder of an intent to forego the right. But express waiver requires much less in the way of formality—there is no need for consideration or for a writing to satisfy the Statute of Frauds. Waiver can also be tacit. An insurer who receives timely oral notification of a claim by an insured who does not remind the insured that the policy requires written notification is likely to be held to have tacitly waived the condition requiring written notification.

A waiver is less permanent than a modification. A waiver affecting an executory part of a contract may be retracted unless the retraction would be unjust in view of the other party's change of position in reliance on the waiver. Also courts are reluctant to find a waiver of a material right in the absence of a clear expression of intent by the right-holder to waive the right.

The rules of classical contract law that give priority to a written contract in determining manifest intent do not apply when a party claims a written contract was modified or that a right was waived. The parol evidence rule applies only to agreements made before and, if the alleged agreement is oral, contemporaneously with, a written contract that constitutes an integration. The rule therefore is inapplicable to a *later* agreement that modifies a written contract. The plain meaning rule prevents the use of evidence of course of performance to interpret an unambiguous term in a written contract. But the rule does not prevent the use of such evidence to establish waiver or to establish a modification, since these do not involve interpreting the written contract.

Often, a written contract includes a provision that the contract cannot be modified except by a writing—a sort of private Statute of Frauds. Such provisions are sometimes referred to as n.o.m. (no oral modification) clauses. The general rule at common law was that an oral modification was enforceable, notwithstanding an n.o.m. clause. The theory was that: (1)

Parties can, by later contracts, change their earlier contracts. (2) An oral modification is a later contract. (3) An implied provision of the later contract is to abrogate the n.o.m. provision of the earlier contract. Section 2–209(2) changes this rule. It provides that if a contract for the sale of goods includes an n.o.m. clause, then modifications of the contract must be in writing. Section 2–209(4) qualifies this rules by providing that an attempt at modification that does not satisfy Section 2–209(2) "can operate as a waiver."

———

SECTION 1. WAIVER

CLARK V. WEST

Court of Appeals of New York, 1908.
193 N.Y. 349, 86 N.E. 1.

On February 12, 1900, the plaintiff and defendant entered into a written contract, under which the former was to write and prepare for publication for the latter a series of law books, the compensation for which was provided in the contract. After the plaintiff had completed a three-volume work known as "Clark & Marshall on Corporations," the parties disagreed. The plaintiff claimed that the defendant had broken the contract by causing the book to be copyrighted in the name of a corporation which was not a party to the contract, and he brought this action to recover what he claims to be due him, for an accounting and other relief. The defendant demurred to the complaint on the ground that it did not state facts sufficient to constitute a cause of action. The Special Term overruled the demurrer, but upon appeal to the Appellate Division that decision was reversed, and the demurrer sustained. [125 App.Div. 654, 110 N.Y.S. 110.]

Those portions of the contract which are germane to the present stage of the controversy are as follows: The plaintiff agreed to write a series of books relating to specified legal subjects. The manuscript furnished by him was to be satisfactory to the defendant. The plaintiff was not to write or edit anything that would interfere with the sale of books to be written by him under the contract, and he was not to write any other books unless requested so to do by the defendant, in which latter event he was to be paid $3,000 a year. The contract contained a clause which provided that "the first party (the plaintiff) agrees to totally abstain from the use of intoxicating liquors during the continuance of this contract, and the payment to him in accordance with the terms of this contract of any money in excess of $2 per page is dependent on the faithful performance of this as well as the other conditions of this contract. . . . " In a later paragraph it further recited that, "in consideration of the above promises of the first party (the plaintiff), the second party (the defendant) agrees to pay to the first party $2 per page, . . . on each book prepared by the first party under this contract and accepted by the second party, and if said first party abstains from the use of intoxicating liquor and otherwise fulfills his agreements as hereinbefore set forth, he shall be paid an additional $4 per page in manner hereinbefore stated." This was followed by a specification of the method and times of payment. . . .

The plaintiff in his complaint alleges completion of the work on Corporations and publication thereof by the defendant, the sale of many copies thereof from which the defendant received large net receipts, the number of pages it contained (3,469), for which he had been paid at the rate of $2 per page, amounting to $6,938, and that defendant has refused to pay him any sum over and above that amount, or any sum in excess of $2 per page. Full performance of the agreement on plaintiff's part is alleged, except that he "did not totally abstain from the use of intoxicating liquor during the continuance of said contract; but such use by the plaintiff was not excessive and did not prevent or interfere with the due and full performance by the plaintiff of all the other stipulations in said contract." The complaint further alleges a waiver on the part of the defendant of the plaintiff's stipulation to totally abstain from the use of intoxicating liquors, as follows: "(12) That defendant waived plaintiff's breach of the stipulation to totally abstain from the use of intoxicating liquors during the continuance of said contract; that long prior to the completion of said manuscript on Corporations, and its delivery to and acceptance by the defendant, the defendant had full knowledge and well knew of plaintiff's said use of intoxicating liquor during the continuance of said contract, but nevertheless acquiesced in and failed to object thereto, and did not terminate the contract on account thereof; that with full knowledge of said breach by the plaintiff defendant continued to exact and require of the plaintiff performance of all the other stipulations and conditions of said contract, and treated the same as still in force, and continued to receive, and did receive, installments of manuscript under said contract, and continued to make and did make payments to plaintiff by way of advancements, and finally accepted and published said manuscript as aforesaid; that at no time during the performance of said contract by the plaintiff did the defendant notify or intimate to the plaintiff that defendant would insist upon strict compliance with said stipulation to totally abstain from the use of intoxicating liquor, or that defendant intended to take advantage of plaintiff's said breach, and on account and by reason thereof refuse to pay plaintiff the royalty stipulated in said contract; that, on the contrary, and with full knowledge of plaintiff's said use of intoxicating liquors, defendant repeatedly avowed and represented to the plaintiff that he was entitled to and would receive said royalty payment, and plaintiff believed and relied on said representation, and in reliance thereon continued in the performance of said contract until the time of the breach thereof by the defendant, as hereinafter specifically alleged, and at all times during the writing of said treatise on Corporations, and after as well as before publication thereof, as aforesaid, it was mutually understood, agreed, and intended by the parties hereto that, notwithstanding plaintiff's said use of intoxicating liquors, he was nevertheless entitled to receive and would receive said royalty as the same accrued under said contract." The defendant's breach of the contract is then alleged, which is claimed to consist in his having taken out a copyright upon the plaintiff's work on Corporations in the name of a publishing company which had no relation to the contract, and the relief asked for is that the defendant be compelled to account, and that the copyright be transferred to the plaintiff, or that he recover its value.

The appeal is by permission of the Appellate Division, and the following questions have been certified to us: (1) Does the complaint herein state facts sufficient to constitute a cause of action? (2) Under the terms of the contract alleged in the complaint, is the plaintiff's total abstinence from the use of intoxicating liquors a condition precedent which can be waived so as to render defendant liable upon the contract notwithstanding plaintiff's use of intoxicating liquors? (3) Does the complaint herein allege facts constituting a valid and effective waiver of plaintiff's nonperformance of such condition precedent?

WERNER, J. . . . Briefly stated, the defendant's position is that the stipulation as to plaintiff's total abstinence is the consideration for the payment of the difference between $2 and $6 per page, and therefore could not be waived except by a new agreement to that effect based upon a good consideration; that the so-called waiver alleged by the plaintiff is not a waiver, but a modification of the contract in respect of its consideration. The plaintiff, on the other hand, argues that the stipulation for his total abstinence was merely a condition precedent, intended to work a forfeiture of the additional compensation in case of a breach, and that it could be waived without any formal agreement to that effect based upon a new consideration.

The subject-matter of the contract was the writing of books by the plaintiff for the defendant. The duration of the contract was the time necessary to complete them all. The work was to be done to the satisfaction of the defendant, and the plaintiff was not to write any other books except those covered by the contract unless requested so to do by the defendant, in which latter event he was to be paid for that particular work by the year. The compensation for the work specified in the contract was to be $6 per page, unless the plaintiff failed to totally abstain from the use of intoxicating liquors during the continuance of the contract, in which event he was to receive only $2 per page. That is the obvious import of the contract construed in the light of the purpose for which it was made, and in accordance with the ordinary meaning of plain language. It is not a contract to write books in order that the plaintiff shall keep sober, but a contract containing a stipulation that he shall keep sober so that he may write satisfactory books. When we view the contract from this standpoint, it will readily be perceived that the particular stipulation is not the consideration for the contract, but simply one of its conditions which fits in with those relating to time and method of delivery of manuscript, revision of proof, citation of cases, assignment of copyrights, keeping track of new cases and citations for new editions, and other details which might be waived by the defendant, if he saw fit to do so. This is made clear, it seems to us, by the provision that, "in consideration of the above promises," the defendant agrees to pay the plaintiff $2 per page on each book prepared by him, and if he "abstains from the use of intoxicating liquor and otherwise fulfills his agreements as hereinbefore set forth, he shall be paid an additional $4 per page in manner hereinbefore stated." The compensation of $2 per page, not to exceed $250 per month, was an advance or partial payment of the whole price of $6 per page, and the payment of the two-thirds, which was to be withheld pending the performance of the contract, was simply made contingent upon the plaintiff's total abstention from the use of intoxicants during the life of the contract. . . .

It is obvious that the parties thought that the plaintiff's normal work was worth $6 per page. That was the sum to be paid for the work done by the plaintiff, and not for total abstinence. If the plaintiff did not keep to the condition as to total abstinence, he was to lose part of that sum. . . . This, we think, is the fair interpretation of the contract, and it follows that the stipulation as to the plaintiff's total abstinence was nothing more nor less than a condition precedent. If that conclusion is well founded, there can be no escape from the corollary that this condition could be waived; and, if it was waived, the defendant is clearly not in a position to insist upon the forfeiture which his waiver was intended to annihilate. The forfeiture must stand or fall with the condition. If the latter was waived, the former is no longer a part of the contract. Defendant still has the right to counterclaim for any damages which he may have sustained in consequence of the plaintiff's breach, but he cannot insist upon strict performance. Dunn v. Steubing, 120 N.Y. 232, 24 N.E. 315; Parke v. Franco-American Trading Co., 120 N.Y. 51, 56, 23 N.E. 996; Brady v. Cassidy, 145 N.Y. 171, 39 N.E. 814.

This whole discussion is predicated, of course, upon the theory of an express waiver. We assume that no waiver could be implied from the defendant's mere acceptance of the books and his payment of the sum of $2 per page without objection. It was the defendant's duty to pay that amount in any event after acceptance of the work. The plaintiff must stand upon his allegation of an express waiver, and if he fails to establish that he cannot maintain his action.

The theory upon which the defendant's attitude seems to be based is that, even if he has represented to the plaintiff that he would not insist upon the condition that the latter should observe total abstinence from intoxicants, he can still refuse to pay the full contract price for his work. The inequity of this position becomes apparent when we consider that this contract was to run for a period of years, during a large portion of which the plaintiff was to be entitled only to the advance payment of $2 per page; the balance being contingent, among other things, upon publication of the books and returns from sales. Upon this theory the defendant might have waived the condition while the first book was in process of production, and yet, when the whole work was completed, he would still be in a position to insist upon the forfeiture because there had not been strict performance. Such a situation is possible in a case where the subject of the waiver is the very consideration of a contract (Organ v. Stewart, 60 N.Y. 413, 420), but not where the waiver relates to something that can be waived. In the case at bar, as we have seen, the waiver is not of the consideration or subject-matter, but of an incident to the method of performance. The consideration remains the same. The defendant has had the work he bargained for, and it is alleged that he has waived one of the conditions as to the manner in which it was to have been done. He might have insisted upon literal performance, and then he could have stood upon the letter of his contract. If, however, he has waived that incidental condition, he has created a situation to which the doctrine of waiver very precisely applies.

The cases which present the most familiar phases of the doctrine of waiver are those which have arisen out of litigation over insurance policies where the defendants have claimed a forfeiture because of the breach of some condition in the contract (Insurance Co. v. Norton, 96 U.S. 234, 24 L.Ed. 689; Titus v. Glens Falls Ins. Co., 81 N.Y. 410; Kiernan v. Dutchess Co. Mut. Insurance Co., 150 N.Y. 190, 44 N.E. 698), but it is a doctrine of general application which is confined to no particular class of cases. A "waiver" has been defined to be the intentional relinquishment of a known right. It is voluntary and implies an election to dispense with something of value, or forego some advantage which the party waiving it might at its option have demanded or insisted upon (Herman on Estoppel & Res Adjudicata, vol. 2, p. 954; Cowenhoven v. Ball, 118 N.Y. 234, 23 N.E. 470), and this definition is supported by many cases in this and other states. In the recent case of Draper v. Oswego Co. Fire R. Ass'n, 190 N.Y. 12, 16, 82 N.E. 755, Chief Judge Cullen, in speaking for the court upon this subject, said: "While that doctrine and the doctrine of equitable estoppel are often confused in insurance litigation, there is a clear distinction between the two. A 'waiver' is the voluntary abandonment or relinquishment by a party of some right or advantage. As said by my Brother Vann in the Kiernan Case, 150 N.Y. 190, 44 N.E. 698: 'The law of waiver seems to be a technical doctrine, introduced and applied by the court for the purpose of defeating forfeitures. . . . While the principle may not be easily classified, it is well established that, if the words and acts of the insurer reasonably justify the conclusion that with full knowledge of all the facts it intended to abandon or not to insist upon the particular defense afterwards relied upon, a verdict or finding to that effect establishes a waiver, which, if it once exists, can never be revoked.' The doctrine of equitable estoppel, or estoppel in pais, is that a party may be precluded by his acts and conduct from asserting a right to the detriment of another party who, entitled to rely on such conduct, has acted upon it. . . . As already said, the doctrine of waiver is to relieve against forfeiture. It requires no consideration for a waiver, nor any prejudice or injury to the other party." To the same effect, see Knarston v. Manhattan Life Ins. Co., 140 Cal. 57, 73 P. 740.

It remains to be determined whether the plaintiff has alleged facts which, if proven, will be sufficient to establish his claim of an express waiver by the defendant of the plaintiff's breach of the condition to observe total abstinence. In the 12th paragraph of the complaint, the plaintiff alleges facts and circumstances which we think, if established, would prove defendant's waiver of plaintiff's performance of that contract stipulation. . . .

The three questions certified should be answered in the affirmative, the order of the Appellate Division reversed, the interlocutory judgment of the Special Term affirmed, with costs in both courts, and the defendant be permitted to answer the complaint within 20 days upon payment of costs.

––––––

RESTATEMENT, SECOND, CONTRACTS § 84

[See Selected Source Materials Supplement]

––––––

RESTATEMENT, SECOND, CONTRACTS § 84, ILLUSTRATIONS 3, 4, 6

3. A employs B to build a house, promising to pay therefor $10,000 on the production of a certificate from A's architect, C, stating that the work has been satisfactorily completed. B builds the house but the work is defective in certain trivial particulars. C refuses to give B a certificate. A says to B, "My architect rightfully refuses to give you a certificate but the defects are not serious; I will pay you the full price which I promised." A is bound to do so, and has no power to restore the requirement of the condition.

4. A, an insurance company, insures B's house for $5000 against loss by fire. The insurance policy provides that it shall be payable only if B gives written notification of any loss within thirty days after its occurrence. An insured loss occurs and B gives only oral notification thereof within thirty days. A tells him, either before or after the lapse of thirty days from the

loss, that this notification is sufficient. A cannot thereafter rely upon B's failure to give written notification as an excuse for failure to pay for the loss. . . .

6.   In Illustration 4, A can restore the requirement of the condition by notifying B of his intention to do so if there still remains a reasonable time for the occurrence of the condition before the expiration of the thirty-day period, unless such action would be unjust in view of a material change of position by B in reliance on A's waiver. If a reasonable time does not remain, A cannot restore the requirement of the condition by extending the time.

Westinghouse Credit Corp. v. Shelton

645 F.2d 869 (1981)

Shelton purchased a mobile home in May 1974, agreeing to pay principal and interest totaling $22,662.71 in 144 installments of $157.38 on the 25th day of every month beginning with June 25, 1974. The dealer assigned the note to Westinghouse. Shelton's payments were habitually late by one, two, and even three months. Westinghouse accepted the late payments. In April 1978, after Shelton failed to make the payments due January, February, and March 1978, Westinghouse filed a complaint that declared Shelton in default, accelerated full payment of the principal remaining due, and requested a writ of replevin to permit repossession of the mobile home. The district court granted Westinghouse's motion for summary judgment. Reversed.

(Seymour, J.) "When Westinghouse filed suit in April 1978 and requested replevin relief, Shelton was indisputedly in default. Also not contested is the fact Westinghouse accepted all late payments in the course of the contract's performance from June 1974 to December 1977, and that almost all of the roughly 40 installments covering this period were paid late. This toleration, Shelton argues, precluded Westinghouse from suddenly declaring default without first apprising Shelton of its insistence on strict compliance with the contract's timeliness terms. Whether or to what extent Shelton was actually apprised of such insistence is a fact vigorously disputed by the parties. Shelton argues this dispute precluded the grant of summary judgment. We conclude that beyond just the question of notification to Shelton, the overall issue whether in this case the parties' course of performance worked a waiver of one or more terms in their contract is a question for the factfinder. Summary judgment was therefore inappropriate. . . .

"Absent an "anti-waiver" clause such as paragraph 6 in Shelton's contract,* courts have uniformly held that a creditor may not fall into a pattern

---

* "The waiver or indulgence of any default by the Buyer of any provision of this Agreement or any promissory note which it secures shall not operate as a waiver of any subsequent default by the Buyer of such provision or as a waiver of any of the other rights of (Westinghouse) herein. Time shall be deemed the essence of this Agreement."

of accepting delinquent installments and then suddenly declare default, without first apprising the debtor of his insistence on strict compliance with the terms of the contract. See, e. g., Knittel v. Security State Bank, 593 P.2d 92, 95–96 (Okl.1979); Lee v. Wood Products Credit Union, 275 Or. 445, 551 P.2d 446, 448 (1976); Nevada National Bank v. Huff, 582 P.2d 364, 369 (Nev.1978). See also Ga.Code Ann. § 20–116 (where parties' course of performance departs from terms of contract, reasonable notice must be given of intention to rely on exact terms of agreement and until such notice departure deemed quasi new agreement). But courts have split over the significance of the parties' course of performance when the contract includes an "anti-waiver" provision, which in effect tells the debtor that the creditor's toleration of one or more defaults should not be taken to mean the creditor would indulge others.

"Some have construed the "anti-waiver" clause strictly according to its terms, thus conclusively precluding a creditor's pattern of accepting late payments from operating as a modification or waiver of the contract's default provisions. See Hale v. Ford Motor Credit Co., 374 So.2d 849, 853 (Ala.1979); Fair v. General Finance Corp., 147 Ga.App. 706, 250 S.E.2d 9 (1978); Universal C.I.T. Credit Corp. v. Middlesboro Motor Sales, Inc., 424 S.W.2d 409, 411 (Ct.App.Ky.1968); Home Finance Co. v. Frazier, 380 S.W.2d 91, 93 (Ky.1964).

"But the weight of authority, and the view we think Oklahoma state courts would follow, is that an "anti-waiver" clause, like any other term in the contract, is itself subject to waiver or modification by course of performance and that whether such waiver or modification has occurred is a question for the factfinder. See Smith v. General Finance Corp., 243 Ga. 500, 255 S.E.2d 14, 15 (1979) (disapproving of Fair v. General Finance Corp., 147 Ga.App. 706, 250 S.E.2d 9); Pierce v. Leasing International, Inc., 142 Ga.App. 371, 235 S.E.2d 752, 754–55 (1977); Van Bibber v. Norris, 404 N.E.2d 1365, 1373–74 (Ct.App.Ind.1980); Cobb v. Midwest Recovery Bureau Co., 295 N.W.2d 232, 237 (Minn.1980). Cf. 12A Okla.Stat.Ann. § 1–205 & Official Comment 2. See also Wade v. Ford Motor Credit Co., 455 F.Supp. 147, 150 (E.D.Mo.1978) (pattern of accepting late payments operates as waiver of default as to previously accepted payments, but not as to yet unaccepted payments); Fontaine v. Industrial National Bank of Rhode Island, 111 R.I. 6, 298 A.2d 521, 523–24 (1973) (acceptance of late payments operates as absolute waiver of contract's default provision as to accepted payments and precludes creditor's declaration of default after timely payments have intervened); Ford Motor Credit Co. v. Waters, 273 So.2d 96, 100 (Ct.App.Fla.1973).

"In Shelton's case the question is whether Westinghouse, by accepting late payments as it did, waived its right to strictly enforce not only the contract's time terms, but also the "anti-waiver" clause itself. Shelton should have the opportunity to prove, if he can, that Westinghouse's conduct in toto regarding timeliness was so pervasive that in the eyes of a reasonable debtor it "spoke louder than (the) word," Van Bibber, 404 N.E.2d at 1374, of the "anti-waiver" clause, which in effect counseled against reliance on conduct indulging default. If waiver by Westinghouse of the contract's timeliness and "anti-waiver" terms were found, the question whether or to what extent Westinghouse apprised

Shelton, before taking him to court in April 1978, of its insistence upon strict adherence to the contract's terms would bear upon whether Westinghouse effectively retracted its waiver. See 12A Okla.Stat.Ann. § 2–209(5). In view of these fact questions, we must vacate the district court's summary judgment and the dismissal of Shelton's counterclaim, and remand for further proceedings."

Nassau Trust Co. v. Montrose Concrete Products Corp.

56 N.Y.2d 175, 451 N.Y.S.2d 663, 436 N.E.2d 1265 (1982), reargument denied, 57 N.Y.2d 674, 454 N.Y.S.2d 1032, 439 N.E.2d 1247 (1982)

"Modification . . . requires consideration. . . . [In contrast, waiver does not rest] upon consideration or agreement. A modification, because it is an agreement based upon consideration, is binding according to its terms and may only be withdrawn by agreement. . . . A waiver, to the extent that it has been executed, cannot be expunged or recalled . . . but, not being a binding agreement, can, to the extent that it is executory, be withdrawn, provided the party whose performance has been waived is given notice of withdrawal and a reasonable time after notice within which to perform. . . . "

UCC §§ 1–306, 2–209(5)
[See Selected Source Materials Supplement]

SECTION 2. NO-ORAL-MODIFICATION TERMS

WISCONSIN KNIFE WORKS V. NATIONAL METAL CRAFTERS
United States Court of Appeals for the Seventh Circuit, 1986
781 F.2d 1280.

POSNER, CIRCUIT JUDGE:

. . . Wisconsin Knife Works, having some unused manufacturing capacity, decided to try to manufacture spade bits for sale to its parent, Black & Decker, a large producer of tools, including drills. A spade bit is made out of a chunk of metal called a spade bit blank; and Wisconsin Knife Works had to find a source of supply for these blanks. National Metal Crafters was eager to be that source. After some negotiating, Wisconsin Knife Works sent National Metal Crafters a series of purchase orders on the back of each of which was printed, "Acceptance of this Order, either by acknowledgment or performance, constitutes an unqualified agreement to the following." A list of "Conditions of Purchase" follows, of which the first is, "No modification of this contract, shall be binding upon Buyer [Wisconsin Knife Works] unless made in writing and signed by Buyer's authorized representative. Buyer shall have the right to make changes in the Order by a notice, in writing, to Seller." There were six purchase orders in all, each with the identical conditions. National Metal Crafters acknowledged the first two orders (which had been placed on August 21, 1981) by letters that said, "Please accept this as our acknowledgment covering the above subject order," followed by a list of delivery dates. The purchase orders had left those dates blank. Wisconsin Knife Works filled them in, after receiving the acknowledgments, with the dates that National Metal Crafters had supplied in the acknowledgments. There were no written acknowledgments of the last four orders (placed several weeks later, on September 10, 1981). Wisconsin Knife Works wrote in the delivery dates that National Metal Crafters orally supplied after receiving purchase orders in which the space for the date of delivery had again been left blank.

Delivery was due in October and November 1981. National Metal Crafters missed the deadlines. But Wisconsin Knife Works did not immediately declare a breach, cancel the contract, or seek damages for late delivery. Indeed, on July 1, 1982, it issued a new batch of purchase orders (later rescinded). By December 1982 National Metal Crafters was producing spade bit blanks for Wisconsin Knife Works under the original set of purchase orders in adequate quantities, though this was more than a year after the delivery dates in the orders. But on January 13, 1983, Wisconsin Knife Works notified National Metal Crafters that the contract was terminated. By that date only 144,000 of the more than 281,000 spade bit blanks that Wisconsin Knife Works had ordered in the six purchase orders had been delivered.

Wisconsin Knife Works brought this breach of contract suit, charging that National Metal Crafters had violated the terms of delivery in the contract that was formed by the acceptance of the six purchase orders. National Metal Crafters replied that the delivery dates had not been intended as firm dates. It also counterclaimed for damages for (among other things) the breach of an alleged oral agreement by Wisconsin Knife Works to pay the expenses of maintaining machinery used by National Metal Crafters to fulfill the contract. The parties later stipulated that the amount of these damages was $30,000.

The judge ruled that there had been a contract but left to the jury to decide whether the contract had been modified and, if so, whether the modified contract had been broken. The jury found that the contract had been modified and not broken. Judgment was entered dismissing Wisconsin Knife Works' suit and awarding National Metal Crafters $30,000 on its counterclaim. Wisconsin Knife Works has appealed from the dismissal of its suit. The appeal papers do not discuss the counterclaim, and the effect on it of our remanding the case for further proceedings on Wisconsin Knife Works' claim will have to be resolved on remand.

The principal issue is the effect of the provision in the purchase orders that forbids the contract to be modified other than by a writing signed by an authorized representative of the buyer. The theory on which the judge sent the issue of modification to the jury was that the contract could be modified orally or by conduct as well as by a signed writing. National Metal Crafters had presented evidence that Wisconsin Knife Works had accepted late delivery of the spade bit blanks and had cancelled the contract not because of the delays in delivery but because it could not produce spade bits at a price acceptable to Black & Decker.

Section 2–209(2) of the Uniform Commercial Code provides that "a signed agreement which excludes modification or rescission except by a signed writing cannot be otherwise modified or rescinded, but except as between merchants such a requirement on a form supplied by the merchant must be separately signed by the other party." ... The meaning of this provision and its proviso is not crystalline and there is little pertinent case law. One might think that an agreement to exclude modification except by a signed writing must be signed in any event by the party against whom the requirement is sought to be enforced, that is, by National Metal Crafters, rather than by the party imposing the requirement. But if so the force of the proviso ("but except as between merchants ...") becomes unclear, for it contemplates that between merchants no separate signature by the party sought to be bound by the requirement is necessary. A possible reconciliation, though not one we need embrace in order to decide this case, is to read the statute to require a separate signing or initialing of the clause forbidding oral modifications, as well as of the contract in which the clause appears. There was no such signature here; but it doesn't matter; this was a contract "between merchants." Although in ordinary language a manufacturer is not a merchant, "between merchants" is a term of art in the Uniform Commercial Code. It means between commercially sophisticated parties (see UCC § 2–104(1); White & Summers, Handbook of the Law Under the Uniform Commercial Code 345 (2d ed. 1980)), which these were.

Of course there must still be a "signed agreement" containing the clause forbidding modification other than by a signed writing, but there was that (see definition of "agreement" and of "signed" in UCC §§ 1–201(3), (39)). National Metal Crafters' signed acknowledgments of the first two purchase orders signified its assent to the printed conditions and naturally and reasonably led Wisconsin Knife Works to believe that National Metal Crafters meant also to assent to the same conditions should they appear in any subsequent purchase orders that it accepted. Those subsequent orders were accepted, forming new contracts on the same conditions as the old, by performance—that is, by National Metal Crafters' beginning the manufacture of the spade bit blanks called for by the orders. See UCC § 2–207(3). So there was an agreement, signed by National Metal Crafters, covering all the purchase orders. The fact that the delivery dates were not on the purchase orders when received by National Metal Crafters is nothing of which it may complain; it was given carte blanche to set those dates.

When National Metal Crafters had difficulty complying with the original specifications for the spade bit blanks, Wisconsin Knife Works modified them; and National Metal Crafters argues that the engineering drawings containing those modifications are the written modification that section 2–209(2), if applicable, calls for. In fact these particular modifications seem to fall within the clause of the contract that allows the buyer (Wisconsin Knife Works) to modify the specifications by notice. The context of this clause makes clear that such notice is not the written modification to which the previous sentence refers. But in any event there was no modification of the delivery dates. The "pert charts" which National Metal Crafters supplied Wisconsin Knife Works, and which showed new target dates for delivery, do not purport to modify the contract and were not signed by Wisconsin Knife Works.

We conclude that the clause forbidding modifications other than in writing was valid and applicable and that the jury should not have been allowed to consider whether the contract had been modified in some other way. This may, however, have been a harmless error. Section 2–209(4) of the Uniform Commercial Code provides that an "attempt at modification" which does not satisfy a contractual requirement that modifications be in writing nevertheless "can operate as a waiver." Although in instructing the jury on modification the judge did not use the word "waiver," maybe he gave the substance of a waiver instruction and maybe therefore the jury found waiver but called it modification. Here is the relevant instruction:

> Did the parties modify the contract? The defendant bears the burden of proof on this one. You shall answer this question yes only if you are convinced to a reasonable certainty that the parties modified the contract.

> If you determine that the defendant had performed in a manner different from the strict obligations imposed on it by the contract, and the plaintiff by conduct or other means of expression induced a reasonable belief by the defendant that strict enforcement was not insisted upon, but that the modified performance was satisfactory and acceptable as equivalent, then you may conclude that the parties have assented to a modification of the original terms of the contract and that the parties have agreed that the different mode of performance will satisfy the obligations imposed on the parties by the contract.

To determine whether this was in substance an instruction on waiver we shall have to consider the background of section 2–209, the Code provision on modification and waiver.

Because the performance of the parties to a contract is typically not simultaneous, one party may find himself at the mercy of the other unless the law of contracts protects him. Indeed, the most important thing which that law does is to facilitate exchanges that are not simultaneous by preventing either party from taking advantage of the vulnerabilities to which sequential performance may give rise. If A contracts to build a highly idiosyncratic gazebo for B, payment due on completion, and when A completes the gazebo B refuses to pay, A may be in a bind—since the resale value of the gazebo may be much less than A's cost—except for his right to sue B for the price. Even then, a right to sue for breach of contract, being costly to enforce, is not a completely adequate remedy. B might therefore go to A and say, "If you don't reduce your price I'll refuse to pay and put you to the expense of suit"; and A might knuckle under. If such modifications are allowed, people in B's position will find it harder to make such contracts in the future, and everyone will be worse off.

The common law dealt with this problem by refusing to enforce modifications unsupported by fresh consideration. See, e.g., Alaska Packers' Ass'n v. Domenico, 117 Fed. 99 (9th Cir.1902), discussed in Selmer Co. v. Blakeslee-Midwest Co., 704 F.2d 924, 927 (7th Cir.1983). Thus in the hypothetical case just put B could not have enforced A's promise to accept a lower price. But this solution is at once overinclusive and underinclusive—the former because most modifications are not coercive and should be enforceable whether or not there is fresh consideration, the latter because, since common law courts inquire only into the existence and not the adequacy of consideration, a requirement of fresh consideration has little bite. B might give A a peppercorn, a kitten, or a robe in exchange for A's agreeing to reduce the contract price, and then the modification would be enforceable and A could no longer sue for the original price. See White & Summers, supra, at 47; Farnsworth, Contracts 271–78 (1982).

The draftsmen of the Uniform Commercial Code took a fresh approach, by making modifications enforceable even if not supported by consideration (see section 2–209(1)) and looking to the doctrines of duress and bad faith for the main protection against exploitive or opportunistic attempts at modification, as in our hypothetical case. See UCC § 2–209, official comment 2. But they did another thing as well. In section 2–209(2) they allowed the parties to exclude oral modifications. National Metal Crafters argues that two subsections later they took back this grant of power by allowing an unwritten modification to operate as a waiver.

The common law did not enforce agreements such as section 2–209(2) authorizes. The "reasoning" was that the parties were always free to agree orally to cancel their contract and the clause forbidding modifications not in writing would disappear with the rest of the contract when it was cancelled. "The most ironclad written contract can always be cut into by the acetylene torch of parol modification supported by adequate proof." Wagner v. Graziano Construction Co., 390 Pa. 445, 448, 136 A.2d 82, 83–84 (1957). This is not reasoning; it is a conclusion disguised as a metaphor. It may have reflected a fear that such clauses, buried in the fine print of form contracts, were traps for the unwary; a sense that they were unnecessary because only modifications supported by consideration were enforceable; and a disinclination to allow parties in effect to extend the reach of the Statute of Frauds, which requires only some types of contract to be in writing. But the framers of the Uniform Commercial Code, as part and parcel of rejecting the requirement of consideration for modifications, must have rejected the traditional view; must have believed that the protection which the doctrines of duress and bad faith give against extortionate modifications might need reinforcement—if not from a requirement of consideration, which had proved ineffective, then from a grant of power to include a clause requiring modifications to be in writing and signed. An equally important point is that with consideration no longer required for modification, it was natural to give the parties some means of providing a substitute for the cautionary and evidentiary function that the requirement of consideration provides; and the means chosen was to allow them to exclude oral modifications.

If section 2–209(4), which as we said provides that an attempted modification which does not comply with subsection (2) can nevertheless operate as a "waiver," is interpreted so broadly that any oral modification is effective as a waiver notwithstanding section 2–209(2), both provisions become superfluous and we are back in the common law—only with not even a requirement of consideration to reduce the likelihood of fabricated or unintended oral modifications. A conceivable but unsatisfactory way around this result is to distinguish between a modification that substitutes a new term for an old, and a waiver, which merely removes an old term. On this interpretation National Metal Crafters could not enforce an oral term of the allegedly modified contract but could be excused from one of the written terms. This would take care of a case such as Alaska Packers, where seamen attempted to enforce a contract modification that raised their wages, but would not take care of the functionally identical case where seamen sought to collect the agreed-on wages without doing the agreed-on work. Whether the party claiming modification is seeking to impose an onerous new term on the other party or to wriggle out of an onerous term that the original contract imposed on it is a distinction without a difference. We can see that in this case. National Metal Crafters, while claiming that Wisconsin Knife Works broke their contract as orally modified to extend the delivery date, is not seeking damages for that breach. But this is small comfort to Wisconsin Knife Works, which thought it had a binding contract with fixed delivery dates. Whether called modification or waiver, what National Metal Crafters is seeking to do is to nullify a key term other than by a signed writing. If it can get away with this merely by testimony about an oral modification, section 2–209(2) becomes very nearly a dead letter.

The path of reconciliation with subsection (4) is found by attending to the precise wording of (4). It does not say that an attempted modification "is" a waiver; it says that "it can operate as a waiver." It does not say in what circumstances it can operate as a waiver; but if an attempted modification is effective as a waiver only if there is reliance, then both sections 2–209(2) and 2–209(4) can be given effect. Reliance, if reasonably induced and reasonable in extent, is a common substitute for consideration in making a promise legally enforceable, in part because it adds something in the way of credibility to the mere say-so of one party. The main purpose of forbidding oral modifications is to prevent the promisor from fabricating a modification that will let him escape his obligations under the contract; and the danger of successful fabrication is less if the promisor has actually incurred a cost, has relied. There is of course a danger of bootstrapping— of incurring a cost in order to make the case for a modification. But it is a risky course and is therefore less likely to be attempted than merely testifying to a conversation; it makes one put one's money where one's mouth is.

We find support for our proposed reconciliation of subsections (2) and (4) in the secondary literature. See Eisler, Oral Modification of Sales Contracts Under the Uniform Commercial Code: The Statute of Frauds Problem, 58 Wash. U.L.Q. 277, 298–302 (1980); Farnsworth, supra, at 476– 77; 6 Corbin on Contracts 211 (1962). It is true that 2 Anderson on the Uniform Commercial Code § 2–209:42 (3d ed. 1982), opines that reliance is not necessary for an attempted modification to operate as a waiver, but he does not explain his conclusion or provide any reason or authority to support it. This provision was quoted along with other material from Anderson in Double-E Sportswear Corp. v. Girard Trust Bank, 488 F.2d 292, 295 (3d Cir.1973), but there was no issue of reliance in that case. 2 Hawkland, Uniform Commercial Code Series § 2–209:05, at p. 138 (1985), remarks, "if clear factual evidence other than mere parol points to that conclusion [that an oral agreement was made altering a term of the contract], a waiver may be found. In the normal case, however, courts should be careful not to allow the protective features of sections 2–209(2) and (3) to be nullified by contested parol evidence." (Footnote omitted.) The instruction given by the judge in this case did not comply with this test, but in any event we think a requirement of reliance is clearer than a requirement of "clear factual evidence other than mere parol."

Our approach is not inconsistent with section 2–209(5), which allows a waiver to be withdrawn while the contract is executory, provided there is no "material change of position in reliance on the waiver." Granted, in (5) there can be no tincture of reliance; the whole point of the section is that a waiver may be withdrawn unless there is reliance. But the section has a different domain from section 2–209(4). It is not limited to attempted modifications invalid under subsections (2) or (3); it applies, for example, to an express written and signed waiver, provided only that the contract is still executory. Suppose that while the contract is still executory the buyer writes the seller a signed letter waiving some term in the contract and then, the next day, before the seller has relied, retracts it in writing; we have no reason to think that such a retraction would not satisfy section 2–209(5), though this is not an issue we need definitively resolve today. In any event we are not suggesting that "waiver" means different things in (4) and (5); it means the same thing; but the effect of an attempted modification as a waiver under (4) depends in part on (2), which (4) (but not 5)) qualifies. Waiver and estoppel (which requires reliance to be effective) are frequently bracketed. See, e.g., Chemetron Corp. v. McLouth Steel Corp., 522 F.2d 469, 472–73 (7th Cir.1975); Hirsch Rolling Mill Co. v. Milwaukee & Fox River Valley Ry., 165 Wis. 220, 161 N.W. 741 (1917).

The statute could be clearer; but the draftsmen were making a big break with the common law in subsections (1) and (2), and naturally failed to foresee all the ramifications of the break. The innovations made in Article 9 of the UCC were so novel that the article had to be comprehensively revised only ten years after its promulgation. See Appendix II to the 1978 Official Text of the Uniform Commercial Code. Article 2 was less innovative, but of course its draftsmanship was not flawless—what human product is? Just a few months ago we wrestled with the mysterious and apparently inadvertent omission of key words in the middle subsection of another section of Article 2. See Jason's Foods, Inc. v. Peter Eckrich & Sons, Inc., 774 F.2d 214 (7th Cir.1985) (section 2–509(2)). Another case of gap-filling in Article 2 is discussed in White & Summers, supra, at 450 (section 2–316(3)(a)). But as a matter of fact we need go no further than section 2–209(5) to illustrate the need for filling gaps in Article 2. In holding that that section allows the retraction of a waiver of the Statute of Frauds, the Third Circuit said in Double-E Sportswear Corp. v. Girard Trust Bank, supra, 488 F.2d at 297 n. 7, "We have found it necessary to fill the interstices of the code," because of "a drafting oversight."

We know that the draftsmen of section 2–209 wanted to make it possible for parties to exclude oral modifications. They did not just want to give "modification" another name—"waiver." Our interpretation gives effect to this purpose. It is also consistent with though not compelled by the case law. There are no Wisconsin cases on point. Cases from other jurisdictions are diverse in outlook. Some take a very hard line against allowing an oral waiver to undo a clause forbidding oral modification. See, e.g., South Hampton Co. v. Stinnes Corp., 733 F.2d 1108, 1117–18 (5th Cir.1984) (Texas law); U.S. Fibres, Inc. v. Proctor & Schwartz, Inc., 358 F.Supp. 449, 460 (E.D.Mich.1972), aff'd, 509 F.2d 1043 (6th Cir.1975) (Pennsylvania law). Others allow oral waivers to override such clauses, but in most of these cases it is clear that the party claiming waiver had relied to his detriment. See, e.g., Gold Kist, Inc. v. Pillow, 582 S.W.2d 77, 79–80 (Tenn.App.1979) (where this feature of the case is emphasized); Linear Corp. v. Standard Hardware Co., 423 So.2d 966 (Fla.App.1982); cf. Rose v. Spa Realty Associates, 42 N.Y.2d 338, 343–44, 397 N.Y.S.2d 922, 925–26, 366 N.E.2d 1279, 1282–83 (1977). In cases not governed by the Uniform Commercial Code, Wisconsin follows the common law rule that allows a contract to be waived orally (unless within the Statute of Frauds) even though the contract provides that it can be modified only in writing. See, e.g., S & M Rotogravure Service, Inc. v. Baer, 77 Wis.2d 454, 468–69, 252 N.W.2d 913, 920 (1977). But of course the Code, which is in force in Wisconsin as in every other state (with the partial exception of Louisiana), was intended to change this rule for contracts subject to it.

Missing from the jury instruction on "modification" in this case is any reference to reliance, that is, to the incurring of costs by National Metal Crafters in reasonable reliance on assurances by Wisconsin Knife Works that late delivery would be acceptable. And although there is evidence of such reliance, it naturally was not a focus of the case, since the issue was cast as one of completed (not attempted) modification, which does not require reliance to be enforceable. National Metal Crafters must have incurred expenses in producing spade bit blanks after the original delivery dates, but whether these were reliance expenses is a separate question. Maybe National Metal Crafters would have continued to manufacture spade bit blanks anyway, in the hope of selling them to someone else. It may be significant that the stipulated counterclaim damages seem limited to the damages from the breach of a separate oral agreement regarding the maintenance of equipment used by National Metal Crafters in fulfilling the contract. The question of reliance cannot be considered so open and shut as to justify our concluding that the judge would have had to direct a verdict for National Metal Crafters, the party with the burden of proof on the issue. Nor, indeed, does National Metal Crafters argue that reliance was shown as a matter of law.

There is no need to discuss most of the other alleged errors in the conduct of the trial; they are unlikely to recur in a new trial. We do however point out that Wisconsin Knife Works' objections to the introduction of parol evidence have no merit once the issue is recast as one of waiver. The purpose of the parol evidence rule is to defeat efforts to vary by oral evidence the terms of a written instrument that the parties intended to be the fully integrated expression of their contract; it has no application when the issue is whether one of the parties later waived strict compliance with those terms. . . .

When a jury instruction is erroneous there must be a new trial unless the error is harmless. On the basis of the record before us we cannot say that the error in allowing the jury to find that the contract had been modified was harmless; but we do not want to exclude the possibility that it might be found to be so, on motion for summary judgment or otherwise, without the need for a new trial. Obviously National Metal Crafters has a strong case both that it relied on the waiver of the delivery deadlines and that there was no causal relationship between its late deliveries and the cancellation of the contract. We just are not prepared to say on the record before us that it is such a strong case as not to require submission to a jury.

REVERSED AND REMANDED.

[Judge Easterbrook's dissenting opinion is omitted.]

BMC Industries, Inc. v. Barth Industries, Inc.

160 F.3d 1322 (11th Cir.1998), certiorari denied, 526 U.S. 1132, 119 S.Ct. 1807, 143 L.Ed.2d 1010 (1999)

(Tjoflat, J.) "As an initial matter, we must determine whether, under the UCC, waiver must be accompanied by detrimental reliance. . . . [C]ourts disagree on whether the UCC retains this requirement. We conclude, however, that the UCC does not require consideration or detrimental reliance for waiver of a contract term.

"Our conclusion follows from the plain language of subsections [2–209(4)] and (5). While subsection (4) states that an attempted modification that fails may still constitute a waiver, subsection (5) provides that the waiver may be retracted unless the non-waiving party relies on the waiver. Consequently, the statute recognizes that waivers may exist in the absence of detrimental reliance—these are the retractable waivers referred to in subsection (5). Only this interpretation renders meaning to subsection (5), because reading subsection (4) to require detrimental reliance for all waivers means that waivers would never be retractable. See Wisconsin Knife Works v. National Metal Crafters, 781 F.2d 1280, 1291 (7th Cir.1986) (Easterbrook, J., dissenting) (noting that reading a detrimental reliance requirement into the UCC would eliminate the distinction between subsections (4) and (5)). Subsection (5) would therefore be meaningless.

"Although [some] courts have held that waiver requires reliance under the UCC, those courts have ignored the UCC's plain language. The leading case espousing this view of waiver is Wisconsin Knife Works v. National Metal Crafters, 781 F.2d 1280 (7th Cir.1986) . . . in which a panel of the Seventh Circuit addressed a contract that included a term prohibiting oral modifications, and considered whether an attempted oral modification could instead constitute a waiver. Writing for the majority, Judge Posner concluded that the UCC's subsection (2), which gives effect to 'no oral modification' provisions, would become superfluous if contract terms could be waived without detrimental reliance. Judge Posner reasoned that if attempted oral modifications that were unenforceable because of subsection (2) were nevertheless enforced as waivers under subsection (4), then subsection (2) is 'very nearly a dead letter.' Id. at 1286. According to Judge Posner, there must be some difference between modification and waiver in order for both subsections (2) and (4) to have meaning. This difference is waiver's detrimental reliance requirement.

"Judge Posner, however, ignores a fundamental difference between modifications and waivers: while a party that has agreed to a contract modification cannot cancel the modification without giving consideration for the cancellation, a party may unilaterally retract its waiver of a contract term provided it gives reasonable notice. The fact that waivers may unilaterally be retracted provides the difference between subsections (2) and (4) that allows both to have meaning. We therefore conclude that waiver under the UCC does not require detrimental reliance."

––––––––

UCC § 2–209(1), (2), (4), (5)

[See Selected Source Materials Supplement]

––––––––

UNIDROIT PRINCIPLES OF INTERNATIONAL COMMERCIAL CONTRACTS ART. 2.1.18

[See Selected Source Materials Supplement]

––––––––

PRINCIPLES OF EUROPEAN CONTRACT LAW ART. 2.106

[See Selected Source Materials Supplement]

––––––––

CHAPTER 15

BATTLE OF THE FORMS

■ ■ ■

The problems raised by form contracts have been a major preoccupation of contract-law scholars since the middle of the twentieth century. The primary areas of concern have been the enforceability of preprinted terms and the import of preprinted terms in determining whether a form sent in response to an offer constitutes an acceptance.

The phenomenon of rational ignorance plays a powerful role in both concerns. The provisions of a contract can be divided into performance and nonperformance terms. Performance terms specify the performance each party must render. All other provisions are normally nonperformance terms. The most important types of performance terms concern the description of the subject-matter of the contract, quantity, price, delivery terms, and payment terms. Nonperformance terms cover a wide range of issues, such as how and when notice of default must be given, limitations on warranties, excuse, and so forth. Most preprinted terms are nonperformance terms that concern low-probability future risks. Nonperformance terms also address matters that are peripheral to the main subject-matter of the contract, such as the right to collect and use an individual's personal data.

Call a party who prepares a form contract a form-giver, and a party who receives a form contract a form-taker. A form-giver typically offers a package consisting of a commodity (using that term in a broadly defined manner, to include goods, realty, and services) and a form contract that states the terms on which the commodity will be purchased or sold. Each part of the package, in turn, consists of a number of attributes: The commodity has physical attributes, such as size, shape, and color. The form contract has business and legal attributes, most of which are nonperformance terms. Typically, the most important performance terms—description, quantity, price, delivery, payment—will be custom-tailored to each transaction, and individually filled into the form. In contrast, the nonperformance terms and the less important performance terms (such as provisions concerning crating or notice of shipment) will typically be preprinted.

To make an optimum substantive decision, a form-taker who is choosing between a variety of commodities of a given type would carefully deliberate not only on the characteristics of the commodities, but also on the business and legal attributes of each form contract that is coupled with each commodity that he is considering. Analyzing all the terms of a form contract in this manner, however, will often be unduly costly. First, a form contract often contains a very large number of terms. Form insurance contracts, for example, often contain forty, fifty, or more terms. Moreover, the meaning and effect of the preprinted terms will very often be inaccessible to laypersons. In part, this is because the terms are often written in highly technical prose. Even if the terms are written clearly, however, the form-taker usually will be unable fully to understand their effects, because preprinted terms characteristically vary the form-taker's baseline legal rights, and most form-takers do not know their baseline legal rights. The verbal and legal obscurity of preprinted terms renders the cost of searching out and deliberating on the preprinted terms of various form contracts exceptionally high. In contrast, the low probability that these nonperformance terms will ever come into play heavily discounts the benefits of search and deliberation.

Furthermore, the length and complexity of a form contract is often not correlated to the dollar value of the transaction. Often, therefore, the cost of thorough search and deliberation on preprinted terms, let alone the cost of legal advice about the meaning and effect of the terms, would be prohibitive in relation to the benefits. A rational form-taker faced with preprinted terms whose effect he knows he will find difficult or impossible to fully understand, which involve risks that probably will never mature, which are unlikely to be worth the cost of search and deliberation, and which probably aren't subject to negotiation in any event, will typically decide to remain ignorant of many or most preprinted terms.

There is, however, a fundamental imbalance in this respect between the form-taker and the form-giver. For the form-taker, any given form contract is normally a one-shot transaction. This is one reason why the costs of searching and deliberating on the preprinted terms, or of retaining a lawyer to evaluate them, will normally far exceed the benefits of search and deliberation. For the form-giver, however, a form contract is a high-volume, repeat transaction. Thus, a rational form-giver will spend a significant amount of time and money, including money for legal services, to prepare a form contract that is optimal from his perspective. These asymmetrical incentives almost always work to heavily slant form contracts in favor of form-givers.

The law has responded to these problems through Section 2–207 of the Uniform Commercial Code, and through the common law doctrines of unfair surprise and reasonable expectations, and through related rules in the Uniform Commercial Code, which sometimes limit the effect of preprinted terms. Section 2–207 is the subject of this Chapter. The latter issues are the subject of Chapter 16.

NOTE ON THE BATTLE OF THE FORMS

When goods are supplied by a commercial seller to a commercial buyer, in most cases there is no document covering the transaction that is called on its face a "contract." Often the buyer will send to the seller a form that the buyer calls a "purchase order." At the bottom of this form, or on the reverse side, there will appear certain preprinted terms, often loosely designated in the form as "conditions." These terms may be fairly extensive, and include shipping instructions, provisions making the order cancellable for delays in delivery, provisions covering crating charges, provisions for the arbitration of disputes, etc. Usually the purchase-order form will state that the order is given subject to the conditions stated. Generally the purchase order will request an acknowledgment, although occasionally the word acceptance is used. The buyer sometimes hopefully provides a tear sheet or a separate form, requesting the seller to sign and return this form as an acknowledgment of the order.

Often the seller, instead of accepting the buyer's purchase order, or returning the buyer's acknowledgment form, sends the buyer the seller's own form, frequently called a sales order. Or the first document may be a sales order sent by the seller to the buyer. This will be like the buyer's purchase order, and will itself be subject to certain preprinted terms or "conditions" printed at the bottom or on the back.

The chances that the preprinted terms in the sales order will coincide with those in the purchase order are negligible. Sometimes, to strengthen its position, the seller will repeat its terms (or perhaps a different set of terms) on an invoice that is sent when the goods are shipped, stating that the goods are shipped "subject to the following conditions." The buyer, anticipating that the seller will decorate the back of its invoice with fine print, may stipulate in its purchase order that if the terms stated in the invoice do not agree with the buyer's purchase order, the terms of the purchase order will control.

The result is that instead of an orderly negotiation of the terms of the sale, we have the parties engaged in a *battle of the forms*, each jockeying for position and each attempting to get the other to indicate assent to its form. Sometimes a seller's sales order is signed by the buyer, and a buyer's purchase order is signed by the seller. Thus, the same transaction is covered by two different forms, stipulating inconsistent terms. More commonly, neither party is willing to sign the other's form, so that each party states in writing its terms of the sale, but neither expressly indicates assent to the terms proposed by the other.

The battle of the forms had a special bite under the mirror-image (or ribbon-matching) rule of classical contract law. Under this rule, any difference between an offer and a purported acceptance, no matter how minor, prevented the formation of a contract. Since the seller's form and the buyer's form seldom if ever matched, the exchange of a purchase order and a sales order (or counterpart forms) would seldom if ever constitute a contract under the mirror-image rule.

But the matter did not end there. Under another common law rule, an offer can be accepted by conduct. Putting the two rules together, if no contract was formed by the exchange of forms because the two forms were not identical, but the seller shipped the goods and the buyer accepted them, a contract was deemed to have been made, consisting of the terms in whichever form was sent last. The theory was that the first form was an offer, the responding form was a counter-offer, and the goods were shipped and accepted pursuant to that counter-offer. For example, suppose the buyer began a transaction by sending a purchase order, and the seller responded by sending back a nonconforming sales order. Under the mirror-image rule, there would be no contract at that point. However, the sales order would not be without legal effect; instead, under traditional principles it would be a counter-offer. Now suppose the seller shipped the goods and the buyer accepted the shipment. The buyer was deemed to have accepted pursuant to the sales order/counter-offer, so that the terms of the resulting contract were those set by the seller. Similarly, suppose the seller began a transaction be sending a sales order, the buyer responded with a nonconforming purchase order, the seller shipped the goods, and the buyer accepted the shipment. In that case, the terms of the contract would be those set in the purchase order, because the buyer's nonconforming purchase order would be a counter-offer, and the seller's shipment would be deemed an acceptance of that counter-offer. This analysis was often called the last-shot approach, because if the goods were shipped and accepted, the terms of the contract were those set by whichever party fired the last shot in the battle of the forms.

UCC §§ 2–204(1), 2–204, 2–207

[See Selected Source Materials Supplement]

ABA Task Force Report on Article 2

16 Del.J.Corp.Law. 981, 1063–64 (1991)

"The premise that underlies [UCC] section 2–207 is that pre-printed boilerplate terms in each party's form are not read. Indeed, they cannot reasonably be expected to be read by the other party."

NOTE ON WHAT CONSTITUTES AN ACCEPTANCE
UNDER UCC § 2–207(1)

UCC § 2–207(1) applies only if there has been a "definite and [seasonable] expression of acceptance," but leaves open what constitutes a definite and seasonable expression of acceptance. In most cases under § 2–207 the offeror has sent a form to the offeree; the offeree has returned to the offeror another form whose individualized (non-preprinted) terms match the individualized terms of the offer; virtually no other terms match; and the courts have explicitly or implicitly held that the return form nevertheless constitutes an "expression of acceptance" under § 2–207. Indeed, that is the paradigm case at which § 2–207 was directed.

Where, however, the parties don't employ forms, even a small difference between the offer and the response may prevent a response from being an acceptance under § 2–207, at least if the parties have been bargaining about that difference.

For example, in Koehring Co. v. Glowacki, 77 Wis.2d 497, 253 N.W.2d 64 (1977), Koehring circulated a letter listing nine items of surplus machinery that were available for sale at its plant on an "as is, where is" basis. The term "as is, where is" meant that the buyer would bear the cost and risk of loading the machinery onto its truck. Glowacki telephoned Koehring, inquiring as to price. Koehring responded that Glowacki must bid $16,500, and that the bid must be in the form of a telegram. Glowacki telegraphed a bid of only $16,000. Koehring called Glowacki, reiterating that the bid must be $16,500. Glowacki then sent a second telegram, which bid $16,500, but including the statement "FOB [free on board], our truck, your plant, loaded." The term "FOB . . . loaded" meant that the seller would bear the cost and risk of loading the machinery onto the buyer's truck. Koehring responded with a telegram "accepting" the bid, but restating that the machinery was sold "as is, where is." In a suit by Koehring, the court held that no contract had been formed:

> As the trial court properly held in the present case, before we reach the question of additional or different terms added to a contract, we must first inquire whether or not any contract ever existed. Here the defendant's telegram was an offer to purchase at a price of $16,500 "FOB, our truck, your plant, loaded." Plaintiff's response was a counteroffer to sell at the price of $16,500 on an "as is, where is" basis. There was no "meeting of the minds" or agreement of the parties prior to the exchange of telegrams. No such "meeting of the minds" or agreement resulted from the exchange of telegrams. This being so, we do not reach the issue as to whether additional or differing terms do or do not destroy an agreement of the parties since there is no valid contract in the first place.

> In the case before us, we deal with an initial and continuing absence of agreement between the parties as to whether the sales price included loading risks and costs. The second telegram of defendant, offering $16,500 "FOB, our truck, your plant, loaded," was

an offer. The responding telegram of plaintiff, all tools sold on an "as is, where is" basis, while labeled an acceptance, was actually a rejection of the defendant's offer and a counteroffer. This being the situation, it follows, as the trial court concluded, that there was here no contract or agreement between these two parties either preceding or derived from their exchange of telegrams.

CISG ART. 19

[See Selected Source Materials Supplement]

UNIDROIT PRINCIPLES OF INTERNATIONAL COMMERCIAL CONTRACTS ARTS. 2.1.12, 2.1.22

[See Selected Source Materials Supplement]

PRINCIPLES OF EUROPEAN CONTRACT LAW ART. 2.209

[See Selected Source Materials Supplement]

GARDNER ZEMKE CO. v. DUNHAM BUSH, INC.

Supreme Court of New Mexico, 1993.
115 N.M. 260, 850 P.2d 319.

FRANCHINI, JUSTICE.

This case involves a contract for the sale of goods and accordingly the governing law is the Uniform Commercial Code—Sales, as adopted in New Mexico. NMSA 1978, §§ 55–2–101 to –2–725 (Orig.Pamp. & Cum.Supp.1992) (Article 2). In the course of our discussion, we will also refer to pertinent general definitions and principles of construction found in NMSA 1978, Sections 55–1–101 to –1–209 (Orig.Pamp. & Cum.Supp.1992). Section 55–2–103(4). The case presents us with our first opportunity to consider a classic "battle of the forms" scenario arising under Section 55–2–207. Appellant Gardner Zemke challenges the trial court's judgment that a Customer's Acknowledgment (Acknowledgment) sent by appellee manufacturer Dunham Bush, in response to a Gardner Zemke Purchase Order (Order), operated as a counteroffer, thereby providing controlling warranty terms under the contract formed by the parties. We find merit in appellants' argument and remand for the trial court's reconsideration.

I.

Acting as the general contractor on a Department of Energy (DOE) project, Gardner Zemke issued its Order to Dunham Bush for air-conditioning equipment, known as chillers, to be used in connection with the project. The Order contained a one-year manufacturer's warranty provision and the requirement that the chillers comply with specifications attached to the Order. Dunham Bush responded with its preprinted Acknowledgment containing extensive warranty disclaimers, a statement that the terms of the Acknowledgment controlled the parties' agreement, and a provision deeming silence to be acquiescence to the terms of the Acknowledgment.

The parties did not address the discrepancies in the forms exchanged and proceeded with the transaction. Dunham Bush delivered the chillers, and Gardner Zemke paid for them. Gardner Zemke alleges that the chillers provided did not comply with their specifications and that they incurred additional costs to install the nonconforming goods. Approximately five or six months after start up of the chillers, a DOE representative notified Gardner Zemke of problems with two of the chillers. In a series of letters, Gardner Zemke requested on-site warranty repairs. Through its manufacturer's representative, Dunham Bush offered to send its mechanic to the job site to inspect the chillers and absorb the cost of the service call only if problems discovered were within any component parts it provided. Further, Dunham Bush required that prior to the service call a purchase order be issued from the DOE, to be executed by Dunham Bush for payment for their services in the event their mechanic discovered problems not caused by manufacturing defects. Gardner Zemke rejected the proposal on the basis that the DOE had a warranty still in effect for the goods and would not issue a separate purchase order for warranty repairs.

Ultimately, the DOE hired an independent contractor to repair the two chillers. The DOE paid $24,245.00 for the repairs and withheld $20,000.00 from its contract with Gardner Zemke.[1] This breach of contract action then ensued, with Gardner Zemke alleging failure by Dunham Bush to provide equipment in accordance with the project plans and specifications and failure to provide warranty service.

II.

On cross-motions for summary judgment, the trial court granted partial summary judgment in favor of Dunham Bush, ruling that its Acknowledgment was a counteroffer to the Gardner Zemke Order and that

---

[1] The government has the right to set off the remaining $4,245.00 from any other Gardner Zemke government contract. *See Project Map, Inc. v. United States*, 203 Ct.Cl. 52, 486 F.2d 1375 (1973) (per curiam).

the Acknowledgment's warranty limitations and disclaimers were controlling. Gardner Zemke filed an application for interlocutory appeal from the partial summary judgment in this Court, which was denied. A bench trial was held in December 1991, and the trial court again ruled the Acknowledgment was a counter-offer which Gardner Zemke accepted by silence and that under the warranty provisions of the Acknowledgment, Gardner Zemke was not entitled to damages.

On appeal, Gardner Zemke raises two issues: (1) the trial court erred as a matter of law in ruling that the Acknowledgment was a counteroffer; and (2) Gardner Zemke proved breach of contract and contract warranty, breach of code warranties, and damages.

III.

Karl N. Llewellyn, the principal draftsman of Article 2, described it as "[t]he heart of the Code." Karl N. Llewellyn, *Why We Need the Uniform Commercial Code,* 10 U.Fla.L.Rev. 367, 378 (1957). Section 2–207 is characterized by commentators as a "crucial section of Article 2" and an "iconoclastic Code section." *Bender's Uniform Commercial Code Service* (Vol. 3, Richard W. Duesenberg & Lawrence P. King, Sales & Bulk Transfers Under The Uniform Commercial Code) § 3.01 at 3–2 (1992). Recognizing its innovative purpose and complex structure Duesenberg and King further observe Section 2–207 "is one of the most important, subtle, and difficult in the entire Code, and well it may be said that the product as it finally reads is not altogether satisfactory." *Id.* § 3.02 at 3–13.

Section 55–2–207 provides:

(1) A definite and seasonable expression of acceptance or a written confirmation which is sent within a reasonable time operates as an acceptance even though it states terms additional to or different from those offered or agreed upon, unless acceptance is expressly made conditional on assent to the additional or different terms.

(2) The additional terms are to be construed as proposals for addition to the contract. Between merchants such terms become part of the contract unless:

(a) the offer expressly limits acceptance to the terms of the offer;

(b) they materially alter it; or,

(c) notification of objection to them has already been given or is given within a reasonable time after notice of them is received.

(3) Conduct by both parties which recognizes the existence of a contract is sufficient to establish a contract for sale although

the writings of the parties do not otherwise establish a contract. In such case the terms of the particular contract consist of those terms on which the writings of the parties agree, together with any supplementary terms incorporated under any other provisions of this act [this chapter].

Relying on Section 2–207(1), Gardner Zemke argues that the trial court erred in concluding that the Dunham Bush Acknowledgment was a counteroffer rather than an acceptance. Gardner Zemke asserts that even though the Acknowledgment contained terms different from or in addition to the terms of their Order, it did not make acceptance expressly conditional on assent to the different or additional terms and therefore should operate as an acceptance rather than a counteroffer.

At common law, the "mirror image" rule applied to the formation of contracts, and the terms of the acceptance had to exactly imitate or "mirror" the terms of the offer. *Idaho Power Co. v. Westinghouse Elec. Corp.,* 596 F.2d 924, 926 (9th Cir.1979). If the accepting terms were different from or additional to those in the offer, the result was a counteroffer, not an acceptance. *Id.; see also Silva v. Noble,* 85 N.M. 677, 678–79, 515 P.2d 1281, 1282–83 (1973). Thus, from a common law perspective, the trial court's conclusion that the Dunham Bush Acknowledgment was a counteroffer was correct.

However, the drafters of the Code "intended to change the common law in an attempt to conform contract law to modern day business transactions." *Leonard Pevar Co. v. Evans Prods. Co.,* 524 F.Supp. 546, 551 (D.Del.1981). As Professors White and Summers explain:

> The rigidity of the common law rule ignored the modern realities of commerce. Where preprinted forms are used to structure deals, they rarely mirror each other, yet the parties usually assume they have a binding contract and act accordingly. Section 2–207 rejects the common law mirror image rule and converts many common law counteroffers into acceptances under 2–207(1).

James J. White & Robert S. Summers, *Handbook of the Law Under the Uniform Commercial Code* § 1–3 at 29–30 (3d ed. 1988) (footnotes omitted).

On its face, Section 2–207(1) provides that a document responding to an offer and purporting to be an acceptance will be an acceptance, despite the presence of additional and different terms. Where merchants exchange preprinted forms and the essential contract terms agree, a contract is formed under Section 2–207(1). Duesenberg & King, § 3.04 at 3–47 to –49. A responding document will fall outside of the provisions of Section 2–207(1) and convey a counteroffer, only when its terms differ radically from the offer, or when "acceptance is expressly made conditional on assent to the additional or different terms"—whether a contract is formed under Section 2–207(1) here turns on the meaning given this phrase.

Dunham Bush argues that the language in its Acknowledgment makes acceptance expressly conditional on assent to the additional or different terms set forth in the Acknowledgment. The face of the Acknowledgment states:

> IT IS UNDERSTOOD THAT OUR ACCEPTANCE OF THIS ORDER IS SUBJECT TO THE TERMS AND CONDITIONS ENUMERATED ON THE REVERSE SIDE HEREOF, IT BEING STRICTLY UNDERSTOOD THAT THESE TERMS AND CONDITIONS BECOME A PART OF THIS ORDER AND THE ACKNOWLEDGMENT THEREOF.

The following was among the terms and conditions on the reverse side of the Acknowledgment.

> Failure of the Buyer to object in writing within five (5) days of receipt thereof to Terms of Sale contained in the Seller's acceptance and/or acknowledgment, or other communications, shall be deemed an acceptance of such Terms of Sale by Buyer.

In support of its contention that the above language falls within the "expressly conditional" provision of Section 2–207, Dunham Bush urges that we adopt the view taken by the First Circuit in *Roto-Lith, Ltd. v. F.P. Bartlett & Co.*, 297 F.2d 497 (1st Cir.1962). There, Roto-Lith sent an order for goods to Bartlett, which responded with an acknowledgment containing warranty disclaimers, a statement that the acknowledgment reflected the terms of the sale, and a provision that if the terms were unacceptable Roto-Lith should notify Bartlett at once. *Id.* at 498–99. Roto-Lith did not protest the terms of the acknowledgment and accepted and paid for the goods. The court held the Bartlett acknowledgment was a counteroffer that became binding on Roto-Lith with its acceptance of the goods, reasoning that "a response which states a condition materially altering the obligation solely to the disadvantage of the offeror" falls within the "expressly conditional" language of 2–207(1). *Id.* at 500.

Dunham Bush suggests that this Court has demonstrated alliance with the principles of *Roto-Lith* in *Fratello v. Socorro Electric Cooperative, Inc.*, 107 N.M. 378, 758 P.2d 792 (1988). *Fratello* involved the terms of a settlement agreement in which one party sent the other party a proposed stipulated order containing an additional term. In the context of the common law, we cited *Roto-Lith* in support of the proposition that the additional term made the proposed stipulation a counteroffer. *Fratello*, 107 N.M. at 381, 758 P.2d at 795.

We have never adopted *Roto-Lith* in the context of the Code and decline to do so now. While ostensibly interpreting Section 2–207(1), the

First Circuit's analysis imposes the common law doctrine of offer and acceptance on language designed to avoid the common law result. *Roto-Lith* has been almost uniformly criticized by the courts and commentators as an aberration on Article 2 jurisprudence. *Leonard Pevar Co.*, 524 F.Supp. at 551 (and cases cited therein); Duesenberg & King, § 3.05[1] at 3–61 to –62; White & Summers, § 1–3 at 36–37.

Mindful of the purpose of Section 2–207 and the spirit of Article 2, we find the better approach suggested in *Dorton v. Collins & Aikman Corp.*, 453 F.2d 1161 (6th Cir.1972). In *Dorton*, the Sixth Circuit considered terms in acknowledgment forms sent by Collins & Aikman similar to the terms in the Dunham Bush Acknowledgment. The Collins & Aikman acknowledgments provided that acceptance of orders was subject to the terms and conditions of their form, together with at least seven methods in which a buyer might acquiesce to their terms, including receipt and retention of their form for ten days without objection. *Id.* at 1167–68.

Concentrating its analysis on the concept of the offeror's "assent," the Court reasoned that it was not enough to make acceptance expressly conditional on additional or different terms; instead, the expressly conditional nature of the acceptance must be predicated on the offeror's "assent" to those terms. *Id.* at 1168. The Court concluded that the "expressly conditional" provision of Section 2–207(1) "was intended to apply only to an acceptance which clearly reveals that the offeree is unwilling to proceed with the transaction unless he is assured of the offeror's assent to the additional or different terms therein." *Id.* This approach has been widely accepted. *Diatom, Inc. v. Pennwalt Corp.*, 741 F.2d 1569, 1576–77 (10th Cir.1984); *Reaction Molding Technologies, Inc. v. General Elec. Co.*, 588 F.Supp. 1280, 1288 (E.D.Pa.1984); *Idaho Power Co.*, 596 F.2d at 926–27.

We agree with the court in *Dorton* that the inquiry focuses on whether the offeree clearly and unequivocally communicated to the offeror that its willingness to enter into a bargain was conditioned on the offeror's "assent" to additional or different terms. An exchange of forms containing identical dickered terms, such as the identity, price, and quantity of goods, and conflicting undickered boilerplate provisions, such as warranty terms and a provision making the bargain subject to the terms and conditions of the offeree's document, however worded, will not propel the transaction into the "expressly conditional" language of Section 2–207(1) and confer the status of counteroffer on the responsive document.

While *Dorton* articulates a laudable rule, it fails to provide a means for the determination of when a responsive document becomes a counteroffer. We adopt the rule in *Dorton* and add that whether an acceptance is made expressly conditional on assent to different or additional terms is dependent on the commercial context of the transaction.

Official Comment 2 to Section 55–2–207 suggests that "[u]nder this article a proposed deal which in commercial understanding has in fact been closed is recognized as a contract." While the comment applies broadly and envisions recognition of contracts formed under a variety of circumstances, it guides us to application of the concept of "commercial understanding" to the question of formation. *See* 2 William D. Hawkland, *Uniform Commercial Code Series* § 2–207:02 at 160 (1992) ("The basic question is whether, in commercial understanding, the proposed deal has been closed.").

Discerning whether "commercial understanding" dictates the existence of a contract requires consideration of the objective manifestations of the parties' understanding of the bargain. It requires consideration of the parties' activities and interaction during the making of the bargain; and when available, relevant evidence of course of performance, Section 55–2–208; and course of dealing and usage of the trade, Section 55–1–205. The question guiding the inquiry should be whether the offeror could reasonably believe that in the context of the commercial setting in which the parties were acting, a contract had been formed. This determination requires a very fact specific inquiry. *See* John E. Murray, Jr., *Section 2–207 Of The Uniform Commercial Code: Another Word About Incipient Unconscionability,* 39 U.Pitt.L.Rev., 597, 632–34 (1978) (discussing *Dorton* and identifying the commercial understanding of the reasonable buyer as the "critical inquiry").

Our analysis does not yield an iron clad rule conducive to perfunctory application. However, it does remain true to the spirit of Article 2, as it calls the trial court to consider the commercial setting of each transaction and the reasonable expectations and beliefs of the parties acting in that setting. *Id.* at 600; § 55–1–102(2)(b) (stating one purpose of the act is "to permit the continued expansion of commercial practices through custom, usage and agreement of the parties").

The trial court's treatment of this issue did not encompass the scope of the inquiry we envision. We will not attempt to make the factual determination necessary to characterize this transaction on the record before us. Not satisfied that the trial court adequately considered all of the relevant factors in determining that the Dunham Bush Acknowledgment functioned as a counteroffer, we remand for reconsideration of the question.

In the event the trial court concludes that the Dunham Bush Acknowledgment constituted an acceptance, it will face the question of which terms will control in the exchange of forms. In the interest of judicial economy, and because this determination is a question of law, we proceed with our analysis.

IV.

The Gardner Zemke Order provides that the "[m]anufacturer shall replace or repair all parts found to be defective during initial year of use at no additional cost." Because the Order does not include any warranty terms, Article 2 express and implied warranties arise by operation of law. Section 55–2–313 (express warranties), § 55–2–314 (implied warranty of merchantability), § 55–2–315 (implied warranty of fitness for a particular purpose). The Dunham Bush Acknowledgment contains the following warranty terms.

> WARRANTY: We agree that the apparatus manufactured by the Seller will be free from defects in material and workmanship for a period of one year under normal use and service and when properly installed: and our obligation under this agreement is limited solely to repair or replacement at our option, at our factories, of any part or parts thereof which shall within one year from date of original installation or 18 months from date of shipment from factory to the original purchaser, whichever date may first occur be returned to us with transportation charges prepaid which our examination shall disclose to our satisfaction to have been defective. THIS AGREEMENT TO REPAIR OR REPLACE DEFECTIVE PARTS IS EXPRESSLY IN LIEU OF AND IS HEREBY DISCLAIMER OF ALL OTHER EXPRESS WARRANTIES, AND IS IN LIEU OF AND IN DISCLAIMER AND EXCLUSION OF ANY IMPLIED WARRANTIES OF MERCHANTABILITY AND FITNESS FOR A PARTICULAR PURPOSE, AS WELL AS ALL OTHER IMPLIED WARRANTIES, IN LAW OR EQUITY, AND OF ALL OTHER OBLIGATIONS OR LIABILITIES ON OUR PART. THERE ARE NO WARRANTIES WHICH EXTEND BEYOND THE DESCRIPTION HEREOF. . . . Our obligation to repair or replace shall not apply to any apparatus which shall have been repaired or altered outside our factory in any way.

The one proposition on which most courts and commentators agree at this point in the construction of the statute is that Section 2–207(3) applies only if a contract is not found under Section 2–207(1) . *Dorton*, 453 F.2d at 1166; Duesenberg & King, § 3.03[1] at 3–40; 2 Hawkland, § 2–207:04 at 178–79; White & Summers, § 1–3 at 35. However, there are courts that disagree even with this proposition. *See Westinghouse Elec. Corp. v. Nielsons, Inc.*, 647 F.Supp. 896 (D.Colo.1986) (dealing with different terms, finding a contract under 2–207(1) and proceeding to apply 2–207(2) and 2–207(3)).

The language of the statute makes it clear that "additional" terms are subject to the provisions of Section 2–207(2). However, a continuing controversy rages among courts and commentators concerning the treatment of "different" terms in a Section 2–207 analysis. While Section 2–207(1) refers to both "additional or different" terms, Section 2–207(2) refers only to "additional" terms. The omission of the word "different" from Section 55–2–207(2) gives rise to the questions of whether "different" terms are to be dealt with under the provisions of Section 2–207(2), and if not, how they are to be treated. That the terms in the Acknowledgment are "different" rather than "additional" guides the remainder of our inquiry and requires that we join the fray. Initially, we briefly survey the critical and judicial approaches to the problem posed by "different" terms.

One view is that, in spite of the omission, "different" terms are to be analyzed under Section 2–207(2). 2 Hawkland, § 2–207:03 at 168. The foundation for this position is found in Comment 3, which provides "[w]hether or not additional or different terms will become part of the agreement depends upon the provisions of Subsection (2)." Armed with this statement in Comment 3, proponents point to the ambiguity in the distinction between "different" and "additional" terms and argue that the distinction serves no clear purpose. *Steiner v. Mobil Oil Corp.,* 20 Cal.3d 90, 141 Cal.Rptr. 157, 165–66 n. 5, 569 P.2d 751, 759–60 n. 5 (1977); *Boese-Hilburn Co. v. Dean Machinery Co.,* 616 S.W.2d 520, 527 (Mo.Ct.App.1981). Following this rationale in this case, and relying on the observation in Comment 4 that a clause negating implied warranties would "materially alter" the contract, the Dunham Bush warranty terms would not become a part of the contract, and the Gardner Zemke warranty provision, together with the Article 2 warranties would control. § 55–2–207(2)(b).

Another approach is suggested by Duesenberg and King who comment that the ambiguity found in the treatment of "different" and "additional" terms is more judicially created than statutorily supported. While conceding that Comment 3 "contributes to the confusion," they also admonish that "the Official Comments do not happen to be the statute." Duesenberg & King, § 3.05 at 3–52. Observing that "the drafters knew what they were doing, and that they did not sloppily fail to include the term 'different' when drafting subsection (2)," Duesenberg and King postulate that a "different" term in a responsive document operating as an acceptance can never become a part of the parties' contract under the plain language of the statute. *Id.* § 3.03[1] at 3–38.

The reasoning supporting this position is that once an offeror addresses a subject it implicitly objects to variance of that subject by the offeree, thereby preventing the "different" term from becoming a part of the contract by prior objection and obviating the need to refer to "different" terms in Section 55–2–207(2). *Id.* § 3.05[1] at 3–77; *Air Prods. & Chems. Inc. v. Fairbanks Morse, Inc.,* 58 Wis.2d 193, 206 N.W.2d 414, 423–25 (1973). Professor Summers lends support to this position. White & Summers, § 1–3 at 34. Although indulging a different analysis, following this view in the case before us creates a result identical to that flowing from application of the provisions of Section 2–207(2) as discussed above—the Dunham Bush warranty provisions fall out, and the stated Gardner Zemke and Article 2 warranty provisions apply.

Yet a third analysis arises from Comment 6, which in pertinent part states:

> Where clauses on confirming forms sent by both parties conflict each party must be assumed to object to a clause of the other conflicting with one on the confirmation sent by himself. As a result the requirement that there be notice of objection which is found in Subsection (2) is satisfied and the conflicting terms do not become a part of the contract. The contract then consists of the terms originally expressly agreed to, terms on which the confirmations agree, and terms supplied by this act, including Subsection (2).

The import of Comment 6 is that "different" terms cancel each other out and that existing applicable code provisions stand in their place. The obvious flaws in Comment 6 are the use of the words "confirming forms," suggesting the Comment applies only to variant confirmation forms and not variant offer and acceptance forms, and the reference to Subsection 55–2–207(2)—arguably dealing only with "additional" terms—in the context of "different" terms. Of course, Duesenberg and King remind us that Comment 6 "is only a comment, and a poorly drawn one at that." Duesenberg & King, § 3.05[1] at 3–79.

The analysis arising from Comment 6, however, has found acceptance in numerous jurisdictions including the Tenth Circuit. *Daitom, Inc. v. Pennwalt Corp.*, 741 F.2d 1569, 1578–79 (10th Cir.1984). Following a discussion similar to the one we have just indulged, the court found this the preferable approach. *Id.* at 1579; *accord Southern Idaho Pipe & Steel Co. v. Cal-Cut Pipe & Supply, Inc.*, 98 Idaho 495, 567 P.2d 1246, 1254–55 (1977), *appeal dismissed and cert. denied*, 434 U.S. 1056, 98 S.Ct. 1225, 55 L.Ed.2d 757 (1978). Professor White also finds merit in this analysis. White & Summers, § 1–3 at 33–35. Application of this approach here cancels out the parties' conflicting warranty terms and allows the warranty provisions of Article 2 to control.

We are unable to find comfort or refuge in concluding that any one of the three paths drawn through the contours of Section 2–207 is more consistent with or true to the language of the statute. We do find that the analysis relying on Comment 6 is the most consistent with the purpose and spirit of the Code in general and Article 2 in particular. We are mindful that the overriding goal of Article 2 is to discern the bargain struck by the contracting parties. However, there are times where the conduct of the parties makes realizing that goal impossible. In such cases, we find guidance in the Code's commitment to fairness, Section 55–1–102(3); good faith, Sections 55–1–203 & –2–103(1)(b); and conscionable conduct, Section 55–2–302.

While Section 2–207 was designed to avoid the common law result that gave the advantage to the party sending the last form, we cannot conclude that the statute was intended to shift that advantage to the party sending the first form. Such a result will generally follow from the first two analyses discussed. We adopt the third analysis as the most even-handed resolution of a difficult problem. We are also aware that under this analysis even though the conflicting terms cancel out, the Code may provide a term similar to one rejected. We agree with Professor White that "[a]t least a term so supplied has the merit of being a term that the draftsmen considered fair." White & Summers, § 1–3 at 35.

Due to our disposition of this case, we do not address the second issue raised by Gardner Zemke. On remand, should the trial court conclude a contract was formed under Section 2–207(1), the conflicting warranty provisions in the parties' forms will cancel out, and the warranty provisions of Article 2 will control.

IT IS SO ORDERED.

BACA, J., and PATRICIO M. SERNA, DISTRICT JUDGE (sitting by designation).

———

NOTE ON GARDNER ZEMKE

The rule approved in *Gardner Zemke*, that when a contract is formed under UCC § 2–207(1), conflicting terms in the offer and acceptance cancel each other out, is commonly referred to as the knockout rule, because under the rule conflicting terms knock each other out of the contract. In Dorton v. Collins & Aikman Corp., 453 F.2d 1161 (6th Cir.1972), the court applied the knockout rule where one of the conflicting terms was implied, rather than express. The alternative to the knockout rule when a contract is formed under § 2–207(1) is a rule that treats the party who sends the apparent acceptance as having assented to all of the terms in the offer, much as if she signed the offer. This has been called the "first-shot" rule. On remand in *Gardner Zemke*, if the trial court did not find a contract was formed by acceptance under § 2–207(1), then it should still find a contract formed by conduct under § 2–207(3). The terms would then be those in both parties' forms and supplementary terms as provided under that section.

———

NOTE ON THE MEANING OF "MATERIALLY ALTER" UNDER UCC § 2–207(2)(b)

Under the common law "last-shot" rule the original offeror (call her A) was treated as having assented to all of the terms in B's writing (i.e., B's counter-offer) when A performs or accepts performance, much as if A had signed B's writing. UCC § 2–207(1) changes this rule but § 2–207(2) still treats A as presumptively assenting to terms in B's writing so long as both parties are merchants and none of the screening rules in § 2–207(2) apply. A term in a writing to which a party has not assented may also become part of the contract by application of § 2–207(2) when a contract is formed by conduct under § 2–207(3) or when a term is in a confirmatory memorandum.

Under § 2–207(2)(b) a term in a writing to which A has not assented does not become part of the contract if the term would "materially alter" the contract. Since this is a rule of presumed assent the answer should turn on whether B could reasonably believe A would have assented to the term, if B had asked A. This will often turn on whether a term is customary and reasonable. Thus the Official Comment to Section 2–207 states:

> 4. Examples of typical clauses which would normally "materially alter" the contract and so result in surprise or hardship if incorporated without express awareness by the other party are: a clause negating such standard warranties as that of merchantability or fitness for a particular purpose in circumstances in which either warranty normally attaches ... [or] a clause requiring that complaints be made in a time materially shorter than customary or reasonable.

> 5. Examples of clauses which involve no element of unreasonable surprise and which therefore are to be incorporated in the contract unless notice of objection is seasonably given are: a clause setting forth and perhaps enlarging slightly upon the seller's exemption due to supervening causes beyond his control, similar to those covered by the provision of this Article on merchant's excuse by failure of presupposed conditions or ... a clause fixing a reasonable time for complaints within customary limits ...; a clause providing for interest on overdue invoices or fixing the seller's standard credit terms where they are within the range of trade practice and do not limit any credit bargained for; a clause limiting the right of rejection for defects which fall within the customary trade tolerances for acceptance "with adjustment" or otherwise limiting remedy in a reasonable manner (see Sections 2–718 and 2–719).

Relying on the test and illustrations set out in the Official Comment, a number of cases have upheld the enforcement of terms, even though the terms were material in the sense of being significant, on the ground that the terms were not surprising. For example, in Aceros Prefabricados, S.A. v. TradeArbed, Inc., 282 F.3d 92 (2d Cir. 2002), the court held that an added term in the acceptance that required all disputes to be arbitrated did not result in a material alteration of the contract under subsection (2)(b):

> A material alteration is one that would "result in surprise or hardship if incorporated without express awareness by the other party." . . . U.C.C. § 2–207 cmt. 4; *Bayway Ref.* [*Co. v. Oxygenated Mktg. & Trading A.G.*, 215 F.3d 219,] 224 (2d. Cir. 2000). Surprise includes both a subjective element of what a party actually knew and an objective element of what a party should have known. *Id.* We have stated that "[a] profession of surprise and raised eyebrows are not enough." *Id.* Instead, "[t]o carry [its] burden . . . [the nonassenting] party must establish that, under the circumstances, it cannot be presumed that a reasonable merchant would have consented to the additional term." *Id.*

Similarly, in Southern Illinois Riverboat Casino Cruises, Inc. v. Triangle Insulation and Sheet Metal Co., 302 F.3d 667 (7th Cir. 2002), the court held that the addition of a term in an acceptance that significantly limited the buyer's remedies did not result in a material alteration of the contract under Subsection 2(b).

But the cases are not consistent in this respect. Some cases have treated "hardship" as a criterion that is independent of surprise in determining whether a term constitutes a material alteration under UCC § 2–207(2)(b) . For example, in Maxon Corp. v. Tyler Pipe Industries, Inc., 497 N.E.2d 570 (Ind.App. 1986), the court said:

> . . . [E]ven if Tyler [the offeror] was not surprised by the indemnity clause in Maxon's invoice, the clause is nevertheless a material alteration if its incorporation without Tyler's express awareness would result in hardship.

> There can be no doubt that Maxon's indemnity clause would impose serious hardship if incorporated without Tyler's express awareness. By its very nature, a clause which shifts liability from a negligent party to an innocent party imposes hardship. Accordingly, we hold that Maxon's indemnity clause constitutes a material alteration as a matter of law.

Similarly, in Horning Co. v. Falconer Glass Industries, Inc., 730 F.Supp. 962 (S.D.Ind.1990), the court held that although a term limiting consequential damages was not surprising because of industry practice, the term did not become part of the contract, because it would result in hardship.

NOTE ON THE EFFECT OF CONFIRMATIONS WITH ADDITIONAL TERMS

Under UCC § 2–207 it is possible for additional terms to become part of a contract even if the terms are not proposed until after the contract is made. As pointed out in Aceros Prefabricados, S.A. v. TradeArbed ["TA"], 282 F.3d 92 (2d Cir. 2002):

> Under [the UCC] an expression of acceptance or written confirmation that sets forth terms in addition to those initially agreed upon will not defeat formation of a binding contract. Instead, a contract will be found and the additional terms . . . are then treated as "proposals" for addition to the contract. . . . [Emphasis added.] An Official Comment to section 2–207 makes clear the applicability of that provision to these two situations:

>> Under this Article a proposed deal which in commercial understanding has in fact been closed is recognized as a contract. Therefore, any additional matter contained *either in the writing intended to close the deal or in a later confirmation* falls within subsection (2) and must be regarded as a proposal for an added term. . . .

> . . . U.C.C. § 2–207 cmt. 2. Therefore, were we to find that the contract between Aceros and TA was formed on January 12, as Aceros claims and as the district court held, then the three confirmation orders would constitute written confirmations stating terms additional to the January 12 agreement, and analysis would proceed under section 2–207(2).*

> Were we to agree instead with TA's argument that each of its order confirmations served as a separate acceptance of individual prior offers by Aceros to purchase steel, the confirmations would then constitute acceptances proposing additional terms and analysis would likewise proceed under section 2–207 (2), albeit of three individual contracts. Both contract formation scenarios lead us to the same conclusion regarding the [effect of the additional term].

Of course, an additional term in a confirmation, like an additional term in an acceptance, will not become part of a contract if it is excluded under section 2–207(2) (a), (b), or (c), or by the knockout rule.

———

DIAMOND FRUIT GROWERS, INC. V. KRACK CORP.

United States Court of Appeals, Ninth Circuit, 1986.
794 F.2d 1440.

Before FLETCHER, ALARCON, and WIGGINS, CIRCUIT JUDGES.

WIGGINS, CIRCUIT JUDGE:

Metal-Matic, Inc. (Metal-Matic) appeals from judgment entered after a jury verdict in favor of Krack Corporation (Krack) on Krack's third-party

---

* Emphasis by the court. (Footnote by eds.)

complaint against Metal-Matic. Metal-Matic also appeals from the district court's denial of its motion for judgment n.o.v. We have jurisdiction under 28 U.S.C. § 1291 (1982) and affirm.

FACTS AND PROCEEDINGS BELOW

Krack is a manufacturer of cooling units that contain steel tubing it purchases from outside suppliers. Metal-Matic is one of Krack's tubing suppliers. At the time this dispute arose, Metal-Matic had been supplying tubing to Krack for about ten years. The parties followed the same course of dealing during the entire ten years. At the beginning of each year, Krack sent a blanket purchase order to Metal-Matic stating how much tubing Krack would need for the year. Then, throughout the year as Krack needed tubing, it sent release purchase orders to Metal-Matic requesting that tubing be shipped. Metal-Matic responded to Krack's release purchase orders by sending Krack an acknowledgment form and then shipping the tubing.[1]

Metal-Matic's acknowledgment form disclaimed all liability for consequential damages and limited Metal-Matic's liability for defects in the tubing to refund of the purchase price or replacement or repair of the tubing. As one would expect, these terms were not contained in Krack's purchase order. The following statement was printed on Metal-Matic's form: "Metal-Matic, Inc.'s acceptance of purchaser's offer or its offer to purchaser is hereby expressly made conditional to purchaser's acceptance of the terms and provisions of the acknowledgment form." This statement and the disclaimer of liability were on the back of the acknowledgment form. However, printed at the bottom of the front of the form in bold-face capitals was the following statement: "SEE REVERSE SIDE FOR TERMS AND CONDITIONS OF SALE."

On at least one occasion during the ten-year relationship between Metal-Matic and Krack, Allen Zver, Krack's purchasing manager, discussed the limitation of warranty and disclaimer of liability terms contained in Metal-Matic's acknowledgment form with Robert Van Krevelen, Executive Vice President of Metal-Matic. Zver told Van Krevelen that Krack objected to the terms and tried to convince him to change them, but Van Krevelen refused to do so. After the discussions, Krack continued to accept and pay for tubing from Metal-Matic.[2]

In February 1981, Krack sold one of its cooling units to Diamond Fruit Growers, Inc. (Diamond) in Oregon, and in September 1981, Diamond

---

[1]   The blanket purchase order apparently did no more than establish Krack's willingness to purchase an amount of tubing during the year. The parties' conduct indicates that they intended to establish their contract based on Krack's release purchase orders and Metal-Matic's acknowledgments sent in response to those purchase orders.

[2]   Krack contends that there is no evidence of when these discussions took place. That is not the case. Van Krevelen testified that at least some discussions were held before this incident arose. That testimony is not contradicted.

installed the unit in a controlled-atmosphere warehouse. In January 1982, the unit began leaking ammonia from a cooling coil made of steel tubing.

After Diamond discovered that ammonia was leaking into the warehouse, Joseph Smith, the engineer who had been responsible for building Diamond's controlled-atmosphere warehouses, was called in to find the source of the leak. Smith testified that he found a pinhole leak in the cooling coil of the Krack cooling unit. Smith inspected the coil while it was still inside the unit. He last inspected the coil on April 23, 1982. The coil then sat in a hall at Diamond's warehouse until May, 1984, when John Myers inspected the coil for Metal-Matic.

Myers cut the defective tubing out of the unit and took it to his office. At his office, he did more cutting on the tubing. After Myers inspected the tubing, it was also inspected by Bruce Wong for Diamond and Paul Irish for Krack.

Diamond sued Krack to recover the loss in value of fruit that it was forced to remove from the storage room as a result of the leak. Krack in turn brought a third-party complaint against Metal-Matic and Van Huffel Tube Corporation (Van Huffel), another of its tubing suppliers, seeking contribution or indemnity in the event it was held liable to Diamond. At the close of the evidence, both Metal-Matic and Van Huffel moved for a directed verdict on the third party complaint. The court granted Van Huffel's motion based on evidence that the failed tubing was not manufactured by Van Huffel. The court denied Metal-Matic's motion.

The jury returned a verdict in favor of Diamond against Krack. It then found that Krack was entitled to contribution from Metal-Matic for thirty percent of Diamond's damages. Metal-Matic moved for judgment n.o.v. The court denied that motion and entered judgment on the jury verdict.

Metal-Matic raises two grounds for reversal. First, Metal-Matic contends that as part of its contract with Krack, it disclaimed all liability for consequential damages and specifically limited its liability for defects in the tubing to refund of the purchase price or replacement or repair of the tubing. Second, Metal-Matic asserts that the evidence does not support a finding that it manufactured the tubing in which the leak developed or that it caused the leak. We address each of these contentions in turn. . . .

DISCUSSION . . .

If the contract between Metal-Matic and Krack contains Metal-Matic's disclaimer of liability, Metal-Matic is not liable to indemnify Krack for part of Diamond's damages. Therefore, the principal issue before us on this appeal is whether Metal-Matic's disclaimer of liability became part of the contract between these parties.

Relying on Uniform Commercial Code (U.C.C.) § 2–207, Or.Rev.Stat. § 72.2070 (1985), Krack argues that Metal-Matic's disclaimer did not become part of the contract. Metal-Matic, on the other hand, argues that section 2–207 is inapplicable to this case because the parties discussed the disclaimer, and Krack assented to it.

Krack is correct in its assertion that section 2–207 applies to this case. One intended application of section 2–207 is to commercial transactions in which the parties exchange printed purchase order and acknowledgment forms. *See* U.C.C. § 2–207 comment 1. The drafters of the U.C.C. recognized that "[b]ecause the [purchase order and acknowledgment] forms are oriented to the thinking of the respective drafting parties, the terms contained in them often do not correspond." *Id.* Section 2–207 is an attempt to provide rules of contract formation in such cases. In this case, Krack and Metal-Matic exchanged purchase order and acknowledgment forms that contained different or additional terms. This, then, is a typical section 2–207 situation. The fact that the parties discussed the terms of their contract after they exchanged their forms does not put this case outside section 2–207. *See* 3 R. Duesenburg & L. King, *Sales and Bulk Transfers under the Uniform Commercial Code* (Bender's U.C.C. Service) § 3.05[2] (1986). Section 2–207 provides rules of contract formation in cases such as this one in which the parties exchange forms but do not agree on all the terms of their contract.

Generally, section 2–207 (1) "converts a common law counteroffer into an acceptance even though it states additional or different terms." *Idaho Power,* 596 F.2d at 926; *see* U.C.C. § 2–207(1). The only requirement under section 2–207(1) is that the responding form contain a definite and seasonable expression of acceptance. The terms of the responding form that correspond to the offer constitute the contract. Under section 2–207(2), the additional terms of the responding form become proposals for additions to the contract. Between merchants the additional terms become part of the contract unless the offer is specifically limited to its terms, the offeror objects to the additional terms, or the additional terms materially alter the terms of the offer. U.C.C. § 2–207(2); *see* J. White & R. Summers, § 1–2 at 32.

However, section 2–207(1) is subject to a proviso. If a definite and seasonable expression of acceptance expressly conditions acceptance on the offeror's assent to additional or different terms contained therein, the parties' differing forms do not result in a contract unless the offeror assents to the additional terms. *See* J. White & R. Summers, § 1–2 at 32–33. If the offeror assents, the parties have a contract and the additional terms are a part of that contract. If, however, the offeror does not assent, but the parties proceed with the transaction as if they have a contract, their performance results in formation of a contract. U.C.C. § 2–207(3). In that case, the terms of the contract are those on which the parties' forms agree plus any terms supplied by the U.C.C. *Id.; see Boise Cascade Corp. v. Etsco,*

Ltd., 39 U.C.C.Rep.Serv. (Callaghan) 410, 414 (D.Or.1984); J. White & R. Summers, § 1–2 at 34.

In this case, Metal-Matic expressly conditioned its acceptance on Krack's assent to the additional terms contained in Metal-Matic's acknowledgment form. That form tracks the language of the section 2–207(1) proviso, stating that "Metal-Matic, Inc.'s acceptance . . . is hereby *expressly made conditional* to purchaser's acceptance of the terms and provisions of the acknowledgment form." (emphasis added). *See C. Itoh & Co.,* 552 F.2d at 1235. Therefore, we must determine whether Krack assented to Metal-Matic's limitation of liability term.

Metal-Matic argues that Krack did assent to the limitation of liability term. This argument is based on the discussions between Zver for Krack and Van Krevelen for Metal-Matic. Some time during the ten-year relationship between the companies, these two men discussed Krack's objections to the warranty and liability limitation terms in Metal-Matic's acknowledgment form. Krack attempted to persuade Metal-Matic to change its form, but Metal-Matic refused to do so. After the discussions, the companies continued to do business as in the past. Metal-Matic contends that Krack assented to the limitation of liability term when it continued to accept and pay for tubing after Metal-Matic insisted that the contract contain its terms.

To address Metal-Matic's argument, we must determine what constitutes assent to additional or different terms for purposes of section 2–207(1). The parties have not directed us to any cases that analyze this question and our research has revealed none. We therefore look to the language and structure of section 2–207 and to the purposes behind that section to determine the correct standard.

One of the principles underlying section 2–207 is neutrality. If possible, the section should be interpreted so as to give neither party to a contract an advantage simply because it happened to send the first or in some cases the last form. *See* J. White & R. Summers, § 1–2 at 26–27. Section 2–207 accomplishes this result in part by doing away with the common law's "last shot" rule. *See* 3 R. Duesenberg & L. King, § 3.05[1][a][iii] at 3–73. At common law, the offeree/counterofferor gets all of its terms simply because it fired the last shot in the exchange of forms. Section 2–207(3) does away with this result by giving neither party the terms it attempted to impose unilaterally on the other. *See id.* at 3–71. Instead, all of the terms on which the parties' forms do not agree drop out, and the U.C.C. supplies the missing terms.

Generally, this result is fair because both parties are responsible for the ambiguity in their contract. The parties could have negotiated a contract and agreed on its terms, but for whatever reason, they failed to do so. Therefore, neither party should get its terms. *See* 3 R. Duesenberg & L.

King, § 3.05[2] at 3–88. However, as White and Summers point out, resort to section 2–207(3) will often work to the disadvantage of the seller because he will "wish to undertake less responsibility for the quality of his goods than the Code imposes or else wish to limit his damages liability more narrowly than would the Code." J. White & R. Summers, § 1–2 at 34. Nevertheless, White and Summers recommend that section 2–207(3) be applied in such cases. *Id.* We agree. Application of section 2–207(3) is more equitable than giving one party its terms simply because it sent the last form. Further, the terms imposed by the code are presumably equitable and consistent with public policy because they are statutorily imposed. *See* 3 R. Duesenberg & L. King, § 3.05[2] at 3–88.

With these general principles in mind, we turn now to Metal-Matic's argument that Krack assented to the disclaimer when it continued to accept and pay for tubing once Metal-Matic indicated that it was willing to sell tubing only if its warranty and liability terms were part of the contract. Metal-Matic's argument is appealing. Sound policy supports permitting a seller to control the terms on which it will sell its products, especially in a case in which the seller has indicated both in writing and orally that those are the only terms on which it is willing to sell the product. Nevertheless, we reject Metal-Matic's argument because we find that these considerations are outweighed by the public policy reflected by Oregon's enactment of the U.C.C.

If we were to accept Metal-Matic's argument, we would reinstate to some extent the common law's last shot rule. To illustrate, assume that the parties in this case had sent the same forms but in the reverse order and that Krack's form contained terms stating that Metal-Matic is liable for all consequential damages and conditioning acceptance on Metal-Matic's assent to Krack's terms. Assume also that Metal-Matic objected to Krack's terms but Krack refused to change them and that the parties continued with their transaction anyway. If we applied Metal-Matic's argument in that case, we would find that Krack's term was part of the contract because Metal-Matic continued to ship tubing to Krack after Krack reaffirmed that it would purchase tubing only if Metal-Matic were fully liable for consequential damages. Thus, the result would turn on which party sent the last form, and would therefore be inconsistent with section 2–207's purpose of doing away with the last shot rule.

That result is avoided by requiring a specific and unequivocal expression of assent on the part of the offeror when the offeree conditions its acceptance on assent to additional or different terms. If the offeror does not give specific and unequivocal assent but the parties act as if they have a contract, the provisions of section 2–207(3) apply to fill in the terms of the contract. Application of section 2–207(3) is appropriate in that situation because by going ahead with the transaction without resolving their dispute, both parties are responsible for introducing ambiguity into the contract. Further, in a case such as this one, requiring the seller to assume more liability than it intends is not altogether inappropriate. The seller is most responsible for the ambiguity because it inserts a term in its form that requires assent to additional terms and then does not enforce that requirement. If the seller truly does not want to be bound unless the buyer assents to its terms, it can protect itself by not shipping until it obtains that assent. *See C. Itoh & Co.*, 552 F.2d at 1238.

We hold that because Krack's conduct did not indicate unequivocally that Krack intended to assent to Metal-Matic's terms, that conduct did not amount to the assent contemplated by section 2–207(1). *See* 3 R. Duesenberg & L. King, § 3.05[1][a][iii] at 3–74. . . .

[The court also concluded that the evidence supported the findings that Metal-Matic manufactured the tubing that failed, and caused the defect.]

The jury verdict is supported by the evidence and consistent with the U.C.C. Therefore, the district court did not err in denying Metal-Matic's motion for a directed verdict.

AFFIRMED.

———

Transwestern Pipeline Co. v. Monsanto Co.

46 Cal.App.4th 502, 53 Cal.Rptr.2d 887 (1996)

Monsanto sold a lubricant called Turbinol to Texas Eastern during a twelve-year period. The Turbinol was sold for use by Texas Eastern's subsidiary, Transwestern, a pipeline company. It turned out that Turbinol contained PCBs, a chemical that poses a substantial risk of environmental contamination. Some of the PCBs ended up in a pipeline owned by SoCalGas. Transwestern paid SoCalGas's cleanup costs, and then sued Monsanto for indemnification.

Monsanto's acceptances of Texas Eastern's purchase orders for Turbinol had been expressly made conditional on Turbinol's assent to the additional terms in Monsanto's sales-invoice forms. These forms disclaimed liability for consequential damages, and limited the buyer's damages to the purchase price. Monsanto contended that no contract was formed under UCC §§ 2–207(1) and (2), because of the expressly-made-conditional provisions, and that under § 2–207 (3) the provisions in the sales invoices became "supplementary terms" of the contracts as a result of the parties' course of dealing over a twelve-year period. Held, for Transwestern:

(Johnson, A.J.) "We agree with Monsanto [that] the 'supplementary terms' referred to in section [2–207(3)] may include terms incorporated as a result of the parties' course of dealing. Subdivision (3) refers to 'supplementary terms incorporated under any other provisions of this code.' Section [1–201], subdivision (3) defines an 'agreement' as: "[T]he bargain of the parties in fact as found in their language or by implication from other circumstances including course of dealing . . .

"Thus, the issue boils down to whether the exchange of forms containing inconsistent provisions as to liability and remedies, over a long period of time, can 'fairly be regarded as establishing a common basis of understanding' between the parties as to their respective liability and remedies.

"Common sense tells us the mere exchange of forms containing inconsistent terms, for however long a period, cannot establish a common understanding between the parties as to which set of conflicting terms is part of their contract. Although Monsanto repeatedly stated in its invoices its acceptance was conditioned on assent to its liability limiters, Texas Eastern never expressed such assent. Moreover, Texas Eastern's purchase orders repeatedly stated terms and conditions which contained no limitations on Monsanto's liability. Under these circumstances, we see no reason why Monsanto's form disclaiming liability and limiting Texas Eastern's remedies should be accepted over Texas Eastern's form which contained no such limitations. Each party is equally entitled to claim its terms and conditions constituted the parties' 'course of dealing.' . . . Furthermore, the fact this battle of the forms went on for 12 years makes Monsanto's argument even less tenable. The longer such a battle continues, the more obvious it is the parties have not reached an agreement over the terms in dispute."

———

CHAPTER 16

CONSUMER FORM CONTRACTS

■ ■ ■

This Chapter concerns rules that often are associated with consumer form contracts though the rules are of more general applicability. In the "battle of the forms," generally both parties are firms and each firm argues its form governs a transaction. In the cases considered in this Chapter, generally one party is an individual and the other party is a firm. The Chapter begins with cases in which a firm seeks to hold an individual to a term in its form that the individual has not read. Section 1 concerns rules that treat everyday actions, such as purchasing a good in a package that contains a form, as the legal equivalent of signing the form. Section 2 concerns UCC rules that guard against unfair surprise and protect reasonable expectations. Section 3 concerns the common law reasonable expectations doctrine and related doctrines. The Chapter closes in Section 4 with cases in which an individual seeks to enforce a term in a document that was promulgated by a firm as a statement of its policies and practices.

LLEWELLYN, THE COMMON LAW TRADITION: DECIDING APPEALS
362–371 (1960).

The impetus to the form-pad is clear, for any business unit: by standardizing terms, and by standardizing even the spot on the form where any individually dickered term appears, one saves all the time and skill otherwise needed to dig out and record the meaning of variant language; one makes check-up, totaling, follow-through, etc., into routine operations; one has duplicates (in many colors) available for the administration of a multidepartment business; and so on more. The content of the standardized terms accumulates experience, it avoids or reduces legal risks and also confers all kinds of operating leeways and advantages, all without need of either consulting counsel from instance to instance or of bargaining with the other parties. Not to be overlooked, either, is the tailoring of the crude misfitting hand-me-down pattern of the "general law" "in the absence of agreement" to the particular detailed working needs of your own line of business—whether apartment rentals, stock brokerage, international grain trade, installment selling of appliances, flour milling, sugar beet raising, or insurance. It would be a heartwarming scene, a triumph of private attention to what is essentially private self-government in the lesser transactions of life or in those areas too specialized for the blunt, slow tools of the legislature—if only all businessmen and all their lawyers would be reasonable.

But power, like greed, if it does not always corrupt, goes easily to the head. So that the form-agreements tend either at once or over the years, and often by whole lines of trade, into a massive and almost terrifying jughandled character; the one party lays his head into the mouth of a lion— either, and mostly, without reading the fine print, or occasionally in hope and expectation (not infrequently solid) that it will be a sweet and gentle lion. The more familiar instances, perhaps, are the United Realtors' Standard Lease, almost any bank's collateral note or agreement, almost any installment sale form, an accident insurance policy, a steamship ticket, a beet sugar refinery contract with a farmer or a flour miller's with its customer; or, on a lesser scale, the standard nonwarranty given by seed companies or auto manufacturers. In regard to such, one notes four things: (1) sometimes language which seems at first sight horrifying may have good human and economic stimulus; thus, suits for loss of crop before a farmer jury are pretty terrible things to face for the price of a few bags of seed; and (2) there are crooked claims and there are irrationally unreasonable ones—each with its jury risk—as well as solid ones; and only a clause which in law bars the claim absolutely can free an outfit like an insurance company to deal fairly though "in its discretion" with the latter class. On the other hand, (3) boiler-plate clauses can and often do run far beyond any such need or excuse, sometimes . . . involving flagrant trickery; and (4) not all "dominant" parties are nice lions, and even nice lions can make mistakes.

There is a fifth and no less vital thing to note: Where the form is drawn with a touch of Mr. Dooley's "gentlemanly restraint," or where, as with the overseas grain contracts or the Pacific Coast dried fruit contracts or the Worth Street Rules on textiles, two-fisted bargainers on either side have worked out in the form a balanced code to govern the particular line or trade or industry, there is every reason for a court to assume both fairness and wisdom in the terms, and to seek in first instance to learn, understand, and fit both its own thinking and its action into the whole design. Contracts of this kind (so long as reasonable in the net) are a road to better than official-legal regulation of our economic life. . . .

. . . [T]he true answer to the whole problem seems, amusingly, to be one which could occur to any court or any lawyer, at any time, as readily as to a scholar who had spent a lifetime on the subject—though I doubt if it could occur to anyone without the inquiry and analysis in depth which we owe to the scholarly work.

The answer, I suggest, is this: Instead of thinking about "assent" to boilerplate clauses, we can recognize that so far as concerns the specific, there is no assent at all. What has in fact been assented to, specifically, are the few dickered terms, and the broad type of the transaction, and but one thing more. That one thing more is a blanket assent (not a specific assent) to any not unreasonable or indecent terms the seller may have on his form, which do not alter or eviscerate the reasonable meaning of the dickered terms. The fine print which has not been read has no business to cut under the reasonable meaning of those dickered terms which constitute the dominant and only real expression of agreement. . . .

The queer thing is that where the transaction occurs without the fine print present, courts do not find this general line of approach too hard to understand: thus . . . [I cannot] see a court having trouble, where a short memo agrees in due course to sign "our standard contract," in rejecting an outrageous form as not being fairly within the reasonable meaning of the term. The clearest case to see is the handing over of a blank check: no court, judging as between the parties, would fail to reach for the circumstances, in determining whether the amount filled in had gone beyond the reasonable.

Why, then, can we not face the fact where boiler-plate is present? There has been an arm's length deal, with dickered terms. There has been accompanying that basic deal another which, if not on any fiduciary basis, at least involves a plain expression of confidence, asked and accepted, with a corresponding limit on the powers granted: the boiler-plate is assented to en bloc, "unsight, unseen," on the implicit assumption and to the full extent that (1) it does not alter or impair the fair meaning of the dickered terms when read alone, and (2) that its terms are neither in the particular nor in the net manifestly unreasonable and unfair. Such is the reality, and I see nothing in the way of a court's operating on that basis, to truly effectuate the only intention which can in reason be worked out as common to the two parties, granted good faith. And if the boiler-plate party is not playing in good faith, there is law enough to bar that fact from benefiting it. We had a hundred years of sales law in which any sales transaction with explicit words resulted in two several contracts for the one consideration: that of sale, and the collateral one of warranty. The idea is applicable here, for better reason: any contract with boiler-plate results in *two* several contracts: the *dickered* deal, and the collateral one of *supplementary* boiler-plate.

Rooted in sense, history, and simplicity, it is an answer which could occur to anyone.

———

SECTION 1. "SHRINKWRAP," "CLICKWRAP," AND "BROWSEWRAP" AGREEMENTS

DeFONTES V. DELL, INC.
Supreme Court of Rhode Island, 2009.
984 A.2d 1061.

WILLIAMS, RETIRED CHIEF JUSTICE. The defendants, Dell, Inc. f/k/a Dell Computer Corp. (Dell), Dell Catalog Sales LP (Dell Catalog), Dell Marketing LP (Dell Marketing), QualxServ, LLC (QualxServ), and BancTec, Inc. (BancTec), collectively (defendants), appeal from a Superior Court order denying their motion to stay proceedings and compel arbitration. This case is the first of two companion cases now before this Court. *See Long v. Dell Inc.*, No. 2007–346–M.P., 984 A.2d 1074 (R.I., filed Dec. 14, 2009) . It arises out of a long-frustrated putative class-action suit brought against the defendants. For the reasons set forth below, we affirm the judgment of the Superior Court.

I

Facts and Travel

This litigation began on May 16, 2003, when Mary E. DeFontes, individually and on behalf of a class of similarly situated persons, brought suit against Dell, alleging that its collection of taxes from them on the purchase of Dell optional service contracts violated the Deceptive Trade Practices Act, G.L.1956 chapter 13.1 of title 6. Ms. DeFontes asserted that service contracts, such as the option service contract offered by Dell, were not taxable within the State of Rhode Island. Nicholas Long joined the suit as a plaintiff, and an amended complaint was filed on July 16, 2003, that also added Dell subsidiaries Dell Catalog and Dell Marketing, and two service providers, QualxServ and BancTec as defendants.

Dell is an international computer hardware and software corporation. Within the Dell corporate umbrella, Dell Catalog and Dell Marketing primarily are responsible for selling computers via the internet, mail-order catalogs, and other means to individual and business consumers. Dell ships these orders throughout all fifty states from warehouses located in Texas and Tennessee. As part of these purchases, Dell offers consumers an optional service contract for on-site repair of its products, with Dell often acting as an agent for third-party service providers, including BancTec and QualxServ. Parties opting to purchase a service contract are charged a "tax," which is either paid to the State of Rhode Island directly or collected by the third-party service provider and then remitted to the state.

The two initial plaintiffs, Ms. DeFontes and Mr. Long, engaged in slightly different transactions. Ms. DeFontes purchased her computer through Dell Catalog and selected a service contract with BancTec. She paid a total of $950.51, of which $13.51 was characterized as tax on the service contract. Mr. Long purchased his computer through Dell Marketing and opted for a service contract managed by Dell. In total, he paid $3,037.73, out of which $198.73 was designated as tax paid on the service contract. There is no allegation that Dell improperly retained any of the collected tax. Several months after plaintiffs filed their amended complaint, defendants filed a motion to stay proceedings and compel arbitration, citing an arbitration provision within the parties' purported agreements.[2] The defendants argued that the arbitration provision was part of a "Terms and Conditions Agreement," which they contended plaintiffs had accepted by accepting delivery of the goods. Specifically, they averred that plaintiffs had three separate opportunities to review the terms and conditions agreement, to wit, by selecting a hyperlink on the Dell website, by reading the terms that were included in the acknowledgment/invoice that was sent to plaintiffs sometime after they placed their orders, or by reviewing the copy of the terms Dell included in the packaging of its computer products.

The hearing justice issued a written decision on January 29, 2004. He first addressed which state law to apply to the parties' dispute. After determining that the choice-of-law provision included in the terms and conditions agreement, which identified Texas as the controlling jurisdiction, was enforceable, he then analyzed whether the parties had, in fact, agreed to be bound by the terms and conditions agreement. The hearing justice found that although plaintiffs had three opportunities to review the terms, none was sufficient to give rise to a contractual obligation. First, he noted that plaintiffs could have reviewed the terms and conditions agreement had they clicked a hyperlink that appeared on Dell's website. The hearing justice found, however, that this link was "inconspicuously located at the bottom of the webpage" and insufficient to

---

[2]   The arbitration clause in Ms. DeFontes' "Terms and Conditions Agreement," quoted by the hearing justice in his decision, provided,

"ANY CLAIM, DISPUTE, OR CONTROVERSY (WHETHER IN CONTRACT, TORT, OR OTHERWISE, WHETHER PREEXISTING, PRESENT OR FUTURE, AND INCLUDING STATUTORY, COMMON LAW, INTENTIONAL TORT AND EQUITABLE CLAIMS) AGAINST DELL, its agents, employees, successors, assigns or affiliates * * * arising from or relating to this Agreement, its interpretation, or the breach, termination or validity thereof, the relationships which result from this Agreement (including, to the full extent permitted by applicable law, relationships with third parties who are not signatories to this Agreement), Dell's advertising, or any related purchase SHALL BE RESOLVED EXCLUSIVELY AND FINALLY BY BINDING ARBITRATION ADMINISTERED BY THE NATIONAL ARBITRATION FORUM (NAF) under its Code of Procedure then in effect * * *. The arbitration * * * will be limited solely to the dispute or controversy between Customer and Dell * * *. Any award of the arbitrator(s) shall be final and binding on each of the parties, and may be entered as a judgment in any court of competent jurisdiction."

The arbitration provision in the terms and conditions agreement sent to Mr. Long contained substantially similar language.

place customers on notice of the terms and conditions.[3] Nevertheless, the hearing justice noted that the terms and conditions agreement also appeared both in the acknowledgment that Dell sent to plaintiffs when they placed their orders and later within the packaging when the computers were delivered.

The hearing justice noted that "courts generally recognize that shrinkwrap agreements,[5] paper agreements enclosed within the packaging of an item, are sufficient to put consumers on inquiry notice of the terms and conditions of a transaction." He also observed, however, that shrinkwrap agreements generally contain an express disclaimer that explains to consumers that they can reject the proposed terms and conditions by returning the product. The crucial test, according to the hearing justice, was "whether a reasonable person would have known that return of the product would serve as rejection of those terms." He looked to the introductory language of the terms and conditions agreement, which he quoted as follows,[6]

> "PLEASE READ THIS DOCUMENT CAREFULLY! IT CONTAINS VERY IMPORTANT INFORMATION ABOUT YOUR RIGHTS AND OBLIGATIONS, AS WELL AS LIMITATIONS AND EXCLUSIONS THAT MAY APPLY TO YOU. THIS DOCUMENT CONTAINS A DISPUTE RESOLUTION CLAUSE.

> "This Agreement contains the terms and conditions that apply to purchases by Home, Home Office, and Small Business customers from the Dell entity named on the invoice ('Dell'). By accepting delivery of the computer systems, related products, and/or services and support, and/or other products described on that invoice. [sic] You ('Customer') agrees [sic] to be bound by and accepts [sic] these terms and conditions * * * These terms and conditions are subject to change without prior written notice at any time, in Dell's sole discretion."

The hearing justice found that this language was insufficient to give a reasonable consumer notice of the method of rejection. He found that defendants' failure to include an express disclaimer meant that they could

---

[3] We also note that Mr. Long appears to have purchased his computer over the telephone and it is unclear from the record whether he viewed the Dell website in relation to his purchase.

[5] A "shrinkwrap agreement" refers to the common commercial practice of including additional terms and conditions either on the outside of a package or within it when it is shipped to the consumer. Often these packages are covered in plastic or cellophane which must be breached to open.

[6] The hearing justice appears to have conflated the slightly different language of the terms and conditions agreements sent to Mr. Long and Ms. DeFontes. Although similar, some differences do exist. Significantly, the documents sent to Ms. DeFontes contained an express disclaimer advising her that "[i]f for any reason Customer is not satisfied with a Dell-branded hardware system, Customer may return the system under the terms and conditions of Dell's Total Satisfaction Return Policy * * * "

not prove that plaintiffs "knowingly consent[ed]" to the terms and conditions of the agreement. Accordingly, the hearing justice found that Plaintiffs could not be compelled to enter arbitration. . . .

II

Discussion

We review the trial court's denial of a motion to compel arbitration *de novo. See Kristian v. Comcast Corp.*, 446 F.3d 25, 31 (1st Cir.2006). The parties acknowledge that because their transactions involved interstate commerce, the Federal Arbitration Act (FAA) is applicable. *See* 9 U.S.C. §§ 1 through 16. Congress enacted the FAA to "overrule the judiciary's longstanding refusal to enforce agreements to arbitrate." *Dean Witter Reynolds Inc. v. Byrd*, 470 U.S. 213, 219–20, 105 S.Ct. 1238, 84 L.Ed.2d 158 (1985). It requires enforcement of privately negotiated arbitration agreements "save upon such grounds as exist at law or in equity for the revocation of any contract." 9 U.S.C. § 2. Thus, once a court is "satisfied that the making of the agreement for arbitration or the failure to comply therewith is not an issue" it "shall make an order directing the parties to proceed to arbitration in accordance with the terms of the agreement." 9 U.S.C. § 4.

Yet, the United States Supreme Court has been equally insistent that "arbitration is a matter of contract and a party cannot be required to submit to arbitration any dispute which he has not agreed so to submit." *Howsam v. Dean Witter Reynolds, Inc.*, 537 U.S. 79, 83, 123 S.Ct. 588, 154 L.Ed.2d 491 (2002) (quoting *United Steelworkers of America v. Warrior & Gulf Navigation Co.*, 363 U.S. 574, 582, 80 S.Ct. 1347, 4 L.Ed.2d 1409 (1960)); *see also Mirra Co. v. School Administrative District No. 35*, 251 F.3d 301, 304 (1st Cir.2001) ("Arbitration is a contractual matter, and no party may be forced to arbitrate a dispute unless she has expressly agreed to do so by contract."). The determination of whether the parties have formed an agreement to arbitrate is a matter of state contract law. *See* 9 U.S.C. § 2; *First Options of Chicago, Inc. v. Kaplan*, 514 U.S. 938, 944, 115 S.Ct. 1920, 131 L.Ed.2d 985 (1995). Moreover, a hearing justice's determination of "[w]hether a party has agreed to be bound by arbitration is a question of law subject to this Court's de novo review." *Stanley-Bostitch, Inc. v. Regenerative Environmental Equipment Co.*, 697 A.2d 323, 325 (R.I.1997) (citing *Providence Teachers' Union v. Providence School Committee*, 433 A.2d 202, 205 (R.I.1981)). . . .

We therefore evaluate whether plaintiffs are bound by the terms and conditions agreement by resorting to a careful review of the provisions of the U.C.C. Under U.C.C. § 2–204, contracts for the sale of goods may be formed "in any manner sufficient to show agreement, including conduct by both parties which recognizes the existence of such a contract." Tex. Bus. & Com.Code Ann. § 2.204 (Vernon 1994). The U.C.C. creates the assumption that, unless circumstances unambiguously demonstrate otherwise, the buyer is the offeror and the seller is the offeree. *See Klocek v. Gateway, Inc.,* 104 F.Supp.2d 1332, 1340 (D.Kan.2000). Moreover, U.C.C. § 2–206 provides in relevant part,

"(a) Unless otherwise unambiguously indicated by the language or circumstances,

"(1) an offer to make a contract shall be construed as inviting acceptance in any manner and by any medium reasonable in the circumstances;

"(2) an order or other offer to buy goods for prompt or current shipment shall be construed as inviting acceptance either by a prompt promise to ship or by the prompt or current shipment of conforming or nonconforming goods * * *." Tex. Bus. & Com.Code Ann. § 2.206 (Vernon 1994).

If contract formation occurred at the moment Dell's sales agents processed the customer's credit card payment and agreed to ship the goods, as plaintiffs argue, then any additional terms would necessarily be treated as "[a]dditional [t]erms in [a]cceptance or [c]onfirmation" under U.C.C. § 2–207 or offers to modify the existing contract under U.C.C. § 2–209. Yet, the modern trend seems to favor placing the power of acceptance in the hands of the buyer after he or she receives goods containing a standard form statement of additional terms and conditions, provided the buyer retains the power to "accept or return" the product.

The eminent Judge Frank Easterbrook has authored what are widely considered to be the two leading cases on so-called "shrinkwrap" agreements. In *ProCD, Inc. v. Zeidenberg,* 86 F.3d 1447, 1452–53 (7th Cir.1996), the court challenged the traditional understanding of offer and acceptance in consumer transactions by holding that a buyer of software was bound by an agreement that was included within the packaging and later appeared when the buyer first used the software.[11] *Id.* The court first held that U.C.C. § 2–207 was inapplicable because in cases involving only one form, the "battle-of-the-forms" provision was irrelevant. *ProCD, Inc.,* 86 F.3d at 1452. It then proceeded to evaluate the agreement under U.C.C. § 2–204 and reasoned that "[a] vendor, as master of the offer, may invite acceptance by conduct, and may propose limitations on the kind of conduct that constitutes acceptance. A buyer may accept by performing the acts the vendor proposes to treat as acceptance." *ProCD, Inc.,* 86 F.3d at 1452. In

---

[11] Although not discussed in the appellate decision, the trial court indicated that the agreement included the language,

"By using the discs and the listings licensed to you, you agree to be bound by the terms of this License. If you do not agree to the terms of this License, promptly return all copies of the software, listings that may have been exported, the discs and the User Guide to the place where you obtained it." *ProCD, Inc. v. Zeidenberg,* 908 F.Supp. 640, 644 (W.D.Wis.1996).

Hill v. Gateway 2000, Inc., 105 F.3d 1147, 1148–49 (7th Cir.1997),* the court expanded its earlier holding in *ProCD* beyond transactions involving software where the consumer is prompted to accept or decline the terms when he first uses the program. It determined that when a merchant delivers a product that includes additional terms and conditions, but expressly provides the consumer the right to either accept those terms or return the product for a refund within a reasonable time, a consumer who retains the goods beyond that period may be bound by the contract. *Id.* Judge Easterbrook explained,

> "Practical considerations support allowing vendors to enclose the full legal terms with their products. Cashiers cannot be expected to read legal documents to customers before ringing up sales. If the staff at the other end of the phone for direct-sales operations such as Gateway's had to read the four-page statement of terms before taking the buyer's credit card number, the droning voice would anesthetize rather than enlighten many potential buyers. Others would hang up in a rage over the waste of their time. And oral recitation would not avoid customers' assertions (whether true or feigned) that the clerk did not read term X to them, or that they did not remember or understand it." *Id.* at 1149.

The defendants argue that *ProCD* represents the majority view and we have found considerable support for their contention. *See, e.g., O'Quin v. Verizon Wireless,* 256 F.Supp.2d 512, 515–16 (M.D.La.2003) ("Terms and Conditions Pamphlet" binding where acceptance expressed by activation and use of wireless services as long as "opportunity to return"); *Bischoff v. DirecTV, Inc.,* 180 F.Supp.2d 1097, 1101 (C.D.Cal.2002) ("Customer Agreement" mailed to each customer along with the first billing statement valid when clearly advised "[i]f you do not accept these terms, please notify us immediately and we will cancel your service"); *Brower v. Gateway 2000, Inc.,* 246 A.D.2d 246, 676 N.Y.S.2d 569, 572 (N.Y.App.Div.1998) (arbitration clause of standard terms and conditions agreement valid where consumer informed that by keeping product beyond thirty days after delivery he was accepting terms); *M.A. Mortenson Co., v. Timberline Software Corp.,* 140 Wash.2d 568, 998 P.2d 305, 308 (2000) (adopting ProCD analysis but noting shrinkwrap agreement explicitly instructed consumers "IF YOU DO NOT AGREE TO THESE TERMS AND CONDITIONS, PROMPTLY RETURN * * * TO THE PLACE OF PURCHASE AND YOUR PURCHASE PRICE WILL BE REFUNDED").

---

*   [Gateway's arbitration term required the arbitration be conducted in Chicago under the rules of the International Chamber of Commerce. The ICC rules required a party filing a claim of less than $50,000 to pay an advance fee of $4,000 half of which was not refundable even if the party prevailed. While the arbitration was conducted in Chicago, all correspondence regarding the arbitration had to be sent to ICC headquarters in France. See Brower v. Gateway 2000, Inc., 246 A.D.2d 246, 676 N.Y.S.2d 569 (1998)(holding provision requiring arbitration before the ICC to be unconscionable and remanding so the trial court could consider whether Gateway's substitution of arbitration before the American Arbitration Association cured the problem). (Footnote by eds.)]

Moreover, as plaintiffs' counsel has initiated nationwide litigation, a number of sister jurisdictions have decided more or less the precise issue put before us in defendants' favor. For instance, in *Stenzel v. Dell, Inc.,* 870 A.2d 133 (Me.2005), the Maine Supreme Judicial Court reviewed a similar terms and conditions agreement sent to Dell customers that included the language,

> "By accepting delivery of the computer systems, related products, and/or services and support, and/or other products described on that invoice[, the customer] agrees to be bound by and accepts these terms and conditions. If for any reason Customer is not satisfied with a Dell-branded hardware system, Customer may return the system under the terms and conditions of Dell's Total Satisfaction Return Policy * * *." *Id,* at 140.

The court held that by "accepting delivery of the computers, and then failing to exercise their right to return the computers as provided by the agreement, [the plaintiffs] expressly manifested their assent to be bound by the agreement * * *." *Id; see also Carideo v. Dell, Inc.,* 520 F.Supp.2d 1241, 1244 (W.D.Wash.2007); *Omstead v. Dell, Inc.,* 473 F.Supp.2d 1018, 1025–26 (N.D.Cal.2007); *Adams v. Dell Computer Corp.,* No. CIV AC–06–089, 2006 WL 2670969 (S.D.Tex. Sept.18, 2006); *Sherr v. Dell Inc.,* No. 05 CV 10097(GBD) 2006 WL 2109436, *3 (S.D.N.Y. July 27, 2006) ("customer need only return the product according to the return policy in order to reject the Agreement"); *Falbe v. Dell, Inc.,* No. 04–C–1425, 2004 WL 1588243, *3 (N.D.Ill.2004) ("Our analysis begins, and could end, with * * * *Hill v. Gateway 2000, Inc.*").

Courts have not been universal in embracing the reasoning of *ProCD* and its progeny, however. In *Step-Saver Data Systems, Inc. v. Wyse Technology,* 939 F.2d 91, 98 (3d Cir.1991), the court determined that when parties exchange the shipment of goods for remuneration the existence of a contract is not in doubt; rather, any dispute relates solely to the nature of its terms. After deciding that U.C.C. § 2–207 applies to situations in which a party sends a confirmatory document that claims to establish additional terms of the contract, the court held that U.C.C. § 2–207 "establishes a legal rule that proceeding with a contract after receiving a writing that purports to define the terms of the parties's contract is not sufficient to establish the party's consent to the terms of the writing to the extent that the terms of the writing either add to, or differ from, the terms detailed in the parties's earlier writings or discussions." *Id.* at 99.[12] The court therefore held that a licensing agreement affixed to the packaging constituted a proposal for additional terms that was not binding unless

---

[12] The official comment to U.C.C. § 2–207 indicates that the provision applies "where an agreement has been reached orally or by informal correspondence between the parties and is followed by one or both of the parties sending formal memoranda embodying the terms so far agreed upon and adding terms not discussed." U.C.C. § 2–207 Official Comment 1 (2001).

expressly agreed to by the purchaser. *Id* at 100; *see also Klocek,* 104 F.Supp.2d at 1339, 1341 (finding buyer's "act of keeping the computer past five days was not sufficient to demonstrate that plaintiff expressly agreed to the Standard Terms" and criticizing the *Hill* court's summary dismissal of U.C.C. § 2–207 by stating "nothing in its language precludes application in a case which involves only one form"); *Licitra v. Gateway, Inc.,* 189 Misc.2d 721, 734 N.Y.S.2d 389, 396 (N.Y.Civ.Ct.2001) (construing arbitration clause of a shrinkwrap agreement as a proposal for additional terms under U.C.C. § 2–207 because it materially altered the existing agreement).

The Supreme Court of Oklahoma, which has also been drawn into this nationwide class-action suit against defendants, has rejected *Hill's* reasoning as well. *See Rogers,* 138 P.3d at 833. Although remanding the case to determine whether the arbitration provision was included in the parties' agreement, it noted,

> "The plaintiffs' accepting the computers and not returning them is consistent with a contract being formed at the time that the orders were placed and cannot be construed as acquiescing in the 'Terms and Conditions of Sale' document whether included with the invoice or acknowledgment or with the computer packaging. If the contracts were formed at the time the orders were placed, *see* U.C.C. § 2–206(1), the 'Terms and Conditions of Sale' document, including the arbitration provision, would be an additional term of the contracts under section 2–207. The arbitration provision would not be part of the contracts but proposals to add it as a term to the contracts." *Rogers,* 138 P.3d at 833 (citing U.C.C. § 2–207).[13]

After reviewing the case law pertaining to so-called "shrinkwrap" agreements, we are satisfied that the *ProCD* line of cases is better reasoned and more consistent with contemporary consumer transactions. It is simply unreasonable to expect a seller to apprise a consumer of every term and condition at the moment he or she makes a purchase. A modern consumer neither expects nor desires to wade through such minutia, particularly when making a purchase over the phone, where full disclosure of the terms would border on the sadistic. Nor do we believe that, after placing a telephone order for a computer, a reasonable consumer would believe that

---

[13] It appears that the drafters of the Uniform Commercial Code were themselves flummoxed by this issue. Amended U.C.C. § 2–207, which, although not adopted, could provide some insight into any evolving consensus among commercial law scholars and practitioners, states in Official Comment 5,

> "The section omits any specific treatment of terms attached to the goods, or in or on the container in which the goods are delivered. This article takes no position on whether a court should follow the reasoning in *Step-Saver Data Systems, Inc. v. Wyse Technology,* 939 F.2d 91 (3d Cir.1991) and *Klocek v. Gateway, Inc.,* 104 F.Supp.2d 1332 (D.Kan.2000) (original 2–207 governs) or the contrary reasoning of *Hill v. Gateway* 2000, 105 F.3d 1147 (7th Cir.1997) (original 2–207 inapplicable)." Amended § 2–207, Comment 5 (2003).

he or she has entered into a fully consummated agreement. *See Axelson, Inc. v. McEvoy-Willis, a Division of Smith International (North Sea), Ltd.,* 7 F.3d 1230, 1232–33 (5th Cir.1993) ("An offer is an act that leads the offeree reasonably to believe that assent (i.e., acceptance) will conclude the deal."). Rather, he or she is aware that with delivery comes a multitude of standard terms attendant to nearly every consumer transaction.

We therefore decline to adopt the minority view, as urged by plaintiffs, that a contract is fully formed when a buyer orders a product and the seller accepts payment and either ships or promises to ship. Instead, formation occurs when the consumer accepts the full terms after receiving a reasonable opportunity to refuse them. Yet in adopting the so-called "layered contracting"[14] theory of formation, we reiterate that the burden falls squarely on the seller to show that the buyer has accepted the seller's terms after delivery. Thus, the crucial question in this case is whether defendants reasonably invited acceptance by making clear in the terms and conditions agreement that (1) by accepting defendants' product the consumer was accepting the terms and conditions contained within and (2) the consumer could reject the terms and conditions by returning the product.

On the first question, defendants notified plaintiffs that "[b]y accepting delivery of the computer systems, related products, and/or services and support, and/or other products described on that invoice[,] You ('Customer') agrees to be bound by and accepts those terms and conditions." This language certainly informed plaintiffs that defendants intended to bind them to heretofore undisclosed terms and conditions, but it did not advise them of the period beyond which they will have indicated their assent to those terms. The defendants argue that the meaning of the term "accepting delivery" is apparent to a reasonable consumer. We are not so sure. *See Licitra,* 734 N.Y.S.2d at 392 ("All terms of the 'Agreement' should not be enforced merely because the consumer retains the equipment for 30 days after receipt, especially because it is unclear when the 30-day period to protest begins. Does it commence upon delivery of the goods to the carrier since the 'Agreement' states that title passes upon 'delivery to the carrier' * * * or does it commence upon receipt by the consumer? Is the time period stayed in the all too common situation where a parent buys the computer as a present for a student and does not give the gift for several weeks or is the clock ticking while the equipment sits in the box?"). "Acceptance of goods" has a technical meaning not easily discernable to the average consumer. A consumer may believe that simply by opening the package he or she has agreed to be bound by the terms and conditions

---

[14] This phrase is taken from the Supreme Court of Washington and is meant to denote that "while some contracts are formed and their terms fully defined at a single point in time, many transactions involve a rolling or layered process." *M.A. Mortenson Co. v. Timberline Software Corp.,* 140 Wash.2d 568, 998 P.2d 305, 313 n. 10 (2000) (quoting the Uniform Computer Information Transactions Act § 208 cmt. 3 (Approved Official Draft)).

contained therein. Indeed, many of the courts that have enforced so-called "approve-or-return" agreements cite language informing the consumer of a specific period after which he or she will have accepted the terms. *See, e.g., Hill,* 105 F.3d at 1148 (terms govern if consumer retains beyond thirty days); *Brower,* 676 N.Y.S.2d at 570 ("By keeping your Gateway 2000 computer system beyond thirty (30) days after the date of delivery, you accept the Terms and Conditions."). The more problematic issue, however, is whether plaintiffs were aware of their power to reject by returning the goods.

Significantly, the agreement sent to Ms. DeFontes, who is no longer a plaintiff in this case, contained additional language advising her of the method of rejection. The introductory provision of the terms and conditions agreement that defendants sent to her stated, "[i]f for any reason Customer is not satisfied with a Dell-branded hardware system, Customer may return the system under the terms and conditions of Dell's Total Satisfaction Return Policy * * *." In doing so, defendants explicitly contrasted acceptance of the terms with rejection of the goods, albeit while retaining some ambiguity whether rejection of defendants' proposed terms could reasonably be construed as dissatisfaction with "Dell-branded hardware." Many of the cases upholding shrinkwrap agreements cite explicit disclaimers advising consumers of their right to reject the terms. *See, e.g., ProCD, Inc. v. Zeidenberg,* 908 F.Supp. 640, 644 (W.D.Wis.1996) ("If you do not agree to the terms of this License, promptly return all copies of the software, listings that may have been exported, the discs and the User Guide to the place where you obtained it."); *Bischoff,* 180 F.Supp.2d at 1101 ("[i]f you do not accept these terms, please notify us immediately and we will cancel your service"); *M.A. Mortenson Co.,* 998 P.2d at 308 ("IF YOU DO NOT AGREE TO THESE TERMS AND CONDITIONS, PROMPTLY RETURN * * * TO THE PLACE OF PURCHASE AND YOUR PURCHASE PRICE WILL BE REFUNDED"). Such explicit language is also present in some of the foreign cases in which defendants have prevailed. *See, e.g., Sherr,* 2006 WL 2109436, at *1 ("[a]greement informs the consumer that by returning the product or refusing delivery in accordance with Dell's return policy, he can reject the terms and conditions"). Although the above language is significantly clearer, the terms and conditions agreement sent to Ms. DeFontes nevertheless made the important connection between acceptance of the terms by accepting delivery and rejection by returning the goods.[16]

That this language is absent in the documents sent to current plaintiffs Mr. Long and Ms. Ricci is troubling and raises the specter that they were unaware of both their power to reject and the method with which to do so. The introductory provision that purportedly bound plaintiffs does

---

[16] We do not decide today whether the disclaimer sent to Ms. DeFontes was sufficient to bind her to the terms and conditions.

not mention either the "Total Satisfaction Return Policy" or the thirty-day period in which a consumer may exercise his or her right to return the product. Rather, this policy is explained, if at all, in a distinct section of the terms and conditions agreement, which confusingly informed plaintiffs that "Dell Branded Hardware systems and parts that are purchased directly from Dell by an end-user Customer may be returned by Customer in accordance with Dell's 'Total Satisfaction Return Policy' in effect on the date of the invoice." Thus, the consumer is left to construe these provisions together and infer that his or her right to reject the terms extends beyond what would commonly be understood as the moment of delivery. This separate provision not only fails to establish a clear relationship between the consumer's acceptance of the terms by retaining the goods and his or her right to reject the terms by returning the product, but it further obscures the matter by forcing the consumer to refer to a separate document if he or she wants to discover the full terms and conditions of the "Total Satisfaction Return Policy." Even if the consumer reviews the total satisfaction return policy, we are not convinced that the policy clearly explains to a reasonable consumer that his or her right to return the product includes rejection of the terms and conditions agreement. We believe the hearing justice rightly concluded that although "Dell does provide a 'total satisfaction policy' whereby a customer may return the computer, this return policy does not mention the customer's ability to return based on their unwillingness to comply with the terms."

In reviewing the language of the terms and conditions agreement it cannot be said that it was reasonably apparent to the plaintiffs that they could reject the terms simply by returning the goods. We believe that too many inferential steps were required of the plaintiffs and too many of the relevant provisions were left ambiguous. We are not persuaded that a reasonably prudent offeree would understand that by keeping the Dell computer he or she was agreeing to be bound by the terms and conditions agreement and retained, for a specified time, the power to reject the terms by returning the product. Because we hold that the hearing justice properly denied the defendants' motion to compel arbitration on the ground that the plaintiffs did not agree to be bound by the terms and conditions agreement, we need not discuss any of the alternative grounds the hearing justice offered for denying the defendants' motion to compel arbitration. We must note, however, that the hearing justice found that the purported agreement "fails to bind Defendants in any genuine way" because it gave the defendants the right to change the terms of the agreement "without prior written notice at any time, in Dell's sole discretion." Although we recognize the existence of a formidable argument that such language rendered the purported agreement illusory, we shall leave the analysis of that argument for another day, in keeping with our general aversion towards reaching issues that prove unnecessary for the disposition of the case at bar. *See Irons v. Rhode Island Ethics Commission*, 973 A.2d 1124, 1135 (R.I.2009).

III

Conclusion

For the reasons set out above, the judgment of the Superior Court is affirmed. The papers of the case are returned to the Superior Court.

CHIEF JUSTICE SUTTELL and JUSTICE ROBINSON did not participate.

ProCD, Inc. v. Zeidenberg

86 F.3d 1447 (7th Cir.1996)

ProCD sold packaged software with a database of information compiled for more than 3,000 telephone directories. A lower-priced package was sold to the general public for personal use. A higher-priced package was sold to trade users. The manual and CD-ROM disks inside the lower-priced package included a license limiting the use of the application program and information in the database to non-commercial purposes. Zeidenberg purchased the lower-priced package at a retail outlet and began to sell the data over the internet. ProCD filed a lawsuit seeking an injunction against this activity based on Zeidenberg's violation of the license. The district court denied the injunction because the terms of the license did not appear on the outside of the package. Reversed.

(Easterbrook, J.) "Transactions in which the exchange of money precedes the communication of detailed terms are common. Consider the purchase of insurance. The buyer goes to an agent, who explains the essentials (amount of coverage, number of years) and remits the premium to the home office, which sends back a policy. On the district judge's understanding, the terms of the policy are irrelevant because the insured paid before receiving them. Yet the device of payment, often with a "binder" (so that the insurance takes effect immediately even though the home office reserves the right to withdraw coverage later), in advance of the policy, serves buyers' interests by accelerating effectiveness and reducing transactions costs. Or consider the purchase of an airline ticket. The traveler calls the carrier or an agent, is quoted a price, reserves a seat, pays, and gets a ticket, in that order. The ticket contains elaborate terms, which the traveler can reject by canceling the reservation. To use the ticket is to accept the terms, even terms that in retrospect are disadvantageous. See Carnival Cruise Lines, Inc. v. Shute, 499 U.S. 585, 111 S.Ct. 1522, 113 L.Ed.2d 622 (1991); see also Vimar Seguros y Reaseguros, S.A. v. M/V Sky Reefer, 515 U.S. 528, 115 S.Ct. 2322, 132 L.Ed.2d 462 (1995) (bills of lading). Just so with a ticket to a concert. The back of the ticket states that the patron promises not to record the concert; to attend is to agree. A theater that detects a violation will confiscate the tape and escort the violator to the exit. One could arrange things so that every concertgoer signs this promise before forking over the money, but that cumbersome way of doing things not only would lengthen queues and raise prices but also would scotch the sale of tickets by phone or electronic data service. . . .

"Some portions of the UCC impose additional requirements on the way parties agree on terms. A disclaimer of the implied warranty of merchantability must be "conspicuous." UCC § 2–316(2), incorporating UCC § 1–201(10). Promises to make firm offers, or to negate oral modifications, must be "separately signed." UCC §§ 2–205, 2–209(2). These special provisos reinforce the impression that, so far as the UCC is concerned, other terms may be as inconspicuous as the forum-selection clause on the back of the cruise ship ticket in *Carnival Lines*. Zeidenberg has not located any Wisconsin case—for that matter, any case in any state—holding that under the UCC the ordinary terms found in shrinkwrap licenses require any special prominence, or otherwise are to be undercut rather than enforced. In the end, the terms of the license are conceptually identical to the contents of the package. Just as no court would dream of saying that SelectPhone (trademark) must contain 3,100 phone books rather than 3,000, or must have data no more than 30 days old, or must sell for $100 rather than $150—although any of these changes would be welcomed by the customer, if all other things were held constant—so, we believe, Wisconsin would not let the buyer pick and choose among terms. Terms of use are no less a part of "the product" than are the size of the database and the speed with which the software compiles listings. Competition among vendors, not judicial revision of a package's contents, is how consumers are protected in a market economy. Digital Equipment Corp. v. Uniq Digital Technologies, Inc., 73 F.3d 756 (7th Cir.1996). ProCD has rivals, which may elect to compete by offering superior software, monthly updates, improved terms of use, lower price, or a better compromise among these elements. As we stressed above, adjusting terms in buyers' favor might help Matthew Zeidenberg today (he already has the software) but would lead to a response, such as a higher price, that might make consumers as a whole worse off. . . ."

NOTE ON THE RESTATEMENT OF THE LAW, CONSUMER CONTRACTS

Section 2(b) of the Restatement of the Law, Consumer Contracts addresses the situation in which a business presents a consumer with a standard contract term after the consumer manifests assent to the transaction to which the term would apply. It provides the standard contract term "is adopted as part of the consumer contract" if the consumer "received a reasonable opportunity to review the standard contract term," and "after the standard contract term is made available for review, the consumer received a reasonable opportunity to terminate the transaction without unreasonable cost, loss of value, or personal burden, and did not exercise that power." Restatement of the Law, Consumer Contracts, Rev. Tentative Draft No. 2 (June 2022). The consumer must also have reasonable notice "before manifesting assent to the transaction" that the term would be provided for their review later, and that they would have the opportunity to terminate the transaction after reviewing the term.

As for what constitutes a "reasonable opportunity to terminate the transaction without unreasonable cost, loss of value, or personal burden," the illustrations take the position that 30 days is sufficient time to return a $500 computer while 5 days is not; that the seller cannot charge a restocking fee "[e]ven if the restocking fee is reasonable from the seller's standpoint in light of the handling and depreciation costs"; and that the seller cannot require the consumer to "bear the return shipping cost" even if "[t]he shipping cost may be reasonable." Id., Section 2, Illustrations 26, 27, and 28.

The Restatement acknowledges that the consumer usually only thinks about what the Restatement describes as "core deal terms":

> When manifesting assent, the consumer is usually aware only of the core deal terms. Such core deal terms often include price and payment methods, a shorthand description of the product, key delivery arrangements, and a few successfully communicated legal rights or limitations (for example, the right to receive refund of airline fares or the length of the duration commitment in service contracts). Id., Section 2, Comment 4.

The Restatement takes a flexible position with respect to when and how a business can present non-core terms for review by the consumer:

> Because the review of the entire body of standard contract terms is an uncommon practice for the great majority of consumers, and because convenience in the method of delivery of the terms benefits consumers and businesses alike, the adoption of standard contract terms can be made either together with or separate from the act of manifesting assent to the transaction. Standard contract terms may be presented to the consumer before the consumer manifests assent to the transaction, at the same time that the consumer manifests assent to the transaction but before the product is delivered or the service is rendered, when the product is delivered, or when the service commences. Standard contract terms may also be presented in some combination of the foregoing. Accordingly, a single consumer contract may contain several "packets" of standard contract terms, each adopted in a different manner and at a different time . . . . Id., Section 2, Comment 3.

The following comment explains the relationship of the rules on the adoption of non-core standard terms to rules that enable courts to police unfair terms:

> The adoption rules in this Section reflect the reality in which the consumer's consent to the standard contract terms is rarely informed. In classic contract law, the requirement of assent was regarded as a meaningful mechanism that protects the contracting party, under the premise that this party, with full knowledge of the terms and with sufficient understanding of their impact, would manifest assent only to a contract that promotes his or her interests. The length and

complexity of standard-form contracts, and the large number of such contracts consumers enter into, have diluted the effectiveness and plausibility of such front-end self-protection. Accordingly, it is widely recognized that adoption procedures designed to achieve informed consent would yield relatively little value to, and might even impose burdensome transaction costs upon, the consumer. Courts have thus recognized the importance of safeguards in consumer-contract law. Primary among these are the rules that strike down unconscionable terms and other standard contract terms that undermine consumers' benefit of the bargain (§ 6). Adding to the protection afforded by the unconscionability doctrine are the good-faith duties that govern contract modification and open discretionary terms (§§ 3 and 4) and rules that police deception and enforce pre-contractual affirmations and promises (§§ 7 to 9). . . . If, despite reasonably communicated disclosures, consumers are not expected to scrutinize the legal terms up front, courts should scrutinize them ex post. The ex post scrutiny is intended to uproot terms that are so one-sided that they would be unlikely to survive in an environment of meaningful assent or that peel off the value that consumers bargained for. Id., Section 2, Comment 14.

Nguyen v. Barnes & Noble Inc.

763 F.3d 1171 (9th Cir. 2014)

Nguyen purchased two heavily discounted Hewlett-Packard Touchpads using Barnes & Noble's website during what was advertised as a "fire sale." He received an email confirming the transaction but the next day he received another email informing that his order had been cancelled due to unexpectedly high demand. Nguyen filed a lawsuit on behalf of himself and a putative class of consumers whose Touchpad orders had been cancelled. Barnes & Noble moved to compel arbitration invoking its "Terms of Use," which required claims be resolved by arbitration on an individual basis. The district court denied the motion. Affirmed.

(Noonan, J.) "Contracts formed on the Internet come primarily in two flavors: "clickwrap" (or "click-through") agreements, in which website users are required to click on an "I agree" box after being presented with a list of terms and conditions of use; and "browsewrap" agreements, where a website's terms and conditions of use are generally posted on the website via a hyperlink at the bottom of the screen. *See Register.com,* 356 F.3d at 428–30. Barnes & Noble's Terms of Use fall in the latter category.

" 'Unlike a clickwrap agreement, a browsewrap agreement does not require the user to manifest assent to the terms and conditions expressly . . . [a] party instead gives his assent simply by using the website.' *Hines v. Overstock.com, Inc.,* 668 F.Supp.2d 362, 366–67 (E.D.N.Y.2009) (citation and quotation marks omitted) (alteration in original). Indeed, "in a pure—form browsewrap agreement, 'the website will contain a notice that—by merely using the services of, obtaining information from, or initiating applications within the website—the user is agreeing to and is bound by the site's terms of service.'" *Fteja v. Facebook, Inc.*, 841 F.Supp.2d 829, 837 (S.D.N.Y.2012) (quoting *United States v. Drew*, 259 F.R.D. 449, 462 n. 22 (C.D.Cal.2009)). Thus, "by visiting the website—something that the user has already done—the user agrees to the Terms of Use not listed on the site itself but available only by clicking a hyperlink." *Id.* "The defining feature of browsewrap agreements is that the user can continue to use the website or its services without visiting the page hosting the browsewrap agreement or even knowing that such a webpage exists." *Be In, Inc. v. Google Inc.*, No. 12–CV–03373–LHK, 2013 WL 5568706, at *6 (N.D.Cal. Oct. 9, 2013). "Because no affirmative action is required by the website user to agree to the terms of a contract other than his or her use of the website, the determination of the validity of the browsewrap contract depends on whether the user has actual or constructive knowledge of a website's terms and conditions." *Van Tassell v. United Mktg. Grp., LLC*, 795 F.Supp.2d 770, 790 (N.D.Ill.2011) (citing *Sw. Airlines Co. v. BoardFirst, LLC*, No. 06–CV–0891–B, 2007 WL 4823761, at *4 (N.D.Tex. Sept. 12, 2007)); *see also* Mark A. Lemley, *Terms of Use*, 91 Minn. L.Rev. 459, 477 (2006) ("Courts may be willing to overlook the utter absence of assent only when there are reasons to believe that the [website user] is aware of the [website owner's] terms.").

"Were there any evidence in the record that Nguyen had actual notice of the Terms of Use or was required to affirmatively acknowledge the Terms of Use before completing his online purchase, the outcome of this case might be different. Indeed, courts have consistently enforced browsewrap agreements where the user had actual notice of the agreement. . . .Courts have also been more willing to find the requisite notice for constructive assent where the browsewrap agreement resembles a clickwrap agreement—that is, where the user is required to affirmatively acknowledge the agreement before proceeding with use of the website. *See, e.g., Zaltz v. JDATE*, 952 F.Supp.2d 439, 451–52 (E.D.N.Y.2013)(enforcing forum selection clause where prospective members had to check box confirming that they both read and agreed to the website's Terms and Conditions of Service to obtain account); *Fteja*, 841 F.Supp.2d at 838–40 (enforcing forum selection clause in website's terms of service where a notice below the "Sign Up" button stated, "By clicking Sign Up, you are indicating that you have read and agree to the Terms of Service," and user had clicked "Sign Up").

"But where, as here, there is no evidence that the website user had actual knowledge of the agreement, the validity of the browsewrap agreement turns on whether the website puts a reasonably prudent user on inquiry notice of the terms of the contract. *Specht*, 306 F.3d at 30–31; *see also In re Zappos.com, Inc. Customer Data Sec. Breach Litig.*, 893 F.Supp.2d 1058, 1064 (D.Nev.2012). Whether a user has inquiry notice of a browsewrap agreement, in turn, depends on the design and content of the website and the agreement's webpage. *Google,* 2013 WL 5568706, at *6. Where the link to a website's terms of use is buried at the bottom of the page or tucked away in obscure corners of the website where users are unlikely to see it, courts have refused to enforce the browsewrap agreement. *See, e.g., Specht,* 306 F.3d at 23 (refusing to enforce terms of use that "would have become visible to plaintiffs only if they had scrolled down to the next screen"); *In re Zappos.com,* 893 F.Supp.2d at 1064 ("The Terms of Use is inconspicuous, buried in the middle to bottom of every Zappos.com webpage among many other links, and the website never directs a user to the Terms of Use."); *Van Tassell,* 795 F.Supp.2d at 792–93 (refusing to enforce arbitration clause in browsewrap agreement that was only noticeable after a "multi-step process" of clicking through non-obvious links); *Hines,* 668 F.Supp.2d at 367 (plaintiff "could not even see the link to [the terms and conditions] without scrolling down to the bottom of the screen—an action that was not required to effectuate her purchase"). On the other hand, where the website contains an explicit textual notice that continued use will act as a manifestation of the user's intent to be bound, courts have been more amenable to enforcing browsewrap agreements. *See, e.g., Cairo, Inc. v. Crossmedia Servs., Inc.,* No. 04–04825, 2005 WL 756610, at *2, *4–5 (N.D.Cal. Apr. 1, 2005) (enforcing forum selection clause in website's terms of use where every page on the website had a textual notice that read: "By continuing past this page and/or using this site, you agree to abide by the Terms of Use for this site, which prohibit commercial use of any information on this site"). *But see Pollstar v. Gigmania, Ltd.,* 170 F.Supp.2d 974, 981 (E.D.Cal.2000) (refusing to enforce browsewrap agreement where textual notice appeared in small gray print against a gray background). In short, the conspicuousness and placement of the "Terms of Use" hyperlink, other notices given to users of the terms of use, and the website's general design all contribute to whether a reasonably prudent user would have inquiry notice of a browsewrap agreement.

"Barnes & Noble argues that the placement of the "Terms of Use" hyperlink in the bottom left-hand corner of every page on the Barnes & Noble website, and its close proximity to the buttons a user must click on to complete an online purchase, is enough to place a reasonably prudent user on constructive notice. It is true that the location of the hyperlink on Barnes & Noble's website distinguishes this case from *Specht,* the leading authority on the enforceability of browsewrap terms under New York law. There, the Second Circuit refused to enforce an arbitration provision in a website's licensing terms where the hyperlink to the terms was located at the bottom of the page, hidden below the "Download" button that users had to click to initiate the software download. *See Specht,* 306 F.3d at 30. Then-Second Circuit Judge Sotomayor, writing for the panel, held that "a reference to the existence of license terms on a submerged screen is not sufficient to place consumers on inquiry or constructive notice of those terms." *Id.* at 32. By contrast, here the "Terms of Use" link appears either directly below the relevant button a user must click on to proceed in the checkout process or just a few inches away. On some pages, the content of the webpage is compact enough that a user can view the link without scrolling. On the remaining pages, the hyperlink is close enough to the "Proceed with Checkout" button that a user would have to bring the link within his field of vision in order to complete his order.

"But the proximity or conspicuousness of the hyperlink alone is not enough to give rise to constructive notice, and Barnes & Noble directs us to no case law that supports this proposition. The most analogous case the court was able to locate is *PDC Labs., Inc. v. Hach Co.,* an unpublished district court order cited by neither party. No. 09–1110, 2009 WL 2605270 (C.D.Ill. Aug. 25, 2009). There, the "Terms [and Conditions of Sale] were hyperlinked on three separate pages of the online . . . order process in underlined, blue, contrasting text." *Id.* at *3. The court held that "[t]his contrasting text is sufficient to be considered conspicuous," thereby placing a reasonable user on notice that the terms applied. *Id.* It also observed, however, that the terms' conspicuousness was reinforced by the language of the final checkout screen, which read, " 'STEP 4 of 4: *Review terms,* add any comments, and submit order,' " and was followed by a hyperlink to the Terms. *Id.* (emphasis added).

"As in *PDC,* the checkout screens here contained "Terms of Use" hyperlinks in underlined, color-contrasting text. But *PDC* is dissimilar in that the final screen on that website contained the phrase "Review terms." *PDC Labs.,* 2009 WL 2605270, at *3. This admonition makes *PDC* distinguishable, despite the court's explanation that the blue contrasting hyperlinks were sufficiently conspicuous on their own. That the *PDC* decision couched its holding in terms of procedural unconscionability rather than contract formation further distinguishes it from our case. *See id.*

"In light of the lack of controlling authority on point, and in keeping with courts' traditional reluctance to enforce browsewrap agreements against individual consumers, we therefore hold that where a website makes its terms of use available via a conspicuous hyperlink on every page of the website but otherwise provides no notice to users nor prompts them to take any affirmative action to demonstrate assent, even close proximity of the hyperlink to relevant buttons users must click on—without more—is insufficient to give rise to constructive notice. While failure to read a contract before agreeing to its terms does not relieve a party of its obligations under the contract, *Gillman v. Chase Manhattan Bank, N.A.,* 73 N.Y.2d 1, 11, 537 N.Y.S.2d 787, 534 N.E.2d 824 (1988), the onus must be on website owners to put users on notice of the terms to which they wish to bind consumers. Given the breadth of the range of technological savvy of online purchasers, consumers cannot be expected to ferret out hyperlinks to terms and conditions to which they have no reason to suspect they will be bound."

NOTE ON UNCONSCIONABILITY AND WAIVER OF ARBITRATION CLAUSES IN FORM CONTRACTS

Discover Bank v. Superior Court, 36 Cal.4th 148, 113 P.3d 1100, 30 Cal. Rptr. 76 (2005), held waiver of class arbitration in a consumer contract of adhesion unconscionable "in a setting in which disputes between the contracting parties predictably involve small amounts of damages, and when it is alleged that the party with the superior bargaining power has carried out a scheme to deliberately cheat large numbers of consumers out of individually small sums of money. . . . " The decision was abrogated by AT&T Mobility LLC v. Concepcion, 563 U.S. 333, 131 S.Ct. 1740, 179 L.E.2d 742 (2011), which held that the Federal Arbitration Act preempts the rule:

> California's Discover Bank rule similarly interferes with arbitration. Although the rule does not require classwide arbitration, it allows any party to a consumer contract to demand it ex post. The rule is limited to adhesion contracts. . . but the times in which consumer contracts were anything other than adhesive are long past. . . . Hill v. Gateway 2000, Inc., 105 F.3d 1147, 1149 (C.A.7 1997). The rule also requires that damages be predictably small, and that the consumer allege a scheme to cheat consumers. . . . The former requirement, however, is toothless and malleable (the Ninth Circuit has held that damages of $4,000 are sufficiently small. . .) and the latter has no limiting effect, as all that is required is an allegation.

State courts continue to evaluate arbitration clauses for unconscionability on a case-by-case basis, reading *Concepcion* to preclude only a "rule classifying most collective-arbitration waivers in consumer contracts as unconscionable." Saleemi v. Doctor's Associates, Inc., 176 Wash.2d 368, 292 P.3d 108 (2013).

SECTION 2. UCC RULES PROTECTING FORM-TAKERS

UCC §§ 1–201(10), 2–302, 2–314, 2–316, 2–719(2), 2–719(3)

[See Selected Source Materials Supplement]

MOSCATIELLO V. PITTSBURGH CONTRACTORS EQUIPMENT CO.

Superior Court of Pennsylvania, 1991.
407 Pa. Super. 363, 595 A.2d 1190.

HESTER, JUDGE: Pittsburgh Contractors Equipment Company ("PCEC") appeals from judgment entered on that portion of the order of August 21, 1990 entered in the Allegheny County Court of Common Pleas which denied the relief sought by PCEC in its post-trial motions. We find appellant's numerous allegations of trial court error to be without merit, and accordingly, we affirm the judgment.

This action arises out of a contract entered between appellant, PCEC, and appellee, Franco Moscatiello, i/a, t/d/b/a Moscatiello Construction

Company ("Moscatiello"), for the purchase of a concrete paving machine ("paver") manufactured by Curbmaster, Inc. Approximately one month before the contract between PCEC and Moscatiello was executed in May, 1987, Franco Moscatiello and his superintendent, Jay Palino, met with the vice president of PCEC to discuss the purchase of the paver. At the time of the meeting, PCEC was aware that Moscatiello had been awarded a contract by the Pennsylvania Department of Transportation ("PennDot") to reconstruct a road, and that PennDot required that the concrete surface of the road be laid by a certain type of paving machine. The manufacturer of the paver, Curbmaster, also participated in these preliminary discussions. The vice president of Curbmaster had a telephone conversation with a representative of PCEC and Moscatiello in which he suggested that either of two machines manufactured by Curbmaster would be suitable for the job and acceptable to PennDot. Reproduced Record ("R.R.") at 92–93a, 340–41a, 432a, 492a.

On or about May 19, 1987, Mr. Palino, Moscatiello's superintendent, executed a contract on a form provided by PCEC for the purchase from PCEC of a Curbmaster concrete spreader-finisher machine for a total price of $85,125.42. PCEC's purchase agreement stated on the reverse side that no warranties were offered on equipment sold and that any implied warranties were excluded in favor of the manufacturer's offer of warranties. The contract also contained a provision which limited a buyer's remedy solely to return of the purchase price, less wear and use of the machine. In addition, all consequential and incidental damages were expressly excluded.

Moscatiello had no previous dealing with PCEC and was not on notice that the sales agreement relinquished warranties and limited damages. During the contract negotiations, neither PCEC's vice president nor the salesman in attendance directed Moscatiello's attention to the reverse side of the contract where the warranty exclusions were printed.

The paver was manufactured by Curbmaster at its plant in Iowa and shipped to Pittsburgh, arriving at Moscatiello's job site on June 15, 1987. When the paver arrived, it contained no warranty information from the manufacturer. It was alleged during trial that Curbmaster's warranty information was attached to Curbmaster's operations and parts manual, which was delivered to PCEC following execution of the sales contract between Curbmaster and PCEC. However, the trial court found that the manual which ultimately was delivered to Moscatiello did not contain Curbmaster's warranty exclusions and disclaimers. A Curbmaster employee was present when the paver arrived, assisted Moscatiello employees in assembling it, instructed Moscatiello employees on how to operate the machine, and was present when the machine was used for the first time. The Curbmaster representative never informed Moscatiello employees that the machine's warranties were limited or excluded.

According to the testimony of four witnesses during trial, from the time it was first used in June, 1987, to on or about November 12, 1987, when it was used last, the paver failed to lay concrete evenly. Furthermore, the product which resulted was unacceptable to PennDot. During the five-month period of the paver's operation, Moscatiello made numerous complaints to PCEC about the paver's failure to produce an acceptable product. During this period, PCEC and Curbmaster unsuccessfully attempted numerous times to remedy the defects in the machine. The machine finally was returned to Curbmaster in December, 1987. As a result of the paver's failure to perform its functions properly, Moscatiello incurred increased labor costs in order to produce a product acceptable to PennDot.

On February 8, 1988, Moscatiello filed a complaint against PCEC asserting breach of contract, breach of express warranty, breach of implied warranty of merchantability, and breach of implied warranty of fitness for a particular purpose. PCEC joined Curbmaster as an additional defendant, asserting breach of express warranty, breach of implied warranties of merchantability and fitness for a particular purpose, and negligence. By agreement of the parties, PCEC dismissed its negligence claim against Curbmaster and amended its complaint to add a claim against Curbmaster for breach of contract.

Following a bench trial, the trial court issued an opinion and order dated March 14, 1990, awarding $146,811.43 in damages, plus interest, to Moscatiello against PCEC and Curbmaster jointly... PCEC filed this timely appeal . . . .

PCEC first argues that the trial court erred in concluding that the disclaimer of warranties contained in the sales agreement was not conspicuous. PCEC contends that the disclaimer contained in the contract between Moscatiello and itself was a binding and effective disclaimer of all warranty liability, which consequently, precludes Moscatiello's claims of breach of warranties and breach of contract.

. . . [W]e concur with the trial court's determination that PCEC's disclaimer of warranties was inconspicuous and therefore ineffective as a bar to Moscatiello's breach of warranty claims.

Counts three and four of Moscatiello's complaint against PCEC consist of claims for breach of implied warranty of merchantability and for breach of implied warranty of fitness for a particular purpose. The Uniform Commercial Code ("U.C.C.") defines the implied warranty of merchantability as a warranty that the goods will pass without objection in the trade and are fit for the ordinary purposes for which such goods are used. 13 Pa.C.S.A. § 2314. Comment 11 to this section of the U.C.C. states that this warranty is so commonly taken for granted that its exclusion from a contract is recognized as a matter threatening surprise and therefore requiring special precaution. Thus, to exclude the implied warranty of merchantability, the exclusionary language must mention the term "merchantability" and be conspicuous. 13 Pa.C.S.A. § 2316(b). As noted in Comment 1 to section 2316(b), this section of the U.C.C. is designed to protect a buyer from unexpected and unbargained for language of disclaimer.

A term or clause is "conspicuous" when it is "so written that a reasonable person against whom it is to operate ought to have noticed it. . . Language in the body of a form is conspicuous if it is in larger or other contrasting type or color. . . " 13 Pa.C.S.A. § 1201. Comment 10 to section 1201 states that the test for conspicuousness is whether attention can reasonably be expected to be called to the exclusions. The primary object of the conspicuousness requirement is to avoid fine print waiver of rights by the buyer. *Greenspun v. American Adhesives, Inc.,* 320 F.Supp. 442 (E.D.Pa.1970).

The exclusionary clause involved herein is located on the reverse side of a standard sales contract. The front of the form contains blank lines in which are typed a customer's name, shipping instructions, detailed description of the machine, price breakdown, and payment terms. All of the information is individually typed on separate lines at least one quarter of an inch wide. Toward the bottom of the form, inside the margins for the price breakdown, is the phrase in capital letters: "TERMS AND CONDITIONS ON REVERSE SIDE ARE AN INTEGRAL PART OF THIS ORDER." Immediately below is a sentence containing the clause, in smaller type, "subject to the provisions hereof and conditions contained on reverse side hereof."

By contrast, the reverse side of the form contains eighteen numbered paragraphs which fill the page, top to bottom and side to side, in extremely small type, approximately one-sixteenth inch in height and one-fourth the size used on the front. The capital letters are slightly larger, but of the same color and in the same type style as the rest of the printing. The type used on the front of the contract is much larger and bolder than that used on the reverse side. The warranty disclaimer is buried in paragraph number sixteen at the bottom of the page. Though the operative language of the disclaimer is set forth in capital letters, the size of the type of even the capital letters is so minute that it simply does nothing to attract attention to the clause. As Moscatiello aptly observes, "to say that the print is 'fine' is an understatement." Appellee's brief at 12.

Upon our review of the agreement, we have no doubt, as the trial court stated, that PCEC's warranty disclaimer "did not adequately put Moscatiello on notice that substantial rights of theirs were being relinquished." Trial court opinion at 5. The disclaimer was set forth in some of the "finest" print this court ever has read. Even the language on the front of the contract referring to terms and conditions on the reverse side of the contract was inconspicuous as well as misleading. The letters are capitalized but are buried in the middle of the contract within the margins of the price breakdown of the goods. In addition, reference is made only to the "terms" and "conditions" on the reverse side rather than to the limitation on warranties and remedies available to the buyer. This language clearly does not meet the letter or the spirit of the U.C.C. requirements.

The evidence during trial was unequivocal that PCEC was fully familiar with the terms of the agreement, having employed it for many years, and had numerous opportunities throughout the purchase negotiations to notify Moscatiello of the exclusion of warranties and the limitation on potential remedies set forth on the reverse side of the contract. It is clear that PCEC failed to take advantage of those opportunities. Instead, as the trial court noted, PCEC "utilized a boiler-plate provision in a standard sales agreement to exclude important warranties that naturally arise in the course of any sale." Trial court opinion at 5. Section 2316 of the U.C.C. protects buyers such as Moscatiello from this type of disclaimer hidden deep within the illegible fine print on the reverse side of a standard sales contract, and that section invalidates such exclusionary language. Thus, we agree with the trial court's finding that the warranty disclaimer was ineffective, and we find no error in the trial court's decision to allow Moscatiello to pursue its cause of action for breach of implied warranty of merchantability.

We also concur with the trial court's finding that PCEC, in fact, did breach its implied warranty of merchantability. Our review of the record in accordance with our standard compels the conclusion that the machine in question could not "pass without objection in the trade under the contract description," nor was it "fit for the ordinary purposes for which such goods are used." 13 Pa.C.S.A. § 2314(b). From the first use of the paver, it failed to lay concrete evenly, which even a lay person would recognize as inadequate for its intended purpose. Further, PennDot's strict requirements regarding its paving were known to PCEC. Testimony during trial established that representatives from PCEC and the manufacturer, Curbmaster, devoted as many as twenty days on site attempting to make the paver perform the functions for which Moscatiello purchased it. They failed, and consequently, the machine was returned. Since the paver never conformed to the contract and obviously was not fit for the ordinary, let alone the specific, purposes for which it was sold, we find no error in the trial court's determination that PCEC breached its implied warranty of merchantability and that Moscatiello was entitled to recover damages from PCEC for that breach.

PCEC next argues that the trial court erred in failing to calculate the damages to which Moscatiello was entitled in a manner consistent with the limitation of remedies provision set forth in the sales agreement. Specifically, PCEC contends that Moscatiello is bound by the limitation of remedies provisions in the contract regardless of whether such provisions were conspicuous "inasmuch as any limitation is a term set forth in a contract executed by [Moscatiello]." Appellant's brief at 22. Moscatiello responds that the provisions in the contract which prohibit recovery of incidental and consequential damages are unconscionable, and therefore, the trial court was correct in refusing to enforce those provisions. We concur and consequently, find no error in the trial court's ruling.

Our examination begins with a review of the applicable sections of the U.C.C. Section 2714(c) provides that incidental or consequential damages may be recovered in an action for breach of contract or breach of warranty. 13 Pa.C.S.A. § 2714(c). Consequential damages include "any loss resulting from general or particular requirements and needs of which the seller at the time of contracting had reason to know . . ." 13 Pa.C.S.A. § 2715(b)(1). Consequential damages may be limited or excluded unless the limitation or exclusion is unconscionable. 13 Pa.C.S.A. § 2719(c). Section 2302 of the U.C.C. allows the court to refuse to enforce the contract as a whole or any single clause or group of clauses if permeated by unconscionability. 13 Pa.C.S.A. § 2302(a). The principle upon which this section rests is one of prevention of oppression and unfair surprise. 13 Pa.C.S.A. § 2302, Comment 1.

The verdict which Moscatiello received from the trial court included the sum of $64,567.93, representing the increased costs it incurred in laying concrete with the defective paver and interest on money borrowed by Moscatiello to purchase the machine. PCEC argues that this portion of the award is erroneous due to the existence of paragraphs seventeen and eighteen in the parties' sales contract which provide the following:

17. If the goods covered by this Order are new, Buyer and Vendor agree that there is no failure of an essential purpose of Buyer's exclusive and limited remedy so long as Vendor is willing and able to repair or replace any part which is not as warranted. If Vendor is not willing and able to repair or replace any such part or if for any reason it is determined that Buyer's exclusive and limited remedy has failed of its essential purpose, Buyer's sole and exclusive remedy shall then be to have its purchase price returned in exchange for the goods, less a reasonable charge for any use by Buyer.

18. It is agreed that Vendor shall not be liable for any incidental or consequential damages occasioned by the sale, possession, operation, maintenance or use of the goods or for any failure of the goods to operate under any claim of breach of warranty or contract, negligence, strict liability or otherwise.

A clause in a contract is considered unconscionable and unenforceable if there is "an absence of meaningful choice on the part of one of the parties together with contract terms which are unreasonably favorable to the other party." *Germantown Manufacturing Co. v. Rawlinson,* 341 Pa.Super. 42, 55, 491 A.2d 138, 145 (1985), quoting E.A. Farnsworth *Contracts* 314 (1982). In *Germantown,* we were asked to determine the enforceability of a confession of judgment clause which was buried, as were the contract provisions at issue here, within the fine print of boilerplate language of a standard form. In finding the clause unenforceable, we were guided by the following analysis contained in section 353 of J. Murray, *Murray on Contracts* (2d ed., 1974):

> Parties to a contract rarely consciously advert to any number of terms which are binding upon them. If such terms allocate the risks of the bargain in a manner which the parties should have reasonably expected, they are enforceable-they are, to use the expression of Karl Llewellyn, decent terms. If the terms of the contract suggest the reallocation of material risks, an attempted reallocation may be so extreme that regardless of apparent and genuine assent, a court will not enforce it. . . The parties will not be found to have agreed to an abnormal allocation of risk if the only evidence thereof is an inconspicuous provision on the boilerplate of a standard form. At a minimum, the reallocation must be physically manifested in a fashion comprehensible to the party against whom it is sought to be enforced. Finally, such party must have had a reasonable choice in relation to such reallocation.

Germantown Manufacturing Company v. Rawlinson, 341 Pa.Super. at 56–57, 491 A.2d at 146.

The question presented in the instant sales agreement, therefore, is whether Mr. Moscatiello and his superintendent reasonably should have expected that if the paver failed to perform as promised, they, rather than the seller, would be responsible for the economic losses which resulted. We cannot agree with appellant that appellee harbored any such expectation.

First, paragraphs seventeen and eighteen of the sales contract are, as appellee aptly states in his brief, "classic examples of physically inconspicuous provisions in the boilerplate of a standard form." Appellee's brief at 21. Neither Mr. Moscatiello nor Mr. Palino understood that buried in the fine print on the reverse side of the contract was a term that shifted to Moscatiello the risk of loss resulting from the purchase of a machine which was unable to perform the operations that it was designed to perform. Neither man was a dealer in concrete-spreader finishers or heavy equipment of any kind. Neither individual had ever dealt with PCEC on any previous occasion, and neither had any knowledge of the standard contracts or business practices of PCEC.

Thus, Moscatiello qualified as neither a merchant, as the term is defined in 13 Pa.C.S.A. § 2104, nor a substantial business concern skilled in the negotiation of sales contracts for goods. It is undisputed that PCEC was both. Courts have upheld limitation of damage provisions in sales contracts between merchants or experienced business concerns because there is no disparity between such entities in either bargaining power or sophistication. *See K & C, Inc. v. Westinghouse Electric Corp.*, 437 Pa. 303, 263 A.2d 390 (1970) (buyers were an experienced attorney and the owner of a used furniture business who dealt with the renovation and sale of the type of machines being purchased); *Chatlos Systems, Inc. v. National Cash Register Corp.*, 635 F.2d 1081 (3rd Cir.1980) (buyer was a manufacturer of complex electronic equipment who purchased a defective computer system).

Appellant places great reliance on *S. M. Wilson and Co. v. Smith International, Inc.*, 587 F.2d 1363 (9th Cir.1978), in support of its argument that the limitation of damages provisions were reasonable. However, just as in *K & C, Inc.* and *Chatlos,* the parties in *Wilson* held equal bargaining positions as experienced business concerns. Moreover, the limitation of damages provision in *Wilson* was agreed to specifically by the buyer during purchase negotiations between the parties, and the damage provision as well as the warranty disclaimer were conspicuously set forth in the contract between the parties.

Similarly, the limitation of damages provision upheld by the court in *Marr Enterprises, Inc. v. Lewis Refrigeration Co.,* 556 F.2d 951 (9th Cir.1977), also was set forth conspicuously in the contract between the parties. The contract provision at issue in the final case cited by appellant, *FMC Finance Corp. v. Murphree,* 632 F.2d 413 (5th Cir.1980), was a warranty disclaimer rather than a limitation of damage provision and therefore, is inapposite to the facts before us.

The contract provisions at issue in the cases cited by appellant are clearly distinguishable from the provisions contained in the contract between the parties herein. Each contract either involved experienced business concerns holding equal bargaining positions or the provision at issue was displayed in a very conspicuous manner in the contract. Appellee was not a dealer or manufacturer of heavy equipment of any kind, and he lacked any prior experience negotiating a contract for the purchase of this type of equipment with PCEC. He had no reason to expect that the contract he signed contained a clause that was buried in the fine print on the reverse side which shifted to him the risk of economic loss resulting from the purchase of a machine which was incapable of performing the job that it was designed to do.

In contrast, PCEC was a well-established dealer engaged in the sale, service, and support of construction equipment to area contractors. It had negotiated many other contracts for the purchase of this type of equipment and was familiar with the "conditions" on the reverse side of its own form which disclaimed warranties and limited damages. PCEC clearly held superior bargaining position with respect to Moscatiello. Moreover, the limitation of damages provisions were classic examples of physically inconspicuous provisions in the boilerplate language of a standard form. Thus, we find the numerous cases cited in appellant's brief inapplicable to the case at bar. Accordingly, we concur with appellee's contention that the limitation of damages provisions contained in its contract with PCEC are unconscionable, and we affirm the trial court's refusal to give effect to those provisions.

Appellant next argues that the integration clause contained in the contract between the parties operates as a waiver of appellee's objections to the terms and conditions of the agreement of sale. While we agree that the terms of an integrated agreement may not be contradicted by evidence of any prior agreement or of a contemporaneous oral agreement, an integration clause cannot validate an unconscionable or otherwise invalid contract provision. The remedies which the trial court afforded appellee were specifically provided to purchasers in the position of appellee by the legislature when it adopted the U.C.C. These remedies cannot be extinguished by the inclusion of an integration clause in a contract which contains invalid provisions. . . .

Judgment affirmed; appellant's request for assessment of attorneys' fees and costs remanded to the trial court; jurisdiction relinquished.

———————

Pierce v. Catalina Yachts, Inc.

2 P.3d 618 (Alaska 2000)

Catalina sold a yacht to the Pierces. The contract included the limited warranty: "Catalina will repair or, at its option, pay for 100% of the labor and material necessary to repair" below-line water blisters. The contract included a separate disclaimer of liability for consequential damages. The Pierces sued after Catalina refused to honor the limited warranty, denying the seriousness of the problem. The Pierces prevailed at trial but their damages were limited to the cost of repair based on these contract terms. The Pierces appealed.

(Bryner, J.) "Courts construing U.C.C. subsection 719(b) agree that a limited warranty to repair 'fails of its essential purpose,' when the seller is either unwilling or unable to conform the goods to the contract. The policy behind the failure of essential purpose rule is to insure that the buyer has 'at least minimum adequate remedies.' Typically, a limited repair/replacement remedy fails of its essential purpose where (1) the seller is unsuccessful in repairing or replacing the defective part, regardless of good or bad faith; or (2) there is unreasonable delay in repairing or replacing defective components.

"Here, by specifically finding that the Pierces' boat experienced gel-coat blisters, that the Pierces gave Catalina timely notice of the problem, that Catalina thereafter breached its obligations under the limited gel-coat warranty, and that the Pierces could not have avoided their damages, the jury effectively determined that the gel-coat warranty had failed of its essential purpose. . .

"[W]hen a warranty fails, a separate provision barring consequential damages will survive under subsection 719(c) as long as the bar itself is not unconscionable. . .[1]

"In the present case, the nature of the Pierces' warranty and the circumstances surrounding Catalina's breach weigh heavily against enforcing the consequential damages bar. The contract at issue was a consumer sale, not a commercial transaction between sophisticated businesses with equivalent bargaining power. Catalina unilaterally drafted the damages bar and evidently included it in a preprinted standard limited warranty. Moreover, the jury's sizable award for the reasonable cost of repairing the boat's gel coat establishes that Catalina's breach deprived the Pierces of a substantial benefit of their bargain. Though some gel-coat blistering might have been foreseeable, a defect of this magnitude does not fit neatly 'within the realm of expectable losses.'

"But the decisive factor in this case is the nature of Catalina's breach, which caused the limited remedy to fail of its essential purpose. The jury specifically found that Catalina acted in bad faith in failing to honor its warranty. This finding virtually establishes a 'circumstance[ ] resulting in failure of performance that makes it unconscionable to enforce the parties' allocation of risk.' Because the jury found that Catalina consciously deprived the Pierces of their rights under the warranty, the company cannot conscionably demand to enforce its own warranty rights against the Pierces . . .

"This Court would be in an untenable position if it allowed the defendant to shelter itself behind one segment of the warranty when it has allegedly repudiated and ignored its very limited obligations under another segment of the same warranty, which alleged repudiation has caused the very need for relief which the defendant is attempting to avoid.

"Moreover, in light of Catalina's bad faith, allowing the company to enforce the consequential damages bar would conflict with the commercial code's imperative that '[e]very contract or duty in the code imposes an obligation of good faith in its performance or enforcement.' Finally, because it is self-evident that the Pierces did not bargain to assume the risk of a bad faith breach by Catalina, enforcing the bar against consequential damages would thwart AS 45.02.719's basic goal of implementing the parties' agreement."

---

[1] The opinion characterizes this "case-by-case" analysis of a term excluding consequential damages as the majority approach while noting that some courts adopt a per se rule allowing for the recovery of consequential damages when a limited remedy fails under UCC § 2–719(2).

SECTION 3. THE REASONABLE EXPECTATIONS DOCTRINE

RESTATEMENT, SECOND, CONTRACTS § 211

[See Selected Source Materials Supplement]

UNIDROIT PRINCIPLES OF INTERNATIONAL COMMERCIAL CONTRACTS ARTS. 2.1.19, 2.1.22

[See Selected Source Materials Supplement]

PRINCIPLES OF EUROPEAN CONTRACT LAW ART. 4.110

[See Selected Source Materials Supplement]

DARNER MOTOR SALES v. UNIVERSAL UNDERWRITERS

Supreme Court of Arizona, En Banc, 1984.
140 Ariz. 383, 682 P.2d 388.

FELDMAN, JUSTICE.

Darner Motor Sales, Inc., dba Darner Leasing Co. (Darner Motors), petitions for review of a memorandum decision of the court of appeals (Darner Motor Sales, Inc. v. Universal Underwriters Insurance Company, No. 1 CA–CIV 5796, filed February 22, 1983). That decision affirmed a summary judgment in favor of Universal Underwriters Insurance Company (Universal) and their agent, John Brent Doxsee (Doxsee), who were the third party defendants impleaded by Darner Motors. We granted review because we believe that the issues presented call into question the clarity and consistency of a large body of Arizona law dealing with insurance coverage. We have jurisdiction pursuant to Ariz. Const. Art. 6, § 5(3) and Rule 23, Rules of Civ.App.P., 17A A.R.S.

FACTS

Darner Motors is in the automobile sales, service and leasing business. Prior to transacting business with Universal, Darner Motors' various operations were insured under several policies issued by The Travelers Company (Travelers). In October of 1973, Doxsee, an insurance agent who was a full-time employee of Universal, contacted Joel Darner to solicit insurance business. The following month, Darner purchased a Universal "U-Drive policy" through Doxsee. This policy insured Darner Motors and the lessees of its cars for automobile liability risk. Darner Motors was covered in limits of $100,000 for any one injury and $300,000 (100/300) for all injuries arising out of any one accident. The lessees were covered in limits of 15/30. The rest of Darner Motors' business risks continued to be insured under a "dealership package policy" issued by Travelers.

It is unclear from the record, but this situation presumably continued until April of 1975, a renewal date of the Travelers policy. In April of 1975, Universal "picked up" the entire insurance "package" for Darner Motors' various business activities. This "package" consisted of a Universal "Unicover" policy which included coverage for garagekeeper's liability, premises liability, property coverage, crime coverage, customer car coverage, and plate glass insurance. The parties describe this as an "umbrella policy," so it is possible that, in addition to covering multiple risks, it also contained excess coverage over other policies which provided primary coverage.[1] In addition to the umbrella policy, Universal also renewed the U-Drive policy, which provided coverage to the lessees of Darner Motors.[2]

Substantial controversy exists with regard to many of the factual allegations. However, according to Darner, he informed Doxsee that renewal of lessee coverage was to be in the same limits as applied to Darner Motors in the original U-Drive policy. When the new U-Drive policy arrived after renewal in April of 1975, Darner examined it and noticed that the limits of coverage for lessees were 15/30. After reading this, Darner claims that he called Doxsee. He was concerned because his rental contract contained a representation of greater coverage (100/300) and because he felt that it would be better for his business operation if his lessees had the higher coverage. Darner told Doxsee that the liability limits of the U-Drive policy did not conform to their prior agreement, and asked Doxsee to come to Darner Motors and discuss the matter. Doxsee did call upon Mr. Darner at the latter's office. Although Doxsee could not recall the subsequent conversation, both Darner and his former sales manager, Jack Hadley, testified about the discussion. Their deposition testimony would support a finding that Doxsee told Darner not to worry about the limits because, although the U-Drive policy provided only 15/30 coverage, the all-risk

---

[1]   It is difficult to tell just what was or was not insured under this "umbrella policy" since a copy of the policy is not part of the record, even though the coverage contained in that policy is the precise issue in the case.

[2]   Lessors are required to provide such insurance to their lessees, A.R.S. § 28–324. The statute also provides that if the lessor fails to do so, it is jointly and severally liable for all damages caused by the lessee while driving the leased vehicle.

clause of the umbrella policy would provide additional coverage to limits of 100/300.[3]

At some time after he received the U-Drive policy and, presumably, also after his discussions with Doxsee, Darner did receive a copy of the umbrella policy. That policy was evidently quite lengthy and forbidding. Darner admits never reading it; he explained this omission by pointing out that "it's like reading a book" and stating that, following his conversations with Doxsee, "I didn't think I needed to." Darner's office manager testified that she never really read the policy either and saw little need to do so in view of the fact that Doxsee would occasionally appear, remove pages from the loose-leaf binder and insert new pages. So far as the record shows, the printed, boiler-plate provisions contained in the loose-leaf type, "book length," all-risk policy were neither negotiated before nor discussed after the policy was delivered. The parties seem to have confined themselves to a discussion of the objectives that would be realized from the purchase of the policy rather than an attempt to negotiate the wording of the policy.

Approximately twenty months after the conversation between Darner and Doxsee concerning coverage under the Universal policies, Darner Motors rented a car to Dwayne Crawford. The transaction was in the ordinary course of business, except that the form used for the rental agreement was the "old type," which contained a representation of coverage in the amount of 100/300. While driving the vehicle under this rental contract, Crawford negligently injured a pedestrian and caused severe injuries. The pedestrian sued Crawford, who looked to Universal for coverage. Universal claimed that lessee's coverage on the "U-Drive" policy was limited to 15/30. Crawford then sued Darner Motors under the rental agreement warranty that coverage was provided in limits of 100/300. Darner Motors called upon Universal to provide additional coverage under the umbrella policy. The umbrella policy did contain the higher limits, but Universal claimed that lessees were not parties "insured" as that term was defined in the all-risk policy. Universal was therefore unwilling to provide coverage in excess of the $15,000 limit of the U-Drive policy. Darner Motors then filed a third-party complaint, naming Universal and Doxsee as third party defendants.

Eventually, the pedestrian recovered $60,000 from Crawford. Universal paid $15,000 of this amount, and Darner Motors has either paid or is liable to Crawford for the remainder. Darner Motors claims that

---

[3] As might be expected, although Doxsee does not remember the substance of the conversation, he is quite sure he could have told Darner no such thing. Darner's testimony was impeached by evidence that he subsequently reduced the limits on his rental forms from 100/300 to 15/30. Darner explains this by stating that Doxsee told him that it was better to represent the coverage limits at the minimum required by the state so as to discourage plaintiffs' lawyers from pursuing claims for their badly injured clients. As in most such cases, who told what to whom is hotly contested, and there is much to be said for both versions of the facts.

Universal and Doxsee are obligated to indemnify it against that loss. To support that contention, Darner Motors advances the following theories:

> (1) Universal is estopped to deny coverage for lessees under the umbrella policy in amounts less than 100/300;

> (2) The umbrella policy should be reformed so that it does contain such coverage;

> (3) If no coverage is found through estoppel or reformation, then the loss incurred by Darner Motors was caused by the negligence of Universal and its agent, Doxsee, and should be borne by them;

> (4) If no coverage exists by way of estoppel or reformation, then the loss incurred by Darner Motors is the result of fraud committed by Universal and its agent, Doxsee.

After considerable discovery, Universal and Doxsee moved for summary judgment, contending that there was no genuine issue of fact and that they were entitled to judgment as a matter of law. The motion was granted and judgment entered against Darner Motors. The court of appeals affirmed; pointing out that Darner Motors had not claimed that the umbrella policy was ambiguous, the court held that the insured's failure to read the policy prevented recovery on any theory, even though the contents of the policy did not comport with the representations of the insurance agent and those same representations were a part of the reason that the insured failed to read the policy.

The court of appeals stated that under Arizona law an insured who had received a copy of an unambiguous policy could not "expand the insurer's liability beyond the terms of the . . . policy issued. . . . " We believe this statement is too broad, though we acknowledge that the law is, at best, confused on this subject. In an attempt to bring some clarity and logic to the question, we have reviewed our cases and will discuss each of the theories advanced by Darner Motors. Before doing so, however, we must consider the inherent nature of an insurance contract and of the issues presented by the fact situation before us.

CONTRACT LAW AND INSURANCE POLICIES

Since this is an appeal from summary judgment, we must view the facts in the light most favorable to the party against whom judgment was taken. *Gulf Insurance Co. v. Grisham,* 125 Ariz. 123, 124, 613 P.2d 283, 284 (1980). Taking the facts in that light, the question we must decide is whether the courts will enforce an unambiguous provision contrary to the negotiated agreement made by the parties because, after the insurer's representations of coverage, the insured failed to read the insurance contract which was in his possession.[5]

Implicit in the reasoning of the court of appeals is the concept that the insurance policies purchased by Darner constitute *the* contract between Darner and Universal. Darner is considered to be bound by the terms contained within the documents. The court of appeals held:

> Because Mr. Darner received a copy of the umbrella policy and made no contention that it was ambiguous or confusing, he cannot expand the insurer's liability beyond the terms of the umbrella policy issued by Universal.

(slip op. at 7). Basic to this holding is the principle that the oral agreement between Doxsee and Darner cannot be shown to vary the terms of the insurance policy. This, indeed, was at one time the majority view. See cases cited in 12 Appleman, *Insurance Law and Practice* § 7155 (1981); similar language is contained in *Parks v. American Casualty Co. of Reading, Pa.,* 117 Ariz. 339, 572 P.2d 801 (1977); *Sellers v. Allstate Insurance Company,* 113 Ariz. 419, 422, 555 P.2d 1113, 1116 (1976); *see also Western Farm Bureau Mut. Ins. Co. v. Barela,* 79 N.M. 149, 441 P.2d 47 (1968). Some cases, including those from our own state, hold that since insurance policies are like other contracts, where the meaning and intent of the parties is "clear" from the words used in the instrument, the courts cannot "rewrite" the policy by considering the actual "words" used in striking the bargain. Thus, the rule of interpretation is stated to be that the intention of the parties as derived from the language used within the four corners of the instrument must prevail. *See, e.g., Rodemich v. State Farm Mutual Auto. Insurance Co.,* 130 Ariz. 538, 539, 637 P.2d 748, 749 (App.1981) (a vehicle which turned over and was damaged when the driver swerved to avoid an animal was not covered under the "upset" clause of a comprehensive risk policy because "upsets" resulting from attempts to avoid collision with animals were not covered unless there was actual contact). . . .

. . . Artificial results derived from application of ordinary rules of contract construction to insurance policies have made courts struggle to find some method of reaching a sensible resolution within the conceptual bounds of treating standardized, formal contracts as if they were traditional "agreements," reached by bargaining between the parties. This

---

[5] In characterizing the issue in this manner, we acknowledge that the insured did read the terms of the policy covering lessees and did discover the error in that policy. He was told by the agent that the umbrella policy provided the additional coverage. He did not read the provisions of the umbrella policy. Although that policy is not part of the record, we assume that it contains a clause or clauses defining the word "insured" in such a manner that lessees are excluded from the class of persons insured by the policy. We assume further that this definitional exclusion is clear and unambiguous. Therefore, it could have been found, read and understood by Darner. Of course we have no way of knowing that these assumptions are correct; however, it was the appellant's burden to make an adequate record on appeal. Since the appellant failed to offer the policy in evidence at the trial, we settle all factual uncertainty in favor of supporting the judgment of the trial court.

difficult task is often accomplished by the use of various constructs which enable courts to reach a desired result by giving lip service to traditional contract rules. One of the most prominent of these methods is the well recognized principle of resolving ambiguities against the insurer. *See Almadova v. State Farm Mutual Automobile Ins. Co.*, 133 Ariz. 81, 649 P.2d 284 (1982). The limitations of this principle have been discussed by Professor Robert Keeton, who comments that

> [t]he principle of resolving ambiguities against the draftsman is simply an inadequate explanation of the results of some cases. The conclusion is inescapable that courts have sometimes invented ambiguity where none existed, then resolved the invented ambiguity contrary to the plainly expressed terms of the contract document.

Keeton, *Insurance Law Rights at Variance with Policy Provisions*, 83 Harv.L.Rev. 961, 972 (1970) (footnotes omitted). Our court of appeals has attempted to avoid the problem of invented ambiguity by stating the principle that courts should not create ambiguities in order to rewrite the policy. Cf. *Barber v. Old Republic Life Ins. Co.*, 132 Ariz. 602, 604, 647 P.2d 1200, 1202 (App.1982) with *State Farm v. Gibbs, supra.* However, we also follow the rule of construction that where different jurisdictions reach different conclusions regarding the language of an insurance contract "ambiguity is established," *Federal Insurance Co. v. P.A.T. Homes, Inc.*, 113 Ariz. 136, 138, 547 P.2d 1050, 1052 (1976); thus, we may find ourselves justly criticized for accepting the inventions of other courts. It is also illogical to hold that an unexpected, unknown ambiguity in a clause which the parties did not negotiate, write or read should permit them to show the true terms of the agreement, but that the lack of such an ambiguity prevents them from so doing.

Such systems of logic—or illogic—have been criticized by Keeton, *supra,* and others for failing to recognize the realities of the insurance business and the methods used in modern insurance practice. *See, e.g., Zuckerman v. Transamerica Ins. Co.*, 133 Ariz. 139, 144–46, 650 P.2d 441, 446–48 (1982); *Harr v. Allstate Insurance Co.*, 54 N.J. 287, 301–04, 255 A.2d 208, 216–18 (1969); Restatement of Contracts (Second) § 211, comment b, and authorities cited in the reporter's note thereto; Abraham, *Judge-Made Law and Judge-Made Insurance: Honoring the Reasonable Expectations of the Insured*, 67 Va.L.Rev. (1981); Murray, *The Parol Evidence Process and Standardized Agreements under the Restatement (Second) of Contracts*, 123 U.Pa.L.Rev. 1342 (1975).

Abraham, *supra,* argues that "insurance law should be brought into the mainstream of our jurisprudence," and notes that "in many states, a principle authorizing the courts to honor the 'reasonable expectations' of the insured is emerging." *Id.* at 1151. "Emergence" is probably an inaccurate description of the use of the reasonable expectations test since, if correctly understood, that doctrine has long been a basic principle in the law of contracts.

> That portion of the field of law that is classified and described as the law of contracts attempts the realization of *reasonable expectations that have been induced* by the making of a promise.

1 Corbin, *Contracts* § 1, at 2 (1963) (emphasis supplied). We have previously recognized the doctrine of "reasonable expectations." *Zuckerman v. Transamerica Ins. Co.*, 133 Ariz. at 146, 650 P.2d at 448; *Sparks v. Republic Nat. Life Ins. Co.*, 132 Ariz. 529, 536–37, 647 P.2d 1127, 1134–35, *cert. denied,* 459 U.S. 1070, 74 L.Ed.2d 632, 103 S.Ct. 490 (1982). Of course, if not put in proper perspective, the reasonable expectations concept is quite troublesome, since most insureds develop a "reasonable expectation" that every loss will be covered by their policy. Therefore, the reasonable expectation concept must be limited by something more than the fervent hope usually engendered by loss. Such a limitation is easily found in the postulate contained in Corbin's work—that the expectations to be realized are those that "have been induced by the making of a promise." 1 Corbin, *supra* § 1 at 2.

We think it better, then, to start the analysis by attempting to determine what expectations have been induced. We note the concept that contracts are not merely printed words. The words, of course, are usually of paramount importance. However, other matters are also significant. 3 Corbin, *supra* §§ 538, 549. It is important to recognize that although the writing "may be coextensive with the agreement, it is not the agreement but only evidence thereof." Murray, *supra,* 123 U.Pa.L.Rev. at 1389. Murray adds that "if the writing is normally executed absent understanding of its fine print provisions, it is less worthy as evidence of the true agreement." *Id.* at 1373. Llewellyn puts the proposition another way:

> The fine print which has not been read has no business to cut under the reasonable meaning of those dickered terms which constitute the dominant and only real expression of agreement, but much of [the writing] commonly belongs in [the contract].

Llewellyn, *The Common Law Tradition* 370 (1960). Thus, Llewellyn concludes, "any contract with boiler-plate results in *two* several contracts: the *dickered* deal and the collateral one of *supplementary* boiler-plate." *Id.* at 371 (emphasis in original).

If we continue to look at an insurance policy as a contract between the insured and insurer, the foregoing analysis compels the conclusion that the problem is simply the application of the parol evidence rule. The traditional view of the law of contracts is that a written agreement adopted by the parties will be viewed as an integrated contract which binds those parties to the terms expressed within the four corners of the agreement. Thus, the parties may not vary or expand the agreement by introducing parol evidence to show understandings or antecedent agreements which are in some way contrary to the terms of the contract. *Restatement (Second) of Contracts* § 215. This rule is applied with varying degrees of exactitude to insurance policies. Cases from this state reflect that attitude. *See Sparks v. Republic Nat. Life Ins. Co., supra; Isaak v. Massachusetts Indemnity Life Ins. Co.,* 127 Ariz. 581, 623 P.2d 11 (1981); *Dairyland Mutual Ins. Co. v. Andersen,* 102 Ariz. 515, 433 P.2d 963 (1967); *but see Southern Casualty v. Hughes,* 33 Ariz. 206, 263 P. 584 (1928); *Ranger Insurance Co. v. Phillips,* 25 Ariz.App. 426, 544 P.2d 250 (1976).

When faced with harsh or illogical results, such as those produced by application of the parol evidence rule to most insurance contracts, the law usually reacts by recognizing exceptions which permit courts to avoid injustice. The ambiguity rule is, of course, one of those exceptions. Others, advanced with varying success, are the doctrines of waiver and estoppel. In our view, a better rationale is to be found by application of *established principles of contract law*. In so doing, however, we must remember that the usual insurance policy is a special kind of contract. It is largely adhesive; some terms are bargained for, but most terms consist of boilerplate, not bargained for, neither read nor understood by the buyer, and often not even fully understood by the selling agent. In contracts, as in other fields, the common law has evolved to accommodate the practices of the marketplace. Thus, in insurance law, as in other areas of contract law, the parol evidence rule has not been strictly applied to enforce an illusory "bargain" set forth in a *standardized contract* when that "bargain" was never really made and would, if applied, defeat the true agreement which was supposedly contained in the policy. *Sparks v. Republic National Life Insurance Co.,* 132 Ariz. at 537, 647 P.2d at 1135. *See also Zuckerman v. Transamerica Insurance Co.,* 133 Ariz. at 144, 650 P.2d at 446.

Sparks and *Zuckerman* reflect this court's attempt to bring some degree of logic and predictability into the field of insurance. What is needed, however, is recognition of a general rule of contract law. We believe that the current formulation of the *Restatement (Second) of Contracts* contains a workable resolution of the problem. The Restatement approach is basically a modification of the parol evidence rule when dealing with contracts containing boiler-plate provisions which are not negotiated, and often not even read by the parties.

Standardized Agreements

(1) Except as stated in Subsection (3), where a party to an agreement signs or otherwise manifests assent to a writing and has reason to believe that like writings are regularly used to embody terms of agreements of the same type, he adopts the

writing as an integrated agreement with respect to the terms included in the writing.

(2) Such a writing is interpreted wherever reasonable as treating alike all those similarly situated, without regard to their knowledge or understanding of the standard terms of the writing.

(3) Where the other party has reason to believe that the party manifesting such assent would not do so if he knew that the writing contained a particular term, the term is not part of the agreement.

Restatement (Second) of Contracts § 211. We believe that the comments to this section of the Restatement support the wisdom of the rule formulated. Comment (a) points out that standardization of agreements is essential

> to a system of mass production and distribution. Scarce and costly time and skill can be devoted to a class of transactions rather than to details of individual transactions.... Sales personnel and customers are freed from attention to numberless variations and can focus on meaningful choice among a limited number of significant features: transaction-type, style, quantity, price, or the like. Operations are simplified and costs reduced, to the advantage of all concerned.

Subsections (1) and (2) of § 211 reflect the reality of the marketplace. Thus, those who make use of a standardized form of agreement neither expect nor desire their customers "to understand or even to read the standard terms." *Id.* comment (b). On the other hand, customers "trust to the good faith of the party using the form [and] ... understand that they are assenting to the terms not read or not understood, subject to such limitations as the law may impose." *Id.* The limitations that the law may impose are that standard terms

> may be superseded by separately negotiated or added terms (§ 203), they are construed against the draftsman (§ 206), and they are subject to the overriding obligation of good faith (§ 205) and to the power of the court to refuse to enforce an unconscionable contract or term (§ 208).

Id. comment (c).[7]

Subsection (3) of § 211 is the Restatement's codification of and limitation on the "reasonable expectation" rule as applied to standardized agreements. The comment reads as follows:

> Although customers typically adhere to standardized agreements and are bound by them without even appearing to

---

[7] The Section numbers in this quote refer to sections in the Restatement (Second) of Contracts.

know the standard terms in detail, they are not bound to unknown terms which are beyond the range of reasonable expectation. . . . [An insured] who adheres to the [insurer's] standard terms does not assent to a term if the [insurer] has reason to believe that the [insured] would not have accepted the agreement if he had known that the agreement contained the particular term. Such a belief or assumption may be shown by the prior negotiations or inferred from the circumstances. Reason to believe may be inferred from the fact that the term is bizarre or oppressive, from the fact that it eviscerates the non-standard terms explicitly agreed to, or from the fact that it eliminates the dominant purpose of the transaction. The inference is reinforced if the adhering party never had an opportunity to read the term, or if it is illegible or otherwise hidden from view. This rule is closely related to the policy against unconscionable terms and the rule of interpretation against the draftsman.

Id. comment (f). We believe the analysis contained in the comments to the cited sections in the Restatement is a sensible rationale for interpretation of the usual type of insuring agreement.[8]

This treatment of insurance law is neither radical nor new. All that is new in the "changed" Restatement is the articulation of the rule. Some cases long ago recognized the underlying principles. . . .

. . . Missing has been the articulation or formulation of some general rule to explain results of many past cases and to provide a pragmatic, honest approach to the resolution of future disputes. Hopefully, the adoption of § 211 of the Restatement as the rule for standardized contracts will provide greater predictability and uniformity of results—a benefit to both the insurance industry and the consumer.

In adopting this rule, we do not create a special field of contract law, we merely adopt a rule of integration which recognizes the method by which people do business. Indeed, the law pertaining to nonstandardized, negotiated contracts long ago began to move in the same direction. "Ordinary" contract law now recognizes that an agreement may be "partially integrated," or "completely integrated," depending upon "the degree to which the parties intended the writing to express their agreement." E. Farnsworth, *Contracts,* § 7.3 at 452 (1982). The relationship between the degree of integration and the application of the parol evidence

---

[8] It would, of course, also be applicable to other transactions handled in a similar manner. We note, for example, that contracts for transport by rail, airline or bus; for rental of cars, trucks and other equipment; credit card and charge account "rules" and terms; bills of lading, invoices and many other commercial documents are "sold" or "made" in the same manner as most insurance policies. On the other hand, there are some insurance transactions which are still the product of negotiation which includes the terms of the policy. Such contracts are not affected by § 211 because it applies only to standardized agreements such as the average automobile, general liability, or fire policy.

rule has been the subject of much scholarly controversy. The authors of the leading contract treatises, Williston and Corbin, present differing views. "The point in dispute is whether the fact that the writing appears on its face to be a complete and exclusive statement of the terms of the agreement establishes conclusively that the agreement is completely integrated." Farnsworth, *supra* at 455. If it does, Williston would restrict interpretation to the four corners of the document. *Id.; See 4 Williston on Contracts* §§ 600A, 629, 633 (3d ed. 1961). Corbin argues that account should always be taken of all the surrounding circumstances to determine the extent of the integration *and* the interpretation of the agreement. Farnsworth, *supra* at 456; 3 Corbin, *supra*, § 582.

Recent decisions, the Uniform Commercial Code and the Restatement (Second) of Contracts have all favored Corbin's view. Farnsworth, *supra* at 453. *See also* Braucher, *Interpretation and Legal Effect in the Second Restatement of Contracts,* 81 Colum.L.Rev. 12 (1981). Arizona has followed the modern trend and adopted the Corbin view. . . .

It would be anomalous, indeed, to follow this view for contracts with bargained terms but to cling to the rejected rule in cases involving standardized form contracts. It would be even more anomalous if reasonable expectations induced by promises or conduct of a party are to be considered in determining integration or interpreting the words of a negotiated . . . agreement but disregarded when dealing with boilerplate, so that regardless of intent or even actual agreement, the parties are bound by provisions that were never discussed, examined, read or understood.

The general rule of contract interpretations adopted by the Restatement and based on Corbin's viewpoint is a modern view which takes into account the realities of present day commercial practice. See, Trakman, *Interpreting Contracts: A Common Law Dilemma,* 59 Canadian Bar Review 241 (1981). The rule which we adopt today for interpretation of standardized contracts recognizes modern commercial practice by business entities which use automated equipment to effect a large volume of transactions through use of standardized forms. It parallels the general rule which applies to all contracts by attempting to discover the intent of the parties, in so far as intent existed, and attempts to ascertain the real agreement so far as it was expressed or conveyed by implication. However, it recognizes that most provisions of standardized agreements are not the result of negotiation; often, neither customer nor salesperson are aware of the contract provisions. The rule adopted today recognizes reality and the needs of commerce; it allows businesses that use such forms to write their own contract. It charges the customer with knowledge that the contract being "purchased" is or contains a form applied to a vast number of transactions and includes terms which are unknown (or even unknowable); it binds the customer to such terms. However, the rule stops short of granting the drafter of the contract license to accomplish any result. It holds the drafter to good faith and terms which are conscionable; it requires drafting of provisions which can be understood if the customer does attempt to check on his rights; it does not give effect to boilerplate terms which are contrary to either the expressed agreement or the purpose of the transaction as known to the contracting parties. From the standpoint of the judicial system, the rule recognizes the true origin of standardized contract provisions, frees the courts from having to write a contract for the parties, and removes the temptation to create ambiguity or invent intent in order to reach a result.

The rule does not set a premium on failure to read. Those who negotiate their transactions will be held to the same rules as have previously obtained with regard to the duty to read. The rule which we adopt applies to contracts (or parts of contracts) made up of standardized forms which, because of the nature of the enterprise, customers will not be expected to read and over which they have no real power of negotiation.[9]

To apply the old rule and interpret such contracts according to the imagined intent of the parties is to perpetuate a fiction which can do no more than bring the law into ridicule. To those troubled by the change in the law, we point out that the fundamental change occurred first in business practice. The change in legal analysis does no more than reflect the change in methods of doing business. To acknowledge standardized contracts for what they are—rules written by commercial enterprises—and to enforce them as written, subject to those reasonable limitations provided by law, is to recognize the reality of the marketplace as it now exists, while imposing just limits on business practice. These, we think, have always been the proper functions of contract law. . . .

[The court also held that Darner might prevail on an equitable estoppel or reformation theory. As to estoppel, the court held: "if the fact finder determines that Darner and Doxsee did agree upon lessee's coverage in limits of 100/300, and if, by justifiably relying on Doxsee's assurances or

---

[9] It cannot be seriously contended, for instance, that airline companies, car rental agencies, and the like expect their customers to line up, demand copies of the various instruments which set forth the "contract" and require explanations of the various terms. The usual "contract" for air transportation provides an example; it begins as follows:

Conditions of Contract

As used in this contract "ticket" means this passenger ticket and baggage check, of which these conditions and the notices form part, "carriage" is equivalent to "transportation", "carrier" means all air carriers that carry or undertake to carry the passenger or his baggage hereunder or perform any other service incidental to such air carriage, "Warsaw Convention" means the convention for the unification of certain rules relating to international carriage by air signed at Warsaw, 12th of October, 1929, or that convention as amended at the Hague, 28th September, 1955, whichever may be applicable.

Uniform Passenger Ticket and Baggage Check, ATC version, printed on the back of the standard form of ticket in general use by airlines in the United States. Fortunately, we have not yet been required to interpret this contract by conjuring up some supposed intent of the passenger.

for some other justifiable reason, Darner was unaware of the limitation in the umbrella policy, Universal would be estopped to assert the definitional exclusion which eliminates Darner's lessee from the class of persons insured." As to reformation, the court held the contract would be formed to be in accord with Darner's understanding if Darner could establish "Doxsee had knowledge of Darner's 'mistaken' understanding of the agreement."

As to Darner's negligence theory, the court held that an insurance agent owes a duty to the insured to exercise reasonable care, skill, and prudence in procuring insurance; that whether the insured's not reading the policies constitutes contributory negligence turns on the reasonableness of not reading the policies and relying on the agent's statements; and that the issue was one for the trier of fact. As to Darner's fraud theory, the court held that it could not say that the allegations on which the fraud count was based were wholly without merit.]

For the foregoing reasons we vacate the decision of the court of appeals and reverse the trial court's summary judgment as to the counts of equitable estoppel, reformation of the contract, negligent misrepresentation and fraud. Because of this disposition of the substantive matters, the court of appeals' award of attorney's fees is vacated.

GORDON, V.C.J., and HAYS, J., concur.

[The concurring opinion of Cameron, J., and the dissenting opinion of Holohan, C.J., are omitted.]

Gordinier v. Aetna Casualty & Surety Co.

154 Ariz. 266, 742 P.2d 277 (1987)

The Arizona Court here elaborated on *Darner* as follows: " . . . As a synthesis of the cases and authorities demonstrates, Arizona courts will not enforce even unambiguous boilerplate terms in standardized insurance contracts in a *limited* variety of situations:

"1. Where the contract terms, although not ambiguous to the court, cannot be understood by the reasonably intelligent consumer who might check on his or her rights, the court will interpret them in light of the objective, reasonable expectations of the average insured (*see* . . . *Wainscott v. Ossenkop,* 633 P.2d 237 (Alaska 1981) (application of "resident of same household" definition, while not technically ambiguous, defeats reasonable expectations of spouse));

"2. Where the insured did not receive full and adequate notice of the term in question, and the provision is either unusual or unexpected, or one that emasculates apparent coverage . . . ;

"3. Where some activity which can be reasonably attributed to the insurer would create an objective impression of coverage in the mind of a reasonable insured . . . ;

"4. Where some activity reasonably attributable to the insurer has induced a particular insured reasonably to believe that he has coverage, although such coverage is expressly and unambiguously denied by the policy. . . .

Farm Bureau Mutual Insurance Co. v. Sandbulte

302 N.W.2d 104 (Iowa 1981)

(Larson, J.) "The rationale of the reasonable expectation doctrine is that, in a contract of adhesion, such as an insurance policy, form must not be exalted over substance, and that the reasonable expectations of the insured may not be frustrated 'even though painstaking study of the policy provisions would have negated those expectations.' Rodman v. State Farm Mutual Insurance Co., 208 N.W.2d at 906 (quoting Keeton, Insurance Law—Basic Text § 6.3(a), at 351 (1971)); *see also* C & J Fertilizer, Inc., 227 N.W.2d at 176–77. Reasonable expectations giving rise to application of the doctrine may be established by proof of the underlying negotiations or inferred from the circumstances. Restatement (Second) of Contracts § 237, at 541 (comment f). The doctrine will apply here if the exclusion (1) is bizarre or oppressive, (2) eviscerates terms explicitly agreed to, or (3) eliminates the dominant purpose of the transaction. *Id.* The doctrine is well illustrated by C & J Fertilizer: Under the terms of a burglary policy the insurer agreed '[t]o pay for loss by burglary or by robbery of a watchman, while the premises are not open for business. . . .' In the definition section of the policy, however, burglary was defined in such a way as to exclude any occurrence which was not evidenced by marks left on the exterior of the premises. This definition was not consistent with a layman's concept of the crime, nor with its legal interpretation. In effect, the definition overrode the dominant purpose for purchasing the policy and in effect eviscerated the coverage specifically bargained for, protecting against burglary. 227 N.W.2d at 176–77."

SECTION 4. COMPANY POLICY
DOCUMENTS AS CONTRACTS

ANDERSON V. DOUGLAS & LOMASON COMPANY

Supreme Court of Iowa, 1995.
540 N.W.2d 277.

TERNUS, JUSTICE.

Defendant, Douglas & Lomason Company (DLC), discharged plaintiff, Terry Anderson, for taking a box of pencils. Anderson responded with a breach-of-contract action claiming DLC failed to follow progressive discipline policies contained in the employee handbook. The district court granted DLC's motion for summary judgment, which argued, in part, that the handbook did not constitute a contract. Anderson appealed.

Although we conclude progressive discipline policies meeting the requirements for a unilateral contract are enforceable, a disclaimer in the handbook given to Anderson prevented the policies from constituting a contract. Therefore, we affirm the district court's grant of summary judgment.

I.   *Background Facts and Proceedings.*

On Anderson's first day of work at DLC he attended a six hour orientation session for new employees. He was informed that DLC had a progressive discipline policy and he was given a fifty-three page employee handbook which included these policies. Anderson read only the first few pages of the handbook; he admits he never read the provisions on progressive discipline.

DLC fired Anderson after three years of employment. His termination was based on an incident which occurred as he was leaving the plant one day. Company personnel stopped his pickup and asked to search it. Anderson gave permission and the workers found a box of company pencils. As a result, they also asked to search his home and garage. Anderson consented and a subsequent search revealed no company property. However, that same day, DLC asked Anderson to resign. He refused and was immediately fired.

Anderson responded by filing this breach-of-contract action against DLC. He claims DLC did not follow the progressive discipline policies outlined in its handbook for unauthorized possession of company property. These progressive discipline policies require a written warning for the first offense, a three-day suspension without pay for the second offense, and discharge for the third offense. Because this was not Anderson's third offense, he claims DLC could not fire him.

DLC filed a motion for summary judgment claiming the handbook did not constitute a contract and therefore Anderson was employed at-will. First, DLC contended the handbook was never communicated to or accepted by Anderson because he did not read it. Second, DLC argued the handbook was not definite enough to constitute an offer. DLC cited two reasons for its vagueness claim: the handbook contains no written guarantees that discharge will occur only for cause or under certain conditions—the rules are mere guidance; and the manual contains a written disclaimer. The district court granted the employer's summary judgment motion without explanation in a calendar entry.

II. *Scope of Review.*

We uphold summary judgment when the moving party shows no genuine issue of material fact exists and it is entitled to judgment as a matter of law. Iowa R.Civ.P. 237(c); *C-Thru Container Corp. v. Midland Mfg. Co.*, 533 N.W.2d 542, 544 (Iowa 1995). To decide if the moving party has met this burden, we review the record in the light most favorable to the party opposing summary judgment. *Hoffnagle v. McDonald's Corp.*, 522 N.W.2d 808, 811 (Iowa 1994).

III. *Indefinite Employment Contracts.*

The central issue presented by this dispute is whether DLC's issuance of a handbook created an employment contract. This question arises because Iowa employment relationships are presumed to be at-will: In the absence of a valid employment contract either party may terminate the relationship without consequence. *See Hunter v. Board of Trustees*, 481 N.W.2d 510, 513 (Iowa 1992). Indeed, the doctrine of employment at-will is merely a gap-filler, a judicially created presumption utilized when parties to an employment contract are silent as to duration. *Butler v. Walker Power, Inc.*, 137 N.H. 432, 629 A.2d 91, 93 (1993); *see also Sorenson v. Kennecott-Utah Copper Corp.*, 873 P.2d 1141, 1145 (Utah App.1994) (at-will rule is mere rule of contract construction); Richard A. Epstein, *In Defense of the Contract at Will*, U.Chi.L.Rev. 947, 951 (1984) ("[at-will] rule of construction [is] in response to the perennial question of gaps"). To understand our interpretation of employment contracts, particularly the nexus between the at-will doctrine and employee handbooks, we provide a brief overview.

A. *Development of employment at will.* The at-will presumption originated in English seasonal servant contract law. *See* Jay M. Feinman, *The Development of the Employment at Will Rule*, 20 Am.J.Legal Hist. 118, 118 (1976) (hereinafter "Feinman Article"). When parties remained silent as to the duration of service, the English courts filled the gap by presuming a certain duration and imposing a notice-of-termination requirement. 1 William Blackstone, *Commentaries on the Laws of England* 413 (U.Chi.Press 1979) ("If the hiring be general without any particular time limited, the law construes it to be a hiring for a year. . . . [Neither side can break the contract] without a quarter's warning.") (hereinafter "Blackstone"). The judicially created doctrine complemented statutes imposing a ban on leaving one's position or firing a worker before the end of the term and reflected the judiciary's concern for fairness between masters and seasonal servants. Feinman Article, 20 Am.J.Legal Hist. at 120; *see* Blackstone, at 413 (relationship continues "throughout all the revolutions of the respective seasons; as well as when there is work to be done, as when there is not").

The doctrine has never been static. As additional statutes were promulgated and the variety of employment situations far removed from the domestic environment increased, the English judiciary varied the amount of notice in accordance with the type of employment. Feinman Article, 20 Am.J.Legal Hist. at 121–22. "English law thus attempted to adapt to changing conditions and new situations. . . . " *Id.* at 121.

American courts relied heavily upon English precedent until the 1870s, when changing economic and social conditions prompted a dissolution of earlier law: the presumption of yearly hiring was seen as anachronistic and the concept of reasonable notice was disavowed. *Id.* at 125; *cf.* Richard J. Pratt, Comment, *Unilateral Modification of Employment Handbooks: Further Encroachments On the Employment-At-Will Doctrine,* 139 U.Pa.L.Rev. 197, 198–99 (1990) (hereinafter "Pratt Article"); Marla J. Weinstein, Comment, *The Limitations of Judicial Innovation: A Case Study of Wrongful Dismissal Litigation in Canada and the United States,* 14 Comp.Lab.L.J. 478 (1993) (comparing Canadian and American at-will jurisprudence; Canada retains the notice requirement). At this juncture, a new approach was suggested that changed the doctrine to a presumption of at-will employment:

> With us the rule is inflexible, that a general or indefinite hiring is *prima facie* a hiring at will, and if the servant seeks to make it out a yearly hiring, the burden is upon him to establish it by proof. . . . [I]t is an indefinite hiring and is determinable at the will of either party, and in this respect there is no distinction between domestic and other servants.

H.G. Wood, *A Treatise on the Law of Master & Servant* § 134, at 272 (1877). As the English presumption was a reflection of the economic and societal conditions in early Britain, Wood's rule was an outgrowth of prevailing American thought: ascendancy of freedom of contract, a reflection of the usual duration of employment contracts, and support for the development of advanced capitalism. Feinman Article, 20 Am.J.Legal Hist. at 130–31; *see also* Pratt Article, 139 U.Pa.L.Rev. at 199–201.

B.   *Iowa jurisprudence.* Wood's version of employment at will quickly spread and was universally adopted. 1 Samuel Williston, *The Law of*

Contracts § 39, at 61–62 (1920) (hereinafter "Williston"). Indeed, it is long established in Iowa case law. *Harrod v. Wineman,* 146 Iowa 718, 720, 125 N.W. 812, 813 (1910) ("it is held by an overwhelming weight of authority that a contract of indefinite employment may be abandoned at will by either party without incurring any liability"); *see also Fogel v. Trustees of Iowa College,* 446 N.W.2d 451, 455 (Iowa 1989); *Wolfe v. Graether,* 389 N.W.2d 643, 652 (Iowa 1986); *Harper v. Cedar Rapids Television Co.,* 244 N.W.2d 782, 791 (Iowa 1976).

Despite the universal acceptance of the employment-at-will doctrine, legislatures and courts have restricted its application. For example, federal labor law gave rise to union contracts that include just cause discharge provisions. Michael J. Phillips, *Disclaimers of Wrongful Discharge Liability: Time for a Crackdown,* 70 Wash.U.L.Q. 1131, 1134 (1992). Similarly, public employees are protected from arbitrary dismissal under civil service statutes. *E.g., City of Des Moines v. Civil Serv. Comm'n,* 540 N.W.2d 52, 58 (Iowa 1995); Iowa Code § 400.18 (1995).

Reflecting the perceived need to protect employees from the harshness of the at-will doctrine, courts began to erode the doctrine with exceptions. Richard Harrison Winters, Note, *Employee Handbooks & Employment-At-Will Contracts,* 1985 Duke L.J. 196, 199; *cf.* Lawrence E. Blades, *Employment at Will vs. Individual Freedom: On Limiting the Abusive Exercise of Employer Power,* 67 Colum.L.Rev. 1404 (1967). These exceptions generally fell within three categories: (1) discharges in violation of public policy, (2) discharges in violation of employee handbooks constituting a unilateral contract, and (3) discharges in violation of a covenant of good faith and fair dealing. Stephen F. Befort, *Employee Handbooks & the Legal Effect of Disclaimers,* 13 Indus.Rel.L.J. 326, 333–34 (1991/1992) (hereinafter "Befort Article"). However, Iowa's strong support of the at-will presumption is demonstrated by our reluctance to undermine the rule with exemptions. We have carved out only two narrow deviations: tort liability when a discharge is in clear violation of a "well-recognized and defined public policy of the State," *Springer v. Weeks & Leo Co.,* 429 N.W.2d 558, 560 (Iowa 1988), and employee handbooks that meet the requirements for a unilateral contract, *French v. Foods, Inc.,* 495 N.W.2d 768, 769–71 (Iowa 1993). We have consistently rejected recognition of a covenant of good faith and fair dealing. *E.g., id.* at 771; *Fogel,* 446 N.W.2d at 456–57.

Our prior handbook decisions concerned only "for-cause" provisions. However, we explicitly left room for future expansion: an employment handbook may guarantee an employee that discharge will occur "only for cause *or under certain conditions.*" *French,* 495 N.W.2d at 770; *accord Hunter,* 481 N.W.2d at 513; *Fogel,* 446 N.W.2d at 455. We now hold "or under certain conditions" to include progressive disciplinary procedures. Such provisions are enforceable if they are part of an employment contract.

Cf. Vaughn v. Ag Processing, Inc., 459 N.W.2d 627, 639 (Iowa 1990) ("We have recognized that written personnel policies providing terms *and procedures to be followed when discharging an employee* would be considered part of an at-will employee's employment contract.") (emphasis added); *Hamilton v. First Baptist Elderly Hous. Found.,* 436 N.W.2d 336, 340–41 (Iowa 1989) (considering whether personnel policies are part of the employment contract). We must now determine whether Anderson's handbook constitutes an enforceable contract. If it does not, we presume the parties intended a contract at will.

   C. *Unilateral contract approach.* When considering whether a handbook creates a contract we utilize unilateral contract theory. *McBride v. City of Sioux City,* 444 N.W.2d 85, 90–91 (Iowa 1989). A unilateral contract consists of an offeror making a promise and an offeree rendering some performance as acceptance. *See Hunter,* 481 N.W.2d at 513; *see also* 1 E. Allan Farnsworth, *Farnsworth on Contracts* § 3.4, at 165 (1990) (hereinafter "Farnsworth"). An employee handbook is a unilateral contract when three elements are present: (1) the handbook is sufficiently definite in its terms to create an *offer;* (2) the handbook is communicated to and accepted by the employee so as to constitute *acceptance;* and (3) the employee provides *consideration. McBride,* 444 N.W.2d at 91.

   As with any contract, the party who seeks recovery on the basis of a unilateral contract has the burden to prove the existence of a contract. *Hawkeye Land Co. v. Iowa Power & Light Co.,* 497 N.W.2d 480, 486 (Iowa App.1993). Therefore, Anderson has the burden to prove DLC's handbook created an enforceable contract. We begin our analysis with a discussion of the communication aspect of the acceptance element of Anderson's claim.

   III. *Was the Employee Manual Communicated Even Though Anderson Never Read the Progressive Discipline Policies Upon Which He Now Relies?*

   Anderson read only a few pages of the employee manual; he did not read the provisions on progressive discipline. DLC contends that under these circumstances, there can be no acceptance. We disagree. DLC distributed its employee handbook to new employees. We think Anderson's receipt of the handbook is sufficient communication.

   A. *Traditional analysis: offeree must know of offer.* Under traditional contract analysis, an offer is not effective until it reaches the offeree. Farnsworth, § 3.10, at 212; Restatement (Second) of Contracts § 51, cmt. a (1981) ("it is ordinarily essential to the acceptance of the offer that the offeree know of the proposal made"); *cf. Iowa Malleable Iron Co. v. Iowa Employment Sec. Comm'n,* 195 N.W.2d 714, 718 (Iowa 1972) ("one cannot be deemed to have declined an offer never communicated to him"). The reason for the rule is clear: The offeree must know of the offer before there can be mutual assent. *Caldwell v. Cline,* 109 W.Va. 553, 554, 156 S.E. 55, 56 (1930); Farnsworth, § 3.10, at 212 ("This requirement has been reinforced by the insistence of the bargain theory of consideration that the acceptance be made in response to the offer.").

The most common illustration of the application of this rule is the general offer of a reward. John P. Dawson et al., *Cases & Comment on Contracts* 360 (5th ed. 1987). The reward-giver, or offeror, bargains for performance, not a reciprocal promise; sometimes the performance is rendered without knowledge of the offer. Some courts resolve this issue using the traditional law of contracts:

> there can be no contract unless the claimant when giving the desired information knew of the offer of the reward and acted with the intention of accepting such offer; otherwise the claimant gives the information not in the expectation of receiving a reward but rather out of a sense of public duty or other motive unconnected with the reward.

Glover v. Jewish War Veterans, 68 A.2d 233, 234 (D.C.1949); *see also Gadsden Times v. Doe*, 345 So.2d 1361, 1363–64 (Ala.Civ.App.1977); *Slattery v. Wells Fargo Armored Serv. Corp.*, 366 So.2d 157, 159 (Fla.Dist.App.1979); *Alexander v. Russo*, 1 Kan.App.2d 546, 571 P.2d 350, 358 (1977); *Braun v. Northeast Stations & Servs., Inc.*, 93 A.D.2d 994, 461 N.Y.S.2d 623, 624 (1983). Courts adopting this traditional approach do so because " 'it is impossible for an offeree actually to assent to an offer unless he knows of its existence.' " *Glover*, 68 A.2d at 234 (quoting Williston, § 33, at 47). On the other hand, one authority has suggested knowledge of a reward-offer need not be a prerequisite to acceptance:

> It is probable, indeed, that the chief reason for enforcing a promise is that it has induced the promisee to act in reliance upon it. One who has rendered a service without knowledge of an offered promise has not so acted. But the chief reason is not necessarily the only reason for enforcing a promise. If it seems fair to the courts to enforce a promise when the promisor has received the desired equivalent, even though the one rendering it knew nothing of the promise and rendered the service from other motives, there is no sufficient reason for refusing to call that enforceable promise a contract.

1 Joseph M. Perillo, *Corbin on Contracts* § 3.5, at 328 (rev. ed. 1993).

Iowa case law on rewards has not addressed this issue. However, we have adopted the traditional position with respect to unilateral contracts in general, that the offeree's performance "must have been induced by the promise made." *St. Peter v. Pioneer Theatre Corp.*, 227 Iowa 1391, 1401, 291 N.W. 164, 169 (1940). Nevertheless, for reasons that follow, we decline to follow the traditional requirement that knowledge of the offer is a prerequisite to acceptance *in the limited context of employee handbook cases.*

B. *Employee handbooks: alteration of traditional rule.* Although we apply the traditional requirement of communication in ordinary contexts, an employment contract based upon an employee handbook "does not always follow the traditional model." Mark Pettit, Jr., *Modern Unilateral Contracts,* 63 B.U.L.Rev. 551, 583 (1983). We believe important policies, which are confined to employee handbook cases, dictate a narrow divergence.

Where a contract is based upon an employee handbook distributed to all employees, the contract is not an individually negotiated agreement; it is a standardized agreement between the employer and a class of employees. *Id.* We analogize to the interpretation of standardized contracts: "A standardized agreement 'is interpreted wherever reasonable as treating alike all those similarly situated, without regard to their knowledge or understanding of the standard terms of the writing.'" *Kinoshita v. Canadian P. Airlines, Ltd.,* 68 Haw. 594, 724 P.2d 110, 116–17 (1986) (quoting Restatement (Second) of Contracts § 211(2) (1981)).

Therefore, we hold it unnecessary that the particular employee seeking to enforce a promise made in an employee manual have knowledge of the promise. Although this holding is a departure from traditional 'bargain-theory' contract analysis, we think it produces "the salutary result that all employees, those who read the handbook and those who did not, are treated alike." E. Allan Farnsworth, *Developments in Contract Law During the 1980's: The Top Ten,* 41 Case W.Res.L.Rev. 203, 209 (1990). Moreover, our deviation from traditional contract theory is consistent with the spirit of the judicially created at-will presumption: It is a common law presumption created in response to statutory and societal demands.

Our decision also finds support in other jurisdictions. *E.g., Kinoshita,* 724 P.2d at 117 ("the plaintiffs' right to compel the company to live up to its promises does not turn on whether they received all of the communications addressed to the employees or not"); *Toussaint v. Blue Cross & Blue Shield,* 408 Mich. 579, 292 N.W.2d 880, 892 (1980) ("nor does it matter that the employee knows nothing of the particulars of the employer's policies and practices"); *Woolley v. Hoffmann-La Roche, Inc.,* 99 N.J. 284, 491 A.2d 1257, 1268 n. 10 (1985), *modified,* 101 N.J. 10, 499 A.2d 515 (1988) ("If reliance is not presumed, a strict contractual analysis might protect the rights of some employees and not the others. . . . [E]mployees neither had to read [the manual], know of its existence, or rely on it to benefit from its provisions any more than employees in a plant that is unionized have to read or rely on a collective-bargaining agreement in order to obtain its benefits."). Thus, the fact that Anderson did not read the employee manual does not prevent him from relying on the promises contained in the manual in this breach-of-contract action.

IV. *Did the Handbook's Progressive Discipline Procedures Constitute an Offer?*

We now consider whether DLC's handbook constituted an offer to Anderson to utilize progressive disciplinary procedures. We believe this aspect of the analysis should be conducted according to traditional contract theory.

A. *Offer.* All contracts must contain mutual assent; mode of assent is termed offer and acceptance. *Kristerin Dev. Co. v. Granson Inv.*, 394 N.W.2d 325, 330 (Iowa 1986); Restatement (Second) of Contracts § 22 (1981); *see also Service Employees Int'l Local No. 55 v. Cedar Rapids Community Sch. Dist.*, 222 N.W.2d 403, 408 (Iowa 1974). An offer is a "manifestation of willingness to enter into a bargain, so made as to justify another person in understanding that his assent to that bargain is invited and will conclude it." Restatement (Second) of Contracts § 24 (1981); *accord* Farnsworth, § 3.10, at 210 (offer is "a promise that is conditional on a manifestation of assent in the form of some action by the offeree and that confers upon the offeree the right to create a contract by taking that action").

We look for the existence of an offer objectively—not subjectively. *Cf. LaFontaine v. Developers & Builders, Inc.*, 261 Iowa 1177, 1183, 156 N.W.2d 651, 655 (1968) (existence of contract determined from words and circumstances). Judge Learned Hand explained this rule:

> A contract has, strictly speaking, nothing to do with the personal, or individual intent of the parties. A contract is an obligation attached by the mere force of law to certain acts of the parties, usually words, which ordinarily accompany and represent a known intent. If, however, it were proved by twenty bishops that either party, when he used the words, intended something else than the usual meaning which the law imposes upon them, he would still be held. . . .

Hotchkiss v. National City Bank, 200 F. 287, 293 (S.D.N.Y.1911), *aff'd sub nom. Ernst v. Mechanics' & Metals Nat'l Bank*, 201 F. 664 (2d Cir.1912), *aff'd sub nom. National City Bank v. Hotchkiss*, 231 U.S. 50, 34 S.Ct. 20, 58 L.Ed. 115 *and aff'd sub nom. Mechanics' & Metals Nat'l Bank v. Ernst*, 231 U.S. 60, 34 S.Ct. 22, 58 L.Ed. 121 (1913); *see also Embry v. Hargadine, McKittrick Dry Goods Co.*, 127 Mo.App. 383, 105 S.W. 777, 778 (1907) ("In so far as their intention is an influential element, it is only such intention as the words or acts of the parties indicate."). "The standard is what a normally constituted person would have understood [the words] to mean, when used in their actual setting." *New York Trust Co. v. Island Oil & Transp. Corp.*, 34 F.2d 655, 656 (2d Cir.1929) (Hand, J.); *cf. Deitrick v. Sinnott*, 189 Iowa 1002, 1010, 179 N.W. 424, 428 (1920) (cannot avoid contract because merely jesting if conduct and words were such as to warrant a reasonable person in believing that he was in earnest). We adopt the following analysis: "The test for an offer is whether it induces a reasonable belief in the recipient that he can, by accepting, bind the sender." *Architectural Metal Sys., Inc. v. Consolidated Sys., Inc.,* 58 F.3d 1227, 1229 (7th Cir.1995).

When objectively examining the handbook to determine intent to create an offer, we look for terms with precise meaning that provide certainty of performance. *Cf. Gildea v. Kapenis,* 402 N.W.2d 457, 459 (Iowa App.1987). This is a definiteness inquiry: if an offer is indefinite there is no intent to be bound. *See Architectural Metal Sys., Inc.,* 58 F.3d at 1229 ("A lack of essential detail would negate such a belief, since the sender could not reasonably be expected to empower the recipient to bind him to a contract of unknown terms. . . . [T]he recipient of a hopelessly vague offer should know that it was not intended to be an offer that could be made legally enforceable by being accepted.").

B.   *DLC's handbook is too vague to constitute an offer.* Here the issue is how a reasonable employee would construe DLC's handbook—a promise of progressive disciplinary procedures or mere guidance? The question resolves to whether the handbook's text was sufficiently definite to constitute an offer to apply certain procedures for discharge. *See Falczynski v. Amoco Oil Co.,* 533 N.W.2d 226, 235 (Iowa 1995). That is a question of law. *French,* 495 N.W.2d at 770; *Fogel,* 446 N.W.2d at 456.

DLC asserts the handbook was not definite enough to constitute an offer for two reasons: It claims there are no guarantees that the company will always follow the progressive discipline procedures, and the handbook includes a written disclaimer that expressly states there is no intent to create a contract. Therefore, DLC contends no offer existed for Anderson to accept.

1.   *Handbook language.* When considering whether a handbook is objectively definite to create a contract we consider its language and context. Our analysis of case law reveals three factors to guide this highly fact-intensive inquiry: (1) Is the handbook in general and the progressive disciplinary procedures in particular mere guidelines or a statement of policy, or are they directives? *See Boulay v. Impell Corp.,* 939 F.2d 480, 482 (7th Cir.1991) (language that was suggestive rather than mandatory lead to conclusion of no promise); *Johnson v. McDonnell Douglas Corp.,* 745 S.W.2d 661, 662 (Mo.1988) (en banc) ("The handbook was merely an informational statement of McDonnell's self-imposed policies"); (2) Is the language of the disciplinary procedures detailed and definite or general and vague? *See Hunt v. I.B.M. Mid America Employees Fed. Credit Union,* 384 N.W.2d 853, 856–58 (Minn.1986) (vague language fails to provide any detailed or definite disciplinary procedure); *Mecurio v. Therm-O-Disc, Inc.,* 92 Ohio App.3d 131, 634 N.E.2d 633, 637 (Ohio App.), *overruled on other*

grounds, 68 Ohio St.3d 1410, 623 N.E.2d 566 (1993) ("From the plain terms of the [progressive discipline] policy . . . reasonable minds could conclude that an implied contract was created."); and (3) Does the employer have the power to alter the procedures at will or are they invariable? *See McDonnell Douglas Corp.,* 745 S.W.2d at 662 (handbook "provided that the rules were subject to change at any time"; thus, there was no contract); *Martin v. Capital Cities Media, Inc.,* 354 Pa.Super. 199, 511 A.2d 830, 838–39 (1986) (because employer could alter plan at will, no contract). We ask these questions to determine whether an employee is reasonably justified in understanding a commitment has been made. *See Bolling v. Clevepak Corp.,* 20 Ohio App.3d 113, 20 O.B.R. 146, 484 N.E.2d 1367, 1373 (1984).

Here, the text of the disciplinary procedures contains language of command: "The following action is prohibited, and the penalties for violation of these Shop Rules *shall* be as follows [progressive discipline steps are then listed]." (Emphasis added.) However, the introduction to the section of the handbook containing the disciplinary procedures states twice that the rules "have been designed for the *information and guidance* of all employees." (Emphasis added.) Second, the procedures themselves are fairly specific. There are four categories that describe in detail the offenses included in each category. In addition, the discipline for each category is also specific: for unauthorized possession of company property, the first offense requires a written warning, the second offense a three day unpaid suspension and the third offense results in discharge. Finally, DLC retained the power to alter the procedures at will. We need not decide whether these factors alone result in a sufficiently definite offer, however, because we must also consider the effect of DLC's disclaimer. *See Johnson v. Morton Thiokol, Inc.,* 818 P.2d 997, 1003 (Utah 1991) ("procedures in the handbook for terminating an employee must be read in light of the language in the disclaimer which clearly reserved the right to discharge for any reason").

2. *Handbook disclaimer.* A disclaimer can prevent the formation of a contract by clarifying the intent of the employer not to make an offer. Befort Article, 13 Indus.Rel.L.J. at 349; Chagares Article, 17 Hofstra L.Rev. at 378. "In the context of employee handbooks, the essential purpose of a disclaimer is to claim at-will status for the employment relationship by repudiating or denying liability for statements expressed in the handbook." Befort Article, 13 Indus.Rel.L.J. at 349. Although in theory disclaimers protect employers, many courts have imposed requirements that make it more difficult to give effect to them. *Id.*

For example, many jurisdictions require the disclaimer be "clear and conspicuous" to be enforceable and negate any contractual relationship between an employer and employee. Chagares Article, 17 Hofstra L.Rev. at 380; *see, e.g., Mace v. Charleston Area Medical Ctr. Found., Inc.,* 188 W.Va. 57, 63, 422 S.E.2d 624, 630 (1992) ("employee handbook which

contains a clear and conspicuous disclaimer of job security will preserve
the at-will status"). While we have never considered whether a disclaimer
in an employee handbook must be clear and conspicuous, our court of
appeals has implicitly endorsed a conspicuous requirement by holding a
disclaimer "[p]rominently displayed in the first page" of a handbook
prevented the formation of a contract. *Palmer v. Women's Christian Ass'n,*
485 N.W.2d 93, 95–96 (Iowa App.1992).

The requirement that a disclaimer be conspicuous has given rise to
much litigation. Compare cases holding disclaimer clear and conspicuous,
Hein v. Kerr-McGee Coal Corp., 809 F.Supp. 84, 86–87 (D.Wyo.1990), *aff'd,*
956 F.2d 278 (10th Cir.1992) (disclaimer at beginning of handbook under
heading "INTRODUCTION" which was one of two paragraphs on page,
both of which were surrounded by open space); *Chambers v. Valley Nat'l
Bank,* 721 F.Supp. 1128, 1131 (D.Ariz.1988) (disclaimer prominently
displayed in bold print in introductory paragraph); *Nettles v. Techplan
Corp.,* 704 F.Supp. 95, 98 (D.S.C.1988) (disclaimer of same type and color
contained in separate paragraph on first page of manual); *Butler v.
Westinghouse Elec. Corp.,* 690 F.Supp. 424, 429 (D.Md.1987) (disclaimer in
bold print at front of handbook); *Investors Premium Corp. v. Burroughs
Corp.,* 389 F.Supp. 39, 45 (D.S.C.1974) (clause set out in separate
paragraph in capital letters); *Hanson v. New Technology, Inc.,* 594 So.2d
96, 99 (Ala.1992) (language found on first page of handbook); *Chesnick v.
Saint Mary of Nazareth Hosp.,* 211 Ill.App.3d 593, 156 Ill.Dec. 69, 71, 570
N.E.2d 545, 547 (1991) (disclaimer on separate page signed by plaintiff);
Eldridge v. Evangelical Lutheran Good Samaritan Soc'y, 417 N.W.2d 797,
800 (N.D.1987) (explicit disclaimer in closing statement located directly
above signature of employee) with cases holding disclaimer not clear and
conspicuous, *Durtsche v. American Colloid Co.,* 958 F.2d 1007, 1010 (10th
Cir.1992) (disclaimer buried in glossary definition and no effort to highlight
existence or effect of disclaimer); *Jimenez v. Colorado Interstate Gas Co.,*
690 F.Supp. 977, 980 (D.Wyo.1988) (disclaimer not set off in any way to
attract attention, was placed under heading "GENERAL
INSTRUCTIONS" and subheading "CONTENTS," was indistinct in print
and type and had no border setting it apart from any other paragraph on
page); *Hicks v. Methodist Medical Ctr.,* 229 Ill.App.3d 610, 170 Ill.Dec. 577,
579–80, 593 N.E.2d 119, 121–22 (1992) (disclaimer located on page thirty-
eight of thirty-nine page manual; not highlighted, printed in capital letters
nor in any way prominently displayed; was not entitled "Disclaimer," but
was located in section headed "Revisions"); *Kumpf v. United Tel. Co.,* 311
S.C. 533, 429 S.E.2d 869, 872 (App.1993) (disclaimer located in "conclusion"
section of handbook and not capitalized, in bold type, set apart with
distinctive border nor in contrasting type or color). While the factual nature
of the definiteness inquiry is partially to blame, too often such litigation is
the product of illusory judicial standards. *See Sanchez v. Life Care Ctrs. of
Am., Inc.,* 855 P.2d 1256, 1260 (Wyo.1993) ("This is yet another case to

CH. 16 CONSUMER FORM CONTRACTS 633

come before us in which an employer has tried to satisfy the court's secret concept of an adequate disclaimer in an employee handbook.") (Cardine, J., dissenting).

We think such uncertainty is unnecessary. A disclaimer should be considered in the same manner as any other language in the handbook to ascertain its impact on our search for the employer's intent. Therefore, we reject any special requirements for disclaimers; we simply examine the language and context of the disclaimer to decide whether a reasonable employee, reading the disclaimer, would understand it to mean that the employer has not assented to be bound by the handbook's provisions. *Cf. Bolling*, 484 N.E.2d at 1373 ("the employees ... must be justified 'in understanding that a commitment has been made.' ") (citations omitted); *Payne v. Sunnyside Community Hosp.*, 78 Wash.App. 34, 894 P.2d 1379, 1384 (1995) ("crucial question is whether the employee has a reasonable expectation the employer will follow the discipline procedure, based upon the language used").

Similar to our consideration of handbook language in general, we believe two factors guide our inquiry. First, is the disclaimer clear in its terms: does the disclaimer state that the handbook does not create any rights, or does not alter the at-will employment status? Second, is the coverage of the disclaimer unambiguous: what is the scope of its applicability? Here the disclaimer appears on page fifty-three, the last page of the handbook, two inches below the preceding paragraph:

This Employee Handbook is not intended to create any contractual rights in favor of you or the Company. The Company reserves the right to change the terms of this handbook at any time.

When examining the disclaimer we first consider the text employed. In no uncertain terms DLC's disclaimer states the handbook "is not intended to create *any* contractual rights." (Emphasis added.) *See Smoot v. Boise Cascade Corp.*, 942 F.2d 1408, 1411 (9th Cir.1991) ("the written materials also contain explicit disclaimers that preclude their forming the basis of an employment agreement"); *Shapiro v. Wells Fargo Realty Advisors*, 152 Cal.App.3d 467, 199 Cal.Rptr. 613, 616 (1984) (agreement stated that it did not confer a right to continued employment); *Tilbert v. Eagle Lock Co.*, 116 Conn. 357, 165 A. 205, 207 (1933) (death benefit plan said "it constitutes no contract with any Employee or any beneficiary, and confers no legal rights on" any party). We believe DLC's disclaimer is clear in its disavowal of any intent to create a contract.

Second, we examine the scope of the disclaimer. There is nothing about the location of DLC's disclaimer or the language used to suggest that the disclaimer does not apply to the progressive discipline policies. The disclaimer is found in the handbook itself and *289 unequivocally applies to the entire employee handbook.

We think a reasonable person reading the handbook could not believe that DLC has assented to be bound to the provisions contained in the manual. *See Smoot,* 942 F.2d at 1411 (finding employment at will as a matter of law: "Although [employer's] termination policies contain promises of specific treatment in specific situations, the written materials also contain explicit disclaimers that preclude their forming the basis of an employment agreement."). Thus, we hold DLC's handbook is not sufficiently definite to constitute a valid offer.

VI. *Summary.*

We hold as a matter of law no contract existed between Anderson and DLC. Anderson was employed at-will. Therefore, the trial court correctly granted summary judgment to DLC.

AFFIRMED.

———

Dyer v. Northwest Airlines Corporations

334 F.Supp.2d 1196 (D.N.D. 2004)

(Hovland, C.J.) "Following September 11, 2001, the National Aeronautical and Space Administration ("NASA") requested system-wide passenger data from Northwest Airlines for a three-month period in order to conduct research for use in airline security studies. Northwest Airlines complied and, unbeknownst to its customers, provided NASA with the names, addresses, credit card numbers, and travel itineraries of persons who had flown on Northwest Airlines between July and December 2001.

"The discovery of Northwest Airlines' disclosure of its customers' personal information triggered a wave of litigation. Eight class actions—seven in Minnesota and one in Tennessee—were filed in federal court prior to March 19, 2004. The seven Minnesota actions were later consolidated into a master file.

"The Plaintiffs initiated the above-entitled action in state court in North Dakota on March 19, 2004. The complaint alleges that Northwest Airlines' unauthorized disclosure of customers' personal information constituted a violation of the Electronic Communications Privacy Act ("ECPA"), 18 U.S.C. §§ 2702(a)(1) and (a)(3), and a breach of contract. . . .

"The Plaintiffs base their breach of contract claim on Northwest Airlines' alleged violation of the privacy policy posted on its website. Northwest Airlines contends that a policy posted on its website does not constitute a contract. In addition, Northwest Airlines argues that even if the policy did constitute a contract, the Plaintiffs claim fails because they have not alleged any contract damages.

"To sustain a breach of contract claim, the Plaintiffs must demonstrate (1) the existence of a contract; (2) breach of the contract; and (3) damages which flow from the breach. *United States v. Basin Elec. Power Co-op.*, 248 F.3d 781, 810 (8th Cir.2001) (applying North Dakota law). The plaintiff bears the burden of proving each element. *Id.*

"Having carefully reviewed the complaint, the Court finds the Plaintiffs' breach of contract claim fails as a matter of law. First, broad statements of company policy do not generally give rise to contract claims. See *Pratt v. Heartview Foundation*, 512 N.W.2d 675, 677 (N.D.1994); accord *Martens v. Minnesota Mining and Manu. Co.*, 616 N.W.2d 732, 740 (Minn.2000). As such, the alleged violation of the privacy policy at issue does not give rise to a contract claim. Second, nowhere in the complaint are the Plaintiffs alleged to have ever logged onto Northwest Airlines' website and accessed, read, understood, actually relied upon, or otherwise considered Northwest Airlines' privacy policy. Finally, even if the privacy policy was sufficiently definite and the Plaintiffs had alleged they did read the policy prior to providing personal information to Northwest Airlines, the Plaintiffs have failed to allege any contractual damages arising out of the alleged breach. A plaintiff cannot recover for a breach of contract claim without showing damages resulting from the breach. The Plaintiffs have failed to allege any facts relating to the breach of contract claim which support the conclusory statements they have suffered damages. The breach of contract claim is subject to dismissal as a matter of law."

———

PART 5

MISTAKE AND UNEXPECTED CIRCUMSTANCES

■ ■ ■

CHAPTER 17

MISTAKE

■ ■ ■

This Chapter concerns rules that determine the legal effect of a party's mistake involving a contract. Section 1 concerns mistakes in transcribing an agreement to writing and the remedy of reformation. Section 2 concerns the doctrine of unilateral mistake, which also covers mistakes regarding the content of a writing as well as certain others types of mistakes. The remedy is to avoid the contract infected by the mistake. Section 3 concerns the doctrine of mutual mistake. It covers mistaken factual assumptions about a present state of the world that affects the value of a contract. Section 4 concerns the duty to disclose. The duty to disclose relates to mistake because the duty sometimes prevents A from taking advantage of B's mistake when A is aware B is mistaken.

SECTION 1. MISTAKES IN TRANSCRIPTION; REFORMATION

TRAVELERS INS. CO. V. BAILEY
Supreme Court of Vermont, 1964.
124 Vt. 114, 197 A.2d 813.

BARNEY, JUSTICE. The plaintiff insurance company has come into equity asking for reformation of the annuity provisions of a life insurance policy on the basis of mistake. Thirty years after issuance of the original policy it tendered the defendant insured an amended policy which he refused. On trial, the chancellor found that the amended policy represented the true insuring agreement originally entered into by the parties and allowed reformation. The defendant appealed.

At the instance of his mother, the defendant, when nineteen, submitted an application to an agent of the plaintiff for a life insurance policy. The plan requested in the application was one insuring the defendant's life for five thousand dollars, with an annuity at age sixty-five for five hundred dollars a year for the balance of his life, ten years certain. When the application was accepted and the policy prepared in the home office of the plaintiff, the correct descriptive information was inserted on the wrong policy form. The printed portion of the form used yielded the

639

correct life insurance contract, but produced an annuity obligation to pay five hundred dollars a month for life, one hundred months certain. The application was made a part of the policy, by its terms. In accordance with its usual practice, the plaintiff did not retain a copy of the policy itself but kept a record of the information permitting reproduction of the policy if the occasion demanded.

The premiums were regularly paid on the policy issued in 1931, and about the middle of 1961 the actual policy came into the possession of the defendant for the first time. The semi-annual premiums charged and paid were identical with the prescribed premium for five thousand dollars of life insurance with annuity at age sixty-five of five hundred dollars annually, with payment for ten years certain. This $40.90 semi-annual premium was applicable only to that policy plan, issued at the defendant's then age of nineteen, and no other. The plaintiff had no rate for and did not sell a policy for five thousand dollars life insurance with an annuity at age sixty-five of five hundred dollars monthly, payment for one hundred months certain.

After being told by a third party that his policy could not have the provisions he claimed for it, the defendant took the policy to the office of the defendant's agent that sold the policy and made inquiry. Shortly thereafter, in late 1961, the amended policy was tendered. There is no evidence that the defendant then knew that his original policy provided for an annuity payment larger than he was entitled to in view of the premium paid and the life insurance coverage purchased.

Vermont law, like that of many jurisdictions, imposes upon the party seeking reformation the duty of establishing, beyond a reasonable doubt, the true agreement to which the contract in question is to be reformed. deNeergaard v. Dillingham, 123 Vt. 327, 331, 187 A.2d 494. That this was accomplished, in the judgment of the chancellor, is demonstrated by this finding in particular:

> "The only agreement that the plaintiff and defendant made was for $5000 insurance with annuity of $500 per year at attained age 65, ten years certain."

Adequate evidentiary support for all findings of fact, including this one, made in this case by the chancellor, appears from the transcript of the evidence.

Indeed, in his appeal, the defendant does not question any of the findings relating to the facts already recited. His principal attack on the decision relates to the chancellor's finding that the mistake in issuing the policy furnished the defendant came about through no fault of the defendant, but solely through the negligence and inattention of the plaintiff. This, says the defendant, is a finding of unilateral mistake, and therefore, under the authority of New York Life Insurance Co. v. Kimball, 93 Vt. 147, 153, 106 A. 676, is not grounds for reformation. . . .

In [that case] Justice Miles commented . . . "The law of a case cannot be determined from a brief quotation of portions of the opinion separate from the facts of a case, especially where the law upon the subject has many exceptions, as in the subject now under consideration." This thought is particularly applicable to cases dealing with mistake and reformation. . . .

One variety of classification [of cases involving mistake] is suggested by the difference between a subsequent erroneous recording or transcription of a contract already in fact agreed to by the parties, and a mistake or misunderstanding [which] occurs while the parties are seeking to arrive at or believe they are arriving at an agreement. In the first case an agreement already exists, while in the second considerations of mutuality, together with knowledge of and responsibility for the mistake, weigh heavily in determining whether or not an enforceable agreement, or a right to relief, exists. Unfortunately, language appropriate to the second situation has sometimes been transposed to the first, where it may be both inappropriate and misleading. See 3 Corbin on Contracts § 608 (1960).

Where, as here, an antecedent contract has been established by the requisite measure of proof, equity will act to bring the erroneous writing into conformity with the true agreement. Burlington Building & Loan Ass'n v. Cummings, 111 Vt. 447, 453, 17 A.2d 319. On the basis of the maxim, "Equity regards that as done which ought to be done," equity will deal generously with the correction of mistakes. Stone v. Blake, 118 Vt. 424, 427, 110 A.2d 702, 704. This power has been regularly and frequently invoked in connection with real estate transactions, but there is nothing that requires that equity limit its application to that kind of case.

Other courts have exercised the equitable power of reformation in similar cases. In New England Mutual Life Insurance Co. v. Jones, D.C., 1 F.Supp. 984, a clerical mistake in the policy was discovered after the death of the insured when a double indemnity benefit claim for accidental death was made. The policy provided for double indemnity on the basis of the face amount of the policy, but in the blank space stating the obligation the figure $5000.00 had been entered. This considerably increased the double indemnity figure above that computed on the face amount of the policy. Premiums had been assessed and paid on the basis of the correct figure. Reformation was allowed.

In Stamen v. Metropolitan Life Insurance Co., 41 N.J.Super. 135, 124 A.2d 328, the insured received a policy, after a series of policy conversions, which inadvertently included a provision for disability benefits. The original application accepted by the company requested a policy without such provision, and the premiums had been assessed on the basis that no such benefits were payable. Reformation was allowed. . . .

Each of these cases speak of the reformation as justified either because there was "mutuality" of mistake or because the policy holder knew or ought to have known that there was a variation between the policy described in the accepted application and the one handed the insured. To insist on enforcement of the contract once knowledge of the error is acquired by the insured is held to be unconscionable, and classified as then a unilateral mistake known to the other party, which supports reformation. If the mistake exists in the writing unknown to both parties, it is classified as "mutual" and reformation is allowed.

Since these cases support reformation irrespective of the insured's knowledge of the existence of the mistake conferring a benefit on him beyond the bargain, talk of "mutual" or "unilateral" mistake seems to be of little help in this kind of situation. . . .

If, in this kind of case, talk of "mutuality" of mistake is unnecessary, much confusion can be avoided. Invariably, two mistakes are involved. There is a natural tendency to concentrate on the making of the clerical error in the writing as the critical mistake involved, when the true crucial error is mistaken belief of the parties about the correctness of the written instrument. When a test of "mutuality" is applied to the clerical error, the confusion is compounded, since the concern of the court should be with the belief or knowledge of the parties. The concept of "mutuality" adds nothing to the right to a remedy in this type of case. It is important as a concept in other, different, reformation situations. Applying to all the common linguistic label of "mutuality" gives to unlike situations an illusion of similarity. This invites the misapplication of principles, sound for one type of situation, to a different type, for which they are unsound.

Accordingly, we hold that where there has been established beyond a reasonable doubt a specific contractual agreement between parties, and a subsequent erroneous rendition of the terms of the agreement in a material particular, the party penalized by the error is entitled to reformation, if there has been no prejudicial change of position by the other party while ignorant of the mistake. If such change of position can equitably be taken into account and adjusted for in the decree, reformation may be possible even then. Mutual Life Ins. Co. of Baltimore v. Metzger, 167 Md. 27, 172 A. 610; see also Brown v. Lamphear, 35 Vt. 252. Mistakes generally occur through some carelessness, and failure to discover a mistake may be in some degree negligent, but unless some prejudice to the other party's rights under the true contract results, so as to make its enforcement inequitable, reformation will not be refused because of the presence of some negligence. Ward v. Lyman, 108 Vt. 464, 471, 188 A. 892; Mutual Life Insurance Co. of Baltimore v. Metzger, supra, 167 Md. 27, 30, 172 A. 610.

Change of position is raised as an issue by the defendant. It cannot be said that the defendant acted in reliance on the terms of the policy which, he testified, were not exactly known by him until he received the policy in 1961. But he argues that the mere passage of time, in this case thirty years, should overcome the chancellor's finding to the contrary and establish a change of position. But clearly this aging process was inevitable, and not a prejudicial act induced by the mistaken term in the policy. The defendant has not demonstrated that he was prejudiced by the existence of the error. Ward v. Lyman, supra, 108 Vt. 464, 471, 188 A. 892.

Reformation was properly granted.

Decree affirmed.

RESTATEMENT, SECOND, OF CONTRACTS § 155

[See Selected Source Materials Supplement]

Chimart Associates v. Paul

66 N.Y.2d 570, 498 N.Y.S.2d 344, 489 N.E.2d 231 (1986)

(Kaye, J.) "Because the thrust of a reformation claim is that a writing does not set forth the actual agreement of the parties, generally neither the parol evidence rule nor the Statute of Frauds applies to bar proof, in the form of parol or extrinsic evidence, of the claimed agreement. . . . However, this obviously recreates the very danger against which the parol evidence rule and Statute of Frauds were supposed to protect—the danger that a party, having agreed to a written contract that turns out to be disadvantageous, will falsely claim the existence of a different, oral contract. . . . To this end . . . reformation has been limited both substantively and procedurally. Substantively, for example, reformation based upon mistake is not available where the parties purposely contract based upon uncertain or contingent events. . . .

"Procedurally, there is a 'heavy presumption that a deliberately prepared and executed written instrument [manifests] the true intention of the parties' . . . and a correspondingly high order of evidence is required to overcome that presumption. . . . The proponent of reformation must 'show in no uncertain terms, not only that mistake or fraud exists, but exactly what was really agreed upon between the parties'. . . . "

SECTION 2. UNILATERAL MISTAKE

This Section concerns the doctrine of unilateral mistake. The principal case involves a mistake about the content of a writing. The problem is described as one of unilateral mistake because the employer was not mistaken about the writing's contents. Do not ascribe much significance to this aspect of the case. If the employer had also been mistaken about the writing's content, or if the employer knew or had reason to know the employee was mistaken about the writing's content, then relief would be available under the doctrine of reformation.

A difference between reformation and unilateral mistake is that the remedy for unilateral mistake is to avoid the contract infected by the mistake. If reformation had been available, then the document would have been reformed so it operated as a release and the employee would have been allowed to keep the money he received when he signed the document. As it was, the employee had to return the money to avoid the release.

Another difference is that relief under the doctrine of unilateral mistake is not limited to a mistake regarding the content of a writing. The doctrine covers mistake in expressing assent more generally. Andrew Kull, Unilateral Mistake in the Baseball Card Case, 70 Wash. U.L.Q. 57 (1992), explains relief typically is given for a unilateral mistake because the mistake "negatives a party's apparent assent." In other words, a person did not intend to agree to the contract she appeared to agree to. Relief also is regularly given for a computational error like that in the *Drennan* case where a subcontractor miscalculated a bid.

The possibility of relief under the doctrine of unilateral mistake for a mistake in expressing assent was an important qualification to objective rules of interpretation under classical contract law. The interests of the other party were protected by rules that limited relief to cases in which the other party was at fault either because he knew or had reason to know of the mistake, or because he caused the mistake, such as by misrepresenting the content of a writing. Modern contract law also allows relief if the other party has not changed his position in reliance on the contract.

———

RICKETTS v. PENNSYLVANIA R. CO.

United States Court of Appeals, Second Circuit, 1946.
153 F.2d 757.

L. HAND, CIRCUIT JUDGE.

The defendant appeals from a judgment awarding damages to the plaintiff—a waiter upon one of its dining cars—for injuries suffered while in its service on February 16, 1943. The action was brought under the Federal Employers' Liability Act, Secs. 51–60, Title 45 U.S.C.A.; but the only question raised upon this appeal concerns the validity of two releases, dated August 23, 1943, by which the plaintiff released all claims against the defendant upon the payment of $600. The plaintiff had already executed a release for $150 in the same words on March 19, 1943, and one of the two releases of August 23, recited a payment of $750, the sum of the two payments; but, as that release plays no part in the result we shall ignore it and speak as though only the second release had been given in

August. The plaintiff testified that he executed the first release after a talk with one, Brown, the defendant's claim agent, who told him that the payment of $150 was only for the tips and wages which he had lost; and that, relying upon this representation, he did not read the release, but signed it as Brown told him to do. Between that time and July he made some efforts to work but still felt incapacitated; and towards the end of that month, or early in August, he went again to Brown asking for more money. They could not agree, and he left, saying to Brown: 'Well, I will have to get somebody to get all my tips and everything, my salary, because that is what I am getting.' He then went to an attorney named Reich, who, after talking to Brown on the telephone, later brought to the plaintiff the release drawn on the defendant's form and told him: 'I was just to sign a receipt for the amount of money that I got for the time I was off, my tips also included, to go back to work and they won't have anything against you * * * he had the word from the Pennsylvania that I will be taken care of.' On his redirect he somewhat amplified this. Reich had told him: 'the $600 is just for my earnings and my tips, because that would be better such and such. He said he did not want to sue. He said that would be better, and the company wants you to sign. That is big money. If you do, they won't have anything against you. Since you stay in the company, you have eligibility to be retired. You will have full retirement pay.' Relaying upon this, and again not reading the release, he signed it and the defendant paid him $600. The plaintiff's wife also testified that Reich had said that 'the money was for his back pay and tips.'

This version of the transaction the defendant denied. It called Reich, who said that Brown, when Reich consulted him agreed to pay $600 for a complete release; and that all this Reich explained to the plaintiff when the release was executed. The judge charged the jury that, if the plaintiff executed the release 'without fraud or misrepresentation, and understanding what he was doing,' it bound him, but that if he 'signed these papers as receipts for wages, if it was as his understanding that that was all he was signing, that he did not sign any general release, then, of course you take up the question of damages.' Again: 'Was it represented to the plaintiff by his lawyer that the papers he signed on August 23, 1943, were releases of all claims or only for lost wages?' . . . .

[Hand's opinion resolves the appeal in favor of Ricketts relying on a rule in the law of agency and without referring to the law of mistake.]

FRANK, CIRCUIT JUDGE (concurring).

1.   Plaintiff, as a result of a railroad accident which occurred while he was working as an employee of the Pennsylvania Railroad Company, suffered personal injuries which turned out to be so serious that the jury returned a verdict in his favor for $7,500, which the Railroad Company does not contest—except on one ground, i.e., that his claim was barred by

a release he gave the company on payment to him of one-tenth that sum, or $750. That smaller sum represents merely the approximate amount of his lost earnings up to the date of the release. When he signed the release, he could not read it because of the effects of the accident, and without negligence on his part—since he relied on his own lawyer who mis-informed him—he understood that it purported to be only a receipt for payment of those lost earnings.

Judge Hand says (and I entirely agree) that the evidence sufficiently shows that the lawyer acted beyond his authority. Accordingly, it is as if a non-lawyer, carefully selected by plaintiff, had erroneously interpreted the release to him. The case thus comes within the category, described by Williston,[1] of non-negligent unilateral mistakes preventing the formation of valid contracts. Accepting Williston's analysis, Judge Hand's rationale Seems to me to be impregnable.

But I am not content to rest the decision on that analysis, because I think that that analysis leads to needless complexities which will confront us in future cases. The Supreme Court recently, in a case (cited by Judge Hand) relating to a release by a seaman, Garrett v. Moore-McCormack Co., 317 U.S. 239, at page 248, 63 S.Ct. 246, 87 L.Ed. 239, note 17, has broadly hinted that the courts should treat non-maritime employees, with respect to releases of personal injury claims, just as they treat seamen. I think we should take that hint, and, in doing so, should reject many of the finespun distinctions made by Williston and expressed in the Restatement of Contracts. Since I believe that not only is an important social policy involved but also that a good opportunity offers itself to uncomplicate an excessively complicated set of legal rules, I shall state, in some detail, my reasons for this conclusion.

2.   In the early days of this century a struggle went on between the respective proponents of two theories of contracts, (a) the 'actual intent' theory—or 'meeting of the minds' or 'will' theory—and (b) the so-called 'objective' theory. Without doubt, the first theory had been carried too far: Once a contract has been validly made, the courts attach legal consequences of which the parties usually never dreamed—as, for instance, where situations arise which the parties had not contemplated. As to such matters, the 'actual intent' theory induced much fictional discourse which imputed to the parties intentions they plainly did not have.

But the objectivists also went too far. They tried (1) to treat virtually all the varieties of contractual arrangements in the same way, and (2), as to all contracts in all their phases, to exclude, as legally irrelevant, consideration of the actual intention of the parties or either of them, as distinguished from the outward manifestation of that intention. The objectivists transferred from the field of torts that stubborn anti-

---

[1] Williston, Contracts (Rev. Ed.) Sec. 95A.

subjectivist, the 'reasonable man'; so that, in part at least, advocacy of the 'objective' standard in contracts appears to have represented a desire for legal symmetry, legal uniformity, a desire Seemingly prompted by aesthetic impulses. Whether (thanks to the 'subjectivity' of the jurymen's reactions and other factors) the objectivists' formula, in its practical workings, could yield much actual objectivity, certainty, and uniformity may well be doubted.[6] At any rate, the sponsors of complete 'objectivity' in contracts largely won out in the wider generalizations of the Restatement of Contracts and in some judicial pronouncements.

Influenced by their passion for excessive simplicity and uniformity, many objectivists have failed to give adequate special consideration to releases of claims for personal injuries, and especially to such releases by employees to their employers. Williston, the leader of the objectivists, insists that, as to all contracts, without differentiation, the objective theory is essential because 'founded upon the fundamental principle of the security of business transaction'.

He goes to great lengths to maintain this theory, using a variety of rather desperate verbal distinctions to that end. Thus he distinguishes between (1) a unilateral non-negligent mistake in executing an instrument (i.e., a mistake of that character in signing an instrument of one kind believing it to be of another kind) and (2) a similar sort of mistake as to the meaning of a contract which one intended to make. The former, he says, renders the contract 'void'; the latter does not prevent the formation of a valid contract. Yet in both instances 'the fundamental principle of the security of business transactions' is equally at stake, for there has been the same 'disappointment of well-founded expectations.' More than that, Williston concedes that a mistaken idea of one party as to the meaning of a valid contract (Williston's second category) 'may, under certain circumstances, be ground for relief from enforcement of the contract.' But he asserts that (a) such a contract is not 'void' but 'voidable,' and (b) that the granting of such relief is no exception to the objective theory, because this relief 'is in its origin equitable,' and 'equity' does not deny the formation of a valid contract but merely acts 'by subsequently * * * rescinding' it. His differentiation, moreover, of 'void' and 'voidable' has little if any practical significance: He says that a 'voidable' contract will be binding unless the mistaken party sets up the mistake as a defense;[15] but

---

[6]   ...Perhaps the most fatuous of all notions solemnly voiced by learned men who ought to know better is that when legal rules are 'clear and complete' litigation is unlikely to occur. See, e.g., Kantorowicz. Some Rationalism about Realism, 43 Yale L.J. (1934) 1240, 1241; Dickinson, Legal Rules, 79 Un. of Pa.L.Rev. (1931) 833, 846, 847.

Such writers surely cannot be unaware that thousands of decisions yearly turn on disputes concerning the facts, i.e., as to whether clear-cut legal rules were in fact violated. It is the uncertainty about the 'facts' that creates most of the unpredictability of decisions. See Frank, If Men Were Angels (1942) Chaps. VI and VII and Appendices II and V. . . .

[15]   ...Williston refused to concede that the mutual-mistake doctrine does not jibe with the 'objective' theory. He perhaps had in mind this comment of Wigmore's on the reformation of a

the same is obviously true of agreements which (because of unilateral mistakes affecting their 'validity') he describes as 'wholly void.'

It is little wonder that a considerable number of competent legal scholars have criticized the extent to which the objective theory, under Williston's influence, was carried in the Restatement of Contracts. One of them, Whittier, says that the theory, in its application to the formation of contracts, is a generalization from the exceptional cases; he points out that the theory of 'actual mutual assent' explains the great majority of the decisions, so that it would be better, he believes to adhere to it, creating an exception for the relatively few instances where one party has reasonably relied on negligent use of words by the other; 'Why not,' asks Whittier, 'say that actual assent communicated is the basis of Mutual assent except where there is careless misleading which induces a reasonable belief in assent?' There may be much in that notion: Williston admits that 'the law generally is expressed in terms of subjective assent, rather than of objective expressions * * * '; and that 'a doctrine which permits the rescission of a contract on account of a unilateral mistake approaches nearly to a contradiction of the objective theory * * * 'As able a judge as Cuthbert Pound said, not long ago 'The meeting of minds which establishes contractual relations must be shown.'

Another critic[21] suggests that, in general, Williston, because he did not searchingly inquire into the practical results of many of his formulations,

---

contract for such a mistake: 'The theory of reformation is to make the instrument state, objectively and in appearance to others, what it did subjectively state to the parties themselves * * * ' Wigmore, Evidence, Sec. 2418; cf. Sec. 2417. Williston, to whom all subjectivity was anathema, insisted that 'the external expression' of the parties' 'will,' no matter how mistaken, results in a contract which 'equity' recognizes as a contract but which, when the mistake is mutual, it sets aside because 'it is just to do so.' See Williston, The Formation of Contracts, 14 Ill.L.Rev. (1919) 85, 92, 94. However (in part because of the formal 'merger' of 'law' and 'equity' but even in jurisdictions where no such merger has occurred) the 'law' courts have often refused to enforce such contracts.

Williston, undoubtedly a master, takes a position here which Seems highly casuistical: Since 'equity'—whether administered in a separate court or in a court of 'law'—departs from the objective appearance, the objective theory, for all practical purposes, cannot be said to be consistently applied in our legal system. It is far more helpful to acknowledge frankly that there exist important exceptions to that theory. Cf. Patterson, The Restatement of The Law of Contracts, 33 Col.L.Rev. (1933) 397, 407–408; Robinson, Law—An Unscientific Science, 44 Yale L.J. 235, 259–261.

There is a danger, that through the merger of 'law' and 'equity,' the latter may lose its desirable elasticity. See Emmerglick, A Century of The New Equity, 23 Tex.L.R. (1945) 244. That danger may be augmented if, via the Restatement, the 'objective' theory of contracts is not recognized as subject to exceptions.

[21] F.S. Cohen says that Williston, 'a master of classical jurisprudence,' in many of his formulations 'has in mind neither the question of * * * prediction which the practical lawyer faces nor the question of values which the conscientious judge faces. If he had in mind the former question, his studies would no doubt reveal the extent to which courts actually enforce various types of contractual obligation. His conclusions would be in terms of probability and statistics. On the other hand, if Professor Williston were interested in the ethical aspects of contractual liability, he would undoubtedly offer a significant account of human values, and social costs involved in different types of agreement and in the means of their enforcement. In fact, however, the discussions of a Williston oscillate between a theory of what courts actually do and a theory of what courts ought to do, without coming to rest either on the plant of social realities or on the

assumed, unwarrantably, without proof, that those results must invariably have a general social value, although (as Williston admits as to the objective theory) they are 'frequently harsh.'

In other realms of thought, attempted over-simplification has yielded complexities in practice. So here, as appears from the following.

Fortunately, most judges are too sensible to allow, for long, a passion for aesthetic elegance, or for the appearance of an abstract consistency, to bring about obviously unjust results. Accordingly, courts not infrequently have departed from the objective theory when necessary to avoid what they have considered an unfair decision against a person who, for a small sum, signed a release without understanding either the seriousness of his injury or the import of the words of the release, provided (1) he was not 'negligent' and (2) the other party (the releasee) had not, in reliance on the release, importantly 'changed his position.' Some courts, in some of the mistake cases, frankly abandon the 'objective' test, saying boldly that a non-negligent unilateral mistake justifies cancellation or rescission of a contract. As New York, a lively center of commerce, at least to some extent allows relief for such unilateral mistakes, it should be obvious that, contrary to Williston & Co., any deviation from the objective theory is not fatal to the functioning of business.

Some courts, however, escape marring the verbal symmetry of the objective theory, while actually abandoning it, thus: They say that a mistake by one party about a striking fact (sometimes called 'palpable') must be deemed to have been known to the other party, that even if the evidence fails to show that he knew it, yet he had 'reason to know it' and is therefore to be treated as if he did; so that there results, by this device, which comes close to a fiction, a 'mutual mistake of fact.' This court, in pre-Erie-Tompkins days, in effect adopted that rule in a case where the plaintiff, before executing the release, had consulted her own physician; That thesis has been utilized especially when an employee has given a release to his employer of all claims for an injury in consideration of a sum which approximates his lost wages (or his lost wages and medical expenses) and no more. Many courts have said that, on such a state of facts, it is impossible to believe that the releasor and releasee had in mind serious consequences of the injury which became apparent after the release was given, and therefore there was a 'mutual mistake of fact.'

Williston, realizing the desire of the courts to escape the objective theory in such cases, describes them as follows: 'Thus, where a release is given by one injured in an accident and more serious injuries develop than were supposed to exist at the time of settlement, it is a question of fact

---

plane of values long enough to come to grips with significant problems. This confused wandering between the world of fact and the world of justice vitiates every argument and every analysis.' Cohen, Transcendental Nonsense and The functional Approach, 25 Col.L.Rev; (1935) 809, 840, 841....

whether the parties assumed as a basis of the release the known injuries, or whether the intent was to make a compromise for whatever injuries from the accident might exist whether known or not.' On a fair interpretation not only of the language of the instrument, but of the intention of the parties, the latter position is more likely, but presumably out of tenderness for injured plaintiffs some courts have gone very far in accordance with the former possibility.' (In the instant case, plaintiff's lawyer testified that he had received the report of a physician to the effect that plaintiff's injury was not serious. The evidence was, then, probably sufficient to bring this case within the mutual mistake rule; but I think the trial judge's instructions were such as not to leave that issue to the jury.)

Two approaches have been suggested which diverge from that of Williston and the Restatement but which perhaps come closer to the realities of business experience. (1) The first utilizes the concept of an 'assumption of risk'. The parties to a contract, it is said, are presumed to undertake the risk that the facts upon the basis of which they entered into the contract might, within a certain margin, prove to be non-existent; accordingly, one who is mistaken about any such fact should not, absent a deliberate assumption by him of that risk, be held for more than the actual expenses caused by his conduct. Otherwise, the other party will receive a windfall to which he is not entitled. (2) The second suggestion runs thus: Business is conducted on the assumption that men who bargain are fully informed as to all vital facts about the transactions in which they engage; a contract based upon a mistake as to any such facts as would have deterred either of the parties from making it, had he known that fact, should therefore be set aside in order to prevent unjust enrichment to him who made the mistake; the other party, on this suggestion also, is entitled to no more than his actual expenses. Each of those suggestions may result in unfairness, if the other party reasonably believing that he has made a binding contract, has lost the benefit of other specific bargains available at the time but no longer open to him. But any such possibility of unfairness will seldom, if ever, exist in the case of a release of liability for personal injury whatever the nature of the mistake (i.e., whether it fits into one or the other of Williston's categories.)

In short, the 'security of business transactions' does not require a uniform answer to the question when and to what extent the non-negligent use of words should give rise to rights in one who has reasonably relied on them. That the answer should be favorable to the relier when the words are used in certain kinds of contracts, does not mean that it should also be when they are used in a release of a claim for personal injury; and there may be still further reasons for an unfavorable answer when the claim is by an employee against him employer.

In all likelihood, it is because the courts have sensed the differentiated character of releases of personal injury claims that the 'modern trend,' as

Alternatives to R2k's objection.

Wigmore describes it, 'is to * * * develop a special doctrine * * * for that class of cases, liberally relieving the party who signed the release.' Surely much is to be said for that liberality, especially in a case where an employee has given a release of personal injury liability, without the fullest comprehension of what he was about, for a relatively small sum which turns out to be wholly inadequate.

In the admiralty cases, such relief has long been accorded seamen; the courts, calling them 'wards of admiralty,' have regarded them, in many of their dealings with their employers, as necessitous persons, under strong economic pressures, who, because of their helplessness, are to be protected from hard bargains, just as 'equity,' for similar reasons, protects mortgagors and beneficiaries of spendthrift trusts. The usual non-maritime employees, because they are under similar economic pressures, are no less helpless in their trafficking with their employers. It can truthfully be said of them what the admiralty decisions say of seamen: 'They are,' remarked Mr. Justice Story, 'considered as placed under the dominion and influence of men, who have naturally acquired a mastery over them; and as they have little of the foresight and caution belonging to persons trained in other pursuits of life, the most rigid scrutiny is instituted into the terms of every contract, in which they engage. If there is any undue inequality in the terms, any disproportion in the bargain, any sacrifice of rights of one side which are not compensated by extraordinary benefits on the other, the judicial interpretation of the transaction is that the bargain is unjust and unreasonable, that advantage has been taken of the situation of the weaker party, and that pro tanto the bargain ought to be set aside as inequitable.' To men like plaintiff here, the following comment about seamen fully applies: 'They are * * * placed too much in the power of the owners (i.e., employers) to be able to negotiate with them on equal terms.'

It is not surprising, then, that many courts—although without such direct expressions as those which adorn the seaman cases—have in fact in the release cases manifested, although obliquely, a not dissimilar guardianship of employees of large corporations. As already noted, the Supreme Court recently gave a broad hint that the admiralty doctrine is not as exceptional as is sometimes supposed; See Garrett v. Moore-McCormack Co., 317 U.S. 239, 248, 63 S.Ct. 246, 87 L.Ed. 239; note 17. For reasons previously indicated, I think we should take that hint. It seems to me that the time has come to give up the elaboration of distinctions found in the judicial opinions relieving non-admiralty employees of their releases.[41] I believe that the courts should now say forthrightly that the

---

[41] As Patterson (28 Col. L. Rev. at 893) observes, 'The courts have been quite willing to find fraud, innocent misrepresentation, or material mistake in these cases.' They have indeed; they have found such facts, in the release cases, on very slight evidence, evidence which in many other types of cases they would consider insufficient. . .

And they have been quick, too, to seize on words in the releases in order to construe them most narrowly. . .

judiciary regards the ordinary employee as one who needs and will receive the special protection of the courts when, for a small consideration, he has given a release after an injury. As Mr. Justice Holmes often urged, when an important issue of social policy arises, it should be candidly, not evasively, articulated. In other contexts, the courts have openly acknowledged that the economic inequality between the ordinary employer and the ordinary individual employee usually means the absence of 'free bargaining.' I think the courts should do so in these employee release cases. And the federal courts, I think, should so hold in respect to liability pursuant to the Federal Employers' Liability Act. I think, therefore, that we should treat the plaintiff here as we would if he were a seaman.

Such a ruling will not produce legal uncertainty but will promote certainty-as anyone can See who reads the large number of cases in this field, with their numerous intricate methods of getting around the objective theory. Such a ruling would simply do directly what many courts have been doing indirectly. It is fairly clear that they have felt, although they have not said, that employers should not, by such releases, rid themselves of obligations to injured employees, obligations which society at large will bear-either, by taxes, through the government or, by donations, through private charitable organizations.

3. The Pennsylvania Railroad Company warns us that, if a release given by an employee, advised by his own lawyer, is disregarded in a case like this, in the absence of fraud on the part of the employer, then employers will never hereafter settle with their employees who, to their grave disadvantage, will always in the future be forced to sue even for minor personal injury claims. That is a glib prediction based upon no evidence and intended to frighten the court. Sometimes judges have been persuaded by such prophecies which later events have shown to have been unfounded. So Choate, in Pollock v. Farmers' Loan & Trust Co., 1895, 157 U.S. 429, 532, 15 S.Ct. 673, 39 L.Ed, 759, seemingly alarmed the majority of the Court by his forecast that a federal income tax would usher in a communist regime in this country. And it is well to recall Lord Abinger's dire prediction when in 1837 he enunciated the fellow-servant rule which the Employers Liability Act has wiped out: 'If the master be liable to the servant in this action, the principle of liability will be found to carry us to an alarming extent * * * The inconvenience, not to say the absurdity of these consequences, afford a sufficient argument against the application of this principle to the present case * * * In fact, to allow this action to prevail would be an encouragement to the servant to omit that diligence and caution which he is in duty bound to exercise on the behalf of his masters, to protect him against the misconduct of others who serve him, and which diligence and caution, while they protect the master, are a much better security against any injury the servant may sustain by the negligence of others engaged under the same master, than any recourse against his

master for damages could possibly afford.' Certainly, that prophecy went astray.

In New York, the rule as to releases is precisely that to which the Pennsylvania Railroad here objects; yet I venture to guess that thousands of settlements yearly are made in New York by employers who take the risk that, on a proper showing, the releases will be judicially disregarded. Where the amount paid in settlement is relatively small, very likely most employers are willing to take such a risk.

One need not be highly imaginative or unduly cynical to surmise that the Pennsylvania Railroad, in seeking here to be rid of a liability of $7,500 to this employee for a payment of $750, is not too strongly motivated by a philanthropic regard for its other employees.

[Circuit Judge Swan's dissent is omitted.]

———

Dylan C. Penningroth, Race in Contract Law

170 U. Pa. L. Rev. 1199, 1256–1262 (2022).

"In the winter of 1943, Sydney George Ricketts, a waiter on the Pennsylvania Railroad, got seriously hurt just outside Newark, New Jersey. After talking with railroad officials and a company lawyer, Ricketts signed a paper that turned out to be a release settling all his claims for $750. It then became clear that he would be crippled for the rest of his life. Ricketts got a different lawyer and sued in the Southern District of New York, claiming that when he signed the release, he was relying on the company lawyer's representation that it was "just . . . a receipt" for his "earnings and tips" during the six months he had missed work, and that the company "will take care of you." He asked $25,000 in damages for lost earnings, "physical and mental pain," and medical costs. Although nothing in the trial record says so, Ricketts was Black.

"Ricketts' testimony, carefully drawn out by the railroad's lawyer, crystallized the debate between objective and subjective theories of contract law in a way that proved irresistible to Frank. The arguments were familiar. The railroad insisted that Ricketts had settled his claim by signing and accepting the $750. His lawyer argued "that the intention of the parties was not reflected in the form of the documents" Ricketts signed "but rather in the express understanding and conduct of the parties." Ricketts himself claimed he "did not even read" the release and "did not know what was going on." And, just as Mississippi lawyers had done with people like Ben Houston and George Reno, the railroad's lawyer made Ricketts read and explain documents in front of the jury, trying to show that he was literate, "intelligent[ ]," and far from ignorant. A jury awarded Ricketts $7,500 and the railroad appealed.

"When *Ricketts* reached the Second Circuit, two of the three judges wanted to reverse. Learned Hand thought that, under New York law, which followed

Samuel Williston's objective approach, it did not matter whether Ricketts's lawyer had misrepresented the paper to him. Ricketts had signed, taken some money, and that was that. In a series of memoranda that winter, Frank managed to talk Hand into switching sides.

"When *Ricketts* was finally published, Frank used a separate concurrence to lay out a full-on critique of the objective theory in contract law, a concurrence that caught the eye of the professoriate and that still appears in some casebooks and treatises today. Rather than "treat virtually all the varieties of contractual arrangements" alike and every bargainer as "the 'reasonable man,'" Frank argued, "the modern trend" was toward "a special doctrine" granting liberal relief from personal injury releases in cases involving extreme inequalities of bargaining power. The objectivists, Frank pointed out, could only preserve their theory as an accurate description of contract law by treating these exceptions as matters of equity, much as we saw Justice Miller do in *Wilkinson*. Frank urged courts to treat the exception as the rule. "[T]he ordinary employee" who signed away his personal injury claim should be treated the same way that sailors and other "necessitous persons" had always been treated: as people "under strong economic pressures, who, because of their helplessness, are to be protected from hard bargains." They were, as Joseph Story wrote in 1823 (and as Freedmen's Bureau officers held in 1865 and George Reno's lawyer argued in 1916), "under the dominion and influence of [other] men"—so much weaker than their employers, Frank insisted, that "free bargaining" was a mirage. To keep companies like the Pennsylvania Railroad from using penny-ante payoffs to escape their liabilities, courts should strictly scrutinize employee releases to find "the actual intention" of the parties.

"Maybe it didn't matter that Sydney Ricketts was Black. After all, *Ricketts* was one of a long line of cases by sailors and train workers and other employees, most of whom were white. And of course, Frank did not want to limit his argument to Black employees.

"But *Ricketts* became a staple of law school teaching, just as Frank intended, and precisely because of his choices about race. In Sydney Ricketts, Frank had tapped a racial icon to be the face of the "modern trend" toward the subjective approach and its frank recognition of unequal bargaining power: the railroad waiter. In those days, waiters and porters on the big eastern and midwestern railroads were almost invariably Black men, and their signature role was to act as personal servants to passengers, who were mostly white. They had two bosses, not one: the railroad and the passengers. Waiters and porters depended on tips for more than half their income, as Ricketts himself pointed out. And they earned those tips by flattering and "mak[ing] a fuss over" passengers, whisking heavy trays across the swaying stage of a speeding railcar, all while smilingly obeying their white stewards, who held "absolute[ ] . . . power" to dock pay, suspend, or fire them for any reason. Justice Story's "helpless" sailors had been far out to sea, where few people could see. By contrast, the friendly Black waiter and porter were such well-known personae that railroads featured them in advertisements. In short, Black railroad waiters were the most visible group of American workers for whom bargaining inequality was not just inherent, but on display, personified in the form of personal "service." We have lost that context today, and even then, the unionizing of porters was weakening their association with personal servitude. But to Jerome Frank and his fellow judges and law professors riding the train between New Haven, New York, and Washington, Sydney Ricketts' Blackness would have been so obvious as to go unspoken, just as students today, steeped in political rhetoric about Black poverty, assume that the defendant in *Williams v. Walker-Thomas Furniture* was Black even though, like *Ricketts*, the reported case does not say so.

"Ricketts' race was essential for establishing Frank's theoretical point, yet simultaneously had to be effaced for that theory to reach beyond "race" cases. Much like the late-nineteenth-century critics of "contract freedom" and the Realist attack on the "voluntaristic fallacy," Frank needed Sydney Ricketts (the man) to be "colored" but *Ricketts* (the case) to be *not* "colored." *Ricketts* provided a useful fact pattern for theorizing inequality of bargaining position because being Black was integral to the railroad waiter's job, because lost tips were the main measure of his damages, and because his ignorant helplessness was the key to Frank's rule requiring strict scrutiny of workers' personal-injury releases. At a moment when "civil rights" was becoming synonymous with a struggle for racial equality—when, as *Life Magazine* put it, "Civil rights . . . means Negro rights"—Frank kept *Ricketts* in the domain of contract law by leaving implicit the fact that Ricketts was Black. Frank used this Black man's weak position to formulate a theory of assent that helped all contracting parties who bargained from a weak position, without claiming, as white union leaders had done in the aftermath of emancipation, that wage labor itself amounted to slavery. As we will see, Frank's formulation appears today in leading casebooks as the paradigmatic Realist approach to contract formation.

"As legal liberals—heirs to the Realist tradition—invented "the law of the poor" in the 1950s and 1960s, they reinvented the "ignorant negro" for the modern age. But now it had lost the complex associations with literacy, common sense, racism, and business custom that had made it such a flawed yet durable tool for Black southerners. Above all, it meant presuming that Black people knew nothing about law, that they were ignorant not only of the intricate terms hidden in fine-print boilerplate but of basic legal concepts and principles. In fact, as we saw in Part I, African Americans had been actively engaged in contract law since before the Civil War. My great-uncle and aunt, Thomas and Annie Holcomb, knew that the words "default," and "due and payable" meant pretty much the same thing on a refrigerator contract in New Jersey as when you bought a farm or a mule back home in Virginia. But if "the law of the poor" was going to have a fighting chance in the courts, the poor could not just be poor. They had to be ignorant, too."

———

Donovan v. RRL Corp.

26 Cal.4th 261, 109 Cal. Rptr.2d 807, 27 P.3d 702 (2001)

Defendant advertised a used 1995 Jaguar with a retail value of over $36,000 for sale at a price of $25,995 as a result of an error by a newspaper in preparing ad copy. Plaintiff went to defendant's dealership, test drove the car, and tried to accept the offer, showing the salesperson the advertisement. Defendant's salesperson immediately informed plaintiff the price in the ad was a mistake. Plaintiff sued for breach of contract when defendant refused to sell him the car at the advertised price. The lower courts held that the advertisement was an offer and that the ad satisfied the statute of frauds. The municipal court held for the defendant on ground of unilateral mistake, finding the mistake was made in good faith and the defendant had not intended to deceive the public. The court of appeals reversed, finding that defendant's failure to review a proof sheet of the advertisement constituted negligence, which precluded relief on ground of unilateral mistake. Reversed.

(George, C.J.) "Under the first Restatement of Contracts, unilateral mistake did not render a contract voidable unless the other party knew of or caused the mistake. (1 Witkin, . . . Contracts, § 370, p. 337; see Rest., Contracts, § 503.) In *Germain etc. Co. v. Western Union etc. Co.* (1902) 137 Cal. 598, 602, 70 P. 658, this court endorsed a rule similar to that of the first Restatement. Our opinion indicated that a seller's price quotation erroneously transcribed and delivered by a telegraph company contractually could bind the seller to the incorrect price, unless the buyer knew or had reason to suspect that a mistake had been made. Some decisions of the Court of Appeal have adhered to the approach of the original Restatement. (See, e.g., *Conservatorship of O'Connor* (1996) 48 Cal.App.4th 1076, 1097–1098, 56 Cal.Rptr.2d 386, and cases cited therein.) Plaintiff also advocates this approach and contends that rescission is unavailable to defendant, because plaintiff was unaware of the mistaken price in defendant's advertisement when he accepted the offer.

". . . California law does not adhere to the original Restatement's requirements for rescission based upon unilateral mistake of fact—i.e., only in circumstances where the other party knew of the mistake or caused the mistake. . . . [T]he Restatement Second of Contracts authorizes rescission for a unilateral mistake of fact where "the effect of the mistake is such that enforcement of the contract would be unconscionable." (Rest.2d Contracts, § 153, subd. (a).)[6] The comment following this section recognizes "a growing willingness to allow avoidance where the consequences of the mistake are so grave that enforcement of the contract would be unconscionable." (*Id.*, com. a, p. 394.) Indeed, two of the illustrations recognizing this additional ground for

---

[6]   Section 153 of the Restatement Second of Contracts states: "Where a mistake of one party at the time a contract was made as to a basic assumption on which he made the contract has a material effect on the agreed exchange of performances that is adverse to him, the contract is voidable by him if he does not bear the risk of the mistake under the rule stated in § 154, and [¶] (a) the effect of the mistake is such that enforcement of the contract would be unconscionable, or [¶] (b) the other party had reason to know of the mistake or his fault caused the mistake."

rescission in the Restatement Second of Contracts are based in part upon this court's decisions in [*M.F. Kemper Const. Co. v. City of L.A.* (1951) 37 Cal.2d 696, 701, 235 P.2d 7 (*Kemper*)] and [*Elsinore Union etc. Sch. Dist. v. Kastorff* (1960) 54 Cal.2d 380, 6 Cal.Rptr. 1, 353 P.2d 713 (*Elsinore*). (Rest.2d Contracts, § 153, com. c, illus. 1, 3, pp. 395, 396, and Reporter's Note, pp. 400–401. . . . Although the most common types of mistakes falling within this category occur in bids on construction contracts, section 153 of the Restatement Second of Contracts is not limited to such cases. (Rest.2d Contracts, § 153, com. b, p. 395.)

"Because the rule in section 153, subdivision (a), of the Restatement Second of Contracts, authorizing rescission for unilateral mistake of fact where enforcement would be unconscionable, is consistent with our previous decisions, we adopt the rule as California law. As the author of one treatise recognized more than 40 years ago, the decisions that are inconsistent with the traditional rule "are too numerous and too appealing to the sense of justice to be disregarded." (3 Corbin, Contracts (1960) § 608, p. 675, fn. omitted.) We reject plaintiff's contention and the Court of Appeal's conclusion that, because plaintiff was unaware of defendant's unilateral mistake, the mistake does not provide a ground to avoid enforcement of the contract. . . .

"Civil Code section 1577, as well as our prior decisions, instructs that the risk of a mistake must be allocated to a party where the mistake results from that party's neglect of a legal duty. (*Kemper, supra,* 37 Cal.2d at p. 701, 235 P.2d 7.) It is well established, however, that ordinary negligence does not constitute neglect of a legal duty within the meaning of Civil Code section 1577. (*Kemper, supra,* 37 Cal.2d at p. 702, 235 P.2d 7.) For example, we have described a careless but significant mistake in the computation of the contract price as the type of error that sometimes will occur in the conduct of reasonable and cautious businesspersons, and such an error does not necessarily amount to neglect of legal duty that would bar equitable relief. (*Ibid.;* see also *Sun 'n Sand, Inc. v. United California Bank* (1978) 21 Cal.3d 671, 700–701, 148 Cal.Rptr. 329, 582 P.2d 920 (plur. opn. of Mosk, J.); *Elsinore, supra,* 54 Cal.2d at pp. 388–389, 6 Cal.Rptr. 1, 353 P.2d 713.)

"A concept similar to neglect of a legal duty is described in section 157 of the Restatement Second of Contracts, which addresses situations in which a party's fault precludes relief for mistake. Only where the mistake results from "a failure to act in good faith and in accordance with reasonable standards of fair dealing" is rescission unavailable. (Rest.2d Contracts, § 157.) This section, consistent with the California decisions cited in the preceding paragraph, provides that a mistaken party's failure to exercise due care does not necessarily bar rescission under the rule set forth in section 153.

" 'The mere fact that a mistaken party could have avoided the mistake by the exercise of reasonable care does not preclude . . . avoidance . . . [on the ground of mistake]. Indeed, since a party can often avoid a mistake by the exercise of such care, the availability of relief would be severely circumscribed if he were to be barred by his negligence. Nevertheless, in *extreme cases* the mistaken party's fault is a proper ground for denying him relief for a mistake that he otherwise could have avoided. . . . [T]he rule is stated in terms of good faith and fair dealing. . . . The terms 'good faith' and 'fair dealing' are used, in this context, in much the same sense as in . . . Uniform Commercial Code § 1–203.' " (Rest.2d Contracts, § 157, com. a, pp. 416–417, italics added.) Section 1201, subdivision (19), of the California Uniform Commercial Code defines "good faith," as used in section 1203 of that code, as "honesty in fact in the conduct or transaction concerned." . . .

"No evidence presented at trial suggested that defendant knew of the mistake before plaintiff attempted to purchase the automobile, that defendant intended to mislead customers, or that it had adopted a practice of deliberate indifference regarding errors in advertisements. Wadsworth regularly reviews proof sheets for the numerous advertisements placed by defendant, and representatives of the newspapers, including the Daily Pilot, also proofread defendant's advertisements to ensure they are accurate. Defendant follows procedures for notifying its sales staff and customers of errors of which it becomes aware. The uncontradicted evidence established that the Daily Pilot made the proofreading error resulting in defendant's mistake.

"Defendant's fault consisted of failing to review a proof sheet reflecting the change made on Thursday, April 24, 1997, and/or the actual advertisement appearing in the April 26 edition of the Daily Pilot—choosing instead to rely upon the Daily Pilot's advertising staff to proofread the revised version. Although, as the Court of Appeal found, such an omission might constitute negligence, it does not involve a breach of defendant's duty of good faith and fair dealing that should preclude equitable relief for mistake. In these circumstances, it would not be reasonable for this court to allocate the risk of the mistake to defendant."

———

In re UAL Corporation

411 F.3d 818 (2005)

UAL filed a motion to vacate on the ground of excusable neglect an order of the bankruptcy court that it had requested. UAL claimed that it had mistakenly elected not to abandon three airplane leases, as was its right under bankruptcy law, because it was unaware that it owed several million dollars on the leases. The bankruptcy court granted the motion. Affirmed, in an opinion drawing on the law of unilateral mistake.

(Posner, J.) "We agree with the bankruptcy court that this is a case of excusable neglect within the meaning of Rule 60(b). United's mistake in failing to abandon the leases was excusable, but not because their number and complexity and the 60-day deadline for sorting through them and figuring out which to abandon and which to keep made mistakes inevitable. That would make it a case not of excusable *neglect,* but of unavoidable error. See *Pioneer Investment Services Co. v. Brunswick Associates Limited Partnership,* 507 U.S. 380, 394–95, 113 S.Ct. 1489, 123 L.Ed.2d 74 (1993). United is a huge company represented by one of the nation's largest law firms (Kirkland & Ellis). Sixty days in which to sort through some 460 leases requires examining on average fewer than eight leases per day, and all that had to be determined was whether United owed any money on the lease; if it did, it would abandon the lease and if not, not.

"Had the beneficiaries of the mistake, the airplanes' owners, relied to their detriment on it, United would not be entitled to relief. *General Electric Capital Corp. v. Central Bank,* 49 F.3d 280, 284–86 (7th Cir.1995); *Equilease Corp. v. Hentz,* 634 F.2d 850, 854 (5th Cir.1981); *Strubbe v. Sonnenschein,* 299 F.2d 185, 192 (2d Cir.1962); *Bank of Naperville v. Catalano,* 86 Ill.App.3d 1005, 42 Ill.Dec. 63, 408 N.E.2d 441, 445–46 (1980). This is a general limitation on restitution unless restitution is sought against a defrauder or other wrongdoer; it is not a limitation that is special to mistake cases. See, e.g., *Amalgamated Ass'n of Street Electric Ry. & Motor Coach Employees of America v. Danielson,* 24 Wis.2d 33, 128 N.W.2d 9, 10–11 (1964); *Restatement of Restitution* § 69 (1937). But the owners do not argue that they relied . . . .

"Even without reliance, it can be argued that United is entitled to no relief because a unilateral mistake by a contract party, as distinct from a mutual mistake, is not a generally recognized excuse for failing to comply with the contract's terms. *Praxair, Inc. v. Hinshaw & Culbertson,* 235 F.3d 1028, 1034–35 (7th Cir.2000); II. E. Allan Farnsworth, *Contracts* § 9.4, p. 614 (3d ed.2004). But the qualification in "generally" is, as so often in law, critical. Nor is the qualification limited to trivial errors in the administration of a contract, as where one party pays the other the wrong amount because of a mistake in calculation. That by the way is a classic case for restitution even if the mistake was careless-always provided, however, that the payee had not relied on it, to his disadvantage if it is corrected. . . .

"Closest to the present case is a line of cases illustrated by *M.F. Kemper Construction Co. v. City of Los Angeles,* 37 Cal.2d 696, 235 P.2d 7 (1951); see also *Donovan v. RRL Corp,* 26 Cal.4th 261, 109 Cal.Rptr.2d 807, 27 P.3d 702, 714–17 (2001) . . . . As succinctly explained in *Donovan v. RRL Corp., supra,* 109 Cal.Rptr.2d 807, 27 P.3d at 715, "the plaintiff in *Kemper* inadvertently omitted a $301,769 item from its bid for the defendant city's public works project-approximately one-third of the total contract price. After discovering the mistake several hours later, the plaintiff immediately notified the city and subsequently withdrew its bid. Nevertheless, the city accepted the erroneous bid, contending that rescission of the offer was unavailable for the plaintiff's unilateral mistake." The court rejected the city's argument. When an innocent mistake can be rectified without harm to anyone (loss of a windfall is not the kind of harm that a court should endeavor to avert), it should be. Especially in a case such as this. If the mistake is not corrected, the cost will be borne not by its maker—United—but by creditors no less innocent than the airplanes' owners. A refusal to correct would serve no deterrent or punitive purpose; it would merely redistribute wealth among creditors capriciously. . . .

"The principle of the mistaken-bid cases must not be pressed too far. Otherwise the courts would be drowned in disputes over whether, for example, a seller had made a mistake in charging such a low price-had he studied market conditions more carefully he would have realized that the buyer would have been willing to pay more. Cases like *Kemper* and *Boise* distinguish between an obvious error, such as an error in computation, and an "error of judgment," which if a ground of restitution would make every contract party a kind of fiduciary of the opposing party, end arm's length bargaining, and make contractual obligations radically uncertain. The present case, however, is closer to the computation-error pole than to the error-of-judgment pole. Indeed, for all we know, it *was* a computation error that precipitated United's decision not to abandon the three leases."

RESTATEMENT, SECOND, CONTRACTS §§ 153, 154

[See Selected Source Materials Supplement]

NOTE ON UNILATERAL MISTAKE IN THE CONTRACTS RESTATEMENTS

Learned Hand may not rely on the doctrine of unilateral mistake in *Ricketts* because relief was not available under Restatement First. It does not allow relief for unilateral mistake as such.[1] A mistake regarding the content of a writing is covered by rules on reformation.[2] A mistake in an expression of agreement is covered by rules on offer and acceptance.[3] Under these rules, Ricketts would have to establish that the railroad company's agent knew Ricketts mistakenly believed the paper he signed was merely a receipt.

The caselaw was more generous than this rule for it also allowed relief from a mistake about the content of a writing (or in an expression of agreement) if the other party had reason to know of the mistake.[4] Restatement First adopts the more generous reason-to-know rule in rules on misrepresentation[5] and duty to disclose,[6] which cover unilateral mistakes that do not involve a mistake regarding the content of a writing or in an expression of agreement. These rules would cover a computational error like that in

---

[1] Restatement First § 503 ("A mistake of only one party that forms the basis on which he enters into a transaction does not of itself render the transaction voidable . . .")

[2] Restatement First §§ 504 and 505.

[3] Restatement First § 71.

[4] See, e.g., Travelers Ins. Co. v. Bailey, 124 Vt. 114, 197 A.2d 813 (1964).

[5] Restatement First § 476.

[6] Restatement First § 503, Comment ("Additional facts stated in the chapter on fraud may render a transaction voidable where one party only is under a mistake, namely, 1, where the mistake of one party is due to the fault of the other (see § 476), or, 2, a party knows or has reason to know there is a mistake when the transaction is entered into (see § 472(b).")

DePrince v. Starboard Cruise Services, Inc.[7] A large diamond with an intended retail price of $4,850,400 was sold to a passenger aboard a cruise ship for $235,000. The clerk, who knew little about diamonds, assumed the per carat price was the price of the diamond. Under Restatement First's duty to disclose rule Starboard could avoid the contract to sell the diamond if DePrince knew or had reason to know the clerk had made a mistake in calculating the price.

The caselaw was more generous than Restatement First in another respect. Some cases allowed relief if the other party had not changed their position in reliance on the contract. Jerome Frank's concurring opinion in *Ricketts* relies on these cases because there was no evidence the railroad company's agent knew or had reason to know Ricketts mistakenly thought the paper he signed was merely a receipt. This is an alternative basis for avoiding the contract in *DePrince* because the mistake was discovered before the ship landed and the diamond was delivered to DePrince.

Restatement Second Section 153 adopts the more generous positions. It allows relief if "the other party had reason of the mistake or his fault caused the mistake,"[8] or if "the effect of the mistake is such that enforcement of the contract would be unconscionable."[9] In addition, the party seeking relief must not bear the risk of the mistake under one of three rules: "the risk is allocated to him by agreement of the parties,"[10] "he is aware at the time the contract is made, that he has only limited knowledge with respect to the facts to which the mistake relates but treats his limited knowledge as sufficient,"[11] or "the risk is allocated to him by the court on the ground that it is reasonable in the circumstances to do so."[12]

The mistake claims in *Ricketts* and *DePrince* do not run afoul of the three risk-allocation rules. They also satisfy two factors identified by the Restatement that go to establishing unconscionability. The mistake caused a large loss and gain[13] and the other party had not changed his position in reliance on the contract.[14] These factors may be necessary to establish "enforcement of the contract would be unconscionable," but they clearly are not sufficient. This position is untenable for it would allow a contract to be avoided

---

[7] 163 So.3d 586 (2015). The court of appeals address rules similar to those in both restatements because Florida law is unsettled.

[8] Restatement Second § 153(b).

[9] Restatement Second § 153(a).

[10] Restatement Second § 154(a).

[11] Restatement Second § 154(b). Restatement, Third, Restitution and Unjust Enrichment § 5(3)(b) expressly this more felicitously as "the claimant has consciously assumed the risk by deciding to act in the face of a recognized uncertainty."

[12] Restatement Second § 154(c). Restatement, Third, Restitution and Unjust Enrichment § 5(3)(b) expressly this as "allocation to the claimant of a risk in question accords with the common understanding of the transaction concerned."

[13] Restatement, Second, Torts § 553, Comment c. If the Restatement had expressed the animating concern as unjust enrichment, rather than unconscionability, this would make the issue clearer.

[14] Restatement Second § 553, Comment d.

in a case like *Wood v. Boynton*.[15] The plaintiff sold a small stone she found to a jeweler for $1. The stone turned out to be a diamond worth about $700.

As for what else is required for relief, Restatement Second never says relief for mistake is readily given for some types of mistakes (e.g., mistakes in an expression of agreement and computational errors) and is rarely given for other types of mistakes (e.g., mistakes about something's value). Andrew Kull, Unilateral Mistake: The Baseball Card Case, 70 Wash. U.L.Q. 59, 74–75 (1992), suggests a plausible reason why Restatement Second's authors left this unsaid. Saying this might have led courts to limit relief to cases involving the types of errors for which courts readily give relief. Kull infers Restatement Second's authors wanted a broader rule to give courts an additional tool to police unfair transactions. They may not have drawn this line for another reason. Courts sometimes allow people to avoid contracts because of a mistake about something's value. Numerous cases allow rescission of a release of a personal injury claim when the releasee's mistake concerned the severity of their injuries.[16]

SECTION 3. MUTUAL MISTAKE

Another important type of mistake in contract law consists of a mistaken factual assumption about the present state of the world that affects the value of an agreed exchange. An example is when an individual releases a personal injury claim for a minor sum of money because they are mistaken about the severity of their injuries.

A mistaken factual assumption may either be shared by both parties to a contract or held by only one of the parties. Traditionally, shared mistaken factual assumptions have been treated under the heading of mutual mistake, meaning a mistake that is shared by both parties. This terminology fails to differentiate among shared mistakes according to their functional characteristics. Some kinds of shared mistakes should provide a basis for relief, while others should not. For example, if Team A trades Player P to Team B, and both teams share a mistake about just how fast or how strong P is, that mistake should not and would not give either team the right to rescind the trade. Even shared mistakes that should provide a basis for relief fall into different functional categories that require differing treatment. For example, in mistranscription cases the parties both mistakenly believe that the writing properly transcribes the bargain. The appropriate remedy here normally is reformation, not recission.

---

[15] 64 Wis. 265, 25 N.W. 42 (1885).

[16] Casey v. Proctor, 378 P.2d 579, 587 (Cal. 1963)(reporting "the majority of jurisdictions permit a releaser under proper circumstances to avoid a release, regardless of its terms, where it appears that unknown injuries existed at the time it was executed."). For an up-to-date report see Grace M. Giesel, A New Look at Contract Mistake Doctrine and Personal Injury Releases, 19 Nev. L.J. 535, 556–565 (2018).

In short, that a mistake is shared is relevant but it is not critical. What is critical is the character of the shared mistake. That character is captured in the term *shared mistaken factual assumptions*.

In analyzing shared mistaken factual assumptions, it is useful to begin with assumptions that are made explicit in a contract. If a contract is explicitly based on a shared mistaken factual assumption, normally the mistake would furnish a basis for relief under a relatively straightforward interpretation of the language of the contract. For example, suppose A agrees to sell a plot of land, Tenacre, to B, and the contract provides, "This agreement is made on the assumption that Tenacre is zoned for commercial use." If it turns out that Tenacre is not zoned for commercial use, it is pretty clear that under the contract, B should be entitled to rescission.

Now suppose a shared mistaken factual assumption is tacit rather than explicit. The concept of a tacit assumption has been explicated as follows by Lon Fuller:

> Words like "intention," "assumption," "expectation" and "understanding" all seem to imply a conscious state involving an awareness of alternatives and a deliberate choice among them. It is, however, plain that there is a psychological state that can be described as a "tacit assumption", which does not involve a consciousness of alternatives. The absent-minded professor stepping from his office into the hall as he reads a book "assumes" that the floor of the hall will be there to receive him. His conduct is conditioned and directed by this assumption, even though the possibility that the floor has been removed does not "occur" to him, that is, is not present in his conscious mental processes.

A more colloquial expression that captures the concept of a tacit assumption is "taken for granted." A tacit assumption is so deeply embedded in an actor's mind that it simply doesn't occur to the actor to make the assumption explicit—any more than it occurs to Fuller's professor to think to himself, every time he is about to walk through a door, "Remember to check that the floor is still in place." Of course, if actors had infinite time and no costs, they would ransack their minds to think through every one of their tacit assumptions, and make each of those assumptions explicit. But actors do not have infinite time and they do have costs. Normally, it would be irrational for a potential contracting party to take the time to determine, and make explicit, every tacit assumption that he holds, because the costs of doing so would often approach or exceed the expected profit from the contract. It would also normally be virtually impossible to make such a determination. As Randy Barnett has stated:

> [When we add] to the infinity of knowledge about the present world the inherent uncertainty of future events ... we immediately can see that the seductive idea that a contract can

... articulate every contingency that might arise before ... performance is sheer fantasy. For this reason, contracts must be silent on an untold number of items. And many of these silent assumptions that underlie every agreement are as basic as the assumption that the sun will rise tomorrow. They are simply too basic to merit mention.

Randy E. Barnett, Contracts: Cases and Doctrine 1163 (2d ed. 1999).

————

SHERWOOD V. WALKER
Supreme Court of Michigan, 1887.
66 Mich. 568, 33 N.W. 919, 11 Am.St.Rep. 531.

MORSE, J. Replevin for a cow. Suit commenced in justice's court; judgment for plaintiff; appealed to circuit court of Wayne county, and verdict and judgment for plaintiff in that court. The defendants bring error, and set out 25 assignments of the same.

The main controversy depends upon the construction of a contract for the sale of the cow. The plaintiff claims that the title passed, and bases his action upon such claim. The defendants contend that the contract was executory, and by its terms no title to the animal was acquired by plaintiff. The defendants reside at Detroit, but are in business at Walkerville, Ontario, and have a farm at Greenfield, in Wayne county, upon which were some blooded cattle supposed to be barren as breeders. The Walkers are importers and breeders of polled Angus cattle. The plaintiff is a banker living at Plymouth, in Wayne county. He called upon the defendants at Walkerville for the purchase of some of their stock, but found none there that suited him. Meeting one of the defendants afterwards, he was informed that they had a few head upon their Greenfield farm. He was asked to go out and look at them, with the statement at the time that they were probably barren, and would not breed. May 5, 1886, plaintiff went out to Greenfield and saw the cattle. A few days thereafter, he called upon one of the defendants with the view of purchasing a cow, known as "Rose 2d of Aberlone." After considerable talk it was agreed that defendants would telephone Sherwood at his home in Plymouth in reference to the price. The second morning after this talk he was called up by telephone, and the terms of the sale were finally agreed upon. He was to pay five and one-half cents per pound, live weight, fifty pounds shrinkage. He was asked how he intended to take the cow home, and replied that he might ship her from King's cattle-yard. He requested defendants to confirm the sale in writing, which they did by sending him the following letter:

"Walkerville, May 15, 1886.

"T.C. Sherwood, President, etc.—Dear Sir: We confirm sale to you of the cow Rose 2d of Aberlone, lot 56 of our catalogue, at five and a half cents per pound, less fifty pounds shrink. We inclose herewith order on Mr. Graham for the cow. You might leave check with him, or mail to us here, as you prefer.

"YOURS TRULY,
HIRAM WALKER & SONS."

The order upon Graham enclosed in the letter read as follows:

"Walkerville, May 15, 1886.

"George Graham: You will please deliver at King's cattle-yard to Mr. T.C. Sherwood, Plymouth, the cow Rose 2d of Aberlone, lot 56 of our catalogue. Send halter with the cow, and have her weighed.

"YOURS TRULY,
HIRAM WALKER & SONS."

On the twenty-first of the same month the plaintiff went to defendants' farm at Greenfield, and presented the order and letter to Graham, who informed him that the defendants had instructed him not to deliver the cow. Soon after, the plaintiff tendered to Hiram Walker, one of the defendants, $80, and demanded the cow. Walker refused to take the money or deliver the cow. The plaintiff then instituted this suit. After he had secured possession of the cow under the writ of replevin, the plaintiff caused her to be weighed by the constable who served the writ, at a place other than King's cattle-yard. She weighed 1,420 pounds.

When the plaintiff, upon the trial in the circuit court, had submitted his proofs showing the above transaction, defendants moved to strike out and exclude the testimony from the case, for the reason that it was irrelevant and did not tend to show that the title to the cow passed, and that it showed that the contract of sale was merely executory. The court refused the motion, and an exception was taken.

The defendants then introduced evidence tending to show that at the time of the alleged sale it was believed by both the plaintiff and themselves that the cow was barren and would not breed; that she cost $850, and if not barren would be worth from $750 to $1,000; that after the date of the letter, and the order to Graham, the defendants were informed by said Graham that in his judgment the cow was with calf, and therefore they instructed him not to deliver her to plaintiff, and on the twentieth of May, 1886, telegraphed plaintiff what Graham thought about the cow being with calf, and that consequently they could not sell her. The cow had a calf in the month of October following.

On the nineteenth of May, the plaintiff wrote Graham as follows:

"Plymouth, May 19, 1886

"Mr. George Graham, Greenfield—Dear Sir: I have bought Rose or Lucy from Mr. Walker, and will be there for her Friday morning, nine or ten o'clock. Do not water her in the morning.

"YOURS, ETC., T.C. SHERWOOD"

Plaintiff explained the mention of the two cows in this letter by testifying that, when he wrote this letter, the order and letter of defendants was at his home, and, writing in a hurry, and being uncertain as to the name of the cow, and not wishing his cow watered, he thought it would do no harm to name them both, as his bill of sale would show which one he had purchased. Plaintiff also testified that he asked defendants to give him a price on the balance of their herd at Greenfield, as a friend thought of buying some, and received a letter dated May 17, 1886, in which they named the price of five cattle, including Lucy, at $90, and Rose 2d at $80. When he received the letter he called defendants up by telephone, and asked them why they put Rose 2d in the list, as he had already purchased her. They replied that they knew he had, but thought it would make no difference if plaintiff and his friend concluded to take the whole herd.

The foregoing is the substance of all the testimony in the case.

The circuit judge instructed the jury that if they believed the defendants, when they sent the order and letter to plaintiff, meant to pass the title to the cow, and that the cow was intended to be delivered to plaintiff, it did not matter whether the cow was weighed at any particular place, or by any particular person; and if the cow was weighed afterwards, as Sherwood testified, such weighing would be a sufficient compliance with the order. If they believed that defendants intended to pass the title by writing, it did not matter whether the cow was weighed before or after suit brought, and the plaintiff would be entitled to recover.

The defendants submitted a number of requests which were refused. The substance of them was that the cow was never delivered to plaintiff, and the title to her did not pass by the letter and order; and that under the contract, as evidenced by these writings, the title did not pass until the cow was weighed and her price thereby determined; and that, if the defendants only agreed to sell a cow that would not breed, then the barrenness of the cow was a condition precedent to passing title, and plaintiff cannot recover. The court also charged the jury that it was immaterial whether the cow was with calf or not. It will therefore be seen that the defendants claim that, as a matter of law, the title of this cow did not pass, and that the circuit judge erred in submitting the case to the jury, to be determined by them, upon the intent of the parties as to whether or not the title passed with the sending of the letter and order by the defendants to the plaintiff. . . .

It appears from the record that both parties supposed this cow was barren and would not breed, and she was sold by the pound for an insignificant sum as compared with her real value if a breeder. She was evidently sold and purchased on the relation of her value for beef, unless the plaintiff had learned of her true condition, and concealed such knowledge from the defendants. Before the plaintiff secured the possession of the animal, the defendants learned that she was with calf, and therefore of great value, and undertook to rescind the sale by refusing to deliver her. The question arises whether they had a right to do so. The circuit judge ruled that this fact did not avoid the sale and it made no difference whether she was barren or not. I am of the opinion that the court erred in this holding. I know that this is a close question, and the dividing line between the adjudicated cases is not easily discerned. But it must be considered as well settled that a party who has given an apparent consent to a contract of sale may refuse to execute it, or he may avoid it after it has been completed, if the assent was founded, or the contract made, upon the mistake of a material fact,—such as the subject-matter of the sale, the price, or some collateral fact materially inducing the agreement; and this can be done when the mistake is mutual. . . .

If there is a difference or misapprehension as to the substance of the thing bargained for; if the thing actually delivered or received is different in substance from the thing bargained for, and intended to be sold,—then there is no contract; but if it be only a difference in some quality or accident, even though the mistake may have been the actuating motive to the purchaser or seller, or both of them, yet the contract remains binding. "The difficulty in every case is to determine whether the mistake or misapprehension is as to the substance of the whole contract, going, as it were, to the root of the matter, or only to some point, even though a material point, an error as to which does not affect the substance of the whole consideration." Kennedy v. Panama, etc., Mail Co., L.R. 2 Q.B. 580, 588. It has been held, in accordance with the principles above stated, that where a horse is bought under the belief that he is sound, and both vendor and vendee honestly believe him to be sound, the purchaser must stand by his bargain, and pay the full price, unless there was a warranty.

It seems to me, however, in the case made by this record, that the mistake or misapprehension of the parties went to the whole substance of the agreement. If the cow was a breeder, she was worth at least $750; if barren, she was worth not over $80. The parties would not have made the contract of sale except upon the understanding and belief that she was incapable of breeding, and of no use as a cow. It is true she is now the identical animal that they thought her to be when the contract was made; there is no mistake as to the identity of the creature. Yet the mistake was not of the mere quality of the animal, but went to the very nature of the thing. A barren cow is substantially a different creature than a breeding one. There is as much difference between them for all purposes of use as there is between an ox and a cow that is capable of breeding and giving milk. If the mutual mistake had simply related to the fact whether she was with calf or not for one season, then it might have been a good sale, but the mistake affected the character of the animal for all time, and for its present and ultimate use. She was not in fact the animal, or the kind of animal, the defendants intended to sell or the plaintiff to buy. She was not a barren cow, and, if this fact had been known, there would have been no contract. The mistake affected the substance of the whole consideration, and it must be considered that there was no contract to sell or sale of the cow as she actually was. The thing sold and bought had in fact no existence. She was sold as a beef creature would be sold; she is in fact a breeding cow, and a valuable one. The court should have instructed the jury that if they found that the cow was sold, or contracted to be sold, upon the understanding of both parties that she was barren, and useless for the purpose of breeding, and that in fact she was not barren, but capable of breeding, then the defendants had a right to rescind, and refuse to deliver, and the verdict should be in their favor.

The judgment of the court below must be reversed, and a new trial granted, with costs of this court to defendants.

CAMPBELL, C.J., and CHAMPLIN, J., concurred.

SHERWOOD, J. (dissenting). I do not concur in the opinion given by my brethren in this case. . . .

As has already been stated by my brethren, the record shows that the plaintiff is a banker and a farmer as well, carrying on a farm, and raising the best breeds of stock, and lived in Plymouth, in the county of Wayne, 23 miles from Detroit; that the defendants lived in Detroit, and were also dealers in stock of the higher grades; that they had a farm at Walkerville, in Canada, and also one in Greenfield in said county of Wayne, and upon these farms the defendants kept their stock. The Greenfield farm was about 15 miles from the plaintiff's. In the spring of 1886 the plaintiff, learning that the defendants had some "polled Angus cattle" for sale, was desirous of purchasing some of that breed, and meeting the defendants, or some of them, at Walkerville, inquired about them, and was informed that they had none at Walkerville, "but had a few head left on their farm in Greenfield, and asked the plaintiff to go and see them, stating that in all probability they were sterile and would not breed." . . . The record further shows that the defendants, when they sold the cow, believed the cow was not with calf, and barren; that from what the plaintiff had been told by defendants (for it does not appear he had any other knowledge or facts from which he could form an opinion) he believed the cow was farrow, but still thought she could be made to breed. The foregoing shows the entire interview and treaty between the parties as to the sterility and qualities of the cow sold to the plaintiff. The cow had a calf in the month of October.

There is no question but that the defendants sold the cow representing her of the breed and quality they believed the cow to be, and that the purchaser so understood it. And the buyer purchased her believing her to be of the breed represented by the sellers, and possessing all the qualities stated, and even more. He believed she would breed. There is no pretense that the plaintiff bought the cow for beef, and there is nothing in the record indicating that he would have bought her at all only that he thought she might be made to breed. Under the foregoing facts,—and these are all that are contained in the record material to the contract,—it is held that because it turned out that the plaintiff was more correct in his judgment as to one quality of the cow than the defendants, and a quality, too, which could not by any possibility be positively known at the time by either party to exist, the contract may be annulled by the defendants at their pleasure. I know of no law, and have not been referred to any, which will justify any such holding, and I think the circuit judge was right in his construction of the contract between the parties.

It is claimed that a mutual mistake of a material fact was made by the parties when the contract of sale was made. There was no warranty in the case of the quality of the animal. When a mistaken fact is relied upon as ground for rescinding, such fact must not only exist at the time the contract is made, but must have been known to one or both of the parties. Where there is no warranty, there can be no mistake of fact when no such fact exists, or, if in existence, neither party knew of it, or could know of it; and that is precisely this case. If the owner of a Hambletonian horse had speeded him, and was only able to make him go a mile in three minutes, and should sell him to another, believing that was his greatest speed, for $300, when the purchaser believed he could go much faster, and made the purchase for that sum, and a few days thereafter, under more favorable circumstances, the horse was driven a mile in 2 min. 16 sec., and was found to be worth $20,000, I hardly think it would be held, either at law or in equity, by any one, that the seller in such case could rescind the contract. The same legal principles apply in each case.

In this case neither party knew the actual quality and condition of this cow at the time of the sale. The defendants say, or rather said, to the plaintiff, "they had a few head left on their farm in Greenfield, and asked plaintiff to go and see them, stating to plaintiff that in all probability they were sterile and would not breed." Plaintiff did go as requested, and found there these cows, including the one purchased, with a bull. The cow had been exposed, but neither knew she was with calf or whether she would breed. The defendants thought she would not, but the plaintiff says that he thought she could be made to breed, but believed she was not with calf. The defendants sold the cow for what they believed her to be, and the plaintiff bought her as he believed she was, after the statements made by the defendants. No conditions whatever were attached to the terms of sale by either party. It was in fact as absolute as it could well be made, and I know of no precedent as authority by which this court can alter the contract thus made by these parties in writing, and interpolate in it a condition by which, if the *defendants should be mistaken in their belief that the cow was barren,* she could be returned to them and their contract should be annulled. It is not the duty of courts to destroy contracts when called upon to enforce them, after they have been legally made. There was no mistake of any material fact by either of the parties in the case as would license the vendors to rescind. There was no difference between the parties, nor misapprehension, as to the substance of the thing bargained for, which was a cow supposed to be barren by one party, and believed not to be by the other. As to the quality of the animal, subsequently developed, both parties were equally ignorant, and as to this each party took his chances. If this were not the law, there would be no safety in purchasing this kind of stock.

I entirely agree with my brethren that the right to rescind occurs whenever "the thing actually delivered or received is different in substance from the thing bargained for, and intended to be sold; but if it be only a difference in some quality or accident, even though the misapprehension may have been the actuating motive" of the parties in making the contract, yet it will remain binding. In this case the cow sold was the one delivered. What might or might not happen to her after the sale formed no element in the contract. . . .

————

Nester v. Michigan Land & Iron Co.

69 Mich. 290, 37 N.W. 278 (1888)

In September 1885, Michigan Land entered into a written contract with Nester, under which Michigan Land sold to Nester all the merchantable pine on certain land. Michigan Land made no representation to Nester that it intended Nester to rely upon, or that he did rely upon, in making his purchase. Prior to the sale, Michigan Land's agent told Nester that if he purchased the timber he had to do so on the basis of his own estimate. Nester had such an estimate made, and knew that an estimate could not be made with any degree of certainty—to use the language of his estimate, that "it is all guesswork any way." After the purchase, Nester sued to reduce the purchase price by 50% on the ground that both parties were mistaken in their estimate of the quality of the timber on the land; that a large portion of the timber was unsound; and that in consequence of the amount of decayed timber, the yield of merchantable pine furnished only about half the quantity of such pine that was anticipated or estimated. The case was decided by the Michigan Supreme Court, one year after Sherwood v. Walker. The opinion was written by Judge Sherwood, who had dissented in Sherwood v. Walker, and then had become Chief Judge of the Court. Held, for Michigan Land.

"We know of no case which will sustain the complainant's case upon the facts before us. That of *Sherwood v. Walker* . . . will come the nearest to it of any referred to. That is, however, somewhat different upon its facts, and the rule applied in that case can never be resorted to except in a case where all the facts and circumstances are precisely the same as in that." There were no dissents.

Wood v. Boynton

64 Wis. 265, 25 N.W. 42 (1885)

Wood had found a small stone about the size of a canary egg. Subsequently, she sold the stone for $1 to Boynton, who was in the jewelry business. Afterwards, it was ascertained that the stone was a rough diamond, worth about $700. After learning this fact, Wood tendered $1 plus 10¢ interest to Boynton, and demanded a return of the stone. Boynton refused, and Wood brought an action for rescission.

At the trial, Wood testified: "The first time Boynton saw that stone he was talking about buying the topaz, or whatever it is, in September or October. I went into the store to get a little pin mended, and I had it in a small box,—the pin,—a small ear-ring; . . . this stone, and a broken sleeve—button were in the box. Mr. Boynton turned to give me a check for my pin. I thought I would ask him what the stone was, and I took it out of the box and asked him to please tell me what that was. He took it in his hand and seemed some time looking at it. I told him I had been told it was a topaz, and he said it might be. He says, 'I would buy this; would you sell it?' I told him I did not know but what I would. What would it be worth? And he said he did not know; he would give me a dollar and keep it as a specimen, and I told him I would not sell it. . . . Afterwards, and about the twenty-eighth of December, I needed money pretty badly, and thought every dollar would help, and I took it back to Mr. Boynton and told him I had brought back the topaz, and he says, 'Well, yes; what did I offer you for it?' and I says, 'One dollar;' and he stepped to the change drawer and gave me the dollar, and I went out." Boynton testified that at the time he bought the stone he had never seen an uncut diamond; "he had no idea this was a diamond, and it never entered his brain at the time." Held, for Boynton:

> In this case, upon the plaintiff's own evidence, there can be no just ground for alleging that she was induced to make the sale she did by any fraud or unfair dealings on the part of Mr. Boynton. Both were entirely ignorant at the time of the character of the stone and of its intrinsic value. Mr. Boynton was not an expert in uncut diamonds, and had made no examination of the stone, except to take it in his hand and look at it before he made the offer of one dollar, which was refused at the time, and afterwards accepted without any comment

or further examination made by Mr. Boynton. The appellant had the stone in her possession for a long time, and it appears from her own statement that she had made some inquiry as to its nature and qualities. If she chose to sell it without further investigation as to its intrinsic value to a person who was guilty of no fraud or unfairness which induced her to sell it for a small sum, she cannot repudiate the sale because it is afterwards ascertained that she made a bad bargain. Kennedy v. Panama, etc., Mail Co., L.R. 2 Q.B. 580. There is no pretense of any mistake as to the identity of the thing sold. It was produced by the plaintiff and exhibited to the vendee before the sale was made, and the thing sold was delivered to the vendee when the purchase price was paid. . . . Suppose the appellant had produced the stone, and said she had been told it was a diamond, and she believed it was, but had no knowledge herself as to its character or value, and Mr. Boynton had given her $500 for it, could he have rescinded the sale if it had turned out to be a topaz or any other stone of very small value? Could Mr. Boynton have rescinded the sale on the ground of mistake? Clearly not. . . .

It is urged, with a good deal of earnestness, on the part of the counsel for the appellant that, because it has turned out that the stone was immensely more valuable than the parties at the time of the sale supposed it was, such fact alone is a ground for the rescission of the sale, and that fact was evidence of fraud on the part of the vendee. Whether inadequacy of price is to be received as evidence of fraud, even in a suit in equity to avoid a sale, depends upon the facts known to the parties at the time the sale is made. When this sale was made the value of the thing sold was open to the investigation of both parties, neither knowing its intrinsic value, and, so far as the evidence in this case shows, both supposed that the price paid was adequate. How can fraud be predicated upon such a sale, even though after-investigation showed that the intrinsic value of the thing sold was hundreds of times greater than the price paid? It certainly shows no such fraud as would authorize the vendor to rescind the contract and bring an action at law to recover the possession of the thing sold. Whether that fact would have any influence in an action in equity to avoid the sale we need not consider. . . .

We can find nothing in the evidence from which it could be justly inferred that Mr. Boynton, at the time he offered the plaintiff one dollar for the stone, had a knowledge of the real value of the stone, or that he entertained even a belief that the stone was a diamond. It cannot, therefore, be said that there was a suppression of knowledge on the part of the defendant as to the value of the stone which a court of equity might seize upon to avoid the sale. . . . However unfortunate the plaintiff may have been in selling this valuable stone for a mere nominal sum, she has failed entirely to make out a case either of fraud or mistake in the sale such as will entitle her to a rescission of such sale so as to recover the property sold in an action at law.

———

RESTATEMENT, SECOND, CONTRACTS §§ 151, 152, 154

[See Selected Source Materials Supplement]

———

UNIDROIT PRINCIPLES OF INTERNATIONAL COMMERCIAL CONTRACTS ARTS. 3.4, 3.5, 3.18

[See Selected Source Materials Supplement]

———

PRINCIPLES OF EUROPEAN CONTRACT LAW ART. 4.103

[See Selected Source Materials Supplement]

———

LENAWEE COUNTY BOARD OF HEALTH V. MESSERLY

Supreme Court of Michigan, 1982.
417 Mich. 17, 331 N.W.2d 203.

RYAN, JUSTICE.

In March of 1977, Carl and Nancy Pickles, appellees, purchased from appellants, William and Martha Messerly, a 600-square-foot tract of land upon which is located a three-unit apartment building. Shortly after the transaction was closed, the Lenawee County Board of Health condemned the property and obtained a permanent injunction which prohibits human habitation on the premises until the defective sewage system is brought into conformance with the Lenawee County sanitation code.

We are required to determine whether appellees should prevail in their attempt to avoid this land contract on the basis of mutual mistake and failure of consideration. We conclude that the parties did entertain a mutual misapprehension of fact, but that the circumstances of this case do not warrant rescission.

I

The facts of the case are not seriously in dispute. In 1971, the Messerlys acquired approximately one acre plus 600 square feet of land. A three-unit apartment building was situated upon the 600-square-foot portion. The trial court found that, prior to this transfer, the Messerlys' predecessor in title, Mr. Bloom, had installed a septic tank on the property without a permit and in violation of the applicable health code. The Messerlys used the building as an income investment property until 1973 when they sold it, upon [a] land contract, to James Barnes who likewise used it primarily as an income-producing investment.

Mr. and Mrs. Barnes, with the permission of the Messerlys, sold approximately one acre of the property in 1976, and the remaining 600 square feet and building were offered for sale soon thereafter when Mr. and Mrs. Barnes defaulted on their land contract. Mr. and Mrs. Pickles evidenced an interest in the property, but were dissatisfied with the terms of the Barnes-Messerly land contract. Consequently, to accommodate the Pickleses' preference to enter into a land contract directly with the Messerlys, Mr. and Mrs. Barnes executed a quit-claim deed which conveyed their interest in the property back to the Messerlys. After inspecting the property, Mr. and Mrs. Pickles executed a new land contract with the Messerlys on March 21, 1977. It provided for a purchase price of $25,500. A clause was added to the end of the land contract form which provides:

> "17. Purchaser has examined this property and agrees to accept same in its present condition. There are no other or additional written or oral understandings."

Five or six days later, when the Pickleses went to introduce themselves to the tenants, they discovered raw sewage seeping out of the ground. Tests conducted by a sanitation expert indicated the inadequacy of the sewage system. The Lenawee County Board of Health subsequently condemned the property and initiated this lawsuit in the Lenawee Circuit Court against the Messerlys as land contract vendors, and the Pickleses, as vendees, to obtain a permanent injunction proscribing human habitation of the premises until the property was brought into conformance with the Lenawee County sanitation code. The injunction was granted, and the Lenawee County Board of Health was permitted to withdraw from the lawsuit by stipulation of the parties.

When no payments were made on the land contract, the Messerlys filed a cross-complaint against the Pickleses seeking foreclosure, sale of the property, and a deficiency judgment. Mr. and Mrs. Pickles then counterclaimed for rescission against the Messerlys, and filed a third-party complaint against the Barneses, which incorporated, by reference, the allegations of the counterclaim against the Messerlys. In count one, Mr. and Mrs. Pickles alleged failure of consideration. Count two charged Mr. and Mrs. Barnes with willful concealment and misrepresentation as a result of their failure to disclose the condition of the sanitation system. Additionally, Mr. and Mrs. Pickles sought to hold the Messerlys liable in equity for the Barneses' alleged misrepresentation. The Pickleses prayed that the land contract be rescinded.

After a bench trial, the court concluded that the Pickleses had no cause of action against either the Messerlys or the Barneses as there was no fraud or misrepresentation. This ruling was predicated on the trial judge's conclusion that none of the parties knew of Mr. Bloom's earlier transgression or of the resultant problem with the septic system until it was discovered by the Pickleses, and that the sanitation problem was not caused by any of the parties. The trial court held that the property was purchased "as is", after inspection and, accordingly, its "negative * * * value cannot be blamed upon an innocent seller". Foreclosure was ordered against the Pickleses, together with a judgment against them in the amount of $25,943.09.[3]

Mr. and Mrs. Pickles appealed from the adverse judgment. The Court of Appeals unanimously affirmed the trial court's ruling with respect to Mr. and Mrs. Barnes but, in a two-to-one decision, reversed the finding of no cause of action on the Pickleses' claims against the Messerlys. *Lenawee County Board of Health v. Messerly,* 98 Mich.App. 478, 295 N.W.2d 903 (1980). It concluded that the mutual mistake between the Messerlys and the Pickleses went to a basic, as opposed to a collateral, element of the contract,[6] and that the parties intended to transfer income-producing rental property but, in actuality, the vendees paid $25,500 for an asset without value.[7]

We granted the Messerlys' application for leave to appeal. 411 Mich. 900 (1981).[8]

II

We must decide initially whether there was a mistaken belief entertained by one or both parties to the contract in dispute and, if so, the resultant legal significance.[9]

---

[3] The parties stipulated that this amount was due on the land contract, assuming that the contract was valid and enforceable.

[6] Mr. and Mrs. Pickles did not appeal the trial court's finding that there was no fraud or misrepresentation by the Messerlys or Mr. and Mrs. Barnes. Likewise, the propriety of that ruling is not before this Court today.

[7] The trial court found that the only way that the property could be put to residential use would be to pump and haul the sewage, a method which is economically unfeasible, as the cost of such a disposal system amounts to double the income generated by the property. There was speculation by the trial court that the adjoining land might be utilized to make the property suitable for residential use, but, in the absence of testimony directed at that point, the court refused to draw any conclusions. The trial court and the Court of Appeals both found that the property was valueless, or had a negative value.

[8] The Court of Appeals decision to affirm the trial court's finding of no cause of action against Mr. and Mrs. Barnes has not been appealed to this Court and, accordingly, the propriety of that ruling is not before us today.

[9] We emphasize that this is a bifurcated inquiry. Legal or equitable remedial measures are not mandated in every case in which a mutual mistake has been established.

A contractual mistake "is a belief that is not in accord with the facts". 1 Restatement Contracts, 2d, § 151, p. 383. The erroneous belief of one or both of the parties must relate to a fact in existence at the time the contract is executed. *Richardson Lumber Co. v. Hoey,* 219 Mich. 643, 189 N.W. 923 (1922); *Sherwood v. Walker,* 66 Mich. 568, 580, 33 N.W. 919 (1887) (Sherwood, J., dissenting). That is to say, the belief which is found to be in error may not be, in substance, a prediction as to a future occurrence or non-occurrence. *Henry v. Thomas,* 241 Ga. 360, 245 S.E.2d 646 (1978); *Hailpern v. Dryden,* 154 Colo. 231, 389 P.2d 590 (1964). But see *Denton v. Utley,* 350 Mich. 332, 86 N.W.2d 537 (1957).

The Court of Appeals concluded, after a *de novo* review of the record, that the parties were mistaken as to the income-producing capacity of the property in question. 98 Mich.App. 487–488, 295 N.W.2d 903. We agree. The vendors and the vendees each believed that the property transferred could be utilized as income-generating rental property. All of the parties subsequently learned that, in fact, the property was unsuitable for any residential use.

Appellants assert that there was no mistake in the contractual sense because the defect in the sewage system did not arise until after the contract was executed. The appellees respond that the Messerlys are confusing the date of the inception of the defect with the date upon which the defect was discovered.

This is essentially a factual dispute which the trial court failed to resolve directly. Nevertheless, we are empowered to draw factual inferences from the facts found by the trial court. GCR 1963, 865.1(6).

An examination of the record reveals that the septic system was defective prior to the date on which the land contract was executed. The Messerlys' grantor installed a nonconforming septic system without a permit prior to the transfer of the property to the Messerlys in 1971. Moreover, virtually undisputed testimony indicates that, assuming ideal soil conditions, 2,500 square feet of property is necessary to support a sewage system adequate to serve a three-family dwelling. Likewise, 750 square feet is mandated for a one-family home. Thus, the division of the parcel and sale of one acre of the property by Mr. and Mrs. Barnes in 1976 made it impossible to remedy the already illegal septic system within the confines of the 600-square-foot parcel.

Appellants do not dispute these underlying facts which give rise to an inference contrary to their contentions.

Having determined that when these parties entered into the land contract they were laboring under a mutual mistake of fact, we now direct our attention to a determination of the legal significance of that finding.

A contract may be rescinded because of a mutual misapprehension of the parties, but this remedy is granted only in the sound discretion of the court. *Harris v. Axline,* 323 Mich. 585, 36 N.W.2d 154 (1949). Appellants argue that the parties' mistake relates only to the quality or value of the real estate transferred, and that such mistakes are collateral to the agreement and do not justify rescission, citing *A & M Land Development Co. v. Miller,* 354 Mich. 681, 94 N.W.2d 197 (1959).

In that case, the plaintiff was the purchaser of 91 lots of real property. It sought partial rescission of the land contract when it was frustrated in its attempts to develop 42 of the lots because it could not obtain permits from the county health department to install septic tanks on these lots. This Court refused to allow rescission because the mistake, whether mutual or unilateral, related only to the value of the property. . . .

Appellees contend, on the other hand, that in this case the parties were mistaken as to the very nature of the character of the consideration and claim that the pervasive and essential quality of this mistake renders rescission appropriate. They cite in support of that view *Sherwood v. Walker,* 66 Mich. 568, 33 N.W. 919 (1887), the famous "barren cow" case. . . .

As the parties suggest, the foregoing precedent arguably distinguishes mistakes affecting the essence of the consideration from those which go to its quality or value, affording relief on a per se basis for the former but not the latter. See, *e.g., Lenawee County Board of Health v. Messerly,* 98 Mich.App. 478, 492, 295 N.W.2d 903 (1980) (Mackenzie, J., concurring in part).

However, the distinctions which may be drawn from *Sherwood* and *A & M Land Development Co.* do not provide a satisfactory analysis of the nature of a mistake sufficient to invalidate a contract. Often, a mistake relates to an underlying factual assumption which, when discovered, directly affects value, but simultaneously and materially affects the essence of the contractual consideration. It is disingenuous to label such a mistake collateral. *McKay v. Coleman,* 85 Mich. 60, 48 N.W. 203 (1891). Corbin, Contracts (One Vol. ed.), § 605, p. 551.

Appellant and appellee both mistakenly believed that the property which was the subject of their land contract would generate income as rental property. The fact that it could not be used for human habitation deprived the property of its income-earning potential and rendered it less valuable. However, this mistake, while directly and dramatically affecting the property's value, cannot accurately be characterized as collateral because it also affects the very essence of the consideration. "The thing sold and bought [income generating rental property] had in fact no existence". *Sherwood v. Walker,* 66 Mich. 578, 33 N.W. 919.

We find that the inexact and confusing distinction between contractual mistakes running to value and those touching the substance of the consideration serves only as an impediment to a clear and helpful analysis for the equitable resolution of cases in which mistake is alleged and proven. Accordingly, the holdings of *A & M Land Development Co.* and *Sherwood* with respect to the material or collateral nature of a mistake are limited to the facts of those cases.

Instead, we think the better-reasoned approach is a case-by-case analysis whereby rescission is indicated when the mistaken belief relates to a basic assumption of the parties upon which the contract is made, and which materially affects the agreed performances of the parties. *Denton v. Utley*, 350 Mich. 332, 86 N.W.2d 537 (1957); *Farhat v. Rassey*, 295 Mich. 349, 294 N.W. 707 (1940); *Richardson Lumber Co. v. Hoey*, 219 Mich. 643, 189 N.W. 923 (1922). 1 Restatement Contracts, 2d, § 152, pp. 385–386. Rescission is not available, however, to relieve a party who has assumed the risk of loss in connection with the mistake. *Denton v. Utley*, 350 Mich. 344–345, 86 N.W.2d 537; *Farhat v. Rassey*, 295 Mich. 352, 294 N.W. 707; Corbin, Contracts (One Vol. ed.), § 605, p. 552; 1 Restatement Contracts, 2d, §§ 152, 154, pp. 385–386, 402–406.

All of the parties to this contract erroneously assumed that the property transferred by the vendors to the vendees was suitable for human habitation and could be utilized to generate rental income. The fundamental nature of these assumptions is indicated by the fact that their invalidity changed the character of the property transferred, thereby frustrating, indeed precluding, Mr. and Mrs. Pickles' intended use of the real estate. Although the Pickleses are disadvantaged by enforcement of the contract, performance is advantageous to the Messerlys, as the property at issue is less valuable absent its income-earning potential. Nothing short of rescission can remedy the mistake. Thus, the parties' mistake as to a basic assumption materially affects the agreed performances of the parties.

Despite the significance of the mistake made by the parties, we reverse the Court of Appeals because we conclude that equity does not justify the remedy sought by Mr. and Mrs. Pickles.

Rescission is an equitable remedy which is granted only in the sound discretion of the court. *Harris v. Axline*, 323 Mich. 585, 36 N.W.2d 154 (1949); *Hathaway v. Hudson*, 256 Mich. 694, 239 N.W. 859 (1932). A court need not grant rescission in every case in which the mutual mistake relates to a basic assumption and materially affects the agreed performance of the parties.

In cases of mistake by two equally innocent parties, we are required, in the exercise of our equitable powers, to determine which blameless party should assume the loss resulting from the misapprehension they shared.[13] Normally that can only be done by drawing upon our "own notions of what is reasonable and just under all the surrounding circumstances".[14]

Equity suggests that, in this case, the risk should be allocated to the purchasers. We are guided to that conclusion, in part, by the standards announced in § 154 of the Restatement of Contracts 2d, for determining when a party bears the risk of mistake. . . . Section 154(a) suggests that the court should look first to whether the parties have agreed to the allocation of the risk between themselves. While there is no express assumption in the contract by either party of the risk of the property becoming uninhabitable, there was indeed some agreed allocation of the risk to the vendees by the incorporation of an "as is" clause into the contract which, we repeat, provided:

> "Purchaser has examined this property and agrees to accept same in its present condition. There are no other or additional written or oral understandings."

That is a persuasive indication that the parties considered that, as between them, such risk as related to the "present condition" of the property should lie with the purchaser. If the "as is" clause is to have any meaning at all, it must be interpreted to refer to those defects which were unknown at the time that the contract was executed.[15] Thus, the parties themselves assigned the risk of loss to Mr. and Mrs. Pickles.

We conclude that Mr. and Mrs. Pickles are not entitled to the equitable remedy of rescission and, accordingly, reverse the decision the Court of Appeals.

WILLIAMS, C.J., and COLEMAN, FITZGERALD, KAVANAGH and LEVIN, JJ., concur.

RILEY, J., not participating.

---

[13] This risk-of-loss analysis is absent in both *A & M Land Development Co.* and *Sherwood,* and this omission helps to explain, in part, the disparate treatment in the two cases. Had such an inquiry been undertaken in *Sherwood,* we believe that the result might have been different. Moreover, a determination as to which party assumed the risk in *A & M Land Development Co.* would have alleviated the need to characterize the mistake as collateral so as to justify the result denying rescission. Despite the absence of any inquiry as to the assumption of risk in those two leading cases, we find that there exists sufficient precedent to warrant such an analysis in future cases of mistake.

[14] *Hathaway v. Hudson,* 256 Mich. 702, 239 N.W. 859, quoting 9 C.J., p. 1161.

[15] An "as is" clause waives those implied warranties which accompany the sale of a new home, *Tibbitts v. Openshaw,* 18 Utah 2d 442, 425 P.2d 160 (1967), or the sale of goods. M.C.L. § 440.2316(3)(a); M.S.A. § 19.2316(3)(a). Since implied warranties protect against latent defects, an "as is" clause will impose upon the purchaser the assumption of the risk of latent defects, such as an inadequate sanitation system, even when there are no implied warranties.

UCC §§ 2–312, 2–313, 2–314, 2–315

[See Selected Source Materials Supplement]

SECTION 4. NONDISCLOSURE

HILL V. JONES

Arizona Court of Appeals, 1986.
151 Ariz. 81, 725 P.2d 1115.

MEYERSON, JUDGE.

Must the seller of a residence disclose to the buyer facts pertaining to past termite infestation? This is the primary question presented in this appeal. Plaintiffs Warren G. Hill and Gloria R. Hill (buyers) filed suit to rescind an agreement to purchase a residence. Buyers alleged that Ora G. Jones and Barbara R. Jones (sellers) had made misrepresentations concerning termite damage in the residence and had failed to disclose to them the existence of the damage and history of termite infestation in the residence. . . .

. . . The trial court granted summary judgment, finding that there was "no genuinely disputed issue of material fact and that the law favors the . . . defendants." . . . Buyers have appealed from the judgment and sellers have cross-appealed from the trial court's ruling on attorney's fees.

I. FACTS

In 1982, buyers entered into an agreement to purchase sellers' residence for $72,000. The agreement was entered after buyers made several visits to the home. The purchase agreement provided that sellers were to pay for and place in escrow a termite inspection report stating that the property was free from evidence of termite infestation. Escrow was scheduled to close two months later.

One of the central features of the house is a parquet teak floor covering the sunken living room, the dining room, the entryway and portions of the halls. On a subsequent visit to the house, and when sellers were present, buyers noticed a small "ripple" in the wood floor on the step leading up to the dining room from the sunken living room. Mr. Hill asked if the ripple could be termite damage. Mrs. Jones answered that it was water damage. A few years previously, a broken water heater in the house had in fact caused water damage in the area of the dining room and steps which necessitated that some repairs be made to the floor. No further discussion on the subject, however, took place between the parties at that time or afterwards.

Mr. Hill, through his job as maintenance supervisor at a school district, had seen similar "ripples" in wood which had turned out to be termite damage. Mr. Hill was not totally satisfied with Mrs. Jones's explanation, but he felt that the termite inspection report would reveal whether the ripple was due to termites or some other cause.

The termite inspection report stated that there was no visible evidence of infestation. The report failed to note the existence of physical damage or evidence of previous treatment. The realtor notified the parties that the property had passed the termite inspection. Apparently, neither party actually saw the report prior to close of escrow.

After moving into the house, buyers found a pamphlet left in one of the drawers entitled "Termites, the Silent Saboteurs." They learned from a neighbor that the house had some termite infestation in the past. Shortly after the close of escrow, Mrs. Hill noticed that the wood on the steps leading down to the sunken living room was crumbling. She called an exterminator who confirmed the existence of termite damage to the floor and steps and to wood columns in the house. The estimated cost of repairing the wood floor alone was approximately $5,000.

Through discovery after their lawsuit was filed, buyers learned the following. When sellers purchased the residence in 1974, they received two termite guarantees that had been given to the previous owner by Truly Nolen, as well as a diagram showing termite treatment at the residence that had taken place in 1963. The guarantees provided for semi-annual inspections and annual termite booster treatments. The accompanying diagram stated that the existing damage had not been repaired. The second guarantee, dated 1965, reinstated the earlier contract for inspection and treatment. Mr. Jones admitted that he read the guarantees when he received them. Sellers renewed the guarantees when they purchased the residence in 1974. They also paid the annual fee each year until they sold the home.

On two occasions during sellers' ownership of the house but while they were at their other residence in Minnesota, a neighbor noticed "streamers" evidencing live termites in the wood tile floor near the entryway. On both occasions, Truly Nolen gave a booster treatment for termites. On the second incident, Truly Nolen drilled through one of the wood tiles to treat for termites. The neighbor showed Mr. Jones the area where the damage and treatment had occurred. Sellers had also seen termites on the back fence and had replaced and treated portions of the fence.

Sellers did not mention any of this information to buyers prior to close of escrow. They did not mention the past termite infestation and treatment to the realtor or to the termite inspector. There was evidence of holes on the patio that had been drilled years previously to treat for termites. The inspector returned to the residence to determine why he had not found evidence of prior treatment and termite damage. He indicated that he had not seen the holes in the patio because of boxes stacked there. It is unclear whether the boxes had been placed there by buyers or sellers. He had not found the damage inside the house because a large plant, which buyers had purchased from sellers, covered the area. After investigating the second time, the inspector found the damage and evidence of past treatment. He acknowledged that this information should have appeared in the report. He complained, however, that he should have been told of any history of termite infestation and treatment before he performed his inspection and that it was customary for the inspector to be given such information.

Other evidence presented to the trial court was that during their numerous visits to the residence before close of escrow, buyers had unrestricted access to view and inspect the entire house. Both Mr. and Mrs. Hill had seen termite damage and were therefore familiar with what it might look like. Mr. Hill had seen termite damage on the fence at this property. Mrs. Hill had noticed the holes on the patio but claimed not to realize at the time what they were for. Buyers asked no questions about termites except when they asked if the "ripple" on the stairs was termite damage. Mrs. Hill admitted she was not "trying" to find problems with the house because she really wanted it. . . .

III. DUTY TO DISCLOSE

The principal legal question presented in this appeal is whether a seller has a duty to disclose to the buyer the existence of termite damage in a residential dwelling known to the seller, but not to the buyer, which materially affects the value of the property. For the reasons stated herein, we hold that such a duty exists.

This is not the place to trace the history of the doctrine of caveat emptor. Suffice it to say that its vitality has waned during the latter half of the 20th century. E.g., Richards v. Powercraft Homes, Inc., 139 Ariz. 242, 678 P.2d 427 (1984) (implied warranty of workmanship and habitability extends to subsequent buyers of homes); see generally Quashnock v. Frost, 299 Pa.Super. 9, 445 A.2d 121 (1982); Ollerman v. O'Rourke Co., 94 Wis.2d 17, 288 N.W.2d 95 (1980). The modern view is that a vendor has an affirmative duty to disclose material facts where:

    1.   Disclosure is necessary to prevent a previous assertion from being a misrepresentation or from being fraudulent or material;

    2.   Disclosure would correct a mistake of the other party as to a basic assumption on which that party is making the contract and if nondisclosure amounts to a failure to act in good faith and in accordance with reasonable standards of fair dealing;

3.   Disclosure would correct a mistake of the other party as to the contents or effect of a writing, evidencing or embodying an agreement in whole or in part;

4.   The other person is entitled to know the fact because of a relationship of trust and confidence between them.

Restatement (Second) of Contracts § 161 (1981) (Restatement); See Restatement (Second) of Torts § 551 (1977).

Arizona courts have long recognized that under certain circumstances there may be a "duty to speak." Van Buren v. Pima Community College Dist. Bd., 113 Ariz. 85, 87, 546 P.2d 821, 823 (1976); Batty v. Arizona State Dental Bd., 57 Ariz. 239, 254, 112 P.2d 870, 877 (1941). As the supreme court noted in the context of a confidential relationship, "[s]uppression of a material fact which a party is bound in good faith to disclose is equivalent to a false representation." Leigh v. Loyd, 74 Ariz. 84, 87, 244 P.2d 356, 358 (1952); National Housing Indus. Inc. v. E.L. Jones Dev. Co., 118 Ariz. 374, 379, 576 P.2d 1374, 1379 (1978).

Thus, the important question we must answer is whether under the facts of this case, buyers should have been permitted to present to the jury their claim that sellers were under a duty to disclose their (sellers') knowledge of termite infestation in the residence. This broader question involves two inquiries. First, must a seller of residential property advise the buyer of material facts within his knowledge pertaining to the value of the property? Second, may termite damage and the existence of past infestation constitute such material facts?

The doctrine imposing a duty to disclose is akin to the well-established contractual rules pertaining to relief from contracts based upon mistake. Although the law of contracts supports the finality of transactions, over the years courts have recognized that under certain limited circumstances it is unjust to strictly enforce the policy favoring finality. Thus, for example, even a unilateral mistake of one party to a transaction may justify rescission. Restatement § 153.

There is also a judicial policy promoting honesty and fair dealing in business relationships. This policy is expressed in the law of fraudulent and negligent misrepresentations. Where a misrepresentation is fraudulent or where a negligent misrepresentation is one of material fact, the policy of finality rightly gives way to the policy of promoting honest dealings between the parties. See Restatement § 164(1).

Under certain circumstances nondisclosure of a fact known to one party may be equivalent to the assertion that the fact does not exist. For example "[w]hen one conveys a false impression by the disclosure of some facts and the concealment of others, such concealment is in effect a false representation that what is disclosed is the whole truth." State v.

Coddington, 135 Ariz. 480, 481, 662 P.2d 155, 156 (App.1983). Thus, nondisclosure may be equated with and given the same legal effect as fraud and misrepresentation. One category of cases where this has been done involves the area of nondisclosure of material facts affecting the value of property, known to the seller but not reasonably capable of being known to the buyer.

Courts have formulated this "duty to disclose" in slightly different ways. For example, the Florida Supreme Court recently declared that "where the seller of a home knows of facts materially affecting the value of the property which are not readily observable and are not known to the buyer, the seller is under a duty to disclose them to the buyer." Johnson v. Davis, 480 So.2d 625, 629 (Fla.1985) (defective roof in three-year old home). In California, the rule has been stated this way:

> [W]here the seller knows of facts materially affecting the value or desirability of the property which are known or accessible only to him and also knows that such facts are not known to, or within the reach of the diligent attention and observation of the buyer, the seller is under a duty to disclose them to the buyer.

Lingsch v. Savage, 213 Cal.App.2d 729, 735, 29 Cal.Rptr. 201, 204 (1963); contra Ray v. Montgomery, 399 So.2d 230 (Ala.1980); see generally W. Prosser & W. Keeton, The Law of Torts § 106 (5th ed.1984). We find that the Florida formulation of the disclosure rule properly balances the legitimate interests of the parties in a transaction for the sale of a private residence and accordingly adopt it for such cases.

As can be seen, the rule requiring disclosure is invoked in the case of material facts.[3] Thus, we are led to the second inquiry—whether the existence of termite damage in a residential dwelling is the type of material fact which gives rise to the duty to disclose. The existence of termite damage and past termite infestation has been considered by other courts to be sufficiently material to warrant disclosure. See generally Annot., 22 A.L.R.3d 972 (1968). . . .

Although sellers have attempted to draw a distinction between live termites[4] and past infestation, the concept of materiality is an elastic one which is not limited by the termites' health. "A matter is material if it is one to which a reasonable person would attach importance in determining his choice of action in the transaction in question." Lynn v. Taylor, 7 Kan.App.2d at 371, 642 P.2d at 134–35. For example, termite damage

---

[3]   Arizona has recognized that a duty to disclose may arise where the buyer makes an inquiry of the seller, regardless of whether or not the fact is material. Universal Inv. Co. v. Sahara Motor Inn, Inc., 127 Ariz. 213, 215, 619 P.2d 485, 487 (1980). The inquiry by buyers whether the ripple was termite damage imposed a duty upon sellers to disclose what information they knew concerning the existence of termite infestation in the residence.

[4]   Sellers acknowledge that a duty of disclosure would exist if live termites were present. Obde v. Schlemeyer, 56 Wash.2d 449, 353 P.2d 672 (1960).

substantially affecting the structural soundness of the residence may be material even if there is no evidence of present infestation. Unless reasonable minds could not differ, materiality is a factual matter which must be determined by the trier of fact. The termite damage in this case may or may not be material. Accordingly, we conclude that buyers should be allowed to present their case to a jury.

Sellers argue that even assuming the existence of a duty to disclose, summary judgment was proper because the record shows that their "silence . . . did not induce or influence" the buyers. This is so, sellers contend, because Mr. Hill stated in his deposition that he intended to rely on the termite inspection report. But this argument begs the question. If sellers were fully aware of the extent of termite damage and if such information had been disclosed to buyers, a jury could accept Mr. Hill's testimony that had he known of the termite damage he would not have purchased the house.

Sellers further contend that buyers were put on notice of the possible existence of termite infestation and were therefore "chargeable with the knowledge which [an] inquiry, if made, would have revealed." Godfrey v. Navratil, 3 Ariz.App. 47, 51, 411 P.2d 470 (1966) (quoting Luke v. Smith, 13 Ariz. 155, 162, 108 P. 494, 496 (1910)). It is also true that "a party may . . . reasonably expect the other to take normal steps to inform himself and to draw his own conclusions." Restatement § 161 comment d. Under the facts of this case, the question of buyers' knowledge of the termite problem (or their diligence in attempting to inform themselves about the termite problem) should be left to the jury.[5]

. . . Reversed and remanded.

CONTRERAS, P.J., and YALE MCFATE, J. (Retired), concur.

———

Weintraub v. Krobatsch

64 N.J. 445, 317 A.2d 68 (1974)

The Krobatschs contracted to purchase a house from Mrs. Weintraub. After making the contract, but before the closing, the Krobatschs discovered that the house was badly infested with roaches. The Krobatschs sought to rescind the contract, and Mrs. Weintraub sued to recover a deposit of $4,250 that the Krobatschs had put into escrow. In their suit, the Krobatschs claimed that Mrs. Weintraub was aware of the infestation and had kept every room in the house illuminated while the Krobatschs inspected the house, to keep the roaches, which are nocturnal, from appearing. The trial court granted

---

[5] Sellers also contend that they had no knowledge of any existing termite damage in the house. An extended discussion of the facts on this point is unnecessary. Simply stated, the facts are in conflict on this issue.

summary judgment for Mrs. Weintraub. The New Jersey Supreme Court reversed:

> "[T]he purchasers here were entitled to withstand the seller's motion for summary judgment. They should have been permitted to proceed with their efforts to establish by testimony that they were equitably entitled to rescind because the house was extensively infested in the manner described by them, the seller was well aware of the infestation, and the seller deliberately concealed or failed to disclose the condition because of the likelihood that it would defeat the transaction. . . .

> "If the trial judge finds such deliberate concealment or nondisclosure of the latent infestation not observable by the purchasers on their inspection, he will still be called upon to determine whether, in the light of the full presentation before him, the concealment or nondisclosure was of such significant nature as to justify rescission. Minor conditions which ordinary sellers and purchasers would reasonably disregard as of little or no materiality in the transaction would clearly not call for judicial intervention. While the described condition may not have been quite as major as in the termite cases which were concerned with structural impairments, to the purchasers here it apparently was of such magnitude and was so repulsive as to cause them to rescind immediately though they had earlier indicated readiness that there be adjustment at closing for damage resulting from a fire which occurred after the contract was signed. We are not prepared at this time to say that on their showing they acted either unreasonably or without equitable justification."

RESTATEMENT, SECOND, CONTRACTS §§ 159, 161

[See Selected Source Materials Supplement]

RESTATEMENT, SECOND, CONTRACTS § 161, ILLUSTRATIONS 7, 10, 11

7.   A, seeking to induce B to make a contract to sell land, knows that B does not know that the land has appreciably increased in value because of a proposed shopping center but does not disclose this to B. B makes the contract. Since B's mistake is not one as to a basic assumption . . . A's non-disclosure is not equivalent to an assertion that the value of the land has not appreciably increased. . . . The contract is not voidable by B. . . .

10. A, seeking to induce B to make a contract to sell A land, learns from government surveys that the land contains valuable mineral deposits

and knows that B does not know this, but does not disclose this to B. B makes the contract. A's non-disclosure does not amount to a failure to act in good faith and in accordance with reasonable standards of fair dealing and is therefore not equivalent to an assertion that the land does not contain valuable mineral deposits. The contract is not voidable by B.

11. The facts being otherwise as stated in Illustration 10, A learns of the valuable mineral deposits from trespassing on B's land and not from government surveys. A's non-disclosure is equivalent to an assertion that the land does not contain valuable mineral deposits, and this assertion is a misrepresentation. . . .

RESTATEMENT, SECOND, TORTS § 551, ILLUSTRATIONS 6, 8

6. A is a violin expert. He pays a casual visit to B's shop, where second-hand musical instruments are sold. He finds a violin which, by reason of his expert knowledge and experience, he immediately recognizes as a genuine Stradivarius, in good condition and worth at least $50,000. The violin is priced for sale at $100. Without disclosing his information or his identity, A buys the violin from B for $100. A is not liable to B. . . .

8. B has a shop in which he sells second-hand musical instruments. In it he offers for sale for $100 a violin, which he knows to be an imitation Stradivarius and worth at most $50. A enters the shop, looks at the violin and is overheard by B to say to his companion that he is sure that the instrument is a genuine Stradivarius. B says nothing, and A buys the violin for $100. B is not liable to A. . . .

CHAPTER 18

THE EFFECT OF UNEXPECTED CIRCUMSTANCES

■ ■ ■

INTRODUCTORY NOTE

The issue considered in this Chapter is when, and to what extent, unexpected circumstances bear on the parties' rights and duties under a contract. In many crucial respects, the modern legal rules that govern this issue are comparable to the rules that govern mutual mistake, in that both sets of rules focus on the effect of shared tacit assumptions that proved to be incorrect. A major difference between the two kinds of cases is practical: In general, mutual-mistake cases usually involve attempts to either rescind the contract, or justify nonperformance, before either party has done much under the contract. In contrast, in unexpected-circumstances cases the relevant circumstances usually become salient only after performance has begun. The legal treatment of unexpected-circumstances cases is often rendered more complex and difficult as a result of this practical difference.

The cases considered in this chapter are generally dealt with under the legal rubrics *impossibility*, *impracticability*, and *frustration*. Historically, the three doctrines arose in roughly that order: First, the courts recognized that impossibility might be a defense; next, that impracticability might be a defense; and finally, that frustration of the purpose of a contract might be a defense. In this Chapter, these three doctrines will be taken up more or less in that order ("more or less," because the doctrines overlap) under the general heading of unexpected circumstances.

———

TAYLOR V. CALDWELL
In the Queen's Bench, 1863.
3 Best & S. 826.

BLACKBURN, J. In this case the plaintiffs and defendants had, on May 27th, 1861, entered into a contract by which the defendants agreed to let the plaintiffs have the use of The Surrey Gardens and Music Hall on four days then to come, viz., June 17th, July 15th, August 5th, and August 19th, for the purpose of giving a series of four grand concerts, and day and night fêtes, at the Gardens and Hall on those days respectively; and the plaintiffs agreed to take the Gardens and Hall on those days, and pay £100 for each day.

The parties inaccurately call this a "letting," and the money to be paid, a "rent"; but the whole agreement is such as to show that the defendants were to retain the possession of the Hall and Gardens so that there was to be no demise of them, and that the contract was merely to give the plaintiffs the use of them on those days. Nothing, however, in our opinion, depends on this. The agreement then proceeds to set out various stipulations between the parties as to what each was to supply for these concerts and entertainments, and as to the manner in which they should be carried on. The effect of the whole is to show that the existence of the Music Hall in the Surrey Gardens in a state fit for a concert was essential for the fulfilment of the contract,—such entertainments as the parties contemplated in their agreement could not be given without it.

After the making of the agreement, and before the first day on which a concert was to be given, the Hall was destroyed by fire. This destruction, we must take it on the evidence, was without the fault of either party, and was so complete that in consequence the concerts could not be given as intended. And the question we have to decide is whether, under these circumstances, the loss which the plaintiffs have sustained is to fall upon the defendants. [The damages claimed in the declaration were for moneys paid by the plaintiffs in advertising the concerts and for sums expended and expenses incurred by them in preparing for the concerts.] The parties when framing their agreement evidently had not present to their minds the possibility of such a disaster, and have made no express stipulation with reference to it, so that the answer to the question must depend upon the general rules of law applicable to such a contract.

There seems no doubt that where there is a positive contract to do a thing, not in itself unlawful, the contractor must perform it or pay damages for not doing it, although in consequence of unforeseen accidents the performance of his contract has become unexpectedly burdensome or even impossible. The law is so laid down in 1 Roll.Abr. 450, Condition (G), and in the note (2) to Walton v. Waterhouse (2 Wms.Saund. 421a, 6th Ed.) and is recognized as the general rule by all the judges in the much discussed case of Hall v. Wright (E.B. & E. 746). But this rule is only applicable when the contract is positive and absolute, and not subject to any condition either express or implied; and there are authorities which, as we think, establish the principle that where, from the nature of the contract, it appears that the parties must from the beginning have known that it could not be fulfilled unless when the time for the fulfilment of the contract arrived some particular specified thing continued to exist, so that, when entering into the contract, they must have contemplated such continuing existence as the foundation of what was to be done; there, in the absence of any express or implied warranty that the thing shall exist, the contract is not to be construed as a positive contract, but as subject to an implied condition that the parties shall be excused in case, before breach, performance becomes impossible from the perishing of the thing without default of the contractor.

There seems little doubt that this implication tends to further the great object of making the legal construction such as to fulfill the intention of those who entered into the contract. For in the course of affairs men in making such contracts in general would, if it were brought to their minds, say that there should be such a condition. . . .

There is a class of contracts in which a person binds himself to do something which requires to be performed by him in person; and such promises, e.g. promises to marry, or promises to serve for a certain time, are never in practice qualified by an express exception of the death of the party; and therefore in such cases the contract is in terms broken if the promisor dies before fulfilment. Yet it was very early determined that, if the performance is personal, the executors are not liable; Hyde v. The Dean of Windsor (Cro.Eliz. 552, 553). See 2 Wms.Exors. 1560 (5th Ed.), where a very apt illustration is given. "Thus," says the learned author, "if an author undertakes to compose a work, and dies before completing it, his executors are discharged from this contract; for the undertaking is merely personal in its nature, and by the intervention of the contractor's death, has become impossible to be performed." For this he cites a dictum of Lord Lyndhurst in Marshall v. Broadhurst (1 Tyr. 348, 349) and a case mentioned by Patteson, J., in Wentworth v. Cock (10 A. & E. 42, 45–46). In Hall v. Wright (E.B. & E. 746, 749), Crompton, J., in his judgment, puts another case. "Where a contract depends upon personal skill, and the act of God renders it impossible, as, for instance, in the case of a painter employed to paint a picture who is struck blind, it may be that the performance might be excused."

It seems that in those cases the only ground on which the parties or their executors can be excused from the consequences of the breach of the contract, is, that from the nature of the contract there is an implied condition of the continued existence of the life of the contractor, and perhaps in the case of the painter, of his eyesight. In the instances just given the person, the continued existence of whose life is necessary to the fulfilment of the contract, is himself the contractor, but that does not seem in itself to be necessary to the application of the principle, as is illustrated by the following example. In the ordinary form of an apprentice deed, the apprentice binds himself in unqualified terms to "serve until the full end and term of seven years to be fully complete and ended," during which term it is covenanted that the apprentice his master "faithfully shall serve," and the father of the apprentice in equally unqualified terms binds himself for the performance by the apprentice of all and every covenant on his part. (See the form, 2 Chitty on Pleading, 370 [7th Ed.] by Greening.) It is undeniable that if the apprentice dies within the seven years, the covenant of the father that he shall perform his covenant to serve for seven years is not fulfilled, yet surely it cannot be that an action would lie against the father. Yet the only reason why it would not is that he is excused because of the apprentice's death.

These are instances where the implied condition is of the life of a human being, but there are others in which the same implication is made as to the continued existence of a thing. For example, where a contract of sale is made amounting to a bargain and sale, transferring presently the property in specific chattels, which are to be delivered by the vendor at a future day; there, if the chattels, without the fault of the vendor, perish in the interval, the purchaser must pay the price, and the vendor is excused from performing his contract to deliver, which has thus become impossible.

That this is the rule of the English law is established by the case of Rugg v. Minett (11 East, 210), where the article that perished before delivery was turpentine, and it was decided that the vendor was bound to refund the price of all those lots in which the property had not passed; but was entitled to retain without deduction the price of those lots in which the property had passed, though they were not delivered, and though in the conditions of sale, which are set out in the report, there was no express qualification of the promise to deliver on payment. It seems in that case rather to have been taken for granted than decided that the destruction of the thing sold before delivery excused the vendor from fulfilling his contract to deliver on payment. . . .

It may, we think, be safely asserted to be now English law, that in all contracts of loan of chattels or bailments if the performance of the promise of the borrower or bailee to return the things lent or bailed, becomes impossible because it has perished, this impossibility (if not arising from the fault of the borrower or bailee from some risk which he has taken upon himself) excuses the borrower or bailee from the performance of his promise to redeliver the chattel.

The great case of Coggs v. Bernard (1 Smith's L.C. 171 [5th Ed.] 2 L.Raym. 909) is now the leading case on the law of bailments, and Lord Holt, in that case, referred so much to the civil law that it might perhaps be thought that this principle was there derived direct from the civilians, and was not generally applicable in English law except in the case of bailments; but the case of Williams v. Lloyd (W. Jones, 179), above cited, shows that the same law had been already adopted by the English law as early as the Book of Assizes. The principle seems to us to be that, in contracts in which the performance depends on the continued existence of a given person or thing, a condition is implied that the impossibility of performance arising from the perishing of the person or thing shall excuse the performance.

In none of these cases is the promise in words other than positive, nor is there any express stipulation that the destruction of the person or thing shall excuse the performance; but that excuse is by law implied, because from the nature of the contract it is apparent that the parties contracted on the basis of the continued existence of the particular person or chattel. In the present case, looking at the whole contract, we find that the parties contracted on the basis of the continued existence of the Music Hall at the time when the concerts were to be given, that being essential to their performance.

We think, therefore, that the Music Hall having ceased to exist, without fault of either party, both parties are excused, the plaintiffs from taking the gardens and paying the money, the defendants from performing their promise to give the use of the Hall and Gardens and other things. Consequently the rule must be absolute to enter the verdict for the defendants.

Rule absolute.

TACIT ASSUMPTIONS—CONTINUED

In *Taylor v. Caldwell* the court says that when framing their agreement the parties "had not present to their minds the possibility" of a disaster affecting the Music Hall, and concludes that "the parties contracted on the basis of the continued existence" of the Hall.

Is there a contradiction here? The court seems to say that the parties did not think of the possibility of the Hall's burning and therefore assumed that it would not burn. But how can the parties assume that no fire will occur when the possibility of a fire was never present to their minds? If this possibility was not present to their minds, would it not be more accurate to say that they assumed nothing about a fire, either that it would or would not occur?

The difficulty here can be resolved through the concept of tacit assumptions, discussed in the previous Chapter. As pointed out in that Chapter, words like "intention," "assumption," "expectation" and "understanding" all seem to imply a *conscious* state involving an awareness of alternatives and a deliberate choice among them. However, there is a psychological state that can be described as a tacit assumption, which does not involve a consciousness of alternatives. In experiments with animals, the relative strength of such assumptions can be roughly measured. If a rat is trained for months to run through a particular maze, the sudden interposition of a barrier in one of the paths will have a very disruptive effect on its behavior. For some time after encountering the barrier, the rat will be likely to engage in random and apparently pointless behavior, running in circles, scratching itself, etc. The degree to which the barrier operates disruptively reflects the strength of the assumption made by the rat that the barrier would not be there. If the maze has been frequently changed, and the rat has only recently become accustomed to the maze's present form, the introduction of a barrier will act less disruptively. In such a case, after a relatively short period of random behavior the rat will begin to act purposively, will retrace its steps, seek other outlets, etc. In this situation the assumption that the path would not be obstructed has not been deeply etched into the rat's nervous system; the rat behaves as if it "half-expected" some such impediment.

In a similar way, where parties have entered into a contract, an unexpected obstacle to performance may operate disruptively in varying degrees, depending on the context. To one who has contracted to carry goods by truck over a road traversing a mountain pass, a landslide filling the pass may be a very disruptive and unexpected event. But one who contracts to build a road through the mountains might view the same event, occurring during the course of construction, as a temporary set-back and a challenge to her resourcefulness. One who contracts to deliver goods a year from now at a fixed price certainly takes into account the possibility of some inflation, but may feel that a ten-fold inflation is contrary to an assumption or expectation that price variations would occur within the normal range, and that this expectation was the foundation of the contract.

In spite of hopeful beginnings that promise a more comprehensive psychological treatment of human behavior, for the time being the only methods available for dealing with problems like that raised by *Taylor v. Caldwell* are essentially those resting on intuition and introspection. We "just know" that the burning of a music hall violates a tacit assumption of the parties who executed a contract for hiring it for a few days in the very near future; we "just know" that a two per cent increase in the price of beans does not violate a tacit assumption underlying a contract to deliver a ton of beans for a fixed price.

———

Ocean Tramp Tankers Corp. v. V/O Sovfracht

[1964] 2 Q.B. 226 (1963)

(Denning, M.R.). "It was originally said that the doctrine of frustration was based on an implied term. In short, that the parties, if they had foreseen the new situation, would have said to one another: 'If that happens, of course, it is all over between us.' But the theory of an implied term has now been discarded by everyone, or nearly everyone, for the simple reason that it does not represent the truth. The parties would not have said: 'It is all over between us.' They would have differed about what was to happen. Each would have sought to insert reservations or qualifications of one kind or another."

Mineral Park Land Co. v. Howard

172 Cal. 289, 156 P. 458 (1916)

Plaintiff owned certain land in a ravine. Defendants had made a contract with public authorities to construct a concrete bridge across the ravine. In August 1911, the parties made a contract under which plaintiff granted defendants the right to haul gravel and earth from its land, and defendants agreed to take from that land all the gravel and earth necessary for the fill and cement work on the bridge. Defendants used 101,000 cubic yards in this work but procured 50,869 of those cubic yards from persons other than plaintiff, and plaintiff sued for breach of contract. The trial court found as follows: Plaintiff's land contained earth and gravel far in excess of 101,000 cubic yards of earth and gravel, but only 50,131 of these cubic yards, the amount taken by defendants, was above the water level. No greater quantity could have been taken by ordinary means, but only by employing a steam dredger, and earth and gravel taken in this way could not have been used without first having been dried. Defendants removed all the earth and gravel from plaintiff's land "that was practical to take and remove from a financial standpoint." Any greater amount could have been taken only at an expense of 10 or 12 times the usual cost per yard. It was not "advantageous or practical" to have taken more material from plaintiff's land, although it was not impossible. Held, defendants were excused:

> ". . . When [the parties] stipulated that all of the earth and gravel needed for this purpose should be taken from plaintiff's land, they contemplated and assumed that the land contained the requisite quantity, available for use. The defendants were not binding themselves to take what was not there. And, in determining whether the earth and gravel were "available," we must view the conditions in a practical and reasonable way. Although there was gravel on the land, it was so situated that the defendants could not take it by ordinary means, nor except at a prohibitive cost. To all fair intents then, it was impossible for defendants to take it.

> ". . . A thing is impossible in legal contemplation when it is not practicable; and a thing is impracticable when it can only be done at an excessive and unreasonable cost." 1 Beach on Contr. § 216. We do not mean to intimate that the defendants could excuse themselves by showing the existence of conditions which would make the performance of their obligation more expensive than they had anticipated, or which would entail a loss upon them. But, where the difference in cost is so great as here, and has the effect, as found, of making performance impracticable, the situation is not different from that of a total absence of earth and gravel.

TRANSATLANTIC FINANCING CORP. V. UNITED STATES

United States Court of Appeals, District of Columbia Circuit, 1966.
363 F.2d 312.

Before DANAHER, WRIGHT and MCGOWAN, CIRCUIT JUDGES.

J. SKELLY WRIGHT, CIRCUIT JUDGE. This appeal involves a voyage charter between Transatlantic Financing Corporation, operator of the SS CHRISTOS, and the United States covering carriage of a full cargo of wheat from a United States Gulf port to a safe port in Iran. The District Court dismissed a libel filed by Transatlantic against the United States for costs attributable to the ship's diversion from the normal sea route caused by the closing of the Suez Canal. We affirm.

On July 26, 1956, the Government of Egypt nationalized the Suez Canal Company and took over operation of the Canal. On October 2, 1956, during the international crisis which resulted from the seizure, the voyage charter in suit was executed between representatives of Transatlantic and the United States. The charter indicated the termini of the voyage but not the route. On October 27, 1956, the SS CHRISTOS sailed from Galveston for Bandar Shapur, Iran, on a course which would have taken her through Gibraltar and the Suez Canal. On October 29, 1956, Israel invaded Egypt. On October 31, 1956, Great Britain and France invaded the Suez Canal Zone. On November 2, 1956, the Egyptian Government obstructed the Suez Canal with sunken vessels and closed it to traffic.

On or about November 7, 1956, Beckmann, representing Transatlantic, contacted Potosky, an employee of the United States Department of Agriculture, who appellant concedes was unauthorized to bind the Government, requesting instructions concerning disposition of the cargo and seeking an agreement for payment of additional compensation for a voyage around the Cape of Good Hope. Potosky advised Beckmann that Transatlantic was expected to perform the charter according to its terms, that he did not believe Transatlantic was entitled to additional compensation for a voyage around the Cape, but that Transatlantic was free to file such a claim. Following this discussion, the CHRISTOS changed course for the Cape of Good Hope and eventually arrived in Bandar Shapur on December 30, 1956.

Transatlantic's claim is based on the following train of argument. The charter was a contract for a voyage from a Gulf port to Iran. Admiralty principles and practices, especially stemming from the doctrine of deviation, require us to imply into the contract the term that the voyage was to be performed by the "usual and customary" route. The usual and customary route from Texas to Iran was, at the time of contract, via Suez, so the contract was for a voyage from Texas to Iran via Suez. When Suez was closed this contract became impossible to perform. Consequently, appellant's argument continues, when Transatlantic delivered the cargo by going around the Cape of Good Hope, in compliance with the Government's demand under claim of right, it conferred a benefit upon the United States for which it should be paid in *quantum meruit.*

The doctrine of impossibility of performance has gradually been freed from the earlier fictional and unrealistic strictures of such tests as the "implied term" and the parties' "contemplation." Page, The Development of the Doctrine of Impossibility of Performance, 18 Mich.L.Rev. 589, 596 (1920). See generally 6 Corbin, Contracts §§ 1320–1372 (rev. ed. 1962); 6 Williston, Contracts §§ 1931–1979 (rev. ed. 1938). It is now recognized that " 'A thing is impossible in legal contemplation when it is not practicable; and a thing is impracticable when it can only be done at an excessive and unreasonable cost.' " Mineral Park Land Co. v. Howard, 172 Cal. 289, 293, 156 P. 458, 460, L.R.A. 1916F, 1 (1916). Accord, Whelan v. Griffith Consumers Company, D.C.Mun.App., 170 A.2d 229 (1961); Restatement, Contracts § 454 (1932); Uniform Commercial Code (U.L.A.) § 2–615, comment 3. The doctrine ultimately represents the ever-shifting line, drawn by courts hopefully responsive to commercial practices and mores, at which the community's interest in having contracts enforced according to their terms is outweighed by the commercial senselessness of requiring performance.[1] When the issue is raised, the court is asked to construct a condition of performance based on the changed circumstances, a process which involves at least three reasonably definable steps. First, a contingency—something unexpected—must have occurred. Second, the risk of the unexpected occurrence must not have been allocated either by agreement or by custom. Finally, occurrence of the contingency must have rendered performance commercially impracticable.[3] Unless the court finds these three requirements satisfied, the plea of impossibility must fail.

The first requirement was met here. It seems reasonable, where no route is mentioned in a contract, to assume the parties expected performance by the usual and customary route at the time of contract. Since the usual and customary route from Texas to Iran at the time of contract[5] was through Suez, closure of the Canal made impossible the

---

[1]   While the impossibility issue rarely arises, as it has here, in a suit to recover the cost of an alternative method of performance, compare Annot., 84 A.L.R.2d 12, 19 (1962), there is nothing necessarily inconsistent in claiming commercial impracticability for the method of performance actually adopted; the concept of impracticability assumes performance was physically possible. Moreover, a rule making nonperformance a condition precedent to recovery would unjustifiably encourage disappointment of expectations.

[3]   Compare Uniform Commercial Code § 2–615 (a). . . .

[5]   . . . It may be that very often the availability of a customary route at the time of performance other than the route expected to be used at the time of contract should result in denial of relief under the impossibility theory; certainly if *no* customary route is available at the time of performance the contract is rendered impossible. But the same customarily used alternative route may be practicable in one set of circumstances and impracticable in another, as where the goods are unable to survive the extra journey. Moreover, . . . the alternative route, in our case around the Cape, may be practicable at some time during performance, for example while the vessel is still in the Atlantic Ocean, and impracticable at another time during performance, for example after the vessel has traversed most of the Mediterranean Sea. . . .

expected method of performance. But this unexpected development raises rather than resolves the impossibility issue, which turns additionally on whether the risk of the contingency's occurrence had been allocated and, if not, whether performance by alternative routes was rendered impracticable.

Proof that the risk of a contingency's occurrence has been allocated may be expressed in or implied from the agreement. Such proof may also be found in the surrounding circumstances, including custom and usages of the trade. See 6 Corbin, supra, § 1339, at 394–397; 6 Williston, supra, § 1948, at 5457–5458. The contract in this case does not expressly condition performance upon availability of the Suez route. Nor does it specify "via Suez" or, on the other hand, "via Suez or Cape of Good Hope." Nor are there provisions in the contract from which we may properly imply that the continued availability of Suez was a condition of performance.[8] Nor is there anything in custom or trade usage, or in the surrounding circumstances generally, which would support our constructing a condition of performance. The numerous cases requiring performance around the Cape when Suez was closed, see e.g., Ocean Tramp Tankers Corp. v. V/O Sovfracht (The Eugenia), [1964] 2 Q.B. 226, and cases cited therein, indicate that the Cape route is generally regarded as an alternative means of performance. So the implied expectation that the route would be via Suez is hardly adequate proof of an allocation to the promisee of the risk of closure. In some cases, even an express expectation may not amount to a condition of performance.[9] The doctrine of deviation supports our assumption that parties normally expect performance by the usual and customary route, but it adds nothing beyond this that is probative of an allocation of the risk.[10]

---

[8] The charter provides that the vessel is "in every way fitted for *the voyage*" (emphasis added), and the "P. & I. Bunker Deviation Clause" refers to "the contract voyage" and the "direct and/or customary route." Appellant argues that these provisions require implication of a voyage by the direct and customary route. Actually they prove only what we are willing to accept—that the parties expected the usual and customary route would be used. The provisions in no way condition performance upon nonoccurrence of this contingency. . . .

[9] [The court here quoted UCC § 2–614(1).]

[10] The deviation doctrine, drawn principally from admiralty insurance practice, implies into all relevant commercial instruments naming the termini of voyages the usual and customary route between those points. 1 Arnould, Marine Insurance and Average § 376, at 522 (10th ed. 1921). Insurance is cancelled when a ship unreasonably "deviates" from this course, for example by extending a voyage or by putting in at an irregular port, and the shipowner forfeits the protection of clauses of exception which might otherwise have protected him from his common law insurer's liability to cargo. See Gilmore & Black [on Admiralty] § 2–6, at 59–60. This practice, properly qualified see id. § 3–41, makes good sense, since insurance rates are computed on the basis of the implied course, and deviations in the course increasing the anticipated risk make the insurer's calculations meaningless. Arnould, supra, § 14, at 26. Thus the route, so far as insurance contracts are concerned, is crucial, whether express or implied. But even here, the implied term is not inflexible. Reasonable deviations do not result in loss of insurance, at least so long as established practice is followed . . . The doctrine's only relevance, therefore, is that it provides additional support for the assumption we willingly make that merchants agreeing to a voyage between two

If anything, the circumstances surrounding this contract indicate that the risk of the Canal's closure may be deemed to have been allocated to Transatlantic. We know or may safely assume that the parties were aware, as were most commercial men with interests affected by the Suez situation, see The Eugenia, supra, that the Canal might become a dangerous area. No doubt the tension affected freight rates, and it is arguable that the risk of closure became part of the dickered terms. Uniform Commercial Code § 2–615, comment 8. We do not deem the risk of closure so allocated, however. Foreseeability or even recognition of a risk does not necessarily prove its allocation.[11] Compare Uniform Commercial Code § 2–615, Comment 1; Restatement, Contracts § 457 (1932). Parties to a contract are not always able to provide for all the possibilities of which they are aware, sometimes because they cannot agree, often simply because they are too busy. Moreover, that some abnormal risk was contemplated is probative but does not necessarily establish an allocation of the risk of the contingency which actually occurs. In this case, for example, nationalization by Egypt of the Canal Corporation and formation of the Suez Users Group did not necessarily indicate that the Canal would be blocked even if a confrontation resulted.[12] The surrounding circumstances do indicate, however, a willingness by Transatlantic to assume abnormal risks, and this fact should legitimately cause us to judge the impracticability of performance by an alternative route in stricter terms than we would were the contingency unforeseen.

We turn then to the question whether occurrence of the contingency rendered performance commercially impracticable under the circumstances of this case. The goods shipped were not subject to harm from the longer, less temperate Southern route. The vessel and crew were fit to proceed around the Cape. Transatlantic was no less able than the United States to purchase insurance to cover the contingency's occurrence. If anything, it is more reasonable to expect owner-operators of vessels to insure against the hazards of war. They are in the best position to calculate the cost of performance by alternative routes (and therefore to estimate the amount of insurance required), and are undoubtedly sensitive to international troubles which uniquely affect the demand for and cost of their services. The only factor operating here in appellant's favor is the

points expect that the usual and customary route between those points will be used. The doctrine provides no evidence of an allocation of the risk of the route's unavailability.

[11] See Note, The Fetish of Impossibility in the Law of Contracts, 53 Colum.L.Rev. 94, 98 n. 23 (1953), suggesting that foreseeability is properly used "as a *factor* probative of assumption of the risk of impossibility." (Emphasis added.)

[12] Sources cited in the briefs indicate formation of the Suez Canal Users Association on October 1, 1956, was viewed in some quarters as an implied threat of force. See N.Y. Times, Oct. 2, 1956, p. 1, col. 1, noting, on the day the charter in this case was executed, that "Britain has declared her freedom to use force as a last resort if peaceful methods fail to achieve a satisfactory settlement." Secretary of State Dulles was able, however, to view the statement as evidence of the canal users' "dedication to a just and peaceful solution." The Suez Problem 369–370 (Department of State Pub.1956).

added expense, allegedly $43,972.00 above and beyond the contract price of $305,842.92, of extending a 10,000 mile voyage by approximately 3,000 miles. While it may be an overstatement to say that increased cost and difficulty of performance never constitute impracticability, to justify relief there must be more of a variation between expected cost and the cost of performing by an available alternative than is present in this case, where the promisor can legitimately be presumed to have accepted some degree of abnormal risk, and where impracticability is urged on the basis of added expense alone.

We conclude, therefore, as have most other courts considering related issues arising out of the Suez closure, that performance of this contract was not rendered legally impossible. Even if we agreed with appellant, its theory of relief seems untenable. When performance of a contract is deemed impossible it is a nullity. In the case of a charter party involving carriage of goods, the carrier may return to an appropriate port and unload its cargo, The Malcolm Baxter, Jr., 277 U.S. 323, 48 S.Ct. 516, 72 L.Ed. 901 (1928), subject of course to required steps to minimize damages. If the performance rendered has value, recovery in *quantum meruit* for the entire performance is proper. But here Transatlantic has collected its contract price, and now seeks *quantum meruit* relief for the additional expense of the trip around the Cape. If the contract is a nullity, Transatlantic's theory of relief should have been *quantum meruit* for the entire trip, rather than only for the extra expense. Transatlantic attempts to take its profit on the contract, and then force the Government to absorb the cost of the additional voyage. When impracticability without fault occurs, the law seeks an equitable solution, see 6 Corbin, supra, § 1321, and *quantum meruit* is one of its potent devices to achieve this end. There is no interest in casting the entire burden of commercial disaster on one party in order to preserve the other's profit. Apparently the contract price in this case was advantageous enough to deter appellant from taking a stance on damages consistent with its theory of liability. In any event, there is no basis for relief.

Affirmed.

Mishara Constr. Co. v. Transit-Mixed Concrete Corp.

365 Mass. 122, 310 N.E.2d 363 (1974)

"With respect to the requirement that performance must have been impracticable, the Official Code Comment to the section stresses that the reference is to 'commercial impracticability' as opposed to strict impossibility. G.L. c. 106, § 2–615, comments 3–4. This is not a radical departure from the common law of contracts as interpreted by this court. Although a strict rule was originally followed denying any excuse for accident or 'inevitable necessity,' e.g., Adams v. Nichols, 19 Pick. 275 (1837), it has long been assumed that circumstances drastically increasing the difficulty and expense of the contemplated performance may be within the compass of 'impossibility.' See Rowe v. Peabody, 207 Mass. 226, 233–234, 93 N.E. 604 (1911) (dictum); Fauci v. Denehy, 332 Mass. 691, 696–697, 127 N.E.2d 477 (1955). By adopting the term 'impracticability' rather than 'impossibility' the drafters of the Code appear to be in accord with Professor Williston who stated that 'the essence of the modern defense of impossibility is that the promised performance was at the making of the contract, or thereafter became, impracticable owing to some extreme or unreasonable difficulty, expense, injury, or loss involved, rather than that it is scientifically or actually impossible.' Williston, Contracts (Rev. ed.) § 1931 (1938). See Restatement: Contracts, § 454 (1932); Corbin, Contracts, § 1339 (1962).

"The second criterion of the excuse, that the intervening circumstance be one which the parties assumed would not occur, is also familiar to the law of Massachusetts. Baetjer v. New England Alcohol Co., 319 Mass. 592, 600, 66 N.E.2d 798 (1946). Boston Plate & Window Glass Co. v. John Bowen Co., Inc., 335 Mass. 697, 699–700, 141 N.E.2d 715 (1957). The rule is essentially aimed at the distribution of certain kinds of risks in the contractual relationship. By directing the inquiry to the time when the contract was first made, we really seek to determine whether the risk of the intervening circumstance was one which the parties may be taken to have assigned between themselves. It is, of course, the very essence of contract that it is directed at the elimination of some risks for each party in exchange for others. Each receives the certainty of price, quantity, and time, and assumes the risk of changing market prices, superior opportunity, or added costs. It is implicit in the doctrine of impossibility (and the companion rule of 'frustration of purpose') that certain risks are so unusual and have such severe consequences that they must have been beyond the scope of the assignment of risks inherent in the contract, that is, beyond the agreement made by the parties. To require performance in that case would be to grant the promisee an advantage for which he could not be said to have bargained in making the contract. 'The important question is whether an unanticipated circumstance has made performance of the promise vitally different from what should reasonably have been within the contemplation of both parties when they entered into the contract. If so, the risk should not fairly be thrown upon the promisor.' Williston, Contracts (Rev. ed.) § 1931 (1938). The emphasis in contracts governed by the Uniform Commercial Code is on the commercial context in which the agreement was made. The question is, given the commercial circumstances in which the parties dealt: Was the contingency which developed one which the parties could reasonably be thought to have foreseen as a real possibility which could affect performance? Was it one of that variety of risks which the parties were tacitly assigning to the promisor by their failure to provide for it explicitly? If it were, performance will be required. If it could not be so considered, performance is excused. The contract cannot be reasonably thought to govern in these circumstances, and the parties are both thrown upon the resources of the open market without the benefit of their contract."

UCC §§ 1–103, 2–509, 2–510, 2–613, 2–614, 2–615, 2–616

[See Selected Source Materials Supplement]

RESTATEMENT, SECOND, CONTRACTS §§ 261–272

[See Selected Source Materials Supplement]

CISG ARTS. 66–69

[See Selected Source Materials Supplement]

UNIDROIT PRINCIPLES OF INTERNATIONAL COMMERCIAL CONTRACTS ARTS. 6.2.1, 6.2.2, 6.2.3, 7.1.7

[See Selected Source Materials Supplement]

PRINCIPLES OF EUROPEAN CONTRACT LAW ARTS. 4.102, 6.111, 8.108

[See Selected Source Materials Supplement]

ALBRE MARBLE & TILE CO. v. JOHN BOWEN CO.
Supreme Judicial Court of Massachusetts, 1959.
338 Mass. 394, 155 N.E.2d 437.

Before SPALDING, WILLIAMS, COUNIHAN and WHITTEMORE, JJ.

SPALDING, JUSTICE. The declaration in this action of contract contains four counts. The plaintiff in counts 1 and 2 seeks damages for the defendant's alleged breach of two subcontracts under which the plaintiff agreed to supply labor and materials to the defendant as general contractor of the Chronic Disease Hospital and Nurses' Home in Boston.[1] In counts 3 and 4 the plaintiff seeks to recover the value of work and labor furnished by it to the defendant at the defendant's request. The defendant's substitute answer in defence to the first two counts states that the

---

[1]   Count 1 relates to tile work and count 2 relates to marble work.

performance of the subcontracts became impossible when the defendant's general contract with the Commonwealth was declared invalid by this court in Gifford v. Commissioner of Public Health, 328 Mass. 608, 105 N.E.2d 476. The defendant's answer to counts 3 and 4 (based on quantum meruit) states that no payment could be demanded because the plaintiff did not possess an architect's certificate for the work done. . . .

The defendant filed a motion, accompanied by an affidavit, for the immediate entry of judgment in its favor. . . . The plaintiff filed a counter affidavit. After hearing, the motion was allowed, and the plaintiff duly claimed an exception.

[The court concluded that the granting of defendant's motion for judgment on counts 1 and 2 was proper.]

We turn now to counts 3 and 4 by which the plaintiff seeks a recovery for the fair value of work and labor furnished to the defendant prior to the termination of the general contract. The plaintiff seeks recovery in count 3 for "preparation of samples, shop drawings, tests and affidavits" in connection with the tile work; in count 4 recovery for similar work in connection with the marble contract is sought.

The defendant in its affidavit maintains that the tile and marble work to be furnished by the plaintiff could not have been done until late in the construction process; that no tile or marble was actually installed in the building; and that the expenses incurred by the plaintiff prior to the time the general contract was declared invalid consisted solely of expenditures in preparation for performance. Relying on the decision in Young v. Chicopee, 186 Mass. 518, 72 N.E. 63, the defendant maintains that where a building contract has been rendered impossible of performance a plaintiff may not recover for expenses incurred in preparation for performance, but may recover only for the labor and materials "wrought into" the structure. Therefore, the defendant says, the plaintiff should take nothing here.

The plaintiff places its reliance upon a clause appearing in both contracts which provides in part: "It is agreed you [the plaintiff] will furnish and submit all necessary or required samples, shop drawings, tests, affidavits, etc., for approval, all as ordered or specified. . . . " The plaintiff in effect concedes that no labor or materials were actually wrought into the structure, but argues that the contract provision quoted above placed its preparatory efforts under the supervision of the defendant, and that this circumstance removes this case from the ambit of those decisions which apply the "wrought-in" principle. . . .

The problem of allocating losses where a building contract has been rendered impossible of performance by a supervening act not chargeable to either party is a vexed one. In situations where the part performance of one party measurably exceeds that of the other the tendency has been to allow recovery for the fair value of work done in the actual performance of the contract and to deny recovery for expenditures made in reliance upon the contract or in preparing to perform. This principle has sometimes been expressed in terms of "benefit" or "lack of benefit." In other words, recovery may be had only for those expenditures which, but for the supervening act, would have enured to the benefit of the defendant as contemplated by the contract. See, e.g. Young v. Chicopee, 186 Mass. 518, 520, 72 N.E. 63. The "wrought-in" principle applied in building contract cases is merely a variant of this principle. It has long been recognized that this theory is unworkable if the concept of benefit is applied literally. In M. Ahern Co. v. John Bowen Co. Inc., 334 Mass. 36, 41, 133 N.E.2d 484, 487, we quoted with approval the statement of Professor Williston that "It is enough that the defendant has actually received in part performance of the contract something for which when completed he had agreed to pay a price." Williston on Contracts (Rev. ed.) § 1976.

Although the matter of denial of reliance expenditures in impossibility situations seems to have been discussed but little in judicial opinions, it has, however, been the subject of critical comment by scholars. See Fuller and Perdue, The Reliance Interest in Contract Damages, 46 Yale L.J. 52, 373, 379–383. Note, 46 Mich.L.Rev. 401. In England the recent frustrated contracts legislation provides that the court may grant recovery for expenditures in reliance on the contract or in preparation to perform it where it appears "*just to do so having regard to all the circumstances of the case*" (emphasis supplied). 6 & 7 George VI, c. 40.

We are of opinion that the plaintiff here may recover for those expenditures made pursuant to the specific request of the defendant as set forth in the contract clause quoted above. A combination of factors peculiar to this case justifies such a holding without laying down the broader principle that in every case recovery may be had for payments made or obligations reasonably incurred in preparation for performance of a contract where further performance is rendered impossible without fault by either party. See Boston Plate & Window Glass Co. v. John Bowen Co. Inc., 335 Mass. 697, 702, 141 N.E.2d 715.

The factors which determine the holding here are these: First, this is not a case of mere impossibility by reason of a supervening act. The opinion of this court in M. Ahern Co. v. John Bowen Co. Inc., 334 Mass. 36, 133 N.E.2d 484, points out that the defendant's involvement in creating the impossibility was greater than that of its subcontractors. The facts regarding the defendant's conduct are set forth in that opinion and need not be restated.* Although the defendant's conduct was not so culpable as to render it liable for breach of contract (Boston Plate & Window Glass Co. v. John Bowen Co. Inc., 335 Mass. 697, 141 N.E.2d 715), nevertheless, it was a contributing factor to a loss sustained by the plaintiff which as

---

*   The defendant had presented its bid for the hospital construction project in such a manner as to cause the bid to appear to be the lowest although in fact it was not. (Footnote by ed.)

between the plaintiff and the defendant the latter ought to bear to the extent herein permitted.

We attach significance to the clause in the contract, which was prepared by the defendant, specifically requesting the plaintiff to submit samples, shop drawings, tests, affidavits, etc., to the defendant. This is not a case in which all efforts in preparation for performance were solely within the discretion and control of the subcontractor. We are mindful that in Young v. Chicopee, 186 Mass. 518, 72 N.E. 63, recovery of the value of materials brought to the construction site at the specific request of the defendant therein was denied. But in that case the supervening act rendering further performance impossible was a fire not shown to have been caused by the fault of either party. We are not disposed to extend that holding to a situation in which the defendant's fault is greater than the plaintiff's.

Moreover, the acts requested here by their very nature could not be "wrought into" the structure. In Angus v. Scully, 176 Mass. 357, 57 N.E. 674, 49 A.L.R. 562, recovery for the value of services rendered by house movers was allowed although the house was destroyed midway in the moving. The present case comes nearer to the rationale of the *Angus* case than to that of the *Young* case. . . .

We hold that the damages to be assessed are limited solely to the fair value of those acts done in conformity with the specific request of the defendant as contained in the contract. Expenses incurred prior to the execution of the contract, such as those arising out of preparing the plaintiff's bid, are not to be considered.

The plaintiff's exceptions as to counts 1 and 2 are overruled and are sustained as to counts 3 and 4; as to those counts the case is remanded to the Superior Court for further proceedings in conformity with this opinion. The appeal is dismissed.

So ordered.

———

NOTE ON THE EQUITABLE APPORTIONMENT
OF LOSSES FOLLOWING IMPOSSIBILITY

Restatement First seemed to adopt the assumption that the reimbursement of reliance is not a proper function of the courts except in tort cases. As a corollary, it was assumed that in contract cases a court has a choice, subject to the applicable rules of law, of (1) denying relief; (2) granting relief measured by the value of the performance promised by the defendant; or (3) granting relief measured by the value of the benefit conferred by the plaintiff on the defendant. The possibility of measuring relief by the plaintiff's losses through reliance was completely passed over, except insofar as it crept in, perhaps unintentionally, in certain of the illustrative cases. As applied to unexpected-circumstances cases, this meant that courts had to go whole hog or none in dealing with the problem of remedies. It is difficult to see anything in the American case law that compelled that assumption. If a court has power to impose an obligation to return benefits, it would seem also to have power to impose equitable conditions and limitations on this obligation. If a court has power to relieve a person from a promise because of an unexpected event, it would seem also to have power to relieve the person on condition that she reimburse all or a part of the other party's reliance on the contract.

Restatement Second takes a considerably different view on this matter than Restatement First. Under Restatement Second Section 272:

> (1) In any case governed by the rules stated in this Chapter [Impracticability and Frustration], either party may have a claim for relief including restitution . . .

> (2) In any case governed by the rules stated in this Chapter, if those rules together with the rules stated in [the chapter on remedies] will not avoid injustice, the court may grant relief on such terms as justice requires, including protection of the parties' reliance interests.

To the same effect is Official Comment 6 to UCC Section 2–615 (the principal UCC section dealing with the problem of unexpected circumstances):

> In situations in which neither sense nor justice is served by either answer when the issue is posed in flat terms of "excuse" or "no excuse," adjustment under the various provisions of this Article is necessary, especially the sections on good faith, on insecurity and assurance and on the reading of all provisions in the light of their purposes, and the general policy of this Act to use equitable principles in furtherance of commercial standards and good faith.

KRELL v. HENRY

In the Court of Appeal, 1903.
[1903] 2 K.B. 740.

Appeal from a decision of DARLING, J.

The plaintiff, Paul Krell, sued the defendant, C.S. Henry, for £50, being the balance of a sum of £75, for which the defendant had agreed to hire a flat at 56A, Pall Mall on the days of June 26 and 27, for the purpose of viewing the processions to be held in connection with the coronation of His Majesty. The defendant denied his liability, and counterclaimed for the return of the sum of £25, which had been paid as a deposit, on the ground that, the processions not having taken place owing to the serious illness of the King, there had been a total failure of consideration for the contract entered into by him.

The facts, which were not disputed, were as follows. The plaintiff on leaving the country in March, 1902, left instructions with his solicitor to let his suite of chambers at 56A, Pall Mall on such terms and for such period (not exceeding six months) as he thought proper. On June 17, 1902, the defendant noticed an announcement in the windows of the plaintiff's flat to the effect that windows to view the coronation processions were to be let. The defendant interviewed the housekeeper on the subject, when it was pointed out to him what a good view of the procession could be obtained from the premises, and he eventually agreed with the housekeeper to take the suite for the two days in question for a sum of £75.

On June 20 the defendant wrote the following letter to the plaintiff's solicitor:—

> "I am in receipt of yours of the 18th instant, inclosing form of agreement for the suite of chambers on the third floor at 56A, Pall Mall, which I have agreed to take for the two days, the 26th and 27th instant, for the sum of £75. For reasons given you I cannot enter into the agreement, but as arranged over the telephone I inclose herewith cheque for £25 as deposit, and will thank you to confirm to me that I shall have the entire use of these rooms during the days (not the nights) of the 26th and 27th instant. You may rely that every care will be taken of the premises and their contents. On the 24th inst. I will pay the balance, viz., £50, to complete the £75 agreed upon."

On the same day the defendant received the following reply from the plaintiff's solicitor:—

> "I am in receipt of your letter of today's date inclosing cheque for £25 deposit on your agreeing to take Mr. Krell's chambers on the third floor at 56A, Pall Mall for the two days, the 26th and 27th June, and I confirm the agreement that you are to have the entire use of these rooms during the days (but not the nights), the balance, £50, to be paid to me on Tuesday next the 24th instant."

The processions not having taken place on the days originally appointed, namely, June 26 and 27, the defendant declined to pay the balance of £50 alleged to be due from him under the contract in writing of June 20 constituted by the above two letters. Hence the present action.

DARLING J., on August 11, 1902, held upon the authority of Taylor v. Caldwell and The Moorcock (1889, 14 P.D. 64), that there was an implied condition in the contract that the procession should take place, and gave judgment for the defendant on the claim and counterclaim.

The plaintiff appealed.

Spencer Bower, K.C., and Holman Gregory, for the plaintiff. In the contract nothing is said about the coronation procession, but it is admitted that both parties expected that there would be a procession, and that the price to be paid for the rooms was fixed with reference to the expected procession. Darling J. held that both the claim and the counterclaim were governed by Taylor v. Caldwell, and that there was an implied term in the contract that the procession should take place. It is submitted that the learned judge was wrong. If he was right, the result would be that in every case of this kind an unremunerated promisor will be in effect an insurer of the hopes and expectations of the promisee. . . . In order that the person who has contracted to pay the price should be excused from doing so, there must be (1) no default on his part; (2) either the physical extinction or the not coming into existence of the subject-matter of the contract; (3) the performance of the contract must have been thereby rendered impossible.

In the present case there has been no default on the part of the defendant. But there has been no physical extinction of the subject-matter, and the performance of the contract was quite possible. . . .

VAUGHAN WILLIAMS, L.J. read the following written judgment:—The real question in this case is the extent of the application in English law of the principle of the Roman law which has been adopted and acted on in many English decisions, and notably in the case of Taylor v. Caldwell. . . . It is said, on the one side, that the specified thing, state of things, or condition the continued existence of which is necessary for the fulfilment of the contract, so that the parties entering into the contract must have contemplated the continued existence of that thing, condition, or state of things as the foundation of what was to be done under the contract, is limited to things which are either the subject-matter of the contract or a condition or state of things, present or anticipated, which is expressly mentioned in the contract. But, on the other side, it is said that the condition or state of things need not be expressly specified, but that it is sufficient if that condition or state of things clearly appears by extrinsic evidence to have been assumed by the parties to be the foundation or basis of the contract, and the event which causes the impossibility is of such a character that it cannot reasonably be supposed to have been in the contemplation of the contracting parties when the contract was made. In such a case the contracting parties will not be held bound by the general words which, though large enough to include, were not used with reference to a possibility of a particular event rendering performance of the contract impossible. I do not think that the principle of the civil law as introduced into the English law is limited to cases in which the event causing the impossibility of performance is the destruction or nonexistence of some thing which is the subject-matter of the contract or of some condition or state of things expressly specified as a condition of it. I think that you first have to ascertain, not necessarily from the terms of the contract, but, if required, from necessary inferences, drawn from surrounding circumstances recognized by both contracting parties, what is the substance of the contract, and then to ask the question whether that substantial contract needs for its foundation the assumption of the existence of a particular state of things. If it does, this will limit the operation of the general words, and in such case, if the contract becomes impossible of performance by reason of the nonexistence of the state of things assumed by both contracting parties as the foundation of the contract, there will be no breach of the contract thus limited. . . .

In my judgment [in this case] the use of the rooms was let and taken for the purpose of seeing the Royal procession. It was not a demise of the rooms, or even an agreement to let and take the rooms. It is a licence to use rooms for a particular purpose and none other. And in my judgment the taking place of those processions on the days proclaimed along the proclaimed route, which passed 56A, Pall Mall, was regarded by both contracting parties as the foundation of the contract; and I think that it cannot reasonably be supposed to have been in the contemplation of the contracting parties, when the contract was made, that the coronation would not be held on the proclaimed days, or the processions not take place on those days along the proclaimed route; and I think that the words imposing on the defendant the obligation to accept and pay for the use of the rooms for the named days, although general and unconditional, were not used with reference to the possibility of the particular contingency which afterwards occurred.

It was suggested in the course of the argument that if the occurrence, on the proclaimed days, of the coronation and the procession in this case were the foundation of the contract, and if the general words are thereby limited or qualified, so that in the event of the non-occurrence of the coronation and procession along the proclaimed route they would discharge both parties from further performance of the contract, it would follow that if a cabman was engaged to take some one to Epsom on Derby Day at a suitable enhanced price for such a journey, say £10, both parties to the contract would be discharged in the contingency of the race at Epsom for some reason becoming impossible; but I do not think this follows, for I do not think that in the cab case the happening of the race would be the foundation of the contract. No doubt the purpose of the engager would be to go to see the Derby, and the price would be proportionately high; but the cab had no special qualifications for the purpose which led to the selection of the cab for this particular occasion. Any other cab would have done as well. Moreover, I think, that under the cab contract, the hirer, even if the race went off, could have said, "Drive me to Epsom; I will pay you the agreed sum; you have nothing to do with the purpose for which I hired the cab," and that if the cabman refused he would have been guilty of a breach of contract, there being nothing to qualify his promise to drive the hirer to Epsom on a particular day. Whereas in the case of the coronation, there is not merely the purpose of the hirer to see the coronation procession, but it is the coronation procession and the relative position of the rooms which is the basis of the contract as much for the lessor as the hirer; and I think that if the King, before the coronation day and after the contract, had died, the hirer could not have insisted on having the rooms on the days named. It could not in the cab case be reasonably said that seeing the Derby race was the foundation of the contract, as it was of the licence in this case. Whereas in the present case, where the rooms were offered and taken, by reason of their peculiar suitability from the position of the rooms for a view of the coronation procession, surely the view of the coronation procession was the foundation of the contract, which is a very different thing from the purpose of the man who engaged the cab—namely, to see the race—being held to be the foundation of the contract.

Each case must be judged by its own circumstances. In each case one must ask oneself, first, what, having regard to all the circumstances, was the foundation of the contract? Secondly, was the performance of the contract prevented? Thirdly, was the event which prevented the performance of the contract of such a character that it cannot reasonably be said to have been in the contemplation of the parties at the date of the contract? If all these questions are answered in the affirmative (as I think they should be in this case), I think both parties are discharged from further performance of the contract. . . .

This disposes of the plaintiff's claim for £50 unpaid balance of the price agreed to be paid for the use of the rooms. The defendant at one time set up a cross-claim for the return of the £25 he paid at the date of the contract. As that claim is now withdrawn it is unnecessary to say anything about it. . . . I think this appeal ought to be dismissed.

[The concurring opinions of Romer, L.J., and Stirling, L.J., are omitted.]

Appeal dismissed.

––––––––

Wladis, Common Law and Uncommon Events: The Development of the Doctrine of Impossibility of Performance in English Contract Law

75 Geo.L.J. 1575, 1609, 1618 (1987)

"The facts giving rise to the coronation cases may be stated briefly: Edward VII was to be crowned on Thursday, June 26, 1902, in Westminster Abbey. There was to be a coronation procession that day between the royal residence at Buckingham Palace and the Abbey, and a lengthier one [on June 27] throughout the city of London. In addition, on Saturday, June 28, a naval review of the fleet was to take place. Flats were let, grandstands erected, and seats sold along the routes of the processions. Boats were also chartered to take the public to the naval review. However, during the morning of June 24 it was determined that Edward, who had been suffering from appendicitis, needed to undergo surgery. Later that day it was announced that the coronation would be postponed and the naval review not held. . . .

" . . . The coronation events were not canceled, but only postponed. The procession [scheduled for] June 26 eventually took place on August 9 and proceeded along the same route as had originally been planned. The procession scheduled for June 27 occurred on October 25 and followed as nearly as possible the original route. Even the naval review that had been canceled was rescheduled and held on August 16."

———

La Cumbre Golf & Country Club v. Santa Barbara Hotel Co.

205 Cal. 422, 271 P. 476 (1928)

Santa Barbara Hotel Co. owned and operated the Ambassador Hotel. Under a contract between Santa Barbara and the La Cumbre Golf and Country Club, La Cumbre extended privileges at its Club to guests at the Ambassador. In 1920, Santa Barbara wanted to purchase and operate a bus between the Ambassador and the Club, provided the golf privileges were extended over an additional period of time. Accordingly, the parties made a contract for a period ending December 31, 1923, under which La Cumbre agreed that it would grant all the privileges of membership to guests at the Ambassador, and Santa Barbara agreed to be responsible for the guests' greens fees and to pay La Cumbre $300 a month. In April 1921, the Ambassador burned down. Santa Barbara stopped making payments under the contract, and La Cumbre sued for the balance due, $7200. Held, for Santa Barbara. It was an implied condition of the contract that there would be guests in the Ambassador.

———

Chase Precast Corp. v. John J. Paonessa Co.

409 Mass. 371, 566 N.E.2d 603 (1991)

In 1982, the Commonwealth of Massachusetts, through the Department of Public Works (the Department), entered into two contracts with Paonessa for resurfacing and improvements on two stretches of Route 128. Part of each contract called for replacing a grass median strip between the north- and south-bound lanes with concrete surfacing and precast concrete median barriers. Paonessa then entered into two contracts with Chase, under which Chase was to supply 25,800 linear feet of precast concrete median barriers according to the Department's specifications. The quantity and type of barriers to be supplied were specified in two purchase orders prepared by Chase.

The highway reconstruction began in the spring of 1983. By late May, the Department was receiving protests from angry residents who objected to use of the concrete median barriers and removal of the grass median strip. Paonessa and Chase became aware of the protest around June 1. On June 6, a group of about 100 citizens filed an action in the Superior Court to stop installation of the concrete median barriers and other aspects of the work. On June 7, anticipating modification of the contracts by the Department, Paonessa notified Chase by letter to stop producing concrete barriers for the projects. Chase did so. On June 17, the Department and the citizens' group entered into a settlement which provided, in part, that no additional concrete median barriers would be installed. On June 23, the Department deleted the concrete-median-barriers item from its contracts with Paonessa.

Before stopping production on June 8, Chase had produced approximately one-half of the barriers required under its contracts with Paonessa, and had delivered most of these to the construction sites. Paonessa paid Chase, at the contract price, for all the barriers that Chase had produced. Chase suffered no out-of-pocket expense as a result of the cancellation of the remaining barriers.

Chase brought an action against Paonessa to recover its anticipated profit on the median barriers called for by its supply contracts with Paonessa but not produced. After a jury-waived trial, a Superior Court judge ruled for Paonessa on the basis of impossibility of performance. The Appeals Court affirmed, noting that the doctrine of frustration of purpose more accurately described the basis of the decision than the doctrine of impossibility. The Massachusetts Supreme Judicial Court agreed:

> Paonessa bore no responsibility for the department's elimination of the median barriers from the projects. Therefore, whether it can rely on the defense of frustration turns on whether elimination of the barriers was a risk allocated by the contracts to Paonessa. *Mishara Constr. Co., supra,* 365 Mass. [122,] at 129, 310 N.E.2d 363 [1974], articulates the relevant test:
>
>> "The question is, given the commercial circumstances in which the parties dealt: Was the contingency which developed one which the parties could reasonably be thought to have foreseen as a real possibility which could affect performance? Was it one of that variety of risks which the parties were tacitly assigning to the promisor by their failure to provide for it explicitly? If it was, performance will be required. If it could not be so considered, performance is excused."

This is a question for the trier of fact. *Id.* at 127, 130, 310 N.E.2d 363.

Power Engineering & Manufacturing, Ltd. v. Krug International

501 N.W.2d 490 (Iowa 1993)

Tripod Laing had contracted to deliver to Iraqi Airways, in Iraq, an aeromedical equipment laboratory. One part of the laboratory was a human centrifuge to train jet pilots, and Tripod Laing contracted with Krug to build the centrifuge. Krug, in turn, contracted with Power Engineering for the construction of a gear box, to be used as a part of the centrifuge, for $149,700.

Power Engineering did not know the identity of either Krug's buyer (Tripod Laing) or the ultimate consumer (Iraqi Airways). During the initial manufacturing stages, Krug paid Power Engineering $75,000. The gear box was completed in late July, and a minor adjustment requested by Krug was completed in early August. On August 7, Krug authorized Power Engineering to ship the gear box.

The Gulf War with Iraq broke out on or about August 6, 1990. The United Nations immediately implemented an embargo against all shipments to Iraq. Reacting to the embargo, on August 7 Tripod Laing directed Krug to carry out no more work and expend no more money until further notice. Several days later, Krug learned that Power Engineering had not yet shipped the gear box, and directed Power Engineering not to ship it. The gear box remained in storage, because Krug refused to have it shipped. Power Engineering then brought suit for the balance of the purchase price. Held, for Power Engineering.

"Under [UCC § 2–615] a buyer wishing to escape from liability for nonperformance must make a three-pronged showing:

(1)   Its performance has become commercially impracticable,

(2)   By either

(a)   the occurrence of an unforeseen contingency the nonoccurrence of which was a basic assumption on which the contract was made, or

(b)   compliance in good faith with any applicable foreign or domestic governmental regulation or order whether or not it later proves to be invalid, and

(3)   It had not assumed the risk of the contingency or governmental regulation.

"We think the theory has no application here. In the first place Krug's performance cannot truly be said to be commercially impracticable.... The embargo does not prevent Krug from fulfilling its contractual obligations with Power Engineering. Although the embargo prevents products from being shipped to Iraq, it does not prohibit a domestic purchaser from buying, from a domestic manufacturer, a machinery component part intended for shipment there.

"We do not believe that the stop order further up the chain of contracts in this case constitutes an 'occurrence of a contingency the nonoccurrence of which was a basic assumption on which the contract was made.' Although Krug may have made assumptions regarding such unforeseen contingencies, Power Engineering was not privy to Krug's planned use of the gear box. Under the circumstances Krug must be found to have assumed the risk that its purchaser would not, or could not, perform."

———

PART 6

CONDITIONS

■ ■ ■

Part 6 of this book concerns conditions.

Chapter 19 concerns several doctrines that often are described as "constructive conditions." These doctrines are default rules that define when a breach by one party discharges the other party from her performance obligation under the contract, or at least allows the other party to suspend performance until the breach is cured.

Chapter 20 concerns express conditions. An express condition differs from a promise in that it imposes no obligation, but instead provides that a contracting party either does not come under a duty to perform unless a certain state of affairs exists, or is released from a duty to perform if a certain state of affairs exists.

CHAPTER 19

CONSTRUCTIVE CONDITIONS

■ ■ ■

This Chapter concerns a set of doctrines that often are described as constructive conditions. When a promise is subject to a condition, non-occurrence of the condition discharges the promisor from her obligation to perform the promise. Suppose A and B make a bargain in which A's achievement of objective x is of vital importance to B. B may encourage A to achieve x, and B may ensure she is not obligated to pay A if x is not achieved, by making A's achievement of x a condition to B's payment obligation. Express conditions tend to be clear cut. B wants condition x to be clearly defined to avoid any dispute about her payment obligation if x is not achieved.

The rules considered in this Chapter generally are not clear cut. They are standards that determine whether a party in B's position is discharged from her performance obligation because of A's nonperformance in the absence of an express condition. These standards generally ask a court to balance the risk the injured party will suffer an uncompensated loss if she is not discharged from her performance obligation and the risk the defaulter will suffer forfeiture if the injured party is discharged from her performance obligation. An important consideration is whether the injured party can be made whole by a damage award. Another important consideration is whether the defaulter has acted in bad faith.

The rules considered in this Chapter rest on the premise that obligations under a contract generally are mutually dependent, so that if one party fails to perform in a substantial or material respect, then the other party is discharged from her obligation. It took a long time for the common law to come around to this point of view. For much of the history of the common law promises were assumed to be independent, in the absence of an express condition. The final break with the old view came in a decision by Mansfield in 1773, Kingston v. Preston, 2 Douglas 689, which established that to recover on a contract claim a plaintiff generally must allege substantial performance of her promise, or some excuse for her failure to perform, such as a material breach by the defendant.

———

SECTION 1. COMMON LAW DOCTRINES

This Section concerns common law doctrines that determine when one party's breach of contract discharges the other party from her performance obligation under the contract. The issue is framed as one of substantial performance when the question is whether a party who has rendered defective or partial performance is entitled to the contract price less damages. More precisely, the doctrine of substantial performance concerns the question, when can a party who has breached a contract nevertheless bring suit under the contract. The doctrine of material breach concerns when a party who has *not* breached a contract has the power to suspend performance or the power to terminate a contract because of the other party's nonperformance.

(A) SUBSTANTIAL PERFORMANCE

JACOB & YOUNGS V. KENT
Court of Appeals of New York, 1921.
230 N.Y. 239, 129 N.E. 889, 23 A.L.R. 1429.

CARDOZO, J. The plaintiff built a country residence for the defendant at a cost of upwards of $77,000, and now sues to recover a balance of $3,483.46, remaining unpaid. The work of construction ceased in June, 1914, and the defendant then began to occupy the dwelling. There was no complaint of defective performance until March, 1915. One of the specifications for the plumbing work provides that "all wrought-iron pipe must be well galvanized, lap welded pipe of the grade known as 'standard pipe' of Reading manufacture."

The defendant learned in March, 1915, that some of the pipe, instead of being made in Reading, was the product of other factories. The plaintiff was accordingly directed by the architect to do the work anew. The plumbing was then encased within the walls except in a few places where it had to be exposed. Obedience to the order meant more than the substitution of other pipe. It meant the demolition at great expense of substantial parts of the completed structure. The plaintiff left the work untouched, and asked for a certificate that the final payment was due. Refusal of the certificate was followed by this suit.

The evidence sustains a finding that the omission of the prescribed brand of pipe was neither fraudulent nor wilful. It was the result of the oversight and inattention of the plaintiff's subcontractor. Reading pipe is distinguished from Cohoes pipe and other brands only by the name of the manufacturer stamped upon it at intervals of between six and seven feet. Even the defendant's architect, though he inspected the pipe upon arrival, failed to notice the discrepancy. The plaintiff tried to show that the brands installed, though made by other manufacturers, were the same in quality,

Same pipe except for brand name

in appearance, in market value, and in cost as the brand stated in the contract—that they were indeed, the same thing, though manufactured in another place. The evidence was excluded, and a verdict directed for the defendant. The Appellate Division reversed, and granted a new trial.

We think the evidence, if admitted would have supplied some basis for the inference that the defect was insignificant in its relation to the project. The courts never say that one who makes a contract fills the measure of his duty by less than full performance. They do say, however, that an omission, both trivial and innocent, will sometimes be atoned for by allowance of the resulting damage, and will not always be the breach of a condition to be followed by a forfeiture. . . . The distinction is akin to that between dependent and independent promises, or between promises and conditions. Anson on Contracts (Corbin's Ed.) § 367; 2 Williston on Contracts, § 842. Some promises are so plainly independent that they can never by fair construction be conditions of one another. Rosenthal Paper Co. v. Nat. Folding Box & Paper Co., 226 N.Y. 313, 123 N.E. 766; Bogardus v. N.Y. Life Ins. Co., 101 N.Y. 328, 4 N.E. 522. Others are so plainly dependent that they must always be conditions. Others, though dependent and thus conditions when there is departure in point of substance, will be viewed as independent and collateral when the departure is insignificant. 2 Williston on Contracts, §§ 841, 842; Eastern Forge Co. v. Corbin, 182 Mass. 590, 592, 66 N.E. 419; Robinson v. Mollett, L.R., 7 Eng. & Ir.App. 802, 814; Miller v. Benjamin, 142 N.Y. 613, 37 N.E. 631. Considerations partly of justice and partly of presumable intention are to tell us whether this or that promise shall be placed in one class or in another. The simple and the uniform will call for different remedies from the multifarious and the intricate. The margin of departure within the range of normal expectation upon a sale of common chattels will vary from the margin to be expected upon a contract for the construction of a mansion or a "skyscraper." There will be harshness sometimes and oppression in the implication of a condition when the thing upon which labor has been expended is incapable of surrender because united to the land, and equity and reason in the implication of a like condition when the subject-matter, if defective, is in shape to be returned. From the conclusion that promises may not be treated as dependent to the extent of their uttermost minutiae without sacrifice of justice, the progress is a short one to the conclusion that they may not be so treated without a perversion of intention. Intention not otherwise revealed may be presumed to hold in contemplation the reasonable and probable. If something else is in view, it must not be left to implication. There will be no assumption of a purpose to visit venial faults with oppressive retribution.

Those who think more of symmetry and logic in the development of legal rules than of practical adaptation to the attainment of a just result will be troubled by a classification where the lines of division are so wavering and blurred. Something doubtless, may be said on the score of consistency and certainty in favor of a stricter standard. The courts have balanced such considerations against those of equity and fairness, and found the latter to be the weightier. The decisions in this state commit us to the liberal view, which is making its way, nowadays, in jurisdictions slow to welcome it. Dakin & Co. v. Lee, 1916, 1 K.B. 566, 579. Where the line is to be drawn between the important and the trivial cannot be settled by a formula. "In the nature of the case precise boundaries are impossible." 2 Williston on Contracts, § 841. The same omission may take on one aspect or another according to its setting. Substitution of equivalents may not have the same significance in fields of art on the one side and in those of mere utility on the other. Nowhere will change be tolerated, however, if it is so dominant or pervasive as in any real or substantial measure to frustrate the purpose of the contract. Crouch v. Gutmann, 134 N.Y. 45, 51, 31 N.E. 271, 30 Am.St.Rep. 608. There is no general license to install whatever, in the builder's judgment, may be regarded as "just as good." Easthampton L. & C. Co., Ltd. v. Worthington, 186 N.Y. 407, 412, 79 N.E. 323. The question is one of degree, to be answered, if there is doubt, by the triers of the facts (Crouch v. Gutmann; Woodward v. Fuller, supra), and, if the inferences are certain, by the judges of the law (Easthampton L. & C. Co., Ltd. v. Worthington, supra). We must weigh the purpose to be served, the desire to be gratified, the excuse for deviation from the letter, the cruelty of enforced adherence. Then only can we tell whether literal fulfillment is to be implied by law as a condition. This is not to say that the parties are not free by apt and certain words to effectuate a purpose that performance of every term shall be a condition of recovery. That question is not here. This is merely to say that the law will be slow to impute the purpose, in the silence of the parties, where the significance of the default is grievously out of proportion to the oppression of the forfeiture. The wilful transgressor must accept the penalty of his transgression. Schultze v. Goodstein, 180 N.Y. 248, 251, 73 N.E. 21; Desmond-Dunne Co. v. Friedman-Doscher Co., 162 N.Y. 486, 490, 56 N.E. 995. For him there is no occasion to mitigate the rigor of implied conditions. The transgressor whose default is unintentional and trivial may hope for mercy if he will offer atonement for his wrong. Spence v. Ham [163 N.Y. 220, 57 N.E. 412].

In the circumstances of this case, we think the measure of the allowance is not the cost of replacement, which would be great, but the difference in value, which would be either nominal or nothing. . . . It is true that in most cases the cost of replacement is the measure. Spence v. Ham, supra. The owner is entitled to the money which will permit him to complete, unless the cost of completion is grossly and unfairly out of proportion to the good to be attained. When that is true, the measure is the difference in value. . . .

The order should be affirmed, and judgment absolute directed in favor of the plaintiff upon the stipulation, with costs in all courts. . . .

[The dissenting opinion of McLaughlin, J. is omitted.]

———

R. Danzig, The Capability Problem in Contract Law

120–23 (1978)

"The contract [in Jacob & Youngs v. Kent] specified a standard of pipe [wrought iron] which cost 30% more than steel pipe—then the most widely used (and now the almost universally used) pipe. The makers of wrought iron pipe, however, claimed that the savings due to durability and low maintenance more than made up for the added expense. . . .

"The Reading Company was by its account the largest manufacturer of wrought iron pipe in the country. . . .

". . . According to a pipe wholesaler interviewed in New York City in 1975, genuine wrought iron pipe was manufactured in the pre-war period by four largely noncompeting companies: Reading, Cohoes, Byers and Southchester. According to this informant, all of these brands 'were of the same quality and price. The manufacturer's name would make absolutely no difference in pipe or in price.' . . .

"Why then was Reading Pipe specified? Apparently because it was the normal trade practice to assure wrought iron pipe quality by naming a manufacturer. In contemporary trade bulletins put out by Byers and Reading, prospective buyers were cautioned that some steel pipe manufacturers used iron pipe and often sold under misleading names like 'wrought pipe.' To avoid such inferior products, Byers warned: 'When wrought iron pipe is desired, the specifications often read "genuine wrought iron pipe" but as this does not always exclude wrought iron containing steel scrap, it is safer to mention the name of a manufacturer known not to use scrap.'"

———

Vincenzi v. Cerro

186 Conn. 612, 442 A.2d 1352 (1982)

"The principal claim of the defendants is that the doctrine of substantial performance was inapplicable in this case because the plaintiffs were guilty of a willful or intentional breach of contract by failing to complete all of the work required. . . . We have in several cases approved the common statement that a contractor who is guilty of a 'willful' breach cannot maintain an action upon the contract. . . . The contemporary view, however, is that even a conscious and intentional departure from the contract specifications will not necessarily defeat recovery, but may be considered as one of the several factors involved in deciding whether there has been full performance. 3A Corbin, Contract § 707;

2 Restatement (Second), Contracts § 237, comment D. The pertinent inquiry is not simply whether the breach was 'willful' but whether the behavior of the party in default 'comports with standard of good faith and fair dealing.' 2 Restatement (Second), Contracts § 241(e); see comment f. Even an adverse conclusion on this point is not decisive but is to be weighted with other factors, such as the extent to which the owner will be deprived of a reasonably expected benefit and the extent to which the builder may suffer forfeiture, in deciding whether there has been substantial performance. Id.; see § 237, comment d."

O.W. Grun Roofing & Constr. Co. v. Cope

529 S.W.2d 258 (Tex.Civ.App.1975)

Grun agreed to install a new russet-colored shingle roof on Cope's home for $648. As actually installed, the roof had yellow streaks but was structurally sound. Cope refused to pay, and Grun filed a mechanic's lien. Cope then sued to set aside the lien and for damages equal to difference between (i) the $648 price under the contract with Grun and (ii) the cost of installing a new roof, which was 20% higher. The trial court set aside the lien and awarded Cope $123, based on the cost to install a new roof ($648 plus 20% for price increases). Affirmed:

> . . . It should not come as a shock to anyone to adopt a rule to the effect that a person has, particularly with respect to his home, to choose for himself and to contract for something which exactly satisfies that choice, and not to be compelled to accept something else. In the matter of homes and their decoration, as much as, if not more than, in many other fields, mere taste or preference, almost approaching whimsy, may be controlling with the homeowner, so that variations which might, under other circumstances, be considered trifling, may be inconsistent with that "substantial performance" on which liability to pay must be predicated. [M]ere incompleteness or deviations which may be easily supplied or remedied after the contractor has finished his work, and the cost of which to the owner is not excessive and readily ascertainable, present less cause for hesitation in concluding that the performance tendered constitutes substantial performance, since in such cases the owner can obtain complete satisfaction by merely spending some money and deducting the amount of such expenditure from the contract price.

> In the case before us there is evidence to support the conclusion that plaintiff can secure a roof of uniform coloring only by installing a completely new roof. We cannot say, as a matter of law, that the evidence establishes that in this case that a roof which so lacks uniformity in color as to give the appearance of a patch job serves essentially the same purpose as a roof of uniform color which has the appearance of being a new roof. We are not prepared to hold that a contractor who tenders a performance so deficient that it can be

remedied only by completely redoing the work for which the contract called has established, as a matter of law, that he has substantially performed his contractual obligation.

A recovery by Grun in quantum meruit for benefit conferred was denied:

. . . [T]he evidence does not conclusively establish that plaintiff has received any benefit from defendant's defective performance. As already pointed out, there is evidence that plaintiff will have to install a completely new roof.

────────

NOTE ON RESTITUTION IN FAVOR OF A PLAINTIFF IN DEFAULT

The quantum meruit claim brought by Grun alongside the claim for the contract price is part of the law of restitution or unjust enrichment. A party who partially performs a contract and then defaults has a claim in restitution to be compensated for the performance rendered, if the plaintiff can establish that the defendant otherwise would receive a windfall, i.e. be in a better position than the defendant would have been on full performance. The restitution claim can be brought by a defaulting purchaser of real property to recover a deposit when the purchaser can establish that the seller suffered a smaller loss as a result of the purchaser's breach. Usually this will be because the seller resells the property for the contract price, or an amount near the contract price. In a sale of goods, U.C.C. § 2–718(2) and (3) give a purchaser the right to recover a deposit if the seller cannot establish damages. A seller is allowed to retain part of the deposit as statutory liquidated damages (the lesser of $500 or 20 percent of the purchase price). Under both the common law rule and U.C.C. § 2–718(2), if the contract provides a deposit is forfeited as liquidated damages, then the rule on penalties determines the seller's right to retain the deposit.

In construction cases a contractor may bring a restitution claim alongside a claim for the contract price. To recover the contract price (less damages), the contractor must persuade the court that his performance satisfies the substantial performance test. The restitution claim gives the contractor a second chance at recovering some compensation for his work. From the perspective of the court, the consequence of finding the contractor's performance satisfies the substantial performance test is that this places the burden on the defendant to establish damages as an offset to the contract price. On the other hand, if the court finds the contractor's performance does not satisfy the substantial performance test, then this places the burden on the contractor to establish that the defendant would be unjustly enriched, if the defendant did not pay for the work done. The defendant can shield himself from a claim of substantial performance and a restitution claim by making his obligation to pay subject to a condition. The contractor would have to look to doctrines covered in Chapter 20 to excuse his nonfulfillment of a condition.

Vines v. Orchard Hills, Inc.

181 Conn. 501, 435 A.2d 1022 (1980)

(Peters, J.) "This case concerns the right of purchasers of real property, after their own default, to recover moneys paid at the time of execution of a valid contract of sale. The plaintiffs, Euel D. Vines and his wife Etta Vines, contracted, on July 11, 1973, to buy Unit No. 10, Orchard Hills Condominium, New Canaan, Connecticut, from the defendant Orchard Hills, Inc. for $78,800. On or before that date, they had paid the defendant $7880 as a down payment toward the purchase. Alleging that the sale of the property was never consummated, the plaintiffs sought to recover their down payment. . . .

". . . The purchasers decided not to take title to the condominium because Euel D. Vines was transferred by his employer to New Jersey; the Vines so informed the seller by a letter dated January 4, 1974. There has never been any claim that the seller has failed, in any respect, to conform to his obligations under the contract, nor does the complaint allege that the purchasers are legally excused from their performance under the contract. In short, it is the purchasers and not the seller whose breach precipitated the present cause of action. . . .

"The right of a contracting party, despite his default, to seek restitution for benefits conferred and allegedly unjustly retained has been much disputed in the legal literature and in the case law. . . . Although earlier cases often refused to permit a party to bring an action that could be said to be based on his own breach . . . many of the more recent cases support restitution in order to prevent unjust enrichment and to avoid forfeiture. . . .

"A variety of considerations, some practical and some theoretical, underlie this shift in attitude toward the plaintiff in breach. As Professor Corbin pointed out in his seminal article, 'The Right of a Defaulting Vendee to the Restitution of Installments Paid,' 40 Yale L.J. 1013 (1931), the anomalous result of denying any remedy to the plaintiff in breach is to punish more severely the person who has partially performed, often in good faith, than the person who has entirely disregarded his contractual obligations from the outset. Only partial performance triggers a claim for restitution, and partial performance will not, in the ordinary course of events, have been more injurious to the innocent party than total nonperformance. Recognition of a claim in restitution is, furthermore, consistent with the economic functions that the law of contracts is designed to serve. See Kessler & Gilmore, Contracts, pp. 4–6 (1970). The principal purpose of remedies for the breach of contract is to provide compensation for loss; see Restatement (Second), Contracts, c. 16, Introductory Note (Tent.Draft No. 14, 1979); Farnsworth, 'Legal Remedies for Breach of Contract,' 70 Colum.L.Rev. 1145 (1970); and therefore a party injured by breach of contract is entitled to retain nothing in excess of that sum which compensates him for the loss of his bargain. . . .

"Recognition that there are circumstances under which a defaulting purchaser may be entitled to restitution for benefits conferred upon the innocent seller of land is consistent with parallel developments elsewhere in the law of contracts. Judicial resistance to enforcement of forfeitures has of course long been commonplace, particularly with regard to contract clauses purporting to liquidate damages. See 5 Corbin, Contracts § 1058 (1964); 5 Williston, Contracts § 788 (3d Ed.1961). Despite the deference afforded by nineteenth-century courts to freedom of contract in other areas; see Weisbrod, The Boundaries of Utopia, pp. 165–67, 210–11 (1980); clauses that might impose forfeitures were invariably carefully scrutinized and frequently denounced as penal. . . .

". . . We . . . conclude that a purchaser whose breach is not willful has a restitutionary claim to recover moneys paid that unjustly enrich his seller. In this case, no one has alleged that the purchasers' breach, arising out of a transfer to a more distant place of employment, should be deemed to have been willful. . . .

"The purchaser's right to recover in restitution requires the purchaser to establish that the seller has been unjustly enriched. The purchaser must show more than that the contract has come to an end and that the seller retains moneys paid pursuant to the contract. To prove unjust enrichment, in the ordinary case, the purchaser, because he is the party in breach, must prove that the damages suffered by his seller are less than the moneys received from the purchaser. Schwasnick v. Blandin, 65 F.2d 354, 358 (2d Cir.1933); Kitchin v. Mori, 84 Nev. 181, 437 P.2d 865, 866 (1968). It may not be easy for the purchaser to prove the extent of the seller's damages, it may even be strategically advantageous for the seller to come forward with relevant evidence of the losses he has incurred and may expect to incur on account of the buyer's breach. Nonetheless, only if the breaching party satisfies his burden of proof that the innocent party has sustained a net gain may a claim for unjust enrichment be sustained. Dobbs, Remedies '12.14 (1973); 1 Palmer, Restitution § 5.4 (1978)."

RESTATEMENT, THIRD, RESTITUTION AND UNJUST ENRICHMENT § 36

[See Selected Source Materials Supplement]

(B) MATERIAL BREACH

This Section considers when breach gives a party the powers to withhold performance and to treat a contract as at an end ("terminate the contract") in the absence of an express condition. Under the Restatement a "material breach" gives a party the power to suspend performance while a "total breach" gives a party the power to terminate a contract. Often when the question is framed as one of material breach both parties will have failed to perform in a tit for tat way and each party will argue the other party's prior nonperformance excuses their own responsive nonperformance, which would allow them to recover contract damages for total breach. In this situation, each party will try to persuade the court the other was the first to materially breach, justifying their own responsive nonperformance and allowing them to recover contract damages.

K & G CONSTR. CO. V. HARRIS
Court of Appeals of Maryland, 1960.
223 Md. 305, 164 A.2d 451.

Before BRUNE, C.J., and HENDERSON, HAMMOND, PRESCOTT and HORNEY, JJ.

PRESCOTT, JUDGE. Feeling aggrieved by the action of the trial judge of the Circuit Court for Prince George's County, sitting without a jury, in finding a judgment against it in favor of a subcontractor, the appellant, the general contractor on a construction project, appealed.[1]

The principal question presented is: Does a contractor, damaged by a subcontractor's failure to perform a portion of his work in a workmanlike manner, have a right, under the circumstances of this case, to withhold, in partial satisfaction of said damages, an installment payment, which, under the terms of the contract, was due the subcontractor, unless the negligent performance of his work excused its payment?

The appeal is presented on a case stated in accordance with Maryland Rule 826g.

The statement, in relevant part, is as follows:

"... K & G Construction Company, Inc. (hereinafter called Contractor), plaintiff and counter-defendant in the Circuit Court and appellant herein, was owner and general contractor of a housing subdivision project being constructed (herein called Project). Harris and Brooks (hereinafter called Subcontractor), defendants and counter-plaintiffs in the Circuit Court and appellees herein, entered into a contract with Contractor to do excavating and earth-moving work on the Project. Pertinent parts of the contract are set forth below:

---

[1] There are two appellees; the statement of the case refers to them as "subcontractor." We shall do likewise.

" 'Section 3. The Subcontractor agrees to complete the several portions and the whole of the work herein sublet by the time or times following:

" '(a) Without delay, as called for by the Contractor.

" '(b) It is expressly agreed that time is of the essence of this contract, and that the Contractor will have the right to terminate this contract and employ a substitute to perform the work in the event of delay on the part of Subcontractor, and Subcontractor agrees to indemnify the Contractor for any loss sustained thereby, provided, however, that nothing in this paragraph shall be construed to deprive Contractor of any rights or remedies it would otherwise have as to damage for delay.

" 'Section 4. (b) Progress payments will be made each month during the performance of the work. Subcontractor will submit to Contractor, by the 25th of each month, a requisition for work performed during the preceding month. Contractor will pay these requisitions, less a retainer equal to ten per cent (10%), by the 10th of the months in which such requisitions are received.[2]

" '(c) No payments will be made under this contract until the insurance requirements of Sec. 9 hereof have been complied with. . . .

" 'Section 8. . . . All work shall be performed in a workmanlike manner, and in accordance with the best practices.

" 'Section 9. Subcontractor agrees to carry, during the progress of the work, . . . liability insurance against . . . property damage, in such amounts and with such companies as may be satisfactory to Contractor and shall provide Contractor with certificates showing the same to be in force.'

"While in the course of his employment by the Subcontractor on the Project, a bulldozer operator drove his machine too close to Contractor's house while grading the yard, causing the immediate collapse of a wall and other damage to the house. The resulting damage to contractor's house was $3,400.00. Subcontractor had complied with the insurance provision (Sec. 9) of the aforesaid contract. Subcontractor reported said damages to their liability insurance carrier. The Subcontractor and its insurance carrier refused to repair damage or compensate Contractor for damage to

---

[2]   This section is not a model for clarity.

the house, claiming that there was no liability on the part of the Subcontractor.

"Contractor gave no written notice to Subcontractor for any services rendered or materials furnished by the Contractor to the Subcontractor . . .

"Contractor was generally satisfied with Subcontractor's work and progress as required under Sections 3 and 8 of the contract until September 12, 1958, with the exception of the bulldozer accident of August 9, 1958.

"Subcontractor performed work under the contract during July, 1958, for which it submitted a requisition by the 25th of July, as required by the contract, for work done prior to the 25th of July, payable under the terms of the contract by Contractor on or before August 10, 1958. Contractor was current as to payments due under all preceding monthly requisitions from Subcontractor. The aforesaid bulldozer accident damaging Contractor's house occurred on August 9, 1958. Contractor refused to pay Subcontractor's requisition due on August 10, 1958, because the bulldozer damage to Contractor's house had not been repaired or paid for. Subcontractor continued to work on the project until the 12th of September, 1958, at which time they discontinued working on the project because of Contractor's refusal to pay the said work requisition and notified Contractor by registered letters of their position and willingness to return to the job, but only upon payment. At that time, September 12, 1958, the value of the work completed by Subcontractor on the project for which they had not been paid was $1,484.50

"Contractor later requested Subcontractor to return and complete work on the Project which Subcontractor refused to do because of nonpayment of work requisitions of July 25 and thereafter. Contractor's house was not repaired by Subcontractor nor compensation paid for the damage.

"It was stipulated that Subcontractor had completed work on the Project under the contract for which they had not been paid in the amount of $1,484.50 and that if they had completed the remaining work to be done under the contract, they would have made a profit of $1,340.00 on the remaining uncompleted portion of the contract. It was further stipulated that it cost the Contractor $450.00 above the contract price to have another excavating contractor complete remaining work required under the contract. It was the opinion of the Court that if judgment were in favor of the Subcontractor, it should be for the total amount of $2,824.50.

"... Contractor filed suit against the Subcontractor in two counts: (1), for the aforesaid bulldozer damage to Contractor's house, alleging negligence of the Subcontractor's bulldozer operator, and (2) for the $450.00 costs above the contract price in having another excavating subcontractor complete the uncompleted work in the contract. Subcontractor filed a counter-claim for recovery of work of the value of $1,484.50 for which they had not received payment and for loss of anticipated profits on uncompleted portion of work in the amount of $1,340.00. By agreement of the parties, the first count of Contractor's claim, i.e., for aforesaid bulldozer damage to Contractor's house, was submitted to jury who found in favor of Contractor in the amount of $3,400.00. Following the finding by the jury, the second count of the Contractor's claim and the counter-claims of the Subcontractor, by agreement of the parties, were submitted to the Court for determination, without jury. All of the facts recited herein above were stipulated to by the parties to the Court. Circuit Court Judge Fletcher found for counter-plaintiff Subcontractor in the amount of $2,824.50 from which Contractor has entered this appeal."

The $3,400 judgment has been paid.

It is immediately apparent that our decision turns upon the respective rights and liabilities of the parties under that portion of their contract whereby the subcontractor agreed to do the excavating and earth-moving work in "a workmanlike manner, and in accordance with the best practices," with time being of the essence of the contract, and the contractor agreed to make progress payments therefor on the 10th day of the months following the performance of the work by the subcontractor.[3] The subcontractor contends, of course, that when the contractor failed to make the payment due on August 10, 1958, he breached his contract and thereby released him (the subcontractor) from any further obligation to perform. The contractor, on the other hand, argues that the failure of the subcontractor to perform his work in a workmanlike manner constituted a material breach of the contract, which justified his refusal to make the August 10 payment; and, as there was no breach on his part, the subcontractor had no right to cease performance on September 12, and his refusal to continue work on the project constituted another breach, which rendered him liable to the contractor for damages. The vital question, more tersely stated, remains: Did the contractor have a right, under the

---

[3]   The statement of the case does not show the exact terms concerning the remuneration to be paid the subcontractor. It does not disclose whether he was to be paid a total lump sum, by the cubic yard, by the day, or in some other manner. It does state that the excavation finally cost the contractor $450 more than the "contract price."

circumstances, to refuse to make the progress payment due on August 10, 1958?

. . . Promises are mutually dependent if the parties intend *performance* by one to be conditioned upon *performance* by the other, and, if they be mutually dependent, they may be (a) precedent, i.e., a promise that is to be performed before a corresponding promise on the part of the adversary party is to be performed, (b) subsequent, i.e., a corresponding promise that is not to be performed until the other party to the contract has performed a precedent covenant, or (c) concurrent, i.e., promises that are to be performed at the same time by each of the parties, who are respectively bound to perform each. . . .

. . . The modern rule, which seems to be of almost universal application, is that there is a presumption that mutual promises in a contract are dependent and are to be so regarded, whenever possible. . . .

Considering the presumption that promises and counter-promises are dependent and the statement of the case, we have no hesitation in holding that the promise and counter-promise under consideration here were mutually dependent, that is to say, the parties intended performance by one to be conditioned on performance by the other; and the subcontractor's promise was, by the explicit wording of the contract, precedent to the promise of payment, monthly, by the contractor. In Shapiro Engineering Corp. v. Francis O. Day Co., 215 Md. 373, 380, 137 A.2d 695, we stated that it is the general rule that where a total price for work is fixed by a contract, the work is not rendered divisible by progress payments. It would indeed present an unusual situation if we were to hold that a building contractor, who has obtained someone to do work for him and has agreed to pay each month for the work performed in the previous month, has to continue the monthly payments, irrespective of the degree of skill and care displayed in the performance of work, and his only recourse is by way of suit for ill-performance. If this were the law, it is conceivable, in fact, probable, that many contractors would become insolvent before they were able to complete their contracts. . . .

We hold that when the subcontractor's employee negligently damaged the contractor's wall, this constituted a breach of the subcontractor's promise to perform his work in a "workmanlike manner, and in accordance with the best practices." Gaybis v. Palm, 201 Md. 78, 85, 93 A.2d 269; Johnson v. Metcalfe, 209 Md. 537, 544, 121 A.2d 825; 17 C.J.S. Contracts § 515; Weiss v. Sheet Metal Fabricators, 206 Md. 195, 203, 110 A.2d 671. And there can be little doubt that the breach was material: the damage to the wall amounted to more than double the payment due on August 10. Speed v. Bailey, 153 Md. 655, 661, 662, 139 A. 534. 3A Corbin, Contracts, § 708, says: "The failure of a contractor's [in our case, the subcontractor's] performance to constitute 'substantial' performance may justify the owner [in our case, the contractor] in refusing to make a progress payment. . . . If the refusal to pay an installment is justified on the owner's [contractor's] part, the contractor [subcontractor] is not justified in abandoning work by reason of that refusal. His abandonment of the work will itself be a wrongful repudiation that goes to the essence, even if the defects in performance did not." See also Restatement, Contracts § 274; F.H. McGraw & Co. v. Sherman Plastering Co., D.C.Conn., 60 F.Supp. 504, 512, affirmed 2 Cir., 149 F.2d 301 . . . and compare Williston, op. cit., §§ 805, 841 and 842. Professor Corbin, in § 954, states further: "The unexcused failure of a contractor to render a promised performance when it is due is always a breach of contract . . . Such failure may be of such great importance as to constitute what has been called herein a 'total' breach. . . . For a failure of performance constituting such a 'total' breach, an action for remedies that are appropriate thereto is at once maintainable. Yet the injured party is not required to bring such action. He has the option of treating the non-performance as a 'partial' breach only. . . ." In permitting the subcontractor to proceed with work on the project after August 9, the contractor, obviously, treated the breach by the subcontractor as a partial one. As the promises were mutually dependent and the subcontractor had made a material breach in his performance, this justified the contractor in refusing to make the August 10 payment; hence, as the contractor was not in default, the subcontractor again breached the contract when he, on September 12, discontinued work on the project, which rendered him liable (by the express terms of the contract) to the contractor for his increased cost in having the excavating done—a stipulated amount of $450. Cf. Keystone Engineering Corp. v. Sutter, 196 Md. 620, 628, 78 A.2d 191. . . .

Judgment against the appellant reversed; and judgment entered in favor of the appellant against the appellees for $450, the appellees to pay the costs.

———

Bartlett v. Bartlett

465 S.W.3d 745 (2015)

William and Lori Bartlett's divorce decree included a provision that William would pay the college expenses of each of their two children "provided the child is a full-time student and maintains at least a "C" or equivalent grade point average . . . " Their son began Trinity College in August 2012. Lori sued William for breach of contract in 2012 when he refused to pay his son's expenses for the fall semester. At trial the son testified his grades dropped below a "C" average to 1.929 after the Spring semester of his freshman year but that after the Summer semester his average was at least a "C." The trial court held the agreement to pay college expenses was enforceable as a contract and that the son's failure to maintain a "C" average at the end of the Spring semester of his first year was not a material breach, discharging William from his obligation to pay college expenses for the year. The court of appeals affirmed, applying the factors in the Restatement.

In view of these factors, the record supports the trial court's deemed finding that any breach by the son was not material and did not excuse William's obligation to pay for expenses incurred before the breach. First, as the trial court expressly found, the son brought his GPA above a "C" average after the Summer 2013 semester. Thus, the son actually cured any failure to perform that occurred by his having a GPA below a "C" after the Spring 2013 semester. The trial court could have concluded that the son's behavior comported with standards of good faith and fair dealing, as he testified his grades dipped below a "C" average because his attendance suffered after surgery on his knee; he also was a football player for the university. Excusing William's performance as to all semesters (including the Fall 2012 semester for which the son's GPA was above a "C") would cause the son significant forfeiture. William was not deprived of the benefit he expected because his son remained a full time student toward a bachelor's degree at a university and maintained a GPA above a "C" by the time of trial. And there was evidence that William's refusal to fulfill his obligations under the agreement had nothing to do with the son's failure to maintain a "C" GPA for the Spring 2013 semester. There is no evidence that the son's one-semester lapse prevented William from making "substitute arrangements." Finally, the agreement itself does not require performance on a semester-by-semester basis, nor does it call for the forfeiture of obligations previously owed to the son (i.e., Fall 2012 expenses) for a breach occurring in a later semester. The agreement itself does not explicitly require the son to reimburse William for expenses incurred for a prior semester if the son ultimately does not obtain a "C" average in a later semester.

Frost, C.J., disagreed with this analysis, arguing that the son maintaining a "C" average was a condition to William's obligation to pay college expenses. He continued: "Even presuming for the sake of argument that a breach-of-contract analysis would be appropriate in this context, the failure to meet the grade requirement was material. . . . A "D" is not a "C." Saying the difference between a "D" and a "C" is immaterial is like saying that almost scoring a touchdown is the same as scoring a touchdown or that "second place" is no different than "first place." Grade-point averages, by nature, are precise measurements that set lines of demarcation between one performance category and the next. The metric reflects an exact and unforgiving standard. Anything that falls short of meeting it is a material failure."

———————

RESTATEMENT, SECOND, CONTRACTS §§ 237, 241, 242

[See Selected Source Materials Supplement]

CISG ARTS. 25, 49

[See Selected Source Materials Supplement]

UNIDROIT PRINCIPLES OF INTERNATIONAL COMMERCIAL CONTRACTS ARTS. 7.3.1, 7.3.5, 7.3.6

[See Selected Source Materials Supplement]

PRINCIPLES OF EUROPEAN CONTRACT LAW ARTS. 9.301, 9.302, 9.305, 9.307–309

[See Selected Source Materials Supplement]

E. Allan Farnsworth, Contracts

§ 8.13 (4th ed. 2004)

"A contract is said to be divisible if the performances to be exchanged can be divided into corresponding pairs of part performances in such a way that a court will treat the parts of each pair as if the parties had agreed that they were equivalents. . . .

"Suppose, for example, that a builder has made a contract to build three houses at $100,000 each for a total price of $300,000. The builder breaks the contract by building only one of the houses and claims its price of $100,000. Will a court allow the builder to recover on the contract to build three houses, even though the builder has not substantially performed it? It will, if it regards the contract as divisible into three pairs of part performances, each pair consisting of the building of a house and the payment of $100,000. The builder is then entitled to recover $100,000 on the contract for the house that was built, less such damages as the owner can prove were suffered by the builder's breach in not building the other two. Indeed, if the contract is divisible, the builder is entitled to recover on the contract for building the first house even if performance of that part of the contract is only substantial. The builder's recovery will then be reduced by damages resulting from the defects in the first house as well as from the failure to build the other two houses.

"How does a court decide whether a contract is divisible? As the Supreme Court of Colorado warned that 'there is no set formula which furnishes a foolproof method for determining in a given case just which contracts are severable and which are entire.' The Restatement Second lays down two requirements: it must be possible to apportion the parties' performances into corresponding pairs of part performances; and it must be proper to regard the parts of each pair as agreed equivalents."

NOTE ON ANTICIPATORY REPUDIATION

A declaration of an intent not to perform a contract in the future is described by UCC Section 2–610 as an "Anticipatory Repudiation." The Restatement addresses the topic under the heading "Prospective Non-Performance" in Sections 250 to 260. The reluctance to describe the conduct as simply a breach of contract reflects an old debate. Wells. J., pithily expressed one side of this debate in Daniels v. Newtown, 114 Mass. 530 (1874):

> A renunciation of the agreement, by declarations or inconsistent conduct, before the time of performance, may give cause for treating it as rescinded, and excuse the other party from making ready for performance on his part, or relieve him from the necessity of offering performance in order to enforce his rights. It may destroy all capacity of the party, so disavowing its obligations to assert rights under it afterwards, if the other party has acted upon such disavowal. But we are unable to see how it can of itself constitute a present violation of any legal rights of the other party, or confer upon him a present right of action. An executory contract ordinarily confers no title or interest in the subject matter of the agreement. Until the time arrives when, by the terms of the agreement, he is or might be entitled to its performance, he can suffer no injury or deprivation which can form a ground of damages. There is neither violation of right, nor loss upon which to found an action. . . .

The other side to this debate overcame this objection by implying a promise not to repudiate. Learned Hand, J., explained this solution in Equitable Trust Co. v. Western Pac. Ry., 244 Fed. 485, 501–502 (S.D.N.Y.1917), remanded for correction and affirmed, 250 Fed. 327 (2d Cir.), cert. denied 246 U.S. 672, 38 S.Ct. 423, 62 L.Ed. 932 (1918):

> [The basis of the doctrine of anticipatory breach] is that a promise to perform in the future by implication includes an engagement not deliberately to compromise the probability of performance. A promise is a verbal act designed as a reliance to the promisee, and so as a means to the forecast of his own conduct. Abstention from any deliberate act before the time of performance which makes impossible that reliance and that forecast ought surely to be included by implication. Such intermediate uncertainties as

arise from the vicissitudes of the promisor's affairs are, of course, a part of the risk, but it is hard to see how, except by mere verbalism, it can be supposed that the promisor may within the terms of his undertaking gratuitously add to those uncertainties by announcing his purpose to default.

Today it is well established that a clear repudiation of a future performance obligation is a breach of contract. It is also well established that it gives rise to an immediate claim for damages. Issues remain. Among these issues is when words and conduct short of a clear repudiation of a future performance obligation will be treated as anticipatory repudiation.

WHOLESALE SAND & GRAVEL, INC. V. DECKER

Supreme Judicial Court of Maine, 1993.
630 A.2d 710.

Before WATHEN, C.J., and ROBERTS, GLASSMAN, CLIFFORD, COLLINS, RUDMAN and DANA, JJ.

ROBERTS, JUSTICE.

Wholesale Sand & Gravel, Inc., appeals from a judgment entered in the Superior Court (Sagadahoc County, *Lipez, J.*) in favor of James Decker on its claim for the breach of their contract. On appeal, Wholesale contends that the court erred in holding that its conduct constituted an anticipatory repudiation of the contract and in deciding the case on a defense that had not been raised in the pleadings. Finding no error, we affirm the judgment.

On June 13, 1989, James Decker and Wholesale Sand & Gravel, Inc., entered into a contract whereby Wholesale agreed to perform earth work, including the installation of a gravel driveway, on Decker's property in Bowdoin. The contract contained no provision specifying a completion date for the work. Indeed, the only time reference made in the contract was that payment was to be made within 90 days. Although Carl Goodenow, Wholesale's president, believed the company had 90 days within which to complete the work, he told Decker that the driveway portion of the work would be completed within one week.

Wholesale began work on the driveway on the weekend after the contract was executed and immediately experienced difficulty because of the wetness of the ground. In fact, Wholesale's bulldozer became stuck in the mud and had to be removed with a backhoe. Wholesale returned to the site the following weekend, when it attempted to stabilize the driveway site by hauling out mud and hauling in gravel. Because the ground was too wet to allow Wholesale to perform the work without substantially exceeding the contract price, Goodenow decided to wait for the ground to dry out before proceeding further.

On July 12, 1989, Decker contacted Goodenow concerning the lack of activity at the site and his urgent need to have the driveway completed. Goodenow responded that he would "get right on it." On July 19, Decker telephoned Goodenow to inquire again about the lack of activity and gave him one week in which to finish the driveway. Again, Goodenow said that he would "get right on it." On July 28, Decker called Goodenow for the purpose of terminating the contract. When Goodenow stated that he would be at the site the next day, Decker decided to give him one more chance. Goodenow, however, did not appear at the site and Decker subsequently terminated the contract. At that point, Goodenow believed Wholesale still had 45 days to complete the job. Decker, however, hired another contractor to finish the driveway and complete the excavation work.

Wholesale commenced this action against Decker by a complaint seeking damages for a breach of their contract. After a jury-waived trial, the court entered a judgment in favor of Decker. Although it found that a reasonable time for the completion of performance was 60 days, the court concluded that Wholesale's conduct constituted an anticipatory repudiation of the contract, permitting Decker to terminate the contract during the 60-day period. This timely appeal followed.

An anticipatory repudiation of a contract is "a definite and unequivocal manifestation of intention on the part of the repudiator that he will not render the promised performance when the time fixed for it in the contract arrives." 4 Corbin, *Corbin on Contracts* § 973 (1951); *Restatement (Second) of Contracts* § 250 (1979). The manifestation of an intention to repudiate a contract may be made and communicated by either words or conduct. *See* 4 Corbin § 973; *Restatement* § 250(b). The words or conduct evidencing such refusal or inability to perform, however, must be definite, unequivocal, and absolute. *See Martell Bros., Inc. v. Donbury, Inc.*, 577 A.2d 334, 337 n. 1 (Me.1990). Wholesale contends that the court erred in concluding that its conduct constituted an anticipatory repudiation of the contract. We disagree. After its second weekend of work at the site, Wholesale removed its equipment and did not return. Moreover, on two occasions Goodenow, responding to Decker's inquiries about the progress of the job, promised to get right to work but did not do so. Indeed, when confronted by the fact that Wholesale would be fired if he did not appear at the job site the following day, Goodenow promised that he would be at the site but did not appear. On this record it was reasonable for Decker to conclude that Wholesale would never complete its performance under the contract. We conclude therefore that the court properly found that Wholesale, through its conduct, manifested an unequivocal and definite inability or unwillingness to perform within a reasonable time. . . .

The entry is:

Judgment affirmed.

GLASSMAN, COLLINS, RUDMAN and DANA, JJ., concur.

WATHEN, CHIEF JUSTICE, with whom CLIFFORD, J., joins, dissenting.

I must respectfully dissent. In my judgment both this Court and the Superior Court misapply the doctrine of anticipatory repudiation. The record is devoid of any words or conduct on the part of plaintiff that distinctly, unequivocally, and absolutely evidence a refusal or inability to perform. *See Martell Bros., Inc. v. Donbury, Inc.*, 577 A.2d 334, 337 n. 1 (Me.1990). There was a disagreement between the parties as to how much time was allowed for performance, but it is clear that plaintiff expected to perform the contract as soon as circumstances permitted. The Superior Court found a repudiation of the contract even though the 60 days it found available for performance had not passed.

I would vacate the judgment.

———

Unique Systems, Inc. v. Zotos International, Inc.

622 F.2d 373 (8th Cir.1980)

On January 30, 1974, Lilja contracted to manufacture and sell to Zotos, for resale by Zotos, 15,000 hair-spray systems that Lilja would develop. In an amendment to the contract, the parties agreed that Zotos's stocking and distribution of the systems would commence in "month one," defined as a "mutually agreed date in the year 1974." Later, Zotos began to fear a softening of the market, and indicated that it would not proceed unless Lilja would agree to a market test of completed systems. In light of Zotos's refusal to proceed without the market-test period, Lilja considered the contract repudiated, and brought suit. Held, for Lilja.

"If a party to a contract demands of the other party a performance to which he has no right under the contract and states definitely that, unless his demand is complied with, he will not render his promised performance, an anticipatory repudiation has been committed. 4 Corbin, Contracts § 973 (1951). When Zotos told Lilja in August of 1975 that it would not proceed until market tests were performed with results subject to Zotos's approval, Zotos repudiated the contract and was in total breach. No market tests were required by the contract, a fact that Zotos admits that it knew."

———

Thermo Electron Corp. v. Schiavone Construction Co.

958 F.2d 1158 (1st Cir.1992)

" . . . Thermo repudiated only if it 'insist[ed] . . . upon terms' . . . to the point where that insistence 'amounts to a statement of intention not to perform except on conditions which go beyond the contract.' Restatement (Second) of Contracts § 250 cmt. b, at 273 (quoting U.C.C. § 2–610 cmt. 2) (emphasis added). Commentators have pointed out that there 'must be a definite and unequivocal manifestation of intention [not to render performance]. . . . A mere request for a change in the terms or a request for cancellation of the contract is not in itself enough to constitute a repudiation.' 4 Arthur L. Corbin, Corbin on Contracts § 973, at 905–06 (1951) (footnotes omitted). A party's statements or actions 'must be sufficiently positive to be reasonably understood as meaning that the breach will actually occur. A party's expressions of doubt as to its willingness or ability to perform do not constitute a repudiation.' E. Allan Farnsworth, Contracts § 8.21, at 663 (2d ed. 1990); accord Restatement (Second) of Contracts § 250 cmt. b, at 273."

SECTION 2. CONTRACTS FOR THE SALE OF GOODS

UCC §§ 2–508, 2–601, 2–608, 2–612

[See Selected Source Materials Supplement]

CISG ARTS. 35(1), 37, 45, 46, 48, 49

[See Selected Source Materials Supplement]

J. White & R. Summers, Uniform Commercial Code
§ 8–2 (5th ed. 2000)

"At the outset one should understand the significance of a self-help remedy which permits the buyer to return the goods to the seller (that is, rejection or revocation of acceptance). In these cases the buyer is freed from its obligation to pay the price, and the buyer has a right to recover that part of the price already paid. Moreover, except in unusual circumstances, the buyer need not resell the goods. One should understand the economic difference between the status of the buyer who has rejected and the status of the buyer who has accepted and sued for breach of warranty. The typical buyer who accepts and sues for breach of warranty under 2–714 will recover only for injury proximately resulting from defects in the goods at the time of sale. If, for example, the purchased automobile had a cracked piston that will cost $500 to repair (and the value of the car is so diminished by $500), buyer will recover that $500. On the other hand, if buyer rejects the goods, buyer is first recompensed for the losses resulting from the seller's failure to perform its end of the contract (for example, by a suit under 2–713 or 2–712); more important, buyer escapes the bargain, and throws any loss resulting from depreciation of the goods back upon the seller.

"The importance of goods oriented remedies can be illustrated by an example from a commodity market. Assume that the seller delivers 10,000 bushels of potatoes and that 100 of those bushels are rotten. If the buyer accepts the potatoes, it will have a cause of action under 2–714, and it will recover money approximately equivalent to the value of those 100 bushels. If, on the other hand, the buyer rejects the entire delivery, if the seller cannot cure, and if the price of the potatoes has fallen substantially, the buyer's rejection may save it thousands of dollars by allowing the purchase of conforming goods on the market at a much lower price than specified in the contract. Rejection avoids the economic injury of a bad bargain as well."

NOTE ON THE PERFECT-TENDER RULE AND THE UCC

Prior to the adoption of the Uniform Commercial Code, the doctrine of substantial performance was not applicable to contracts for the sale of goods. Instead, at least in theory and often in practice, a buyer could refuse to accept a delivery of goods that in any way failed to conform to the contract. This rule was known as the perfect-tender rule, because a buyer of goods could reject any tender of delivery that was not perfect. A leading case was Norrington v. Wright, 115 U.S. 188, 6 S.Ct. 12, 29 L.Ed. 366 (1885). UCC § 2–601 nominally preserves the perfect-tender rule for the sale of goods. However, other provisions of the UCC strip away much or most of the significance of this Section.

1. *Revocation of acceptance.* First, UCC § 2–601 applies only where a buyer rejects goods. It does not apply where the buyer accepts goods and then discovers a defect. Under UCC § 2–608, a buyer may revoke acceptance in such a case, but only if the nonconformity substantially impairs the value of the goods to her.

There are other limitations on the buyer's right to revoke acceptance under § 2–608, even if the nonconformity does substantially impair the value of the goods to him. If the buyer accepted the goods knowing that they were nonconforming, she can revoke her acceptance only if she accepted on the reasonable assumption that the nonconformity would be cured (for example, because the seller promised cure), and the nonconformity was not seasonably cured. If the buyer accepted the goods without knowing that they were nonconforming, she can revoke her acceptance only if her acceptance was reasonably induced either by the difficulty of discovering the defect before acceptance or by the seller's assurances.

2. *Installment contracts.* Section 2–601 is also inapplicable to installment contracts, that is, contracts that require or authorize the delivery of goods in separate lots, to be separately accepted. Such contracts are covered by Section 2–612. Under Section 2–612(2), a buyer normally can reject a

nonconforming installment only if the nonconformity substantially impairs the value of the installment and cannot be cured. Furthermore, under Section 2–612(3) a buyer cannot treat the whole installment contract as breached on the ground of a nonconformity or default with respect to one or more installments, unless those nonconformities or defaults substantially impair the value of the whole contract.

3. *Cure.* The perfect-tender rule is also significantly ameliorated by Section 2–508, the "cure" provision. Under Section 2–508(1), in the case of a single-delivery (non-installment) contract, if a tender of goods is rejected because it is nonconforming, and the time for performance has not yet expired, the seller may cure the defect by making a conforming delivery within the contract time. Even more significantly, under Section 2–508(2) if a tender of goods is rejected because it is nonconforming, and the seller had reasonable grounds to believe that the tender would be acceptable with a money allowance or otherwise, the seller has a further reasonable time to substitute a conforming tender even if the time for performance has expired.

4. *Good faith.* The obligation of good faith under the UCC requires "honesty in fact and the observance of reasonable commercial standards of fair dealing." The obligation and this definition are in Sections 1–304 and 1–201(20) of the 2001 version of the UCC. In the pre-2001 version of the UCC, Sections 1–203, 1–201(19), and 2–103(1)(b) required honesty of fact of everyone but only merchants to observe reasonable commercial standards. A buyer who seized on a minor defect to justify a rejection that was really based on the fact that the contract is no longer favorable to her might not satisfy this obligation. As stated in Printing Center of Texas, Inc. v. Supermind Publishing Co., 669 S.W.2d 779 (Tex.App.1984):

> Once the contract of the parties has been determined, the evidence must be reviewed to see if the right goods were tendered at the right time and place. If the evidence does establish nonconformity in some respect, the buyer is entitled to reject if he rejects in good faith. [UCC] § 1–203 provides that, "Every contract or duty within this Act imposes an obligation of good faith in its performance or enforcement." Since the rejection of goods is a matter of performance, the buyer is obligated to act in good faith when he rejects the goods. When the buyer is a merchant, his standard of good faith rejection requires honesty in fact and observance of reasonable commercial standards of fair dealing in the trade. [UCC § 2–103(2)]. . . . Evidence of circumstances which indicate that the buyer's motivation in rejecting the goods was to escape the bargain, rather than to avoid acceptance of a tender which in some respect impairs the value of the bargain to him, would support a finding of rejection in bad faith. Neumiller Farms Inc. v. Cornett, 368 So.2d 272 (Ala.1979). Thus, evidence of rejection of the goods on account of a minor defect in a falling market would in some instances be sufficient to support a finding that the buyer acted in bad faith when he rejected the goods.

Ramirez v. Autosport

88 N.J. 277, 440 A.2d 1345 (1982)

"In the nineteenth century, sellers were required to deliver goods that complied exactly with the sales agreement. See Filley v. Pope, 115 U.S. 213, 220, 6 S.Ct. 19, 21, 29 L.Ed. 372, 373 (1885) (buyer not obliged to accept otherwise conforming scrap iron shipped to New Orleans from Leith, rather than Glasgow, Scotland, as required by contract); Columbia Iron Works & Dry-Dock Co. v. Douglas, 84 Md. 44, 47, 34 A. 1118, 1120–1121 (1896) (buyer who agreed to purchase steel scrap from United States cruisers not obliged to take any other kind of scrap). That rule, known as the 'perfect tender' rule, remained part of the law of sales well into the twentieth century. By the 1920's the doctrine was so entrenched in the law that Judge Learned Hand declared '[t]here is no room in commercial contracts for the doctrine of substantial performance.' Mitsubishi Goshi Kaisha v. J. Aaron & Co., Inc., 16 F.2d 185, 186 (2 Cir.1926).

"The harshness of the rule led courts to seek to ameliorate its effect and to bring the law of sales in closer harmony with the law of contracts, which allows rescission only for material breaches. LeRoy Dyal Co. v. Allen, 161 F.2d 152, 155 (4 Cir.1947). See 5 Corbin, Contracts § 1104 at 464 (1951); 12 Williston, Contracts § 1455 at 14 (3 ed. 1970). Nevertheless, a variation of the perfect tender rule appeared in the Uniform Sales Act. N.J.S.A. 46:30–75 (purchasers permitted to reject goods or rescind contracts for any breach of warranty). . . . The chief objection to the continuation of the perfect tender rule was that buyers in a declining market would reject goods for minor non-conformities and force the loss on surprised sellers. . . .

"To the extent that a buyer can reject goods for any nonconformity, the UCC retains the perfect tender rule. . . . Section 2–601 authorizes a buyer to reject goods if they 'or the tender of delivery fail in any respect to conform to the contract.' . . . The Code, however, mitigates the harshness of the perfect tender rule and balances the interests of buyer and seller."

T.W. OIL, INC. v. CONSOLIDATED EDISON CO.

Court of Appeals of New York, 1982.
57 N.Y.2d 574, 457 N.Y.S.2d 458, 443 N.E.2d 932.

FUCHSBERG, JUDGE.

In the first case to wend its way through our appellate courts on this question, we are asked, in the main, to decide whether a seller who, acting in good faith and without knowledge of any defect, tenders nonconforming goods to a buyer who properly rejects them, may avail itself of the cure provision of subdivision (2) of section 2–508 of the Uniform Commercial

Code. We hold that, if seasonable notice be given, such a seller may offer to cure the defect within a reasonable period beyond the time when the contract was to be performed so long as it has acted in good faith and with a reasonable expectation that the original goods would be acceptable to the buyer.

The factual background against which we decide this appeal is based on either undisputed proof or express findings at Trial Term. In January, 1974, midst the fuel shortage produced by the oil embargo, the plaintiff (then known as Joc Oil USA, Inc.) purchased a cargo of fuel oil whose sulfur content was represented to it as no greater than 1%. While the oil was still at sea en route to the United States in the tanker *MT Khamsin*, plaintiff received a certificate from the foreign refinery at which it had been processed informing it that the sulfur content in fact was .52%. Thereafter, on January 24, the plaintiff entered into a written contract with the defendant (Con Ed) for the sale of this oil. The agreement was for delivery to take place between January 24 and January 30, payment being subject to a named independent testing agency's confirmation of quality and quantity. The contract, following a trade custom to round off specifications of sulfur content at, for instance, 1%, .5% or .3%, described that of the *Khamsin* oil as .5%. In the course of the negotiations, the plaintiff learned that Con Ed was then authorized to buy and burn oil with a sulfur content of up to 1% and would even mix oils containing more and less to maintain that figure.

When the vessel arrived, on January 25, its cargo was discharged into Con Ed storage tanks in Bayonne, New Jersey.[2] In due course, the independent testing people reported a sulfur content of .92%. On this basis, acting within a time frame whose reasonableness is not in question, on February 14 Con Ed rejected the shipment. Prompt negotiations to adjust the price failed; by February 20, plaintiff had offered a price reduction roughly responsive to the difference in sulfur reading, but Con Ed, though it could use the oil, rejected this proposition out of hand. It was insistent on paying no more than the latest prevailing price, which, in the volatile market that then existed, was some 25% below the level which prevailed when it agreed to buy the oil.

The very next day, February 21, plaintiff offered to cure the defect with a substitute shipment of conforming oil scheduled to arrive on the *S.S. Appollonian Victory* on February 28. Nevertheless, on February 22, the very day after the cure was proffered, Con Ed, adamant in its intention to avail itself of the intervening drop in prices, summarily rejected this proposal too. The two cargos were subsequently sold to third parties at the best price obtainable, first that of the *Appollonian* and, sometime later,

---

[2] The tanks already contained some other oil, but Con Ed appears to have had no concern over the admixture of the differing sulfur contents. In any event, the efficacy of the independent testing required by the contract was not impaired by the commingling.

after extraction from the tanks had been accomplished, that of the
Khamsin.[3]

There ensued this action for breach of contract,[4] which, after a
somewhat unconventional trial course, resulted in a nonjury decision for
the plaintiff in the sum of $1,385,512.83, essentially the difference between
the original contract price of $3,360,667.14 and the amount received by the
plaintiff by way of resale of the *Khamsin* oil at what the court found as a
matter of fact was a negotiated price which, under all the circumstances,[5]
was reasonably procured in the open market. To arrive at this result, the
Trial Judge, while ruling against other liability theories advanced by the
plaintiff, which, in particular, included one charging the defendant with
having failed to act in good faith in the negotiations for a price adjustment
on the *Khamsin* oil (Uniform Commercial Code, § 1–203), decided as a
matter of law that subdivision (2) of section 2–508 of the Uniform
Commercial Code was available to the plaintiff even if it had no prior
knowledge of the nonconformity. Finding that in fact plaintiff had no such
belief at the time of the delivery, that what turned out to be a .92% sulfur
content was "within the range of contemplation of reasonable acceptability"
to Con. Ed., and that seasonable notice of an intention to cure was given,
the court went on to hold that plaintiff's "reasonable and timely offer to
cure" was improperly rejected (*sub nom. Joc Oil USA v. Consolidated
Edison Co. of N.Y.*, 107 Misc.2d 376, 390, 434 N.Y.S.2d 623 [Shanley N.
Egeth, J.]). The Appellate Division, 84 A.D.2d 970, 447 N.Y.S.2d 572,
having unanimously affirmed the judgment entered on this decision, the
case is now here by our leave (CPLR 5602, subd. [a], par. 1, cl. [i]).

In support of its quest for reversal, the defendant now asserts that the
trial court erred . . . in failing to interpret subdivision (2) of section 2–508
of the Uniform Commercial Code to limit the availability of the right to
cure after date of performance to cases in which the seller knowingly made
a nonconforming tender and . . . in calculating damages on the basis of the
resale of the nonconforming cargo rather than of the substitute offered to
replace it. For the reasons which follow, we find [these assertions]
unacceptable. . . .

. . . Fairly interpreted, did subdivision (2) of section 2–508 of the
Uniform Commercial Code require Con Ed to accept the substitute

---

[3] Most of the *Khamsin* oil was drained from the tanks and sold at $10.75 per barrel. The
balance was retained by Con Ed in its mixed form at $10.45 per barrel. The original price in
January had been $17.875 per barrel.

[4] The plaintiff originally also sought an affirmative injunction to compel Con Ed to accept
the *Khamsin* shipment or, alternatively, the *Appollonian* substitute. However, when a preliminary
injunction was denied on the ground that the plaintiff had an adequate remedy at law, it amended
its complaint to pursue the latter remedy alone.

[5] These circumstances included the fact that the preliminary injunction was not denied until
April so that, by the time the *Khamsin* oil was sold in May, almost three months had gone by since
its rejection.

shipment plaintiff tendered? In approaching this question, we, of course, must remember that a seller's right to cure a defective tender, as allowed by both subdivisions of section 2–508, was intended to act as a meaningful limitation on the absolutism of the old perfect tender rule, under which, no leeway being allowed for any imperfections, there was, as one court put it, just "no room * * * for the doctrine of substantial performance" of commercial obligations (*Mitsubishi Goshi Kaisha v. Aron & Co.,* 16 F.2d 185, 186 [Learned Hand, J.]; see Note, Uniform Commercial Code, § 2–508; Seller's Right to Cure Non-Conforming Goods, 6 Rutgers—Camden L.J. 387–388).

In contrast, to meet the realities of the more impersonal business world of our day, the code, to avoid sharp dealing, expressly provides for the liberal construction of its remedial provisions (§ 1–102) so that "good faith" and the "observance of reasonable commercial standards of fair dealing" be the rule rather than the exception in trade (see § 2–103, subd. [1], par. [b]), "good faith" being defined as "honesty in fact in the conduct or transaction concerned" (Uniform Commercial Code, § 1–201, subd. [19]). As to section 2–508 in particular, the code's Official Comment advises that its mission is to safeguard the seller "against surprise as a result of sudden technicality on the buyer's part" (Uniform Commercial Code, § 2–106, Comment 2; see, also, Peters, Remedies for Breach of Contracts Relating to the Sale of Goods under the Uniform Commercial Code: A Roadmap for Article Two, 73 Yale L.J. 199, 210; 51 N.Y.Jur., Sales, § 101, p. 41).

Section 2–508 may be conveniently divided between provisions for cure offered when "the time for performance has not yet expired" (subd. [1]), a precode concept in this State (*Lowinson v. Newman,* 201 App.Div. 266, 194 N.Y.S. 253), and ones which, by newly introducing the possibility of a seller obtaining "a further reasonable time to substitute a conforming tender" (subd. [2]), also permit cure beyond the date set for performance. In its entirety the section reads as follows:

> "(1) Where any tender or delivery by the seller is rejected because non-conforming and the time for performance has not yet expired, the seller may seasonably notify the buyer of his intention to cure and may then within the contract time make a conforming delivery.

> "(2) Where the buyer rejects a non-conforming tender which the seller had reasonable grounds to believe would be acceptable with or without money allowance the seller may if he seasonably notifies the buyer have a further reasonable time to substitute a conforming tender."

Since we here confront circumstances in which the conforming tender came after the time of performance, we focus on subdivision (2) . On its face, taking its conditions in the order in which they appear, for the statute to apply (1) a buyer must have rejected a nonconforming tender, (2) the seller must have had reasonable grounds to believe this tender would be acceptable (with or without money allowance), and (3) the seller must have "seasonably" notified the buyer of the intention to substitute a conforming tender within a reasonable time.[7]

In the present case, none of these presented a problem. The first one was easily met for it is unquestioned that, at .92%, the sulfur content of the *Khamsin* oil did not conform to the .5% specified in the contract and that it was rejected by Con Ed. The second, the reasonableness of the seller's belief that the original tender would be acceptable, was supported not only by unimpeached proof that the contract's .5% and the refinery certificate's .52% were trade equivalents, but by testimony that, by the time the contract was made, the plaintiff knew Con Ed burned fuel with a content of up to 1%, so that, with appropriate price adjustment, the *Khamsin* oil would have suited its needs even if, at delivery, it was, to the plaintiff's surprise, to test out at .92%. Further, the matter seems to have been put beyond dispute by the defendant's readiness to take the oil at the reduced market price on February 20. Surely, on such a record, the trial court cannot be faulted for having found as a fact that the second condition too had been established.

As to the third, the conforming state of the *Appollonian* oil is undisputed, the offer to tender it took place on February 21, only a day after Con Ed finally had rejected the *Khamsin* delivery and the *Appollonian* substitute then already was en route to the United States, where it was expected in a week and did arrive on March 4, only four days later than expected. Especially since Con Ed pleaded no prejudice (unless the drop in prices could be so regarded), it is almost impossible, given the flexibility of the Uniform Commercial Code definitions of "seasonable" and "reasonable" (n. 7, *supra*), to quarrel with the finding that the remaining requirements of the statute also had been met.

Thus lacking the support of the statute's literal language, the defendant nonetheless would have us limit its application to cases in which a seller *knowingly* makes a nonconforming tender which it has reason to believe the buyer will accept. For this proposition, it relies almost entirely on a critique in Nordstrom, Law of Sales (§ 105), which rationalizes that, since a seller who believes its tender is conforming would have no reason to think in terms of a reduction in the price of the goods, to allow such a seller to cure after the time for performance had passed would make the

---

[7]   Essentially a factual matter, "seasonable" is defined in subdivision (3) of section 1–204 of the Uniform Commercial Code as "at or within the time agreed or if no time is agreed at or within a reasonable time". At least equally factual in character, a "reasonable time" is left to depend on the "nature, purpose and circumstances" of any action which is to be taken (Uniform Commercial Code, § 1–204, subd. [2]).

statutory reference to a money allowance redundant.[8] Nordstrom, interestingly enough, finds it useful to buttress this position by the somewhat dire prediction, though backed by no empirical or other confirmation, that, unless the right to cure is confined to those whose nonconforming tenders are knowing ones, the incentive of sellers to timely deliver will be undermined. To this it also adds the somewhat moralistic note that a seller who is mistaken as to the quality of its goods does not merit additional time (Nordstrom, *loc. cit.*). Curiously, recognizing that the few decisions extant on this subject have adopted a position opposed to the one for which it contends, Con Ed seeks to treat these as exceptions rather than exemplars of the rule (e.g., *Wilson v. Scampoli,* 228 A.2d 848 (D.C.App.) [goods obtained by seller from their manufacturer in original carton resold unopened to purchaser; seller held within statute though it had no reason to believe the goods defective]; *Appleton State Bank v. Lee,* 33 Wis.2d 690, 148 N.W.2d 1 [seller mistakenly delivered sewing machine of wrong brand but otherwise identical to one sold; held that seller, though it did not know of its mistake, had a right to cure by substitution]).[9]

That the principle for which these cases stand goes far beyond their particular facts cannot be gainsaid. These holdings demonstrate that, in dealing with the application of subdivision (2) of section 2–508, courts have been concerned with the reasonableness of the seller's belief that the goods would be acceptable rather than with the seller's pretender knowledge or lack of knowledge of the defect (*Wilson v. Scampoli, supra;* compare *Zabriskie Chevrolet v. Smith,* 99 N.J.Super. 441, 240 A.2d 195).

It also is no surprise then that the aforementioned decisional history is a reflection of the mainstream of scholarly commentary on the subject. . . .

White and Summers, for instance, put it well, and bluntly. Stressing that the code intended cure to be "a remedy which should be carefully cultivated and developed by the courts" because it "offers the possibility of conforming the law to reasonable expectations and of thwarting the chiseler who seeks to escape from a bad bargain" . . ., the authors conclude, as do we, that a seller should have recourse to the relief afforded by

---

[8]   The premise for such an argument, which ignores the policy of the code to prevent buyers from using insubstantial remediable or price adjustable defects to free themselves from unprofitable bargains (Hawkland, Sales and Bulk Sales Under the Uniform Commercial Code, pp. 120–122), is that the words "with or without money allowance" apply only to sellers who believe their goods will be acceptable with such an allowance and not to sellers who believe their goods will be acceptable without such an allowance. But, since the words are part of a phrase which speaks of an otherwise unqualified belief that the goods will be acceptable, unless one strains for an opposite interpretation, we find insufficient reason to doubt that it intends to include both those who find a need to offer an allowance and those who do not.

[9]   The only New York case to deal with this section involved a seller who knowingly tendered a "newer and improved version of the model that was actually ordered" on the contract delivery date. The court held he had reasonable grounds to believe the buyer would accept the newer model (*Bartus v. Riccardi,* 55 Misc.2d 3, 284 N.Y.S.2d 222 [Utica City Ct., Hymes, J.]).

subdivision (2) of section 2–508 of the Uniform Commercial Code as long as it can establish that it had reasonable grounds, tested objectively, for its belief that the goods would be accepted (*ibid.*, at p 321). It goes without saying that the test of reasonableness, in this context, must encompass the concepts of "good faith" and "commercial standards of fair dealing" which permeate the code (Uniform Commercial Code, § 1–201, subd. [19] ; §§ 1–203, 2–103, subd. [1], par. [b]).

As to the damages issue raised by the defendant, we affirm without reaching the merits. At no stage of the proceedings before the trial court did the defendant object to the plaintiff's proposed method for their calculation. . . .

COOKE, C.J., and JASEN, GABRIELLI, JONES, WACHTLER and MEYER, JJ., concur.

Order affirmed.

––––––––––

Zabriskie Chevrolet v. Smith

99 N.J.Super. 441, 240 A.2d 195 (1968)

Zabriskie Chevrolet, a new-car dealership, sold a new 1966 Chevrolet to Smith. As soon as Smith's wife drove off from the dealership, it became evident that the car had very serious problems. As a result, Smith stopped payment on his check and notified Zabriskie that the sale was canceled. Zabriskie then towed the car back, determined that the transmission was defective, replaced the transmission with a transmission it removed from a car on its showroom floor, and asked Smith to take delivery of the repaired car under the contract. When Smith refused to take delivery, Zabriskie brought suit. Held, Zabriskie did not have a right to cure the defective delivery:

"A 'cure' which endeavors by substitution to tender a chattel not within the agreement or contemplation of the parties is invalid.

"For a majority of people the purchase of a new car is a major investment, rationalized by the peace of mind that flows from its dependability and safety. Once their faith is shaken, the vehicle loses not only its real value in their eyes, but becomes an instrument whose integrity is substantially impaired and whose operation is fraught with apprehension. The attempted cure in the present case was ineffective."

––––––––––

Manassas Autocars v. Couch

274 Va. 82, 645 S.E.2d 443 (2007)

The Couches agreed to purchase a new red minivan from Manassas Autocars. The dealership did not have the van in stock so they arranged to have one delivered from another dealership. When the Couches came to pick up the van and do paperwork to complete the purchase they noticed "a grey circular 'splotch' approximately seven to eight inches in diameter with a 'drip' mark streaking three to four inches down to the wheel well of the passenger side rear panel." The salesperson persuaded the Couches to take the van and return to the dealership later to have the stain removed. When the Couches brought the van in for the repair the dealership was unable to remove the stain. Without asking the Couches' permission, the dealership repainted the stained area. The Couches returned the van to the dealership as soon as they realized what had been done, stating they had purchased a new vehicle and not a repainted vehicle. The dealership had the van towed back to the Couches' home. The Couches also notified the lender of the revocation. Eventually the lender repossessed the van. When the Couches returned the van it had been driven approximately 1,100 miles. The Couches brought a claim for damages. The jury returned a verdict in favor of the Couches on the revocation claim and awarded damages. Held, affirmed:

Manassas claims that the trial court erred in denying its motions to strike the Couches' revocation claim because the evidence did not establish that the nonconformity substantially impaired the vehicle's value to the Couches. Specifically, Manassas argues that under *Gasque v. Mooers Motor Car Co.*, 227 Va. 154, 313 S.E.2d 384 (1984), the measure of substantial impairment of value to the buyer is not diminution in the value of the goods on the open market; rather, unless the evidence establishes otherwise, the usual and customary purpose of the goods—in this case, transportation—is presumed to be the reason for the purchase and the measure by which the value of the goods is determined. Considering this purpose, Manassas points out that there was no evidence that the nonconformity adversely affected the vehicle's "driveability." The only evidence offered at trial regarding value was the Couches' expert witness who testified that the repainting diminished the value of the vehicle by 20 percent. Manassas contends that the Couches therefore failed to carry their burden of proof on their revocation claim and the trial court erred in submitting this issue to the jury. We disagree with Manassas' proposed application of *Gasque*.

The plaintiffs in *Gasque* sought to revoke their acceptance of a new 1979 Fiat vehicle based on a number of problems such as a water leak, heater malfunction, inoperative clock and interior light, automatic choke problems, excessive oil consumption, loud vibrations, and other noises and rattles. The plaintiffs had driven the vehicle with these various defects for at least 4,500 miles prior to revocation, and the vehicle had been driven over 8,000 miles at the time of trial. The trial court struck the plaintiffs' evidence and entered judgment for the defendant dealer, holding that, under a 'driveability' test, there was no substantial diminution in the value of the vehicle to the plaintiffs and the plaintiffs did not notify the dealer of the revocation within a reasonable time.

On appeal to this Court, one issue was whether the "driveability" test used by the trial court was correct. The plaintiffs argued that the appropriate test was a subjective test, "under which the buyers need only persuade the fact-finder that their 'faith has been shaken' in the product." 227 Va. at 160, 313 S.E.2d at 389. We rejected this argument, holding that while a "driveability" test "would not be of universal application," the application of the test in that case was not erroneous "where the buyers failed to prove any need for the car beyond ordinary transportation." *Id.* at 161, 313 S.E.2d at 389.

The record in this case shows that Mr. Couch testified he wanted to purchase a new vehicle, not a repainted vehicle, and that the repainted vehicle was not the vehicle they purchased. Mrs. Couch testified that, if she had been told that Manassas intended to cure the defect in the vehicle by repainting it, she would not have given permission because she "purchased a vehicle at new car standards and if you paint it, then, it is no longer a new car." The Couches' expert witness then testified that the vehicle lost 20 percent of its value in its repainted condition.

This record thus demonstrates that the Couches intended to buy not only a means of transportation but a *new* vehicle. When the nonconforming condition was repaired by repainting, the value of the vehicle to the Couches—as a new vehicle—was impaired. The expert's testimony that the repainting caused a 20 percent decrease in value supports a determination that the impairment was substantial. Therefore the trial court did not err in submitting the Couches' revocation of acceptance claim to the jury.

CHAPTER 20

EXPRESS CONDITIONS

■ ■ ■

SECTION 1. INTRODUCTION

NOTE ON THE DIFFERENCE BETWEEN PROMISES AND CONDITIONS

Up to now, the materials in this casebook have chiefly concerned promises. This Chapter concerns another basic set of contractual building blocks—express conditions. As previously discussed, the term "express condition" normally refers to an explicit contractual provision that either: (1) A party to the contract does not come under a duty to perform unless and until some designated state of affairs occurs or fails to occur; or (2) If some designated state of affairs occurs or fails to occur, a party's duty to perform is suspended or terminated. For example, Corporation A may agree to merge with Corporation B, but only on condition that the Commissioner of Internal Revenue rules that the transaction will be tax-free. Or, C may agree to purchase D's house, but only on condition that a termite-inspection report shows no infestation.

Why would parties use an express condition rather than a promise? In some cases, it is because neither party is willing to promise that the state of affairs in question will occur. In the merger hypothetical, for example, neither A nor B would normally be willing to promise that the Commissioner will issue a favorable ruling. In the sale-of-the-house hypothetical, D may not know whether the house is infested with termites, and therefore may not be willing to promise that there is no infestation.

Another possible reason for using express conditions, rather than promises, is to avoid—or at least attempt to avoid—the doctrine of substantial performance. Under that doctrine, if A promises to perform construction for B according to agreed-upon specifications, a slight deviation from the specifications will render A liable to a claim for damages by B, but may not prevent A from holding B to his promise to pay for the job, with an offset for the damages. On the other hand, if the contract expressly states that it is a condition to B's liability to A that A's performance meets the designated specifications, then B's chance of escaping liability for the contract price because of a departure from the specifications is improved.

As the next several cases illustrate, it is not always easy to determine whether a given contractual provision is a promise or a condition. The issue is further confused by the fact that under modern contract terminology, where A and B have a contract, A's substantial performance of *his* promises may be an *implied condition* to B's obligation to perform *her* promises. The doctrine of substantial performance and the doctrine of material breach (both taken up in Chapter 19, supra), are often described as constructive conditions.

The organization of this Chapter is as follows: Section 2 will explore the differences between the operation of promises and conditions. Section 3 concerns issues of interpretation in determining whether a contractual provision is a promise or a condition. Sections 4 and 5 concern the prevention doctrine, which denies effect to a condition when the obligor wrongfully prevents its fulfillment, and conditions of satisfaction, in which a duty to pay for a performance is made conditional on satisfaction with the performance. A common theme is the interplay of the duty of good faith with conditions. Section 6 concerns excuses for the nonfulfillment of conditions that do not turn on the obligor's misconduct or bad faith.

———

SECTION 2. THE DISTINCTIONS BETWEEN THE OPERATION OF A PROMISE AND THE OPERATION OF A CONDITION

OPPENHEIMER & CO. V. OPPENHEIM, APPEL, DIXON & CO.
Court of Appeals of New York, 1995.
86 N.Y.2d 685, 660 N.E.2d 415, 636 N.Y.S.2d 734.

CIPARICK, JUSTICE.

The parties entered into a letter agreement setting forth certain conditions precedent to the formation and existence of a sublease between them. The agreement provided that there would be no sublease between the parties "unless and until" plaintiff delivered to defendant the prime landlord's written consent to certain "tenant work" on or before a specified deadline. If this condition did not occur, the sublease was to be deemed "null and void." Plaintiff provided only oral notice on the specified date. The issue presented is whether the doctrine of substantial performance applies to the facts of this case. We conclude it does not for the reasons that follow.

I.

In 1986, plaintiff Oppenheimer & Co. moved to the World Financial Center in Manhattan, a building constructed by Olympia & York Company (O & Y). At the time of its move, plaintiff had three years remaining on its existing lease for the 33rd floor of the building known as One New York Plaza. As an incentive to induce plaintiff's move, O & Y agreed to make the rental payments due under plaintiff's rental agreement in the event plaintiff was unable to sublease its prior space in One New York Plaza.

In December 1986, the parties to this action entered into a conditional letter agreement to sublease the 33rd floor. Defendant already leased space on the 29th floor of One New York Plaza and was seeking to expand its operations. The proposed sublease between the parties was attached to the letter agreement. The letter agreement provided that the proposed sublease would be executed only upon the satisfaction of certain conditions. Pursuant to paragraph 1(a) of the agreement, plaintiff was required to obtain "the Prime Landlord's written notice of confirmation, substantially to the effect that [defendant] is a subtenant of the Premises reasonably acceptable to Prime Landlord." If such written notice of confirmation were not obtained "on or before December 30, 1986, then this letter agreement and the Sublease shall be deemed null and void and of no further force and effect and neither party shall have any rights against nor obligations to the other."

Assuming satisfaction of the condition set forth in paragraph 1(a), defendant was required to submit to plaintiff, on or before January 2, 1987, its plans for "tenant work" involving construction of a telephone communication linkage system between the 29th and 33rd floors. Paragraph 4(c) of the letter agreement then obligated plaintiff to obtain the prime landlord's "written consent" to the proposed "tenant work" and deliver such consent to defendant on or before January 30, 1987. Furthermore, if defendant had not received the prime landlord's written consent by the agreed date, both the agreement and the sublease were to be deemed "null and void and of no further force and effect," and neither party was to have "any rights against nor obligations to the other." Paragraph 4(d) additionally provided that, notwithstanding satisfaction of the condition set forth in paragraph 1(a), the parties "agree not to execute and exchange the Sublease unless and until the conditions set forth in paragraph (c) above are timely satisfied."

The parties extended the letter agreement's deadlines in writing and plaintiff timely satisfied the first condition set forth in paragraph 1(a) pursuant to the modified deadline. However, plaintiff never delivered the prime landlord's written consent to the proposed tenant work on or before the modified final deadline of February 25, 1987. Rather, plaintiff's attorney telephoned defendant's attorney on February 25 and informed defendant that the prime landlord's consent had been secured. On February 26, defendant, through its attorney, informed plaintiff's attorney that the letter agreement and sublease were invalid for failure to timely deliver the prime landlord's written consent and that it would not agree to an extension of the deadline. The document embodying the prime landlord's written consent was eventually received by plaintiff on March 20, 1987, 23 days after expiration of paragraph 4(c)'s modified final deadline.

Plaintiff commenced this action for breach of contract, asserting that defendant waived and/or was estopped by virtue of its conduct[1] from insisting on physical delivery of the prime landlord's written consent by the February 25 deadline. Plaintiff further alleged in its complaint that it had substantially performed the conditions set forth in the letter agreement.

At the outset of trial, the court issued an order in *limine* barring any reference to substantial performance of the terms of the letter agreement. Nonetheless, during the course of trial, the court permitted the jury to consider the theory of substantial performance, and additionally charged the jury concerning substantial performance. Special interrogatories were submitted. The jury found that defendant had properly complied with the terms of the letter agreement, and answered in the negative the questions whether defendant failed to perform its obligations under the letter agreement concerning submission of plans for tenant work, whether defendant by its conduct waived the February 25 deadline for delivery by plaintiff of the landlord's written consent to tenant work, and whether defendant by its conduct was equitably estopped from requiring plaintiff's strict adherence to the February 25 deadline. Nonetheless, the jury answered in the affirmative the question, "Did plaintiff substantially perform the conditions set forth in the Letter Agreement?," and awarded plaintiff damages of $1.2 million.

Defendant moved for judgment notwithstanding the verdict. Supreme Court granted the motion, ruling as a matter of law that "the doctrine of substantial performance has no application to this dispute, where the Letter Agreement is free of all ambiguity in setting the deadline that plaintiff concededly did not honor." The Appellate Division reversed the judgment on the law and facts, and reinstated the jury verdict. The Court concluded that the question of substantial compliance was properly submitted to the jury and that the verdict should be reinstated because plaintiff's failure to deliver the prime landlord's written consent was inconsequential.

This Court granted defendant's motion for leave to appeal and we now reverse.

II.

Defendant argues that no sublease or contractual relationship ever arose here because plaintiff failed to satisfy the condition set forth in paragraph 4(c) of the letter agreement. Defendant contends that the doctrine of substantial performance is not applicable to excuse plaintiff's failure to deliver the prime landlord's written consent to defendant on or

---

[1] Plaintiff argued that it could have met the deadline, but failed to do so only because defendant, acting in bad faith, induced plaintiff into delaying delivery of the landlord's consent. Plaintiff asserted that the parties had previously extended the agreement's deadlines as a matter of course.

before the date specified in the letter agreement and that the Appellate Division erred in holding to the contrary. Before addressing defendant's arguments and the decision of the court below, an understanding of certain relevant principles is helpful.

A condition precedent is "an act or event, other than a lapse of time, which, unless the condition is excused, must occur before a duty to perform a promise in the agreement arises" (Calamari and Perillo, Contracts § 11–2, at 438 [3d ed.]; see, Restatement [Second] of Contracts § 224; see also, Merritt Hill Vineyards v. Windy Hgts. Vineyard, 61 N.Y.2d 106, 112–113, 472 N.Y.S.2d 592, 460 N.E.2d 1077). Most conditions precedent describe acts or events which must occur before a party is obliged to perform a promise made pursuant to an existing contract, a situation to be distinguished conceptually from a condition precedent to the formation or existence of the contract itself (see, M.K. Metals v. Container Recovery Corp., 645 F.2d 583). In the latter situation, no contract arises "unless and until the condition occurs" (Calamari and Perillo, Contracts § 11–5, at 440 [3d ed]).

Conditions can be express or implied. Express conditions are those agreed to and imposed by the parties themselves. Implied or constructive conditions are those "imposed by law to do justice" (Calamari and Perillo, Contracts § 11–8, at 444 [3d ed]). Express conditions must be literally performed, whereas constructive conditions, which ordinarily arise from language of promise, are subject to the precept that substantial compliance is sufficient. The importance of the distinction has been explained by Professor Williston:

> "Since an express condition depends for its validity on the manifested intention of the parties, it has the same sanctity as the promise itself. Though the court may regret the harshness of such a condition, as it may regret the harshness of a promise, it must, nevertheless, generally enforce the will of the parties unless to do so will violate public policy. Where, however, the law itself has imposed the condition, in absence of or irrespective of the manifested intention of the parties, it can deal with its creation as it pleases, shaping the boundaries of the constructive condition in such a way as to do justice and avoid hardship". (5 Williston, Contracts § 669, at 154 [3d ed.].)

In determining whether a particular agreement makes an event a condition courts will interpret doubtful language as embodying a promise or constructive condition rather than an express condition. This interpretive preference is especially strong when a finding of express condition would increase the risk of forfeiture by the obligee (see, Restatement [Second] of Contracts § 227 [1]).

Interpretation as a means of reducing the risk of forfeiture cannot be employed if "the occurrence of the event as a condition is expressed in unmistakable language" (Restatement [Second] of Contracts § 229, comment a, at 185; see, § 227, comment b [where language is clear, "(t)he policy favoring freedom of contract requires that, within broad limits, the agreement of the parties should be honored even though forfeiture results"]). Nonetheless, the nonoccurrence of the condition may yet be excused by waiver, breach or forfeiture. The Restatement posits that "[t]o the extent that the non-occurrence of a condition would cause disproportionate forfeiture, a court may excuse the non-occurrence of that condition unless its occurrence was a material part of the agreed exchange" (Restatement [Second] of Contracts § 229).

Turning to the case at bar, it is undisputed that the critical language of paragraph 4(c) of the letter agreement unambiguously establishes an express condition precedent rather than a promise, as the parties employed the unmistakable language of condition ("if," "unless and until"). There is no doubt of the parties' intent and no occasion for interpreting the terms of the letter agreement other than as written.

Furthermore, plaintiff has never argued, and does not now contend, that the nonoccurrence of the condition set forth in paragraph 4(c) should be excused on the ground of forfeiture.[2] Rather, plaintiff's primary argument from the inception of this litigation has been that defendant waived or was equitably estopped from invoking paragraph 4(c). Plaintiff argued secondarily that it substantially complied with the express condition of delivery of written notice on or before February 25th in that it gave defendant oral notice of consent on the 25th.

Contrary to the decision of the Court below, we perceive no justifiable basis for applying the doctrine of substantial performance to the facts of this case. The flexible concept of substantial compliance "stands in sharp contrast to the requirement of strict compliance that protects a party that has taken the precaution of making its duty expressly conditional" (2 Farnsworth, Contracts § 8.12, at 415 [2d ed 1990]). If the parties "have made an event a condition of their agreement, there is no mitigating standard of materiality or substantiality applicable to the non-occurrence of that event" (Restatement [Second] of Contracts § 237, comment d, at 220). Substantial performance in this context is not sufficient, "and if relief is to be had under the contract, it must be through excuse of the non-occurrence of the condition to avoid forfeiture" (id.; see, Brown-Marx Assocs. v. Emigrant Sav. Bank, 703 F.2d 1361, 1367–1368 [11th Cir.]; see also, Childres, Conditions in the Law of Contracts, 45 NYU L.Rev. 33, 35).

---

[2]   The Restatement defines the term "forfeiture" as "the denial of compensation that results when the obligee loses [its] right to the agreed exchange after [it] has relied substantially, as by preparation or performance on the expectation of that exchange" (§ 229, comment b).

Here, it is undisputed that plaintiff has not suffered a forfeiture or conferred a benefit upon defendant. Plaintiff alludes to a $1 million licensing fee it allegedly paid to the prime landlord for the purpose of securing the latter's consent to the subleasing of the premises. At no point, however, does plaintiff claim that this sum was forfeited or that it was expended for the purpose of accomplishing the sublease with defendant. It is further undisputed that O & Y, as an inducement to effect plaintiff's move to the World Financial Center, promised to indemnify plaintiff for damages resulting from failure to sublease the 33rd floor of One New York Plaza. Consequently, because the critical concern of forfeiture or unjust enrichment is simply not present in this case, we are not presented with an occasion to consider whether the doctrine of substantial performance is applicable, that is, whether the courts should intervene to excuse the nonoccurrence of a condition precedent to the formation of a contract.

The essence of the Appellate Division's holding is that the substantial performance doctrine is universally applicable to all categories of breach of contract, including the nonoccurrence of an express condition precedent. However, as discussed, substantial performance is ordinarily not applicable to excuse the nonoccurrence of an express condition precedent . . .

III.

In sum, the letter agreement provides in the clearest language that the parties did not intend to form a contract "unless and until" defendant received written notice of the prime landlord's consent on or before February 25, 1987. Defendant would lease the 33rd floor from plaintiff only on the condition that the landlord consent in writing to a telephone communication linkage system between the 29th and 33rd floors and to defendant's plans for construction effectuating that linkage. This matter was sufficiently important to defendant that it would not enter into the sublease "unless and until" the condition was satisfied. Inasmuch as we are not dealing here with a situation where plaintiff stands to suffer some forfeiture or undue hardship, we perceive no justification for engaging in a "materiality-of-the-nonoccurrence" analysis. To do so would simply frustrate the clearly expressed intention of the parties. Freedom of contract prevails in an arm's length transaction between sophisticated parties such as these, and in the absence of countervailing public policy concerns there is no reason to relieve them of the consequences of their bargain. If they are dissatisfied with the consequences of their agreement, "the time to say so [was] at the bargaining table" [Maxton Bldrs. v. Lo Galbo, 68 N.Y.2d 373, 509 N.Y.S.2d 507, 502 N.E.2d 184].

Finally, the issue of substantial performance was not for the jury to resolve in this case. A determination whether there has been substantial performance is to be answered, "if the inferences are certain, by the judges of the law" (Jacob & Youngs v. Kent, 230 N.Y. 239, 243, 129 N.E. 889 supra).

Accordingly, the order of the Appellate Division should be reversed, with costs, and the complaint dismissed.

CHIEF JUDGE KAYE, C.J., and JUDGES SIMONS, TITONE, BELLACOSA, SMITH and LEVINE, JJ., concur.

Order reversed, etc.

———

NOTE ON STRICT ENFORCEMENT OF CONDITIONS

One distinction between a promise and a condition is that conditions are supposed to be strictly enforced. Courts often say a default need not be material and substantial performance will not satisfy a condition. Sometimes conditions are strictly enforced. For example, in Union Eagle Ltd. v. Golden Achievement Ltd, [1997] 2 All E.R. 215, an agreement to purchase a flat required the purchaser to pay the balance of the purchase price by 5:00PM or forfeit a 10 percent deposit as liquidated damages. A messenger with a check arrived 10 minutes late. The seller was allowed to terminate the contract and retain the deposit. Under modern contract law in the U.S. several rules temper the enforcement of conditions to avoid unjust results so we are not sure this case would come out the same way in a U.S. court. Some of these rules are covered in Sections 4, 5, and 6. And sometimes courts will stretch find a term ambiguous and then apply an interpretive presumption against treating a term as a condition when this would lead to an unjust result. These rules are covered in Section 3.

———

MERRITT HILL VINEYARDS, INC. V.
WINDY HEIGHTS VINEYARD, INC.
Court of Appeals of New York, 1984.
61 N.Y.2d 106, 472 N.Y.S.2d 592, 460 N.E.2d 1077.

KAYE, JUDGE. . .

In September, 1981, plaintiff, Merritt Hill Vineyards, entered into a written agreement with defendants, Windy Heights Vineyard and its sole shareholder Leon Taylor, to purchase a majority stock interest in respondents' Yates County vineyard, and tendered a $15,000 deposit. The agreement provides that "[i]f the sale contemplated hereby does not close, Taylor shall retain the deposit as liquidated damages unless Taylor or Windy Heights failed to satisfy the conditions specified in Section 3 thereof." Section 3, in turn, lists several "conditions precedent" to which the obligation of purchaser to pay the purchase price and to complete the purchase is subject. Among the conditions are that, by the time of the closing, Windy Heights shall have obtained a title insurance policy in a form satisfactory to Merritt Hill, and Windy Heights and Merritt Hill shall have received confirmation from the Farmers Home Administration that certain mortgages on the vineyard are in effect and that the proposed sale does not constitute a default.

In April, 1982, at the closing, plaintiff discovered that neither the policy nor the confirmation had been issued. Plaintiff thereupon refused to close and demanded return of its deposit. When defendants did not return the deposit, plaintiff instituted this action, asserting two causes of action, one for return of the deposit, and one for approximately $26,000 in consequential damages allegedly suffered as a result of defendants' failure to perform.

Special Term denied plaintiff's motion for summary judgment on both causes of action. The Appellate Division unanimously reversed Special Term's order, granted plaintiff's motion for summary judgment as to the cause of action for return of the deposit, and ... granted summary judgment in favor of defendants, dismissing plaintiff's second cause of action for consequential damages. Both plaintiff and defendants appealed from that decision. . . .

... [P]laintiff's right to return of its deposit or to consequential damages depends upon whether the undertaking to produce the policy and mortgage confirmation is a promise or a condition.

A promise is "a manifestation of intention to act or refrain from acting in a specified way, so made as to justify a promisee in understanding that a commitment has been made." (Restatement, Contracts 2d, § 2, subd. [1].) A *condition,* by comparison, is "an event, not certain to occur, which must occur, unless its non-occurrence is excused, before performance under a contract becomes due." (Restatement, Contracts 2d, § 224.) Here, the contract requirements of a title insurance policy and mortgage confirmation are expressed as conditions of plaintiff's performance rather than as promises by defendants. The requirements are contained in a section of the agreement entitled "Conditions Precedent to Purchaser's Obligation to Close," which provides that plaintiff's obligation to pay the purchase price and complete the purchase of the vineyard is "subject to" fulfillment of those requirements. No words of promise are employed.*

---

*   Plaintiff contends that the failure to produce the policy and confirmation is also a breach of section 5, entitled "Representations, Warranties and Agreements." A provision may be both a condition and a promise, if the parties additionally promise to perform a condition as part of their bargain. Such a promise is not present here. The only provision of section 5 conceivably relevant is that "Windy Heights has good and marketable title to the Property and all other properties and assets * * * as of December 31, 1980". But this is quite different from the conditions of section 3 that a title insurance policy and mortgage confirmation be produced at the closing, which took place in April, 1982. Both the complaint and plaintiff's affidavits are premised on nonperformance of section 3 of the agreement, not section 5. [Footnote by the court.]

Defendants' agreement to sell the stock of the vineyard, not those conditions, was the promise by defendants for which plaintiff's promise to pay the purchase price was exchanged.

Defendants' failure to fulfill the conditions of section 3 entitles plaintiff to a return of its deposit but not to consequential damages. While a contracting party's failure to fulfill a condition excuses performance by the other party whose performance is so conditioned, it is not, without an independent promise to perform the condition, a breach of contract subjecting the nonfulfilling party to liability for damages (Restatement, Contracts 2d, § 225, subds. [1], [3]; 3A Corbin, Contracts, § 663; 5 Williston, Contracts [Jaeger—3d ed.], § 665). This is in accord with the parties' expressed intent, for section 1 of their agreement provides that if defendants fail to satisfy the conditions of section 3 plaintiff's deposit will not be returned. It does not provide for payment of damages.

On the merits of this case the Appellate Division thus correctly determined that plaintiff was entitled to the return of its deposit but not to consequential damages.

Accordingly, the order of the Appellate Division should be affirmed.

COOKE, C.J., and JASEN, JONES, WACHTLER and MEYER, JJ., concur.

SIMONS, J., taking no part.

Order affirmed, without costs.

SECTION 3. PROBLEMS OF INTERPRETATION IN DISTINGUISHING BETWEEN CONDITIONS AND PROMISES

HOWARD V. FEDERAL CROP INSURANCE CORP.

United States Court of Appeals, Fourth Circuit, 1976.
540 F.2d 695.

Before RUSSELL, FIELD and WIDENER, CIRCUIT JUDGES.

WIDENER, CIRCUIT JUDGE:

Plaintiff-appellants sued to recover for losses to their 1973 tobacco crop due to alleged rain damage. The crops were insured by defendant-appellee, Federal Crop Insurance Corporation (FCIC). Suits were brought in a state court in North Carolina and removed to the United States District Court. The three suits are not distinguishable factually so far as we are concerned here and involve identical questions of law. They were combined for disposition in the district court and for appeal. The district court granted summary judgment for the defendant and dismissed all three actions. We remand for further proceedings. Since we find for the plaintiffs as to the construction of the policy, we express no opinion on the procedural questions.

Federal Crop Insurance Corporation, an agency of the United States, in 1973, issued three policies to the Howards, insuring their tobacco crops, to be grown on six farms, against weather damage and other hazards.

The Howards (plaintiffs) established production of tobacco on their acreage, and have alleged that their 1973 crop was extensively damaged by heavy rains, resulting in a gross loss to the three plaintiffs in excess of $35,000. The plaintiffs harvested and sold the depleted crop and timely filed notice and proof of loss with FCIC, but, prior to inspection by the adjuster for FCIC, the Howards had either plowed or disked under the tobacco fields in question to prepare the same for sowing a cover crop of rye to preserve the soil. When the FCIC adjuster later inspected the fields, he found the stalks had been largely obscured or obliterated by plowing or disking and denied the claims, apparently on the ground that the plaintiffs had violated a portion of the policy which provides that the stalks on any acreage with respect to which a loss is claimed shall not be destroyed until the corporation makes an inspection.

The holding of the district court is best capsuled in its own words:

"The inquiry here is whether compliance by the insureds with this provision of the policy was a condition precedent to the recovery. The court concludes that it was and that the failure of the insureds to comply worked a forfeiture of benefits for the alleged loss."

... Paragraph 5 of the tobacco endorsement is entitled *Claims*. Pertinent to this case are subparagraphs 5(b) and 5(f), which are as follows:

"5(b) *It shall be a condition precedent* to the payment of any loss that the insured establish the production of the insured crop on a unit and that such loss has been directly caused by one or more of the hazards insured against during the insurance period for the crop year for which the loss is claimed, and furnish any other information regarding the manner and extent of loss as may be required by the Corporation. (Emphasis added)"

"5(f) The tobacco stalks on any acreage of tobacco of types 11a, 11b, 12, 13, or 14 with respect to which a loss is claimed *shall not be destroyed until the Corporation makes an inspection.* (Emphasis added)"

The arguments of both parties are predicated upon the same two assumptions. First, if subparagraph 5(f) creates a condition precedent, its violation caused a forfeiture of plaintiffs' coverage. Second, if subparagraph 5(f) creates an obligation (variously called a promise or covenant) upon plaintiffs not to plow under the tobacco stalks, defendant may recover from plaintiffs (either in an original action, or, in this case, by a counterclaim, or as a matter of defense) for whatever damage it sustained because of the elimination of the stalks. However, a violation of subparagraph 5(f) would not, under the second premise, standing alone, cause a forfeiture of the policy.

Generally accepted law provides us with guidelines here. There is a general legal policy opposed to forfeitures. *United States v. One Ford Coach,* 307 U.S. 219, 226, 59 S.Ct. 861, 83 L.Ed. 1249 (1939); *Baca v. Commissioner of Internal Revenue,* 326 F.2d 189, 191 (5th Cir.1963). Insurance policies are generally construed most strongly against the insurer. *Henderson v. Hartford Accident & Indemnity Co.,* 268 N.C. 129, 150 S.E.2d 17, 19 (1966). When it is doubtful whether words create a promise or a condition precedent, they will be construed as creating a promise. *Harris and Harris Const. Co. v. Crain and Denbo, Inc.,* 256 N.C. 110, 123 S.E.2d 590, 595 (1962). The provisions of a contract will not be construed as conditions precedent in the absence of language plainly requiring such construction. *Harris,* 123 S.E.2d at 596. And *Harris,* at 123 S.E.2d 590, 595, cites *Jones v. Palace Realty Co.,* 226 N.C. 303, 37 S.E.2d 906 (1946), and *Restatement of the Law, Contracts,* § 261.

Plaintiffs rely most strongly upon the fact that the term "condition precedent" is included in subparagraph 5(b) but not in subparagraph 5(f). It is true that whether a contract provision is construed as a condition or an obligation does not depend entirely upon whether the word "condition" is expressly used. Appleman, *Insurance Law and Practice* (1972), vol. 6A, § 4144. However, the persuasive force of plaintiffs' argument in this case is found in the use of the term "condition precedent" in subparagraph 5(b) but not in subparagraph 5(f). Thus, it is argued that the ancient maxim to be applied is that the expression of one thing is the exclusion of another. . . .

The *Restatement [First] of the Law of Contracts* states:

"§ 261.   Interpretation of Doubtful Words as Promise or Condition.

Where it is doubtful whether words create a promise or an express condition, they are interpreted as creating a promise; but the same words may sometimes mean that one party promises a performance and that the other party's promise is conditional on that performance."

Two illustrations (one involving a promise, the other a condition) are used in the *Restatement:*

"2. A, an insurance company, issues to B a policy of insurance containing promises by A that are in terms conditional on the happening of certain events. The policy contains this clause: 'provided, in case differences shall arise touching any loss, *the matter shall be submitted to impartial arbitrators,* whose award shall be binding on the parties.' This is a promise to arbitrate and does not make an award a condition precedent of the insurer's duty to pay.

"3. A, an insurance company, issues to B an insurance policy in usual form containing this clause: 'In the event of disagreement as to the amount of loss it shall be ascertained by two appraisers and an umpire. The loss shall *not be payable until 60 days after the award of the appraisers when such an appraisal is required.*' This provision is not merely a promise to arbitrate differences but makes an award a condition of the insurer's duty to pay in case of disagreement." (Emphasis added)

We believe that subparagraph 5(f) in the policy here under consideration fits illustration 2 rather than illustration 3. Illustration 2 specifies something to be done, whereas subparagraph 5(f) specifies something not to be done. Unlike illustration 3, subparagraph 5(f) does not state any conditions under which the insurance shall "not be payable," or use any words of like import. We hold that the district court erroneously held, on the motion for summary judgment, that subparagraph 5(f) established a condition precedent to plaintiffs' recovery which forfeited the coverage.

From our holding that defendant's motion for summary judgment was improperly allowed, it does not follow the plaintiffs' motion for summary judgment should have been granted, for if subparagraph 5(f) be not construed as a condition precedent, there are other questions of fact to be determined. At this point, we merely hold that the district court erred in holding, on the motion for summary judgment, that subparagraph 5(f) constituted a condition precedent with resulting forfeiture.

The explanation defendant makes for including subparagraph 5(f) in the tobacco endorsement is that it is necessary that the stalks remain standing in order for the Corporation to evaluate the extent of loss and to determine whether loss resulted from some cause not covered by the policy. However, was subparagraph 5(f) inserted because without it the Corporation's opportunities for proof would be more difficult, or because they would be impossible? Plaintiffs point out that the Tobacco Endorsement, with subparagraph 5(f), was adopted in 1970, and crop insurance goes back long before that date. Nothing is shown as to the Corporation's prior 1970 practice of evaluating losses. Such a showing might have a bearing upon establishing defendant's intention in including 5(f). Plaintiffs state, and defendant does not deny, that another division of the Department of Agriculture, or the North Carolina Department, urged that tobacco stalks be cut as soon as possible after harvesting as a means of pest control. Such an explanation might refute the idea that plaintiffs plowed under the stalks for any fraudulent purpose. Could these conflicting directives affect the reasonableness of plaintiffs' interpretation of defendant's prohibition upon plowing under the stalks prior to adjustment?

We express no opinion on these questions because they were not before the district court and are mentioned to us largely by way of argument rather than from the record. No question of ambiguity was raised in the court below or here and no question of the applicability of paragraph 5(c) to this case was alluded to other than in the defendant's pleadings, so we also do not reach those questions. Nothing we say here should preclude FCIC from asserting as a defense that the plowing or disking under of the stalks caused damage to FCIC if, for example, the amount of the loss was thereby made more difficult or impossible to ascertain whether the plowing or disking under was done with bad purpose or innocently. To repeat, our narrow holding is that merely plowing or disking under the stalks does not of itself operate to forfeit coverage under the policy.

The case is remanded for further proceedings not inconsistent with this opinion.

VACATED AND REMANDED.

_____

RESTATEMENT, SECOND, CONTRACTS § 227

[See Selected Source Materials Supplement]

_____

SECTION 4. PREVENTION; THE IMPLICATION OF A DUTY TO FULFILL A CONDITION

JOHNSON V. COSS

Supreme Court of South Dakota, 2003.
667 N.W.2d 701, 2003 SD 86.

ZINTER, JUSTICE. Lawrence Coss entered into an agreement to purchase George Johnson's, auto dealership. The agreement was conditioned on Ford Motor Company's transfer of its franchise from Johnson to Coss. After several months, Coss notified both Johnson and Ford that the agreement could not be completed because Coss could not meet Ford's franchise transfer requirements. Johnson subsequently commenced this action for breach of contract and breach of the covenant of good faith and fair dealing. The circuit court granted summary judgment for Johnson reasoning that Coss's actions prevented Ford's transfer of the franchise. Coss appeals. Because we find material issues of disputed fact relating to the cause of the failure to transfer the franchise, we reverse and remand.

FACTS AND PROCEDURAL HISTORY

On January 7, 2000, Johnson and Coss entered into an Asset Purchase Agreement for the sale of Johnson Ford Lincoln-Mercury, Inc. The sale included the dealership assets, the real estate upon which the car business was located, as well as the inventory, parts, and other related items.

The agreement was expressly conditioned upon Ford Motor Company's approval of the transfer of the Ford franchise from Johnson to Coss. Paragraph 16 of the agreement provided:

> All transactions described in this agreement are subject to the consent and approval of Seller's franchisor, Ford Motor Company, and any of its subsidiaries or member companies. Transfer, or written approval of transfer, of the Ford Lincoln-Mercury franchise, is a condition precedent to closing of the transactions herein. In the event the consent and approval of Ford Motor Company or any other entity necessary to approve and effectively transfer the Ford Lincoln-Mercury franchise to Purchaser is not obtained, then this transaction in its entirety and this agreement in its entirety is null and void.

Paragraph 17 of the agreement also conditioned the agreement on: "[r]eceipt of the consent and approval [sic] the Corporation's franchisor, Ford Motor Company, in regard to the transfer of the Corporation's Ford Lincoln-Mercury franchise to Purchaser[.]"

Coss hired Steven Grodahl, an attorney and CPA, to assist Coss with the franchise transfer. According to Grodahl's affidavit in opposition to Johnson's motion for summary judgment, Ford identified several requirements that Coss needed to satisfy before Ford would approve the transfer. Those requirements included an on site manager that was approved by Ford. That manager was required to demonstrate, to Ford's satisfaction, the ability to operate a dealership successfully. The manager was also required to own a substantial interest in the business.

Viewing the facts most favorably to Coss as we must do on summary judgment, Grodahl indicated that Ford would not approve Coss as the manager/co-owner. Because Ford would not transfer the franchise if Coss were the sole owner, Coss decided that the success of the agreement depended upon finding a manager willing to run the day-to-day operations of the dealership. That person would also have to acquire a substantial ownership in the business.

Mark Goodrich was identified as such a manager/co-owner. Originally, Coss proposed a 50/50 ownership arrangement with Goodrich and a joint capitalization of $1 million. However, Ford indicated that they required a majority owner. Pursuant to that requirement, Coss revised the plan so that he would own 50.1% of the dealership. In addition to the ownership requirements, Ford required that the potential owners develop a New Dealer Operating Plan, and that each owner submit personal and financial information. Ford further advised that it would require an initial capitalization of $1.476 million instead of the $1 million Coss had initially proposed.

Grodahl's affidavit indicates that despite Coss's attempts to comply with these requirements, Coss could not meet them. Although it is undisputed that Ford did not issue a written denial of the transfer after a formal request by Coss, Grodahl asserted that it became clear after several conversations with Ford representatives that they would refuse to approve the transfer to Coss if a formal request were made. Consequently, Grodahl sent letters to Ford and Johnson informing them that, because Coss could not meet Ford's requirements, the agreement was null and void under paragraph 16.

After receiving Grodahl's letter, Johnson commenced this action against Coss. Johnson filed a motion for partial summary judgment on Count 1 (breach of contract) and Count 2 (breach of the covenant of good faith and fair dealing). Coss filed a cross motion for summary judgment. After a hearing, the circuit court granted partial summary judgment in favor of Johnson and denied judgment for Coss. The circuit court reasoned that: "the agreement was not performed and the transaction was not consummated according to its terms 'due to an act of the Purchaser,' and was not a result of the denial of the application by Ford Motor Co." Coss appeals . . . .

The dispositive issue in this appeal is whether the condition precedent (Ford's approval of the franchise transfer) failed because of an act for which Coss was legally responsible, or because of a discretionary act of Ford Motor Co. . . . Ford held the ultimate right to determine if the condition precedent was fulfilled by approval of the franchise transfer. By affidavit opposing summary judgment, Grodahl stated that the terms and conditions imposed by Ford could not be met. However, Johnson argues, and the circuit court concluded, that under the prevention doctrine, the failure of the condition precedent was caused by Coss, and therefore, Coss should be prevented from relying on the unfulfilled condition.

"The prevention doctrine . . . operates as an exception to the general rule that one has no duty to perform under a contract containing a condition precedent until the condition occurs." *Williston* § 39:4; *see also Moore Brothers Co. v. Brown & Root, Inc.,* 207 F.3d 717, 725 (4th Cir.2000). "[P]revention is similar to the concept of 'waiver by estoppel' in the context of excuses for nonperformance of contractual duties. An individual who prevents the occurrence of a condition may be said to be 'estopped' from benefiting from the fact that the condition precedent to his or her obligation failed to occur." *Williston* § 39:7. As the Restatement (Second) of Contracts explains:

> Where a duty of one party is subject to the occurrence of a condition, the additional duty of good faith and fair dealing imposed on him . . . may require some cooperation on his part, either by refraining from conduct that will prevent or hinder the occurrence of that condition or by taking affirmative steps to cause its occurrence. . . [N]on-performance of that duty when performance is due is a breach. . . [I]t has the further effect of excusing the non-occurrence of the condition itself, so that performance of the duty that was originally subject to its occurrence can become due in spite of its non-occurrence.

Restatement (Second) of Contracts § 245 cmt. (a) (1981). Similarly, *Williston* explains that if a party to a contract hinders the occurrence of a condition precedent, that condition is waived.

> If a promisor prevents or hinders the occurrence or fulfillment of a condition to his or her duty of performance, the condition is excused. In other words, "the nonoccurrence or nonperformance of a condition is excused where the failure of the condition is caused by the party against whom the condition operates to impose a duty." Accordingly, the liability of the promisor is fixed regardless of the failure to fulfill the condition.

Williston, § 39:4. (citing *Rohde v. Massachusetts Mut. Life Ins. Co.*, 632 F.2d 667 (6th Cir.1980)). "The prevention doctrine does not require proof that the condition would have occurred 'but for' the wrongful conduct of the promisor; instead it only requires that the conduct have 'contributed materially' to the non-occurrence of the condition." *Moore Brothers*, 207 F.3d at 725. "Whether interference by one party to a contract amounts to prevention so as to excuse performance by the other party and constitute a breach by the interfering party is a question of fact to be decided by the jury under all of the proved facts and circumstances." *Williston*, § 39:3.

Because this is a summary judgment under review, the question then is whether there are genuine issues of material fact whether Coss contributed materially to the failure of the condition. According to Grodahl's affidavit, one of Ford's requirements for transfer of the franchise was that the dealership be managed and operated by a person who could run the business, on site, on a day-to-day basis. That person had to demonstrate, to Ford's satisfaction, the ability to manage a dealership successfully. That person also had to have a substantial ownership interest in the business. According to Grodahl, Ford indicated that Coss was not acceptable or qualified for these purposes. Therefore, to satisfy the agreement's conditions precedent, it was reasonably necessary for Coss to locate a manager/co-owner who could meet Ford's requirement.

Although the trial court did not believe that Coss could rely on the Goodrich co-ownership arrangement to satisfy the condition precedent, that manager/co-owner contingency was envisioned by the agreement. Even before the agreement's execution, the parties were aware that Ford would require someone other than Coss to be the on-site manager. Consequently, in October 1999, Coss identified Goodrich as a potential co-owner and manager. In fact, Coss produced an October 25, 1999 letter from Coss's attorney to Goodrich outlining the potential co-owner relationship between Coss and Goodrich. That October letter emphasized that the "entire series of transactions [was] all contingent on Ford approving the transfer of the franchise." At that time, Coss proposed that he and Goodrich would each own a 50% interest in the business, and each would contribute $500,000 toward its initial capitalization.

However, following the execution of the agreement, Ben Waite, a Ford District Representative, advised Grodahl that Ford would not approve the ownership arrangement expressed in the October letter to Goodrich. Waite stated that one of the owners had to have a majority interest in the business. Pursuant to this requirement, Coss revised the plan so he would be the majority owner with the 50.1% interest in the business.

However, Waite also advised Grodahl that Ford required an initial capitalization of $1.476 million instead of the contemplated $1 million. According to Grodahl, even after this added capitalization requirement, Coss continued to work towards the consummation of the transaction and was willing to satisfy that requirement. Coss established a new South Dakota corporation called "21st Century Motor Company, Inc." to operate the business. Coss also submitted his completed personal and financial information. Waite later advised Grodahl that the information provided was sufficient for Ford's purposes.

Ultimately, however, Coss asserts that he could not comply with all of Ford's requirements for the franchise transfer. According to the Grodahl affidavit, "Ford imposed requirements relating to ownership and capitalization that Mark Goodrich and Lawrence Coss were unable to meet to Ford's satisfaction." Although there was no written rejection from Ford, Grodahl's affidavit asserted that Waite had verbally advised him of the requirements from which Ford would not deviate. The alleged fact that Coss, working with Goodrich, could not meet these requirements, led Coss to the conclusion that the conditions could not be met. We believe that these alleged facts were sufficient to create genuine issues of dispute whether Coss spent sufficient time, energy, and expense to satisfy the condition precedent. Under those circumstances, a trier of fact must determine whether Coss's conduct contributed materially to the failure to obtain Ford's approval. . . .

Johnson finally argues that Coss's failure to deposit $100,000 into an escrow account, as required by paragraph 9 of the agreement, demonstrates Coss's abandonment of the contract from the very beginning. However, Coss submitted evidence indicating that a check for that amount was outstanding. Moreover, even if there was a total failure to tender $100,000, that failure was only some evidence of Coss's abandonment of the contract, and Grodahl's affidavit raised other facts indicating that Coss did not intend to abandon the contract. Therefore, Coss's showing was sufficient to preclude summary judgment. Any alleged abandonment must ultimately be determined by trial.

Because Coss raised disputed issues of material fact concerning the cause of the failure of the condition precedent, we reverse the summary judgment and remand for further proceedings.

———

Lach v. Cahill

138 Conn. 418, 85 A.2d 481 (1951)

Lach signed an agreement with Cahill to purchase Cahill's house for $18,000, and paid a deposit of $1,000. The contract contained the following provision: "This agreement is contingent upon buyer being able to obtain mortgage in the sum of $12,000 on the premises. . . . " Lach then applied to six banks for a $12,000 mortgage, but was denied. Thereafter, Lach wrote to Cahill that he was unable to secure a mortgage in the amount of $12,000, and requested the return of the deposit. Cahill offered to take back a purchase-money mortgage payable on demand, or to obtain a mortgage from another person, but he specified no terms. Lach had already made a deposit on another house, and declined Cahill's offer. Lach then sued for the return of his deposit. The trial court held for Lach. Affirmed.

" . . . The decisive issues in the case are whether the ability of the plaintiff to secure a $12,000 mortgage was a condition precedent to his duty to perform his promise to purchase and whether he made a reasonable effort to secure the mortgage.

"The . . . language used, read in the light of the situation of the parties, expressed an intention that the plaintiff should not be held to an agreement to purchase unless he could secure a mortgage for $12,000 on reasonable terms as to the amount and time of instalment payments.

"The condition in the contract implied a promise by the plaintiff that he would make reasonable efforts to secure a suitable mortgage. . . . The performance or nonperformance of this implied promise was a matter for the determination of the trial court. The conclusion reached upon the facts was proper."

———

SECTION 5. CONDITIONS OF SATISFACTION

INTRODUCTORY NOTE

Often a contract provides that one party, A, need not pay for the performance of the other party, B, unless A is satisfied with the performance. The question then arises whether A may escape liability even though his dissatisfaction, while honest, is unreasonable. In the determination of this question, the following factors would probably be influential:

(1) The language used. Did the contract say, for example, that A must be "personally satisfied," or merely that the performance must be "satisfactory"?

(2) The degree to which it is possible to apply an objective standard to the performance in question. For example, there is a decided difference in this respect between a contract to install a furnace and a contract to paint a portrait. The inclination to interpret "satisfaction" as the actual personal satisfaction of A would obviously be stronger in the latter case.

(3) The degree to which A will be enriched at B's expense if the contract is interpreted to require A's personal satisfaction. If A retains and uses in his house a furnace installed by B, and seeks to escape liability to pay anything for the furnace by declaring that he is not satisfied with its performance, the case would be a very strong one for B. Recovery in B's favor might be supported either on the basis of interpretation—the word "satisfaction" being interpreted to mean satisfaction of a reasonable person—or on the theory that one who has failed to comply with a condition may nevertheless recover the value of the benefit conferred on the other party. The case is less strong for B if he has, for example, painted a portrait under a contract whereby A is not to pay unless he is satisfied, and A refuses to accept the portrait. Here B has lost the value of his own performance, but A has not been enriched.

(4) The degree of forfeiture that will be imposed on B if A escapes liability to pay for B's performance.

The chief lesson that the draftsman should derive from the cases in this field is that even though the words used in the contract may seem clearly to imply that the actual, personal satisfaction of the defendant is a condition to his liability, in certain cases the courts may nevertheless construe the contract to require only such performance as would satisfy a reasonable person.

McCartney v. Badovinac

62 Colo. 76, 160 P. 190 (1916)

A diamond had been stolen from Mrs. Ragsdale. Her husband, Dr. Ragsdale, accused Mrs. McCartney of the theft. Mr. McCartney then hired Badovinac, a private detective, to investigate the affair. Badovinac was to receive $500 for his services when he had "to the satisfaction of the said McCartney" determined whether the diamond was stolen, and if so, who had taken it. Badovinac's investigations led him to the uncomforting conclusion that Mrs. McCartney had in fact stolen the diamond, and he put his proofs before McCartney. On McCartney's refusal to pay, Badovinac brought suit. The case was tried without a jury. The trial judge found that Badovinac had clearly established that Mrs. McCartney had taken the jewel. McCartney, however, testified on the stand that he was not satisfied that his wife was the thief. Held, McCartney's statement that he is not satisfied is not conclusive of the issue. On these facts the trial judge properly found that McCartney's answers on the stand were "a mere subterfuge and pretext." A judgment for Badovinac was affirmed.

MORIN BUILDING PRODUCTS CO. v. BAYSTONE CONSTRUCTION, INC.

United States Court of Appeals, Seventh Circuit, 1983.
717 F.2d 413.

Before POSNER and COFFEY, CIRCUIT JUDGES and FAIRCHILD, SENIOR CIRCUIT JUDGE.

POSNER, CIRCUIT JUDGE.

This appeal from a judgment for the plaintiff in a diversity suit requires us to interpret Indiana's common law of contracts. General Motors, which is not a party to this case, hired Baystone Construction, Inc., the defendant, to build an addition to a Chevrolet plant in Muncie, Indiana. Baystone hired Morin Building Products Company, the plaintiff, to supply and erect the aluminum walls for the addition. The contract required that the exterior siding of the walls be of "aluminum type 3003, not less than 18 B & S gauge, with a mill finish and stucco embossed surface texture to match finish and texture of existing metal siding." The contract also provided "that all work shall be done subject to the final approval of the Architect or Owner's [General Motors'] authorized agent, and his decision in matters relating to artistic effect shall be final, if within the terms of the Contract Documents"; and that "should any dispute arise as to the quality or fitness of materials or workmanship, the decision as to acceptability shall rest strictly with the Owner, based on the requirement that all work done or materials furnished shall be first class in every respect. What is usual or customary in erecting other buildings shall in no wise enter into any consideration or decision."

Morin put up the walls. But viewed in bright sunlight from an acute angle the exterior siding did not give the impression of having a uniform finish, and General Motors' representative rejected it. Baystone removed Morin's siding and hired another subcontractor to replace it. General Motors approved the replacement siding. Baystone refused to pay Morin the balance of the contract price ($23,000) and Morin brought this suit for the balance, and won.

The only issue on appeal is the correctness of a jury instruction which, after quoting the contractual provisions requiring that the owner (General Motors) be satisfied with the contractor's (Morin's) work, states: "Notwithstanding the apparent finality of the foregoing language, however, the general rule applying to satisfaction in the case of contracts for the construction of commercial buildings is that the satisfaction clause must be determined by objective criteria. Under this standard, the question is not whether the owner was satisfied in fact, but whether the owner, as a reasonable person, should have been satisfied with the materials and workmanship in question." There was much evidence that General Motors' rejection of Morin's exterior siding had been totally unreasonable. Not only was the lack of absolute uniformity in the finish of the walls a seemingly trivial defect given the strictly utilitarian purpose of the building that they enclosed, but it may have been inevitable; "mill finish sheet" is defined in the trade as "sheet having a nonuniform finish which may vary from sheet to sheet and within a sheet, and may not be entirely free from stains or oil." If the instruction was correct, so was the judgment. But if the instruction was incorrect—if the proper standard is not whether a reasonable man would have been satisfied with Morin's exterior siding but whether General Motors' authorized representative in fact was—then there must be a new trial to determine whether he really was dissatisfied, or whether he was not and the rejection therefore was in bad faith.

Some cases hold that if the contract provides that the seller's performance must be to the buyer's satisfaction, his rejection—however unreasonable—of the seller's performance is not a breach of the contract unless the rejection is in bad faith. See, e.g., *Stone Mountain Properties, Ltd. v. Helmer,* 139 Ga.App. 865, 869, 229 S.E.2d 779, 783 (1976). But most cases conform to the position stated in section 228 of the Restatement (Second) of Contracts (1979): if "it is practicable to determine whether a reasonable person in the position of the obligor would be satisfied, an interpretation is preferred under which the condition [that the obligor be satisfied with the obligee's performance] occurs if such a reasonable person in the position of the obligor would be satisfied." See Farnsworth, Contracts 556–59 (1982); Annot., 44 A.L.R.2d 1114, 1117, 1119–20 (1955). *Indiana Tri-City Plaza Bowl, Inc. v. Estate of Glueck,* 422 N.E.2d 670, 675 (Ind.App.1981), consistently with hints in earlier Indiana cases, see *Andis v. Personett,* 108 Ind. 202, 206, 9 N.E. 101, 103 (1886); *Semon, Bache & Co. v. Coppes, Zook & Mutschler Co.,* 35 Ind.App. 351, 355, 74 N.E. 41, 43 (1905), adopts the majority position as the law of Indiana.

We do not understand the majority position to be paternalistic; and paternalism would be out of place in a case such as this, where the subcontractor is a substantial multistate enterprise. The requirement of reasonableness is read into a contract not to protect the weaker party but to approximate what the parties would have expressly provided with respect to a contingency that they did not foresee, if they had foreseen it. Therefore the requirement is not read into every contract, because it is not always a reliable guide to the parties' intentions. In particular, the presumption that the performing party would not have wanted to put himself at the mercy of the paying party's whim is overcome when the nature of the performance contracted for is such that there are no objective standards to guide the court. It cannot be assumed in such a case that the parties would have wanted a court to second-guess the buyer's rejection. So "the reasonable person standard is employed when the contract involves commercial quality, operative fitness, or mechanical utility which other knowledgeable persons can judge.... The standard of good faith is employed when the contract involves personal aesthetics or fancy." *Indiana Tri-City Plaza Bowl, Inc. v. Estate of Glueck, supra,* 422 N.E.2d at 675; see also *Action Engineering v. Martin Marietta Aluminum,* 670 F.2d 456, 460–61 (3d Cir.1982).

We have to decide which category the contract between Baystone and Morin belongs in. The particular in which Morin's aluminum siding was found wanting was its appearance, which may seem quintessentially a matter of "personal aesthetics," or as the contract put it, "artistic effect." But it is easy to imagine situations where this would not be so. Suppose the manager of a steel plant rejected a shipment of pig iron because he did not think the pigs had a pretty shape. The reasonable-man standard would be applied even if the contract had an "acceptability shall rest strictly with the Owner" clause, for it would be fantastic to think that the iron supplier would have subjected his contract rights to the whimsy of the buyer's agent. At the other extreme would be a contract to paint a portrait, the buyer having reserved the right to reject the portrait if it did not satisfy him. Such a buyer wants a portrait that will please him rather than a jury, even a jury of connoisseurs, so the only question would be his good faith in rejecting the portrait. *Gibson v. Cranage,* 39 Mich. 49 (1878).

This case is closer to the first example than to the second. The building for which the aluminum siding was intended was a factory—not usually intended to be a thing of beauty. That aesthetic considerations were decidedly secondary to considerations of function and cost is suggested by the fact that the contract specified mill-finish aluminum, which is unpainted. There is much debate in the record over whether it is even possible to ensure a uniform finish within and among sheets, but it is at least clear that mill finish usually is not uniform. If General Motors and Baystone had wanted a uniform finish they would in all likelihood have ordered a painted siding. Whether Morin's siding achieved a reasonable uniformity amounting to satisfactory commercial quality was susceptible of objective judgment; in the language of the Restatement, a reasonableness standard was "practicable."

But this means only that a requirement of reasonableness would be read into this contract if it contained a standard owner's satisfaction clause, which it did not; and since the ultimate touchstone of decision must be the intent of the parties to the contract we must consider the actual language they used. The contract refers explicitly to "artistic effect," a choice of words that may seem deliberately designed to put the contract in the "personal aesthetics" category whatever an outside observer might think. But the reference appears as number 17 in a list of conditions in a general purpose form contract. And the words "artistic effect" are immediately followed by the qualifying phrase, "if within the terms of the Contract Documents," which suggests that the "artistic effect" clause is limited to contracts in which artistic effect is one of the things the buyer is aiming for; it is not clear that he was here. The other clause on which Baystone relies, relating to the quality or fitness of workmanship and materials, may seem all-encompassing, but it is qualified by the phrase, "based on the requirement that all work done or materials furnished shall be first class in every respect"—and it is not clear that Morin's were not. This clause also was not drafted for this contract; it was incorporated by reference to another form contract (the Chevrolet Division's "Contract General Conditions"), of which it is paragraph 35. We do not disparage form contracts, without which the commercial life of the nation would grind to a halt. But we are left with more than a suspicion that the artistic-effect and quality-fitness clauses in the form contract used here were not intended to cover the aesthetics of a mill-finish aluminum factory wall.

If we are right, Morin might prevail even under the minority position, which makes good faith the only standard but presupposes that the contract conditioned acceptance of performance on the buyer's satisfaction in the particular respect in which he was dissatisfied. Maybe this contract was not intended to allow General Motors to reject the aluminum siding on the basis of artistic effect. It would not follow that the contract put Morin under no obligations whatsoever with regard to uniformity of finish. The contract expressly required it to use aluminum having "a mill finish . . . to match finish . . . of existing metal siding." The jury was asked to decide whether a reasonable man would have found that Morin had used aluminum sufficiently uniform to satisfy the matching requirement. This was the right standard if, as we believe, the parties would have adopted it had they foreseen this dispute. It is unlikely that Morin intended to bind itself to a higher and perhaps unattainable standard of achieving whatever perfection of matching that General Motors' agent insisted on, or that General Motors would have required Baystone to submit to such a standard. Because it is difficult—maybe impossible—to achieve a uniform finish with mill-finish aluminum, Morin would have been running a considerable risk of rejection if it had agreed to such a condition, and it therefore could have been expected to demand a compensating increase in the contract price. This would have required General Motors to pay a premium to obtain a freedom of action that it could not have thought terribly important, since its objective was not aesthetic. If a uniform finish was important to it, it could have gotten such a finish by specifying painted siding.

All this is conjecture; we do not know how important the aesthetics were to General Motors when the contract was signed or how difficult it really would have been to obtain the uniformity of finish it desired. The fact that General Motors accepted the replacement siding proves little, for there is evidence that the replacement siding produced the same striped effect, when viewed from an acute angle in bright sunlight, that Morin's had. When in doubt on a difficult issue of state law it is only prudent to defer to the view of the district judge, *Murphy v. White Hen Pantry Co.*, 691 F.2d 350, 354 (7th Cir.1982), here an experienced Indiana lawyer who thought this the type of contract where the buyer cannot unreasonably withhold approval of the seller's performance.

Lest this conclusion be thought to strike at the foundations of freedom of contract, we repeat that if it appeared from the language or circumstances of the contract that the parties really intended General Motors to have the right to reject Morin's work for failure to satisfy the private aesthetic taste of General Motors' representative, the rejection would have been proper even if unreasonable. But the contract is ambiguous because of the qualifications with which the terms "artistic effect" and "decision as to acceptability" are hedged about, and the circumstances suggest that the parties probably did not intend to subject Morin's rights to aesthetic whim.

AFFIRMED.

———————

Forman v. Benson

112 Ill.App.3d 1070, 68 Ill.Dec. 629, 446 N.E.2d 535 (1983)

Buyer made an offer to purchase certain real estate owned by seller, with the purchase price to be paid over a ten-year period. Before accepting the offer, seller expressed concern over buyer's creditworthiness. Seller's broker thereupon added the following provision to the offer: "subject to seller's approving buyer's credit report, oral on March 24, 1981, and written when ready." Seller accepted the offer, but thereafter refused to convey the property on the ground that he was not satisfied with buyer's credit. The court held that the subjective rather than the objective standard should be applied to interpret this provision, but nevertheless held for buyer:

"The personal judgment standard . . . does not allow the defendant to exercise unbridled discretion in rejecting plaintiff's credit, but rather is subject to the requirement of good faith. . . . In the instant case the trial court made no specific finding whether defendant Benson rejected plaintiff's credit in good faith. However, the trial court did find that between the time the contract was executed and the time the offer was rejected, defendant attempted to renegotiate the purchase price of the building as well as the interest rate. . . . [W]e hold that while defendant may have had a basis in his personal judgment for rejecting plaintiff's credit (i.e., outstanding debts and a $2,000 loss reflected in an income tax return), his attempted renegotiation demonstrates that his rejection was based on reasons other than plaintiff's credit rating and was, therefore, in bad faith."

Fursmidt v. Hotel Abbey Holding Corp.

10 A.D.2d 447, 200 N.Y.S.2d 256 (1960)

On February 1, 1958, Fursmidt entered into a contract with a hotel, which provided that Fursmidt would furnish valet and laundry services to guests at the hotel for a three-year period, and would pay the hotel $325 per month for the valet-and-laundry franchise. The agreement provided that "it is distinctly understood and agreed that the services to be rendered by [Fursmidt] shall meet with the approval of the [hotel], who shall be the sole judge of the sufficiency and propriety of the services."

In September 1958, the hotel informed Fursmidt that he was to discontinue his services as of October 1, 1958. Fursmidt then sued for breach of contract. The hotel counterclaimed for damages that it said it sustained by reason of Fursmidt's failure to render adequate and proper service. The trial court charged the jury that it had to decide not only whether the hotel was in fact dissatisfied but also whether the dissatisfaction was reasonable. Judgment was rendered for Fursmidt. Reversed.

(Rabin, J.) "[A] literal construction of . . . 'satisfaction' provisions is made where the agreements provide for performance involving 'fancy, taste, sensibility, or judgment' of the party for whose benefit it was made. . . . Such a result obtains in cases calling for performance to one's satisfaction in the making of a garment, the giving of a course of instruction, the services of an orchestra, the making of recordings by a singer and the painting of a portrait. . . .

"The resolution of the issue here presented lies with the determination of whether the instant agreement is one relating to operative fitness, utility or marketability or one involving fancy, taste, sensibility or judgment. We find that it comes within the rules applicable to the latter class and thus conclude that the court erred in its charge. . . .

"[I]t appears that the primary and overriding objective of the defendant in entering into this agreement was to ensure to its guests proper, efficient, courteous and reasonable valet and laundry facilities as an integral part of the overall personal services rendered by the hotel to the end that the good will of the guests be retained. . . . No objective standards of reasonableness can be set up by which the effectiveness of the plaintiff's performance in achieving the effect sought can be measured. It is for that reason that in cases of this nature the honest judgment of the party rather than that of a jury is all that is required and it was in order to make sure that that would be the measure of performance that the defendant inserted in the contract that it was to be the sole judge. . . .

"It may very well be that the charge of the Court is correct for the purpose of determining whether the plaintiff breached the agreement so as to entitle the defendant to damages on its counterclaim as distinguished from its right to terminate the contract. Honest dissatisfaction on the part of the defendant, although entitling it to terminate will not, in and of itself, entitle it to recover damages on its counterclaim. Such determination will depend on the facts surrounding the manner of the plaintiff's performance in relation to what he was obliged to do under the agreement and accordingly we do not pass on that phase of the case at this time."

———

E. Allan Farnsworth, Contracts

§ 8–4 (3d ed. 1999)

"The risk to the contractor in conditioning the owner's duty to pay on even reasonable satisfaction can be avoided by making the condition the satisfaction of an independent third person. When this is done, courts have generally been willing to read 'satisfaction' to mean 'honest satisfaction.' In construction contracts, the owner's duty to pay as the work progresses is often conditioned on the satisfaction of the architect, evidenced by issuance of architects' certificates. If a certificate is refused, the fact that the architect's dissatisfaction may be unreasonable does not give the contractor a claim to payment as long as the dissatisfaction is honest. However, the requirement of a certificate will be dispensed with if the refusal can be characterized as 'not in good faith' or as 'dishonest' or 'fraudulent.' If the third party's dissatisfaction is unreasonable in the extreme, courts have sometimes dispensed with the requirement by using justifications that include characterizing the refusal as 'constructive fraud.' "

———

RESTATEMENT, SECOND, CONTRACTS § 227, ILLUSTRATIONS 5–8

"5. A contracts with B to repair B's building for $20,000, payment to be made 'on the satisfaction of C, B's architect, and the issuance of his certificate.' A makes the repairs, but C refuses to issue his certificate, and explains why he is not satisfied. Other experts in the field consider A's performance to be satisfactory and disagree with C's explanation. A has no claim against B. . . . If C is honestly not satisfied, B is under no duty to pay A, and it makes no difference if his dissatisfaction was not reasonable.

"6. The facts being otherwise as stated in Illustration 5, C refuses to issue his certificate although he admits that he is satisfied. A has a claim against B for $20,000. The quoted language will be interpreted so that the requirement of the certificate is merely evidentiary and the condition occurs when there is, as here, adequate evidence that C is honestly satisfied.

"7. The facts being otherwise as stated in Illustration 5, C does not make a proper inspection of the work and gives no reasons for his dissatisfaction. A has a claim against B for $20,000. In using the quoted language, A and B assumed that C would exercise an honest judgment and by failing to make a proper inspection, C did not exercise such a judgment. . . .

"8. The facts being otherwise as stated in Illustration 5, C makes a gross mistake with reference to the facts on which his refusal to give a certificate is based. A has a claim against B for $20,000. In using the quoted language, A and B assumed that C would exercise his judgment without a gross mistake as to the facts. . . . "

SECTION 6.   EXCUSE

INTRODUCTORY NOTE

Earlier materials concern several rules that temper conditions in specific circumstances that make enforcement of a condition unjust. The rules on waiver (Chapter 14) and interference (Section 4 of this Chapter) address cases where an obligor's conduct makes enforcement of a condition unjust. The requirement of good faith that attaches to a condition of satisfaction (Section 5 of this Chapter) addresses a specific type of condition that is susceptible to misuse by the obligor. The impracticability rule excuses nonfulfillment of a condition when circumstances beyond the obligee's control prevent the obligee from fulfilling a condition. Restatement Second § 271.

In applying these tempering rules, courts generally consider the same factors that bear on whether a breach is material and performance is substantial (i.e., the harm to the obligor from nonfulfillment of the condition, the loss to the obligee from enforcement of the condition, and the obligee's fault). Thus, a condition will be excused on ground of impracticability only "if the occurrence of the condition is not a material part of the agreed exchange and forfeiture would otherwise result." Restatement Second § 271. This is in addition to the requirement of impracticability. And in deciding whether a condition has been waived, courts consider the extent of prejudice to the obligor from non-fulfillment of the condition and the extent of forfeiture by the obligee if the condition is enforced. Clark v. West, 86 N.E. 1 (N.Y. 1908). This is in addition to the requirement of words or conduct by the obligor that manifests a decision to waive a condition.

This Section concerns the doctrine of disproportionate forfeiture. The doctrine empowers courts to excuse nonfulfillment of a condition to avoid forfeiture in the absence of the sort of specific circumstances that make enforcement of a condition unjust that would bring one of these other rules into play.

CAPISTRANT V. LIFETOUCH NATIONAL SCHOOLS STUDIO, INC.

Supreme Court of Minnesota, 2018.
916 N.W.2d 23.

GILDEA, CHIEF JUSTICE.

We are asked to decide whether a former employee's delay in returning his employer's property excuses the employer from paying a commission otherwise due to the employee. Respondent John J. Capistrant argues that he was due the commission when his employment relationship with appellant Lifetouch National School Studios, Inc. ("Lifetouch") ended. Lifetouch contends that because Capistrant did not return Lifetouch's property immediately upon leaving the company, Lifetouch is excused from paying the commission.

The district court agreed with Lifetouch, determining that the return-of-property clause in the employment contract between the parties was a condition precedent to Lifetouch's contractual obligation to pay the residual commission, and that Capistrant's failure to comply with the clause excused Lifetouch's obligation to pay that commission. The court of appeals reversed, applying Restatement (Second) of Contracts § 229 (Am. Law Inst. 1981), and concluding, as a matter of law, that the loss of the commission was a disproportionate forfeiture for Capistrant's failure to comply with the return-of-property clause in the employment contract. We agree with the court of appeals that in the circumstances of this case, the guidance provided by section 229 of the Restatement is consistent with our precedent that disfavors forfeitures. But we disagree with the court of appeals that the materiality and proportionality analysis contemplated by section 229 can be decided as a matter of law on this record. We therefore reverse the court of appeals in part, affirm in part, and remand to the district court for further proceedings.

FACTS

Lifetouch sells photography services to schools and other organizations across the nation. In 1980, Capistrant began working as a photographer and sales representative for Lifetouch in its Minneapolis office. In 1981, Capistrant transferred within the company to the California office. Capistrant took over as Territory Manager of the San Francisco Bay Area in 1986 and entered into the contract with Lifetouch that is at issue in this appeal. The pertinent portions of the contract for our purposes include Paragraphs 8 and 11, and Exhibit B.

The contract provides that Capistrant would manage certain territory. In exchange for his management, Paragraph 8 provides that he would be compensated as described in exhibits attached to the agreement. One of those exhibits, Exhibit B, clarifies that Lifetouch would compensate Capistrant entirely with "commissions."

Section III of Exhibit B, entitled "Residual Commission and Payments For Restriction Against Competition," explains Capistrant's right to, and the calculation of, a post-employment "residual commission." This paragraph also specifically makes reference to Paragraph 11 of the contract, acknowledging that "the provisions of Paragraph 11 of the Agreement shall be extended and shall apply during the period Territory Manager is entitled to receive Residual Commission payments." The parties also agreed that if, "at any time," Capistrant "breaches the provisions of Paragraph 11 of the Agreement, in addition to Lifetouch's other remedies, Lifetouch shall be entitled to terminate Lifetouch's obligation to make any payments of Residual Commission that have not yet been paid by giving Territory Manager written notice of such termination."

[margin note: Alleged Condition Precedent]

Under Paragraph 11, entitled "Restriction Against Competition," Capistrant agreed for a period of 24 months after his employment that he would not "[d]isclose any trade secrets and confidential information," "solicit or deal with any school included in Lifetouch's Business," or "solicit any present or future employee of Lifetouch for the purpose of hiring or attempting to hire such employee." A separate clause at the end of Paragraph 11 additionally provides that Capistrant would "immediately deliver to Lifetouch all of Lifetouch's property" that was in Capistrant's possession or control at the end of his employment. We refer to this last clause of Paragraph 11 as "the return-of-property clause."

[margin note: Return-of-property Clause (alleged violation)]

The present dispute stems from a disagreement between Capistrant and Lifetouch about the interpretation of the residual commission provision described in Exhibit B. Over the years, Capistrant and Lifetouch disagreed about how his commissions, including the residual commission, were or would be calculated. The disputes arose as Lifetouch expanded

Capistrant's territory or asked Capistrant to execute new agreements regarding his commissions. Capistrant refused to sign a new agreement.

By 2014, Capistrant was planning for retirement, and some of these past disputes remained unresolved. In September of 2014, Capistrant commenced a declaratory-judgment action in district court requesting a declaration of the parties' respective rights and duties under the employment contract, including the proper calculation of the residual commission he was to be paid under the contract.

In March of 2015, while this litigation was still in the discovery phase, Capistrant retired. Three months later, in response to Lifetouch's discovery requests, Capistrant's counsel disclosed that Capistrant had in his possession a large number of Lifetouch's documents, including customer lists, sales data, payroll records, financial statements, and business plans that he had kept after his retirement.

On June 26, 2015, Lifetouch demanded that Capistrant return the documents he had retained. Capistrant returned the documents within three business days of this request.

On August 4, 2015, Lifetouch also demanded that Capistrant give it access to his e-mail account; Capistrant complied. Lifetouch's forensic expert then determined from a review of electronic files that the Lifetouch materials Capistrant had sent to his personal e-mail account had not been shared with outside sources.

In January of 2016, the parties each moved for summary judgment on the issue of Capistrant's right to a residual commission. Capistrant asserted in his motion that he is entitled to summary judgment against Lifetouch because it is contractually obligated to pay him a residual commission. Lifetouch argued in its motion that its obligation to pay the residual commission was excused because Capistrant failed to comply with the return-of-property clause.

The district court concluded that the return-of-property clause was a condition precedent to Lifetouch's payment of the residual commission. The court rejected Capistrant's argument that the court should not enforce the condition because to do so would result in an inequitable forfeiture. Specifically, the court concluded that the language of the contract is "clear," and "[e]quity cannot rescue [Capistrant] from his contractual obligations." The court granted summary judgment to Lifetouch on this issue, holding that Capistrant was not entitled to the residual commission under Exhibit B, Section III because he failed to satisfy his obligations under the return-of-property clause.

Capistrant appealed, and the court of appeals reversed. *Capistrant v. Lifetouch Nat'l Sch. Studios, Inc.*, 899 N.W.2d 844 (Minn.App. 2017). The court of appeals concluded that the district court did not err in considering the return-of-property clause as a "condition precedent to Lifetouch's duty to pay [Capistrant] his residual commission." *Id.* at 854. But the court of appeals determined that the district court did err in failing to recognize that, read as a whole, the non-compete provisions and the residual commission provision "function as a non-compete agreement with a forfeiture clause." *Id.* And the court of appeals also determined that the district court erred in not applying "binding precedent on the unenforceability of disproportionate forfeiture clauses and overbroad non-compete agreements." *Id.*

The court of appeals turned to section 229 of the Restatement (Second) of Contracts, and held that the "the timing of the return of property was not a material part of the contract" and "a forfeiture of potentially $2.6 million for retaining proprietary documents and e-mails, when there is no evidence of an intent to compete and when it is undisputed that there is no evidence of any dissemination of the retained documents" would cause a disproportionate forfeiture. 899 N.W.2d at 857. The court of appeals therefore concluded that Capistrant's failure to immediately return Lifetouch's property was excused as a matter of law. *Id.* at 859–60. We granted Lifetouch's petition for review.[2]

ANALYSIS

This case comes to us after the district court granted Lifetouch's motion for summary judgment. On appeal from summary judgment, we review de novo whether there are any genuine issues of material fact and whether the district court erred in its application of the law to the facts. *Commerce Bank v. W. Bend Mut. Ins. Co.*, 870 N.W.2d 770, 773 (Minn. 2015). Lifetouch contends that Capistrant's knowing failure to immediately return Lifetouch's property at the end of his employment relieves Lifetouch of its contractual obligation to pay the residual commission to Capistrant. Specifically, Lifetouch asserts that the return-of-property clause operates as an absolute precondition to its duty to pay the residual commission. Capistrant argues that his immediate return of Lifetouch's property was not a material term of the contract, and thus any breach cannot excuse

---

[2] We also granted Capistrant's request for cross-review on two issues. Based on our review of the record, we affirm the court of appeals on both of these issues. First, we reject Capistrant's argument that under a broad definition of "immediately," he complied with the return-of-property clause. We agree with the court of appeals that no definition of "immediately," as that term is used here and under the facts of this case, can encompass an almost three-month delay in the return of Lifetouch's property. *See* Capistrant, 899 N.W.2d at 851 (" 'Immediately' is an unambiguous term"). Second, we reject Capistrant's claim that Lifetouch's contractual right to terminate the payment of the residual commission is an illegal penalty. The illegal-penalty argument that Capistrant makes is grounded in our liquidated-damages jurisprudence. *See Gorco Constr. Co. v. Stein*, 256 Minn. 476, 99 N.W.2d 69, 75 (1959) (holding that a penalty is an agreed-to sum that is greatly disproportionate to the actual damages). This case is not about liquidated damages because Lifetouch does not contend that the residual commission amount forfeited by Capistrant's breach accurately represents the damages caused by Capistrant's failure to return its property. The liquidated-damages or penalty analysis therefore is not applicable to the forfeiture clause at issue in this case.

Lifetouch's performance. The court of appeals agreed with Capistrant, holding that "immediate" compliance with the return-of-property clause was not a material term of the parties' contract, and thus Capistrant's non-compliance could be excused. 899 N.W.2d at 860. Both the court of appeals and the district court concluded that the return-of-property clause "created a condition precedent to Lifetouch's duty to pay Capistrant any residual commission." 899 N.W.2d at 853.

A condition precedent is a contract term that "calls for the performance of some act or the happening of some event after the contract is entered into, and upon the performance or happening of which [the promisor's] obligation is made to depend." *Lake Co. v. Molan*, 269 Minn. 490, 131 N.W.2d 734, 740 (1964) (citation omitted) (internal quotation marks omitted); *see also Carl Bolander & Sons, Inc. v. United Stockyards Corp.*, 298 Minn. 428, 215 N.W.2d 473, 476 (1974) (explaining that a condition precedent is a fact that must occur before the promisor is obligated to perform). We have said that "if the event required by the condition does not occur, there [is] no breach of contract." *451 Corp. v. Pension Sys. for Policemen & Firemen*, 310 N.W.2d 922, 924 (Minn. 1981); *see also Crossroads Church of Prior Lake MN v. Cty. of Dakota*, 800 N.W.2d 608, 616 (Minn. 2011) (explaining that several conditions of the parties' oral contract were "unfulfilled," and thus performance under the contract was not required); *Nat'l City Bank v. St. Paul Fire & Marine Ins. Co.*, 447 N.W.2d 171, 178 (Minn. 1989) ("[N]o legal principle permits violation of a contract condition to be completely ignored."). Our precedent reflects the "general rule" that "conditions . . . must be literally met or exactly fulfilled, or no liability can arise on the promise qualified by the condition." 13 Richard A. Lord, *Williston on Contracts* § 38.6 (4th ed. 2013). But we have never explicitly decided whether the breach of a condition precedent must be material in order to relieve the non-breaching party of its obligation under the contract.

Lifetouch, citing to the general rule regarding conditions precedent, contends that conditions precedent are always material, and so the court of appeals erred in excusing Capistrant's failure to perform the material condition of returning Lifetouch's property immediately upon his retirement. But the return-of-property clause at issue here operates differently than the conditions at issue in our cases applying the general rule. Here, the parties had been performing under the contract for 28 years before the condition became operative, and the condition came into play only as the parties' employment relationship was ending. Moreover, the consequence of failing to comply with the return-of-property clause would be the forfeiture of millions of dollars.

In this unique context, we agree with the court of appeals that guidance can be drawn from the Restatement. Section 229 provides: "To the extent that the non-occurrence of a condition would cause

[handwritten margin note: Why? That's how much P was owed in residual commissions?]

disproportionate forfeiture, a court may excuse the non-occurrence of that condition unless it was a material part of the agreed exchange." Restatement (Second) of Contracts § 229. Section 229 is consistent with our precedent regarding forfeitures.

We look with disfavor on forfeitures of all kinds, *see Harris v. Bolin*, 310 Minn. 391, 247 N.W.2d 600, 602 (1976) (discussing how covenants against competition with forfeitures attached are not favored and those claiming them must show the equities are on their side), and we will avoid forfeitures when reasonably possible to do so. *Naftalin v. John Wood Co.*, 263 Minn. 135, 116 N.W.2d 91, 100 (1962); *Tomasko v. Cotton*, 200 Minn. 69, 273 N.W. 628, 632 (1937) (explaining that we try to avoid forfeiture when reasonably possible); *Warren v. Driscoll*, 186 Minn. 1, 242 N.W. 346, 347 (1932) (stating a forfeiture cannot be enforced when "great injustice is done thereby and the one seeking a forfeiture is adequately protected without"). Because section 229 reflects our reluctance to enforce forfeitures, the court of appeals properly looked to it for guidance in resolving this case.

While we agree with the court of appeals that section 229 provides helpful guidance given the context presented here, we disagree with the court's conclusion "as a matter of law" that section 229 excuses Capistrant's failure to comply with the condition. *Capistrant*, 899 N.W.2d at 857. Section 229 consists of two prongs: (1) whether the occurrence of the condition was a material part of the agreed exchange and (2) a proportionality analysis that balances the risk to be protected with the amount to be forfeited. *See* Restatement (Second) of Contracts § 229, cmts. b–c (explaining that the rule applies "only where occurrence of the condition was not a material part of the agreed exchange" and requires weighing to determine "whether the forfeiture is 'disproportionate' "); *see also Varel v. Banc One Capital Partners, Inc.*, 55 F.3d 1016, 1018 (5th Cir. 1995) (discussing how courts applying the Restatement must examine "whether performing the condition precedent was the object of the contract or merely incidental to it" and then weigh whether the penalty is extreme when "measured against the purpose" of the condition). Application of the second prong (proportionality) depends on whether the first prong (materiality) is met. Restatement (Second) of Contracts § 229 cmt. c ("The rule of this Section applies only where occurrence of the condition was not a material part of the agreed exchange."). In other words, if the occurrence of the condition is a material part of the agreement, then the proportionality analysis is not applied and the forfeiture cannot be prevented. But if the condition is not material, then the court is to engage in the proportionality analysis.

With respect to the materiality prong, the court of appeals concluded, as a matter of law, that the "immediate" time frame of the occurrence of the return of property was not a material part of the agreed exchange.

Disagreement about whether the return of-property clause was a material part of the exchange

Capistrant, 899 N.W.2d at 859. Lifetouch contends that this determination was erroneous.

Lifetouch argues that the immediacy requirement was material because Lifetouch needed to prevent "its confidential, proprietary, and trade-secret information from passing out of its control" and the risk of that harm "begins immediately upon an employee's departure." Thus, Lifetouch contends, Capistrant's return of the property *immediately* upon his departure from the company was important so that Lifetouch continued to have exclusive control of its property and confidential information. Lifetouch points to the testimony of its Senior Vice President of Sales who explained that the documents Capistrant kept included information about Lifetouch's "selling methods" and "sales commission and profit performance." Such information, the Vice President said, could help Lifetouch's competitors "target our accounts" and give competitors "a hand up in . . . competing with [Lifetouch]."

For his part, Capistrant argues that his retention of Lifetouch's property for a few months was a minor, temporary delay that should be excused as immaterial. Capistrant asserts that any delay in his return of the property was immaterial because materiality goes to the "very root or essence of the contract" and it is impossible to find a material difference between the return of Lifetouch's property on the day of his retirement as compared to a few months later. Accordingly, Capistrant argues, the court of appeals properly resolved the materiality question as a matter of law.[4]

We have resolved cases involving conditions precedent as a matter of law. *See, e.g.*, *Crossroads Church*, 800 N.W.2d at 615 (affirming summary judgment and concluding that because the condition precedent was unfulfilled, the contract could not be enforced). But the record in this case does not allow resolution of the materiality question as matter of law. Specifically, the condition at issue—a post-employment return-of-property clause—is included in a provision that imposes ongoing noncompetition obligations on Capistrant after the employment relationship defined by the contract has ended.

Lifetouch cites *St. Louis Produce Market v. Hughes*, a case that also involved a condition precedent that arose at the end of the parties'

---

[4] Capistrant additionally asserts, separate from his section 229 argument, that Minnesota case law supports his assertion that immaterial delays are excused to the extent necessary to prevent forfeiture, citing *Trollen v. City of Wabasha*, 287 N.W.2d 645, 648 (Minn. 1979) and *Jostens, Inc. v. CNA Ins./Cont'l Cas. Co.*, 403 N.W.2d 625, 629 (Minn. 1987), *overruled in part by N. States Power Co. v. Fidelity & Cas. Co. of N.Y.*, 523 N.W.2d 657 (Minn. 1994). Lifetouch contends that these cases do not extend past the realm of immaterial delays in giving notice and that these principles have never been applied to substantive duties. In *Jostens*, we excused the failure to give timely notice of an insurance claim. 403 N.W.2d at 629. In *Trollen*, we excused the immaterial delay in giving a renewal notice under a lease. 287 N.W.2d at 648. We have not relied on *Jostens* outside of the insurance context and have not relied on *Trollen* outside of the real property context. We decline to import forfeiture principles from these notice cases into the context of the contractual employment relationship at issue here.

employment relationship. 735 F.3d 829 (8th Cir. 2013). That contract provided that "[a]s a condition precedent to Company's obligations . . . and prior to Company making any additional separation payments," the employee agreed to return the company's property. *Id.* at 831. Because the employee did not return the company's property, the *Hughes* court held that the company was relieved of its obligation to make additional payments to the employee. *Id.* at 832. In so holding, the court rejected the employee's argument that his nonperformance should be excused because it was immaterial. *Id.* ("Hughes is correct that one party's *breach* of a contract term must be material to excuse the other party's performance, but the failure to fulfill a condition precedent need not." (citation omitted)).

Hughes applies Missouri law. In addition, the case is not helpful here because the return-of-property clause is not as clearly tied to Lifetouch's performance as the condition was tied to the company's performance in *Hughes*. The return-of-property clause is included in Paragraph 11, a paragraph imposing continuing non-compete and non-disclosure obligations on Capistrant for years after his retirement. Yet, as the court of appeals recognized, the return-of-property clause "is a one-time event," and Lifetouch relies on the failure to comply with this one-time event—at least for a period of time—to forfeit the entire residual commission that would otherwise be paid during the entire period of non-disclosure and non-competition that Paragraph 11 encompasses. *Capistrant*, 899 N.W.2d at 855.

Moreover, the materiality of the return-of-property clause to the residual commission payments is subject to conflicting inferences. It could be that the return-of-property clause is material to Capistrant's receipt of *any* residual commission, as Lifetouch argues. After all, the condition is a stand-alone obligation in Paragraph 11, and in Exhibit B, Capistrant plainly agreed that if he "breaches the provisions of Paragraph 11," that breach "terminate[s]" Lifetouch's obligation to pay the residual commission.

On the other hand, and also consistent with Exhibit B, the amount of the residual commission is determined based on Capistrant's sales during his last year with Lifetouch. This part of the agreement supports an inference that Capistrant's right to the residual commission is independent of his obligation to return Lifetouch's property. And the fact that the return-of-property clause is contained in the "Restriction against Competition" paragraph reinforces the inference that the return of property was material only to Capistrant's noncompetition with Lifetouch. In other words, as long as Capistrant did not disclose or use Lifetouch's property to compete with Lifetouch, his retention of the property for some period of time may not be material to his receipt of the residual commission.

[handwritten margin note: Different ways of interpreting the return-of-property clause]

Given these conflicting inferences, we conclude that the materiality determination should not be resolved as a matter of law on appeal. This is especially true in this case because the district court did not make any findings on materiality. Accordingly, we conclude that a remand is necessary to allow the district court to resolve the materiality question in the first instance.

On the proportionality prong, the court of appeals also concluded, as a matter of law, that because the forfeiture was disproportionate, Lifetouch was not relieved of its obligation to pay the residual commission. We reverse this aspect of the court's decision as well because we have concluded that a remand on the materiality issue is necessary, and the proportionality prong is reached only after there is a conclusion on the materiality prong.

If the district court determines that the immediate return of property under the contract was not material, the district court then must turn to the proportionality prong of section 229 to determine if the forfeiture was disproportionate. Comment b to section 229 explains that "[t]he rule . . . is, of necessity, a flexible one, and its application is within the sound discretion of the court." Restatement (Second) of Contracts § 229 cmt. b; *see also Acme Markets, Inc. v. Fed. Armored Express, Inc.*, 437 Pa.Super. 41, 648 A.2d 1218, 1222 (1994) (remanding for an evidentiary hearing where the district court "did not consider whether the forfeiture would be disproportionate, [or] decide if the [condition precedent] constituted a material part of the exchange" and requiring the court on remand to "engage in the necessary weighing analysis").

CONCLUSION

For the foregoing reasons, we affirm the decision of the court of appeals in part, reverse that decision in part, and remand to the district court for further proceedings consistent with this opinion.

Affirmed in part, reversed in part, and remanded.

RESTATEMENT, SECOND, CONTRACTS § 229

[See Selected Source Materials Supplement]

RESTATEMENT, SECOND, CONTRACTS § 229, ILLUSTRATIONS 1, 2

1. A contracts to build a house for B, using pipe of Reading manufacture. In return, B agrees to pay $75,000 in progress payments, each payment to be made "on condition that no pipe other than that of

Reading manufacture has been used." Without A's knowledge, a subcontractor mistakenly uses pipe of Cohoes manufacture which is identical in quality and is distinguishable only by the name of the manufacturer which is stamped on it. The mistake is not discovered until the house is completed, when replacement of the pipe will require destruction of substantial parts of the house. B refuses to pay the unpaid balance of $10,000. A court may conclude that the use of Reading rather than Cohoes pipe is so relatively unimportant to B that the forfeiture that would result from denying A the entire balance would be disproportionate, and may allow recovery by A subject to any claim for damages for A's breach of his duty to use Reading pipe.

2. A, an ocean carrier, carries B's goods under a contract providing that it is a condition of A's liability for damage to cargo that "written notice of claim for loss or damage must be given within 10 days after removal of goods." B's cargo is damaged during carriage and A knows of this. On removal of the goods, B notes in writing on the delivery record that the cargo is damaged, and five days later informs A over the telephone of a claim for that damage and invites A to participate in an inspection within the ten day period. A inspects the goods within the period, but B does not give written notice of its claim until 25 days after removal of the goods. Since the purpose of requiring the condition of written notice is to alert the carrier and enable it to make a prompt investigation, and since this purpose had been served by the written notice of damage and the oral notice of claim, the court may excuse the non-occurrence of the condition to the extent required to allow recovery by B.

Clementi v. Nationwide Mutual Fire Ins. Co.

16 P.3d 223 (Colo. 2001)

Clementi appeals from a decision holding that he forfeited uninsured motorist ("UIM") coverage under a Nationwide policy when he failed to notify of the claim "as soon as practicable." The trial court determined this time was no later than 12 months after the accident when Clementi learned his damages exceeded the other driver's policy limits. Clementi notified Nationwide 17 months after the accident. Held, reversed.

(Rice, J.) ". . . This case presents an opportunity for us to address the status of the so-called notice-prejudice rule in Colorado. Nearly twenty years ago, this court refused to adopt the notice-prejudice rule in a liability insurance case, holding that in denying benefits, an insurer is not required to demonstrate that it was prejudiced by an insured's failure to comply with a policy's notice requirements. . . ."

"Traditionally, courts did not consider prejudice in late-notice cases. . . .The traditional approach is grounded upon a strict contractual interpretation of insurance policies under which delayed notice was viewed as constituting a breach of contract, making the issue of insurer prejudice immaterial. . . .

"Few courts today strictly adhere to the traditional approach which allowed for no consideration of insurer prejudice in determining whether benefits should be denied due to noncompliance with an insurance policy's notice requirements. . . . While some courts continue to apply the traditional approach to late-notice liability cases, the vast majority of courts have joined the modern trend in the context of a UIM case. . . .

"Courts that have joined the modern trend by adopting the notice-prejudice rule consider insurer prejudice in determining whether the insurer may deny benefits in late-notice cases. Although many courts that have adopted the notice-prejudice rule have failed to supply a definition of prejudice, generally, an insurer is prejudiced by an insured's breach of a policy requirement when the purposes of the requirement are defeated. Since the purpose of a policy's notice requirement is to allow an insurer to adequately investigate and defend a claim, courts that have adopted the notice-prejudice rule have permitted an insurer to deny benefits only where its ability to investigate or defend the insured's claim was compromised by the insured's failure to provide timely notice. . . .

"Courts have articulated three policy justifications for departing from the traditional approach. These justifications can be generally described as follows: (1) the adhesive nature of insurance contracts, (2) the public policy objective of compensating tort victims, and (3) the inequity of the insurer receiving a windfall due to a technicality. . . .

"In [*Brakeman v. Potomac Insurance Co.*, 371 A.2d 193 (Pa. 1977)], the Pennsylvania Supreme Court rationalized its departure from the traditional approach in part by noting that such an approach fails to recognize the true nature of the relationship between insurance companies and their insureds. 371 A.2d at 196. "An insurance contract is not a negotiated agreement; rather its conditions are by and large dictated by the insurance company to the insured." *Id*. Thus, the *Brakeman* court concluded that a strict contractual approach was inappropriate in deciding a late-notice case. . . .

"Courts that have adopted the notice-prejudice rule have also recognized the public interest in enforcing automobile insurance contracts to further the goal of compensating tort victims, including innocent third parties. . . . They note that this public interest is thwarted by the traditional approach, which would deny an accident victim who provided late notice from recovering, even if the insurer suffered no prejudice. . . .

"Courts that have adopted the notice-prejudice rule have also expressed concern for the severity of forfeiting one's insurance benefits based on the technical violation of a notice provision. . . . Some courts that have taken this position have pointed to the Restatement (Second) of Contracts, which states that: "To the extent that the non-occurrence of a condition would cause disproportionate forfeiture, a court may excuse the non-occurrence of that condition unless its occurrence was a material part of the agreed exchange." Restatement (Second) of Contracts § 229 (1981). These courts hold that when an insurer is not prejudiced, an insured's failure to comply with a notice requirement is excused, since a "disproportionate forfeiture" ensues from enforcing such a requirement. . . .

"Courts that have adopted the notice-prejudice rule by considering insurer prejudice in determining whether a denial of benefits is justified by noncompliance with a policy's notice requirements have done so in various ways. A plurality of courts have held that once it is evident that the insured breached the notice provision, the burden of proof should fall upon the insurer to prove that it has been prejudiced by the breach. . . .

"In *Brakeman,* the court reasoned that "although it may be difficult for the insurance company to prove it suffered prejudice as a consequence of an untimely notice, it appears to us that it would be at least as difficult for the claimant to prove a lack of prejudice." 371 A.2d at 198. Other courts agree, concluding that the insurer is in a much better position to prove that it has been prejudiced, especially since the insured would otherwise be forced to prove a negative. . . .The *Brakeman* court chose to place the burden of showing prejudice on the insurance company because of the adhesive nature of an insurance contract, the severity of forfeiture and the fact that it was the insurance company who is choosing to disclaim its obligations under the policy. 371 A.2d at 198.

"Some courts have held that when the insured fails to comply with a policy's notice requirements, a presumption that the insurer was prejudiced by the breach arises. . . .

"These courts reason that the insured is the party seeking to be excused from the consequences of violating a contract provision. These courts take the opposite position from those choosing to place the burden on the insurer, arguing that the insured is in a better position to demonstrate that vital witnesses are still available and crucial information has not been lost.

"A few courts have held that prejudice is a factor to be considered along with the insured's excuse for the delay, the length of delay, and the sophistication of the insured, in determining the reasonableness of a delay in notice. . . . [T]he Alabama Supreme Court held that in UIM cases, the insured must, at a minimum, put on evidence showing the reason for not complying with the insurer's notice requirement. Once such evidence is presented, the insurer may then demonstrate that it was prejudiced by the insured's failure to comply with the policy's notice requirements.

"We find this approach problematic because we believe that insurer prejudice is not relevant to the reasonableness of the insured's delayed notice, and thus should not be considered as a factor. . . . Rather, we find that a two-step approach to late-notice cases is appropriate. This approach would require a preliminary determination of whether an insured's notice was timely. Such a determination should include an evaluation of the timing of the notice, and the reasonableness of any delay. Once a court has determined that an insured's notice was untimely, and that the delay was unreasonable, it should then turn to the issue of whether the insured was prejudiced by such untimely notice. Indeed, such an approach comports with that of the majority of courts that have adopted the notice-prejudice rule.

"Having rejected the prejudice-as-a-factor approach, we now determine whether the burden of proving prejudice should be placed on the insurer or on the insured. We agree with the courts that have concluded that it is more difficult for an insured to prove a negative, that is, that the insurer was not prejudiced, than it would be for the insurer to demonstrate that it was hampered in its ability to investigate or defend a claim because of the insured's failure to provide timely notice. . . . Therefore, while we agree that consideration should be given to the fact that the insured is the party seeking to be excused from the consequences of violating a contract provision, we reject the presumption of prejudice approach in favor of placing the burden on the insurer to demonstrate that it was prejudiced. Thus, we now hold that once it has been established that an insured has unreasonably provided delayed notice to an insurer, an insurer may only deny benefits if it can prove by a preponderance of the evidence that it was prejudiced by the delay. . . ."

APPENDIX

THE STATUTE OF FRAUDS

■ ■ ■

Analysis

Sec.

————

SECTION 1. INTRODUCTION.

The law does not require all contracts to be in writing, but the Statute of Frauds (sometimes hereafter "the Statute"), which was adopted in England in 1677 and is in force in almost every American state, provides that certain kinds of contracts are unenforceable against the party to be charged—that is, the party sought to be held liable—unless the contract is evidenced by a writing or, today, in an electronic record, signed by that party.

The Statute of Frauds is subject to a number of exceptions. If a contract is of a type that is covered by the Statute and is not in writing or electronic form, or not signed by the party to be charged, the contract is said to be *within* the Statute, and therefore unenforceable against that party. If an exception to the Statute applies the contract is said to be *taken out of* the Statute and therefore enforceable against the party to be charged even though it is not evidenced by a signed writing or other record.

[handwritten margin note: Statute of Frauds (SoF) only applies to contracts covered by the Statute]

SECTION 2. THE STATUTE COVERS CONTRACTS THAT WERE IMPORTANT IN 1677.

The principles by which the Statute's drafters decided what contracts deserved the protection of a writing were based on the needs of the seventeenth century, not those of modern commerce. Accordingly, in the modern business world the Statute does not apply to many very important types of contracts, but does apply to some unimportant contracts, as illustrated by the next three examples:

Turf I. Bertram Builder and Teresa Turf enter a complex oral agreement under which Builder promises to construct a commercial building according to certain plans and specifications, commencing work on January 1 and finishing by December 1. Turf agrees to pay Builder $15 million for the job. This important contract is enforceable despite being oral because it does not come within any Section of the Statute.

Turf II. After the completion of the building in *Turf I* Terese Turf enters into an oral agreement with Rock of Ages Insurance Company under which Rock of Ages insures the building against fire in the amount of $15 million, for one year effective immediately, and Turf agrees to pay a premium of $200,000. This contract is also enforceable despite being oral, because this contract too does not come within any Section of the Statute.

Redacre. Jim Joad orally agrees with Jane Jukes that he will sell her his eroded tract, Redacre, for ten dollars. This relatively insignificant contract is unenforceable by virtue of Section 4(4) of the 1677 Statute, the sale-of-land provision.

The Statute of Frauds has a number of sections, the most important of which concern contracts for the sale of an interest in land, contracts for the sale of goods, and contracts not to be performed within a year.

SECTION 3. CONTRACTS FOR THE SALE OF AN INTEREST IN LAND.

Section 4(4) of the 1677 Statute covers contracts for the sale of an interest in land, including by implication, sales of interests in buildings and other improvements on land. The price, value, or extent of the interest is immaterial. In determining what constitutes an interest in land for purposes of the Statute normally the test is how the interest is treated by the law of property.

Shortcut. To obtain a shortcut from his farm to the highway Paul Pass wants the right to drive through Bilbo Block's land. The parties orally agree that in consideration of the payment of $1,000, Pass shall have that right during his life.

The agreement falls within the statute and is therefore unenforceable, because the agreement would give Pass an easement, which is an interest in land under property law.

Leases. In very general terms, the first three Sections of the original Statute state that a writing is necessary to create or transfer an interest in land, except that a tenancy at will and, under certain conditions, a lease not to exceed three years, may be created orally. The substance of these provisions is very generally carried over into American Statutes of Frauds, but the exception for oral short-term leases is usually reduced to either one year or two years.

SECTION 4. CONTRACTS FOR THE SALE OF GOODS.

a.   Coverage

Contracts for the sale of goods are governed by UCC Section 2–201(1), which provides that "a contract for the sale of goods for the price of $500 or more is not enforceable by way of action or defense unless there is some writing sufficient to indicate that a contract for sale has been made between the parties and signed by the party against whom enforcement is sought or by his authorized agent or broker." "Goods" are defined as physical property other than realty, or what the Official Comment calls movables. Section 2–201(1) does not cover the sale of intangibles. And Section 2–201 applies only if the price is $500 or more. There is a separate and similar statute of frauds for leases of goods in Article 2A, Section 2A–201.

b.   Exceptions

The basic requirement of Section 2–201(1) is subject to several important exceptions.

i.   Part performance. Section 2–201(3)(c) provides that "A contract which does not satisfy the requirements of [Section 2–201(1)] but which is valid in other respects is enforceable . . . with respect to goods for which payment has been made and accepted or which have been received and accepted . . . ."

ii.   Goods made specially to order. Suppose A orally orders a custom-made suit from his tailor and agrees to pay $1,500. The tailor prepares the suit but A refuses to accept it. If this contract was unenforceable a serious injustice would be done to the tailor, who will have some difficulty finding a market for the suit since it was custom-made for A. Subsection (3)(a) deals with this problem by providing that "A contract which does not satisfy the requirements of [Section 2–201(1)] but which is valid in other respects is enforceable . . . if the goods are to be specially manufactured for the buyer and are not suitable for sale to others in the ordinary course of the seller's business and the seller, before notice of repudiation is received and under circumstances which reasonably indicate that the goods are for the buyer, has made either a substantial beginning of their manufacture or commitments for their procurement . . . ."

iii. Receipt of confirmation. UCC Section 2–201(2) provides that "Between merchants if within a reasonable time a writing in confirmation of the contract and sufficient against the sender is received and the party receiving it has reason to know its contents, it satisfies the requirements of [Section 2–201(1)] against such party unless written notice of objection to its contents is given within ten days after it is received." UCC Section 2–104(1) defines the term *merchant* to mean "a person who deals in goods of the kind or otherwise by his occupation holds himself out as having knowledge or skill peculiar to the practices or goods involved in the transaction or to whom such knowledge or skill may be attributed by his employment of an agent or broker or other intermediary who by his occupation holds himself out as having such knowledge or skill."

iv. Admissions. UCC Section 2–201(3)(b) provides that "A contract which does not satisfy the requirements of [Section 2–201(1)] but which is valid in other respects is enforceable . . . if the party against whom enforcement is sought admits in his pleading, testimony or otherwise in court that a contract for sale was made, but the contract is not enforceable under this provision beyond the quantity of goods admitted . . . ." Under the weight of authority the admission may be either voluntary or involuntary. Accordingly, a plaintiff can bring suit on an oral contract and then try to make the defendant admit, in discovery proceedings or on cross-examination, that the oral contract was in fact made. If the defendant admits that the oral contract was made the admission takes the contract out of the Statute. If the defendant falsely denies that the oral contract was made he is guilty of perjury.

v. The CISG. Many international contracts for the sale of goods are governed by the Convention for the International Sale of Goods (the CISG) rather than by the UCC. CISG Article 11 provides that a contract of sale need not be concluded in or evidenced by writing and is not subject to any other requirement as to form: it may be proved by any means, including witnesses.

SECTION 5.   AGREEMENTS NOT TO BE PERFORMED WITHIN ONE YEAR FROM THE MAKING THEREOF.

Section 4(5) of the 1677 Statute provides that actions "upon any agreement that is not to be performed within the space of one year from the making thereof" must be based on a writing or other record signed by the party to be charged. The applicability of this provision depends not on what the parties *thought* would happen, or on how long the contract would *probably* take to perform, or on how long the contract *actually took* to perform, but on whether, when the oral contract was made, there was a *possibility* that by its terms it could have been performed within a year. If so, the contract is not within the Statute, and therefore is enforceable. However, if an oral contract *by its terms* could not possibly be performed within one year it is within the Statute and therefore unenforceable against the party to be charged. On this basis an oral agreement to hire an octogenarian for thirteen months is within the Statute, and therefore unenforceable unless in a writing or other record, but an oral agreement by A to hire B for life is not within the Statute because there is a possibility that the agreement can be performed within a year through the death of A before that time. It is immaterial that in fact A lives and works on the job for another twenty years. If A is discharged at that point he can sue B under the oral agreement made twenty years earlier. (However, in some states the legislature has provided that a contract that is not to be completed before the end of a lifetime *is* within the Statute. A few cases reach the same result.)

SECTION 6.   WHAT KIND OF WRITING WILL SATISFY THE STATUTE.

1.   If a writing or other record is to satisfy the Statute it must state the terms of the contract with reasonable adequacy. A writing or other record that failed to identify the parties, the subject-matter, and the essential terms of the contract normally would not be sufficient. On the other hand, the courts do not demand perfection, and some degree of ambiguity or ellipsis is not fatal.

2.   Even where no single writing exists that is sufficient to satisfy the Statute the Statute may be satisfied by piecing together several writings together. If the writings are physically attached or contain internal references to one another, there is no difficulty in piecing the writings together. There is a division of authority on whether a contract can be pieced together by other means. In Crabtree v. Elizabeth Arden Sales Corp. 110 N.E.2d 551, 553–554 (N.Y. 1953), the court stated "The courts of some jurisdictions insist that there be a reference, of varying degrees of specificity, in the signed writing to that unsigned, and, if there is no such reference, they refuse to permit consideration of the latter in determining whether the memorandum satisfies the statute .... The other position which has gained increasing support over the years is that a sufficient connection between the papers is established simply by a reference in them to the same subject matter or transaction.... The view last expressed impresses us as the more sound ... and we now definitively adopt it, permitting the signed and unsigned writings to be read together, provided that they clearly refer to the same subject matter or transaction ...."

3. A principal will normally be bound by the signature of an authorized agent on the principal's behalf even if the agent's authority is not evidenced by a writing or other record. However, some state statutes provide that if a contract signed by an agent is within the Statute of Frauds the agent's authority must be evidenced in a record signed by the principal. The doctrine embodied in such legislation is called the "equal-dignity rule"—meaning that the authority of an agent to enter into a contract on behalf of a principal must be evidenced by a formality equal to that required for the contract itself. The equal-dignity rule is applicable only in states where it has been specifically adopted by statute.

4. As to contracts for the sale of goods, UCC Section 2–201(1) changes this whole corner of the law in a fairly substantial way. Recall that under Section 2–201(1):

> Except as otherwise provided in this Section a contract for the sale of goods for the price of $500 or more is not enforceable by way of action or defense unless there is some writing sufficient to indicate that a contract for sale has been made between the parties and signed by the party against whom enforcement is sought or by his authorized agent or broker. A writing is not insufficient because it omits or incorrectly states a term agreed upon but the contract is not enforceable under this paragraph beyond the quantity of goods shown in such writing.

And the Official Comment to this Section provides:

> ... The required writing need not contain all the material terms of the contract and such material terms as are stated need not be precisely stated. All that is required is that the writing afford a basis for believing that the offered oral evidence rests on a real transaction. It may be written in lead pencil on a scratch pad. It need not indicate which party is the buyer and which the seller. The only term which must appear is the quantity term which need not be accurately stated but recovery is limited to the amount stated. The price, time and place of payment or delivery,

the general quality of the goods, or any particular warranties may
all be omitted . . . .

SECTION 7.   WHAT COUNTS AS A SIGNATURE.

The requirement of a signed writing does not mean that the document
must be signed by the party in his own hand and with his full name. Any
symbol used with an intent to authenticate a document will suffice. For
example, O.K. with initials is sufficient. Even a photocopied or computer-
printed name will count as a signature if it reflects an intent to
authenticate a document. The UCC defines the term "signed" to include
"any symbol executed or adopted by a party with present intention to
authenticate a writing." The Comment to UCC Section 1–201 states: ". . .
as the term 'signed' is used in the Uniform Commercial Code, a complete
signature is not necessary. The symbol may be printed, stamped or written;
it may be by initials or by thumbprint. It may be on any part of the
document and in appropriate cases may be found in a billhead or
letterhead. No catalog of possible situations can be complete and the court
must use common sense and commercial experience in passing upon these
matters. The question always is whether the symbol was executed or
adopted by the party with present intention to adopt or authenticate the
writing." The approach of Restatement Second Section 134 is somewhat
broader, because it allows either actual or apparent intent to suffice. In
Donovan v. RRL Corp., 27 P.3d 702, 713–714 (Cal. 2001), the court held
that "When an advertisement constitutes an offer, the printed name of the
merchant is intended to authenticate the advertisement as that of the
merchant. . . . In other words, where the advertisement reasonably justifies
the recipient's understanding that the communication was intended as an
offer, the offeror's intent to authenticate his or her name as a signature can
be established from the face of the advertisement."

SECTION 8.   ELECTRONIC CONTRACTING
AND THE STATUTE OF FRAUDS.

Under the Uniform Electronic Transactions Act (UETA), which was
promulgated in 1999 by the National Conference of Commissioners on
Uniform State Laws and has been adopted by most states, a record or
signature may not be denied legal effect or enforceability solely because it
is in electronic form; a contract may not be denied legal effect or
enforceability solely because an electronic record was used in its formation;
and if a law requires a record to be in writing, an electronic record satisfies
the law; and if a law requires a signature, an electronic signature satisfies
the law.

UETA Section 2(13) provides that the term *record* means "information that is inscribed on a tangible medium or that is stored in an electronic or other medium and is retrievable in perceivable form." The Official Comment to Section 2(13) states:

> This is a standard definition designed to embrace all means of communicating or storing information except human memory. It includes any method for storing or communicating information, including "writings." A record need not be indestructible or permanent, but the term does not include oral or other communications which are not stored or preserved by some means. Information that has not been retained other than through human memory does not qualify as a record. . . .

UETA has a terminological and a substantive impact on the Statute of Frauds. Terminologically, UETA effectively replaces the term *writing* with the term *record*. Substantively, UETA makes it much easier to satisfy the Statute of Frauds because the term *record* is given a very expansive definition, so as to denote any means, other than human memory, for storing information—including, for example, a message that was recorded on voicemail or an answering machine. In light of UETA today the best way to describe the requirements of the Statute of Frauds today would be to use the term *record* rather than *writing*.

SECTION 9.   PERFORMANCE AND RELIANCE-BASED CLAIMS UPON AN ORAL AGREEMENT WITHIN THE STATUTE.

1.   Introduction

The rise of the action of assumpsit create the need for the 1677 Statute because this opened the door to a claim for breach of an informal promise in a wholly executory agreement. The legal system at the time was ill-equipped to handle these claims because it had primitive rules of evidence and civil procedure. The statute was not intended to cut off a claim seeking payment for performance rendered under an oral agreement. The sale of goods provision in the 1677 Statute required a writing only in the absence of part performance. UCC Section 2–201(3)(c) carries this rule forward. Most service agreements were not within the statute. If a service agreement was within the statute under the one-year rule, then what is now called a restitution claim was available to recover payment for performance rendered. And English courts quickly allowed a claim under a contract to convey an interest in land based on part performance. This Section concerns the modern forms of these performance-based claims. It also concerns reliance-based claims, which are a more recent development.

2. *Restitution*

It is well settled that normally a plaintiff may recover a reasonable price (typically the market price) for performance rendered under a contract that is unenforceable against the defendant under the Statute of Frauds. Take the following example:

> *A Mural.* Under an oral contract with Marion Means, Steven Smock, an artist, agrees to paint a mural in Means's home in exchange for a conveyance of Passacre. After full performance by Smock, Means refuses to convey Passacre.

Although this transaction is a contract for the sale of land within the Statute of Frauds, and therefore unenforceable against Means, Smock can recover a reasonable price for the mural on a restitution claim. This does not require Smock establish Means actually has benefitted from the performance.

2. *Enforcement based on performance*

Over the centuries the courts have read exceptions into certain provisions of the Statute under which the plaintiff can bring a suit to enforce a contract even though the contract is within the Statute, where the contract has been fully or even partly performed on one side. These part-performance exceptions vary.

The Land Section. In the case of contracts for the sale of an interest in land a part-performance exception—perhaps more accurately, a part-performance-and-reliance exception—has become institutionalized and has been built into an imposing body of case law. Traditionally, the cases in this area set out two bases for enforcing land contracts that would fall within the Statute except for the fact that they have been partly performed: (1) The equity in favor of a party who has acted under the oral contract and who will suffer hardship if the contract is not enforced. (2) The evidentiary value of acts of reliance or part performance in pointing to the existence of a contract. Because these considerations may appear in varying degrees there are strict and liberal applications of the part-performance exception in the land contract context. Furthermore, some decisions place greater weight on the evidentiary significance of part performance while others place greater weight on the element of hardship.

In considering the part-performance exception for land contracts it is necessary to distinguish between acts under the contract by the vendor (seller) and acts under the contract by the purchaser.

A vendor is entitled to recover the purchase price under an oral contract for the sale of land as soon as he has actually conveyed the land to the purchaser. Thus the vendor can obtain the price promised by the purchaser instead of being thrown back upon either an action in restitution for the reasonable value of the land conveyed or a suit in specific restitution to compel a reconveyance of the land.

Where it is the purchaser who acts under a contract that is otherwise within the Statute the law is more complicated. A good summary of the traditional rule in this area was set out in Restatement First Section 197, which provided that an oral agreement for the sale of an interest in land becomes *specifically enforceable* if "the purchaser with the assent of the vendor (a) makes valuable improvements on the land, or (b) takes possession thereof or retains a possession thereof existing at the time of the bargain, and also pays a portion or all of the purchase price."

As indicated by Restatement First Section 197, under the traditional rule payment of all or part of the purchase price, without more, usually does not itself make the contract enforceable, on the ground that such a payment does not identify the land sold. (However, the payment can be recovered in a suit for restitution.) Similarly, under the traditional rule the purchaser's act of taking possession, without more, does not make the contract enforceable by the purchaser, on the ground that taking possession is just as consistent with a lease as with a purchase and may not involve a serious change of position by the purchaser.

These limitations are not universally respected by the courts. Some cases indicate that taking possession is sufficient even without payment of the purchase price, and many cases hold that the rendition of services by the purchaser over a long period will suffice to take the contract out of the Statute. This holding is typically found in situations involving contracts involving a promise to leave a farm or a house to someone in return for providing care until the promisor's death.

The traditional rule that certain acts by the purchaser under a land contract may make the contract specifically enforceable was developed by courts of equity and therefore only gives the purchaser a right to specific performance, not to recover damages measured by the value of the land. In contrast, the vendor's right to the price after conveying the land is a right to sue at law.

Restatement Second Section 129 completely reconceptualizes and reformulates the part-performance exception for land contracts by making the exception center on reliance. This Section provides that a contract for the transfer of an interest in land may be specifically enforced notwithstanding failure to comply with the Statute of Frauds if it is established that the party seeking enforcement, in reasonable reliance on the contract and on the continuing assent of the party against whom enforcement is sought, has so changed his position that injustice can be avoided only by specific enforcement.

The One-Year Section. Under Restatement Second Section 130, and many cases, as soon as one party has fully performed, notwithstanding the one-year provision the promise of the other party becomes binding even if that promise cannot be performed within one year. Putting this exception together with the basic rule for interpreting the one-year provision, an oral contract is either not within, or is taken out of, the one-year section if the whole contract *could* have been performed within one year, or if one party has fully performed, no matter how long it took for that performance to take place.

However, some cases hold that if the defendant's performance will require more than a year the fact that the plaintiff has fully performed is immaterial and the plaintiff's only relief is in restitution. Still other cases hold that full performance on one side will take the contract out of the Statute only the performance takes place within a year.

3. *Reliance*

Suppose a plaintiff seeks recovery, under a contract that is unenforceable by virtue of the Statute of Frauds, for losses that were incurred in reliance under the contract, but which did not result in a benefit to the defendant. Under classical contract law the prevailing view was that it would be contrary to the Statute to allow a recovery for losses through reliance on a contract that is unenforceable under the Statute if those losses did not benefit the defendant. Today that view is gradually changing. Two of the leading cases are Monarco v. Lo Greco, 220 P.2d 737 (Cal. 1950), and Alaska Airlines v. Stephenson, 217 F.2d 295 (9th Cir. 1954).

In *Monarco v. Lo Greco* Christie Lo Greco's mother and stepfather orally promised Christie that if he would stay on the family farm and help in its management they would leave him the bulk of their property. Christie did as they asked and the family farm prospered, but the farm was left to the stepfather's grandson. The agreement was covered by both the land provision of the statute of frauds and the provision covering an agreement to make a testamentary bequest. A claim was not available under the equitable doctrine of part performance because the requirements of possession or improvements were not satisfied. And a restitution claim would only be for the wages paid a day laborer and the value of room and board would be subtracted. Nevertheless, the court held for Christie on the basis of his reliance. The opinion qualified the reliance exception to the Statute by stating that reliance was a ground for overcoming the Statute only "where either an unconscionable injury or unjust enrichment would result from refusal to enforce the contract."

In *Alaska Airlines v. Stephenson* Alaska Airlines orally promised to give a pilot a two-year written employment contract as soon as the airline obtained a required certificate to fly between Seattle and Alaska. In reliance on this promise the pilot let his right to return to his previous employer expire. Alaska broke its promise. The agreement was covered by the one-year provision of the statute. A restitution claim would not have helped the pilot because he was seeking salary beyond the time he was terminated. Nevertheless, the court held for the pilot on the ground that his reliance overcame the Statute.

Restatement Second Section 139 gives full recognition to the reliance principle in the Statute of Frauds cases:

Section 139. Enforcement by Virtue of Action in Reliance

(1) A promise which the promisor should reasonably expect to induce action or forbearance on the part of the promisee or a third person and which does induce the action or forbearance is enforceable notwithstanding the Statute of Frauds if injustice can be avoided only by enforcement of the promise. The remedy granted for breach is to be limited as justice requires.

(2) In determining whether injustice can be avoided only by enforcement of the promise, the following circumstances are significant:

(a) the availability and adequacy of other remedies, particularly cancellation and restitution;

(b) the definite and substantial character of the action or forbearance in relation to the remedy sought;

(c) the extent to which the action or forbearance corroborates evidence of the making and terms of the promise, or the making and terms are otherwise established by clear and convincing evidence;

(d) the reasonableness of the action or forbearance;

(e) the extent to which the action or forbearance was foreseeable by the promisor . . . .

Not all courts adopt this exception. Furthermore, some courts that adopt the reliance exception qualify the exception in the same manner as *Monarco.*

A special problem is presented where a party invokes the reliance exception in the case of a contract for the sale of goods. The UCC Statute of Frauds provision, Section 2–201, includes a number of exceptions. Reliance is not one of these exceptions. Some cases take the position that the exceptions included in Section 2–201 should be deemed to be exclusive of any others, including reliance. *See, e.g.,* Lige Dickson Co. v. Union Oil Co., 635 P.2d 103 (Wash. 1981). Other cases take the position that the reliance exception applies to cases that fall under Section 2–201 because UCC Section 1–103 provides that "Unless displaced by the particular provisions of this Act, the principles of law and equity, including . . . the law relative to . . . estoppel . . . or other validating or invalidating cause shall supplement its provisions." *See, e.g.,* Allen M. Campbell Co. v. Virginia Metal Indus., 708 F.2d 930, 932–934 (4th Cir. 1983).

SECTION 10.   THE EFFECT OF NON-COMPLIANCE—LEGAL CONSEQUENCES OF THE UNENFORCEABLE AGREEMENT.

Noncompliance with the statute makes an affirmative defense available to a claim to enforce a contract. The defense is waived if it is not asserted. Noncompliance with the statute does not otherwise make a contract void or ineffective. For example, a person who transfers an interest in land pursuant to an oral contract cannot assert noncompliance with the statute as a basis to avoid the contract and recover the land.

The Statute of Frauds affects only the legal relations of the contracting parties. Accordingly, that a contract is oral and therefore unenforceable between the parties makes it no less a binding contract so far as third persons are concerned. Restatement Second § 144. Accordingly, persuading a party to break an oral contract may constitute the tort of inducing breach of contract even though the contract is within the Statute.

SECTION 11.   ORAL RESCISSION.

The problem of the validity of an oral rescission arises chiefly in connection with the following situation: Under the Statute of Frauds the original contract had to be and was in a writing or other record. Subsequently, however, the contract was orally rescinded by mutual agreement. As a general proposition, rescission in such cases is effective even if not in writing, on the theory that the rescission does not call for the performance of any duties and therefore does not fall within any of the classes covered by the Statute. However, there are two qualifications on this general proposition:

1.   *Sale of land.* Where the rescinded contract was for the sale of land and was fully executed, rescission is effectively a conveyance—albeit a reconveyance—and therefore falls within the Statute. However, Restatement Second Section 148 comment c states that the prevailing rule, which is adopted by Restatement Second, is that an executory land contract may be rescinded orally, like other contracts within the Statute.

2.   *Sale of goods.* Where the original contract was for the sale of goods and ownership had already passed to the buyer a rescission is really a resale of the goods and falls within UCC Section 2–201 if the amount involved is $500 or more.

SECTION 12.   ORAL MODIFICATIONS.

Generally speaking, a modification of a contract falls within the Statute of Frauds if but only if the new agreement that results from putting together the original agreement and the modification falls within the Statute. However, the rule regarding modifications of contracts for the sale of goods is more complex. UCC Section 2–209(3) provides that the requirements of Section 2–201 must be satisfied if a contract for the sale of goods as modified is within its provisions. Zemco Mfg. Inc. v. Navistar Int'l Transp. Corp., 186 F.3d 815 (7th Cir. 1999), decided by the Seventh Circuit under Indiana law, discusses the law on this issue.

In 1983 the parties entered into a written contract for the sale of parts. Originally, the contract was to last one year, but it was extended until 1987 by written agreements. After 1987 the parties orally agreed to extend the contract once more. Zemco and Navistar argued that the oral contract extensions were unenforceable under the Statute of Frauds even though UCC Section 2–201 (the UCC Statute of Frauds) is triggered only by the price, not by the duration, of the contract. The Seventh Circuit agreed:

> We begin our analysis of this question with [UCC § 2–209(3)], which generally applies to contract modifications. It states that "[t]he requirements of the statute of frauds . . . must be satisfied if the contract as modified is within its provisions." . . . The interpretation of this provision . . . has generated controversy among courts and commentators. One view is that all contract modifications must be in writing; another view is that only modifications of terms that are required to be in writing under UCC § 2–201 must be in writing. Under the second view, the time extension would not need to be in writing because the length of a contract is not a type of term that needs to be in writing.
>
> Indiana courts have not interpreted the meaning of [UCC § 2–209(3)]. A substantial number of the courts in other jurisdictions that have considered identical UCC provisions have held that every contract modification must be in writing . . . . Although these courts have provided little analysis, they essentially interpret § 2–209(3) to mean that, if the post-modification contract fits within the terms of § 2–201 (i.e., it is a sale of goods for more than $500), then any modification of it must be in writing . . . .
>
> At least one court has held that the writing requirement for modifications applies only to either a change in consideration, or a change in a term that the UCC statute of frauds requires to be

in writing. *See Costco Wholesale Corp. v. World Wide Licensing Corp.*, 78 Wash.App. 637, 898 P.2d 347, 351 & n. 5 (1995). This view also appears to be favored among commentators. The general theory behind this approach is that it would be anomalous, if not inconsistent, to require that a modification be in writing if the same term in the original contract could be proven by parol evidence. Moreover, proponents of this view argue, § 2–209(3) explicitly invokes only the writing requirements contained in § 2–201—nothing less and nothing more . . . .

We need not decide in the abstract the correct interpretation of § 2–209(3). Because the jurisdiction of the district court was based on the diversity of citizenship of the parties, it was obligated to apply the law of Indiana . . . . Although the Indiana courts have not spoken directly on the matter, we believe . . . that Indiana would follow the majority of jurisdictions and hold that the extension of the contract needed to be in writing . . . .

———

INDEX

References are to Pages